ARCHITECTURAL
GRAPHIC STANDARDS
STUDENT EDITION

D1159009

ARCHITECTURAL
GRAPHIC STANDARDS
STUDENT EDITION

ELEVENTH EDITION

EDITED BY
BRUCE BASSLER, NCARB
IOWA STATE UNIVERSITY

AUTHORED BY
THE AMERICAN INSTITUTE OF ARCHITECTS

SMITH MARAN ARCHITECTURE
AND INTERIORS
GRAPHICS EDITOR

WITH ADDITIONAL ILLUSTRATIONS FROM
THE MAGNUM GROUP

JOHN WILEY & SONS, INC.
WILEY

Designed by Bruce Mau Design, Inc.

This book is printed on acid-free paper. ∞

Copyright ©2008 by John Wiley & Sons, Inc. All rights reserved

Published by John Wiley & Sons, Inc., Hoboken, New Jersey
Published simultaneously in Canada

No part of this publication may be reproduced, stored in a retrieval system, or transmitted in any form or by any means, electronic, mechanical, photocopying, recording, scanning, or otherwise, except as permitted under Section 107 or 108 of the 1976 United States Copyright Act, without either the prior written permission of the Publisher, or authorization through payment of the appropriate per-copy fee to the Copyright Clearance Center, 222 Rosewood Drive, Danvers, MA 01923, (978) 750-8400, fax (978) 646-8600, or on the web at www.copyright.com. Requests to the Publisher for permission should be addressed to the Permissions Department, John Wiley & Sons, Inc., 111 River Street, Hoboken, NJ 07030, (201) 748-6011, fax (201) 748-6008, or online at www.wiley.com/go/permissions.

Limit of Liability/Disclaimer of Warranty: While the publisher and the author have used their best efforts in preparing this book, they make no representations or warranties with respect to the accuracy or completeness of the contents of this book and specifically disclaim any implied warranties of merchantability or fitness for a particular purpose. No warranty may be created or extended by sales representatives or written sales materials. The advice and strategies contained herein may not be suitable for your situation. You should consult with a professional where appropriate. Neither the publisher nor the author shall be liable for any loss of profit or any other commercial damages, including but not limited to special, incidental, consequential, or other damages.

For general information about our other products and services, please contact our Customer Care Department within the United States at (800) 762-2974, outside the United States at (317) 572-3993 or fax (317) 572-4002.

Wiley also publishes its books in a variety of electronic formats. Some content that appears in print may not be available in electronic books. For more information about Wiley products, visit our web site at www.wiley.com.

Library of Congress Cataloging-in-Publication Data:

Architectural graphic standards : student edition / edited by Bruce Bassler;
authored by the American Institute of Architects; Smith Maran Architecture and
Interiors, graphics editor; with Additional illustrations from the Magnum Group.
— Student ed.
        p. cm.
  Includes bibliographical references and index.
  ISBN: 978-0-470-08546-2 (cloth)
1. Building—Details—Drawings—Standards. 2. Architectural drawing—Standards.
3. Building—Standards. I. Bassler, Bruce L. II. American Institute of Architects.

TH2031.A84257 2008
690—dc22
                                                                    2007034299

Printed in the United States of America
10 9 8 7 6 5 4 3 2 1

ACKNOWLEDGMENTS

JOHN WILEY & SONS, INC.

AMANDA L. MILLER
VICE PRESIDENT AND PUBLISHER

KATHRYN MALM BOURGOINE
ACQUISITIONS EDITOR

LAUREN POPLAWSKI
EDITORIAL ASSISTANT

KERSTIN NASDEO
PRODUCTION MANAGER

JACQUELINE BEACH
PRODUCTION EDITOR

JUSTIN MAYHEW
SENIOR MARKETING MANAGER

DESIGN/PRODUCTION

BRUCE MAU DESIGN, INC.
DESIGNER

LUCINDA GEIST
COMPOSITION

JANICE BORZENDOWSKI
COPYEDITOR

BRUCE BASSLER
STUDENT EDITION EDITOR

AGS EDITORS

DENNIS J. HALL, FAIA, FCSI
SENIOR EXECUTIVE EDITOR

NINA M. GIGLIO, ASSOC. AIA, CSI
EXECUTIVE EDITOR

RICHARD L. HAYES, PHD, AIA
EXECUTIVE EDITOR

KEVIN SHAFER
DEVELOPMENT EDITOR

WANDA MADRID-DIAZ, ASSOC. AIA
ASSISTANT EDITOR

LESLIE H. SCHLESINGER, CSI-I
ASSISTANT EDITOR

GRAPHICS EDITOR

SMITH MARAN ARCHITECTURE AND INTERIORS

  IRA SMITH, PROJECT PRINCIPAL
  ERIK MARAN, PRINCIPAL
  KIMBERLY MURRAY, GRAPHICS MANAGER
  PETER GREENBERG, GREENBERG DESIGN

  DANIEL D'AGOSTINO
  CAROLINE GUSTUS
  MICHEALLA LEE
  JOHN PETULLO

ADDITIONAL ILLUSTRATIONS

THE MAGNUM GROUP
  LUCKY BALARAMAN
  V.P. RAJAGOPAL
  S. RAJESHKUMAR
  V. KARTHIKEYAN

STUDENT EDITION ADVISORY BOARD

MARK BARNHOUSE, AIA, RA
ELIZABETH BOWEN
KEITH HEDGES, AIA
MEGAN LUENEBURG
BRUCE MCMILLAN, AIA
JONATHAN OCHSHORN

AGS 11TH EDITION ADVISORY BOARD

DAVID W. ALTENHOFEN, AIA, CSI
RENEE CHENG, AIA
WILLIAM MCDONOUGH, FAIA
J. ROBERT HILLIER, FAIA
KIERAN TIMBERLAKE ASSOCIATES, LLP
RICHARD POLLACK, FAIA, FIIDA
CATHY J. SIMON, FAIA

SUBJECT EDITORS/AUTHORS

DAVID W. ALTENHOFEN, AIA, CSI
LEONARD R. BACHMAN, RA
RENEE CHENG, AIA
JOSEPH DEMKIN, AIA
THOMAS FISHER
CARL GALIOTO, FAIA
ROBIN GUENTHER, FAIA
DENNIS J. HALL, FAIA, FCSI
STEPHEN HARBY
REBECCA INGRAM, RA
GEORGE B. JOHNSTON
KAREN J. KING, RA
JOHN P. MCCARTHY, PE, SE
WILLIAM MCDONOUGH, FAIA
MARYROSE MCGOWEN, AIA
BARBARA NADEL, FAIA
MARK RYLANDER, AIA
WILLIAM SARAMA, AIA
TIMOTHY SHEA, AIA
ALF SIMON, PhD, FCSLA, ASLA
NANCY SOLOMON, AIA

CONTRIBUTORS

GEOFFREY C. ADAMS, RA
RICHARD O. ANDERSON, PE, HON. M. ASCE
JOAN BLUMENFELD
MARK CHILDS
CHARLES CULP, PHD, PE
BRUCE FERGUSON
ANTHONY GOLEBIEWSKI, AIA
WALTER GRONDZIK, PE
HENRY GROSSBARD
JEFF HABERL, PhD, PE
CODY HICKS
RESHMA HOLLA
LACHMI KHEMLANI, PHD
STEVE MARANOWSKI
WALTER MOBERG, ASSOC. AIA
JAMES W. NIEHOFF, PE
FAITH OKUMA, ASLA
ELAINE OSTROFF, HON. AIA
LISA PASSAMONTE GREEN
JON PEARSON
JOHN ROWE
GANPAT SINGHVI, PHD, PE, SE
MICHAEL J. SMITH, AIA
MARC SWACKHAMER
DENNIS WILKINSON, ASLA

CONTENTS

PUBLISHER'S NOTES ON THE 11TH EDITION

Unless a hidden stash of documents suddenly turns up, we will never know why John Wiley, my grandfather's grandfather, developed an interest in architecture. Without documents, we are forced to parse the logic of John's publishing program, which was shaped in part by his experiences working with his father, Charles, the founder of the company. We do know two things. Soon after John revived his father's faltering publishing house, he developed an interest in what we publishers like to call "need to know" information. Both John and his father played formative roles in the origins of American literature, publishing writers such as James Fenimore Cooper, Washington Irving, Nathaniel Hawthorne, Herman Melville, and Edgar Allan Poe. Working with his partner, George Palmer Putnam, John evinced an interest in more practical subjects, such as architecture, engineering, landscape design, and surveying, and consequently, Wiley & Putnam would come to play a comparable role in the development of an American architecture.

Wiley's 200-year history is filled with important publications that have helped shape the built environment. Wiley & Putnam published Andrew Jackson Downing's *Theory and Practice of Landscape Gardening with a View to the Improvement of Country Residences and Cottage Residences* in 1841 and 1842, respectively. Downing was an important figure in the development of a distinctive American architecture, one closely associated with the country's early suburbs, where John would move in the 1850s. Downing also influenced the shape of the urban landscape perusing large-scale urban park designs with his assistant, Calvin Vaux.

John Wiley's other interest, which looks something like a personal obsession, was John Ruskin, the renowned British aesthete, artist, social reformer, and architectural critic. Beginning in 1851, and for the rest of John's active publishing life, he and his offspring, as John Wiley & Sons, published endless sets and single monographs penned by Ruskin.

Soon after John split amicably with Putnam in 1848, he gave up on fiction and moved slowly but decidedly into publishing for the academy and the professions, a move that was accelerated by the arrival in the business of a second son, William Halsted Wiley, a civil engineer. John published books that would be used by carpenter-builders, draftsmen, and architects and then, with his sons, branched out more and more into related engineering professions. As with the history of Architectural Graphic Standards, one can trace the evolution of home, commercial, and industrial construction—railroad and bridge building, ship and fortification design, highway construction, all of those physical features associated with the industrialization of America—by delving into Wiley books.

Our company was particularly adept at handbook publishing, and Frank E. Kidder's *Architects' and Builders' Pocket-book*, later rewritten by Harry Parker, went through 18 editions between its original publication in 1884 and 1986, when it finally went out of print.

The arrival of *Architectural Graphic Standards* in 1932 was part of a natural progression. It was very much in the tradition of Wiley's century-long commitment to quality publishing for a particular profession or group of professions. Charles G. Ramsey and Harold R. Sleeper authored and designed the first edition and continued to do so until Sleeper's death. Sleeper, as George B. Johnston points out in his introductory essay, published other books with Wiley. At one point in the 1950s, when Wiley was beginning to outgrow its offices at 440 Park Avenue South, my father asked Sleeper to design a building for the company. However, Wiley was neither large nor profitable enough at the time to undertake such an ambitious project, and the project was not realized.

From the start, *AGS* acquired the reputation as an indispensable tool for architects and others, a reputation that has been sustained by constant revision to assure that the content keeps up with changes in all aspects of design and construction. I must add that even from the perspective of a nonprofessional, the book itself is an appealing work of art. Beginning in the mid-1990s, constant revision has been supplemented by the delivery of *AGS*'s content in a digital format. The fourth release of the CD-ROM coincides with the publication of this 11th edition. *AGS* offers its readers not only must have content, but also now provides tools to work with that content.

We at Wiley are proud of our role in the birthing of *AGS* and of our association with the AIA. *AGS* represents our very finest work while demonstrating our continuing commitment to meeting the needs of our readers.

Peter Booth Wiley
Chairman of the Board
John Wiley & Sons Inc.

FOREWORD TO THE 11TH EDITION

As part of a graduate project at Yale, I went to Ireland during the autumn of 1975 to design and build a solar house in rural County Cork. I had never built a building before, and no one had ever built a modern solar house in Ireland, so I quickly realized that my ambition surpassed my knowledge. There I was, shivering in a cold drizzle, one moment dreaming of a solar-powered world, the next trying to figure out how to build a sturdy, dry, and warm rural house by hand. Thankfully, I remembered to bring my *Architectural Graphic Standards*.

Indeed, *Architectural Graphic Standards* was my bible. When I needed to know how to lay out a wall, I found it here. To figure out the loads on the slate roof, I found it here. Day after day, I wore out the pages of my third edition, poring over its rich collection of details and drawings. Studying the book, as much as making the building, was my initiation into the world of the practical, experienced architect.

As deeply personal as that experience was, it was not unique. If you are a professional architect, this book has, at one time or another, been your mentor. Its encyclopedic representation of architecture's best ideas and practices has not only shaped your understanding of what it means to make a building, but also it has helped you make better buildings, for what you find here is the tried and true, rock-solid, indispensable wisdom that underlies our craft and our art.

Yet *Architectural Graphic Standards* can also be seen as a living document. While the book's time-honored reliability makes it an able keeper of rich traditions, its content is always evolving. The volume I carried with me to Ireland, for example, is not the same as the one you hold in your hands. Like preceding editions, this 11th edition preserves the detailed knowledge of the past; however, it contains forward-looking sections on solar collectors, porous paving, and green roofs, which I could only wish for while I was searching and innovating relentlessly thirty years ago. There is also a wealth of new information that shows the importance of considering the specific qualities of each site—its geography and climate, its ecology and cultural history—when applying the universal standards illustrated in these pages. Gone are the days of Le Corbusier's "one single building for all nations and climates."

The evolution of *Architectural Graphic Standards*, then, represents more than a simple accumulation of facts; it actually enables change in the way we think about and practice architecture; not change for change sake, but intelligent innovations that answer the needs of the future and introduce a new layer of quality to building design. Consider the new chapter on sustainability. Here we find a treasury of ideas and practices that enables designers to respond to a diverse range of economic, social, and environmental concerns. Indeed, archi-

tecture has always been a multidisciplinary profession, but appreciating the rich connectivity of economy, ecology, and equity has become a crucial dimension of our work as we have come to see each building as a part of a complex community of events affecting everything from the health of architecture's provisioners, makers, and users all the way to the long-term prospects of the planet.

Too often, the news from this expanded purview—how buildings waste energy and resources or contribute to climate change, for example—has either been ignored or read too narrowly. Ignoring this news is negligence, plain and simple—a strategy of tragedy. But a narrow response, like trying to limit the negative impacts of architecture by using an environmentally damaging energy source more efficiently, doesn't get to the heart of the matter either. Rather than creatively addressing the design flaws that create pollution and waste in the first place, minimizing strategies only make architecture "less bad." Or "differently bad," as we saw in the 1970s when a single-minded response to the shortage of fossil fuels yielded a host of energy-efficient buildings that made their occupants sick. Less is not more in this context.

If we have come far since then, we still need a principled framework for good design that offers a positive, regenerative course for the future of architecture. The new case studies presented here offer just that. Illustrating the many ways in which architects, landscape designers, and engineers have been effectively applying the intelligence of natural systems to building and site design, the case studies show that we can create architecture that is not simply less polluting or less energy intensive, but architecture that generates a wide spectrum of positive effects, enhancing environmental health, social well-being, and economic vitality. This is the work Vitruvius began millennia ago.

In each of these examples, we see a design process built on a dialogue with natural processes, a creative interaction with the flows of sunlight, wind, water, and nutrient cycles in a particular place. By integrating this dialogue into our technological discourse on building and energy systems, architects and designers are developing magnificent innovations. We see safe, healthful materials designed to be perpetually recycled or returned to the earth to nourish the soil, effectively closing the loop on material flows. We see durable public buildings powered by the energy of the sun and private residences heated and cooled by geothermal currents rising from underground. We see green-roofed manufacturing plants that create habitat, restore landscapes, and cost-effectively filter storm water while providing safe, comfortable places to work. We see a profusion of inspired designs that are not only surpassing conventional standards of cost and performance, but also are creating beautiful, deeply satisfying places to live, work, learn, and participate in community life.

As ecological design principles become a part of *Architectural Graphic Standards*, they become a part of our culture; if a practice appears between the covers of this book, it has been done and will be done again. That's not to say that *Architectural Graphic Standards* is prone to the whims of fashion. On the contrary, showing how to construct a human habitat in harmony with nature is an important act of historical and cultural restoration, for the story of architecture and building—from the Roman Pantheon to the University of Virginia, from the cathedral to the vernacular house—can be read as a long, fruitful dialogue between our buildings and the sun.

It seems, somehow, in the last century, much of this knowledge was lost or ignored. In 1975, when I was designing the first of my solar buildings, a visiting professor at Yale, a celebrated modernist, admonished me, saying "solar energy has nothing to do with architecture." Twenty-five years later, at a joint meeting of the American Institute of Architects and the International Union of Architects, less than a dozen of thousands of architects in attendance raised their hands when I asked who knew how to find true south. But that skill is the true cornerstone of building intelligence. We see it in the deep history of building in places like Athens or Mykonos, where orientation and the play of light and shadow were fundamental elements of design and human celebration. The Mediterranean house was built with thick walls that transferred the heat of the winter sun or the coolness of the summer night into the interior, while deep, whitewashed window reveals reflected sunlight coolly and deeply into the space. In Vitruvius's 1st century BC encyclopedia of architecture, a seminal antecedent to *Architectural Graphic Standards*, these vernacular skills become the art of building, and one finds entire chapters devoted to the profound significance of the sun's movement in relation to the location of rooms, the size of apertures, and thermal mass. Fourteen hundred years later, Palladio was deeply influenced by Vitruvius, and Thomas Jefferson, in turn, studied them both, drawing inspiration from the masters' classical forms as well as from their keen attention to site and solar flux. Indeed, Monticello and the University of Virginia make art of an intense engagement with history, landscape, and the movement of the sun. Armed with the technology and ecological insights of our age, 21st century architects can surely do the same.

One can imagine the self-taught Jefferson studying his Vitruvius as we study our *Architectural Graphic Standards*. And one can imagine the architects of the future poring over this book as we pore over Vitruvius. That is the singular place *Architectural Graphic Standards* holds in our profession: It is, all at once,

a repository of our stories, a comprehensive resource for practicing architects, a record of what it means to make a building in our time, and a signal to forthcoming generations that we stayed in touch with our sources as we anticipated the needs of the future. Feedback and feed-forward all in one volume.

In that sense, *Architectural Graphic Standards* plays a pivotal role in both cultural memory and cultural evolution. In the absence of time and practical mentors, it fills the role of the elder craftsman, much like the father or grandfather on the intergenerational teams that build temples in Japan. There, wooden temples are deconstructed and rebuilt each generation so that the local building arts are never lost. The grandfather's third time building the temple is the grandson's first, and board by board, cut by cut, joint by joint, the grandfather transfers ancestral knowledge and skills into living memory. At the same time, high-speed change is a 21st century reality, which demands that we practice anticipatory design—a strategic, purposeful approach to architecture that uses sophisticated, regenerative technologies, and a new architectural language to nurture and celebrate the future of life.

Both of these roles are value-laden, and so, they begin to suggest a value-based framework for the application of the tools of our trade. Quite simply, architects need to follow all of the laws of nature as diligently as we follow the laws of gravity. This is a blessing, not a burden. We live on a wondrous, biologically rich planet daily renewed by sunlight and new growth. Working with, rather than against, all of the processes that make the surface of our world a dynamic living biosphere—the energy of the sun, wind and waves; the vital synergies of biochemistry; the dynamics of photosynthesis—we can create buildings that celebrate our interdependence with other living systems and make architecture itself a regenerative force. Imagine a building that makes oxygen, sequesters carbon, fixes nitrogen, distills water, provides habitat for thousands of species, accrues solar energy as fuel, builds soil, creates microclimates, changes with the seasons, and is beautiful. Such buildings already exist, and they show how our tools can serve a principled, creative dialogue with Earth that generates a living architectural language for our time—an aesthetically rich, technologically sophisticated language that celebrates sunlight and landscape, people and place, community and creativity, as well as the immensely rich traditions of the past. At this fertile crossroads is *Architectural Graphic Standards*, preserver and creator of architecture's dynamic legacy.

William McDonough, FAIA
Founder and Principal
William McDonough + Partners

INTRODUCTION

FROM THE INTRODUCTION TO *ARCHITECTURAL GRAPHIC STANDARDS, 11TH EDITION*

Dennis J. Hall, FAIA, FCSI

Architectural Graphic Standards (*AGS*) has long been revered as an indispensable resource in architectural offices, presenting design and technical information on building subject matter. It is also a historic record of the materials, construction practices, and techniques commonly in use at each edition's time of publication, in effect creating a snapshot of the era's standards of practice. *AGS* celebrates its 75th anniversary in 2007. In recognition of this milestone, the 11th edition builds on its venerable tradition to cover contemporary issues of architectural practice in this age of exploding design technology, thereby, establishing *AGS* as documentation of past, present, and future standards of practice in architecture.

Our vision for this edition was to create a volume that is more relevant to today's practicing architects and related practitioners. It is intended to be used as a design and reference tool during the earliest stages of project conception through production of detailed construction documents. A new content paradigm and updated design enables *AGS* to achieve this goal and remain the flagship architectural title that it has always been. This edition of *AGS* is divided into three sections and completely reorganized. The contents of each section are organized using established construction classification systems.

Section 1, "Building Elements," applies the Construction Specifications Institute (CSI)/Construction Specifications Canada (CSC) *UniFormat*™, a classification system for organizing construction information by functional building elements. It is the primary organizational structure used by architects and contractors for preliminary design documentation, which includes schematic design drawings, preliminary project descriptions, and preliminary cost estimates. *UniFormat*™ characterizes building systems and assemblies by their function without identifying specific products or work results that compose them. Joseph Demkin, AIA, provides a discussion on the advantages of this organizational structure over CSI/CSC *MasterFormat*™ for *AGS* on page xiv.

Additionally, Section 1 addresses emerging strategies in building design, such as rainscreen wall design, heat, air and moisture considerations, and the impact of climatic differences. It also introduces case studies for each building element that demonstrate architectural responses to specific design considerations and serve to foster critical thinking in design by providing examples of the standards at work.

Section 2, "Materials," uses four of the *MasterFormat*™ division titles to organize information on the primary building materials—concrete, masonry, metals, and wood—used in construction. These chapters focus on the characteristics and properties of these materials and associated work results without regard for the types of building elements in which they may be used. For example, Chapter 9, "Masonry" includes such subjects as masonry mortaring and grouting, masonry anchorage, reinforcing, and accessories, unit masonry, glass unit masonry, and stone assemblies.

Section 3, "Issues in Contemporary Practice," includes four current issues of architectural practice that influence design and the development of construction documents. These issues represent current challenges facing all architects in an ever-changing profession. These topics include, a framework for environmentally-sensitive and sustainable design as a design philosophy; expanded and updated coverage of inclusive, universal, and accessible design strategies, using real-world examples to highlight key principles; emerging project-delivery methods, including Building Information Modeling and CAD/CAM, focusing on the movement from site-built construction processes to shop-fabricated/site-erected projects; and finally, the value of conducting, disseminating, and applying architectural research. By inclusion and expansion of this information from previous *AGS* editions, the hope is to provoke creative thought and analysis of design solutions that will advance the practice of architecture.

Careful attention has been paid to ensure the consistent use of proper construction terminology throughout *AGS*. Terminology has been coordinated with the 2004 edition of *MasterFormat*™ and the *OmniClass Construction Classification System*™ tables, which are being used by the National Institute of Building Sciences as the basis of terminology for the National Building Information Model Standard. At the end of each topic is a listing of *MasterFormat*™ titles that are found in that portion of the chapter. These are identified as "See Also" and are intended to assist users in finding subject matter and transitioning between the preliminary design organizational structure and work results titles used in specifications. The electronic version of the professional edition of *AGS* may be searched by construction entities, spaces, elements, work results, or products as defined in *OmniClass*™.

Also new to this edition is the updated design. Our colleagues at Bruce Mau Design, Inc. of Toronto were instrumental in evaluating *AGS* and creating a bold new look and feel. Inspired by the floor plan of the Abbey of St.

Gaul, the design of *AGS* was achieved by an underlying grid of squares. The design, in most simple terms, provides a logical place for everything. Using a grid system and a new typeface, the pages are liberated; topics are no longer confined to one page, allowing content to flow across pages and providing more room for additional information. The numbering system and the bold new second color provide a wayfinding tool for the reader. The color highlights key elements of the page—chapter titles appear in red on every page followed by the topic in black, and the use of red on the printed page highlights the start of a new subtopic. All details, drawings, and tables have been numbered by chapter for easy reference, and notes to those images are now located at the bottom of the page.

The new generation of *Architectural Graphic Standards* is a first step in the evolution of presenting building information that will inspire critical thinking about design solutions, and uphold the profession's highest standards of care for the health, safety, and welfare of the public.

ORGANIZATION OF *AGS* CORE CONTENT

Joseph A. Demkin, AIA

The intrinsic value of a technical reference such as *Architectural Graphic Standards* lies in the quality of its content, and that value is undoubtedly what has made *AGS* so well-respected and widely used for the past 75 years. Because of the extensive amount of information that *AGS* embodies, how that information is organized also contributes, at least in part, to the value and utility of this venerable work. To enhance its ease of use, the 11th edition has adopted a new organizational framework. After a brief overview of how past *AGS* editions addressed content organization, the framework for organizing content in the 11th edition is described.

ORGANIZATION OF PAST EDITIONS

Each of the first four *AGS* editions (published between 1932 and 1956) organized material based on the general sequence of construction for buildings. The preface of the first edition explains, "The progression of the book follows the usual building construction procedure from foundation to furniture, with the most-needed miscellaneous sheets placed at the end." A shortcoming of this arrangement was that it lacked any kind of hierarchy. The table of contents at the front of the book is presented in a long continuous list, which became increasingly harder to use as the 213 pages of the first edition

expanded to 566 pages in the fourth edition. Fortunately, the comprehensive and extensive indexes accompanying the first four editions compensated for this shortcoming.

The fifth edition (published in 1956) adopted a new organizational approach based on construction trades and practices. This approach—first formalized in 1963 in *CSI Format for Building Specifications*—later evolved into the CSI 16-division classification system that formed the basis for the *Uniform System for Construction Specifications* and the *MasterFormat*™ system. Despite a strong orientation toward construction trades and practices, the 16-division *MasterFormat*™ framework would be widely adopted over the next four decades for many design-related uses, including the content organization of publications such as *AGS*.

As the number of *AGS* pages ballooned, a considerable amount of the new material did not easily fit into the *MasterFormat*™ work results classifications. Consequently, in the sixth through tenth editions, new chapters containing information on subjects not readily accommodated within *MasterFormat*'s™ 16 divisions were progressively tacked on at the end of the book. By the release of the tenth edition in 2000, *AGS* had grown to 21 chapters.

ORGANIZATION OF 11th EDITION

To address the limitations and shortcomings of *MasterFormat*™ for organizing *AGS* content, the 11th edition incorporates the *UniFormat*™ classification system. The *Project Resource Manual: CSI Manual of Practice* (fifth edition) defines *UniFormat*™ as "a uniform classification system for organizing preliminary construction information into a standard order or sequence on the basis of systems and assemblies." The *UniFormat*™ system describes building components starting from the ground up and from the outside to the inside of a building. *UniFormat*™ is organized by the function performed by each building element, rather than the products and materials specified for it. Thus, a metal roof and a wood shake roof are found in the same section, rather than in chapters on metal and wood. The functional orientation of *UniFormat*™ makes it particularly suited for planning, conceptual, and early design tasks (e.g., preparing preliminary project descriptions, developing preliminary cost estimates, and evaluating alternative schematic building elements).

To align *AGS* with the functional aspects of building elements, the organization of the 11th edition's core content of building details in Section 1,

"Building Elements," tracks with *UniFormat*™ categories A through G as list-ed below:

(A) Substructure
(B) Shell
(C) Interiors
(D) Services
(E) Equipment and Furnishings
(F) Special Construction and Demolition
(G) Building Sitework

Each of the categories contains both classes and subclasses. For example, Category B, Shell, includes classes for superstructure, exterior enclosure, and roof-ing. Each class, in turn, contains subclass elements. The exterior enclosure class, for example, includes subclasses for exterior walls, exterior windows, and exteri-or doors. [Note: The 11th edition carries only the letter tags for the *UniFormat*™ categories. The letter-number tags for *UniFormat*™ classes and subclasses are not used. This allows greater flexibility to modify class and subclass elements and simplifies the referencing of *AGS* details in non-*UniFormat*™ chapters].

AN ENHANCED *AGS*

The use of *UniFormat*™ promises to make the 11th edition more "user-friendly." The organization by functional building elements better accommo-dates the visually delineated components that make up *AGS* core content. Additionally, because *UniFormat*™ generically defines a total facility by func-tional components, users can find information for developing a specific build-ing element in one location. In a broader sense, *AGS* use of *UniFormat*™ tracks with the AEC community's efforts to develop design-related databas-es for application in powerful digital technologies such as object-oriented programming, industry foundation classes (IFCs), and building information modeling (BIM). The 11th edition repositions *AGS* as a resource suited to planning and design tasks, and anyone tapping into its rich and extensive content will benefit from the new organizational structure.

PREFACE

We are flooded daily it seems with stories in magazines, newspapers, and e-publications describing newly designed buildings that stretch the limits of construction technology, and profiling the designers who have become experts in sustainable design or in generating unique forms and aesthetic finishes. In recognition of these accomplishments, the American Institute of Architects (AIA) designates a firm of the year and gives awards for outstanding achievements in design and technology for a variety of building types.

Thus enthralled by beautiful photographs and tales of success, the fledgling design student may wonder what distinguishes a successful career in the design and construction professions. More poignantly, they may ask how can they set out on a career in design, and what can they do to facilitate success? The answer to these questions is at least partly obvious—get an education, read about architecture and architects, visit notable buildings, study architectural details, become familiar with materials, work around construction sites, study human behavior, understand energy issues and sustainability, work with color and light, and so on.

Equally essential for design students is to spend time around seasoned professionals with expertise in very specific areas of design, technology, and construction. That is precisely what the new *Architectural Graphic Standards Student Edition* makes possible, for it makes available to the beginning design student a wealth of professional expertise. Hundreds of design and construction professionals, educators, editors, publishers, and graphic designers were instrumental in the development of the 11th Edition of *Architectural Graphic Standards* and this new *Student Edition*.

For example, the student having difficulty understanding the relationships between climate and cladding/fenestration need only seek out the climatic design considerations guidelines offered in the work by Hillier Architecture of Philadelphia, Pennsylvania. The student confused by the new *International Building Code* can refer to the code-based superstructure considerations developed by Hansen Lind Meyer of Orlando, Florida, for help in developing a schematic structural concept. For understanding something as specific as stair details, Krommehoek/McKeown and Associates of San Diego, California, and Karlsberger and Companies of Columbus, Ohio, show code-compliant stair and landing widths, proper nosing, tread and riser details, and headroom clearances. And for contemporary insight into the "hot" topic of sustainability, William McDonough + Partners of Charlottesville, Virginia, relates the principles of sustainable design and sustainable design process.

I encourage you, the design student, to search through this new edition, for you will find a trove of design and detailing treasures. Take time to examine the guidelines and details that have facilitated the success of the numerous contributing professionals. Do not hesitate to utilize their expertise in your design process and detail development. Be sure to check out the section on environmental impact and material life cycles. The diagram showing energy systems utilizing photovoltaics, passive water preheaters, and cloches is very informative, as are the diagrams of constant-volume multizone HVAC systems.

Best wishes as you advance in your career, with the coaching of some of the best in the profession. Perhaps one day, you, too, will be asked to contribute your own expertise in green design or building diagnostics, facilitating success for those a few rungs lower on the ladder of experience.

Bruce Bassler
NCARB

SECTION 1

BUILDING ELEMENTS

ELEMENT A: SUBSTRUCTURE

1

INTRODUCTION

Well-designed foundations are a necessity to building design. A basic understanding of factors that influence facility substructure design — bearing strata, settlement, and the effects of adjacent structures, slopes, and building modification that either physically expand the structure or change the use of a structure—is essential for good building design.

This chapter provides a basic vocabulary for the design team to use to communicate when assisting in the design of the optimum foundation system to satisfy cost, schedule, and building constraints. This chapter also focuses on the work of the geotechnical engineer, who, together with the structural engineer, creates solutions to complex design constraints. When engineering insight is combined with practical construction methods to produce structures that support increasingly larger loads in more efficient way, it reduces the risk that the effectiveness of structures above grade will be diminished by a misunderstanding or lack of attention to an important detail below grade.

In addition to exploring soils and geotechnical investigation, this chapter examines climatic and seismic considerations relating to the facility substructure and provides a review of special foundations, including basement construction. The topic of basement construction addresses basement excavation, soil support, shoring strategies, and basement wall construction, using both concrete and masonry, and methods of waterproofing or dampproofing these elements.

Contributor:
John P. McCarthy, PE, SE, Smith Group Architecture, Engineering, Interiors, Planning, Detroit, Michigan.

SOILS AND SOILS EXPLORATIONS

Bringing together project team design professionals, including geotechnical engineers, structural engineers, and architects to discuss the matter of soils and foundations is fundamental to ensure that the foundation selected satisfies the constraints of the project budget as well as the functionality of the structure.

Understanding the vocabulary of geotechnical science (for example, the difference between "cohesive" and "cohesionless" soils) is the first step toward fostering collaborative communication, which becomes increasingly important as the process continues. What should be tested, what the test should be, why it is important, and what the limitations of the test are must be addressed. Likewise, identifying foundation and ground modification alternatives (as well as their pros and cons) will aid in the preliminary design phase, when the building foundations are being developed.

Understanding the geotechnical investigation report and geographical variations such as climate and seismic conditions will assist the design professionals in discussing important foundation issues.

SOILS DEFINITIONS: TERMS AND CLASSIFICATIONS

It is critical that geotechnical and structural engineering information be understood properly; to that end, the following definitions of common soils and other terms are included for reference:

- *Clay*: Determined by the size of particles and composition, clays are chemically different from their parent materials as a result of weathering. Clays are typically inorganic and have grain sizes less then 0.0002 in. in diameter. This material contains charged particles and has an affinity for water. Because of their size and chemical composition, clays exhibit cohesion and plasticity. Clays can be classified as stiff, medium, or soft, depending on the moisture content, with drier clays typically being stiffer. Clays make a satisfactory bearing material under some conditions. Long-term settlement can sometimes control the allowable bearing pressure. Because of the cohesive nature of clay, excavations can have steep slopes for short periods of time.
- *Silt*: Silt consists of inorganic particles between 0.003 in. and 0.0002 in. in diameter. These fine-grained particles are similar in composition to the rocks from which they are derived, and are not plastic in nature. Organic silt is found on the bottom of lakes and river deltas.
- *Sand*: Classifications of sand vary from fine to coarse, these rock particles range in size from 0.003 in. to 0.079 in. in diameter. Adequately compacted, sand makes an ideal bearing material. The coarser the sand, the higher the allowable bearing pressures. Fine sands are susceptible to becoming quick when subjected to unbalanced hydrostatic pressures, and may liquify when they are loose, saturated, or subjected to seismic forces. Settlement is usually immediate, with little long-term settlement.
- *Gravel*: Classifications of gravel vary from fine to coarse, and these unconsolidated rock fragments range from .75 in. to about 3 in. Except for gravels composed of shale, this material makes a good foundation material. Depending on the compactness and the underling material, very high bearing pressures are allowed by some building codes.
- *Cobbles*: Ranging in size from about 3 in. to about 10 in., these rock fragments can make reliable foundation-bearing materials, but can be difficult to properly compact when used for fill. Cobble-sized materials can interfere with pile driving and drilled-pier construction causing significant problems.
- *Boulders*: Typically classified as rock fragments greater than 10 in., boulders can be used as part of a fill mass if the voids between the boulders are filled with finer-grained sands and silts. These materials are generally not considered suitable for direct foundation support because of their size and shape, and the difficulty in excavating the material to desired shapes. As with cobbles, boulders can cause significant problems during construction.

- *Bedrock*: Unbroken hard rock that is not over any other material is considered bedrock. Depending upon its composition, it can be capable of withstanding extremely high bearing pressure, and is desirable for foundations supporting high loads. If the rock has been weathered or is cracked, its bearing capacity may be compromised. Settlement of buildings on bedrock is primarily limited to the elastic settlement of the foundation.
- *Residuum*: Residuum consists of soil derived from the in-place decomposition of bedrock materials. In general, these soils are more weathered near the surface, and gradually transition to a more rocklike material with depth. Where residual soils reveal evidence of the stratification and structure of the parent rock, they are known as *saprolitic* materials.
- *Alluvial soils*: Because materials are eroded, transported, and deposited through the action of flowing water, these soils are typically loose and saturated, hence often are unsuitable for support of structures or pavements.
- *Colluvial soils*: Because materials are transported by gravity, typically associated with landslides, these soils are generally irregular in composition and loose. They require improvement prior to being used to support buildings and pavements.
- *Aeolian soils*: These soils are transported and deposited by the wind. Typically, they consist of silt or sand-sized soils. Loess, one of the more common types of aeolian soils, is composed of fine cemented silt. While this material may be competent in place, it loses much of its strength when disturbed or recompacted.
- *Till*: Till is a mixture of clay, silt, sand, gravel, and boulders deposited by glaciers. Consolidated tills that are well graded (indicated by a uniform distribution of particle size) are exceptionally strong and make excellent foundation strata. Loose tills can cause differential settlements if used as a bearing material.
- *Loam:* This organic material, made up of humus and sand, silt, or clay, provides excellent material for agriculture but should not be used for foundations. Organic materials will settle a great deal over time, and even lightly loaded slabs on grade will settle if bearing on loam.
- *Cohesionless soils*: These types of soils consist of cobbles, gravels, sands, and nonplastic silts. They are generally formed from the mechanical weathering of bedrock brought about by water, ice, heat, and cold. They are typically composed of the same minerals as the parent rock. The strength of cohesionless materials is derived primarily from interparticle friction.
- *Cohesive soils*: These types of soils contain clay minerals with an unbalanced chemical charge. As a result, they tend to attract

SOIL TYPES AND THEIR PROPERTIES
1.1

DIVISION	SYMBOLS			SOIL DESCRIPTION	VALUE AS A FOUNDATION MATERIAL	FROST ACTION	DRAINAGE
	LETTER	HATCHING	COLOR				
Gravel and gravelly soils	GW		Red	Well-graded gravel, or gravel sand mixture; little or no fines	Excellent	None	Excellent
	GP		Red	Poorly graded gravel, or gravel-sand mixtures; little or no fines	Good	None	Excellent
	GM		Yellow	Silty gravels, gravel sand-silt mixtures	Good	Slight	Poor
	GC		Yellow	Clayey gravels, gravel clay-sand mixtures	Good	Slight	Poor
Sand and sandy soils	SW		Red	Well-graded sands, or gravelly sands; little or no fines	Good	None	Excellent
	SP		Red	Poorly graded sands, or gravelly sands; little or no fines	Fair	None	Excellent
	SM		Yellow	Silty sands, sand-silt mixtures	Fair	Slight	Fair
	SC		Yellow	Clayey sands, sand-clay mixtures	Fair	Medium	Poor
Silts and clays Liquid Limit	ML		Green	Inorganic silt, rock flour, silty or clayey fine sands, or clayey silts with slight plasticity	Fair	Very high	Poor
	CL		Green	Inorganic clays of low to medium plasticity, gravelly clays, silty clays, lean clays	Fair	Medium	Impervious
	OL		Green	Organic silt-clays of low plasticity	Poor	High	Impervious
Silts and clays Liquid Limit >50	MH		Blue	Inorganic silts, micaceous ordiatamaceous fine sandy or silty soils, elastic silts	Poor	Very high	Poor
	CH		Blue	Inorganic clays of high plasticity, fat clays	Very poor	Medium	Impervious
	OH		Blue	Organic clays of medium to high plasticity, organic silts	Very poor	Medium	Impervious
Highly organic soils	Pt		Orange	Peat and other highly organic soil	Not suitable	Slight	Poor

water and bond together. The strength of cohesive materials is derived from a combination of these chemical bonds and from interparticle friction.

- *Consolidation*: When soils are subjected to loads, water within the void spaces initially supports the change in stress through an increase in pressure. Excess pressures gradually dissipate in proportion to the permeability of the soil. Coarse-grained materials drain rapidly, while finer-grained silts and clays drain more slowly. As the excess pore pressures dissipate, the void spaces compress and transfer the loads to the soil grains. The resulting reduction in volume over time is known as *consolidation*.
- *Underconsolidated soils*: Soils that have built up in river deltas and other water bodies are deposited in a very loose state. These soils are often underconsolidated, in that they have never experienced stresses equal to or greater than current overburden stresses. These materials tend to consolidate under their own weight over time, until all excess pore pressures have been dissipated and the soils become "normally consolidated." Foundations bearing on underconsolidated soils can typically expect large short- and long-term settlement.
- *Overconsolidated soils*: Unlike many other types of materials, soils are not elastic. When stresses are applied to soils, they compress. However, when the same stress is removed, they do not rebound to the same height. When reloaded, the soils "remember" previously loaded conditions and compress to their historical level of stress. Soils that have previously been loaded to stresses above those created by the current soil overburden are considered to be overconsolidated. Foundations bearing on overconsolidated soils can typically expect less short- and long-term settlements.
- *Desiccation*: All soils typically contain some moisture within the voids between soil particles. When soils are dried, capillary tension tends to pull the soil grains together, causing the soil to shrink and lose volume. This action can cause the soil to become overconsolidated, as the capillary tension results in stress.

SOIL STUDIES AND REPORTS

READING A SOILS REPORT

A geotechnical report helps the design team understand the site on which the structure is to be built. Most geotechnical reports contain the following information, based on the previously defined scope of exploration:

- Report summary
- Project information
- Exploration methods
- Description of soil and groundwater conditions
- Design recommendations
- Construction considerations
- Appendix
- Location diagram
- Soil-boring or test pit logs
- Soil profiles
- Laboratory test results

The report summary is generally one to two pages long, and provides the most salient information and recommendations of the report. Use the summary as quick reference, but read the entire report for details and qualifications/limitations. Most reports can be read within 30 minutes. Check and verify the project information and criteria (i.e., building height, structural loads, floor/basement levels, and so on). The scope of the evaluation and recommendations are based on this information. Also included in the report would be project information describing the building and site characteristics such as number of stories, building construction materials, foundation loadings, basement data if applicable, and grades. The exploration section defines how the geotechnical engineer obtained the soil information required to describe the foundation this would include number, location and depth of soil borings and test pits, and laboratory and field testing to be performed.

The general soil and groundwater conditions include a general overview of the results of the geotechnical engineer's tests. More detailed information is contained in the soil-boring and test pit logs, which can be reviewed when required.

The design recommendations section is of greatest interest to the project design team, as it makes specific recommendations concerning the design of foundations, grade slab, walls, drainage requirements, and other key building components. It should be read together with the section on construction considerations, which identifies potential problems during construction that can be avoided or minimized by both the design team and contractor when everyone understands the challenges for the project.

Often reports will provide a transverse section of the soil profile, combining the soil-boring information in a convenient picture. This will enable the reader to better understand approximately how the soil properties vary across the site.

CLIMATIC FOUNDATION ISSUES

DESIGNING FOR COLD AND UNDERHEATED CLIMATES

Cold and underheated climate conditions occur over the northern half of the United States and in mountainous regions. These conditions can be generally quantified as where the frost depth is 12 in. or greater. Designing foundations for these conditions is treated in a more typical manner, such as: providing a foundation below the frost depth, including a basement, and providing insulation on the exterior to reduce the chances of cold ground temperatures reaching the structure.

**SLAB-ON-GRADE CONSTRUCTION IN COLD CLIMATES
1.2**

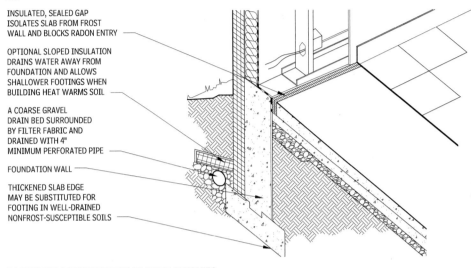

INSULATED, SEALED GAP ISOLATES SLAB FROM FROST WALL AND BLOCKS RADON ENTRY

OPTIONAL SLOPED INSULATION DRAINS WATER AWAY FROM FOUNDATION AND ALLOWS SHALLOWER FOOTINGS WHEN BUILDING HEAT WARMS SOIL

A COARSE GRAVEL DRAIN BED SURROUNDED BY FILTER FABRIC AND DRAINED WITH 4" MINIMUM PERFORATED PIPE

FOUNDATION WALL

THICKENED SLAB EDGE MAY BE SUBSTITUTED FOR FOOTING IN WELL-DRAINED NONFROST-SUSCEPTIBLE SOILS

**BASEMENT CONSTRUCTION IN COLD CLIMATES
1.3**

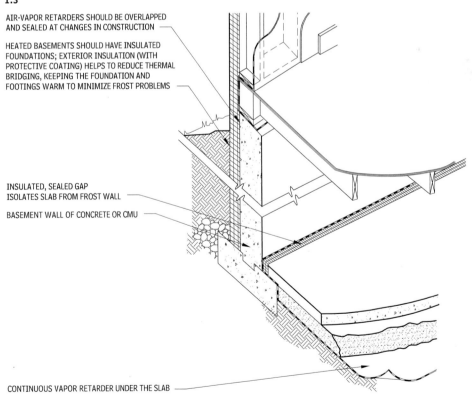

AIR-VAPOR RETARDERS SHOULD BE OVERLAPPED AND SEALED AT CHANGES IN CONSTRUCTION

HEATED BASEMENTS SHOULD HAVE INSULATED FOUNDATIONS; EXTERIOR INSULATION (WITH PROTECTIVE COATING) HELPS TO REDUCE THERMAL BRIDGING, KEEPING THE FOUNDATION AND FOOTINGS WARM TO MINIMIZE FROST PROBLEMS

INSULATED, SEALED GAP ISOLATES SLAB FROM FROST WALL

BASEMENT WALL OF CONCRETE OR CMU

CONTINUOUS VAPOR RETARDER UNDER THE SLAB

ENERGY-EFFICIENT WALL SECTIONS FOR UNDERHEATED CLIMATES
1.4

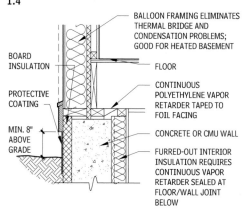

BALLOON FRAMING ELIMINATES THERMAL BRIDGE AND CONDENSATION PROBLEMS; GOOD FOR HEATED BASEMENT

BOARD INSULATION

FLOOR

PROTECTIVE COATING

CONTINUOUS POLYETHYLENE VAPOR RETARDER TAPED TO FOIL FACING

MIN. 8" ABOVE GRADE

CONCRETE OR CMU WALL

FURRED-OUT INTERIOR INSULATION REQUIRES CONTINUOUS VAPOR RETARDER SEALED AT FLOOR/WALL JOINT BELOW

INSULATION ON INSIDE OF CONSTRUCTION

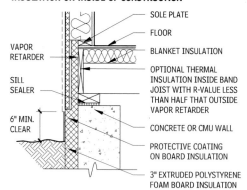

SOLE PLATE

FLOOR

VAPOR RETARDER

BLANKET INSULATION

SILL SEALER

OPTIONAL THERMAL INSULATION INSIDE BAND JOIST WITH R-VALUE LESS THAN HALF THAT OUTSIDE VAPOR RETARDER

6" MIN. CLEAR

CONCRETE OR CMU WALL

PROTECTIVE COATING ON BOARD INSULATION

3" EXTRUDED POLYSTYRENE FOAM BOARD INSULATION

INSULATION ON OUTSIDE OF CONSTRUCTION

FROST ISSUES

Detrimental frost action in soils is obviously limited to those areas of the United States where subfreezing temperatures occur on a regular basis and for extended periods of time. "Frost action," as used in this context, is the lateral or vertical movement of structures supported on or in the soil. Frozen soil is, in itself, not necessarily detrimental to the supported structures. It becomes detrimental when, through the growth of ice lenses, the soil, and whatever is resting on the soil above the ice lenses, heaves upward. This causes foundations and the structures supported by the foundations to distort and suffer distress. Other common problems are the heaving of sidewalks, pavements, steps, retaining walls, fence poles, and architectural features.

The depth of frost penetration is directly related to the intensity and duration of the freezing conditions, a measure that is termed the *freezing degree day index*. In milder climates in the United States, the local building codes might stipulate a frost protection depth for foundations of 12 in. In the northern portions of the United States, the frost protection depth might be 42 to 60 in. as required by local building codes. These guidelines are usually conservative, but there are situations where deeper frost protection depths are warranted. For instance, if the emergency entrance to a hospital is on the north side of the hospital, where the sun never warms the pavement adjacent to the building, and the pavement is kept 100 percent snow-free for safety reasons, then the frost penetration can easily exceed the code requirements.

Carefully evaluate exposure conditions to see if a special condition exists. Grass and snow are very effective insulators for the ground below. Avoid the use of sloping exterior faces on grade beams or foundations that give the freezing forces something to push against when the frost heave situation develops.

AVERAGE DEPTH OF FROST PENETRATION (IN.)
1.5

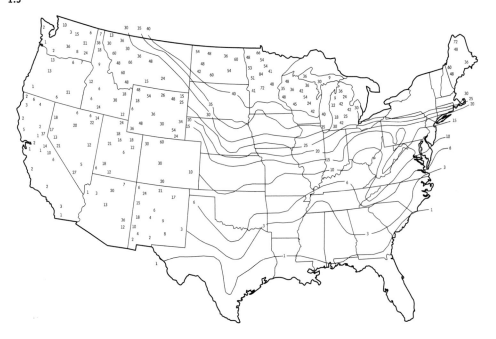

DESIGNING FOR HOT, ARID CLIMATES

CLIMATE IMPLICATIONS

Though classified as arid and overheated, severe desert climates in the United States typically have four distinct periods for determining comfort strategies:

- The *hot dry season*, occurring in late spring, early summer, and early fall, has dry, clear atmospheres that provide high insulation levels, high daytime air temperatures, very high sol-air temperatures, and large thermal radiation losses at night, producing a 30° to 40°F daily range. Nighttime temperatures may fall below the comfort limits and are useful for cooling. Low humidity allows effective evaporative cooling.
- The *hot humid season* occurs in July and August. In addition to high insulation, it is characterized by high dew point temperatures (above 55°F), reducing the usefulness of evaporative cooling for comfort conditioning. Cloudiness and haze prevent nighttime thermal reradiation, resulting in only a 20°F or less daily range. Lowest nighttime temperatures are frequently higher than the comfort limits. Thus, refrigeration or dehumidification may be needed to meet comfort standards.
- The *winter season* typically has clear skies, cold nights, very low dew point temperatures, a daily range of nearly 40°F, and the opportunity for passively meeting all heating requirements from isolation.
- The *transitional* or *thermal sailing season* occurs before and after the winter season and requires no intervention by environmental control systems. This season can be extended by the passive features of the building. Other desert climates have similar seasons but in different proportions and at cooler scales.

CONSTRUCTION DETAILS

Capitalize on conditions climatic conditions by incorporating construction practices that respond in beneficial ways to the environment, including:

- Insulate coolant and refrigerant pipes from remote evaporative towers and condensers for their entire length.
- In hot locations, use roof construction similar to the cold climate roof detail.

- Do not use exposed wood (especially in small cross sections) and many plastics, as they deteriorate from excessive heat and high ultraviolet exposure.
- Although vapor retarders may not be critical to control condensation, implement them as a building wrap or wind shield, both to control dust penetration and to avoid convective leaks from high temperature differentials.
- Avoid thermal bridges such as extensive cantilevered slabs.
- Radiant barriers and details appropriate to humid overheated climates are at least as effective as vapor retarders, but avoid holes in assembly where convection would leak their thermal advantage.
- Ventilate building skin (attic or roof, walls) to relieve sol-air heat transfer.

DESIGNING FOR HUMID, OVERHEATED CLIMATES

Humid, overheated conditions are most severe along the Gulf Coast, but occur across the entire southeastern United States. Atmospheric moisture limits radiation exchange, resulting in daily temperature ranges less than 20°F. High insulation gives first priority to shading. Much of the overheated period is only a few degrees above comfort limits, so air movement can cool the body. Ground temperatures are generally too high for the Earth to be useful as a heat sink, although slab-on-grade floor mass is useful. The strategies are to resist solar and conductive heat gains and to take best advantage of ventilation.

Contributors:
Richard O. Anderson, PE, Somat Engineering, Taylor, Michigan; Eric K. Beach, Rippeteau Architects, PC, Washington DC; Stephen N. Flanders and Wayne Tobiasson, U.S. Army Corps of Engineers, Hanover, New Hampshire; Donald Watson, FAIA, Rensselaer Polytechnic Institute, Troy, New York; Kenneth Labs, New Haven, Connecticut; Jeffrey Cook, Arizona State University, Tempe, Arizona; K. Clark and P. Paylore, *Desert Housing: Balancing Experience and Technology for Dwelling in Hot Arid Zones,* Office of Arid Land Studies, University of Arizona, Tucson, Arizona, 1980. J. Cook, *Cool Houses for Desert Suburbs,* Arizona Solar Energy Commission, Phoenix, Arizona, 1984.

TYPICAL WALL SECTIONS FOR HOT, ARID CLIMATES
1.6

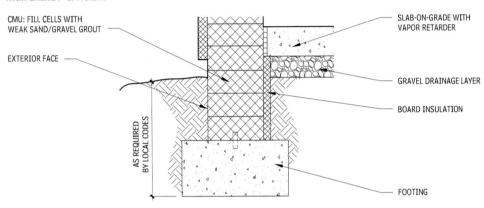

EXTERIOR FACE

SLAB-ON-GRADE WITH VAPOR RETARDER

GRAVEL DRAINAGE LAYER

AS REQUIRED BY LOCAL CODES

BOARD INSULATION

FOOTING

HIGH ENERGY-EFFICIENT

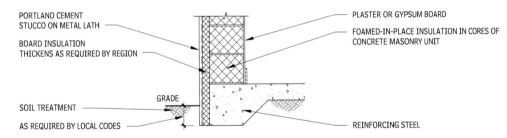

CMU: FILL CELLS WITH WEAK SAND/GRAVEL GROUT

SLAB-ON-GRADE WITH VAPOR RETARDER

EXTERIOR FACE

GRAVEL DRAINAGE LAYER

BOARD INSULATION

AS REQUIRED BY LOCAL CODES

FOOTING

ECONOMIC ENERGY-EFFICIENT

ENERGY-EFFICIENT WALL SECTION: VENTED SKIN MASONRY WALL WITH INSIDE INSULATION FOR HUMID, OVERHEATED CLIMATES
1.7

PORTLAND CEMENT STUCCO ON METAL LATH

PLASTER OR GYPSUM BOARD

BOARD INSULATION THICKENS AS REQUIRED BY REGION

FOAMED-IN-PLACE INSULATION IN CORES OF CONCRETE MASONRY UNIT

GRADE

SOIL TREATMENT

AS REQUIRED BY LOCAL CODES

REINFORCING STEEL

ENERGY-EFFICIENT WALL SECTION: VENTED SKIN WALL WITH RADIANT BARRIER FOR HUMID, OVERHEATED CLIMATES
1.8

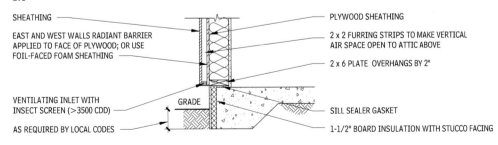

SHEATHING

PLYWOOD SHEATHING

EAST AND WEST WALLS RADIANT BARRIER APPLIED TO FACE OF PLYWOOD; OR USE FOIL-FACED FOAM SHEATHING

2 x 2 FURRING STRIPS TO MAKE VERTICAL AIR SPACE OPEN TO ATTIC ABOVE

2 x 6 PLATE OVERHANGS BY 2"

VENTILATING INLET WITH INSECT SCREEN (>3500 CDD)

GRADE

AS REQUIRED BY LOCAL CODES

SILL SEALER GASKET

1-1/2" BOARD INSULATION WITH STUCCO FACING

SEISMIC FOUNDATION ISSUES

INTRODUCTION TO SEISMIC DESIGN

According to the theory of plate tectonics, the Earth's crust is divided into constantly moving plates. Earthquakes occur when, as a result of slowly accumulating pressure, the ground slips abruptly along a geological fault plane on or near a plate boundary. The resulting waves of vibration within the Earth create ground motions at the surface, which, in turn, induce movement within buildings. The frequency, magnitude, and duration of the ground motion; physical characteristics of the building; and geology of a site determine how these forces affect a building.

DESIGN JUDGMENT

During a seismic event, buildings designed to the minimum levels required by model codes often sustain damage, even significant structural damage. Early discussions with an owner should explore the need to limit property loss in an earthquake, and the desirability of attempting to ensure continued building operation immediately afterward. To achieve these results, it may be necessary to make design decisions that are more carefully tuned to the seismic conditions of a site than the code requires.

The relationship between the period of ground motion and the period of building motion is of great importance to building design. Fundamental periods of motion in structures range from 0.1 second for a one-story building to 4.0 seconds or more for a high-rise building. Ground generally vibrates for a period of between 0.5 and 1.0 second. If the period of ground motion and the natural period of motion in a building coincide, the building may resonate, and the loads will be increased. Theoretically, one part of the seismic design solution is to "tune" the building so that its own period of motion falls outside the estimated range of ground motion frequency. In practice, this tuning is very seldom carried out. Rather, design professionals rely on increased load effects required by the applicable code to take care of the problem.

SEISMIC CODES

The building code adopted in most jurisdictions in the United States is International Building Code (IBC). There are some significant changes to the seismic forces determined by this code compared to seismic forces determined by previous building codes. The IBC 2006 code seismic provisions are designed around a level of earthquake that is expected to be exceeded only 2 percent of the time in the next 50 years. The level of seismic design for most structures, per the IBC, is based on a "collapse protection" strategy (commonly referred to as a "life safety" level), which assumes that there may be significant damage to the structure up to the point of collapse but that the structure does not collapse.

The structural engineer will design a lateral force-resisting structural assembly to resist a design-level earthquake. These designs are developed from detailed maps that indicate the ground spectral accelerations of buildings, which are based upon known past seismic events, in combination with probability studies. These maps typically include known fault locations, which help to determine the distance of the building from any known fault. The ground accelerations can typically be found down to the county level in the United States. The geotechnical engineer works with the design team to develop the site coefficient, which is dependent on the local soils layers and depths.

The following information is based on the requirements in the IBC 2006 Building Code, which in turn is based on the 2000 National Earthquake Hazards Reduction Program (NEHRP). Detached one- and two-family dwellings are exempt from seismic regulations in areas other than those with high seismicity. (Note: Seismic codes are constantly evolving, so consult the applicable code before beginning a project.)

Contributors:
Donald Watson, FAIA, Rensselaer Polytechnic Institute, Troy, New York; Kenneth Labs, New Haven, Connecticut; Subrato Chandra, Philip W. Fairey, Michael M. Houston, and Florida Solar Energy Center, *Cooling with Ventilation*, Solar Energy Research Institute, Golden, Colorado. 1982.; K. E. Wilkes, *Radiant Barrier Fact Sheet*, CAREIRS, Silver Spring, Maryland; P. Fairey, S. Chandra, A. Kerestecioglu, *Ventilative Cooling in Southern Residences: A Parametric Analysis*, PF-108-86, Florida, Solar Energy Center, Cape Canaveral, Florida 1986; William W. Stewart, FAIA, Stewart-Schaberg Architects, Clayton, Missouri.

MAIN CAUSES OF FOUNDATION FAILURE
1.9

GROUND RUPTURE   **GROUND SHAKING**   **DIFFERENTIAL SUBSIDENCE**   **LIQUEFACTION**

FUNDAMENTAL PERIODS
1.10

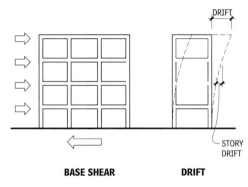

FREQUENCY

MAGNITUDE

SEISMIC GROUND MOTION

0.10   0.50   1-2   4
PERIOD OF BUILDING MOTION

SEISMIC ACCELERATION FOR LOW BUILDINGS EXPRESSED AS A PERCENTAGE OF GRAVITY
1.11

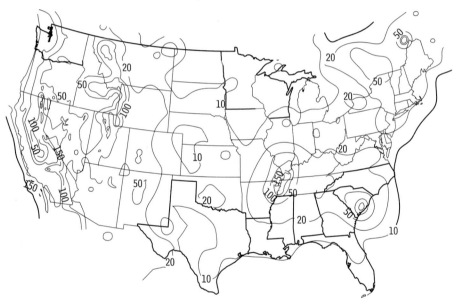

Source: Map courtesy of the U.S. Geological Survey, National Seismic Hazard Mapping Project (June 1996)

TERMS

The seismic community has an extensive set of terms that describe common conditions in the field. Here is a short list of these terms and their definitions:

- *Base shear (static analysis)*: Calculated total shear force acting at the base of a structure, used in codes as a static representation of lateral earthquake forces. Also referred to as *equivalent lateral force*.

BASE SHEAR AND DRIFT
1.12

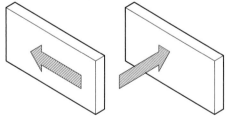

DRIFT

STORY DRIFT

BASE SHEAR   **DRIFT**

- *Design earthquake*: Earthquake ground motion for which a building is designed. This is typically about two-thirds of the maximum considered earthquake (MCE) (defined below) when designing per the IBC codes.
- *Drift and story drift*: Lateral deflection of a building or structure. Story drift is the relative movement between adjacent floors.
- *Ductility*: The ability of a structural frame to bend, but not break. Ductility is a major factor in establishing the ability of a building to withstand large earthquakes. Ductile materials (steel, in particular) fail only after permanent deformation has taken place. Good ductility requires special detailing of the joints.
- *Dynamic analysis*: A structural analysis based on the vibration motion of a building. Dynamic analysis is time-consuming, and normally reserved for complex projects.
- *Forces, in-plane*: Forces exerted parallel to a wall or frame.
- *Forces, out-of-plane*: Forces exerted perpendicular to a wall or frame.

FORCE DIAGRAMS
1.13

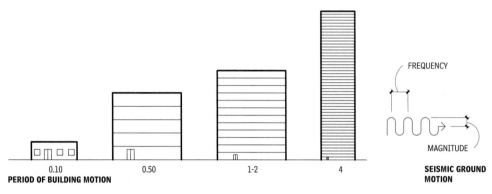

IN-PLANE   **OUT-OF-PLANE**

- *Maximum considered earthquake (MCE)*: The greatest ground-shaking expected to occur during an earthquake at a site. These values are somewhat higher than those of the design earthquake, particularly in areas where seismic events are very infrequent. The code maps are based on earthquakes of this magnitude.
- *Reentrant corner*: The inside building corner of an L-, H-, X-, or T-shaped plan.

ESTABLISHING SEISMIC FORCES

The equivalent lateral force procedure is the most common method used to determine seismic design forces. In it, the seismic load, V (base shear), is determined by multiplying the weight of the build-

Contributors:
Donald Watson, FAIA, Rensselaer Polytechnic Institute, Troy, New York; Kenneth Labs, New Haven, Connecticut; Subrato Chandra, Philip W. Fairey, Michael M. Houston, and Florida Solar Energy Center, *Cooling with Ventilation,* Solar Energy Research Institute, Golden, Colorado. 1982.; K. E. Wilkes, *Radiant Barrier Fact Sheet,* CAREIRS, Silver Spring, Maryland; P. Fairey, S. Chandra, A. Kerestecioglu, *Ventilative Cooling in Southern Residences: A Parametric Analysis,* PF-108-86, Florida, Solar Energy Center, Cape Canaveral, Florida 1986; William W. Stewart, FAIA, Stewart-Schaberg Architects, Clayton, Missouri.

ing by a factor of Cs ($V = C_s W$). The value of C_s depends on the size of the design earthquake, the type of soil, the period of the building, the importance of the building, and the response-modification factor (a variable that accounts for different levels of ductility for different types of lateral force-resisting systems used). This force is applied at the base of the structure then is distributed vertically throughout the building according to the mass, and horizontally throughout the building according to the stiffness of the lateral elements of the structure (for a "rigid" diaphragm), or according to tributary width of the lateral elements of the structure (for a "flexible" diaphragm).

DESIGN FOR RESISTING SEISMIC FORCES AND FOUNDATION ISSUES

A design that resists seismic forces for a structure makes use of the lateral systems' ductility. Such ductile lateral systems are designed to deflect more under seismic loading than what would be expected from something such as wind loading. This allows for the use of smaller effective seismic design forces and more reasonably sized members. It is important, however, that the overall design still be capable of handling the expected deflections. Story drifts that are too large can result in secondary forces and stresses for which the structure was not designed, as well as increase the damage to the interior and exterior building components, and hinder the means of egress from the building.

Typical means of resisting these forces include the use of moment frames, shear walls, and braced frames. Each of these types of lateral systems can be made up of one of the main structural materials (such as steel or reinforced concrete moment frames; masonry, wood, or reinforced concrete shear walls; or steel or reinforced concrete-braced frames). The building configuration and design parameters will have a major effect on which system to chose and, subsequently, the lateral system chosen will have a major impact on the foundations required to resist the loads.

Moment frames typically are distributed more evenly over the building footprint and have little or no uplift; they also generally have large base moments that can be difficult to resist. In addition, moment frames will tend to have greater lateral deflections than other stiffer systems (such as shear walls or braced frames). Concrete shear walls and steel-braced frames are more localized, not only concentrating lateral shear at the base but also having a high potential for net uplift forces to be resisted. These forces are difficult to resist with some foundation systems and should be reviewed extensively before selecting the lateral load-resisting system.

Tall, narrow structures tend to have overturning issues before they will face sliding issues, whereas short structures face sliding problems rather than overturning problems. Seismic motion rocks the building, increasing overturning loads, and can act in any direction. Thus, resistance to overturning is best achieved at a building's perimeter, rather than at its core.

Building foundations must be designed to resist the lateral forces transmitted through the earth and the forces transmitted from the lateral load-resisting system to the earth. In general, softer soils amplify seismic motion.

SHEAR WALLS AND DIAPHRAGMS
1.14

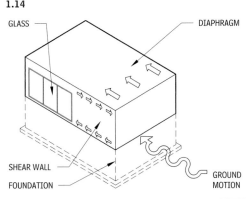

OUT-OF-PLANE VERTICAL OFFSETS
1.15

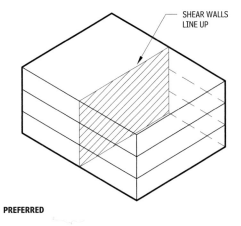

SHEAR WALLS LINE UP

PREFERRED

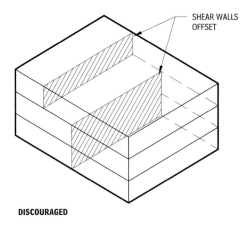

SHEAR WALLS OFFSET

DISCOURAGED

TORSION IN PLAN
1.16

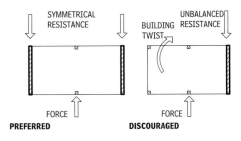

SYMMETRICAL RESISTANCE

UNBALANCED RESISTANCE

BUILDING TWIST

FORCE

FORCE

PREFERRED   **DISCOURAGED**

REENTRANT CORNERS
1.17

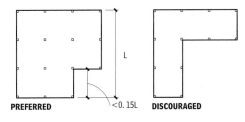

L

<0.15L

PREFERRED   **DISCOURAGED**

MASS IRREGULARITY
1.18

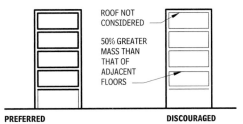

ROOF NOT CONSIDERED

50% GREATER MASS THAN THAT OF ADJACENT FLOORS

PREFERRED   **DISCOURAGED**

SOFT STORY
1.19

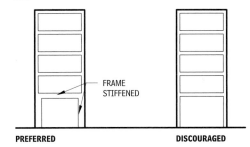

FRAME STIFFENED

PREFERRED   **DISCOURAGED**

IN-PLANE DISCONTINUITY
1.20

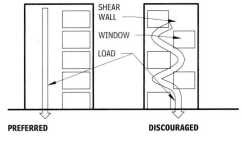

SHEAR WALL

WINDOW

LOAD

PREFERRED   **DISCOURAGED**

NOTES

1.16 The lateral force-resisting system for a symmetrical building is much easier to design than that for an asymmetrical building. Because the source of an earthquake cannot be known, symmetry in both directions should be considered.
1.17 This is a variation of the symmetry issue. When the notch gets too big, the building tends to tear at the inside corner.
1.18 Not all floors have to be the same; nevertheless, it is important that no floor has much more mass than those adjacent.
1.19 When a taller (inherently softer) first floor is desired, anticipate

using much heavier first-floor framing to equalize the stiffness with that of the floors above.
1.20 Although both drawings illustrate shear walls in the same plane, one arrangement is discouraged because the load path is not direct.

Contributor:
William W. Stewart, FAIA, Stewart-Schaberg Architects, Clayton, Missouri; Scott Maxwell, PE, SE, Adrian, Michigan.

FOUNDATION STRATEGIES FOR HIGH-SEISMIC LOADS

UPLIFT

Braced buildings typically end up with high-tension loads at the foundations. Shallow foundations are difficult to design with high-tension loads. Some strategies are available to resist these uplift forces:

- Increase the dead load by removing adjacent columns, increasing the tributary area.
- Deepen the footing, increasing the soil load.
- Increase the footing dimensions, to increase the soil and concrete loads.
- Decrease column spacing, to decrease the brace forces.
- Change the foundation type (typically, to a deep foundation that can resist the uplift more effectively).

SHEAR

Braces and shear walls tend to collect the lateral forces and concentrate the loads in a few locations. Shallow and deep foundations have limited lateral load-resisting capability. By combining several foundations together, it is possible to effectively increase the lateral load resistance. The concrete tie beams are typically designed to distribute the lateral loads through tension or compression of the beam.

**BRACE WITH UPLIFT
1.21**

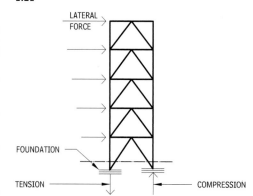

FOUNDATIONS

GENERAL

Foundations, because they are hidden below the surface, are often overlooked and their importance minimized by the design team. A great deal of scientifically guided creativity is often necessary to produce a foundation that supports the loads of the structure in such a way as to economically maintain the aesthetics and function of a facility. The wide variety of soil types and conditions across the United States—from the bedrock near the surface in New York to the sink holes and coral in Florida to the deep soft clays in the Midwest and South, and expansive soils in the Southwest to the seismically active areas of the country such as the West Coast—pose a challenge to the design team. The most popular and economical foundation solution is the spread footing. Spread footings are typically shallow, simple to design and construct, and perform well under many conditions. When properly designed, load is spread from a column to the soil at a bearing pressure that causes neither excessive settlement nor failure of the soil.

Should the soil conditions near the surface be weak, poorly compacted, filled with debris or organic material, or too compressible, deep foundations are warranted. The effect is to extend the foundation through the weak strata to a soil type that can withstand the loadings with tolerable settlement. Deep foundations come in several types and, depending on the soil conditions, may include driven piles, bored piles (bored, augered or drilled) or caissons. Deep foundations resist imposed loads either by end bearing or side friction or some combination. It is not necessary to drive or drill a deep foundation to rock, only to the depth required to reach a suitable stratum.

A spread footing is not always appropriate, such as when the property line limits the extent of the foundation in one direction, or when the soil conditions are very weak and suitable soil strata too deep to reach with a deep foundation. In these cases, other types of special foundations (such as combined footings, strap footings, and raft foundations) are sometimes required.

Two basic criteria should be met for all foundations:

- *Soil strength (bearing capacity)*: The ability of a soil to support a load without experiencing failure is known as the bearing capacity and is a function of the foundation size as well as the inherent strength properties of the soil. If the pressures exerted by a foundation exceed the strength of a soil, the soil mass experiences a shear failure leading to gross movements of both the soil and the supporting foundation element.
- *Limitations of settlement*: Settlement can happen either immediately (foundations on sands), or over period of time, short or long term (foundations on clays). Some settlement is expected, over various parts of the country, typical and acceptable settlement is usually less then 1 in. Settlement is not as important with a solitary structure, but becomes more important when: (1) buildings adjacent to an existing structure need to be interconnected, (2) long utility runs need to be connected to the structure, or (3) there is sensitive equipment in the building. Uniform settlement is somewhat better tolerated than differential settlement that is uneven across several columns. Differential settlement distorts the structure and causes cracking of the exterior skin and interior partitions, broken windows, and doors that don't open. Allowable differential settlement may be dependant on the material of the skin and structure; for example, brick and concrete masonry buildings tolerate less differential settlement than curtain wall buildings. Differential settlement of 1/4 in. is typically considered tolerable for most building types.

The importance of proper foundation design and detailing cannot be overemphasized. Working with the geotechnical engineer, familiar with the soil conditions in the area, and a structural engineer, familiar with the proposed design and detailing of the foundation, will help ensure the building functions as intended for its life cycle.

SETTLEMENT AND DIFFERENTIAL SETTLEMENT

Often, settlement governs the allowable bearing pressure, which is set at an intensity that will yield a settlement within tolerable levels for the building type. Allowable settlement is typically building and use-specific. Total and differential settlement, as well as the time rate of the occurrence of the settlement, must be considered when evaluating whether the settlement is tolerable. For example, in the case of a conventional steel frame structure, in typical practice a total maximum settlement of 1 in. is usually acceptable, and differential settlement of one-half of the total settlement is also usually tolerable.

ANGULAR DISTORTION

Settlement tolerance is commonly referred to in terms of angular distortion in the building or settlement between columns. Typically, an angular distortion of 1:480 is used for conventional structures. This equates to 1 in. in 480 in., or 1 in. in 40 ft. Depending on the type of structure, the allowable angular distortion might vary from 1:240 for a flexible structure (such as a wood frame, single-story structure) to 1:1000 for a more "brittle" or sensitive structure.

EFFECTS OF SOIL TYPES

When load is applied to granular soils, the grains of soil are able to respond almost immediately, and they will densify as the packing of the grains becomes tighter.

Clay soils exhibit a time-dependent relationship associated with the consolidation of the clay soil. In order for the clay to consolidate, and the overlying soil or structure to settle, the excess pressures that are induced in the water in the clay must dissipate, and this takes time because of the low permeability of the clay. Depending on the drainage characteristics of the clay, the time required for 90 percent of the consolidation (and settlement) to occur may vary from a few months to several years. If there is a high frequency of sand layers or seams within the clay mass, then the consolidation will be quicker, because the excess pore water pressure can be dissipated faster.

Both sand and clay soils have a built-in "memory" that, in effect, remember the maximum load that was applied to the soil at some time in the past. This memory is referred to as the *preconsolidation pressure*. If 10 ft of soil has been removed (by excavation or erosion) from a soil profile then the equivalent weight of that 10 ft of soil (approximately 1250 lbs per square foot) could be reapplied to the soil profile without the soil below sensing any difference. Depending on the process that deposited the soil, weathering processes, past climatological changes, or human activities, the preconsolidation pressure of the soil may be far in excess of the pressures induced by the current soil profile. When that is the case, settlement of conventional structures is rarely a significant concern. But when the soil has not been preconsolidated, the addition of any new load may result in excessive settlement.

Contributor:
James W. Niehoff, PE, Chief Engineer, PSI, Wheat Ridge, Colorado.

MINIMUM SPECIFIED COMPRESSIVE STRENGTH AT 28 DAYS F'C, AND MAXIMUM SLUMP OF CONCRETE
1.22

| | WEATHERING PROBABILITY | | | |
| | NEGLIGIBLE | MODERATE | SEVERE | MAXIMUM |
TYPE OF LOCATION OF CONCRETE CONSTRUCTION	f'$_c$ PSI	f'$_c$ PSI	f'$_c$ PSI	SLUMP (IN.)
Type 1: Walls and foundations not exposed to weather; interior slabs-on-ground, not including garage floor slabs.	2500	2500	2500	6
Type 2: Walls, foundations, and other concrete work exposed to weather, except as noted in Type 3.	2500	3000	3000	6
Type 3: Driveways, curbs, walk-ways, ramps, patios, porches, steps, and stairs exposed to weather and garage floors, slabs.	2500	3500	4500	5

Source: Based on ACI 332 *Requirements for Residential Concrete Construction and Commentary*, Table 4.1, Reprinted with permission of the American Concrete Institute.

AIR CONTENT FOR TYPE 2 AND TYPE 3 CONCRETE UNDER MODERATE OR SEVERE WEATHERING PROBABILITY
1.23

| NOMINAL MAXIMUM AGGREGATE SIZE (IN.) | AIR CONTENT (TOLERANCE ±0.015) | |
	MODERATE	SEVERE
3/8	0.06	0.075
1/2	0.055	0.07
3/4	0.05	0.07
1	0.045	0.06
1-1/2	0.045	0.055

Source: Based on ACI 332 *Requirements for Residential Concrete Construction and Commentary*, Table 4.2, Reprinted with permission of the American Concrete Institute.

FOOTING MINIMUM DIMENSIONAL REQUIREMENTS
1.24

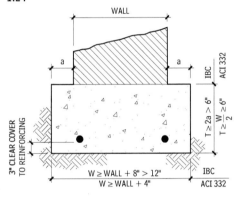

DOWEL AND KEYWAY REQUIREMENTS FOR FOOTINGS
1.25

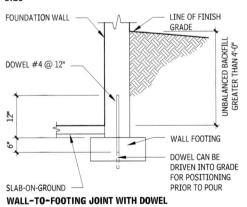

WALL-TO-FOOTING JOINT WITH DOWEL

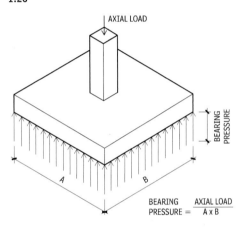

WALL-TO-FOOTING JOINT WITH KEYWAY

Source: Based on ACI 332 *Requirements for Residential Concrete Construction and Commentary*, Figures R6.5 and R 6.6. Reprinted with permission of the American Concrete Institute.

SHALLOW FOUNDATIONS

Shallow foundations are typically the most economical foundations to construct where soil and loading conditions permit. Coordination with local codes for frost depth and with the underground utilities is required. The thickness of the footing has to be coordinated with anchor bolt and dowel embedment. Typically, one layer of steel in the bottom of the footing is required to resist the bending of the footing caused by soil-bearing pressures.

AXIALLY LOADED SPREAD FOOTING
1.26

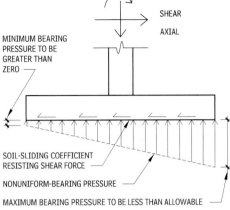

$$\text{BEARING PRESSURE} = \frac{\text{AXIAL LOAD}}{A \times B}$$

Axial loads are distributed in a uniform manner under the footing. The allowable bearing pressure necessary to resist the load determines footing size.

SPREAD FOOTING RESISTING MOMENT, SHEAR, AND AXIAL LOADS
1.27

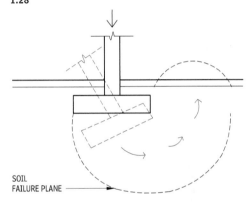

Axial loads, combined with shear and overturning forces can be resisted by spread footings. The combination of axial load and moment forces on the foundation need to be balanced to keep the calculated loads on the footing less than the allowable bearing pressure of the soil as determined by the geotechnical engineer.

SPREAD FOOTING SIZE LIMITATIONS
1.28

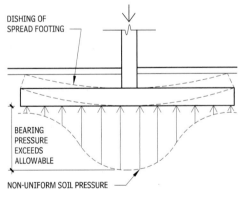

MINIMUM FOOTING WIDTHS TYPICALLY 3'-0" SQUARE

MAXIMUM FOOTING WIDTHS TYPICALLY 20'-0" SQUARE

Minimum sizes of spread footings are specified by the geotechnical engineer, to reduce the possibility of local soil failures by punching shear of an overall movement of soil mass. Maximum sizes of spread footings keep the nonuniform bearing pressure from becoming extreme and overstressing the soil.

NOTES

1.22 Maximum slump refers to the characteristics of the specified mixture proportion based on water cement ratio only. Midrange and high-range water-reducing admixtures can be used to increase the slump beyond these maximums.

1.23 American Concrete Institute (ACI) and International Building Code (IBC) have requirements for the minimum footing dimensions.

Contributor:
American Concrete Institute, www.concrete.org.

SPREAD FOOTING—CONCRETE COLUMN
1.29

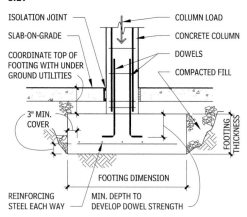

ISOLATION JOINT

SLAB-ON-GRADE

COORDINATE TOP OF FOOTING WITH UNDER GROUND UTILITIES

COLUMN LOAD

CONCRETE COLUMN

DOWELS

COMPACTED FILL

3" MIN. COVER

FOOTING THICKNESS

FOOTING DIMENSION

REINFORCING STEEL EACH WAY

MIN. DEPTH TO DEVELOP DOWEL STRENGTH

SPREAD FOOTING—STEEL COLUMN
1.30

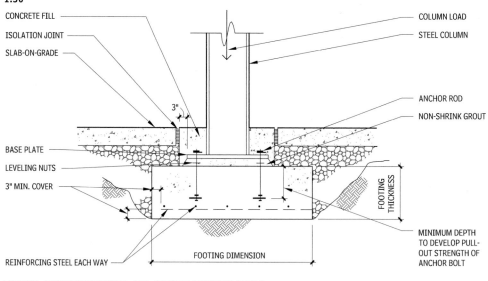

CONCRETE FILL

ISOLATION JOINT

SLAB-ON-GRADE

BASE PLATE

LEVELING NUTS

3" MIN. COVER

REINFORCING STEEL EACH WAY

COLUMN LOAD

STEEL COLUMN

ANCHOR ROD

NON-SHRINK GROUT

3"

FOOTING THICKNESS

FOOTING DIMENSION

MINIMUM DEPTH TO DEVELOP PULL-OUT STRENGTH OF ANCHOR BOLT

TYPICAL FOUNDATION WALL AND SPREAD FOOTING DETAIL
1.31

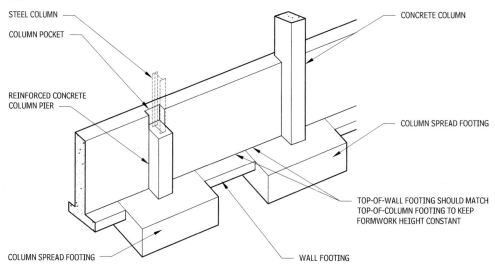

STEEL COLUMN

COLUMN POCKET

REINFORCED CONCRETE COLUMN PIER

CONCRETE COLUMN

COLUMN SPREAD FOOTING

TOP-OF-WALL FOOTING SHOULD MATCH TOP-OF-COLUMN FOOTING TO KEEP FORMWORK HEIGHT CONSTANT

COLUMN SPREAD FOOTING

WALL FOOTING

FOUNDATIONS AT GRADE
1.32

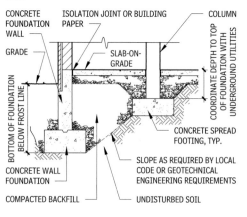

CONCRETE FOUNDATION WALL

GRADE

ISOLATION JOINT OR BUILDING PAPER

SLAB-ON-GRADE

COLUMN

COORDINATE DEPTH TO TOP OF FOUNDATION WITH UNDERGROUND UTILITIES

BOTTOM OF FOUNDATION BELOW FROST LINE

CONCRETE WALL FOUNDATION

COMPACTED BACKFILL

CONCRETE SPREAD FOOTING, TYP.

SLOPE AS REQUIRED BY LOCAL CODE OR GEOTECHNICAL ENGINEERING REQUIREMENTS

UNDISTURBED SOIL

FOUNDATIONS AT BASEMENT
1.33

FLOOR

COLUMN

GRADE

BASEMENT WALL

ISOLATION JOINT OR BUILDING PAPER

SLAB ON GRADE

CONCRETE WALL FOOTING

FOUNDATION DRAIN

COMPACTED BACKFILL

COORDINATE TOP OF FOOTING WITH UNDERGROUND UTILITIES

CONCRETE SPREAD FOOTING, TYP.

UNDISTURBED SOIL

NOTES

1.29 a. Soil below footing should not be disturbed after excavation.
b. Footing size based on allowable bearing pressure.
c. Thickness based on bending and shear requirements.
d. Reinforcing steel based on bending and minimum steel requirements.
e. Dowels as required to transfer load.
1.30 a. Provide concrete fill after all dead load has been applied to column.
b. Thickness of nonshrink grout to accommodate unevenness of footing surface and leveling nuts.
c. Anchor bolts designed to resist moments and shears from axial loads, as well as lateral loads.

Contributors:
Anthony L. Felder, Concrete Reinforcing Steel Institute, Schaumburg, Illinois; Kenneth D. Franch, AIA, PE, Phillips Swager Associates, Inc, Dallas, Texas; Donald Neubauer, PE, Neubauer Consulting Engineers, Potomac, Maryland; Mueser Rutledge Consulting Engineers, New York City, New York; SmithGroup, Architecture, Engineering, Interiors, Planning, Detroit, Michigan.

SPECIAL FOUNDATIONS

PILE TYPES
1.34

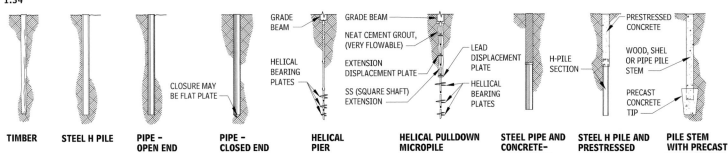

| TIMBER | STEEL H PILE | PIPE – OPEN END | PIPE – CLOSED END | HELICAL PIER | HELICAL PULLDOWN MICROPILE | STEEL PIPE AND CONCRETE-FILLED SHELL | STEEL H PILE AND PRESTRESSED CONCRETE | PILE STEM WITH PRECAST CONCRETE TIP |

TIMBER   STEEL   COMPOSITE

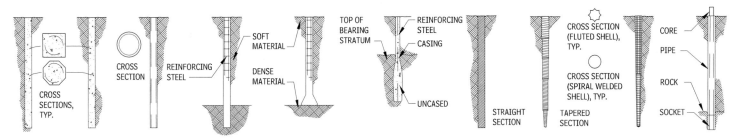

| PRECAST CONCRETE | PRESTRESSED CONCRETE | CYLINDER | DRILLED PIER WITH SOCKET | DRILLED PIER WITH BELL | MINIPILE | SHELL WITH MANDREL | SHELL, NO MANDREL | DRILLED CAISSON |

CONCRETE

GENERAL PILE DATA
1.35

PILE TYPE	MAXIMUM LENGTH (FT)	OPTIMUM LENGTH (FT)	SIZE (IN.)	MAXIMUM CAPACITY (TONS)	OPTIMUM LOAD RANGE (TONS)	USUAL SPACING
TIMBER						
Timber	110	45–65	5–10 tip; 12–20 butt	40	15–25	2'–6" to 3'–0"
STEEL						
Steel H pile	250	40–150	8–14	200	50–200	2'–6" to 3'–6"
Pipe—open end, concrete-filled	200	40–120	7–36	250	50–200	3'–0" to 4'–0"
Pipe—closed end, concrete-filled	200	30–80	10–30	200	50–70	3'–0" to 4'–0"
Shell—mandrel, concrete-filled; straight or taper	100	40–80	8–18	75	40–60	3'–0" to 3'–6"
Shell—no mandrel, concrete-filled	150	30–80	8–18	80	30–60	3'–0" to 3'–6"
Drilled caisson, concrete-filled	250	60–120	24–48	3500	1000–2000	6'–0" to 8'–0"
CONCRETE						
Precast concrete	100	40–50	10–24	100	40–60	3'–0"
Prestressed concrete	270	60–80	10–24	200	100–150	3'–0" to 3'–6"
Cylinder pile	220	60–80	36–54	500	250–400	6'–0" to 9'–0"
Drilled pier with socket	120	10–50	30–120	500	30–300	3'–0" to 8'–0"
Drilled pier with bell	120	25–50	30–120	500	30–200	6'–0"
Auger cast grout or CFA (Continuous Flight Auger) pile	120	40–80	12 - 40	500	75–150	3'–0"
Minipiles	200	25–70	2.5–7	100	5–40	2'–0" to 4'–0"
COMPOSITE						
Helical pier	120	20–70	1-1/2" sq. to 4-1/2 dia.	100	15–60	4'-0" to 15'–0"
Helical pulldown micropile	100	20–70	4" dia. to 7" dia.	150	20–80	4'-0" to 15'–0"
Concrete—pipe	180	60–120	10–23	150	40–80	3'–0" to 4'–0"
Steel H pile and prestressed concrete	200	100–150	20–24	200	120–150	3'–6" to 4'–0"
Pile stem with precast concrete tip	80	40	13–35 tip; 19–41 butt	180	30–150	4'–6"

DRILLED PIER WITH BELL
1.36

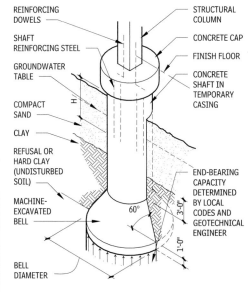

NOTES

1.35 a. Applicable material specifications: Concrete ACI 318; Timber ASTM D 25; Structural Sections ASTM A 36, A 572, and A 690. For selection of type of pile, consult a geotechnical engineer.
b. A mandrel is a member inserted into a hollow pile to reinforce the pile shell while it is driven into the ground.
c. Timber piles must be treated with wood preservative when any portion is above the groundwater table.
1.36 a. Test soils to determine their allowable bearing capacity.
b. "H" (depth of shaft reinforcing, below concrete cap) is the function of the passive resistance of the soil, generated by the moment applied to the pier cap.
c. Piers may be used under grade beams or concrete walls. For very heavy loads, pier foundations may be more economical than piles.

Contributors:
Mueser Rutledge Consulting Engineers, New York City, New York; John P. McCarthy, PE, SE, SmithGroup, Architects, Engineers, Interiors, Planners, Detroit, Michigan; AB Chance, Centralia, Missouri.

DRILLED PIER WITH SOCKET
1.37

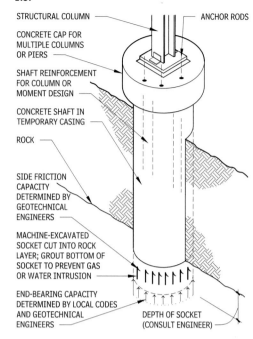

STRUCTURAL COLUMN

ANCHOR RODS

CONCRETE CAP FOR MULTIPLE COLUMNS OR PIERS

SHAFT REINFORCEMENT FOR COLUMN OR MOMENT DESIGN

CONCRETE SHAFT IN TEMPORARY CASING

ROCK

SIDE FRICTION CAPACITY DETERMINED BY GEOTECHNICAL ENGINEERS

MACHINE-EXCAVATED SOCKET CUT INTO ROCK LAYER; GROUT BOTTOM OF SOCKET TO PREVENT GAS OR WATER INTRUSION

END-BEARING CAPACITY DETERMINED BY LOCAL CODES AND GEOTECHNICAL ENGINEERS

DEPTH OF SOCKET (CONSULT ENGINEER)

CONSTRUCTION ISSUES WITH DRILLED PIERS
1.38

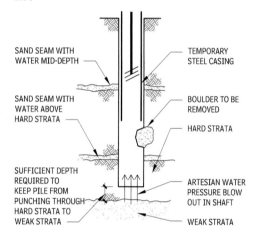

SAND SEAM WITH WATER MID-DEPTH

TEMPORARY STEEL CASING

SAND SEAM WITH WATER ABOVE HARD STRATA

BOULDER TO BE REMOVED

HARD STRATA

SUFFICIENT DEPTH REQUIRED TO KEEP PILE FROM PUNCHING THROUGH HARD STRATA TO WEAK STRATA

ARTESIAN WATER PRESSURE BLOW OUT IN SHAFT

WEAK STRATA

REINFORCING AXIALLY LOADED DRILLED PIERS
1.39

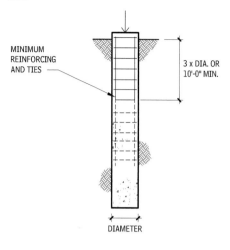

MINIMUM REINFORCING AND TIES

3 x DIA. OR 10'-0" MIN.

DIAMETER

DRILLED CONCRETE PIER

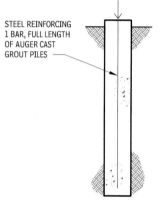

STEEL REINFORCING 1 BAR, FULL LENGTH OF AUGER CAST GROUT PILES

AUGER CAST GROUT PILE

PILE CAPS

Typically, more than one deep foundation element is required to resist the gravity and lateral loads; in order to distribute the loads from the single point column to the multiple foundation elements, a pile cap is required. Pile caps are thick, reinforced concrete blocks that distribute the load from the column to the foundations through a combination of flexure and shear.

Other applications of the pile caps include providing a method of connecting the columns to the foundations, and easing the construction tolerance issues that occur when installing deep foundations. These pile caps are designed and detailed to encase a small portion of the deep foundation, and transition to the column support elevation, thus providing a convenient location to position anchor bolts and column dowels.

PILE SUPPORTED FOUNDATIONS
1.40

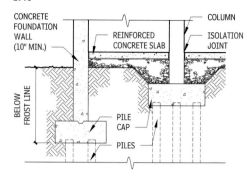

CONCRETE FOUNDATION WALL (10" MIN.)

REINFORCED CONCRETE SLAB

COLUMN

ISOLATION JOINT

BELOW FROST LINE

PILE CAP

PILES

SECTION

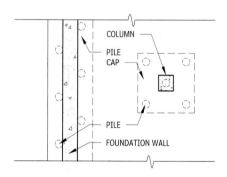

COLUMN

PILE CAP

PILE

FOUNDATION WALL

PLAN – INDIVIDUAL PILE CAPS

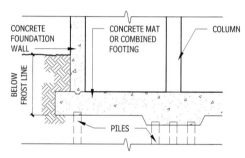

CONCRETE FOUNDATION WALL

CONCRETE MAT OR COMBINED FOOTING

COLUMN

BELOW FROST LINE

PILES

SECTION

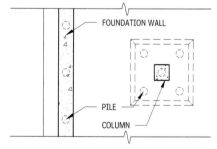

FOUNDATION WALL

PILE

COLUMN

PLAN – MAT OR COMBINED FOOTING PILE CAPS

NOTES

1.37 a. Set pier into a socket in rock to transmit high compression or tension lads into rock by side friction and end bearing.
b. Pier shaft should be poured in dry conditions if possible, but tremie pours can be used.

TYPICAL JOINT DETAILS
1.41

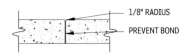

- 1/8" RADIUS
- PREVENT BOND

BUTT JOINT CONSTRUCTION JOINT

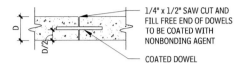

- 1/4" x 1/2" SAW CUT AND FILL FREE END OF DOWELS TO BE COATED WITH NONBONDING AGENT
- COATED DOWEL

BUTT-TYPE CONSTRUCTION JOINT WITH DOWELS

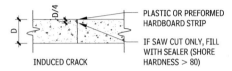

- PLASTIC OR PREFORMED HARDBOARD STRIP
- IF SAW CUT ONLY, FILL WITH SEALER (SHORE HARDNESS > 80)

INDUCED CRACK

SAWED OR PREMOLDED CONTRACTION JOINT

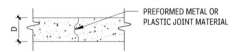

- PREFORMED METAL OR PLASTIC JOINT MATERIAL

TONGUE-AND-GROOVE JOINT

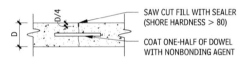

- SAW CUT FILL WITH SEALER (SHORE HARDNESS > 80)
- COAT ONE-HALF OF DOWEL WITH NONBONDING AGENT

CONTRACTION JOINT WITH DOWELS

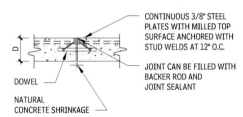

- CONTINUOUS 3/8" STEEL PLATES WITH MILLED TOP SURFACE ANCHORED WITH STUD WELDS AT 12" O.C.
- JOINT CAN BE FILLED WITH BACKER ROD AND JOINT SEALANT

DOWEL

NATURAL CONCRETE SHRINKAGE

TYPICAL ARMORED CONSTRUCTION JOINT DETAIL

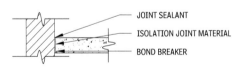

- JOINT SEALANT
- ISOLATION JOINT MATERIAL
- BOND BREAKER

ISOLATION JOINT

Source: Armored Construction Joint Detail based on ACI 302.1R *Guide for Concrete Floor Construction and Slab Construction*, Figure 3.15, reprinted with permission of the American Concrete Institute.

DIAMOND-SHAPED LOAD PLATES AT SLAB CORNER
1.42

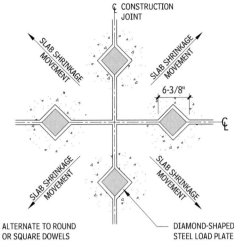

CONSTRUCTION JOINT

SLAB SHRINKAGE MOVEMENT

SLAB SHRINKAGE MOVEMENT

6-3/8"

SLAB SHRINKAGE MOVEMENT

SLAB SHRINKAGE MOVEMENT

ALTERNATE TO ROUND OR SQUARE DOWELS

DIAMOND-SHAPED STEEL LOAD PLATE

Source: Based on ACI 302.1R *Guide for Concrete Floor Construction and Slab Construction*, Figure 3.13, reprinted with permission of the American Concrete Institute.

DOWELED JOINT DETAIL FOR MOVEMENT PARALLEL AND PERPENDICULAR TO THE JOINT
1.43

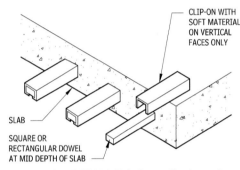

- CLIP-ON WITH SOFT MATERIAL ON VERTICAL FACES ONLY

SLAB

SQUARE OR RECTANGULAR DOWEL AT MID DEPTH OF SLAB

Source: Based on ACI 302.1R *Guide for Concrete Floor Construction and Slab Construction*, Figure 3.14, reprinted with permission of the American Concrete Institute.

FINISH AND FLOOR FLATNESS

In general, concrete floor slabs are monolithically finished by floating and troweling, to achieve a smooth and dense surface finish. ACI 302 provides guidance for appropriate finishing procedures to control achievable floor flatness. ACI 302, ACI 360, and ACI 117 provide guidance for flatness selection, as well as techniques by which flatness and levelness are produced and measured.

Floor finish tolerance is measured by placing a freestanding 10-ft straightedge on the slab surface, or by F-Numbers. The preferred method of measuring flatness and levelness is the F-Number System. Special finishes are available to improve appearance, as well as surface properties. These include sprinkled (shake) finishes or high-strength toppings, either as monolithic or separate surfaces.

TYPICAL ISOLATION JOINTS AT TUBE COLUMNS
1.44

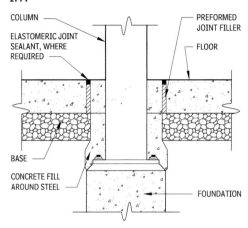

- COLUMN
- ELASTOMERIC JOINT SEALANT, WHERE REQUIRED
- PREFORMED JOINT FILLER
- FLOOR
- BASE
- CONCRETE FILL AROUND STEEL
- FOUNDATION

SECTION

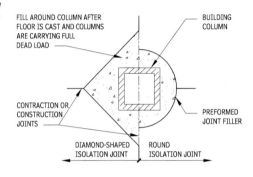

- FILL AROUND COLUMN AFTER FLOOR IS CAST AND COLUMNS ARE CARRYING FULL DEAD LOAD
- BUILDING COLUMN
- CONTRACTION OR CONSTRUCTION JOINTS
- PREFORMED JOINT FILLER
- DIAMOND-SHAPED ISOLATION JOINT
- ROUND ISOLATION JOINT

PLAN

Source: Based on ACI 302.1R *Guide for Concrete Floor Construction and Slab Construction*, Figure 3.3, reprinted with permission of the American Concrete Institute.

PROTECTIVE AND DECORATIVE COATINGS

Concrete surfaces may require a sealer or coating for the following:

- To protect against severe weather, chemicals, or abrasions.
- To prevent dusting of the surface layer.
- To harden the surface layer.
- To add a decorative finish.

Sealers are usually clear and are expected to penetrate the surface without leaving a visible film. Coatings are clear or opaque, and, though they may have some penetration, they leave a visible film on the surface. Sealers and coatings should allow vapor emission from the concrete but, at the same time, prevent moisture from penetrating after curing.

Decorative coatings usually protect as well, and are formulated in a wide selection of colors. Decorative coatings include the following:

- Water-based acrylic emulsion
- Elastomeric acrylic resin
- Liquid polymer stain
- Solvent-based acrylic stain
- Portland cement-based finish coating
- Water-based acidic stain (a solution of metallic salts)

NOTE

1.42 Alternate to round or square dowels.

Contributor:
American Concrete Institute, www.concrete.org.

BASEMENT CONSTRUCTION

BASEMENT EXCAVATION

TRENCHING

Trenches are narrow vertical cuts in soil used to place utilities and to construct continuous foundations. For short periods of time, many trenches may appear to be stable, but then collapse suddenly. Unsupported trenches can be dangerous to workers, as the early-warning signs of a trench collapse cannot be seen from the bottom of the trench. Moreover, in a narrow trench, there is nowhere to escape, if a sudden collapse of the trench wall occurs. And, because 1 to 2 cu ft of soil weighs as much as 100 to 250 lbs., even a relatively small collapse can severely injure or kill a worker. For safety purposes, therefore, OHSA requires trenches more than 5 ft deep be supported with shoring, or protected with a trench box, before allowing worker access.

TIMBER-BRACED TRENCH
1.45

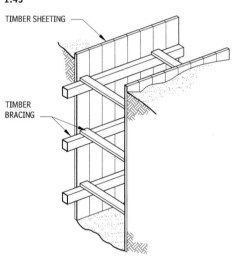

TIMBER SHEETING

TIMBER BRACING

HYRAULICALLY BRACED TRENCH
1.46

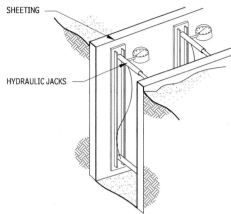

SHEETING

HYDRAULIC JACKS

TRENCH BOX
1.47

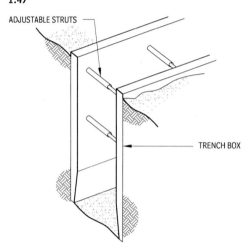

ADJUSTABLE STRUTS

TRENCH BOX

LATERAL SUPPORT

Walls that extend to depths of 10 to 15 ft can generally be self-supported or cantilevered and do not require additional lateral support. This is accomplished by extending the shoring sufficient depth below the excavation. These "cantilevered" walls resist the lateral pressures from the soil and groundwater, although some deflection at the top of the wall should be expected. However, walls that extend deeper or have significant surcharge loads, or where deflection is a concern, will require some type of additional lateral support (known as "braced walls").

INTERNAL SUPPORT

The lateral support can be internal to the excavation, in the form of wales, struts, or rakers. Internal bracing is very effective but interferes with the construction of the permanent structure.

INTERNALLY BRACED EXCAVATIONS
1.48

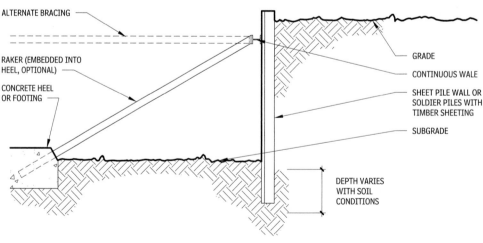

ALTERNATE BRACING

RAKER (EMBEDDED INTO HEEL, OPTIONAL)

CONCRETE HEEL OR FOOTING

GRADE

CONTINUOUS WALE

SHEET PILE WALL OR SOLDIER PILES WITH TIMBER SHEETING

SUBGRADE

DEPTH VARIES WITH SOIL CONDITIONS

RAKER BRACE

INTERNALLY BRACED EXCAVATION SCHEMES
1.49

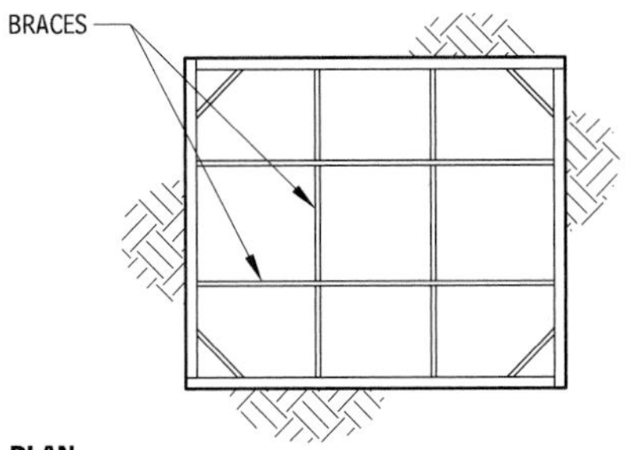

BRACES

PLAN

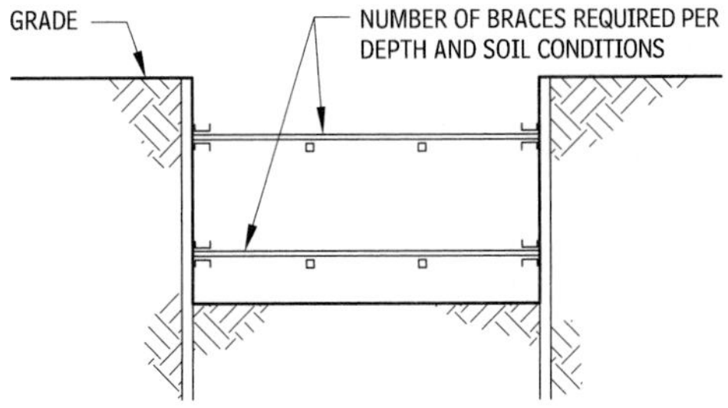

GRADE

NUMBER OF BRACES REQUIRED PER DEPTH AND SOIL CONDITIONS

SECTION

CROSS BRACING

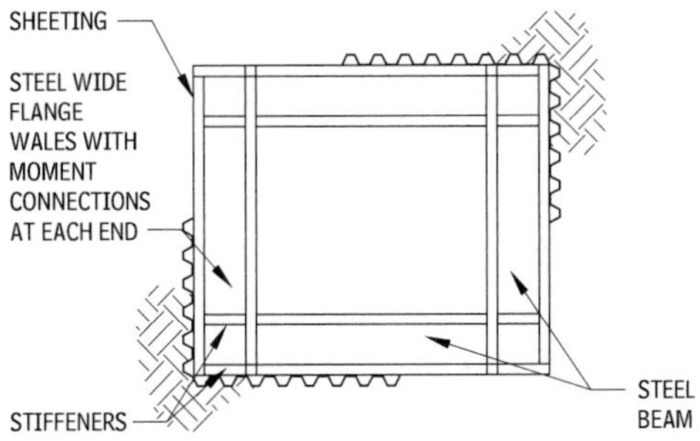

SHEETING

STEEL WIDE FLANGE WALES WITH MOMENT CONNECTIONS AT EACH END

STIFFENERS

STEEL BEAM

MOMENT-RESISTING FRAME

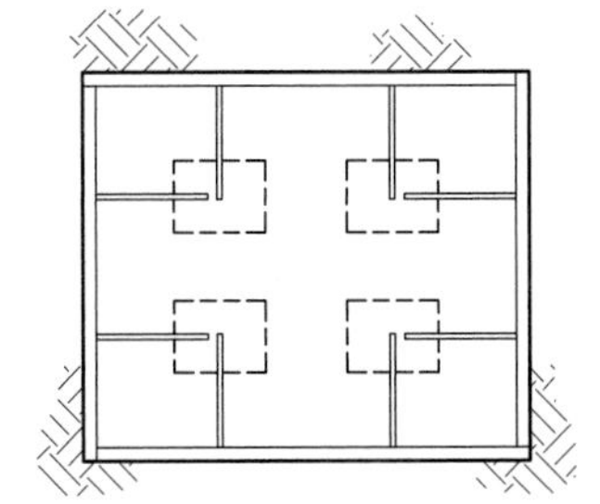

PLAN

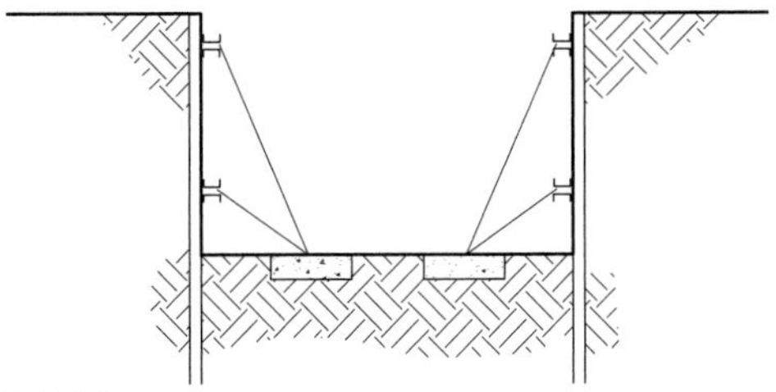

SECTION

RAKER – BRACING

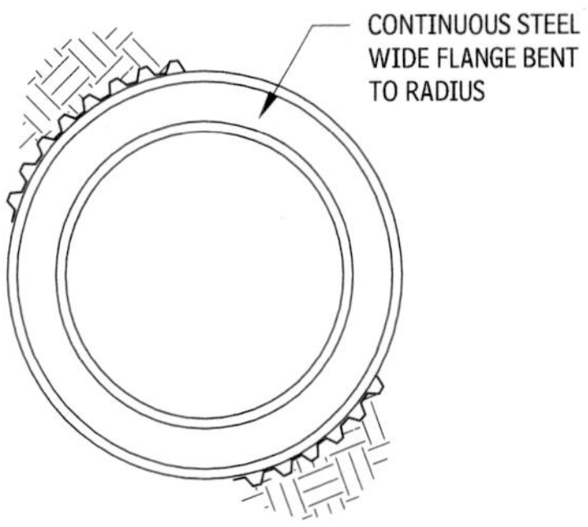

CONTINUOUS STEEL WIDE FLANGE BENT TO RADIUS

RING GIRDER

EXTERNAL SUPPORT

External bracing of the excavation is usually in the form of drilled tieback (ground) anchors. The use of tieback anchors to support the wall enables a clear and unencumbered excavation, but requires access to areas beyond the building, which may extend outside the property line. For this reason, tieback anchors are almost always the most desirable method of lateral support if the owner controls the property around the excavation, or if temporary easements can be obtained from private owners or public municipalities.

EXTERNALLY BRACED EXCAVATION DETAILS
1.50

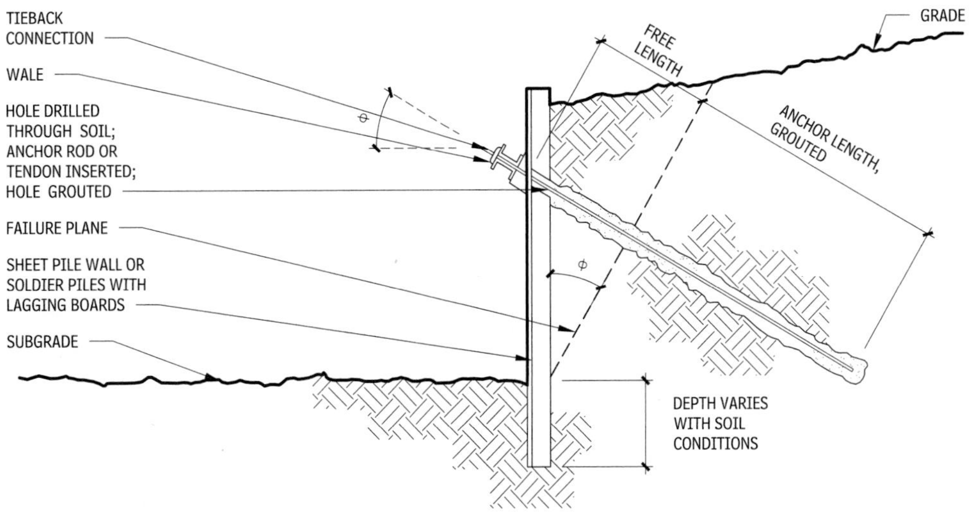

TIEBACK CONNECTION

WALE

HOLE DRILLED THROUGH SOIL; ANCHOR ROD OR TENDON INSERTED; HOLE GROUTED

FAILURE PLANE

SHEET PILE WALL OR SOLDIER PILES WITH LAGGING BOARDS

SUBGRADE

FREE LENGTH

GRADE

ANCHOR LENGTH, GROUTED

φ

DEPTH VARIES WITH SOIL CONDITIONS

EARTH ANCHOR BRACE

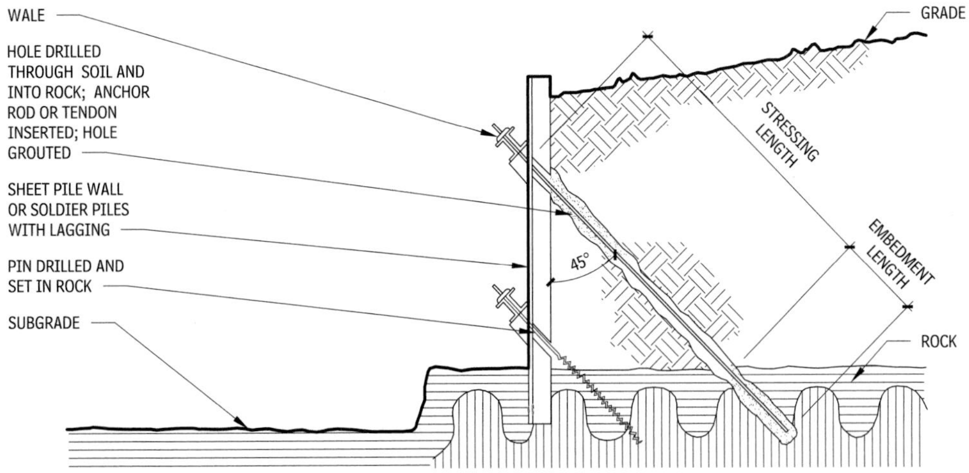

WALE

HOLE DRILLED THROUGH SOIL AND INTO ROCK; ANCHOR ROD OR TENDON INSERTED; HOLE GROUTED

SHEET PILE WALL OR SOLDIER PILES WITH LAGGING

PIN DRILLED AND SET IN ROCK

SUBGRADE

GRADE

STRESSING LENGTH

EMBEDMENT LENGTH

45°

ROCK

ROCK ANCHOR BRACE

EXTERNALLY BRACED EXCAVATION
1.51

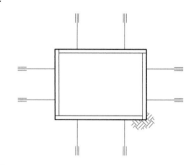

PLAN

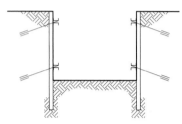

SECTION

TEMPORARY TIEBACK SECTION
1.52

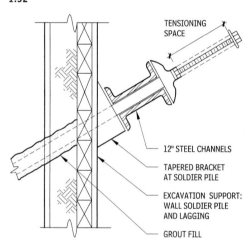

TENSIONING SPACE

12" STEEL CHANNELS

TAPERED BRACKET AT SOLDIER PILE

EXCAVATION SUPPORT: WALL SOLDIER PILE AND LAGGING

GROUT FILL

PERMANENT TIEBACK AT FOUNDATION WALL
1.53

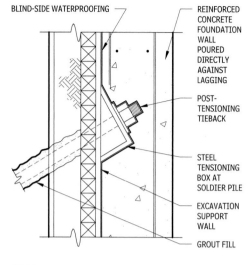

BLIND-SIDE WATERPROOFING

REINFORCED CONCRETE FOUNDATION WALL POURED DIRECTLY AGAINST LAGGING

POST-TENSIONING TIEBACK

STEEL TENSIONING BOX AT SOLDIER PILE

EXCAVATION SUPPORT WALL

GROUT FILL

SOIL STABILIZATION

Soil stabilization is sometimes called soil modification or soil conditioning. For deep excavations in very soft soils, the construction of earth support systems can be quite massive and expensive because of the higher lateral soil and hydrostatic pressures. Furthermore, in some situations, wall installation can be difficult to accomplish because of space requirements.

Various techniques have been developed to improve the effective strength or resistance of the soils around and below the excavations. Improving the in-situ soil strength or resistance reduces or eliminates the net pressure at the face of the excavation. The underground construction industry has developed the following techniques for improving or reinforcing soil.

SOIL-MIXING STABILIZATION
Soil mixing stabilization is the mixing the soils in the ground with asphalt, cement, lime, fly ash, or lime–fly ash to stabilize and strengthen the soil. Often, only a selected portion of soil mass must be treated to provide a significant increase in overall soil strength or resistance.

PRESSURE GROUTING SOIL STABILIZATION
Pressure grouting soil stabilization is the injection of cement or chemicals into the pores of the soil. Soil particles are then "glued" together to form a hardened solid mass of grouted soil. The spacing of the injection points and the grout mixture is varied to achieve a specific pattern and grout coverage, depending on the requirements of the project.

GROUND FREEZING
Ground freezing uses the natural moisture in the soil and artificial cooling methods to freeze and harden the soil. The ambient temperature of nearly all soil is above freezing (except for permafrost regions). Lowering the soil temperature to below freezing causes the water in the pores of the soil to freeze and "cement" the soil particles together. This results in a very hard, impermeable condition. However, soil has a relatively low thermal conductivity. Liquid Nitrogen may be used to freeze the soil in a timely manner. A continual flow of a brine solution through a series of embedded refrigeration pipes must be used to maintain the soil in a frozen state.

SOIL NAILING
Soil nailing is a method used for both temporary excavation bracing and for permanent retaining walls. This technique employs closely spaced, high-strength steel anchors grouted into the soil, and may include a reinforced shotcrete facing. The major advantages of soil nail wall construction over more traditional excavation bracing methods include relatively low cost and the ability to con-

struct the wall system from the top down, as the excavation proceeds. A typical installation sequence for grouted soil nailing is as follows:

1. Excavation begins by exposing a cut about 3 to 5 ft in depth.
2. A borehole (typically 4 to 6 in. in diameter) is drilled into the face of the excavation at a downward angle of approximately 15° to the horizontal. The length of the borehole is dependent on the height of the cut and the nature of the material exposed in the excavation. Typical lengths range from 60 to 70 percent of the wall height.
3. A high-strength, threaded reinforcing bar is inserted into the borehole, then the borehole is grouted to the excavation face.
4. After the grout has cured, a wire mesh is placed over the exposed face of the cut, and reinforcement is placed to span over the borehole and reinforcing bar. When groundwater is a concern, a geosynthetic drainage mat is typically placed against the soil face to intercept water and direct it to the base of the wall.
5. The exposed excavation face is sprayed with shotcrete, typically 8 to 10 in. thick.
6. A bearing plate is fitted over the reinforcing bar, and a nut is screwed into place to tension the soil nail.
7. If the method is to be used as a permanent wall, a second application of shotcrete is used to cover the soil nail head and bearing plate.
8. After completion of the first level, the excavation extends downward an additional 4 to 6 ft, and the process is repeated.

SLOPE STABILITY WITH SOIL NAILS
1.54

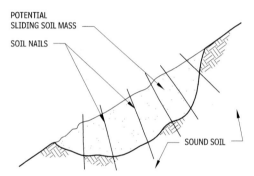

POTENTIAL SLIDING SOIL MASS

SOIL NAILS

SOUND SOIL

EXCAVATION SUPPORT WITH SOIL NAILS
1.55

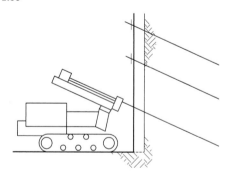

SOIL NAIL WALL DETAIL
1.56

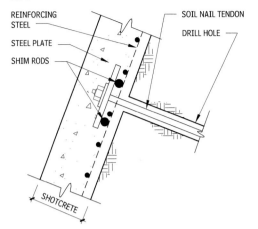

MOISTURE-DENSITY RELATIONSHIP
1.57

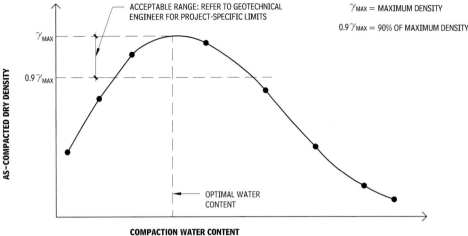

BACKFILL AND COMPACTION

FILL AND BACKFILL

Fill is typically used to raise or level site grades. Backfill is used to fill in spaces around below-grade structural elements, such as around basement walls, The fill must have sufficient strength or resistance and low compressibility to support its own weight and any other overlying structures pavements, floor slabs, foundations, etc.) without excessive settlement. When soils are excavated, they become loosened and disturbed. If they are suitable for reuse as structural fill or backfill, the soils must be placed in thin layers and compacted to achieve the required strength, resistance and stability.

COMPACTION

Compaction is the process by which mechanical energy is applied to a soil to increase its density. The degree to which soil can be densified depends on the amount and type of compactive effort, type of soil, and moisture content. Soil is made up of solids and the void spaces between the solid particles. The void space almost always contains some water. If the water completely fills the void, the soil is considered to be totally saturated. During compaction, the total volume of the soil is decreased by reducing the volume of voids, while the volume of solids remains essentially unchanged. If the soil is saturated or nearly saturated during compaction, water must be expelled to decrease the void space.

MOISTURE-DENSITY RELATIONSHIP

Nearly all soil exhibits a defined moisture-density relationship for a specific level of compactive effort.

These relationships can be graphed in a nearly bell-shaped curve, with the maximum density at the apex, corresponding to the *optimum moisture content.*

Standard laboratory tests, such as the Standard Proctor (ASTM D 698) and Modified Proctor (ASTM D 1557), use a standard-size mold and a specific level of compactive energy to develop the moisture density curve for a specific soil. The maximum density from these curves defines the 100 percent level of compaction for a given soil. Compaction requirements for fill and backfill are generally specified as a percentage of the maximum density, typically between 90 to 95 percent, as determined using one of the standard laboratory tests mentioned above. The low and high moisture contents are usually represented as a horizontal line connecting opposite sides of the Proctor curve for a given density. This represents the range of moisture content within which the soil can be compacted most readily.

FIELD DENSITY TESTS

Field density tests are performed on compacted soil to verify that a specific level of compaction has been achieved. There are several methods for determining the in-place density of soil. Today, the most commonly used method involves the nuclear density gauge, a device that measures the reflection of atomic particles from a tiny radioactive source material to determine the soil density and moisture content. The test is performed at the surface without any excavation, and results can be obtained faster than with other test methods.

MOISTURE CONTROL

Moisture content of the fill and backfill should be near the optimum moisture content. Otherwise, the minimum required field density is very difficult (or impossible) to obtain, no matter how much energy is used for compaction. If the soil is too wet, the water in the pores cannot be expelled fast enough to allow for a sufficient decrease in volume. If the soil is too dry, the capillary forces around the soil particles are too large to be broken down by the compactive energy. Therefore, controlling the moisture of the fill and backfill to within specific limits near the optimum moisture content is necessary to achieve the required level of compaction.

SOIL TYPE AND COMPACTION EQUIPMENT

To be most effective, the compaction equipment must match the type of soil to be compacted. In general, compaction equipment can be divided into two basic groups: rollers or plates. Rollers come in large variations in size, but all use a weighted wheel or drum to impart energy to the soil. In addition, some rollers use an electric rotor to vibrate the drum, thereby increasing the energy to the soil. Other drums have protrusions called *sheepsfoots,* which impart a kneading action to the soils. Some plate compactors also use vibratory energy to compact the soils, while other plate compactors, called *tampers*, move up and down, imparting a vertical dynamic load to the soil.

In general, coarse-grained granular soils such as sands and gravels are more easily compacted than fine-grained soils such as clays and clayey silts. Vibratory energy is very effective in densifying sands and gravels, since the interparticle bonds are relatively weak. When the granular soils are vibrated at the correct frequency, the soil particles rearrange themselves into a denser state under their own weight and the weight of the compactor. Vibratory steel drum rollers and vibratory plate compacters are considered the most effective compaction equipment for granular soils.

Fine-grained soils hold more moisture and have higher internal interparticle forces. Vibratory energy is much less effective for these soils. Clayey soils require more mechanical energy to break down the internal forces during compaction. The kneading action of a sheepsfoot roller is very effective in this regard.

Fine-grained soils generally have a narrower range of moisture contents for optimum compaction. Often, the clayey soils are too wet to compact and the moisture content must be reduced. Reducing the moisture content in clay is typically done by allowing water to evaporate from the surface of the clay. The rate of evaporation is dependent on the ambient air temperature and wind conditions. However, the drying process can be enhanced by using a process called *aeration* in which steel discs are used to periodically turn the soil, thus exposing more of the soil to the atmosphere.

BASEMENT WALLS

Basement walls may be constructed of various materials, including, concrete, masonry, and wood.

BASEMENT WALL CONSTRUCTION

CONCRETE BASEMENT WALLS

Concrete basement walls may be either cast-in-place or precast. Cast-in-place concrete basement walls provide a cost-effective means of supporting a floor and resisting soil pressures. Commercial and residential applications of cast-in-place concrete basement walls are prevalent. Forms are easily placed in the excavation on the footings. Reinforcing steel may be tied on or off-site, and is placed within the wall formwork. Depending on the soil and groundwater conditions, dampproofing should typically be used on foundations walls and waterproofing is generally required on basement walls prior to backfilling. Unless lateral bracing is utilized, the top of the basement wall must be supported by the first floor and the base of the wall by the footing or slab-on-grade before backfilling against the wall can begin. Keeping the wall heights uniform, as well as reducing the number of penetrations and maintaining a simple plan configuration, will help reduce the final cost of the wall.

Precast concrete basement walls enable basement construction in less time than conventional cast-in-place concrete. In addition to time and construction methods other advantages of precast concrete include the ability of the precast supplier to utilize concrete admixtures that focus on ultimate strength, rather than cure time and temperature. Precast concrete manufacturers are able to produce mixes that cure to 5000 psi, which is stronger than concrete unit masonry or cast-in-place concrete walls. Additionally, better control of the concrete mixture and curing environment allows the use of low water/cement ratios, which results in a dense material that reduces water penetration.

NOTE

1.57 Reinforcing is based on unbraced backfill height, soil pressure, and groundwater conditions.

Contributors:
Donald Neubauer, PE, Neubauer Consulting Engineers, Potomac, Maryland; Mueser Rutledge Consulting Engineers, New York City, New York; James W. Niehoff, PE, PSI, Wheat Ridge, Colorado; Timothy H. Bedenis, PE, Soil and Materials Engineers, Inc., Plymouth, Michigan; American Concrete Institute; Grace S. Lee, Rippeteau Architects, PC,

Washington DC; Stephen S. Szoke, PE, National Concrete Masonry Association, Herndon, Virginia; Daniel Zechmeister, PE, Masonry Institute of Michigan, Livonia, Michigan; Paul Johnson, AIA, Senior Architect, SmithGroup, Detroit, Michigan.

CONCRETE BASEMENT WALLS
1.58

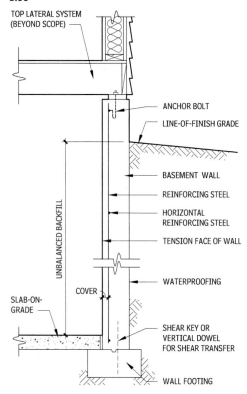

RESIDENTIAL CONSTRUCTION

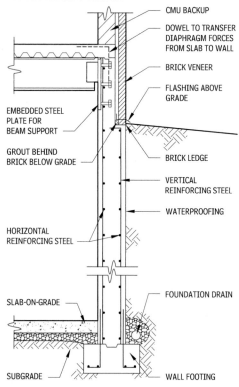

COMMERCIAL CONSTRUCTION

Source: Based on ACI 332 *Requirements for Residential Concrete Construction and Commentary*, Figure R7.1. Reprinted with permission of the American Concrete Institute.

MASONRY BASEMENT WALLS

Masonry walls have long served as foundations for structures. Today, most masonry basement walls consist of a single wythe, or hollow, solid concrete masonry units, depending on the required bearing capacity. The walls are reinforced as necessary to resist lateral loads. Generally, such reinforcing should be held as close to the interior face shell as possible, to provide the maximum tensile strength.

Basement walls should protect against heat and cold, insect infestation (particularly termites), fire, and penetration of water and soil gases.

If radon is a major concern, the top course of the masonry and the course of masonry at or below the slab should be constructed of solid units or fully grouted hollow units using foundation drain to collect and drain condensation moisture from basements, should be avoided in areas where soil-gas entry is a concern.

Architectural masonry units may be used to improve the appearance of the wall. Masonry units with architectural finishes facing the interior can be used for economical construction of finished basement space.

Masonry easily accommodates any floor plan, and returns and corners increase the structural performance of the wall for lateral load resistance.

TYPICAL MASONRY BASEMENT WALL
1.59

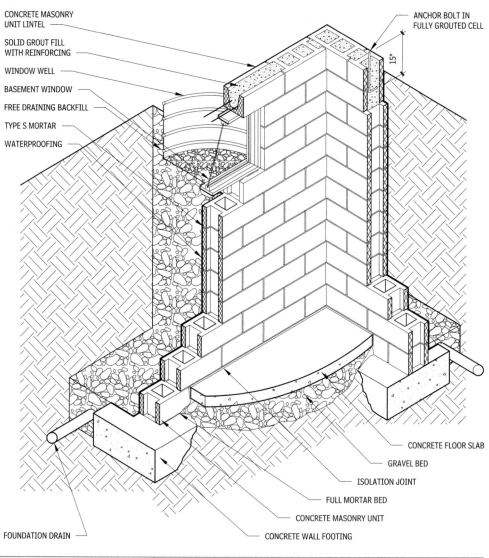

THICKNESS OF CMU BASEMENT WALLS
1.60

BASEMENT WALL CONSTRUCTION	NOMINAL THICKNESS (IN.)	MAXIMUM DEPTH OF UNBALANCED FILL (FT)
CMU – hollow units, ungrouted	8	5
	10	6
	12	7
CMU – solid units	8	5
	10	7
	12	7
CMU – hollow or solid units, fully grouted	8	7
	10	8
	12	8

NOTES

1.58 a. Drainage must be provided on surface and below grade to remove groundwater from the basement wall. The backfill must be granular, and the soil conditions nonexpansive.
b. Backfill pressure on wall is assumed to be 30 psf/ft of depth of wall. Soil pressures may be higher, and greater thicknesses required at a given location. Consult with local code officials or geotechnical engineers.

VERTICAL REINFORCEMENT SPACING
1.61

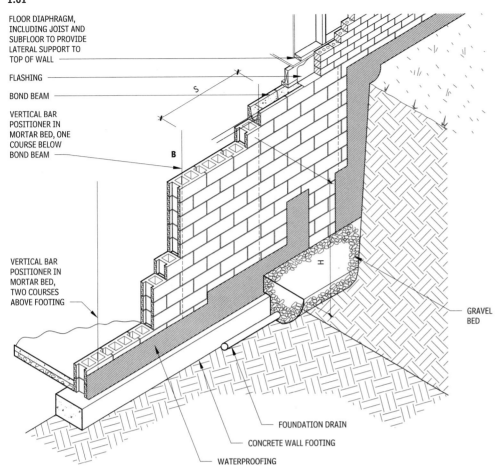

FLOOR DIAPHRAGM, INCLUDING JOIST AND SUBFLOOR TO PROVIDE LATERAL SUPPORT TO TOP OF WALL

FLASHING

BOND BEAM

VERTICAL BAR POSITIONER IN MORTAR BED, ONE COURSE BELOW BOND BEAM

VERTICAL BAR POSITIONER IN MORTAR BED, TWO COURSES ABOVE FOOTING

GRAVEL BED

FOUNDATION DRAIN

CONCRETE WALL FOOTING

WATERPROOFING

S = spacing of vertical reinforcing bars
B = bar size
H = height of backfill

CMU BASEMENT WALL REINFORCEMENT (BAR SIZE AND MAXIMUM BAR SPACING)
1.62

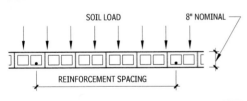

SOIL LOAD   8" NOMINAL

REINFORCEMENT SPACING

	HEIGHT OF BACKFILL, H				
	8'	7'	6'	5'	4'
Bar size, B	#6	#6	#5	#5	#4
Spacing, S	64"	56"	64'	72'	72'

CMU BASEMENT WALL: HORIZONTAL JOINT REINFORCEMENT
1.63

MORTAR JOINT	HEIGHT OF BACKFILL, H				
	8'	7'	6'	5'	4'
13	—	—	—	—	—
12	—	—	—	—	—
11	W2.1	W1.7	W1.7	W1.7	W1.7
10	—	—	—	—	—
9	W2.1	W1.7	W1.7	W1.7	—
8	—	—	—	—	W1.7
7	W2.1	W1.7	W1.7	W1.7	—
6	—	—	—	—	—
5	W2.1	W1.7	W1.7	W1.7	—
4	—	W1.7	W1.7	W1.7	W1.7
3	W2.1	W1.7	W1.7	W1.7	W1.7
2	—	—	—	—	—
1	—	—	—	—	—

NOTES

1.63 a. The empirical design method of the *Building Code Requirements for Masonry Structures*, ACI 530/ASCE 5, Chapter 9, allows up to 5 ft of backfill on an 8-in., nonreinforced concrete masonry wall.
b. As an alternate, W1.7 joint reinforcement placed in joints numbers 3, 4, 5, 7, 8, and 11 may be used.
c. Use of vapor retarders should be verified by proper analysis.
d. Backfill pressure on wall is assumed to be 30 psf/ft of depth of wall. Soil pressures may be higher, and greater thicknesses required at a given location. Consult with local code officials or geotechnical engineers.

TREATED WOOD BASEMENT WALLS

The construction of treated wood foundations and basements is similar to the construction of standard wood light-frame walls except for two factors:

- The wood used is pressure-treated with wood preservatives.
- The extra loading and stress requirements caused by below-grade conditions must be accommodated in the design and detailing of the fasteners, connections, blocking, and wall corners.

As with standard masonry or concrete foundations, treated wood foundations require good drainage to maintain dry basements and crawl spaces. However, the drainage system typically used with treated wood foundations is different from that used with masonry or concrete systems. The components of a drainage system suitable for use with a treated wood foundation include:

- A highly porous backfill material, which directs water down to a granular drainage layer.
- A porous granular drainage layer under the entire foundation and floor to collect and discharge water.
- Positive discharge of water by means of a sump designed for the soil type. This drainage system (developed for treated wood foundations) takes the place of a typical porous backfill over a perimeter drainage pipe.

Benefits of a treated wood foundation include system:

- All framing is standard 2 by construction.
- Treated wood foundations can be erected in any weather and when site access for other methods is difficult.
- Deep wall cavities allow use of high R-value thermal insulation without loss of interior space.
- Wiring and finishing are easily achieved.

Considerations when working with treated wood foundations:

- Treated wood foundations are not appropriate for all sites. Selection of the proper foundation for a project depends on site conditions, including soil types, drainage conditions, groundwater, and other factors. Wet sites in low areas (especially areas with coarse-grained soil) should be avoided if a full basement is desired, although a crawl space type foundation can be used in these cases. Consult a geotechnical engineer to determine the viability of any foundation system. Also, refer to the wood deterioration zones indicated in Figure 1.150. Lumber and plywood used in treated wood foundations must be grade-stamped for foundation use. These are typically pressure treated with chromated copper arsenate. Treated wood products used in foundation construction are required to contain more preservatives than treated wood used in applications such as fencing and decking. Codes generally call for hot-dipped, galvanized fasteners above grade and stainless steel fasteners below grade.

- Avoid skin contact and prolonged or frequent inhalation of sawdust when handling or working with any pressure-treated wood product.
- Consult applicable building codes and the American Forest & Paper Association's *Permanent Wood Foundation System—Design, Fabrication, Installation Manual* for requirements and design guidelines. In the early stages of a project, consult with the building code officials for the area or jurisdiction to assess their familiarity with and willingness to approve this type of construction.
- The vertical and horizontal edge-to-edge joints of all plywood panels used in these systems should be sealed with a suitable sealant.
- Correct materials and details of construction are very important for treated wood foundations. If the contractor to be used for the installation is unfamiliar with this foundation type, the design should include the use of shop-fabricated foundation panels. Most problems with treated wood foundations can be traced to improper installation by inexperienced workers.
- This type of foundation depends especially on the first-floor deck to absorb and distribute any backfill loads; therefore, backfilling cannot occur until the first floor deck is complete unless lateral bracing is utilized.

WOOD DETERIORATION ZONES
1.64

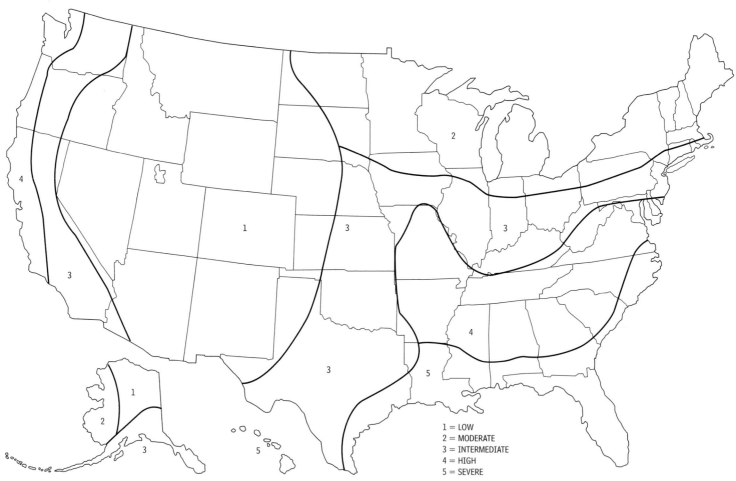

1 = LOW
2 = MODERATE
3 = INTERMEDIATE
4 = HIGH
5 = SEVERE

Source: Based on AWPA Book of Standards 1997.

TYPICAL TREATED WOOD BASEMENT WALL
1.65

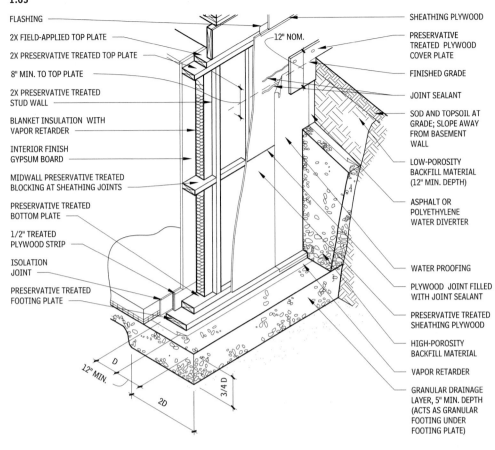

FLASHING

2X FIELD-APPLIED TOP PLATE

2X PRESERVATIVE TREATED TOP PLATE

8" MIN. TO TOP PLATE

2X PRESERVATIVE TREATED STUD WALL

BLANKET INSULATION WITH VAPOR RETARDER

INTERIOR FINISH GYPSUM BOARD

MIDWALL PRESERVATIVE TREATED BLOCKING AT SHEATHING JOINTS

PRESERVATIVE TREATED BOTTOM PLATE

1/2" TREATED PLYWOOD STRIP

ISOLATION JOINT

PRESERVATIVE TREATED FOOTING PLATE

12" NOM.

SHEATHING PLYWOOD

PRESERVATIVE TREATED PLYWOOD COVER PLATE

FINISHED GRADE

JOINT SEALANT

SOD AND TOPSOIL AT GRADE; SLOPE AWAY FROM BASEMENT WALL

LOW-POROSITY BACKFILL MATERIAL (12" MIN. DEPTH)

ASPHALT OR POLYETHYLENE WATER DIVERTER

WATER PROOFING

PLYWOOD JOINT FILLED WITH JOINT SEALANT

PRESERVATIVE TREATED SHEATHING PLYWOOD

HIGH-POROSITY BACKFILL MATERIAL

VAPOR RETARDER

GRANULAR DRAINAGE LAYER, 5" MIN. DEPTH (ACTS AS GRANULAR FOOTING UNDER FOOTING PLATE)

12" MIN.   2D   D   3/4 D

TREATED WOOD BASEMENT WALL WITH EXTERIOR KNEE WALL
1.66

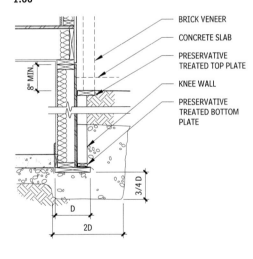

BRICK VENEER

CONCRETE SLAB

PRESERVATIVE TREATED TOP PLATE

KNEE WALL

PRESERVATIVE TREATED BOTTOM PLATE

8" MIN.

3/4 D

D

2D

WOOD SLEEPER FLOOR SYSTEM
1.67

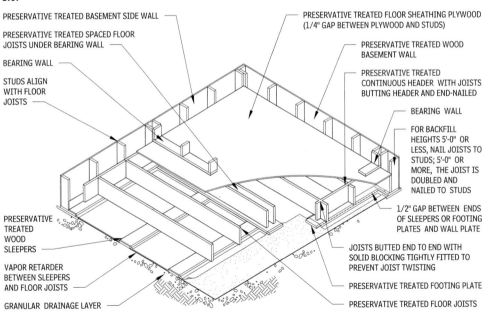

PRESERVATIVE TREATED BASEMENT SIDE WALL

PRESERVATIVE TREATED SPACED FLOOR JOISTS UNDER BEARING WALL

BEARING WALL

STUDS ALIGN WITH FLOOR JOISTS

PRESERVATIVE TREATED WOOD SLEEPERS

VAPOR RETARDER BETWEEN SLEEPERS AND FLOOR JOISTS

GRANULAR DRAINAGE LAYER

PRESERVATIVE TREATED FLOOR SHEATHING PLYWOOD (1/4" GAP BETWEEN PLYWOOD AND STUDS)

PRESERVATIVE TREATED WOOD BASEMENT WALL

PRESERVATIVE TREATED CONTINUOUS HEADER WITH JOISTS BUTTING HEADER AND END-NAILED

BEARING WALL

FOR BACKFILL HEIGHTS 5'-0" OR LESS, NAIL JOISTS TO STUDS; 5'-0" OR MORE, THE JOIST IS DOUBLED AND NAILED TO STUDS

1/2" GAP BETWEEN ENDS OF SLEEPERS OR FOOTING PLATES AND WALL PLATE

JOISTS BUTTED END TO END WITH SOLID BLOCKING TIGHTLY FITTED TO PREVENT JOIST TWISTING

PRESERVATIVE TREATED FOOTING PLATE

PRESERVATIVE TREATED FLOOR JOISTS

NOTES

1.65 a. Geotextile material may be used under and around drainage layers and backfill, if soil conditions warrant.
b. Stud size and spacing vary with material grade and backfill depth. In general, 42-in. backfill requires 2 by 4 at 12 in. o.c., 64-in. requires 2 by 6 at 16 in. o.c., and 84-in. requires 2 by 6 at 12 in. o.c.
1.67 a. Joists to be butted end to end over pressure-treated wood sleepers.
b. Floor stiffness will be increased by blocking between each joist above each sleeper.
c. Check with applicable code for underfloor ventilation requirements.

BASEMENT—WATERPROOFING/ DAMPPROOFING/INSULATION

Consult a geotechnical engineer to determine soil types and groundwater levels, as well as their effect on drainage and waterproofing methods. Consult a waterproofing specialist to determine a specific design approach for problem soils and conditions. Sites may have groundwater contamination that will degrade the durability of the waterproofing materials. Generally, waterproofing will be necessary if a head of water is expected against the basement wall or under the slab. Because groundwater levels can vary with seasons, it is important to understand these seasonal fluctuations and design for the maximum expected head.

Foundation drainage is recommended when the groundwater level may rise above the top of the floor slab or when the foundation is subject to hydrostatic pressure after heavy rain. Geosynthetic drainage material conveys water to the drainage piping, thus reducing hydrostatic pressure. It is important to understand the hydrostatic pressures exerted on the floor slab and wall systems if the drainage system is not adequate to remove all the water.

Special negative-side coatings on interior face of foundation wall, such as metallic oxide, are recommended only when the exterior is not accessible (such as pits and trenches, and in particular, elevator pits).

BASEMENT WALL VERTICAL WATERPROOFING

The grading around the building is an important part of the overall water management plan. The backfilling operation usually results in a more porous material than the adjacent undisturbed soil, which makes it easier for water to collect next to the building. The finished grade should slope away from the building, and an impervious layer of soil placed on top of the backfill against the building. Drainage from downspouts should be diverted away from the foundations.

Types of waterproofing include built-up bituminous, sheet, fluid-applied, cementitious and reactive, and bentonite.

- *Built-up bituminous*: Composed of alternating layers of bituminous sheets and viscous bituminous coatings. Bituminous waterproofing includes built-up asphalt and cold-tar waterproofing systems.
- *Sheet waterproofing*: Formed with sheets of elastomeric, bituminous, modified bituminous or thermoplastic materials. Sheet waterproofing may be either mechanically attached or self-adhered. Sheet waterproofing provides an impermeable surface to water penetration.
- *Fluid-applied*: Applied in a hot or cold viscous state. Includes hot fluid-applied rubberized asphalt. As with sheet waterproofing, fluid-applied waterproofing will bridge minor cracks in a concrete surface.
- *Cementitious and reactive*: Types of waterproofing that achieve waterproof qualities through chemical reaction and include polymer modified cement, crystalline, and metal-oxide waterproofing systems. Metal oxide is recommended for use when the exterior surface is not accessible, as in the case of an elevator pit.
- *Bentonite*: Formed from clay into panels and composite sheets. When moistened, the clay swells and takes on a gel-like consistency, forming an impermeable retarder when confined. Bentonite clay works well only when moistened. For applications where the water table fluctuates, there may be a time lag between the rising water table and when the bentonite takes effect, during which time there is the possibility of water infiltration. Therefore, when the water table varies, caution is in order when relying on bentonite clay for waterproofing. Proper coordination between the wall construction details and the waterproofing termination is required.

At the interface of the foundation wall and slab, waterstops are placed on top of the footing, at vertical concrete keyed wall joints.

Most waterproofing materials require a stable, rigid, and level substrate. Generally, a mud slab (subslab that is nonreinforced and nonstructural) is used when the waterproofing material is placed below the structural slab and/or when a solid working surface is needed on unstable soils. When waterproofing materials are placed on top of the structural slab, a protective cover, such as another concrete slab, is required.

**WATERPROOFING APPLICATIONS AT BASEMENT CONDITIONS
1.68**

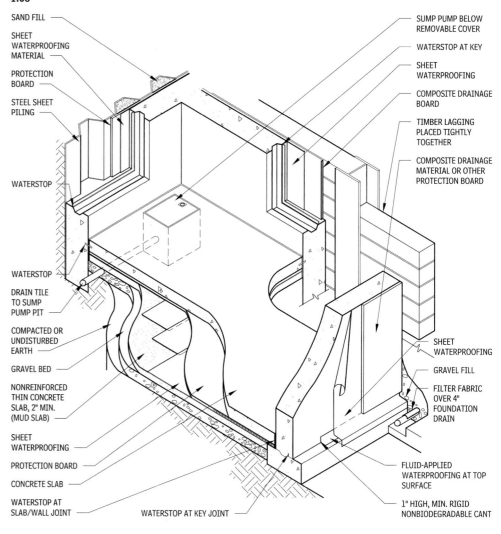

- SAND FILL
- SHEET WATERPROOFING MATERIAL
- PROTECTION BOARD
- STEEL SHEET PILING
- WATERSTOP
- WATERSTOP
- DRAIN TILE TO SUMP PUMP PIT
- COMPACTED OR UNDISTURBED EARTH
- GRAVEL BED
- NONREINFORCED THIN CONCRETE SLAB, 2" MIN. (MUD SLAB)
- SHEET WATERPROOFING
- PROTECTION BOARD
- CONCRETE SLAB
- WATERSTOP AT SLAB/WALL JOINT
- WATERSTOP AT KEY JOINT
- SUMP PUMP BELOW REMOVABLE COVER
- WATERSTOP AT KEY
- SHEET WATERPROOFING
- COMPOSITE DRAINAGE BOARD
- TIMBER LAGGING PLACED TIGHTLY TOGETHER
- COMPOSITE DRAINAGE MATERIAL OR OTHER PROTECTION BOARD
- SHEET WATERPROOFING
- GRAVEL FILL
- FILTER FABRIC OVER 4" FOUNDATION DRAIN
- FLUID-APPLIED WATERPROOFING AT TOP SURFACE
- 1" HIGH, MIN. RIGID NONBIODEGRADABLE CANT

**WATERPROOFING AT FOOTINGS
1.69**

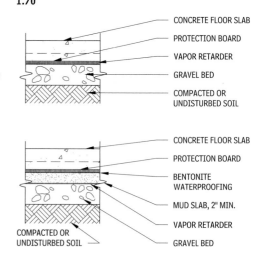

- 6" MIN.
- JOINT SEALANT AND BACKER ROD AT ISOLATION JOINT
- 2" MIN.
- WATER STOP
- 1" HIGH, MIN. RIGID NONBIODEGRADABLE CANT WITH FLUID-APPLIED WATERPROOFING AT TOP SURFACE
- SLOPE GRADE AWAY FROM WALL
- WATERSTOP
- BOARD INSULATION OR OTHER PROTECTION BOARD MATERIAL; IN WET SOILS, PROVIDE A COMPOSITE DRAINAGE BOARD, WHICH ACTS AS A PROTECTION BOARD
- WATERPROOFING
- FILTER FABRIC OVER 4" FOUNDATION DRAIN
- SHAPE SOIL TO FORM GUTTER
- GRAVEL FILL

**WATERPROOFING UNDERSLAB
1.70**

- CONCRETE FLOOR SLAB
- PROTECTION BOARD
- VAPOR RETARDER
- GRAVEL BED
- COMPACTED OR UNDISTURBED SOIL
- CONCRETE FLOOR SLAB
- PROTECTION BOARD
- BENTONITE WATERPROOFING
- MUD SLAB, 2" MIN.
- VAPOR RETARDER
- COMPACTED OR UNDISTURBED SOIL
- GRAVEL BED

NOTE

1.68 Place 12-in. neoprene strips over joints in sheet piling.

ELEMENT B: SHELL

2

INTRODUCTION

In the last analysis, everything turns as much on exactly how something is realized as on an overt manifestation of its form. This is not to deny spatial ingenuity but rather to heighten its character through its precise realization. Thus the presencing of a work is inseparable from the manner of its foundation in the ground and the ascendency of its structure through the interplay of support, span, seam, and joint—the rhythm of its revetment and the modulation of its fenestration.

—Kenneth Frampton, *Studies in Tectonic Culture: The Poetics of Construction in Nineteenth and Twentieth Century Architecture*

This chapter on the shell of a building—the structure rising from the foundation; the exterior walls with doors, windows, louvers, and shading; the roof with openings and lights—describes what, arguably, are the most significant architectural form-givers and expressive elements. As Frampton points out in the epigraph here, the realization of the individual components and their interplay is as important as the overall spatial concept.

The information contained in this chapter is meant to serve as the starting point for an exploration of the poetic and tectonic expression of a building's shell, in concert with its environment, rather than against it, to provide for human occupancy while elevating the emotional and spiritual experience.

In addition to the requirements to be warm and dry, humans need protection from a variety of natural and cultural vicissitudes. In 1963, in *Canadian Building Digest,* Dr. Neil Hutcheon categorized the purposes of architectural enclosure, which are paraphrased as follows:

• Control heat flow.
• Control airflow.
• Control water vapor flow.
• Control rain penetration.
• Control light, solar, and other radiation.
• Control noise and vibration.
• Control fire.
• Provide strength and rigidity (resist gravity, snow, wind, seismic, blast, impact, and ballistic loads).
• Be durable.
• Be of economic value.
• Be of aesthetic value.

Satisfying the requirements to be warm, safe, and dry is only the beginning, however; without appealing to the human intellect and addressing sociocultural conditions, mere building results. For architecture to occur, poetics and art must be brought into the realization of the enclosure. Therefore, the last purpose listed is the key to the creation of architecture.

Frampton points out the other determinants with tectonics: the type and topos (or the function or commodity, and the site). The enclosure mediates two distinct environments: the interior and the exterior. The building type is a major determinant in the required interior environment, while the topos—the site and its distinct local climatic conditions—determines the exterior environment. The consideration of these two environments is essential to the architectural solution, and their impact is evident throughout the chapter.

Architecture is not a collection of standard details, but neither is it a maquette assembled without regard for the realities of service and function. Whether a building is expressive of its tectonics or tells a story based on other aesthetic and cultural aspirations, it must provide the basics of support and environmental control over time. Certainly, many details contained in this chapter represent tried-and-true solutions to common problems, but the underlying principles of their functionality have been given in hopes of expanding, modifying, and adapting their usage to inform and influence the overall design concept.

Contributor:
David Altenhofen, AIA, Hillier ArchICEcture, Philadelphia, Pennsylvania.

DESIGN CONSIDERATIONS

CLIMATE AND ENERGY

Of primary importance to the shell of a building is the mediation between the exterior and interior environment. Proper design and detailing of the building enclosure requires an understanding of the specific characteristics of both the desired interior environmental conditions and specific exterior environmental conditions, on both a macro and micro scale.

DEFINITIONS

When reading the content of this chapter, keep in mind the following definitions of concepts and principles:

- *Air barriers*: Materials or combinations of materials that form a continuous envelope around all sides of the conditioned space to resist the passage of air. Joints, seams, transitions, penetrations, and gaps must be sealed. The air barrier must be capable of withstanding combined positive and negative wind load and fan and stack pressure without damage or displacement. The air barrier must be at least as durable as the overlying construction and be detailed to accommodate anticipated building movement. An air barrier may or may not be a vapor retarder.
- *Vapor barriers and retarders*: Without industrywide consensus, materials with a perm rating less than 1 are interchangeably

called vapor barriers or vapor retarders (IBC and IEC 2003 use "vapor retarder"). More important than the term is to understand a few basic principles:

- Vapor diffusion through materials with perm ratings less than 1 is nearly inconsequential, but even small gaps or holes can easily transport many times as much water vapor.
- All materials have some greater or lesser degree of resistance to diffusion, and their placement in an enclosure assembly, whether intended as a retarder or not, will affect wetting and, more importantly, drying of an assembly.
- *Insulation*: A material that slows the flow of heat through conduction.
- *Radiant barriers*: A material, usually metallic or shiny, that reflects radiant thermal energy.
- *Weather barrier (water-resistant barrier)*: A material that is resistant to the penetration of water in the liquid state, or is waterproof. It may or may not be an air barrier or vapor retarder. The face of the weather barrier is sometimes called the *drainage plane*.
- *Barrier wall*: A wall assembly that resists moisture with a continuous waterproof membrane or with a plane of weather barrier material thick enough to prevent absorbed moisture from penetrating to the interior.

- *Drained cavity wall*: A wall assembly with an outer water-shedding layer over an air cavity, and with a weather barrier. The cavity is flashed and weeped to drain incidental water.
- *Drainage plane wall*: A wall assembly with a continuous water-resistant barrier under an outer water-shedding layer. The lack of a cavity limits the amount of water that can be quickly drained.
- *Pressure-equalized rainscreen wall*: A wall assembly that resists all the physical forces that can transport water across a joint in the outer or "rainscreen" layer. Kinetic energy forces are controlled by venting a cavity behind the rainscreen and, thus, allowing the pressure differential across the joint to be equalized. An air barrier and compartmentalization of the cavity are required to control the pressure equalization. The cavity is flashed and weeped to drain incidental moisture.

EXTERIOR CLIMATIC INFLUENCE

The United States has widely varying climates. More than the obvious extremes of Miami and Alaska are the subtler—and just as important variations—within the contingent states. The ANSI/ASHRAE/IESNA Standard 90.1 Map of Climate Zones for the United States reproduced in Figure 2.1 dictates zones based on heating and cooling requirements. (Note: A simplified map of climatic zones can be found in the book, *Moisture Control Handbook: Principles*

CLIMATE ZONES FOR UNITED STATES LOCATIONS
2.1

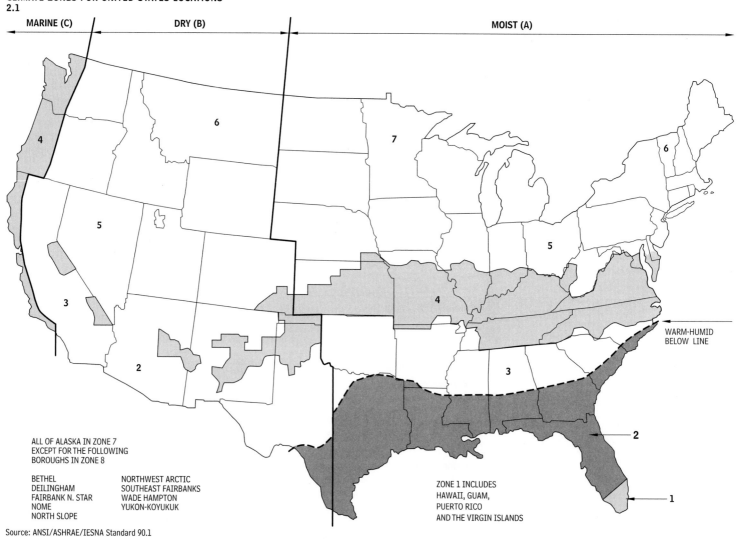

MARINE (C)   DRY (B)   MOIST (A)

WARM-HUMID
BELOW LINE

ALL OF ALASKA IN ZONE 7
EXCEPT FOR THE FOLLOWING
BOROUGHS IN ZONE 8

BETHEL   NORTHWEST ARCTIC
DEILINGHAM   SOUTHEAST FAIRBANKS
FAIRBANK N. STAR   WADE HAMPTON
NOME   YUKON-KOYUKUK
NORTH SLOPE

ZONE 1 INCLUDES
HAWAII, GUAM,
PUERTO RICO
AND THE VIRGIN ISLANDS

Source: ANSI/ASHRAE/IESNA Standard 90.1

and Practices for Residential and Small Commercial Buildings, by Joseph W. Lstiburek and John Carmody, 1996.) There are six zones within the continental states and Hawaii, plus two more for Alaska. Within these zones are subzones for moist, dry, marine, and warm-humid.

As this chapter will demonstrate, solutions appropriate for one zone may be totally unsuited for another. SEI/ASCE 7, "Minimum Design Loads for Buildings and Other Structures," and other similar standards establish the wind, snow, and seismic structural loads on buildings. Again, there is wide variation in wind speed, snowfall, and ground movement. In addition to the base loads, localized conditions such as surrounding topography and adjacent buildings can cause wide variances in the environmental influences. Figure 2.2 shows the annual precipitation for North America. Suggested types of exterior enclosure systems that will meet the minimum level of service and reliability are correlated to the rainfall levels.

INTERIOR CLIMATIC INFLUENCE

Environmental conditions to be maintained within the building also influence the design of the shell. Buildings with requirements for high or low levels of humidity, tight temperature tolerances, pressure differentials to the exterior, high-reliability containment, acoustic isolation, protection from blast or forced entry, high indoor air quality, or other extraordinary requirements will require particular attention to system selection and detailing, in concert with consideration of the exterior climate.

HEAT, AIR, AND MOISTURE

In addition to the obvious structural loads, the building enclosure must resist the transfer of heat, air, and moisture (HAM). The laws of physics dictate that heat always flows from hot to cold. Air moves through building enclosures by passing through porous materials, or through holes and gaps in nonporous materials, based on differential air pressures. Moisture, as water in the liquid state (such as rain, snow, and groundwater), moves through enclosures by four methods: capillary action, surface tension, gravity, and kinetic energy (e.g., wind-driven rain). Moisture in the vapor state moves through enclosures from zones of higher to lower vapor pressures, by diffusion through solid materials or by air transport through holes.

CONTROL OF HAM

Control of the flow of HAM across the building enclosure is an interrelated problem, in that air movement can create the kinetic energy that pulls water through joints, dramatically reduce thermal insulation effectiveness, or cause massive vapor transport. Improper thermal insulation can cause condensation on uncontrolled surfaces.

To control HAM, three components must be considered separately: heat, air, and moisture.

Heat is most commonly controlled by thermal insulation. Keep in mind the following:

- Air movement around thermal insulation can seriously degrade its effectiveness, so avoid systems that ventilate the conditioned side of the thermal insulation.
- Radiant barriers may be effective, particularly in hot climates, but they must have an airspace on the warm side. Generally speaking, radiant barriers have virtually no insulating value and should not replace but, instead, enhance typical thermal insulation and conductive losses.
- Thermal short circuits can dramatically reduce the U-value of thermal insulation. The most common example is metal studs, which may reduce the effective value of thermal insulation between the studs by half.

Air transfer is controlled by a coordinated and continuous system of air barriers for all six sides of the enclosure (i.e., the lowest grade level, foundation walls, exterior walls, and the roof).

- Common approaches to wall air barriers are continuous membranes applied to sheathing and sealed to windows, doors, and penetrations.
- Below-grade assemblies can utilize either the concrete walls and slabs or applied waterproofing membranes.
- Most typical low-slope roof membranes will provide an air barrier, except for mechanically fastened systems that may not be able to resist all of the required loads.
- It is possible to design the gypsum board as an air barrier, if all joints and cracks are sealed.
- Many air barrier systems require a combination of a membrane and a structural panel to resist loading, such as spun-bond poly-olefin membranes stapled to sheathing or bituminous membranes adhered to CMU.

Moisture management consists of controlling moisture entry, moisture accumulation, and allowing for drying.

- Perfect barriers to moisture are virtually impossible to achieve; therefore, it is important that measures taken to keep out moisture do not also trap moisture—for example, waterproofing membranes that trap thermal insulation between a vapor retarder.
- It is essential to maintain a balance of the moisture that is able to accumulate in an assembly between drying cycles. Accumulation and drying are extremely dependent on the local climate. Some materials such as wood-framed walls and masonry have the capacity to absorb relatively large quantities of moisture and to then later dry out without damage or deterioration. Other systems such as gypsum board on metal studs have very little capacity for the storage of moisture.
- The source of water is primarily rain, which should be limited by a reasonably detailed assembly based on the expected amount of precipitation. The precipitation map in Figure 2.2 shows recommended enclosure types along with the required performance to minimize water entry.

ANNUAL PRECIPITATION IN NORTH AMERICA
2.2

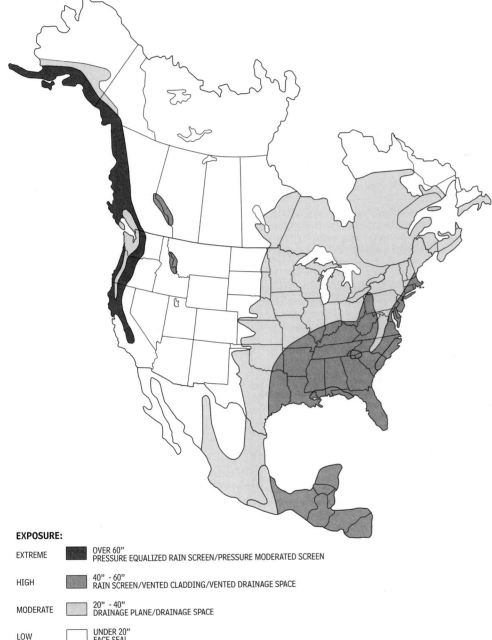

EXPOSURE:

EXTREME	■	OVER 60" PRESSURE EQUALIZED RAIN SCREEN/PRESSURE MODERATED SCREEN
HIGH	▨	40" - 60" RAIN SCREEN/VENTED CLADDING/VENTED DRAINAGE SPACE
MODERATE	▨	20" - 40" DRAINAGE PLANE/DRAINAGE SPACE
LOW	□	UNDER 20" FACE SEAL

Source: ASHRAE Journal, February 2002

- Below grade, the primary source of moisture is through capillary action that can be controlled through membranes and capillary breaks.
- Sources of vapor may be in the interior or exterior environment. Vapor retarders have been the traditional method used to control vapor movement, but their use in mixed heating and cooling climates must be carefully evaluated to allow drying.
- Moisture control in the solid state (i.e., ice) depends on not letting liquid water freeze; or, if it does, allowing room for expansion. For example, cold roof surfaces that eliminate thawing also prevent ice buildup, and air-entrained concrete provides room for ice crystals to expand.

Figures 2.3 and 2.4 show details of wall assemblies that can be used for analysis of drying under various climatic conditions. The various assemblies are somewhat independent of the cladding type. Other wall assemblies, including face-sealed or massive barrier assemblies, should receive similar analysis of HAM control. Two useful tools for this purpose are:

- *Computerized modeling of wetting and drying of walls*: This is widely available and is very helpful to understanding moisture accumulation and drying. Analysis is recommended for large projects and any assembly that requires seasonal drying. Mixed climates may be the most difficult to predict by rule of thumb or empirical analysis. WUFI, developed by the Fraunhofer Institute for Building Physics in Germany with a North American version developed jointly with Oak Ridge National Laboratory (www.ornl.gov) is widely recognized modeling tool. Similar software is available through www.virtual-north.com/download/OrderForm.pdf and www.architects.org/emplibrary/HAMtoolbox.pdf.
- *Manual analysis of simple two-dimensional diagrams of wall sections*: This involves using temperature gradients plotted against dew point temperature or vapor-pressure gradients plotted against saturation pressure. For instructions refer to "Design Tools," by Anton TenWolde (Chapter 11 in the manual *Moisture Control in Buildings* [MNL18], Heinz R. Trechsel, editor, published by ASTM, 1994).

CONSIDERATIONS FOR CLIMATE ZONES
GENERAL

- Refer to specific information for each material for more information regarding selection criteria and proper detailing.
- Include only one vapor retarder in a wall assembly, and ensure that all other materials are increasingly permeable from the vapor retarder out.
- It is acceptable (and sometimes desirable) to provide more than one air barrier in a wall assembly.
- It is generally desirable to protect blanket insulation from air-washing with an air barrier on the cold side.

ALL CLIMATES

- Highly reliable enclosure system to control HAM in all climate zones, without relying on building mechanical systems to dry interior air.
- Thermal insulation located outside of structure and wall framing allows easy installation of continuous air barriers and vapor retarders.
- Thermal insulation must be continuous to prevent the vapor retarder from reaching the dew point.
- Excellent choice for masonry veneer over CMU or metal stud backup systems.
- If metal stud backup systems are used, do not place thermal insulation between the studs.
- Any paint or wall covering is allowed on interior finish.

COLD CLIMATES (Zones 5 to 8)

- Materials should be progressively more permeable, because they are located closer to exterior face.
- Any paint or wall covering is allowed on interior finish.
- Mechanical system is not required to dry interior air.
- Failure of the building paper may allow moisture accumulation that cannot be overcome by drying.
- Elements penetrating thermal insulation, (such as beams supporting a projecting canopy or the sump pan of roof drains) can cause condensation problems, unless they are insulated with closed-cell thermal insulation or a thermal insulation with a vapor

ALL CLIMATES AND COLD CLIMATES
2.3

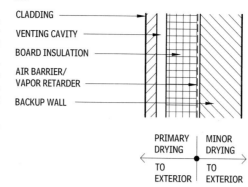

CLADDING
VENTING CAVITY
BOARD INSULATION
AIR BARRIER/ VAPOR RETARDER
BACKUP WALL

PRIMARY DRYING | MINOR DRYING
TO EXTERIOR | TO EXTERIOR

ALL CLIMATES

INTERIOR AIRTIGHT GYPSUM WALL BOARD, EXTERIOR SHEATHING, OR PERMEABLE MEMBRANE APPLIED TO SHEATHING OR COMBINATION TO PROVIDE AIR BARRIER

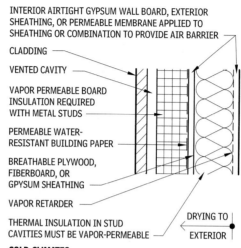

CLADDING
VENTED CAVITY
VAPOR PERMEABLE BOARD INSULATION REQUIRED WITH METAL STUDS
PERMEABLE WATER-RESISTANT BUILDING PAPER
BREATHABLE PLYWOOD, FIBERBOARD, OR GPYSUM SHEATHING
VAPOR RETARDER
THERMAL INSULATION IN STUD CAVITIES MUST BE VAPOR-PERMEABLE

DRYING TO EXTERIOR

COLD CLIMATES

retarder to keep moisture-laden air from getting to these surfaces. This is particularly true for occupancies with high humidity, (including residences, hospitals, museums, swimming pools,).

HOT CLIMATES (Zones 1, 2, and 3)

- The mechanical system must provide dehumidification of interior air for drying.
- Avoid any vapor-impermeable interior finishes (e.g., a vinyl wall covering that will trap moisture).
- A radiant barrier may be incorporated into the cavity.
- Taped joints in sheathing, board insulation, or a combination may provide air barrier.
- An air barrier is crucial to limit moisture transport through imperfections in the vapor retarder.

MIXED CLIMATES (Zones 3 and 4)

- All materials must be relatively vapor-permeable to allow drying in both directions, because seasons change direction of heat flow and vapor drive.
- Detail system with interior and exterior side-permeable air barriers to limit moisture transport and infiltration/exfiltration.
- May be possible to use board insulation with taped joints as sheathing, which will form a vapor retarder if board and blanket insulation have approximately the same U-value.

SUSTAINABILITY AND ENERGY

The building shell should be a major part of the sustainable strategy. At a minimum, the shell should:

- Contribute to minimizing energy usage.
- Incorporate environmentally sensitive materials.

HOT, HUMID CLIMATES AND MIXED CLIMATES
2.4

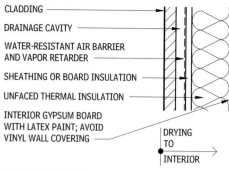

CLADDING
DRAINAGE CAVITY
WATER-RESISTANT AIR BARRIER AND VAPOR RETARDER
SHEATHING OR BOARD INSULATION
UNFACED THERMAL INSULATION
INTERIOR GYPSUM BOARD WITH LATEX PAINT; AVOID VINYL WALL COVERING

DRYING TO INTERIOR

HOT, HUMID CLIMATES

CLADDING
DRAINAGE CAVITY
PERMEABLE WEATHER BARRIER
PERMEABLE FIBERBOARD, PERMEABLE PLYWOOD, GYPSUM OR WOOD FIBERBOARD SHEATHING
INTERIOR AIRTIGHT GYPSUM BOARD, EXTERIOR SHEATHING, OR BOTH, TO PROVIDE AIR BARRIER

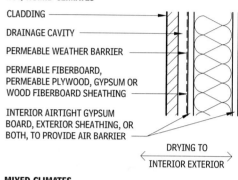

DRYING TO INTERIOR EXTERIOR

MIXED CLIMATES

- Ensure good indoor air quality and occupant comfort.
- Be durable.

For high-performance building projects, the enclosure could help generate energy, return nutrients to the environment, and filter pollutants.

One area of special concern for the building shell is durability, even though it currently is not included in LEED evaluations in the United States. (It is included in Canadian LEED programs). The building superstructure and enclosure are frequently portions of the building that should last the longest and are the most difficult to repair or replace. Buildings that perform well for many years slow or reduce the consumption of resources and the wastestream. Failures of the enclosure can lead not only to water-damaged materials needing repair or replacement but also to unnecessary long-term energy consumption, toxic mold, and sick buildings.

Buildings are major consumers of energy, so the enclosures should be part of a strategy to reduce energy consumption. In fact, creating a well-performing enclosure is considered to be the first step in reducing energy usage, ahead of other more sophisticated strategies, such as high-performance mechanical systems. A thorough understanding of the interior and exterior environments is paramount. For residential buildings in cold climates, heat loss through the enclosure may be the largest component of total energy consumption. For large commercial buildings in a moderate environment, daylighting schemes may save more energy, even as they may result in an enclosure with lower thermal resistance.

Most jurisdictions require compliance with an energy conservation code. ASHRAE 90.1 and the International Energy Code (in various editions) are common model codes. These minimum standards should be exceeded by 20 to 50 percent, if possible.

Consult the following references:

- *Designing the Exterior Wall: An Architectural Guide to the Vertical Envelope* by Linda Brock (John Wiley & Sons, Inc., 2005)
- *Moisture Control Handbook: Principles and Practices for Residential and Small Commercial Buildings* by Joseph W. Lstiburek and John Carmody (John Wiley & Sons, Inc. 1996)
- *Water in Buildings: An Architect's Guide to Moisture and Mold* by William B. Rose (John Wiley & Sons, Inc., 2005)

NOTES

2.3 and 2.4 Provide an air barrier in the assembly at one or more of the locations noted by properly detailing either the inner layer of gypsum board, the sheathing layer, or the permeable weather barrier. The inner gypsum board can be made an air barrier by sealing the perimeter, penetrations, and transitions to adjacent air barrier assemblies. The sheathing can be made an air barrier through similar means of sealing all joints, penetrations, and transitions. Using a membrane over the sheathering (either fluid-applied or sheet material) that is vapor permeable, weather-resistant, anmd airtight is extremely effective for providing an air barries with the added benefits of simple installation and inspection.

SUPERSTRUCTURE

FLOOR CONSTRUCTION

This section of the chapter examines common floor construction assemblies. Consult literature from manufacturers and trade associations for more details on the information presented in the accompanying tables.

FLOOR STRUCTURAL FRAME

CONCRETE CONSTRUCTION

The information presented here is intended only as a preliminary design guide. All structural dimensions for slab thickness, beam and joint sizes, column sizes, should be calculated and analyzed for each project condition by a licensed professional engineer.

Spans shown in the accompanying figures and tables are approximate and are based on use of mild reinforcing steel. For spans greater than 40 ft, consider post-tensioning.

Consider embedded items such as conduits and penetrations for ducts and pipes when coordinating a structural system. Concrete floor construction may have less flexibility for locating large duct openings close to beam lines or small penetrations immediately adjacent to columns.

FLAT PLATE
2.5

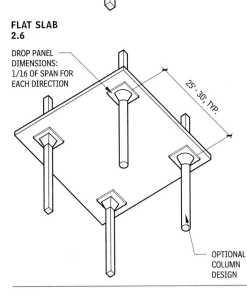

FLAT SLAB
2.6

DROP PANEL
DIMENSIONS:
1/16 OF SPAN FOR
EACH DIRECTION

25' - 30', TYP.

OPTIONAL
COLUMN
DESIGN

BANDED SLAB
2.7

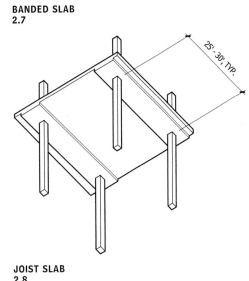

25' - 30', TYP.

JOIST SLAB
2.8

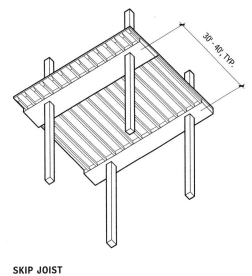

30' - 40', TYP.

SKIP JOIST
2.9

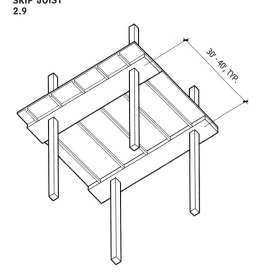

30' - 40', TYP.

WAFFLE SLAB
2.10

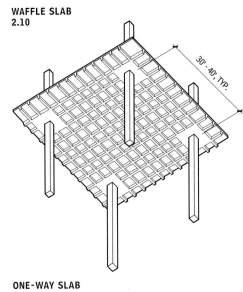

30' - 40', TYP.

ONE-WAY SLAB
2.11

UP TO 60'-0"

18' - 27', TYP.

TWO-WAY SLAB
2.12

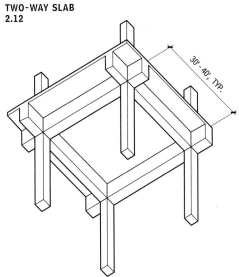

30' - 40', TYP.

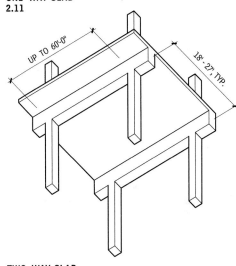

Contributor:
Russell S. Fling, PE, Columbus, Ohio.

FLOOR STRUCTURE ASSEMBLIES
2.13

		DEPTH OF ASSEMBLY (IN.)	STANDARD MEMBER SIZES (IN.)	DEAD LOAD OF STRUCTURE (PSF)	SUITABLE LIVE LOAD RANGE (PSF)	SPAN RANGE (FT)	DIMENSIONAL STABILITY AFFECTED BY
Wood joist	SUBFLOORING / WOOD JOIST / CEILING	7–13	Nominal joist 2 × 6, 8, 10, and 12	5–8	30–40	Up to 18	Deflection
Wood I-joists or shop-fabricated wood trusses	SUBFLOORING / WOOD I-JOIST (OR SHOP-FABRICATED WOOD TRUSS) / CEILING	13–21	12, 14, 16, 18, and 20	6–12	30–40	12–30	Deflection
Wood beam and plank	WOOD PLANK / WOOD BEAM	10–22	Nominal plank 2, 3, and 4	6–16	30–40	10–22	—
Glue-Laminated beam and plank	WOOD PLANK / GLUE-LAMINATED BEAM	8–22	Nominal plank 2, 3, and 4	6–20	30–40	8–34	—
Steel joist	SUBFLOORING / WOOD NAILER / STEEL JOIST / CEILING	9–31	Steel joists 8–30	8–20	30–40	16–40	Deflection
Steel joist	CONCRETE SLAB / STEEL DECKING / STEEL JOIST / CEILING	11–75	Steel joists 8–72	30–110	30–100	16–60 (up to 130)	Deflection
Lightweight steel frame	SUBFLOORING / STRUCTURAL STEEL FRAME / CEILING	7–12	Consult manufacturers' literature	6–20	30–60	10–22	—
Structural steel frame	CONCRETE SLAB / STEEL DECKING / STEEL BEAM / CEILING	9–15	—	35–60	30–100	16–35	Deflection
Structural steel frame	CONCRETE TOPPING / PRECAST STRUCTURAL CONCRETE / STEEL BEAM / CEILING	8–16	Precast Structural Concrete 16–48 W 4–12 D	40–75	60–150	Up to 50; generally below 35	Deflection and creep
Precast concrete	CONCRETE TOPPING / PRECAST STRUCTURAL CONCRETE / CONCRETE BEAM	6–12	Precast Structural Concrete 16–48 W 4–12 D	40–75	60–150	Up to 60; generally below 35	Deflection and creep
One-way concrete slab	CONCRETE SLAB / CONCRETE BEAM	4–10	—	50–120	40–150	10–20; more with post-tensioning	—
Two-way concrete slab	CONCRETE SLAB / CONCRETE BEAM	4–10	—	50–120	40–250	10–30; more with post-tensioning	—

Contributors:
Roger K. Lewis, FAIA, and Mehmet T. Ergene, architect, Roger K. Lewis & Associates, Washington, DC.

FLOOR STRUCTURE ASSEMBLIES (continued)
2.13

BAY SIZE CHARACTERISTICS	REQUIRES FINISHED FLOOR SURFACE	REQUIRES FINISHED CEILING SURFACE	SERVICE PLENUM	COMPARATIVE RESISTANCE TO SOUND TRANSMISSION		REMARKS
				IMPACT	AIRBORNE	
—	Yes	Visual or fire protection purposes	Between joists—one way	Poor	Fair	Economical, light, easy to construct; limited to low-rise construction
—	Yes	Visual for fire protection purposes	Between trusses and joists—two ways	Poor	Fair	Close dimensional tolerances; cutting holes through web permissible
Maximum beam spacing 8'-0"	Optional	No	Under structure—one way	Poor	Fair	Most efficient with planks continuous over more than one span
—	Optional	No	Under structure— one way	Poor	Fair	—
Light joists, 16" to 30" o.c.; heavy joists, 4'–12' o.c.	Yes	Visual or fire protection purposes	Between joists—two ways	Poor	Poor	—
Light joists, 16" to 30" o.c.; heavy joists, 4'–12' o.c.	No	Visual or fire protection purposes	Between joists—two ways	Poor	Fair	Economical system; selective partition placement required; cantilevers difficult
—	Yes	Visual or fire protection purposes	Under structure	Poor	Poor	—
—	No	Visual or fire protection purposes	Under structure	Poor	Fair	—
—	Optional	Visual or fire protection purposes	Under structure	Fair	Fair	—
—	Optional	No	Under structure	Fair	Fair	—
—	No	No	Under structure	Good	Good	Restricted to short spans because of excessive dead load
L 1.33 W	No	No	Under structure	Good	Good	Suitable for concentrated loads; easy partition placement

FLOOR STRUCTURE ASSEMBLIES (continued)
2.13

		DEPTH OF ASSEMBLY (IN.)	STANDARD MEMBER SIZES (IN.)	DEAD LOAD OF STRUCTURE (PSF)	SUITABLE LIVE LOAD RANGE (PSF)	SPAN RANGE (FT)	DIMENSIONAL STABILITY AFFECTED BY
One-way ribbed concrete slab	CONCRETE SLAB / RIB (JOIST)	8–22	Standard pan forms 20 and 30 W, 6–20 D	40–90	40–150	15–50; more with post-tensioning	Creep
Two-way ribbed concrete slab	CONCRETE SLAB / RIB (JOIST)	8–22	Standard dome forms 19 × 19, 30 × 30 6–20 D	75–105	60–200	25–60; more with post-tensioning	Creep
Concrete flat slab	CONCRETE SLAB / DROP PANEL / CAPITAL / COLUMN	6–16	Minimum slab thickness 5, without drop panel; 4 with drop panel	75–170	60–250	20–40; up to 70 with post-tensioning	Creep
Precast double tee	CONCRETE TOPPING / PRECAST DOUBLE TEE	8–18	48, 60, 72, 96, and 120 W 6–16 D	50–80	40–150	20–50	Creep
Precast tee	CONCRETE TOPPING / PRECAST SINGLE TEE	18–38	16–36 D	50–90	40–150	25–65	Creep
Composite	CONCRETE SLAB / COMPOSITE METAL DECKING / WELDED STUD (SHEAR CONNECTOR) / STEEL BEAM	4–6	—	35–70	60–200	Up to 35	Deflection
Concrete flat plate	COLUMN / CONCRETE FLAT PLATE	5–14	—	60–175	60–200	18–35; more with post-tensioning	Creep

CONCRETE FLOOR SYSTEM COMPARISON
2.14

FLOOR SYSTEM	ADVANTAGES	DISADVANTAGES	APPROPRIATE BUILDING TYPES	COMMENTS
Flat plate	Inexpensive formwork; ceilings may be exposed; minimum thickness; fast erection; flexible column location.	Excess concrete for longer spans; low shear capacity; greater deflections.	Hotels, motels, dormitories, condominiums, hospitals.	A flat plate is best for moderate spans because it is the most economical floor system and has the lowest structural thickness. Avoid penetrations for piping and ductwork through the slab near the columns. Spandrel beams may be necessary.
Flat slab	Economical for design loads greater than 150 psf.	Formwork is costly.	Warehouses, industrial structures, parking structures.	Flat slabs are most commonly used today for buildings supporting very heavy loads. When live load exceeds 150 lb per sq ft, this scheme is by far the most economical.
Banded slab	Longer spans than flat plate; typically post-tensioned; minimum thickness.	Must reuse formwork many times to be economical.	High-rise buildings; same use as flat plates, if flying forms can be used more than 10 times.	A banded slab has most of the advantages of a flat plate, but permits a longer span in one direction. It can resist greater lateral loads in the direction of the beams.
Joist slab	Minimum concrete and steel; minimum weight, hence reduced column and footing size; long spans in one direction; accommodates poke-through electrical systems.	Unattractive for a ceiling; formwork may cost more than flat plate.	Schools, offices, churches, hospitals, public and institutional buildings, buildings with moderate loadings and spans.	This is the best scheme if slabs are too long for a flat plate and the structure is not exposed. The slab thickness between joists is determined by fire requirements. Joists are most economical if beams are the same depth as the joists. Orient joists in the same direction throughout the building and in the long direction of long rectangular bays.
Skip joist	Uses less concrete than joist slab; lower rebar placing costs; joist space used for mechanical systems; permits lights and equipment to be recessed between joists.	Similar to joist slab; joists must be designed as beams; forms may require special order.	Same as for joist slabs, especially for longer fire ratings.	Ensure the availability of formwork before specifying skip joists. For larger projects, a skip joist slab should be less expensive than a joist slab, and it permits lights and equipment recessed between joists.
Waffle slab	Longer two-way spans; attractive exposed ceilings; heavy load capacity.	Formwork costs more and uses more concrete and steel than a joist slab.	Prominent buildings with exposed ceiling structure; same types as are suitable for flat slab, but with longer spans.	Column spacing should be multiples of span spacing to ensure uniformity of drop panels at each column. Drop panels can be diamond-shaped, square, or rectangular.
One-way slab	Long span in one direction.	Beams interfere with mechanical services; more expensive forms than flat plate.	Parking garages, especially with post-tensioning.	This scheme is most favored for parking garages, but the long span of about 60' must be post-tensioned, unless beams are quite deep. Shallow beams will deflect excessively.
Two-way slab	Long span in two directions; small deflection; can carry concentrated loads.	Same as for one-way beams, only more so.	Portions of buildings in which two-way beam framing is needed for other reasons; industrial buildings with heavy concentrated loads.	The high cost of the formwork and structural interference with mechanical systems make this scheme unattractive, unless heavy concentrated loads must be carried.

Contributors:
Russell S. Fling, PE, Columbus, Ohio; Roger K. Lewis, FAIA, and Mehmet T. Ergene, architect, Roger K. Lewis & Associates, Washington, DC.

FLOOR STRUCTURE ASSEMBLIES (continued)
2.13

BAY SIZE CHARACTERISTICS	REQUIRES FINISHED FLOOR SURFACE	REQUIRES FINISHED CEILING SURFACE	SERVICE PLENUM	COMPARATIVE RESISTANCE TO SOUND TRANSMISSION		REMARKS
				IMPACT	AIRBORNE	
—	No	No	Between ribs—one way	Good	Good	Economy through reuse of forms; shear at supports controlling factor
L 1.33 W	No	No	Under structure	Good	Good	For heavy loads, columns should be equidistant; not good for cantilevers
L 1.33 W	No	No	Under structure	Good	Good	Drop panels against shear required for spans above 12′
—	Optional	Visual purposes; differential camber	Between ribs—one way	Fair	Good	Most widely used prestressed concrete product in the medium-span range
—	Optional	Visual purposes; differential camber	Between ribs—one way	Fair	Good	Easy construction; lacks continuity; poor earthquake resistance
—	No	Visual or fire protection purposes	Under structure	Good	Good	—
L 1.33 W	No	No	Under structure	Good	Good	Uniform slab thickness; economical to form; easy to cantilever

PRESTRESSED AND POST-TENSIONED CONCRETE

Concrete by itself is inherently strong in tension and weak in compression. There are two procedures used for placing concrete in compression. Prestressing of the reinforcing steel occurs prior to placement of concrete and is used almost exclusively with precast concrete. Post-tensioning is the permanent tensioning of reinforcing steel for cast-in-place concrete.

- Concrete strength is usually 5000 psi at 28 days, and at least 3000 psi at the time of post-tensioning. Use hard-rock aggregate or lightweight concrete. Low-slump-controlled mix concrete is required to reduce shrinkage. Concrete shrinkage after post-tensioning decreases strength gains.
- Post-tensioning systems can be divided into three categories depending on whether the tendon is *wire, strand,* or *bar.* Wire systems use 0.25-in. diameter wires that have a minimum strength of 240,000 psi, and are usually cut to length in the shop. Strand systems use tendons (made of seven wires wrapped together) that have a minimum strength of 270,000 psi, and are cut in the field. Bar systems use bars ranging from 5/8- to 13/8-in. diameter, with a minimum strength of 145,000 psi, and may be smooth or deformed. The system used determines the type of anchorage used, which in turn affects the size of blockout required (in the edge of slab or beam) for the anchorage to be recessed.
- Grease and wrap tendons, or place in conduits, to reduce frictional losses during stressing operations. Limit the length of continuous tendons to about 10 ft if stressed from one end. Long tendons require simultaneous stressing from both ends to reduce friction loss. Tendons may be grouted after stressing, or left unbonded. Bonded tendons have structural advantages that are more important for beams and primary structural members.
- Minimum average post-tensioning (net force per area of concrete) equals 150 to 250 psi for flat plates and 200 to 500 psi for beams. Exceeding these values by much causes excessive post-tension loss because of creep.

POST-TENSIONING ANCHOR
2.15

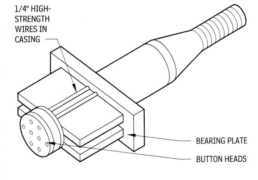

1/4" HIGH-STRENGTH WIRES IN CASING

BEARING PLATE
BUTTON HEADS

PRESTRESSED OR POST-TENSIONED BEAM
2.16

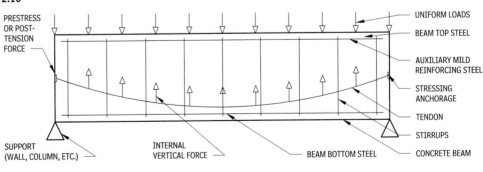

PRESTRESS OR POST-TENSION FORCE

UNIFORM LOADS
BEAM TOP STEEL
AUXILIARY MILD REINFORCING STEEL
STRESSING ANCHORAGE
TENDON
STIRRUPS
CONCRETE BEAM

SUPPORT (WALL, COLUMN, ETC.)
INTERNAL VERTICAL FORCE
BEAM BOTTOM STEEL

- Field inspection of post-tensioned concrete is critical to ensure proper size and location of tendons, and to monitor the tendon stress. Check tendon stress by measuring the elongation of the tendon and by monitoring gauge pressures on the stressing jack.
- Make provisions for the shortening of post-tensioned beams and slabs caused by elastic compression, shrinkage, and creep. After the post-tensioning is complete, build shear walls, curtain walls, or other stiff elements that adjoin post-tensioned members and isolate them with an expansion joint. Otherwise, additional post-tensioning force will be required to overcome the stiffness of the walls and prevent cracking.
- Fire tests have been conducted on prestressed beam and slab assemblies according to ASTM E 119, "Standard Test Methods for Fire Tests of Building Construction and Material," test procedures. They compare favorably with reinforced cast-in-place concrete. There is little difference between beams using grouted tendons and those using ungrouted tendons.

Contributor:
Leo A. Daly, Planning/Architecture/Engineering/Interiors, Omaha, Nebraska.

Consult the following references:

- Post-Tensioning Institute, *Post-Tensioning Manual.*
- Precast/Prestressed Concrete Institute, *PCI Design Handbook - Precast and Prestressed Concrete.*
- *Design of Prestressed Concrete Structures*, 1981, T.Y. Lin and Ned H. Burns, Wiley
- American Concrete Institute, *Building Code Requirements for Structural Concrete and Commentary* (ACI-318)

When working with a prestressed or post-tensioned beam, keep the following in mind:

- Prestressing force compresses the entire cross section of the beam, thereby reducing unwanted tension cracks.
- Permanent tension is introduced into the tendon and "locked in" with the stressing anchorage in one of two ways, though the principle in both cases is the same. In prestressed concrete, the tendon is elongated in a stressing bed before the concrete is poured. In post-tensioned concrete, the tendon is elongated after concrete has been poured and allowed to cure by means of hydraulic jacks pushing against the beam itself. Post-tensioned beams permit casting at the site for members too large or heavy for transporting from the factory to the site.
- Internal vertical forces within the beam are created by applying tension on the tendon, making the tendon begin to "straighten out." The tension reduces downward beam deflection and allows for shallower beams and longer spans than in conventionally reinforced beams.
- Auxiliary reinforcing steel provides additional strength, and controls cracking and produces more ductile behavior.
- Use stirrups to provide additional shear strength in the beam and to support the tendons and longitudinal reinforcing steel. Stirrups should be open at the top to allow the reinforcing to be placed before the tendon is installed. After the tendons are placed, "hairpins" that close the stirrups may be used, when required.

UNBONDED SINGLE STRAND TENDON ANCHORAGE
2.19

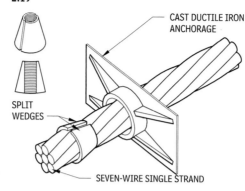

SPLIT WEDGES

CAST DUCTILE IRON ANCHORAGE

SEVEN-WIRE SINGLE STRAND

GROUTED THREAD BAR ANCHORAGE
2.20

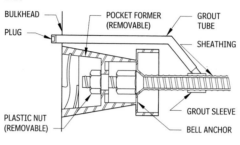

BULKHEAD

PLUG

POCKET FORMER (REMOVABLE)

GROUT TUBE

SHEATHING

PLASTIC NUT (REMOVABLE)

GROUT SLEEVE

BELL ANCHOR

PRECAST CONCRETE FRAME

Precast concrete frame systems are ideal for highly repetitive structural frames such as parking garages and hotel/apartment/dormitory buildings. Precast concrete members can be precast structural concrete or precast architectural concrete in exposed locations.

Detailing of connections for both aesthetics and to protect embedded steel members from corrosion is crucial. Typically, welded or bolted connections are grouted after final adjustment and anchorage.

Using shear walls in both directions is the most common method to resist lateral loads. Stair/elevator cores and dwelling unit separation may also serve as shear walls.

PRECAST CONCRETE COLUMN
2.21

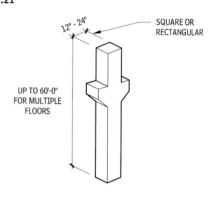

12" - 24"

SQUARE OR RECTANGULAR

UP TO 60'-0" FOR MULTIPLE FLOORS

POST-TENSIONED CONCRETE BEAM AND SLAB
2.17

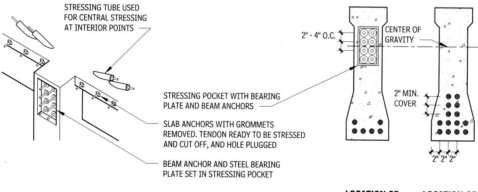

STRESSING TUBE USED FOR CENTRAL STRESSING AT INTERIOR POINTS

2" - 4" O.C.

CENTER OF GRAVITY

STRESSING POCKET WITH BEARING PLATE AND BEAM ANCHORS

SLAB ANCHORS WITH GROMMETS REMOVED. TENDON READY TO BE STRESSED AND CUT OFF, AND HOLE PLUGGED

BEAM ANCHOR AND STEEL BEARING PLATE SET IN STRESSING POCKET

2" MIN. COVER

2" 2" 2"

LOCATION OF TENDONS AT SUPPORT

LOCATION OF TENDONS AT MIDSPAN

UNBONDED SINGLE-STRAND TENDON INSTALLATION AT SLAB
2.18

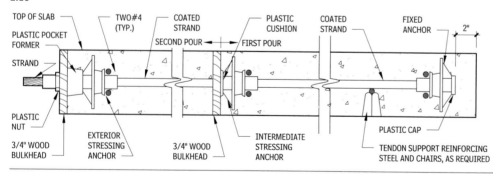

TOP OF SLAB

PLASTIC POCKET FORMER

STRAND

PLASTIC NUT

3/4" WOOD BULKHEAD

EXTERIOR STRESSING ANCHOR

TWO #4 (TYP.)

COATED STRAND

SECOND POUR

FIRST POUR

PLASTIC CUSHION

3/4" WOOD BULKHEAD

INTERMEDIATE STRESSING ANCHOR

COATED STRAND

FIXED ANCHOR

2"

PLASTIC CAP

TENDON SUPPORT REINFORCING STEEL AND CHAIRS, AS REQUIRED

Contributor:
Leo A. Daly, Planning/Architecture/Engineering/Interiors, Omaha, Nebraska.

PRECAST CONCRETE FRAME
2.22

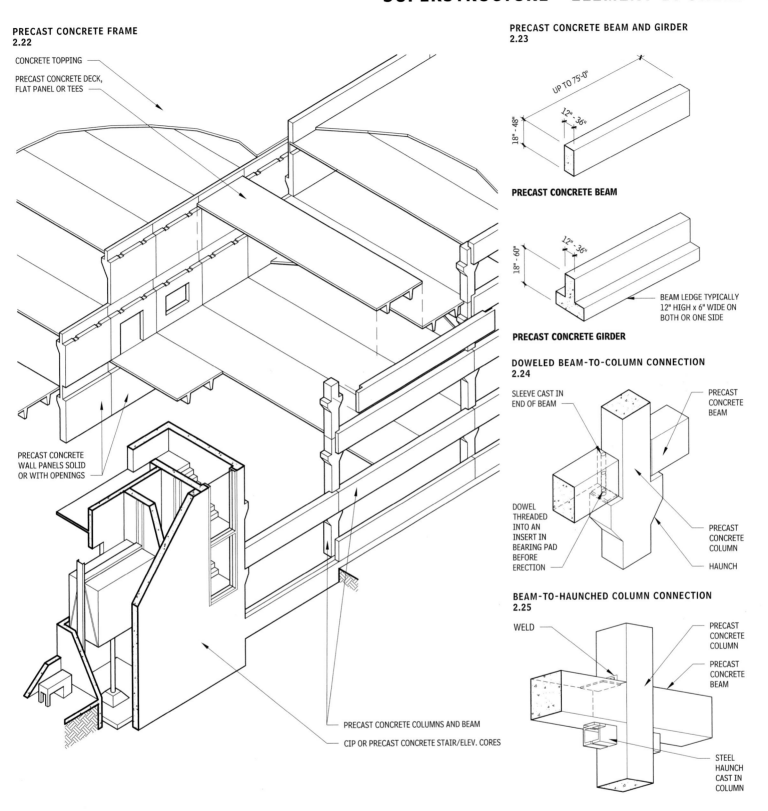

CONCRETE TOPPING

PRECAST CONCRETE DECK, FLAT PANEL OR TEES

PRECAST CONCRETE WALL PANELS SOLID OR WITH OPENINGS

PRECAST CONCRETE COLUMNS AND BEAM

CIP OR PRECAST CONCRETE STAIR/ELEV. CORES

PRECAST CONCRETE BEAM AND GIRDER
2.23

UP TO 75'-0"

18" – 48"

12" – 36"

PRECAST CONCRETE BEAM

18" – 60"

12" – 36"

BEAM LEDGE TYPICALLY 12" HIGH x 6" WIDE ON BOTH OR ONE SIDE

PRECAST CONCRETE GIRDER

DOWELED BEAM-TO-COLUMN CONNECTION
2.24

SLEEVE CAST IN END OF BEAM

PRECAST CONCRETE BEAM

DOWEL THREADED INTO AN INSERT IN BEARING PAD BEFORE ERECTION

PRECAST CONCRETE COLUMN

HAUNCH

BEAM-TO-HAUNCHED COLUMN CONNECTION
2.25

WELD

PRECAST CONCRETE COLUMN

PRECAST CONCRETE BEAM

STEEL HAUNCH CAST IN COLUMN

NOTES

2.24 The beam sits on the bearing pad, which provides uniform bearing and accommodates small movements caused by shrinkage, creep, and temperature changes.

2.25 Steel haunches are smaller than concrete bearing pads, which is important if headroom is critical.

Contributor:
Richard J. Vitullo, AIA, Oak Leaf Studio, Crownsville, Maryland.

SPANDREL CONNECTION
2.26

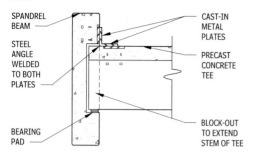

SPANDREL BEAM

STEEL ANGLE WELDED TO BOTH PLATES

CAST-IN METAL PLATES

PRECAST CONCRETE TEE

BEARING PAD

BLOCK-OUT TO EXTEND STEM OF TEE

STRUCTURAL STEEL FRAMING

MOMENT-RESISTING FRAME

A moment-resisting frame's lateral stability and resistance to wind and seismic forces depend on a fixed connection of beams and columns. A moment-resisting connection is achieved when the top and bottom flanges of each beam are welded to the flanges of the connecting columns with full-depth welds. By directly welding the beam web to the column flange, the beam's horizontal reaction to wind forces is transferred to the column. (A connection using web angles and high-strength bolts is also permitted.) The building's floors are designed to act as diaphragms that connect all of the columns and beams, enabling the building to react as a unit.

Moment-resisting frames are uneconomical in tall steel buildings because the larger lateral forces in such structures can be handled more efficiently by compression and tension diagonal members, as found in braced frames. To save costs, often the upper stories of a braced-frame building use moment-resisting beam-column connections to resist wind loads.

MOMENT-RESISTING FRAME
2.27

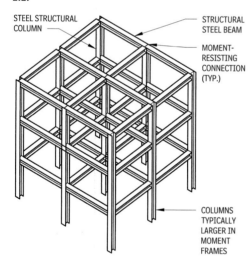

STEEL STRUCTURAL COLUMN

STRUCTURAL STEEL BEAM

MOMENT-RESISTING CONNECTION (TYP.)

COLUMNS TYPICALLY LARGER IN MOMENT FRAMES

BRACED CORE

In the braced core system, walls around elevator shafts and stairwells are designed to act as vertical trusses that cantilever up from the foundation. The chords of each truss are building columns; the floor beams act as ties. Diagonals placed in a K pattern (occasionally, in an X pattern) complete the truss. A system employing knee braces is used in seismic areas because of its greater capability to dissipate earthquake energy.

Braced core systems can be used efficiently in single-story buildings, as well as in buildings over 50 stories.

BRACED CORE
2.28

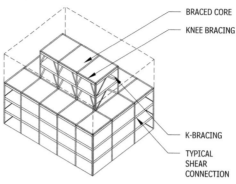

BRACED CORE

KNEE BRACING

K-BRACING

TYPICAL SHEAR CONNECTION

BRACING DIAGRAM
2.29

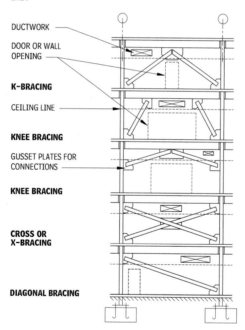

DUCTWORK

DOOR OR WALL OPENING

K-BRACING

CEILING LINE

KNEE BRACING

GUSSET PLATES FOR CONNECTIONS

KNEE BRACING

CROSS OR X-BRACING

DIAGONAL BRACING

Following are characteristics and principles to keep in mind when working with structural steel framing:

- The high strength of steel provides for economical construction of relatively large structural bays.
- Major framing elements are typically W-shaped sections, or round, square, and rectangular hollow structural sections. Angles or channels may be used for architectural expression.
- Building codes require protection of the steel from fire, except for small or low-rise structures in some low-hazard occupancies.
- Horizontal loads from wind and seismic events must be resisted, typically by diagonal bracing, moment connections, or shear walls.
- Moment frames allow maximum floor plan flexibility, but typically increase weight and cost of the structural steel framing.
- Braced frames are cost-effective, but disrupt the floor plan if not carefully located around typical core elements such as stairs, shafts, and toilet rooms. Bracing typically is provided by angles or W-shapes, as well as hollow structural shapes. Rods and cables may be used for architectural expression.
- Shear walls, typically around shafts for stairs, ducts, and elevators, can be an effective lateral load design option. Shear walls can be constructed of steel plate, concrete, or reinforced CMU. Minimize openings in shear walls for doors and services.
- It may be effective to mix different lateral restraint methods. For a long, narrow building, bracing in the short direction with moment frames in the long direction may be effective.
- The floor or roof deck typically is designed to act as a diaphragm to transmit loads to the lateral restraint elements. Structures without a deck capable of transmitting loads (such as bar grating or metal roofing) may require diagonal bracing in the floor or roof framing.
- Open-web steel joists may be used within a main frame of structural steel for economy.

For more information, refer to the *AISC Manual of Steel Construction*.

FABRICATED FIREPROOFED STEEL COLUMNS

Fabricated fireproofed steel columns, (lally columns) are structural units that consist of load-bearing steel columns filled with concrete. This creates a column with increased load-bearing capacity in a space no larger than a standard column. Lally columns have fire-resistant characteristics when a layer of fireproofing material encases the structural column. Fire ratings typically range from two to four hours.

NOTES

2.28 Bracing design to be determined by structural engineer based on specific loading configurations.
2.29 a. Knee bracing introduces bending into columns and beams and may increase their size, but allows largest openings.
b. Cross or diagonal bracing is very efficient but limits opening location and size.

Contributors:
Donald J. Neubauer, PE, Neubauer-Sohn Consulting Engineers, Potomac, Maryland; Richard J. Vitullo, AIA, Oak Leaf Studio, Crownsville, Maryland.

FABRICATED FIREPROOFED STEEL COLUMNS
2.30

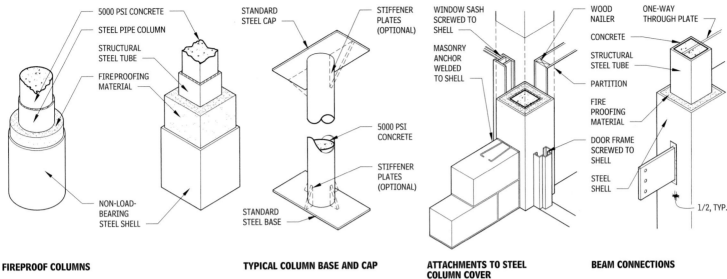

FIREPROOF COLUMNS

- 5000 PSI CONCRETE
- STEEL PIPE COLUMN
- STRUCTURAL STEEL TUBE
- FIREPROOFING MATERIAL
- NON-LOAD-BEARING STEEL SHELL

TYPICAL COLUMN BASE AND CAP

- STANDARD STEEL CAP
- STIFFENER PLATES (OPTIONAL)
- 5000 PSI CONCRETE
- STIFFENER PLATES (OPTIONAL)
- STANDARD STEEL BASE

ATTACHMENTS TO STEEL COLUMN COVER

- WINDOW SASH SCREWED TO SHELL
- MASONRY ANCHOR WELDED TO SHELL
- WOOD NAILER
- CONCRETE
- STRUCTURAL STEEL TUBE
- PARTITION
- FIRE PROOFING MATERIAL
- DOOR FRAME SCREWED TO SHELL
- STEEL SHELL

BEAM CONNECTIONS

- ONE-WAY THROUGH PLATE
- 1/2, TYP.

ARCHITECTURALLY EXPOSED STRUCTURAL STEEL FRAMING

The characteristics and principles to keep in mind when working with architecturally-exposed structural steel (AESS) include the following:

- AESS is structural steel superstructure, supporting all or portions of a building, which is left exposed in the finished work. Through layout and detailing, AESS is meant to contribute to the architectural expression.
- The challenge to successful use of AESS is to clearly specify and detail the level of quality required, which is substantially beyond the requirements for normal structural steel. Primary areas of concern are the quality of finish of the individual members, the quality of the methods of joining members together (particularly of welds), and the tolerances of the finished work.
- AESS frequently incorporates a variety of tension members fabricated of stainless steel and proprietary fittings.
- AESS may need special fire protection, such as intumescent coating or deluge sprinkler systems.
- For economy, it is worthwhile to carefully identify which portions of the AESS will be viewed in close proximity versus those that are farther away. Locate defects, welds, and connections on the side of assembly away from view, for economy.

Refer to *AESS Supplement* to "Modern Steel Construction" (May 2003), for explanation of how to specify AESS.

AESS WELDS
2.32

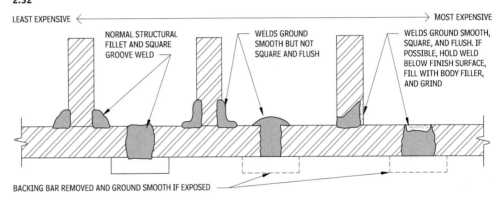

LEAST EXPENSIVE ← → MOST EXPENSIVE

- NORMAL STRUCTURAL FILLET AND SQUARE GROOVE WELD
- WELDS GROUND SMOOTH BUT NOT SQUARE AND FLUSH
- WELDS GROUND SMOOTH, SQUARE, AND FLUSH. IF POSSIBLE, HOLD WELD BELOW FINISH SURFACE, FILL WITH BODY FILLER, AND GRIND

BACKING BAR REMOVED AND GROUND SMOOTH IF EXPOSED

AESS CONNECTION
2.31

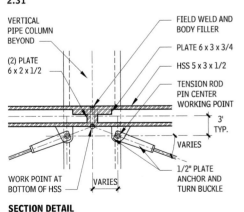

SECTION DETAIL

- VERTICAL PIPE COLUMN BEYOND
- (2) PLATE 6 x 2 x 1/2
- FIELD WELD AND BODY FILLER
- PLATE 6 x 3 x 3/4
- HSS 5 x 3 x 1/2
- TENSION ROD PIN CENTER WORKING POINT
- 3' TYP.
- VARIES
- 1/2" PLATE ANCHOR AND TURN BUCKLE
- WORK POINT AT BOTTOM OF HSS
- VARIES

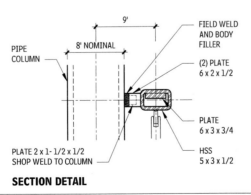

SECTION DETAIL

- PIPE COLUMN
- 9'
- 8' NOMINAL
- FIELD WELD AND BODY FILLER
- (2) PLATE 6 x 2 x 1/2
- PLATE 6 x 3 x 3/4
- HSS 5 x 3 x 1/2
- PLATE 2 x 1-1/2 x 1/2 SHOP WELD TO COLUMN

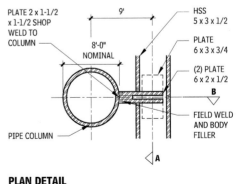

PLAN DETAIL

- PLATE 2 x 1-1/2 x 1-1/2 SHOP WELD TO COLUMN
- 9'
- 8'-0" NOMINAL
- PIPE COLUMN
- HSS 5 x 3 x 1/2
- PLATE 6 x 3 x 3/4
- (2) PLATE 6 x 2 x 1/2
- B
- FIELD WELD AND BODY FILLER
- A

NOTE

2.31 Locate HSS seam away from line of sight, or grind smooth.

Contributors:
Anthony Golebiewski, AIA, Kling, Philadelphia, Pennsylvania; Eric Gastier, Alexandria, Virginia.

STEEL JOIST FLOOR FRAMING

Design consideration of steel joist floor framing should include:

- *Ceilings*: Ceiling supports can be suspended from or mounted directly to the bottom chords of joists. Suspended systems are recommended, because of dimensional variations in actual joist depths.
- *Floor construction*: Joists are usually covered by 2-1/2 to 3 in. of concrete on steel decking. Concrete thickness may be increased to accommodate electrical conduit or electrical/communications raceways. Precast concrete, gypsum planks, or plywood can also be used for the floor system.
- *Vibration*: Objectionable vibrations can occur in open web joist and 2-1/2-in. concrete slab designs for open floor areas at spans between 20 and 40 ft, in particular at 28 ft. When a floor area cannot have partitions, objectionable vibrations can be prevented or reduced by increasing slab thickness or modifying the joist span. Attention should also be given to support for framing beams, which can magnify a vibration problem when unsupported.
- *Openings in floor or roof systems*: Small openings between joists are framed with angles or channels supported on the adjoining two joists. Larger openings necessitating interruption of joists are framed with steel angle or channel headers.
- *Adaptability*: It is more difficult to alter joists, add openings, or change loading than with structural steel framing.
- *Fireproofing*: Applying fireproofing to joists is more difficult and expensive than to structural steel.

SECTION-THROUGH OPEN WEB STEEL JOIST BEARING
2.33

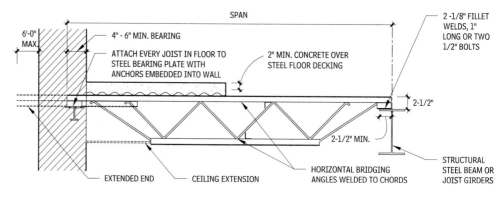

SECTION-THROUGH OPEN WEB STEEL JOISTS
2.34

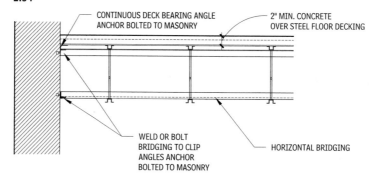

JOIST PROFILES

SECTION-THROUGH LONG SPAN STEEL JOIST BEARING
2.35

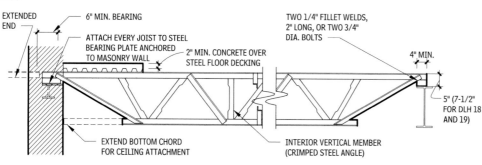

SECTION-THROUGH LONG-SPAN STEEL JOIST
2.36

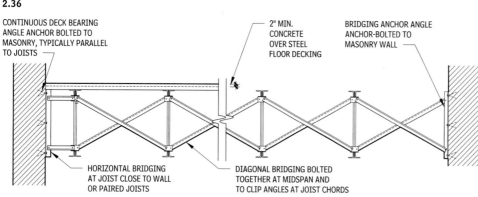

BOTTOM CHORD BEARING AT SQUARE END
2.37

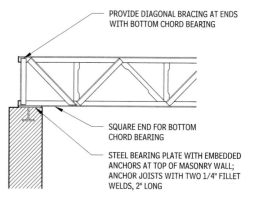

PROVIDE DIAGONAL BRACING AT ENDS WITH BOTTOM CHORD BEARING

SQUARE END FOR BOTTOM CHORD BEARING

STEEL BEARING PLATE WITH EMBEDDED ANCHORS AT TOP OF MASONRY WALL; ANCHOR JOISTS WITH TWO 1/4" FILLET WELDS, 2" LONG

BOTTOM CHORD EXTENSION DETAIL
2.38

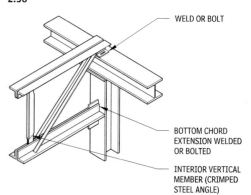

WELD OR BOLT

BOTTOM CHORD EXTENSION WELDED OR BOLTED

INTERIOR VERTICAL MEMBER (CRIMPED STEEL ANGLE)

NOTE

2.35 Web-member type depends on span and load characteristics.

Contributors:
Kenneth D. Franch, PE, AIA, Aguirre, Inc., Dallas, Texas; Charles M. Ault, Setter, Leach, & Lindstrom, Architects & Engineers, Minneapolis, Minnesota.

COLD-FORMED METAL FLOOR JOIST FRAMING

Cold-formed steel (CFS) floor framing uses C-shaped members that are cold-rolled from a steel sheet. CFS framing is laid out similar to traditional wood joist floor framing. Finishes may be a hot-dipped galvanized coating or shop primed. Fastening is typically self-drilling, self-tapping screws, or welded.

Final engineering of CFS framing is commonly provided by a structural engineer hired by the installing contractor, based on a performance specification prepared by the architect and project structural engineer. This delivery method, known as delegated design, allows an optimization of the design of the CFS system. CFS framing characteristic vary by manufacturer. Based on preliminary investigation and other project design requirements, the design professional may select certain characteristics of the joists, for example depth or minimum spacing. The installer's engineer will then select specific joists that conform to the design characteristics that also meet the structural performance criteria, including yield strength (33 or 50 ksi), joist gauge and flange width. CFS rim joists, plates, and other framing may require continuous insulation outside of the CFS element, to reduce thermal bridging and to comply with energy code.

BRIDGING
2.39

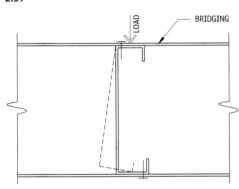

Joists are subject to twisting under load. Bracing of the top and bottom flange is required at approximately 1/3 points or 6 to 8 ft on center, depending on final design. Bridging is, typically, continuous top and bottom straps with solid blocking at ends, and periodically spaced. Structural sheathing or decking may reduce some or all of the bridging.

WEB STIFFENERS
2.40

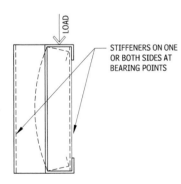

Point loads at bearing points or from applied loads may cause crushing of the flange or folding of the web. Stiffeners from short lengths of a vertical joist, a sistered joist, or angles attached to the rim track may be required, as determined by final engineering.

OPENINGS
2.41

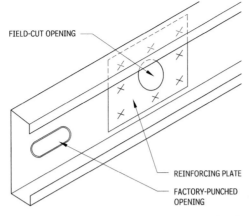

Joists may come factory-punched, with openings of approximately 1-1/2 by 4 in. at 24 in. on center, though this will vary by manufacturer. Additional openings, generally not larger than half the joist depth, may be added if individually analyzed during final engineering. Reinforcing plates may be required.

COLD-FORMED METAL JOISTS
2.42

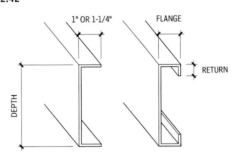

Common Depths: 6, 7-1/4, 8, 9-1/4, 10, 11-1/2, 12, 14, and 16 in., consult manufacturers for available sizes.

Lengths up to 60 ft.

FLANGE (IN.)	RETURN (IN.)
1-3/8	5/16 to 3/8
1-5/8	1/2 to 9/16
2 or 2-1/2	9/16 to 11/16
3 or 3-1/2	1

FRAMING OF FLOOR OPENING
2.43

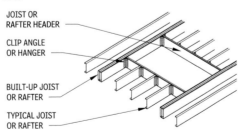

FLOOR JOISTS AT CONTINUOUS WALLS
2.44

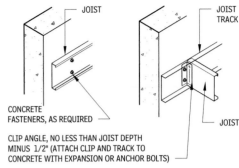

CLIP ANGLE, NO LESS THAN JOIST DEPTH MINUS 1/2" (ATTACH CLIP AND TRACK TO CONCRETE WITH EXPANSION OR ANCHOR BOLTS)

FLOOR JOISTS PARALLEL TO WALL   **FLOOR JOIST SUPPORT AT WALL**

JOISTS OVER BEAM OR BEARING WALL (CONTINUOUS SPAN)
2.45

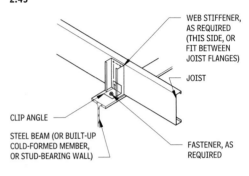

FLOOR FRAMING AT EXTERIOR WALL
2.46

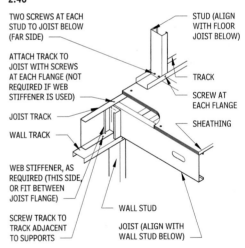

Consult the following reference:

- "Product Technical Information," the Steel Stud Manufacturers Association (www.ssma.com)

NOTES

2.44 Provide solid blocking and bridging as required.

2.45 a. Continuous bridging is required between each joist above a beam. Solid blocking in other spaces may be used in lieu of bridging.

b. When a bearing wall is above, the studs must align with the joists below.

c. Web stiffeners are not required when continuous solid blocking is used.

Contributor:
American Iron and Steel Institute, Washington, DC.

FLOOR JOISTS SUPPORTED BY BEAM OR BEARING WALL (OVERLAPPED)
2.47

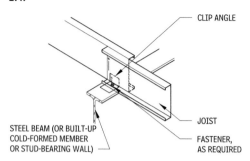

CLIP ANGLE

JOIST

FASTENER, AS REQUIRED

STEEL BEAM (OR BUILT-UP COLD-FORMED MEMBER OR STUD-BEARING WALL)

FLOOR JOISTS BEARING ON FOUNDATION
2.48

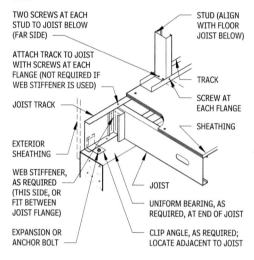

TWO SCREWS AT EACH STUD TO JOIST BELOW (FAR SIDE)

ATTACH TRACK TO JOIST WITH SCREWS AT EACH FLANGE (NOT REQUIRED IF WEB STIFFENER IS USED)

JOIST TRACK

EXTERIOR SHEATHING

WEB STIFFENER, AS REQUIRED (THIS SIDE, OR FIT BETWEEN JOIST FLANGE)

EXPANSION OR ANCHOR BOLT

STUD (ALIGN WITH FLOOR JOIST BELOW)

TRACK

SCREW AT EACH FLANGE

SHEATHING

JOIST

UNIFORM BEARING, AS REQUIRED, AT END OF JOIST

CLIP ANGLE, AS REQUIRED; LOCATE ADJACENT TO JOIST

WOOD FLOOR FRAMING

This section examines the use of wood in floor framing assemblies.

WOOD FLOOR FRAMING MEMBERS
2.49

SHORT SPAN, LESS THAN 24'

DIMENSION LUMBER

DIMENSIONAL LUMBER 2 x 8, 2 x 10, 2 x 12

SMALL TO MEDIUM, 16' TO 30'

5-1/2" - 18"

LAMINATED VENEER LUMBER

1-3/4" THICK LAMINATED JOISTS

SMALL TO MEDIUM, 20' TO 60'

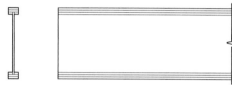

WOOD I-JOISTS

LIGHTWEIGHT 3/8" LAMINATED STRAND LUMBER, OSB, OR PLYWOOD WEB 1-1/2", 2" OR 3" WIDE LVL OR LUMBER FLANGE

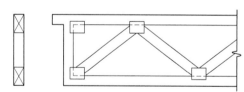

SHOP-FABRICATED WOOD TRUSSES

2x4 TRUSSES

MEDIUM, SPAN 40' TO 60'

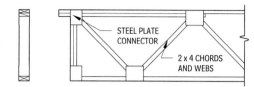

STEEL PLATE CONNECTOR

2 x 4 CHORDS AND WEBS

SHOP-FABRICATED WOOD TRUSSES

WOOD CHORDS AND WEBS, STEEL PLATE CONNECTORS

MEDIUM TO LONG, SPAN 40' TO 60'

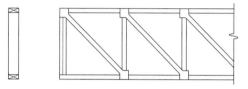

WOOD CHORDS, 20-GA. STEEL WEBS

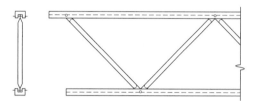

WOOD CHORDS, 1" TO 1-1/2" DIA. TUBING WEBS; DEPTHS TO 40"

LONG TO VERY LONG, SPAN 60' TO 100'

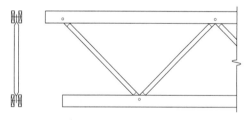

DOUBLE 2x6 CHORDS, 2" DIA. WEBS; DEPTH TO 63"

METAL-WEB WOOD JOISTS

FLOOR FRAMING WOOD BEAMS
2.50

HEAVY TIMBER BEAM   **LAMINATED VENEER LUMBER (LVL) BEAM**   **PARALLEL STRAND LUMBER (PSL) BEAM**   **GLUE-LAMINATED BEAM**   **BUILT-UP BEAM**   **FLITCH BEAM**   **BOX BEAM**

NOTES

2.47 a. Continuous bridging is required between each joist above a beam. Solid blocking in other space may be used in lieu of bridging.
b. When a bearing wall is above, studs must align with joists below.
2.50 a. *Heavy timber beam*: Timber beams are available in a variety of species and grades; Douglas fir is the strongest. Heavy timber uses rectangular solid-wood framing members that are a nominally a minimum of 5 in., in both dimensions.
b. *Laminated veneer lumber (LVL) beam*: Vertical factory-laminated sections are glued together. Actual widths are multiples of 1-3/4 in. (two

pieces match thickness of 2 × 4 wall). Actual heights range from 5-1/2 to 18 in.
c. *Parallel strand lumber (PSL) beam*: Factory-glued composite beam made with long narrow strips of veneer, oriented along beam length. Actual widths are 3-1/2, 5-1/4, and 7 in. Heights range from 9-1/4 to 18 in.
d. *Glue-laminated beam*: Horizontal factory-glued laminations make a knot-free and very stable beam. Actual widths are 3-1/8, 5-1/8, 7-1/8 in., and so on. Heights are in multiples of 1-1/2 in.
e. *Built-up beam*: Dimension lumber is nailed together to form a single beam (four pieces maximum). Widths are multiples of 1-1/2 in. Height follows dimension lumber.

f. *Flitch beam*: A steel plate sandwiched between two pieces of lumber adds strength without substantially increasing the beam size. The lumber prevents buckling of the steel and provides a nailing surface. Widths are 3 to 3-1/2 in. Heights follow dimension lumber.
g. *Box beam*: 2 × 4 lumber is sandwiched between two plywood skins. Plywood is both nailed and glued to 2 × 4s and at all edges. Plywood joints must be offset.

WESTERN OR PLATFORM WOOD FRAMING

Before any of the superstructure is erected, the first-floor framing and subflooring is put down, making a platform on which the walls and partitions can be assembled and tilted into place. Because floor framing and wall frames do not interlock, adequate sheathing must act as bracing and provide the necessary lateral resistance. Where required for additional stiffness or bracing, metal strapping, or 1 × 4 may be let into the outer face of studs at 45° angles,

secured at top, bottom, and to studs. The process is repeated for each story of the building.

Bridging may be omitted when flooring is nailed adequately to the joist. However, where nominal depth-to-thickness ratio of joists exceeds 6, bridging would be installed at 8-ft-0-in. intervals. Building codes may allow omission of bridging under certain conditions. Steel bridging is available. Some types do not require nails.

For firestopping, all concealed spaces in framing, with the exception of areas around flues and chimneys, are to be fitted with 2-in. blocking arranged to prevent drafts between spaces.

Platform framing has essentially replaced balloon framing. Balloon framing with studs continuous from wood sill to top plate is rarely used, except in special locations (such as two-story spaces, at parapets, and similar situations where a structural cantilever of the wall is required).

PLATFORM FRAMING
2.51

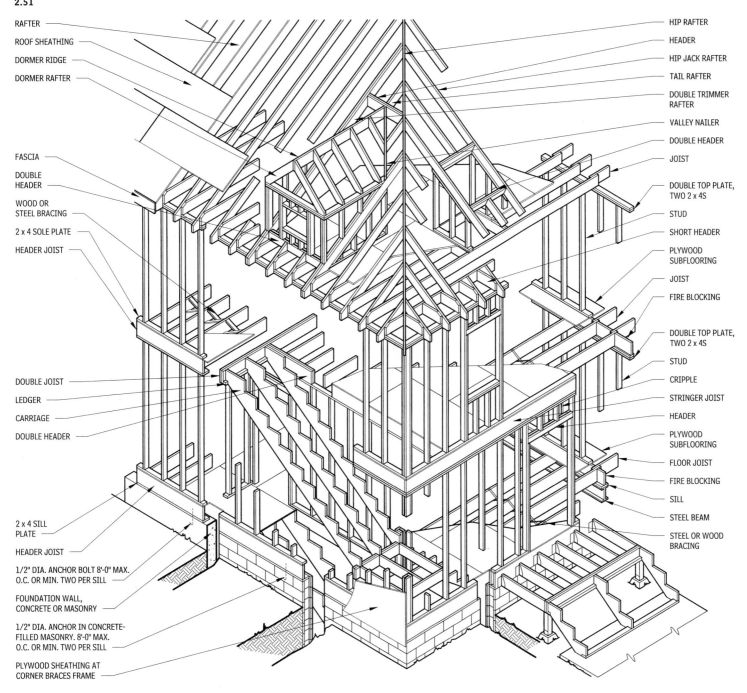

RAFTER
ROOF SHEATHING
DORMER RIDGE
DORMER RAFTER

FASCIA
DOUBLE HEADER
WOOD OR STEEL BRACING
2 x 4 SOLE PLATE
HEADER JOIST

DOUBLE JOIST
LEDGER
CARRIAGE
DOUBLE HEADER

2 x 4 SILL PLATE
HEADER JOIST
1/2" DIA. ANCHOR BOLT 8'-0" MAX. O.C. OR MIN. TWO PER SILL
FOUNDATION WALL, CONCRETE OR MASONRY
1/2" DIA. ANCHOR IN CONCRETE-FILLED MASONRY. 8'-0" MAX. O.C. OR MIN. TWO PER SILL
PLYWOOD SHEATHING AT CORNER BRACES FRAME

HIP RAFTER
HEADER
HIP JACK RAFTER
TAIL RAFTER
DOUBLE TRIMMER RAFTER
VALLEY NAILER
DOUBLE HEADER
JOIST
DOUBLE TOP PLATE, TWO 2 x 4S
STUD
SHORT HEADER
PLYWOOD SUBFLOORING
JOIST
FIRE BLOCKING
DOUBLE TOP PLATE, TWO 2 x 4S
STUD
CRIPPLE
STRINGER JOIST
HEADER
PLYWOOD SUBFLOORING
FLOOR JOIST
FIRE BLOCKING
SILL
STEEL BEAM
STEEL OR WOOD BRACING

NOTES

2.14 a. Roof framing may be level, I-joist, or trusses, shown in Figure 2.116.
b. Floor joists may be any of the framing members shown in Figure 2.50.

Contributor:
Timothy B. McDonald, Washington, DC.

PLATFORM FRAMING SECTION
2.52

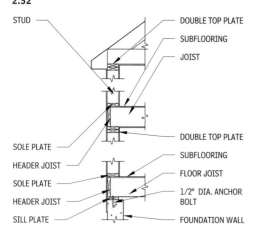

- STUD
- DOUBLE TOP PLATE
- SUBFLOORING
- JOIST
- SOLE PLATE
- DOUBLE TOP PLATE
- HEADER JOIST
- SUBFLOORING
- SOLE PLATE
- FLOOR JOIST
- HEADER JOIST
- 1/2" DIA. ANCHOR BOLT
- SILL PLATE
- FOUNDATION WALL

FRAMING DETAILS FOR JOISTS AND SILLS

WOOD JOISTS SUPPORTED ON STEEL BEAM
2.53

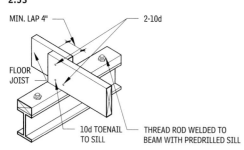

MIN. LAP 4"

2-10d

FLOOR JOIST

10d TOENAIL TO SILL

THREAD ROD WELDED TO BEAM WITH PREDRILLED SILL

LAPPED OVER WOOD SILL

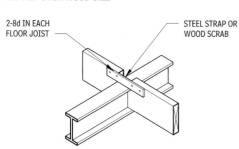

2-8d IN EACH FLOOR JOIST

STEEL STRAP OR WOOD SCRAB

ON LOWER FLANGE

BRIDGING
2.56

STEEL BRIDGING

2-10d TOENAILS EACH END

1 x 3 CROSS BRIDGING

WOOD JOISTS SUPPORTED ON WOOD BEAM
2.54

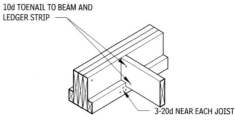

10d TOENAIL TO BEAM AND LEDGER STRIP

3-20d NEAR EACH JOIST

JOIST NOTCHED OVER LEDGER STRIP

BEAM AND JOIST NOTCHED FOR HANGER

JOIST IN JOIST HANGER

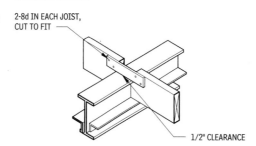

2-8d IN EACH JOIST

THREAD ROD WELDED TO BEAM WITH PREDRILLED SILL

APPROXIMATE THICKNESS SAME AS EXTERIOR SILL TO EQUALIZE SHRINKAGE

1/2" CLEARANCE

ON WOOD LEDGER

2-8d IN EACH JOIST, CUT TO FIT

1/2" CLEARANCE

ON STEEL ANGLES

2-16d TOENAILS EACH END

SOLID BRIDGING

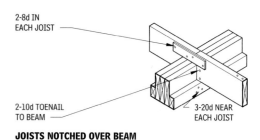

2-10d

10d TOENAIL TO BEAM

3-20d NEAR EACH JOIST

OVERLAPPING JOISTS NOTCHED OVER BEAM

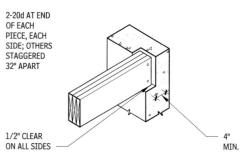

2-8d IN EACH JOIST

2-10d TOENAIL TO BEAM

3-20d NEAR EACH JOIST

JOISTS NOTCHED OVER BEAM

BEAMS
2.55

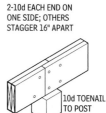

2-10d EACH END ON ONE SIDE; OTHERS STAGGER 16" APART

10d TOENAIL TO POST EACH SIDE

TWO-PIECE BUILT-UP BEAM

2-20d AT END OF EACH PIECE, EACH SIDE; OTHERS STAGGERED 32" APART

1/2" CLEAR ON ALL SIDES

4" MIN.

THREE-PIECE BUILT-UP BEAM

SILL FOR PLATFORM FRAMING
2.57

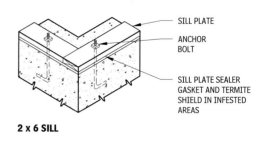

- SILL PLATE
- ANCHOR BOLT
- SILL PLATE SEALER GASKET AND TERMITE SHIELD IN INFESTED AREAS

2 x 6 SILL

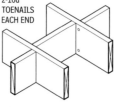

Contributor:
Joseph A. Wilkes, Wilkes and Faulkner, Washington, DC.

WOOD I-JOIST FLOOR FRAMING DETAILS
2.58

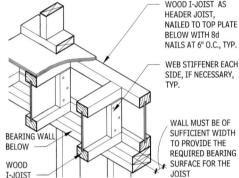

WOOD I-JOIST BLOCKING NAILED TO TOP PLATE BELOW WITH 8d NAILS AT 6" O.C., TYP.

WOOD I-JOIST

WEB STIFFENER EACH SIDE, IF NECESSARY, TYP.

BEARING WALL BELOW

WOOD I-JOIST BLOCKING

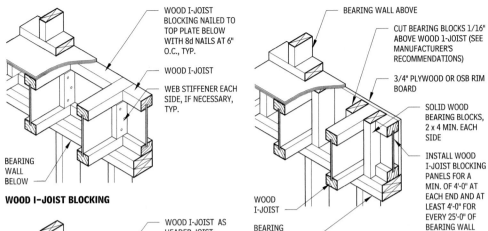

BEARING WALL ABOVE

CUT BEARING BLOCKS 1/16" ABOVE WOOD I-JOIST (SEE MANUFACTURER'S RECOMMENDATIONS)

3/4" PLYWOOD OR OSB RIM BOARD

SOLID WOOD BEARING BLOCKS, 2 x 4 MIN. EACH SIDE

INSTALL WOOD I-JOIST BLOCKING PANELS FOR A MIN. OF 4'-0" AT EACH END AND AT LEAST 4'-0" FOR EVERY 25'-0" OF BEARING WALL LENGTH

WOOD I-JOIST

BEARING WALL BELOW

BEARING BLOCKS

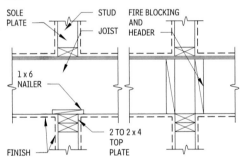

WOOD I-JOIST AS HEADER JOIST, NAILED TO TOP PLATE BELOW WITH 8d NAILS AT 6" O.C., TYP.

WEB STIFFENER EACH SIDE, IF NECESSARY, TYP.

WALL MUST BE OF SUFFICIENT WIDTH TO PROVIDE THE REQUIRED BEARING SURFACE FOR THE JOIST

BEARING WALL BELOW

WOOD I-JOIST

WOOD I-JOIST AS HEADER JOIST

BEARING WALL BELOW

TWO LAYERS OF 3/4" PLYWOOD OR OSB RIM BOARDS

END JOINT MUST BE AT WOOD I-JOIST LOCATION

WEB STIFFENERS EACH SIDE, WHEN REQUIRED

BEARING WALL BELOW

WOOD I-JOIST

STANDARD 2X RIM BOARDS

FLOOR DETAILS AT BEARING INTERIOR PARTITIONS
2.59

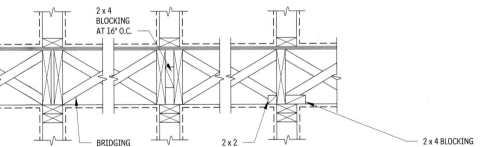

SOLE PLATE

STUD

JOIST

FIRE BLOCKING AND HEADER

1 x 6 NAILER

2 TO 2 x 4 TOP PLATE

FINISH

PARTITIONS PERPENDICULAR TO JOISTS

JOIST

BALLOON AND BRACED

2 x 4 BLOCKING AT 16" O.C.

BRIDGING

2 x 2

2 x 4 BLOCKING

PARTITIONS PARALLEL TO JOISTS

Contributors:
Joseph A. Wilkes, Wilkes and Faulkner, Washington, DC; John Ray Hoke, Jr., FAIA, Washington, DC.

FLOOR DETAILS AT NONBEARING INTERIOR PARTITIONS
2.60

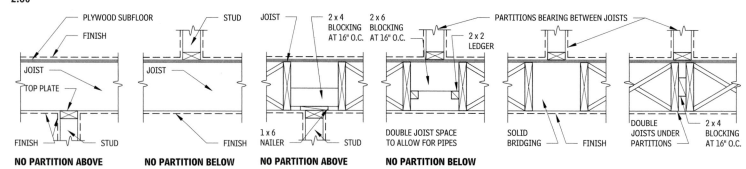

NO PARTITION ABOVE　　　**NO PARTITION BELOW**　　　**NO PARTITION ABOVE**　　　**NO PARTITION BELOW**

PARTITIONS PERPENDICULAR TO JOISTS　　　**PARTITIONS PARALLEL TO JOISTS**

FLOOR CANTILEVERS
2.61

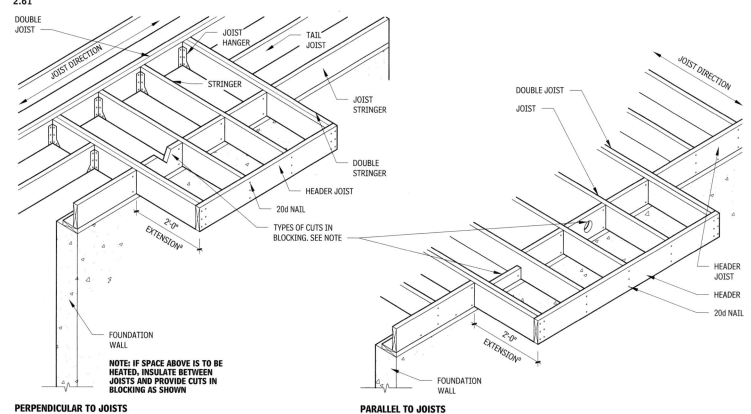

NOTE: IF SPACE ABOVE IS TO BE HEATED, INSULATE BETWEEN JOISTS AND PROVIDE CUTS IN BLOCKING AS SHOWN

PERPENDICULAR TO JOISTS　　　**PARALLEL TO JOISTS**

NOTE

2.61 a. Any extension greater than 2′ must be engineered.

Contributors:
Joseph A. Wilkes, Wilkes and Faulkner, Washington, DC; John Ray Hoke, Jr., FAIA, Washington, DC.

SHOP-FABRICATED WOOD TRUSSES
2.62

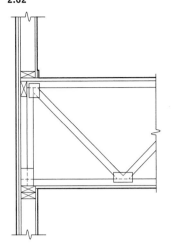

BOTTOM CHORD BEARING ON STUD WALL

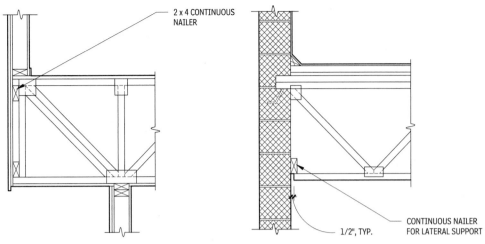

2 x 4 CONTINUOUS NAILER

CANTILEVERED FLOOR TRUSS

1/2", TYP.

CONTINUOUS NAILER FOR LATERAL SUPPORT

TOP CHORD BEARING ON MASONRY WALL

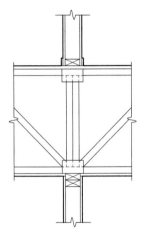

BOTTOM CHORD BEARING

HEAVY TIMBER CONSTRUCTION

Heavy timber construction is characterized by large, exposed timber columns, beams, and other structural members, joined together by traditional pegged mortise-and-tenon or similar joints. Heavy timber uses rectangular solid-wood framing members that are nominally a minimum of 5 in., in both dimensions. Heavy timber fabricated timber frame modules are called bents. Bents run perpendicular to the ridge, and include the primary columns, beams, girders, and rafters, and knee braces. Bents are typically spaced 10 to 16 ft on center. Note that alternate framing methods running parallel to the ridge, or utilizing systems similar in concept to platform framing, are available from some timber framers. Knee braces typically provide bracing against lateral loads.

Heavy timber structures are typically enclosed with stressed-skin insulated panels, leaving the frame totally exposed on the interior. Heavy timber construction is being updated with modern materials such as glulam members and proprietary concealed metal connections.

TYPICAL TIMBER FRAME (SHOWING TWO-ROOF AND FLOOR TYPES)
2.63

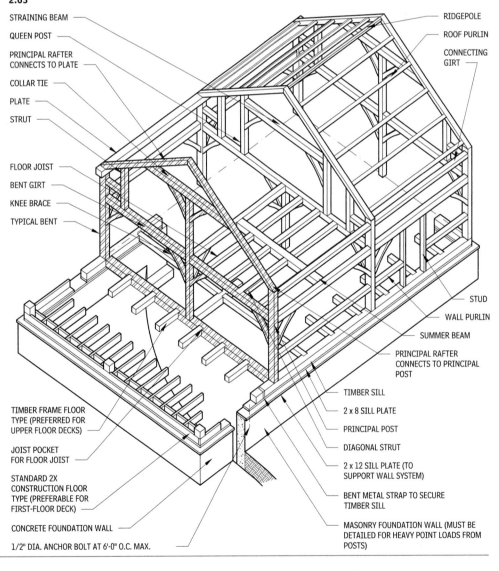

STRAINING BEAM
QUEEN POST
PRINCIPAL RAFTER CONNECTS TO PLATE
COLLAR TIE
PLATE
STRUT
FLOOR JOIST
BENT GIRT
KNEE BRACE
TYPICAL BENT

RIDGEPOLE
ROOF PURLIN
CONNECTING GIRT
STUD
WALL PURLIN
SUMMER BEAM
PRINCIPAL RAFTER CONNECTS TO PRINCIPAL POST
TIMBER SILL
2 x 8 SILL PLATE
PRINCIPAL POST
DIAGONAL STRUT
2 x 12 SILL PLATE (TO SUPPORT WALL SYSTEM)
BENT METAL STRAP TO SECURE TIMBER SILL
MASONRY FOUNDATION WALL (MUST BE DETAILED FOR HEAVY POINT LOADS FROM POSTS)

TIMBER FRAME FLOOR TYPE (PREFERRED FOR UPPER FLOOR DECKS)
JOIST POCKET FOR FLOOR JOIST
STANDARD 2X CONSTRUCTION FLOOR TYPE (PREFERABLE FOR FIRST-FLOOR DECK)
CONCRETE FOUNDATION WALL
1/2" DIA. ANCHOR BOLT AT 6'-0" O.C. MAX.

NOTE

2.63 Shaded members represent components of a typical bent.

Contributors:
Tedd Benson and Ben Brungraber, PhD, PE, Benson Woodworking Co., Inc., Alstead, New Hampshire; Timothy B. McDonald, Washington, DC; Richard J. Vitullo, AIA, Oak Leaf Studio, Corwnsville, Maryland.

SHOULDERED MORTISE-AND-TENON JOINT
2.64

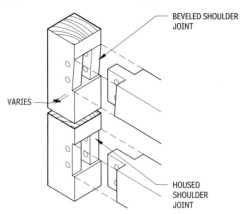

BEVELED SHOULDER JOINT

VARIES

HOUSED SHOULDER JOINT

A beveled shoulder or housed joint is used to connect all load-bearing beams (such as bent and connecting girts and summer beams) to posts. Angled variations can be used when principal rafters join to posts or for diagonal braces. The depth of the shoulder depends on loading, torsion, other joinery in the area, and wood species.

BASIC MORTISE-AND-TENON JOINT
2.65

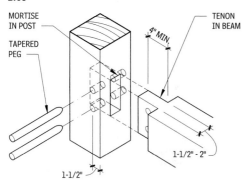

MORTISE IN POST

TAPERED PEG

4" MIN.

TENON IN BEAM

1-1/2" - 2"

1-1/2"

The basic mortise-and-tenon joint can be very effective in resisting both tension and compression forces. To increase tensile strength, increase the depth and thickness of the tenon and use additional pegs if the width and length of the tenon allow.

TUSK AND SOFFIT TENON JOINT
2.66

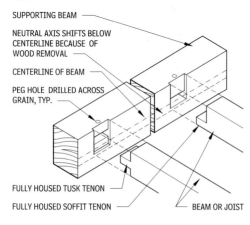

SUPPORTING BEAM

NEUTRAL AXIS SHIFTS BELOW CENTERLINE BECAUSE OF WOOD REMOVAL

CENTERLINE OF BEAM

PEG HOLE DRILLED ACROSS GRAIN, TYP.

FULLY HOUSED TUSK TENON

FULLY HOUSED SOFFIT TENON

BEAM OR JOIST

OPEN MORTISE-AND-TENON JOINTS
2.67

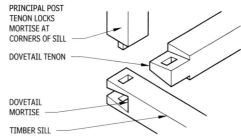

PRINCIPAL POST TENON LOCKS MORTISE AT CORNERS OF SILL

DOVETAIL TENON

DOVETAIL MORTISE

TIMBER SILL

DOVETAIL MORTISE-AND-TENON JOINT

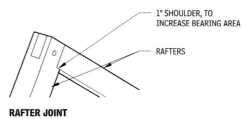

1" SHOULDER, TO INCREASE BEARING AREA

RAFTERS

RAFTER JOINT

LAP JOINTS
2.68

HOUSED DOVETAIL LAP

LAP MUST NOT CUT ACROSS ENTIRE TOP OF BEAM

WEDGES TIGHTEN JOINT TO REDUCE EFFECTS OF SHRINKAGE, PREVENTING WITHDRAWAL

BEAM

STRAIGHT LAP

FLOOR JOIST OR ROOF PURLIN

WEDGED DOVETAIL LAP (TENON TAPERED BOTTOM TO TOP)

Contributors:
Tedd Benson and Ben Brungraber, PhD, PE, Benson Woodworking Co., Inc., Alstead, New Hampshire; Richard J. Vitullo, AIA, Oak Leaf Studio, Corwnsville, Maryland.

GLUED-LAMINATED CONSTRUCTION

The term glued-laminated construction refers to an engineered, stress-rated product made of wood laminations bonded with adhesives, with the grain approximately parallel lengthwise. Laminated pieces can be end-joined to form any length, be glued edge to edge to make wider pieces, or be of bent pieces curved during the laminating process.

STANDARD DEPTHS

Dimension lumber surfaced to 1-1/2 in. is used to laminate straight members and members that have a curvature within the bending radius limitations for the species. Boards surfaced to 3/4 in. are recommended for laminating curved members when the bending radius is too short to permit the use of dimension lumber, provided that the bending radius limitations for the species are observed. Other lamination thicknesses may be used to meet special requirements.

STANDARD WIDTHS
2.69

NOMINAL WIDTH (IN.)	NET FINISHED WIDTH (IN.)
3	2-1/8
4	3-1/8a
6	5-1/8a
8	6-3/4
10	8-3/4a
12	10-3/4a
14	12-1/4
16	14-1/4

CONNECTION DESIGN

The design of connections for glued-laminated construction is similar to the design of connections for dimension lumber. Since glued-laminated members often are much larger than dimension lumber, and the loads transferred are larger, the effect of increased size should be taken into account in the design of connections. In addition to being designed for strength to transfer loads, connections also should be designed to avoid splitting of the member, as well as to accommodate swelling and shrinking of the wood.

FIRE SAFETY

Similar in nature to those of heavy timber, the self-insulating qualities of glued-laminated construction cause the members to burn slowly. Good structural details, elimination of concealed spaces, and use of vertical fireblocking contribute to its fire resistance and ability to retains its strength longer than unprotected metals.

Therefore, building codes generally classify glued-laminated construction as heavy timber construction if certain minimum dimensional requirements are met. Codes also allow for calculation of one-hour fire ratings for exposed glue-laminated members.

It is not recommended that fire-retardant treatments be applied to glued-laminated members because they do not substantially increase the fire resistance. In considering fire-retardant treatments, it is essential to investigate the following: reduction of strength related to type and penetration of treatment, compatibility of treatment and adhesive, use of special gluing methods, difficulty of application, and effect on wood color and fabrication process.

PROPRIETARY CONNECTIONS
2.70

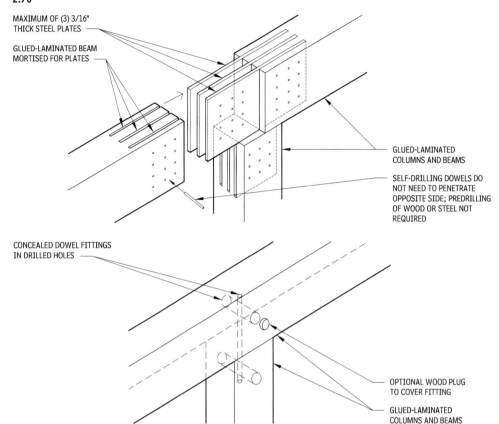

MAXIMUM OF (3) 3/16" THICK STEEL PLATES

GLUED-LAMINATED BEAM MORTISED FOR PLATES

GLUED-LAMINATED COLUMNS AND BEAMS

SELF-DRILLING DOWELS DO NOT NEED TO PENETRATE OPPOSITE SIDE; PREDRILLING OF WOOD OR STEEL NOT REQUIRED

CONCEALED DOWEL FITTINGS IN DRILLED HOLES

OPTIONAL WOOD PLUG TO COVER FITTING

GLUED-LAMINATED COLUMNS AND BEAMS

PURLIN-TO-BEAM CONNECTION
2.71

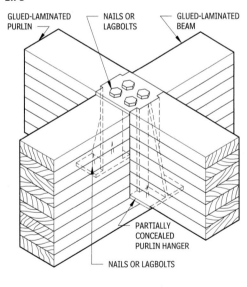

GLUED-LAMINATED PURLIN

NAILS OR LAGBOLTS

GLUED-LAMINATED BEAM

PARTIALLY CONCEALED PURLIN HANGER

NAILS OR LAGBOLTS

BEAM-TO-GIRDER CONNECTION
2.72

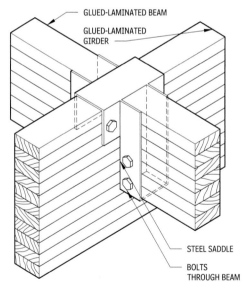

GLUED-LAMINATED BEAM

GLUED-LAMINATED GIRDER

STEEL SADDLE

BOLTS THROUGH BEAM

NOTES

2.69 a. Widths are 3, 5, 8-1/2, and 10-1/2 in. for southern pine.
2.70 a. Most typical connections can be accomplished with concealed or semiconcealed fasteners.
b. Final engineering is by manufacturer.

Contributor:
Timothy B. McDonald, Washington, DC.

FLOOR DECKS AND SLABS

PRECAST CONCRETE DECKS AND SLABS

Normal weight (150 pcf) or lightweight concrete (115 pcf) is used in standard precast concrete slab construction. Concrete topping is usually normal-weight concrete with a cylinder strength of 3000 psi. All units are prestressed with strand release once concrete strength is 3500 psi. Strands are available in various sizes, strengths, and placements, according to individual manufacturers.

Camber varies substantially depending on slab design, span, and loading. Nonstructural components attached to members may be affected by camber variations. Calculations of topping quantities should recognize camber variations. Safe superimposed surface loads include a dead load of 10 psf for untopped concrete and 15 psf for topped concrete. The remainder is live load.

FLAT DECKS
2.75

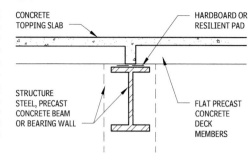

CONCRETE TOPPING SLAB

HARDBOARD OR RESILIENT PAD

STRUCTURE STEEL, PRECAST CONCRETE BEAM OR BEARING WALL

FLAT PRECAST CONCRETE DECK MEMBERS

TEE DECKS
2.76

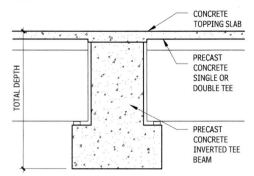

CONCRETE TOPPING SLAB

PRECAST CONCRETE SINGLE OR DOUBLE TEE

PRECAST CONCRETE INVERTED TEE BEAM

TOTAL DEPTH

FLAT DECK MEMBERS
2.73

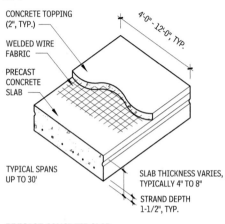

CONCRETE TOPPING (2", TYP.)

WELDED WIRE FABRIC

PRECAST CONCRETE SLAB

4'-0" - 12'-0", TYP.

TYPICAL SPANS UP TO 30'

SLAB THICKNESS VARIES, TYPICALLY 4" TO 8"

STRAND DEPTH 1-1/2", TYP.

PRECAST CONCRETE SLAB

CONCRETE TOPPING (2", TYP.)

WELDED WIRE FABRIC REINFORCING

PRECAST CONCRETE HOLLOW CORE PLANK

2'-0", 4'-0" AND 8'-0", TYP.

TYPICAL SPANS UP TO 40'

SLAB THICKNESS VARIES, TYPICALLY 6" TO 12"

STRAND DEPTH 1-1/2", TYP.

HOLLOW CORE PLANK

TEE DECKS DAPPED
2.77

CONCRETE POUR STRIP TO CONCEAL CONNECTIONS

PRETOPPED PRECAST CONCRETE DOUBLE TEE

TOTAL DEPTH

PRECAST CONCRETE INVERTED TEE BEAM

DAPPED TEE LEG

SINGLE OR DOUBLE TEE MEMBERS
2.74

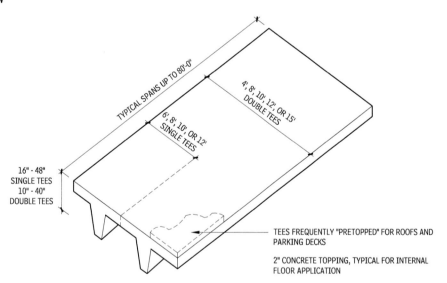

TYPICAL SPANS UP TO 80'-0"

4', 8', 10', 12', OR 15' DOUBLE TEES

6', 8', 10', OR 12' SINGLE TEES

16" - 48" SINGLE TEES
10" - 40" DOUBLE TEES

TEES FREQUENTLY "PRETOPPED" FOR ROOFS AND PARKING DECKS

2" CONCRETE TOPPING, TYPICAL FOR INTERNAL FLOOR APPLICATION

Contributor:
Timothy B. McDonald, Washington, DC.

FILIGREE SLABS

Filigree slabs combine desirable characteristics of cast-in-place and precast concrete. The precast filigree panels act as permanent forms for the field-placed reinforcing and cast-in-place (CIP) topping. Slabs can be used with CIP frame, precast frame, or steel frame or with bearing wall construction. The underside of the filigree panels is smooth enough to remain exposed.

METAL FLOOR DECKING

When designing with metal decking, two guidelines are important to follow:

- When lightweight concrete is used in the construction, use galvanized deck material.
- In a fire-resistant assembly, ensure that metal components are unprimed.

These are some advantages of metal floor decks:

- They provide a working platform, eliminating temporary wood planking in high-rise use.
- Composite decks provide positive reinforcement for concrete slabs.
- Both noncomposite and composite decks serve as forms for concrete, eliminating the need for forming and stripping.
- Acoustical treatment is possible.
- Electric raceways may be built into the floor slab.
- Metal floor decking provides economical floor assemblies.

Consult independent testing laboratory directories for specific fire-rating requirements.

FILIGREE FLAT PLATE
2.78

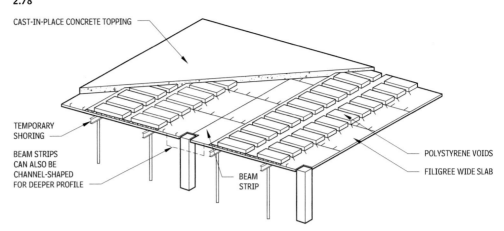

CAST-IN-PLACE CONCRETE TOPPING

TEMPORARY SHORING

BEAM STRIPS CAN ALSO BE CHANNEL-SHAPED FOR DEEPER PROFILE

BEAM STRIP

POLYSTYRENE VOIDS

FILIGREE WIDE SLAB

FILIGREE ON STEEL
2.79

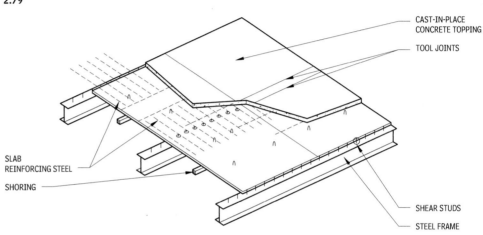

CAST-IN-PLACE CONCRETE TOPPING

TOOL JOINTS

SLAB REINFORCING STEEL

SHORING

SHEAR STUDS

STEEL FRAME

COMPOSITE FLOOR DECK WITH CONCRETE FILL
2.80

TYPE	PROFILE	REMARKS	SPAN	WIDTH	MAXIMUM LENGTH
Shallow deck	6" 2-1/2" 3-1/2"–6" 1-1/2" EMBOSSMENT CONCRETE FILL	Convex embossments bond with concrete fill; reverse deck for concave embossments	5'-0" to 12'-0"	36"	42'-0"
Intermediate deck	5" 7" 4"–6-1/2" 2"	Convex embossments	6'-0" to 13'-0"	24" or 36"	42'-0"
Deep deck	4-3/4" 7-1/4" 5"–7-1/2" 3"	Convex embossments	7'-0" to 14'-0"	24" or 36"	42'-0"

NOTE

2.78 Required field placed reinforcing steel not shown for clarity.

Contributors:
Midstate Filigree Systems, www.filigreein.com; Donald J. Neubauer, PE, Neubauer-Sohn, Consulting Engineers, Potomac, Maryland; Walter D. Shapiro, PE, Tor, Shapiro & Associates, New York City, New York.

NONCOMPOSITE FLOOR DECK WITH CONCRETE FILL
2.81

TYPE	PROFILE	REMARKS	SPAN	WIDTH	MAXIMUM LENGTH
Shallow deck	CONCRETE FILL, TYP. — 9/16" — 2"–5"	Narrow rib	2'-0" to 5'-6"	30", 35", 36"	42'-0"
Intermediate deck	3-5/8" - 4" 2-3/4" - 3" 1" 2-1/2" - 5-1/2"	Narrow rib	3'-0" to 10'-0"	32", 33"	42'-0"
Intermediate deck	4-5/8" 1-5/16" 3-1/4" - 6-1/4"	Narrow rib	4'-0" to 11'-0"	32"	42'-0"
Intermediate deck	6" 2 -1/2" 1-1/2" 3-1/2" - 6-1/2"	Narrow rib	4'-0" to 11-0"	30", 36"	42'-0"
Deep deck	6" 2"– 3" 4-1/2" – 8"	Wide rib	5'-6" to 14'-0"	24", 36"	42'-0"

COMPOSITE AND NONCOMPOSITE CELLULAR FLOOR DECK WITH CONCRETE FILL
2.82

TYPE	PROFILE	SPAN	WIDTH	CELL CROSS-SECTIONAL AREA
3" × 12" cellular deck (for steel frames requiring studs)	STUD OPTIONAL 12" WIDE RIB ALLOWS STUDS 3"	12'-0" to 15'-0"	24", 36"	17.7 sq in./cell (35 sq in./sheet)
3" × 8" cellular deck (not suitable for structural studs)	2-1/2" CONCRETE COVER, TYP. 8" NARROW RIB 3"	12'-0" to 15'-0"	24"	17.4 sq in./cell (52.2 sq in./sheet)
1.5" × 6" cellular deck (for thinner total slabs)	6" 1-1/2"	4'-0" to 8'-0"	24", 30", 36"	6 sq in./cell (24 sq in./sheet)

ELECTRICAL TRENCH DUCT
2.83

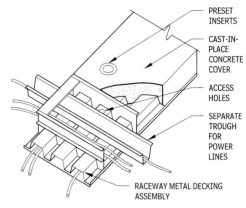

PRESET INSERTS

CAST-IN-PLACE CONCRETE COVER

ACCESS HOLES

SEPARATE TROUGH FOR POWER LINES

RACEWAY METAL DECKING ASSEMBLY

FLOOR DECK ACCESSORIES
2.84

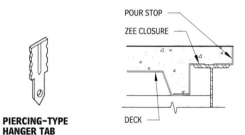

POUR STOP

ZEE CLOSURE

DECK

CELL CLOSURE

GIRDER FILLER

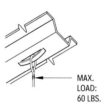

MAX. LOAD: 60 LBS. PER TAB

PIERCING-TYPE HANGER TAB

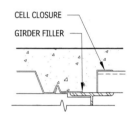

INTEGRAL HANGER TAB

POUR STOPS AND CLOSURES

WOOD DECKING

POST AND BEAM CONNECTIONS
2.85

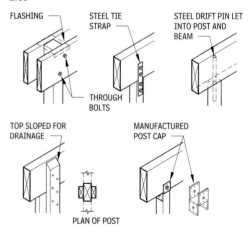

FLASHING

STEEL TIE STRAP

STEEL DRIFT PIN LET INTO POST AND BEAM

THROUGH BOLTS

TOP SLOPED FOR DRAINAGE

MANUFACTURED POST CAP

PLAN OF POST

NOTES

2.83 a. Electric raceways may be built into floor slabs by using cellular deck or special units that are blended with plain deck. Two-way distribution is achieved by using trench ducts that sit astride the cellular units at right angles.

b. Using trench ducts with composite floor deck may reduce or eliminate entirely the effectiveness of composite action at the trench duct. This is also true for composite action between steel floor beams and concrete fill. Trench duct locations must be taken into account in deciding whether composite action is possible.

2.84 A convenient, economical means of supporting lightweight acoustical ceilings is to attach a suspension system to hanger tabs at side laps, pierce tabs driven through the deck, or prepunch tabs in the roof deck. Do not use this tab-and-metal deck arrangement to support plaster ceilings, piping, ductwork, electrical equipment, or other heavy loads. Such elements must be suspended directly from structural members or supplementary subframing.

Contributors:
Donald Neubauer, PE, Neubauer Consulting Engineers, Potomac, Maryland; Walter D. Shapiro, PE, Tor, Shapiro & Associates, New York City, New York; The Bumgardner Architects, Seattle, Washington.

RAILINGS
2.86

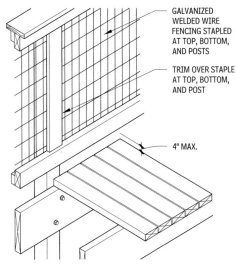

- GALVANIZED WELDED WIRE FENCING STAPLED AT TOP, BOTTOM, AND POSTS
- TRIM OVER STAPLE AT TOP, BOTTOM, AND POST
- 4" MAX.

FENCING INFILL RAILING

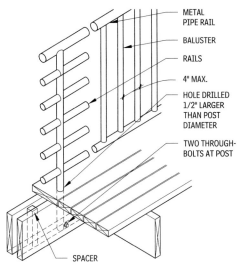

- METAL PIPE RAIL
- BALUSTER
- RAILS
- 4" MAX.
- HOLE DRILLED 1/2" LARGER THAN POST DIAMETER
- TWO THROUGH-BOLTS AT POST
- SPACER

PIPE RAILING

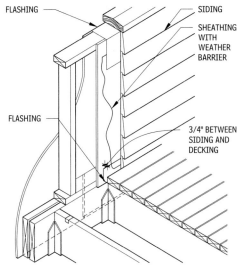

- FLASHING
- SIDING
- SHEATHING WITH WEATHER BARRIER
- FLASHING
- 3/4" BETWEEN SIDING AND DECKING

SOLID RAILING

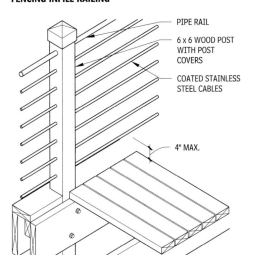

- PIPE RAIL
- 6 x 6 WOOD POST WITH POST COVERS
- COATED STAINLESS STEEL CABLES
- 4" MAX.

TENSION CABLE RAILING

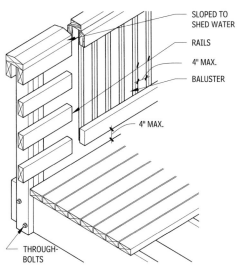

- SLOPED TO SHED WATER
- RAILS
- 4" MAX.
- BALUSTER
- 4" MAX.
- THROUGH-BOLTS

WOOD RAILING

DECKING APPLICATIONS
2.88

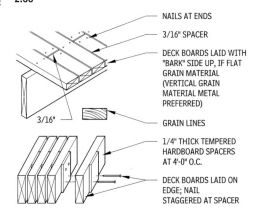

- NAILS AT ENDS
- 3/16" SPACER
- DECK BOARDS LAID WITH "BARK" SIDE UP, IF FLAT GRAIN MATERIAL (VERTICAL GRAIN MATERIAL METAL PREFERRED)
- 3/16"
- GRAIN LINES
- 1/4" THICK TEMPERED HARDBOARD SPACERS AT 4'-0" O.C.
- DECK BOARDS LAID ON EDGE; NAIL STAGGERED AT SPACER

WOOD SELECTION

When it comes to selecting wood for decking, characteristics should include effective resistance to decay, nonsplintering, stiffness, strength, hardness, and warp resistance. Species selection will vary according to local climate and structure.

CONNECTIONS AT BUILDING
2.87

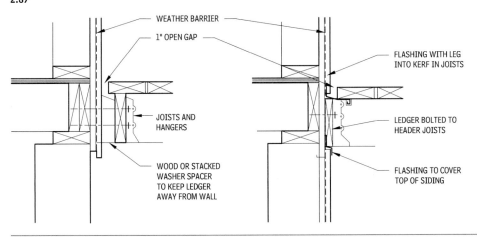

- WEATHER BARRIER
- 1" OPEN GAP
- JOISTS AND HANGERS
- WOOD OR STACKED WASHER SPACER TO KEEP LEDGER AWAY FROM WALL
- FLASHING WITH LEG INTO KERF IN JOISTS
- LEDGER BOLTED TO HEADER JOISTS
- FLASHING TO COVER TOP OF SIDING

NOTE

2.88 Spacing of 1/4 in. is not recommended for walking surfaces where high heels are anticipated.

Contributor:
The Bumgardner Architects, Seattle, Washington.

RELATIVE COMPARISON OF VARIOUS QUALITIES OF WOOD USED IN DECK CONSTRUCTION
2.89

	DOUGLAS FIR LARCH[d]	SOUTHERN PINE[d]	HEMLOCK FIR[a, d]	SOFT PINE[b, d]	WESTERN RED CEDAR	REDWOOD	SPRUCE	CYPRESS	IPE[e]
Hardness	Fair	Fair	Poor	Poor	Poor	Fair	Poor	Fair	Good
Warp resistance resistance	Fair	Fair	Fair	Good	Good	Good	Fair	Fair	Good
Ease of working	Poor	Fair	Fair	Good	Good	Fair	Fair	Fair	Difficult
Paint holding	Poor	Poor	Poor	Good	Good	Good	Fair	Good	—
Stain acceptance[c]	Fair	Fair	Fair	Fair	Good	Good	Fair	Fair	Good
Nail holding	Good	Good	Poor	Poor	Poor	Fair	Fair	Fair	—
Heartwood decay resistance	Fair	Fair	Poor	Poor	Good	Good	Poor	Good	Excellent
Proportion of heartwood	Good	Poor	Poor	Fair	Good	Good	Poor	Good	Excellent
Bending strength	Good	Good	Fair	Poor	Poor	Fair	Fair	Fair	Good
Stiffness	Good	Good	Good	Poor	Poor	Fair	Fair	Fair	Good
Strength as a post	Good	Good	Fair	Poor	Fair	Good	Fair	Fair	—
Freedom from pitch	Fair	Poor	Good	Fair	Good	Good	Good	Good	Good

DECK EDGES
2.92

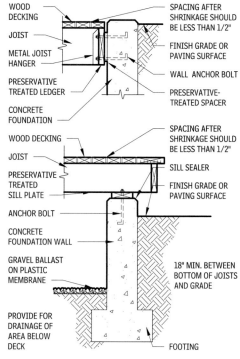

WOOD DECKING
JOIST
METAL JOIST HANGER
PRESERVATIVE TREATED LEDGER
CONCRETE FOUNDATION
SPACING AFTER SHRINKAGE SHOULD BE LESS THAN 1/2"
FINISH GRADE OR PAVING SURFACE
WALL ANCHOR BOLT
PRESERVATIVE-TREATED SPACER

WOOD DECKING
JOIST
PRESERVATIVE TREATED SILL PLATE
ANCHOR BOLT
CONCRETE FOUNDATION WALL
GRAVEL BALLAST ON PLASTIC MEMBRANE
PROVIDE FOR DRAINAGE OF AREA BELOW DECK
SPACING AFTER SHRINKAGE SHOULD BE LESS THAN 1/2"
SILL SEALER
FINISH GRADE OR PAVING SURFACE
18" MIN. BETWEEN BOTTOM OF JOISTS AND GRADE
FOOTING

WALKWAYS AND RAMPS
2.90

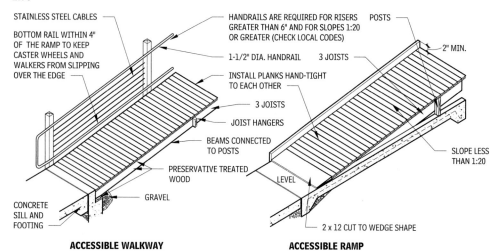

STAINLESS STEEL CABLES
BOTTOM RAIL WITHIN 4" OF THE RAMP TO KEEP CASTER WHEELS AND WALKERS FROM SLIPPING OVER THE EDGE
CONCRETE SILL AND FOOTING
GRAVEL
3 JOISTS
JOIST HANGERS
BEAMS CONNECTED TO POSTS
PRESERVATIVE TREATED WOOD

HANDRAILS ARE REQUIRED FOR RISERS GREATER THAN 6" AND FOR SLOPES 1:20 OR GREATER (CHECK LOCAL CODES)
POSTS
1-1/2" DIA. HANDRAIL
INSTALL PLANKS HAND-TIGHT TO EACH OTHER
3 JOISTS
2" MIN.
SLOPE LESS THAN 1:20
LEVEL
2 x 12 CUT TO WEDGE SHAPE

ACCESSIBLE WALKWAY   **ACCESSIBLE RAMP**

POST BASES
2.91

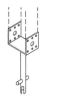

POST KERFED FOR ANCHOR
PIPE OR BAR WELDED TO ANCHOR
POST AND ANCHOR BOLT HOLES SHOULD BE SHOP-DRILLED TO ENSURE ALIGNMENT

STEPS AND STAIRS
2.93

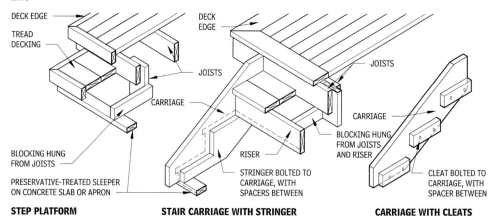

DECK EDGE
TREAD DECKING
BLOCKING HUNG FROM JOISTS
PRESERVATIVE-TREATED SLEEPER ON CONCRETE SLAB OR APRON
JOISTS
CARRIAGE

DECK EDGE
JOISTS
RISER
STRINGER BOLTED TO CARRIAGE, WITH SPACERS BETWEEN

JOISTS
CARRIAGE
BLOCKING HUNG FROM JOISTS AND RISER
CLEAT BOLTED TO CARRIAGE, WITH SPACER BETWEEN

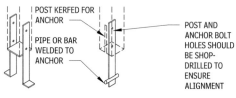

STEP PLATFORM   **STAIR CARRIAGE WITH STRINGER**   **CARRIAGE WITH CLEATS**

NOTES

2.89 a. Includes West Coast and eastern hemlocks.
b. Includes western and northeastern pines.
c. Categories refer to semitransparent oil-base stain.
d. Use pressure-preservative-treated material only. All materials below deck surfaces should be pressure-treated.
e. Ipe used typically for decking only, not framing.

Contributors:
The Bumgardner Architects, Seattle, Washington; Mark J. Mazz, AIA, CEA, Inc., Hyattsville, Maryland.

POSTS AND FOOTINGS
2.94

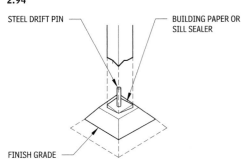

PRECAST CONCRETE PLINTH/PRESERVATIVE TREATED WOOD POST

- STEEL DRIFT PIN
- BUILDING PAPER OR SILL SEALER
- FINISH GRADE

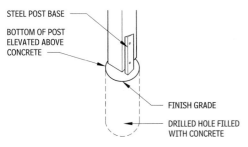

POURED FOOTING/PRESERVATIVE TREATED WOOD POST

- STEEL POST BASE
- BOTTOM OF POST ELEVATED ABOVE CONCRETE
- FINISH GRADE
- DRILLED HOLE FILLED WITH CONCRETE

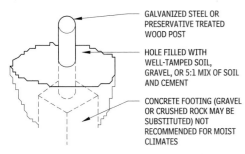

POURED OR PRECAST CONCRETE FOOTING/PRESERVATIVE TREATED WOOD POST

- GALVANIZED STEEL OR PRESERVATIVE TREATED WOOD POST
- HOLE FILLED WITH WELL-TAMPED SOIL, GRAVEL, OR 5:1 MIX OF SOIL AND CEMENT
- CONCRETE FOOTING (GRAVEL OR CRUSHED ROCK MAY BE SUBSTITUTED) NOT RECOMMENDED FOR MOIST CLIMATES

FASTENERS

Guidelines for selecting fasteners include:

- Use hot-dipped galvanized fasteners to avoid corrosion and staining.
- Preservative treated wood requires stainless steel fasteners or special heavy galvanized coating recommended by the treatment manufacturer.
- To reduce board splitting by nailing, do the following: blunt nail points, predrill (3/4 of nail diameter), stagger nailing, and place nails no closer to the edge than one-half of board thickness.
- Avoid end-grain nailing and toenailing, if possible.
- Use flat washers under heads of lag screws and bolts, and under nuts.

In addition, note that hot-dipped galvanized casing nails or stainless steel deck screws are typically the best type of decking fasteners, and plated ring shank or spiral groove shank nails are suitable for arid climates.

PRESERVATIVE WOOD TREATMENT

To protect wood decking from moisture, follow these guidelines:

- Protect wood members from weather by preservative wood treatment.
- Treat wood in direct contact with soil or concrete with preservative.
- Ensure that the bottoms of posts on piers are 6 in. above grade.

Contributors:
The Bumgardner Architects, Seattle, Washington; Mark J. Mazz, AIA, CEA, Inc., Hyattsville, Maryland; David S. Collins, FAIA, American Forest and Paper Association, Cincinnati, Ohio; Timothy B. McDonald, Washington, DC.

- Sterilize or cover soil with membrane to keep plant growth away from wood members, to minimize moisture exchange.
- Treat ends, cuts, and holes, with preservative before placement.
- Kerf decking and flat-trim boards, 2 by 6 and wider, on the underside with 3/4-in.-deep saw cuts at 1 in. o.c., to prevent cupping.
- Avoid horizontal exposure of end grain, or provide adequate protection by flashing or sealing. Avoid or minimize joint conditions where moisture may be trapped by using spacers and/or flashing, caulking, sealant, or plastic roofing cement.

BRACING

On large decks or decks where post heights exceed 5 ft, lateral stability should be achieved with horizontal bracing (metal or wood diagonal ties on top or bottom of joists or diagonal application of decking), in combination with vertical bracing (rigid bolted or gusseted connections at tops of posts, knee bracing, or cross bracing between posts), and/or connection to a braced building wall. Lateral stability should be assessed by a structural engineer.

MACHINE-SHAPED DECKING TYPES
2.95

SINGLE TONGUE-AND-GROOVE

SPLINE   **PATTERNED**

SIZES				
THICKNESSES		**WIDTH**		**MAXIMUM SPAN**
NOMINAL (IN.)	ACTUAL (IN.)	NOMINAL (IN.)	ACTUAL (IN.)	TYPICAL (FT)
2	1-1/2	5, 6, 8, 10, 12	4, 5, 6-3/4, 8-3/4, 10-3/4	8
3	2-1/2	6	5-1/4, 7-1/8	12
4	3-1/2	6	5-1/4, 7-1/8	16

LAMINATED DECKING
2.96

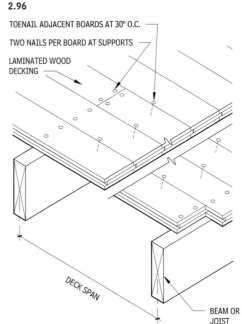

- TOENAIL ADJACENT BOARDS AT 30" O.C.
- TWO NAILS PER BOARD AT SUPPORTS
- LAMINATED WOOD DECKING
- DECK SPAN
- BEAM OR JOIST

WOOD DECKING JOINT PATTERNS
2.97

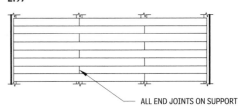

- ALL END JOINTS ON SUPPORT

SIMPLE SPAN

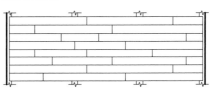

CONTINUOUS SPAN WITH RANDOM LENGTHS

DECKING JOINTS
2.98

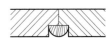

GROOVED PLANK MOLDED SPLINE   **RABBETED PLANK BATTEN INSERT**

GROOVED PLANK WITH SPLINE   **GROOVED PLANK WITH EXPOSED SPLINE**

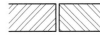

SQUARE EDGE   **TONGUE-AND-GROOVE (MOST COMMON)**

FLOOR CONSTRUCTION VAPOR RETARDERS, AIR BARRIERS, AND INSULATION

CRAWL SPACE INSULATION AND VENTILATION

The best understanding of the interrelated issues surrounding control of heat, air, and moisture (HAM) inside crawl spaces and the transfer of HAM to the building interior suggests that it is preferable to treat the crawl space as part of the interior conditioned environment.

Arguments against ventilating crawl spaces include:

- Venting of a crawl space is meant to keep moisture within acceptable levels, pulling hot, humid air into the space is counterproductive, especially when it is likely that the ground surface temperatures may be below the dew point temperature.
- Insulated floor assemblies are rarely constructed airtight and, allow air infiltration/exfiltration.
- Insulated floor assemblies are rarely as warm or as comfortable as floors with a conditioned environment on both sides.
- Conditioned spaces above hot, humid, ventilated crawl spaces create a vapor drive, which may result in excess load on the HVAC, uncontrolled condensation, and potentially rot and mold.
- Crawl spaces are frequently used for distribution of mechanical ductwork. The distribution ductwork is outside of the thermal envelope and, therefore, experiences greater loss than if interior to the thermal envelope. The penetrations required for the ductwork create more opportunities for air leakage between the conditioned and unconditioned space. In hot, humid conditions, there is a likelihood that the vapor retarder on the duct insulation will not be perfect, causing condensation on the ductwork to occur, thereby adding more moisture to an already damp environment.
- Sanitary sewer and domestic water supply lines likely pass through the unconditioned crawl space and may be susceptible to freezing and condensation.

Recommendations for crawl spaces include the following:

- Codes generally require ventilation of crawl spaces; however, they also provide exemptions for a variety of conditions, specifically: "where warranted by climatic conditions," "where continuously operated mechanical ventilation is provided," and "when the perimeter walls are insulated." Most exemptions require the ground surface to be covered with a vapor retarder. Refer to the specific building codes in effect for all requirements.
- Cover the ground surface in the crawl space with a vapor retarder. Tape seams and seal penetrations. Consider protecting the vapor retarder with a rough concrete mud slab. Mechanically fasten the retarder to the foundation at the perimeter with a nailing strip. In cold climates, it may be desirable to insulate the entire ground surface.
- Insulate the crawl space walls as required by code. Follow recommendations for exterior walls regarding the permeability of insulation materials, air sealing, and the use of vapor retarders. Insulation may need to be fire-rated, especially board insulation; or use noncombustible-type insulation. If possible, locate insulation outside of the dampproofing on the foundation wall.
- Ventilate the crawl space, typically with a small supply duct at code-specified rate, normally 1 cfm for each 50 sq ft, and provide connection to the return air plenum, either directly or through the interior space above via transfer grilles. Locate the supply and return points to evenly mix and distribute the air.
- Alternative crawl space drying methods include a permanent dehumidifier or exhaust fans controlled by humidistats, with makeup air from the interior and ducted to the exterior. However, this solution may use a large amount of energy.
- Pay attention to exterior wall detailing and proper drainage to keep water away from the crawl space.
- Crawl spaces used as the supply plenum to the remainder of the house require special treatment to maintain air quality.

CRAWL SPACE VENTILATION MATERIALS
2.99

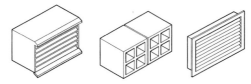

FOUNDATION VENT   HOLLOW TILE   LOUVER

VENTILATED CRAWL SPACE
2.100

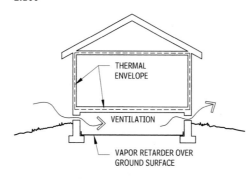

THERMAL ENVELOPE

VENTILATION

VAPOR RETARDER OVER GROUND SURFACE

CONDITIONED CRAWL SPACE
2.101

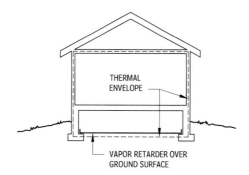

THERMAL ENVELOPE

VAPOR RETARDER OVER GROUND SURFACE

WOOD FRAME OVER CRAWL SPACE (COLD CLIMATE)
2.102

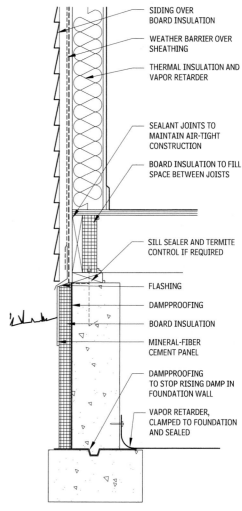

SIDING OVER BOARD INSULATION

WEATHER BARRIER OVER SHEATHING

THERMAL INSULATION AND VAPOR RETARDER

SEALANT JOINTS TO MAINTAIN AIR-TIGHT CONSTRUCTION

BOARD INSULATION TO FILL SPACE BETWEEN JOISTS

SILL SEALER AND TERMITE CONTROL IF REQUIRED

FLASHING

DAMPPROOFING

BOARD INSULATION

MINERAL-FIBER CEMENT PANEL

DAMPPROOFING TO STOP RISING DAMP IN FOUNDATION WALL

VAPOR RETARDER, CLAMPED TO FOUNDATION AND SEALED

Contributors:
Joe Lstriburek, Building Sciences Corporation, Richard J. Vitullo, AIA, Oak Leaf Studio, Crownsville, Maryland; Eric Gastier, Alexandria, Virginia.

**WOOD FRAME OVER CRAWL SPACE (MIXED CLIMATE)
2.103**

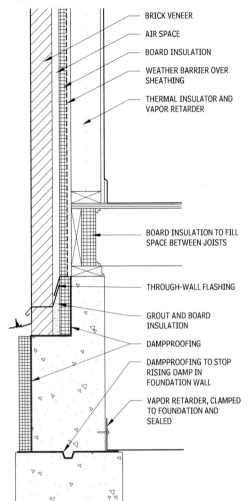

- BRICK VENEER
- AIR SPACE
- BOARD INSULATION
- WEATHER BARRIER OVER SHEATHING
- THERMAL INSULATOR AND VAPOR RETARDER
- BOARD INSULATION TO FILL SPACE BETWEEN JOISTS
- THROUGH-WALL FLASHING
- GROUT AND BOARD INSULATION
- DAMPPROOFING
- DAMPPROOFING TO STOP RISING DAMP IN FOUNDATION WALL
- VAPOR RETARDER, CLAMPED TO FOUNDATION AND SEALED

**INSULATING UNDERSIDE OF STEEL AND CONCRETE FLOOR STRUCTURES
2.104**

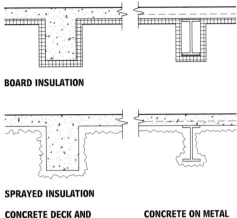

BOARD INSULATION

SPRAYED INSULATION

CONCRETE DECK AND STRUCTURE   **CONCRETE ON METAL DECK ON STEEL FRAME**

Two primary difficulties encountered with the insulation of floor assemblies are providing a continuous vapor retarder on the warm side, and keeping the floor warm, even with insulation. In cold climates, the floor will be uncomfortable for any long-term occupancy. If possible, it is best to avoid insulation applied directly to the bottom of floor assemblies; instead, use an insulated soffit. If direct application is unavoidable, consider the following two following methods:

- Board insulation is typically applied to the underside of the structure by impaling over adhesive-applied stickpins and crimped with large washers. Mineral wool insulation is a good choice because it is noncombustible and performs well even if it becomes slightly damp from condensation.
- Sprayed insulation can be cellulose-based, mineral-based, or foam. Closed-cell foam can eliminate the need for a separate vapor barrier.
- Consult the following reference: www.buildingscience.com.

ROOF CONSTRUCTION

This section examines common systems used in roof construction. Consult literature from manufacturers and trade associations for more details on the information presented in the accompanying tables.

Contributors:
Joe Lstriburek, Building Sciences Corporation, Richard J. Vitullo, AIA, Oak Leaf Studio, Crownsville, Maryland; Eric Gastier, Alexandria, Virginia.

ROOF STRUCTURE ASSEMBLIES
2.105

		DEPTH OF SYSTEM (IN.)	STANDARD MEMBER SIZES (IN.)	DEAD LOAD OF STRUCTURE (PSF)	SUITABLE LIVE LOAD RANGE (PSF)	SPAN RANGE (FT)	BAY SIZE CHARACTERISTICS	DIMENSIONAL STABILITY AFFECTED BY
Wood rafter	SHEATHING / WOOD RAFTER / CEILING	5–13	Nominal joist 2 × 6, 8, 10, and 12	4–8	10–50	Up to 22	—	Deflection
Wood beam and plank	WOOD ROOF DECKING / WOOD BEAM (OR GLUED-LAMINATED BEAM)	8–22	Nominal planks 2, 3, and 4	5–12	10–50	8–34	Maximum beam spacing 8'–0"	—
Stress skin panel	STRESSED SKIN PANELS	3-1/4 and 8-1/4	—	3–6	10–50	8–32	4'–0" modules	—
Shop-fabricated wood truss	SHEATHING / SHOP-FABRICATED WOOD TRUSS / CEILING	Varies 12–120	—	5–15	10–50	30–50	2'–8" between trusses	Deflection
Cold-formed metal truss	STEEL DECKING / PURLIN / COLD-FORMED METAL TRUSS	Varies	—	15–25	10–60	100–200	—	Deflection
Steel joist	CONCRETE / METAL DECKING / STEEL JOIST / CEILING	11–75	Steel joists 8–72	10–28	10–50	Up to 96	Light joists 16"–30" o.c.; heavy joists 4'–12' o.c.	Deflection
Steel joist	WOOD ROOF DECKING / WOOD NAILER / STEEL JOIST / CEILING	10–32	Steel joists 8–30	8–20	10–50	Up to 96	Light joists 16"–30" o.c.; heavy joists 4'–12' o.c.	Deflection
Steel joist	BOARD INSULATION / STEEL DECKING / STEEL JOIST / CEILING	11–75	Steel joists 8–72	6–24	10–50	Up to 96	—	Deflection
Steel frame	PRECAST CONCRETE SLAB / STEEL BEAM / CEILING	4–12, plus	Concrete plank	40–75	30–70	20–60; generally below 35	—	Deflection and creep
Precast concrete	PRECAST CONCRETE PLANK / CONCRETE BEAM	4–12, plus beam depth	Concrete plank 16–48 W, 4–12 D	40–75	30–70	20–60; generally below 35	—	Deflection and creep
One-way concrete slab	CONCRETE SLAB / CONCRETE BEAM	4–10 slab, plus	—	50–120	Up to 100	10–25; more with post-tensioning	—	—
Two-way concrete slab	CONCRETE SLAB / CONCRETE BEAM	4–10 slab, plus beam depth	—	50–120	Up to 100	10–30; more with post-tensioning	L 1.33 W	—

Contributors:
Roger K. Lewis, FAIA, and Mehmet T. Ergene, architect, Roger K. Lewis and Associates, Washington, DC.

ROOF STRUCTURE ASSEMBLIES (continued)
2.105

SUITABLE FOR INCLINED ROOFS	REQUIRES FINISHED CEILING SURFACE	SERVICE PLENUM	RELATIVE THERMAL CAPACITY	COMPARATIVE RESISTANCE TO SOUND TRANSMISSION		REMARKS
				IMPACT	AIRBORNE	
Yes	For visual or fire protection purposes	Between rafters—one way	Low	Poor	Fair	
Yes	For fire protection purposes	Under structure—one way	Medium	Poor	Fair	
Yes	No	Under structure only	Low	Poor	Fair	
Yes	For visual or fire protection	Between trusses	Low	Poor	Fair	Truss depth to span ratio 1:5 to 1:10
Yes; pitched trusses usually used for short spans	For visual or fire protection purposes	Between trusses	Low	Fair	Fair	Truss depth to span ratio 1:5 to 1:15
No	For visual or fire protection purposes	Between joists	Medium	Fair	Fair	
Yes	For visual or fire protection purposes	Between joists	Low	Poor	Fair	
Yes	For visual or fire protection purposes	Between joists	High	Excellent	Good	
Yes	For visual or fire protection purposes	Under structure	High	Fair	Fair	Easy to design; quick erection
Yes	No	Under structure	High	Fair	Fair	Provides finished flush ceiling; may be used with any framing system
No	No	Under structure	High	Good	Good	
No	No	Under structure	High	Good	Good	

Contributors:
Roger K. Lewis, FAIA, and Mehmet T. Ergene, architect, Roger K. Lewis and Associates, Washington, DC.

ROOF STRUCTURE ASSEMBLIES (continued)
2.105

		DEPTH OF SYSTEM (IN.)	STANDARD MEMBER SIZES (IN.)	DEAD LOAD OF STRUCTURE (PSF)	SUITABLE LIVE LOAD RANGE (PSF)	SPAN RANGE (FT)	BAY SIZE CHARACTER-ISTICS	DIMENSIONAL STABILITY AFFECTED BY
One-way ribbed concrete slab	CONCRETE SLAB / RIB (JOIST)	8–22	Standard pan forms 20 and 30 W, 6–20 D	40–90	Up to 100	15–50; more with prestressing	—	Creep
Two-way ribbed concrete slab	CONCRETE SLAB / RIB (JOIST)	8–24	Standard dome forms 19 × 19, 30 × 30, 6–20 D	75–105	Up to 100	25–60; more with prestressing	L 1.33 W	Creep
Precast concrete single tee		16–36	16–36 D	65–85	20–80	30–100	—	Creep
Precast concrete double tee		6–16	48, 60, 72, 96, and 120 W, 6–16 D	35–55	25–60	20–75	—	Creep
Concrete flat plate	CONCRETE FLAT PLATE / COLUMN	4–14	—	50–160	Up to 100	Up to 35; more with prestressing	L 1.33 W	Creep
Concrete flat slab	CONCRETE SLAB / DROP PANEL / CAPITAL / COLUMN	5–16	Minimum slab thickness 5 without drop panel, 4 with drop panel	50–200	Up to 100	Up to 40; more with prestressing	L 1.33 W equal column spacing required	Creep
Gypsum concrete roof deck	GYPSUM CONCRETE / BOARD INSULATION / SUBPURLIN / CEILING	3–6	—	5–20	Up to 50	Up to 10	Up to 8' between subpurlins	Deflection and creep

ROOF STRUCTURE ASSEMBLIES (continued)
2.105

SUITABLE FOR INCLINED ROOFS	REQUIRES FINISHED CEILING SURFACE	SERVICE PLENUM	RELATIVE THERMAL CAPACITY	COMPARATIVE RESISTANCE TO SOUND TRANSMISSION		REMARKS
				IMPACT	AIRBORNE	
No	For visual purposes	Between ribs—one way	High	Good	Good	
No	No	Under structure	High	Good	Good	Economy in forming; suitable for two-way cantilevering
Yes	For visual or fire protection purposes	Between ribs—one way	High	Fair	Good	Generally used for long spans
Yes	For visual or fire protection purposes	Between ribs—one way	High	Fair	Good	Most widely used prestressed concrete element
No	No	Under structure	High	Good	Good	Uniform slab thickness; easy to form; suitable for vertical expansion of building
No	No	Under structure	High	Good	Good	Suitable for heavy roof loads
No	For visual or fire protection purposes	Under structure	High	Good	Good	Provides resistance to wind and seismic loads

LONG-SPAN AND TENSILE STRUCTURES

DESIGN CONSIDERATION FACTORS

Examples of long-span structures shown in Table 2.126 are rated for their capability to address the following design factor conditions.

NATURAL CONDITIONS

A. *Uneven or excessive snow and ice loads*: Geometry, equipment, or surrounding structure may contribute to snow drifting or ice buildup.

B. *Ponding*: Provide positive drainage to remove water from the structure when roof drains clog.

C. *Wind*: Evaluate potential of wind-induced destructive vibration in members or connections.

D. *Thermal*: Daily and seasonal temperature cycles can cause significant changes in structural shape and member stresses, and may lead to fatigue failure.

E. *Freeze/thaw cycles or corrosive atmosphere*: Evaluate long-term effects on structural performance, particularly for exposed concrete structures.

PRIMARY STRESSES

F. *Load paths*: Two or more load paths for all loads should be provided wherever possible. The greater the area a single member supports, the greater should be its safety factor.

G. *Compression failure*: Resistance to lateral buckling of long members is crucial. Use members that ensure initial and verifiable alignment.

H. *Tension failure*: Dynamic stability under wind or other vibration loading should be carefully verified.

SECONDARY STRESSES

I. *Deflection:* Changes in orientation of members at joints can increase distructive stresses from loads.

J. *Member interaction*: Load flows through structures in such a way as to minimize strength. Check all possible load paths of complex geometric structures.

K. *Nonstructural connections*: Assemblies attached to a structure will influence structural load flow and even become part of the load flow if the attachment changes the deflected shape.

L. *Scale*: Most members have a span limit, beyond which weight of the member itself becomes a limiting factor.

M. *Stress concentration*: Check stresses at changes of cross sections, holes, and connections. High-strength materials are particularly sensitive.

TOLERANCES

N. *Erection alignment*: True member length and spatial position are crucial for proper alignment and load flow.

O. *Creep*: Length changes over time will influence both primary and secondary stresses.

P. *Supports and foundations*: Supports must accept movements due to deflections from primary and secondary stresses and differential foundation settlement.

QUALITY CONTROL

Q. *Design*: Engineering design must not be compromised by time, scheduling, design changes, or building codes.

R. *Methods*: Construction methods should be selected carefully to safely and accurately locate the structural components.

S. *Site observation*: Only when the structure is properly established in space should it be accepted. Changes in construction materials or methods should be carefully evaluated.

T. *Structural building maintenance*: Conditions and alignment of various members, especially crucial nonredundant members, should be verified on a regular schedule. Consider using equipment to detect excessive deflection.

U. *Nonstructural building maintenance*: The condition of building components should not adversely affect the structure (e.g., keep roof drains open, prevent excessive equipment vibration, and maintain expansion joints).

LONG-SPAN COMPONENTS
2.106

COMPONENTS	MATERIAL (OR SHAPE)	ONE-WAY	TWO-WAY	FLAT SURFACE	PITCHED PLANE	CURVED PLANE	CURVED SURFACE	SPAN RANGE (FT) 50	100	150	300	600	SPAN/DEPTH RATIO (FT)	FACTORS STRONG AGAINST	FACTORS SENSITIVE TO
Joist	Steel	•		•	—								24	P, Q, S	A, B, F, G
Truss	Steel	•		•	•	—							22		A, B, F, G, M, T
		•		•		—							20	A, B, F	M
	Wood	•		•	•	—							12		A, B, F, G
		•		•		—							12	B, F	
Space frame	Steel	•	•	•									20	F	A, B, I, J, M, N, P, Q, S, U
Stressed skin	Steel		•	•		—							18	F	A, B, I, J, M, N, P, Q, S, U
Beam	Steel	•	—	•									22	A, Q	B, F, T
	Wood	•		•									20		B, F, T
	Prestressed concrete	•	—	•									26		B, F, T
Rigid frame	Steel	•	—	•	—								20–24	A, B	F
	Wood	•		•	—								18–22		F
	Prestressed concrete	•	—	•	—								24–28		F
Cable-stayed														I, P	C, E, H, Q, T
Folded plate	Steel	•			•								22	B	A, F, M
	Wood	•			•								6	B	A, F, M
	Concrete	•			•								14	B	A, F, L, M
Cylindric shell	Concrete	•				•							14	B	A, L, M, O
Vault	Concrete	•	•			•							10	B	C, O
Arch	Steel	•	•			•							8	B	A, D, F, G
	Wood	•	•			•							7	B	A, D, F, G
	Concrete	•	•			•							7	B	A, D, F, G
Dome	Radial steel		•				•						8	B, C	A, D, F, G
	Geodesic dome		•				•						5	A, B, C, F, G	D, N, R
	Radial wood		•				•						6	B, C	A, D, F, G
	Lamella wood		•				•						6	A, B, C, F, G	D, N, R
	Concrete		•				•						8	B, C, F, G	A, D, L, O
Pneumatics	Steel		•				•						7	D	A, B, C, E
Cable	Parallel	•				•							16	D	A, B, C, F
	Radial		•				•						12	D	A, B, C, F
	Hyperbolic		•										8	B, D, F	A, C
	Tent		•										6	B, F	A, C
Hyperbolic	Concrete		•				•						6	F	A, D, L, O

NOTES

2.106 a. Steel is A-36; wood is laminated, sometimes heavy timber; concrete is reinforced with steel; prestressed concrete is prestressed with steel.

b. Cable-stayed system can give auxiliary support to trusses, beams, or frames, greatly reducing span and member sizes, but providing additional tensional strength.

c. Lamella arches provide two-way arch structures and improve redundancy.

d. Domes may also be constructed of aluminum.

e. Pneumatics are fabric roofs, pressurized, and stabilized with steel cables.

f. For each system, the following notation applies: the bullet (•) indicates the typical configuration; the dash (—) indicates occasionally used.

Contributor:
William C. Bauman, Jr., University of Oklahoma, Norman, Oklahoma.

SPACE FRAMES

A space frame is a three-dimensional truss with linear members that form a series of triangulated polyhedrons. It can be seen as a plane of constant depth that can sustain fairly long spans and varied configurations of shape.

Space frames prime attributes include:

- Light weight
- Inherent rigidity
- Wide variety of form, size, and span
- Compatible interaction with services, primarily HVAC

Most space frames are designed for specific applications, and a structural engineer with specific experience should be consulted. Manufacturers can provide the full range of capabilities (loading, spans, shapes, specific details) for their products. Standardized structural assemblies in 4- and 5-ft modules are available.

Metal space frames are classified as noncombustible construction, and can usually be exposed when 20 ft above the floor. However, a fire suppression or a rated ceiling assembly may be required. Consult codes.

Common finishes include paint, thermoset polyester, galvanized, stainless steel, and metal plating.

MODULE SELECTION AND CHARACTERISTICS
2.109

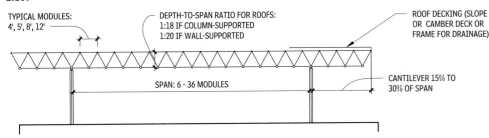

TYPICAL MODULES: 4', 5', 8', 12'

DEPTH-TO-SPAN RATIO FOR ROOFS:
1:18 IF COLUMN-SUPPORTED
1:20 IF WALL-SUPPORTED

ROOF DECKING (SLOPE OR CAMBER DECK OR FRAME FOR DRAINAGE)

SPAN: 6 - 36 MODULES

CANTILEVER 15% TO 30% OF SPAN

Select a space frame module that is compatible with the structural module in shape (e.g., a square module with orthogonal plan) and size (a multiple of the structural module), is consistent with the limitations of the interfacing systems (e.g., the maximum span of the roof deck or mullion spacing of the glazing system), and satisfies the spatial and aesthetic effects in scale and form.

MEMBER SHAPES
2.110

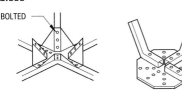

SUPPORT TYPES
2.107

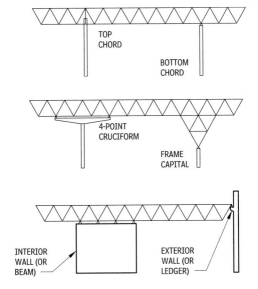

TOP CHORD

BOTTOM CHORD

4-POINT CRUCIFORM

FRAME CAPITAL

INTERIOR WALL (OR BEAM)

EXTERIOR WALL (OR LEDGER)

NODE CONNECTIONS
2.111

BOLTED

BENT PLATE

FLAT PLATE

FLAT PLATE

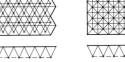
SCREW-IN

FOR DIRECT ATTACHMENT OF CLADDING OR GLAZING

FULL SPHERE

WELDED

BOX SECTION OUTER CHORD

SCREW-IN

PARTIAL SPHERE

SLOPED GLAZING
2.112

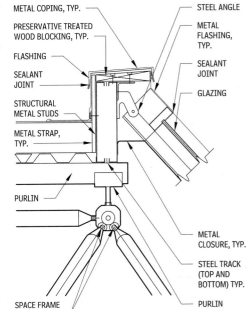

METAL COPING, TYP.

PRESERVATIVE TREATED WOOD BLOCKING, TYP.

FLASHING

SEALANT JOINT

STRUCTURAL METAL STUDS

METAL STRAP, TYP.

PURLIN

SPACE FRAME STRUCTURE

STEEL ANGLE

METAL FLASHING, TYP.

SEALANT JOINT

GLAZING

METAL CLOSURE, TYP.

STEEL TRACK (TOP AND BOTTOM) TYP.

PURLIN SUPPORT

COMMON PATTERNS
2.108

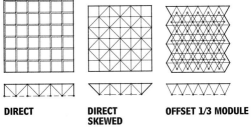

DIRECT   **DIRECT SKEWED**   **OFFSET 1/3 MODULE**   **OFFSET 1/2 MODULE**   **OFFSET SKEWED**   **SHAPE CHANGE**

NOTES

2.108 Many proprietary node systems are available for specific applications and budgets. Keep field connections to a minimum; welded connections often eliminate joint pieces.

2.110 Square tubes or angles within their span range are often the most economical.

2.111 Space frame supports are at joints only, not along members.

Contributor:
Severud Associates, New York City, New York.

GRID SHAPES
2.113

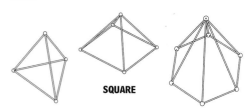

TETRAHEDRON   **SQUARE**   **HEXAGONAL**

SPACE FRAME FORM TYPES
2.114

PLATE   **MULTIFACETED**

FOLDED PLATE   **DOME**

PYRAMID   **HYPERBOLIC PARABOLOID**

COLD-FORMED METAL ROOF FRAMING

Cold-formed steel (CFS) framing members can be used to frame roofs in essentially the same manner as wood rafters or trusses. Note that thermal bridging can be a problem in cold climates when CFS members are not covered by continuous insulation.

Similarly cold-formed metal floor joist framing, including the use of delegated design, the following considerations should be considered when utilizing CFS for roof framing:

- Cold-formed metal roof framing uses C-shaped members, in sizes approximating wood framing, with special details for sloped bearing conditions.
- CFS framing is laid out similar to traditional wood joist framing.
- CFS roof trusses are available in virtually all of the configurations available for wood trusses.
- Proprietary roof truss systems use various shapes for chords and webs designed to allow higher productivity in fabrication and optimization of structural performance. It is generally not advisable to design around any single system, but instead to provide a general shape that many fabricators can provide.

For more information, consult the reference "Product Technical Information," Steel Stud Manufacturers Association, www.ssma.com.

COLD-FORMED METAL ROOF FRAMING DETAILS

COLD-FORMED STEEL ROOF TRUSSES
2.116

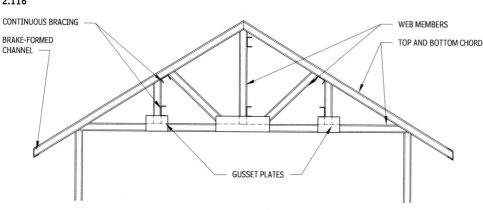

CONTINUOUS BRACING
BRAKE-FORMED CHANNEL
WEB MEMBERS
TOP AND BOTTOM CHORD
GUSSET PLATES

WEB MEMBERS
2.117

CHORDS   **WEB**

ROOF AND FLOOR CONNECTIONS
2.115

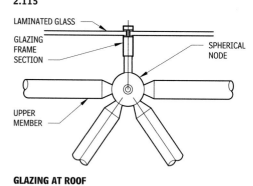

LAMINATED GLASS
GLAZING FRAME SECTION
SPHERICAL NODE
UPPER MEMBER

GLAZING AT ROOF

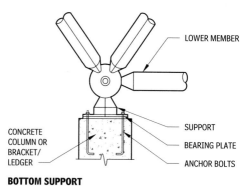

LOWER MEMBER
CONCRETE COLUMN OR BRACKET/LEDGER
SUPPORT
BEARING PLATE
ANCHOR BOLTS

BOTTOM SUPPORT

RIDGE BOARD
2.118

JOIST AND TRACK AS RIDGE BOARD
ALIGN RAFTERS
RAFTER, TYP.

NOTES

2.116 a. Chords and webs can be typical CFS C-shapes or a variety of proprietary special shapes.
b. Bracing is typically channel or track.
c. Gusset plates from flat plate or section of large C-shape.

Contributors:
American Iron and Steel Institute, Washington, DC; Severud Associates, New York City, New York.

ROOF EAVE AT CATHEDRAL CEILING
2.119

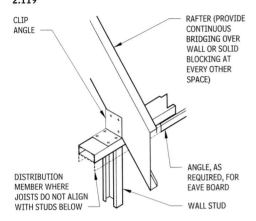

CLIP ANGLE

RAFTER (PROVIDE CONTINUOUS BRIDGING OVER WALL OR SOLID BLOCKING AT EVERY OTHER SPACE)

DISTRIBUTION MEMBER WHERE JOISTS DO NOT ALIGN WITH STUDS BELOW

ANGLE, AS REQUIRED, FOR EAVE BOARD

WALL STUD

ROOF TRUSS EAVE DETAIL
2.120

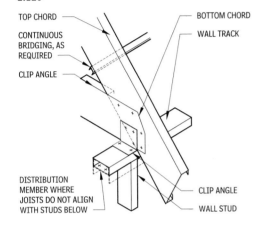

TOP CHORD

CONTINUOUS BRIDGING, AS REQUIRED

CLIP ANGLE

BOTTOM CHORD

WALL TRACK

DISTRIBUTION MEMBER WHERE JOISTS DO NOT ALIGN WITH STUDS BELOW

CLIP ANGLE

WALL STUD

ROOF EAVE DETAIL
2.121

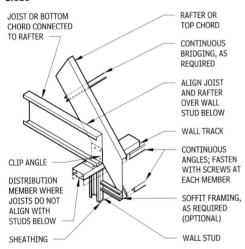

JOIST OR BOTTOM CHORD CONNECTED TO RAFTER

RAFTER OR TOP CHORD

CONTINUOUS BRIDGING, AS REQUIRED

ALIGN JOIST AND RAFTER OVER WALL STUD BELOW

WALL TRACK

CLIP ANGLE

DISTRIBUTION MEMBER WHERE JOISTS DO NOT ALIGN WITH STUDS BELOW

CONTINUOUS ANGLES; FASTEN WITH SCREWS AT EACH MEMBER

SOFFIT FRAMING, AS REQUIRED (OPTIONAL)

SHEATHING

WALL STUD

ROOF END DETAILS
2.122

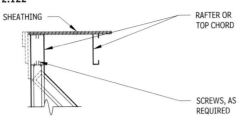

SHEATHING

RAFTER OR TOP CHORD

SCREWS, AS REQUIRED

ROOF GABLE END

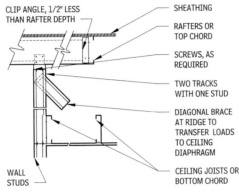

CLIP ANGLE, 1/2" LESS THAN RAFTER DEPTH

SHEATHING

RAFTERS OR TOP CHORD

SCREWS, AS REQUIRED

TWO TRACKS WITH ONE STUD

DIAGONAL BRACE AT RIDGE TO TRANSFER LOADS TO CEILING DIAPHRAGM

WALL STUDS

CEILING JOISTS OR BOTTOM CHORD

CANTILEVERED ROOF GABLE END

COLLAR TIE DETAIL
2.123

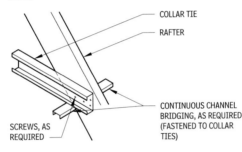

COLLAR TIE

RAFTER

SCREWS, AS REQUIRED

CONTINUOUS CHANNEL BRIDGING, AS REQUIRED (FASTENED TO COLLAR TIES)

FRAMING DETAILS FOR WOODROOFS

These figures illustrate details of common types of roof framing.

GABLE ROOF
2.124

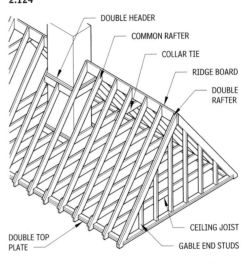

DOUBLE HEADER

COMMON RAFTER

COLLAR TIE

RIDGE BOARD

DOUBLE RAFTER

DOUBLE TOP PLATE

CEILING JOIST

GABLE END STUDS

GAMBREL ROOF
2.125

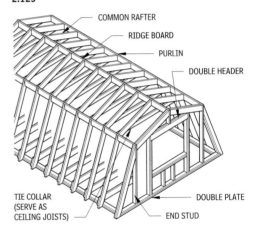

COMMON RAFTER

RIDGE BOARD

PURLIN

DOUBLE HEADER

TIE COLLAR (SERVE AS CEILING JOISTS)

DOUBLE PLATE

END STUD

HIP ROOF
2.126

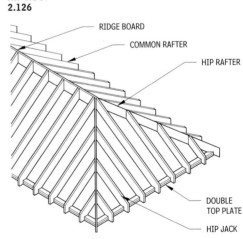

RIDGE BOARD

COMMON RAFTER

HIP RAFTER

DOUBLE TOP PLATE

HIP JACK

NOTE

2.122 Provide bridging at ceiling joists and roof rafters, and continuous bridging between rafters at the wall.

Contributors:
American Iron and Steel Institute, Washington, DC.; Timothy B. McDonald, Washington, DC.

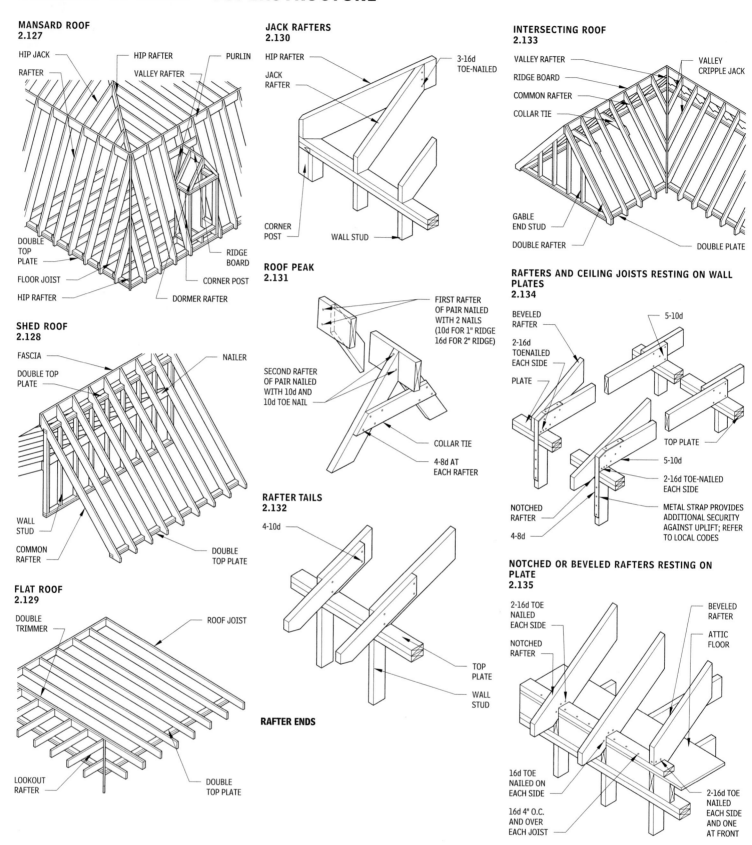

MANSARD ROOF
2.127

HIP JACK
RAFTER
HIP RAFTER
PURLIN
VALLEY RAFTER
DOUBLE TOP PLATE
FLOOR JOIST
HIP RAFTER
CORNER POST
DORMER RAFTER
RIDGE BOARD

SHED ROOF
2.128

FASCIA
DOUBLE TOP PLATE
NAILER
WALL STUD
COMMON RAFTER
DOUBLE TOP PLATE

FLAT ROOF
2.129

DOUBLE TRIMMER
ROOF JOIST
LOOKOUT RAFTER
DOUBLE TOP PLATE

JACK RAFTERS
2.130

HIP RAFTER
JACK RAFTER
3-16d TOE-NAILED
CORNER POST
WALL STUD

ROOF PEAK
2.131

FIRST RAFTER OF PAIR NAILED WITH 2 NAILS (10d FOR 1" RIDGE 16d FOR 2" RIDGE)
SECOND RAFTER OF PAIR NAILED WITH 10d AND 10d TOE NAIL
COLLAR TIE
4-8d AT EACH RAFTER

RAFTER TAILS
2.132

4-10d
TOP PLATE
WALL STUD

RAFTER ENDS

INTERSECTING ROOF
2.133

VALLEY RAFTER
RIDGE BOARD
COMMON RAFTER
COLLAR TIE
VALLEY CRIPPLE JACK
GABLE END STUD
DOUBLE RAFTER
DOUBLE PLATE

RAFTERS AND CEILING JOISTS RESTING ON WALL PLATES
2.134

BEVELED RAFTER
5-10d
2-16d TOENAILED EACH SIDE
PLATE
TOP PLATE
5-10d
2-16d TOE-NAILED EACH SIDE
NOTCHED RAFTER
4-8d
METAL STRAP PROVIDES ADDITIONAL SECURITY AGAINST UPLIFT; REFER TO LOCAL CODES

NOTCHED OR BEVELED RAFTERS RESTING ON PLATE
2.135

2-16d TOE NAILED EACH SIDE
NOTCHED RAFTER
16d TOE NAILED ON EACH SIDE
16d 4" O.C. AND OVER EACH JOIST
BEVELED RAFTER
ATTIC FLOOR
2-16d TOE NAILED EACH SIDE AND ONE AT FRONT

Contributors:
Timothy B. McDonald, Washington, DC.; Joseph A. Wilkes, FAIA, Wilkes and Associates, Washington, DC.

CURB FOR SKYLIGHT
2.136

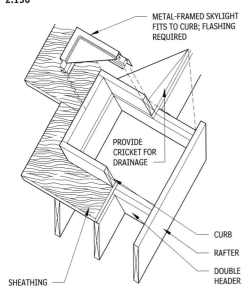

METAL-FRAMED SKYLIGHT FITS TO CURB; FLASHING REQUIRED

PROVIDE CRICKET FOR DRAINAGE

CURB

RAFTER

DOUBLE HEADER

SHEATHING

WOOD I-JOIST CONSTRUCTION DETAILS

WOOD I-JOIST RAFTER AT RIDGE BEAM DETAIL
2.137

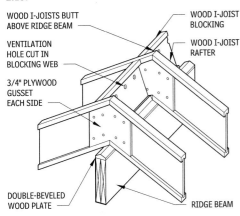

WOOD I-JOISTS BUTT ABOVE RIDGE BEAM

WOOD I-JOIST BLOCKING

VENTILATION HOLE CUT IN BLOCKING WEB

WOOD I-JOIST RAFTER

3/4" PLYWOOD GUSSET EACH SIDE

DOUBLE-BEVELED WOOD PLATE

RIDGE BEAM

WOOD I-JOIST RAFTER AT RIDGE BEAM DETAIL
2.138

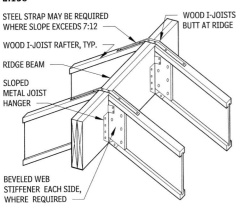

STEEL STRAP MAY BE REQUIRED WHERE SLOPE EXCEEDS 7:12

WOOD I-JOISTS BUTT AT RIDGE

WOOD I-JOIST RAFTER, TYP.

RIDGE BEAM

SLOPED METAL JOIST HANGER

BEVELED WEB STIFFENER EACH SIDE, WHERE REQUIRED

WOOD I-JOIST RAFTER AT RIDGE BEAM DETAIL
2.139

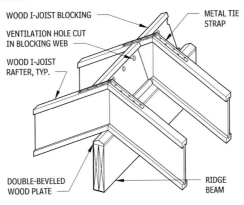

WOOD I-JOIST BLOCKING

VENTILATION HOLE CUT IN BLOCKING WEB

WOOD I-JOIST RAFTER, TYP.

METAL TIE STRAP

DOUBLE-BEVELED WOOD PLATE

RIDGE BEAM

LAPPED WOOD I-JOIST RAFTER AT RIDGE BEAM
2.140

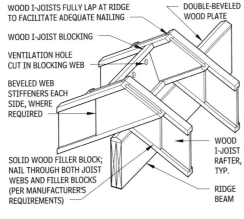

WOOD I-JOISTS FULLY LAP AT RIDGE TO FACILITATE ADEQUATE NAILING

WOOD I-JOIST BLOCKING

VENTILATION HOLE CUT IN BLOCKING WEB

BEVELED WEB STIFFENERS EACH SIDE, WHERE REQUIRED

DOUBLE-BEVELED WOOD PLATE

WOOD I-JOIST RAFTER, TYP.

RIDGE BEAM

SOLID WOOD FILLER BLOCK; NAIL THROUGH BOTH JOIST WEBS AND FILLER BLOCKS (PER MANUFACTURER'S REQUIREMENTS)

WOOD I-JOIST RAFTER AT OVERHANG
2.141

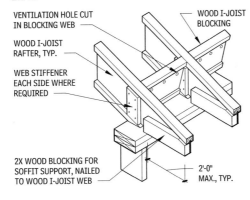

VENTILATION HOLE CUT IN BLOCKING WEB

WOOD I-JOIST RAFTER, TYP.

WEB STIFFENER EACH SIDE WHERE REQUIRED

WOOD I-JOIST BLOCKING

2X WOOD BLOCKING FOR SOFFIT SUPPORT, NAILED TO WOOD I-JOIST WEB

2'-0" MAX., TYP.

WOOD I-JOIST RAFTER AT OVERHANG
2.142

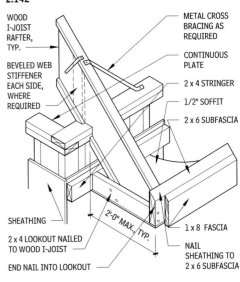

WOOD I-JOIST RAFTER, TYP.

BEVELED WEB STIFFENER EACH SIDE, WHERE REQUIRED

SHEATHING

2 x 4 LOOKOUT NAILED TO WOOD I-JOIST

END NAIL INTO LOOKOUT

METAL CROSS BRACING AS REQUIRED

CONTINUOUS PLATE

2 x 4 STRINGER

1/2" SOFFIT

2 x 6 SUBFASCIA

2'-0" MAX., TYP.

1 x 8 FASCIA

NAIL SHEATHING TO 2 x 6 SUBFASCIA

WOOD I-JOIST RAFTER AT OVERHANG
2.143

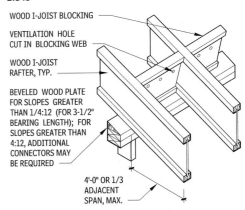

WOOD I-JOIST BLOCKING

VENTILATION HOLE CUT IN BLOCKING WEB

WOOD I-JOIST RAFTER, TYP.

BEVELED WOOD PLATE FOR SLOPES GREATER THAN 1/4:12 (FOR 3-1/2" BEARING LENGTH); FOR SLOPES GREATER THAN 4:12, ADDITIONAL CONNECTORS MAY BE REQUIRED

4'-0" OR 1/3 ADJACENT SPAN, MAX.

TYPICAL BIRD'S MOUTH I-JOIST CUT DETAIL
2.144

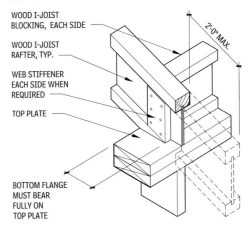

WOOD I-JOIST BLOCKING, EACH SIDE

WOOD I-JOIST RAFTER, TYP.

WEB STIFFENER EACH SIDE WHEN REQUIRED

TOP PLATE

BOTTOM FLANGE MUST BEAR FULLY ON TOP PLATE

2'-0" MAX.

NOTES

2.137 Uplift connections may be required.
2.138 Uplift connections may be required.
2.139 Uplift connections may be required.
2.140 Uplift connections may be required.
2.141 Uplift connections may be required.
2.142 Uplift connections may be required.
2.143 a. Uplift connections may be required.
b. Special sloped seat-bearing metal connectors can be used in lieu of beveled wood plate in some sloped applications. See manufacturer's recommendations.

2.144 Uplift connections may be required.

Contributor:
Richard J., Vitullo, AIA, Oak Leaf Studio, Crownsville, Maryland.

WOOD I-JOIST RAFTER WITH OUTRIGGER
2.145

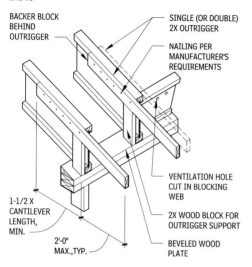

BACKER BLOCK BEHIND OUTRIGGER

SINGLE (OR DOUBLE) 2X OUTRIGGER

NAILING PER MANUFACTURER'S REQUIREMENTS

VENTILATION HOLE CUT IN BLOCKING WEB

2X WOOD BLOCK FOR OUTRIGGER SUPPORT

BEVELED WOOD PLATE

1-1/2 X CANTILEVER LENGTH, MIN.

2'-0" MAX.,TYP.

WOOD I-JOIST RAFTER AT OUTRIGGER
2.146

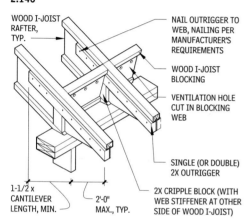

WOOD I-JOIST RAFTER, TYP.

NAIL OUTRIGGER TO WEB, NAILING PER MANUFACTURER'S REQUIREMENTS

WOOD I-JOIST BLOCKING

VENTILATION HOLE CUT IN BLOCKING WEB

SINGLE (OR DOUBLE) 2X OUTRIGGER

2X CRIPPLE BLOCK (WITH WEB STIFFENER AT OTHER SIDE OF WOOD I-JOIST)

1-1/2 x CANTILEVER LENGTH, MIN.

2'-0" MAX., TYP.

FLY RAFTER DETAIL
2.147

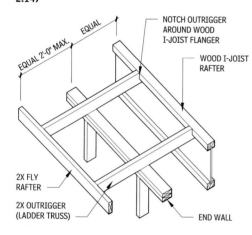

NOTCH OUTRIGGER AROUND WOOD I-JOIST FLANGER

WOOD I-JOIST RAFTER

EQUAL 2'-0" MAX.   EQUAL   EQUAL

2X FLY RAFTER

2X OUTRIGGER (LADDER TRUSS)

END WALL

WOOD I-JOIST SKYLIGHT FRAMING DETAIL
2.148

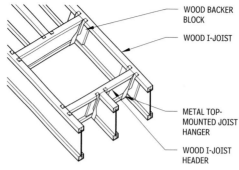

WOOD BACKER BLOCK

WOOD I-JOIST

METAL TOP-MOUNTED JOIST HANGER

WOOD I-JOIST HEADER

SHOP-FABRICATED WOOD TRUSSES

Shop-fabricated wood trusses have been used in building construction since 1953, when the metal connector plate was invented. Metal plates are available in a range of styles and tooth orientations. The metal plates are punched with barbs that grab onto the wood truss, thus reducing the hand-nailing required to fabricate a structure. Plate size for a given truss is based on a combination of

PITCHED CHORD TRUSSES
2.149

MIN. SLOPE = 1.75:12, TYP.

KING POST (TYP. MAX. SPAN = 37' APPROX.)

HOWE (TYP. MAX. SPAN = 37' APPROX.)

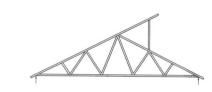

MODIFIED QUEEN POST (TYP. MAX. SPAN = 47' APPROX.)

FINK (TYP. MAX. SPAN = 27' APPROX.)

DOUBLE FINK (TYP. MAX. SPAN = 37' APPROX.)

DOUBLE FINK (TYP. MAX. SPAN = 37' APPROX.)

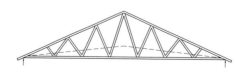

CANTILEVER (TYP. MAX. SPAN = 20' APPROX.)

CLERESTORY (TYP. MAX. SPAN = 37' APPROX.)

INVERTED (TYP. MAX. SPAN = 37' APPROX.)

the tooth withdrawal strength of the plate, the tensile and shear strength of the steel, and the net sectional area of the lumber.

This system is primarily used for roofs with either pitched or parallel chord trusses. It is occasionally employed for floors with parallel chord trusses. Individual trusses are cut from 2-by-4-in. or 2-by-6-in. dimension lumber and can be spaced 24 in. or 48 in. o.c. For typical residential construction, 24 in. o.c. is used. Exceptionally long spans are possible with shop-fabricated wood trusses, allowing the large, unencumbered interior spaces often required in commercial, agricultural, and other nonresidential building types.

Camber is designed for dead load only: Camber (in.) = Length (ft)/60

BRACING

Providing adequate bracing for trusses is essential, both during installation and as a component of the overall roof design. Truss members must be held in place with supports that meet them at right angles. Truss chords and web members are placed in a vertical, plumb position, and maintain that position, resisting applied design loads throughout the life of the structure. Permanent bracing and anchorage are expected to be an integral part of construction, and strongbacks are often used for this purpose.

Movement by crane can damage trusses. Crane spreader bars are used to avoid this "out-of-plane" buckling. Special stiffening may be applied to trusses during erection.

NOTES

2.146 Uplift connections may be required.

2.148 Check code and manufacturer's requirements for all ventilation hole sizes cut in blocking web.

2.149 a. The average spacing for light trusses (trussed rafters) is 2 ft o.c., but it varies, up to 4 ft. The average combined dead and live loads is 45 lb per sq ft. Spans are usually between 20 and 32 ft, but can be as much as 50 ft.

b. Early in the design process, consult an engineer or truss supplier for preengineered truss designs to establish the most economical and effi-

cient truss proportions. The supplier may provide final truss engineering design.

c. Permanent and temporary erection bracing must be installed as specified to prevent failure of properly designed trusses.

d. Some locales require an engineer's stamp when prefab trusses are used. Check local codes.

e. Member forces in a truss rise rapidly as the lower chord is raised above the horizontal.

Contributor:
Richard J. Vitullo, AIA, Oak Leaf Studio, Crownsville, Maryland.

TYPICAL METAL PLATE CONNECTOR
2.150

PLATE TOOTH PUNCHED THROUGH PLATE HAS PARTICULAR LENGTH, SHAPE, AND TWIST; ALL AFFECT WITHDRAWAL STRENGTH (TOOTH LATERAL RESISTANCE)

GAUGE NET AREA OF STRUCTURAL STEEL LEFT IN PLATE AFTER PUNCHED TEETH ARE FORMED; RESIDUAL STRENGTH OF THIS UNPUNCHED STEEL IS USED TO TRANSFER FORCES IN TRUSS JOINT

PLATE CONNECTOR PRESSED BY PNEUMATIC, HYDRAULIC, OR ROLLER PRESS INTO BOTH SIDES OF TRUSS

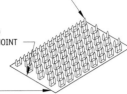

PITCHED TRUSSES
2.151

SCISSORS (TYP. MAX. SPAN = 45'-0" APPROX.)

VAULTED CEILING (TYP. MAX. SPAN = 42'-0" APPROX.)

MONO-PITCH (TYP. MAX. SPAN = 23'-0" APPROX.)

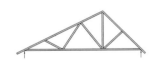

DUAL PITCH (TYP. MAX. SPAN = 32'-0" APPROX.)

PITCHED WARREN (TYP. MAX. SPAN = 42'-0" APPROX.)

SCISSORED WARREN (TYP. MAX. SPAN = 42'-0" APPROX.)

BOWSTRING (TYP. MAX. SPAN = 30'-0" APPROX.)

PARALLEL TRUSSES
2.152

4X2 TRUSS (FLOOR)   **CHORD/WEB ORIENTATION**

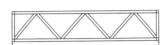

2X4 TRUSS (ROOF)   **CHORD/WEB ORIENTATION**

OVERHANG DETAILS
2.153

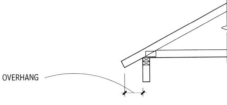
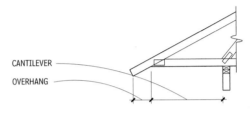

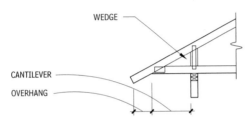
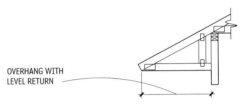

TYPICAL PITCHED CHORD ROOF TRUSS
2.154

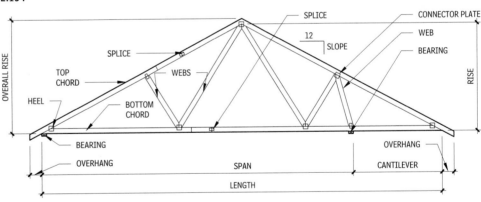

QUEENPOST AND KINGPOST
2.155

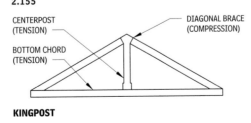
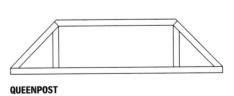

KINGPOST   **QUEENPOST**

SPLIT-RING WOOD TRUSSES

The first wood trusses were developed for bridge design, with the kingpost truss being the earliest form. It uses a primary engineering principle: a triangle will hold its shape under a load until its side members or its joints are crushed. Next came the queenpost truss, in which the peak of the kingpost was replaced by a horizontal crosspiece to allow a longer base.

Further amplifications permitted greater flexibility, to overcome different spanning challenges and to integrate various combinations of inclined wood braces, wood arches, steel tension rods, and other structural members.

When working with these trusses, keep the following in mind:

- A built-in camber of approximately 1 in. per 40-ft span will be introduced in the top and bottom chords during fabrication.
- When lumber is not adequately seasoned, the trusses should be inspected periodically, and adjusted, if necessary, until moisture equilibrium is reached.

Contributors:
Richard J. Vitullo, AIA, Oak Leaf Studio, Crownsville, Maryland; TECO Products, Collier, West Virginia.

- Pitched trusses are very economical for spans up to 70 ft (with an average spacing of 15 ft), for three reasons: the member sizes are small, the joint details are relatively simple, and the trusses are easily fabricated. All pitched trusses require either knee braces to columns or some other provision for lateral restraint against wind or other forces.
- A typical span (l) to depth (d) ratio for the Pratt, Howe, or Belgian truss is 4 to 6, which gives a relatively normal slope of 4:12 to 6:12. Fink trusses are preferred where the slope is steep (over 7:12). Scissors trusses and other types of raised lower-chord pitched roof trusses are used for special conditions where clearance or appearance requires an arched bottom chord.

PITCHED TRUSSES
2.156

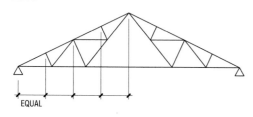

EQUAL

CONNECTORS
2.157

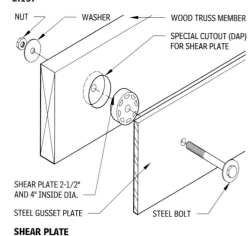

NUT — WASHER — WOOD TRUSS MEMBER

SPECIAL CUTOUT (DAP) FOR SHEAR PLATE

SHEAR PLATE 2-1/2" AND 4" INSIDE DIA.

STEEL GUSSET PLATE

STEEL BOLT

SHEAR PLATE

SPLIT-RING CONNECTOR
2.158

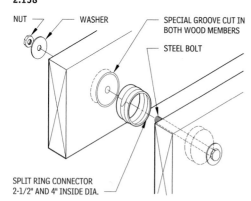

NUT — WASHER — SPECIAL GROOVE CUT IN BOTH WOOD MEMBERS

STEEL BOLT

SPLIT RING CONNECTOR 2-1/2" AND 4" INSIDE DIA.

GLUED-LAMINATED CONSTRUCTION

STRUCTURAL GLUED-LAMINATED SHAPES
2.159

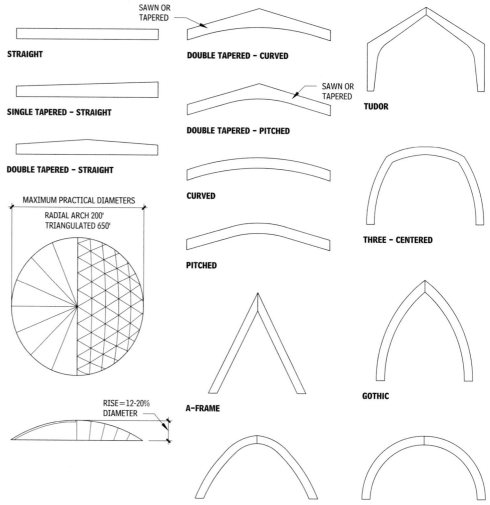

STRAIGHT

SINGLE TAPERED – STRAIGHT

DOUBLE TAPERED – STRAIGHT

SAWN OR TAPERED

DOUBLE TAPERED – CURVED

SAWN OR TAPERED

DOUBLE TAPERED – PITCHED

CURVED

PITCHED

TUDOR

THREE – CENTERED

GOTHIC

A–FRAME

PARABOLIC

RADIAL

MAXIMUM PRACTICAL DIAMETERS

RADIAL ARCH 200'
TRIANGULATED 650'

RISE=12-20% DIAMETER

LAMINATED DOME

When examining the shapes of structural glued-laminated members, note the following:

- Beam names describe top and bottom surfaces of the beam. Sloped or pitched surfaces should be used on the tension side of the beam.
- The three-hinged arches and frames shown in Figure 2.175 produce horizontal reactions requiring horizontal ties or modified foundations.
- The triangulated and the radial arch are the two basic types of structural glued-laminated wood dome systems available. Both require a tension ring at the dome spring line to convert axial thrusts to vertical loads. Consideration must be given to the

perimeter bond beam design, as wind forces will produce loads in this member. The lengths of the main members of the radial arch system, which must span a distance greater than half the dome diameter, limit the maximum practical dome diameter. The much smaller members of the triangulated dome result in the greater diameters. The triangulated system can be designed for five or more segments, with an equal number of peripheral supports at each segment.

- More complicated shapes may be fabricated. Contact the American Institute of Timber Construction (AITC) and APA – Engineered Wood Association.

NOTE

2.157 Shear plate connectors are commonly used to connect wood truss members to steel gusset plates, but they may be used to connect wood to wood, as well.

Contributors:
TECO Products, Collier, West Virginia; Richard J. Vitullo, AIA, Oak Leaf Studio, Crownsville, Maryland; Roger W. Kipp, AIA, Thomas Hodne Architects, Inc., Minneapolis, Minnesota.

GLUED-LAMINATED COLUMN WITH ROOF BEAM
2.160

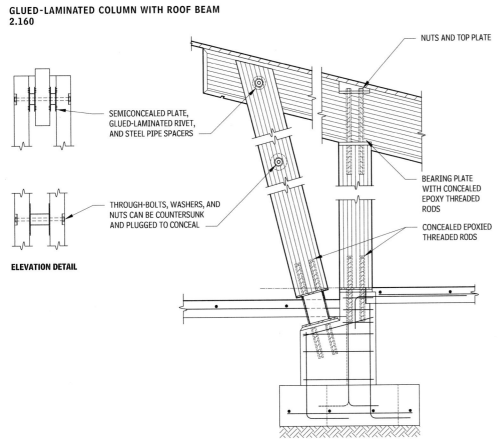

SEMICONCEALED PLATE, GLUED-LAMINATED RIVET, AND STEEL PIPE SPACERS

NUTS AND TOP PLATE

BEARING PLATE WITH CONCEALED EPOXY THREADED RODS

CONCEALED EPOXIED THREADED RODS

THROUGH-BOLTS, WASHERS, AND NUTS CAN BE COUNTERSUNK AND PLUGGED TO CONCEAL

ELEVATION DETAIL

GLUED-LAMINATED BEAM/CONCEALED DOUBLE COLUMN
2.161

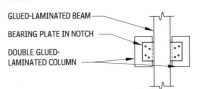

GLUED-LAMINATED BEAM

BEARING PLATE IN NOTCH

DOUBLE GLUED-LAMINATED COLUMN

PLAN VIEW

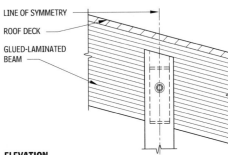

LINE OF SYMMETRY

ROOF DECK

GLUED-LAMINATED BEAM

ELEVATION

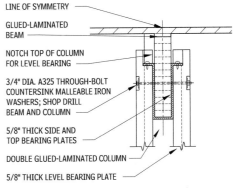

LINE OF SYMMETRY

GLUED-LAMINATED BEAM

NOTCH TOP OF COLUMN FOR LEVEL BEARING

3/4" DIA. A325 THROUGH-BOLT COUNTERSINK MALLEABLE IRON WASHERS; SHOP DRILL BEAM AND COLUMN

5/8" THICK SIDE AND TOP BEARING PLATES

DOUBLE GLUED-LAMINATED COLUMN

5/8" THICK LEVEL BEARING PLATE

SECTION

GLUED-LAMINATED RIVET CONNECTION AND INSTALLATION DETAILS
2.162

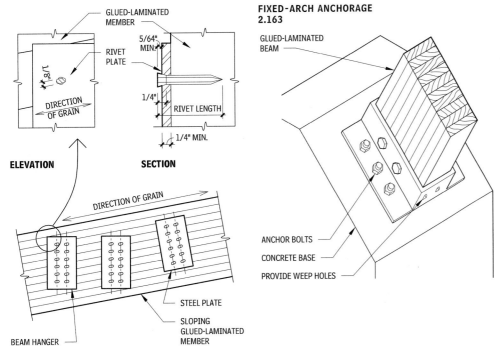

GLUED-LAMINATED MEMBER

RIVET PLATE

5/64" MIN.

1/8"

DIRECTION OF GRAIN

1/4"

RIVET LENGTH

1/4" MIN.

ELEVATION

SECTION

DIRECTION OF GRAIN

STEEL PLATE

SLOPING GLUED-LAMINATED MEMBER

BEAM HANGER

GLUED-LAMINATED CONSTRUCTION: CONNECTIONS

FIXED-ARCH ANCHORAGE
2.163

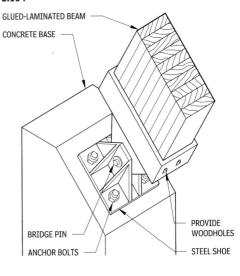

GLUED-LAMINATED BEAM

ANCHOR BOLTS

CONCRETE BASE

PROVIDE WEEP HOLES

TRUE HINGE ANCHORAGE FOR ARCHES
2.164

GLUED-LAMINATED BEAM

CONCRETE BASE

BRIDGE PIN

ANCHOR BOLTS

PROVIDE WOODHOLES

STEEL SHOE

NOTES

2.162 a. Rivets must be installed with their long axis parallel to the grain of the wood.
b. Rivets must be driven so that the conical head is firmly seated in the hole, but not flush.
c. Side plates must be at least 1/4-in. thick and must be hot dipped galvanized for use in wet service conditions.
d. Steel plates must be drilled (not punched) with 17/64- to 9/32-in. holes to accommodate the rivets.

Contributors:
David Nairne-Associates Ltds., North Vancouver, British Columbia;
Timothy B. McDonald, Washington, DC.

ARCH PEAK CONNECTION
2.165

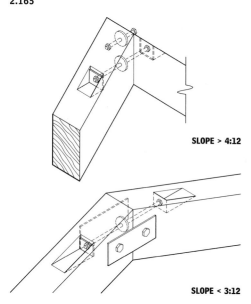

SLOPE > 4:12

SLOPE < 3:12

RAFTER TO BEARING WALL
2.167

SLOTTED HOLES IN SIDE
PLATES TO ALLOW FOR
MOVEMENT

BEAM CANTILEVER
TO FORM EAVE

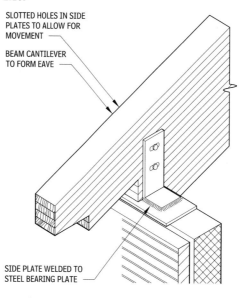

SIDE PLATE WELDED TO
STEEL BEARING PLATE

STEEL COMPRESSION BOX
2.169

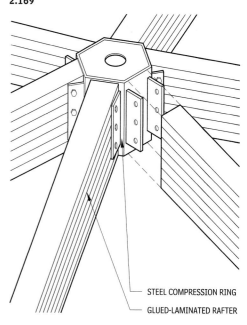

STEEL COMPRESSION RING

GLUED-LAMINATED RAFTER

RAFTER TO COLUMN CONDITION
2.166

GLUED
LAMINATED
BEAM

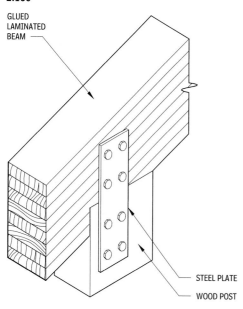

STEEL PLATE

WOOD POST

NOTCHED BEARING CONDITION
2.168

PURLIN

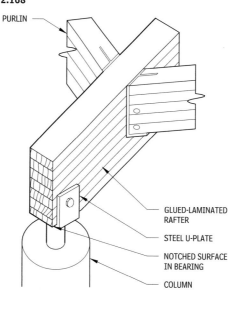

GLUED-LAMINATED
RAFTER

STEEL U-PLATE

NOTCHED SURFACE
IN BEARING

COLUMN

SPECIAL CONNECTION
2.170

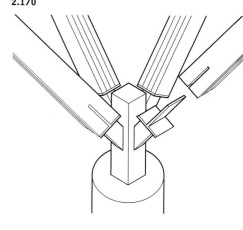

GLUED-LAMINATED COLUMNS
2.171

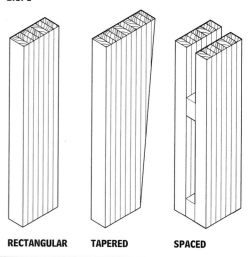

RECTANGULAR   TAPERED   SPACED

NOTES

2.168 a. An abrupt notch in the end of a wood member reduces the effective shear strength of the member and may permit a more rapid migration of moisture in the lower portion of the member, potentially causing splitting.
b. The shear strength of the end of the member is reduced, and the exposed end grain may also result in splitting because of drying. At inclined beams, the taper cut should be loaded in bearing.
2.170 One of a large variety of special connections and connection assemblies that are possible using structural glued-laminated timber. It is critical that connections be designed carefully in accordance with good engineering practice.

Contributors:
Roger W. Kipp, AIA, Thomas Hodne Architects, Inc., Minneapolis, Minnesota; Timothy B. McDonald, Washington, DC.

ROOF DECKING

This section examines common types of roof decking, including metal decking, grouted roof decking, and timber frame roof decking.

METAL ROOF DECKING

Some of the many types of available metal roof decking include:

- Roof decking
- Composite deck
- Permanent forms for self-supporting concrete slabs
- Raceway (composite or noncomposite)
- Acoustical metal decking
- Acoustical cellular deck (composite or noncomposite)
- Vented roof deck (used with lightweight insulating concrete fill)

INSTALLATION AND DESIGN

Metal roof decks must be secured to supports, generally by means of welds made through the decking to supporting steel. Steel sheet lighter than 22 gauge should be secured by use of welding washers.

Side laps between adjacent sheets of deck must be secured by button-punching standing seams, welding, or screws, in accordance with the manufacturer's recommendations.

Decks used as lateral diaphragms must be welded to steel supports around their entire perimeter to ensure development of diaphragm action. More stringent requirements may govern the size and/or spacing of attachments to supports and side lap fasteners or welds.

Roof deck selection must consider construction and maintenance loads, as well as the capacity to support uniformly distributed live loads. Consult the Steel Deck Institute's recommendations and Factory Mutual Global's requirements.

Heavy roof-mounted mechanical equipment should not be placed directly on a metal roof deck. Equipment on curbs should be supported directly on main and supplementary structural members, and the deck must be supported along all free edges. Heavy items such as cooling towers that must be elevated should be supported directly onto structural members below the deck.

FIRE-RESISTANCE RATINGS

Fire-resistance ratings for roof assemblies are published by Code authorities, Underwriters Laboratories and Factory Mutual. Fire-Resistance ratings may be achieved by various methods including applied fireproofing, rated acoustical ceilings, and gypsum board enclosures.

ADVANTAGES OF METAL ROOF DECKS

There are a number of advantages to using metal roof decks:

- A high strength-to-weight ratio reduces roof dead load.
- They can be erected in most weather conditions.
- A variety of depths and rib patterns are available.

ROOF DECK ACCESSORIES
2.172

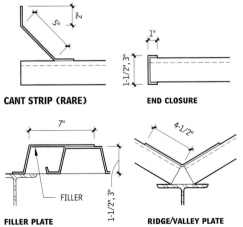

CANT STRIP (RARE) **END CLOSURE**

FILLER PLATE **RIDGE/VALLEY PLATE**

- Acoustical treatment is possible.
- They can serve as the base for insulation and roofing.
- Fire ratings can be obtained with standard assemblies.
- They can provide a lateral diaphragm.
- They can be erected quickly and economically.
- Using them makes it easy and economical to create roof slopes for drainage when mounted over sloped structural steel.

OPENINGS IN DECK
2.173

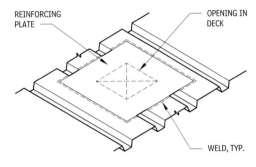

REINFORCING PLATE

OPENING IN DECK

WELD, TYP.

RECESSED SUMP PAN
2.174

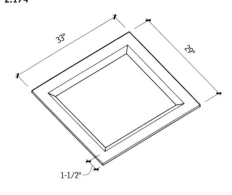

33" 29" 1-1/2"

METAL ROOF DECK TYPES
2.175

TYPE	PROFILE	REMARKS	SPAN	WIDTH	MAXIMUM LENGTH
Economy	3-5/8", 4" 2-3/4", 3" 1"	Most economical deck for shorter spans; use with 1" or more insulation	2'-6" to 8'-0"	32" to 33"	42'-0"
Narrow rib (1" wide)	6" 1" 1-1/2"	Use with 1/2" insulation; maximum surface area on top for adhering insulation	4'-0" to 11'-0"	36"	42'-0"
Intermediate rib (1-3/4" wide)	6" 1-3/4" 1-1/2"	Use with 1" insulation	4'-0" to 11'-0"	36"	42'-0"
Wide rib (2-1/2" wide)	6" 2-1/2" 1-1/2"	Use with 1" insulation	5'-0" to 12'-0"	36"	42'-0"
Acoustical metal decking	2-5/8" 8" 3" SOUND INSULATION (OPTIONAL) SIDES PERFORATED (OPTIONAL)	Perforated type for sound absorption only	10'-0" to 20'-0"	24"	42'-0"
Raceway decking assemblies	2-1/2" 6" 1-1/2"	For use as electrical raceway or as acoustical ceiling; bottom plate is perforated for sound absorption	9'-0" to 12'-0"	24"	40'-0"
Raceway decking assemblies	2-5/8" 8" 3"		10'-0" to 13'-0"	24"	40'-0"
Raceway decking assemblies	3" 12" 4-1/2", 6", 7-1/2" SOUND INSULATION (OPTIONAL)		20'-0" to 30'-0"	24"	30'-0"

NOTES

2.173 a. Small openings (up to 6 by 6 in. or 6 in. in diameter) usually may be cut in a roof or floor deck without reinforcing the deck.
b. Openings up to 10 by 10 in. or 10 in. in diameter require reinforcing of the deck either by welding a reinforcing plate to the deck all around the openings or providing channel-shaped headers and/or supplementary reinforcing parallel to the deck span. Reinforcing plates should be 14-gauge sheets with a minimum projection of 6 in. beyond all sides of the opening, and they should be welded to each cell of the deck.
c. Larger openings should be framed with supplementary steel members so that all free edges of the deck are supported.

2.174 Preformed recessed sump pans are available from deck manufacturers for use at roof drains.

Contributors:
Donald Neubauer, PE, Neubauer Consulting Engineers, Potomac, Maryland; Walter D. Shapiro, PE, Tor, Shapiro & Associates, New York City, New York.

TIMBER FRAME ROOF DECKING

WOOD SLEEPERS AND TONGUE-AND-GROOVE CEILING ON ROOF PURLINS
2.176

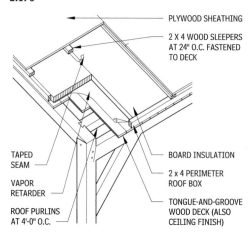

- PLYWOOD SHEATHING
- 2 X 4 WOOD SLEEPERS AT 24" O.C. FASTENED TO DECK
- TAPED SEAM
- VAPOR RETARDER
- ROOF PURLINS AT 4'-0" O.C.
- BOARD INSULATION
- 2 x 4 PERIMETER ROOF BOX
- TONGUE-AND-GROOVE WOOD DECK (ALSO CEILING FINISH)

WOOD NAILERS ON ROOF PURLINS
2.177

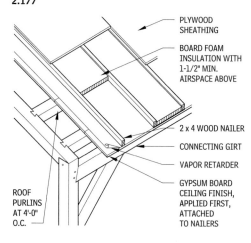

- PLYWOOD SHEATHING
- BOARD FOAM INSULATION WITH 1-1/2" MIN. AIRSPACE ABOVE
- 2 x 4 WOOD NAILER
- CONNECTING GIRT
- VAPOR RETARDER
- GYPSUM BOARD CEILING FINISH, APPLIED FIRST, ATTACHED TO NAILERS
- ROOF PURLINS AT 4'-0" O.C.

ROOF SHEATHING AND PANELS

OPEN SOFFIT
2.178

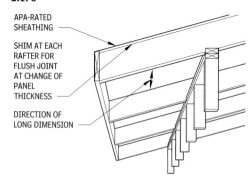

- APA-RATED SHEATHING
- SHIM AT EACH RAFTER FOR FLUSH JOINT AT CHANGE OF PANEL THICKNESS
- DIRECTION OF LONG DIMENSION

CLOSED SOFFIT
2.179

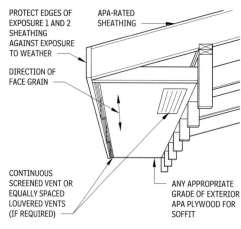

- PROTECT EDGES OF EXPOSURE 1 AND 2 SHEATHING AGAINST EXPOSURE TO WEATHER
- APA-RATED SHEATHING
- DIRECTION OF FACE GRAIN
- CONTINUOUS SCREENED VENT OR EQUALLY SPACED LOUVERED VENTS (IF REQUIRED)
- ANY APPROPRIATE GRADE OF EXTERIOR APA PLYWOOD FOR SOFFIT

GABLE ROOF
2.180

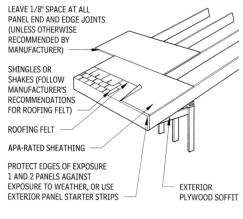

- LEAVE 1/8" SPACE AT ALL PANEL END AND EDGE JOINTS (UNLESS OTHERWISE RECOMMENDED BY MANUFACTURER)
- SHINGLES OR SHAKES (FOLLOW MANUFACTURER'S RECOMMENDATIONS FOR ROOFING FELT)
- ROOFING FELT
- APA-RATED SHEATHING
- PROTECT EDGES OF EXPOSURE 1 AND 2 PANELS AGAINST EXPOSURE TO WEATHER, OR USE EXTERIOR PANEL STARTER STRIPS
- EXTERIOR PLYWOOD SOFFIT

FLAT LOW-PITCHED ROOF
2.181

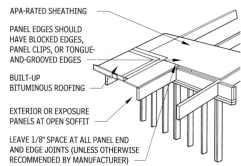

- APA-RATED SHEATHING
- PANEL EDGES SHOULD HAVE BLOCKED EDGES, PANEL CLIPS, OR TONGUE-AND-GROOVED EDGES
- BUILT-UP BITUMINOUS ROOFING
- EXTERIOR OR EXPOSURE PANELS AT OPEN SOFFIT
- LEAVE 1/8" SPACE AT ALL PANEL END AND EDGE JOINTS (UNLESS OTHERWISE RECOMMENDED BY MANUFACTURER)

CONNECTIONS TO STEEL JOIST
2.182

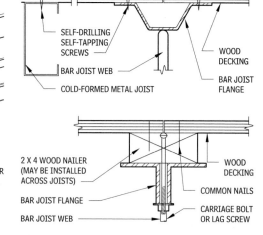

- SELF-DRILLING SELF-TAPPING SCREWS
- BAR JOIST WEB
- COLD-FORMED METAL JOIST
- WOOD DECKING
- BAR JOIST FLANGE

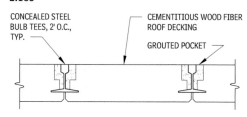

- 2 X 4 WOOD NAILER (MAY BE INSTALLED ACROSS JOISTS)
- BAR JOIST FLANGE
- BAR JOIST WEB
- WOOD DECKING
- COMMON NAILS
- CARRIAGE BOLT OR LAG SCREW

CAST ROOF DECKS
Cement panels may be used instead of oriented strand board (OSB)/plywood for noncombustible construction.

CAST ROOF DECKS
2.183

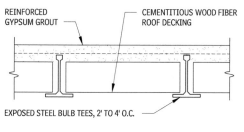

- CONCEALED STEEL BULB TEES, 2' O.C., TYP.
- CEMENTITIOUS WOOD FIBER ROOF DECKING
- GROUTED POCKET

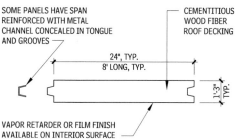

- REINFORCED GYPSUM GROUT
- CEMENTITIOUS WOOD FIBER ROOF DECKING
- EXPOSED STEEL BULB TEES, 2' TO 4' O.C.

- SOME PANELS HAVE SPAN REINFORCED WITH METAL CHANNEL CONCEALED IN TONGUE AND GROOVES
- CEMENTITIOUS WOOD FIBER ROOF DECKING
- 24", TYP.
- 8' LONG, TYP.
- 1'-3" TYP.
- VAPOR RETARDER OR FILM FINISH AVAILABLE ON INTERIOR SURFACE

NOTE

2.178 Any appropriate exterior or exposure panel grade of adequate span rating to carry design roof loads, refer to Chapter 11.

Contributors:
APA–Engineered Wood Association, Tacoma, Washington; BSB Design, Des Moines, Iowa; Richard J. Vitullo, AIA, Oak Leaf Studio, Crownsville, Maryland; Tedd Benson and Ben Brungraber, PhD, PE, Benson Woodworking Co., Inc., Alstead, New Hampshire.

STRUCTURAL INSULATED PANELS (SIP)
2.184

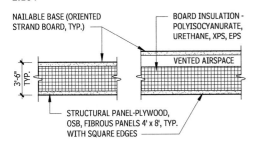

NAILABLE BASE (ORIENTED STRAND BOARD, TYP.)

BOARD INSULATION - POLYISOCYANURATE, URETHANE, XPS, EPS

VENTED AIRSPACE

3'-6" TYP.

STRUCTURAL PANEL-PLYWOOD, OSB, FIBROUS PANELS 4' x 8', TYP. WITH SQUARE EDGES

ROOF FRAMING WITH RAFTERS AND TRUSSES
2.185

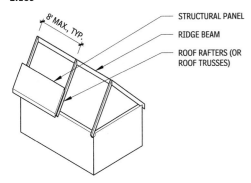

8' MAX., TYP.

STRUCTURAL PANEL

RIDGE BEAM

ROOF RAFTERS (OR ROOF TRUSSES)

ROOF FRAMING WITH RIDGE BEAM
2.186

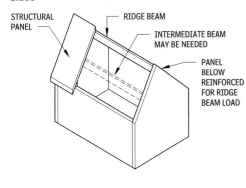

STRUCTURAL PANEL

RIDGE BEAM

INTERMEDIATE BEAM MAY BE NEEDED

PANEL BELOW REINFORCED FOR RIDGE BEAM LOAD

ROOF EAVE DETAIL WITH SLOPED CEILING
2.187

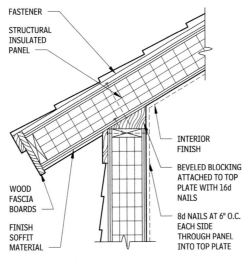

FASTENER

STRUCTURAL INSULATED PANEL

WOOD FASCIA BOARDS

FINISH SOFFIT MATERIAL

INTERIOR FINISH

BEVELED BLOCKING ATTACHED TO TOP PLATE WITH 16d NAILS

8d NAILS AT 6" O.C. EACH SIDE THROUGH PANEL INTO TOP PLATE

PANEL AT RIDGE CONNECTION
2.188

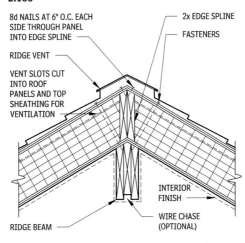

8d NAILS AT 6" O.C. EACH SIDE THROUGH PANEL INTO EDGE SPLINE

RIDGE VENT

VENT SLOTS CUT INTO ROOF PANELS AND TOP SHEATHING FOR VENTILATION

RIDGE BEAM

2x EDGE SPLINE

FASTENERS

INTERIOR FINISH

WIRE CHASE (OPTIONAL)

CONTINUOUS PANEL DETAIL AT ROOF
2.189

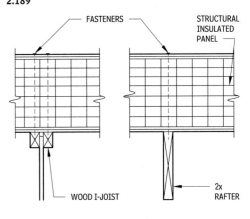

FASTENERS

STRUCTURAL INSULATED PANEL

WOOD I-JOIST

2x RAFTER

GABLE END OVERHANG AT ROOF PANEL DETAIL
2.190

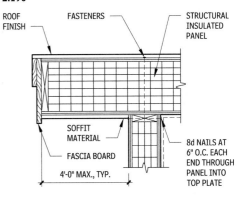

ROOF FINISH

FASTENERS

STRUCTURAL INSULATED PANEL

SOFFIT MATERIAL

FASCIA BOARD

4'-0" MAX., TYP.

8d NAILS AT 6" O.C. EACH END THROUGH PANEL INTO TOP PLATE

Contributor:
Richard J. Vitullo, AIA, Oak Leaf Studio, Crownsville, Maryland.

GLASS CANOPIES

FABRICATED GLASS CANOPY
2.191

CUSTOM GLASS CANOPY WITH ARCHITECTURALLY EXPOSED STRUCTURAL STEEL (AESS)
2.192

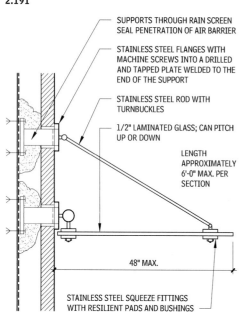

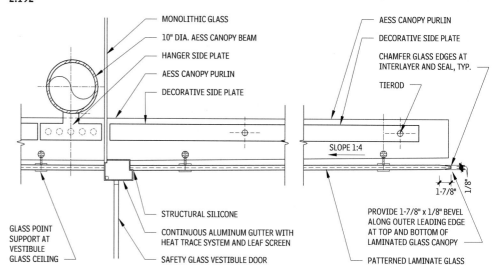

Labels for fabricated glass canopy:
- SUPPORTS THROUGH RAIN SCREEN SEAL PENETRATION OF AIR BARRIER
- STAINLESS STEEL FLANGES WITH MACHINE SCREWS INTO A DRILLED AND TAPPED PLATE WELDED TO THE END OF THE SUPPORT
- STAINLESS STEEL ROD WITH TURNBUCKLES
- 1/2" LAMINATED GLASS; CAN PITCH UP OR DOWN
- LENGTH APPROXIMATELY 6'-0" MAX. PER SECTION
- STAINLESS STEEL SQUEEZE FITTINGS WITH RESILIENT PADS AND BUSHINGS
- 48" MAX.

Labels for AESS canopy:
- MONOLITHIC GLASS
- 10" DIA. AESS CANOPY BEAM
- HANGER SIDE PLATE
- AESS CANOPY PURLIN
- DECORATIVE SIDE PLATE
- GLASS POINT SUPPORT AT VESTIBULE GLASS CEILING
- STRUCTURAL SILICONE
- CONTINUOUS ALUMINUM GUTTER WITH HEAT TRACE SYSTEM AND LEAF SCREEN
- SAFETY GLASS VESTIBULE DOOR
- AESS CANOPY PURLIN
- DECORATIVE SIDE PLATE
- CHAMFER GLASS EDGES AT INTERLAYER AND SEAL, TYP.
- TIEROD
- SLOPE 1:4
- 1-7/8"
- 1/8"
- PROVIDE 1-7/8" x 1/8" BEVEL ALONG OUTER LEADING EDGE AT TOP AND BOTTOM OF LAMINATED GLASS CANOPY
- PATTERNED LAMINATE GLASS

VIEW OF CANOPY FROM ABOVE
2.193

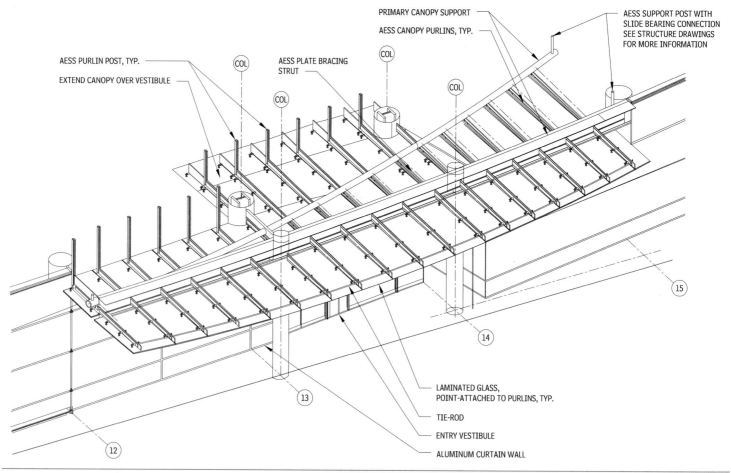

Labels:
- AESS PURLIN POST, TYP.
- EXTEND CANOPY OVER VESTIBULE
- AESS PLATE BRACING STRUT
- PRIMARY CANOPY SUPPORT
- AESS CANOPY PURLINS, TYP.
- AESS SUPPORT POST WITH SLIDE BEARING CONNECTION SEE STRUCTURE DRAWINGS FOR MORE INFORMATION
- COL
- LAMINATED GLASS, POINT-ATTACHED TO PURLINS, TYP.
- TIE-ROD
- ENTRY VESTIBULE
- ALUMINUM CURTAIN WALL
- 12
- 13
- 14
- 15

NOTES

2.191 Laminated glass requires edge protection, or edge may discolor. Protect with clear silicone or adhere a structural silicone on a metal edge.

2.192 Carefully consider monolithic glass and structural steel supports for condensation.

2.193 Second floor and curtain wall not shown, for clarity.

Contributor:
Anthony Golebiewski AIA, Kling, Philadelphia, Pennsylvania.

PROTECTIVE COVERS
2.194

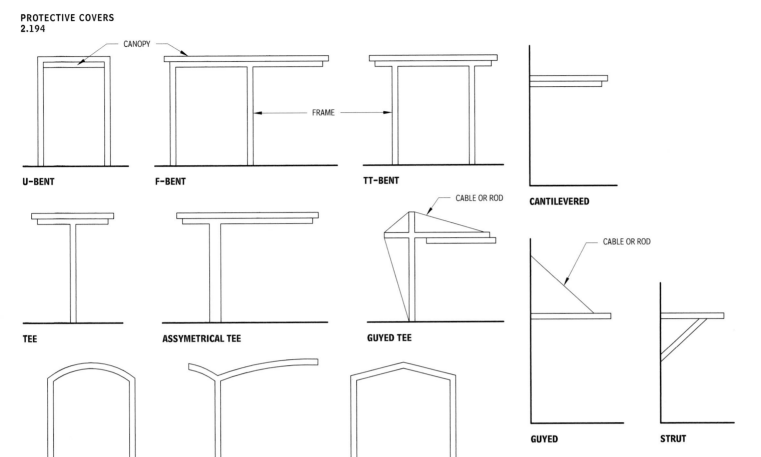

U-BENT   F-BENT   TT-BENT   CANTILEVERED

TEE   ASSYMETRICAL TEE   GUYED TEE   GUYED   STRUT

BARREL   GULL WING   GABLE

ROOF, EAVE, AND ATTIC VENTILATION

Ventilation of attics can cause as many problems as it solves, if not designed and constructed carefully. The best understanding of the interrelated issues surrounding control of heat, air, and moisture (HAM) inside attics, and the transfer of HAM to the building interior, suggests that, like crawl spaces, it may be preferable to treat the attic as part of the interior conditioned environment. This is especially true when HVAC equipment and ductwork are located in the attic.

The following are recommendations for insulated and conditioned attics.

- Codes require ventilation of "enclosed attics and enclosed rafter spaces where ceilings are applied directly to the underside of roof rafters," but this does not specifically exclude installing insulation within rafter spaces exposed in a conditioned attic. Verify with local building codes in effect for all requirements.
- From a practical standpoint, it is much more difficult to install a vapor barrier on the inside face of batt or sprayed insulation between joists and especially roof trusses because of the many penetrations. Therefore, control of the temperature of the first condensing surface is crucial to the success of many of these systems.
- Attic ventilation has a much smaller impact on asphalt shingle temperatures than roof orientation and shingle color.
- Provide heating and cooling to attic.

CONTROL OF FIRST CONDENSATION SURFACE TEMPERATURE

The following assemblies control vapor by ensuring that the surface temperature of the first surface on which condensation would form is above the predicted dew point, with some margin of safety. These assemblies allow for some seasonal wetting and drying of interior materials.

- *Blanket insulation between joists/trusses*: Cover roof sheathing with board insulation to raise the inside temperature of sheathing above dew point. Determine the thickness of both insulations, based on external and internal environmental conditions. Provide an air barrier with building felts, or by offsetting joints in board insulation. Detail for continuity.
- *Board and blanket insulation between joists/trusses*: Fill space between joists with board insulation located tight against the underside of the sheathing. Carefully seal all joints and penetrations with sealant. Determine the thickness of board insulation based on external and internal environmental conditions to raise inside surface above dew point. Provide blanket insulation over joist space to thickness required for total R-value.
- *Sprayed insulation*: Closed-cell high-density sprayed insulation will act as an air barrier and does not require an applied vapor barrier. Open-cell, low-density sprayed insulation may require covering with latex paint or gypsum board to limit vapor transfer. Control of vapor flow.

The assemblies described here control vapor by installing a vapor retader on the warm side, except in mixed climates where no vapor barrier is installed and the system is allowed to dry to both the interior and exterior, depending on the season. Plywood is recommended over oriented-strand board (OSB) in mixed climates because of plywood's greater capability to store moisture.

- *Vented compact roof assemblies*: Board insulation applied above roof sheathing with a vented space above the insulation allows for continuous installation of vapor retarders at the proper location for the climate zone. Venting ensures drying insulation from condensation. Venting can help moderate roof temperatures. The thickness of insulation is crucial for performance of a cold roof design to minimize ice dams, and may need to be R-40 in cold climates and R-48 in very cold climates.
- *Unvented compact roof assemblies*: When board insulation is applied above the roof sheathing with no venting either the sheathing must be sealed to form an air barrier or a separate layer should be installed between the insulation and sheathing. In cold climates, the air barrier should also be a vapor retarder. In mixed or hot climates, the air barrier should be permeable. The underlayment layer under shingles must be breathable in cold climates, and under metal roofing in mixed climates; it must be a vapor retarder in hot climates, and under asphalt shingles in mixed or hot climates.

These are common methods to properly ventilate an attic or rafter space:

- Separate the attic from the conditioned portion of the home with a continuous air barrier, with joints and penetrations sealed.
- Provide a weather barrier with joints and penetrations sealed airtight to the warm side of the insulation, unless analysis reveals it is not required in mixed climates. In hot or mixed climates, the underlayment for asphalt shingles must be vapor-impermeable.
- Do not install any HVAC equipment or ductwork in the attic.
- Do not install any water pipes within the attic.
- Ensure that all vents from clothes dryers, kitchen exhausts, bathroom exhausts, and similar sources of conditioned air do not discharge in the attic and that any ducts for such vents routed through the attic are carefully sealed.
- Use baffles to ensure that eave and cornice vents have a free airspace to the attic past insulation at narrow points.

Refer to www.buildingscience.com for further information.

NOTES

2.194 a. Frames welded from rolled or extruded tubes into rigid frames or bents.
b. Canopy formed from corrugated sheet or translucent plastic panels.
c. Fascia from formed sheet or extruded aluminum; square, bullnose, or profiled.
d. Drainage typically directed to tube columns.
e. Materials typically aluminum or galvanized steel with factory finishes.

VENT APPLICATIONS
2.195

CONTINUOUS RIDGE VENT (OPTIONAL)

GABLE LOUVER AT EACH END

EXHAUST DUCT (MUST NOT EXHAUST INTO ATTIC: EXTEND TO OUTSIDE)

EAVE VENT

INSULATION

GABLE ROOF WITH UNOCCUPIED ATTIC

CONTINUOUS RIDGE VENT

GABLE LOUVER AT EACH END

VENT SPACE (MAINTAIN 1-1/2" CLEAR PATH ABOVE INSULATION FROM EAVE TO RIDGE)

INSULATION

EAVE VENT

VAPOR BARRIER

GABLE WITH OCCUPIED SPACE UNDER ROOF

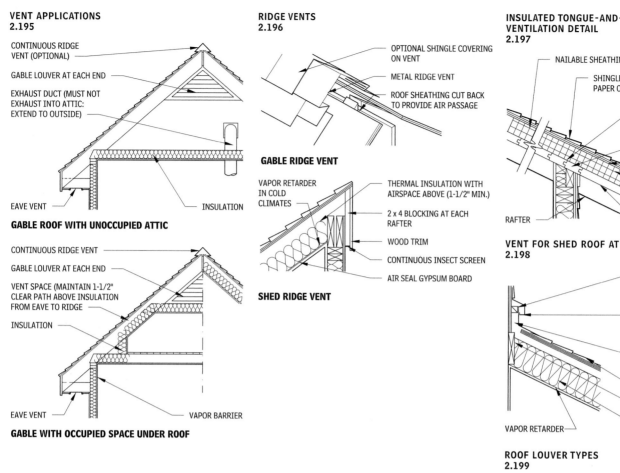

RIDGE VENTS
2.196

OPTIONAL SHINGLE COVERING ON VENT

METAL RIDGE VENT

ROOF SHEATHING CUT BACK TO PROVIDE AIR PASSAGE

GABLE RIDGE VENT

VAPOR RETARDER IN COLD CLIMATES

THERMAL INSULATION WITH AIRSPACE ABOVE (1-1/2" MIN.)

2 x 4 BLOCKING AT EACH RAFTER

WOOD TRIM

CONTINUOUS INSECT SCREEN

AIR SEAL GYPSUM BOARD

SHED RIDGE VENT

INSULATED TONGUE-AND-GROOVE ROOF VENTILATION DETAIL
2.197

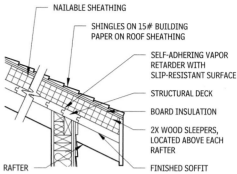

NAILABLE SHEATHING

SHINGLES ON 15# BUILDING PAPER ON ROOF SHEATHING

SELF-ADHERING VAPOR RETARDER WITH SLIP-RESISTANT SURFACE

STRUCTURAL DECK

BOARD INSULATION

2X WOOD SLEEPERS, LOCATED ABOVE EACH RAFTER

RAFTER

FINISHED SOFFIT

VENT FOR SHED ROOF AT WALL
2.198

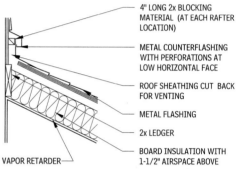

4" LONG 2x BLOCKING MATERIAL (AT EACH RAFTER LOCATION)

METAL COUNTERFLASHING WITH PERFORATIONS AT LOW HORIZONTAL FACE

ROOF SHEATHING CUT BACK FOR VENTING

METAL FLASHING

2x LEDGER

BOARD INSULATION WITH 1-1/2" AIRSPACE ABOVE

VAPOR RETARDER

ROOF LOUVER TYPES
2.199

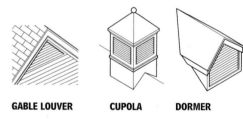

GABLE LOUVER   **CUPOLA**   **DORMER**

NOTES

2.197 a. Provide ridge vent to complete cavity ventilation detail.
b. In hot, humid climates, vapor barrier should be on top of rigid insulation.
c. A vapor retarder is typically not desirable in mixed climates.
d. A properly detailed air barrier is important.

Contributors:
Richard J. Vitullo, AIA, Oak Leaf Studio, Crownsville, Maryland; Erik K. Beach, Rippeteau Architects, PC, Washington, DC.

INSULATION BLOCKING AND BAFFLE
2.200

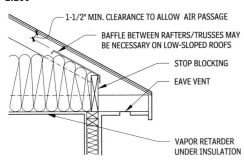

1-1/2" MIN. CLEARANCE TO ALLOW AIR PASSAGE

BAFFLE BETWEEN RAFTERS/TRUSSES MAY BE NECESSARY ON LOW-SLOPED ROOFS

STOP BLOCKING

EAVE VENT

VAPOR RETARDER UNDER INSULATION

EAVE VENTILATION TYPES
2.201

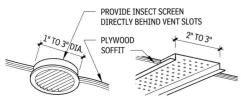

PROVIDE INSECT SCREEN DIRECTLY BEHIND VENT SLOTS

PLYWOOD SOFFIT

1" TO 3" DIA.

2" TO 3"

CIRCULAR VENTS

STAMPED OR EXTRUDED VENT STRIPS

SEE ALSO

Contributors:
Richard J. Vitullo, AIA, Oak Leaf Studio, Crownsville, Maryland; Erik K. Beach, Rippeteau Architects, PC, Washington, DC.

EXTERIOR ENCLOSURE

EXTERIOR WALLS

This section discusses exterior wall and their construction. For additional information about the material presented in the tables and graphics in this section, consult literature from individual manufacturers and trade associations.

DESIGN CONSIDERATIONS

EXTERIOR WALL ASSEMBLIES
2.202

EXTERIOR WALL ASSEMBLY		WALL THICKNESS, NOMINAL (IN.)	WEIGHT (PSF)	VERTICAL SPAN RANGE (UNSUPPORTED HEIGHT) (FT)	RACKING RESISTANCE	SERVICE PLENUM SPACE	HEAT TRANSMISSION COEFFICIENT (U-FACTOR) (BTU/HR-SQ FT °F)
CMU	CMU	8	55	Up to 13	Good	None	0.56
		12	85	Up to 20			0.49
CMU (insulated)	CMU / BOARD INSULATION / INTERIOR WALL FINISH	8 +	60	Up to 13	Good	Through insulation	0.21
		12 +	90	Up to 20			0.20
CMU and brick veneer (interior insulation)	BRICK VENEER AND AIR SPACE / CMU / BOARD INSULATION / INTERIOR WALL FINISH	4 + 2 + 4 +	75	Up to 13 (with filled cavity)	Good	Through insulation	0.19
		4 + 2 + 8 +	100	Up to 20 (with filled cavity)			0.18
CMU and brick veneer (cavity insulation)	BRICK VENEER / AIR SPACE (2" MIN.) / INSULATION OVER VAPOR RETARDER / CMU / INTERIOR WALL FINISH	4 + 4 + 4	75	Up to 9	Fair	None	0.07
		4 + 4 + 8	100	Up to 13			0.11
CMU and portland cement stucco (insulated)	PORTLAND CEMENT STUCCO / CMU / BOARD INSULATION / INTERIOR WALL FINISH	8 +	67	Up to 13	Good	Through interior insulation	0.16
Wood stud	EXTERIOR WALL FINISH / SHEATHING WITH WEATHER BARRIER / WOOD STUD / INSULATION / INTERIOR WALL FINISH	4	12	Up to 14	Poor to fair	Between studs	0.06
		6	16	Up to 20 (L/d < 50)			0.04
Brick veneer on wood stud	BRICK VENEER AND AIRSPACE / SHEATHING WITH WEATHER BARRIER / WOOD STUD / INSULATION / INTERIOR WALL FINISH	4 + 4	52	Up to 14	Poor to fair	Between studs	0.07
Metal stud	EXTERIOR WALL FINISH / SHEATHING WITH WEATHER BARRIER / METAL STUD / INSULATION / INTERIOR WALL FINISH	5	14	Up to 13	Poor	Between studs	0.10
		7	18	Up to 17			0.08

EXTERIOR WALL ASSEMBLIES (continued)
2.202

WALL ASSEMBLY TYPE	VAPOR RETARDER LOCATION AND TYPE			RECOMMENDED CLIMATE AND PRECIPITATION ZONES (SEE FIGURES 2.1 AND 2.2)[a]	PERFORMANCE COMMENTS (HAM = HEAT, AIR, AND MOISTURE)	RESISTANCE TO EXTERIOR AIRBORNE SOUND TRANSMISSION	EXTERIOR MAINTENANCE REQUIREMENTS	REMARKS
	EXTERIOR SIDE	NONE	INTERIOR SIDE					
Mass barrier wall	Coating			Hot; low-precipitation climate only	Very poor control of HAM.	Good	Washing, repointing joints, painting, sandblasting	Properties of nonengineered masonry are drastically reduced.
		None		Mild; low-precipitation climate only				
			Coating	Cold; low-precipitation climate only				
Mass barrier wall	Coating or insulation facing			Mixed or hot; low precipitation	Very poor control of, air and moisture. Average control of heat.	Good	Washing, repointing joints, painting, sandblasting	Interior insulation is discontinuous.
		None		Mixed; low precipitation				
			Sheet or insulation facing	Cold; low precipitation				
Drainage cavity	Coating or insulation or insulation facing			Mixed or hot; low to moderate precipitation	Poor control of air, water and transmission. Adding vapor retarder on cavity face of CMU improves performance to high precipitation	Excellent	Washing, repointing joints, sandblasting	Interior insulation is discontinuous.
		None		Mixed or hot; low to moderate precipitation				
			Coating or insulation facing	Cold; low to moderate precipitation				
Drainage cavity	As noted			All climates; extreme precipitation	Excellent control of heat, air and moisture.	Excellent	Washing, repointing joints, sandblasting	Cavity allows installation of continuous insulation and vapor retarder.
Mass barrier	Vapor retarder insulation			Mixed or hot; low precipitation	Average control of HAM. Adding weather barrier under stucco increases control of driving rain.	Good	Washing, painting, and re-stuccoing	Assembly with insulation on exterior and added WRB provides better control of HAM.
		None		Mixed or hot; low precipitation				
			Sheet or insulation facing	Cold; low precipitation				
Internal drainage plane	Weather barrier or vapor retarder insulation for sheathing			Hot; low to moderate precipitation	Average control of HAM. Upgrading weather barrier to air barrier increases control of driving rain.	Poor to fair	Washing, painting, and replacing exterior finish	Exterior wall finishes: wood, plywood, aluminum siding, stucco.
		None		Mixed; low to moderate precipitation				
			Sheet or insulation facing	Cold; low to moderate precipitation				
Drainage cavity	Weather barrier or vapor retarder insulation for sheathing			Hot; moderate precipitation	Average control of HAM. Upgrading weather barrier to air barrier to increase control of driving rain.	Good	Washing, repointing joints	Note that brick veneer holds moisture that can be forced into insulation, allow for drying.
				Mixed; moderate precipitation				
			Sheet or insulation facing	Cold; moderate precipitation				
Internal drainage plane	Weather barrier or vapor retarder insulation for sheathing			Hot; low to moderate precipitation	Average control of air and moisture. Add insulation over sheathing to increase thermal performance. Upgrading weather barrier to air barrier to increase control of rain.	Poor to fair	Washing, painting, and replacing exterior finish	Exterior wall finishes: wood, plywood, aluminum siding, stucco.
		None		Mixed; low to moderate precipitation				
			Sheet or insulation facing	Cold; low to moderate precipitation				

NOTE

2.202 [a] The climate recommendations are dependent on the relative location of the vapor retarder as indicated in the three previous columns. Review recommendations for vapor retarder on pages 173 through 175 for a more complete discussion on placement of vapor retarder within a wall assembly and the effect on the performance of the wall assembly.

EXTERIOR WALL ASSEMBLIES (continued)
2.202

EXTERIOR WALL ASSEMBLY		WALL THICKNESS, NOMINAL (IN.)	WEIGHT (PSF)	VERTICAL SPAN RANGE (UNSUPPORTED HEIGHT) (FT)	RACKING RESISTANCE	SERVICE PLENUM SPACE	HEAT TRANSMISSION COEFFICIENT (U-FACTOR) (BTU/HR-SQ FT °F)
Brick veneer on metal stud	BRICK VENEER AND AIRSPACE / SHEATHING WITH WEATHER BARRIER / METAL STUD / INSULATION / INTERIOR WALL FINISH	4 + 2 + 6	54	Up to 15	Good	Between studs	0.10
Insulated sandwich panel	METAL SKIN / AIR SPACE / INSULATING CORE / METAL SKIN	5	6	(See manufacturers' literature.)	Fair to good	None	0.05 (See manufacturers' literature.)
Concrete	CONCRETE	8	92	Up to 13 (with reinforcement, 17)	Excellent	None	0.68
		12	138	Up to 20 (with reinforcement, 25)			0.55
Concrete (insulated)	CONCRETE / BOARD INSULATION / INTERIOR WALL FINISH	8 +	97	Up to 13 (with reinforcement, 17)	Excellent	Through insulation	0.13
Concrete and brick veneer (insulated)	BRICK VENEER AND AIR SPACE / CONCRETE / BOARD INSULATION / INTERIOR WALL FINISH	4 + 2 + 8 +	112	Up to 13 (with reinforcement, 17)	Excellent	Through insulation	0.13
Precast concrete	PRECAST CONCRETE (REINFORCED) / BOARD INSULATION / INTERIOR WALL FINISH	2 +	23	Up to 6	Fair to good	Through insulation	0.99
		4 +	46	Up to 12			0.85
Precast concrete sandwich	CONCRETE / BOARD INSULATION	5	45	Up to 14	Fair to good	None	0.14
Rainscreen on metal studs	RAINSCREEN / AIR SPACE / BOARD INSULATION OVER WEATHER BARRIER / EXTERIOR SHEATHING / METAL STUD / INTERIOR WALL FINISH	12 +	15-20	Up to 20	Poor to fair	Between studs	0.05
Brick veneer on metal stud	BRICK VENEER / AIR SPACE / INSULATION OVER WEATHER BARRIER / EXTERIOR SHEATHING / METAL STUD / INTERIOR WALL FINISH	4 + 4 + 6	54	Up to 15	Good	Between studs	0.05
EIFS on metal stud	EIFS / WEATHER BARRIER / SHEATHING / METAL STUDS / INTERIOR WALL FINISH	8	15	Up to 20	Poor to fair	Between studs	0.05

EXTERIOR WALL ASSEMBLIES (continued)
2.202

WALL ASSEMBLY TYPE	VAPOR RETARDER LOCATION AND TYPE			RECOMMENDED CLIMATE AND PRECIPITATION ZONES (SEE FIGURES 2.1 AND 2.2)[a]	PERFORMANCE COMMENTS (HAM = HEAT, AIR AND MOISTURE)	RESISTANCE TO EXTERIOR AIRBORNE SOUND TRANSMISSION	EXTERIOR MAINTENANCE REQUIREMENTS	REMARKS
	EXTERIOR SIDE	NONE	INTERIOR SIDE					
Drainage cavity	Weather barrier or vapor retarder insulation for sheathing			Hot; moderate precipitation	Average control of air and moisture. Add insulation over sheathing to increase thermal performance. Upgrading water-resistant barrier to weather barrier to increase control of rain.	Good	Washing, repointing joints	Note that brick veneer holds moisture that can be forced into insulation. Advisable to move all insulation into air cavity and add continuous board insulation and weather barrier.
		None		Mixed; moderate precipitation				
			Sheet or insulation facing	Cold; moderate precipitation				
Internal drainage plane. Some factory-insulated panels provide pressure-equalized rainscreen joint design.		None		All except extremely cold; low precipitation	Field assembled systems generally lower performance, factory-insulated systems offer average performance.	Poor to good (See manufacturers' literature.)	Washing, steam cleaning, painting, replacing joint sealers	Temperature change critical; minimize metal through connections.
Mass barrier wall		None		Mild; low precipitation only	Very poor control of heat, poor control of moisture, average control of air.	Good	Washing, sandblasting	Concrete walls have very high-heat-storage capacity.
Mass barrier wall	Coating or insulation facing			Mixed or hot; low to moderate precipitation	Poor control of moisture. Average control of heat and air.	Good	Washing, sandblasting	Insulation on interior minimizes advantage of heat-storage capacity.
		None		Mixed or hot; low to moderate precipitation				
			Coating or insulation facing	Cold; low to moderate precipitation				
Drainage cavity	Coating or insulation facing			Mixed or hot; moderate precipitation	Average control of moisture. Average control of heat and air. Adding weather barrier on cavity face of concrete improves performance for high precipitation	Excellent	Washing, repointing joints, sandblasting	Move insulation into cavity maximizes heat-storage of concrete.
		None		Mixed; moderate precipitation				
			Coating or insulation facing	Cold; moderate precipitation				
Mass barrier wall	Coating or insulation facing			Mixed or hot; low to moderate precipitation	Poor control of moisture. Average control of heat and air.	Good	Washing, sandblasting, replacing joint sealers	Large-size economical (fewer joints) units available with various finishes. Joints are weak point for control of air and moisture.
		None		Mixed or hot; low to moderate precipitation				
			Coating or insulation facing	Cold; low to moderate precipitation				
Mass barrier wall		None		All climates; low to moderate precipitation	Poor control of HAM.	Fair	Washing, sandblasting, replacing joint sealers	Panels warp from differential temperatures unless one side is dramatically thickened. Control of vapor is difficult. Joints are weak point for control of air and moisture.
Drainage cavity	As noted			All climates; extreme precipitation	Excellent control of HAM. Upgrade to pressure-equalized rainscreen system for even higher performance	Good	Minimal washing	Rainscreens can be metal panels, wood siding, cement panel siding, resin panels, or terra cotta.
Drainage cavity	As noted			All climates; extreme precipitation	Excellent control of HAM. Upgrade to pressure-equalized rainscreen system for even higher performance	Good to excellent	Washing, repointing joints	
Internal drainage plane		None		All climates; low to moderate precipitation	Poor control of moisture. Average control of air. Good control of heat.	Fair to good	Check sealants frequently. Repair of sealants is extremely difficult and will likely alter appearance of building, so select highest-quality sealant.	System is highly dependent on quality installation. Barrier-type EIFS system not advised except at CMU or concrete back-up.

NOTE

2.202 [a] The climate recommendations are dependent on the relative location of the vapor retarder as indicated in the three previous columns. Review recommendations for vapor retarder on pages 122 through 125 for a more complete discussion on placement of vapor retarder within a wall assembly and the effect on the performance of the wall assembly.

BASIC EXTERIOR WALL ASSEMBLY TYPES

Exterior wall assemblies can be defined in three basic categories:

- Barrier walls
- Drainage walls
- Pressure-equalized walls

BARRIER WALLS

Mass barrier walls rely on thickness of water-resistant materials to absorb moisture and then dry when precipitation stops. Typical assemblies include:

- Cast-in-place concrete
- Precast concrete
- Concrete masonry units

Face-sealed barrier walls rely on a perfect continuous seal at the exterior face. Common assemblies include:

- Exterior insulation and finish systems (EIFS)
- Windows with a single sealant bead

BARRIER WALLS 2.203

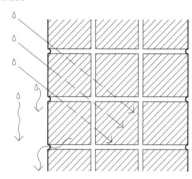

MASS WALL

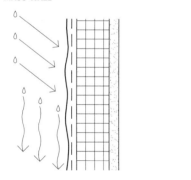

FACE SEALED

DRAINAGE WALLS

Drainage walls resist air and moisture penetration with an outer layer, to block the bulk of precipitation, and an inner water barrier. At drainage cavity walls, a cavity of 3/4 in. or more is present in front of the drainage plane. If the water barrier is not also an air barrier, then another layer of the wall assembly must serve as an air barrier.

Common drainage cavity walls include:

- Brick veneer
- Some metal panels

Mineral-fiber cement siding can be detailed to function as a drainage cavity wall, usually by adding 1 by 3 vertical furring strips.

Typical internal drainage plane walls include:

- Portland cement stucco over lath and a weather barrier
- Wood or vinyl siding
- Water-drainage EIFS

DRAINAGE WALLS 2.204

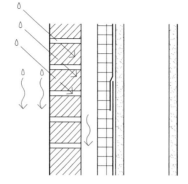

DRAINAGE CAVITY

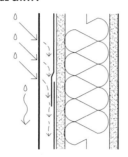

DRAINAGE PLANE

PRESSURE-EQUALIZED WALL

Pressure-equalized (PE) rainscreen walls use a drainage cavity, with the air pressure in the cavity, similar to the exterior air pressure. Proper detailing of joints and the PE chamber eliminates the migration of water across the cavity. PE rainscreen walls must include an air barrier at the inner face of the cavity, venting, and compartmentalization of the cavity.

Typical pressure-equalized rainscreen walls include:

- Some unitized stone or metal panels
- Many curtain wall systems

Through careful detailing, brick veneer and many siding products can be made into PE rainscreen assemblies.

PRESSURE-EQUALIZED WALL 2.205

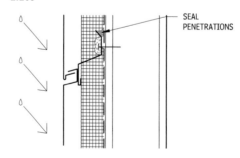

SEAL PENETRATIONS

FORCES MOVING WATER ACROSS JOINTS 2.206

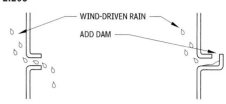

WIND-DRIVEN RAIN
ADD DAM

KINETIC ENERGY

ADD DRIP

SURFACE TENSION

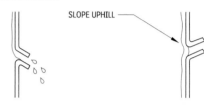

SLOPE UPHILL

GRAVITY

INCREASE JOINT TO 3/8" AND/OR ADD CAVITY

CAPILLARY

ADD AIR BARRIER TO EQUALIZE PRESSURE ACROSS JOINT

PRESSURE DIFFERENTIAL

EXTERIOR WALL SKIN

TILT-UP CONCRETE

Tilt-up concrete construction is a fast, economical method of enclosing a building with durable, load-bearing walls. The wall panel units are formed and cast horizontally at the job site, on either the building slab floor or a temporary casting slab. The panels do not have to be transported, so there are fewer restrictions on panel size. Wood formwork is typically used to define the edges, reveals, details, and openings in the panel. Once the concrete has reached sufficient strength, the panels are lifted (or tilted up) by crane and placed on isolated or continuous foundations (usually grade beams). The panels are braced against the floor slab or a brace foundation until they are tied to the roof and floor system, and then become an integral part of the completed structure. Although tilt-up concrete construction is primarily restricted to buildings of one story, walls up to four stories tall have been cast and lifted into position.

DESIGN

Panel thickness varies from 5-1/2 to 11-1/4 in., depending on height, loads, span, depth of reveals, surface finish, local codes, and construction practices. Full-height panel widths of 20 ft and weights of 30,000 to 50,000 lbs are typical. Spans of 30 ft are common for spandrel panels, as are cantilevers of 10 to 15 ft. Panels are designed structurally to resist lifting stresses, which frequently exceed in-place loads. Floor slab design must accommodate panel and crane loads.

FINISH

Panels can be cast either face down or face up, depending on desired finish and formwork methods. The face-down method, however, is usually easier to erect. Casting method, desired finish, and available aggregates affect concrete mix design. Control of the concrete mix design and placement of the concrete in the forms are more difficult than with factory-cast units. Discoloration occurs if cracks and joints in the casting are not sealed.

HEAT, AIR, AND MOISTURE (HAM)

Tilt-up concrete controls HAM in the same way as precast concrete.

TILT-UP CONCRETE
2.207

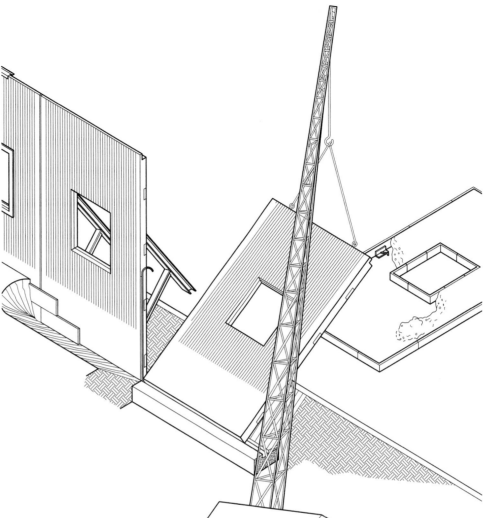

TILT-UP CONCRETE PANEL TYPES
2.208

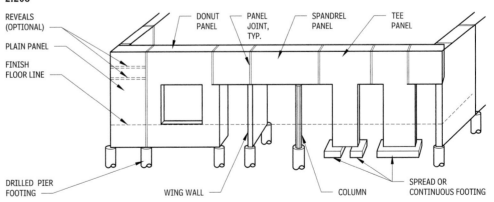

REVEALS (OPTIONAL)

PLAIN PANEL

FINISH FLOOR LINE

DRILLED PIER FOOTING

DONUT PANEL

PANEL JOINT, TYP.

SPANDREL PANEL

TEE PANEL

WING WALL

COLUMN

SPREAD OR CONTINUOUS FOOTING

TILT-UP CONCRETE PANEL CONNECTIONS AT ROOF
2.209

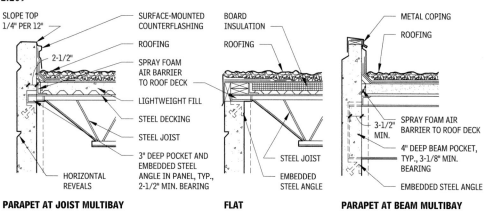

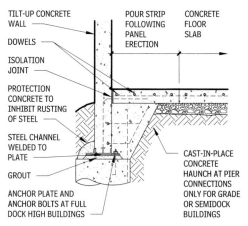

PARAPET AT JOIST MULTIBAY   **FLAT**   **PARAPET AT BEAM MULTIBAY**

PIER CONNECTION (SECTION)
2.211

TILT-UP CONCRETE PANEL DETAILS
2.210

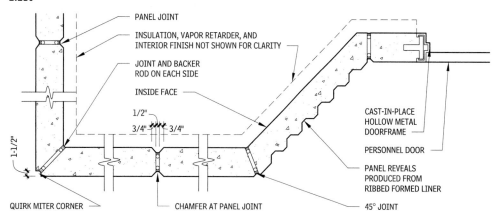

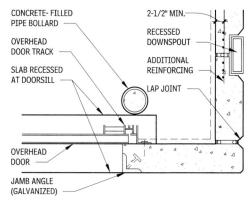

PRECAST CONCRETE

It is important to carefully distinguish between the more specialized architectural wall panel and the structural wall panel that is a derivative of floor systems. Work with fabricators early in the design process, giving careful attention to manufacturing and joint tolerance. Thoroughly examine joint sealants for adhesion and expected joint movement between the panels.

FINISHES

Form liner molds provide a wide variety of smooth and textured finishes. Finishes after casting (but prior to hardening) include exposed aggregate, broom, trowel, screed, float, or stippled. After hardening, finishes include acid-etched, sandblasted, honed, polished, and hammered rib.

COLORS

Select a color range, as complete uniformity cannot be guaranteed. White cement offers the best color uniformity, as gray cement is subject to color variations even when supplied from one source. Pigments require high-quality manufacturing and curing standards. Fine aggregate color requires control of the mixture graduation; coarse aggregate color provides the best durability and appearance.

HEAT, AIR, AND MOISTURE

Control of heat flow through the panel is typically accomplished by adding insulation to the interior side (except insulated sandwich panels). The insulation is best installed immediately adjacent to the inside face of the panel, using board insulation installed with adhesive, stickpins, or Z-shaped furring channels. Because the insulation may be exposed to moisture penetrating the concrete, insulation should be selected that will withstand occasional moisture.

Blanket insulation may be used between stud walls erected inside of the precast panel, but thermal loss through the studs must be accounted for. Effectiveness of the insulation is dependent on close contact with the weather barrier, so the interior gypsum board should be sealed.

The precast concrete panels function as an air barrier. To complete the air barrier assembly, joints and penetrations should be double-sealed and allowance made for weepholes.

Precast concrete wall panels typically perform as mass barrier walls. The density and thickness of the concrete controls the penetration of water. In cold climates, a vapor retarder is typically applied over the interior face of the insulation. (Blanket insulation installed in a stud wall will probably need the vapor retarder to be sealed around electrical and other types of junction boxes.)

However, even with the vapor retarder applied directly to the inside face of the insulation that is adhered to the inside panel, sealing joints is unlikely at the spandrel beams and columns, making the system less desirable in very cold climates. In hot climates, a vapor barrier can be applied to the interior face of the panel before adhering the insulation.

Access to the joints for sealing of the vapor retarder is difficult. In mixed climates, it is best to select an insulation that can tolerate wetting, provide no vapor retarder, and allow the assembly to dry to both the interior and exterior. Precast concrete may not perform well in areas of high precipitation or situations with an extreme vapor drive.

Joints between precast concrete panels are very susceptible to HAM problems. Therefore, joints should be designed as a two-stage sealant joints as indicated in Figure 2.214.

Contributors:
Haynes Whaley Associates, Structural Engineers, Houston, Texas;
Robert P. Foley, PE, Con/Steel Tilt-up Systems, Dayton, Ohio.

PANEL VARIATIONS
2.212

VERIFY COLOR AND FINISH AVAILABLE

8'-0", TYP.

8'-0" TYP.

SPECIAL FINISH

WINDOW OPENING

BOARD INSULATION LAYER

8'-0", TYP.

6" - 12"

4'-0", TYP.

10" - 12"

FLAT OR V-GROOVE

DOUBLE TEE

SCULPTURED

WINDOW MULLION

SANDWICH PANEL

HOLLOW CORE SANDWICH PANEL

LOCATE JOINTS TO CHANNEL WATER

TRUSS TYPE

SPANDREL AND COLUMN CLADDING

DRIP

MULLION WALL

TWO-STAGE SEALANT JOINTS
2.214

DISCONTINUE JOINT SEALANT AT VERTICAL JOINTS TO DRAIN JOINT

JOINT SEALANT CONTINUES AT HORIZONTAL JOINTS

1/2" MIN.

VERTICAL JOINT

HORIZONTAL JOINT

JOINT DETAILS
2.215

JOINT SEALANT AND BACKER ROD

TAPER OR REVEAL

3/4" MIN.

RECESSED JOINT

QUIRK DETAIL

SANDWICH PANEL CONSTRUCTION
2.213

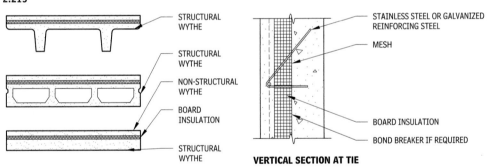

STRUCTURAL WYTHE

STRUCTURAL WYTHE

NON-STRUCTURAL WYTHE

BOARD INSULATION

STRUCTURAL WYTHE

STAINLESS STEEL OR GALVANIZED REINFORCING STEEL

MESH

BOARD INSULATION

BOND BREAKER IF REQUIRED

VERTICAL SECTION AT TIE

NOTE

2.213 Evaluate the capability of the structural wall to resist bowing caused by differential thermal expansion of inner and outer layers.

Contributor:
Sidney Freedman, Precast/Prestressed Concrete Institute, Chicago, Illinois.

SUSPENDED PRECAST PANEL ANCHORAGE
2.216

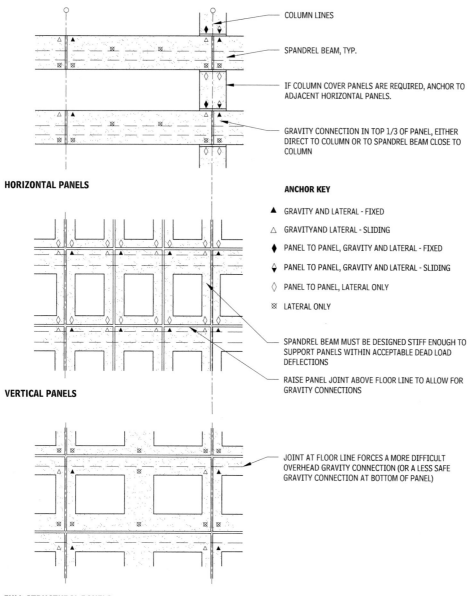

— COLUMN LINES

— SPANDREL BEAM, TYP.

— IF COLUMN COVER PANELS ARE REQUIRED, ANCHOR TO ADJACENT HORIZONTAL PANELS.

— GRAVITY CONNECTION IN TOP 1/3 OF PANEL, EITHER DIRECT TO COLUMN OR TO SPANDREL BEAM CLOSE TO COLUMN

HORIZONTAL PANELS

ANCHOR KEY

▲ GRAVITY AND LATERAL - FIXED

△ GRAVITY AND LATERAL - SLIDING

◆ PANEL TO PANEL, GRAVITY AND LATERAL - FIXED

◇ PANEL TO PANEL, GRAVITY AND LATERAL - SLIDING

◇ PANEL TO PANEL, LATERAL ONLY

⊠ LATERAL ONLY

— SPANDREL BEAM MUST BE DESIGNED STIFF ENOUGH TO SUPPORT PANELS WITHIN ACCEPTABLE DEAD LOAD DEFLECTIONS

— RAISE PANEL JOINT ABOVE FLOOR LINE TO ALLOW FOR GRAVITY CONNECTIONS

VERTICAL PANELS

— JOINT AT FLOOR LINE FORCES A MORE DIFFICULT OVERHEAD GRAVITY CONNECTION (OR A LESS SAFE GRAVITY CONNECTION AT BOTTOM OF PANEL)

FULL STRUCTURAL PANELS

WINDOW IN PRECAST PANEL
2.217

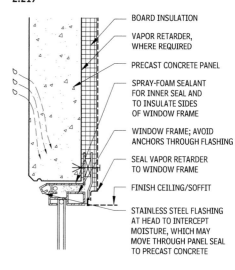

— BOARD INSULATION

— VAPOR RETARDER, WHERE REQUIRED

— PRECAST CONCRETE PANEL

— SPRAY-FOAM SEALANT FOR INNER SEAL AND TO INSULATE SIDES OF WINDOW FRAME

— WINDOW FRAME; AVOID ANCHORS THROUGH FLASHING

— SEAL VAPOR RETARDER TO WINDOW FRAME

— FINISH CEILING/SOFFIT

— STAINLESS STEEL FLASHING AT HEAD TO INTERCEPT MOISTURE, WHICH MAY MOVE THROUGH PANEL SEAL TO PRECAST CONCRETE

PRECAST CONCRETE CONNECTIONS

DIRECT BEARING CONNECTION
2.218

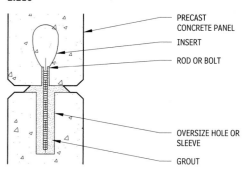

— PRECAST CONCRETE PANEL

— INSERT

— ROD OR BOLT

— OVERSIZE HOLE OR SLEEVE

— GROUT

SPANDREL CONDITION
2.221

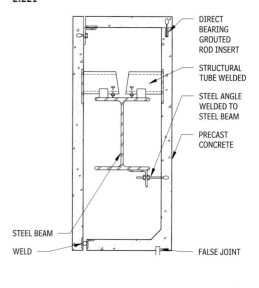

— DIRECT BEARING GROUTED ROD INSERT

— STRUCTURAL TUBE WELDED

— STEEL ANGLE WELDED TO STEEL BEAM

— PRECAST CONCRETE

— STEEL BEAM

— WELD

— FALSE JOINT

BOLTED TIEBACK
2.219

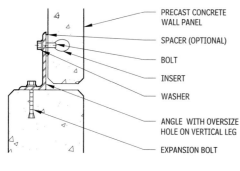

— PRECAST CONCRETE WALL PANEL

— SPACER (OPTIONAL)

— BOLT

— INSERT

— WASHER

— ANGLE WITH OVERSIZE HOLE ON VERTICAL LEG

— EXPANSION BOLT

BOLTED ALIGNMENT
2.220

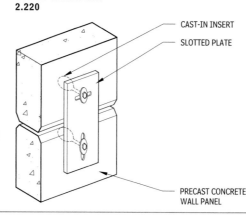

— CAST-IN INSERT

— SLOTTED PLATE

— PRECAST CONCRETE WALL PANEL

NOTES

2.216 Each panel has only one three-way fixed gravity and lateral anchor. All other anchors must allow differential structural and thermal movement.
2.218 Shim stacks occur at two points per panel adjacent to connection.
2.219 This tieback accommodates a large tolerance with expansion bolts.

Contributors:
Precast/Prestressed Concrete Institute, Chicago, Illinois; Architectural Precast Association, Ft. Myers, Florida.

COLUMN COVER CONNECTION
2.222

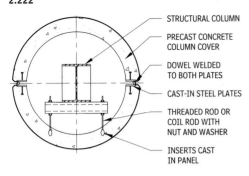

- STRUCTURAL COLUMN
- PRECAST CONCRETE COLUMN COVER
- DOWEL WELDED TO BOTH PLATES
- CAST-IN STEEL PLATES
- THREADED ROD OR COIL ROD WITH NUT AND WASHER
- INSERTS CAST IN PANEL

DIRECT BEARING CONNECTION
2.223

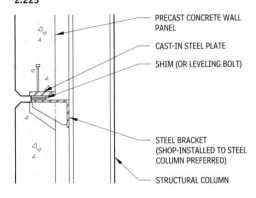

- PRECAST CONCRETE WALL PANEL
- CAST-IN STEEL PLATE
- SHIM (OR LEVELING BOLT)
- STEEL BRACKET (SHOP-INSTALLED TO STEEL COLUMN PREFERRED)
- STRUCTURAL COLUMN

BOLTED TIEBACK CONNECTION
2.224

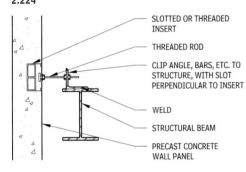

- SLOTTED OR THREADED INSERT
- THREADED ROD
- CLIP ANGLE, BARS, ETC. TO STRUCTURE, WITH SLOT PERPENDICULAR TO INSERT
- WELD
- STRUCTURAL BEAM
- PRECAST CONCRETE WALL PANEL

SLAB-TO-WALL CONNECTION
2.225

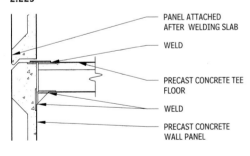

- PANEL ATTACHED AFTER WELDING SLAB
- WELD
- PRECAST CONCRETE TEE FLOOR
- WELD
- PRECAST CONCRETE WALL PANEL

ECCENTRIC BEARING CONNECTION
2.226

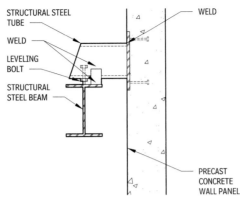

- STRUCTURAL STEEL TUBE
- WELD
- LEVELING BOLT
- STRUCTURAL STEEL BEAM
- WELD
- PRECAST CONCRETE WALL PANEL

WELDED TIEBACK CONNECTION
2.227

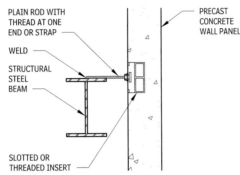

- PLAIN ROD WITH THREAD AT ONE END OR STRAP
- WELD
- STRUCTURAL STEEL BEAM
- SLOTTED OR THREADED INSERT
- PRECAST CONCRETE WALL PANEL

WELDED ALIGNMENT
2.228

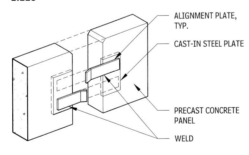

- ALIGNMENT PLATE, TYP.
- CAST-IN STEEL PLATE
- PRECAST CONCRETE PANEL
- WELD

PRECAST PERMANENT FORMWORK
2.229

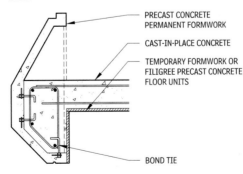

- PRECAST CONCRETE PERMANENT FORMWORK
- CAST-IN-PLACE CONCRETE
- TEMPORARY FORMWORK OR FILIGREE PRECAST CONCRETE FLOOR UNITS
- BOND TIE

GLASS-FIBER-REINFORCED CONCRETE

Glass-fiber-reinforced concrete (GFRC) is a composite material manufactured under controlled conditions and consisting of portland cement, fine aggregate, water, alkali-resistant glass fibers, and additives. It can be used for cladding applications, especially where weight is a significant factor. GFRC is categorized into two primary applications:

- *Architectural cladding panels* are very similar in application, strength, and performance to architectural precast concrete panels, except for providing a significant reduction in weight.
- *Decorative shapes* are generally smaller elements not part of the building enclosure.

GFRC ARCHITECTURAL PANELS

GFRC panels consist of a GFRC skin supported by a structural support frame, usually constructed of cold-formed steel members or a small structural channel, angles, and tubes. The GFRC skin is typically sprayed into a mold approximately 1/2 to 3/4 in. thick. After spraying, the structural frame backup is suspended over the skin, and anchors are embedded in the wet mix, which must be applied while the skin is still green. The anchors are designed to allow for a relatively large amount of differential movement between the backup and the skin.

GFRC MIX

The GFRC mix is typically designed by the manufacturer's engineers in a process called delegated design. The mix is designed to comply with the performance requirements indicated by the design team of record. The characteristics of GFRC differ from architectural concrete mixes often influencing the final design.

- The strength of GFRC is typically very high: 10,000 psi is not unusual, which is cost effective because a relatively small amount of material is required. The high strength results in a more dense material that is necessary to resist water penetration.
- Aggregates are generally small, 3/8 in. or less. Such small aggregate limits some of the surface textures available in architectural concrete.
- Because small amounts of aggregate are required, it is possible to carefully control the quality and moisture content. Oven-dried aggregate is available, which allows for very precise control of the moisture content of the finished mix and, therefore, better control over the finished color.

DESIGN AND FINISH

GFRC can be very similar to architectural precast panels, but the manufacturing process, assembly, and inherent qualities of GFRC allow for a slightly different design expression.

The fine aggregate, high cement ratio, and spray application allow for a fine level of finish, which is very effective at imitating the appearance of limestone and other tight-grained uniform stone. The finish and detailing can also produce a very precise and machinelike appearance. Other characteristics include the following:

- The low weight of the panels makes large overhangs, cornices, and other horizontal projections possible.
- Shipping of the panels is relatively inexpensive if the design allows for four to six panels to be shipped on each truckload.
- Relatively flat panels, articulated with joints, is the most cost-effective, but large three-dimensional configurations with reveals, returns, and setbacks can be economically produced because the lightweight material requires less structural support and limited backforming.
- The skin has relatively large amounts of thermal movement, so it is generally broken into multiple segments when more than 30 feet long, even when mounted on a longer steel backup frame.

HEAT, AIR, AND MOISTURE

GFRC panels typically perform as thin barrier walls. The density of the thin concrete layer controls the penetration of water. GFRC panels may not perform well in areas of high precipitation or situations with an extreme vapor drive.

NOTES

2.225 a. Avoid use of this detail at both ends of slab to prevent excessive restraint.
b. Consider rotation of wall elements and effects on bracing wall connections and volume changes.
2.228 Alignment plate is welded to one plate only to allow for possible volume change of panels.
2.229 One-piece spandrels may require support, and restrict placement of concrete.

Contributor:
Sidney Freedman, Precast/Prestressed Concrete Institute, Chicago, Illinois.

Joints between GFRC panels are very susceptible to HAM problems. As with precast, a double line of joint sealant is preferred, as indicated in Figure 2. 262. Control of heat flow through the panel is typically accomplished by adding insulation between the studs of the backup frame. Reduction of effectiveness of the insulation because of conductive loss through the studs must be accounted for. In cold climates, a vapor retarder is typically applied over the interior face of the insulation. Fasteners joining the GFRC members may be in an environment that may get moist because of condensation. Therefore, stainless steel fasteners and careful touch-up of welds is very important.

The GFRC skin typically functions as an air barrier. To complete the air barrier assembly, joints and penetrations must also be sealed. Consult the following reference: *GFRC Handbook*, published by the Architectural Precast Association (www.archprecast.org/GFRC_handbook.htm).

TYPICAL GFRC ARCHITECTURAL PANEL
2.230

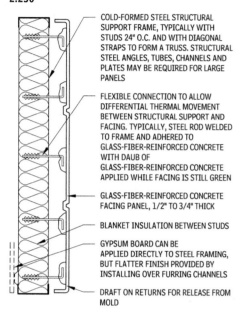

COLD-FORMED STEEL STRUCTURAL SUPPORT FRAME, TYPICALLY WITH STUDS 24" O.C. AND WITH DIAGONAL STRAPS TO FORM A TRUSS. STRUCTURAL STEEL ANGLES, TUBES, CHANNELS AND PLATES MAY BE REQUIRED FOR LARGE PANELS

FLEXIBLE CONNECTION TO ALLOW DIFFERENTIAL THERMAL MOVEMENT BETWEEN STRUCTURAL SUPPORT AND FACING. TYPICALLY, STEEL ROD WELDED TO FRAME AND ADHERED TO GLASS-FIBER-REINFORCED CONCRETE WITH DAUB OF GLASS-FIBER-REINFORCED CONCRETE APPLIED WHILE FACING IS STILL GREEN

GLASS-FIBER-REINFORCED CONCRETE FACING PANEL, 1/2" TO 3/4" THICK

BLANKET INSULATION BETWEEN STUDS

GYPSUM BOARD CAN BE APPLIED DIRECTLY TO STEEL FRAMING, BUT FLATTER FINISH PROVIDED BY INSTALLING OVER FURRING CHANNELS

DRAFT ON RETURNS FOR RELEASE FROM MOLD

GFRC PROFILED PANEL
2.231

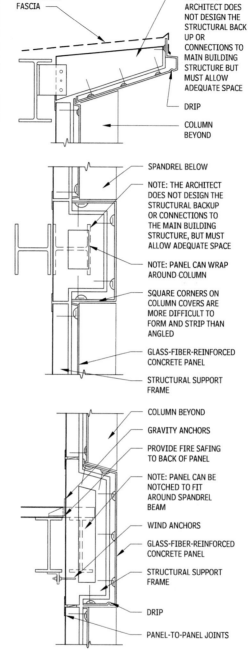

ROOFING AND FASCIA

NOTE: THE ARCHITECT DOES NOT DESIGN THE STRUCTURAL BACK UP OR CONNECTIONS TO MAIN BUILDING STRUCTURE BUT MUST ALLOW ADEQUATE SPACE

DRIP

COLUMN BEYOND

SPANDREL BELOW

NOTE: THE ARCHITECT DOES NOT DESIGN THE STRUCTURAL BACKUP OR CONNECTIONS TO THE MAIN BUILDING STRUCTURE, BUT MUST ALLOW ADEQUATE SPACE

NOTE: PANEL CAN WRAP AROUND COLUMN

SQUARE CORNERS ON COLUMN COVERS ARE MORE DIFFICULT TO FORM AND STRIP THAN ANGLED

GLASS-FIBER-REINFORCED CONCRETE PANEL

STRUCTURAL SUPPORT FRAME

COLUMN BEYOND

GRAVITY ANCHORS

PROVIDE FIRE SAFING TO BACK OF PANEL

NOTE: PANEL CAN BE NOTCHED TO FIT AROUND SPANDREL BEAM

WIND ANCHORS

GLASS-FIBER-REINFORCED CONCRETE PANEL

STRUCTURAL SUPPORT FRAME

DRIP

PANEL-TO-PANEL JOINTS

GFRC JOINT DETAILS
2.232

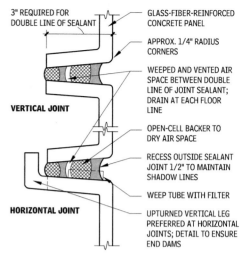

3" REQUIRED FOR DOUBLE LINE OF SEALANT

VERTICAL JOINT

HORIZONTAL JOINT

GLASS-FIBER-REINFORCED CONCRETE PANEL

APPROX. 1/4" RADIUS CORNERS

WEEPED AND VENTED AIR SPACE BETWEEN DOUBLE LINE OF JOINT SEALANT; DRAIN AT EACH FLOOR LINE

OPEN-CELL BACKER TO DRY AIR SPACE

RECESS OUTSIDE SEALANT JOINT 1/2" TO MAINTAIN SHADOW LINES

WEEP TUBE WITH FILTER

UPTURNED VERTICAL LEG PREFERRED AT HORIZONTAL JOINTS; DETAIL TO ENSURE END DAMS

CONCRETE MASONRY UNITS

Single-wythe CMU walls may be either load-bearing or non-load-bearing supported by the building frame. CMU walls are subject to significant movement from shrinkage caused by initial drying and then ongoing movement caused by temperature and moisture content variations. Therefore, control joints within the masonry must be provided at approximately 30-ft centers, near corners, and at changes in the strength of the wall (e.g., chases, changes of thickness, door openings, and window openings).

Masonry units for the wall may be structural, though architectural units may provide more design options. Architectural units include split-faced, scored, integrally colored, ground-faced, and specially shaped/sized. Glazed CMU and structural clay tile also may be used and are advantageous because they are less absorptive.

NOTES

2.230 Panel size is limited by shipping availability—usually a over the road truck, 10 by 40 ft is common.

2.231 For clarity, insulation, vapor retarder, and interior finishes are not shown.

SINGLE-WYTHE MASONRY WALL DETAILS
2.233

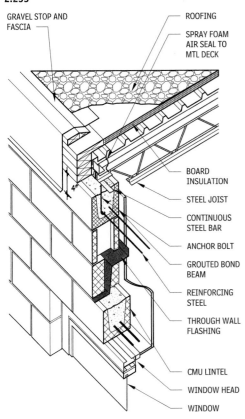

GRAVEL STOP AND FASCIA
ROOFING
SPRAY FOAM AIR SEAL TO MTL DECK
BOARD INSULATION
STEEL JOIST
CONTINUOUS STEEL BAR
ANCHOR BOLT
GROUTED BOND BEAM
REINFORCING STEEL
THROUGH WALL FLASHING
CMU LINTEL
WINDOW HEAD
WINDOW

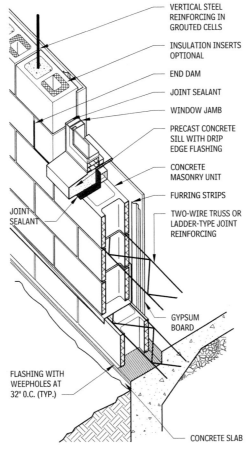

VERTICAL STEEL REINFORCING IN GROUTED CELLS
INSULATION INSERTS OPTIONAL
END DAM
JOINT SEALANT
WINDOW JAMB
PRECAST CONCRETE SILL WITH DRIP EDGE FLASHING
CONCRETE MASONRY UNIT
FURRING STRIPS
TWO-WIRE TRUSS OR LADDER-TYPE JOINT REINFORCING
GYPSUM BOARD
JOINT SEALANT
FLASHING WITH WEEPHOLES AT 32" O.C. (TYP.)
CONCRETE SLAB

SINGLE-WYTHE MASONRY WALL SECTION
2.234

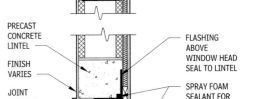
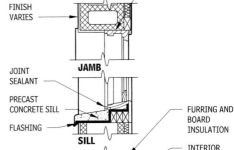
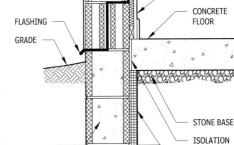

BLANKET INSULATION
2" DIA. WASHER (TYP.)
1/2" DIA. ANCHOR EMBEDDED 15" AT 6" O.C. (TYP.)
INTERIOR FINISH OPTIONAL
CORES FILLED WITH GROUT
VENT
METAL LATH TO RESTRAIN GROUT
PRECAST CONCRETE LINTEL
FINISH VARIES
JOINT SEALANT
FLASHING ABOVE WINDOW HEAD SEAL TO LINTEL
SPRAY FOAM SEALANT FOR INNER AIR SEAL

HEAD

FINISH VARIES

JAMB

JOINT SEALANT
PRECAST CONCRETE SILL
FLASHING
FURRING AND BOARD INSULATION

SILL

FLASHING
GRADE
INTERIOR FINISH
CONCRETE FLOOR
STONE BASE
ISOLATION JOINT (TYP.)
FILL CORES WITH GROUT
BOARD INSULATION (IF REQUIRED)

HEAT, AIR, AND MOISTURE

Single-wythe masonry walls function as mass barrier walls. They absorb moisture during precipitation and then dry out. Control of heat flow is typically accomplished by adding insulation to the interior side or by inserting insulation into the cores of the CMU. Board insulation is best installed immediately adjacent to the inside face of the panel using stickpins, or Z-shaped furring channels. Because the insulation may be exposed to moisture, which penetrates the concrete; the insulation should be capable of withstanding occasional moisture. Blanket insulation may be used between stud walls erected inside of the CMU, but thermal loss through the studs must be accounted for, along with the use of a weather barrier. Insulation inside of the CMU cores can be factory-installed foam inserts, foamed-in-place insulation, or poured fill. Note, however, that insulation in the cores is less effective because it cannot cover the entire area. For both insulation applied to the interior face or in the cores, the advantage of the thermal mass of the masonry is largely lost because it is outside the thermal envelope.

CMU is generally too porous to function as an air barrier; therefore, a different layer of the assembly must provide that function. A membrane may be applied to the interior surface or plaster may be applied to the exterior, or an interior gypsum board layer may be detailed as components of the air barrier.

Single-wythe CMU assemblies are very susceptible to water penetration. The porous nature of the CMU itself, the large number of joints that are only as deep as the thickness of the outer face, cracks caused by thermal movement, control joints, and lack of a dependable drainage path once moisture penetrates make single-wythe walls a poor choice in relationship to heat, air, and moisture.

IMPROVED PERFORMANCE

A variety of proprietary water-repellant additives both for the concrete used to manufacture the CMU and in the mortar can help reduce water absorption. Flashing systems to provide internal drainage of the cores of the CMU at the base are also available, and may improve performance. The application of water-repellant coatings may help, but will need maintenance coatings over the life of the structure.

Applying a three-coat stucco system over the CMU may help minimize absorption. Exterior insulation and finish systems (EIFS) applied over the CMU will help with both minimizing absorption and continuity of the insulation layer. Providing a drainage mat and weather barrier to the inside face of the CMU can substantially improve performance.

Consult the following references:

- Boston Building Enclosure Council, a committee of the Boston Society of Architects for the Massachusetts Bureau of Building Regulations and Standards.

Contributors:
Grace S. Lee, Rippeteau Architects, PC, Washington, DC; Stephen S. Szoke, PE, National Concrete Masonry Association, Herndon, Virginia; Brian F. Trimble, Brick Industry Association, Reston, Virginia.

HORIZONTAL SUPPORT FOR NON-LOAD-BEARING WALLS—STEEL FRAME
2.235

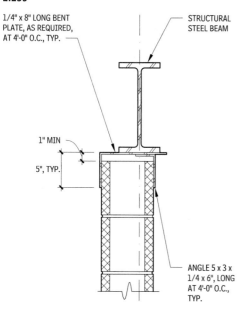

1/4" x 8" LONG BENT PLATE, AS REQUIRED, AT 4'-0" O.C., TYP.

STRUCTURAL STEEL BEAM

1" MIN

5", TYP.

ANGLE 5 x 3 x 1/4 x 6", LONG AT 4'-0" O.C., TYP.

CONCEALED FLASHING
2.237

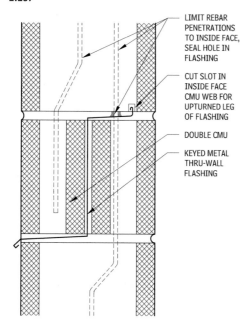

LIMIT REBAR PENETRATIONS TO INSIDE FACE, SEAL HOLE IN FLASHING

CUT SLOT IN INSIDE FACE CMU WEB FOR UPTURNED LEG OF FLASHING

DOUBLE CMU

KEYED METAL THRU-WALL FLASHING

HORIZONTAL SUPPORT FOR NON-LOAD-BEARING WALLS—METAL DECK
2.236

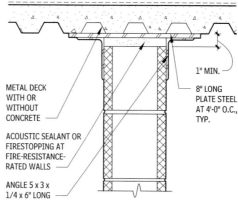

1" MIN.

8" LONG PLATE STEEL AT 4'-0" O.C., TYP.

METAL DECK WITH OR WITHOUT CONCRETE

ACOUSTIC SEALANT OR FIRESTOPPING AT FIRE-RESISTANCE-RATED WALLS

ANGLE 5 x 3 x 1/4 x 6" LONG

WALL ANCHORAGE DETAILS
2.238

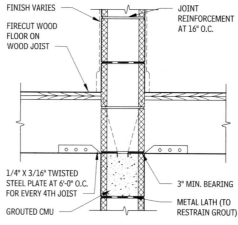

FINISH VARIES

FIRECUT WOOD FLOOR ON WOOD JOIST

JOINT REINFORCEMENT AT 16" O.C.

1/4" X 3/16" TWISTED STEEL PLATE AT 6'-0" O.C. FOR EVERY 4TH JOIST

GROUTED CMU

3" MIN. BEARING

METAL LATH (TO RESTRAIN GROUT)

CMU WALL TO WOOD JOIST ANCHORAGE

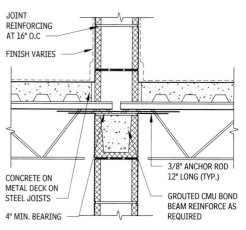

JOINT REINFORCING AT 16" O.C

FINISH VARIES

3/8" ANCHOR ROD 12" LONG (TYP.)

CONCRETE ON METAL DECK ON STEEL JOISTS

4" MIN. BEARING

GROUTED CMU BOND BEAM REINFORCE AS REQUIRED

CMU WALL TO STEEL JOIST ANCHORAGE

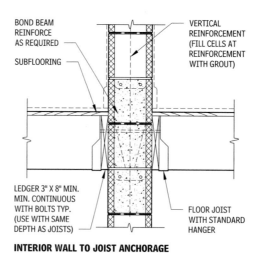

BOND BEAM REINFORCE AS REQUIRED

SUBFLOORING

VERTICAL REINFORCEMENT (FILL CELLS AT REINFORCEMENT WITH GROUT)

LEDGER 3" X 8" MIN. MIN. CONTINUOUS WITH BOLTS TYP. (USE WITH SAME DEPTH AS JOISTS)

FLOOR JOIST WITH STANDARD HANGER

INTERIOR WALL TO JOIST ANCHORAGE

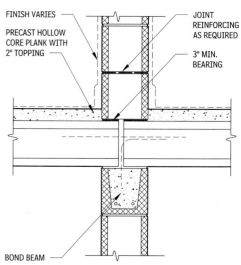

FINISH VARIES

PRECAST HOLLOW CORE PLANK WITH 2" TOPPING

JOINT REINFORCING AS REQUIRED

3" MIN. BEARING

BOND BEAM

CMU WALL TO CONCRETE JOIST ANCHORAGE

Contributors:
Grace S. Lee, Rippeteau Architects, PC, Washington, DC; Stephen S. Szoke, PE, National Concrete Masonry Association, Herndon, Virginia; Brian F. Trimble, Brick Industry Association, Reston, Virginia.

METHODS OF REINFORCING
2.239

BOND BEAM COURSE EVERY 48" O.C. (TYP.)

HORIZONTAL REINFORCING
STEEL IN BOND BEAM

PLACE METAL LATH OR WIRE SCREEN
UNDER BOND BEAM TO RESTRAIN GROUT

VERTICAL REINFORCING STEEL

CELLS CONTAINING REINFORCING
STEEL ARE FILLED SOLIDLY WITH
GROUT: VERTICAL CELLS SHOULD
PROVIDE A CONTINUOUS SPACE,
FREE OF MORTAR DROPINGS, AND
AT LEAST 1-1/2" x 2" IN SIZE (TYP.)
(SEE GROUT TABLE 9.3)

PLACE MORTAR ON CROSS WEBS
ADJACENT TO CELLS THAT WILL
BE GROUTED TO FORM DAMS

CLAY MASONRY

Clay masonry, including brick used in veneer walls can provide some of the most cost-effective, high-performance exterior wall assemblies available. The wall may function as a drainage cavity wall or, possibly, as a pressure-equalized wall, when properly detailed and constructed. The brick veneer must be supported by a structural backup, most typically CMU, wood studs, or cold-formed steel framing, but may also be placed over structural concrete or precast concrete.

Architectural concrete masonry units (e.g., split-faced, scored, integrally colored, ground-faced, and specially shaped/sized) stone, cast stone, or most other masonry units may be substituted for the brick, with little or no effect on total performance.

STRUCTURAL BACKUP

- *CMU*: CMU provides a nearly ideal backup to brick veneer. It matches structural stiffness, is resistant to minor wetting, and has similar movement characteristics. The veneer is typically anchored with loose pintels attached to eyes on crosspieces of the horizontal reinforcing.
- *Cold-formed steel framing*: CFS framing should be designed stiff enough to limit cracks caused by deflection: L/600 is minimum, but L/720 or L/900 might be appropriate for longer performance. Veneer ties not only must provide structural anchorage but must also be able to seal penetrations through the sheathing.
- *Wood framing*: Wood framing is typically limited to residential and very light commercial construction without the benefit of structural engineering. Stud framing should be limited to normal limits dictated by codes. Sheathing varies widely from plywood, OSB, board insulation, wood fiberboard, and gypsum sheathing. Ties are normally light-gauge, corrugated galvanized steel tabs nailed to the studs.

HEAT, AIR, AND MOISTURE

Brick veneer walls in commercial construction should always be detailed as drained cavity walls, and in high-rise situations or where very high performance is required, they may be upgraded to pressure-equalized walls. This wall assembly performs very well in all climates. The application of the weather barrier and insulation outside the backup allows for a continuous application with a minimum of breaks or gaps. If CMU backup is used, the mass stays within the insulation, providing a thermal reservoir.

Incorporate the following recommendations:

- 2 in. air space. If air space is reduced to 1 in., take extra care to keep air space clear of mortar droppings, or add proprietary products.

REINFORCED LOAD-BEARING MASONRY WALLS
2.240

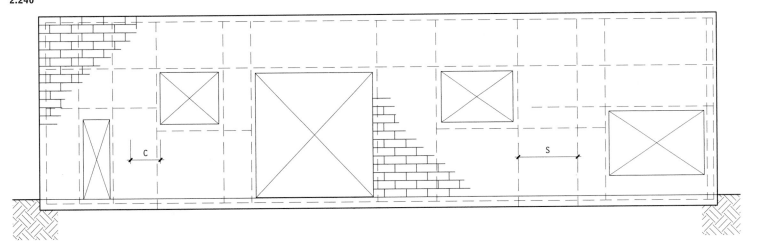

NOTE

2.240 C = 24 in., minimum, but not less than 40 bar diameters. In seismic performance category C, S = 10 ft maximum; in seismic performance categories D and E, S = 4 ft maximum.

Contributors:
Grace S. Lee, Rippeteau Architects, PC, Washington, DC; Stephen S. Szoke, PE, National Concrete Masonry Association, Herndon, Virginia; Brian F. Trimble, Brick Industry Association, Reston, Virginia.

- Functional weeps above every line of through-wall flashing.
- Through-wall flashing to direct any moisture within the air space to the exterior.
- A continuous weather barrier applied to the air space face of the backup. Coordinate the membrane into through-wall flashing, window frames, and other penetrations.
- Board insulation installed in the air space.
- Movement capability of the veneer and of the structure, while maintaining continuity of the weather barrier.

In cold-formed steel studs, avoid insulation in the stud space, unless dictated by economics. If required, evaluate the assembly for the proper location of the vapor barrier, the loss of effectiveness of the insulation because of thermal bridges through the studs, and the location of the air barrier. A water-resistant membrane must be installed over the sheathing, and if it also performs as a weather barrier, it may have to be vapor-permeable.

In residential wood-framed brick veneer walls, blanket insulation is typically installed in the stud space. The sheathing, board insulation, weather barrier, and detailing must all be carefully considered and balanced in relationship to the local climate.

For pressure-equalized walls, divide the air space behind the brick veneer into zones approximately one story high by 15 or 20 ft wide. Divide the cavity at inside and outside corners approximately 5 ft wide, because these are areas of large pressure changes. Extra venting at the top of the cavity is required. Ensure cavity is divided from roof at parapets.

BRICK VENEER ON STUDS

STEEL STUD VENEER ANCHORS
2.241

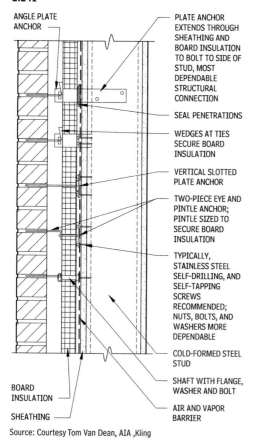

Source: Courtesy Tom Van Dean, AIA ,Kling

STRUCTURAL STEEL STUD BACKUP
2.242

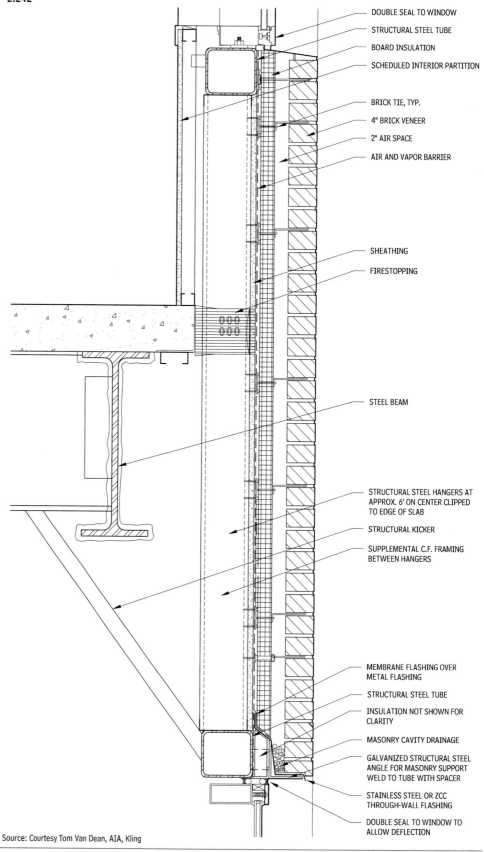

Source: Courtesy Tom Van Dean, AIA, Kling

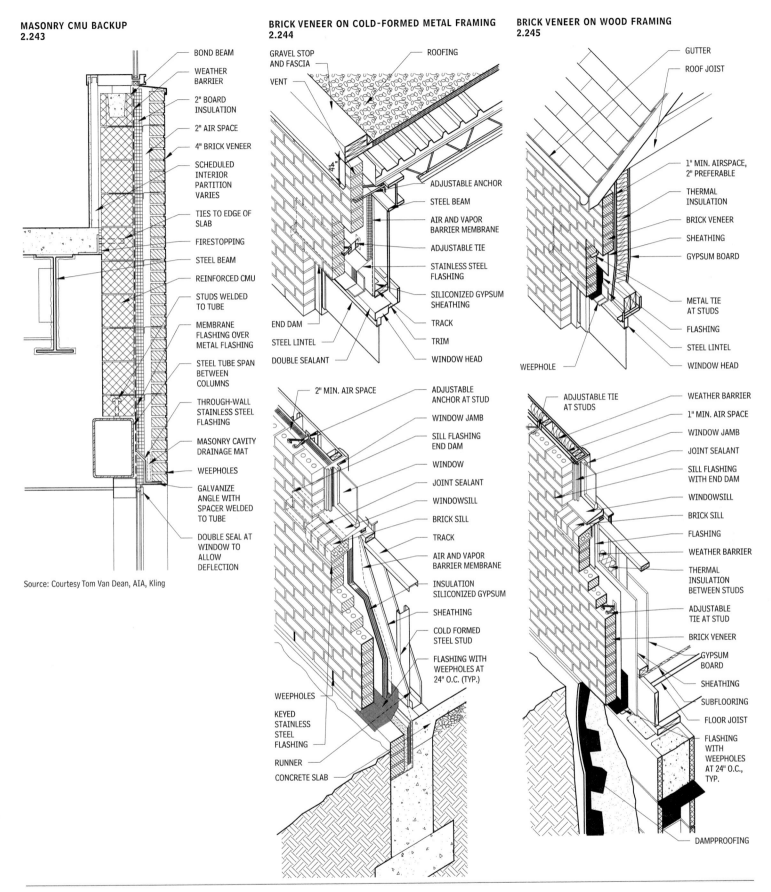

MASONRY CMU BACKUP
2.243

- BOND BEAM
- WEATHER BARRIER
- 2" BOARD INSULATION
- 2" AIR SPACE
- 4" BRICK VENEER
- SCHEDULED INTERIOR PARTITION VARIES
- TIES TO EDGE OF SLAB
- FIRESTOPPING
- STEEL BEAM
- REINFORCED CMU
- STUDS WELDED TO TUBE
- MEMBRANE FLASHING OVER METAL FLASHING
- STEEL TUBE SPAN BETWEEN COLUMNS
- THROUGH-WALL STAINLESS STEEL FLASHING
- MASONRY CAVITY DRAINAGE MAT
- WEEPHOLES
- GALVANIZE ANGLE WITH SPACER WELDED TO TUBE
- DOUBLE SEAL AT WINDOW TO ALLOW DEFLECTION

Source: Courtesy Tom Van Dean, AIA, Kling

BRICK VENEER ON COLD-FORMED METAL FRAMING
2.244

- GRAVEL STOP AND FASCIA
- VENT
- ROOFING
- ADJUSTABLE ANCHOR
- STEEL BEAM
- AIR AND VAPOR BARRIER MEMBRANE
- ADJUSTABLE TIE
- STAINLESS STEEL FLASHING
- SILICONIZED GYPSUM SHEATHING
- END DAM
- STEEL LINTEL
- DOUBLE SEALANT
- TRACK
- TRIM
- WINDOW HEAD

- 2" MIN. AIR SPACE
- ADJUSTABLE ANCHOR AT STUD
- WINDOW JAMB
- SILL FLASHING END DAM
- WINDOW
- JOINT SEALANT
- WINDOWSILL
- BRICK SILL
- TRACK
- AIR AND VAPOR BARRIER MEMBRANE
- INSULATION SILICONIZED GYPSUM
- SHEATHING
- COLD FORMED STEEL STUD
- FLASHING WITH WEEPHOLES AT 24" O.C. (TYP.)
- WEEPHOLES
- KEYED STAINLESS STEEL FLASHING
- RUNNER
- CONCRETE SLAB

BRICK VENEER ON WOOD FRAMING
2.245

- GUTTER
- ROOF JOIST
- 1" MIN. AIRSPACE, 2" PREFERABLE
- THERMAL INSULATION
- BRICK VENEER
- SHEATHING
- GYPSUM BOARD
- METAL TIE AT STUDS
- FLASHING
- STEEL LINTEL
- WINDOW HEAD
- WEEPHOLE

- ADJUSTABLE TIE AT STUDS
- WEATHER BARRIER
- 1" MIN. AIR SPACE
- WINDOW JAMB
- JOINT SEALANT
- SILL FLASHING WITH END DAM
- WINDOWSILL
- BRICK SILL
- FLASHING
- WEATHER BARRIER
- THERMAL INSULATION BETWEEN STUDS
- ADJUSTABLE TIE AT STUD
- BRICK VENEER
- GYPSUM BOARD
- SHEATHING
- SUBFLOORING
- FLOOR JOIST
- FLASHING WITH WEEPHOLES AT 24" O.C., TYP.
- DAMPPROOFING

Contributors:
Grace S. Lee, Rippeteau Architects, PC, Washington, DC; Brian F. Trimble, Brick Industry Association, Reston, Virginia.

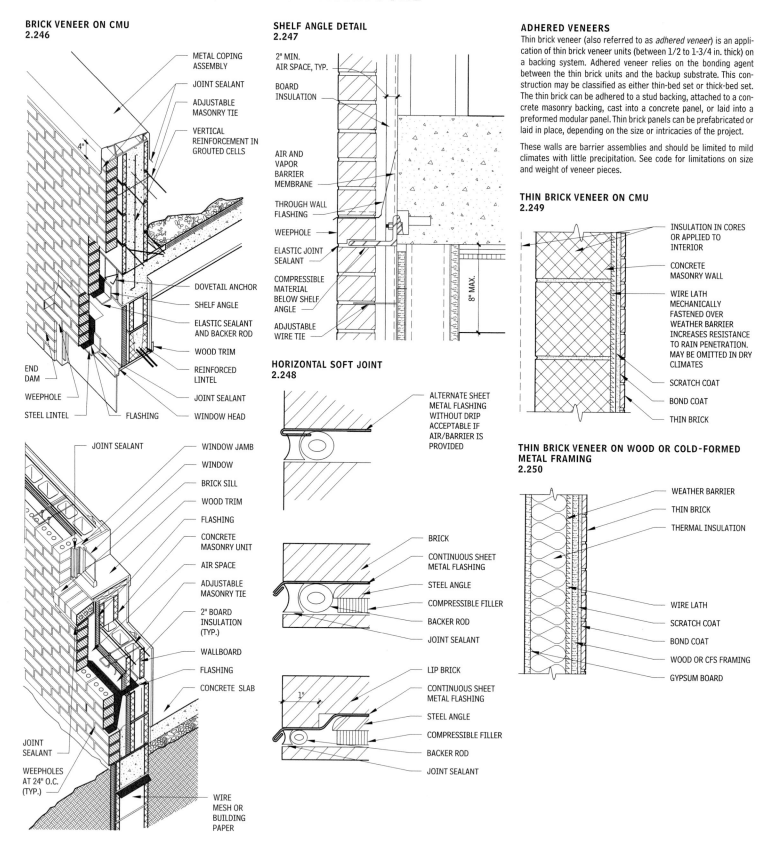

BRICK VENEER ON CMU
2.246

- METAL COPING ASSEMBLY
- JOINT SEALANT
- ADJUSTABLE MASONRY TIE
- VERTICAL REINFORCEMENT IN GROUTED CELLS
- 4"
- DOVETAIL ANCHOR
- SHELF ANGLE
- ELASTIC SEALANT AND BACKER ROD
- WOOD TRIM
- REINFORCED LINTEL
- JOINT SEALANT
- WINDOW HEAD
- END DAM
- WEEPHOLE
- STEEL LINTEL
- FLASHING

- JOINT SEALANT
- WINDOW JAMB
- WINDOW
- BRICK SILL
- WOOD TRIM
- FLASHING
- CONCRETE MASONRY UNIT
- AIR SPACE
- ADJUSTABLE MASONRY TIE
- 2" BOARD INSULATION (TYP.)
- WALLBOARD
- FLASHING
- CONCRETE SLAB
- JOINT SEALANT
- WEEPHOLES AT 24" O.C. (TYP.)
- WIRE MESH OR BUILDING PAPER

SHELF ANGLE DETAIL
2.247

- 2" MIN. AIR SPACE, TYP.
- BOARD INSULATION
- AIR AND VAPOR BARRIER MEMBRANE
- THROUGH WALL FLASHING
- WEEPHOLE
- ELASTIC JOINT SEALANT
- COMPRESSIBLE MATERIAL BELOW SHELF ANGLE
- ADJUSTABLE WIRE TIE
- 8" MAX.

HORIZONTAL SOFT JOINT
2.248

- ALTERNATE SHEET METAL FLASHING WITHOUT DRIP ACCEPTABLE IF AIR/BARRIER IS PROVIDED

- BRICK
- CONTINUOUS SHEET METAL FLASHING
- STEEL ANGLE
- COMPRESSIBLE FILLER
- BACKER ROD
- JOINT SEALANT

- LIP BRICK
- CONTINUOUS SHEET METAL FLASHING
- STEEL ANGLE
- COMPRESSIBLE FILLER
- BACKER ROD
- JOINT SEALANT
- 1"

ADHERED VENEERS

Thin brick veneer (also referred to as *adhered veneer*) is an application of thin brick veneer units (between 1/2 to 1-3/4 in. thick) on a backing system. Adhered veneer relies on the bonding agent between the thin brick units and the backup substrate. This construction may be classified as either thin-bed set or thick-bed set. The thin brick can be adhered to a stud backing, attached to a concrete masonry backing, cast into a concrete panel, or laid into a preformed modular panel. Thin brick panels can be prefabricated or laid in place, depending on the size or intricacies of the project.

These walls are barrier assemblies and should be limited to mild climates with little precipitation. See code for limitations on size and weight of veneer pieces.

THIN BRICK VENEER ON CMU
2.249

- INSULATION IN CORES OR APPLIED TO INTERIOR
- CONCRETE MASONRY WALL
- WIRE LATH MECHANICALLY FASTENED OVER WEATHER BARRIER INCREASES RESISTANCE TO RAIN PENETRATION. MAY BE OMITTED IN DRY CLIMATES
- SCRATCH COAT
- BOND COAT
- THIN BRICK

THIN BRICK VENEER ON WOOD OR COLD-FORMED METAL FRAMING
2.250

- WEATHER BARRIER
- THIN BRICK
- THERMAL INSULATION
- WIRE LATH
- SCRATCH COAT
- BOND COAT
- WOOD OR CFS FRAMING
- GYPSUM BOARD

NOTES

2.247 A common mistake is to seal the flashing to the brick above, which blocks the drainage.

Contributors:
Grace S. Lee, Rippeteau Architects, PC, Washington, DC; Stephen S. Szoke, PE, National Concrete Masonry Association, Herndon, Virginia; Brian F. Trimble, Brick Industry Association, Reston, Virginia.

WALL-TO-FLOOR ANCHORAGE AT CAVITY WALLS
2.251

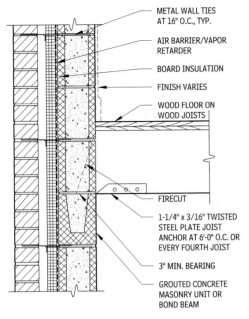

- METAL WALL TIES AT 16" O.C., TYP.
- AIR BARRIER/VAPOR RETARDER
- BOARD INSULATION
- FINISH VARIES
- WOOD FLOOR ON WOOD JOISTS
- FIRECUT
- 1-1/4" x 3/16" TWISTED STEEL PLATE JOIST ANCHOR AT 6'-0" O.C. OR EVERY FOURTH JOIST
- 3" MIN. BEARING
- GROUTED CONCRETE MASONRY UNIT OR BOND BEAM

WOOD FLOOR

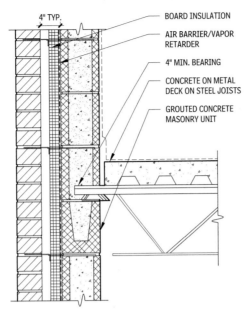

- 4" TYP.
- BOARD INSULATION
- AIR BARRIER/VAPOR RETARDER
- 4" MIN. BEARING
- CONCRETE ON METAL DECK ON STEEL JOISTS
- GROUTED CONCRETE MASONRY UNIT

STEEL JOIST FLOOR

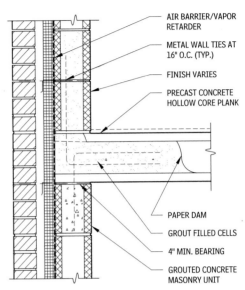

- AIR BARRIER/VAPOR RETARDER
- METAL WALL TIES AT 16" O.C. (TYP.)
- FINISH VARIES
- PRECAST CONCRETE HOLLOW CORE PLANK
- PAPER DAM
- GROUT FILLED CELLS
- 4" MIN. BEARING
- GROUTED CONCRETE MASONRY UNIT

PRECAST HOLLOW CORE FLOOR

SPANDREL DETAIL
2.252

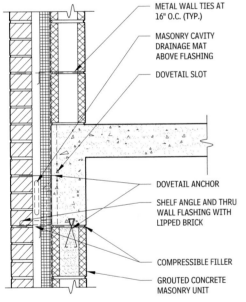

- METAL WALL TIES AT 16" O.C. (TYP.)
- MASONRY CAVITY DRAINAGE MAT ABOVE FLASHING
- DOVETAIL SLOT
- DOVETAIL ANCHOR
- SHELF ANGLE AND THRU WALL FLASHING WITH LIPPED BRICK
- COMPRESSIBLE FILLER
- GROUTED CONCRETE MASONRY UNIT

DOVETAIL ANCHORS AT CORNER
2.253

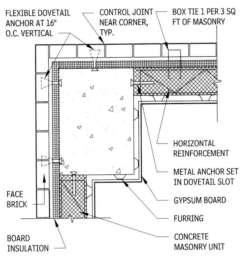

- FLEXIBLE DOVETAIL ANCHOR AT 16" O.C. VERTICAL
- CONTROL JOINT NEAR CORNER, TYP.
- BOX TIE 1 PER 3 SQ FT OF MASONRY
- HORIZONTAL REINFORCEMENT
- METAL ANCHOR SET IN DOVETAIL SLOT
- GYPSUM BOARD
- FURRING
- CONCRETE MASONRY UNIT
- FACE BRICK
- BOARD INSULATION

Contributors:
Grace S. Lee, Rippeteau Architects, PC, Washington, DC; Stephen S. Szoke, PE, National Concrete Masonry Association, Herndon, Virginia; Brian F. Trimble, Brick Industry Association, Reston, Virginia.

CAVITY WALL FLASHING
2.254

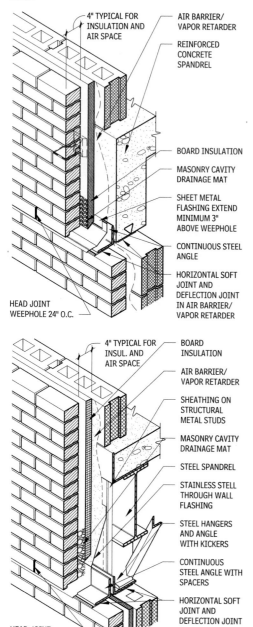

4" TYPICAL FOR INSULATION AND AIR SPACE
AIR BARRIER/VAPOR RETARDER
REINFORCED CONCRETE SPANDREL
BOARD INSULATION
MASONRY CAVITY DRAINAGE MAT
SHEET METAL FLASHING EXTEND MINIMUM 3" ABOVE WEEPHOLE
CONTINUOUS STEEL ANGLE
HORIZONTAL SOFT JOINT AND DEFLECTION JOINT IN AIR BARRIER/VAPOR RETARDER
HEAD JOINT WEEPHOLE 24" O.C.

4" TYPICAL FOR INSUL. AND AIR SPACE
BOARD INSULATION
AIR BARRIER/VAPOR RETARDER
SHEATHING ON STRUCTURAL METAL STUDS
MASONRY CAVITY DRAINAGE MAT
STEEL SPANDREL
STAINLESS STELL THROUGH WALL FLASHING
STEEL HANGERS AND ANGLE WITH KICKERS
CONTINUOUS STEEL ANGLE WITH SPACERS
HORIZONTAL SOFT JOINT AND DEFLECTION JOINT IN AIR BARRIER/VAPOR RETARDER
HEAD JOINT WEEPHOLES 24" O.C.

GLASS MASONRY UNITS

When specifying supports and shelf angles, the installed weight and deflection limitation of the glass block should be taken into account, and local building codes checked for any limits on panel sizes or installation details.

INSTALLED WEIGHT OF GLASS BLOCK
2.255

TYPE OF UNIT	INSTALLED WEIGHT (LB/SQ FT)
Regular	20
Thin	16
Thick	26
Solid	38

DEFLECTION LIMITATIONS

Maximum deflection of structural members supporting glass block panels must not exceed:

L/600

where L = distance between vertical supports.

ELEVATION
2.256

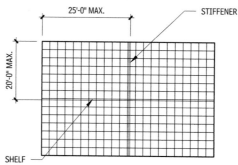

25'-0" MAX.
STIFFENER
20'-0" MAX.
SHELF

SECTIONS AT SUPPORTS
2.257

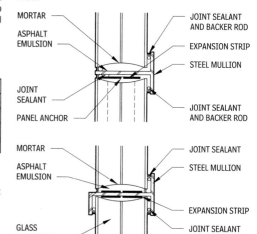

MORTAR
ASPHALT EMULSION
JOINT SEALANT
PANEL ANCHOR
JOINT SEALANT AND BACKER ROD
EXPANSION STRIP
STEEL MULLION
JOINT SEALANT AND BACKER ROD

MORTAR
ASPHALT EMULSION
GLASS BLOCK UNIT
JOINT SEALANT
STEEL MULLION
EXPANSION STRIP
JOINT SEALANT AND BACKER ROD

SHELF ANGLES IN MULTIPLE VERTICAL PANELS

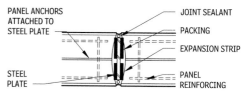

PANEL ANCHORS ATTACHED TO STEEL PLATE
STEEL PLATE
JOINT SEALANT
PACKING
EXPANSION STRIP
PANEL REINFORCING

SUPPORT IN MULTIPLE HORIZONTAL PANELS

NOTES

2.257 Panels with an expansion joint stiffener incorporating a concealed vertical plate should be limited to 10 ft maximum height.

Contributors:
Grace S. Lee, Rippeteau Architects, PC, Washington, DC; Brian F. Trimble, Brick Industry Association, Reston, Virginia; Theodore D. Sherman, AIA, Lev Zetlin Associates, Engineers and Designers, New York City, New York.

EXTERIOR CONNECTION DETAILS
2.258

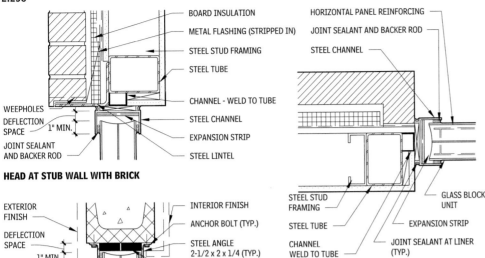

HEAD AT STUB WALL WITH BRICK

- BOARD INSULATION
- METAL FLASHING (STRIPPED IN)
- STEEL STUD FRAMING
- STEEL TUBE
- CHANNEL - WELD TO TUBE
- STEEL CHANNEL
- EXPANSION STRIP
- STEEL LINTEL
- WEEPHOLES
- DEFLECTION SPACE
- 1" MIN.
- JOINT SEALANT AND BACKER ROD

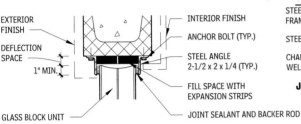

HEAD AT CONCRETE MASONRY UNIT WALL

- EXTERIOR FINISH
- DEFLECTION SPACE
- 1" MIN.
- GLASS BLOCK UNIT
- INTERIOR FINISH
- ANCHOR BOLT (TYP.)
- STEEL ANGLE 2-1/2 x 2 x 1/4 (TYP.)
- FILL SPACE WITH EXPANSION STRIPS
- JOINT SEALANT AND BACKER ROD

SILL AT CONCRETE MASONRY UNIT WALL

- GLASS BLOCK UNIT
- PRECAST CONCRETE SILL
- MORTAR
- ASPHALT EMULSION
- INTERIOR FINISH

JAMB AT STUD WALL WITH BRICK

- HORIZONTAL PANEL REINFORCING
- JOINT SEALANT AND BACKER ROD
- STEEL CHANNEL
- GLASS BLOCK UNIT
- EXPANSION STRIP
- JOINT SEALANT AT LINER (TYP.)
- STEEL STUD FRAMING
- STEEL TUBE
- CHANNEL WELD TO TUBE

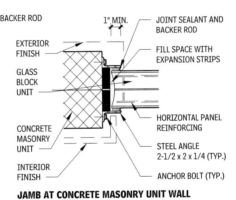

JAMB AT CONCRETE MASONRY UNIT WALL

- 1" MIN.
- EXTERIOR FINISH
- GLASS BLOCK UNIT
- CONCRETE MASONRY UNIT
- INTERIOR FINISH
- JOINT SEALANT AND BACKER ROD
- FILL SPACE WITH EXPANSION STRIPS
- HORIZONTAL PANEL REINFORCING
- STEEL ANGLE 2-1/2 x 2 x 1/4 (TYP.)
- ANCHOR BOLT (TYP.)

CUTAWAY OF A TYPICAL ICF GRID WALL
2.260

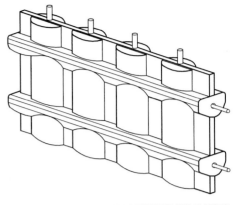

WAFFLE GRID CORE WITH FORM REMOVED FOR CLARITY

CUTAWAY OF A TYPICAL ICF POST-AND-BEAM WALL
2.261

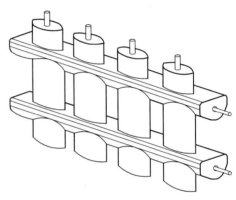

SCREEN GRID CORE WITH FORM REMOVED FOR CLARITY

INSULATING CONCRETE FORMING

ICFs are basically forms for poured concrete walls that stay in place as a permanent part of the wall assembly.

The forms, made of foam insulation, are either formed interlocking blocks or separate panels connected with plastic ties. The left-in-place forms not only provide a continuous insulation and sound barrier, but also provide a backing for gypsum board on the inside and stucco cements, plaster, lap siding, or brick on the outside.

Although all ICF are identical in principle, the various brands differ widely in the details of their shapes, cavities, and component parts.

Block assemblies have the smallest individual units, ranging from 8in. x 1 ft -4 in. (height x length) to 1 ft 4 in. x 41 in. A typical ICF block is 10 in. in overall width, with a 6 in. cavity for the concrete. The units are factory-molded with special interlocking edges that allow them to fit together much like plastic children's blocks.

Panel systems have the largest units, ranging from roughly 1 ft x 8 ft to 4 ft x 12 ft. Their foam edges are flat, and interconnection requires attachment of a separate connector or "tie." Panels are assembled into units before setting in place—either on-site or prior to delivery.

Plank systems are similar to panel systems, but generally use smaller faces of foam, ranging in height from 8 in. to 12 in. and in width from 4 ft to 8 ft. The major difference between planks and panels is assembly. The foam planks are outfitted with ties as part of the setting sequence, rather than being assembled into units.

Within these broad categories of ICF, individual brands vary in their cavity design. "Flat wall" systems yield a continuous thickness of concrete, like a conventional poured wall. "Grid wall" systems have a waffle pattern where the concrete is thicker at some points than others. "Post and beam" systems have widely spaced horizontal and vertical columns of concrete that are completely encapsulated in the foam form. Whatever the differences among ICF brands, all major ICF systems are engineer designed, code accepted, and field proven.

INSULATING CONCRETE FORMING
2.259

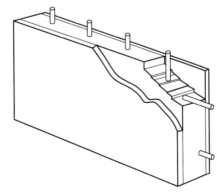

FLAT WALL CORE WITH FORM IN PLACE

RAINSCREEN PANELS

Panels are used in a drained cavity exterior wall system by mounting over a suspension system with air space, a weather barrier, and a structural backup (usually sheathing over studs). The panels come in a wide variety of base materials, sizes, and colors. Most manufacturers sell the tiles together with the suspension system as a proprietary system.

PANELS

Panels are available in a large variety of types. Some are homogeneous through the thickness, while others have the decorative finish applied to one or both faces. Common panel types include:

- *Solid phenolic resin panels with wood-fiber binder*: These have a decorative face on one or both sides, with a black core.
- *Engineered wood panels, with veneers and/or cores in clear resin*: In these, the exposed face is available in a variety of high-quality wood veneers.
- *Resin panels with mineral filler*: These panels are generally integrally colored through the entire thickness.

SIZES

Panels range from 4 by 8 ft to 5 by 12 ft. Thickness ranges from 5/16 to 1/2 in.

FINISHES

Not all panel types are available in all finishes.

- *Solid colors with smooth surfaces and satin gloss*: Standard color ranges are wide, and custom colors are available for larger runs.

Contributor:
Grace S. Lee, Rippeteau Architects, PC, Washington, DC.

- *Wood grain*: Real wood or printed wood veneer.
- *Speckled*: Stone look or decorative speckled patterns.

WALL ASSEMBLY COMPONENTS

- *Panel:* Panel should be mounted to allow for relatively large amounts of thermal movement. Exposed fastener systems must provide oversized holes. Concealed clip systems should allow sliding of connections.
- *Structural backup*: CMU or gypsum sheathing over cold-formed metal framing.
- *Weather barrier*: Continuous barrier applied over sheathing or CMU.
- *Insulation*: Board or blanket insulation installed in the air space between suspension system members.
- *Suspension system*: Commonly extruded aluminum or formed galvanized steel furring with mounting clips, that may be propriety to the panel manufacturer. Wood battens can be used in residential or light commercial construction.
- *Through-wall flashing*: Stainless steel or aluminum sheet incorporated with the weather barrier. Flashing must incorporate openings to allow ventilation and weeping of cavity.

HEAT, AIR, AND MOISTURE

In commercial construction, high-rise situations, or where very high performance is required, rainscreen panel walls should be detailed as drained cavity walls, though they can also be pressure-equalized walls. This wall system performs very well in all climates. The application of the air barrier or vapor retarder and insulation outside the backup wall allows for a continuous application with a minimum of breaks or gaps. If CMU backup is used, the mass stays within the insulation, providing thermal dampening.

PHENOLIC PANEL HORIZONTAL JOINTS
2.262

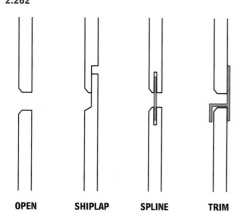

OPEN   **SHIPLAP**   **SPLINE**   **TRIM**

PHENOLIC PANEL VERTICAL JOINTS
2.263

TRIM

SPLINE

BACKED

OPEN

Avoid insulation in the stud space, unless dictated by economics. If required, evaluate the assembly for the proper location of the vapor retarder and the loss of effectiveness of the insulation because of thermal bridges through the studs. An air barrier should be installed over the sheathing; dependent on climatic conditions the air barrier may need to be vapor-permeable.

CONCEALED CLIPS ON ALUMINUM GRID
2.264

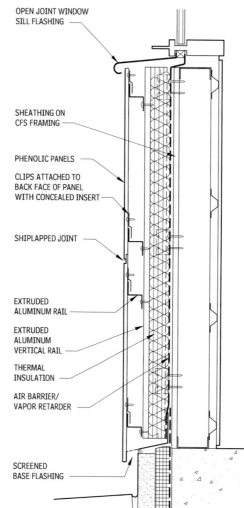

OPEN JOINT WINDOW
SILL FLASHING

SHEATHING ON
CFS FRAMING

PHENOLIC PANELS

CLIPS ATTACHED TO
BACK FACE OF PANEL
WITH CONCEALED INSERT

SHIPLAPPED JOINT

EXTRUDED
ALUMINUM RAIL

EXTRUDED
ALUMINUM
VERTICAL RAIL

THERMAL
INSULATION

AIR BARRIER/
VAPOR RETARDER

SCREENED
BASE FLASHING

EXPOSED SCREWS INTO WOOD
2.265

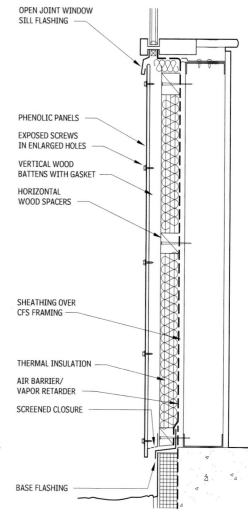

OPEN JOINT WINDOW
SILL FLASHING

PHENOLIC PANELS

EXPOSED SCREWS
IN ENLARGED HOLES

VERTICAL WOOD
BATTENS WITH GASKET

HORIZONTAL
WOOD SPACERS

SHEATHING OVER
CFS FRAMING

THERMAL INSULATION

AIR BARRIER/
VAPOR RETARDER

SCREENED CLOSURE

BASE FLASHING

NOTE

2.263 It is preferable to use open joints in a rainscreen assembly that has been engineered by the manufacturer.

EXPOSED RIVETS INTO ALUMINUM SUPPORTS
2.266

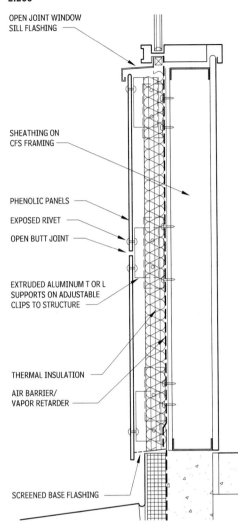

OPEN JOINT WINDOW
SILL FLASHING

SHEATHING ON
CFS FRAMING

PHENOLIC PANELS

EXPOSED RIVET

OPEN BUTT JOINT

EXTRUDED ALUMINUM T OR L
SUPPORTS ON ADJUSTABLE
CLIPS TO STRUCTURE

THERMAL INSULATION

AIR BARRIER/
VAPOR RETARDER

SCREENED BASE FLASHING

STRUCTURAL PANELS

Structural building panels are factory-assembled composite panels ready for installation as a complete structural and/or insulating wall section. The material of each component of the panel system is very important when selecting a panel manufacturer. Components include the skin, foam core, adhesive, and optional exterior or interior finish. The application for which the panel is intended determines the materials used. Consult manufacturers for specifications.

Sizes vary from 4-by-8-ft panels weighing about 100 lbs, to 8-by-28-ft panels that must be installed using a crane.

PANEL TYPES

There are two main types of structural building panels:

- *Stressed skin panels*: These are manufactured by gluing and nailing plywood skins to both sides of a wood frame, resulting in a unit that performs like an I-beam. Stressed skin panels are not necessarily insulated.
- *Structural foam core panels*: These fall into two groups: sandwich panels and unfaced panels. Sandwich panels are rigid-foam panels faced with two structural-grade skins, usually made of oriented-strand board (OSB) or plywood. Depending on the application and the manufacturer, these foam-core panels may or may not include framing members within the core. Unfaced structural foam core panels look like panels of stick-framing

with thermal insulation between the members, instead of blanket insulation. Interior and exterior finishes are applied to these panels in the field.

The skins of structural building panels (such as I-beam flanges) resist tension and compression, while the wood frame or core (such as an I-beam web) resists shear and prevents buckling of the skins.

All structural foam-core panels are insulated with a core of expanded polystyrene (EPS), extruded polystyrene, or urethane foam, from 3-1/2 to 11-1/4 in. thick. Urethane panels are either glue-laminated like polystyrene or foamed in place, either in the factory or in the field. Urethane has an R-value of 6 or 7 per inch, versus R-5 for extruded polystyrene and R-4 for EPS foam. Urethane is about twice as strong in compression as polystyrene, and has a perm rating of less than 1, which technically qualifies it as a vapor retarder. EPS has a perm rating of from 1 to 3 and may require an additional vapor retarder. EPS, however, is inert, non-toxic (if ingested), and resilient; it doesn't feed microorganisms and is generally cheaper than urethane.

Consult manufacturers on CFC and formaldehyde content in the foam core and skin material because it varies among manufacturers. Regarding flammability of both foam-core types, consult with the manufacturer about the individual product.

CHARACTERISTICS

Using structural panels generally speeds construction because the panels replace three standard steps: framing, sheathing, and insulation. Panel assemblies offer superior energy performance compared to a conventional framing. This is largely because the thermal insulation has higher R-values, there are fewer seams to seal, and conductive heat is not lost through air infiltration around the framing. Structural building panels also offer good resistance to lateral loads.

These panels can, however, be susceptible to infestation by insects such as carpenter ants and termites, which eat through wood and tunnel through the insulation material, reducing insulation value and even compromising structural integrity. Use of termite shields, foam cores treated with insect repellant, and other strategies should be considered.

Structural building panels are components of a relatively new building system, therefore it is important to consult code officials early to prevent any misunderstandings or delays in the code approval process. Also, check with manufacturers to determine whether their products have received compliance approval from authorities having jurisdiction.

The seams between the panels are the part of of the assembly most prone to infiltration and weakness, hence most likely to show the results of expansion and contraction. Tight spline connections with sealant at all edges (top, bottom, and sides) can greatly increase thermal efficiency.

In very cold climates, the seams of the panels should be taped and sealed against air infiltration and to prevent condensation and rotting inside joints.

TYPICAL INTERMEDIATE PANEL SPLINE DETAILS
2.267

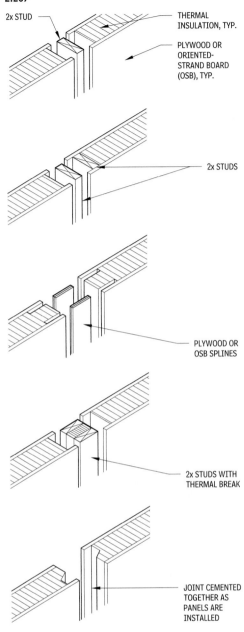

2x STUD

THERMAL INSULATION, TYP.

PLYWOOD OR ORIENTED-STRAND BOARD (OSB), TYP.

2x STUDS

PLYWOOD OR OSB SPLINES

2x STUDS WITH THERMAL BREAK

JOINT CEMENTED TOGETHER AS PANELS ARE INSTALLED

TYPICAL WIRE CHASE LOCATIONS IN PANELS
2.268

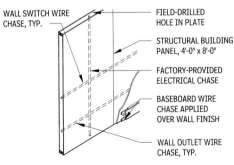

WALL SWITCH WIRE CHASE, TYP.

FIELD-DRILLED HOLE IN PLATE

STRUCTURAL BUILDING PANEL, 4'-0" x 8'-0"

FACTORY-PROVIDED ELECTRICAL CHASE

BASEBOARD WIRE CHASE APPLIED OVER WALL FINISH

WALL OUTLET WIRE CHASE, TYP.

NOTES

2.266 Revise base detail for termite control where protection is required.
2.267 Studs and splines are screwed, and usually glued, to panels from both sides. Consult manufacturer's literature. Joints are typically sealed with expanding foam.
2.268 Consult local codes for all electrical installations.

Contributor:
Richard J. Vitullo, AIA, Oak Leaf Studio, Crownsville, Maryland.

WINDOW DETAILS
2.269

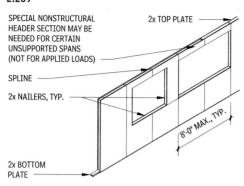

SPECIAL NONSTRUCTURAL HEADER SECTION MAY BE NEEDED FOR CERTAIN UNSUPPORTED SPANS (NOT FOR APPLIED LOADS)

2x TOP PLATE

SPLINE

2x NAILERS, TYP.

8'-0" MAX., TYP.

2x BOTTOM PLATE

REINFORCED DOOR OPENING DETAIL
2.270

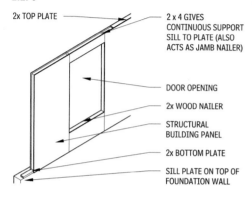

2x TOP PLATE

2 x 4 GIVES CONTINUOUS SUPPORT SILL TO PLATE (ALSO ACTS AS JAMB NAILER)

DOOR OPENING

2x WOOD NAILER

STRUCTURAL BUILDING PANEL

2x BOTTOM PLATE

SILL PLATE ON TOP OF FOUNDATION WALL

CONNECTION WITH FLOOR JOIST BETWEEN PANELS
2.271

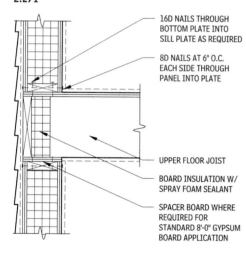

16D NAILS THROUGH BOTTOM PLATE INTO SILL PLATE AS REQUIRED

8D NAILS AT 6" O.C. EACH SIDE THROUGH PANEL INTO PLATE

UPPER FLOOR JOIST

BOARD INSULATION W/ SPRAY FOAM SEALANT

SPACER BOARD WHERE REQUIRED FOR STANDARD 8'-0" GYPSUM BOARD APPLICATION

CONNECTION WITH FLOOR JOIST ADJACENT TO PANEL
2.272

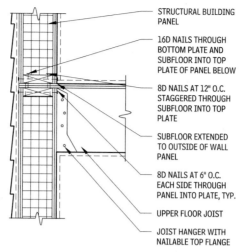

STRUCTURAL BUILDING PANEL

16D NAILS THROUGH BOTTOM PLATE AND SUBFLOOR INTO TOP PLATE OF PANEL BELOW

8D NAILS AT 12" O.C. STAGGERED THROUGH SUBFLOOR INTO TOP PLATE

SUBFLOOR EXTENDED TO OUTSIDE OF WALL PANEL

8D NAILS AT 6" O.C. EACH SIDE THROUGH PANEL INTO PLATE, TYP.

UPPER FLOOR JOIST

JOIST HANGER WITH NAILABLE TOP FLANGE

PANEL AT SILL, WITH FLOOR JOIST BELOW CONNECTION
2.273

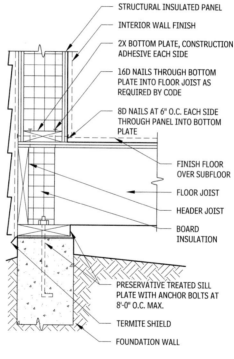

STRUCTURAL INSULATED PANEL

INTERIOR WALL FINISH

2X BOTTOM PLATE, CONSTRUCTION ADHESIVE EACH SIDE

16D NAILS THROUGH BOTTOM PLATE INTO FLOOR JOIST AS REQUIRED BY CODE

8D NAILS AT 6" O.C. EACH SIDE THROUGH PANEL INTO BOTTOM PLATE

FINISH FLOOR OVER SUBFLOOR

FLOOR JOIST

HEADER JOIST

BOARD INSULATION

PRESERVATIVE TREATED SILL PLATE WITH ANCHOR BOLTS AT 8'-0" O.C. MAX.

TERMITE SHIELD

FOUNDATION WALL

PANEL AT SILL CONNECTION, WITH FLOOR JOIST ADJACENT
2.274

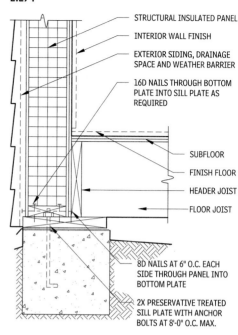

STRUCTURAL INSULATED PANEL

INTERIOR WALL FINISH

EXTERIOR SIDING, DRAINAGE SPACE AND WEATHER BARRIER

16D NAILS THROUGH BOTTOM PLATE INTO SILL PLATE AS REQUIRED

SUBFLOOR

FINISH FLOOR

HEADER JOIST

FLOOR JOIST

8D NAILS AT 6" O.C. EACH SIDE THROUGH PANEL INTO BOTTOM PLATE

2X PRESERVATIVE TREATED SILL PLATE WITH ANCHOR BOLTS AT 8'-0" O.C. MAX.

PORTLAND CEMENT STUCCO

Stucco is a traditional exterior finish material, typically three coats of portland cement plaster, applied over weather barrier to create a drainage plane wall system. It is impact and fire resistant, and because it is applied in a plastic state, it can be made to conform to virtually any shape. Durable stucco is, however, highly dependent on knowledgeable and skilled application, as many of the problems attributed to stucco (e.g., cracking, delamination, water leakage) are not inherent to the product but are the result of improper installation.

Stucco is applied in three coats: scratch, brown, and finish.

- The scratch and brown coats are portland cement plaster, typically each approximately 3/8-in. thick; together they are called the base coat. The base coat must be moist-cured for two days, then further cured for five days before application of the finish coat. In very hot or windy conditions, it may be necessary to protect the base coat with tarps or sheeting.
- The scratch coat is so called because, after application, the surface is roughened with a rake or other device to promote a mechanical bonding of the brown coat.
- The brown coat is applied after the scratch coat has set up. IBC requires a minimum or 24 hours between coats if damp-curing is used, or 48 hours without. In the recent past, one week was common for curing. It is important that the scratch coat be properly cured before the application of the brown coat, to minimize the cracking. The brown coat may be reinforced with a variety of fibers, and it must be trowel-floated while still moist but after taking an initial set, to densify the surface and further reduce cracking. Application of the brown coat before the scratch coat has properly cured, and failure to make the additional trowel-float pass, are common causes of cracking in the finished stucco.
- The finish coat may be either portland cement plaster or acrylic, typically 1/8-in. thick. Portland cement-based finish coats are likely to be more durable, but acrylic finish coats generally have better color consistency. Factory mixed finish coat mixes improve the color consistency of cement-based finish coats.

NOTES

2.273 a. Check perm rating of insulation to determine whether additional vapor retarder is required.
b. Assembly where the panel sits on top of the floor joist is easier to construct but is less energy efficient than the method indicated in Figure 2.274.
2.274 Assembly where the panel adjacent to joist is more energy efficient, but more difficult to construct than method indicated in Figure 2.273.

Contributor:
Richard J. Vitullo, AIA, Oak Leaf Studio, Crownsville, Maryland.

LATH/ACCESSORIES:

Lath is typically expanded metal or welded wire mesh of galvanized steel. Self-furring lath has crimps or dimples to space it off the substrate, allowing proper embedment of the stucco. Lath is available with a paper backing, but this should be avoided, because it is extremely difficult to create laps in the paper to properly control the flow of water.

Accessories should be formed from rust-resistant materials. Zinc is preferred, but depending on the application and conditions, galvanized steel may be acceptable. Plastic accessories are also available. All accessories that are used at the base of the system (such as edge screeds, control joints, and expansion joints) must be perforated to allow drainage of water from within the stucco.

WEATHER BARRIER

Stucco requires a weather barrier behind the lath to control the penetration of water. The paper must be continuous and properly shingled over each sheet and accessories, to direct the flow of water. The weather barrier gets wet during application of the stucco and, after drying, pulls away from stucco, creating the drainage plane.

HEAT, AIR, AND MOISTURE

Stucco should be applied over a weather barrier to create a drainage plane wall assembly. Stucco applied directly to CMU or concrete, which functions as a barrier system, should be limited to very dry climates. The performance of stucco assemblies can be upgraded by detailing the wall as a drainage cavity with insulation.

WALL ASSEMBLIES

Wall assemblies fall into five categories:

- *Stucco on CMU*: Limit the use of this assembly to very dry climates. Insulation needs to be added within the CMU cores or applied to the inside surface. (Refer to the analysis for single wythe masonry.)
- *Stucco on studs*: Application of stucco over open studs is possible, but not recommended, as proper installation of the weather barrier is very difficult. Without a backup, it is difficult to maintain a consistent thickness of the stucco, resulting in increased cracking. A reasonable amount of moisture will be introduced into insulation in the stud space, so drying of the entire assembly must be analyzed. The location or need of a vapor retarder must be analyzed to allow for drying. The interior gypsum board will need to be detailed as a continuous weather barrier.
- *Stucco on sheathing*: In this assembly, the sheathing provides for a better substrate for both the weather barrier and the stucco, resulting in improved performance of the drainage plane; moreover, the sheathing can be appropriately detailed as the weather barrier. Insulation in the stud space is susceptible to wetting and must be analyzed for moisture accumulation. The location or need of a vapor retarder must be analyzed to also allow for drying. In hot climates, the weather barrier can be changed to a weather barrier for improved performance.
- *Stucco on board insulation*: Moving the insulation to the outside of the sheathing allows for the installation of a continuous weather barrier, and improves performance of the drainage plane. Wetting of insulation within the stud space is eliminated, so this assembly is more appropriate for colder and wetter climates.
- *Stucco on furring*: Spacing the stucco away from the insulation creates a drainage cavity and improves the performance of the system. However, because a solid layer does not continuously back the lath, it is difficult to maintain consistent thickness of the stucco. Paper-faced lath is helpful.

STUCCO ON CMU
2.275

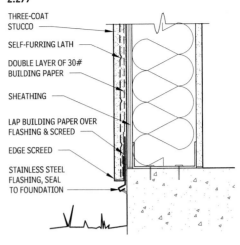

TWO-COAT STUCCO DIRECT TO CMU

DRIP EDGE SCREED

STUCCO ON STUDS
2.276

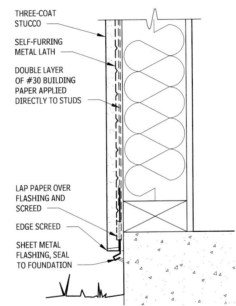

THREE-COAT STUCCO

SELF-FURRING METAL LATH

DOUBLE LAYER OF #30 BUILDING PAPER APPLIED DIRECTLY TO STUDS

LAP PAPER OVER FLASHING AND SCREED

EDGE SCREED

SHEET METAL FLASHING, SEAL TO FOUNDATION

PORTLAND CEMENT STUCCO ON SHEATHING
2.277

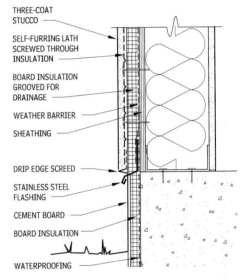

THREE-COAT STUCCO

SELF-FURRING LATH

DOUBLE LAYER OF 30# BUILDING PAPER

SHEATHING

LAP BUILDING PAPER OVER FLASHING & SCREED

EDGE SCREED

STAINLESS STEEL FLASHING, SEAL TO FOUNDATION

PORTLAND CEMENT STUCCO ON BOARD INSULATION
2.278

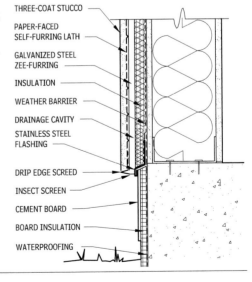

THREE-COAT STUCCO

SELF-FURRING LATH SCREWED THROUGH INSULATION

BOARD INSULATION GROOVED FOR DRAINAGE

WEATHER BARRIER

SHEATHING

DRIP EDGE SCREED

STAINLESS STEEL FLASHING

CEMENT BOARD

BOARD INSULATION

WATERPROOFING

PORTLAND CEMENT STUCCO ON FURRING
2.279

THREE-COAT STUCCO

PAPER-FACED SELF-FURRING LATH

GALVANIZED STEEL ZEE-FURRING

INSULATION

WEATHER BARRIER

DRAINAGE CAVITY

STAINLESS STEEL FLASHING

DRIP EDGE SCREED

INSECT SCREEN

CEMENT BOARD

BOARD INSULATION

WATERPROOFING

NOTES

2.275 Not recommended for use in wet climates.
2.276 Not recommended for use in wet climates.

SIDING

PLYWOOD SIDING PRODUCTS

The types of plywood recommended for exterior siding are APA grade trademarked, medium-density overlay (MDO), Type 303 siding; or Texture 1-11 (T1-11 special 303 siding). T1-11 plywood siding is manufactured with 3/8-in.-wide parallel grooves and shiplapped edges. MDO, which is recommended for paint finishes, is available in a variety of surfaces. The 303 plywood panels are also available in a wide variety of surfaces. The most common APA plywood siding panel dimensions are 4 by 8 ft, but the panels are also available in 9- and 10-ft lengths, with lap siding to 16 ft.

MINERAL-FIBER-REINFORCED CEMENTITIOUS PANELS

These panels, typically 5/16-in. thick, are available smooth or with a texture and factory finished or primed. Cement panels are extremely resistant to damage from moisture and come with warranties up to 50 years.

WOOD-FIBER PANELS

Hardboard, fiberboard, and other engineered cellulose-based products are available.

PLYWOOD SIDING—TYPES AND PROFILES
2.280

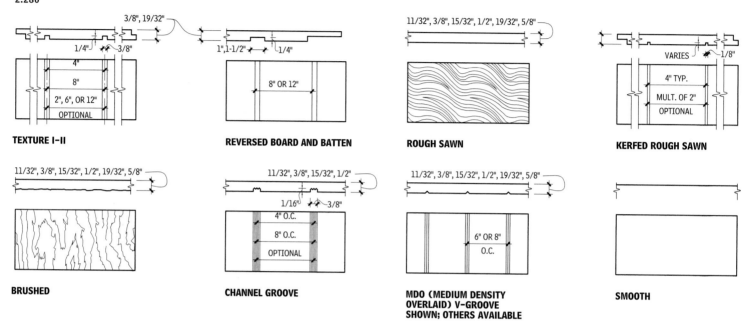

TEXTURE I–II

REVERSED BOARD AND BATTEN

ROUGH SAWN

KERFED ROUGH SAWN

BRUSHED

CHANNEL GROOVE

MDO (MEDIUM DENSITY OVERLAID) V-GROOVE SHOWN; OTHERS AVAILABLE

SMOOTH

PANEL SIDING – VERTICAL APPLICATION
2.281

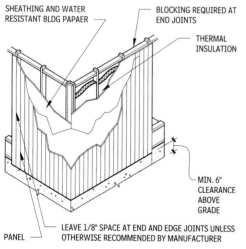

SHEATHING AND WATER RESISTANT BLDG PAPAER

BLOCKING REQUIRED AT END JOINTS

THERMAL INSULATION

MIN. 6" CLEARANCE ABOVE GRADE

PANEL

LEAVE 1/8" SPACE AT END AND EDGE JOINTS UNLESS OTHERWISE RECOMMENDED BY MANUFACTURER

LAP SIDING APPLICATION
2.282

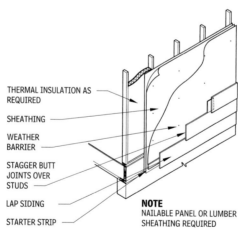

THERMAL INSULATION AS REQUIRED

SHEATHING

WEATHER BARRIER

STAGGER BUTT JOINTS OVER STUDS

LAP SIDING

STARTER STRIP

NOTE
NAILABLE PANEL OR LUMBER SHEATHING REQUIRED

PANEL SIDING – HORIZONTAL
2.283

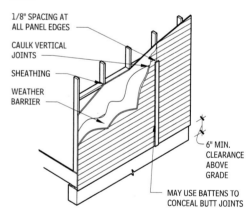

1/8" SPACING AT ALL PANEL EDGES

CAULK VERTICAL JOINTS

SHEATHING

WEATHER BARRIER

6" MIN. CLEARANCE ABOVE GRADE

MAY USE BATTENS TO CONCEAL BUTT JOINTS

NOTE

2.282 Nailable panel or lumber sheathing is required.

Contributors:
BSB Design, Des Moines, Iowa; APA–Engineered Wood Association, Tacoma, Washington.

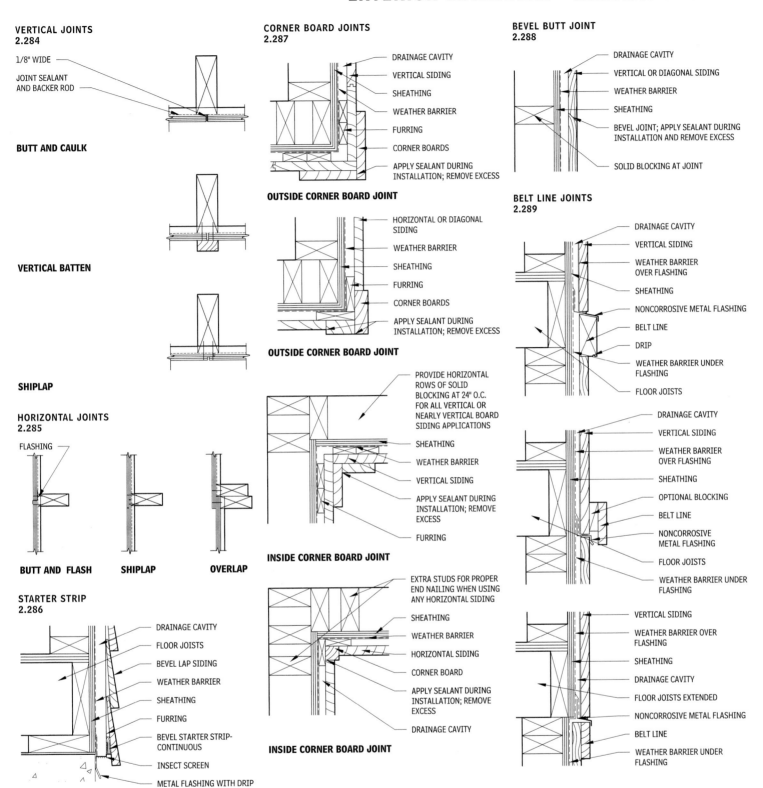

VERTICAL JOINTS
2.284

1/8" WIDE

JOINT SEALANT
AND BACKER ROD

BUTT AND CAULK

VERTICAL BATTEN

SHIPLAP

HORIZONTAL JOINTS
2.285

FLASHING

BUTT AND FLASH   **SHIPLAP**   **OVERLAP**

STARTER STRIP
2.286

DRAINAGE CAVITY
FLOOR JOISTS
BEVEL LAP SIDING
WEATHER BARRIER
SHEATHING
FURRING
BEVEL STARTER STRIP-
CONTINUOUS
INSECT SCREEN
METAL FLASHING WITH DRIP

CORNER BOARD JOINTS
2.287

DRAINAGE CAVITY
VERTICAL SIDING
SHEATHING
WEATHER BARRIER
FURRING
CORNER BOARDS
APPLY SEALANT DURING
INSTALLATION; REMOVE EXCESS

OUTSIDE CORNER BOARD JOINT

HORIZONTAL OR DIAGONAL
SIDING
WEATHER BARRIER
SHEATHING
FURRING
CORNER BOARDS
APPLY SEALANT DURING
INSTALLATION; REMOVE EXCESS

OUTSIDE CORNER BOARD JOINT

PROVIDE HORIZONTAL
ROWS OF SOLID
BLOCKING AT 24" O.C.
FOR ALL VERTICAL OR
NEARLY VERTICAL BOARD
SIDING APPLICATIONS
SHEATHING
WEATHER BARRIER
VERTICAL SIDING
APPLY SEALANT DURING
INSTALLATION; REMOVE
EXCESS
FURRING

INSIDE CORNER BOARD JOINT

EXTRA STUDS FOR PROPER
END NAILING WHEN USING
ANY HORIZONTAL SIDING
SHEATHING
WEATHER BARRIER
HORIZONTAL SIDING
CORNER BOARD
APPLY SEALANT DURING
INSTALLATION; REMOVE
EXCESS
DRAINAGE CAVITY

INSIDE CORNER BOARD JOINT

BEVEL BUTT JOINT
2.288

DRAINAGE CAVITY
VERTICAL OR DIAGONAL SIDING
WEATHER BARRIER
SHEATHING
BEVEL JOINT; APPLY SEALANT DURING
INSTALLATION AND REMOVE EXCESS
SOLID BLOCKING AT JOINT

BELT LINE JOINTS
2.289

DRAINAGE CAVITY
VERTICAL SIDING
WEATHER BARRIER
OVER FLASHING
SHEATHING
NONCORROSIVE METAL FLASHING
BELT LINE
DRIP
WEATHER BARRIER UNDER
FLASHING
FLOOR JOISTS

DRAINAGE CAVITY
VERTICAL SIDING
WEATHER BARRIER
OVER FLASHING
SHEATHING
OPTIONAL BLOCKING
BELT LINE
NONCORROSIVE
METAL FLASHING
FLOOR JOISTS
WEATHER BARRIER UNDER
FLASHING

VERTICAL SIDING
WEATHER BARRIER OVER
FLASHING
SHEATHING
DRAINAGE CAVITY
FLOOR JOISTS EXTENDED
NONCORROSIVE METAL FLASHING
BELT LINE
WEATHER BARRIER UNDER
FLASHING

NOTE

2.288 A similar detail with square cuts would apply to vertical joints in bevel lap siding.
2.284–2.289 Typically preferred to detail either the sheathing or the weather barrier to function as the air barrier. Alternatively, or additionally, the interior gypsum board may be detailed as an air barrier.

Contributors:
Reshema Holla, University of Pennsylvania; BSB Design, Des Moines, Iowa; APA–Engineered Wood Association, Tacoma, Washington; Gerald D. Graham, CTA Architects Engineers, Billings, Montana.

PLAIN BEVEL
2.290

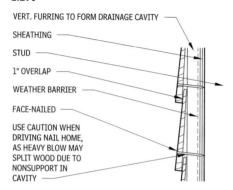

VERT. FURRING TO FORM DRAINAGE CAVITY

SHEATHING

STUD

1" OVERLAP

WEATHER BARRIER

FACE-NAILED

USE CAUTION WHEN
DRIVING NAIL HOME,
AS HEAVY BLOW MAY
SPLIT WOOD DUE TO
NONSUPPORT IN
CAVITY

TONGUE-AND-GROOVE (VERTICAL OR HORIZONTAL)
2.291

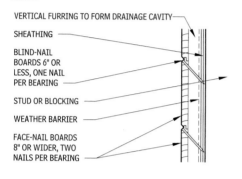

VERTICAL FURRING TO FORM DRAINAGE CAVITY

SHEATHING

BLIND-NAIL
BOARDS 6" OR
LESS, ONE NAIL
PER BEARING

STUD OR BLOCKING

WEATHER BARRIER

FACE-NAIL BOARDS
8" OR WIDER, TWO
NAILS PER BEARING

RABBETED BEVEL
2.292

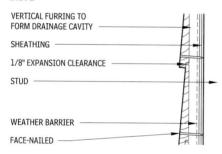

VERTICAL FURRING TO
FORM DRAINAGE CAVITY

SHEATHING

1/8" EXPANSION CLEARANCE

STUD

WEATHER BARRIER

FACE-NAILED

CHANNEL (VERTICAL)
2.293

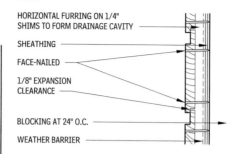

HORIZONTAL FURRING ON 1/4"
SHIMS TO FORM DRAINAGE CAVITY

SHEATHING

FACE-NAILED

1/8" EXPANSION
CLEARANCE

BLOCKING AT 24" O.C.

WEATHER BARRIER

SHIPLAP (VERTICAL OR HORIZONTAL)
2.294

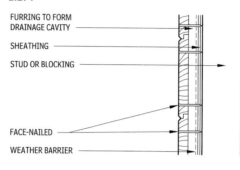

FURRING TO FORM
DRAINAGE CAVITY

SHEATHING

STUD OR BLOCKING

FACE-NAILED

WEATHER BARRIER

BOARD AND BATTEN (VERTICAL)
2.295

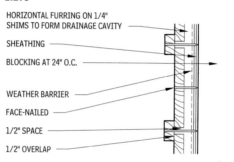

HORIZONTAL FURRING ON 1/4"
SHIMS TO FORM DRAINAGE CAVITY

SHEATHING

BLOCKING AT 24" O.C.

WEATHER BARRIER

FACE-NAILED

1/2" SPACE

1/2" OVERLAP

STONE PANELS
STONE PANELS ON STEEL FRAMING

Detailing stone panels wall assemblies is important; consider the
following recommendations:

- Because of the cost and weight of stone, a highly reliable back-
up and support system is recommended.
- Provide a continuous weather barrier over face of the sheathing.
- Insulation is located in the cavity, not in the stud space.
- CMU may be used for backup, instead of studs and sheathing.
- Bolt anchors to steel studs.
- Design considerations for bearing and retaining anchors
include: width of cavity, adjustability of slotted connections, shim
systems, avoidance of down-turned slots, and minimum thick-
ness between anchor slot and face of stone

NOTES

2.290–2.295 Typically preferred to detail either the sheathing or the
weather barrier to function as the air barrier. Alternatively, or additionally,
the interior gypsum board may be detailed as an air barrier.

Contributors:
Reshema Holla, University of Pennsylvania; Gerald D. Graham, CTA
Architects Engineers, Billings, Montana.

STONE PANEL SECTIONS AT ROOF PARAPET
2.296

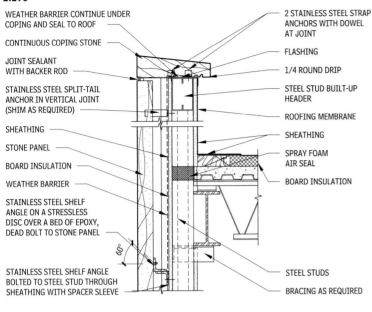
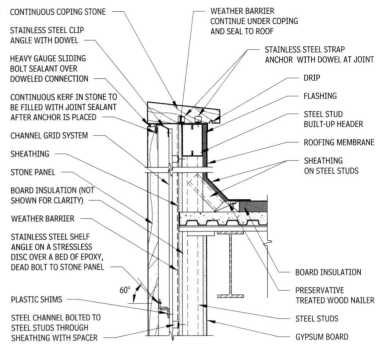

Left detail labels (left side):
- WEATHER BARRIER CONTINUE UNDER COPING AND SEAL TO ROOF
- CONTINUOUS COPING STONE
- JOINT SEALANT WITH BACKER ROD
- STAINLESS STEEL SPLIT-TAIL ANCHOR IN VERTICAL JOINT (SHIM AS REQUIRED)
- SHEATHING
- STONE PANEL
- BOARD INSULATION
- WEATHER BARRIER
- STAINLESS STEEL SHELF ANGLE ON A STRESSLESS DISC OVER A BED OF EPOXY, DEAD BOLT TO STONE PANEL
- STAINLESS STEEL SHELF ANGLE BOLTED TO STEEL STUD THROUGH SHEATHING WITH SPACER SLEEVE
- 60°

Left detail labels (right side):
- 2 STAINLESS STEEL STRAP ANCHORS WITH DOWEL AT JOINT
- FLASHING
- 1/4 ROUND DRIP
- STEEL STUD BUILT-UP HEADER
- ROOFING MEMBRANE
- SHEATHING
- SPRAY FOAM AIR SEAL
- BOARD INSULATION
- STEEL STUDS
- BRACING AS REQUIRED

Right detail labels (left side):
- CONTINUOUS COPING STONE
- STAINLESS STEEL CLIP ANGLE WITH DOWEL
- HEAVY GAUGE SLIDING BOLT SEALANT OVER DOWELED CONNECTION
- CONTINUOUS KERF IN STONE TO BE FILLED WITH JOINT SEALANT AFTER ANCHOR IS PLACED
- CHANNEL GRID SYSTEM
- SHEATHING
- STONE PANEL
- BOARD INSULATION (NOT SHOWN FOR CLARITY)
- WEATHER BARRIER
- STAINLESS STEEL SHELF ANGLE ON A STRESSLESS DISC OVER A BED OF EPOXY, DEAD BOLT TO STONE PANEL
- PLASTIC SHIMS
- STEEL CHANNEL BOLTED TO STEEL STUDS THROUGH SHEATHING WITH SPACER
- 60°

Right detail labels (right side):
- WEATHER BARRIER CONTINUE UNDER COPING AND SEAL TO ROOF
- STAINLESS STEEL STRAP ANCHOR WITH DOWEL AT JOINT
- DRIP
- FLASHING
- STEEL STUD BUILT-UP HEADER
- ROOFING MEMBRANE
- SHEATHING ON STEEL STUDS
- BOARD INSULATION
- PRESERVATIVE TREATED WOOD NAILER
- STEEL STUDS
- GYPSUM BOARD

STONE SPANDREL AT WINDOW HEAD AND SILL
2.297

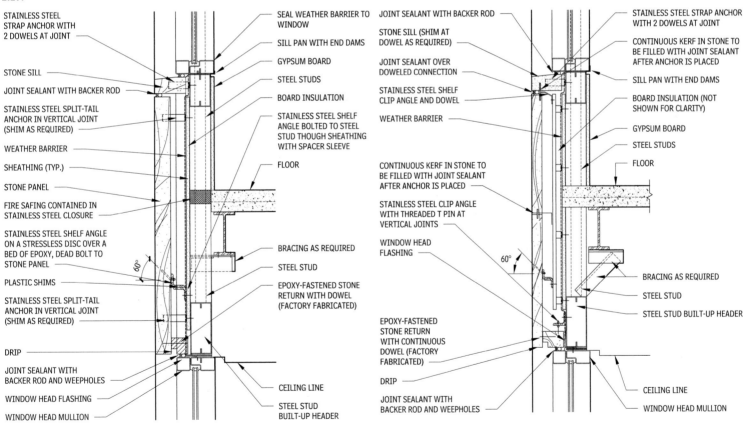

Left detail labels (left side):
- STAINLESS STEEL STRAP ANCHOR WITH 2 DOWELS AT JOINT
- STONE SILL
- JOINT SEALANT WITH BACKER ROD
- STAINLESS STEEL SPLIT-TAIL ANCHOR IN VERTICAL JOINT (SHIM AS REQUIRED)
- WEATHER BARRIER
- SHEATHING (TYP.)
- STONE PANEL
- FIRE SAFING CONTAINED IN STAINLESS STEEL CLOSURE
- STAINLESS STEEL SHELF ANGLE ON A STRESSLESS DISC OVER A BED OF EPOXY, DEAD BOLT TO STONE PANEL
- PLASTIC SHIMS
- STAINLESS STEEL SPLIT-TAIL ANCHOR IN VERTICAL JOINT (SHIM AS REQUIRED)
- DRIP
- JOINT SEALANT WITH BACKER ROD AND WEEPHOLES
- WINDOW HEAD FLASHING
- WINDOW HEAD MULLION
- 60°

Left detail labels (right side):
- SEAL WEATHER BARRIER TO WINDOW
- SILL PAN WITH END DAMS
- GYPSUM BOARD
- STEEL STUDS
- BOARD INSULATION
- STAINLESS STEEL SHELF ANGLE BOLTED TO STEEL STUD THROUGH SHEATHING WITH SPACER SLEEVE
- FLOOR
- BRACING AS REQUIRED
- STEEL STUD
- EPOXY-FASTENED STONE RETURN WITH DOWEL (FACTORY FABRICATED)
- CEILING LINE
- STEEL STUD BUILT-UP HEADER

Right detail labels (left side):
- JOINT SEALANT WITH BACKER ROD
- STONE SILL (SHIM AT DOWEL AS REQUIRED)
- JOINT SEALANT OVER DOWELED CONNECTION
- STAINLESS STEEL SHELF CLIP ANGLE AND DOWEL
- WEATHER BARRIER
- CONTINUOUS KERF IN STONE TO BE FILLED WITH JOINT SEALANT AFTER ANCHOR IS PLACED
- STAINLESS STEEL CLIP ANGLE WITH THREADED T PIN AT VERTICAL JOINTS
- WINDOW HEAD FLASHING
- EPOXY-FASTENED STONE RETURN WITH CONTINUOUS DOWEL (FACTORY FABRICATED)
- DRIP
- JOINT SEALANT WITH BACKER ROD AND WEEPHOLES
- 60°

Right detail labels (right side):
- STAINLESS STEEL STRAP ANCHOR WITH 2 DOWELS AT JOINT
- CONTINUOUS KERF IN STONE TO BE FILLED WITH JOINT SEALANT AFTER ANCHOR IS PLACED
- SILL PAN WITH END DAMS
- BOARD INSULATION (NOT SHOWN FOR CLARITY)
- GYPSUM BOARD
- STEEL STUDS
- FLOOR
- BRACING AS REQUIRED
- STEEL STUD
- STEEL STUD BUILT-UP HEADER
- CEILING LINE
- WINDOW HEAD MULLION

NOTES

2.296 Fireproofing of steel has been omitted for clarity.
2.296 and 2.297 Typically preferred to detail either the sheathing or the weather barrier to function as the air barrier.

Contributor:
The Spector Group, North Hills, New York.

STONE SPANDREL AT FOUNDATION
2.298

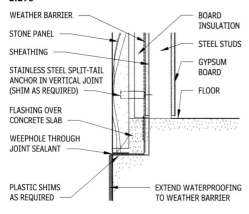

Labels (left diagram):
- WEATHER BARRIER
- STONE PANEL
- SHEATHING
- STAINLESS STEEL SPLIT-TAIL ANCHOR IN VERTICAL JOINT (SHIM AS REQUIRED)
- FLASHING OVER CONCRETE SLAB
- WEEPHOLE THROUGH JOINT SEALANT
- PLASTIC SHIMS AS REQUIRED
- BOARD INSULATION
- STEEL STUDS
- GYPSUM BOARD
- FLOOR
- EXTEND WATERPROOFING TO WEATHER BARRIER

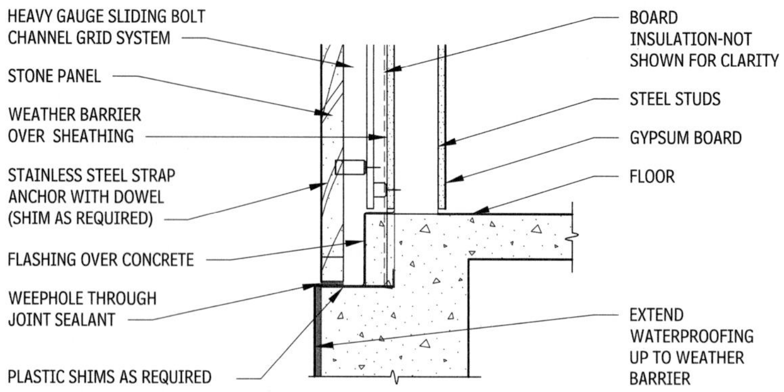

Labels (right diagram):
- HEAVY GAUGE SLIDING BOLT CHANNEL GRID SYSTEM
- STONE PANEL
- WEATHER BARRIER OVER SHEATHING
- STAINLESS STEEL STRAP ANCHOR WITH DOWEL (SHIM AS REQUIRED)
- FLASHING OVER CONCRETE
- WEEPHOLE THROUGH JOINT SEALANT
- PLASTIC SHIMS AS REQUIRED
- BOARD INSULATION-NOT SHOWN FOR CLARITY
- STEEL STUDS
- GYPSUM BOARD
- FLOOR
- EXTEND WATERPROOFING UP TO WEATHER BARRIER

FABRICATED STONE PANELS

Fabricated stone panel technology offers savings in on-site labor and accuracy of component stone unit joining.

Shipping and erection stresses on the stone panels and stone anchorage system of the fabricated units should be evaluated.

Design of sealant joints between fabricated units should include at least the following:

- Thermal movement
- Fabrication and erection tolerances
- Irreversible material growth or shrinkage
- Sealant movement potential

STONE ON STEEL FRAME WITH EPOXY JOINTS

Stone panels are mounted in a steel frame, with expansion anchors and dowel pins (as recommended by the fabricator). Joints between the panels are sealed with epoxy, maintaining a gap of approximately 1/8 in. Stone panels in the assembly are anchored as a unit to the building structure. Fabricated stone panel installation reduces individual leveling, plumbing, and aligning, and on-site joint sealing is not as extensive as with individual stone panels.

FABRICATED STONE PANELS
2.299

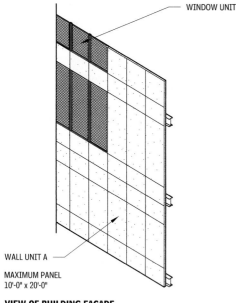

- WINDOW UNIT
- WALL UNIT A
- MAXIMUM PANEL 10'-0" x 20'-0"

VIEW OF BUILDING FACADE

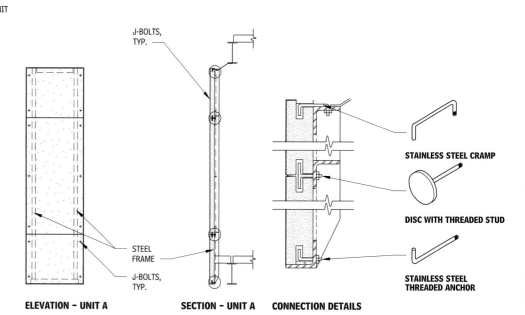

Labels:
- J-BOLTS, TYP.
- STEEL FRAME
- J-BOLTS, TYP.
- STAINLESS STEEL CRAMP
- DISC WITH THREADED STUD
- STAINLESS STEEL THREADED ANCHOR

ELEVATION – UNIT A   **SECTION – UNIT A**   **CONNECTION DETAILS**

Contributors:
The Spector Group, North Hills, Neww York; George M. Whiteside, III, AIA, and James D. Lloyd, Kennett Square, Pennsylvania; Building Stone Institute, New York City, New York; Alexander Keyes, Rippeteau Architects, PC, Washington, DC.

UNITIZED RAINSCREEN PANELS
2.300

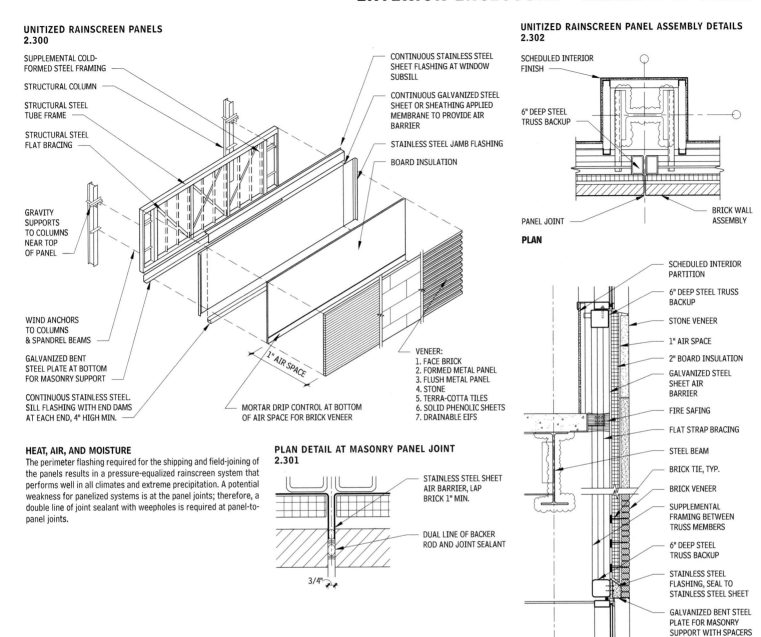

SUPPLEMENTAL COLD-FORMED STEEL FRAMING

STRUCTURAL COLUMN

STRUCTURAL STEEL TUBE FRAME

STRUCTURAL STEEL FLAT BRACING

GRAVITY SUPPORTS TO COLUMNS NEAR TOP OF PANEL

WIND ANCHORS TO COLUMNS & SPANDREL BEAMS

GALVANIZED BENT STEEL PLATE AT BOTTOM FOR MASONRY SUPPORT

CONTINUOUS STAINLESS STEEL. SILL FLASHING WITH END DAMS AT EACH END, 4" HIGH MIN.

CONTINUOUS STAINLESS STEEL SHEET FLASHING AT WINDOW SUBSILL

CONTINUOUS GALVANIZED STEEL SHEET OR SHEATHING APPLIED MEMBRANE TO PROVIDE AIR BARRIER

STAINLESS STEEL JAMB FLASHING

BOARD INSULATION

1" AIR SPACE

MORTAR DRIP CONTROL AT BOTTOM OF AIR SPACE FOR BRICK VENEER

VENEER:
1. FACE BRICK
2. FORMED METAL PANEL
3. FLUSH METAL PANEL
4. STONE
5. TERRA-COTTA TILES
6. SOLID PHENOLIC SHEETS
7. DRAINABLE EIFS

HEAT, AIR, AND MOISTURE

The perimeter flashing required for the shipping and field-joining of the panels results in a pressure-equalized rainscreen system that performs well in all climates and extreme precipitation. A potential weakness for panelized systems is at the panel joints; therefore, a double line of joint sealant with weepholes is required at panel-to-panel joints.

PLAN DETAIL AT MASONRY PANEL JOINT
2.301

STAINLESS STEEL SHEET AIR BARRIER, LAP BRICK 1" MIN.

DUAL LINE OF BACKER ROD AND JOINT SEALANT

3/4"

UNITIZED RAINSCREEN PANEL ASSEMBLY DETAILS
2.302

SCHEDULED INTERIOR FINISH

6" DEEP STEEL TRUSS BACKUP

PANEL JOINT

BRICK WALL ASSEMBLY

PLAN

SCHEDULED INTERIOR PARTITION

6" DEEP STEEL TRUSS BACKUP

STONE VENEER

1" AIR SPACE

2" BOARD INSULATION

GALVANIZED STEEL SHEET AIR BARRIER

FIRE SAFING

FLAT STRAP BRACING

STEEL BEAM

BRICK TIE, TYP.

BRICK VENEER

SUPPLEMENTAL FRAMING BETWEEN TRUSS MEMBERS

6" DEEP STEEL TRUSS BACKUP

STAINLESS STEEL FLASHING, SEAL TO STAINLESS STEEL SHEET

GALVANIZED BENT STEEL PLATE FOR MASONRY SUPPORT WITH SPACERS 24" O.C., FILL VOID WITH FORMED-IN-PLACE INSULATION

SECTION

Contributors:
Rich Cianfrini, AIA, and Dan Swiegart, Kling, Philadelphia, Pennsylvania.

INSULATED METAL PANEL WALL ASSEMBLIES

Metal wall panels fall into two primary categories: field-assembled and factory-formed. Metal wall panels span between 4 and 15 ft, depending on gauge of metal, panel thickness, and wind load. Finish on metal panels can be raw galvanized sheet or any number of various factory-applied finishes. ranging from baked-on enamel to high-performance polyvinyldene flouride (PVDF) coatings.

FIELD-ASSEMBLED PANELS

The order of assembly for these panels is as follows:

1. Metal liner panels are secured to structural girts with self-drilling, self-tapping screws. Liner panels are typically 24 in. wide. The depth of the liner panel is determined by required insulation (2 to 4 in.).
2. Semirigid mineral wool insulation located on the inside liner panel.
3. Subgirts are screwed to liner panel flanges.
4. Outer metal panels are screwed to subgirts. Outer panels can be corrugated, standing seam, batten, or formed into box shapes. Fasteners that are typically exposed, but concealed fasteners are available.

FIELD-ASSEMBLED WALL PANELS
2.304

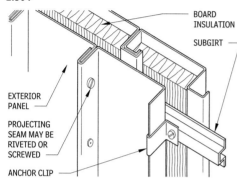

BOARD INSULATION
SUBGIRT
EXTERIOR PANEL
PROJECTING SEAM MAY BE RIVETED OR SCREWED
ANCHOR CLIP

TYPICAL INSULATED

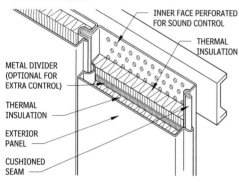

INNER FACE PERFORATED FOR SOUND CONTROL
THERMAL INSULATION
METAL DIVIDER (OPTIONAL FOR EXTRA CONTROL)
THERMAL INSULATION
EXTERIOR PANEL
CUSHIONED SEAM

ACOUSTICAL

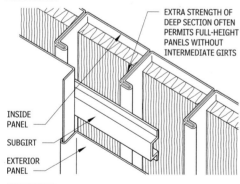

EXTRA STRENGTH OF DEEP SECTION OFTEN PERMITS FULL-HEIGHT PANELS WITHOUT INTERMEDIATE GIRTS
INSIDE PANEL
SUBGIRT
EXTERIOR PANEL

EXTRARIGID

METAL PANEL WALL SECTIONS
2.303

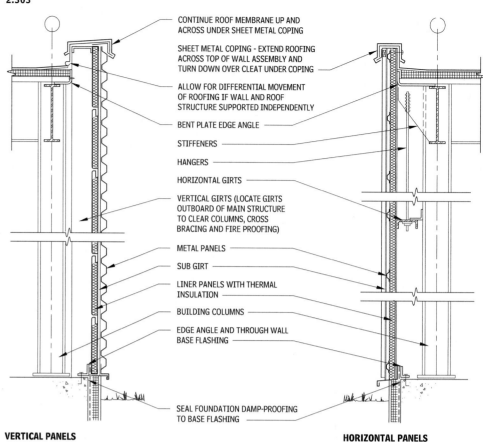

CONTINUE ROOF MEMBRANE UP AND ACROSS UNDER SHEET METAL COPING
SHEET METAL COPING - EXTEND ROOFING ACROSS TOP OF WALL ASSEMBLY AND TURN DOWN OVER CLEAT UNDER COPING
ALLOW FOR DIFFERENTIAL MOVEMENT OF ROOFING IF WALL AND ROOF STRUCTURE SUPPORTED INDEPENDENTLY
BENT PLATE EDGE ANGLE
STIFFENERS
HANGERS
HORIZONTAL GIRTS
VERTICAL GIRTS (LOCATE GIRTS OUTBOARD OF MAIN STRUCTURE TO CLEAR COLUMNS, CROSS BRACING AND FIRE PROOFING)
METAL PANELS
SUB GIRT
LINER PANELS WITH THERMAL INSULATION
BUILDING COLUMNS
EDGE ANGLE AND THROUGH WALL BASE FLASHING
SEAL FOUNDATION DAMP-PROOFING TO BASE FLASHING

VERTICAL PANELS

HORIZONTAL PANELS

FACTORY-FORMED METAL PANELS

Panels are typically between 24 and 36 in wide, up to 40 ft long, and between 2 and 4 in. thick. Panels are fabricated either by laminating inner and outer sheet metal skins to rigid insulation or by injecting expanding foam between the two skins. Panels can be oriented horizontally or vertically and are available in a large number of profiles. Horizontally oriented panels provide rainscreen design joints.

FACTORY-ASSEMBLED WALL PANEL
2.305

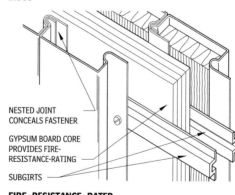

NESTED JOINT CONCEALS FASTENER
GYPSUM BOARD CORE PROVIDES FIRE-RESISTANCE-RATING
SUBGIRTS

FIRE-RESISTANCE-RATED

FACTORY-FORMED INSULATED METAL PANELS
2.306

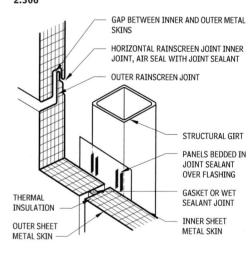

GAP BETWEEN INNER AND OUTER METAL SKINS
HORIZONTAL RAINSCREEN JOINT INNER JOINT, AIR SEAL WITH JOINT SEALANT
OUTER RAINSCREEN JOINT
STRUCTURAL GIRT
PANELS BEDDED IN JOINT SEALANT OVER FLASHING
GASKET OR WET SEALANT JOINT
INNER SHEET METAL SKIN
THERMAL INSULATION
OUTER SHEET METAL SKIN

Contributor:
Eric K. Beach, Rippeteau Architects, PC, Washington, DC.

HEAT, AIR, AND MOISTURE

Field-assembled insulated metal panels are drainage-cavity-type walls. Water that may penetrate the outer skin is weeped to the outside by through-wall flashing. Factory-foamed panels are available with pressure-equalized rainscreen-type joints or shingled overlap joints. For both types of systems, the inner sheet metal skin functions as the air barrier and must be sealed to make the system perform. Most panels accomplish this with a factory-installed gasket or bead of noncuring sealant inside of the receiving groove that is then compressed by the tongue during installation. Relatively slight misalignment of panels will not provide the proper compression of this inside seal, resulting in a large air leak and loss of function of the rainscreen joint. Joints across the short direction of the panel cannot be fabricated with the tongue and groove. Typically, the joints are backed up with girts or flashing, and the panels are bedded in sealant and an outer wet seal or dry gasket is added.

METAL WALL PANELS

Metal wall panels are made in a wide variety of shapes, sizes, etc.. However, if properly designed as part of a drained cavity wall or drainage plane wall, all of them can perform well. Most of the panels, except interlocking tiles, can span several feet over a spaced support system.

Following is a list of cladding panel types:

- *Formed sheet metal*: Made up of aluminum, galvanized steel, and, less commonly, stainless steel, zinc, or copper, these panels are formed into corrugated, standing seam, batten, or box shapes with exposed or concealed fasteners.
- *Aluminum composite material (ACM)*: These types of panels con-

sist of two gauge metal layers of aluminum bonded to a rigid plastic core. These panels are very flat and easily fabricated into a variety of configurations and mounting methods.

- *Plate*: Typically made up of 1/8 in. thick solid aluminum or stainless steel, this panel is stretcher leveled and fabricated with folded back perimeter frames.
- *Interlocking flat lock seam tiles*: These panels are made from light-gauge copper, zinc, lead-coated copper, titanium, and stainless steel; they are shop formed into small interlocking tiles for installation over a continuous substrate.
- *ACM and plate systems*: A wide variety of proprietary mounting methods for large-scale architectural panels are available, with associated pros and cons.
- *Staggered clip mounting*: Clips around the perimeter of the panels are spaced so that clips of adjacent panels do not overlap. ACM and plate systems can be formed for this mounting system, with wet sealant joints or dry gaskets. The primary advantage of this system is that it allows for nonsequential erection and repair of isolated panels without disturbing the remainder of the field.
- *Tongue-and-groove clip mounting*: Perimeter panel extrusions are supported by spaced tongue-and-groove type clips. Each clip supports the gravity load of only one panel while restraining the other panel against wind and allowing movement. Joints can be wet sealed or dry gasketed but are more commonly dry-splined with the same material as the panel fitting into the perimeter extrusion, though the spline can be the same or a contrasting finish. While requiring sequential erection, this system provides for less oil-canning of the panel and better joint alignment.
- *Hook-and-pin mounting*: This is the most common plate system; each panel has hooks in the vertical edge that engage pins in vertical channels mounted to the support grid. The horizontal joints include a shingled overlapping joint that directs water to

the vertical channel. Fabrication costs tend to make this system more expensive, but the free movement for flatness and nonsequential erection are positives.

- *Route and return*: Route and return is a method to fold ACM, and sometimes plates, to a very tight corner. A V-groove is routed out of the back of the panel, leaving only the thin outer skin intact, and then the edges are folded (or returned). Perimeter frames may or may not be added.
- *Continuous edge grip*: ACM panels have an extremely small groove routed in the plastic interlayer around the full perimeter of the panels. Aluminum extrusions with a small tongue are glued into this groove to hold the panel. A very small edge of the perimeter extrusion is visible.
- *Wet seals*: Joint sealant and backer rod in the joints may be the least expensive option to finish joints, but typically, they are not required for weather-tightness and can result in a loss of crisp shadow lines. The joint sealant may attract dirt and cause staining of the panels.
- *Dry gasketed joints*: Soft silicone, EPDM, or neoprene extruded gaskets provide a neater joint, easier future access to fasteners under the joint, and good weather performance.
- *Dry splined joints*: Joints splined with ACM or plates may provide the sharpest corners and cleanest edges.
- *Open joint systems*: These panel systems consist of baffles and shingled flashing for pressure-equalized rainscreen systems.
- *Finishes*: Some metals have inherent finishes such as zinc, copper, and galvanized steel. Most metals require applied finishes that include anodized, color anodized, polyvinylidene fluoride (PVDF), baked-on enamels, powder coatings, and many others. PVDF coatings have become very common because of their wide range of colors and metallic finishes, extreme durability, and color consistency.

FLATLOCK METAL PANEL WALL ASSEMBLIES
2.307

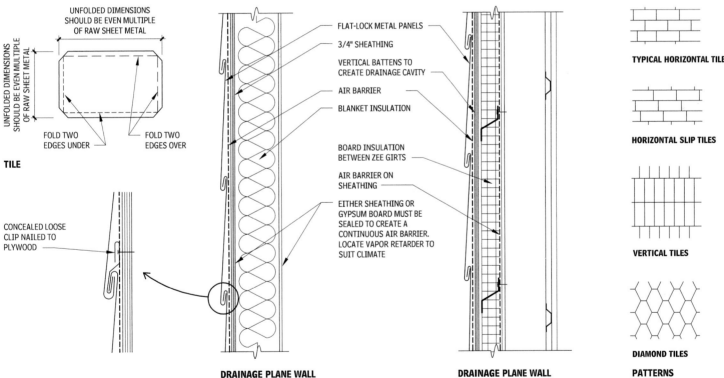

UNFOLDED DIMENSIONS SHOULD BE EVEN MULTIPLE OF RAW SHEET METAL

UNFOLDED DIMENSIONS SHOULD BE EVEN MULTIPLE OF RAW SHEET METAL

FOLD TWO EDGES UNDER

FOLD TWO EDGES OVER

TILE

CONCEALED LOOSE CLIP NAILED TO PLYWOOD

FLAT-LOCK METAL PANELS

3/4" SHEATHING

VERTICAL BATTENS TO CREATE DRAINAGE CAVITY

AIR BARRIER

BLANKET INSULATION

BOARD INSULATION BETWEEN ZEE GIRTS

AIR BARRIER ON SHEATHING

EITHER SHEATHING OR GYPSUM BOARD MUST BE SEALED TO CREATE A CONTINUOUS AIR BARRIER. LOCATE VAPOR RETARDER TO SUIT CLIMATE

DRAINAGE PLANE WALL

DRAINAGE PLANE WALL

TYPICAL HORIZONTAL TILES

HORIZONTAL SLIP TILES

VERTICAL TILES

DIAMOND TILES

PATTERNS

NOTE

2.307 Exterior air barriers can help reduce wind-driven rain penetration. Interior air barriers can help reduce convection air currents in insulation in stud spaces. Consider utilizing multiple air barriers to maximize performance. Typically preferred to detail either the sheathing or the weather barrier to function as the air barrier. Alternatively or additionally, the interior gypsum may be detailed as an air barrier.

METAL WALL PANEL – DRY SPLINE JOINT
2.308

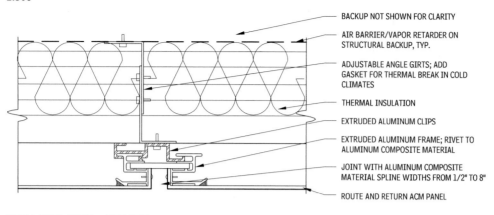

BACKUP NOT SHOWN FOR CLARITY

AIR BARRIER/VAPOR RETARDER ON STRUCTURAL BACKUP, TYP.

ADJUSTABLE ANGLE GIRTS; ADD GASKET FOR THERMAL BREAK IN COLD CLIMATES

THERMAL INSULATION

EXTRUDED ALUMINUM CLIPS

EXTRUDED ALUMINUM FRAME; RIVET TO ALUMINUM COMPOSITE MATERIAL

JOINT WITH ALUMINUM COMPOSITE MATERIAL SPLINE WIDTHS FROM 1/2" TO 8"

ROUTE AND RETURN ACM PANEL

METAL WALL PANEL – WET SEAL
2.309

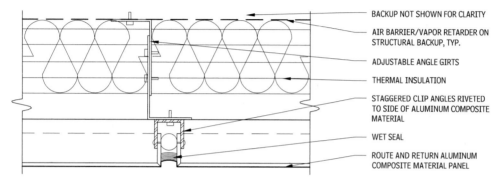

BACKUP NOT SHOWN FOR CLARITY

AIR BARRIER/VAPOR RETARDER ON STRUCTURAL BACKUP, TYP.

ADJUSTABLE ANGLE GIRTS

THERMAL INSULATION

STAGGERED CLIP ANGLES RIVETED TO SIDE OF ALUMINUM COMPOSITE MATERIAL

WET SEAL

ROUTE AND RETURN ALUMINUM COMPOSITE MATERIAL PANEL

METAL WALL PANEL – HOOK-AND-PIN
2.310

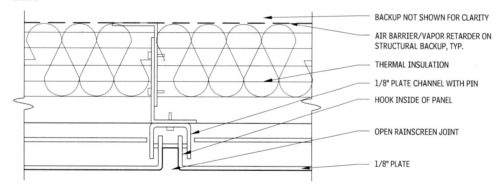

BACKUP NOT SHOWN FOR CLARITY

AIR BARRIER/VAPOR RETARDER ON STRUCTURAL BACKUP, TYP.

THERMAL INSULATION

1/8" PLATE CHANNEL WITH PIN

HOOK INSIDE OF PANEL

OPEN RAINSCREEN JOINT

1/8" PLATE

METAL WALL PANEL – DRY GASKET
2.311

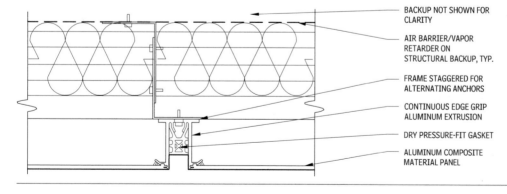

BACKUP NOT SHOWN FOR CLARITY

AIR BARRIER/VAPOR RETARDER ON STRUCTURAL BACKUP, TYP.

FRAME STAGGERED FOR ALTERNATING ANCHORS

CONTINUOUS EDGE GRIP ALUMINUM EXTRUSION

DRY PRESSURE-FIT GASKET

ALUMINUM COMPOSITE MATERIAL PANEL

DRAINAGE CAVITY WALL
2.312

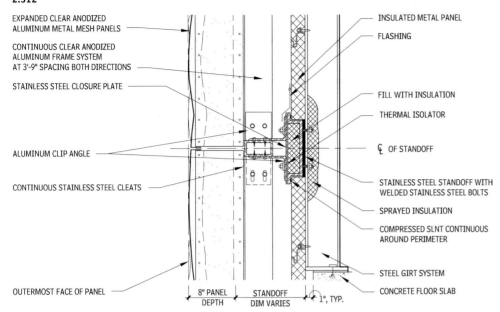

EXPANDED CLEAR ANODIZED
ALUMINUM METAL MESH PANELS

CONTINUOUS CLEAR ANODIZED
ALUMINUM FRAME SYSTEM
AT 3'-9" SPACING BOTH DIRECTIONS

STAINLESS STEEL CLOSURE PLATE

ALUMINUM CLIP ANGLE

CONTINUOUS STAINLESS STEEL CLEATS

OUTERMOST FACE OF PANEL

8" PANEL DEPTH

STANDOFF DIM VARIES

1", TYP.

INSULATED METAL PANEL

FLASHING

FILL WITH INSULATION

THERMAL ISOLATOR

℄ OF STANDOFF

STAINLESS STEEL STANDOFF WITH
WELDED STAINLESS STEEL BOLTS

SPRAYED INSULATION

COMPRESSED SLNT CONTINUOUS
AROUND PERIMETER

STEEL GIRT SYSTEM

CONCRETE FLOOR SLAB

HEAT, AIR, AND MOISTURE

None of the metal cladding panels may provide a waterproof system by themselves. In fact, many of the ACM and plate systems require an air barrier to function fully. Note that a common standard for testing performance of the panels does not exist yet. The panels should always be installed over a water-resistant substrate that allows drainage and weeping of any water that may penetrate the joints. The most dependable method is to install the panels as a drainage cavity assembly by mounting the panels on a support grid spaced away from the sheathing line with an applied air barrier/vapor retarder and insulation between the supports. Alternative systems may place some or all of the insulation inside stud cavities if proper evaluation of heat loss, vapor flow, and wetting and drying are considered. Interlocking flat lock seam tiles require a continuous nailable substrate, and, therefore, the provision of a proper drainage cavity can require multiple layers.

For high-rise or high-wind applications, the systems can be stepped up to a true pressure-equalized system by partitioning the drainage cavity behind the metal panels. Either the joint system should admit air (such as dry splines or hook and pin) or vents will be required in addition to the weeps. Joints must be designed to resist kinetic energy with sloped or vertical dams, break surface tension with drips, and eliminate capillary draw with joints at least 3/8 in. wide.

EXTERIOR INSULATION AND FINISH SYSTEMS (EIFS)

EXTERIOR INSULATION AND FINISH SYSTEM (POLYMER-BASED DRAINAGE PLANE WALL)
2.313

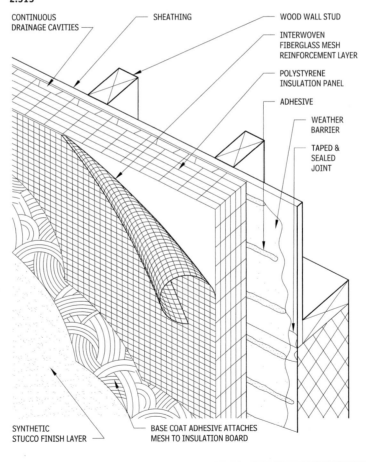

CONTINUOUS
DRAINAGE CAVITIES

SHEATHING

WOOD WALL STUD

INTERWOVEN
FIBERGLASS MESH
REINFORCEMENT LAYER

POLYSTYRENE
INSULATION PANEL

ADHESIVE

WEATHER
BARRIER

TAPED &
SEALED
JOINT

SYNTHETIC
STUCCO FINISH LAYER

BASE COAT ADHESIVE ATTACHES
MESH TO INSULATION BOARD

NOTE

2.313 Substrate and weather barrier typically are designed as air barrier.

Contributors:
HGA Architects & Engineers, Minneapolis, Minnesota; Richard J. Vitullo, AIA, Oak Leaf Studio, Crownsville, Maryland.

EIFS OVER WOOD FRAME DETAILS
2.314

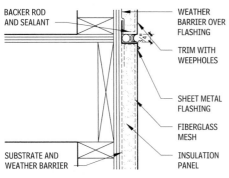

BACKER ROD AND SEALANT
WEATHER BARRIER OVER FLASHING
TRIM WITH WEEPHOLES
SHEET METAL FLASHING
FIBERGLASS MESH
SUBSTRATE AND WEATHER BARRIER
INSULATION PANEL

EXPANSION JOINT DETAIL AT FLOOR LEVEL

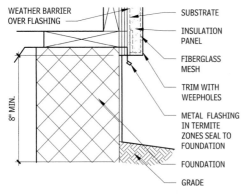

WEATHER BARRIER OVER FLASHING
SUBSTRATE
INSULATION PANEL
FIBERGLASS MESH
TRIM WITH WEEPHOLES
METAL FLASHING IN TERMITE ZONES SEAL TO FOUNDATION
FOUNDATION
GRADE
8" MIN.

DETAIL AT GRADE

EIFS OVER MASONRY DETAILS
2.315

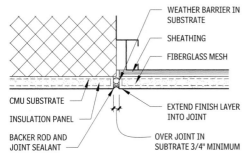

WEATHER BARRIER IN SUBSTRATE
SHEATHING
FIBERGLASS MESH
CMU SUBSTRATE
INSULATION PANEL
BACKER ROD AND JOINT SEALANT
EXTEND FINISH LAYER INTO JOINT
OVER JOINT IN SUBTRATE 3/4" MINIMUM

EXPANSION JOINT AT DISSIMILAR SUBSTRATES

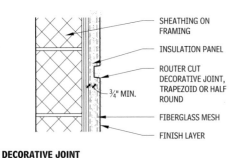

SHEATHING ON FRAMING
INSULATION PANEL
ROUTER CUT DECORATIVE JOINT, TRAPEZOID OR HALF ROUND
FIBERGLASS MESH
FINISH LAYER
3/4" MIN.

DECORATIVE JOINT

Exterior insulation and finish systems (EIFS) provide an uninterrupted layer of board insulation, mechanically fastened but more typically adhered over a water-resistive membrane to the exterior walls of the building and then covered with a very thin layer of reinforced polymer-modified cement membrane (lamina).

LAMINA
The lamina consists of a base coat, reinforcing, and a finish coat. An EIFS is categorized by the lamina, either polymer-modified (PM) or polymer-based (PB). PM systems are thicker (3/16 in. or more) and have a higher cement content resulting in a harder finish. PB systems have a much higher proportion of polymer to cement and have a total thickness less than 1/8 in.

- *Reinforcing*: Reinforcing is typically fiberglass mesh and is available in several weights. Heavier weights are used where impact resistance is required but puncture is still likely at sidewalks or other high traffic zones. It may be better to use a more durable material for the first floor or provide a wainscot.
- *Finishes*: Many colors are available in textures ranging from very smooth to medium rough. The smoothest finishes tend to telegraph more imperfections of the base coats. Some base coats now have silicone or other additives to help keep the surface clean.

INSULATION
Typically expanded polystyrene is used but extruded polystyrene or other noncombustible types may be incorporated dependent on construction classification. Insulation thickness ranges from 1 to 6 in. The insulation should be grooved or spaced away from the substrate to create a drainage plane. Mechanical fasteners are generally limited to polymer-modified (PM) systems. Polymer-based (PB) systems, especially with a weather barrier, are typically applied with adhesive. Note that while mechanical fasteners may seem to be a good safeguard, they can limit the flexibility of the PB lamina or cause ghosting.

WATER-RESISTIVE BARRIER
The substrate should be prepared with sealants, tapes, and primer to receive a water-resistive barrier membrane. The substrate and membrane together will provide an air barrier.

JOINTS
Joints in EIFS must be carefully located and detailed for their intended purpose. Aesthetic reveal joints provide for movement of the lamina and should be trapezoid or half-round shapes. V-shaped or square joints may flex and crack the lamina. Control joints should be detailed to extend completely through the system and be wide enough to allow for anticipated movement. Note that the bond of the sealant may be stronger than the bond of the finish to the base coats, so carefully select low-modulus sealant paired with proper joint width and detail joints for adhesion to base coat, not finish coat. Also, note that it is nearly impossible to properly reseal EIFS because it is very difficult to remove joint sealant from the lamina. Therefore, it is imperative to select the joint sealant and detail the joint.

HEAT, AIR, AND MOISTURE
EIFS are based on a face-sealed, thin-barrier system to resist moisture. Except for EIFS applied over CMU or concrete in structures where interior moisture control is not necessary, systems that utilize an internal drainage plane to add moisture protection are highly recommended. The location of the insulation layer fully outside the structure and supporting walls provides continuous and dependable barrier to heat loss/gain. EIFS does not breathe well; consequently, it is very important not to trap vapor within a wall assembly. Most EIFS manufacturers provide analysis of the complete wall assembly to decide whether a separate vapor barrier is necessary and if so, it's proper location. The sheathing of the typical backup wall system needs to provide the air barrier, so it must be designed continuous and detailed to meet windows, doors, penetrations and transitions to other systems. The water barrier membrane supplied with drainage plane EIFS will typically require that the joints in the sheathing be taped or sealed.

RECOMMENDATIONS FOR SUCCESSFUL EIFS
Properly installed EIFS does not allow water to penetrate the system. However, many buildings clad with EIFS have suffered from problems. From the design professional's (and, more importantly, the owner's) point of view, it is meaningless whether the problems are caused by the EIFS itself or are the result of poor construction at penetrations and transitions. Therefore, the following recommendations should be followed to increase the likelihood of a successful installation:

- Use a reputable manufacturer.
- Enlist the assistance of the manufacturer during design and detailing process
- Do not allow the installation of "accidental" vapor retarders such as vinyl wall covering.
- Ensure that all products within the system are from one manufacturer and that the manufacturer confirms compatibility and recommends use of the products in the exact configuration intended for the project.
- Ensure that the manufacturer has adequately trained and certified the installer.
- Arrange to have a manufacturer's technical representative visit the site periodically during installation.
- Use an internal drainage plane, and avoid face-sealed barrier walls. Detail the drainage indicating flashing and weepholes.
- Utilize a moisture-resistant substrate. Do not use paper-faced gypsum sheathing or OSB.
- Provide a continuous weather barrier behind the EIFS.
- Do not expose any portions of the EIFS at horizontal areas. Flash windowsills, copings, and projections with sheet metal.
- For joints:
  - Understand the limitations and best profiles of aesthetic joints within the system.
  - Honor movement joints in the substrate through the EIFS.
  - Joints between EIFS should use a double line of low-modulus silicone joint sealant with closed-cell backer rods.
- Performance of EIFS depends strictly on adherence to the manufacturer's instructions. Quality measures beyond the requirements of other systems are reasonable.
- Require a large-scale mockup, including typical joints, plus a window and other typical penetrations.
- Require inspection of the weather barrier prior to covering with insulation.
- Require periodic or continuous third-party inspections appropriate to the complexity of the project.

WATER REPELLANTS
A variety of thin membranes are available, which, under laboratory conditions, may be waterproof, but actually only slow water absorption because of their inability to bridge large cracks, accelerated weathering, and thin application. Because of this inevitable leakage, water repellants cannot replace proper detailing and construction of truly waterproof wall assemblies. Water repellants may provide passable performance on existing structures where retrofit of flashings, drainage plane, and weather barriers are not feasible.

CLEAR REPELLANTS
Clear repellants are typically used for concrete, CMU, brick, stone, and sometimes wood. Clear repellants come in two basic types: penetrating and film-forming sealers.

- Penetrating sealers typically include siloxanes, silanes, or combinations of the two. Advantages include resistance to UV degradation, vapor permeability, low color change, and usability on walkable surfaces.
- Film-forming surfaces include acrylics and urethanes. There is a relatively high risk of unsightly failure if vapor pressure is present under the film. However, they can fill larger cracks and work over rougher concrete and wood.
- Clear repellants are typically applied by sprayed-on flood coating in one or two coats.

Comparisons of manufacturers marketing claims of the many varieties and concentrations of clear water repellants can be difficult. Review generic evaluations relative to the specific product type

Contributor:
Richard J. Vitullo, AIA, Oak Leaf Studio, Crownsville, Maryland.

and check for proven performance on similar substrates in similar situations. Test an inconspicuous sample panel for performance and appearance before finalizing materials selection.

CEMENTITIOUS COATINGS

Cementitious coatings are typically portland cement-based with fine aggregate and additives to enhance bond, water and freeze-thaw resistance, and color. Cementitious coatings are generally brittle and will not bridge cracks. They are breathable, and have excellent bonding strengths and weathering capabilities, but may cause a substantial change in the appearance of the building. Crystalline waterproofing is also available, which fills the microscopic pores of concrete and CMU.

Cementitious coatings are usually applied by spray, but may also be brushed or troweled. For mortar between brick, the brick must be either masked individually or wiped clean after spraying (so-called bagged because of the burlap bags used).

ELASTOMERIC COATINGS

Elastomeric coatings are essentially high-build elastomeric paint, either water- or solvent-based. Some products are breathable. Elastomeric coatings have the highest crack-bridging capabilities, and can be applied over most substrates, but they have a drastic effect on the appearance of the building, may fade, and may require relatively frequent reapplication.

JOINT SEALANTS

Joint sealants are essential to the watertightness of buildings. Joints between the various enclosure assemblies, as well as joints to accommodate movement, penetrations, and transitions, require joint sealant.

SEALANT TYPES

Together, polyurethane and silicone joint sealants account for the largest percentage of exterior joint sealants in commercial construction. Butyls, epoxies, and polysulfides are used less frequently. Acrylic or latex sealants are generally not used on the exterior of commercial construction, but may be suitable for small-scope residential projects.

- *Polyurethane*: Available as either single or multicomponent types in many colors, polyurethane sealants have very good movement capabilities and excellent adhesion. Polyurethanes, while still requiring priming on surfaces, tolerate less-than-perfect surface prep better than silicone. Polyurethane is well-suited for horizontal, traffic-bearing surfaces, and below grade.
- *Silicone*: Available as either single or multicomponent types in many colors, silicone joint sealants have excellent movement capabilities and excellent adhesion. Ultralow-modulus silicone has the highest movement capacity. Medium- and high-modulus silicones have progressively less movement capacity, but higher hardness and compressive strength. Silicone joint sealant requires fastidious surface cleaning, and, frequently, they also require priming. Silicone can be used on horizontal surfaces, but not below grade.
- *Extruded precured silicone strips*: Silicone is extruded in a factory into various widths, approximately 1/8-in. thick. The strips are adhered in the field with silicone sealant. Precured strips are frequently used for repairing failed joints.
- *Butyl*: Butyl sealants have relatively low movement capabilities, but have excellent adhesion, and require minimal surface prep and no priming. Butyl works in relatively thin layers and stays flexible, making it a good choice for lap joints in metal such as sheet metal flashing and curtain wall. Butyl cannot be exposed to daylight in the finished work.
- *Epoxies*: Epoxy sealants are used for very specialized applications such as where sealant must not be "pickable," as in a detention facility or zoo. However, epoxy sealants generally have limited movement capacity, UV resistance, and weathering ability, and, therefore, must be carefully selected for exterior work.

- *Acrylic/latex*: Acrylic, latex, and siliconized latex sealants have very low movement capabilities and limited weathering capability, hence should be used only in areas of limited movement that require painting.
- *Polysulfide*: Polysulfide sealants have limited movement capabilities and are, therefore, not selected as often as silicone or polyurethane. However, they are excellent for immersion and below-grade situations. Primers are required.
- *Foamed-in-place sealant (FIP)*: Available in single-component or multicomponent, open-cell and closed-cell, high and low expansion rates, and with flame spread and smoke development ratings, FIP sealant is useful to fill complicated large voids that will not be exposed in the finished work. Priming and backers are not required. FIP sealants also can be used as secondary air seals around windows, and as the inner line in double sealant systems; but they are difficult to inspect for a continuous seal.
- *Precompressed foam*: Flexible foam is impregnated with sealant and adhesive on one side. The foam is held in a compressed state, either in rolls or long straight lengths, and is quickly installed in the joint before the slowly expanding foam swells and bonds to the substrates. Splices between lengths are usually made with beveled butt joints. Precompressed foam is usually covered by other sealants or waterproofing, or comes factory-faced with a layer of precured silicone. Joints widths up to 6 in. are common.

JOINT DESIGN

- *Shape of joint*: The cross-sectional profile of the joint is crucial to proper functioning of the joint sealant. The classic joint profile is an hourglass shape, with a depth one-half its width. Fillet and banded profiles are also possible with proper bond breakers.
- *Backer*: Backer rod and bond-breaker tapes prevent improper three-sided adhesion. Backer rod is available in closed- and open-cell materials, and the sealant manufacturer recommends the use of each. Generally, open-cell is not used in horizontal or submerged joints, and closed-cell is not used with moisture-cured sealants. Bond-breaker tapes are used where there is insufficient depth for a rod.
- *Size of joint*: Conservatively, the width of joints should be four times the anticipated movement, based on a minimum 150°F temperature change (up to 200 for dark materials), plus anticipated structural movement. If the joint width becomes aesthetically objectionable, the distance between joints can be decreased, as can the structural movement; and, possibly, a higher-performing sealant can be selected; or a combination of the three.

Horizontal joints in traffic surfaces present special issues, particularly if the joint is wide. The selected joint sealant should have high shore hardness, and the joint backup should structurally support the joint sealant and have a bond-breaker tape to more firmly support the sealant. Avoid foam backer rods, which are too soft to provide structural support to the joint.

APPLICATION

Proper application of joint sealant is extremely dependent on a wide number of skills and decisions of the installer. Dimensional tolerances are very tight, often within 1/8 in. of ideal location, and seemingly minor mistakes can result in systemic failure. Factors to consider include:

- *Environmental conditions*: Application should take place between 50°F and 80°F, without rain before, during, and after installation, until curing is complete, as recommended by the manufacturer.
- *Joint preparation*: Joints may need to be mechanically ground to remove loose materials, contaminants such as form release oils, and old joint sealants. After mechanical grinding, all dust must be removed, and then the bonding surfaces must be carefully wiped clean with solvents.
- *Priming*: Primers improve adhesion, and should be used unless proven not necessary by project testing. Note that two different sides of the joint may require different primers.

- *Backer*: The width of the backer, either backer rod or bond-breaker tape, must be carefully selected to suit the width of the joint, and then carefully placed to the proper depth. A roller tool is recommended to control depth of rod.
- *Joint sealant*: While the joint is still clean, and while the primer is within the recoat period, sufficient sealant must be forced into the joint and then tooled to form the proper profile, push the joint sealant against the substrates, and eliminate bubbles. Multicomponent sealants will need to be mixed in carefully controlled quantities.

DOUBLE LINE JOINT SEALANTS

Considering the high level of quality and attention to detail required at every step of the process to select and install joint sealants, it is not prudent to conclude that the joint sealant will be installed perfectly on the job site. Therefore, it is desirable to provide a double line of sealant at joints that extend completely through the exterior enclosure, to provide redundancy and long-term performance. Note that joints in the outer layer of a drained cavity wall or pressure-equalized rainscreen assembly do not require a double line—assuming the inner weather barrier is properly sealed.

Requirements are as follows:

- The backer rods selected for double lines of joint sealant must accommodate the gasses emitted during curing.
- The space between the inner and outer line of sealant must be weeped periodically.
- Precompressed foam joint sealant or foamed-in-place joint sealants can be used for an inner secondary seal, but because the main sealant is in direct contact with the inner seal, no cavity results without provision for drainage. Precompressed foam generally is for joints 1 in. and larger.

PROJECT TESTING

Modern joint sealants are the result of sophisticated chemical engineering. Unfortunately, many other uncontrolled and difficult-to-predict chemicals exist on any construction project, and chemical interactions are possible and difficult to predict, the manufacturer should test all possible combinations of joint sealant and project specific substrates to eliminate potential incompatibility and to select the best primer. It is crucial that the substrates be exact replicas of those intended for use on the project.

For example, if precast concrete will have a curing sealer applied in the finished work, then the sample must have the same sealer. Likewise, exact copies of aluminum extrusions, complete with the exact finish applied in the identical fashion, should be tested, not samples of sheets of aluminum.

After project specific testing has been completed, periodic testing in the field should be completed to verify proper installation. Simple pull tests can help ensure diligent quality control

JOINT SEALANT REPLACEMENT AND REPAIR

The key to successful repair or replacement of joint sealant is highly dependent on rigorous preparation of the existing conditions and selection of the correct replacement joint sealant. Most sealants will not adhere to another sealant, so it is best that the replacement sealant match the existing one, as it is nearly impossible to remove all traces from the substrate. Cleaning of the substrate usually requires abrasive removal of the old joint sealant and a thin layer of the substrate. For soft substrates such as EIFS, proper removal of the existing joint sealant is nearly impossible. For these systems, a "band-aid" repair is typically required.

EXTERIOR WALL CONSTRUCTION

This section examines common types of framing used for exterior wall systems.

COLD-FORMED METAL FRAMING AND BRACING

Lightweight steel framing is cold-formed, which means the components are manufactured by brake forming and punching galvanized coil and sheet stock. Cold-formed framing members consist of two basic types of components that are C-shaped in section: one type has 1/4-in. flanges folded inward; the other has no flanges. Studs, joists, and rafters are made with flanges to stiffen them so they will more readily stand vertically. Components without flanges (called *tracks*) have unpunched solid webs. For added strength, tracks are sized slightly larger than the flanged members so the tracks will fit snugly inside them as sill or top plates or as part of posts or headers.

Cold-Formed metal framing is strong and versatile. The strength and load-carrying capacity of a member can be increased simply by increasing the thickness, or gauge, of the metal; the dimensions of the member, or the spacing, do not necessarily have to be increased. There is little limitation on the length of steel framing members; joists or studs may be fabricated in lengths up to 40 ft. If handled with care, steel framing is straight and consistent; also, it is not affected by moisture content.

Disadvantages of cold-formed metal framing include lack of insulating qualities; difficulty in cutting, compared to wood; and dangerously sharp edges. Consult the American Iron and Steel Institute (AISI) for further information.

BRACING

Buildings must be properly braced to resist racking under wind and seismic loads. Diagonal strap bracing is sloped to resist forces in tension, and fastened by screws or welds to studs and plates. Properly spaced lateral steel bracing resists stud rotation and minor axis bending under wind, seismic, and axial loads; this is especially critical during construction, before sheathing or finishes are installed.

DIAGONAL STABILITY BRACING ANCHORAGE DETAILS
2.316

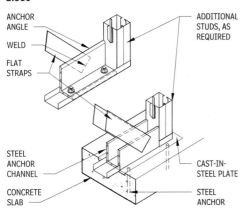

LATERAL BRACING ATTACHMENTS
2.317

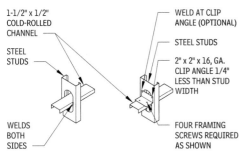

WELD ATTACHMENT (FOR 3-5/8" OR SMALLER STUDS; 16-GA. OR HEAVIER)   **SCREW ATTACHMENT (FOR 3-5/8" TO 8" STUDS)**

WALL BRIDGING
2.318

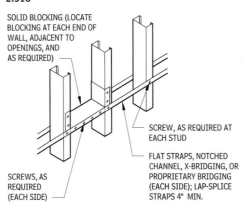

DIAGONAL STABILITY BRACING ANCHORAGE
2.319

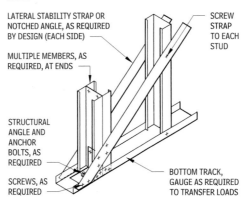

DIAGONAL STABILITY BRACING AT INTERMEDIATE FLOOR
2.320

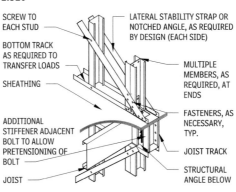

COLD-FORMED METAL FRAMING – OPENING DETAILS

WINDOW OPENING
2.321

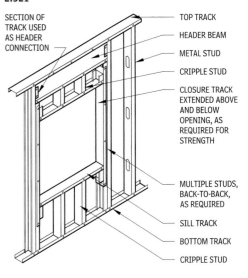

DOOR OPENING
2.322

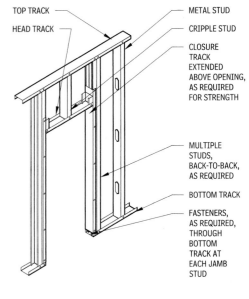

NOTES

2.316 The top detail is for one-to-two story buildings; the bottom detail is for buildings more than two stories. Steel channel, plate, and anchor size depend on applied uplift and horizontal shear forces.

2.317 Channels to be spaced as required by design.

2.318 Number of required rows of bridging is dependent on structural design.

2.319 Strap forces may require additional stiffening of the bottom track or structural angle.

2.320 Strap forces may require additional stiffening of top and bottom track or structural angle.

Contributor:
American Iron and Steel Institute, Washington, DC.

DOOR JAMB BASE AT FLOOR FRAMING
2.323

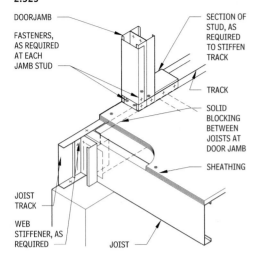

DOORJAMB

FASTENERS, AS REQUIRED AT EACH JAMB STUD

SECTION OF STUD, AS REQUIRED TO STIFFEN TRACK

TRACK

SOLID BLOCKING BETWEEN JOISTS AT DOOR JAMB

SHEATHING

JOIST TRACK

WEB STIFFENER, AS REQUIRED

JOIST

HEAD AT OPENING LESS THAN 4 FT WIDE IN LOAD-BEARING WALL CONDITION
2.324

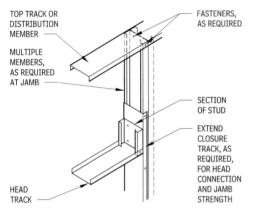

TOP TRACK OR DISTRIBUTION MEMBER

MULTIPLE MEMBERS, AS REQUIRED AT JAMB

FASTENERS, AS REQUIRED

SECTION OF STUD

EXTEND CLOSURE TRACK, AS REQUIRED, FOR HEAD CONNECTION AND JAMB STRENGTH

HEAD TRACK

HEAD AT OPENING 4 FT WIDE OR WIDER IN LOAD-BEARING WALL CONDITION
2.325

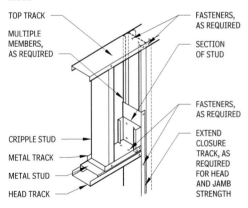

TOP TRACK

MULTIPLE MEMBERS, AS REQUIRED

FASTENERS, AS REQUIRED

SECTION OF STUD

CRIPPLE STUD

METAL TRACK

METAL STUD

HEAD TRACK

FASTENERS, AS REQUIRED

EXTEND CLOSURE TRACK, AS REQUIRED FOR HEAD AND JAMB STRENGTH

DETAILS FOR COLD-FORMED METAL FRAMING

HEAVY FIXTURE ATTACHMENT
2.326

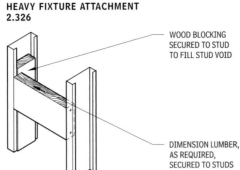

WOOD BLOCKING SECURED TO STUD TO FILL STUD VOID

DIMENSION LUMBER, AS REQUIRED, SECURED TO STUDS WITH SCREWS, AS REQUIRED

TRACK SPLICE
2.327

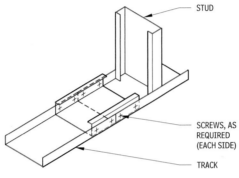

STUD

SCREWS, AS REQUIRED (EACH SIDE)

TRACK

BACKING FOR CABINETS
2.328

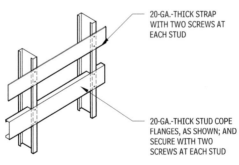

20-GA.-THICK STRAP WITH TWO SCREWS AT EACH STUD

20-GA.-THICK STUD COPE FLANGES, AS SHOWN; AND SECURE WITH TWO SCREWS AT EACH STUD

NAILABLE BASEPLATE
2.329

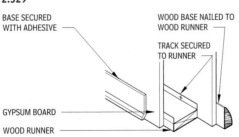

BASE SECURED WITH ADHESIVE

WOOD BASE NAILED TO WOOD RUNNER

TRACK SECURED TO RUNNER

GYPSUM BOARD

WOOD RUNNER

TOP PLATE INTERSECTION
2.330

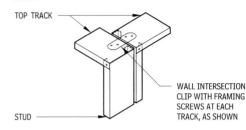

TOP TRACK

WALL INTERSECTION CLIP WITH FRAMING SCREWS AT EACH TRACK, AS SHOWN

STUD

STUD-TO-TRACK CONNECTION
2.331

STUD

ONE SCREW EACH FLANGE, MIN.

TRACK

MECHANICAL FASTENERS

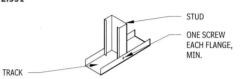

WELDS, AS REQUIRED

WELDED CONNECTION

WALL INTERSECTION FRAMING
2.332

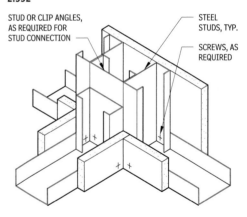

STUD OR CLIP ANGLES, AS REQUIRED FOR STUD CONNECTION

STEEL STUDS, TYP.

SCREWS, AS REQUIRED

CORNER FRAMING
2.333

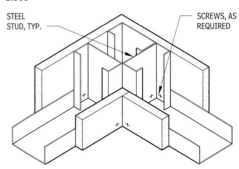

STEEL STUD, TYP.

SCREWS, AS REQUIRED

NOTES

2.324 Detail may be applicable to larger openings in partitions with non-axial loads.

2.328 Dimension lumber may also be used for backing.

Contributor:
American Iron and Steel Institute, Washington, DC.

CORNER POST
2.334

16d TO FILLER BLOCK

FILLER BLOCK

3-16d TO FILLER BLOCK

16d STAGGERED 12" O.C. VERTICAL

10d TOENAILED TO SOLE

3-16d TO FILLER BLOCK

SOLE

TOP PLATE AND BRACING
2.335

16d

16d STAGGERED 16 O.C.

10d

8 d

1 x 4 MIN. OR 1-1/4" WIDE 16-GA. STEEL STRAP BRACE AT 45°; OR PLYWOOD PANELS

SOLE PLATE

10d

PLYWOOD SUBFLOOR

10d TOENAILED

PARTITION-TO-WALL CONNECTION
2.336

DOUBLE TOP PLATE

2-16d

16d 12" O.C. TO SPACER STUD

16d 12" O.C. STAGGERED

WALL STUD

SOLE PLATE

JOISTS BEARING ON RIBBON
2.337

WALL STUD

JOIST

10d

2-8d

RIBBON

BALLOON FRAMING
2.338

CANTILEVER STUDS FOR LOW WALL AT ATTIC

CANTILEVER STUDS FOR PARAPET

JOISTS ON RIBBON

MODIFIED BALLOON FRAME WALLS USED IN MODERN CONSTRUCTION ONLY WHEN CANTILEVERED STUDS ARE REQUIRED FOR STRUCTURAL REASONS

TYPICAL PLATFORM FRAMING

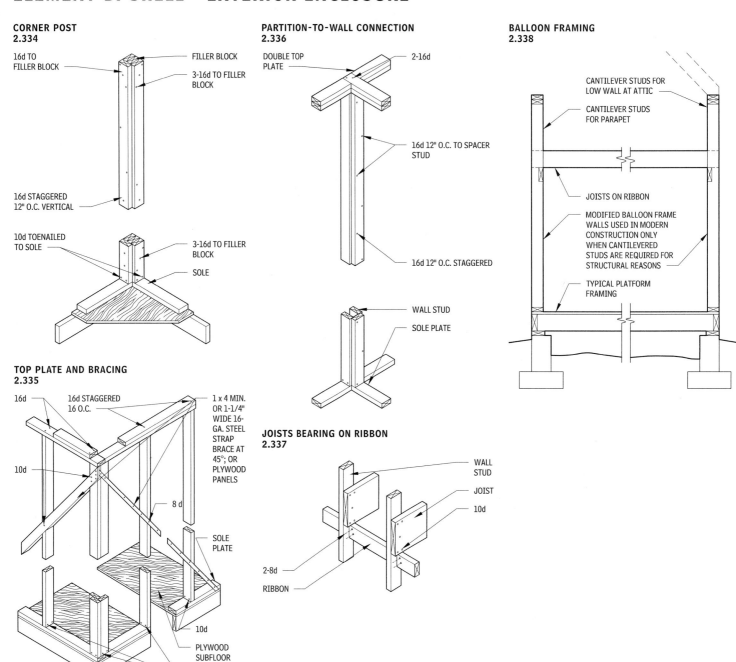

NOTE

2.337 Two nails on each joist are sufficient if a full story exists above ribbon.

Contributor:
Joseph A. Wilkes, FAIA, Wilkes and Faulkner, Washington, DC.

FRAMING DETAILS FOR OPENINGS

Steel lintels are selected from steel beam design tables on the basis of floor, wall, and roof openings. Wood lintels over openings in bearing walls may be engineered as beams. Composite beams, such as glued-laminated beams, also are appropriate in some applications. Plywood box beams are used for garage doors. Steel flitch plates can add strength without adding extra width to a composite beam.

Check with local codes and standards for fire-resistance requirements.

DOOR OPENING
2.339

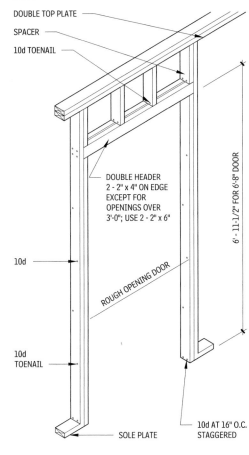

DOUBLE TOP PLATE

SPACER

10d TOENAIL

DOUBLE HEADER 2 - 2" x 4" ON EDGE EXCEPT FOR OPENINGS OVER 3'-0"; USE 2 - 2" x 6"

6' -11-1/2" FOR 6'-8" DOOR

10d

ROUGH OPENING DOOR

10d TOENAIL

10d AT 16" O.C. STAGGERED

SOLE PLATE

LINTELS FOR WIDE OPENINGS
2.340

TOP PLATE

USE SINGLE HEADER ALONGSIDE WOOD I-JOIST FOR FULL FRAMING

LAMINATED WOOD JOIST

NOTE:
DOUBLE TRIMMER REQUIRED FOR ADEQUATE BEARING ON OPENINGS LARGER THAN 9'-0"

TOP PLATE

LAMINATED HEADERS

BOLTS AT 2'-0" O.C. DOUBLE AT EACH END

STEEL FLITCH PLATE

FRAMING BOLTED TO STEEL CHANNEL

WINDOW OPENING
2.341

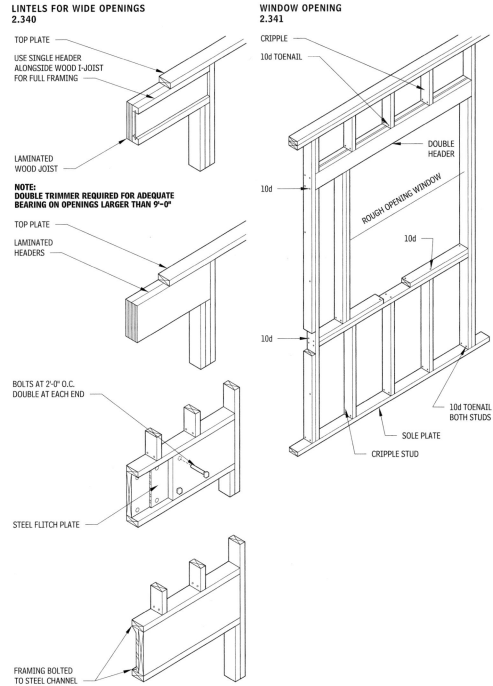

CRIPPLE

10d TOENAIL

DOUBLE HEADER

10d

ROUGH OPENING WINDOW

10d

10d

10d TOENAIL BOTH STUDS

SOLE PLATE

CRIPPLE STUD

Contributor:
Joseph A. Wilkes, FAIA, Wilkes and Faulkner, Washington, DC.

INTERSECTING WALL DETAILS
2.342

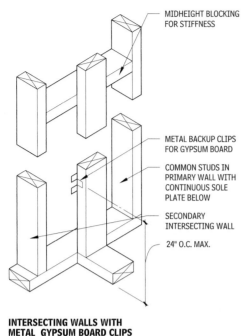

MIDHEIGHT BLOCKING FOR STIFFNESS

METAL BACKUP CLIPS FOR GYPSUM BOARD

COMMON STUDS IN PRIMARY WALL WITH CONTINUOUS SOLE PLATE BELOW

SECONDARY INTERSECTING WALL

24" O.C. MAX.

INTERSECTING WALLS WITH METAL GYPSUM BOARD CLIPS

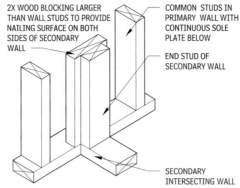

2X WOOD BLOCKING LARGER THAN WALL STUDS TO PROVIDE NAILING SURFACE ON BOTH SIDES OF SECONDARY WALL

COMMON STUDS IN PRIMARY WALL WITH CONTINUOUS SOLE PLATE BELOW

END STUD OF SECONDARY WALL

SECONDARY INTERSECTING WALL

INTERSECTING WALLS WITH BLOCKING

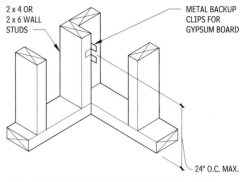

2 x 4 OR 2 x 6 WALL STUDS

METAL BACKUP CLIPS FOR GYPSUM BOARD

24" O.C. MAX.

WALL CORNER WITH METAL GYPSUM BOARD CLIPS

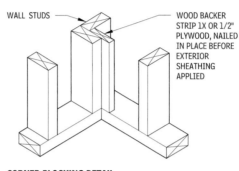

WALL STUDS

WOOD BACKER STRIP 1X OR 1/2" PLYWOOD, NAILED IN PLACE BEFORE EXTERIOR SHEATHING APPLIED

CORNER BLOCKING DETAIL

REDUCED WOOD FRAMING DETAILS
2.343

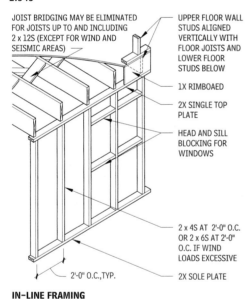

JOIST BRIDGING MAY BE ELIMINATED FOR JOISTS UP TO AND INCLUDING 2 x 12S (EXCEPT FOR WIND AND SEISMIC AREAS)

UPPER FLOOR WALL STUDS ALIGNED VERTICALLY WITH FLOOR JOISTS AND LOWER FLOOR STUDS BELOW

1X RIMBOAED

2X SINGLE TOP PLATE

HEAD AND SILL BLOCKING FOR WINDOWS

2 x 4S AT 2'-0" O.C. OR 2 x 6S AT 2'-0" O.C. IF WIND LOADS EXCESSIVE

2'-0" O.C.,TYP.

2X SOLE PLATE

IN-LINE FRAMING

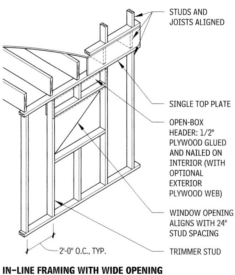

STUDS AND JOISTS ALIGNED

SINGLE TOP PLATE

OPEN-BOX HEADER: 1/2" PLYWOOD GLUED AND NAILED ON INTERIOR (WITH OPTIONAL EXTERIOR PLYWOOD WEB)

WINDOW OPENING ALIGNS WITH 24" STUD SPACING

2'-0" O.C., TYP.

TRIMMER STUD

IN-LINE FRAMING WITH WIDE OPENING

RIM BOARD (MAY BE 1X WOOD MATERIAL WITH IN-LINE FRAMING; MAY BE ELIMINATED IF BLOCKING IS USED)

FLOOR JOIST

NAIL ANCHOR STRAPS DIRECTLY TO EACH FLOOR JOIST

SILL PLATE MAY BE ELIMINATED IF FOUNDATION IS LEVEL AND ACCURATE

HEADER JOIST

CONCRETE OR SOLID (TOP) CMU FOUNDATION WALL

ANCHOR STRAP NAILED TO PRESERVATIVE TREATED SILL PLATE

NOTES

2.343 a. Some framing details rely on techniques that reduce the amount of lumber in wood construction. Among these are in-line framing details and corner details with metal framing clips for gypsum board. These types of details were developed to conserve wood resources, reduce material cost and job-site waste, and enhance energy efficiency by reducing thermal bridging across wall systems and increasing insulation cavities. When wood levels are to be reduced, a structural engineer should first be consulted. b. Gypsum board installed at inside corners with metal clips or wood backers does not get fastened to either. The sheet resting against the backer or clips is installed first so the second sheet (which is nailed to the stud) will lock the first sheet in place. The "floating joint" that results is recommended, to reduce cracks in the corner.

Contributor:
Richard J. Vitullo, AIA, Oak Leaf Studio, Crownsville, Maryland.

WIND AND SEISMIC CONNECTOR FRAMING
2.344

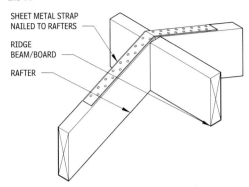

SHEET METAL STRAP
NAILED TO RAFTERS

RIDGE
BEAM/BOARD

RAFTER

RIDGE UPLIFT STRAP

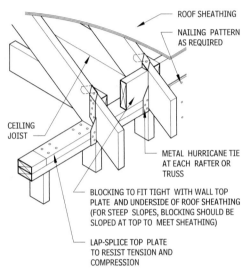

ROOF SHEATHING

NAILING PATTERN
AS REQUIRED

CEILING
JOIST

METAL HURRICANE TIE
AT EACH RAFTER OR
TRUSS

BLOCKING TO FIT TIGHT WITH WALL TOP
PLATE AND UNDERSIDE OF ROOF SHEATHING
(FOR STEEP SLOPES, BLOCKING SHOULD BE
SLOPED AT TOP TO MEET SHEATHING)

LAP-SPLICE TOP PLATE
TO RESIST TENSION AND
COMPRESSION

ROOF DIAPHRAGM PERIMETER

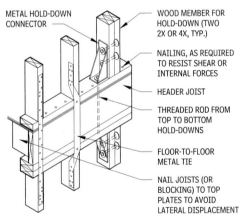

METAL HOLD-DOWN
CONNECTOR

WOOD MEMBER FOR
HOLD-DOWN (TWO
2X OR 4X, TYP.)

NAILING, AS REQUIRED
TO RESIST SHEAR OR
INTERNAL FORCES

HEADER JOIST

THREADED ROD FROM
TOP TO BOTTOM
HOLD-DOWNS

FLOOR-TO-FLOOR
METAL TIE

NAIL JOISTS (OR
BLOCKING) TO TOP
PLATES TO AVOID
LATERAL DISPLACEMENT

TIES BETWEEN FLOORS

WIND AND SEISMIC CONNECTIONS

It is essential to provide a continuous path of resistance from roof to foundation to dissipate both lateral and uplift forces. Connections along this load path will guarantee uninterrupted resistance. Seismic and wind forces are transferred from the roof diaphragm to shear walls and through the walls into the ground at the foundation. Shear walls resist horizontal forces in the roof and floor diaphragms and so must be connected to them. It is important to apply wall sheathing to the full wall height, nailing it to the top plate, blocking, or rim joist, as well as to the mud sill or bottom plate. Shear wall height/width ratios are an important consideration; consult a structural engineer for their design. The details illustrated show several connection paths; for each specific design, a structural engineer familiar with seismic and wind-resistant construction should be consulted. Many of the requirements for high-wind situations apply to seismic loading as well, except in shear wall design.

HEAVY TIMBER WALL CONSTRUCTION

INFILL WOOD STUD ASSEMBLY
2.345

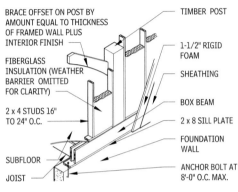

BRACE OFFSET ON POST BY
AMOUNT EQUAL TO THICKNESS
OF FRAMED WALL PLUS
INTERIOR FINISH

FIBERGLASS
INSULATION (WEATHER
BARRIER OMITTED
FOR CLARITY)

2 x 4 STUDS 16"
TO 24" O.C.

SUBFLOOR

JOIST

TIMBER POST

1-1/2" RIGID
FOAM

SHEATHING

BOX BEAM

2 x 8 SILL PLATE

FOUNDATION
WALL

ANCHOR BOLT AT
8'-0" O.C. MAX.

FOAM CORE PANEL WALL SYSTEM
2.346

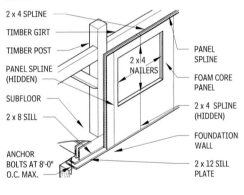

2 x 4 SPLINE

TIMBER GIRT

TIMBER POST

PANEL SPLINE
(HIDDEN)

SUBFLOOR

2 x 8 SILL

ANCHOR
BOLTS AT 8'-0"
O.C. MAX.

2 x 4
NAILERS

PANEL
SPLINE

FOAM CORE
PANEL

2 x 4 SPLINE
(HIDDEN)

FOUNDATION
WALL

2 x 12 SILL
PLATE

EXTERIOR WOOD STUD SYSTEM
2.347

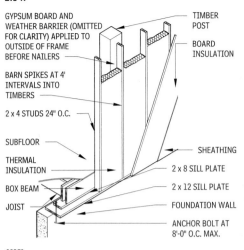

GYPSUM BOARD AND
WEATHER BARRIER (OMITTED
FOR CLARITY) APPLIED TO
OUTSIDE OF FRAME
BEFORE NAILERS

BARN SPIKES AT 4'
INTERVALS INTO
TIMBERS

2 x 4 STUDS 24" O.C.

SUBFLOOR

THERMAL
INSULATION

BOX BEAM

JOIST

TIMBER
POST

BOARD
INSULATION

SHEATHING

2 x 8 SILL PLATE

2 x 12 SILL PLATE

FOUNDATION WALL

ANCHOR BOLT AT
8'-0" O.C. MAX.

HEAVY TIMBER SILL AND JOIST ASSEMBLY
2.348

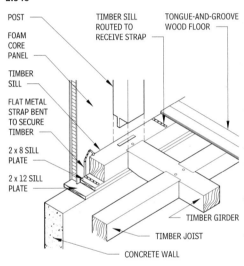

POST

FOAM
CORE
PANEL

TIMBER
SILL

FLAT METAL
STRAP BENT
TO SECURE
TIMBER

2 x 8 SILL
PLATE

2 x 12 SILL
PLATE

TIMBER SILL
ROUTED TO
RECEIVE STRAP

TONGUE-AND-GROOVE
WOOD FLOOR

TIMBER GIRDER

TIMBER JOIST

CONCRETE WALL

HORIZONTAL NAILER WALL ASSEMBLY
2.349

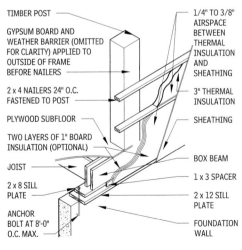

TIMBER POST

GYPSUM BOARD AND
WEATHER BARRIER (OMITTED
FOR CLARITY) APPLIED TO
OUTSIDE OF FRAME
BEFORE NAILERS

2 x 4 NAILERS 24" O.C.
FASTENED TO POST

PLYWOOD SUBFLOOR

TWO LAYERS OF 1" BOARD
INSULATION (OPTIONAL)

JOIST

2 x 8 SILL
PLATE

ANCHOR
BOLT AT 8'-0"
O.C. MAX.

1/4" TO 3/8"
AIRSPACE
BETWEEN
THERMAL
INSULATION
AND
SHEATHING

3" THERMAL
INSULATION

SHEATHING

BOX BEAM

1 x 3 SPACER

2 x 12 SILL
PLATE

FOUNDATION
WALL

NOTES

2.344 Ties between floors: Wood members (studs) must be sized for the load-carrying capacity at the critical net section.

2.345 This assembly reduces the exposure of the heavy timber frame by partially concealing the frame in the wall system. It allows air infiltration due to shrinkage and movement, and requires an exterior board insulation layer to minimize the potential for air movement and condensation.

2.346 Structural foam-core panels (with wood sheathing on both sides of the foam core) may be needed at areas that may have excess stress or loading, with interior finish attached to the frame before the panels are attached.

Contributors:
Richard J. Vitullo, AIA, Oak Leaf Studio, Crownsville, Maryland; Tedd Benson and Ben Brungraber, PhD, Benson Woodworking company, Inc., Alstead, New Hampshire.

STANDARD 2X LUMBER SILL
2.350

INSULATED WALL PANEL

TIMBER POST

2 x 8 WOOD CAP CUT AROUND POST TO PREVENT LATERAL MOVEMENT

ANCHOR BOLT AT 6'-0" O.C. MAX.

CONCRETE FOUNDATION WALL

METAL HOLD-DOWN STRAP FASTENED TO POST

2 x 8 SILL PLATE

2 x 12 PRESERVATIVE TREATED SILL PLACE

EXTERIOR LIGHTWEIGHT WOOD TRUSS WALL ASSEMBLY
2.351

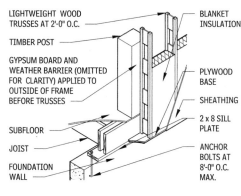

LIGHTWEIGHT WOOD TRUSSES AT 2'-0" O.C.

TIMBER POST

GYPSUM BOARD AND WEATHER BARRIER (OMITTED FOR CLARITY) APPLIED TO OUTSIDE OF FRAME BEFORE TRUSSES

SUBFLOOR

JOIST

FOUNDATION WALL

BLANKET INSULATION

PLYWOOD BASE

SHEATHING

2 x 8 SILL PLATE

ANCHOR BOLTS AT 8'-0" O.C. MAX.

STICK FRAME SILL AND FLOOR DECK
2.352

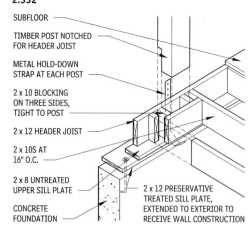

SUBFLOOR

TIMBER POST NOTCHED FOR HEADER JOIST

METAL HOLD-DOWN STRAP AT EACH POST

2 x 10 BLOCKING ON THREE SIDES, TIGHT TO POST

2 x 12 HEADER JOIST

2 x 10S AT 16" O.C.

2 x 8 UNTREATED UPPER SILL PLATE

CONCRETE FOUNDATION

2 x 12 PRESERVATIVE TREATED SILL PLATE, EXTENDED TO EXTERIOR TO RECEIVE WALL CONSTRUCTION

HEAVY TIMBER POST OR RAFTER AT FOAM-CORE PANEL—WIRE CHASE DETAIL
2.353

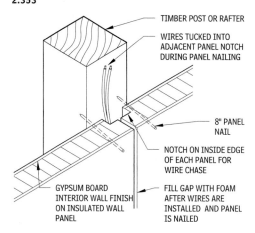

TIMBER POST OR RAFTER

WIRES TUCKED INTO ADJACENT PANEL NOTCH DURING PANEL NAILING

8" PANEL NAIL

NOTCH ON INSIDE EDGE OF EACH PANEL FOR WIRE CHASE

GYPSUM BOARD INTERIOR WALL FINISH ON INSULATED WALL PANEL

FILL GAP WITH FOAM AFTER WIRES ARE INSTALLED AND PANEL IS NAILED

HEAVY TIMBER SILL—WIRE CHASE DETAIL
2.354

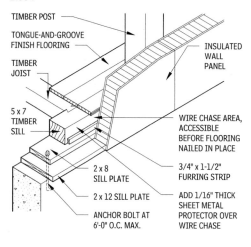

TIMBER POST

TONGUE-AND-GROOVE FINISH FLOORING

TIMBER JOIST

5 x 7 TIMBER SILL

INSULATED WALL PANEL

WIRE CHASE AREA, ACCESSIBLE BEFORE FLOORING NAILED IN PLACE

3/4" x 1-1/2" FURRING STRIP

2 x 8 SILL PLATE

2 x 12 SILL PLATE

ANCHOR BOLT AT 6'-0" O.C. MAX.

ADD 1/16" THICK SHEET METAL PROTECTOR OVER WIRE CHASE

BOX BEAM SILL—WIRE CHASE DETAIL
2.355

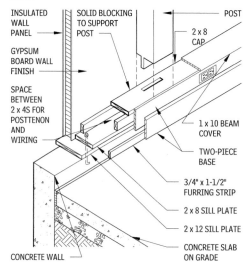

INSULATED WALL PANEL

GYPSUM BOARD WALL FINISH

SPACE BETWEEN 2 x 4S FOR POSTTENON AND WIRING

SOLID BLOCKING TO SUPPORT POST

POST

2 x 8 CAP

1 x 10 BEAM COVER

TWO-PIECE BASE

3/4" x 1-1/2" FURRING STRIP

2 x 8 SILL PLATE

2 x 12 SILL PLATE

CONCRETE SLAB ON GRADE

CONCRETE WALL

SURFACE-MOUNTED WIRE CHASES AT FOAM-CORE PANEL
2.356

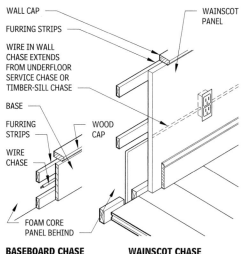

WALL CAP

FURRING STRIPS

WIRE IN WALL CHASE EXTENDS FROM UNDERFLOOR SERVICE CHASE OR TIMBER-SILL CHASE

BASE

FURRING STRIPS

WIRE CHASE

WAINSCOT PANEL

WOOD CAP

FOAM CORE PANEL BEHIND

BASEBOARD CHASE   **WAINSCOT CHASE**

WALL SHEATHING

SHEATHING
2.357

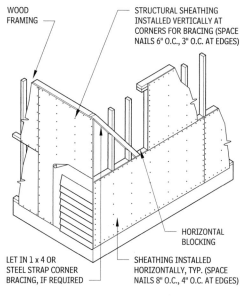

WOOD FRAMING

STRUCTURAL SHEATHING INSTALLED VERTICALLY AT CORNERS FOR BRACING (SPACE NAILS 6" O.C., 3" O.C. AT EDGES)

HORIZONTAL BLOCKING

LET IN 1 x 4 OR STEEL STRAP CORNER BRACING, IF REQUIRED

SHEATHING INSTALLED HORIZONTALLY, TYP. (SPACE NAILS 8" O.C., 4" O.C. AT EDGES)

NOTES

2.351 This assembly allows a great deal of insulation to be packed into the nonstructural wall cavity between trusses. The foundation wall may be off-set to the outside of the truss system (with pilasters added on the inside to support timber posts) to avoid the appearance of excess overhang.

Contributors:
Richard J. Vitullo, AIA, Oak Leaf Studio, Crownsville, Maryland; Tedd Benson and Ben Brungraber, PhD, PE, Benson Woodworking Co., Inc., Alstead, New Hampshire; David S. Collins, FAIA, American Forest & Paper Association, Cincinnati, Ohio.

BOARD INSULATION SHEATHING
2.358

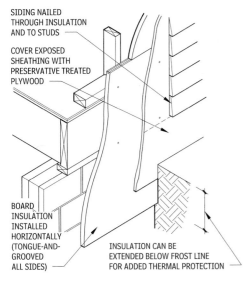

SIDING NAILED THROUGH INSULATION AND TO STUDS

COVER EXPOSED SHEATHING WITH PRESERVATIVE TREATED PLYWOOD

BOARD INSULATION INSTALLED HORIZONTALLY (TONGUE-AND-GROOVED ALL SIDES)

INSULATION CAN BE EXTENDED BELOW FROST LINE FOR ADDED THERMAL PROTECTION

WOOD SHINGLES AND SHAKES

SHEATHING MATERIALS
2.359

CHARACTERISTICS	STRUCTURAL SHEATHING	GYPSUM	FIBERBOARD	PLASTIC
Nailable base	Yes	No	Only high-density	No
Vapor retarder	No	No	If asphalt-treated	Yes
Insulation R-value (1/2″ thickness)	1.2	0.7	2.6	Varies with manufacturer
Corner bracing provided	Yes	Yes (See manufacturers' recommendations.)	Only high-density	No
Panel sizes (feet; except plastic, in inches)	4 × 8, 4 ×, 4 × 10	2 × 8, 4 × 8, 4 × 10, 4 × 12, 4 × 14	4 × 8, 4 × 9, 4 × 10, 4 × 12	16 × 96, 24 × 48, 224 × 96, 48 × 96, 48 × 108
Panel thickness (in.)	5/16, 3/8, 7/16, 15/32, 1/2, 19/32, 5/8, 23/32, 3/4, 7/8, 1, 1-1/8	1/4, 3/8, 1/2, 5/8	1/2, 25/32	1/2 to 6 (for roof)
Other remarks	Plywood grades commonly used for roof and wall sheathing have span ratings of 12/0, 16/0, 20/0, 24/0, 24/16, 32/16, 40/20, and 48/24; exposure durability classifications are Exposure 1 and Exterior. For unsupported edges, refer to manufacturers' recommendations. Oriented-strand board may be used instead of plywood, with appropriate span ratings.	Fire-rated panels are available in1/2″ and 5/8″ thicknesses. Panels are noncombustible and not damaged by occasional exposure to weather. Avoid traditional paper-faced gypsum sheathing.	Also called insulation board. Can be treated or impregnated with asphalt. Available in regular and high-density panels.	Considered an effective vapor barrier, so walls must be well vented. Some products emit toxic fumes when burned; refer to manufacturers' specifications.

PANEL SYSTEMS
2.360

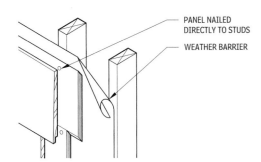

PANEL NAILED DIRECTLY TO STUDS

WEATHER BARRIER

SIDEWALL PANEL APPLIED TO STUDS

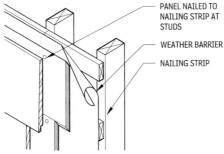

PANEL NAILED TO NAILING STRIP AT STUDS

WEATHER BARRIER

NAILING STRIP

SIDEWALL PANEL APPLIED TO NAILING STRIPS

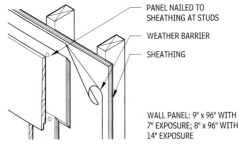

PANEL NAILED TO SHEATHING AT STUDS

WEATHER BARRIER

SHEATHING

WALL PANEL: 9″ x 96″ WITH 7″ EXPOSURE; 8″ x 96″ WITH 14″ EXPOSURE

SIDEWALL PANEL APPLIED TO SHEATHING (RECOMMENDED)

EXPOSURE FOR SHINGLES AND SHAKES USED FOR SIDING
2.361

LENGTH OF SHINGLES (IN.)	EXPOSURE OF SHINGLES (IN.)	
	SINGLE COURSE	DOUBLE COURSE
16	6 to 7-1/2	8 to 12
18	6 to 8-1/2	9 to 14
24	8 to 11-1/2	12 to 20

SHEATHING NOTES
- Sheathing may be strip type, solid 1 by 6 in., and diagonal type, in plywood, fiberboard, or gypsum board. Horizontal wood nailing strips (1 by 2 in.) should be used over fiberboard and gypsum sheathing. Space strips equal to shingle exposure.
- Many finishes can be used on red cedar shakes and shingles: solid color or semitransparent ("weathering") stains, exterior latex paint with primer, wood preservative, and bleaches.
- Breather mats, to allow shingles to be spaced off weather barrier, provide a drainage cavity and vent behind shingles. Mat provides better resistance to weather and longer life for shingles.
- Preferred method: detail sheathing or weather barrier to function as air barrier.

NOTES

2.360 a. With the panel system, shakes and shingles, plus sheathing, go up in one operation: 8-ft roof panels have 16 hand-split shakes bonded to 6- by 1/2-in. plywood strip, which forms a solid deck when the panels are nailed. A 4 to 12 or steeper roof pitch is recommended.
b. After application of starter panels, attach panels directly to rafters. Although designed to center on 16- or 24-in. spacing, they may meet between rafters. Use two 6d nails at each rafter.
c. The 8-ft sidewall panels are of two-ply construction: The surface layer

is of individual #1 grade shingles or shakes. The backup, of exterior-grade plywood shakes or shingles, is bonded under pressure with exterior-type adhesives to plywood backup.
d. Install weather barrier behind panels, lap a minimum of 3 in. vertically and horizontally. Stagger joints between panels.
e. Application types are determined by local building codes.
f. Matching factory-made corners for sidewall or roof panels are available.

Contributors:
David S. Collins, FAIA, American Forest & Paper Association, Cincinnati, Ohio; Richard J. Vitullo, AIA, Oak Leaf Studio, Crownsville, Maryland.

WOOD SHINGLES AND SHAKES FOR SIDING
2.362

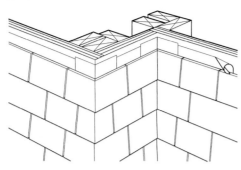

MITERED OUTSIDE AND INSIDE CORNERS (RECOMMENDED)

WOVEN OUTSIDE AND INSIDE CORNERS (MORE ECONOMICAL)

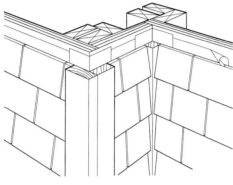

CORNER BOARDS AT OUTSIDE AND INSIDE CORNERS

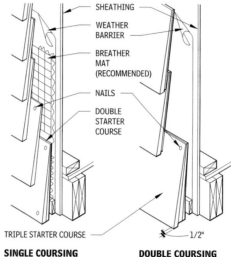

SHEATHING
WEATHER BARRIER
BREATHER MAT (RECOMMENDED)
NAILS
DOUBLE STARTER COURSE
TRIPLE STARTER COURSE
1/2"

SINGLE COURSING APPLICATION

DOUBLE COURSING APPLICATION

EXTERIOR WALL VAPOR RETARDERS, AIR BARRIERS AND INSULATION

BUILDING SECTION ANALYSIS FOR POTENTIAL CONDENSATION

Any building section may be analyzed using simple calculations to determine where condensation might occur and what might be done in selecting materials or their method of assembly to eliminate that possibility. The section may or may not contain a vapor barrier, or it may contain an inadequate one; the building section may include cold-side materials of comparatively high resistance to the passage of vapor (which is highly undesirable). With few exceptions, the vapor resistance at or near the warm surface should be five times that of any components. Table 2.414 supplies permeance and permeability of common building and vapor retarder materials. These values can be used in analyzing building sections by the following simple method:

1. List the materials, without surface films or air spaces, in the order of their appearance in the building section, beginning with the inside surface material and working to the outside.
2. Against each material, list the permeance (or permeability) value from the table, or a more accurate value if available from tests or manufacturers' data. Where a range is given, select an average value or use judgment in assigning a value based on the character and potential installation method of the material proposed for use.
3. Start at the top of the list and note any material that has less permeance than the materials above it on the list. At that point, the possibility exists that vapor leaking through the first material may condense on the second, provided the dew point (condensation point) is reached and the movement is considerable. In that case, provide ventilation through the cold-side material or modify the design to eliminate or change the material to one of greater permeance.

PERMEANCE AND PERMEABILITY OF MATERIALS TO WATER VAPOR
2.363

MATERIAL	PERM (IN.)[e]
MATERIALS USED IN CONSTRUCTION	
Concrete (1:2:4 mix)	3.2[e]
Brick-masonry (4" thick)	0.8 to 1.1
Concrete masonry (8" cored, limestone aggregate)	2.4
Plaster on metal lath (3/4")	15
Plaster on plain gypsum lath (with studs)	20
Gypsum board (3/8" plain)	50
Structural insulating board (sheathing quality	20 to 50[e]
Structural insulating board (interior, uncoated, 1/2")	50 to 90
Hardboard (1/8" standard)	11
Hardboard (1/8" tempered)	5
Built-up roofing (hot-mopped)	0.0
Wood, fir sheathing, 3/4"	2.9
Plywood (Douglas fir, exterior glue, 1/4")	0.7
Plywood (Douglas fir, interior glue, 1/4")	1.9
Acrylic, glass-fiber-reinforced sheet, 56 mil	0.12
Polyester, glass-fiber-reinforced sheet, 48 mil	0.05
THERMAL INSULATIONS	
Cellular glass	0.0[e]
Mineral wool, unprotected	29.0
Expanded polyurethane (R-11 blown)	0.4 to 1.65
Expanded polystyrene—extruded	1.2[e]
Expanded polystyrene—bead	2.0 to 5.8[e]
PLASTIC AND METAL FOILS AND FILMS[b]	
Aluminum foil (1 mil)	0.0
Polyethylene (4 mil)	0.08
Polyethylene (6 mil)	0.06
Polyethylene (8 mil)	0.04
Polyester (1 mil)	0.7
Polyvinylchloride, unplasticized (2 mil)	0.68
Polyvinylchloride, plasticized (4 mil)	0.8 to 1.4
BUILDING PAPERS, FELTS, ROOFING PAPERS[c]	
Duplex sheet, asphalt-laminated, aluminum foil one side (43)[d]	0.176
Saturated and coated roll roofing (326)4	0.24
Kraft paper and asphalt-laminated, reinforced 30-120-30 (34)[d]	1.8
Asphalt-saturated, coated vapor barrier paper (43)[d]	0.6
Asphalt-saturated, not coated sheathing paper (22)[d]	20.2
15-lb asphalt felt (70)[d]	5.6
15-lb tar felt (70)[d]	18.2
Single kraft, double-infused (16)[d]	42
LIQUID-APPLIED COATING MATERIALS	
Paint—two coats	
Aluminum varnish on wood	0.3 to 0.5
Enamels on smooth plaster	0.5 to 1.5
Primers and sealers on interior insulation board	0.9 to 2.1
Miscellaneous primers, plus one coat flat oil paint on plastic	1.6 to 3.0
Flat paint on interior insulation board	4
Water emulsion on interior insulation board	
Paint—three coats	30 to 85
Styrene-butadiene latex coating, 2 oz/sq ft	11
Polyvinyl acetate latex coating, 4 oz/sq ft	5.5
Asphalt cutback mastic	
1/16" dry	0.14
3/16" dry	0.0
Hot-melt asphalt	
2 oz/sq ft	0.5
3.5 oz/sq ft	0.1

NOTES

2.363 a. The vapor transmission rates listed will permit comparisons of materials, but selection of vapor retarder materials should be based on rates obtained from the manufacturer or from laboratory tests. The range of values shown indicates variations among mean values for materials that are similar but of different density. Values are intended for design guidance only.
b. Usually installed as vapor retarders. If used as exterior finish and elsewhere near cold side, special considerations are required.

c. Low-permeance sheets used as vapor retarders. High-permeance used elsewhere in construction.
d. Bases (weight in lb/500 sq ft).
e. Permeability (perm, in.)
f. Based on data from *ASHRAE Handbook*.

Contributor:
Richard J. Vitullo, AIA, Oak Leaf Studio, Crownsville, Maryland.

ESTIMATED PERMEANCE—WOOD
2.364

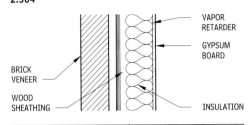

Gypsum Board (3/8 in.)	50.0
Vapor retarder	0.06 (lowest permeance)
Insulation	29.0
Wood sheathing	2.9
4-in. brick veneer	1.1 (next lowest permeance)

In this example, the vapor barrier transmits one grain of moisture per square foot per hour for each unit of vapor pressure difference, or one perm; and nothing else transmits less. However, since the cold brick veneer is nearly as low in permeance, it is advisable to make certain that the vapor barrier is expertly installed, with all openings at pipes and with outlet boxes or joints carefully fitted or sealed. Alternatively, the brick veneer may have open mortar joints near the top and bottom to serve both as weep holes and as vapor release openings. They will also ventilate the wall and help reduce heat gain in summer.

ESTIMATED PERMEANCE—CMU
2.365

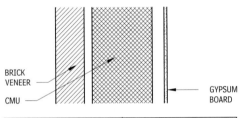

Gypsum Board (3/8 in.) Furred space	50.0
8-in. CMU	2.4
4-in. brick veneer	1.1 (lowest permeance)

Vapor (under pressure) would easily pass through the interior gypsum board finish, be slowed by the concrete masonry unit, and be nearly stopped by the cold brick veneer. Unless this design is radically improved, the masonry will become saturated and, in cold weather, may cause serious water stains or apparent "leaks." In addition, alternating freezing and thawing of condensation within the masonry wall can physically damage the construction.

These types of analysis are not appropriate for buildings in mixed-climate areas. For additional instructions see Chapter 11, "Design Tools," by Anton TenWolde, in *Moisture Control in Buildings*, (ASTM Manual, No. 18) Heinz R. Trechsel (ed.), published by ASTM, 1984.

COMPUTERIZED ANALYSIS
The Figures 2.415 and 2.416 are simple graphical section analyses are limited in reliability. They are two-dimensional, and do not include issues such as thermal bridging at insulation in stud cavities.

Computerized modeling is recommended for large projects, assemblies that require seasonal drying, and for projects located in mixed climates. WUFI, by Oak Ridge National Laboratory (www.ornl.gov), is one strong and widely recognized modeling tool.

AIR LEAKAGE CONSEQUENCES
2.366

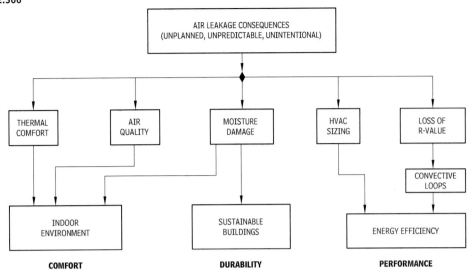

AIR BARRIERS
An air barrier is a combination of interconnected materials, flexible sealed joints, and components of the building envelope that provide the airtightness of the building envelope. The main function of air barriers is to prevent unintentional air and moisture flow through the building enclosure. Leakage can affect the occupants' comfort, as well as thermal performance and durability of the building.

BUILDING ENCLOSURE SEALING
The complete building envelope must be designed and constructed with a continuous air barrier to control air and moisture leakage into or out of the conditioned space. This includes the lowest-level slab-on-grade or crawl space surface, foundation walls, exterior walls, and roof.

Performance of the air barrier for the opaque envelope can be demonstrated by:

- Using individual materials that have an air permeance not to exceed 0.004 cfm/ft^2 under a pressure differential of 0.3 in. water gage (w.g.) (1.57 psf) when tested in accordance with ASTM E 2178.
- Using assemblies of materials and components that have an average air leakage not to exceed 0.04 cfm/ft^2 under a pressure differential of 0.3 in. w.g. (1.57 psf) when tested in accordance with ASTM E 1677.
- Testing the completed building and demonstrating that the air leakage rate of the building envelope does not exceed 0.40 cfm/sf at a pressure differential of 0.3 in. w.g. (1.57 psf) (2.0 L/s perm2 at 75 Pa) in accordance with ASTM E 779 or an equivalent approved method.

CHARACTERISTICS
The air barrier is required to have the following characteristics:

- Be continuous throughout the envelope (at the lowest floor, exterior walls, and ceiling or roof), with sealed connections between all transitions in planes and changes in materials, at all joints and seams, and at all penetrations.
- Be joined and sealed in a flexible manner to the air barrier component of adjacent assemblies, allowing for the relative movement of these assemblies and components.
- Be capable of withstanding positive and negative combined design wind, fan, and stack pressures on the air barrier without damage or displacement, and transfer the load to the structure. It must not displace adjacent materials under full load.
- Where lighting fixtures or other similar devices are to be installed in such a way as to penetrate the air barrier, provisions must be made to maintain the integrity of the barrier.

AIR BARRIER SYSTEMS
Many common building materials (concrete, plywood, roofing membranes, rigid insulation, and gypsum board) are capable of functioning as a weather barrier. For small-scale and residential construction, it is common to utilize either the sheathing or interior drywall as the weather barrier. Special sealing of these materials is required, but otherwise construction does not differ substantially from traditional frame construction. In commercial construction, the use of air barriers, applied over sheathing that fulfill the structural requirement is common. Common building materials that are not air barriers include CMU, board and blanket insulation (even if compressed), and polyethylene sheets.

AIR BARRIER MEMBRANES
Air barrier membranes are airtight materials specifically designed to control airflow through the building enclosure. The main types of air barrier membranes are summarized here. In addition to the primary membranes, air barrier systems must include installation and continuity accessories such as primers, mechanical fasteners, tapes, joint sealants, flashing, and transition membranes.

Based on the application method, air barrier membranes are classified into five categories:

- *Self-adhered (or peel-and-stick) membranes* are fabricated sheets consisting of rubber-modified asphalt bonded to a carrier film, and protected by release paper on the membrane side. These membranes are applied by self-adhesion to a dry, clean, and primed substrate. Self-adhered membranes are vapor-nonpermeable.
- *Fluid-applied membranes* are one- or two-component formulations in organic solvents or water dispersions, which are spray or trowel applied to a dry, clean, and primed substrate. Most fluid-applied membranes are vapor-nonpermeable. A few fluid-applied membranes are vapor-permeable, even though their permeability is quite low (<6 to 7 perms) and depend on the dry film thickness.
- *Mechanically fastened membranes* are, lightweight sheets installed typically with mechanical fasteners. Their installation does not require special surface preparation such as drying, priming, or taping of sheathing joints. Building wraps are vapor-permeable membranes, even though their vapor permeability varies widely depending on the membrane type and the manufacturer. The main types of building wraps are: (1) spunbonded polyolefins, (2) microporous films, (3) perforated films, and (4) asphalt-impregnated papers and felt. The seams and fasteners typically need to be taped or otherwise sealed.
- *Torch-applied membranes* are rubber-modified bitumen, laminated on a nonwoven substrate. The membrane is designed to be fused to a dry, clean, and primed substrate by heating the bitumen side with a propane torch. Torch-applied membranes are vapor-nonpermeable.

Contributors:
David F. Hill, Kosar, Rittolmann Associates, Buttler, Pennsylvania; Marc A. Giagceardo, College of Architecture, Texas Tech Universtiy, Lubbock, Texas; Maria Spinu, PhD, Dupont, Wilmington, Delaware.

- *Sprayed polyurethane foams (SPF)* are two-component foam membranes that combine thermal insulation and weather barrier properties. Only a few closed-cell SPF insulation foams have the required air infiltration resistance to qualify as air barriers.

Based on vapor permeability, air barrier membranes are classified into vapor-permeable and vapor-nonpermeable membranes (air barrier and vapor retarder). Building wraps and a few fluid-applied membranes are vapor-permeable though permeability varies widely among the different types. All other air barrier membranes described previously are vapor-nonpermeable.

Vapor permeability of the air barrier must be carefully considered when selecting a air barrier for the building enclosure.

- *Vapor-permeable* air barrier membranes can be placed anywhere in the wall assembly, based on ease of detailing. The membrane is often installed on the outer side of the exterior sheathing. In addition, there are no climate limitations for vapor-permeable air barriers. Air barriers can and should be used in all climates.
- *Vapor-nonpermeable* air barrier membranes generally must be located on the warm side of the wall assembly to avoid moisture accumulation. "The warm side of the wall assembly" is climate-specific. In the United States, with widely varying climates, it could be on different sides of the wall during different seasons. Consequently, the air barrier could end up on the cold side of the enclosure for part of the year, leading to moisture accumulation.

In summary, take into account the considerations listed in Table 2.367 when selecting an air barrier membrane.

AIR BARRIER CONSIDERATIONS
2.367

TYPE OF AIR BARRIER	LOCATION WITHIN BUILDING ENCLOSURE	CLIMATE CONSIDERATIONS AND LIMITATIONS
Vapor-permeable	Anywhere	No climate limitations; use in all climates
Vapor-nonpermeable (air barrier and vapor retarder)	Warm side	Consider climate to avoid condensation and moisture accumulation

When they are part of a drainage or pressure-equalized wall assembly, air barriers must also be resistant to the passage of water. Air barriers are crucial to the functioning of a pressure-equalized wall assembly. See Figure 2.368 for integration of flashings into these wall types.

The application of the flashing falls into two categories: through-wall flashing and flexible membrane flashing.

- *Through-wall flashing* must typically bridge the open air space and, therefore, is typically sheet metal. Stainless steel, aluminum, galvanized steel, and copper are most common.
- *Flexible membrane flashing* is used to bridge gaps, while allowing movement, and as a transition to other materials, assemblies, and systems. Flexible flashing can be self-adhered peel-and-stick membranes, but their use is limited to applications that do not require bridging a gap larger than 1/2 in. For larger gaps, and where more substantial movement is anticipated, neoprene sheets or extruded cured silicone sheets are common. Note that the membrane flashing sheets must be compatible with all of the adjacent materials they contact.

VAPOR RETARDERS

WATER VAPOR MIGRATION
Water is present as vapor in indoor and outdoor air and as absorbed moisture in many building materials. Within the range of temperatures encountered in buildings, water may exist in the liquid, vapor, or solid states. Moisture-related problems may arise from changes in moisture content, from the presence of excessive moisture, or from the effects of changes of state (such as freezing within walls, or deterioration of materials because of rotting or corrosion).

RAINSCREEN FLASHING
2.368

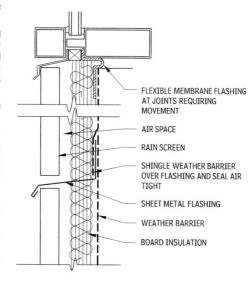

FLEXIBLE MEMBRANE FLASHING AT JOINTS REQUIRING MOVEMENT

AIR SPACE

RAIN SCREEN

SHINGLE WEATHER BARRIER OVER FLASHING AND SEAL AIR TIGHT

SHEET METAL FLASHING

WEATHER BARRIER

BOARD INSULATION

In the design and construction of the thermal envelope of buildings (the enclosure of desired temperatures and humidity), the behavior of moisture must be considered, particularly the change of state from vapor to liquid (condensation). Problems arise when moisture comes into contact with a relatively cold surface (temperature below the dew point), such as a window, or within outdoor walls or under-roof/ceilings. Excessive condensation within indoor walls that enclose cold spaces must be considered.

Although vapor moves by vapor pressure differences, it is important to recognize that moisture moved in air will move much larger quantities of water. Consequently, the causes of air motion must be considered, especially the infiltration/exfiltration at undesirable leakage rates at windows, doors, and other penetrations through the thermal envelope of the building.

Moisture problems generally occur in seasons when the outdoor temperature and vapor pressure are low and there are many indoor vapor sources. These sources may be occupant-induced, such as cooking, laundering, bathing, breathing, and perspiration, or machine-induced, including automatic washers and dryers, dishwashers, and humidifiers. All of these sources combine to cause vapor pressure indoors to be much higher than outdoors, so that the vapor tends to migrate outward through the building envelope. Vapor cannot permeate glazed windows or metal doors, but many other building materials are permeable to some extent. Walls are particularly susceptible to this phenomenon and such migration must be prevented, or at least minimized, by the use of low-permeance membranes, called *vapor retarders*. A vapor retarder is a material that has a flow rating of one perm or less (1 perm = 1 grain/hr ft–in. Hg vapor pressure difference).

Vapor barriers, when installed along with properly treated joints and penetrations, form a vapor retarder assembly, though it does not stop all vapor transmission. Vapor retarder assemblies should be installed as close as possible to the side of the wall through which moisture enters. Therefore, it is important to establish the side of moisture entrance in walls of controlled rooms within buildings. Also note that the beneficial effects of good vapor retarders will be lost without adequate weather barriers.

Moisture in building materials usually increases their thermal conductance significantly and unpredictably. Porous materials that become saturated with moisture lose most of their insulating capability and may not regain it when they dry out. Dust, which usually settles in airspaces, may become permanently affixed to originally reflective surfaces. Moisture migration by evaporation, vapor flow, and condensation can transport significant quantities of latent heat, particularly through fibrous insulating materials.

Positive steps should be taken to prevent migration of moisture in the form of vapor, and accumulation in the form of water or ice within building components. Vapor retarders, correctly located near the source of the moisture, are an effective means of preventing such migration. Venting of moisture-laden air from bathrooms, laundry rooms, and kitchens will reduce indoor vapor pressure, as will the introduction of outdoor air with low moisture content.

PARAPETS, COPINGS, AND GRAVEL STOPS

Parapets, copings, and gravel stops are problematic areas. Roofing and wall assemblies come together at an area that also experiences large amounts of thermal and structural movement. Detailing for long-term performance must be carefully considered to address each issue.

PARAPETS
Parapets experience many problems, as indicated in Figure 2.420. However, parapets do provide safety to rooftop maintenance personnel, allow for sloping roof structures without showing the slope on the elevation, and allow for the most dependable detailing of the interface with the roof system. The wall assembly weather barrier must connect to the roofing assembly.

PARAPET PROBLEMS
2.369

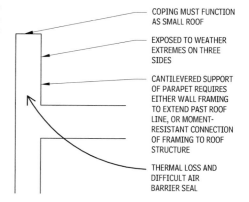

COPING MUST FUNCTION AS SMALL ROOF

EXPOSED TO WEATHER EXTREMES ON THREE SIDES

CANTILEVERED SUPPORT OF PARAPET REQUIRES EITHER WALL FRAMING TO EXTEND PAST ROOF LINE, OR MOMENT-RESISTANT CONNECTION OF FRAMING TO ROOF STRUCTURE

THERMAL LOSS AND DIFFICULT AIR BARRIER SEAL

The structural system of the wall (typically CMU or stud framing) must cantilever past the roof to support the parapet against high wind loads. Two common options include allowing the wall structure to continue from a lower level past the roof framing (balloon frame), or, cantilevering off the roof framing with a rigid moment-resisting connection. When tall parapets are required in wood or CFS construction, it is best to use the balloon frame method.

Detail membranes and closed-cell spray-applied foam to control air leaks and thermal bridging through parapets. Ensure that steel members that penetrate to parapet will not reach dew point within interior environment.

The structure for very short parapets may be included within the HAM enclosure, but because of limited air circulation, framing members more than 12 in. above the roof in cold climates will fall below the dew point because of the exposure to the exterior on three sides.

Contributor:
Maria Spinu, PhD, DuPont, Wilmington, Delaware.

GENERIC PARAPETS
2.370

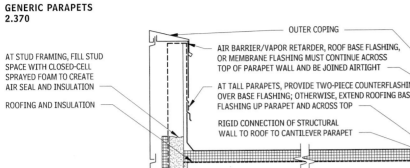

AT STUD FRAMING, FILL STUD SPACE WITH CLOSED-CELL SPRAYED FOAM TO CREATE AIR SEAL AND INSULATION

ROOFING AND INSULATION

AT CMU, PROVIDE BOND BEAM TO CAP CELLS, AND SPRAY FOAM AIR SEAL TO ROOF DECK

CONTINUE STRUCTURAL WALL PAST ROOF STRUCTURE TO CANTILEVER PARAPET

OUTER COPING

AIR BARRIER/VAPOR RETARDER, ROOF BASE FLASHING, OR MEMBRANE FLASHING MUST CONTINUE ACROSS TOP OF PARAPET WALL AND BE JOINED AIRTIGHT

AT TALL PARAPETS, PROVIDE TWO-PIECE COUNTERFLASHING OVER BASE FLASHING; OTHERWISE, EXTEND ROOFING BASE FLASHING UP PARAPET AND ACROSS TOP

RIGID CONNECTION OF STRUCTURAL WALL TO ROOF TO CANTILEVER PARAPET

EXTEND AIR BARRIER/VAPOR RETARDER UNDER PARAPET AND CONNECT TO ROOF VAPOR BARRIER OR TURN UP AND CONNECT TO ROOFING

RAINSCREEN

AIR SPACE

AIR BARRIER/VAPOR RETARDER

THERMAL INSULATION

STRUCTURAL WALL

THERMAL INSULATION THREE SIDES OF PARAPET

12" MAX.

ROOFING AND THERMAL INSULATION

SHORT PARAPET FRAMING INSIDE HAM ENCLOSURE; ALLOW INTERIOR AIR UP INTO STUD SPACE

PARAPET CAP SPLICE JOINT
2.371

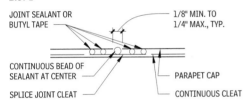

JOINT SEALANT OR BUTYL TAPE

CONTINUOUS BEAD OF SEALANT AT CENTER

SPLICE JOINT CLEAT

1/8" MIN. TO 1/4" MAX., TYP.

PARAPET CAP

CONTINUOUS CLEAT

SECTION THROUGH SPLICE JOINT

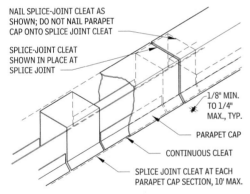

NAIL SPLICE-JOINT CLEAT AS SHOWN; DO NOT NAIL PARAPET CAP ONTO SPLICE JOINT CLEAT

SPLICE-JOINT CLEAT SHOWN IN PLACE AT SPLICE JOINT

1/8" MIN. TO 1/4" MAX., TYP.

PARAPET CAP

CONTINUOUS CLEAT

SPLICE JOINT CLEAT AT EACH PARAPET CAP SECTION, 10' MAX.

COPINGS

Copings are small roof areas and, as such, joints in sheet metal or masonry copings are not sufficiently reliable. Provide a waterproof backup of the air/vapor barrier, the roof base flashing, or a layer of membrane flashing.

Coping materials are commonly sheet metal, cast stone, and cut stone. Metals can have inherent finishes such as zinc, copper, and galvanized steel or aluminum; or steel with an applied finish that includes anodized, color-anodized, polyvinylidene fluoride (Kynar), baked-on enamels, powder coatings, and many others. PVDF coatings have become very common because of their wide range of colors and metallic finishes, extreme durability, and color consistency.

EDGE DETAIL
2.372

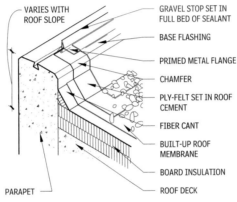

VARIES WITH ROOF SLOPE

GRAVEL STOP SET IN FULL BED OF SEALANT

BASE FLASHING

PRIMED METAL FLANGE

CHAMFER

PLY-FELT SET IN ROOF CEMENT

FIBER CANT

BUILT-UP ROOF MEMBRANE

BOARD INSULATION

ROOF DECK

PARAPET

GRAVEL STOP
2.373

IF ROOFING ASSEMBLY HAS AIR BARRIER/VAPOR RETARDER, TURN ONTO ROOF DECK AND SEAL

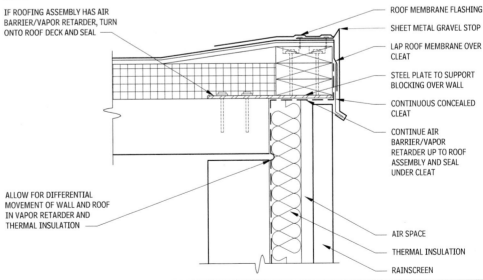

ALLOW FOR DIFFERENTIAL MOVEMENT OF WALL AND ROOF IN VAPOR RETARDER AND THERMAL INSULATION

ROOF MEMBRANE FLASHING

SHEET METAL GRAVEL STOP

LAP ROOF MEMBRANE OVER CLEAT

STEEL PLATE TO SUPPORT BLOCKING OVER WALL

CONTINUOUS CONCEALED CLEAT

CONTINUE AIR BARRIER/VAPOR RETARDER UP TO ROOF ASSEMBLY AND SEAL UNDER CLEAT

AIR SPACE

THERMAL INSULATION

RAINSCREEN

Sheet metal copings can be formed at a local shop or be a standard manufactured system. Manufactured copings provide improved appearance and engineered wind performance, whereas shop-fabricated copings are easier to obtain for small jobs or to customize.

GRAVEL STOPS

Gravel stops terminate the roof edge and cover the top of the wall. In rainscreen walls, the gravel stop covers the top of the air space and provides venting. The air barrier/vapor retarder membrane must be sealed to the roofing assembly under the gravel stop.

Gravel stops are available shop-made or manufactured in the same materials as metal copings.

They must be sealed into the roofing membrane, but the two systems have different coefficients of thermal expansion. Shop-fabricated gravel stop is nailed in two rows at 3 in. o.c to restrict the movement of the metal. Manufactured systems either anchor the system in a similar method or use spring metal systems to allow differential movement.

Contributor:
Joseph J. Williams, AIA, A/R/C/ Associates, Inc., Orlando, Florida.

GRAVEL STOP SPLICE JOINT
2.374

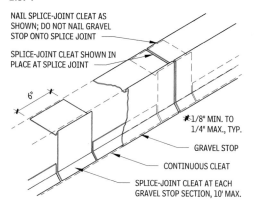

NAIL SPLICE-JOINT CLEAT AS SHOWN; DO NOT NAIL GRAVEL STOP ONTO SPLICE JOINT

SPLICE-JOINT CLEAT SHOWN IN PLACE AT SPLICE JOINT

6"

1/8" MIN. TO 1/4" MAX., TYP.

GRAVEL STOP

CONTINUOUS CLEAT

SPLICE-JOINT CLEAT AT EACH GRAVEL STOP SECTION, 10' MAX.

GRAVEL STOP OUTSIDE CORNER FABRICATION
2.375

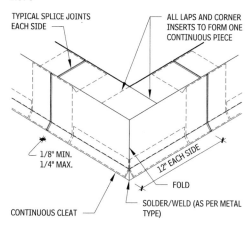

TYPICAL SPLICE JOINTS EACH SIDE

ALL LAPS AND CORNER INSERTS TO FORM ONE CONTINUOUS PIECE

1/8" MIN. 1/4" MAX.

12" EACH SIDE

FOLD

SOLDER/WELD (AS PER METAL TYPE)

CONTINUOUS CLEAT

EXTERIOR WINDOWS

Although architects choose fenestration products based on many unique priorities and circumstances, a number of common considerations apply to most situations. Here are the factors that affect window choice:

- *Appearance*: Size and shape, operating type and style, frame materials, glass color and clarity
- *Function*: Visible light transmittance (provision of daylight), glare control, reduction in fading from ultraviolet radiation, thermal comfort, resistance to condensation, ventilation, sound control, maintenance, and durability
- *Energy performance*: U-value, solar heat gain coefficient (SHGC) (which is replacing the shading coefficient), air leakage, annual heating and cooling season performance, and peak load impacts
- *Cost*: Initial cost of window units and installation, maintenance and replacement costs, effect on heating and cooling plant costs, and cost of annual heating and cooling energy

Many designers and homeowners find it difficult to assess the value of choosing a more energy-efficient window. Although some basic thermal and optical properties (e.g., U-factor, solar heat gain coefficient, and air leakage rate) can be identified if a window is properly labeled, this information does not tell how these properties influence annual energy use for heating and cooling. This must be determined by using an annual energy rating system or by computer simulation.

WINDOW CONFIGURATIONS
2.376

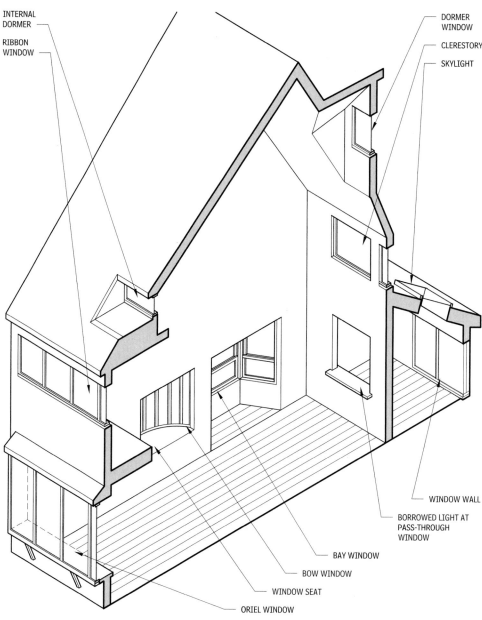

INTERNAL DORMER

RIBBON WINDOW

DORMER WINDOW

CLERESTORY

SKYLIGHT

WINDOW WALL

BORROWED LIGHT AT PASS-THROUGH WINDOW

BAY WINDOW

BOW WINDOW

WINDOW SEAT

ORIEL WINDOW

WINDOW BASICS

Any discussion on exterior windows must begin by defining these key terms:

- *Borrowed light*: An interior wall opening or window that allows light to be transferred into another space.
- *Clerestory*: The portion of a wall above an adjacent roof level; also, a fixed or operable window located in this part of a wall.
- *Dormer*: A vertical window set above the line of a sloped roof in a small projecting space with triangular side walls.
- *Internal dormer:* A vertical window set below the line of a sloped roof.
- *Oriel window*: A bay window supported by brackets, corbeling, or cantilevers.
- *Window wall*: A continuous series of fixed or operable sashes, separated by mullions that form an entire nonload-bearing wall surface.
- *Ribbon window*: A horizontal band of fixed or operable windows extending across a significant portion of the façade.
- *Mullion*: A slender vertical member separating lights, sashes, windows, or doors.
- *Muntin*: Nonstructural members separating panes within a sash; also called a *glazing bar* or *sash bar*.
- *Sash*: The basic unit of a window, consisting of frame, glazing, and gasketing; may be stationary or operable.

Contributors:
Joseph J. Williams, AIA, A/R/C/ Associates, Inc., Orlando, Florida; Richard J. Vitullo, AIA, Oak Leaf Studio, Crownsville, Maryland; John Carmody, University of Minnesota, Minneapolis, Minnesota; Stephen Selkowitz, Lawrence Berkeley National Laboratory, Berkeley, California.

PARTS OF A WINDOW
2.377

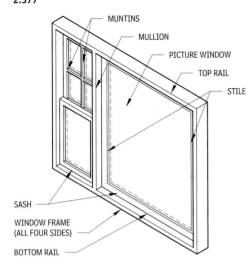

MUNTINS

MULLION

PICTURE WINDOW

TOP RAIL

STILE

SASH

WINDOW FRAME
(ALL FOUR SIDES)

BOTTOM RAIL

PERFORMANCE
Performance standards can be divided in three categories:

- Structural, air filtration, and water leakage
- Thermal and condensation
- Specialized

STRUCTURAL, AIR INFILTRATION, AND WATER LEAKAGE PERFORMANCE
These elements are standardized through ANSI/AAMA/WDMA 101/I.S. 2-97, "Voluntary Performance Specifications for Windows, Skylights, and Glass Doors." The 101 specification establishes five classes for windows and doors: R, LC, C, HC, and AW (i.e., residential, light commercial, commercial, heavy commercial, and architectural, respectively). This specification was updated in 2002 and 2005. In brief, the specification says:

- Select the class based on the project. The class titles are somewhat self-explanatory, but not limiting. AW class windows are typically used for institutional type projects, but they can also be used on a very high-quality house, for example.
- Performance is designated by a number that follows the type and class. For example, "DH-AW 40" designates a double-hung architectural window with a design pressure of 40 psf.
- The number is based on the anticipated structural wind load acting on the window, as determined from ASCE 7 and as required by the building code. Each type and class has minimum performance grades; optional grades increase in 5 psf increments.

- The designation is based on testing of samples for structural performance, air infiltration, and water leakage according to standardized methods. The higher the class, the more difficult the test.
- Windows can be selected of various grades to suit the field pressure and higher wind pressures at corners and higher elevations, or the windows for the entire building can be based on the highest wind pressure.

The 101 specification also provides standards for durability, operating forces, safety, materials, hardware, and overall quality.

Note that the ratings are based on specific test sizes, so it is necessary to verify that the tested size is at least as large as the windows required for the project. Also note that the tested window rarely includes perimeter pan flashing, receivers, mulled assemblies, or other nonstandard configurations, so it's important to ask the manufacturer how these conditions affect performance.

THERMAL AND CONDENSATION PERFORMANCE
Specific exterior climate and desired interior conditions affect the thermal performance of windows the most. Carefully evaluate these conditions to determine acceptable performance criteria, and then select windows that meet the criteria.

- Thermal performance of windows is rated according to NFRC 100, through standardized tests of windows. Note that glazing can dramatically affect the thermal performance, so verify the glazing used in the test versus project requirements.
- Condensation resistance is determined by AAMA test 1503.1; the higher the number, the better the performance. CRF (condensation resistance factor) testing is performed on standard-sized samples and includes glazing, which can influence the results. Note that the CRF test averages out a large number of temperature readings, meaning that a high-reported value may still include areas that perform relatively poorly. If absolutely no condensation is acceptable, then greater scrutiny of the actual test data versus the final CRF value is recommended.
- Assuming frames have thermally resistive materials or have thermal breaks, the glazing may be the major determinant of CRF and overall thermal performance. See the "Condensation Potential" chart, Figure 2.398.
- Thermal and CRF performance affect not only energy usage but also occupant comfort. Analyze the area of glazing, the location and activity of the occupant, and the use of supplemental heating for adequate protection.

SPECIALIZED PERFORMANCE
Standardized test procedures are available to evaluate a great many specialized performance criteria, including acoustic isolation, blast resistance, forced-entry resistance, and safety impact. Refer to the AAMA.

DETAILING
Manufacturers of windows provide only generic details for installation. Adjacent construction is frequently shown as a hatched single line. Therefore, it is necessary to detail the window frame in project-specific assemblies.

WALL ASSEMBLIES
Window installation must be detailed as appropriate for the generic wall assembly type, as described below.

- *Barrier walls*: Seal the window to the barrier. Use a subsill flashing to avoid introducing water into the wall. For massive barrier walls such as precast concrete, head flashing may be required to ensure that water seepage does not get behind the window.
- *Drainage plane walls*: Provide the primary seal of the window to the water-resistant drainage plane, and an outer seal in line with the wallcovering. The subsill flashing should extend past the outer wallcovering.
- *Drainage cavity walls*: Provide the primary seal of the window to the waterproof inner line of protection and an outer seal to the outer wallcovering. The subsill flashing may be detailed to weep into the drainage cavity because only incidental water should leak around the window.
- *Pressure-equalized (PE) rainscreen walls*: Use windows that incorporate PE rainscreen technology. Seal the air barrier of the window to the wall air barrier; likewise for the rainscreen. The subsill flashing may be detailed to seal to the air barrier.

AIR AND VAPOR BARRIERS
Detail the window installation so that the line of the air barrier and/or vapor barrier (if required) extends uninterrupted across the gap at the perimeter of the window. In windows with glass installed using wiggle glazing, or if interior removable stops are used, a heel bead may be required to maintain continuity of the air barrier between the frame and glass.

MOVEMENT
Window installation details must accommodate movement of the surrounding structure. Window heads (particularly at strip windows) often are located at shelf angles, and must accommodate movement typically in the range of 1/2 in. from above.

THERMAL CONTINUITY
Detail the windows to maintain a line of thermal insulation in the same plane as in the tested configuration and as intended by the window manufacturer. Windows installed over an air space in a drainage cavity wall may be exposed to cold on sides for which proper thermal breaks are not provided.

ADDITIONAL INFORMATION
For more information, see the *AAMA Window Selection Guide*.

Contributors:
John Carmody, University of Minnesota, Minneapolis, Minnesota; Stephen Selkowitz, Lawrence Berkeley National Laboratory, Berkeley, California.

WINDOW OPERATION TYPES

Accessibility issues for windows are important for present and future occupants. See *Beautiful Universal Design: A Visual Guide* (John Wiley & Sons, Hoboken, NJ), by Cynthia Leibrock and James Evan Terry for a complete discussion.

WINDOW OPERATION TYPES
2.378

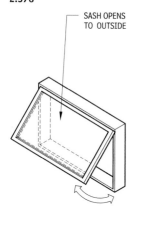
SASH OPENS TO OUTSIDE

AWNING/PROJECTED

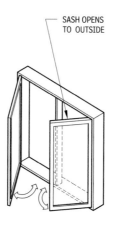
SASH OPENS TO OUTSIDE

DOUBLE CASEMENT/ PROJECTED

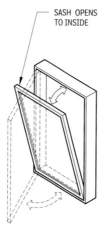
SASH OPENS TO INSIDE

DUAL ACTION

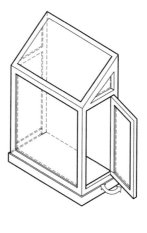

GREENHOUSE

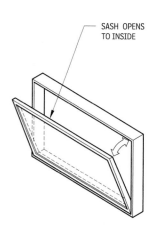
SASH OPENS TO INSIDE

HOPPER

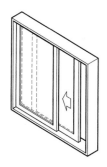

HORIZONTAL SLIDER

JALOUSIE

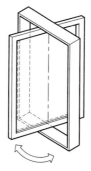

VERTICALLY PIVOTED

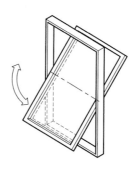

HORIZONTALLY PIVOTED

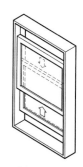

VERTICAL SLIDING (SINGLE- AND DOUBLE-HUNG)

CHARACTERISTICS OF WINDOW OPERATION TYPES
2.379

OPERATION TYPE	DIRECTION	SCREEN LOCATION	MAXIMUM OPENING (%)	WEATHER PROTECTION (WHEN OPEN)	EGRESS (CLEAR OPENING SIZE GOVERNS)	CLEANABILITY (EXTERIOR FROM INTERIOR)	UNIVERSAL OPERATION	NOTES
Awning/projected	Swings outward from hinge or pivot at top	Interior	100	Limited	Not possible without special hardware	Difficult	Acceptable	Not for use adjacent to walkways
Casement/projected	Swings outward or inward from a hinge or pivot on the side	Interior or exterior	100	Poor (wind-buffeting)	Good	Single units are difficult; paired windows easier	Acceptable	When outswinging, not suitable for use adjacent to walkways
Dual-action	Swings inward from hinge or pivot on bottom (hopper for ventilation, casement for cleaning)	Exterior	10, usually; 100, when casement	Good	Good	Easy	Acceptable	
Greenhouse (may be combined with other operation types)	May swing outward but may not be operable	Depends on window operation type	Depends on window operation type	Good	Poor	Difficult	Difficult	Unit projects from building; primarily residential use
Hopper/projected	Swings inward with hinge or pivot at bottom	Exterior	100	Good, with side vents	Not without special hardware	Easy	Acceptable	
Horizontal sliding	Slides sideways with a guide at top and bottom	Exterior	50, for equal-sized sash	Poor	Good	Difficult (easy with tilt-in feature)	Acceptable	Horizontal or square units operate more easily than tall units
Jalousie	Swings outward from pivots on the side	Interior	100	Limited (interior storm windows available)	Poor	Tedious	Acceptable	Translucent/opaque panes provide additional sunscreening; high air leakage
Pivoted/reversible (horizontally and vertically pivoted)	Swings around vertical or horizontal axis	Rare, but special-shaped screens	100	Poor (wind-buffeting)	Poor (size of clear opening restrictions)	Easy	Difficult	
Vertical sliding (single- and double-hung)	Slides up and down along guide on the side	Exterior	50, for equal-sized sash	Poor (but good with hospital sills)	Good	Difficult (easy with tilt-in feature)	Difficult	

Contributors:
John Carmody, University of Minnesota, Minneapolis, Minnesota; Stephen Selkowitz, Lawrence Berkeley National Laboratory, Berkeley, California; Daniel F.C. Hayes, AIA, Washington, DC.

GLASS PRODUCTS

Glass is a hard, brittle, amorphous substance made by melting silica (sometimes combined with oxides of boron or phosphorus) with certain basic oxides (notably sodium, potassium, calcium, magnesium, and lead) to produce annealed flat glass by a controlled cooling process. Most glasses soften at 932°F to 2012°F (500°C to 1100°C). The brittleness of glass is such that minute surface scratches in manufacturing greatly reduce its strength.

INDUSTRY-QUALITY STANDARDS

A number of industry-quality standards apply to glass products:

- Glazing Association of North America (GANA) *Glazing Manual*
- ASTM C 1036: "Specification for Flat Glass"
- ASTM C 1048: "Specification for Heat-treated Flat Glass—Kind HS, Kind FT Coated and Uncoated"
- UL Standard 752: Bullet-Resisting Equipment
- UL Standard 752: Bullet-Resisting Glazing Material
- AAMA Curtain Wall and Storefront Publications: *Glass and Glazing*
- ASTM E 1300: "Practice for Determining Load Resistance of Glass in Buildings"
- CPSC Standard 16CFR 1201: Safety Standard for Architectural Glazing Materials
- ANSI Z97.1: Safety Glazing Materials Used in Buildings—Safety Performance Specification and Methods of Test
- ASTM C 1172: "Specification for Laminated Architectural Flat Glass"

More information can also be found in these two books: *Glass in Building* by David Button and Brian Pye (Pilkington, with Butterworth Architecture, 1993) and *Glass in Architecture* by Michael Wiggington (Phaidon Press Ltd., 1996). Also, be sure to consult glass manufacturers for current information because processes, qualities, finishes, colors, sizes, thicknesses, and limitations are revised continually. The information presented here represents one or more manufacturers' guidelines.

BASIC TYPES OF CLEAR GLASS

The following are basic types of clear glass:

- *Sheet glass*: Sheet glass is manufactured by a horizontal flat or vertical draw process, and then annealed slowly to produce a natural flat-fired, high-gloss surface. It generally is used in residential and industrial applications. Because it is not mechanically polished, inherent surface waves are noticeable in sizes larger than 4 sq ft. For minimum distortion, larger sizes are installed with the wave running horizontally. The width is listed first when specifying. For architectural applications, sheet glass is either single-strength (0.101 in. thick) or double-strength (0.134 in. thick). Very little glass is produced in the United States by this process; almost all sheet glass is produced by the float process.
- *Float glass*: Generally accepted as the successor to polished plate glass, float glass has become the quality standard of the glass industry. It is manufactured by floating molten glass on a surface of molten tin, then annealing it slowly to produce a transparent flat glass, thus eliminating grinding and polishing. This process produces a glass with very uniform thickness and flatness, making it suitable for applications requiring excellent optical properties, such as architectural windows, mirrors, and specialty applications. It is available in thicknesses ranging from 1/8 to 7/8 in.. Float glass is made to the specification requirements of ASTM C 1036, and its minimum thickness to resist wind load is established using ASTM E 1300.
- *Plate glass*: Transparent flat glass is ground and polished after rolling to make plate glass. Cylindrical and conical shapes can be bent to a desired curvature (within limits). Only glass for specialty applications is produced by this method; it is not produced for widespread use in architectural applications.

VARIATIONS OF BASIC GLASS TYPES

Several variations of the basic glass types are in use today.

- *Patterned glass*: Patterned glass is known also as *rolled* or *figured glass*. It is made by passing molten glass through rollers that are etched to produce the design. Designs include flutes, ribs, grids, and other regular and random patterns, which provide translucency and a degree of obscurity. Usually, only one side of the glass is imprinted with a pattern. Patterned glass is available in thicknesses of 1/8, 3/16, and 7/32 in.
- *Wire glass*: Wire glass is available as clear polished glass or in various patterns such as square-welded mesh, diamond-welded mesh, and linear parallel wires. Some distortion, wire discoloration, and misalignment are inherent. Some 1/4-in. wired glass products are recognized as certified safety glazing materials for use in hazardous locations (e.g., fire-rated windows, doors, and skylights). For applicable fire and safety codes that govern their use, refer to ANSI Z97.1. Note that wire glass is no longer exempt from regulations for locations requiring safety glass (i.e., doors and sidelights). Therefore, it is better to avoid wire glass entirely. Consider using other laminated and specialty fire-rated and safety-rated products. If wire glass must be used, ensure that the submitted product complies with the indicated requirement for special wire glass that does comply with safety regulations. Verify application of patterned wire glass to avoid applications requiring safety glazing.
- *Cathedral glass*: Cathedral glass is known also as *art glass*, *stained glass*, or *opalescent glass*. It is produced in many colors, textures, and patterns. Cathedral glass is usually 1/8 in. thick, and is used primarily in decorating leaded glass windows. Specialty firms usually contract this type of glass.
- *Obscure glass*: Obscure glass is used to obscure a view or create a design. The entire surface on one or both sides of the glass can be sandblasted, acid-etched, or both. When a glass surface is altered by any of these methods, the glass is weakened, and may be difficult to clean.

STRENGTHENED GLASS

Glass can be strengthened either by a controlled heating and cooling process, or by immersion in a chemical bath. Both processes have glass thickness, size, and use restrictions that should be verified.

HEAT-TREATED GLASS

Heat-strengthened (Kind HS) and tempered (Kind FT) glass are produced by reheating annealed float glass close to its softening point and then rapidly quenching (cooling) it with high-velocity blasts of air. Both types have greatly increased mechanical strength and resistance to thermal stresses. Before it is heat-treated, the glass must be fabricated to its exact size and shape (including any holes), because neither type of glass can be altered after heat treatment.

Most manufacturers heat-treat the glass using a horizontal process that can introduce warpage, kinks, and bowing into the finished product, which may create aesthetic or technical concerns. A vertical process may still be available that produces tong marks or depressions into the glass surface near the suspended edge. Vertical processing may produce large amounts of warping and distortion. The heat treatment quenching pattern on the surface of the glass can become visible as a pattern of light and dark areas at certain oblique viewing angles and with polarized light. This effect can be more pronounced with thicker glass and may be an aesthetic consideration. Refer to ASTM C 1048 for allowable tolerances and other properties.

Heat-strengthened glass is generally two to three times stronger than annealed glass. It cannot be cut, drilled, or altered after fabrication. Unlike tempered glass, it breaks into large, sharp shards similar to broken annealed glass. Heat-strengthened glass is not acceptable for safety glazing applications.

TEMPERED GLASS

Tempered glass is generally four to five times stronger than annealed glass. It breaks into innumerable small, cube-shaped fragments. It cannot be cut, drilled, or altered after fabrication; the precise size required and any special features (such as notches, holes, edge treatments, and so on) must be specified when ordering.

Tempered glass can be used as a safety-glazing material provided it complies with the ANSI and CPSC references listed in the "Laminated Glass" section, below. Tempered glass can be used in insulating and laminated assemblies and in wired, patterned, and coated processes. All float and sheet glass 1/8 in. or thicker may be tempered.

CHEMICALLY TREATED GLASS

Chemically treated glass is produced by submerging annealed float glass in a bath of molten potassium salts. The larger potassium ions in the bath exchange places with the smaller sodium ions in the glass surface, creating a surface compression layer that strengthens the glass. Chemically treated glass breaks into large, sharp shards similar to broken annealed glass. It does not have the visual distortion that can be caused by a heat-treated strengthening process. At present, chemical strengthening is primarily limited to the glass lights of laminated security glass.

ULTRACLEAR GLASS

The high clarity and high visible light transmittance that characterize ultraclear glass comes from the special soda lime mixture it is made from, which minimizes the iron content that normally gives a slight greenish color to clear flat glass. Ultraclear glass is generally available in thicknesses from 1/8 to 3/4 in. It can be heat-strengthened, tempered, sandblasted, etched, or assembled into laminated glass. Ultraclear glass is used for commercial display cases, museum cases, display windows, frit-coated spandrel glass, aquariums, mirrors, shelving, security glass, and other uses in which clarity and better color transmittance are required.

HEAT-ABSORBING OR TINTED GLASS

This type of float glass was developed to help control solar heat and glare in large areas of glass. It is available in blue, bronze, gray, or green, and in thicknesses ranging from 1/8 to 1/2 in. The glass absorbs a portion of the sun's energy because of its admixture contents and thickness; it then dissipates the heat to both the exterior and interior. The exterior glass surface rejects some heat, depending on the sun's position. Heat-absorbing glass has a higher temperature than clear glass when exposed to the sun; thus, the central area expands more than the cooler, shaded edges, causing edge tensile stress buildup. When designing heat-absorbing or tinted glass windows, consider the following:

SOLAR PERFORMANCE OF HEAT-ABSORBING OR TINTED GLASS
2.380

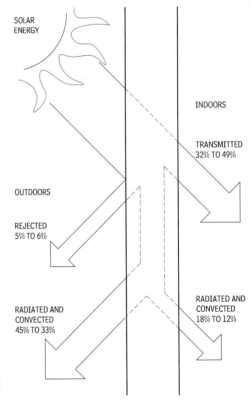

SOLAR ENERGY

INDOORS

TRANSMITTED 32% TO 49%

OUTDOORS

REJECTED 5% TO 6%

RADIATED AND CONVECTED 45% TO 33%

RADIATED AND CONVECTED 18% TO 12%

Contributor:
Thomas F. O'Connor, AIA, FASTM, Smith, Hinchman & Grylls, Detroit, Michigan.

- To minimize shading problems and tensile stress buildup at the edges, provide conditions in which glass edges warm as rapidly as the exposed glass.
- The thicker the glass, the greater the solar energy absorption.
- Indoor shading devices such as blinds and draperies reflect energy back through the glass, thus increasing the temperature of the glass. Spaces between indoor shading devices and the glass, including ceiling pockets, should be vented adequately. Heating elements always should be located on the interior side of shading devices, directing warm air away from the glass.
- The glass can be heat-treated to increase its strength and resistance to edge tensile stress buildup.

INSULATING GLASS

Insulated glass is constructed from two or more panes of glass separated by spacer bars to form a hermetically sealed void between the panes. This arrangement greatly enhances the insulating thermal and acoustic properties of the glass unit. The most common insulated units are filled with air, and employ a hollow spacer bar containing a desiccant to absorb moisture vapor inside the unit. The void can be filled with an inert gas such as argon, and the spacer can be changed to a "warm edge" type to further improve the insulating value of the unit. The spacer bar is sealed to the glass with a continuous joint sealant (typically, butyl or silicone) forming an airtight seal. Structural joint sealant, usually silicone or polyurethane, is applied outboard of the spacer bar to hold the panes of glass together, especially during transport and handling. For coastal environments, in structural silicone glazing systems and when otherwise recommended by the manufacturer, the architect may limit both sealants to silicone type. By varying the make-up of the individual panes of glass in the insulating unit, its insulating, shading and visual characteristics can be greatly enhanced.

Durability for insulating glass is established through ASTM E 774, "Standard Specification for the Durability of Sealed Insulated Glass Units," for Class C, CB, or CBA. Class CBA is the most durable and is typically selected for most commercial and institutional work.

SOUND CONTROL GLASS

Laminated, insulating, laminated insulating, and double laminated-insulating glass products commonly are used for sound control. STC ratings from 31 to 51 are available, depending on glass thicknesses, airspace size, polyvinyl butyral film thickness, and number of laminated units used in insulating products.

SPANDREL GLASS

Spandrel glass is available tinted or with a variety of coatings, including reflective, ceramic frit (patterned and solid colors), and direct-to-glass polyvinylidene fluoride (PVDF) coatings. It can be heat-treated or laminated, and is available as insulating glass units. Insulation and vapor retarders can be added to spandrel glass. Consult with spandrel glass manufacturers for guidelines.

SECURITY GLASS

Security glass is composed of multiple layers of glass and/or polycarbonate plastic that are laminated together under heat and pressure with a polyvinyl butyral (for glass) or polyurethane plastic (for polycarbonate) film. It is available in multilayer laminated glass, insulating, laminated insulating, and double-laminated insulating or spaced configurations, generally in thicknesses from 3/8 in. to 2-1/2 in. as a laminated product and up to about 4-3/4 inches for insulating and spaced construction products. Bullet-resistant glass should be tested to UL 752, and burglar-resistant to UL 972. Consult manufacturers for blast-resistant glass. Security glass products, depending on type, are subject to size limitations, and some are not recommended for exterior applications. Consult with the manufacturer for glazing requirements and restrictions on use.

TYPICAL INSULATING OR SPACED CONSTRUCTION SECURITY GLASS PROFILE
2.381

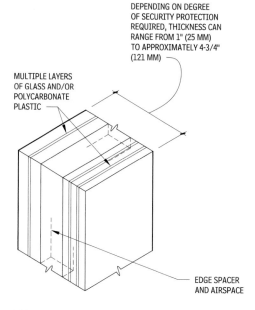

DEPENDING ON DEGREE OF SECURITY PROTECTION REQUIRED, THICKNESS CAN RANGE FROM 1" (25 MM) TO APPROXIMATELY 4-3/4" (121 MM)

MULTIPLE LAYERS OF GLASS AND/OR POLYCARBONATE PLASTIC

EDGE SPACER AND AIRSPACE

TYPICAL MULTILAYER SECURITY GLASS PROFILE
2.382

DEPENDING ON DEGREE OF SECURITY PROTECTION REQUIRED, THICKNESS CAN RANGE FROM 3/8" TO APPROXIMATELY 2-1/2"

BONDING LAYER, POLYVINYL BUTYRAL (PVB) FOR GLASS LAYERS AND POLYURETHANE FOR POLYCARBONATE PLASTIC LAYERS

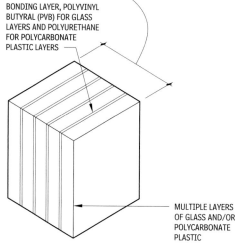

MULTIPLE LAYERS OF GLASS AND/OR POLYCARBONATE PLASTIC

COATED GLASS

A reflective or low-emissivity coating can be applied to the surface of monolithic glass. Generally, only pyrolitically applied "hard" coatings (which have scratch resistance) are used on exposed glass surfaces. During glass manufacture, pyrolitic coatings are sprayed onto the glass before it cools, which integrates them with the glass surface. Magnetically sputtered or "soft" coatings can also be applied to the glass surface, but they must be protected from the elements as part of an insulating or laminated glass product. The range of coating types, aesthetic appearances, and thermal performance available for pyrolitic coatings is generally less than for sputtered coatings.

LAMINATED GLASS

To produce laminated glass, a tough, clear plastic polyvinyl butyral (PVB) sheet (interlayered), ranging in thickness from 0.015 to 0.090 in., is sandwiched, under heat and pressure, between lights of sheet, plate, float, wired, heat-absorbing, tinted, reflective, low-emissivity, or heat-treated glass, or combinations of each. When laminated glass breaks, the particles tend to adhere to the plastic film.

Laminated glass is manufactured to the specification requirements of ASTM C 1172. Laminated safety glass should be manufactured to comply with ANSI Z97.1 and CPSC 16CFR 1201.

LAMINATED GLASS PROFILE
2.383

DEPENDING ON PVB AND GLASS LIGHT THICKNESS, LAMINATED GLASS CAN VARY FROM 1/4" TO 3/4" IN THICKNESS

POLYVINYL BUTYRAL (PVB) THICKNESS RANGES FROM 0.03" TO 0.09"

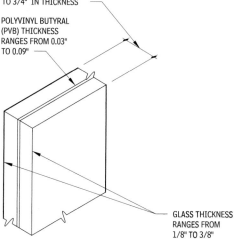

GLASS THICKNESS RANGES FROM 1/8" TO 3/8"

BENT GLASS

Clear, tinted, ceramic frit-coated spandrel, pyrolitically coated, patterned, laminated, and wire glass are among glass types that can be bent in thicknesses to about 1 in. and to a minimum radius of about 4 in. Sharp angle bends to 90°, edgework, pattern cutting, and tempering (meeting safety glazing standards), and heat-strengthening are also available. Bent glass can be fabricated into insulating glass units. Bent glass tolerances must be compatible with the glazing system. Size, configuration, and product availability vary by fabricator.

PHOTOVOLTAIC (PV) GLASS

There are two types of photovoltaic (PV) glass: crystalline silicon (sandwiched between two lights of glass) and thin-film amorphous silicon (applied to an interior-facing glass surface). When these arrangements are exposed to sunlight, they generate either DC or AC power, which is transferred by concealed wiring to the building's power system. Pressure bar or structural silicone flush-glazed curtain walls and skylights, awnings, sunshades, light shelves, and roof panels are some of the systems that can incorporate PV glass. For curtain walls and skylights, the pressure bar type allows easy concealment of the wiring. Shadow patterns from the cap on the PV glass surface must be considered in system design. Flush-glazed systems have no shadow patterns, but wiring concealment is more difficult, and the PV module on the glass must be kept from reacting with the structural silicone sealant. Both types of PV glass are used for opaque curtain wall spandrel panels and can be used for curtain wall or skylight vision glass if the quality of daylighting and visibility is acceptable. Consult PV glass and metal-framing system manufacturers to determine availability, suitability, and cost for a particular application.

Contributors:
Thomas F. O'Connor, AIA, FASTM; Smith, Hinchman and Grylis, Detroit, Michigan.

PHOTOVOLTAIC GLASS (IN A PRESSURE BAR FRAMING SYSTEM)
2.384

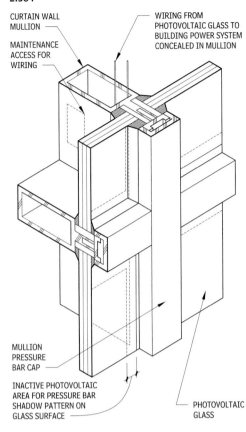

CURTAIN WALL MULLION

MAINTENANCE ACCESS FOR WIRING

WIRING FROM PHOTOVOLTAIC GLASS TO BUILDING POWER SYSTEM CONCEALED IN MULLION

MULLION PRESSURE BAR CAP

INACTIVE PHOTOVOLTAIC AREA FOR PRESSURE BAR SHADOW PATTERN ON GLASS SURFACE

PHOTOVOLTAIC GLASS

DECORATIVE SILK-SCREENED (OR FRIT) GLASS
Annealed clear or tinted glass is washed and ceramic frit paint (in standard or custom color) silk-screened on its surface in a standard or custom pattern or design (such as dots, holes, lines, or a logo) and then dried in an oven. The frit-coated glass is then subjected to very high temperatures in a tempering furnace to fire the ceramic frit permanently to the glass surface. As a result, silk-screened glass will be either heat-strengthened or tempered after firing. Reflective and low-emissivity coatings can also be applied to the glass surface. Silk-screened glass can be used monolithically or for insulating or laminated glass products.

LEADED STAINED GLASS
Decorative stained glass is characterized by pieces of glass joined together with cames (H-shaped strips) of various widths. Varying the widths adds to the window's decorative effect. Joints are sol-

dered on both sides of the panel. To prevent leakage, a mastic waterproofing material is inserted between the glass and came flange.

Another method of joining the pieces of glass is to band the edges of the glass with a copper foil tape, burnished to the glass and then soldered with a continuous bead of solder on both sides.

Bracing bars are fastened to the sash at frequent intervals to strengthen and support the leaded glass. Round bars tied to the leaded glass with twisted copper wires are the most flexible and resilient, allowing for great amounts of thermal movement. Where this system is not suitable, galvanized steel flat bars can be soldered to the surface of the leaded glass.

When the glass requires detail painting, shading, or texturing, it must be done with special mineral pigments and fired at temperatures of 1000°F to 1200°F or higher to ensure absolute permanency.

OUTSIDE PROTECTION GLASS
Properly made decorative glass does not necessarily need additional glazing to make it waterproof, but it is valuable for insulating purposes and to afford some protection from external damage. Frames should be designed with a 3/4-in. ventilated space between glass, and should be arranged for the protection glass to be installed from the exterior, and the decorative glass from the interior. Clear glass or textured glass 3/16 to 1/4 in. thick is most successful.

GLAZING SEALANTS
Exterior decorative glass must be pressed into a deep back bed of mastic compound or glazing tape. When outside protection glass is used, a watertight seal is not required, and foam tape compressed between the glazing bead and glass may suffice.

SIZE LIMITATIONS
Decorative glass panels should not exceed 12 sq ft, making it necessary to divide larger openings with metal division bars: tee bars for single glazed windows, and special channel bars for windows with outside protection glass.

GLASS COLORS
Machine-made and blown glass from the United States, England, France, and Germany are available in most solid colors, as wells as mixed colors and textures. Uniformity of color will vary from glass of different batches. Special colors are derived by "sumping," or kiln firing.

FACETED STAINED GLASS
A twentieth-century development in the art of stained glass introduced the use of glass dalles, 8 by 12 by 1 in., cast in hundreds of different colors. These can be cut to any shape and used in combination with an opaque matrix of epoxy resin or reinforced concrete 5/8 to 1 in. in thickness, to create translucent windows and walls of great beauty. Sizes are limited, and an outer protection glass is required.

Further information is available from the Stained Glass Association of America.

DECORATIVE GLASS PANELS
2.386

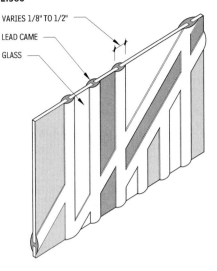

VARIES 1/8" TO 1/2"

LEAD CAME

GLASS

FACETED STAINED GLASS
2.387

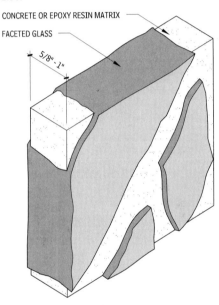

CONCRETE OR EPOXY RESIN MATRIX

FACETED GLASS

5/8" - 1"

WINDOW GLAZING

Important window glazing considerations are as follows: :

- Dry glazing methods are generally less expensive than wet methods.
- Cap beads make glazing watertight and weathertight and are required for face-sealed glazing systems. Cap beads can also be used to increase the performance of existing windows.
- Pressure-plate glazing systems are common for many site-fabricated curtain wall systems.
- Four-sided structural silicone work is generally required to be shop fabricated.
- Two-sided structural silicone glazing usually has the other two sides either pressure-plate glazed or wet/dry glazed.
- Heel beads can be added at the bottom edge and turned up 6 to 8 in. to protect against water leaks caused by differential pressures between the interior and exterior.
- Heel beads at the full perimeter may be required to provide a continuous air barrier in a pressure-equalized rainscreen curtain wall system.

AVERAGE PERFORMANCE VALUES OF 1/4-IN. UNCOATED GLASS
2.385

GLASS TYPE	PERCENT TRANSMITTANCE				
	AVERAGE DAYLIGHT	TOTAL SOLAR	ULTRAVIOLET	PERCENT REFLECTANCE AVERAGE DAYLIGHT	SHADING COEFFICIENT
Ultraclear	91	89	85	8	1.04
Clear	89–88	78–76	71–62	9–8	0.95–0.94
Clear laminated	86–84	67–64	< 1	8–7	0.86–0.83
Green	77–75	42–47	42–30	8–7	0.70–0.67
Blue-green	75–71	49–35	32–28	7	0.72–0.60
Blue	55	47	41	6	0.70
Bronze	55–51	51–48	23–31	6	0.74–0.71
Gray	46–43	49–42	25–32	5–6	0.72–0.66

Contributors:
Thomas F. O'Connor, AIA, FASTM, Smith, Hinchman & Grylls, Detroit, Michigan; Randall S. Lindstrom, AIA, Ware Associates, Inc., Chicago, Illinois; Joseph A. Wilkes, FAIA, Annapolis, Maryland; Bobbie Burnett Studio, Annapolis, Maryland.

- Skylights generally use wet glazing methods, cap beads, or structural silicone glazing.
- "Wiggle" or "jiggle" glazed systems use dry glazing with a removable stop along only one side of the frame or sash. After installing the outer line of gaskets, the pane of glass is wiggled into oversized glazing pockets, the removable stop is installed, and the inner gaskets are installed.

WET GLAZING
2.388

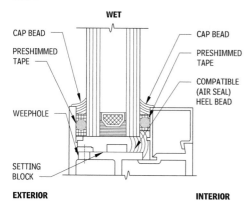

WET

CAP BEAD
PRESHIMMED TAPE
WEEPHOLE
SETTING BLOCK

CAP BEAD
PRESHIMMED TAPE
COMPATIBLE (AIR SEAL) HEEL BEAD

EXTERIOR   INTERIOR

INSULATING GLASS IN WOOD SASH
2.389

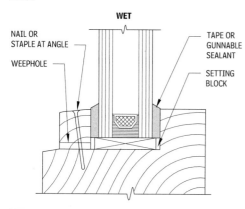

WET

NAIL OR STAPLE AT ANGLE
WEEPHOLE

TAPE OR GUNNABLE SEALANT
SETTING BLOCK

EXTERIOR   INTERIOR

BUTT JOINT GLAZING
2.390

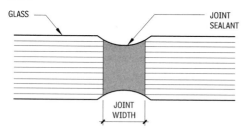

GLASS
JOINT SEALANT

JOINT WIDTH

Butt-joint glazing generally is not acceptable for insulating glass unless a careful review has been conducted in concert with the manufacturer of the insulating unit, because excessive deflection of unsupported edge may cause premature failure.

DRY GLAZING
2.391

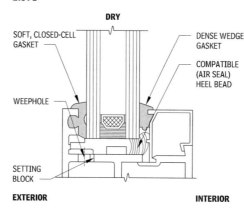

DRY

SOFT, CLOSED-CELL GASKET
WEEPHOLE
SETTING BLOCK

DENSE WEDGE GASKET
COMPATIBLE (AIR SEAL) HEEL BEAD

EXTERIOR   INTERIOR

PRESSURE-GLAZED SYSTEM
2.392

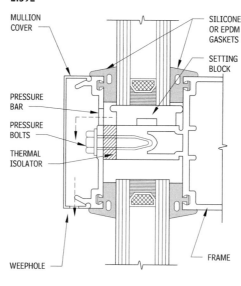

MULLION COVER
PRESSURE BAR
PRESSURE BOLTS
THERMAL ISOLATOR
WEEPHOLE

SILICONE OR EPDM GASKETS
SETTING BLOCK
FRAME

STRUCTURAL SILICONE GLAZING
2.393

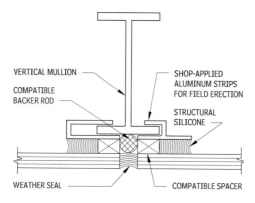

VERTICAL MULLION
COMPATIBLE BACKER ROD
WEATHER SEAL

SHOP-APPLIED ALUMINUM STRIPS FOR FIELD ERECTION
STRUCTURAL SILICONE
COMPATIBLE SPACER

WET/DRY GLAZING SYSTEM
2.394

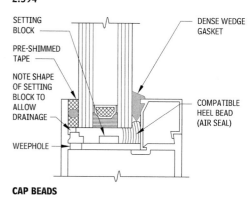

SETTING BLOCK
PRE-SHIMMED TAPE
NOTE SHAPE OF SETTING BLOCK TO ALLOW DRAINAGE
WEEPHOLE

DENSE WEDGE GASKET
COMPATIBLE HEEL BEAD (AIR SEAL)

CAP BEADS

WET/DRY GLAZING WITH CAP BEAD
2.395

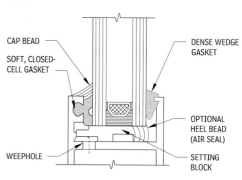

CAP BEAD
SOFT, CLOSED-CELL GASKET
WEEPHOLE

DENSE WEDGE GASKET
OPTIONAL HEEL BEAD (AIR SEAL)
SETTING BLOCK

STRUCTURAL SILICONE GLAZING—TYPICAL VERTICAL MULLION FOR TWO-SIDED SYSTEM
2.396

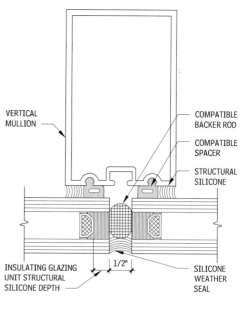

VERTICAL MULLION
INSULATING GLAZING UNIT STRUCTURAL SILICONE DEPTH
1/2"

COMPATIBLE BACKER ROD
COMPATIBLE SPACER
STRUCTURAL SILICONE
SILICONE WEATHER SEAL

STRUCTURAL SILICONE GLAZING—TYPICAL HORIZONTAL MULLION FOR FOUR-SIDED SYSTEM
2.397

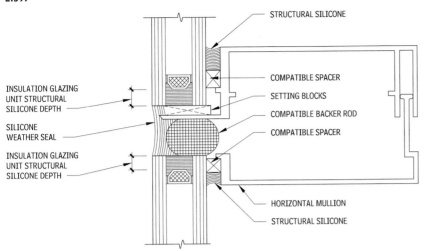

- STRUCTURAL SILICONE
- COMPATIBLE SPACER
- SETTING BLOCKS
- COMPATIBLE BACKER ROD
- COMPATIBLE SPACER
- HORIZONTAL MULLION
- STRUCTURAL SILICONE

- INSULATION GLAZING UNIT STRUCTURAL SILICONE DEPTH
- SILICONE WEATHER SEAL
- INSULATION GLAZING UNIT STRUCTURAL SILICONE DEPTH

GLASS THERMAL RESISTANCE VALUES
2.399

MATERIAL AND DESCRIPTION	OVERALL HEAT TRANSMISSION COEFFICIENT (U)	SEASONS	RESISTANCE (R)
VERTICAL PANELS—EXTERIOR			
Flat Glass:			
Single glass	1.10	Winter	0.91
	1.04	Summer	0.96
Insulating glass: two lights of glass, 3/16" airspace	0.62	Winter	1.61
	0.65	Summer	1.54
1/4" airspace	0.58	Winter	1.72
	0.61	Summer	1.64
1/2" airspace	0.49	Winter	2.04
	0.56	Summer	1.79
Insulating glass: three lights of glass, 1/4" airspace	0.39	Winter	2.56
	0.44	Summer	2.22
1/2" airspace	0.31	Winter	3.23
	0.39	Summer	2.56
1/2" airspace; low-emittance coating e = 0.20	0.32	Winter	3.13
	0.38	Summer	2.63
e = 0.40	0.38	Winter	2.63
	0.45	Summer	2.22
e = 0.60	0.43	Winter	2.33
	0.51	Summer	1.96
Storm windows: 1/4" airspace	0.50	Winter	2.00
	0.50	Summer	2.00
Single Plastic Sheet:			
1/8" thick (nominal)	1.06	Winter	0.94
	0.98	Summer	1.02
1/4" thick (nominal)	0.96	Winter	1.04
	0.89	Summer	1.12
HORIZONTAL PANELS—EXTERIOR			
Flat glass single glass	1.23	Winter	0.81
	0.83	Summer	1.20
Insulating glass: two lights of glass, 3/16" airspace	0.70	Winter	1.43
	0.57	Summer	1.75
1/4" airspace	0.65	Winter	1.54
	0.54	Summer	1.85
1/2" airspace	0.59	Winter	1.69
	0.49	Summer	2.04

CONDENSATION POTENTIAL

Figure 2.484 shows the potential for condensation on glazing (at the center of glass) at various outdoor temperatures and indoor relative humidity conditions. Condensation can occur at any point on or above the curves. (Note: All airspaces are 1/2 in.; all coatings are E = 0.10.)

For example, at 20°F outside, condensation will form on the inner surface of double glazing when the indoor relative humidity is 52 percent or higher. It will form at an indoor relative humidity of 70 percent or higher if a double-pane window with a low-E coating and argon fill is used.

CONDITIONS THAT LEAD TO CONDENSATION ON WINDOWS
2.398

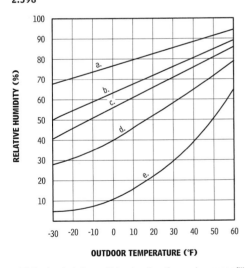

a. Triple-glazed windows with two low-E coatings and argon gas fill.
b. Double-glazed windows with a low-E coating and argon gas fill.
c. Double-glazed windows with a low-E coating.
d. Double-glazed windows.
e. Single-glazed windows.

THERMAL RESISTANCE VALUES OF GLAZING MATERIALS

The thermal conductivity of glass is relatively high (k = 7.5); and for single glazing, most of the thermal resistance is imposed at the indoor and outdoor surfaces. Indoors, approximately two-thirds of the heat flows by radiation to the room surfaces; only one-third flows by convection. This can be materially affected by the use of forced airflow from induction units, for example. The inner surface coefficient of heat transfer, hi, can be substantially reduced by applying a low-emittance metallic film to the glass.

For glazing with airspaces, the U-value can be reduced to a marked degree by the use of low-emittance films. This process imparts a variable degree of reflectance to the glass, thereby reducing its shading coefficient.

Manufacturers' literature should be consulted for more details on this important subject. Also consult the *ASHRAE Handbook*.

SOLAR GAIN THROUGH FENESTRATION SYSTEMS

Heat gains through sunlit fenestration constitute major sources of cooling load in summer. In winter, discomfort is often caused by excessive amounts of solar radiation entering through south-facing windows. By contrast, passive solar design depends largely on admission and storage of the radiant energy falling on south-facing and horizontal surfaces. Admission takes place both by transmission through glazing and by inward flow of absorbed energy. With or without the sun, heat flows through glazing, either inwardly or outwardly, whenever there is a temperature difference between the indoor and outdoor air. These heat flows may be calculated in the following manner.

The solar heat gain is estimated by a two-step process. The first step is to find, either from tabulated data or by calculation, the rate at which solar heat would be admitted under the designated conditions through a single square foot of double strength (1/8-in.) clear sheet glass. This quantity, called the solar heat gain factor (SHGF), is set by (a) the local latitude; (b) the date, hence the declination; (c) the time of day (solar time should be used); (d) the orientation of the window. Tabulated values of SHGF are given in the *ASHRAE Handbook*, for latitudes from 0° (the equator) to 64° N by 8° increments and for orientations around the compass from N to NNW, by 22.5° increments. Selected values from the 40° table are given in an adjacent column.

Each individual fenestration system, consisting of glazing and shading devices, has a unique capability to admit solar heat. This property is evaluated in terms of its shading coefficient (SC), which is the ratio of the amount of solar heat admitted by the system under consideration to the solar heat gain factor for the same conditions. In equation form, this becomes:

$$\text{Solar heat gain (Btu/sq ft} \cdot \text{hr)} = \text{SC} \times \text{SHGF}$$

Values of the shading coefficient also are given in the *ASHRAE Handbook* for the most widely used glazing materials alone and in combination with internal and external shading devices.

NOTES

2.399 a. Resistances are representative values for dry materials and are intended as design (not specification) values for materials in normal use. Unless shown otherwise in descriptions of materials, all values are for 167°F mean temperature.

b. Includes paper backing and facing, if any. In cases where insulation forms a boundary (highly reflective or otherwise) of an airspace, refer to the appropriate table for the insulating value of the airspace. Some manufacturers of batt and blanket insulation mark their products with an R-value, but they can ensure only the quality of the material as shipped.

c. Average values only are given, as variations depend on density of the board and on the type, size, and depth of perforations.

d. Thicknesses supplied by different manufacturers may vary, depending on the particular material.

e. Values will vary if density varies from that listed.

f. Data on rectangular core concrete blocks differ from the data for oval core blocks because of core configuration, different mean temperature, and different unit weight. Weight data on oval core blocks are not available.

g. Weight of units approximately 75/a high by 155/s long are given to describe blocks tested. Values are for 1 sq ft area.

h. Thermal resistance of metals is so low that in building constructions it is usually ignored. Values shown emphasize relatively easy flow of heat along or through metals so that they are usually heat leaks, inward or outward.

i. Spaces of uniform thickness are bounded by moderately smooth surfaces.

j. Values shown are not applicable to interior installations of materials listed.

k. Winter is heat flow up; summer is heat flow down, based on area of opening, not on total surface area. Derived from data from ASHRAE Handbook of Fundamentals (1977), Chapter 22.

Contributor:
John I. Yellott, PE, College of Architecture, Arizona State University, Tempe, Arizona.

WINDOW FRAME TYPES

WINDOW FRAME DETAILS
2.400

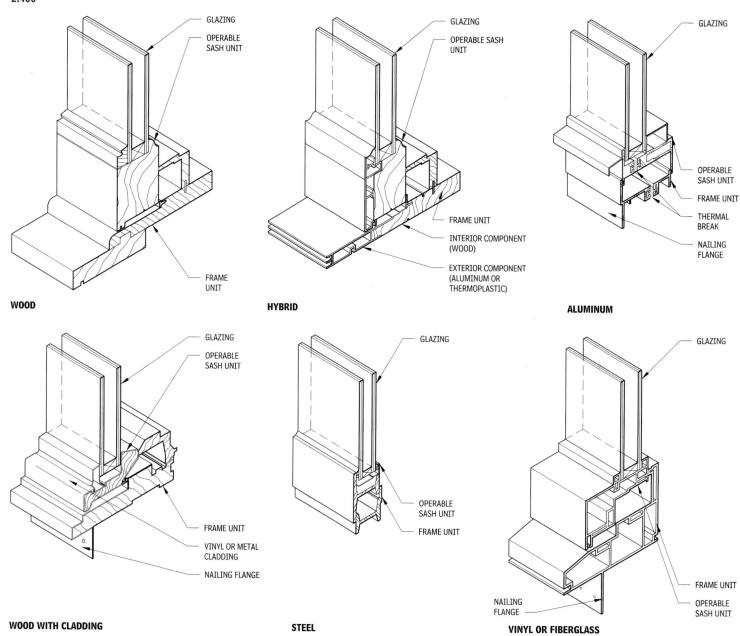

GLAZING
OPERABLE SASH UNIT
FRAME UNIT

WOOD

GLAZING
OPERABLE SASH UNIT
FRAME UNIT
INTERIOR COMPONENT (WOOD)
EXTERIOR COMPONENT (ALUMINUM OR THERMOPLASTIC)

HYBRID

GLAZING
OPERABLE SASH UNIT
FRAME UNIT
THERMAL BREAK
NAILING FLANGE

ALUMINUM

GLAZING
OPERABLE SASH UNIT
FRAME UNIT
VINYL OR METAL CLADDING
NAILING FLANGE

WOOD WITH CLADDING

GLAZING
OPERABLE SASH UNIT
FRAME UNIT

STEEL

GLAZING
NAILING FLANGE
FRAME UNIT
OPERABLE SASH UNIT

VINYL OR FIBERGLASS

Contributors:
John Carmody, University of Minnesota, Minneapolis, Minnesota;
Stephen Selkowitz, Lawrence Berkeley National Laboratory, Berkeley,
California.

WINDOW FRAME TYPES
2.401

FRAME TYPE	CHARACTERISTICS	MAINTENANCE	FINISHES	HEAT TRANSFERENCE	SUSTAINABILITY	NOTES
Wood	Solid members; ease of milling into complex shapes; attractive and traditional appearance U-factor: 0.3–0.5	Rot prevention: refinish in 5- to 10-year cycle, or use permanent finish	Oil or latex paint, stains, oils, or varnishes; preservatives; polyurethane resin coatings; prefinished or site-finished	Low	Renewable resource; requires high-quality solid stock	Traditional and typical material; variety of species available; easy repair
Wood with cladding	Metal- or plastic-clad wood U-factor for vinyl clad: 0.3–0.5; for metal clad, 0.4–0.6	Minimal	See metal and plastic frames.	Low with vinyl cladding, slightly higher with metal	Use of less desirable wood materials; salvageable cladding	Wood for stability/strength, cladding for maintenance
Hybrids	Wood interior, metal or plastic exterior U-factor for vinyl/wood: 0.3–0.5; for metal/wood, 0.4–0.6	See wood, metal, and plastic categories.	See other categories.	Low with vinyl/wood hybrid, slightly higher with metal/wood hybrid	Use of lower quantities of any one material	Good interior look with good exterior performance and low maintenance
Steel	Thin bar/angle steel profiles; cast, extruded, forged U-factor: similar to that of aluminum	Rust prevention: refinish in 5- to 10-year cycle or use permanent finish	Galvanizing, zinc-phosphate coatings; primed; painted; factory finishes: baked enamel, fluoropolymer, polyurethane coatings	Moderate, unless thermal break is installed	Nonrenewable, salvageable	High strength/smallest frame profiles of all types; stainless steel available but expensive
Aluminum	Box profiles; extrusions; lightweight U-factor: 1.0 with thermal break; 1.9–2.2 without thermal break	Minimal	Natural; factory-applied: baked enamel, epoxy, anodized, electrostatic (powder), fluoropolymer coatings	High, unless thermal break is installed	Nonrenewable, salvageable	High strength, no maintenance
Vinyl (PVC)	High impact resistance; box profiles; multichambered extrusions U-factor for hollow: 0.3–0.5; for insulated, 0.2–0.4	Minimal	Integral when fabricated (limited colors)	Low	Nonrenewable, petroleum-based	UV/sun protection from discoloration may be required; acid- and salt-air-resistant
Fiberglass	Box profiles, polymer-based thermoplastic; dimensionally stable U-factor for hollow: 0.3–0.5; for insulated, 0.2–0.4	Minimal	Integral when fabricated	Low	Spun glass in resin binders	More expensive but more structurally stable than vinyl

WINDOW INSTALLATION

Regardless of the quality of the window unit, ultimate performance depends on proper installation. The intersection of the window frame with surrounding walls has always been a difficult detail, and light modern materials have exacerbated the problem. AAMA 2400, "Standard Practice for Installation of Windows with a Mounting Flange in Stud Frame Construction," and ASTM E 2112-01, "Standard Practice for Installation of Exterior Windows, Doors and Skylights," both establish a variety of methods for quality installations.

The architect may desire to exceed the standard installation practices for more durable and dependable service. In particular, it is recommended that you always provide a subsill of sheet metal or other impervious material, with watertight end dams and a slope to the exterior, and avoid penetrations in the horizontal portion of the sill.

Qualified installers who understand the importance of many detailed tasks to the overall level of quality are essential. Consider AAMA Certified "Installation Masters" or similar independently trained and certified installers.

For more information, see the AAMA *Window Selection Guide*.

WOOD WINDOW WEATHERPROOFING DETAILS
2.402

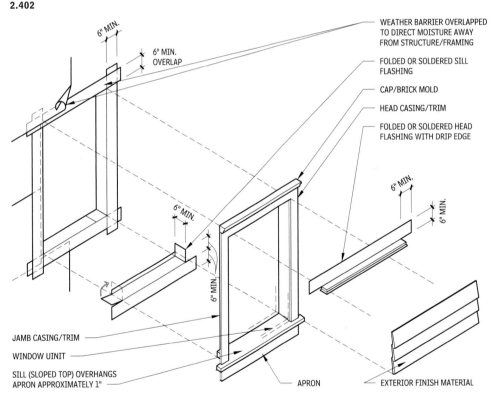

6" MIN.

6" MIN. OVERLAP

WEATHER BARRIER OVERLAPPED TO DIRECT MOISTURE AWAY FROM STRUCTURE/FRAMING

FOLDED OR SOLDERED SILL FLASHING

CAP/BRICK MOLD

HEAD CASING/TRIM

FOLDED OR SOLDERED HEAD FLASHING WITH DRIP EDGE

6" MIN.

6" MIN.

6" MIN.

6" MIN.

JAMB CASING/TRIM

WINDOW UINIT

SILL (SLOPED TOP) OVERHANGS APRON APPROXIMATELY 1"

APRON

EXTERIOR FINISH MATERIAL

NOTES

2.402 a. Caulking, sealant, adhesive, or gasket seals window framing and wall joints to form air barrier.
b. These principles are also applicable to door weatherproofing.

Contributors:
John Carmody, University of Minnesota, Minneapolis, Minnesota;
Stephen Selkowitz, Lawrence Berkeley National Laboratory, Berkeley, California.

SEALING MOUNTING FLANGES
2.403

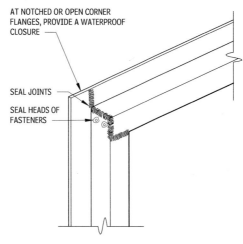

FILLET BEAD TO SEAL MOUNTING FLANGE TO FRAME

FACE SEAL AT BUTT JOINT BETWEEN MOUNTING FLANGES

FRAME CORNERS
2.404

AT NOTCHED OR OPEN CORNER FLANGES, PROVIDE A WATERPROOF CLOSURE

SEAL JOINTS

SEAL HEADS OF FASTENERS

RESIDENTIAL WOOD WINDOW HEAD DETAIL
2.406

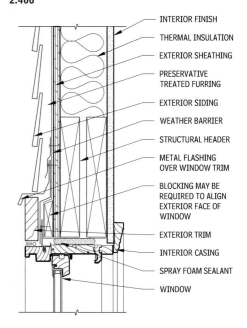

INTERIOR FINISH

THERMAL INSULATION

EXTERIOR SHEATHING

PRESERVATIVE TREATED FURRING

EXTERIOR SIDING

WEATHER BARRIER

STRUCTURAL HEADER

METAL FLASHING OVER WINDOW TRIM

BLOCKING MAY BE REQUIRED TO ALIGN EXTERIOR FACE OF WINDOW

EXTERIOR TRIM

INTERIOR CASING

SPRAY FOAM SEALANT

WINDOW

FLANGED RESIDENTIAL WINDOW WEATHERPROOFING
2.405

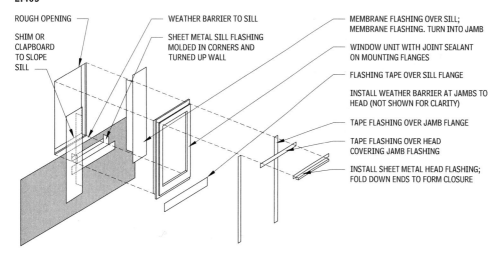

ROUGH OPENING

SHIM OR CLAPBOARD TO SLOPE SILL

WEATHER BARRIER TO SILL

SHEET METAL SILL FLASHING MOLDED IN CORNERS AND TURNED UP WALL

MEMBRANE FLASHING OVER SILL; MEMBRANE FLASHING. TURN INTO JAMB

WINDOW UNIT WITH JOINT SEALANT ON MOUNTING FLANGES

FLASHING TAPE OVER SILL FLANGE

INSTALL WEATHER BARRIER AT JAMBS TO HEAD (NOT SHOWN FOR CLARITY)

TAPE FLASHING OVER JAMB FLANGE

TAPE FLASHING OVER HEAD COVERING JAMB FLASHING

INSTALL SHEET METAL HEAD FLASHING; FOLD DOWN ENDS TO FORM CLOSURE

RESIDENTIAL WOOD WINDOW SILL DETAIL
2.408

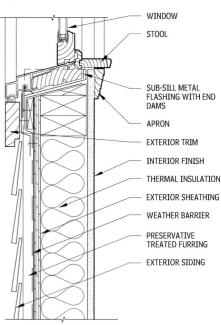

WINDOW

STOOL

SUB-SILL METAL FLASHING WITH END DAMS

APRON

EXTERIOR TRIM

INTERIOR FINISH

THERMAL INSULATION

EXTERIOR SHEATHING

WEATHER BARRIER

PRESERVATIVE TREATED FURRING

EXTERIOR SIDING

RESIDENTIAL WOOD WINDOW JAMB DETAIL
2.407

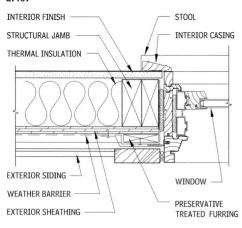

INTERIOR FINISH

STRUCTURAL JAMB

THERMAL INSULATION

STOOL

INTERIOR CASING

EXTERIOR SIDING

WEATHER BARRIER

EXTERIOR SHEATHING

WINDOW

PRESERVATIVE TREATED FURRING

NOTES

2.403 Follow manufacturer's instructions.
2.404 Inspect frames, and add sealant to increase resistance to water penetration.
2.405 a. Install weather barrier above head (not shown, for clarity).
b. Install expanding foam seal between rough opening and window frame on four sides (not shown).

Contributors:
John F. Kaulbach, AIA, Kling, Philadelphia, Pennsylvania.

TYPICAL HEAD AT CAVITY WALL
2.409

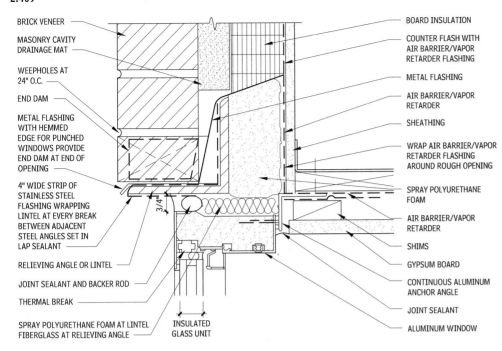

BRICK VENEER

MASONRY CAVITY
DRAINAGE MAT

WEEPHOLES AT
24" O.C.

END DAM

METAL FLASHING
WITH HEMMED
EDGE FOR PUNCHED
WINDOWS PROVIDE
END DAM AT END OF
OPENING

4" WIDE STRIP OF
STAINLESS STEEL
FLASHING WRAPPING
LINTEL AT EVERY BREAK
BETWEEN ADJACENT
STEEL ANGLES SET IN
LAP SEALANT

RELIEVING ANGLE OR LINTEL

JOINT SEALANT AND BACKER ROD

THERMAL BREAK

SPRAY POLYURETHANE FOAM AT LINTEL
FIBERGLASS AT RELIEVING ANGLE

3/4"

INSULATED
GLASS UNIT

BOARD INSULATION

COUNTER FLASH WITH
AIR BARRIER/VAPOR
RETARDER FLASHING

METAL FLASHING

AIR BARRIER/VAPOR
RETARDER

SHEATHING

WRAP AIR BARRIER/VAPOR
RETARDER FLASHING
AROUND ROUGH OPENING

SPRAY POLYURETHANE
FOAM

AIR BARRIER/VAPOR
RETARDER

SHIMS

GYPSUM BOARD

CONTINUOUS ALUMINUM
ANCHOR ANGLE

JOINT SEALANT

ALUMINUM WINDOW

TYPICAL WINDOW JAMB AT CAVITY WALL
2.410

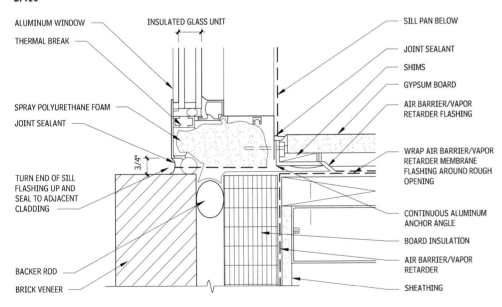

ALUMINUM WINDOW

THERMAL BREAK

INSULATED GLASS UNIT

SPRAY POLYURETHANE FOAM

JOINT SEALANT

3/4"

TURN END OF SILL
FLASHING UP AND
SEAL TO ADJACENT
CLADDING

BACKER ROD

BRICK VENEER

SILL PAN BELOW

JOINT SEALANT

SHIMS

GYPSUM BOARD

AIR BARRIER/VAPOR
RETARDER FLASHING

WRAP AIR BARRIER/VAPOR
RETARDER MEMBRANE
FLASHING AROUND ROUGH
OPENING

CONTINUOUS ALUMINUM
ANCHOR ANGLE

BOARD INSULATION

AIR BARRIER/VAPOR
RETARDER

SHEATHING

TYPICAL SILL AT CAVITY WALL
2.411

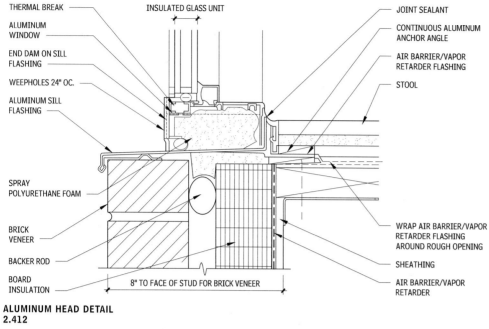

THERMAL BREAK

ALUMINUM WINDOW

END DAM ON SILL FLASHING

WEEPHOLES 24" OC.

ALUMINUM SILL FLASHING

INSULATED GLASS UNIT

SPRAY POLYURETHANE FOAM

BRICK VENEER

BACKER ROD

BOARD INSULATION

8" TO FACE OF STUD FOR BRICK VENEER

JOINT SEALANT

CONTINUOUS ALUMINUM ANCHOR ANGLE

AIR BARRIER/VAPOR RETARDER FLASHING

STOOL

WRAP AIR BARRIER/VAPOR RETARDER FLASHING AROUND ROUGH OPENING

SHEATHING

AIR BARRIER/VAPOR RETARDER

ALUMINUM HEAD DETAIL
2.412

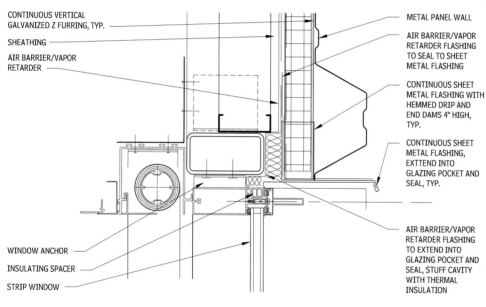

CONTINUOUS VERTICAL GALVANIZED Z FURRING, TYP.

SHEATHING

AIR BARRIER/VAPOR RETARDER

WINDOW ANCHOR

INSULATING SPACER

STRIP WINDOW

METAL PANEL WALL

AIR BARRIER/VAPOR RETARDER FLASHING TO SEAL TO SHEET METAL FLASHING

CONTINUOUS SHEET METAL FLASHING WITH HEMMED DRIP AND END DAMS 4" HIGH, TYP.

CONTINUOUS SHEET METAL FLASHING, EXTTEND INTO GLAZING POCKET AND SEAL, TYP.

AIR BARRIER/VAPOR RETARDER FLASHING TO EXTEND INTO GLAZING POCKET AND SEAL, STUFF CAVITY WITH THERMAL INSULATION

Contributor:
Bernard E. Suber, Kling, Washington, DC.

ALUMINUM SILL DETAIL
2.413

ALUMINUM STRIP WINDOW

INSULATING SPACER

INTERIOR FINISH

WINDOW ANCHOR

PRESSIVE BAR

MULLION COVER, PROVIDE VARIES

CONTINUOUS SHEET METAL SILL; EXTEND INTO GLAZING POCKET AND SEAL

WEATHER BARRIER MEMBRANE FLASHING; EXTEND INTO GLAZING POCKET AND SEAL; STUFF CAVITY WITH THERMAL INSULATION

TYPICAL STOREFRONT
2.414

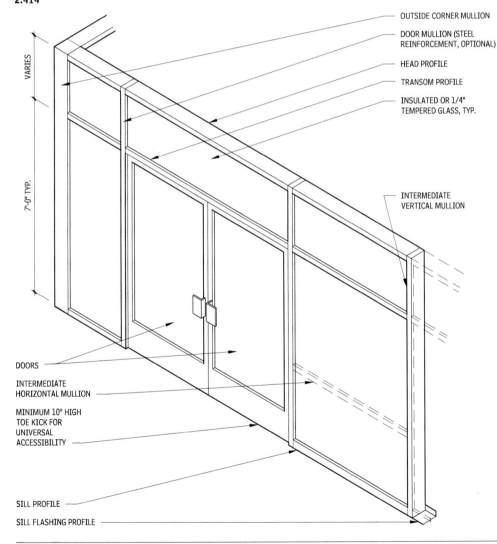

VARIES

7'-0" TYP.

OUTSIDE CORNER MULLION

DOOR MULLION (STEEL REINFORCEMENT, OPTIONAL)

HEAD PROFILE

TRANSOM PROFILE

INSULATED OR 1/4" TEMPERED GLASS, TYP.

INTERMEDIATE VERTICAL MULLION

DOORS

INTERMEDIATE HORIZONTAL MULLION

MINIMUM 10" HIGH TOE KICK FOR UNIVERSAL ACCESSIBILITY

SILL PROFILE

SILL FLASHING PROFILE

STOREFRONT DESIGN AND DETAILS

Glass and metal frame storefront systems typically are designed to allow good views into and out of ground-level commercial spaces. Metal members and glass sections are assembled on-site to form both wall and entrance systems, which typically are attached to the floor structure below and the bottom of structure above, or to a suspended structural frame above the ceiling. Storefront systems typically have lower resistance to air and water infiltration, and less structural performance. Most storefront systems are not pressure-equalized, but do manage water that penetrates into the glazing pocket. Watertight subsills with end dams are required.

Storefront systems design involves these considerations:

- Storefront systems are available in a variety of attachment/ assembly types, depending on the structural or aesthetic design and on the manufacturer. Glass and metal materials come in various shapes, colors, profiles, and structural capabilities.
- Applicable codes must be consulted for safety requirements, glass size, thickness, and tempering. Consult all applicable codes, standards, and regulations for accessibility requirements. These may include requirements for hardware, thresholds, opening forces, and closing speeds.
- Manufacturers' data on structural adequacy must be consulted for required loads, and for frame and transom bar reinforcement. Calculations for deflection and wind-load stresses must be considered in the design of storefront systems. Reinforcing for required loads can be provided by steel reinforcing inserts or by use of a heavier metal mullion profile. Consult a structural engineer for analysis and design.
- The height of entrance doors is typically 7 ft 0 in. Typical door widths are 3 ft 0 in., 3 ft 6 in., pair of 2 ft 6 in., pair of 3 ft 0 in. For accessible doors, at least one leaf of a pair must be 32 in. minimum clear width.
- Perimeters of storefront systems are difficult to detail for both an outer seal and an inner air/vapor barrier seat. Therefore, limit use to low-rise construction, preferably under canopies or overhangs in areas of heavy rainfall.
- Select systems with thermal break and condensation resistance factor (CRF) to suit interior and exterior conditions.

SNAP-TOGETHER/SCREW SPLINE STOREFRONT ASSEMBLY
2.415

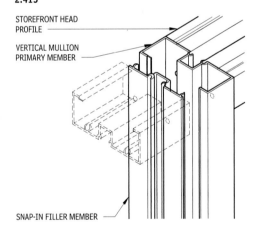

STOREFRONT HEAD PROFILE

VERTICAL MULLION PRIMARY MEMBER

SNAP-IN FILLER MEMBER

NOTE

2.415 The head, intermediate horizontal profile, and sill members are screwed to vertical members at predrilled locations.

Contributor:
Daniel F. C. Hayes, AIA, Washington, DC.

SHEAR BLOCK STOREFRONT ASSEMBLY
2.416

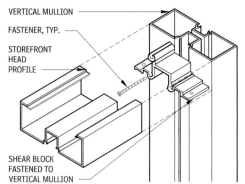

VERTICAL MULLION

FASTENER, TYP.

STOREFRONT HEAD PROFILE

SHEAR BLOCK FASTENED TO VERTICAL MULLION

WALL SECTION AT STOREFRONT
2.417

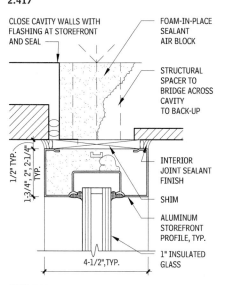

CLOSE CAVITY WALLS WITH FLASHING AT STOREFRONT AND SEAL

FOAM-IN-PLACE SEALANT AIR BLOCK

STRUCTURAL SPACER TO BRIDGE ACROSS CAVITY TO BACK-UP

1/2" TYP., 2", 2-1/4" TYP.

1-3/4" TYP.

INTERIOR JOINT SEALANT FINISH

SHIM

ALUMINUM STOREFRONT PROFILE, TYP.

1" INSULATED GLASS

4-1/2", TYP.

HEAD/JAMB

SLIDING STOREFRONTS AND MULTIPLE SLIDING DOORS

When working with sliding storefronts and multiple sliding doors, these considerations apply:

- Sliding glass door wood finishes are available in clear pine with natural varnish, primed, or painted finishes.
- Cladding for wood doors is available in vinyl or aluminum with electrostatic paint or in anodized aluminum.
- Aluminum frames are available anodized or with electrostatic paint finishes.
- Check with manufacturer's literature for material, cladding, and color options.
- For pocket doors required to be accessible, refer to all applicable codes, standards, and regulations for specific requirements.
- Refer to all applicable codes, standards, and regulations for specific requirements for doors that must be accessible.

BYPASS DOOR DETAILS
2.418

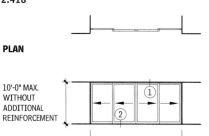

PLAN

10'-0" MAX. WITHOUT ADDITIONAL REINFORCEMENT

①

②

PANEL WIDTH 10'-0" MAX.

ELEVATION

①

②

FINISH FLOOR

SECTION

POCKET DOOR DETAILS
2.419

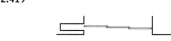

PLAN

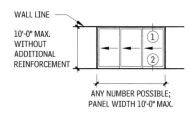

WALL LINE

10'-0" MAX. WITHOUT ADDITIONAL REINFORCEMENT

①

②

ANY NUMBER POSSIBLE; PANEL WIDTH 10'-0" MAX.

ELEVATION

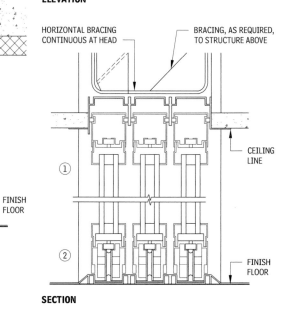

HORIZONTAL BRACING CONTINUOUS AT HEAD

BRACING, AS REQUIRED, TO STRUCTURE ABOVE

CEILING LINE

①

②

FINISH FLOOR

SECTION

Contributor:
Daniel F. C. Hayes, AIA, Washington, DC; Joseph A. Wilkes, FAIA, Wilkes and Faulkner, Annapolis, Maryland.

MULTIPLE SLIDING DOOR DETAILS
2.420

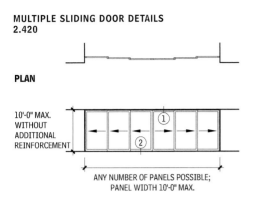

PLAN

10'-0" MAX. WITHOUT ADDITIONAL REINFORCEMENT

ANY NUMBER OF PANELS POSSIBLE; PANEL WIDTH 10'-0" MAX.

ELEVATION

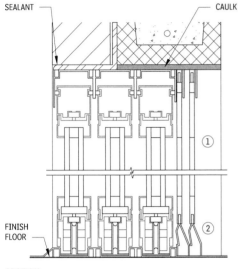

SEALANT

CAULK

①

FINISH FLOOR

②

SECTION

ALL-GLASS STOREFRONT
2.421

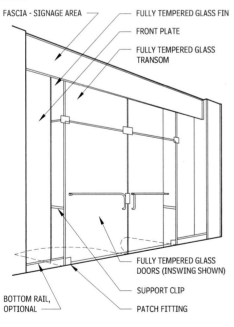

FASCIA - SIGNAGE AREA

FULLY TEMPERED GLASS FIN

FRONT PLATE

FULLY TEMPERED GLASS TRANSOM

FULLY TEMPERED GLASS DOORS (INSWING SHOWN)

SUPPORT CLIP

BOTTOM RAIL, OPTIONAL

PATCH FITTING

STOREFRONT SYSTEMS

Keep the following in mind when working with storefront systems:

- Storefront systems typically require a watertight sill or subsill to direct water within the system to the exterior, unless interior or protected by a large overhang. Verify the manufacturer's details and customize the system to suit the project.
- Review tinted- and coated-glass applications and details to eliminate the possibility of thermal breakage caused by shading devices and shadow patterns.
- Review setting-block spacing, size, and hardness to prevent glass slippage and breakage.
- Weep holes are required at sill for double glazing.
- Other materials such as hollow metal or wood can be used for custom work and in saltwater atmospheres where aluminum will corrode.
- Various aluminum anodized color finishes are available. Class I (0.7 mil) and Class II (0.4 mil) in black, bronze, or clear, are standard with most manufacturers. Class I is recommended for most exterior applications.
- To extend life of aluminum and to reduce the tendency of surface pitting, wash aluminum periodically with water and mild detergent.
- Glass edges mitered at corners are not recommended. Maximum vertical span for butt glazing is 10 ft by 8 ft wide.
- Mullions are clear glass. Tinted or coated glass lights may be considered for small areas. Maximum vertical span is 30 ft.
- Care should be taken to protect the public from the possibility of overhead glass breakage. Laminated glass provides the highest level of protection, but fully tempered glass may be acceptable.
- Higher bulkheads can be built up with aluminum tubing and applied stops. Locate expansion mullions 20 ft o.c.
- Use receptor for deflection or dimensional tolerance.

Refer to manufacturer's current recommendations for specific applications.

CENTER GLAZED
2.422

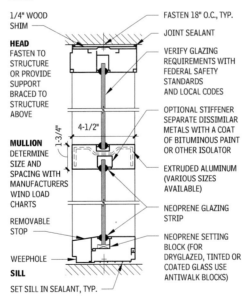

1/4" WOOD SHIM

HEAD
FASTEN TO STRUCTURE OR PROVIDE SUPPORT BRACED TO STRUCTURE ABOVE

MULLION
DETERMINE SIZE AND SPACING WITH MANUFACTURERS WIND LOAD CHARTS

REMOVABLE STOP

WEEPHOLE

SILL

SET SILL IN SEALANT, TYP.

FASTEN 18" O.C., TYP.

JOINT SEALANT

VERIFY GLAZING REQUIREMENTS WITH FEDERAL SAFETY STANDARDS AND LOCAL CODES

OPTIONAL STIFFENER SEPARATE DISSIMILAR METALS WITH A COAT OF BITUMINOUS PAINT OR OTHER ISOLATOR

EXTRUDED ALUMINUM (VARIOUS SIZES AVAILABLE)

NEOPRENE GLAZING STRIP

NEOPRENE SETTING BLOCK (FOR DRYGLAZED, TINTED OR COATED GLASS USE ANTIWALK BLOCKS)

4-1/2"

1-3/4"

OFF-CENTER GLAZED
2.423

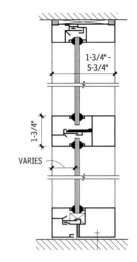

1-3/4" - 5-3/4"

1-3/4"

VARIES

FACE GLAZED
2.424

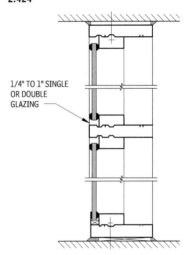

1/4" TO 1" SINGLE OR DOUBLE GLAZING

APPLIED STOPS
2.425

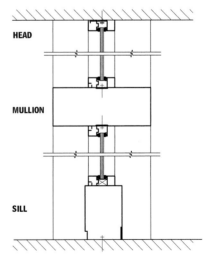

HEAD

MULLION

SILL

Contributor:
Joseph A. Wilkes, FAIA, Annapolis, Maryland; Eric K. Beach, Rippeteau Architects, PC, Washington, DC.

BUTT-GLAZED WITH FLUSH HEAD AND JAMB
2.426

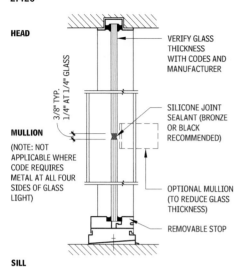

HEAD

VERIFY GLASS THICKNESS WITH CODES AND MANUFACTURER

3/8" TYP. 1/4" AT 1/4" GLASS

MULLION

(NOTE: NOT APPLICABLE WHERE CODE REQUIRES METAL AT ALL FOUR SIDES OF GLASS LIGHT)

SILICONE JOINT SEALANT (BRONZE OR BLACK RECOMMENDED)

OPTIONAL MULLION (TO REDUCE GLASS THICKNESS)

REMOVABLE STOP

SILL

GLASS MULLION
2.427

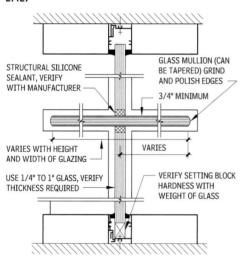

STRUCTURAL SILICONE SEALANT, VERIFY WITH MANUFACTURER

GLASS MULLION (CAN BE TAPERED) GRIND AND POLISH EDGES

3/4" MINIMUM

VARIES WITH HEIGHT AND WIDTH OF GLAZING

VARIES

USE 1/4" TO 1" GLASS, VERIFY THICKNESS REQUIRED

VERIFY SETTING BLOCK HARDNESS WITH WEIGHT OF GLASS

THERMAL GLAZING
2.428

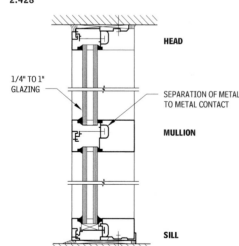

1/4" TO 1" GLAZING

HEAD

SEPARATION OF METAL TO METAL CONTACT

MULLION

SILL

SLOPED GLAZING
2.429

WALL TRANSITION

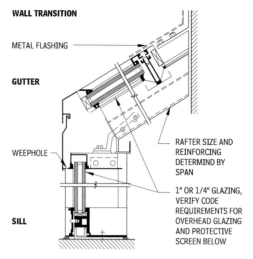

METAL FLASHING

GUTTER

WEEPHOLE

SILL

RAFTER SIZE AND REINFORCING DETERMIND BY SPAN

1" OR 1/4" GLAZING, VERIFY CODE REQUIREMENTS FOR OVERHEAD GLAZING AND PROTECTIVE SCREEN BELOW

ANGLED CORNER
2.430

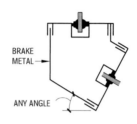

BRAKE METAL

ANY ANGLE

BULKHEAD SILL
2.431

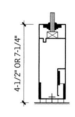

4-1/2" OR 7-1/4"

EXPANSION MULLION
2.432

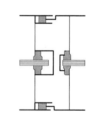

DOOR TRANSOM WITH CLOSER AND ILLUMINATED EXIT SIGN
2.433

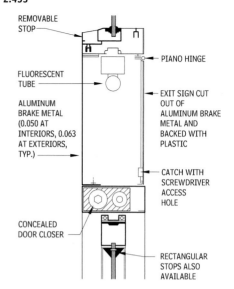

REMOVABLE STOP

FLUORESCENT TUBE

ALUMINUM BRAKE METAL (0.050 AT INTERIORS, 0.063 AT EXTERIORS, TYP.)

CONCEALED DOOR CLOSER

PIANO HINGE

EXIT SIGN CUT OUT OF ALUMINUM BRAKE METAL AND BACKED WITH PLASTIC

CATCH WITH SCREWDRIVER ACCESS HOLE

RECTANGULAR STOPS ALSO AVAILABLE

HEAD WITH RECEPTOR
2.434

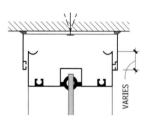

VARIES

GLAZED CURTAIN WALL

The term *curtain wall* was used in the early days of modern architecture to describe virtually any enclosure system that was supported by the building frame, as opposed to masonry or other bearing walls. A modern curtain wall is most typically thought of as a metal frame, usually aluminum, with large areas of glass. Other materials of metal or stone can be used to infill the frame at opaque areas (such as spandrels at floor framing). The frames span past, and are supported by, the floor edges, as opposed to bearing on the floors or spandrel beams. Gravity loads are frequently supported at every other floor, with lateral supports for lateral load only at floors between.

CHARACTERISTICS

A curtain wall is typically manufactured using one of the following methods:

- *Standard commercial systems* use collections of typical mullion sections and accessories, which are selected, fabricated, reinforced, and assembled into custom-sized walls to suit the project.
- *Custom systems* are designed specifically for the project, using specially designed mullions, parts, and accessories. The cost of custom design and engineering is offset by the efficiency of scale inherent with large projects.

Curtain wall water-penetration management methods:

- The highest-performing systems are fully pressure-equalized rainscreen systems, with the glazing pocket around each individual light a pressure-equalization chamber that is separated from other lights, weeped, and vented.
- Nonpressurized systems tend to direct water that penetrates the outer seals to vertical mullions, and then weeps at the base of wall.

Curtain wall installation methods:

- *Stick systems* assemble individual vertical and horizontal mullions on-site, and infill with glass, metal, stone, or other panels. Stick systems require careful attention to sealing the intersecting members.
- *Unitized systems* are substantially factory assembled off-site, complete with frames, glazing, and as much trim or accessories as reasonable. The panels are typically between 5 and 10 ft wide, and one or two stories high. The unitized panels are hoisted onto the wall and anchored in place. Unitized panels are more often a custom system than stick systems, and are used more often on large or high-rise projects. Because the sealing of the intersecting members takes place in a shop or factory, they are more likely to be well made. However, the connections between units are blind and, therefore, must be carefully engineered and verified by mockup testing.

Curtain wall glazing types:

- *Pressure plate glazing*: In this system, the glass and infill panels are installed from the exterior of the building. Pressure plate glazing allows for sealing of all joints in the framing and easy integration with an air/vapor barrier. Toe beads, cap beads, or complete wet glazing are possible to improve performance. However, all of the glass must be handled from scaffolding or lifts.
- *Dry glazing*: In this system, the glass and infill panels are installed from the interior. The exterior frame is fixed and glazing gaskets are installed. Typically, only the top mullion has a removable interior stop. The glass unit is slid into a deep glazing pocket on one jamb far enough to allow clearing the opposite jamb, then slid back and dropped into the sill glazing pocket. The removable interior stop is applied and, finally, an interior wedge gasket is installed. Sometimes this method is called "jiggle" or "wiggle" glazing because of the manipulation necessary to get the glass into place. Installation of the glass units from inside the building is desirable from a constructability standpoint, but performance is slightly reduced because dry metal-to-metal joints result at the removable stop at a point that should be airtight and watertight. Heel beads will improve performance, and some systems incorporate an extra gasket to form an air seal between frame and glass. Installation of spandrel areas may have to be done from the exterior because of limited access space on the interior side.
- *Structural silicone glazing (SSG)*: This system depends on adhering the glass to the frame or other glazing with a bead of silicone. Outer silicone weather seals supplement the structural seal. Unitized systems are frequently structural silicone-glazed because this allows work from one side only, and is highly reliable. Two-sided SSG can be completed in the field with either pressure plate or jiggle-glazed frames in the other direction. Four-sided SSG should only be done under controlled conditions in a factory. If the frames are stick-built, then an aluminum subframe is adhered to the glass at the factory, and the resulting assembly is mechanically fastened to the main frame in the field.

Water management for nearly all curtain walls utilizes pressure-equalized rainscreen technology.

PERFORMANCE

Standardized levels of performance for curtain walls are not commonly available in the industry, but standardized test procedures and ranges of typical values are relatively well known.

- Structural capacity of a curtain wall is tested according to ASTM E 330, "Standard Test Method for Structural Performance of Exterior Windows, Curtain Walls, and Doors by Uniform Static Air Pressure Difference." The loads required for the project are determined by code, normally ASCE-7. For large projects, boundary-condition wind-tunnel testing may be performed to establish more accurate wind loads. Wind-tunnel testing may lower the average field loads and may also help identify hot spots of higher loads.
- Air infiltration is tested according to ASTM E 283, "Standard Test Method for Rate of Air Leakage Through Exterior Windows, Curtain Walls, and Doors," with values of leakage tested at certain differential pressures. Common leakage values are 0.06 cfm per sq ft of wall area. Common test pressures are 1.56 psf (25 mph wind) for low-rise, 6.24 psf (50 mph) or 10 psf (63 mph) for midrise construction, and 12 psf (70 mph) and up for high-rise or monumental buildings. Pressures are also selected at approximately 20 percent of the structural loads.
- Water leakage is tested according to ASTM E 331, "Standard Test Method for Water Penetration of Exterior Windows, Curtain Walls, and Doors by Uniform Static Air Pressure Difference," and AAMA 501.1, "Standard Test Method for Metal Curtain Walls for Water Penetration Using Dynamic Pressure." Test pressures usually match those for air infiltration. The architect should establish leakage criteria—frequently acceptable are water amounts appearing on interior sills small enough to not run off the mullion. The static pressure test is more common, but might give an optimistic result because the test procedure may suck glass against gaskets, making a better than expected seal. Dynamic testing, which may help reveal leaks that would occur under the buffeting conditions of variable winds, is particularly effective at operable sash.
- Thermal performance is tested according to AAMA 501.5, "Test Method for Thermal Cycling of Exterior Walls." U-values should be specified by the design team. Condensation performance is extrapolated from the thermal performance.

Standardized test procedures also are available to evaluate numerous specialized performance criteria, including acoustic isolation, blast resistance, forced-entry resistance, hardware, and safety impact. Refer to AAMA. Standardized tests such as cyclical structural loading, frame racking, and thermal cycling are available to rapidly simulate aging of the sample. The tests for air and water infiltration are repeated after the accelerated aging to determine the likely long-term performance of the wall.

Manufacturers' standard systems are tested for performance in a range of sizes. The design professional must determine the applicability of the tests to specific project conditions. Custom testing may be necessary to accurately predict acceptable performance. Custom systems or unusual configurations of standard systems require testing of job-specific mockups. Testing protocols for custom markups are specified by the design professional and should include confirmation of all criteria.

DETAILING

Manufacturers of curtain walls typically provide generic details for installation. Adjacent construction is frequently shown as a hatched single line. Detail the curtain wall frame in project-specific assemblies.

- *Mullions and covers*: Standard rectangular commercial mullions are available from manufacturers in widths from 2 to 3 in. (2-1/2 in. is most common), in depths from 1 to 12 in. from the inside face of glass. Snap-on mullion covers are available in many shapes, and can be easily customized because they have limited impact on the performance of the curtain wall. Large external mullion covers, however, may seriously affect the thermal performance of systems without complete thermal breaks.
- *Interface with adjacent assemblies*: Seal the air barrier of the curtain wall to the wall air barrier; likewise the rainscreen. Utilize subsill flashing at the base of the wall, detailed to seal to the air barrier. At the interface with barrier walls, provide a dual line of sealant.
- *Air barriers*: Detail the curtain wall installation so that the line of air barrier (if required) extends uninterrupted across the gap at the perimeter of the curtain wall by connecting to the inner shoulder of the glazing pocket.
- *Anchoring*: Curtain walls are typically anchored to each floor slab or spandrel beam. Every other floor is a gravity and wind anchor, with a wind-only slip anchor in between. The anchorage scheme should be determined by the architect and structural engineer, and indicated on the drawings. Unitized panels commonly have a wind and gravity anchor at each floor, with slip joints providing wind load resistance at the stack joints. Anchors for stick systems are commonly mounted on the side of beams or slab edge. Anchors for unitized panels are commonly mounted in pockets on the top of slabs. Manufacturers have a variety of proprietary anchors that allow three-dimensional adjustment and fixed or slip connection.
- *Movement*: Because curtain wall spans floor-to-floor from slab or spandrel beam, it must accommodate differential movement of the spandrel beams and lateral drift of the structure along with the large thermal movement inherent with aluminum. Curtain wall heads (particularly at strip curtain wall) often are located at shelf angles and must accommodate movement typically in the range of 1/2 in. from above.
- *Thermal continuity*: Detail the curtain wall to maintain a line of thermal insulation in the same plane as in the tested configuration, and as intended by the curtain wall manufacturer.
- *Firestopping*: The intersection of a floor slab with curtain wall requires firestopping.
- *Spandrel/shadowboxes*: Where curtain wall is in front of a structure or areas that otherwise need to be opaque, spandrel glass or a shadowbox is used. Spandrel glass is composed of single or insulated glass units, with the inside layer opacified by a film or fired-on ceramic frit. Reflective coating can be used. If an insulated glass unit is used, the second or third surface can be coated with patterned ceramic frit. Shadowboxes are more effective at blending spandrel areas with vision areas, especially if the back panel is reflective. As opposed to spandrel areas, the cavity inside the shadowbox is typically vented and weeped, but there are differences of opinion among experts and manufacturers regarding venting of the cavity. Vented airspaces shift the thermal enclosure to the back of the curtain wall and may result in thermal short circuits and uncontrolled condensation; and, in time, the inside surface may get dirty. Unvented shadowboxes may overheat, especially with clear glass. Note that heat buildup within shadowbox cavity can cause offgassing of sealants and plastics of some materials and may deform composite materials and insulation. The manufacturer can assist with analysis.
- *Parapets and copings*: When curtain wall extends past the edge of the roof, the curtain wall becomes a parapet. Special care must be taken to stop air movement through hollow mullions and to control the thermal conduction to the exterior. Most curtain wall systems are not designed for exposure to weather from the back side, but they can be modified to properly function. If a spandrel of shadowbox is used for an opaque parapet, the back of the curtain wall can be furred, sheathed, and waterproofed with roofing base flashing. Transparent or translucent parapets can be provided by terminating the roof base flashing at a mullion approximately 8 in. above the roof. Special precautions must be taken because the back surface of curtain wall is typically not watertight. Curtain walls extending past the conditioned space into the parapet can create thermal short circuits and uncontrolled condensation. Provide air seals to prevent moisture-laden air from contacting cold surfaces, both inside the mullions and between the mullions and the roof structure. Foam-in-place sealants work well. Because of the inherent thermal break with extending a curtain wall to form a parapet, it is best avoided in cold climates. Thermal analyses can check insulation and air/vapor barriers design to verify that temperatures never reach dew points. Extend roof base flashing or membrane flashing across the top of the parapet and seal into the glazing pocket. Cap with brake metal coping, which is also sealed into the glazing pocket.

INSTALLATION

Whatever the quality of the curtain wall, ultimate performance depends on proper installation. The intersection of the curtain wall frame with surrounding walls has always been a difficult detail, and light modern materials have exacerbated the problem.

Stick systems require a high level of quality control in the field, as there are numerous extremely important and detailed steps in the assembly of the curtain wall.

- Anchors and mullions must be installed to allow movement.
- Joints at the mullion intersection must be made airtight and be properly compartmentalized for pressure-equalized systems.
- Glazing gaskets must be cut precisely and the corners sealed.
- Pressure plates must be torqued to specified values to compress the gaskets sufficiently for watertight performance.

Even unitized systems require attention to detail during field installation but because more assembly takes place in the factory there are fewer crucial requirements. The most important point is the flashing of the four-way intersection.

STICK AND UNITIZED CURTAIN WALL CONSTRUCTION
2.435

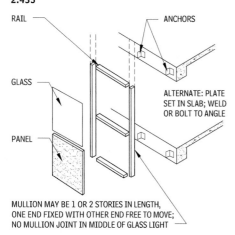

RAIL

ANCHORS

GLASS

ALTERNATE: PLATE SET IN SLAB; WELD OR BOLT TO ANGLE

PANEL

MULLION MAY BE 1 OR 2 STORIES IN LENGTH, ONE END FIXED WITH OTHER END FREE TO MOVE; NO MULLION JOINT IN MIDDLE OF GLASS LIGHT

STICK SYSTEM
FRAMING MEMBERS VISUALLY PROMINENT. COMPONENTS INSTALLED PIECE BY PIECE.

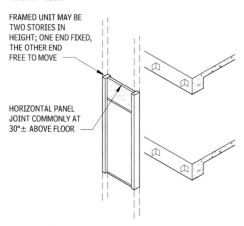

FRAMED UNIT MAY BE TWO STORIES IN HEIGHT; ONE END FIXED, THE OTHER END FREE TO MOVE

HORIZONTAL PANEL JOINT COMMONLY AT 30"± ABOVE FLOOR

UNITIZED SYSTEM
COMPLETELY PREASSEMBLED UNITS MAY OR MAY NOT INCLUDE INTERIOR FINISH

ATTACHMENT AND ANCHORAGE DETAILS
2.436

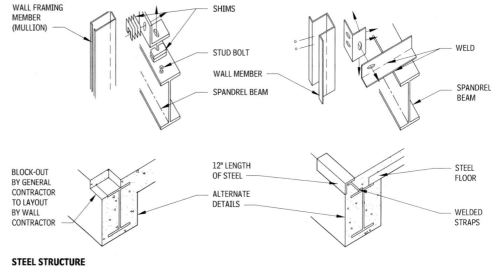

WALL FRAMING MEMBER (MULLION)

SHIMS

STUD BOLT

WALL MEMBER

SPANDREL BEAM

WELD

SPANDREL BEAM

BLOCK-OUT BY GENERAL CONTRACTOR TO LAYOUT BY WALL CONTRACTOR

12" LENGTH OF STEEL

ALTERNATE DETAILS

STEEL FLOOR

WELDED STRAPS

STEEL STRUCTURE

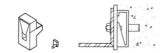

MALLEABLE CAST IRON INSERT PROVIDES ADJUSTABLE SUPPORT

CONTINUOUS GALVANIZED STEEL CHANNEL, INSERT IN LENGTHS TO 20' PROVIDING ATTACHMENT AT ANY POINT; ANCHORAGE AT 4" INTERVALS

THREADED MALLEABLE IRON INSERT WITH BOLTS 1/4" TO 3/4" DIA.

FLASHING

CLIPS

IN COLD CLIMATES CONSIDER SPF AT CLIPS

INSULATION

CONCRETE STRUCTURE

TYPICAL PRESSURE-PLATE MULLION
2.437

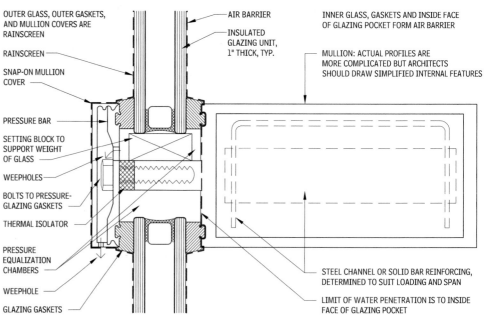

OUTER GLASS, OUTER GASKETS, AND MULLION COVERS ARE RAINSCREEN

RAINSCREEN

SNAP-ON MULLION COVER

PRESSURE BAR

SETTING BLOCK TO SUPPORT WEIGHT OF GLASS

WEEPHOLES

BOLTS TO PRESSURE-GLAZING GASKETS

THERMAL ISOLATOR

PRESSURE EQUALIZATION CHAMBERS

WEEPHOLE

GLAZING GASKETS

AIR BARRIER

INSULATED GLAZING UNIT, 1" THICK, TYP.

INNER GLASS, GASKETS AND INSIDE FACE OF GLAZING POCKET FORM AIR BARRIER

MULLION: ACTUAL PROFILES ARE MORE COMPLICATED BUT ARCHITECTS SHOULD DRAW SIMPLIFIED INTERNAL FEATURES

STEEL CHANNEL OR SOLID BAR REINFORCING, DETERMINED TO SUIT LOADING AND SPAN

LIMIT OF WATER PENETRATION IS TO INSIDE FACE OF GLAZING POCKET

NOTES

2.436 a. Anchorage devices must permit three-dimensional adjustment. Metal-to-metal connections subject to unintentional movement should be designed to eliminate noise caused by movement due to temperature change.
b. Anchors must be designed to withstand wind loads acting outward and inward.
c. Anchors must be permanently secured in position after final assembly and adjustment of wall components.
d. All anchorage members must be corrosion-resistant or otherwise be protected against corrosive forces.

e. Shim plates may be installed between vertical angle anchor and concrete structure, as required.

TYPICAL DRY-GLAZED MULLION
2.438

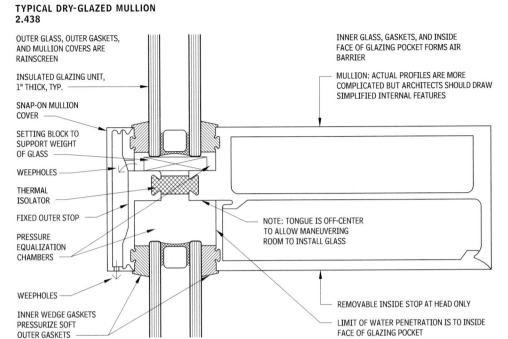

OUTER GLASS, OUTER GASKETS, AND MULLION COVERS ARE RAINSCREEN

INSULATED GLAZING UNIT, 1" THICK, TYP.

SNAP-ON MULLION COVER

SETTING BLOCK TO SUPPORT WEIGHT OF GLASS

WEEPHOLES

THERMAL ISOLATOR

FIXED OUTER STOP

PRESSURE EQUALIZATION CHAMBERS

WEEPHOLES

INNER WEDGE GASKETS PRESSURIZE SOFT OUTER GASKETS

INNER GLASS, GASKETS, AND INSIDE FACE OF GLAZING POCKET FORMS AIR BARRIER

MULLION: ACTUAL PROFILES ARE MORE COMPLICATED BUT ARCHITECTS SHOULD DRAW SIMPLIFIED INTERNAL FEATURES

NOTE: TONGUE IS OFF-CENTER TO ALLOW MANEUVERING ROOM TO INSTALL GLASS

REMOVABLE INSIDE STOP AT HEAD ONLY

LIMIT OF WATER PENETRATION IS TO INSIDE FACE OF GLAZING POCKET

MULLION SNAP-ON COVER OPTIONS
2.439

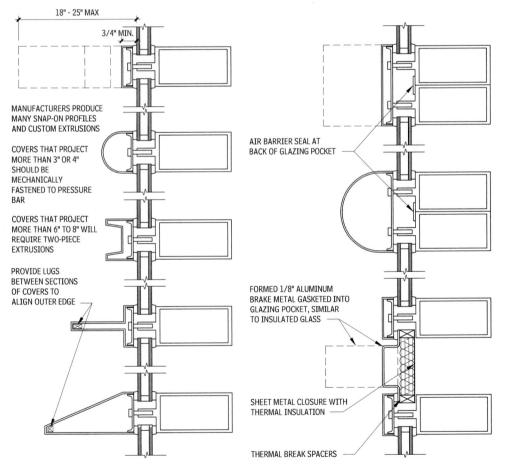

18" - 25" MAX

3/4" MIN.

MANUFACTURERS PRODUCE MANY SNAP-ON PROFILES AND CUSTOM EXTRUSIONS

COVERS THAT PROJECT MORE THAN 3" OR 4" SHOULD BE MECHANICALLY FASTENED TO PRESSURE BAR

COVERS THAT PROJECT MORE THAN 6" TO 8" WILL REQUIRE TWO-PIECE EXTRUSIONS

PROVIDE LUGS BETWEEN SECTIONS OF COVERS TO ALIGN OUTER EDGE

AIR BARRIER SEAL AT BACK OF GLAZING POCKET

FORMED 1/8" ALUMINUM BRAKE METAL GASKETED INTO GLAZING POCKET, SIMILAR TO INSULATED GLASS

SHEET METAL CLOSURE WITH THERMAL INSULATION

THERMAL BREAK SPACERS

TWO-SIDED STRUCTURAL GLAZING SYSTEM WITH STRUCTURAL SILICONE JOINT SEALANT
2.440

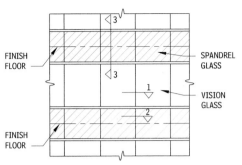

FINISH FLOOR

FINISH FLOOR

SPANDREL GLASS

VISION GLASS

TYPICAL ELEVATION

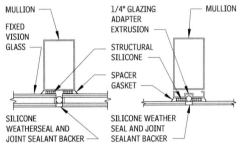

MULLION

FIXED VISION GLASS

SILICONE WEATHERSEAL AND JOINT SEALANT BACKER

1/4" GLAZING ADAPTER EXTRUSION

STRUCTURAL SILICONE

SPACER GASKET

MULLION

SILICONE WEATHER SEAL AND JOINT SEALANT BACKER

SECTION 1   **SECTION 2**

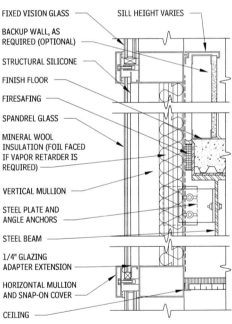

FIXED VISION GLASS

BACKUP WALL, AS REQUIRED (OPTIONAL)

STRUCTURAL SILICONE

FINISH FLOOR

FIRESAFING

SPANDREL GLASS

MINERAL WOOL INSULATION (FOIL FACED IF VAPOR RETARDER IS REQUIRED)

VERTICAL MULLION

STEEL PLATE AND ANGLE ANCHORS

STEEL BEAM

1/4" GLAZING ADAPTER EXTENSION

HORIZONTAL MULLION AND SNAP-ON COVER

CEILING

SILL HEIGHT VARIES

SECTION 3-3

GRID SYSTEM (STICK OR STUD), ALUMINUM PRESSURE BAR
2.441

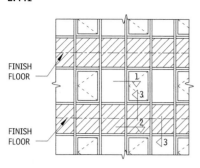

FINISH FLOOR

FINISH FLOOR

TYPICAL ELEVATION – WINDOW AND PANEL TYPES OPTIONAL

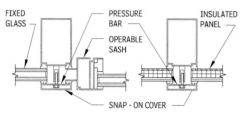

FIXED GLASS

PRESSURE BAR

OPERABLE SASH

INSULATED PANEL

SNAP - ON COVER

SECTION 1   **SECTION 2**

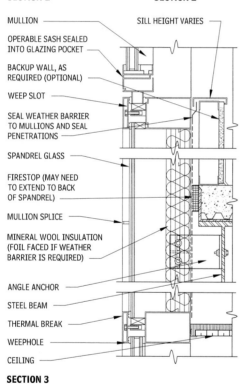

MULLION

SILL HEIGHT VARIES

OPERABLE SASH SEALED INTO GLAZING POCKET

BACKUP WALL, AS REQUIRED (OPTIONAL)

WEEP SLOT

SEAL WEATHER BARRIER TO MULLIONS AND SEAL PENETRATIONS

SPANDREL GLASS

FIRESTOP (MAY NEED TO EXTEND TO BACK OF SPANDREL)

MULLION SPLICE

MINERAL WOOL INSULATION (FOIL FACED IF WEATHER BARRIER IS REQUIRED)

ANGLE ANCHOR

STEEL BEAM

THERMAL BREAK

WEEPHOLE

CEILING

SECTION 3

TYPICAL FOUR-SIDED STRUCTURAL SILICONE GLAZING, CUSTOM-UNITIZED SYSTEM
2.442

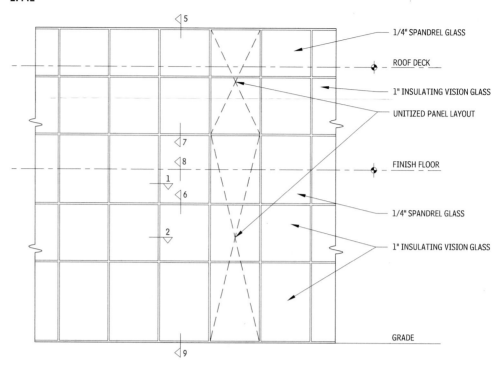

1/4" SPANDREL GLASS

ROOF DECK

1" INSULATING VISION GLASS

UNITIZED PANEL LAYOUT

FINISH FLOOR

1/4" SPANDREL GLASS

1" INSULATING VISION GLASS

GRADE

MULLION DETAIL 1 AT SPANDREL GLASS—VERTICAL PANEL JOINT
2.443

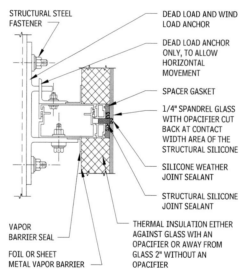

STRUCTURAL STEEL FASTENER

DEAD LOAD AND WIND LOAD ANCHOR

DEAD LOAD ANCHOR ONLY, TO ALLOW HORIZONTAL MOVEMENT

SPACER GASKET

1/4" SPANDREL GLASS WITH OPACIFIER CUT BACK AT CONTACT WIDTH AREA OF THE STRUCTURAL SILICONE

SILICONE WEATHER JOINT SEALANT

STRUCTURAL SILICONE JOINT SEALANT

VAPOR BARRIER SEAL

FOIL OR SHEET METAL VAPOR BARRIER

THERMAL INSULATION EITHER AGAINST GLASS WIH AN OPACIFIER OR AWAY FROM GLASS 2" WITHOUT AN OPACIFIER

MULLION DETAIL 2 AT VISION GLASS—VERTICAL PANEL JOINT
2.444

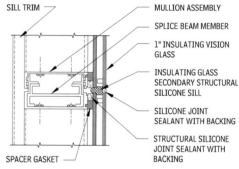

SILL TRIM

MULLION ASSEMBLY

SPLICE BEAM MEMBER

1" INSULATING VISION GLASS

INSULATING GLASS SECONDARY STRUCTURAL SILICONE SILL

SILICONE JOINT SEALANT WITH BACKING

STRUCTURAL SILICONE JOINT SEALANT WITH BACKING

SPACER GASKET

MULLION DETAIL 3 AT OUTSIDE CORNER—VERTICAL PANEL JOINT
2.445

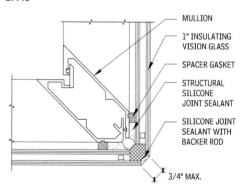

MULLION

1" INSULATING VISION GLASS

SPACER GASKET

STRUCTURAL SILICONE JOINT SEALANT

SILICONE JOINT SEALANT WITH BACKER ROD

3/4" MAX.

NOTE

2.441 Horizontals are weeped for positive performance against water infiltration, with slots at glazing pressure plate and holes at cover.

MULLION DETAIL 4 AT INSIDE CORNER—VERTICAL PANEL JOINT
2.446

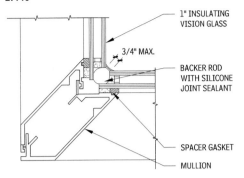

1" INSULATING VISION GLASS

3/4" MAX.

BACKER ROD WITH SILICONE JOINT SEALANT

SPACER GASKET

MULLION

COPING DETAIL 5
2.447

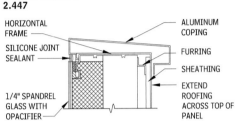

HORIZONTAL FRAME

SILICONE JOINT SEALANT

1/4" SPANDREL GLASS WITH OPACIFIER

ALUMINUM COPING

FURRING

SHEATHING

EXTEND ROOFING ACROSS TOP OF PANEL

HEAD DETAIL 6
2.448

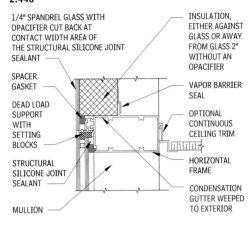

1/4" SPANDREL GLASS WITH OPACIFIER CUT BACK AT CONTACT WIDTH AREA OF THE STRUCTURAL SILICONE JOINT SEALANT

SPACER GASKET

DEAD LOAD SUPPORT WITH SETTING BLOCKS

STRUCTURAL SILICONE JOINT SEALANT

MULLION

INSULATION, EITHER AGAINST GLASS OR AWAY FROM GLASS 2" WITHOUT AN OPACIFIER

VAPOR BARRIER SEAL

OPTIONAL CONTINUOUS CEILING TRIM

HORIZONTAL FRAME

CONDENSATION GUTTER WEEPED TO EXTERIOR

SILL DETAIL 7, AT HORIZONTAL
2.449

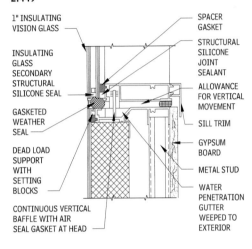

1" INSULATING VISION GLASS

INSULATING GLASS SECONDARY STRUCTURAL SILICONE SEAL

GASKETED WEATHER SEAL

DEAD LOAD SUPPORT WITH SETTING BLOCKS

CONTINUOUS VERTICAL BAFFLE WITH AIR SEAL GASKET AT HEAD

SPACER GASKET

STRUCTURAL SILICONE JOINT SEALANT

ALLOWANCE FOR VERTICAL MOVEMENT

SILL TRIM

GYPSUM BOARD

METAL STUD

WATER PENETRATION GUTTER WEEPED TO EXTERIOR

FLOOR SLAB DETAIL 8
2.450

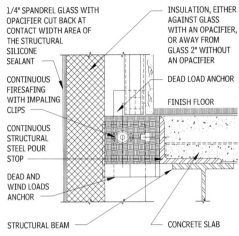

1/4" SPANDREL GLASS WITH OPACIFIER CUT BACK AT CONTACT WIDTH AREA OF THE STRUCTURAL SILICONE SEALANT

CONTINUOUS FIRESAFING WITH IMPALING CLIPS

CONTINUOUS STRUCTURAL STEEL POUR STOP

DEAD AND WIND LOADS ANCHOR

STRUCTURAL BEAM

INSULATION, EITHER AGAINST GLASS WITH AN OPACIFIER, OR AWAY FROM GLASS 2" WITHOUT AN OPACIFIER

DEAD LOAD ANCHOR

FINISH FLOOR

CONCRETE SLAB

GRADE DETAIL 9
2.451

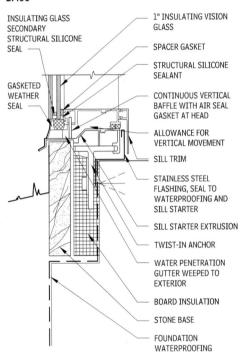

INSULATING GLASS SECONDARY STRUCTURAL SILICONE SEAL

GASKETED WEATHER SEAL

1" INSULATING VISION GLASS

SPACER GASKET

STRUCTURAL SILICONE SEALANT

CONTINUOUS VERTICAL BAFFLE WITH AIR SEAL GASKET AT HEAD

ALLOWANCE FOR VERTICAL MOVEMENT

SILL TRIM

STAINLESS STEEL FLASHING, SEAL TO WATERPROOFING AND SILL STARTER

SILL STARTER EXTRUSION

TWIST-IN ANCHOR

WATER PENETRATION GUTTER WEEPED TO EXTERIOR

BOARD INSULATION

STONE BASE

FOUNDATION WATERPROOFING

SHADOWBOX AND SPANDREL ASSEMBLIES
2.452

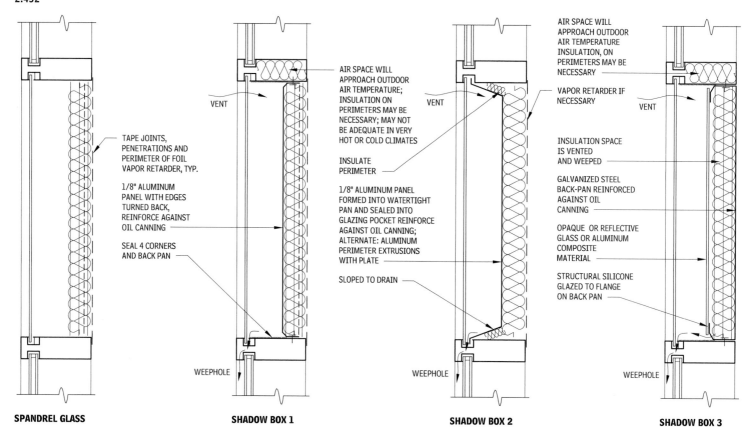

AIR SPACE WILL APPROACH OUTDOOR AIR TEMPERATURE INSULATION, ON PERIMETERS MAY BE NECESSARY

VENT

VAPOR RETARDER IF NECESSARY

VENT

AIR SPACE WILL APPROACH OUTDOOR AIR TEMPERATURE; INSULATION ON PERIMETERS MAY BE NECESSARY; MAY NOT BE ADEQUATE IN VERY HOT OR COLD CLIMATES

VENT

TAPE JOINTS, PENETRATIONS AND PERIMETER OF FOIL VAPOR RETARDER, TYP.

INSULATE PERIMETER

INSULATION SPACE IS VENTED AND WEEPED

1/8" ALUMINUM PANEL WITH EDGES TURNED BACK, REINFORCE AGAINST OIL CANNING

1/8" ALUMINUM PANEL FORMED INTO WATERTIGHT PAN AND SEALED INTO GLAZING POCKET REINFORCE AGAINST OIL CANNING; ALTERNATE: ALUMINUM PERIMETER EXTRUSIONS WITH PLATE

GALVANIZED STEEL BACK-PAN REINFORCED AGAINST OIL CANNING

SEAL 4 CORNERS AND BACK PAN

OPAQUE OR REFLECTIVE GLASS OR ALUMINUM COMPOSITE MATERIAL

SLOPED TO DRAIN

STRUCTURAL SILICONE GLAZED TO FLANGE ON BACK PAN

WEEPHOLE

WEEPHOLE

WEEPHOLE

SPANDREL GLASS **SHADOW BOX 1** **SHADOW BOX 2** **SHADOW BOX 3**

SILL AT GLAZED PARAPETS
2.453

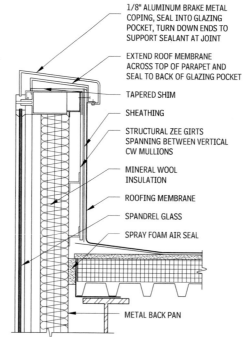

WET-SEAL ALL GLAZING AND ALUMINUM JOINTS EXPOSED ON BACK SIDE OF CURTAIN WALL PARAPET

1/8" ALUMINUM BRAKE METAL SLOPED SILL COVER; NOTCH AROUND VERTICAL MULLIONS AND TURN DOWN ENDS TO SUPPORT BACKER-SEAL PERIMETER

TRANSLUCENT OR PATTERNED TEMPERED GLASS

CAP BACK OF MULLIONS WITH ALUMINUM OR PRECURED SILICONE FLASHING

CONCEALED CLIPS; SEAL FASTENERS

FILL VERTICAL MULLIONS WITH FOAM-IN-PLACE SEALANT

ROOFING BASE FLASHING; EXTEND ACROSS TOP OF MULLION AND SEAL PERIMETER

SPANDREL GLASS

SHEET METAL BACKER

SPRAY FOAM AIR SEAL

CURTAIN WALL PARAPET
2.454

1/8" ALUMINUM BRAKE METAL COPING, SEAL INTO GLAZING POCKET, TURN DOWN ENDS TO SUPPORT SEALANT AT JOINT

EXTEND ROOF MEMBRANE ACROSS TOP OF PARAPET AND SEAL TO BACK OF GLAZING POCKET

TAPERED SHIM

SHEATHING

STRUCTURAL ZEE GIRTS SPANNING BETWEEN VERTICAL CW MULLIONS

MINERAL WOOL INSULATION

ROOFING MEMBRANE

SPANDREL GLASS

SPRAY FOAM AIR SEAL

METAL BACK PAN

SPECIALIZED CURTAIN WALL

Design professionals have been challenging the traditional assumptions regarding the support and glazing of curtain walls. These walls have frequently been utilized in large lobbies, atria, and other monumental-scale spaces, but they have also been used to enclose entire buildings. More sophisticated, lightweight, and visually transparent wall support structures have been developed, including architectural exposed structural steel trusses, trusses with cable and rod tension members, tension grid supports, glass mullions and support fins, the use of the glass itself as part of the load-resisting components, and other innovative solutions. The glazing of these systems frequently depends on point support devices or patch fittings at corners, and silicone butt glazing, resulting in a frameless, visually uninterrupted surface.

Specialized curtain walls require extremely close coordination between the architect, structural engineer, manufacturer, installer, and other contractors. In particular, if the glass is used structurally, there are relatively few engineers qualified to perform the analysis and few installers who understand the difficult sequencing required to temporarily hold the wall in place until all components can be tensioned to design values. The following are issues:

- Heat gain/loss and glare control can become sizable problems with large areas of glass. Shading and specialized glass are required.
- The adjacent building structure may need to accommodate large loads resulting from suspending walls that might otherwise be gravity-loaded to a foundation or to resist large tension loads.
- The interface with surrounding walls, copings, and roofs may need to accommodate significant movement within and between the systems.

NOTES

2.452 a. A spandrel and shadowbox typically occurs at anchorage points. Coordinate size and location of anchors with insulation and panels, and seal penetrations.
b. Shadowbox 2 provides the best thermal isolation of the cavity.

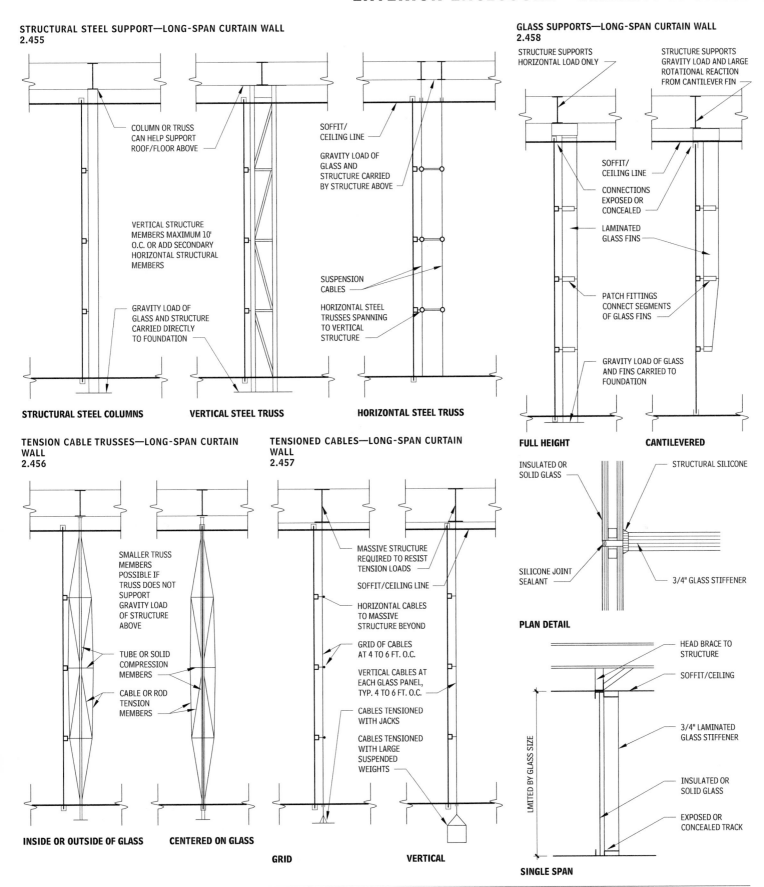

STRUCTURAL STEEL SUPPORT—LONG-SPAN CURTAIN WALL
2.455

COLUMN OR TRUSS CAN HELP SUPPORT ROOF/FLOOR ABOVE

VERTICAL STRUCTURE MEMBERS MAXIMUM 10' O.C. OR ADD SECONDARY HORIZONTAL STRUCTURAL MEMBERS

GRAVITY LOAD OF GLASS AND STRUCTURE CARRIED DIRECTLY TO FOUNDATION

SOFFIT/ CEILING LINE

GRAVITY LOAD OF GLASS AND STRUCTURE CARRIED BY STRUCTURE ABOVE

SUSPENSION CABLES

HORIZONTAL STEEL TRUSSES SPANNING TO VERTICAL STRUCTURE

STRUCTURAL STEEL COLUMNS   **VERTICAL STEEL TRUSS**   **HORIZONTAL STEEL TRUSS**

TENSION CABLE TRUSSES—LONG-SPAN CURTAIN WALL
2.456

SMALLER TRUSS MEMBERS POSSIBLE IF TRUSS DOES NOT SUPPORT GRAVITY LOAD OF STRUCTURE ABOVE

TUBE OR SOLID COMPRESSION MEMBERS

CABLE OR ROD TENSION MEMBERS

INSIDE OR OUTSIDE OF GLASS   **CENTERED ON GLASS**

TENSIONED CABLES—LONG-SPAN CURTAIN WALL
2.457

MASSIVE STRUCTURE REQUIRED TO RESIST TENSION LOADS

SOFFIT/CEILING LINE

HORIZONTAL CABLES TO MASSIVE STRUCTURE BEYOND

GRID OF CABLES AT 4 TO 6 FT. O.C.

VERTICAL CABLES AT EACH GLASS PANEL, TYP. 4 TO 6 FT. O.C.

CABLES TENSIONED WITH JACKS

CABLES TENSIONED WITH LARGE SUSPENDED WEIGHTS

GRID   **VERTICAL**

GLASS SUPPORTS—LONG-SPAN CURTAIN WALL
2.458

STRUCTURE SUPPORTS HORIZONTAL LOAD ONLY

STRUCTURE SUPPORTS GRAVITY LOAD AND LARGE ROTATIONAL REACTION FROM CANTILEVER FIN

SOFFIT/ CEILING LINE

CONNECTIONS EXPOSED OR CONCEALED

LAMINATED GLASS FINS

PATCH FITTINGS CONNECT SEGMENTS OF GLASS FINS

GRAVITY LOAD OF GLASS AND FINS CARRIED TO FOUNDATION

FULL HEIGHT   **CANTILEVERED**

INSULATED OR SOLID GLASS

STRUCTURAL SILICONE

SILICONE JOINT SEALANT

3/4" GLASS STIFFENER

PLAN DETAIL

HEAD BRACE TO STRUCTURE

SOFFIT/CEILING

3/4" LAMINATED GLASS STIFFENER

INSULATED OR SOLID GLASS

EXPOSED OR CONCEALED TRACK

LIMITED BY GLASS SIZE

SINGLE SPAN

NOTES

2.455 a. Weather and thermal barriers must continue above curtain wall. They are not shown, for clarity.
b. Some or all of the steel components may be solid or laminated timber.
c. Structure above must accommodate large horizontal loads from vertical members.
2.456 Weather and thermal barriers must continue above curtain wall. They are not shown, for clarity.
2.457 Weather and thermal barriers must continue above curtain wall. They are not shown, for clarity.

2.458 Weather and thermal barriers must continue above curtain wall. They are not shown, for clarity.

POINT SUPPORT
2.459

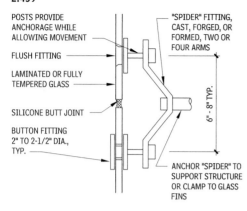

POSTS PROVIDE ANCHORAGE WHILE ALLOWING MOVEMENT

FLUSH FITTING

LAMINATED OR FULLY TEMPERED GLASS

SILICONE BUTT JOINT

BUTTON FITTING 2" TO 2-1/2" DIA., TYP.

"SPIDER" FITTING, CAST, FORGED, OR FORMED, TWO OR FOUR ARMS

6"–8" TYP.

ANCHOR "SPIDER" TO SUPPORT STRUCTURE OR CLAMP TO GLASS FINS

DOUBLE FAÇADE CURTAIN WALL

A double façade curtain wall, as the name suggests, utilizes two layers of a separate wall system with a cavity between. The cavity creates a mediating environment between the interior and exterior, resulting in warmer interior glass surface temperatures, for improved occupant comfort and better acoustic performance. The cavity can also be used to provide natural or mechanically induced ventilation, especially on high-rise buildings where natural ventilation might otherwise be impossible. Shading devices can be installed in the cavity. Cavity size varies, with two primary approaches. The first approach is with small cavities of approximately 6 in. with one of the wall layers having an operable sash to access the cavity. The second approach is with cavities wide enough, generally around 3 ft, for maintenance access.

The value of double façade curtain walls outside of Europe has not been clearly proven, as they are very expensive and payback periods for energy savings may be long. There are other, more cost-effective ways to gain most of the performance enhancements offered by double façades—double façades as retrofits of existing curtain wall may be a good choice. Older curtain wall is frequently single glazed, and the gaskets may be dried. However, removal of the existing curtain wall may cause unacceptable disruptions to existing activities. Adding a new layer of wall outside the existing may be a cost-effective and minimally invasive solution.

CHANNEL GLASS CURTAIN WALL
2.462

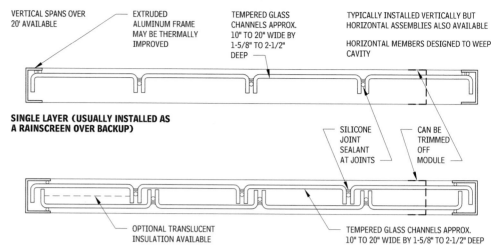

VERTICAL SPANS OVER 20' AVAILABLE

EXTRUDED ALUMINUM FRAME MAY BE THERMALLY IMPROVED

TEMPERED GLASS CHANNELS APPROX. 10" TO 20" WIDE BY 1-5/8" TO 2-1/2" DEEP

TYPICALLY INSTALLED VERTICALLY BUT HORIZONTAL ASSEMBLIES ALSO AVAILABLE

HORIZONTAL MEMBERS DESIGNED TO WEEP CAVITY

SINGLE LAYER (USUALLY INSTALLED AS A RAINSCREEN OVER BACKUP)

SILICONE JOINT SEALANT AT JOINTS

CAN BE TRIMMED OFF MODULE

OPTIONAL TRANSLUCENT INSULATION AVAILABLE

TEMPERED GLASS CHANNELS APPROX. 10" TO 20" WIDE BY 1-5/8" TO 2-1/2" DEEP

DOUBLE LAYER

CHANNEL GLASS CURTAIN WALL

Channel glass walls are composed of single or double layers of extruded glass channels, silicone-sealed together and held at head and sill in an extruded track. The walls are translucent rather than transparent. The double-layer walls are thermally efficient if frames are also thermally broken.

Consult the following references:

- *Double-Skin Façades* by Eberhard Oesterle, Rolf-dieter Lieb, Martin Lutz, and Winfried Heusler (Munich, Germany: Prestel Verlag, 2001)
- *Glass in Architecture* by Michael Wigginton (New York City, NY: Phaidon Press Ltd, 1996)

DOUBLE FAÇADE CURTAIN WALL 1
2.460

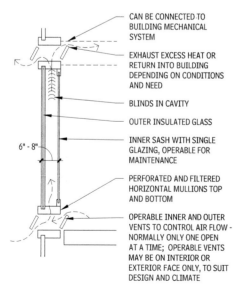

CAN BE CONNECTED TO BUILDING MECHANICAL SYSTEM

EXHAUST EXCESS HEAT OR RETURN INTO BUILDING DEPENDING ON CONDITIONS AND NEED

BLINDS IN CAVITY

OUTER INSULATED GLASS

INNER SASH WITH SINGLE GLAZING, OPERABLE FOR MAINTENANCE

6"–8"

PERFORATED AND FILTERED HORIZONTAL MULLIONS TOP AND BOTTOM

OPERABLE INNER AND OUTER VENTS TO CONTROL AIR FLOW - NORMALLY ONLY ONE OPEN AT A TIME; OPERABLE VENTS MAY BE ON INTERIOR OR EXTERIOR FACE ONLY, TO SUIT DESIGN AND CLIMATE

DOUBLE FAÇADE CURTAIN WALL 2
2.461

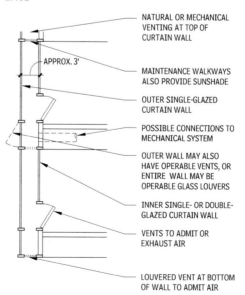

NATURAL OR MECHANICAL VENTING AT TOP OF CURTAIN WALL

APPROX. 3'

MAINTENANCE WALKWAYS ALSO PROVIDE SUNSHADE

OUTER SINGLE-GLAZED CURTAIN WALL

POSSIBLE CONNECTIONS TO MECHANICAL SYSTEM

OUTER WALL MAY ALSO HAVE OPERABLE VENTS, OR ENTIRE WALL MAY BE OPERABLE GLASS LOUVERS

INNER SINGLE- OR DOUBLE-GLAZED CURTAIN WALL

VENTS TO ADMIT OR EXHAUST AIR

LOUVERED VENT AT BOTTOM OF WALL TO ADMIT AIR

EXTERIOR DOORS

DESIGN CONSIDERATIONS

Exterior doors allow access and egress, while maintaining a separation between the interior and exterior environments. Doors must also provide security from intrusion, and may need to be fire rated.

Doors and frame types include:

- *Hollow metal doors and frames*: These comply with performance standards in the *Hollow Metal Manual*, by the Hollow Metal Manufacturers Association (HMMA) and NAAMM and the Steel Door Institute (SDI).
- *Residential prehung doors*: These include insulated. metal-skinned, fiberglass-skinned, and wood doors in wood or metal frames. Refer to AAMA/WDMA/CSA 101/I.S.2/A440, "Standard/Specification for Windows, Doors, and Unit Skylights." Drafts and heat loss from residential doors present a larger problem than for commercial buildings. It is likely that the comfort of the occupants will be affected to a greater degree, and that the energy loss will result in a greater impact on the overall energy usage.
- *Aluminum and glass entrance doors*: This type includes door frames of extruded aluminum with glass or insulated aluminum infill panels. Standardized test procedures are available to evaluate many specialized performance criteria, including acoustic isolation, blast-resistance, forced-entry-resistance, and safety impact. Refer to AAMA.
- *Specialty entrance doors*: Tempered safety-glass doors, frameless with patch fittings, with top and bottom rails or with solid metal frames, are available on a custom basis for monumental entrances. Refer to GANA.

ACCESSIBILITY

Entrance doors are not limited by IBC or ADAAG for operating force for accessibility, primarily because the low force is not sufficient to keep the doors closed against wind pressures. However, this should be verified, as some local codes do have maximum operating forces.

It is good practice to provide automatic doors at entrances to public buildings to allow for universal access. Overhead concealed and exposed operators, as well as operators concealed in the floor, are available. Push button, card key, or motion sensor activators can be used.

Thresholds must provide a continuous walkable surface, with minimal vertical offsets to allow for universal access that is free from tripping hazards and impediments to wheeled traffic. The lack of vertical offset can create an opportunity for water to be pushed under doors by wind pressure, so compensate with generous canopies or overhangs and ensure that the paving slopes away. Trench drains with closely spaced grilles immediately in front of doors will also stop water.

INSTALLATION

Regardless of the quality of the door and frame, ultimate performance depends on proper installation. The intersection of the doorframe with surrounding walls has always been a difficult detail, and light modern materials have exacerbated the problem.

ASTM E 2112, "Standard Practice for Installation of Exterior Windows, Doors, and Skylights," establishes a variety of methods for quality installations of prehung residential doors. The architect may exceed the standard installation practices for more durable and dependable service. In particular, it is recommended that you

coordinate waterproofing, dampproofing, and flashing below grade with the threshold.

Door installation must be detailed as appropriate for the generic wall assembly types, which include:

- *Barrier walls*: Seal the door frame to the barrier. Use a subsill flashing to avoid introducing water into the wall. For massive barrier walls such as precast concrete, head flashing may be required to ensure that water seepage does not get behind the window.
- *Drainage plane walls*: Provide the primary seal of the doorframe to the water-resistant drainage plane, and an outer seal in line with the wallcovering. The flashing below the threshold should extend past the doorframes and be lapped by the water-resistant drainage plane in the wall. Ensure continuity of the air barrier, wherever it is located in the wall assembly.
- *Drainage cavity walls*: Provide the primary seal of the doorframe to the waterproof inner line of protection, and an outer seal to the outer wallcovering. The flashing below the threshold should extend past the doorframes and be lapped by the water-resistant barrier in the wall. Ensure continuity of the air barrier if it is not located at the inner line of protection.
- *Pressure-equalized (PE) rainscreen walls*: Use doorframes that incorporate PE rainscreen technology. Seal the air barrier of the door frame to the wall air barrier; likewise for the rainscreen. The flashing below the threshold should extend past the doorframes and be lapped by the air/vapor barrier in the wall.
- *Air and vapor barriers*: Detail the door installation so that the line of the air barrier and/or vapor barrier (if required) extends uninterrupted across the gap at the perimeter of the doorframes.

These organizations can be contacted for more information:

- Hollow Metal Manufacturers Association (HMMA)
- Steel Door Institute (SDI)
- American Architectural Manufacturers Association (AAMA)
- Window and Door Manufacturers Association (WDMA)

GLASS ENTRANCE DOORS

Keep the following in mind when working with glass entrance doors:

- Consult applicable codes for safety requirements, glass size, thickness, and tempering.
- Frameless 1/2-in. glass doors are available in clear, gray, or bronze tints, in sizes up to 60 by 108 in. Frameless 3/4-in. glass doors are available only in clear tint in sizes up to 48 by 108 in.
- Consult manufacturers' data on structural adequacy for required loads and for frames and transom bars reinforcement.
- Aluminum doors and frames are available in all standard aluminum finishes in sizes up to 6 by 7 ft.
- Frameless doors may not permit adequate weather stripping. The use of frameless doors in exterior walls in northern climates should be evaluated for energy efficiency and comfort.
- Refer to all applicable codes, standards, and regulations for specific requirements for doors that must be accessible.

HOLLOW METAL JAMB DETAIL
2.463

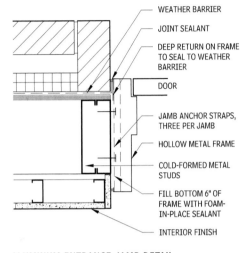

- WEATHER BARRIER
- JOINT SEALANT
- DEEP RETURN ON FRAME TO SEAL TO WEATHER BARRIER
- DOOR
- JAMB ANCHOR STRAPS, THREE PER JAMB
- HOLLOW METAL FRAME
- COLD-FORMED METAL STUDS
- FILL BOTTOM 6" OF FRAME WITH FOAM-IN-PLACE SEALANT
- INTERIOR FINISH

ALUMINUM ENTRANCE JAMB DETAIL
2.464

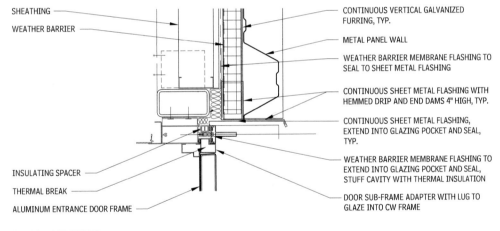

- SHEATHING
- WEATHER BARRIER
- INSULATING SPACER
- THERMAL BREAK
- ALUMINUM ENTRANCE DOOR FRAME
- CONTINUOUS VERTICAL GALVANIZED FURRING, TYP.
- METAL PANEL WALL
- WEATHER BARRIER MEMBRANE FLASHING TO SEAL TO SHEET METAL FLASHING
- CONTINUOUS SHEET METAL FLASHING WITH HEMMED DRIP AND END DAMS 4" HIGH, TYP.
- CONTINUOUS SHEET METAL FLASHING, EXTEND INTO GLAZING POCKET AND SEAL, TYP.
- WEATHER BARRIER MEMBRANE FLASHING TO EXTEND INTO GLAZING POCKET AND SEAL, STUFF CAVITY WITH THERMAL INSULATION
- DOOR SUB-FRAME ADAPTER WITH LUG TO GLAZE INTO CW FRAME

GLASS DOOR TYPES
2.465

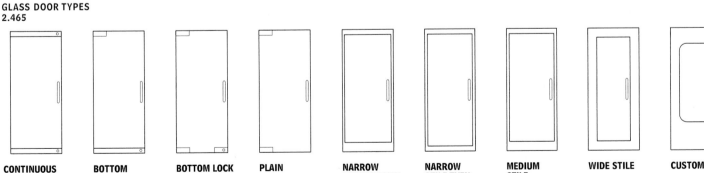

CONTINUOUS TOP AND BOTTOM LOCK | BOTTOM CONTINUOUS | BOTTOM LOCK BOLT SETTING | PLAIN | NARROW STILE/UNEVEN RAILS | NARROW STILE/EVEN RAILS | MEDIUM STILE | WIDE STILE | CUSTOM

NOTE

2.465 Doors with narrow stiles should not be used in heavily trafficked areas.

ELEVATION—TYPICAL GLASS ENTRANCE DOORS
2.466

BALANCED DOOR
2.468

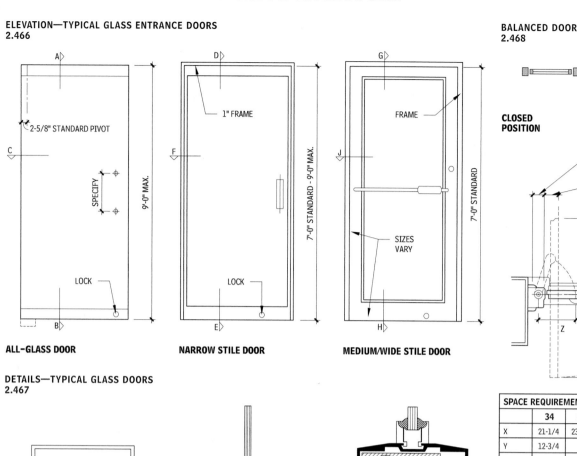

ALL-GLASS DOOR

NARROW STILE DOOR

MEDIUM/WIDE STILE DOOR

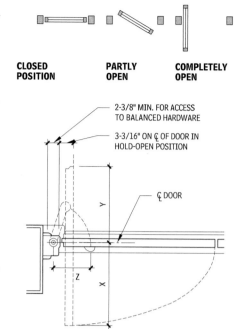

CLOSED POSITION PARTLY OPEN COMPLETELY OPEN

2-3/8" MIN. FOR ACCESS TO BALANCED HARDWARE

3-3/16" ON ℄ OF DOOR IN HOLD-OPEN POSITION

℄ DOOR

DETAILS—TYPICAL GLASS DOORS
2.467

TRANSOM BAR OR HEAD JAMB

HEAD SECTION A

SILL SECTION B

3/16" CLEARANCE

1/8" CLEARANCE WHEN CLOSED OR OPEN AT ANY POSITION

JAMB SECTION C

HEAD SECTION D

SIZE FOR CONCEALED CLOSER OR OPERATOR

SILL SECTION E

JAMB SECTION G

HEAD SECTION G

SILL SECTION H

JAMB SECTION J

SPACE REQUIREMENTS—VARIOUS DOOR WIDTHS (IN.)						
	34	36	38	40	42	44
X	21-1/4	23-1/4	25-1/4	23-1/4	25-1/4	27-1/4
Y	12-3/4			16-1/4		
Z	7-1/8			8-7/8		

REVOLVING DOORS ENTRANCES

The are points to consider when working with revolving doors:

- Circular glass enclosure walls may be annealed 1/4-in. glass. However, this varies with different government bodies. Some jurisdictions require laminated glass. Tempered glass is not available for this use. Refer to the Consumer Products Safety Commission's standards for glazing.
- Practical capacity equals 25 to 35 people per minute.
- Doors fabricated from stainless steel, aluminum, or bronze sections are available. Stainless steel is the most durable; lead times vary with construction techniques. Stainless steel is available in a number of satin and polished finishes. Aluminum is the most common and economical. It is available in anodized or painted finishes. Bronze is most difficult to maintain; satin, polished, or statuary finishes must have a protective lacquer coating. Doors are available, with only top and bottom stiles to be used with all-glass storefront doors. Wall enclosures may be all metal, all glass, partial glass, or housed-in construction.
- Optional heating and cooling source should be placed immediately adjacent to the enclosure.
- For general planning, use 6-ft 6-in. diameter. For hotels, department stores, airports, or other large traffic areas, use a 7-ft or greater diameter.
- Codes may allow 50 percent of legal exiting requirements by means of revolving doors. Some do not credit any, and require hinged doors adjacent. Verify with local authorities.

TYPES AND APPLICATIONS

Revolving door types and applications include:

- Automated revolving doors for large-size doors
- Motorized oval doors for small groups or grocery carts
- Security revolving doors that are noncollapsible until a magnetic shear lock is automatically released in an emergency

- Sliding night door of solid metal construction to close off open quadrant at exterior opening
- Manually operated

DESIGN CONSIDERATIONS
Revolving door design guidelines include the following:

- Mount entirely on one slab.
- Do not attach to adjacent walls.
- Floor must be level.

Swing doors may be required in addition to revolving doors by code or for good practice to provide egress, to meet accessibility requirements, or for off-hours security operation.

TYPICAL REVOLVING DOOR
2.469

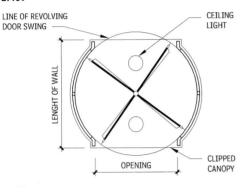

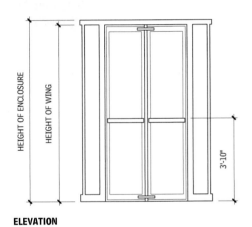

PLAN

ELEVATION

REVOLVING DOOR ENCLOSURE DIMENSIONS
2.470

DIAMETER	OPENING		WALL LENGTH		RECOMMENDED MAXIMUM HEIGHT
	FOUR-WING	THREE-WING	FOUR-WING	THREE-WING	
6'–0 inches	4'–1"		4'–7-5/8"		10'–0"
6'–2"	4'–2-1/2"		4'–9-1/8"		9'–10"
6'–4"	4'–3-7/8"		4'–10-1/2"		9'–8"
*6'–6"	*4'–5-1/4"	3'–1/4"	*4'–11-7/8"	6'–1/4"	9'–6"
6'–8"	4'–6-5/8"	3'–1-1/4"	5'–1-1/4"	6'–2-1/32"	9'–4"
6'–10"	4'–8-1/8"	3'–2-1/4"	5'–1-1/4"	6'–3-3/4"	9'–2"
7'–0"	4'–9-1/2"	*3'–3-1/4"	5'–4-1/8"	*6'–5-1/2"	9'–0"
7'–6"	5'–1-3/4"	3'–6-1/4"	5'–8-3/4"	6'–10-11/16"	8'–6"
8'–0"	5'–6"	3'–9-1/4"	6'–5/8"	7'–3-7/8"	8'–0"
9'–0"		4'–3/4"		8'–2-1/8"	8'–0"
10'–0"		4'–9-1/4"		9'–9/16"	8'–0"
14'–0"	9'–8-7/8"	6'–9-1/4"	10'–3-1/4"	12'–6-1/8"	8'–0"
16'–0"	11'–1-7/8"	7'–9-1/4"	11'–8-1/4"	14'–2-7/8"	8'–0"

LAYOUT TYPES
2.471

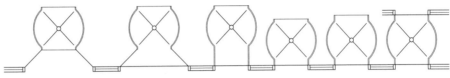

NOTE: A SWINGING DOOR MAY BE PROVIDED
AS WELL, FOR EGRESS AND ACCESSIBILITY

NOTE

2.471 A swinging door may be provided as well, for egress accessibility.

Contributor:
Jane Hansen, AIA, DeStefano & Partners, Chicago, Illinois.

SPECIAL DOORS

COILING OVERHEAD DOOR SECTION
2.472

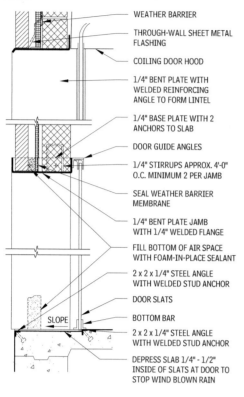

- WEATHER BARRIER
- THROUGH-WALL SHEET METAL FLASHING
- COILING DOOR HOOD
- 1/4" BENT PLATE WITH WELDED REINFORCING ANGLE TO FORM LINTEL
- 1/4" BASE PLATE WITH 2 ANCHORS TO SLAB
- DOOR GUIDE ANGLES
- 1/4" STIRRUPS APPROX. 4'-0" O.C. MINIMUM 2 PER JAMB
- SEAL WEATHER BARRIER MEMBRANE
- 1/4" BENT PLATE JAMB WITH 1/4" WELDED FLANGE
- FILL BOTTOM OF AIR SPACE WITH FOAM-IN-PLACE SEALANT
- 2 x 2 x 1/4" STEEL ANGLE WITH WELDED STUD ANCHOR
- DOOR SLATS
- BOTTOM BAR
- 2 x 2 x 1/4" STEEL ANGLE WITH WELDED STUD ANCHOR
- DEPRESS SLAB 1/4" - 1/2" INSIDE OF SLATS AT DOOR TO STOP WIND BLOWN RAIN

SLOPE

SECTIONAL DOORS

INSTALLATION DETAILS
2.474

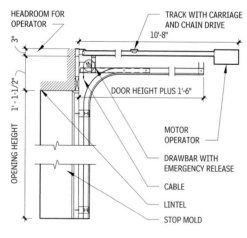

- HEADROOM FOR OPERATOR
- 3"
- TRACK WITH CARRIAGE AND CHAIN DRIVE 10'-8"
- DOOR HEIGHT PLUS 1'-6"
- 1' - 1-1/2"
- OPENING HEIGHT
- MOTOR OPERATOR
- DRAWBAR WITH EMERGENCY RELEASE
- CABLE
- LINTEL
- STOP MOLD

UPWARD-ACTING SECTIONAL DOORS
2.473

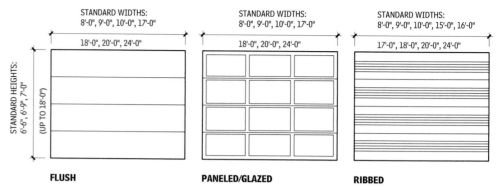

STANDARD WIDTHS:
8'-0", 9'-0", 10'-0", 17'-0"
18'-0", 20'-0", 24'-0"

STANDARD HEIGHTS:
6'-6", 6'-9", 7'-0"
(UP TO 18'-0")

FLUSH

STANDARD WIDTHS:
8'-0", 9'-0", 10'-0", 17'-0"
18'-0", 20'-0", 24'-0"

PANELED/GLAZED

STANDARD WIDTHS:
8'-0", 9'-0", 10'-0", 15'-0", 16'-0"
17'-0", 18'-0", 20'-0", 24'-0"

RIBBED

WOOD SECTIONAL DOORS
2.475

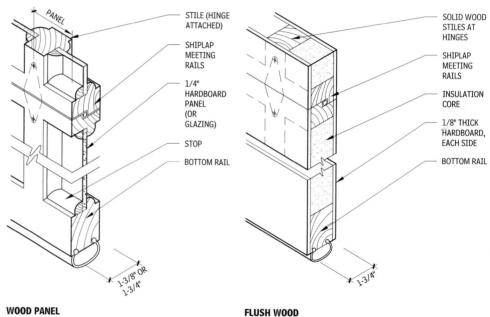

- PANEL
- STILE (HINGE ATTACHED)
- SHIPLAP MEETING RAILS
- 1/4" HARDBOARD PANEL (OR GLAZING)
- STOP
- BOTTOM RAIL
- 1-3/8" OR 1-3/4"

WOOD PANEL

- SOLID WOOD STILES AT HINGES
- SHIPLAP MEETING RAILS
- INSULATION CORE
- 1/8" THICK HARDBOARD, EACH SIDE
- BOTTOM RAIL
- 1-3/4"

FLUSH WOOD

SECTIONAL DOOR DETAILS
2.476

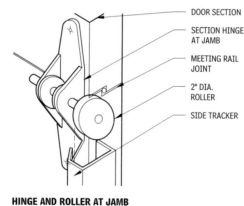

- DOOR SECTION
- SECTION HINGE AT JAMB
- MEETING RAIL JOINT
- 2" DIA. ROLLER
- SIDE TRACKER

HINGE AND ROLLER AT JAMB

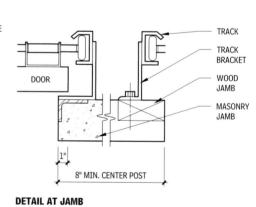

- TRACK
- TRACK BRACKET
- WOOD JAMB
- MASONRY JAMB
- DOOR
- 1"
- 8" MIN. CENTER POST

DETAIL AT JAMB

NOTES

2.472 a. Standard commercial doors are designed to wind loads of 20 lb/sq ft.
b. Glazing may be safety glass, plexiglas, or wired glass.
c. Motor operators may be turned on and off by remote electrical switch, radio signal, photoelectrical control, or key lock switch, for security.
2.473 Consult manufacturers for other door track configurations and clearances.

2.475 a. Typical maximum width for wood panel sectional doors is 24 ft (6 panels); typical maximum height is 18 ft (9 sections).
b. Typical maximum width for flush wood sectional doors is 24 ft (6 panels); typical maximum height is 18 ft (9 sections).

Contributors:
Richard J. Vitullo, AIA, Oak Leaf Studio, Crownsville, Maryland; Daniel F. C. Hayes, AIA, Washington, DC.

METAL SECTIONAL DOORS
2.477

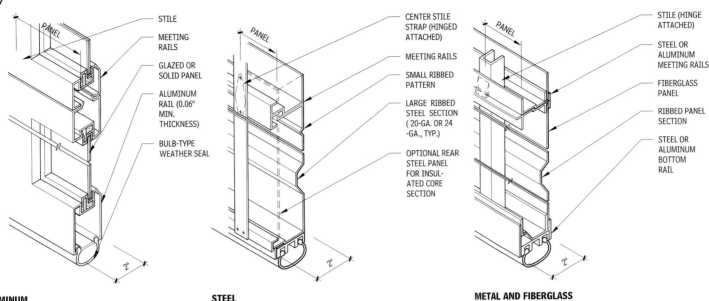

ALUMINUM

Labels (left detail): STILE; MEETING RAILS; GLAZED OR SOLID PANEL; ALUMINUM RAIL (0.06" MIN. THICKNESS); BULB-TYPE WEATHER SEAL; PANEL; 2"

STEEL

Labels (center detail): CENTER STILE STRAP (HINGED ATTACHED); MEETING RAILS; SMALL RIBBED PATTERN; LARGE RIBBED STEEL SECTION (20-GA. OR 24-GA., TYP.); OPTIONAL REAR STEEL PANEL FOR INSULATED CORE SECTION; PANEL; 2"

METAL AND FIBERGLASS

Labels (right detail): STILE (HINGE ATTACHED); STEEL OR ALUMINUM MEETING RAILS; FIBERGLASS PANEL; RIBBED PANEL SECTION; STEEL OR ALUMINUM BOTTOM RAIL; PANEL; 2"

STANDARD HEADROOM —2″ OR 3″ TRACK
2.478

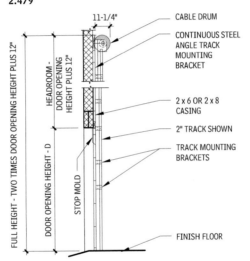

Labels: TENSION SPRING; 2" TRACK; CEILING LINE; HEAD ROOM; DOOR HEIGHT +18"; 2 x 6 OR 2 x 8 CASING; STOP MOLD; TRACK MOUNTING BRACKET; 2" TRACK SHOWN; FINISH FLOOR; DOOR OPENING HEIGHT - D

HEADROOM		
TRACK	**TORSION**	**EXTENSION**
Size	Springs	Springs
2"	16-1/2"	18"
3"	18-1/2"	22"

FULL VERTICAL TRACK
2.479

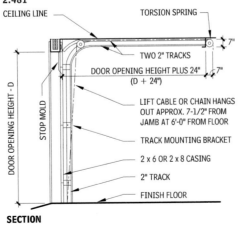

Labels: 11-1/4"; CABLE DRUM; CONTINUOUS STEEL ANGLE TRACK MOUNTING BRACKET; 2 x 6 OR 2 x 8 CASING; 2" TRACK SHOWN; TRACK MOUNTING BRACKETS; STOP MOLD; FINISH FLOOR; FULL HEIGHT - TWO TIMES DOOR OPENING HEIGHT PLUS 12"; HEADROOM - DOOR OPENING HEIGHT PLUS 12"; DOOR OPENING HEIGHT - D

LOW-HEADROOM TRACK—2 IN.
2.481

Labels: CEILING LINE; TORSION SPRING; 7"; TWO 2" TRACKS; DOOR OPENING HEIGHT PLUS 24" (D + 24"); 7"; LIFT CABLE OR CHAIN HANGS OUT APPROX. 7-1/2" FROM JAMB AT 6'-0" FROM FLOOR; TRACK MOUNTING BRACKET; 2 x 6 OR 2 x 8 CASING; 2" TRACK; FINISH FLOOR; DOOR OPENING HEIGHT - D; STOP MOLD

SECTION

LIFT CLEARANCE TRACK—2 OR 3 IN.
2.480

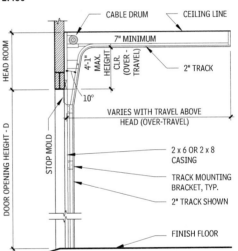

Labels: CABLE DRUM; CEILING LINE; 7" MINIMUM; 4'-1" MAX. HEIGHT; CLR. (OVER-TRAVEL); 2" TRACK; 10°; VARIES WITH TRAVEL ABOVE HEAD (OVER-TRAVEL); 2 x 6 OR 2 x 8 CASING; TRACK MOUNTING BRACKET, TYP.; 2" TRACK SHOWN; FINISH FLOOR; HEAD ROOM; DOOR OPENING HEIGHT - D; STOP MOLD

NOTES

2.477 a. Typical maximum width for aluminum sectional doors is 18 ft (5 panels); typical maximum height is 14 ft (7 sections).

b. Typical maximum width for steel sectional doors is 24 ft (7 panels); typical maximum height is 18 ft (9 sections).

c. Typical maximum width for metal and fiberglass sectional doors is 20 ft (6 panels); typical maximum height is 16 ft (8 sections).

2.478 Available with torsion or extension spring counterbalance. Vertical tracks can be bracket- or angle-mounted.

2.479 Torsion spring or weight counterbalance. Tracks can be bracket- or angle-mounted.

2.480 Torsion spring counterbalance only. Tracks can be bracket- or angle-mounted. Maximum usable headroom is 11 ft 6 in.

2.481 a. Available with torsion or extension spring counterbalance. Vertical tracks can be bracket or angle mounted.

b. Low-headroom track used on doors to 18C sq ft., 500 lbs, or 13 ft 1 in. high.

c. Headroom up to 144 sq ft. is 6 in.

d. Headroom from 144 sq. ft. to 180 sq ft. is 10 in.

Contributor:
Daniel F.C. Hayes, AIA, Washington, DC.

ROOFING

DESIGN CONSIDERATIONS

Roofing generally falls into two broad categories, steep slope and low slope. Selecting the appropriate roof assembly is dependent on many factors, including:

- Initial and life-cycle cost
- Reliability
- Substrate material
- Structural capacity of the deck
- Fire-resistance
- Environmental conditions including wind speed, seasonal weather (hail, snow, and rain)
- Building height
- Future access
- Roof mounted equipment
- Complexity of the building geometry
- Number of penetrations
- Thermal performance
- Construction sequencing
- Building codes

STEEP SLOPE ROOFING

Steep slope roofing is generally designated as roofing with slopes greater than 3 in 12. Steep slope roofing is a water-shedding roof, typically composed of many small overlapping units; as such, it is not a continuous waterproof membrane. The slope must be steep enough so that water runs off by gravity and cannot be pushed uphill by wind or capillary action. Some steep slope roof assemblies can be installed at slopes less than 3 in 12 in accordance with the manufacturer's recommendations.

CHARACTERISTICS AND CONSIDERATIONS

Steep slope roofing is typically a ventilated or "cold" roof design, with insulation below the roof deck and the surface temperature of the roofing system near outdoor conditions. The insulation and weather barrier are typically located at the ceiling below the attic cavity.

Steep slope roofing assemblies can be designed as a compact "warm" or "unvented" roof design with insulation between the shingles or covering and the structural deck. Evaluate the manufacturer's recommendations for compact roof design, because there may be concerns about the possibility of elevated surface temperatures causing premature failure of the assembly. Forensic investigation has shown that roof orientation (south versus north slopes) and material color have a major impact on surface temperature.

Steep slope roofing is most commonly used for residential and light commercial construction. Although it provides long-term performance at competitive costs, it is generally cost-effective for use on large commercial buildings because it does not provide a platform for roof-mounted HVAC or window cleaning equipment, nor is it as easy to maintain or replace on tall buildings. For buildings with large footprints, steep slope roofing can result in excessive internal volume that is not usable.

Roof warranties are offered by most manufacturers of synthetic roof shingle materials, but not for natural products such as slate and wood. However, these warranties are primarily a means for manufacturers to limit their liability, rather than to protect an owner. Furthermore, some products are promoted as having extremely long warranty periods, but the fine print limits coverage to replacement of defective materials on a prorated cost basis to the original owner. Defective installation is not covered, nor is there any value available for the cost of labor to make repairs. Therefore, design professionals should read the warranty carefully, and not rely on it as a basis for product selection. In the end, keep in mind that no piece of paper will keep water out of a building, and a warranty only provides a road map to fixing a leak after it has occurred.

Selecting the steep slope roof system is dependent on many factors, including initial and life-cycle costs, appearance, reliability, historical accuracy, structural capacity of the deck, fire-resistance, wind speed, resistance to weather conditions including hail, rain, and snow, building codes.

Selection recommendations include:

- Consider light-colored, highly reflective roofs to reduce heat island effect in cities and, in warm climates, energy costs for the building.
- In areas susceptible to forest fires, select noncombustible roofing such as concrete or clay tiles, or slate.
- Consider recycled material content, life span, reuse, embodied energy, distance to source, and other sustainable criteria.

Steep slope roofing consists of four major components: the roof covering; the weather barrier; the structural roof deck; and flashing at the edges, transitions, and penetrations.

WEATHER BARRIER

Steep slope roofing is almost always installed over a weather barrier that provides temporary protection until the roofing is installed and serves as a second layer of defense against water penetration.

The traditional material for a weather barrier is building felt. Considering the relatively low material cost of felt, it is recommended to invest in heavier grades, double coverage, or both, to provide more robust performance, especially at shallower slopes.

Self-adhering (peel-and-stick) modified bituminous weather barriers provides an increased level of moisture protection. They are frequently used to seal seams and are flexible enough to form to complicated configurations. Self-adhering membranes are typically recommended at for use at edges, eaves, rakes, valleys, hips, ridges, crickets, and other difficult areas. It is important to consider that modified bituminous membranes are vapor barriers, and in cold or mixed climates their placement should be carefully designed to avoid trapping moisture in the roof assembly.

Slip sheets are necessary under metal roofs to keep them from sticking to the felt weather barrier. Some modified bituminous membranes may come with a surfacing that can be used under metal roofing

Ice dams are a problem for many shingle roofs in cold climates. The first defense against ice dams is to detail the roof framing to allow full thickness of insulation to the edge of the roof, and proper venting to ensure that the roof deck stays cold. Additional protection can be provided by installing a modified bituminous membrane at eaves and up the roof surface past location of building wall.

ROOF DECK

Roof decks under steep slope roofing are almost always plywood or oriented-strand board (OSB) panels. Proper installation of the panels, especially spacing between panels to allow expansion without telegraphing through the shingles, is important.

In some commercial construction, steep slope roofing may be installed over metal decking or, occasionally, concrete planks. In these cases, board insulation is typically installed over the metal or concrete deck, and a nailable panel is added over the insulation. Up to slopes of 6 in 12, the panels may be simply screwed through the insulation layer. With steeper slopes, it may be necessary to install wood sleepers to avoid pulling the fasteners downslope, depending on the weight of the roof covering and the thickness of the insulation.

FLASHING

Flashing is an additional component of steep slope roofing assemblies used at edges, transitions, and penetrations, to provide a watertight assembly. Flashing has traditionally been sheet metal, but elastomeric sheets are replacing some sheet metals for the purpose of flashing, particularly at penetrations. Sheet metal, especially when installed in long lengths, must be allowed to expand and contract independent of the roof deck and the roof cov-

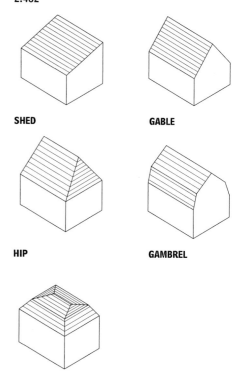

COMMON STEEP SLOPE ROOF SHAPES
2.482

SHED   GABLE

HIP   GAMBREL

MANSARD

ering. Running lengths of sheet metal should be installed with clips and not directly nailed. Where flashing is installed at points that interrupt the flow of water, it must be carefully detailed to control and redirect the water. Crimped dams at valleys and folded crickets are two examples.

LOW SLOPE ROOFING

Low slope roofing is generally designated as roofing with slopes at or less than 3 in 12. Low slope roofing is typically composed of a continuous waterproof membrane. Low slope roofs are not flat; most have a minimum slope of 1/4 in. in 12. Many low slope roof assemblies can be installed at slopes from 3 in 12 up to vertical in accordance with manufacturers' recommendations. Low slope roofing is typically designed as a compact "warm" roof design, with insulation between the roof covering and the structural deck and with no ventilation.

Consult the following reference:

- NRCA Roofing and Waterproofing Manual

CHARACTERISTICS AND CONSIDERATIONS

Low slope roofing provides long-term performance at competitive costs and a platform for roof-mounted HVAC and window cleaning equipment. Low slope roofing is relatively easy to maintain and replace on tall buildings. This is no panacea, however, as metal roofing will suffer equally from poor design and installation. With proper detailing and installation low slope roofing assembly with can deliver 20 or more years of service with minimal maintenance.

Low slope roofing consists of five major components: the roof covering, the insulation with a cover board, a vapor barrier (if present) and sheathing to support the vapor barrier over metal deck; the structural roof deck, and flashing at the edges, transitions, and penetrations: Everything above the roof deck constitutes the roofing system.

TYPICAL LOW SLOPE ROOF ASSEMBLY
2.483

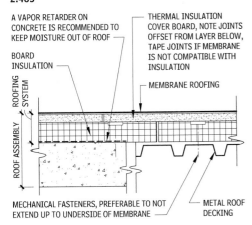

A VAPOR RETARDER ON CONCRETE IS RECOMMENDED TO KEEP MOISTURE OUT OF ROOF

BOARD INSULATION

ROOFING SYSTEM

ROOF ASSEMBLY

THERMAL INSULATION COVER BOARD, NOTE JOINTS OFFSET FROM LAYER BELOW, TAPE JOINTS IF MEMBRANE IS NOT COMPATIBLE WITH INSULATION

MEMBRANE ROOFING

MECHANICAL FASTENERS, PREFERABLE TO NOT EXTEND UP TO UNDERSIDE OF MEMBRANE

METAL ROOF DECKING

INSULATION

Roof insulation not only reduces the energy required to condition the building, but it also helps to control condensation, provides a smooth substrate for the roof membrane, and can be used to slope the surface for drainage.

The ideal low slope roof insulation would be compatible with the membrane, adhesives, and substrates; be dimensionally stable and strong enough for anchorage, uplift, traffic, and impact; be fire-resistant; have a high and stable thermal value; and not be affected by moisture. No single material embodies all of these attributes, however, so the use of two or more layers with complementary properties is recommended.

- *Polyisocyanurate foam*: This is one of the most common commercial roof insulation boards. It is fire- and moisture-resistant, compatible with nearly all membranes and adhesives, and has excellent thermal properties. A more rigid cover board is recommended. Use the more conservative, aged R-value to evaluate long-term thermal performance.
- *Polystyrene foam*: Both extruded and expanded types are available. Polystyrene has a very high R-value and is unaffected by wetting; however, it is combustible and may require an weather barrier of gypsum board to comply with building codes. Moreover, polystyrene is difficult to install with hot asphalt adhesives and may not have sufficient rigidity for mechanical fasteners. Nevertheless, it is very commonly used in ballasted systems and inverted roof membrane assemblies (extruded type). A cover board is recommended to isolate asphalt-based membranes. Polystyrene foam may be recycled.
- *Perlite*: Manufactured from expanded minerals and binders, perlite insulation is noncombustible and has moderate thermal resistance, good strength, and excellent compatibility with most roofing materials. The perlite will absorb moisture.
- *Wood fiberboard*: Manufactured from wood or cane fibers and binders, wood fiberboard shares many traits with perlite. Its disadvantages are that it can burn and degrades when wet.
- *Insulating concrete*: Portland cement or gypsum with lightweight aggregates (possibly with foaming agents), and usually supplemented with expanded polystyrene, provide strength, thermal resistance, and no gaps, and readily produces a sloped, finished surface. Density is between typically between 20 and 40 psf. The system inherently introduces moisture into an assembly that should be dry, thereby creating an opportunity for trapped moisture and resulting failures. Venting of the completed assembly is recommended, which may affect the interior ceiling plenum and create leaks. Careful control of the drying time before installation must be maintained while also protecting the insulating concrete from precipitation.
- *Gypsum sheathing*: While not technically insulation, gypsum sheathing is a high-quality cover, providing a strong substrate for attaching the roof membrane, which is both fireproof and resistant to moisture. Pre-primed boards are available for hot-asphalt applications.

- *Miscellaneous boards*: Other types of insulation include cellular glass, fibrous glass, mineral fiber, and others used for specialized applications.
- *Composite Boards*: Composite boards that combine two insulation materials laminated into one board are available; commonly polyisocyanurate or polystyrene foam bonded to plywood, OSB or gypsum sheathing.

Insulation should be installed in at least two layers, with joints offset between the two. The offset joints reduce air leaks that waste energy and could result in condensation on the cold underside of the membrane.

Insulation is mechanically fastened, set in adhesive or hot asphalt, or ballasted. It is preferable to not have mechanical fasteners extend through the entire assembly to the bottom of the roof membrane because the anchors may puncture or abrade the membrane. Therefore, limit mechanical fasteners to the bottom layer of insulation and install subsequent layers with adhesive.

Also, it is best to limit the size of insulation boards to 4 ft by 4 ft to reduce the size of cracks that may develop from shrinkage. Tapered insulation can be used to build up the roof slope and crickets.

Provide a cover board over the insulation if the top layer is not a composite board or lightweight concrete. Cover boards are typically gypsum sheathing, perlite, or wood fiberboard, to provide the physical rigidity and strength that most insulations do not possess. The cover board can count as the second layer of insulation.

WATER VAPOR CONTROL

Water vapor moves through low slope roof assemblies under two methods: air leakage and water vapor diffusion. Just as in walls, air leakage can carry much more moisture than diffusion. Use offset joints in multiple layers of foam insulation and air seals at edges and penetrations to limit the flow of cold interior air to the underside of the membrane, where it will likely condense. For buildings in cold climates with high interior winter humidity, the vapor drive may be strong enough that a vapor retarder on the warm underside of the insulation may be required, in addition to air sealing.

Additional water vapor control recommendations include:

- Most roof membranes are also vapor retarders, so adding a separate vapor retarder on the inside face may trap moisture in the insulation. Therefore, avoid a separate vapor retarder, unless it is actually required.
- The NRCA recommends a vapor retarder over concrete decks to protect the roof system from the effects of latent moisture.
- An inverted roof membrane assembly places the roof membrane on the warm side of the insulation and, therefore, is an ideal system for control of water vapor in cold climates.
- Vapor retarder membranes can be two- or three-ply built-up roofing, modified bituminous membranes, self-adhering peel-and-stick membranes, polyethylene sheets, or aluminum foils. It is best to select a membrane that will seal around mechanical anchors, or even better, select a membrane over which all subsequent layers of the assembly can be set in hot asphalt or other adhesive.
- On a metal deck, a weather barrier board of gypsum sheathing or a thin layer of insulation may be required to provide a smooth substrate for the installation of the vapor retarder, although some membranes can be installed directly on metal deck.
- At the perimeter of roof vapor retarder, it may be best to connect to wall air and vapor retarders. Otherwise, ensure that the vapor retarder at the perimeter keeps moisture out of the roof assembly. Detail penetrations to be vaportight, similar to details for the roof membrane.

ROOF DECK

Roof decks for low slope roof assemblies must support the gravity loads from snow, rain, and rooftop equipment, and must resist wind uplift loads that may be greater than the gravity loads. The deck also is frequently sloped to provide drainage, and must be stiff enough to ensure that deflection does not result in localized water ponding.

Metal deck, concrete, and plywood are the three most common roof deck materials, but other materials are available. Concrete and poured gypsum decks must be cured before installing roof covering.

FLASHING

Similar in use to flashing for steep slope roofing, flashing includes additional components for lowslope roofing systems and is used at edges, transitions, and penetrations to provide a watertight assembly. Particularly at penetrations, traditional sheet metal has been replaced with elastomeric sheets and preformed cones. Sheet metal moves more with temperature change than roofing. Therefore, it is better to avoid embedding long lengths of sheet metal directly into the roof membrane. At gravel stops and other similar conditions, constrain the movement of the metal by nailing in two rows, with nails 3 in. apart.

LOW SLOPE ROOF ASSEMBLY DESIGN

Roof membrane manufacturers produce standards and recommendations for their roof assemblies. These standards will typically include details for standard conditions, such as penetrations, edges, and terminations. Modifications to these details, such as increased roof slope and the use of tapered edge strips at the base flashing can extend the service life of the roof and should be considered by the design professional.

Many assemblies have specific detailing, and installation procedures that are required to obtain a 20-year warranty. These details should be adhered to even if the warranty is not required. No single low slope roof assembly solution is appropriate for every roofing condition.

Design guidelines and recommendations include:

- Consider light-colored, highly reflective roofs, to reduce the heat island effect in cities and, in warm climates, energy costs for the building.
- Avoid gravel-coated or ballasted systems on buildings in high-wind areas where the stone may become projectiles, causing collateral damage by breaking out windows.
- Consider recycled material content, life span, reuse, embodied energy, distance to source, and other sustainable criteria.
- Consider planted green roofs to slow water runoff, reduce the heat island effect, and increase thermal performance.

ROOF SLOPE AND DRAINAGE

Positive drainage increases roof life and is mandated at 1/4 in. in 12 in most codes, although some large governmental and corporate owners require 1/2 in. in 12. All surfaces of the finished roof should be sloped sufficiently so that no ponding occurs 48 hours after a rain.

Design guidelines include:

- Consider deflection of deck, particularly at long spans. Deflection may be sufficient to negate the roof slope. If the deflection creates a low spot, ponding may increase the deflection, progressively increasing until failure. Structural engineers should check for this failure mode.

LOW SLOPE ROOF ASSEMBLY WITH VAPOR RETARDER
2.484

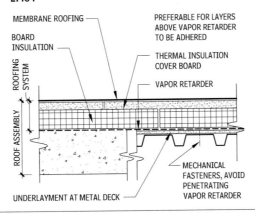

MEMBRANE ROOFING

BOARD INSULATION

ROOFING SYSTEM

ROOF ASSEMBLY

PREFERABLE FOR LAYERS ABOVE VAPOR RETARDER TO BE ADHERED

THERMAL INSULATION COVER BOARD

VAPOR RETARDER

MECHANICAL FASTENERS, AVOID PENETRATING VAPOR RETARDER

UNDERLAYMENT AT METAL DECK

ROOF SLOPE SCHEMES
2.485

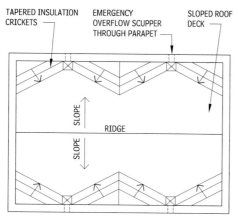

SLOPE TO PARAPET

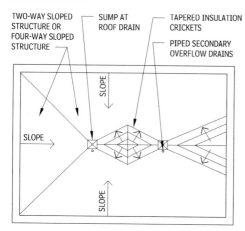

SLOPE TO CENTER

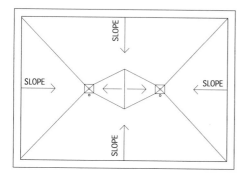

- It is typically less expensive to slope the roof deck and use tapered insulation to create crickets in small areas. If the roof deck is planned as a future floor and is flat, then tapered insulation should be used to build up the slope.
- In addition to primary drains, the roof must have provisions for secondary drainage. Overflow scuppers are the most reliable, but piped secondary drains are an option in most jurisdictions. Requirements for piped secondary drains may be include the size to be twice as large as primary to avoid clogging, or that the rainwater conductors discharge near an entrance so that building personnel will be alerted to the fact the roof is not draining properly. The height of the scupper and the resulting impounded water should be checked against the structural capacity of the deck.

WEATHER BARRIER
The roof system frequently also functions as the weather barrier on the top of the building. Roofs over concrete roof decks may function as a weather barrier, but the roof membrane or a vapor barrier is more frequently chosen as the air barrier. Some manufacturers will not warrant their membrane when it is to be used as an air barrier, particularly mechanically fastened single-ply membranes.

WIND SPEED
Wind speed is the primary determinant of the uplift forces acting on a roof, ASCE 7, "Minimum Design Loads for Buildings and Other Structures," and Factory Mutual Global (FMG) Loss Prevention Data Sheet, "Wind Loads to Roof Systems and Roof Deck Securements" both provide site maps with historical gusts. Adjustments for terrain, building height, parapets, wall openings, and hurricane exposure will result in an uplift classification. Note that wind speeds in miles per hour (mph) and uplift values in pounds per square foot (psf) often are very similar, but should not be confused. The uplift value applies to the field of the roof. Perimeter zones and corner zones have increased uplift, typically at 1.5 and 2 times, respectively, of the field value.

COOL ROOFS
Lightly colored, reflective, and high-emissivity roof systems reduce cooling loads and heat island effect in urban areas. Refer to the ENERGY STAR listing at www.energystar.gov.

INSURANCE COVERAGE
Some owners' insurance coverage (Factory Mutual Global is the most common) will place more stringent requirements on a roof assembly design than the building code or the membrane manufacturer. Verify requirements with the owner at the beginning of the roof design process and for compliance at each subsequent step. The primary impact of FMG is the use of higher design wind speeds, resulting in higher uplift loads on the roof assembly, including the roof deck and perimeter, and limitations on choices of listed materials and assemblies.

FIRE-RATED ROOF ASSEMBLIES
For most fire-rated roof assemblies, a Class A roof covering and listed insulation is acceptable, but verify with the roofing manufacturer and authority having jurisdiction. Note that unlike floor assemblies, penetrations through roofs do not need to be firestopped, except in portions of roofs where openings are not permitted (such as near firewalls).

FALL PROTECTION
An advantage of low-slope roofs is their use as a platform for maintenance of the facility, which may include roof mounted equipment or equipment used for maintenance of windows and walls below the roof. Verify code requirements and related equipment requirements. Other protection recommendations include

- Use of warning signs and locks at roof access points.
- Use of emergency fall-arrest anchors. A worker should be able to tie off a line to a safety harness and be able to access the entire roof edge without being exposed to an excessive fall. Consultants and manufacturers are available to assist in design. Refer to OSHA and local regulations for worker and window-washer safety requirements.
- Provide a continuous cable on structural post supports around the perimeter of the roof and approximately 10 ft back from the edge. The cable allows workers to tie off their safety harnesses at any point. The cable also serves as a physical warning that a worker is approaching the edge of the roof; signs can be added with further instructions.
- Provide fall-arrest anchors, which can be posts mounted on the roof or "eyes" mounted on penthouse walls. Spacing of the anchors should be determined by projecting a 30° cone and ensuring total coverage of the perimeter. Provide additional anchors around obstructions.
- Note that emergency tie-offs are also required for workers on window-washing staging.

WARRANTIES
Roofing manufacturers offer warranties, ranging from a two-year material-defect-only coverage to no-dollar-limit (NDL), 20-year full system replacement.

Some products are promoted as having extremely long warranty periods, but they lack in-place proven performance to back up these claims. Design professionals should read the warranty provisions carefully and not rely too heavily on the warranty as a basis for product selection.

Note that warrantable roof assemblies and details reflect a compromise chosen by the manufacturer between dependable service and a low initial cost, to remain competitive in the open market. Therefore, do not automatically assume that the offer of a warranty implies the highest quality.

Consult the following references:

The NRCA Roofing and Waterproofing Manual; (National Roofing Contractors Association, 2006)

*Roofing Design and Practice (*Pearson Education, 2000), Stephen Patterson and Madan Mehta.

ROOF EMERGENCY FALL PROTECTION
2.486

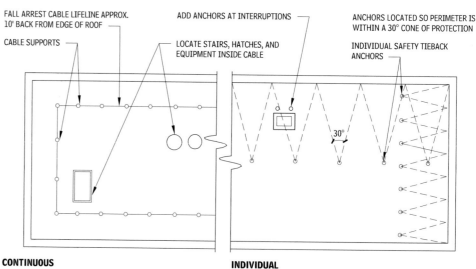

NOTE

2.485 Slopes can be accomplished with tapered insulation on flat roof decks.

ROOF COVERINGS

STEEP SLOPE ROOF COVERINGS

WOOD SHINGLES AND SHAKES

Wood shingles and shakes are cut from wood species that are naturally resistant to water, sunlight, rot, and hail (i.e., red cedar, redwood, and tidewater red cypress). They are typically installed in the natural state, although stains, primers, and paint may be applied.

Nails must be hot dipped in zinc or aluminum. Nail heads should be driven flush with the surface of the shingle or shake but never into the wood.

Weather barrier and sheathing should be designed to augment the protection provided by the shingles or shakes, depending on roof pitch and climate. A low-pitched roof subject to wind-driven snow should have solid sheathing and an additional weather barrier.

Use self-sealing peel-and-stick modified bituminous membrane weather barrier at eaves valley, rake, and other detail areas. Modified bituminous weather barrier is a vapor retarder, so is it not recommended for continuous application where the weather barrier needs to breathe.

WOOD SHAKES APPLIED TO EXISTING ROOF
2.487

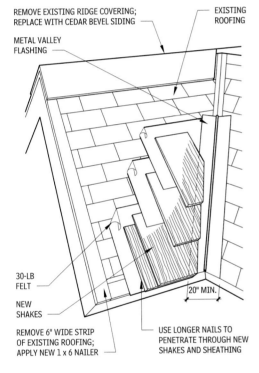

REMOVE EXISTING RIDGE COVERING; REPLACE WITH CEDAR BEVEL SIDING

EXISTING ROOFING

METAL VALLEY FLASHING

30-LB FELT

NEW SHAKES

REMOVE 6" WIDE STRIP OF EXISTING ROOFING; APPLY NEW 1 x 6 NAILER

USE LONGER NAILS TO PENETRATE THROUGH NEW SHAKES AND SHEATHING

20" MIN.

RED CEDAR HAND-SPLIT SHAKES
2.488

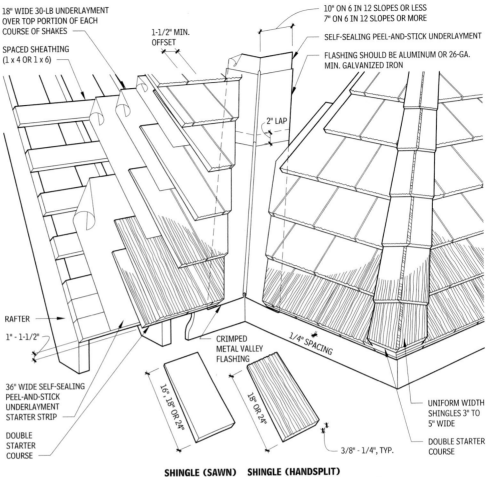

18" WIDE 30-LB UNDERLAYMENT OVER TOP PORTION OF EACH COURSE OF SHAKES

SPACED SHEATHING (1 x 4 OR 1 x 6)

1-1/2" MIN. OFFSET

10" ON 6 IN 12 SLOPES OR LESS
7" ON 6 IN 12 SLOPES OR MORE

SELF-SEALING PEEL-AND-STICK UNDERLAYMENT

FLASHING SHOULD BE ALUMINUM OR 26-GA. MIN. GALVANIZED IRON

2" LAP

RAFTER

1" - 1-1/2"

36" WIDE SELF-SEALING PEEL-AND-STICK UNDERLAYMENT STARTER STRIP

DOUBLE STARTER COURSE

CRIMPED METAL VALLEY FLASHING

1/4" SPACING

16", 18" OR 24"

18" OR 24"

3/8" - 1/4", TYP.

UNIFORM WIDTH SHINGLES 3" TO 5" WIDE

DOUBLE STARTER COURSE

SHINGLE (SAWN)   SHINGLE (HANDSPLIT)

RED CEDAR HANDSPLIT SHAKES
2.489

GRADE	LENGTH AND THICKNESS	DESCRIPTION
No. 1 hand-split and resawn	15″ starter-finish	These shakes have split faces and sawn backs. Cedar logs are first cut into desired lengths. Blanks or boards of proper thickness are split and then run diagonally through a bandsaw to produce two tapered shakes from each blank.
	18″ × 1/2″ medium	
	18″ × 3/4″ heavy	
	24″ × 3/8″	
	24″ × 1/2″ medium	
	24″ × 3/4″ heavy	
No. 1 taper-split	24″ × 1/2″	Produced largely by hand, using a sharp-bladed steel froe and a wooden mallet. The natural shingle-like taper is achieved by reversing the block, end for end, with each split.
No. 1 straight	18″ × 3/8″ side wall	Produced in the same manner as taper-split shakes, except that by splitting from the same end of the block, the shakes acquire the same thickness throughout.
	18″ × 3/8″	
	24″ × 3/8″	

RED CEDAR SHINGLES
2.490

	NO. 1 BLUE LABEL			NO. 2 RED LABEL			NO. 3 BLACK LABEL		
	MAXIMUM EXPOSURE RECOMMENDED FOR ROOFS (IN.)								
ROOF PITCH	16	18	24	16	18	24	16	18	24
3 in 12 to 4 in 12	3-3/4	4-1/4	5-3/4	3-1/2	4	5-1/2	3	3-1/2	5
4 in 12 and steeper	5	5-1/2	7-1/2	4	4-1/2	6-1/2	3-1/2	4	5-1/2

NOTES

2.487 Shakes can also be applied over an existing wall or roof. Brick or other masonry requires vertical frame boards and horizontal nailing strips. Nails should penetrate sheathing or studs. Over wood, apply shakes directly, as on new sheathing.
2.488 Copper flashing should not be used with red cedar.

Contributor:
Richard J. Vitullo, AIA, Oak Leaf Studio, Ceoqnsville, Maryland.

UNDERLAYMENT AND ROOF SHEATHING
2.491

ROOFING TYPE	SHEATHING	UNDERLAYMENT	NORMAL SLOPE		LOW SLOPE	
Wood shakes and shingles	Solid or spaced	No. 30 asphalt saturated felt (interlayment)	4 in 12 and up	Underlayment starter course; interlayment over entire roof	3 in 12 to 4 in 12	Single layer unlayment over entire roof; interlayment over entire roof

FANCY BUTT RED CEDAR SHINGLE SHAPES
2.492

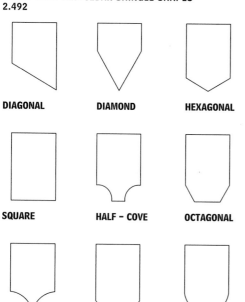

DIAGONAL   DIAMOND   HEXAGONAL

SQUARE   HALF – COVE   OCTAGONAL

ARROW   FISH SCALE   ROUND

SCHEDULE OF UNDERLAYMENT
2.493

SLOPE	TYPE OF UNDERLAYMENT
Normal slope: 4 in 12 and up	Single layer of 15 lb. asphalt saturated felt over entire roof
Low slope: 3 in 12 to 4 in 12	Two layers of 15 lb. asphalt saturated felt over entire roof

APPLICATION OF UNDERLAYMENT ON STEEP SLOPE ROOFS
2.494

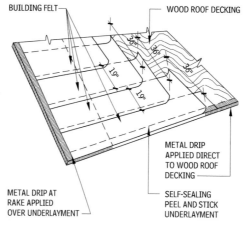

BUILDING FELT

WOOD ROOF DECKING

METAL DRIP APPLIED DIRECT TO WOOD ROOF DECKING

SELF-SEALING PEEL AND STICK UNDERLAYMENT

METAL DRIP AT RAKE APPLIED OVER UNDERLAYMENT

SCHEDULE OF ASPHALT AND COMPOSITION SHINGLE TYPES[a]
2.496

DESCRIPTION	DESIGN	MATERIAL	UL RATING	WEIGHT	SIZE
Three-tab square butt		Fiberglass	A[d]	205–225 lb/sq	36″ × 12″
		Organic felts	C[d]	235–300 lb/sq	36″ × 12″
Two-tab square butt		Fiberglass	A[d]	260–325 lb/sq	36″ × 12″ ″
		Organic felts	C[d]	300 lb/sq	36″ × 12″
Laminated overlay[b]		Fiberglass	A[c]	300 lb/sq	36″ × 14″
		Organic felts	C[c]	330–380 lb/sq	36″ × 14″
Random edge cut		Fiberglass	A[c]	225–260 lb/sq	36″ × 12″
		Organic felts	C[c]	250 lb/sq	36″ × 12″

EAVE FLASHING
2.495

EAVES FLASHING STRIP PREVENTS BACKUP DAMAGE

ALL LAPS SHOULD BE OUTSIDE WALL LINE

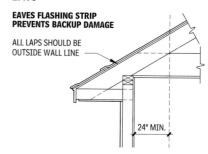

24" MIN.

NORMAL SLOPE

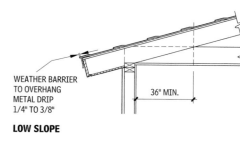

WEATHER BARRIER TO OVERHANG METAL DRIP 1/4" TO 3/8"

36" MIN.

LOW SLOPE

NOTES

2.492 Fancy butt shingles are 5 in. wide and 7-1/2 in. long, and custom-produced to individual orders.

2.495 Eave flashing is required whenever the January daily average temperature is 30°F or less or where there is a possibility of ice forming along the eaves.

2.496 a. For all designs, exposure, 5 in.; edge lap, 2 in.
b. More than one thickness, for varying surface texture.
c. Many rated as wind-resistant.
d. All rated as wind-resistant.

Contributors:
Richard J. Vitullo, AIA, Oak Leaf Studio, Crownsville, Maryland; Robert E. Fehlberg, AIA, CTA Architects Engineers, Billings, Montana.

SHINGLE APPLICATION DIAGRAMS
2.497

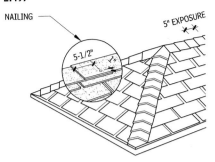

HIP AND RIDGE

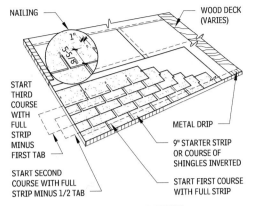

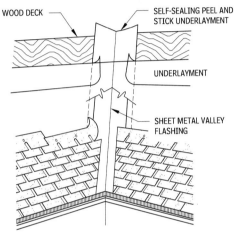

OPEN VALLEY

THREE TAB SQUARE BUTT STRIP SHINGLES

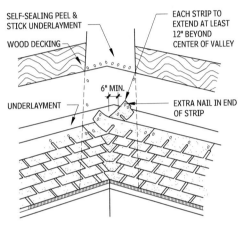

CLOSED VALLEY

NAIL TYPES
2.498

SMOOTH

ANNULAR THREADED

SCREW THREADED

NAILING OF SHINGLES RECOMMENDATION
2.499

DECK TYPE	NAIL LENGTH
1" wood sheathing	1-1/4"
3/8" plywood	7/8"
1/2" plywood	1"
Reroofing over asphalt shingles	1-3/4"

SPANISH TILE
2.500

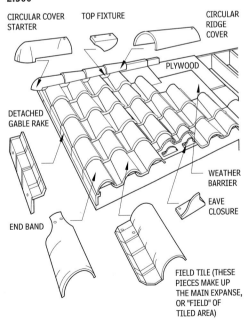

FLAT INTERLOCKING TILES
2.501

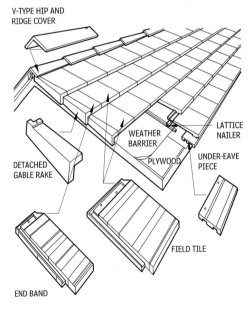

TILE ROOFING

Tile roofs can make a long-lasting, durable roof if well detailed and constructed. Roofing tiles are available in either clay or concrete and in a large number of profiles, sizes, colors, and textures. All tiles absorb moisture and, generally, the more porous, the less strong and durable the tile. Concrete tile is generally more porous than clay, and may require a sealer. The sealer may require reapplication that is inconsistent with tile's otherwise durable quality. Typical 1/2-in. thick tiles weigh approximately 10 psf, with proportional increases for thicker tiles.

Tile is made from two basic materials, clay and concrete:

- *Clay:* Clay tiles are formed from natural material, so color uniformity is dependent on the uniformity of the raw clay—unless glazed. Unglazed tile weathers only slightly over time. Glazed tiles are available in a larger number of colors, including bright blues, greens, reds, and oranges.
- *Concrete:* Concrete tiles are pressed in molds under high pressure. The synthetic oxide compounds color the surface. Tiles are sometimes painted, which may fade with time.

PROFILES

Tiles are typically available in three profiles, flat, barrel, and S-shaped. Barrel and S-shaped are also called *mission tiles.*

- *Flat:* These are sized approximately 10 by 13 up to 13 by 20 in. Flat tiles may be very simple, requiring a doubled shingled overlap, or may be interlocking, with approximately a 3-in. head overlap. Tiles may be fluted on the back to reduce weight, or lugged to hang on battens.
- *Barrel:* Barrel tile sizes are typically 16 by 8, 19 by 10, or 18 by 12 in., punched for one hole.
- *S-shaped:* These tiles are approximately 10 by 13 up to 13 by 20 in. S-shaped tiles are essentially the pan and cover portions of barrel tiles in one piece.

INSTALLATION

- *Underlayment:* Tile roofs in areas of high rain or wind driven rain are likely to allow some water under the tiles and the underlayment provides the final defense against water intrusion. Therefore, the underlayment must be more robust and detailed more thoroughly than in some other steep roofing systems. The minimum underlayment is a double layer of No. 30 unperforated

---

Contributor:
Robert E. Fehlberg, FAIA, CTA Architects Engineers, Billings, Montana;
Darrel Downing, Rippeteau Architects, PC, Washington, DC.

asphalt saturated felt except single coverage allowed at slopes over 20:12. In comparison to the cost of the tiles, the felts are inexpensive; consider using heavier No. 45 or 60 felts. For all edges and detail areas, such as eaves, valleys, rakes, crickets, it is recommended that you install self-sealing, peel-and-stick modified bituminous underlayment. The modified bituminous membrane provides an additional level of protection by sealing around the nails and stopping migration of water under loose felts. Self-sealing membrane is especially important for protection against ice dams in cold climates. Modified bituminous membranes are vapor retarders and should not be used across the entire roof substrate if a continuous vapor retarder is not desired.

- *Flashing*: Sheet metal flashing embedded in the tile should be minimum 24 oz. copper or lead-coated copper or 26-gage stainless steel, fabricated to allow differential thermal movement.
- *Wood nailers*: Although the simplest and least expensive method to install tiles is to nail them directly to the wood deck, nailers can help secure the tiles and provide drainage. For tiles with lugs, horizontal battens with a 1/2 in. space every 48 in. is recommended. Mission tiles may require vertical nailers of 2 by 3's or 2 by 4's, spacing to suit tiles plus nailers at ridges and hips. For maximum reliability and long-term performance it is recommended that you install vertical nailers at 24 inches on center

with horizontal nailers to suit the tiles. This lattice arrangement allows maximum drainage and drying below tiles. Nailers should preservative treated.

- *Tiles*: Barrel tiles are typically secured with a single nail each. Flat and S-shaped tiles typically are installed with two nails. Nailing may be reduced in the field of the roof depending on slope and wind conditions; verify with local code. Some tiles, especially barrel tiles are laid in cement.
- *Low-slope tile roofing*: Tile roofing may be used in some areas of limited rain and wind at slopes lower than 4 in 12, if the lattice nailer system is installed over a continuous waterproof membrane of double-layer modified bituminous roofing. The tiles basically shield the membrane roofing (which provides the actual waterproofing) from UV exposure.
- *High-wind areas*: For high-wind areas, refer to *The Concrete and Clay Tile Installation Manual,* published by the Florida Roofing, Sheet Metal, and Air Conditioning Contractors Association and the Roof Tile Institute.

SLATE ROOFING

Slate roofs are extremely durable, sometimes lasting 75 or 100 years. Due to the expense and durability of the slates, it is important to select all supporting and accessory materials for a similar life span. Use the following as selection guidelines:

- *Commercial standard*: The quarry run of 3/16-in. thickness; includes tolerable variations above and below 3/16 in.

- *Textural*: A rough-textured slate roof with uneven buts. The slates vary in thickness and size, which is generally not true of slate more than 3/8-in. thick.
- *Graduated*: A textural roof of large slates. Greater variation in thickness, size, and color.
- *A square of roofing slate*: A number of slates of any size sufficient to cover 100 sq ft with a 3-in. lap. Weight per square: 3/16 in., 800 lb; 1/4 in., 900 lb; 3/8 in., 1100 lb; 1/2 in., 1700 lb; 3/4 in., 2500 lb.
- *Standard nomenclature for slate color*: Black, blue-black, mottled gray, purple, green, mottled purple and green, purple variegated, and red. These should be preceded by the word "Unfading" or "Weathering." Other colors and combinations are available.
- *Durability*: Durability of slates is rated for their expected service life according to ASTM C 406 as: S1 for over 75 years, S2 for 40 to 75 years, or S3 for 20 to 40 years.
- *Weather barrier*: The minimum weather barrier is a single layer of No. 30 un-perforated asphalt saturated felt with double coverage up to 20 in 12 slopes. Use No. 45, 50 or 60 felts under textural or graduated slates. In comparison to the cost of the slates, the felts are inexpensive; consider using heavier No. 45 or 60 felts. For all edges and detail areas, such as eaves, valleys, rakes, crickets, it is recommended that you install self-sealing, peel and stick modified bituminous underlayment. The modified bituminous membrane provides an additional level of protection by sealing around the nails, stopping migration of water under loose felts, and is especially important for protec-

TILE ROOFING DETAILS
2.502

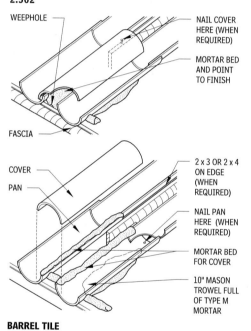

WEEPHOLE

NAIL COVER HERE (WHEN REQUIRED)

MORTAR BED AND POINT TO FINISH

FASCIA

BARREL TILE

COVER

PAN

2 x 3 OR 2 x 4 ON EDGE (WHEN REQUIRED)

NAIL PAN HERE (WHEN REQUIRED)

MORTAR BED FOR COVER

10" MASON TROWEL FULL OF TYPE M MORTAR

SADDLE RIDGE
2.503

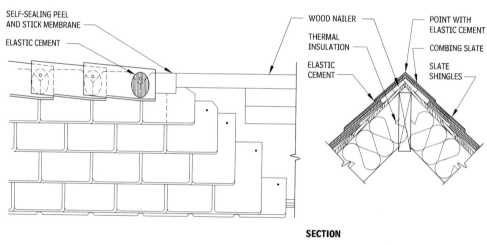

SELF-SEALING PEEL AND STICK MEMBRANE

ELASTIC CEMENT

WOOD NAILER

THERMAL INSULATION

ELASTIC CEMENT

POINT WITH ELASTIC CEMENT

COMBING SLATE

SLATE SHINGLES

SECTION

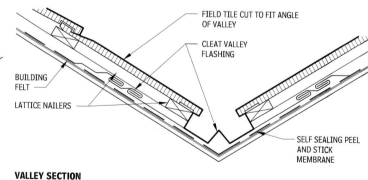

FIELD TILE

EAVE CLOSURE

VALLEY FLASHING

BUILDING FELT

NAILER

SELF SEALING PEEL AND STICK MEMBRANE

VALLEY SECTION

FIELD TILE CUT TO FIT ANGLE OF VALLEY

CLEAT VALLEY FLASHING

BUILDING FELT

LATTICE NAILERS

SELF SEALING PEEL AND STICK MEMBRANE

VALLEY SECTION

NOTES

2.502 a. In climates where snow and ice buildup occurs, valleys should be avoided.
b. Building felt laps over valley flashing.

Contributors:
National Roofing Contractors Association, Rosemont, Illinois; Grace S. Lee and Darrel Downing, Rippeteau Architects, PC, Washington, DC; Domenic F. Valente, AIA, Architects & Planners, Medford, Massachusetts.

tion against ice dams in cold climates. Note that the modified bituminous membrane is a vapor retarder, and it should not be used across the entire roof substrate if a continuous vapor retarder is not desired.

- *Nail fastener*: Use large-head, hard copper wire nails, cut copper, cut brass, or cut yellow metal slating nails. Each slate punched with two nail holes. Use nails that are 1 in. longer than thickness of slate. Cover all exposed heads with elastic cement. In dry climates, hot-dipped galvanized nails may be used.
- *Flashing*: Sheet metal flashing embedded in the slates should be minimum 20 oz. copper or lead-coated copper, fabricated to allow differential thermal movement.
- *Imitation slates*: Slates manufactured from recycled tires, mineral fiber, portland cement, and a variety of other proprietary materials are available, generally at a lower cost than true slate. However, the appearance varies greatly and is rarely the same as true slate, and the expected service life is not as long.

BOSTON HIP
2.506

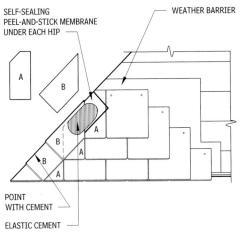

MITERED HIP
2.507

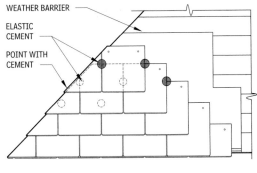

DIAGRAM OF PROPER LAP FOR RISE/RUN
2.504

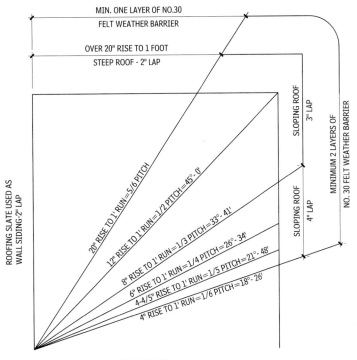

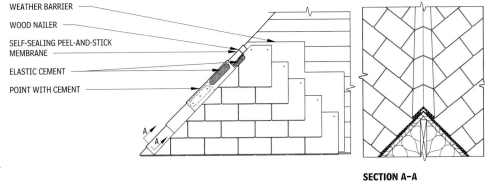

DIAGRAM OF PROPER LAP FOR RISE/RUN

SADDLE HIP
2.505

SECTION A-A

OPEN VALLEY
2.508

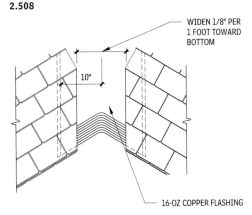

Contributor:
Domenic F. Valente, AIA, Architects & Planners, Medford, Massachusetts.

EAVE
2.509

SLATE SHINGLES OVER UNDERLAYMENT

SHORT STARTER SLATE SHINGLES COURSE LAID SMOOTH SIDE UP

WOOD EDGE STRIP

DRIP

WOOD EDGE STRIP ENSURES THAT SLATE SHINGLES LAY FLAT, IN CONTINUOUS CONTACT TO AVOID BRIDGING BY INDIVIDUAL SLATE SHINGLES

FASCIA ALTERNATE TO EXTEND FASCIA UP AS HIGH AS WOOD EDGE STRIP

SLATING CLIPS
2.510

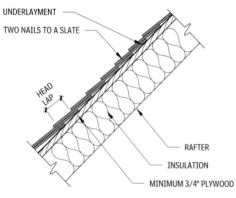

ONE CLIP PER SLATE SHINGLE LOCATED IN THE JOINT BETWEEN SLATES BELOW

ADJOINING SLATE SHINGLE BEYOND

SUCCEEDING SLATE SHINGLE COURSE

APPROXIMATELY 1/8" CLEAR

WOOD RAFTER TO RECEIVE SLATE
2.6511

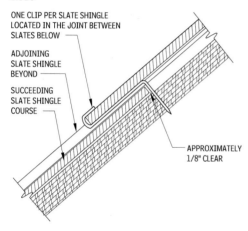

UNDERLAYMENT

TWO NAILS TO A SLATE

HEAD LAP

RAFTER

INSULATION

MINIMUM 3/4" PLYWOOD

METAL DECK TO RECEIVE SLATE
2.512

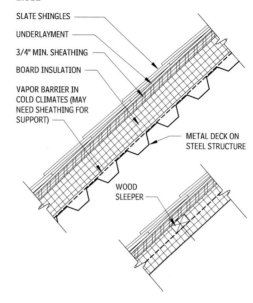

SLATE SHINGLES

UNDERLAYMENT

3/4" MIN. SHEATHING

BOARD INSULATION

VAPOR BARRIER IN COLD CLIMATES (MAY NEED SHEATHING FOR SUPPORT)

METAL DECK ON STEEL STRUCTURE

WOOD SLEEPER

ROOFING SLATE
2.513

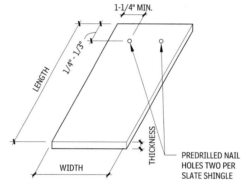

1-1/4" MIN.

LENGTH

1/4" - 1/3"

THICKNESS

WIDTH

PREDRILLED NAIL HOLES TWO PER SLATE SHINGLE

COMPOSITE ROOFING TILES

Fiber cement, cement wood, galvanized steel with acrylic coating, and ceramic slate roofing tiles are popular alternatives to clay or concrete roofing tiles. These composite tiles have been designed to be lighter, stronger, and easier to install than traditional, "natural" tiles. Their strength and combination of materials make them more fire-retardant and wind-resistant than conventional tiles.

Underlayment is similar as that required for asphalt shingles.

MINERAL-FIBER CEMENT

Mineral-fiber cement tiles combine organic fiber with cement, silica, water, and other additives. The resulting product is a roof slate that is lightweight, strong, versatile, and easy to install. The tiles can be made in a variety of distinctive shapes, colors, and textures that mimic natural materials such as slate and patterned wood shingles. Mineral-fiber cement tiles resist deterioration and moisture penetration, and are immune to pests and fungal growth. They are well suited for coastal regions and other areas with high humidity.

Mineral-fiber cement tiles should be applied to nailable decks only. For plywood decks with rafters spaced 20 in. or less, the plywood should be at least 1/2 in. thick. If rafters are spaced greater than 20 in., 5/8 in. plywood is recommended. To fasten, use standard 1-1/2 in. galvanized 11-gauge flat-head roofing nails with 3/8 in. heads. Flashing should be of a noncorrosive metal not lighter than 28 gauge.

When wood fibers are used the tiles are lightweight and can be used for reroofing as well as for new construction. They have excellent impact resistance and are easily sawn and nailed. As a richly textured, composite product, mineral-fiber tiles create an aesthetic similar to that of heavy cedar shakes, yet provide the fire protection associated with cementitious products. The portland cement is noncombustible and allows for Class A fire ratings, and the wood fibers provide excellent tensile strength and a light weight when compared to standard concrete tiles.

NOTES

2.510 Stainless steel clips properly space slates, allow movement, and eliminate nailing through slate and associated problems of broken slates caused by improper nailing.

2.512 a. Where slope exceeds 8:12, it is recommended that you add wood sleepers between insulation to support plywood.

b. In hot climates, the weather barrier may need to also be a vapor retarder.

Contributor:
Domenic F. Valente, AIA, Architects & Planners, Medford, Massachusetts.

CEMENT WOOD TILES
2.514

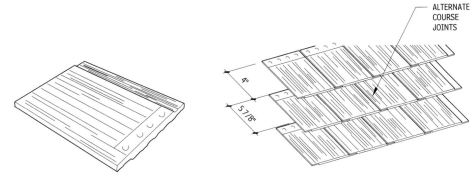

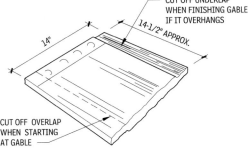

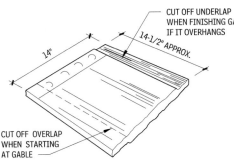

ALTERNATE
COURSE
JOINTS

4"

5 7/8"

BOTTOM RIBBED SIDE OF MINERAL-FIBER CEMENT SHINGLE

MINERAL-FIBER CEMENT SHINGLE TILE LAYOUT

CUT OFF UNDERLAP
WHEN FINISHING GABLE
IF IT OVERHANGS

14-1/2" APPROX.

14"

CUT OFF OVERLAP
WHEN STARTING
AT GABLE

TOP SIDE OF FIELD SHAKE

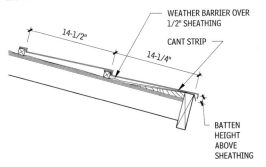

3" EAVE
FLASHING

OPTIONAL

TWO LAYERS OF
WEATHER BARRIER

EAVE DETAIL

METAL ROOFING TILES AT PITCH CHANGE
2.516

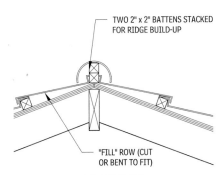

2" x 2" TILE BATTEN
AT PITCH CHANGE

BENT
TILE

FRAMING

FRAMING

CERAMIC SLATE
Ceramic slate tiles combine the look of natural slate with the fired-in strength and durability of ceramic tile. These tiles have the thickness, texture, and appearance of older slate but at a fraction of the weight and cost. They are impervious to freeze-thaw cycles, fire, moisture, and efflorescence.

METAL ROOFING TILES
The advantage of metal roofing tiles over traditional clay or concrete tiles is that they are lightweight, easier to handle, and quicker to install, and because they require fewer building components, they are less costly. Minimum recommended roof pitch for use of metal roofing tiles is a slope of 3 in 12. Roofs with shallower slopes require sealant in all side laps.

Metal roofing tiles usually come in sheets and have a base material of roll-formed 24- to 26-gauge painted galvanized or Galvalume steel. First, a layer of crushed and graded stone granules is bonded to the steel panels with an acrylic resin formula, and then a clear acrylic glaze is applied. Slow oven curing completes the process, and the underside of the tile is protected with a final coat of polyester paint.

Panels can be installed quickly and are secured to either wood or steel battens, creating a strong, weatherproof construction. The panels can be installed directly over existing roofs, unlike clay or concrete tiles, and are thus ideally suited for retrofitting roofs.

METAL ROOFING TILES
2.515

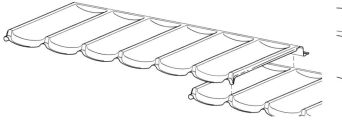

VERTICAL LAP

END CAP
(SECURE WITH
3/16" x 1/2"
SCREWS

RIDGE AT GABLE

METAL ROOFING TILES DETAILS AT EAVE AND RIDGE
2.517

WEATHER BARRIER OVER
1/2" SHEATHING

CANT STRIP

14-1/2"

14-1/4"

BATTEN
HEIGHT
ABOVE
SHEATHING

TWO 2" x 2" BATTENS STACKED
FOR RIDGE BUILD-UP

"FILL" ROW (CUT
OR BENT TO FIT)

SOLID SHEATHING AT EAVE

SOLID SHEATHING RIDGE DETAIL

NOTES

2.516 When an equal number of full courses cannot be accommodated at the pitch change, a full panel can be bent to suit. When the roofline changes dramatically, install a batten at the pitch change.
2.517 The fascia must be positioned above the roof deck sheathing or rafters by the height of the batten. The fascia becomes the first panel batten.

Contributor:
Grace S. Lee, Rippeteau Architects, PC, Washington, DC.

BUILT-UP BITUMINOUS ROOFING

A built-up bituminous roofing assembly is composed of a base sheet attached to the roof substrate, two or more reinforcing felt ply sheets, and a surfaced cap sheet. Asphalt and coal tar are the primary bituminous materials used for built-up roofing. Coal-tar bitumen has a history of maintaining functional characteristics for a very long period, but there are some questions regarding safety from coal-tar fumes, and this is generally more expensive. As the heated mopping bitumen fuses with the saturating bitumen in the roofing felts, the layers are welded together. Surfacing include aggregate, minerals, protective or reflective coatings, and smooth surface. Built-up bituminous roofing can be a very durable and high-quality roof, but requires more skill to install than some other assemblies. If the owner is willing to invest in frequent independent inspection of the roof, then a BUR is an excellent choice.

Four types of asphalt and two types of coal tar are presently used as bitumen in built-up roofing assemblies. The grade of asphalt used for BUR systems should be appropriate for the slope of the

COAL-TAR TYPES
2.518

TYPE NO. PER ASTM D 450	TYPE OF COAL TAR	SOFTENING POINT (°F)	
		MINIMUM	MAXIMUM
I	Coal-tar pitch	126	140
II	Waterproofing pitch	106	126
III	Coal-tar bitumen	133	147

ASPHALT TYPES
2.519

TYPE	KIND OF ASPHALT	SOFTENING POINT (°F)		MAXIMUM TEMPERATURE (°F)
		MINIMUM	MAXIMUM	
I	Dead-level asphalt	151	135	475
II	Flat asphalt	176	158	500
III	Steep asphalt	205	185	525
IV	Special steep asphalt	225	210	525

roof. Backnailing of felts is recommended for built-up roofing whenever the roof slope exceeds 1/2 in. in 12. Aggregate-surfaced built-up roofing should not be used on slopes exceeding 3 in. in 12.

Reinforcing felts for BUR may be saturated, coated, or impregnated with bitumen and are manufactured from both organic and inorganic materials. Organic felts are manufactured from the fiber of paper, wood, or rags. Saturated felts are saturated with asphalt or coal tar bitumen. Impregnated roofing felts are generally lighter in weight and termed "impregnated" because their surface is not completely covered (coated) with asphalt. Saturated and coated roofing felts are generally factory-coated on both sides and surfaced on one or both sides with fine mineral sand or other release agents to prevent adhesion inside the roll prior to application.

Prepared roofing felts have been saturated and coated with talc, mica, sand, or ceramic granules incorporated into the weather surface of the felts, both to provide weather protection and for decorative purposes. Reinforced flashing membrane consists of a glass-fiber base felt that is laminated with cotton, or glass-fiber fabric coated with asphalt. Rosin-sized sheathing paper is a rosin-coated building paper generally used in built-up bituminous roofing to separate felts from wood roof decking.

BITUMEN TEMPERATURE

Proper application temperatures are vital to the creation of a quality built-up bituminous roofing assembly. Temperatures that are too high can lead to incomplete coverage, voids, and lack waterproofing qualities. Temperatures that are too low can lead to poor adhesion, high expansion properties, and low tensile strength.

Bitumen can be heated at high temperatures for short periods of time without damage; in fact, they must be heated at high temperatures to achieve complete fusion and strong bonding of the plies. There is an optimum viscosity range and an optimum temperature range at the point of application that allow complete fusion, optimum wetting and mopping properties, and the desirable inter-ply bitumen weight called the *equiviscous temperature* (EVT). Excessive and prolonged heating of asphalt and coal tar products may have a deleterious effect on the quality of the product.

BUILT-UP ROOF SURFACING

Surfacing protects the bitumen and felts of a built-up bituminous roof from direct sunlight and weather exposure, and may provide other properties such as fire-resistance or reflectivity. Surfacing types include aggregate, smooth surfacing, and mineral cap sheet.

- *Aggregate surfacing*: The aggregate in roofing serves as an opaque covering that improves the appearance and fire-resistance of the roof and helps resist premature aging and damage from weather, temperature fluctuations, and ultraviolet rays. Aggregate also increases the wind uplift resistance of the roof membrane and permits much heavier application of bitumen than would otherwise be possible.
- *Smooth surfacing*: Built-up bituminous roofing may be left smooth, surfaced with a top coating of hot asphalt. Smooth surfacing should not be confused with a built-up membrane left unsurfaced (exposed felts). Smooth surfaced built-up roofing should be specified only in those circumstances where aggregate-surfaced built-up bituminous roofing is impractical, such as when the slope of the roof surface exceeds 3 in. in 12, where the proximity of air-intake or exhaust equipment may cause loose aggregate, and where appropriate aggregate is not available
- *Mineral-surfaced (cap sheet):* Some areas of the country (particularly the far western and southern states) use mineral-surfaced cap sheets as the final surfacing for built-up roofing membranes. These assemblies are similar to aggregate and smooth-surfaced except that a final layer of roofing material with a finished surface is installed on top of the multi-ply roof assembly. This assembly is not popular in colder climates, primarily because it requires phased construction of the final layer of roofing material.

BUILT-UP BITUMINOUS ROOFING — AGGREGATE SURFACE
2.520

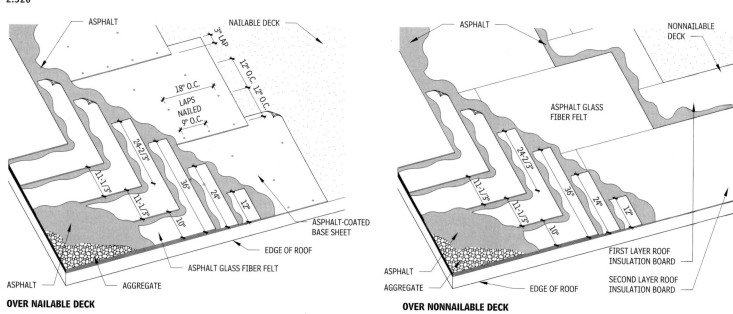

OVER NAILABLE DECK

OVER NONNAILABLE DECK

NOTES

2.520 a. If applied over wood sheathing, add rosin-sized sheathing paper between the sheathing and base bitumen sheet.
b. In lieu of asphalt, coal tar is an acceptable product.
c. For a more conservative system, specify four plies rather than three.

Contributors:
National Roofing Contractors Association, Rosemont, Illinois; Valerie Eickelberger, Rippeteau Architects, PC, Washington, DC.

ELASTOMERIC AND THERMOPLASTIC MEMBRANE ROOFING

Elastomeric membrane roofing and thermoplastic membrane roofing assemblies are both types of single-ply membrane roofing. Single-ply membrane roofing utilizes large sheets that are joined into a continuous roof membrane. In these assemblies the seams and flashing may be vulnerable to defects in workmanship, thus representing a primary weakness of the system. Single-ply membranes are also generally less resistant to physical abuse and cannot as easily be resurfaced as other types.

Single-ply membranes are available in two types: thermoset and thermoplastic. Thermoset materials cure during manufacture and can only be bonded at seams with adhesive. Ethylene propylene diene monomer (EPDM) is the most common thermoset membrane; chlorosulfonated polyethylene (CSPE) and polyisobutylene (PIB) are also available, but not as common. Thermoplastic membrane roofing materials are uncured and, therefore, are capable of being hot-air-welded or solvent-welded. Polyvinyl chloride (PVC) and thermo-plastic polyolefin (TPO) are the common thermoplastic membranes.

Single-ply membranes may be installed using three methods:

- *Loose-laid ballasted assemblies*: Loose-laid assemblies are the least expensive and require the least skills of the installer. There are, however, a number of disadvantages. First, membrane is susceptible to puncture from ballast when maintenance staff walks across the roof. Second, leaks are very hard to find because the water is free to travel horizontally within the insulation before appearing on the interior, and the membrane is covered with stones. Third, the loose ballast is problematic because it can be moved around on the roof by the wind, leaving some areas of the membrane unsecured, ballast may also fly off the roof as dangerous projectiles. Size and weight of ballast should be designed for the specific project site, with increased weights at perimeter and corner zones. Specially designed light-weight concrete roof pavers that are cast for use as roof ballast may be used in place of regular aggregate ballast for some or the entire roof, refer to Figures 2.654 and 2.723. Avoid ballasted roofs in hurricane areas and on high-rise structures. The ballast can be a light color, but is generally not as reflective as white single-ply membrane roofing.
- *Fully adhered assemblies*: Fully adhered assemblies are generally the most expensive of the three applications and offer the highest-level of performance. Fully adhered assemblies may use nonreinforced or reinforced sheets, which generally take longer to wear through. Leaks are relatively easy to find because an area of wet insulation usually forms immediately below the gap in the membrane.
- *Mechanically attached assemblies*: Membranes for mechanically attached assemblies should be reinforced to resist the tearing forces generated by uplift. Because a relatively large amount of seaming is required, thermoplastic sheets are becoming more popular. The level of difficulty of finding leaks within mechanically attached systems is between the loose-laid and fully adhered systems.

LOOSE-LAID BALLASTED SHEETS
2.521

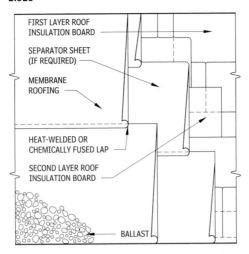

Membrane sheets and insulation are laid loose with the membrane secured at the perimeter and around penetrations only. The membrane is then covered with a ballast of river-washed stones (typically 10 lb/sq ft) or appropriate pavers. This system works efficiently with insulation approved by the membrane manufacturer and on roofs with a slope not exceeding 2 in 12.

FULLY ADHERED SHEETS
2.522

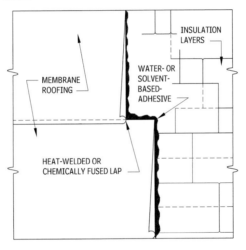

Fully adhered membrane assemblies are not limited by slope, because the membrane is secured to the substrate with bonding adhesive and by mechanically fastening the membrane to perimeter and penetrations. This assembly is appropriate for contoured roofs and roofs that cannot withstand the weight of a ballasted assembly. The membrane can be directly applied to numerous types of roof deck surfaces including concrete and wood and may be compatible with insulation or protection board.

MECHANICALLY ATTACHED SHEETS
2.523

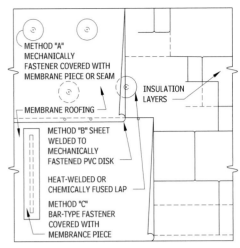

A mechanically attached roof assembly is appropriate for roofs that cannot carry the loads imposed by ballasted roof assemblies. Assemblies are available with fasteners that penetrate the membrane, or that require no membrane penetration. The membrane is anchored to the roof using metal bars or individual clips, and it may be installed over concrete, wood, metal, or compatible insulation.

EPDM ROOFING

Ethylene-propylene-diene-monomer (EPDM) membranes are typically 30 to 60 mils in thickness, single-sheet roofing materials. The membranes are available either nonreinforced or reinforced with fabric. Seams in the membrane are spliced and cemented. EPDM membranes are highly resistant to degradation from certain chemicals, ozone, and ultraviolet radiation, and have excellent resilience, tensile strength, abrasion resistance, hardness, and weathering properties.

EPDM membranes may be loose laid, mechanically fastened, or fully adhered to either nailable or nonnailable decks. For loose-laid systems, ballast provides resistance against wind uplift forces. Field application of surfacing or coatings may enhance the weather-resistance properties, or may be simply aesthetic. Terminations at roof edges, parapets, and other flashings utilize material identical to the roof membrane material shaped to conform to the substrate and area being flashed.

PVC ROOFING

Polyvinyl chloride (PVC) membranes may be nonreinforced or reinforced with glass fibers or polyester fabric the membranes are typically 45 to 60 mils in thickness Seams are sealed by heat or chemical welding, and may require additional caulking. PVC membranes are resistant to bacterial growth, industrial chemical atmospheres, root penetration, and extreme weather conditions. PVC membranes also have excellent fire-resistance and seaming capabilities.

ASTM D 4434 classes PVC materials into several types and classes, depending on the construction of the sheet material:

- *Type I*: Unreinforced sheet
- *Type II, Class I*: Unreinforced sheet containing fibers
- *Type II, Class II*: Unreinforced sheet containing fabrics
- *Type III*: Reinforced sheet containing fibers or fabrics

PVC membranes may be loose laid, mechanically fastened, or fully adhered to either nailable or nonnailable decks. For loose-laid systems, ballast provides resistance against wind uplift forces. Some PVC membranes have a factory-applied coating to enhance weather-resistance or aesthetics. Field application of the coatings may be an option and is dependent on the membrane manufacturer.

Contributors:
CTA Architects Engineers, Billings, Montana.

TPO ROOFING

Thermoplastic polyolefin (TPO) membranes are blended from polypropylene and ethylene-propylene rubber polymers, and may include flame retardants, pigments, UV absorbers, and other modifiers. Membrane sheets are available reinforced and unreinforced in thickness from 40 to 100 mils. TPO membranes range from stiff and "boardy" to soft and flexible. Seams are heat-welded and may require additional caulking to protect wicking of the reinforcing. TPO is resistant to animal fats, some hydrocarbons, and vegetable oils.

TPO membranes may be loose laid, mechanically fastened or fully adhered. Some membranes are white or light in color, or field coatings may be applied.

COATED FOAM ROOFING

Polyurethane foam roofing is spray-applied, seamless, and fully adhered. The foam is made by mixing isocyanate and resin components at a 1:1 ratio. Spray polyurethane foam is a closed-cell foam that provides good insulation and water resistance. These assemblies are used with a protective coating or stone ballast covering, which protects the foam from ultraviolet rays and mechanical damage.

These assemblies can be applied in varying thicknesses to eliminate ponding, to improve drainage, and to meet required R-values (approximately R-6.25 per inch). One advantage of coated foam systems is that they can be used over highly irregular surfaces, unusual geometries, or existing sloped metal assemblies. They are also inherently lightweight and offer good wind-uplift-resistance.

Keep the following in mind when working with coated foam roofing:

- Before sprayed polyurethane foam roofing is applied, all surfaces must be clean, free of contaminants, securely fastened to the substrate, and completely dry. Moisture-sensitive indicators may be needed to detect any moisture within the existing roof assembly. Vapor retarders may be necessary; consult with the manufacturer to coordinate a specific roofing condition with a foam application.
- Most polyurethane foam manufacturers produce three seasonal grades: winter (fast), regular, and summer (slow).
- During application wind may affect quality; use windscreens or discontinue application. The surface texture of sprayed polyurethane foam can vary because of wind, equipment adjustment, spray technique, and characteristics of the materials used. Foam that will be elastomeric-coated should have a smooth texture, resembling orange peel. For an aggregate covering, the texture should be no rougher than popcorn.

Protection of sprayed polyurethane foam falls into two general classifications: protective elastomeric coatings and aggregate. There are seven generic types of elastomeric protective coatings: acrylic, silicone, urethane, butyl, hypalon, neoprene, and modified asphalt. The physical properties of these coatings may vary, and the coating manufacturer should be consulted for recommendations on specific needs. Aggregate granules may be applied to the wet, uncured protective topcoat to enhance the resistance of the coating systems to UV or mechanical damage.

COATED FOAM ROOFING
2.524

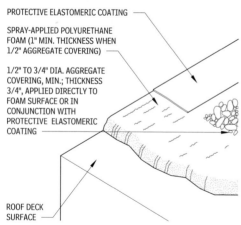

PROTECTIVE ELASTOMERIC COATING

SPRAY-APPLIED POLYURETHANE FOAM (1" MIN. THICKNESS WHEN 1/2" AGGREGATE COVERING)

1/2" TO 3/4" DIA. AGGREGATE COVERING, MIN.; THICKNESS 3/4", APPLIED DIRECTLY TO FOAM SURFACE OR IN CONJUNCTION WITH PROTECTIVE ELASTOMERIC COATING

ROOF DECK SURFACE

SINGLE PIPE PENETRATION
2.525

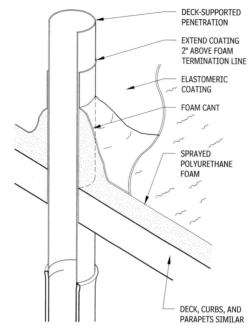

DECK-SUPPORTED PENETRATION

EXTEND COATING 2" ABOVE FOAM TERMINATION LINE

ELASTOMERIC COATING

FOAM CANT

SPRAYED POLYURETHANE FOAM

DECK, CURBS, AND PARAPETS SIMILAR

FLUID-APPLIED ROOFING

Fluid-applied roofing assemblies may be applied at ambient temperatures or heated in kettles. Most of them have some sort of reinforcing fabric that is applied along with the liquid component. Fluid-applied roofing applied over existing roofs is not generally accepted as a "membrane," but as a coating.

Acrylic latex and urethane are the two main types of cold liquid-applied roofing. Acrylic latex refers to a family of products that use water-based polymers and cure by water evaporation. Liquid-applied urethane roof coatings are chemically cured to form an elastomeric membrane. Because these coatings are applied as liquids, installation is relatively simple, even for roofs with irregular geometries or multiple penetrations. For assemblies using a reinforcing fabric, a coating is applied to an acceptable surface. While the coating is still wet, a layer of polyester or fiberglass is laid into it, followed by an additional layer of coating. Subsequent layers may be added as desired or necessary.

Fluid-applied roofing is appropriate for new construction but is most commonly used as enhancements or for repairs to existing roofs, including modified bituminous roofs and built-up roofs.

The advantages of fluid-applied roofing are that it conforms very well to irregular surfaces, is easily applied, and comes in various colors. However, it is sensitive to the skills of the installer, and is best used in sloped roof situations.

HOT FLUID-APPLIED ROOFING

Most commonly, hot fluid-applied membranes are composed of rubberized asphalt applied at 150 to 210 mils in two coats with a reinforcing sheet between the layers. Although the membrane has limited puncture resistance, because it is most often applied directly to a concrete substrate and protected by insulation, puncture resistance is less critical. The membrane is self-healing to minor punctures, has crack-bridging ability, is relatively forgiving of rough substrates, and can be protected shortly after installation. Moreover, fluid-applied membranes allow for easier penetration flashing, so they are particularly suited to complicated roof shapes with many penetrations.

FLUID-APPLIED ROOFING
2.526

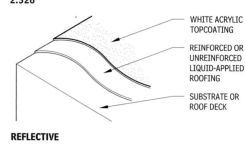

WHITE ACRYLIC TOPCOATING

REINFORCED OR UNREINFORCED LIQUID-APPLIED ROOFING

SUBSTRATE OR ROOF DECK

REFLECTIVE

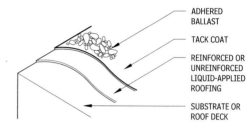

ADHERED BALLAST

TACK COAT

REINFORCED OR UNREINFORCED LIQUID-APPLIED ROOFING

SUBSTRATE OR ROOF DECK

ADHERED BALLAST

Fluid-applied roofing may also be used under board insulation and ballast for further protection.

FLUID-APPLIED ROOFING OVER EXISTING METAL ROOF
2.527

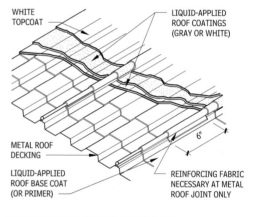

WHITE TOPCOAT

LIQUID-APPLIED ROOF COATINGS (GRAY OR WHITE)

METAL ROOF DECKING

LIQUID-APPLIED ROOF BASE COAT (OR PRIMER)

REINFORCING FABRIC NECESSARY AT METAL ROOF JOINT ONLY

6'

PROTECTED MEMBRANE ROOFING (PRM)

In a typical roofing assembly, the waterproof membrane (built-up, modified bitumen, or single-ply) is applied over the insulation, which is on top of the substrate and/or structural deck. The membrane in this situation is exposed to temperature extremes, as well as wear and tear from people walking or working on the roof. In a protected membrane roof (sometimes called the *inverted* or *insulated roof membrane assembly*, or *IRMA*), a layer of extruded polystyrene insulation board protects the membrane. Extruded polystyrene is the only material generally approved for this application because it does not absorb moisture. This roofing system is best used in extreme climates, where it is important to protect the membrane from the elements, or where the rooftop will receive heavy use (e.g., plaza or parking deck applications).

NOTE

2.527 Roof slope minimum is 1/4 in. in 12, or 2 percent; there is no maximum.

Contributors:
National Roofing Contractors Association, Rosemont, Illinois; Valerie Eickelberger, Rippeteau Architects, PC, Washington, DC; Richard J. Vitullo, AIA, Oak Leaf Studio, Crownsville, Maryland; Rich Boon, the Roofing Industry Educational Institute, Englewood, Colorado.

PROTECTED MEMBRANE ROOF SYSTEM
2.528

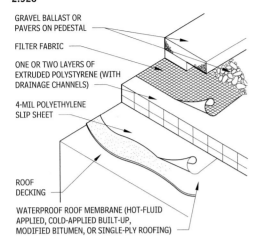

GRAVEL BALLAST OR
PAVERS ON PEDESTAL

FILTER FABRIC

ONE OR TWO LAYERS OF
EXTRUDED POLYSTYRENE (WITH
DRAINAGE CHANNELS)

4-MIL POLYETHYLENE
SLIP SHEET

ROOF
DECKING

WATERPROOF ROOF MEMBRANE (HOT-FLUID
APPLIED, COLD-APPLIED BUILT-UP,
MODIFIED BITUMEN, OR SINGLE-PLY ROOFING)

VEGETATED ROOFING

Varying approaches have been taken to vegetated roofing design, so-called green roofing. The type of assembly selected will depend in part on the job conditions, including climate, plant community desired, and load-bearing capacity of the roof deck. Green roof assemblies are compatible with both conventional and protected roof membrane (PRM) waterproofing systems. All assemblies will include the following characteristics:

- Protection of the waterproofing membrane from root and biological attach
- Protection of the waterproofing membrane from physical abuse and accident
- Base drainage layer
- Separation layer, to prevent fine-grained engineered soils from fouling or clogging the drainage layer system
- Engineered soil, to support the vegetation

Some waterproofing membranes do not require supplemental root protection. Assemblies 6 in. and thinner are referred to as *extensive;* assemblies 12 in. and thicker are referred to as *intensive.*

Optional components can be incorporated, among them:

- Irrigation
- Slope-stabilizing elements
- Root-reinforcement elements
- Enhancements to retain rainfall moisture
- Air layers to dehumidify the insulation layer (some PRM systems)
- Self-contained modules
- Ballasts to resist wind uplift

Most engineered soils intended for green roof use are manufactured from lightweight mineral aggregates. These materials typically have wet densities between 60 and 90 lbs per cu ft, measured according to ASTM E 2399.

Green roof assemblies can be classified into five categories:

- *Category I:* Single-layer assemblies usually installed with a fabric or foam mat to provide physical protection and improve drainage. The overall thicknesses of these assemblies are rarely greater than 4 in. These assemblies are associated with pitched roof installations. They also offer the least expensive option for roof greening.
- *Category II:* Two-layer assemblies in which the engineered soil is placed over an efficient geo-composite drainage layer. A common variation utilizes a drainage layer that can also retain some water. To reduce plant stress during drought conditions, the drainage layer should not be thicker than 1 in. Typical overall assembly thicknesses range from 3 to 6 in. These are probably the most commonly encountered extensive assemblies in the United States.

VEGETATED COVER SYSTEMS FOR ROOFS
2.529

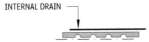

INTERNAL DRAIN

THERMAL INSULATION AND PRIMARY WATERPROOFING
MEMBRANE PLACED HERE IN PRM CONFIGURATIONS

I
FOLIAGE: SUCCULANTS TYPICAL THICKNESS
2-4 INCHES

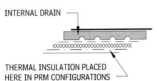

INTERNAL DRAIN

THERMAL INSULATION PLACED
HERE IN PRM CONFIGURATIONS

II
FOLIAGE: SUCCULANTS-HERBS TYPICAL
THICKNESS 3-6 INCHES

THERMAL INSULATION AND PRIMARY WATERPROOFING
MEMBRANE PLACED HERE IN PRM CONFIGURATIONS

III
FOLIAGE: SUCCULANTS-MEADOW GRASS-HERBS
TYPICAL THICKNESS 4-8 INCHES

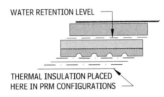

WATER RETENTION LEVEL

THERMAL INSULATION PLACED
HERE IN PRM CONFIGURATIONS

IV
FOLIAGE: MEADOW GRASS-HERBS- WILDFLOWERS
-TURF TYPICAL THICKNESS 6-24 INCHES

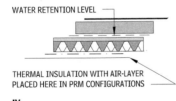

WATER RETENTION LEVEL

THERMAL INSULATION WITH AIR-LAYER
PLACED HERE IN PRM CONFIGURATIONS

IV
FOLIAGE: MEADOW GRASS-HERBS- WILDFLOWERS
-TURF TYPICAL THICKNESS 6-24 INCHES

LEGEND

—————————	WIND PROTECTION
– – – – –	FILTER FABRIC
xxxxxxxxxxxxxxxxxx	GEOCOMPOSITE DRAINAGE LAYER
—–—–—–—	MAT (PROTECTION, MOISTURE MANAGEMENT, OR DRAINAGE)
—————————	MAT (PROTECTION, MOISTURE MANAGEMENT, OR DRAINAGE)

* AIR-LAYER IS A GEOCOMPOSITE DRAINAGE SHEET

- *Category III:* Two-layer assemblies in which a highly permeable coarse granular material is used to create the drainage zone. Typical overall assembly thicknesses range from 4 to 8 in. Compared to a Category II assembly of comparable thickness, a Category III assembly would be markedly more drought-tolerant and accommodate a broader plant selection.
- *Category IV:* Similar to Category III assemblies but with a deeper drainage layer to accommodate base (bottom-up) irrigation methods. The minimum thickness for this assembly is 6 in.
- *Category V:* These assemblies involve the use of a water retention panel that is filled with coarse granular material. As in the Category III and Category IV assemblies, a surface layer of engineered soil is placed over the granular layer and separated from it by a filter fabric. This assembly introduces an air layer at the bottom of the profile. The minimum thickness for this system is 6 in.

Category IV and V systems are irrigated and are most frequently associated with intensive applications. Irrigation enhances landscape design opportunities, and in warm climates can also enhance cooling effects. These assemblies are well represented in deep plaza landscapes that can support large perennial plants and trees.

CATEGORY III
2.530

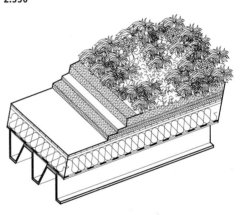

CATEGORY V
2.531

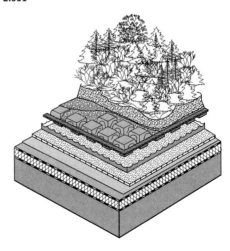

NOTES

2.528 a. Ballast weight is a minimum of 10 lbs per square foot.
b. Refer to ANSI/SPRI/RMA RP-4 for wind design guidance.
c. In lieu of aggregate or concrete ballast, proprietary insulation boards with concrete topping are available. These boards weigh between 4.5 lbs per square foot and 10 lbs per square foot, depending on the product selected.
2.529 The air layer is a generally composed of a geocomposite drainage sheet.

Contributors:
Charlie Miller, PE, Roofscapes, Inc., Philadelphia, Pennsylvania.

ENVIRONMENTAL BENEFITS

Vegetated roofing provides three important environmental benefits. It:

- Prolongs the life expectancy of the underlying waterproofing materials, which will reduce waste generation and the amount of embedded energy associated with the roof.
- Restores a natural hydrologic balance to developed sites, including reducing flooding and promoting more effective water utilization by plants.
- Improves the energy performance of buildings.

The scale of the energy benefit will, of course, depend greatly on the climate; northern temperate and semitropical climates will benefit most. When selecting green roof systems, ask the following questions:

- What contained materials are manufactured from recycled materials or, alternatively, are recyclable?
- How durable is the combined waterproofing and green cover system likely to be? How can its longevity be enhanced?
- To what extent can irrigation be eliminated through appropriate selection of the engineered soil, system configuration, and plant selection?

SPECIAL CONSIDERATIONS

With appropriate precautions, vegetated roofs have been successfully installed in combination with all major waterproofing system types. These membranes do not require supplemental root-protection layers. Also, ASTM E 2397 provides a standardized procedure to established maximum combined assembly weights for use when determining dead loads.

A critical part of all vegetated roof design is protection for the drains and flashings that is comparable to that offered by the vegetated cover elsewhere. The flashing, in particular, are typically the weak link in the overall roofing assembly. As a result, it is considered good practice to armor flashings with metal counterflashing or to protect the flashings with "sacrificial" layers of membrane.

Green roof techniques have been employed with great success in Europe for more than 40 years. In most German cities, for example, vegetated roofing is an indispensable part of the country's urban runoff management and water treatment strategies. Very effective methods for protecting underlying waterproofing membranes have been developed. Also, electrical techniques are available that make it possible to locate even small leaks with pinpoint accuracy.

Methods of installing plants include:

- Plugs
- Reinforced vegetated mats
- Seed and cuttings
- Modules planted in the nursery

Consult the following references:

- www.wbdg.org/designgreenroofs.php
- www.greenroofs.com
- www.greenroofs.org.
- *Planting Green Roofs and Living Walls*, by Nigel Dunnett and Noel Kingsbury (Timber Press, 2004)
- *Green Roof Plants: A Resource Guide*, by Edmund C. Snodgrass and Lucie L. Snodgrass (Timber Press, 2006)

METAL ROOFING

There are four types of metal roofing, in two major categories. The first category is the traditional metal roofing, which needs continuous structural deck support and is sometimes called architectural metal roofing. The second category is structural metal roofing, which is capable of spanning over open purlins. Structural metal roofing includes

- Standing seam
- Bermuda
- Batten seam
- Corrugated or formed sheet metal

STANDING SEAM ROOFING

Standing seam roofing may be installed on slopes as gentle as 1/4 in. in 12. Because of the architectural appearance of the roof system, it is more commonly used on steeper roof slopes, allowing the panels to be seen as part of the overall design.

STANDING SEAM METAL ROOF
2.532

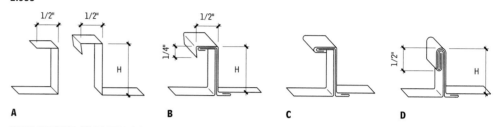

PAN METHOD OF FORMING STANDING SEAM
2.533

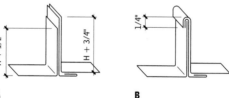

A   B   C   D

FIELD METHOD OF FORMING STANDING SEAM
2.534

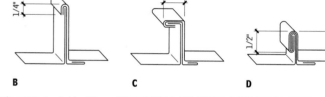

A   B   C   D

The spacing of seams may vary to suit the architectural style of the facility. Formed sheets (used with metal building systems) have seam spacing set by locations of punched holes in the structural framing members.

Two methods of forming a standing seam are used: the pan method and the roll method. In the pan method, the top, bottom, and sides of the individual sheets are preformed to allow locking together at each edge. Seams at the top and bottom of each sheet are called *transverse seams*. In the roll method, a series of long sheets are joined together at their ends with double flat-lock seams. These field-formed seams can be executed either manually or with a seaming machine (a wheeled electronic device that runs along the sheet joint forming the seam). In either method, cleats (spaced as recommended by the manufacturer) are formed into the standing seam. Seam terminations are usually soldered.

MOVABLE CLEAT
2.535

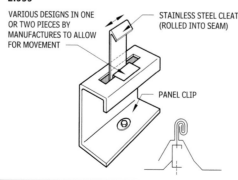

To allow for expansion and contraction movement in roof panels, some manufacturers set movable cleats into a stationary panel clip system, particularly for structural standing seam metal roofing. Note that the cleat must be anchored to a rigid substrate to limit rotation of the clip that constrains movement. If mounted over insulation, provide a layer of plywood or OSB board or provide the manufacturers' large anchoring plate to distribute the load over a large area.

STRUCTURAL STANDING SEAM METAL ROOFING
2.536

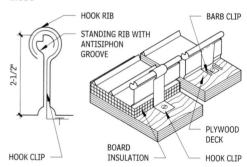

POWER SEAM CLOSURE

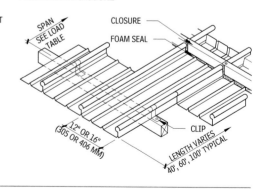

Contributors:
Raso-Greanes, Ian Architecture Corporation, Waco, Texas; Straub Associates/Architects, Troy, Missouri; Emory F. Hinkel, Jr., Odell Associates, Charlotte, North Carolina; John A. Sculte, HOK, St. Louis, Missouri.

CORRUGATED OR FORMED SHEET METAL ROOFING

Sheet metal panels are formed from aluminum, galvanized sheet steel, Galvalume, and zinc. These are relatively low-performing systems relying on gaskets at exposed fasteners and minimal sealant to accommodate movement and remain watertight. A highly reliable weather barrier is preferred for best performance. The following requirements apply:

- Endlaps for roofing and siding must be at least 6 in. and fastened at every rib. Two fasteners may be required when designing for a negative (uplift) loading condition.
- Minimum sidelaps must be equal to one rib or corrugation and laid away from prevailing wind. Fasteners must be spaced a maximum of 12 in. o.c. for all types of roofing and siding.
- For roofing, fasteners may pierce only the high corrugation. For siding, fasteners may pierce either the high or low corrugation. Consult manufacturer for proper sheet metal fasteners and accessories.
- Minimum slopes for sheet roofing are: 1-in. depth corrugated—3 in 12; 1-1/2-in. depth ribbed—2 in 12; 1-3/4-in. V-corrugated—2 in 12.

METAL ROOFING—LOCKS AND SEAMS

The method for joining sheet metal depends on thickness of metal, anticipated movement, appearance, watertightness and cost. Refer to SMACNA for full information on balancing of all requirements.

CORRUGATED OR FORMED SHEET METAL ROOFING
2.537

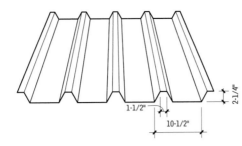

BOLD RIB

L: 3'-0" TO 39'-0"
W: 3'-6" COVERAGE

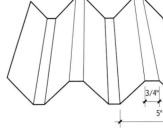

V-BEAM

L: 3'-0" TO 39'-0"
W: 3'-3" COVERAGE

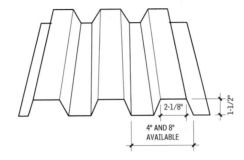

BOX RIB

L: 3'-0" TO 39'-0"
W: 3'-4" COVERAGE

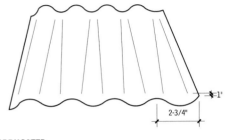

CORRUGATED

L: 3'-0" TO 39'-0"
W: 2'-8" COVERAGE

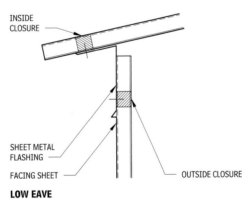

LOW EAVE

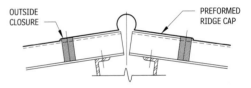

RIDGE

Contributors:
John A. Sculte, HOK, St. Louis, Missouri.

ROOF DETAILING

- Elevate base flashing and penetration flashing above any standing water by using tapered edge strips. This detail is not required by most manufacturers but is a small amount of additional dependability.
- Provide crickets behind any interruption to the downhill flow of water such as at curbs, rails, and rooftop mounted equipment.
- Depress roof drains in large sumps approximately 3 to 4 feet square and minimum 1-1/2 inches deep using tapered insulation to ensure that there is no standing water at drains. In cold climates the underside of the drain body should be insulated with spray foam or else cold rainwater could cause condensation. The rainwater conductor should also be insulated, at least for a length sufficient to allow warming of drain water.
- Verify that roof decks and the adjacent parapet wall or penetrating element are supported together. If they are not, then the base flashing must be detailed to accommodate the anticipated movement.
- Heavy pieces of roof-mounted equipment may need to have curbs mounted directly on the structural frame of the opening or the flutes of metal deck may need to be blocked full to prevent crushing.
- Base flashing should be carried up and across the top of parapets and curbs if possible to ensure that water does not get behind the base flashing and under the roofing. If the wall includes an air barrier or water-resistant drainage plane, then connect base flashing to membrane.
- Pitch pockets should be avoided. Detail penetrations through the roof using square or round shapes that are nearly perpendicular to the plane of the roof.
- Detail lightning protection systems to provide adequate anchorage of air terminals and support of cables without penetrating roof membrane. Air terminals and cable at perimeter should be mounted to inside face of parapet or on coping. Air terminals in the field should be adhered to precast concrete pavers. Cable running across the field of the roof should be supported on traffic walkways or pavers. Cable laying on bituminous roof membrane will eventually become embedded in the softened membrane.
- Detail for replacement of the roof membrane. The membrane will need to be topped or replaced several times over the life of the building. It should be possible to install a new membrane under counterflashing and copings by removing and replacing the sheet metal without damage.
- Joints and fasteners in sheet metal flashing are notoriously susceptible to leakage after expansion and contraction. Back up sheet metal flashing with flexible membrane flashing.
- Expansion joints and area dividers should be detailed above the plane of the roof.
- Expansion joints should be specifically designed for the purpose and should have factory-fabricated intersections, tees, transitions and intersections. Joints made in the field should be simple, straight butt joints.
- Expansion joints fabricated from roof membrane do not maintain continuity of the expansion joint as well as factory-fabricated systems.
- Roof expansion joints must transition without leaks into vertical expansion joints in parapets and walls.
- Expansion joints should be provided with a second line of defense, usually of a watertight vapor barrier membrane. Systems are available with secondary drains.
- Area dividers are similar to expansion joints but do extend through the building structure. Area dividers are recommended at 200 to 300 feet centers, located at ells, tees, changes of deck span and other similar conditions where movement will damage the roof membrane. Note that many roof membranes are flexible enough to not require area dividers but the underlying coverboard and insulation are not flexible and allowing space for their thermal movement will prevent telegraphing of the substrate.
- Sources for Roof Details: A primary source for information regarding roof details is the *NRCA Roofing and Waterproofing Manual*, which covers most detail conditions for nearly every type of roofing system. NRCA details are nearly universally accepted. The second source for roofing details is the roof membrane manufacturer.

- Note however that the manufacturer will publish details that are selected to be less expensive, sometimes resulting in lesser performance. Pitch pockets are an excellent example. For more dependable details, review manufacturers data for details required for an extended 20 year warranty and compare against NRCA.
- Note that details from NRCA or the manufacturer need to be customized to suit the specific project conditions.

FULLY ADHERED ROOF AT PARAPET OR WALL
2.538

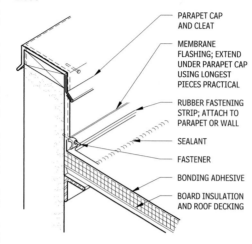

- PARAPET CAP AND CLEAT
- MEMBRANE FLASHING; EXTEND UNDER PARAPET CAP USING LONGEST PIECES PRACTICAL
- RUBBER FASTENING STRIP; ATTACH TO PARAPET OR WALL
- SEALANT
- FASTENER
- BONDING ADHESIVE
- BOARD INSULATION AND ROOF DECKING

ROOF EDGE AT NONSUPPORTING WALL
2.539

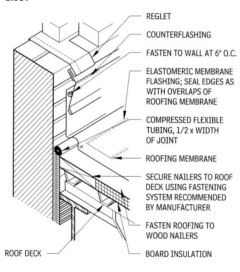

- REGLET
- COUNTERFLASHING
- FASTEN TO WALL AT 6" O.C.
- ELASTOMERIC MEMBRANE FLASHING; SEAL EDGES AS WITH OVERLAPS OF ROOFING MEMBRANE
- COMPRESSED FLEXIBLE TUBING, 1/2 x WIDTH OF JOINT
- ROOFING MEMBRANE
- SECURE NAILERS TO ROOF DECK USING FASTENING SYSTEM RECOMMENDED BY MANUFACTURER
- FASTEN ROOFING TO WOOD NAILERS
- ROOF DECK
- BOARD INSULATION

METAL ROOF EDGE
2.540

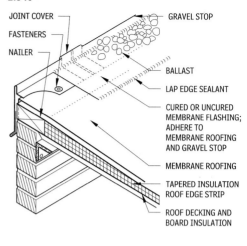

- JOINT COVER
- FASTENERS
- NAILER
- GRAVEL STOP
- BALLAST
- LAP EDGE SEALANT
- CURED OR UNCURED MEMBRANE FLASHING; ADHERE TO MEMBRANE ROOFING AND GRAVEL STOP
- MEMBRANE ROOFING
- TAPERED INSULATION ROOF EDGE STRIP
- ROOF DECKING AND BOARD INSULATION

FULLY-ADHERED ROOF SCUPPER
2.541

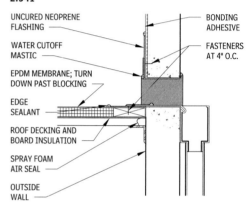

- UNCURED NEOPRENE FLASHING
- WATER CUTOFF MASTIC
- EPDM MEMBRANE; TURN DOWN PAST BLOCKING
- EDGE SEALANT
- ROOF DECKING AND BOARD INSULATION
- SPRAY FOAM AIR SEAL
- OUTSIDE WALL
- BONDING ADHESIVE
- FASTENERS AT 4" O.C.

FABRICATED VENT PIPE FLASHING
2.542

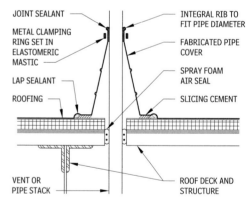

- JOINT SEALANT
- METAL CLAMPING RING SET IN ELASTOMERIC MASTIC
- LAP SEALANT
- ROOFING
- VENT OR PIPE STACK
- INTEGRAL RIB TO FIT PIPE DIAMETER
- FABRICATED PIPE COVER
- SPRAY FOAM AIR SEAL
- SLICING CEMENT
- ROOF DECK AND STRUCTURE

ROOF DRAIN
2.543

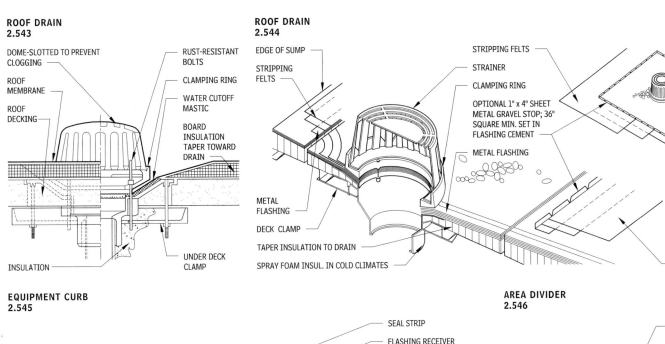

- DOME-SLOTTED TO PREVENT CLOGGING
- ROOF MEMBRANE
- ROOF DECKING
- RUST-RESISTANT BOLTS
- CLAMPING RING
- WATER CUTOFF MASTIC
- BOARD INSULATION TAPER TOWARD DRAIN
- INSULATION
- UNDER DECK CLAMP

ROOF DRAIN
2.544

- EDGE OF SUMP
- STRIPPING FELTS
- METAL FLASHING
- DECK CLAMP
- TAPER INSULATION TO DRAIN
- SPRAY FOAM INSUL. IN COLD CLIMATES
- STRIPPING FELTS
- STRAINER
- CLAMPING RING
- OPTIONAL 1" x 4" SHEET METAL GRAVEL STOP; 36" SQUARE MIN. SET IN FLASHING CEMENT
- METAL FLASHING
- STRIPPING FELTS

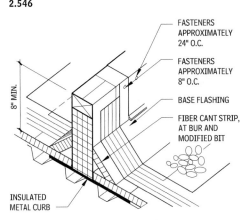

EQUIPMENT CURB
2.545

- 10" NOMINAL MIN.
- 3-1/2" MIN.
- ALTERNATE FRAME LOCATION FOR HEAVY UNITS
- SEAL STRIP
- FLASHING RECEIVER
- COUNTERFLASHING FASTENED APPROXIMATELY 18" O.C.
- FASTENERS APPROXIMATELY 8" O.C.
- 14" STANDARD MANUFACTURED HEIGHT
- COUNTERFLASHING EXTENDED DOWN TO PROTECT AGAINST FOOT DAMAGE (OPTIONAL)
- BASE FLASHING
- INSULATED METAL CURB
- FIBER CANT STRIP, AT BUR AND MODIFIED BIT
- WOOD BLOCKING FASTENED TO DECK (OPTIONAL)

AREA DIVIDER
2.546

- 8" MIN.
- INSULATED METAL CURB
- FASTENERS APPROXIMATELY 24" O.C.
- FASTENERS APPROXIMATELY 8" O.C.
- BASE FLASHING
- FIBER CANT STRIP, AT BUR AND MODIFIED BIT

PIPE SUPPORT
2.547

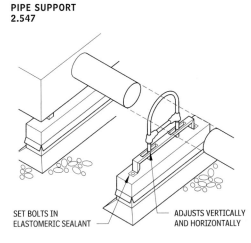

- SET BOLTS IN ELASTOMERIC SEALANT
- ADJUSTS VERTICALLY AND HORIZONTALLY

MULTIPLE PIPE PENETRATION
2.548

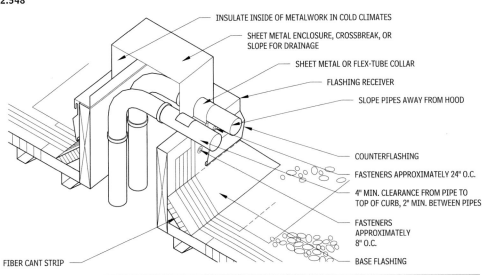

- INSULATE INSIDE OF METALWORK IN COLD CLIMATES
- SHEET METAL ENCLOSURE, CROSSBREAK, OR SLOPE FOR DRAINAGE
- SHEET METAL OR FLEX-TUBE COLLAR
- FLASHING RECEIVER
- SLOPE PIPES AWAY FROM HOOD
- COUNTERFLASHING
- FASTENERS APPROXIMATELY 24" O.C.
- 4" MIN. CLEARANCE FROM PIPE TO TOP OF CURB, 2" MIN. BETWEEN PIPES
- FASTENERS APPROXIMATELY 8" O.C.
- BASE FLASHING
- FIBER CANT STRIP

NOTES

2.544 a. Minimum 30 in. square, 2-1/2 to 4-lb lead or 16-oz soft copper flashing set on finished roof felts set in mastic. Prime top surface before stripping.
b. Membrane plies, metal flashing, and flash-in plies extend under the clamping ring.
c. Stripping felts extend 4 in. and 6 in. beyond edge of flashing sheet, but not beyond edge of sump.
d. The use of metal deck sump pans is not recommended
2.546 An area divider is designed simply as a raised insulated metal curb or double wood member attached to a properly flashed wood base

plate that is anchored to the roof deck. Area dividers should be located between the roof's expansion joints at 200 to 300 ft intervals, depending upon climatic conditions and area practices. They should never restrict the flow of water. Even though many single-ply roof membranes are flexible enough not to require an area divider, the insulation and protection board are not.
2.547 This detail allows for expansion and contraction of pipes without roof damage.
2.548 This detail illustrates another method of eliminating pitch pockets and a satisfactory method of grouping piping that must come up above the roof surface.

Contributors:
Valerie Eickelberger, Rippeteau Architects, PC, Washington, DC; National Roofing Contractors Association, Rosemont, Illinois.

SINGLE-PIPE PENETRATION
2.549

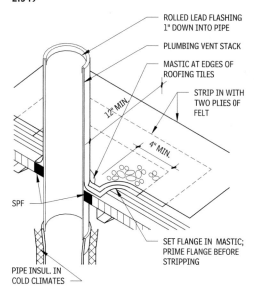

ROLLED LEAD FLASHING 1" DOWN INTO PIPE

PLUMBING VENT STACK

MASTIC AT EDGES OF ROOFING TILES

STRIP IN WITH TWO PLIES OF FELT

12" MIN.

4" MIN.

SPF

SET FLANGE IN MASTIC; PRIME FLANGE BEFORE STRIPPING

PIPE INSUL. IN COLD CLIMATES

SITE-FABRICATED DETAIL

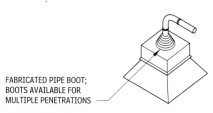

FABRICATED PIPE BOOT; BOOTS AVAILABLE FOR MULTIPLE PENETRATIONS

PREFABRICATED DETAIL

FLASHING AND SHEET METAL

Flashings is a thin material inserted in an assembly to direct the flow of water to the exterior. Flashing has traditionally been sheet metal, but modern elastomeric sheets are gaining in usage. Sheet metal flashing has traditionally been prone to leakage at joints. The joints can be soldered or welded, but this is not recommended for long lengths. In long lengths, joints have been water-proofed with sealant, but the joint design is not ideal and is also prone to fail. Therefore, it is recommended to back up the sheet metal flashing with a layer of an elastomeric membrane.

GUTTERS AND DOWNSPOUTS

Important notes regarding the design of gutters and downspouts are as follows:

- Continuous gutters may be formed at the installation site with cold-forming equipment, thus eliminating joints in long runs of gutter.
- Gutters and downspouts are available in aluminum, galvanized steel, copper, and stainless steel. Consult manufacturers for custom materials.
- *Girth* is the width of the sheet metal from which a gutter is fabricated.
- Although all joining methods are applicable to most gutter shapes, lap joints are more commonly used. Seal all joints with mastic or by soldering. Lock, slip, or lap joints do not provide for expansion.
- Expansion joints should be used on all straight runs over 40 ft. In a 10-ft section of gutter that will undergo a 100° temperature change, linear expansion will follow these coefficients of expansion (CE) and movements: aluminum: CE, .00128, movement, .15 in.; copper: CE, .00093; movement, .11 in.; galvanized steel: CE, .0065, movement, .08 in.
- Always keep the front of the gutter lower than the back.

- Use a minimum width of 4 in., except for canopies and small porches. The minimum ratio of depth to width should be 3 to 4.
- Many custom shapes for gutters and downspouts are available; consult manufacturers' design manuals.

For more information on gutter sizing and details, refer to the Sheet Metal and Air Conditioning Contractors National Association (SMACNA) *Architectural Sheet Metal Manual.* For more on rainfall intensity, sizing of gutter, and sizing and spacing of downspouts, contact the Sheet Metal and Air Conditioning Contractors National Association (SMACNA).

TYPICAL GUTTER SHAPES AND SIZES
2.550

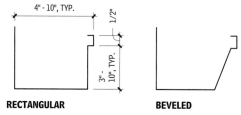

4" - 10", TYP.

1/2"

3" - 10", TYP.

RECTANGULAR

BEVELED

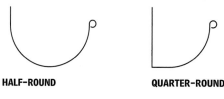

HALF-ROUND

QUARTER-ROUND

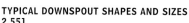

COVE MOLD

OGEE

TYPICAL DOWNSPOUT SHAPES AND SIZES
2.551

FORMED

EXTRUDED

CORRUGATED

ROUND

GUTTER
2.552

SPACER

VARIES

METAL GUTTER LINER

VARIES

DECORATIVE GUTTER COVER

SUPPORT BRACKET

FASTENERS (TOP AND BOTTOM)

CONCEALED DRAINAGE (OPTIONAL)

PARTS OF A GUTTER/DOWNSPOUT ASSEMBLY
2.553

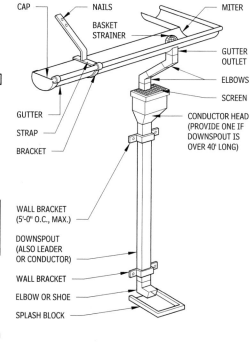

CAP

NAILS

MITER

BASKET STRAINER

GUTTER OUTLET

ELBOWS

SCREEN

GUTTER

STRAP

BRACKET

CONDUCTOR HEAD (PROVIDE ONE IF DOWNSPOUT IS OVER 40' LONG)

WALL BRACKET (5'-0" O.C., MAX.)

DOWNSPOUT (ALSO LEADER OR CONDUCTOR)

WALL BRACKET

ELBOW OR SHOE

SPLASH BLOCK

NOTES

2.549 a. Sheet lead minimum of 2-1/2 lb per sq ft.
b. Minimum clearance of 12 in. from cant strips and other curbs or pipes.
2.551 a. Formed and extruded downspout sizes are 3 by 4 to 6 by 6; round sizes are 3, 4, or 5 in. diameter. (Extruded downspouts are for heavy traffic.)
b. Generally, space downspouts a minimum of 20 ft and a maximum of 50 ft apart.
c. A downspout of 7 sq in. minimum should be used, except for canopies or small porches.

d. Corrugated shapes resist breakage due to freezing better than straight profiles.
e. Elbows are available in 45°, 60°, 75°, and 90° angles.

Contributor:
National Roofing Contractors Association, Rosemont, Illinois; Valerie Eickelberger, Rippeteau Architects, PC, Washington, DC; Jones/Richards and Associates, Ogden, Utah; Lawrence W. Cobb, Columbia, South Carolina.

GUTTER PROTECTION
2.554

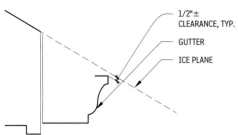

- 1/2"± CLEARANCE, TYP.
- GUTTER
- ICE PLANE

GUTTER PLACEMENT IN SNOW ZONES

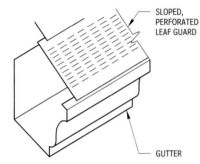

- SLOPED, PERFORATED LEAF GUARD
- GUTTER

LEAF GUARD

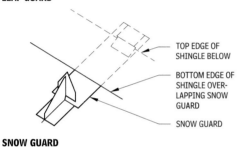

- TOP EDGE OF SHINGLE BELOW
- BOTTOM EDGE OF SHINGLE OVER-LAPPING SNOW GUARD
- SNOW GUARD

SNOW GUARD

GUTTER HANGERS
2.555

BRACKET

BAR HANGER

STRAP

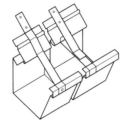

SHANK

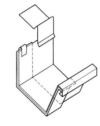

BRACKET HANGER

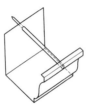

SPIKE AND FERRULE

GUTTER BRACKET OR STRAP SIZES (IN.)
2.556

GIRTH	GALVANIZED STEEL	COPPER	ALUMINUM	STAINLESS
Up to 15	1/8 × 1	1/8 × 1	3/16 × 1	1/8 × 1
15 to 20	3/16 × 1	1/4 × 1	1/4 × 1	1/8 × 1-1/2
20 to 24	1/4 × 1-1/2	1/4 × 1-1/2	1/4 × 2	1/8 × 2

NOTES

2.554 a. Gutters should be placed below the slope line, so snow and ice can slide clear. A steeper pitch requires less clearance.

b. Snow guards are installed on roofs to protect gutters from snow slides and snow overloading. They hold the snow in place evenly over the entire roof, allowing it to melt gradually into the gutter system. They also help prevent snow from collecting over the eaves, where it may thaw and refreeze, potentially causing damage.

c. Snow guard placement depends on the roof slope, local snow conditions, the insulation at the roof below, and the length of the rafters.

Snow guards typically are staggered on the roof, with the first row starting 2 ft from the eave.

2.556 a. Gutter hangers are normally spaced 3 ft o.c.; reduce spacing to 1 ft-6 in. o.c. where snow and ice are prevalent.

b. Spike and ferrule hangers are not recommended if girth is greater than 15 in.

c. Hangers are available in many sizes, shapes, and materials, and are matched to the design of the gutter used. Consult manufacturers' design manuals.

Contributors:
Jones/Richards and Associates. Ogden, Utah; Lawrence W. Cobb, Columbia, South Carolina.

FLAT ROOF DRAINAGE

The size and number of scuppers should be carefully determined to control ponding on roofs. Rectangular shapes convey more water (per inch of water depth on the roof) than round shapes. The performance of rectangular shapes approximates that of a broad-crested weir. Standard equations for channel flow are based on test models larger than typical roof scuppers. Downspout sizes normally are based on draining a given area of roof, but that flow rate may not pass through a scupper that has been sized to have a cross-sectional area equal to the downspout area.

The scupper sizing procedures are:

- Determine the head (H) in inches of water (typically 1 in. minimum by code) at a point 6 ft back from the scupper opening.
- Determine the roof drainage area in square feet (SF).
- Using rainfall intensity in inches per hour (IPH) from a rainfall data table, determine discharge capacity in gallons per minute (GPM). GPM = SF of roof area $\times$ IPH $\times$ 0.0104. The constant is 7.48 gallons per cubic foot divided by 12 in. per foot divided by 60 minutes per hour: GPM = (0.0104) IPH $\times$ SF.
- Using H and the GPM, find the aggregate scupper length (L) in the Scupper Capacity table (Table 2.699).
- Select enough individual scuppers to satisfy the total GPM requirement and locate them proportionately.

TYPICAL CONDUCTOR HEAD
2.558

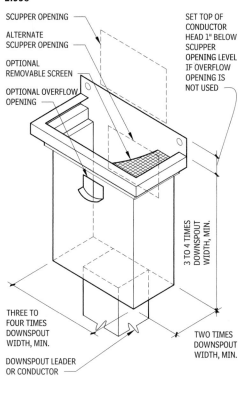

SCUPPER OPENING

ALTERNATE SCUPPER OPENING

OPTIONAL REMOVABLE SCREEN

OPTIONAL OVERFLOW OPENING

SET TOP OF CONDUCTOR HEAD 1" BELOW SCUPPER OPENING LEVEL IF OVERFLOW OPENING IS NOT USED

3 TO 4 TIMES DOWNSPOUT WIDTH, MIN.

THREE TO FOUR TIMES DOWNSPOUT WIDTH, MIN.

TWO TIMES DOWNSPOUT WIDTH, MIN.

DOWNSPOUT LEADER OR CONDUCTOR

SCUPPER AND CONDUCTOR HEAD DETAIL AT PARAPET WALL
2.557

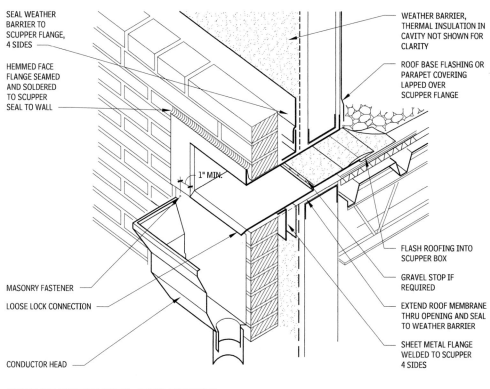

SEAL WEATHER BARRIER TO SCUPPER FLANGE, 4 SIDES

HEMMED FACE FLANGE SEAMED AND SOLDERED TO SCUPPER SEAL TO WALL

1" MIN.

MASONRY FASTENER

LOOSE LOCK CONNECTION

CONDUCTOR HEAD

WEATHER BARRIER, THERMAL INSULATION IN CAVITY NOT SHOWN FOR CLARITY

ROOF BASE FLASHING OR PARAPET COVERING LAPPED OVER SCUPPER FLANGE

FLASH ROOFING INTO SCUPPER BOX

GRAVEL STOP IF REQUIRED

EXTEND ROOF MEMBRANE THRU OPENING AND SEAL TO WEATHER BARRIER

SHEET METAL FLANGE WELDED TO SCUPPER 4 SIDES

OVERFLOW SCUPPER DETAIL AT PARAPET WALL
2.559

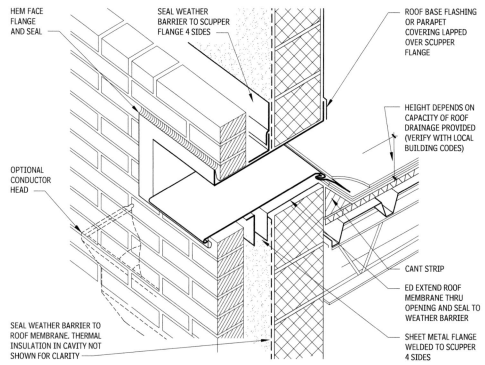

HEM FACE FLANGE AND SEAL

SEAL WEATHER BARRIER TO SCUPPER FLANGE 4 SIDES

OPTIONAL CONDUCTOR HEAD

SEAL WEATHER BARRIER TO ROOF MEMBRANE. THERMAL INSULATION IN CAVITY NOT SHOWN FOR CLARITY

ROOF BASE FLASHING OR PARAPET COVERING LAPPED OVER SCUPPER FLANGE

HEIGHT DEPENDS ON CAPACITY OF ROOF DRAINAGE PROVIDED (VERIFY WITH LOCAL BUILDING CODES)

CANT STRIP

ED EXTEND ROOF MEMBRANE THRU OPENING AND SEAL TO WEATHER BARRIER

SHEET METAL FLANGE WELDED TO SCUPPER 4 SIDES

NOTES

2.559 a. Use overflow scuppers when roof is completely surrounded by parapets and drainage depends on scuppers or internal damage.
b. Precast concrete panels with scuppers do not need closure flanges on face; all penetrations should be seated.

Contributor:
Richard J. Vitullo, AIA, Oak Leaf Studio, Crownsville, Maryland.

SCUPPER CAPACITY IN GPM
2.560

HEAD (H) (IN.)	LENGTH (L) OF WEIR (IN.)									
	4	6	8	10	12	18	24	30	36	48
1	11.0	17.4	23.40	29.3	35.4	53.4	71.5	89.5	107.5	143.2
2	30.5	47.5	64.4	81.4	98.3	149.1	200.0	251.1	302.0	403.4
3	52.9	84.1	115.2	146.3	177.5	270.9	364.3	457.7	551.1	737.9
4	76.7	124.6	172.6	220.5	269.0	412.3	556.1	700.0	843.7	1133.3
6	123.3	211.4	299.4	387.5	475.5	739.7	1003.9	1268.1	1532.3	2060.7

*Based on the Francis formula: $Q = 3.33 (L - 0.2H) H1.5$, in which

  Q = Flow rate, cubic ft per second
  L = Length of scupper opening, ft (should be 4 to 8 times H)
  H = Head on scupper, ft (measured 6 ft back from opening)
GPM = 448.8 CFS

COMBINATION SCUPPER AND GUTTER
2.561

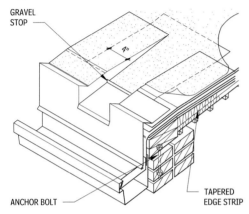

Scuppers that empty into a gutter may be integrated with a roof edge. The scuppers are soldered into a formed gravel-stop fascia system. The suggested maximum scupper interval is 10 ft. The front rim of the gutter must be 1 in. below the back edge, and it should be below the nailers used to elevate the roof edge. The drip edge on the fascia should lap the back edge of the gutter a minimum of 1 in. The gutter must be free to move behind the fascia.

CHIMNEY FLASHING

STEPPED-PAN THROUGH WALL FLASHING
2.562

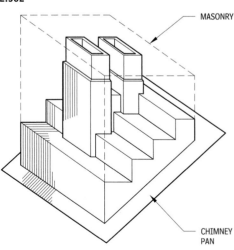

STEPPED-PAN THROUGH WALL FLASHING

FLASHING AT RIDGE
2.563

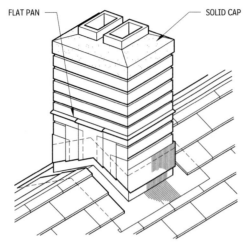

FLASHING AT RIDGE

FLASHING WITH CRICKET
2.564

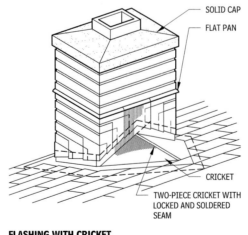

FLASHING WITH CRICKET

ALTERNATE ONE-PIECE CRICKET
2.565

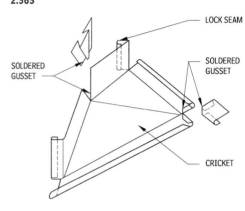

ALTERNATE ONE-PIECE BASE FLASHING
2.566

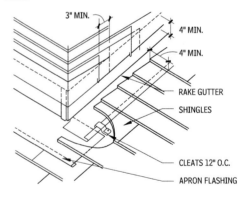

NOTE

2.562 Recommended for chimneys built of stone, rubble, ashlar, and any porous material.

Contributors:
SMACNA, Inc., Chantilly, Virginia; Grace S. Lee, Rippeteau Architects, PC, Washington, DC.

BASE AND COUNTERFLASHING AT FRAME WALL
2.567

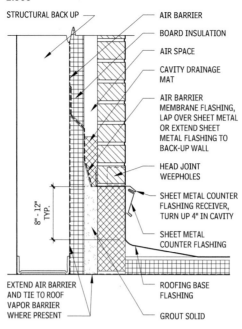

- SHEATHING OVER FRAMING
- AIR BARRIER LAP OVER COUNTERFLASHING
- EXTERIOR FINISH VARIES
- BLOCKING IF SHEATHING IS NOT NAILABLE
- SELF-ADHERING PEEL AND STICK MEMBRANE FLASHING UNDER FELTS AND OVER BASE FLASHING
- SHEET METAL COUNTERFLASHING RECEIVER
- SHEET METAL COUNTERFLASHING
- ROOFING BASE FLASHING
- TAPERED EDGE STRIP

8" – 12" TYPICAL

BASE AND COUNTERFLASHING AT BRICK VENEER
2.568

- STRUCTURAL BACK UP
- AIR BARRIER
- BOARD INSULATION
- AIR SPACE
- CAVITY DRAINAGE MAT
- AIR BARRIER MEMBRANE FLASHING, LAP OVER SHEET METAL OR EXTEND SHEET METAL FLASHING TO BACK-UP WALL
- HEAD JOINT WEEPHOLES
- SHEET METAL COUNTER FLASHING RECEIVER, TURN UP 4" IN CAVITY
- SHEET METAL COUNTER FLASHING
- ROOFING BASE FLASHING
- GROUT SOLID

8" – 12" TYP.

- EXTEND AIR BARRIER AND TIE TO ROOF VAPOR BARRIER WHERE PRESENT

BASE AND COUNTERFLASHING, WITH WALL AND ROOF DECK INDEPENDENTLY SUPPORTED
2.569

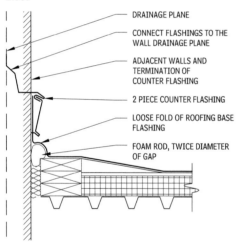

- DRAINAGE PLANE
- CONNECT FLASHINGS TO THE WALL DRAINAGE PLANE
- ADJACENT WALLS AND TERMINATION OF COUNTER FLASHING
- 2 PIECE COUNTER FLASHING
- LOOSE FOLD OF ROOFING BASE FLASHING
- FOAM ROD, TWICE DIAMETER OF GAP

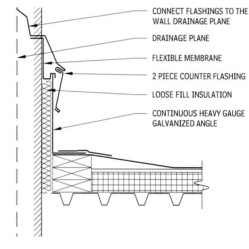

- CONNECT FLASHINGS TO THE WALL DRAINAGE PLANE
- DRAINAGE PLANE
- FLEXIBLE MEMBRANE
- 2 PIECE COUNTER FLASHING
- LOOSE FILL INSULATION
- CONTINUOUS HEAVY GAUGE GALVANIZED ANGLE

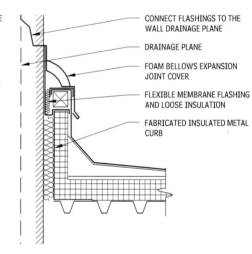

- CONNECT FLASHINGS TO THE WALL DRAINAGE PLANE
- DRAINAGE PLANE
- FOAM BELLOWS EXPANSION JOINT COVER
- FLEXIBLE MEMBRANE FLASHING AND LOOSE INSULATION
- FABRICATED INSULATED METAL CURB

COUNTERFLASHING DIAGRAM
2.570

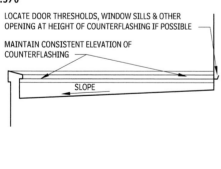

- LOCATE DOOR THRESHOLDS, WINDOW SILLS & OTHER OPENING AT HEIGHT OF COUNTERFLASHING IF POSSIBLE
- MAINTAIN CONSISTENT ELEVATION OF COUNTERFLASHING
- SLOPE

SURFACE-MOUNTED COUNTERFLASHING
2.571

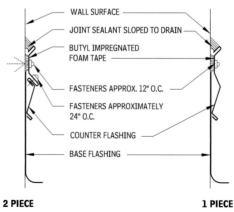

- WALL SURFACE
- JOINT SEALANT SLOPED TO DRAIN
- BUTYL IMPREGNATED FOAM TAPE
- FASTENERS APPROX. 12" O.C.
- FASTENERS APPROXIMATELY 24" O.C.
- COUNTER FLASHING
- BASE FLASHING

2 PIECE   **1 PIECE**

NOTES

2.571 Not for walls with internal drainage plain.

Contributors:
SMACNA, Inc., Chantilly, Virginia; Valerie Eickelberger, Rippeteau Architects, PC, Washington, DC.

ROOF OPENINGS

SKYLIGHTS

Skylights provide daylight to interior spaces and can reduce dependence on electrical lighting. In passive solar designs, skylights are used to admit direct solar radiation, enhancing space heating, and when vented properly, to induce convective airflow, reducing cooling loads through natural ventilation.

Skylights are available as units (which are shipped to the site ready to be installed) or as framed assemblies of stock components (which arrive fabricated for site assembly). Both fixed and hinged skylights are manufactured. The hinged variety can be opened manually or by remote control devices for venting. Frames are typically mounted on a built-up fabricated or site-built curb, with integral counterflashing; they can be assembled with or without insulation.

Self-flashing skylight units are available with or without curbs. Those without curbs are intended only for pitched roof assemblies and are not recommended for roof assemblies with finished spaces below.

Framed skylight assemblies are custom-designed by manufacturers to meet the necessary wind, roof, and dead loads of the assembly itself. When a skylight is pitched beyond a certain angle, it must be designed to resist environmental factors, as does a curtain wall assembly. Roof drainage for rainwater and storm water can limit skylight dimensions. Many skylights are face-sealed as a barrier system, but some are available as a pressure-equalized rainscreen system. Condensate gutters are needed in the body of the skylight assembly and around its perimeter. Gutters should be designed to evaporate collected water or be drained to the building plumbing system. Condensate drains through the skylight curb, common to many systems, violate the air barrier, resulting in energy losses and possible condensation.

Finishes for aluminum frame components are available as mill finish, clear anodized, duranodic bronze or black, acrylic enamel, and fluorocarbon.

In determining the desired form and size of the skylight unit/assembly, consideration should be given to:

- Environmental conditions, including orientation and winter and summer solar penetration angles at the site
- Prevailing wind direction and patterns
- Precipitation quantity and patterns
- Adjacent topography and landscaping (shade trees, etc.)
- Coordination with the HVAC system

PERCENTAGE OF ROOF AREA REQUIRED FOR SKYLIGHTING
2.572

	LIGHT DESIGN LEVELS (FC)		
LIGHT ZONE	30	60	120
1	3.3	5.2	13.3
2	2.8	4.3	10.8
3	1.8	3.2	6.9
4	1.5	2.8	4.0

- Use of shading, screening, or light reflecting/bouncing devices
- Views desired relative to view obstructions, streetlights

FRAMING, GLAZING, AND GASKETS

The heart of a well-designed skylight lies the detailing of frames, glazing, and sealant systems. The thickness, size, and geometric profile of all glass and acrylic glazing materials should be carefully selected for compliance with building codes and manufacturers' recommendations. The following glazing materials are considered resistant to impact and breakage and are generally approved by codes (listed in descending order of cost):

- Formed acrylic with mar-resistant finish
- Formed acrylic
- Polycarbonates
- Flat acrylic
- Laminated glass
- Insulated glass units
- Insulated glass units have a laminated glass inner light and tempered or heat-strengthened outer light.

Framed skylights require somewhat greater mullion widths when glazed with acrylics in order to accommodate the expansion and contraction characteristics of plastics. For economy, tinted acrylics should be limited to 1/4-in. thickness. A combination fiberglass sheet and aluminum frame system with high insulating value and good light diffusion can be a cost-effective alternative. Domed acrylic glazing is almost self-cleaning, as the sloped shapes facilitate rain washing of the surface.

Gaskets are especially subject to degradation from solar ultraviolet rays. Excessive expansion and contraction of acrylic glazing can cause "rolling" of the gasket between metal framing. Small valleys created at the bottom of the sloped glazing and the horizontal glazing cap will hold water, which increases the chance of gasket breakdown and subsequent water infiltration.

SHADING AND GLARE CONTROL

Skylights can introduce too much uncontrolled light, especially in areas where video screens and computers will be used. Skylights also can allow excessive heat buildup. To mitigate these issues:

- Select extent of skylight, glazing, and shading devices to balance the gains of daylighting against heat gain.
- Select glass with low-E coatings, tint, reflective coatings, frits, or combinations to lower the solar heat gain coefficient.
- Approximately 40 to 50 percent visible light transmission in a skylight will appear as bright as vertical glazing with 60 to 70 percent visible light transmission.
- Shading devices such as louvers, grilles, and shades should be added to control direct sun. Movable systems, particularly if fully automated to track the sun are more effective than fixed systems, for controlling glare while maximizing daylighting.

DOME UNIT SKYLIGHT—FLAT ROOF
2.573

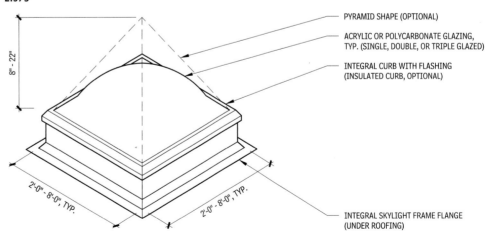

PYRAMID SHAPE (OPTIONAL)

ACRYLIC OR POLYCARBONATE GLAZING, TYP. (SINGLE, DOUBLE, OR TRIPLE GLAZED)

INTEGRAL CURB WITH FLASHING (INSULATED CURB, OPTIONAL)

INTEGRAL SKYLIGHT FRAME FLANGE (UNDER ROOFING)

8" - 22"

2'-0" - 8'-0", TYP.

2'-0" - 8'-0", TYP.

SECURITY AND SAFETY

Frames or screens to protect glazing from impact, fire, or forced entry may be designed into the skylight assembly. To avoid forced entry, a framed skylight should include deterrents to disassembling the framing, removing the snap-on cover, and melting the glazing (acrylics can easily be burned with a torch). Metal security screens may be required.

UNIT SKYLIGHTS

UNIT SKYLIGHT SECTION
2.574

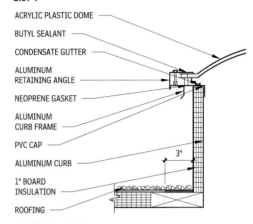

ACRYLIC PLASTIC DOME
BUTYL SEALANT
CONDENSATE GUTTER
ALUMINUM RETAINING ANGLE
NEOPRENE GASKET
ALUMINUM CURB FRAME
PVC CAP
ALUMINUM CURB
1" BOARD INSULATION
ROOFING

3"

INSULATED CURB

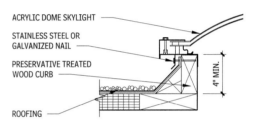

ACRYLIC DOME SKYLIGHT
STAINLESS STEEL OR GALVANIZED NAIL
PRESERVATIVE TREATED WOOD CURB
ROOFING

4" MIN.

WOOD CURB

NOTES

2.573 Glazing is typically clear, tinted transparent, or white translucent.

Contributor:
Richard J. Vitullo, AIA, Oak Leaf Studio, Crownsville, Maryland.

FLAT PANEL UNIT SKYLIGHT—SLOPED ROOF
2.575

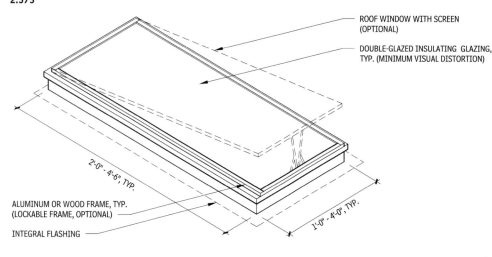

ROOF WINDOW WITH SCREEN (OPTIONAL)

DOUBLE-GLAZED INSULATING GLAZING, TYP. (MINIMUM VISUAL DISTORTION)

2'-0" - 4'-6", TYP.

1'-0" - 4'-0", TYP.

ALUMINUM OR WOOD FRAME, TYP. (LOCKABLE FRAME, OPTIONAL)

INTEGRAL FLASHING

FLAT PANEL UNIT—SKYLIGHT SECTION
2.576

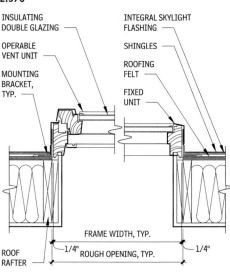

INSULATING DOUBLE GLAZING

OPERABLE VENT UNIT

MOUNTING BRACKET, TYP.

INTEGRAL SKYLIGHT FLASHING

SHINGLES

ROOFING FELT

FIXED UNIT

ROOF RAFTER

FRAME WIDTH, TYP.

1/4" ROUGH OPENING, TYP.

1/4"

FRAMED SKYLIGHT TYPES

Framed skylights are available in two different structural types, three glazing types, and two water management systems. Most manufacturers only provide systems in a limited number of the possible combinations.

STRUCTURAL TYPES, STRUCTURAL OR SKIN
- Structural skylights span the skylight opening and support all loads.
- Skin systems have a frame that performs glazing and water-proofing functions. They are applied to a separate structural system, typically of wood or steel. Skin systems frequently resemble structural systems, except that the members are much more shallow.

GLAZING TYPES
- Four-sided retained systems have pressure plates or other glazing stops on the full perimeter of each pane of glass. Glazing should be a wet/dry type or, preferably, a fully wet glazing for maximum reliability. Avoid systems (especially face-sealed systems) that use dry gaskets.
- Two-sided structural silicone-glazed (SSG) assemblies have pressure plates or glazing stops on the mullions that run parallel to the slope, and structural silicone glazing on mullions running across the slope. Because the SSG has no mullion cover above the plane of the glass, no water is trapped to cause potential leaks or stains from the evaporated water. Two-sided SSG systems are recommended for most framed skylights.
- Four-sided structural silicone glazed assemblies provide the advantages of two-sided SSG systems, plus a more streamlined appearance.

WATER MANAGEMENT SYSTEMS
- Face-sealed systems rely on a perfect watertight seal at the exterior face of glazing. Gutters and weeps on the interior side of the glazing are provided to control condensation only.
- Rainscreen systems employ redundant pressure-equalized rainscreen technology to control both air and water penetration. Drainage channels and weeps on the interior face drain not only condensation but also any minor leaks that get past the exterior seals. Although less common, PE rainscreen systems are more reliable.

POINT-SUPPORTED FRAMELESS SKYLIGHT SYSTEMS
- Frameless skylights supported on point glazing mounts are the most transparent and expensive skylights. They provide a nearly invisible separation between the interior and exterior. The systems rely on perfect silicone butt-joint glazing. The structural support can be one-way or two-way trusses of steel, aluminum, wood, laminated glass, tension cables, or combinations of these.

TYPICAL TUBULAR ALUMINUM FRAMING
2.577

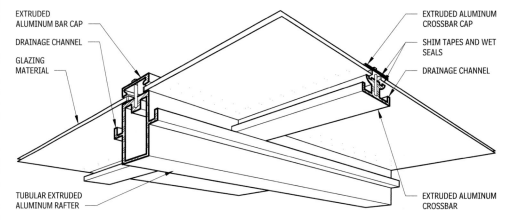

EXTRUDED ALUMINUM BAR CAP

DRAINAGE CHANNEL

GLAZING MATERIAL

TUBULAR EXTRUDED ALUMINUM RAFTER

EXTRUDED ALUMINUM CROSSBAR CAP

SHIM TAPES AND WET SEALS

DRAINAGE CHANNEL

EXTRUDED ALUMINUM CROSSBAR

RAFTER AND SIDEWALL DETAIL
2.578

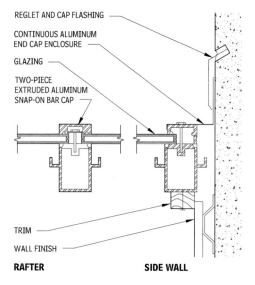

REGLET AND CAP FLASHING

CONTINUOUS ALUMINUM END CAP ENCLOSURE

GLAZING

TWO-PIECE EXTRUDED ALUMINUM SNAP-ON BAR CAP

TRIM

WALL FINISH

RAFTER   **SIDE WALL**

NOTES

2.575 a. Clear and tinted transparent glass is typical, but tempered, laminated, and wire glass also are available.
b. Manual and powered vent operation, venetian blinds, shades, and exterior awnings are available. Consult manufacturers for available options.

Contributor:
Richard J. Vitullo, AIA, Oak Leaf Studio, Crownsville, Maryland.

PYRAMID FRAMED SKYLIGHT ASSEMBLY
2.579

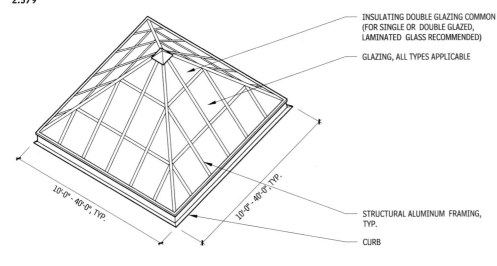

INSULATING DOUBLE GLAZING COMMON (FOR SINGLE OR DOUBLE GLAZED, LAMINATED GLASS RECOMMENDED)

GLAZING, ALL TYPES APPLICABLE

STRUCTURAL ALUMINUM FRAMING, TYP.

CURB

10'-0" - 40'-0", TYP.

10'-0" - 40'-0", TYP.

CURB DETAIL AT SLOPED FRAMED ASSEMBLY
2.580

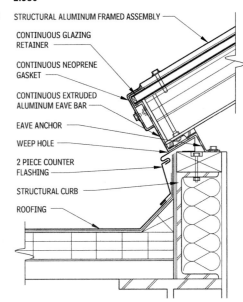

STRUCTURAL ALUMINUM FRAMED ASSEMBLY

CONTINUOUS GLAZING RETAINER

CONTINUOUS NEOPRENE GASKET

CONTINUOUS EXTRUDED ALUMINUM EAVE BAR

EAVE ANCHOR

WEEP HOLE

2 PIECE COUNTER FLASHING

STRUCTURAL CURB

ROOFING

VERTICAL FRAME CURB DETAIL
2.581

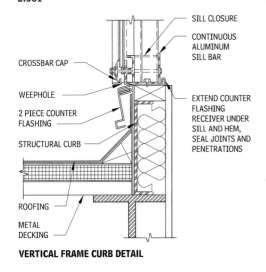

SILL CLOSURE

CONTINUOUS ALUMINUM SILL BAR

CROSSBAR CAP

WEEPHOLE

2 PIECE COUNTER FLASHING

STRUCTURAL CURB

ROOFING

METAL DECKING

EXTEND COUNTER FLASHING RECEIVER UNDER SILL AND HEM, SEAL JOINTS AND PENETRATIONS

VERTICAL FRAME CURB DETAIL

DOUBLE-PITCH FRAMED SKYLIGHT ASSEMBLY
2.582

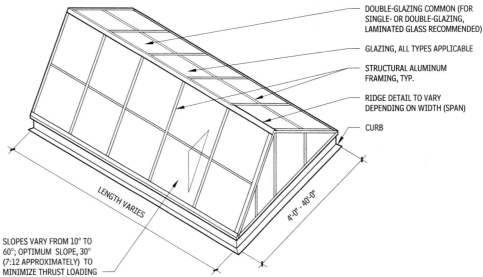

DOUBLE-GLAZING COMMON (FOR SINGLE- OR DOUBLE-GLAZING, LAMINATED GLASS RECOMMENDED)

GLAZING, ALL TYPES APPLICABLE

STRUCTURAL ALUMINUM FRAMING, TYP.

RIDGE DETAIL TO VARY DEPENDING ON WIDTH (SPAN)

CURB

LENGTH VARIES

4'-0" - 40'-0"

SLOPES VARY FROM 10° TO 60°; OPTIMUM SLOPE, 30° (7:12 APPROXIMATELY) TO MINIMIZE THRUST LOADING

NOTE

2.582 Options for a pitched skylight include: (1) integration of skylight with roof structure at ridge, with slope of skylight to match slope of roof, and no end glazing; (2) hip end glazing; and (3) vaulted framing, with minimum rise at 22 percent.

Contributor:
Richard J. Vitullo, AIA, Oak Leaf Studio, Crownsville, Maryland.

3 ELEMENT C: INTERIORS

INTRODUCTION

Interior construction is a formidable component of architecture. After all, people spend more time inside buildings than outside. A main purpose of architecture is to provide sheltered interior space. Compliance with life safety requirements, functional needs of myriad building users, and aesthetic concepts all influence the design, detailing, and construction of interior space. In addition, the rate of change for a building's interior is often frequent, and could be as rapid as every few years for a commercial space. This practice only serves to escalate the required attention to interior construction detailing in support of flexibility.

This chapter provides a foundation of interior detailing basics for various primary building components and systems for use with most building types, answering the question, "What does a design professional need to know about interiors to think critically about interior detailing and related construction documents?" The material, however, does not attempt to address specific manufacturer's systems or products, as interior building components and finishes are constantly evolving. The design professional is encouraged to investigate interior systems and products through Web-based resources or readily available manufacturers' product literature and samples. At the same time, the design professional is encouraged to consider utilizing sustainable products, especially as many of these manufacturers have taken the industry lead in the development of sustainable and recycled-content products for interior construction.

One significant criterion for interior finish selection should involve environmental considerations such as indoor air quality, sustainability, and environmental consequences. Refer to Chapter 12 for an overview.

Contributor:
Tim Shea, AIA

INTERIOR CONSTRUCTION

PARTITIONS

This section discusses common types of partitions, in particular, gypsum board assemblies and glass-reinforced gypsum assemblies, as well as the design of fire-resistant partitions.

GYPSUM BOARD ASSEMBLIES

Gypsum board assemblies consist of gypsum board and framing, which can be wood or metal, and may include sound attenuation, and fireproofing materials.

WOOD-FRAME GYPSUM BOARD PARTITIONS
3.1

FIRE-RESISTANCE RATING	SOUND TRANSMISSION CLASS (STC)	WALL THICKNESS IN.	CONSTRUCTION DESCRIPTION	PLAN VIEW
One-hour	30–34	4-7/8	One layer, 1/2-in. Type X veneer base nailed to each side of 2 × 4 in. wood studs, 16 in. o.c. with 5d coated nails 8 in. o.c.; minimum 3/32-in. gypsum veneer plaster. Joints staggered vertically 16 in., and horizontal joints each side at 12 in.	
		4-7/8	One layer 5/8-in. Type X gypsum board or veneer base nailed to each side of 2 × 4 in. wood studs, 16 in. o.c. with 6d coated nails 7 in. o.c. Stagger joints 24 in. on each side.	
	35–39	5-1/8	Two layers 3/8-in. regular gypsum board or veneer base nailed to each side of 2 × 4 in. wood studs, 16 in. o.c. First layer attached with 4d coated nails; second layer applied with laminating compound and nailed with 5d coated nails 8 in. o.c. Stagger joints 16 in. o.c. each side.	
	45–49	5-3/8 (137)	Base layer 3/8-in. regular gypsum board or veneer base nailed to each side of 2 × 4 in. wood studs, 16 in. o.c. Face layer 1/2 in. (same as base layer). Use 5d coated nails 24 in. o.c. for base layer, 8d coated nails 12 in. o.c. to edge, and 24 in. o.c. to intermediate studs. Stagger joints 16 in. o.c. each layer and side.	
		5-7/8	Base layer 1/2-in. wood fiberboard to each side of 2 × 4 in. wood studs, 16 in. o.c. with 5d coated nails 24 in. o.c. on vertical joints and 16 in. o.c. to top and bottom plates. Face layer 5/8-in. Type X gypsum board or veneer base applied to each side with laminating compound and nailed with 8d coated nails 24 in. o.c. on vertical joints, and 16 in. o.c. to top and bottom plates. Stagger joints 24 in. o.c. each layer and side.	
		5-7/8	Both sides resilient channels 24 in. o.c., attached with gypsum board 54 gypsum board nails to each side of 2 × 4 in. wood studs, 16 in. o.c. One layer 5/8-in. Type X gypsum board or veneer base attached with 1-in. Type S gypsum board screws 12 in. o.c. to each side, and vertical joints back-blocked. Gypsum board filler strips along floor and ceiling, both sides. Stagger joints 24 in. o.c. each side.	
	50–54	5-3/8	Base layer 1/4-in. proprietary gypsum board applied to each side of 2 × 4 in. wood studs, 16 in. o.c. with 4d coated nails 12 in. o.c. Face layer 5/8-in. gypsum board or veneer base applied with laminating compound and nailed with 6d coated nails 16 in. o.c. to each side; 1-1/2-in. mineral fiber insulation in cavity. Stagger joints 24 in. o.c. each side.	
		5-3/8	One side resilient channel 24-in. o.c. with 1-1/4-in. Type S gypsum board screws to 2 × 4 in. wood studs, 16 in. o.c. Both sides 5/8-in. gypsum board or veneer base attached to resilient channel with 1-in. Type S gypsum board screws 12 in. o.c., and gypsum board to stud with 1-1/4-in. Type W gypsum board screws; 1-1/2-in. mineral fiber insulation in cavity. Stagger joints 48 in. each side.	
	60–64	6-7/8	One side resilient channel 24 in. o.c. attached with 1-in. Type S gypsum board screws to 2 × 4 in. wood studs, 16 in. o.c. Two layers of 5/8-in. Type X gypsum board or veneer base. First layer attached with 1-in. Type S gypsum board screws; second layer applied with laminating compound. Other side, one layer each of 5/8-in. and 1/2-in. gypsum board or veneer base, plus top 3/8-in. gypsum board applied with laminating compound. Use 5d coated nails 32 in. o.c. for base, 8d for 1/2-in. center layer, 2-in. glass fiber insulation in cavity. Stagger all joints 16 in. o.c.	
Two-hour	40–44	6-1/8	Two layers 5/8-in. Type X gypsum board or veneer base applied to each side of 2 × 4 in. wood studs, 24 in. o.c. Use 6d coated nails 24 in. o.c. for base layer, and 8d coated nails 8 in. o.c. for face layer. Stagger joints 24 in. o.c. for each layer and side.	

Contributors:
Ted Kollaja, AIA, Gensler, Dallas, Texas; Lohan Caprile Goettsch Architects, Chicago, Illinois; Any Adams, Anshen + Allen, Architects, San Francisco, California; Jim Johnson, Wrightson, Johnson, Haddon & Williams, Inc., Dallas, Texas.

WOOD-FRAME GYPSUM BOARD PARTITIONS (continued)
3.1

FIRE-RESISTANCE RATING	SOUND TRANSMISSION CLASS (STC)	WALL THICKNESS IN.	CONSTRUCTION DESCRIPTION	PLAN VIEW
Two-hour	50–54	8	Two layers 5/8-in. Type X gypsum board or veneer base applied to each side of 2 × 4 in. wood studs, 16 in. o.c. staggered 8 in. o.c. on 2 × 6 in. wood plates. Use 6d coated nails 24 in. o.c. for base layer, and 8d coated nails for face layer. Stagger vertical joints 16 in. o.c. each layer and side.	
	55–59	10-3/4	Two layers 5/8-in. Type X gypsum board or veneer base applied to each side of double row of 2 × 4 in. wood studs, 16 in. o.c. on separate plates 1 in. apart. Use 6d coated nails 24 in. o.c. for base layer, and 8d coated nails for face layer; 3-1/2 in. glass-fiber insulation in cavity. Stagger joints 16 in. o.c. each layer and side. Gypsum board firestop continuous in spaces between plates.	

Contributors:
Ted Kollaja, AIA, Gensler, Dallas, Texas; Lohan Caprile Goettsch Architects, Chicago, Illinois; Andy Adams, Anshen+Allen, Architects, San Francisco, California; Jim Johnson, Wrightson, Johnson, Haddon & Williams, Inc., Dallas, Texas.

METAL-FRAME GYPSUM BOARD PARTITIONS
3.2

FIRE RATING	SOUND TRANSMISSION CLASS (STC)	WALL THICKNESS IN.	CONSTRUCTION DESCRIPTION	PLAN VIEW
One-hour	35–39	2-7/8	One layer 5/8-in. Type X gypsum board or veneer base applied to each side of 1-5/8-in. metal studs, 24 in. o.c. with 1-in. Type S gypsum board screws 8 in. o.c. to edges, and 12 in. o.c. to intermediate studs. Stagger joints 24 in. o.c. each side.	
	40–44	3-3/8	Base layer 3/8-in. regular gypsum board or veneer base applied to each side of 1-5/8-in. metal studs, 24 in. o.c. with 1-in. Type S gypsum board screws 27 in. o.c. to edges and 54 in. o.c. to intermediate studs. Face layer 1/2 in. attached on each side to studs with 1-5/8-in. Type S gypsum board screws 12 in. o.c. to perimeter and 24 in. o.c. to intermediate studs. Stagger joints 24 in. o.c. each layer and side.	
		4-7/8	One layer 5/8-in. Type X gypsum board or veneer base applied to each side of 3-5/8-in. metal studs, 24 in. o.c. with 1-in. Type S gypsum board screws 8 in. o.c. to vertical edges, and 12 in. o.c. to intermediate studs. Stagger joints 24 in. o.c. each layer and side.	
	45–49	3-1/8	Two layers 1/2-in. regular gypsum board or veneer base applied to each side of 1-5/8-in. metal studs, 24 in. o.c. Use 1-in. Type S gypsum board screws 12 in. o.c. for base layer, and 1-5/8-in. Type S gypsum board screws 12 in. o.c. for face layer. Stagger joints 24 in. o.c. each layer and side.	
		3-1/8	Base layer 1/4-in. gypsum board applied to each side of 1-5/8-in. metal studs, 24 in. o.c. with 1-in. Type S gypsum board screws 24 in. o.c. to edges, and 36 in. o.c. to intermediate studs. Face layer 1/2-in. Type X gypsum board or veneer base applied to each side of studs with 1 5/8 in. Type S gypsum board screws 12 in. o.c. Stagger joints 24 in. o.c. each layer and side.	
		5-1/2	One layer 5/8-in. Type X gypsum board or veneer base applied to each side of 3-5/8-in. metal studs 24 in. o.c. with 1-in. Type S gypsum board screws 8 in. o.c. to edge and vertical joints, and 12 in. o.c. to intermediate stud. Face layer 5/8-in. (same as other layer) applied on one side to stud with laminating compound and attached with 1-5/8-in. Type S gypsum board screws, 8 in. o.c. to edges and sides, and 12 in. o.c. to intermediate studs; 3-1/2-in. glass-fiber insulation in cavity. Stagger joints 24 in. o.c. each layer and side.	
	50–54	4	Base layer 1/4-in. regular gypsum board applied to each side of 2-1/2-in. metal studs, 24 in. o.c. with 1-in. Type S gypsum board screws 12 in. o.c. Face layer 1/2-in. Type X gypsum board or veneer base applied to each side of studs with laminating compound and with 1-5/8-in. Type S gypsum board screws in top and bottom runners 8 in. o.c.; 2-in. glass-fiber insulation in cavity. Stagger joints 24 in. o.c. each layer and side.	
		4	Two layers 1/2-in. Type X gypsum board or veneer base applied to one side of 2-1/2-in. metal studs, 24 in. o.c. Base layer 1-in. and face layer 1-5/8-in. gypsum board screws 8 in. o.c. to edge and adhesive beads to intermediate studs. Opposite side layer 1/2-in. Type X gypsum board or veneer base applied with 1-in. Type S gypsum board screws 8 in. o.c. to vertical edges, and 12 in. o.c. to intermediate studs; 3-in. glass-fiber insulation in cavity. Stagger joints 24 in. each layer and face.	
	55–59	4-1/4	Base layer 1/4-in. gypsum board applied to each side of 2-1/2-in. metal studs, 24 in. o.c. with 7/8-in. Type S gypsum board screws 12 in. o.c. Face layer 5/8-in. Type X gypsum board or veneer base applied on each side of studs with 1-5/16-in. Type S gypsum board screws 12 in. o.c.; 1-1/2-in. glass-fiber insulation in cavity. Stagger joints 24 in. o.c. each layer and side.	
Two-hour	40–44	5	Two layers 5/8-in. Type X gypsum board or veneer base applied to each side of 2-1/2-in. metal studs 16 in. o.c., braced laterally. Use 1 in. for base layer and 1-5/8 in. for face layer. Type S-12 gypsum board screws 12 in. o.c. for face layer; 1-1/2-in. glass-fiber insulation in cavity. Stagger joints 24 in. o.c. each layer and side.	
	50–54	3-5/8	Base layer 1/2-in. Type X gypsum board or veneer base applied to each side of 1-5/8-in. metal studs, 24 in. o.c. Use 1-in. Type S gypsum board screws, 12 in. o.c. for base layer, and 1-5/8-in. Type S gypsum board screws 12 in. o.c. for face layer; 1-1/2-in. glass-fiber insulation in cavity. Stagger joints 24 in. o.c. each layer and side.	
	55–59	6-1/4	Two layers 5/8-in. Type X gypsum board or veneer base applied to each side of 3-5/8-in. metal studs, 24 in. o.c. Use 1-in. Type S gypsum board screws 32 in. o.c. for base layer, and 1-5/8-in. Type S gypsum board screws 12 in. o.c. to edge and, 24 in. o.c. to intermediate studs. One side, third layer, 1/4- or 3/8-in. gypsum board or veneer base applied with laminating compound. Stagger joints 24 in. o.c. each layer and side.	

FIRE-RESISTANT DESIGN

Several methods, both active (fire suppression) and passive, are possible for protecting building structures from fire. Designing for fire protection may include dividing a building into isolated modules with a limited number of penetrations for openings, electrical conduits, and ducts. Modules could be protected with applied fireproofing, sprinklers, or both, depending on use, occupancy, potential exposure to abuse, and requirements of authorities having jurisdiction. Costs of a fire suppression system may be offset by savings from less restrictive requirements for construction and finishes.

Avoiding fire-rated doorways reduces costs for doors, hardware, and signs. Avoiding penetrations for electrical and mechanical work reduces the need for and expense of penetration firestopping, fire safing, and fire dampers.

APPLIED FIREPROOFING

Applied fireproofing materials protect structural steel in both concealed and exposed applications. There are many types of applied fireproofing, including cementitious and cement aggregate, and mineral-fiber cementitious products, used predominantly for concealed locations. There also materials used for exposed locations that require a more finished appearance.

Fire-resistance design decisions can affect the cost, scheduling, and complexity of the application. For example, to forestall problems with warranty limitations and with the vulnerability of roof assemblies protected by applied, fire-resistive materials when subject to construction, maintenance, or repair activities on the roof, roof-ceiling designs might be limited to those assemblies protected by materials other than sprayed fire-resistive materials applied to the underside of steel deck or to those not requiring additional protection.

On a project-by-project basis, floor-ceiling assemblies, which are usually stiffer than roof-ceiling assemblies, may or may not require protection by sprayed fire-resistive materials applied on the underside of steel deck. It may be possible to eliminate the need to directly apply fire-resistive materials to the underside of steel deck by comparing design options with the same ratings, then selecting a design that results in thicker concrete slabs and requires no other protection of the steel deck. The resulting stiffer floors will have the additional benefit of being better substrates for thin, rigid flooring, such as tile for restrooms.

If constraints, such as weather, aesthetic appearance, construction scheduling, environmental concerns, or the design program, make using sprayed fire-resistive materials inappropriate, alternative methods of protection may eliminate or reduce their extent. Alternative methods can include:

- Protecting structural steel with concrete
- Masonry; fire-safing insulation
- Mineral-fiberboard fire protection
- Sprinklers
- Assemblies of gypsum plaster, portland cement plaster, gypsum board, veneer-plaster gypsum board, and rated acoustical ceiling panels

EXPOSED APPLICATIONS

For exposed applications, fire-resistive materials are higher in density, compressive strength, bond strength, and hardness than those for concealed applications. Suggestions for high-density products include exposed interior areas protected by deluge sprinkler systems and areas subject to contact, physical abuse, high impact, chemical exposure, high humidity, air, and erosion. Examples of areas where denser fire-resistive materials might be considered are parking garages, loading docks, piers, cargo facilities, warehouses, manufacturing plants, mechanical rooms, elevator machine rooms, shafts, air-handling plenums, stairwells, clean rooms, gymnasiums, and swimming pools.

The following products are used for exposed applications:

- Cementitious fireproofing
- Mineral-fiber cementitious fireproofing
- Magnesium cement fireproofing
- Intumescent mastic fireproofing, including water-based formulations, nonwater-based formulations, and thin films

ENCAPSULANTS

Encapsulants include materials that are applied either over previously applied fire-resistive fibrous and cementitious formulations or to structural members from which previously applied materials have been removed. The latter are called *lockdown encapsulants.* Typically, encapsulants are part of a separate asbestos-abatement contract.

SEALERS AND TOPCOATS

Sealers and topcoats, mandatory or optional, are offered by some manufacturers to enhance product performance and to improve specific physical property limitations of individual formulations, such as resistance to chemicals and to growth of bacteria, fungus, mildew, and mold. Sealers and topcoats must be compatible with the manufacturer's formulation for sprayed fire-resistive materials. They should be applied at rates that maintain fire-resistance ratings; the saturation of sprayed fire-resistive materials with sealers and topcoats would probably negate fire-resistance performance.

BOARD FIREPROOFING

Board fireproofing includes calcium-silicate and slag-fiberboards, and is used for fire protection of steel columns, steel beams, metal and wood framed walls, and solid walls. Another use for mineral-fiberboard fireproofing is the protection of HVAC ducts.

The use of board fireproofing instead of applied fireproofing eliminates the cleanup of a wet residue and possible delays for drying that result from using applied materials. Board fireproofing is also less likely to corrode metal substrates.

CALCIUM SILICATE BOARDS

Calcium silicate board is manufactured either from xonotlite or a combination of xonotlite and tobomorite. Xonotlite differs from tobomorite in crystalline structure and in physical properties. Xonotlite is designed for continuous service at 1700°F, and tobomorite at 1200°F , although both must withstand higher temperatures during testing per ASTM E 119, "Standard Test Methods for Fire Tests of Building Construction and Materials," to attain UL-listed fire-resistance ratings. Most, if not all, board fireproofing systems are typically concealed behind other construction; however, the higher-density forms of calcium silicate can be left exposed, and painted.

SLAG-FIBERBOARD FIREPROOFING

Slag-fiberboard consists of fibers made from slag, which is a by-product of the production of steel, copper, and lead. Slag is the mineral waste that rises to the top of molten metal. Its uses include thermal insulation, curtain-wall insulation, and safing insulation to establish fire barriers in the space between floor edges and curtain-wall spandrel panels. Slag-fiberboards are more prone to damage and deterioration than calciumsilicate boards; they are also softer, lighter, more absorbent, and more compressible.

PENETRATION FIRESTOPPING

Fire-test-response characteristics of penetration firestopping are measured in terms of F- and T-ratings. These are determined by testing according to ASTM E 814, "Standard Test Method for Fire Tests of Through-Penetration Fire Stops."

- *F-ratings* indicate that the firestop system withstood the fire test for the rating period without the following taking place: flames passing through openings, flaming of any element on the unexposed side of the firestop system, and the development of any openings that permit water from the hose stream to project beyond the unexposed side.
- *T-ratings* signify that heat transmitted through the firestop system during the rating period did not raise the temperature of any thermocouple on the unexposed firestop system surface or on any penetrating item by more than 325°F above its initial temperature.

When selecting penetration firestopping assemblies, the design professional must understand both what the building code requirements are and how authorities having jurisdiction will interpret and enforce its provisions.

INTERIOR DOORS

This section begins by introducing the basic concepts and terminology encountered when working with interior doors. It goes on to examine common types of doors and special considerations such as fire safety.

BASIC DOOR TERMINOLOGY

These are basic terms and concepts inherent to door design:

- *Active leaf:* The primary operating leaf of a door pair.
- *Air curtain:* A mechanically produced downward stream of air across a door opening intended to prevent transmission of heat and weather.
- *Automatic closing:* A door that is normally open, but that closes without the necessity for human intervention, and is activated as a result of a predetermined temperature rise, rate of temperature rise, or combustion products.
- *Automatic door bottom:* A device applied to the back side of a door at the bottom, or mortised into the bottom edge of a door, which seals the undercut of a door as it is closed.
- *Balanced door:* A door equipped with double-pivoted hardware designed to cause a semicounterbalanced swing action when opening.
- *Buck:* A subframe of wood or metal set in a wall or partition to support the finish frame of a door.
- *Casing:* The finished, often decorative framework around a door opening, especially that which is parallel to the surrounding surface and at right angles to the jamb.
- *Coordinator:* A device used on a pair of doors to ensure that the inactive leaf is permitted to close before the active leaf.
- *Door bevel:* The slight angle given to the lock stile (vertical edge) of a door, which prevents the door from touching the lock jamb as it swings. Typical bevels are:
  - 1-3/8-in. door—none
  - 1-3/4-in. door—7/64 in.
  - 2-1/4-in.—9/64 in.
- *Double-egress door:* A pair of doors within a single special frame that swing in opposite directions to allow emergency egress from either side. Typically used where a fire or smoke partition crosses a corridor.
- *Flush bolt:* A door bolt set flush with the face or edge of the door.
- *Fire-door assembly:* Any combination of a fire door, frame, hardware, and other accessories that together provide a specific degree of fire protection.
- *Fire exit hardware:* Panic hardware that is listed for use on fire-door assemblies.
- *Head:* The horizontal portion of a door frame above the door opening.
- *Jamb:* The vertical members at the sides of a door opening.
- *Labeled:* Equipment, products, or materials marked with the label, symbol, or other identifying mark of an approved testing organization that indicates compliance with standards for manufacture and testing.
- *Listed:* Equipment, devices, materials, or services included in a list published by a testing agency that have been shown to meet applicable standards for use in fire-rated assemblies or that have been tested and found suitable for use for a specified purpose.
- *Panic hardware:* A door-latching assembly incorporating a device that releases the latch upon the application of a force in the direction of egress travel.
- *Power-assisted door:* A door with a mechanism that helps to open the door or to relieve the opening resistance of the door.
- *Prehung door:* Door and frame combination fabricated and assembled by the manufacturer and shipped to the site.
- *Sill:* The horizontal members at the bottom of a door opening.
- *Subcasing:* The finish frame components that support and guide the door.
- *Undercut:* The space between the bottom edge of a door and the sill or threshold.

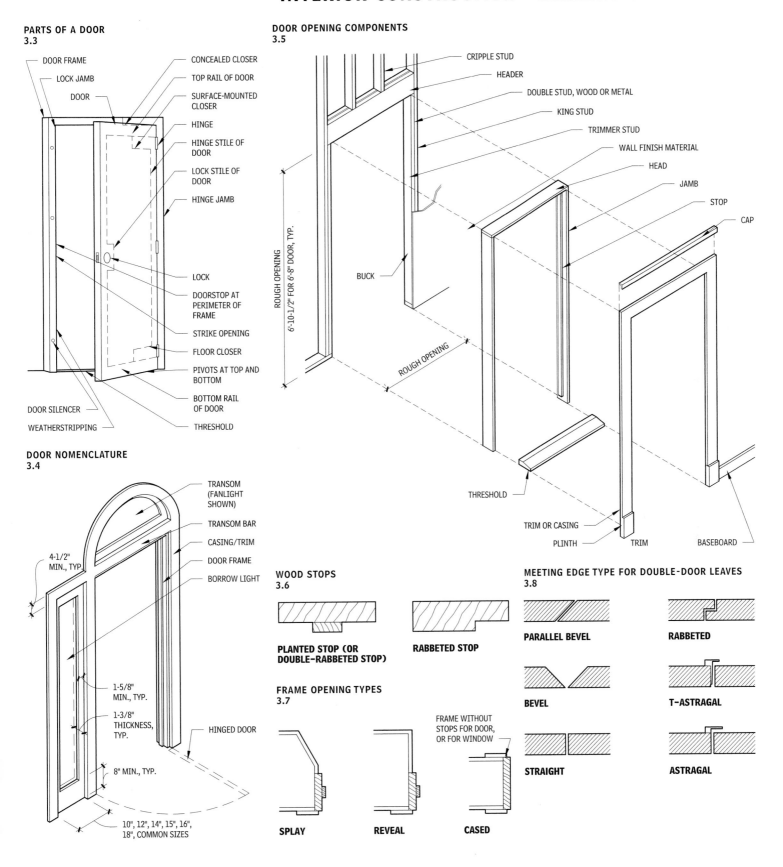

PARTS OF A DOOR
3.3

- DOOR FRAME
- LOCK JAMB
- DOOR
- CONCEALED CLOSER
- TOP RAIL OF DOOR
- SURFACE-MOUNTED CLOSER
- HINGE
- HINGE STILE OF DOOR
- LOCK STILE OF DOOR
- HINGE JAMB
- LOCK
- DOORSTOP AT PERIMETER OF FRAME
- STRIKE OPENING
- FLOOR CLOSER
- PIVOTS AT TOP AND BOTTOM
- BOTTOM RAIL OF DOOR
- DOOR SILENCER
- WEATHERSTRIPPING
- THRESHOLD

DOOR NOMENCLATURE
3.4

- TRANSOM (FANLIGHT SHOWN)
- TRANSOM BAR
- CASING/TRIM
- DOOR FRAME
- BORROW LIGHT
- 4-1/2" MIN., TYP.
- 1-5/8" MIN., TYP.
- 1-3/8" THICKNESS, TYP.
- HINGED DOOR
- 8" MIN., TYP.
- 10", 12", 14", 15", 16", 18", COMMON SIZES

DOOR OPENING COMPONENTS
3.5

- CRIPPLE STUD
- HEADER
- DOUBLE STUD, WOOD OR METAL
- KING STUD
- TRIMMER STUD
- WALL FINISH MATERIAL
- HEAD
- JAMB
- STOP
- CAP
- BUCK
- ROUGH OPENING
- ROUGH OPENING 6'-10-1/2" FOR 6'-8" DOOR, TYP.
- THRESHOLD
- TRIM OR CASING
- PLINTH
- TRIM
- BASEBOARD

WOOD STOPS
3.6

PLANTED STOP (OR DOUBLE-RABBETED STOP)

RABBETED STOP

FRAME OPENING TYPES
3.7

FRAME WITHOUT STOPS FOR DOOR, OR FOR WINDOW

SPLAY

REVEAL

CASED

MEETING EDGE TYPE FOR DOUBLE-DOOR LEAVES
3.8

PARALLEL BEVEL

RABBETED

BEVEL

T-ASTRAGAL

STRAIGHT

ASTRAGAL

DESIGN CONSIDERATIONS

DOOR HANDING

The *hand*, or the *handing*, of a door refers to the standard method of describing the way a door swings. Handing is used in the industry to communicate how a door swings and the kind of hardware that must be supplied for a specific opening. Some hardware is specific to the hand of the door due to the bevel on the strike side of the door. Hardware that works on any hand of door is called *reversible* or *nonhanded*.

Handing is determined by standing on the outside of the door looking at the door. If the door hinges on the left and swings away, it is a left-hand door.

The *corridor side* is considered the outside of a room door, as is the *lobby side* of a door opening into a room or the room side of a closet door. When the distinction between outside and inside is not clear, the outside is considered the side of the door where the hinge is located.

HANDS OF DOORS
3.9

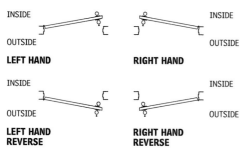

LEFT HAND   RIGHT HAND

LEFT HAND REVERSE   RIGHT HAND REVERSE

In the architectural door hardware industry, the position of the hinges on a door—right or left as viewed from outside the entryway—determines the handing.

SINGLE-ACTING DOOR
3.10

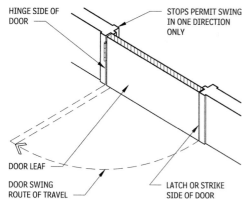

The single-acting door, the most common door type, has a leaf that operates in a swinging or sliding motion in only one direction.

DOUBLE-ACTING DOOR
3.11

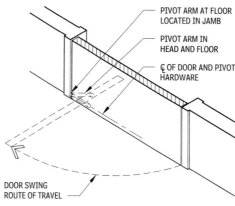

Double-acting doors have a leaf that operates in two directions. There is usually no stop present to restrict the motion of the door, but when the door can be stopped, it can be released mechanically to permit access in an emergency.

BALANCED DOOR
3.12

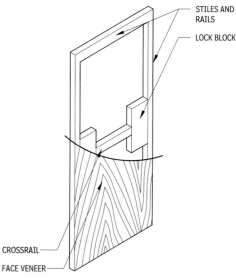

A balanced door is a single-action swinging door mounted on offset pivots. The leaf operates independently of the jamb, and the elliptical trajectory of the leaf requires less clear floor space than a conventional swinging door.

DOOR CORES

Working with door cores requires an understanding of these concepts:

- *Hollow-core versus solid-core doors*: Hollow-core doors are typically used in residential construction and for commercial doors subject only to light use. Institutional hollow-core doors, with heavier stiles and rails and with additional blocking, have increased strength and resistance to warping, but may cost as much as some solid-core doors. Solid-core doors are more secure, more durable, more resistant to warping, and allow less acoustical transmission. They are used in most institutional and commercial projects.
- *Door bevel*: Doors are beveled to allow the door to open past the jamb without binding. The standard bevel is 1/8 in. in 2 in. Generally, *unit locksets* are only available with the standard bevel; *cylindrical locksets* are available with either flat or standard bevel, and *mortise locksets* are available with bevels adjustable from flat to standard.
- *Bonded versus nonbonded cores*: Solid-core doors can either be bonded or nonbonded. With a bonded core, the stiles and rails are glued to the core material and the whole assembly is sanded as a unit before the faces are applied. This reduces the likelihood of telegraphing. With a nonbonded core, the elements can vary slightly in thickness and can telegraph noticeably through the faces. Five-ply doors are typically made with a bonded core, whereas seven-ply doors are made with a nonbonded core.

HOLLOW CORE
3.13

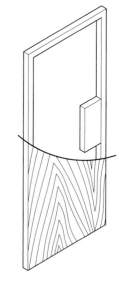

STANDARD

INSTITUTIONAL

Contributor:
Richard J. Vitullo, AIA, Oak Leaf Studio, Crownsville, Maryland.

PARTICLEBOARD CORE
3.14

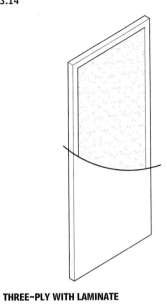

THREE-PLY WITH LAMINATE

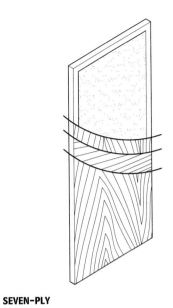

SEVEN-PLY

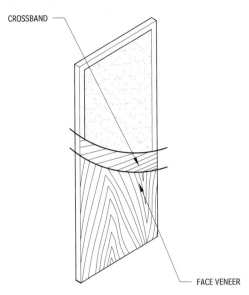

CROSSBAND

FACE VENEER

FIVE-PLY

STAVED LUMBER CORE
3.15

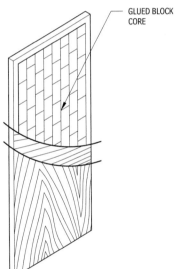

GLUED BLOCK CORE

FIVE-PLY

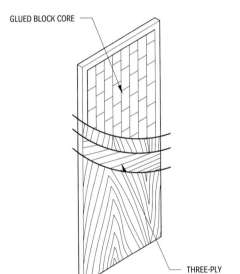

GLUED BLOCK CORE

THREE-PLY HARDWOOD SKIN

SEVEN-PLY

MINERAL COMPOSITION CORE
3.16

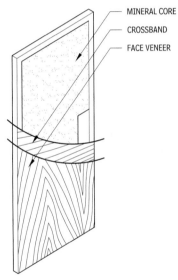

MINERAL CORE

CROSSBAND

FACE VENEER

FIVE-PLY

Figures 3.13 through 3.16 show the most common core types. Other options are available, including structural composite lumber (or laminated strand lumber). The following are specialized cores that may be desired, dependent on the project requirements:

- *Sound-insulating core:* A special core available in thicknesses of 1-3/4 in. and 2-1/4 in. The 1-3/4-in. core can provide a Sound Transmission Class (STC) rating of 36; the 2-1/4-in. core can achieve an STC of 42. Barrier faces are separated by a void or damping compound to keep the faces from vibrating in unison. Special stops, gaskets, and threshold devices are also required.
- *Lead-lined core:* A special core consisting of 1/32-in. to 1/2-in. continuous lead sheeting edge to edge inside the door construction. This material may be reinforced with lead bolts or glued.

DOOR SIZES

Both wood and hollow metal doors are available in a variety of standard widths. Custom doors can be fabricated in any size, but it is generally best to design around standard door sizes.

STANDARD DOOR SIZES
3.17

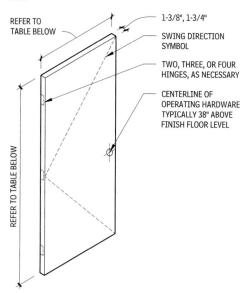

REFER TO TABLE BELOW

1-3/8", 1-3/4"

SWING DIRECTION SYMBOL

TWO, THREE, OR FOUR HINGES, AS NECESSARY

CENTERLINE OF OPERATING HARDWARE TYPICALLY 38" ABOVE FINISH FLOOR LEVEL

REFER TO TABLE BELOW

DOOR TYPE	DOOR THICK-NESS (IN.)	DOOR HEIGHT	DOOR WIDTH[a]
Wood or Metal	1- 3/8	6 ft-8 in	2 ft-0 in
		7 ft-0 in	2 ft-4 in.
		7 ft-2 in.	2 ft-6 in.
	1- 3/4	6 ft-8 in	2 ft-8 in.
		7 ft-0 in	2 ft-10 in.
		7 ft-2 in.	3 ft-0 in.
		8 ft-0 in.	3 ft-4 in.
			3 ft-6 in.
			3 ft-8 in.
			3 ft-10 in.
			4 ft-0 in

PANELS

Flat panels are typically three-ply hardwood or softwood. Raised panels are constructed of solid hardwood or softwood built up of two or more plies. Doors 1 ft-6 in. wide or less are one panel wide.

STILES AND RAILS

Panel doors consist of a framework of vertical (stile) and horizontal (rail) members that hold solid-wood or plywood panels, glass lights, or louvers in place.

The doors are made of solid or built-up stiles, rails, and vertical members (*muntins*), typically doweled per applicable standards. Dependent of location, common species include ponderosa pine, fir, hemlock, or spruce and hardwood veneers. Hardboard, metal, and plastic facings are available in various patterns.

STILE AND RAIL TERMINOLOGY
3.18

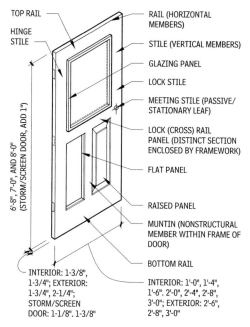

TOP RAIL

HINGE STILE

6'-8", 7'-0", AND 8'-0" (STORM/SCREEN DOOR, ADD 1")

RAIL (HORIZONTAL MEMBERS)

STILE (VERTICAL MEMBERS)

GLAZING PANEL

LOCK STILE

MEETING STILE (PASSIVE/STATIONARY LEAF)

LOCK (CROSS) RAIL PANEL (DISTINCT SECTION ENCLOSED BY FRAMEWORK)

FLAT PANEL

RAISED PANEL

MUNTIN (NONSTRUCTURAL MEMBER WITHIN FRAME OF DOOR)

BOTTOM RAIL

INTERIOR: 1-3/8", 1-3/4"; EXTERIOR: 1-3/4", 2-1/4"; STORM/SCREEN DOOR: 1-1/8". 1-3/8"

INTERIOR: 1'-0", 1'-4", 1'-6". 2'-0", 2'-4", 2'-8", 3'-0"; EXTERIOR: 2'-6", 2'-8", 3'-0"

STILE AND RAIL DOOR DETAILS
3.20

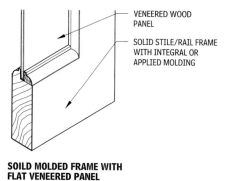

VENEERED WOOD PANEL

SOLID STILE/RAIL FRAME WITH INTEGRAL OR APPLIED MOLDING

SOILD MOLDED FRAME WITH FLAT VENEERED PANEL

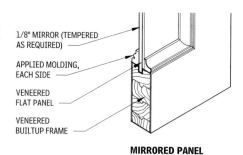

1/8" MIRROR (TEMPERED AS REQUIRED)

APPLIED MOLDING, EACH SIDE

VENEERED FLAT PANEL

VENEERED BUILTUP FRAME

MIRRORED PANEL

STILE AND RAIL RAISED PANEL
3.19

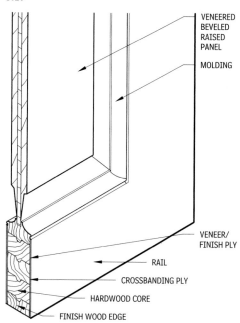

VENEERED BEVELED RAISED PANEL

MOLDING

VENEER/FINISH PLY

RAIL

CROSSBANDING PLY

HARDWOOD CORE

FINISH WOOD EDGE

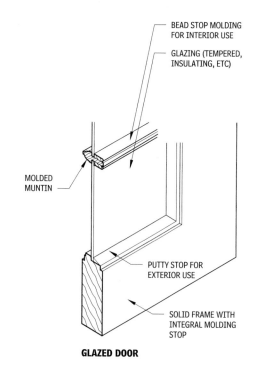

BEAD STOP MOLDING FOR INTERIOR USE

GLAZING (TEMPERED, INSULATING, ETC)

MOLDED MUNTIN

PUTTY STOP FOR EXTERIOR USE

SOLID FRAME WITH INTEGRAL MOLDING STOP

GLAZED DOOR

NOTE

3.17 a. Door width is independent of door height and thickness.

WOOD SLATS
3.21

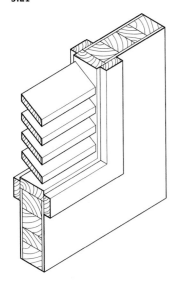

METAL CHEVRONS AND METAL FUSIBLE-LINK LOUVERS ALSO AVAILABLE FOR FIRE-RESISTANCE-RATED DOORS

WOOD CHEVRONS
3.22

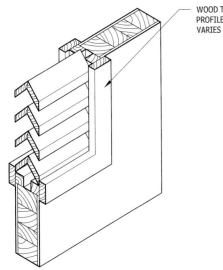

WOOD TRIM; PROFILE VARIES

- *Cylinder (of a lock)*: The cylindrical-shaped assembly containing the tumbler mechanism and the keyway, which can be actuated only by the correct keys.
- *Cylinder lock*: A lock in which the locking mechanism is controlled by a cylinder.
- *Deadbolt (of a lock)*: A lock bolt having no spring action or bevel, and which is operated by a key or turnpiece.
- *Door bolt*: A manually operated rod or bar attached to a door, providing means of locking.
- *Doorstop*: A device to stop the swing or movement of a door at a certain point.
- *Electric strike*: An electrical device that permits releasing of the door from a remote control.
- *Exit device*: A door-locking device that grants instant exit when someone presses a crossbar to release the locking bolt or latch.
- *Flush bolt*: A door bolt set flush with the face or edge of the door.
- *Lockset*: A lock, complete with trim, such as handles, escutcheons, or knobs.
- *Mortise*: A cavity made to receive a lock or other hardware; also the act of making such a cavity.
- *Mortise lock (or latch)*: A lock designed to be installed in a mortise rather than applied to the door's surface.

- *Rabbet*: The abutting edges of a pair of doors or windows, shaped to provide a tight fit.
- *Reversible lock*: A lock that, by reversing the latch bolt, may be used by any hand. On certain types of locks, other parts must also be changed.
- *Rose*: A trim plate attached to the door under the handle; sometimes acts as a handle bearing.
- *Shank (of a handle)*: The projecting stem of handle into which the spindle is fastened.
- *Spindle (of a handle)*: The bar or tube connected with the knob or lever handle that passes through the hub of the lock or otherwise engages the mechanism to transmit the handle action to the bolt(s).
- *Stop (of a lock)*: The button or other small device that serves to lock the latch bolt against the outside handle or thumb piece, or unlock it if locked. Another type holds the bolt retracted.
- *Strike*: A metal plate or box that is pierced or recessed to receive the bolt or latch when projected; sometimes called the *keeper*.
- *Three-point lock*: A device sometimes required on three-hour fire doors to lock the active leaf of a pair of doors at three points.

ACCESSIBLE DOOR
3.23

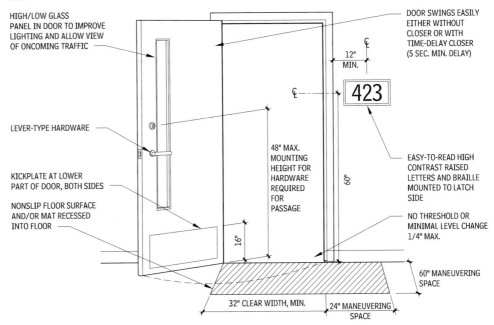

HIGH/LOW GLASS PANEL IN DOOR TO IMPROVE LIGHTING AND ALLOW VIEW OF ONCOMING TRAFFIC

LEVER-TYPE HARDWARE

KICKPLATE AT LOWER PART OF DOOR, BOTH SIDES

NONSLIP FLOOR SURFACE AND/OR MAT RECESSED INTO FLOOR

DOOR SWINGS EASILY EITHER WITHOUT CLOSER OR WITH TIME-DELAY CLOSER (5 SEC. MIN. DELAY)

12" MIN.

423

48" MAX. MOUNTING HEIGHT FOR HARDWARE REQUIRED FOR PASSAGE

60"

16"

EASY-TO-READ HIGH CONTRAST RAISED LETTERS AND BRAILLE MOUNTED TO LATCH SIDE

NO THRESHOLD OR MINIMAL LEVEL CHANGE 1/4" MAX.

60" MANEUVERING SPACE

32" CLEAR WIDTH, MIN.

24" MANEUVERING SPACE

GLAZING
Most building codes require all glass in doors to be safety glazed. Insulated safety glazing is available for increased thermal or acoustical performance.

BUILT-UP MEMBERS
The core and edge strip materials are similar to those used in flush doors. Face veneer is typically hardwood at 1/8-in. minimum thickness.

GLASS STOPS AND MUNTINS
Typical profiles used for trim work include cove, bead, or ovolo.

DOOR HARDWARE
Following are common terms used when discussing and defining door hardware:

- *Coordinator*: A device used on a pair of doors to ensure that the inactive leaf is permitted to close before the active leaf.

BOLT MECHANISMS
3.24

EXTENSION FLUSH BOLT   **MORTISE BOLT**

A mortise bolt is a miniature deadlock, with the bolt projected or retracted by a turn of the small knob. Face the outside of the door to determine its hand. The outside of the door is the *key side*, or that side which would be secured should a lock be used. This would usually be the exterior of an entrance door or the corridor side of an office door.

Contributor:
Richard J. Vitullo, AIA, Oak Leaf Studio, Crownsville, Maryland.

HINGE TYPE
3.25

TYPE OF BUILDING AND DOOR	DAILY FREQUENCY	HINGE TYPE
HIGH FREQUENCY		
Large department store entrance	5000	Heavyweight
Large office building entrance	4000	
School entrance	1250	
School toilet room	1250	
Store or bank entrance	500	
Office building toilet door	400	
AVERAGE FREQUENCY		
School corridor door	80	Standard-weight antifriction bearing (except on heavy doors)
Office building corridor door	75	
Store toilet door	60	
Dwelling entrance	40	
LOW FREQUENCY		
Dwelling toilet door	25	Plain bearing hinges may be used on light doors
Dwelling corridor door	10	
Dwelling closet door	6	

ELEMENTS OF A HINGE
3.26

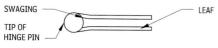

SWAGING
TIP OF HINGE PIN
LEAF

OPEN HINGE WIDTH (VARIES INDEPENDENT OF HEIGHT)

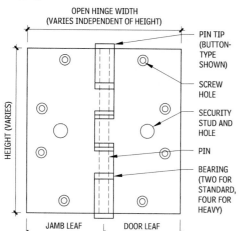

PIN TIP (BUTTON-TYPE SHOWN)
SCREW HOLE
SECURITY STUD AND HOLE
PIN
BEARING (TWO FOR STANDARD, FOUR FOR HEAVY)

HEIGHT (VARIES)

JAMB LEAF   DOOR LEAF

SPECIALTY HINGES
3.27

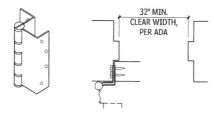

SWING CLEAR

32" MIN. CLEAR WIDTH, PER ADA

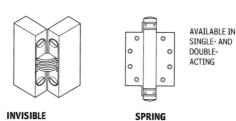

INVISIBLE

AVAILABLE IN SINGLE- AND DOUBLE-ACTING

SPRING

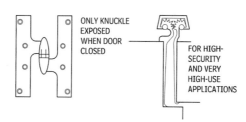

ONLY KNUCKLE EXPOSED WHEN DOOR CLOSED

FOR HIGH-SECURITY AND VERY HIGH-USE APPLICATIONS

OLIVE KNUCKLE   **CONTINUOUS GEAR**

HINGE HEIGHT
3.28

THICKNESS (IN.)	WIDTH OF DOORS (IN.)	HEIGHT OF HINGES (IN.)
Doors 3/4 to 1 (cabinet door)	Any	2-1/2
1-1/8 (screen door)	To 36	3
1-3/8	To 36	3-1/2
	Over 36	4
1-3/4	To 41	4-1/2
	Over 41	4-1/2 heavy
1-3/4 to 2-1/4	Any	5 heavy
TRANSOMS		
1-1/4 and 1-3/8		3
1-3/4		3-1/2
2, 2-1/4, and 2-1/2		4

TYPES OF HINGE PINS
3.29

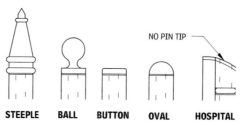

NO PIN TIP

STEEPLE   BALL   BUTTON   OVAL   HOSPITAL

TYPES OF HINGES
3.30

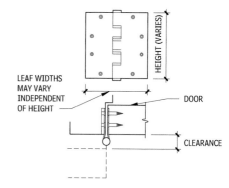

HEIGHT (VARIES)
LEAF WIDTHS MAY VARY INDEPENDENT OF HEIGHT
DOOR
CLEARANCE

FULL MORTISE

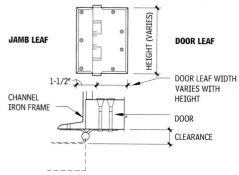

JAMB LEAF   HEIGHT (VARIES)   DOOR LEAF
1-1/2"
CHANNEL IRON FRAME
DOOR LEAF WIDTH VARIES WITH HEIGHT
DOOR
CLEARANCE

HALF-MORTISE

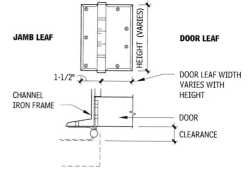

JAMB LEAF   HEIGHT (VARIES)   DOOR LEAF
1-1/2"
CHANNEL IRON FRAME
DOOR LEAF WIDTH VARIES WITH HEIGHT
DOOR
CLEARANCE

FULL SURFACE

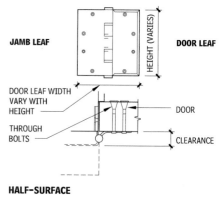

JAMB LEAF   HEIGHT (VARIES)   DOOR LEAF
DOOR LEAF WIDTH VARY WITH HEIGHT
THROUGH BOLTS
DOOR
CLEARANCE

HALF-SURFACE

NOTES

3.26 a. Swaging is a slight offset of the hinge at the barrel, which permits the leaves to come closer together and improves the operation and appearance of the door.
b. A leaf is one of the two attaching plates that when fastened together by the hinge pin from a complete hinge.
c. Bearings (ball, oil-impregnated, or antifriction) offer the best ease of operation and durability.
d. Nonrising pins are a feature of quality hinges. Also available are non-removable pins (NRP), with set screws, spun pins (FSP) without tips, and floating pins (FTP) with tips driven in both ends.
e. Close tolerances, especially in the pins, prevent excessive wear and are characteristic of high-quality, heavy-duty hinges.
f. A security stud, with matching hole in opposite leaf, is attached to a hinge to prevent door removal even if the pin is removed.
g. Hinges are available in brass, bronze, stainless steel, and carbon steel.

Contributor:
Richard J. Vitullo, AIA, Oak Leaf Studio, Crownsville, Maryland.

DOOR TYPES

This section discusses these common types of doors:

- Wood
- Hollow metal
- Glass
- Overhead coiling
- Coiling fire
- Floor, wall, and ceiling access

WOOD DOORS

Wood doors are available with *face materials* of wood veneer, composite veneer, high-density plastic laminate, medium-density overlay, and hardboard. Wood veneer on manufactured doors is available only in the species offered by the manufacturer, but custom doors may be faced with any veneer available on the world market. Both reference standards listed later in this discussion require face veneers of at least 1/50 in., but thicker veneers may be specified. Veneers may be rotary cut, plain sliced, quarter-sliced, or rift cut, and may be matched with random, slip, and book-matched methods.

- *Composite veneers* are manufactured by slicing sustainably grown hardwoods, and then vat-dying and pressing them into new, composite "logs." The composite logs are then sliced to form new veneers that replicate other natural woods. By using various colors of natural veneers and slicing angles of the composite log, a nearly unlimited number of simulated wood species and veneer patterns can be created. These veneers can be applied to doors in the same way as natural veneers.
- *Plastic laminate veneers* provide a durable surface and are available in hundreds of available colors and patterns.
- *Medium-density overlay (MDO)* faces are used to provide a smooth, paintable surface that resists grain raising and moisture. For this reason, they are often used for exterior doors.
- *Hardboard* is used with three-ply construction for interior doors that are to be painted, and as a lower-cost option for MDO.

WOOD DOOR STANDARDS

The two main wood door standards are WDMA, I.S. 1-A, "Wood Flush Doors," published by the Window and Door Manufacturers Association, and the "AWI Architectural Woodwork Quality Standards," published by the Architectural Woodwork Institute. Generally, the WDMA standard is used to specify standard manufacturers' doors, while the AWI standards are used to specify custom doors. The Woodwork Institute of California also publishes standards in its *Manual of Millwork*.

WOOD DOOR GRADES

Both WDMA and AWI standards classify doors into three grades: Premium, Custom, and Economy.

- *Premium grade* is specified when the highest level of materials, workmanship, and installation is required.
- *Custom grade* is suitable for most installations and is intended for high-quality work.
- *Economy grade* is the lowest grade and is intended for work where price is a primary factor.

Despite these common grade names, however, there are some differences between the WDMA and AWI standards, which should be recognized during project design.

WOOD DOORS
3.31

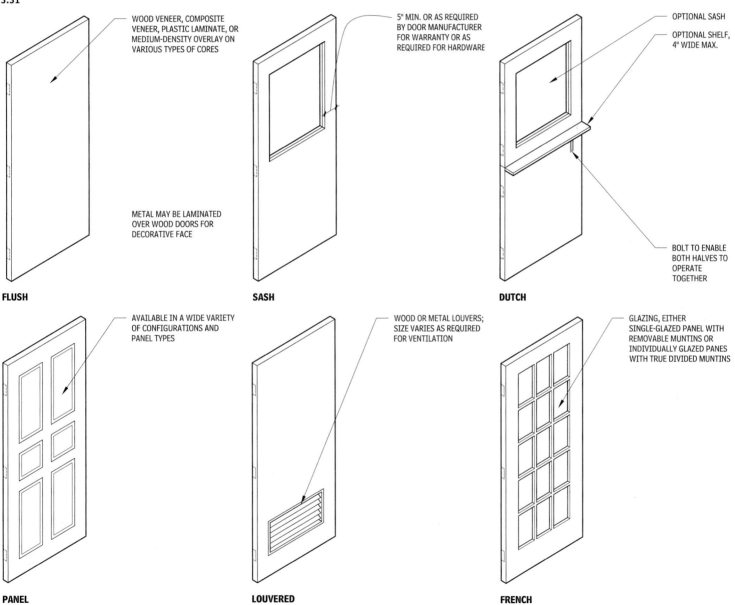

WOOD VENEER, COMPOSITE VENEER, PLASTIC LAMINATE, OR MEDIUM-DENSITY OVERLAY ON VARIOUS TYPES OF CORES

METAL MAY BE LAMINATED OVER WOOD DOORS FOR DECORATIVE FACE

FLUSH

5" MIN. OR AS REQUIRED BY DOOR MANUFACTURER FOR WARRANTY OR AS REQUIRED FOR HARDWARE

SASH

OPTIONAL SASH

OPTIONAL SHELF, 4" WIDE MAX.

BOLT TO ENABLE BOTH HALVES TO OPERATE TOGETHER

DUTCH

AVAILABLE IN A WIDE VARIETY OF CONFIGURATIONS AND PANEL TYPES

PANEL

WOOD OR METAL LOUVERS; SIZE VARIES AS REQUIRED FOR VENTILATION

LOUVERED

GLAZING, EITHER SINGLE-GLAZED PANEL WITH REMOVABLE MUNTINS OR INDIVIDUALLY GLAZED PANES WITH TRUE DIVIDED MUNTINS

FRENCH

WOOD DOOR FRAME INSTALLATION DETAILS

FRAME DETAILS IN WOOD WALL CONSTRUCTION
3.32

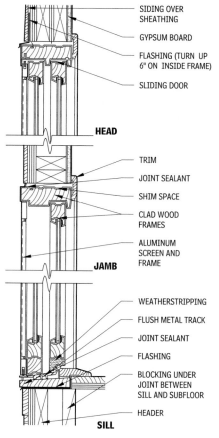

SIDING OVER SHEATHING
GYPSUM BOARD
FLASHING (TURN UP 6" ON INSIDE FRAME)
SLIDING DOOR

HEAD

TRIM
JOINT SEALANT
SHIM SPACE
CLAD WOOD FRAMES
ALUMINUM SCREEN AND FRAME

JAMB

WEATHERSTRIPPING
FLUSH METAL TRACK
JOINT SEALANT
FLASHING
BLOCKING UNDER JOINT BETWEEN SILL AND SUBFLOOR
HEADER

SILL

SLIDING DOOR IN WOOD FRAME

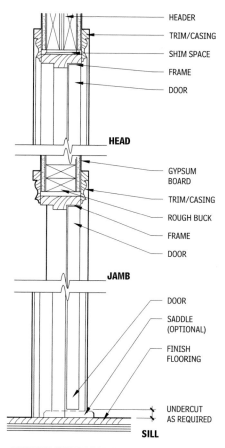

HEADER
TRIM/CASING
SHIM SPACE
FRAME
DOOR

HEAD

GYPSUM BOARD
TRIM/CASING
ROUGH BUCK
FRAME
DOOR

JAMB

DOOR
SADDLE (OPTIONAL)
FINISH FLOORING
UNDERCUT AS REQUIRED

SILL

INTERIOR SWING DOOR IN WOOD FRAME

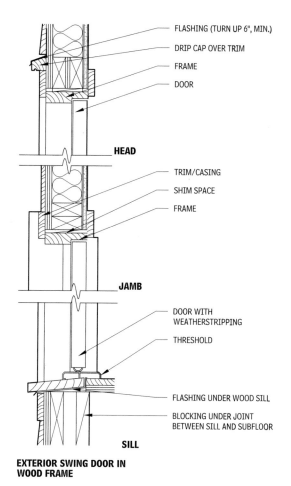

FLASHING (TURN UP 6", MIN.)
DRIP CAP OVER TRIM
FRAME
DOOR

HEAD

TRIM/CASING
SHIM SPACE
FRAME

JAMB

DOOR WITH WEATHERSTRIPPING
THRESHOLD
FLASHING UNDER WOOD SILL
BLOCKING UNDER JOINT BETWEEN SILL AND SUBFLOOR

SILL

EXTERIOR SWING DOOR IN WOOD FRAME

FRAME DETAILS IN MASONRY WALL CONSTRUCTION
3.33

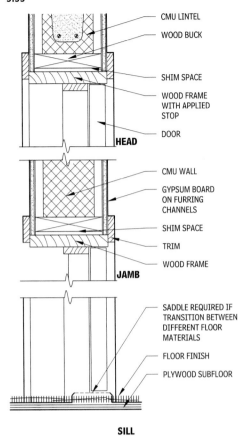

INTERIOR SWING DOOR IN MASONRY WALL

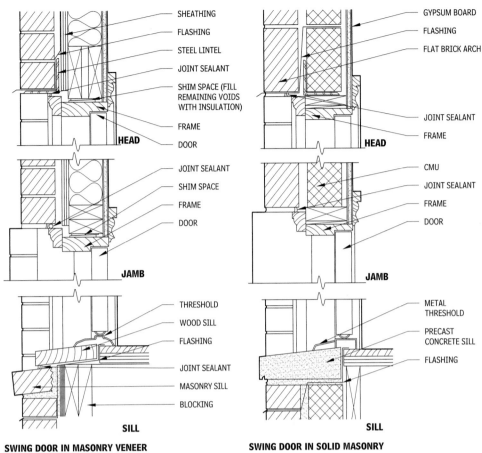

SWING DOOR IN MASONRY VENEER

SWING DOOR IN SOLID MASONRY

HOLLOW METAL DOORS

Hollow metal doors are doors constructed from sheet steel attached to various types of cores. They are generally used in steel frames, also constructed of sheet steel bent into various profiles.

To identify each of the several types of steel doors, the Steel Door Institute (SDI) uses a standard door design nomenclature. Many of these are shown in the accompanying Figure 3.34. Refer to SDI 106, "Recommended Standard Door Type Nomenclature," by the Steel Door Institute for a complete listing and for more information on door nomenclature and construction.

STEEL DOOR TYPES ACCORDING TO SDI
3.34

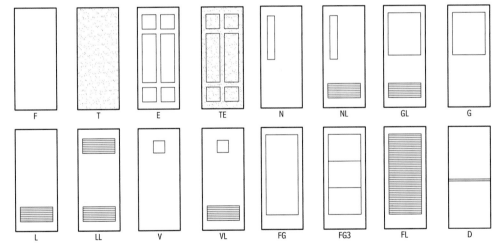

Nomenclature letter symbols and their meaning are:

F: Flush
T: Textured
E: Embossed
TE: Textured and embossed
L: Louvered (top or bottom)
LL: Louvered (top and bottom)
V: Vision lite
VL: Vision lite and louvered

N: Narrow lite
NL: Narrow lite and louvered
GL: Half glass and louvered
G: Half glass (several options available)
FG: Full glass
FG3: Full glass, three panes
FL: Full louver
D: Dutch door

Contributors:
Daniel F. C. Hayes, AIA, Washington, DC; Richard J. Vitullo, AIA, Oak Leaf Studio, Crownsville, Maryland.

HOLLOW METAL DOOR CONSTRUCTION
3.35

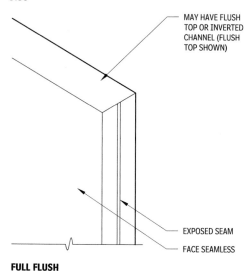

MAY HAVE FLUSH TOP OR INVERTED CHANNEL (FLUSH TOP SHOWN)

EXPOSED SEAM

FACE SEAMLESS

FULL FLUSH

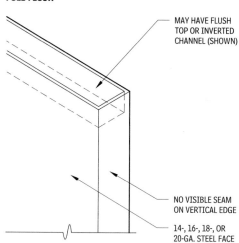

MAY HAVE FLUSH TOP OR INVERTED CHANNEL (SHOWN)

NO VISIBLE SEAM ON VERTICAL EDGE

14-, 16-, 18-, OR 20-GA. STEEL FACE

SEAMLESS

STANDARD STEEL DOOR GRADES AND MODELS
3.36

LEVEL		MODEL	FULL FLUSH OR SEAMLESS		
			GAUGE	IN.	CONSTRUCTION
I	Standard duty	1	20	0.032	Full flush
		2			Seamless
II	Heavy-duty	1	18	0.042	Full flush
		2			Seamless
III	Extra heavy-duty	1	16	0.053	Full flush
		2			Seamless
		3			Site and rail[a]
IV	Maximum duty	1	14	0.067	Full flush
		2			Seamless

Source: Steel Door Institute, SDI-108, Cleveland, Ohio

KNOCKDOWN FRAME CORNER CONSTRUCTION
3.37

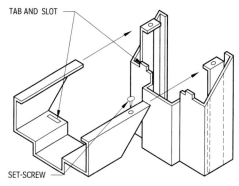

TAB AND SLOT

SET-SCREW

STANDARD HOLLOW METAL FRAMES
3.38

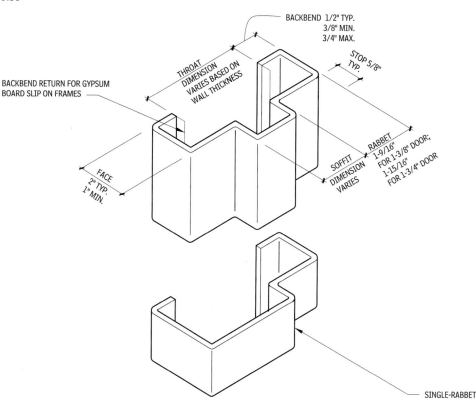

BACKBEND 1/2" TYP. 3/8" MIN. 3/4" MAX.

STOP 5/8" TYP.

THROAT DIMENSION VARIES BASED ON WALL THICKNESS

BACKBEND RETURN FOR GYPSUM BOARD SLIP ON FRAMES

RABBET 1-9/16" FOR 1-3/8" DOOR; 1-15/16" FOR 1-3/4" DOOR

FACE 2" TYP. 1" MIN.

SOFFIT DIMENSION VARIES

SINGLE-RABBET

Door and frame thicknesses should be indicated in minimum thickness of uncoated steel rather than by the older method of gauges. Common frame thicknesses include those listed in Table 3.66.

GAUGE/DECIMAL THICKNESS EQUIVELANTS
3.39

INCHES	GAUGE
0.042	18
0.053	16
0.067	14
0.093	12

FLUSH FRAME
3.40

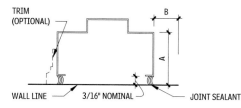

TRIM (OPTIONAL)

B

A

WALL LINE   3/16" NOMINAL   JOINT SEALANT

Use anchors appropriate for the type of wall construction; a minimum of three per jamb is required. Grout frame with mortar or plaster as used in wall. Caulk frame at wall. Dimension A is minimum 3 in. in area of pull or knob hardware. Trim may be used to cover joint at wall line. Check dimension B on hinge side for door swing greater than 90°.

WRAPAROUND FRAME
3.41

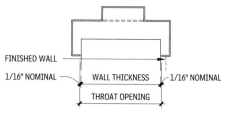

FINISHED WALL

1/16" NOMINAL   WALL THICKNESS   1/16" NOMINAL

THROAT OPENING

The basic wall dimension is less than the throat-opening dimension. Use anchors appropriate for the type of wall construction; a minimum of three per jamb is required. Fill frame with mortar or plaster as used in the wall. Grout frame at masonry wall.

NOTE

3.36 Stiles and rails are 16-gauge; flush panels, when specified, are 18-gauge.

STANDARD STEEL FRAME
3.42

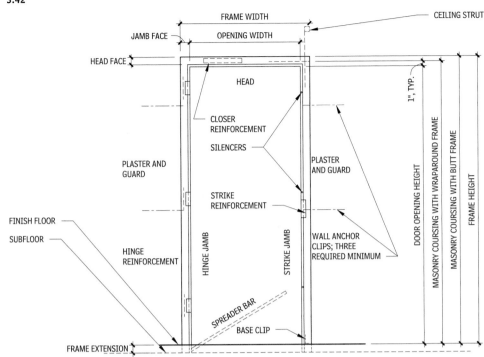

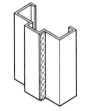

FRAME WIDTH

JAMB FACE

OPENING WIDTH

CEILING STRUT

HEAD FACE

HEAD

CLOSER REINFORCEMENT

SILENCERS

PLASTER AND GUARD

PLASTER AND GUARD

STRIKE REINFORCEMENT

FINISH FLOOR

SUBFLOOR

HINGE REINFORCEMENT

HINGE JAMB

STRIKE JAMB

WALL ANCHOR CLIPS; THREE REQUIRED MINIMUM

1", TYP.

DOOR OPENING HEIGHT

MASONRY COURSING WITH WRAPAROUND FRAME

MASONRY COURSING WITH BUTT FRAME

FRAME HEIGHT

SPREADER BAR

BASE CLIP

FRAME EXTENSION

FLOOR ANCHORS
3.43

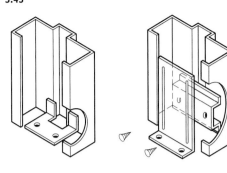

GLASS DOOR CONFIGURATIONS
3.45

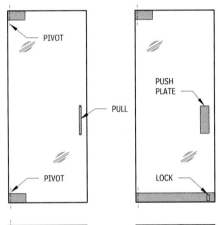

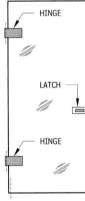

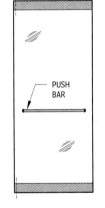

PIVOT

PULL

PIVOT

PUSH PLATE

LOCK

PUSH BAR

HINGE

LATCH

HINGE

HOLLOW METAL FRAME STOPS AND SEALS
3.44

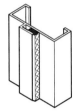

SDI DOOR LEVELS
SDI 108, "Recommended Selection and Usage Guide for Standard Steel Doors," provides recommendations for levels of doors within a variety of building types and usages. In general, these levels should be used:

- *Level 1 Standard Duty*: Doors for interior use in residences, dormitories, and hotels, except for entrances; individual office doors in office buildings and other commercial structures; and closets in most buildings.
- *Level 2 Heavy Duty*: Doors for entrances to apartments, dormitories, and hotels, stairways, toilet rooms, hospital patient and operating rooms, and school classrooms.
- *Level 3 Extra Heavy Duty*: Entrance and stairwell doors in most buildings; in commercial and industrial buildings and schools, except closets; and in hospital kitchens.
- *Level 4 Maximum Duty*: Doors for high-traffic entrances and stairwells in commercial and industrial buildings and entrances requiring increased security. Entrance and gymnasium doors in schools.

HOLLOW METAL FRAME FINISHES
Hollow metal frames should receive at least one shop coat of rust-inhibitive primer before delivery to the job site. In very corrosive atmospheres such as saltwater beach locations, is it advisable to have doors and frames hot-dipped-galvanized for additional protection. If doors are used in severe, humid environments or in humid areas such as pools or kitchens, a galvanized coating should be used either the hot-dip or electrolytic process.

Frames with factory-applied paint finishes in various colors are available from several manufacturers.

GLASS DOORS
Glass doors are constructed primarily of glass, with fittings to hold the pivots and other hardware. Their strength depends on the glass rather than the framing. Glass doors are generally constructed of 1/2-in. or 3/4-in. tempered glass.

Glass doors may be installed within an opening or as part of an all-glass entrance system. If used alone, glass doors may be set within a wall opening with or without a frame, or they can be installed between glass sidelights. The same type of fitting used on the door is generally used for sidelights. Although jamb frames of aluminum, wood, or ornamental metal can be used, they are not necessary, and the glass sidelights can be butted directly to the partition.

The minimum configuration for a glass door requires some type of door pull and a corner fitting at the top and bottom (sometimes called the *shoe*) to hold the pivots. Some manufacturers provide hinge fittings that clamp on the glass and support the door in much the same way as a standard hinged door.

If the door is used for egress, the local building code may require the use of special hardware that allows the door to be locked from the outside but still allows the door to be unlatched and opened from the inside with a single push on a push bar. Glass doors are heavy and may require a power operator or a balanced door system.

FIRE-RESISTANCE-RATED OPENINGS

Fire-resistance-rated assemblies for openings, used to protect against the spread of fire and smoke, consist of a fire-rated door or window with frame, hardware, and accessories, including gasketing. Each component is crucial to the overall performance of the assembly as a fire barrier. Choices to be made regarding the enclosure of openings in fire-rated walls include:

- Fire-resistance rated wall requirements
- Size of opening
- Means of egress
  - Required size per occupancy
  - Quantity and location
  - Direction of egress flow and operation of enclosure
  - Hardware requirements
  - Window egress requirements
- Materials and finishes
- Security
- Visibility and glazing

DEFINITIONS

The terms defined here are commonly used in relation to fire-resistance-rated openings:

- *Automatic:* Providing a function without the necessity of human intervention.
- *Fire barrier:* A continuous membrane, either vertical or horizontal (e.g., a wall, floor, or ceiling assembly), that is designed and constructed with a specified fire-resistance rating to limit the spread of fire and restrict the movement of smoke.
- *Fire resistance:* The property of materials or their assemblies that prevents or retards the passage of excessive heat, hot gas, or flames under conditions of use.
- *Fire-resistance rating:* The time, in minutes or hours, that materials or assemblies have withstood fire exposure in accordance with the test procedure of NFPA 252.
- *Labeled:* Equipment or materials marked with the label, symbol, or other identifying mark of an organization concerned with product evaluation, and acceptable to the local jurisdiction. This organization must periodically inspect the production of labeled equipment.

The manufacturer, by labeling the product, indicates compliance in a specified manner with appropriate standards or performance.

- *Noncombustible:* A material that, in the form in which it is used and under the conditions anticipated, will not aid combustion or add appreciable heat to an ambient fire.
- *Self-closing:* As applied to a fire door or other protective opening, self-closing means the door is normally closed and is equipped with an approved device that will ensure closure after the door has been opened.
- *Smoke barrier:* A continuous membrane, either vertical or horizontal (e.g., a wall, floor, or ceiling assembly), that is designed and constructed to restrict the movement of smoke. A smoke barrier may or may not have a fire-resistance rating.

FIRE PROTECTION CRITERIA

NFPA 80, "Standard for Fire Doors and Fire Windows," is a consensus standard that establishes minimum criteria for installing and maintaining assemblies and devices used to protect openings in walls, ceilings, and floors from the spread of fire and smoke. The degree of fire protection (in hours) required for a given opening is referenced in the building codes and the Life Safety Code (NFPA 101). Fire doors are classified by hourly references determined by testing done in accordance with NFPA 252, "Standard Method of Fire Tests of Door Assemblies" (also known as UL 10B). Further information is available in the NFPA's *Fire Protection Handbook*.

TYPES OF OPENINGS

The hourly protection rating for openings depends on the use of the barrier—whether as exit enclosures, vertical openings in buildings, building separation walls, corridor walls, smoke barriers, and hazardous locations. In most codes, class designations have been replaced by hour classifications such as these:

- *4-hour and 3-hour openings:* Located in fire walls or in walls that divide a single building into fire areas.
- *1-1/2-hour and 1-hour openings:* Located in multistory vertical communication enclosures and in 2-hour-rated partitions providing horizontal fire separations.
- *3/4-hour and 20-minute openings:* Located in walls or partitions between rooms and corridors with a fire-resistance rating of one hour or less.

FIRE-RESISTANCE-RATED STEEL FRAME ELEVATIONS
3.46

OPTIONAL MULLION
VARIES
10'-0" MAX.
4'-0" MAX.   4'-0" MAX.

PAIR

SOLID PANEL (3-, 1 1/2-, 1-, AND 3/4-HR) WIRE GLASS
MAX. GLASS AREA 1296 SQ FT
80 SQ FT MAX. OPENING
10'-0" MAX.
8'-0" MAX.
8'-0" MAX.

PAIR WITH TRANSOM BAR

40 SQ FT MAX. OPENING
11'-2" MAX.
9'-0" MAX.
4'-0" MAX.

SINGLE FLUSH TRANSOM

DOOR OPENINGS FOR MEANS OF EGRESS
3.47

40 SQ. FT. MAX. OPENING
CLEAR HEIGHT 6'-8" MIN. (10'-0" MAX.)
CLEAR WIDTH (4'-0" MAX.)
CLEARANCE BOTTOM OF FRAME TO FLOOR, 3/4" MAX.

WINDOW EGRESS REQUIREMENTS
3.48

20" MIN. CLEAR OPENING
OPERABLE SASH
24" MIN. CLEAR OPENING
44" MAX. ABOVE FLOOR

TESTING LABELS
3.49

DOOR LABEL

FRAME LABEL

Various agencies test and rate fire door and window units and assemblies. Manufacturers locate metal labels in accessible, but concealed, locations—the hinge edge of doors, for example. These labels must remain in place, unpainted, uncovered, and unaltered.

NOTES

3.47 The minimum width of each door opening must be sufficient for the occupant load it serves. Verify the following general guidelines for door width with local codes: (1) dwelling units that are not required to be accessible or adaptable—29-3/4 in.; (2) hospital and other medical facilities—36 in.; (3) standard openings—32 in.

3.48 When required for egress, such as in sleeping areas in residences, windows must meet the following criteria: (1) clear opening per sash must be a minimum of 5.7 sq ft; (2) bars, grilles, or screens must be releasable from inside without use of tools or key; (3) windows opening onto fire escapes have additional requirements, so refer to codes; (4) check with manufacturers for integral release hardware options for awning, casement, pivot, or other windows; (5) double-hung window units with fully removable sash that do not require special tools, force, or knowledge to operate may offer greater flexibility in unit selection to meet size requirements for egress openings, so verify with manufacturers and code officials.

Contributors:
National Fire Protection Association, Quincy, Massachusetts; Daniel F. C. Hayes, AIA, Washington, DC.

FIRE-RESISTANCE-RATED DOOR CLASSIFICATIONS
3.50

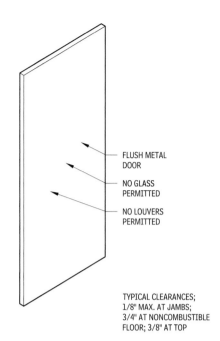

FLUSH METAL DOOR

NO GLASS PERMITTED

NO LOUVERS PERMITTED

TYPICAL CLEARANCES;
1/8" MAX. AT JAMBS;
3/4" AT NONCOMBUSTIBLE FLOOR; 3/8" AT TOP

4-HOUR/3-HOUR FIRE-RESISTANCE-RATING

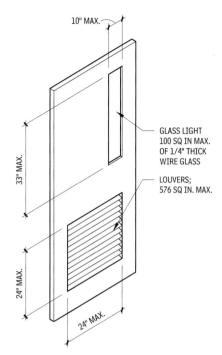

10" MAX.

33" MAX.

24" MAX.

24" MAX.

GLASS LIGHT 100 SQ IN MAX. OF 1/4" THICK WIRE GLASS

LOUVERS; 576 SQ IN. MAX.

1-1/2" - HOUR/1-HOUR FIRE-RESISTANCE-RATING

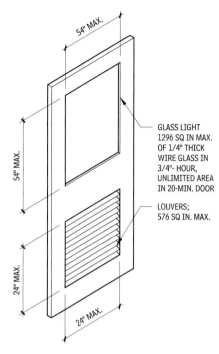

54" MAX.

54" MAX.

24" MAX.

24" MAX.

GLASS LIGHT 1296 SQ IN MAX. OF 1/4" THICK WIRE GLASS IN 3/4"- HOUR, UNLIMITED AREA IN 20-MIN. DOOR

LOUVERS; 576 SQ IN. MAX.

3/4-HOUR/20-MIN. FIRE-RESISTANCE-RATING

TYPES OF FRAMES

Fire-rated frames can be assembled at the factory or in the field. Frames must be adequately anchored at the jambs and floor according to the manufacturer's specifications. Codes require doors to be installed in accordance with NFPA 80; Section 2-5, "Frames," indicates only labeled frames are to be used.

- *Light-gauge metal frame*: Head and jamb members with or without transom panel made from aluminum (45-minute maximum rating) or light-gauge steel (1-1/2-hour maximum rating); installed over finished wall
- *Pressed steel (hollow metal)*: Head and jamb members with or without solid or glazed transoms or sidelights made from 18-gauge or heavier steel (3-hour maximum rating); required for most metal doors

FRAMES FOR FIRE-RESISTANCE-RATED OPENINGS
3.51

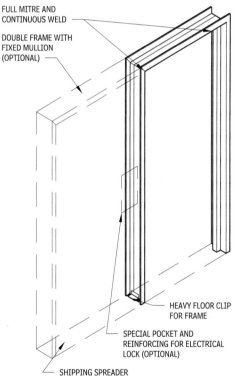

FULL MITRE AND CONTINUOUS WELD

DOUBLE FRAME WITH FIXED MULLION (OPTIONAL)

HEAVY FLOOR CLIP FOR FRAME

SPECIAL POCKET AND REINFORCING FOR ELECTRICAL LOCK (OPTIONAL)

SHIPPING SPREADER

GLAZED FIRE-RESISTANCE-RATED OPENING
3.52

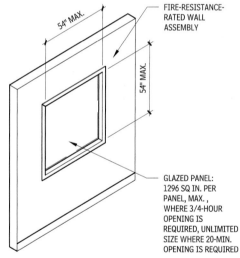

FIRE-RESISTANCE-RATED WALL ASSEMBLY

54" MAX.

54" MAX.

GLAZED PANEL: 1296 SQ IN. PER PANEL, MAX. , WHERE 3/4-HOUR OPENING IS REQUIRED, UNLIMITED SIZE WHERE 20-MIN. OPENING IS REQUIRED

Glazed openings in fire-resistance-rated walls must conform to size limitations using rated glass and other approved material requirements. Multiple panels are permitted, but the aggregate area of all panels and openings must not exceed 25 percent of the wall surface. Refer to specific codes for details.

NOTES

3.50 a. All hinges or pivots must be steel. Two hinges are required on doors up to 5 ft in height; an additional hinge is required for each additional 2 ft-6 in. of door height or fraction thereof. The same requirement holds for pivots.
b. Wired glass 1/4-in. thick is the most common material used for glass lights, but other materials have been listed and approved for installation.
c. Consult all authorities with jurisdiction before installation of glass lights and louvers.

d. Fusible-link/automatic closing louvers are permitted in fire-rated doors with restrictions; they are not permitted in smoke-barrier doors.

Contributors:
National Fire Protection Association, Quincy, Massachusetts; Daniel F. C. Hayes, AIA, Washington, DC.

STAIRS

DESIGN CONSIDERATIONS

TREADS, RISERS, AND NOSINGS

Riser and tread dimensions must be uniform for the entire length of the stair. Americans with Disabilities Act (ADA)—Architectural Barriers Act (ABA) Guidelines for Buildings and Facilities; the Americans with Disabilities Act Accessibility Guidelines (ADAAG); and the International Building Code (IBC), which references the ICC/ANSI A117.1 Accessible and Usable Buildings and Facilities all indicate a minimum tread dimension of 11 in., nosing to nosing; a maximum riser height of 7 in.; and a maximum overhang dimension of 1-1/2 in. Open risers are not permitted on stairs accessible to persons with disabilities.

OSHA standards require tread finishes to be "reasonably slip resistant" by using nosing material with a slip-resistant finish. Treads without nosings are acceptable, provided that the tread is serrated or other slip-resistant design. Uniform color and texture are recommended for clear delineation of edges.

Nosings without abrupt edges that project no more than 1-1/2 in. beyond the edge of the riser are recommended. A safe stair uses a 1/2-in.-radius abrasive nosing that is firmly anchored to the tread, with no overhangs and a clearly visible edge.

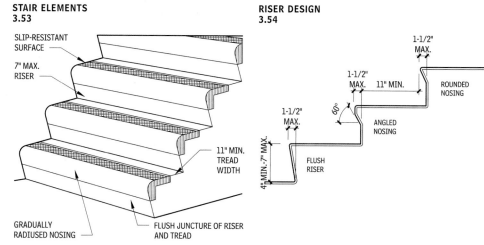

STAIR ELEMENTS
3.53

SLIP-RESISTANT SURFACE

7" MAX. RISER

11" MIN. TREAD WIDTH

GRADUALLY RADIUSED NOSING

FLUSH JUNCTURE OF RISER AND TREAD

RISER DESIGN
3.54

1-1/2" MAX.

ROUNDED NOSING

1-1/2" MAX.

11" MIN.

ANGLED NOSING

60°

1-1/2" MAX.

4" MIN.-7" MAX.

FLUSH RISER

Contributor:
Walter Moberg, Moberg Fireplaces, Inc., Portland, Oregon.

STAIR CONSTRUCTION

CONCRETE STAIRS

A common method of stair construction is the utilization of concrete, which can be cast-in-place or precast concrete.

U-TYPE CONCRETE STAIRS
3.55

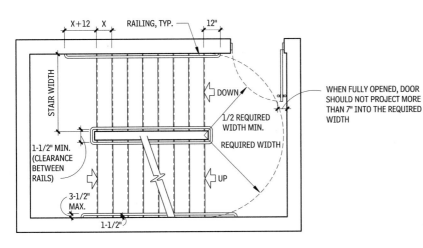

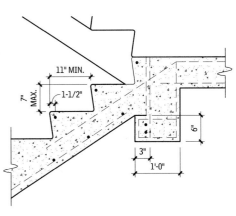

DETAIL A

PLAN

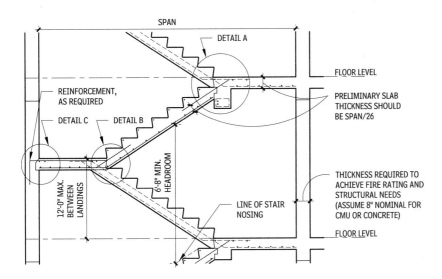

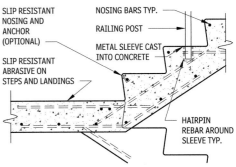

DETAIL B

SECTION

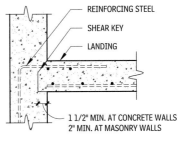

DETAIL C

FREESTANDING CONCRETE STAIR
3.56

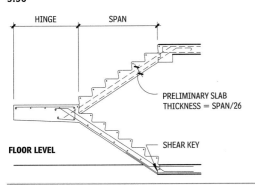

FLOOR LEVEL

NOTES

3.55 a. Consult structural engineer for reinforcing steel placement.
b. Verify required dimensions and clearances for code compliance.
3.56 Limit hinge dimension to requirements of stair.

Contributors:
Krommehoek/McKeown and Associates, San Diego, California;
Karlsberger and Companies, Columbus, Ohio.

HELICOIDAL CONCRETE STAIR
3.57

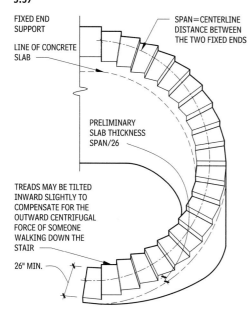

FIXED END SUPPORT

LINE OF CONCRETE SLAB

SPAN=CENTERLINE DISTANCE BETWEEN THE TWO FIXED ENDS

PRELIMINARY SLAB THICKNESS SPAN/26

TREADS MAY BE TILTED INWARD SLIGHTLY TO COMPENSATE FOR THE OUTWARD CENTRIFUGAL FORCE OF SOMEONE WALKING DOWN THE STAIR

26" MIN.

CANTILEVER CONCRETE STAIR
3.58

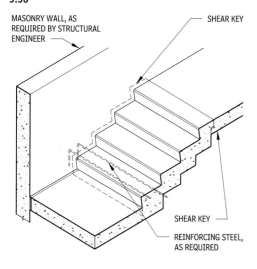

MASONRY WALL, AS REQUIRED BY STRUCTURAL ENGINEER

SHEAR KEY

SHEAR KEY

REINFORCING STEEL, AS REQUIRED

METAL STAIRS

Metal stairs are frequently constructed of steel, and fabricated in the shop to fit the required dimensions.

Treads and landings are may be filled with 1-1/2 to 2 in. of concrete. Many finish materials can then be applied to the concrete. Balusters are anchored by welding, bolting, or screwing to the stringers. Glass balusters are often anchored into a special U-shaped channel, which is attached to the edge of the stringer. A similar detail can be used for glass railings.

DESIGN GUIDELINES FOR METAL STAIRS

General design guidelines for metal stairs are itemized in the following lists.

WIDTH OF STAIR
- Dwelling stairs: minimum 36-in. treads
- Public exit stairs: minimum 44-in. treads
- Rescue assistance area (ADA): 48 in. between handrails

TREADS
- Dwellings: 9 in. minimum (nosing to nosing)
- Other (ADA): 11 in. minimum (nosing to nosing)
- Uniform depth within one flight

RISERS
- Dwellings: 8-1/4 in. maximum
- Other: minimum 4 in.; maximum 7 in.
- Uniform height within one flight

NOSING
- Maximum 1-1/2 in. with 60° under nosing; maximum 1/2-in. radius at edge.
- Minimum: none required

STAIR RAILS
- Height in dwellings: 36 in.
- Height in exit stairs: 42 in.
- Arrange rails so that a sphere 4 in. in diameter cannot be passed through.
- Arrange rails to discourage climbing.
- Concentrated load nonconcurrently applied at the top rail must be 200 lbf in vertical downward and horizontal direction. The test loads are applicable for railings with supports not more than 8 ft apart.

HANDRAILS
- Dwellings: required on one side only
- Other : required on both sides
- Height: 34 to 38 in.
- Grip surface: 1-1/4 to 1-1/2 in.
- Clearance at wall: 1-1/2 in.
- Projecting or recessed
- Extension at top of run: 12 in.
- Extension at bottom of run: 12 in., plus depth of tread
- When a guardrail more than 38 in. high is used, a separate handrail should be installed.
- Nothing should interrupt the continuous sliding of hands.

REGULATORS AND STANDARDS
- ADA-ABA ASTM, ICC/ANSI, NFPA, OSHA, ADAAS, and local building codes.

METAL PAN STAIR SECTION
3.59

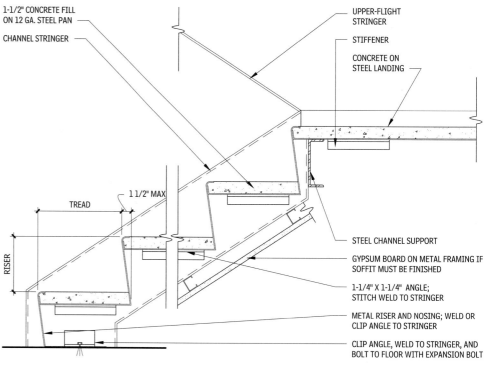

1-1/2" CONCRETE FILL ON 12 GA. STEEL PAN

CHANNEL STRINGER

TREAD

1 1/2" MAX

RISER

UPPER-FLIGHT STRINGER

STIFFENER

CONCRETE ON STEEL LANDING

STEEL CHANNEL SUPPORT

GYPSUM BOARD ON METAL FRAMING IF SOFFIT MUST BE FINISHED

1-1/4" X 1-1/4" ANGLE; STITCH WELD TO STRINGER

METAL RISER AND NOSING; WELD OR CLIP ANGLE TO STRINGER

CLIP ANGLE, WELD TO STRINGER, AND BOLT TO FLOOR WITH EXPANSION BOLT

NOTES

3.57 Use of helicoidal concrete stairs depends on a fixed-end support and small support deflection.

3.58 a. Reinforcing steel must develop full bond in masonry walls and have full development length in concrete walls.

b. Detail of shear key is similar to Figure 3.56 Detail C.

Contributors:
Krommenhoek/McKeown and Associates, San Diego, California; Karlsberger and Companies, Columbus, Ohio; Thomas A. Sabol, PhD, SE, Englekirk & Sabol Consulting Structural Engineers, Inc., Los Angeles, California

WOOD STAIRS

Wood stairs used in private, residential applications usually are not governed by the ADA; however, wood stairs in commercial facilities and places of public accommodation must conform to the accessibility guidelines adopted in the local jurisdiction.

The following are general recommendations; verify specific requirements that may vary from these:

- A minimum interior stair width of 36 in. should be provided.
- Minimum headroom is 6 ft-8 in. as measured vertically from a diagonal line connecting tread nosings to the underside of the finished ceiling or stair landing directly above the stair run.
- Recommended headroom is 7 ft.

Only handrails and stair stringers may project into the required width of a stair. Use the following guidelines:

- The maximum handrail projection is 3-1/2 in.
- The maximum stringer projection is 1-1/2 in.
- The width of a landing or platform should be at least as wide as the stair.
- The maximum vertical rise of a stair between landings is 12.
- Riser height should be between 4 in. minimum and 7 in. maximum.
- Tread depth should be 11 in. minimum, measured from riser to riser or nosing to nosing.
- Variation in adjacent treads or risers should not exceed 3/16 in. The maximum variation allowed in the tread depth or riser height within a flight of stairs is 3/8 in.
- Nosings project 1-1/2 in. maximum.

CLOSED RISER WOOD RISER DETAIL
3.60

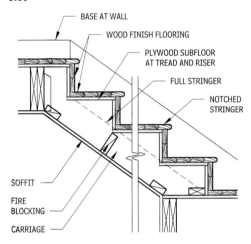

WOOD STAIR SECTION
3.61

DIMENSION LUMBER STAIR
3.62

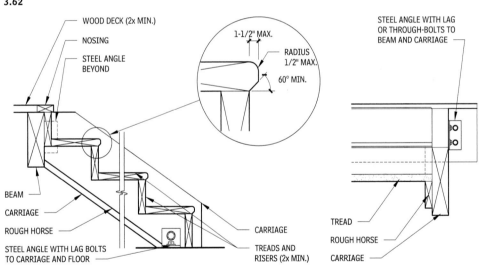

Contributors:
The Bumgardner Architects, Seattle, Washington; Janet B. Rankin, AIA, Rippeteau Architects, PC, Washington, DC.

CLOSED RISER WOOD STAIR WITH CARPET FINISH
3.63

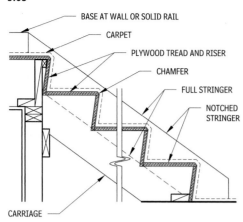

- BASE AT WALL OR SOLID RAIL
- CARPET
- PLYWOOD TREAD AND RISER
- CHAMFER
- FULL STRINGER
- NOTCHED STRINGER
- CARRIAGE

OPEN RISER WOOD STAIR
3.64

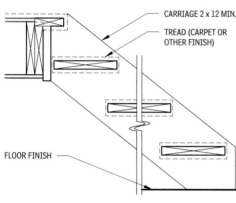

- CARRIAGE 2 x 12 MIN.
- TREAD (CARPET OR OTHER FINISH)
- FLOOR FINISH

Open riser stairs do not comply with code accessibility requirements for non-residential applications.

TREADS AND RISERS AT HOUSED STRINGER
3.65

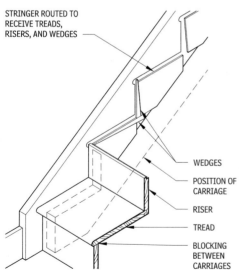

- STRINGER ROUTED TO RECEIVE TREADS, RISERS, AND WEDGES
- WEDGES
- POSITION OF CARRIAGE
- RISER
- TREAD
- BLOCKING BETWEEN CARRIAGES

WOOD NOSINGS
3.66

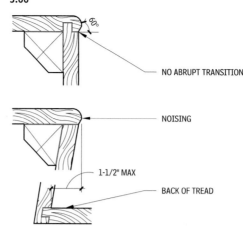

- 60°
- NO ABRUPT TRANSITION
- NOISING
- 1-1/2" MAX
- BACK OF TREAD

ALTERNATE STAIR TYPES

Alternate stair types include *winding stairs*, *circular stairs*, and *spiral stairs*. Generally, the IBC does not allow these types of stairs to be used for egress except within private dwelling units. Spiral stairs may also be used as egress from a space not more than 250 sq ft and serving not more than five occupants. When these alternate stair types are allowed, they must meet the minimum dimensional requirements of the codes.

- Riser heights for circular and winding stairs must meet the code maximums of 7 in. for commercial stairs and 7-3/4 in. for residential stairs.
- Riser heights for spiral stairs must be such that clear headroom of 78 in. is provided.

Spiral stairs are composed of wedge-shaped treads supported from a central column, usually 4 in. in diameter. Fabricated spiral stairs are commonly made from steel.

Spiral stairs are available in custom sizes. To meet building code requirements as a means of egress, stairs must be at least 5 ft in diameter to meet the 26-in. clear width requirement, assuming a 4-in. center post. Larger diameters increase perceived comfort, ease of use, and safety. Treads are available with 22-1/2°, 27°, and 30° angle treads. The most common are 27° and 30° tread angles because these can maintain at least a 7-1/2-in. dimension 12 in. from the center pole. Tread selection depends on the riser height desired, the total rise, the headroom clearance requirements, and the top and bottom riser orientation.

Critical minimum headroom dimensions should be calculated based on a three-quarter turn of the stair, even if a full 360° turn is being used to travel the full rise.

Design considerations for circular stairs are similar to those for spiral stairs. A fabricated steel tube serves as a one-piece stringer to which treads are bolted or welded. Risers may be open or closed.

SPIRAL STAIR
3.67

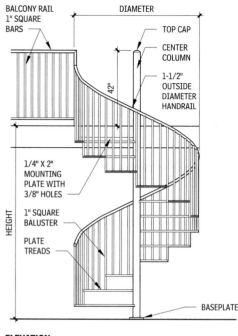

- BALCONY RAIL 1" SQUARE BARS
- DIAMETER
- TOP CAP
- CENTER COLUMN
- 1-1/2" OUTSIDE DIAMETER HANDRAIL
- 42"
- 1/4" X 2" MOUNTING PLATE WITH 3/8" HOLES
- 1" SQUARE BALUSTER
- PLATE TREADS
- HEIGHT
- BASEPLATE

ELEVATION

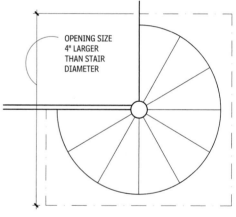

- OPENING SIZE 4" LARGER THAN STAIR DIAMETER

PLAN

Contributors:
The Bumgardner Architects, Seattle, Washington; Janet B. Rankin, AIA;
Rippeteau Architects, PC, Washington, DC.

CIRCULAR STAIR
3.68

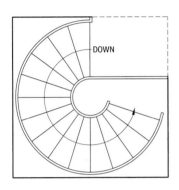

HANDRAILS

BALUSTER

BALCONY RAIL

DIAMETER 60", 80", 102", OR 112", TYP.

HEIGHT

STRINGERS

ELEVATION

DOWN

PLAN

SPIRAL STAIR FRAMING DIMENSIONS (IN.)
3.69

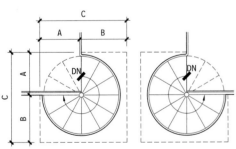

PLAN: RIGHT-HAND UP   **PLAN: LEFT-HAND UP**

STAIR DIAMETER									
	40	48	52	60	64	72	76	88	96
A	20	24	26	30	32	36	38	44	48
B	24	28	30	34	36	40	42	48	52
C	44	52	56	64	68	76	80	92	100

SPIRAL STAIR DESIGN DIMENSIONS (IN.)
3.70

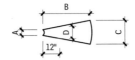

DIAMETER	40	48	52	60	64	72	76	88	96
Center column	4	4	4	4	4	4	4	6-5/8	6-5/8
Tread detail A	4	4	4	4	4	4	4	6-5/8	6-5/8
Tread detail B	18	22	24	28	32	34	36	42	48
27° tread detail C	9-1/4	11-1/8	12-1/8	13-15/16	14-7/8	16-3/4	17-5/8	20-1/2	22-5/16
27° tread detail D	7-5/8	8	8-1/4	8-3/8	8-1/2	8-5/8	8-3/4	10	10-1/2
30° tread detail C	10-1/2	12-9/16	13-5/8	15-3/4	16-3/4	18-7/8	19-7/8	231/8	25-1/8
30° tread detail D	8-1/2	8-5/8	8-3/4	8-7/8	9	9-1/4	9-3/8	11-3/8	11-1/2
Landing size	22	26	28	32	34	38	40	46	52

22-1/2" TREAD SPIRAL STAIRS: FLOOR-TO-FLOOR TREAD COUNT
3.71

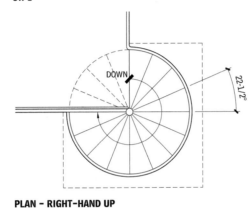

PLAN – RIGHT-HAND UP

FINISH FLOOR HEIGHT (IN.)	NUMBER OF TREADS	CIRCLE CIRCUMFERENCE
84–91	12	270°
92–98	13	292-1/2°
99–105	14	315°
106–112	15	337-1/2°
113–119	16	360°
120–126	17	382-1/2°
127–133	18	405°
134–140	19	427-1/2°
141–147	20	450°
148–154	21	472-1/2°

27" TREAD SPIRAL STAIRS: FLOOR-TO-FLOOR TREAD COUNT
3.72

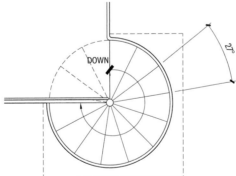

PLAN – RIGHT-HAND UP

FINISH FLOOR HEIGHT (IN.)	NUMBER OF TREADS	CIRCLE CIRCUMFERENCE
90–96	11	297°
97–104	12	324°
105–112	13	351°
113–120	14	375°
121–128	15	405°
129–136	16	432°
137–144	17	459°
145–152	18	486°
153–160	19	513°
161–168	20	540°

NOTES

3.69 a. For spiral stairs, larger diameters increase perceived comfort, ease of use, and safety.

b. The most common tread and platform materials are steel (regular and galvanized), aluminum, and wood. Steel and aluminum can be smooth plate, checker plate, pan type, and bar. A variety of hardwoods can be used, although many manufacturers use steel substructures to support the wood finish surface.

c. Refer to local and national codes for dimension and construction requirements and allowable uses.

3.71 There are 16 treads per circle and the riser height is 6-1/2 to 7 in.
3.72 There are 13-1/2 treads per circle and the riser height is 7-1/2 to 8 in.

Contributors:
David Ballast, AIA, Architectural Research Consulting, Denver, Colorado; Sukamorn Prasithrathsint, Rhode Island School of Design, Providence, Rhode Island; David W. Johnson, Washington, DC; The Bumgardner Architects, Seattle, Washington; Janet B. Rankin, AIA, Rippeteau Architects, PC, Washington, DC; Charles A. Szoradi, AIA, Washington, DC.

30° TREAD SPIRAL STAIRS: FLOOR-TO-FLOOR TREAD COUNT
3.73

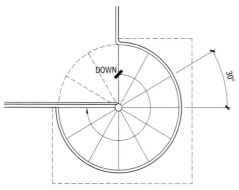

PLAN – RIGHT–HAND UP

FINISH FLOOR HEIGHT (IN.)	NUMBER OF TREADS	CIRCLE CIRCUMFERENCE
85–95	9	270°
96–104	10	300°
105–114	11	330°
115–123	12	360°
124–133	13	390°
134–142	14	420°
143–152	15	450°
153–161	16	480°
162–171	17	510°
172–180	18	540°

STAIR FINISHES

STAIR HANDRAILS

Design recommendations for stair handrails include:

- The height of a handrail above the stair nosings should be 34 to 38 in.. The guardrail height at landings should be 36 or 42 in.; check local code.

- Design handrails should be easy to grip and fit the hand. Recommended diameter is 1-1/4 to 1-1/2 in. for round handrails and a similar size for an elliptical or rounded square-edge section. Handrails should be structurally designed in consideration of both downward (vertical) and lateral (horizontal) thrust loads.
- Extensions of the handrail at the top and bottom of a stair may affect total length of required run, so verify extensions required by codes when designing a stair.

ELEVATION OF FACE STRINGER
3.74

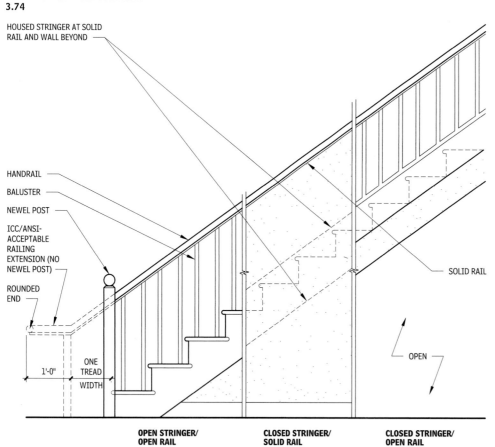

HOUSED STRINGER AT SOLID RAIL AND WALL BEYOND

HANDRAIL

BALUSTER

NEWEL POST

ICC/ANSI-ACCEPTABLE RAILING EXTENSION (NO NEWEL POST)

ROUNDED END

1'-0"

ONE TREAD WIDTH

SOLID RAIL

OPEN

OPEN STRINGER/ OPEN RAIL　　　**CLOSED STRINGER/ SOLID RAIL**　　　**CLOSED STRINGER/ OPEN RAIL**

WALL SECTION STAIRS
3.75

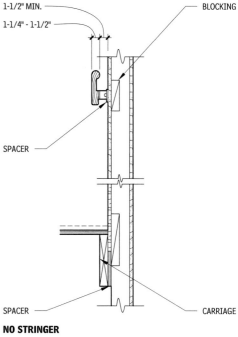

1-1/2" MIN.

1-1/4" - 1-1/2"

BLOCKING

SPACER

SPACER

CARRIAGE

NO STRINGER

1-1/2" MIN.

1-1/4" - 1-1/2"

BLOCKING

METAL BRACKET

SPACER

STRINGER

CARRIAGE

FULL STRINGER

SEE ALSO

Metal Stair Nosing

NOTE

3.73 There are 12 treads per circle and the riser height is 8-1/2 to 9-1/2 in.

Contributors:
David W. Johnson; Washington, DC; The Bumgardner Architects, Seattle, Washington; Janet B. Rankin, AIA, Rippeteau Architects, PC, Washington, DC.

INTERIOR FINISHES

WALL FINISHES

PLASTER WALL FINISHES

For centuries, prior to the advent of gypsum board, plaster was the primary interior wall and ceiling finish. Conventional plaster provides superior wear resistance to gypsum board assemblies, and is preferred to attain a uniform, monolithic surface; however, plaster finishes are more labor-intensive, require greater skill, and can take as long as two days to cure, compared to gypsum board assemblies. For these reasons, plaster finishes are most commonly used in restoration to match existing conditions and in high-end installations.

Three-coat plaster applications are required on all metal lath and on edge-supported gypsum lath used in ceilings. In addition, three-coat applications are preferred, although two-coat applications are acceptable where gypsum lath is properly supported, and on masonry plaster bases such as porous brick, clay tiles, and rough concrete masonry units.

Keene's cement plaster is a specialty finish coat of gypsum plaster primarily used where a smooth, dense, vandal-resistant, white finish is desired.

Thickness, proportion of mixes of various plastering materials, and finishes vary. Methods of application also vary widely, depending on local traditions and innovations promoted by the industry.

PLASTER TERMINOLOGY
When working with plaster, it is important to know these terms:

- *Basecoat*: A plaster coat applied before finish coat, scratch coat, and blow coats in three-coat plaster.
- *Brown coat*: In three-coat plaster, the second coat; in two-coat plaster, the first coat.
- *Fibered plaster*: Gypsum plaster containing fibers of hair, glass, nylon, or sisal.
- *Finish coat*: The final coat of plaster, which provides the decorative surface.
- *Furring*: Generally, channels or Z-shapes attached to the underlying wall (or structure for ceilings) for attaching gypsum or metal lath while allowing an airspace. Often used on cementitious substrate, resilient furring is used to reduce sound transmission.
- *Gypsum*: Hydrous calcium sulphate, a natural mineral in crystalline form.
- *Gypsum lath*: A base for plaster; a sheet having a gypsum core, faced with paper. Also perforated for interior use.
- *Hydrated lime*: Quicklime mixed with water, at the site, to form a lime putty.
- *Lime*: Obtained by burning various types of limestone, consisting of oxides or hydroxides of calcium and magnesium.
- *Lime plaster*: Basecoat plaster of hydrated lime and an aggregate.
- *Neat plaster*: Basecoat plaster, fibered or unfibered, used for site-mixing with aggregates.
- *Perlite*: Siliceious volcanic glass containing silica and alumina, expanded by heat for use as a lightweight plaster aggregate.
- *Plaster*: Cementitious material or combination of cementitious materials and aggregate, which when mixed with water forms a plastic mass that sets and hardens when applied to a surface.
- *Portland cement*: Manufactured combination of limestone and an argillaceous substance for exterior or wet-atmosphere applications.
- *Scratch coat*: In three-coat plastering, the first coat, which is then scratched to provide a bond for the second, or brown, coat.
- *Stucco portland cement*: Plaster used in exterior application. This plaster requires a waterset and must not be applied to a smooth dense surface or gypsum lath; it requires control joints, and cannot have a Keene's cement-lime putty finish.
- *Three-coat plaster*: Preferred application for all substrates; required over metal lath.
- *Two-coat plaster*: Acceptable on lath and on the interior face of rough concrete block, clay tile, or porous brick.
- *Vermiculite*: Micaceous mineral of silica, magnesium, and alumina oxides made up in a series of parallel plates, or laminae, and expanded by heat for use as a lightweight plaster aggregate.

METAL LATH TYPES
3.76

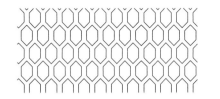

FRONT VIEW   SIDE VIEW

DIAMOND MESH EXPANDED METAL

FRONT VIEW   SIDE VIEW

SELF-FURRING DIAMOND MESH

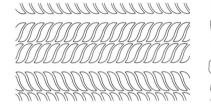

FRONT VIEW   SIDE VIEW

RIB-EXPANDED METAL

JOINT REINFORCEMENT
3.77

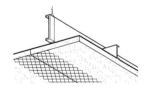

CORNER LATH

4" OR 6"

STRIP LATH

CORNER BEADS
3.78

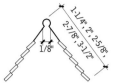

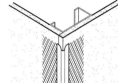

EXPANDED WING

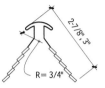

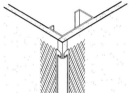

BULLNOSE

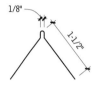

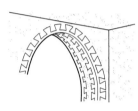

ARCH OR FLEXIBLE

BASE SCREEDS
3.79

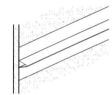

SOLID

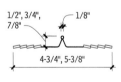

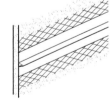

EXPANDED WING

Contributor:
The Marmom Mok Partnership, San Antonio, Texas.

EXPANSION SCREEDS
3.80

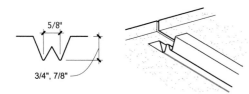

5/8"
3/4", 7/8"

3/4", 1", 1-1/2", 2", 2-1/2"
3/4", 7/8"

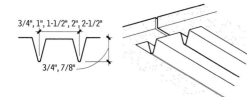

CONTROL JOINTS
3.81

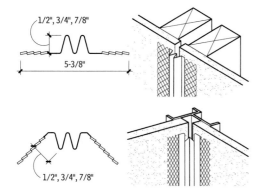

1/2", 3/4", 7/8"
5-3/8"

1/2", 3/4", 7/8"

METAL STUD PARTITION WITH PLASTER AND LATH
3.82

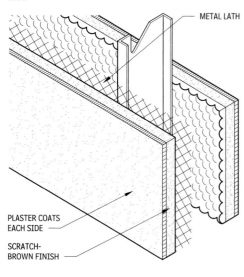

METAL LATH

PLASTER COATS
EACH SIDE

SCRATCH-
BROWN FINISH

SUSPENDED PLASTER CEILING DETAILS
3.83

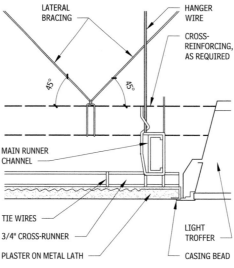

LATERAL
BRACING

HANGER
WIRE

CROSS-
REINFORCING,
AS REQUIRED

45°   45°

MAIN RUNNER
CHANNEL

TIE WIRES

3/4" CROSS-RUNNER

PLASTER ON METAL LATH

LIGHT
TROFFER

CASING BEAD

SOFFIT

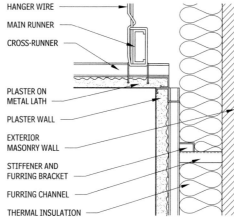

HANGER WIRE

MAIN RUNNER

CROSS-RUNNER

PLASTER ON
METAL LATH

PLASTER WALL

EXTERIOR
MASONRY WALL

STIFFENER AND
FURRING BRACKET

FURRING CHANNEL

THERMAL INSULATION

When interior walls are furred from an exterior masonry wall and insulated, the ceiling should stop short of the furred space. This allows wall insulation to continue above the ceiling line to ceiling or roof insulation, thus forming a complete insulation envelope. In a suspension system that abuts masonry walls, provide 1-in. clearance between the ends of main runners or furring channels and the wall face.

PLASTER OVER METAL RIB LATH
3.84

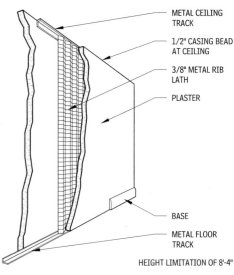

METAL CEILING
TRACK

1/2" CASING BEAD
AT CEILING

3/8" METAL RIB
LATH

PLASTER

BASE

METAL FLOOR
TRACK

HEIGHT LIMITATION OF 8'-4"

CUTAWAY WALL SECTION

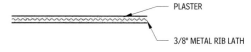

PLASTER

3/8" METAL RIB LATH

PLAN

PLASTER OVER METAL LATH AND CHANNEL STUDS
3.85

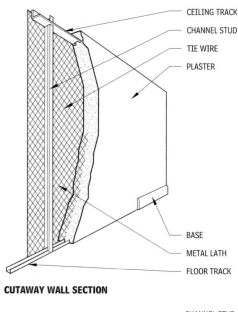

CEILING TRACK

CHANNEL STUD

TIE WIRE

PLASTER

BASE

METAL LATH

FLOOR TRACK

CUTAWAY WALL SECTION

CHANNEL STUD

METAL LATH

PLASTER

PLAN

Contributors:
The Marmom Mok Partnership, San Antonio, Texas; James E. Phillips, AIA, Enwright Associates, Inc., Greenville, South Carolina; United States Gypsum Company, Chicago, Illinois; Walter H. Sobel, FAIA, Walter H. Sobel and Associates, Chicago, Illinois.

PLASTER OVER SOLID GYPSUM LATH
3.86

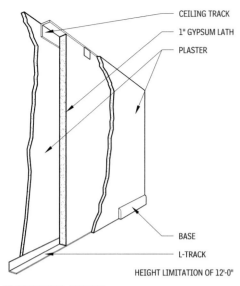

- CEILING TRACK
- 1" GYPSUM LATH
- PLASTER
- BASE
- L-TRACK
- HEIGHT LIMITATION OF 12'-0"

CUTAWAY WALL SECTION

- PLASTER
- PLASTER
- GYPSUM LATH

PLAN

PLASTER OVER METAL OR GYPSUM LATH AND METAL STUDS
3.87

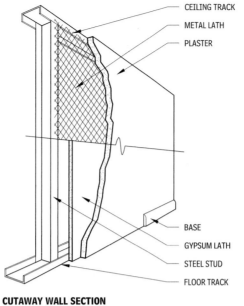

- CEILING TRACK
- METAL LATH
- PLASTER
- BASE
- GYPSUM LATH
- STEEL STUD
- FLOOR TRACK

CUTAWAY WALL SECTION

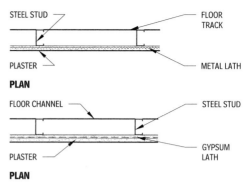

- STEEL STUD
- FLOOR TRACK
- PLASTER
- METAL LATH

PLAN

- FLOOR CHANNEL
- STEEL STUD
- PLASTER
- GYPSUM LATH

PLAN

FURRED AND SUSPENSION SYSTEM COMPONENT SELECTION DETAIL
3.93

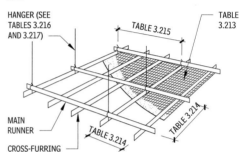

- HANGER (SEE TABLES 3.216 AND 3.217)
- TABLE 3.215
- TABLE 3.213
- MAIN RUNNER
- CROSS-FURRING
- TABLE 3.214
- TABLE 3.214
- TABLE 3.214

DIRECTIONS FOR USING TABLES

Follow these steps to use Tables 3.88 through 3.92:

1. Select lath and plaster assembly.
2. Determine the spacing of the cross-furring channels from Table 3.88, "Lath Span."
3. Determine the spacing of the main runners from Table 3.89, "Maximum Spacing between Runners."
4. Determine hanger support spacing for the main runner from Table 3.89, "Maximum Spacing between Hangers."
5. Calculate the area of ceiling supported per hanger.
6. Select the hanger type from Table 3.91, "Hanger Selection."
7. Select the tie wire size from Table 3.92 "Tie Wire Selection."

LATH SPAN
3.88

	LATH TYPE (IN.)	WEIGHT (LB PER SQ FT)	SPAN (IN.)
Gypsum lath	3/8 plain	1.5	16
	1/2 plain	2.0	16
	1/2 veneer	1.8	16
	5/8 veneer	2.25	16
	3/8 perforated	1.4	16
Metal lath	Diamond mesh	0.27	12
	Diamond mesh	0.38	16
	1/8 flat rib	0.31	12
	1/8 flat rib	0.38	19
	3/8 flat rib	0.38	24

MAXIMUM SPACING BETWEEN RUNNERS
3.89

CROSS FURRING TYPE	CROSS-FURRING SPACING (IN.)			
	12	16	19	24
1/4" diameter pencil rod	24	—	—	—
3/8" diameter pencil rod	30	—	24	—
3/4" CRC, HRC (0.3 lb/ft)	—	54	42	36
1" HRC (0.41 lb/ft)	60	—	54	48

MAXIMUM SPACING BETWEEN HANGERS
3.90

MAIN RUNNER TYPE	MAIN RUNNER SPACING (FT)				
	3	3.5	4	4.5	5
3/4" CRC (0.3 lb/ft)	2	—	—	—	—
1-1/2" CRC (0.3 lb/ft)	3a	—	—	—	—
1-1/2" CRC (0.875 lb/ft)	4	3.5	3	—	—
1-1/2" HRC (1.12 lb/ft)	—	—	—	4	—
2" CRC (0.59 lb/ft)	—	—	5	—	—
2" HRC (1.26 lb/ft)	—	—	—	—	5
1/2 × 1/2 × 3/16"	—	5	—	—	—

HANGER SELECTION
3.91

MAXIMUM CEILING AREA (SQ FT)	MINIMUM HANGER SIZE
12	9-gauge galvanized wire
16	8-gauge galvanized wire
18	3/16" steel rod[a]
25	1/4" steel rod[a]
25	3/16" × 1" steel flat[a]

TIE WIRE SELECTION
3.92

	SUPPORT	MAXIMUM CEILING AREA (SQ FT)	MINIMUM HANGER SIZE
Cross-furring		8	14-gauge wire
		8	16-gauge wire (two loops)
Main runners	Single hangers between beams	8	12-gauge wire
		12	10-gauge wire
		16	8-gauge wire
	Double-wire loops at supports	8	14-gauge wire
		12	12-gauge wire
		16	11-gauge wire

NOTES

3.89 CRC is the abbreviation for cold-rolled channel; HRC is the abbreviation for hot-rolled channel.
3.90 a. For concrete construction only, a 10-gauge wire may be inserted in the joint before concrete is poured.
3.91 a. Rods galvanized or painted with rust-inhibitive paint and galvanized straps are recommended under severe moisture conditions.

Contributors:
United States Gypsum Company, Chicago, Illinois; Walter H. Sobel, FAIA, Walter H. Sobel and Associates, Chicago, Illinois; James E. Phillips, AIA, Enwright Associates, Inc., Greenville, South Carolina.

PAINTS AND STAINS
3.94

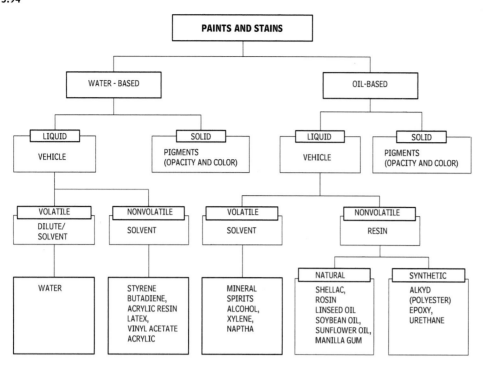

PRIMERS

Primers make a surface more paintable by providing improved adhesion for coatings. They are selected in relation to the characteristics of the selected topcoat, and serve the following functions:

- Conceal the substrate surface so that the existing coating color does not "read" through.
- Provide a barrier to prevent moisture from destroying the paint bond.
- Bind the substrate surface with the topcoat.
- Limit the paint absorption of a porous substrate, such as a skim coat of plaster.
- Recondition old paint to receive future paint coatings.
- Act as a rust inhibitor.

ALKYD PAINTS

The solvent-thinned resin in alkyd paint is made from synthetic oils. Alkyd resins are oil-modified polyesters made primarily from alcohol and acid. They are the most common paint resin. Alkyd paints are faster drying, harder, and more durable, and have better color-retention properties than oil-based paints. They are easy to apply, are washable, and have fewer odors than other paints using solvent thinners. However, alkyd paints have poor resistance to alkaline surfaces, such as masonry, and should not be used unless these substrates are properly primed.

LATEX PAINTS

Most water-based paints are referred to as *latex paint*. Latex paints have very little odor and a fast drying time. Their water-base thinner makes them easy to apply, clean up, and discard. Latex paints are porous, meaning that when applied a latex coating retains microscopic openings that allow it to breathe. Adhesion failure is prevented because moisture that might become trapped beneath the paint's surface can evaporate through these openings. The disadvantage of latex paints is that they have a greater blistering tendency when high levels of tinting color are present.

OIL-BASED PAINTS

The solvent-thinned resin in oil-based paint is made from natural oils, such as linseed oil (from flax seed), soya oil (from soybeans), and tung oil (from china wood tree fruit).

CATALYZED EPOXY PAINTS

Catalyzed epoxy coatings resist chemicals, solvents, stains, physical abrasion, traffic, and cleaning materials. They have good adhesion and color retention. Catalyzed epoxies come in two parts: resin and catalyst. They have a limited "pot life," hence are required to be mixed just prior to use. When applied to a substrate, a chemical action occurs that causes a dense hard film to form, similar to baked enamel. Adequate ventilation must be provided during and after application.

Three types of catalyzed epoxies are commonly used in commercial interiors:

- *Polyester epoxies*, which produce a tough glossy surface.
- *Polyamide epoxies*, which provide a flexible but durable film.
- *Urethane epoxies*, which are the most versatile of the epoxy coatings.

EPOXY ESTER PAINTS

Epoxy esters are similar to catalyzed epoxy, but have no pot-life restrictions and are packaged like conventional paint. The paint film occurs due to oxidation, rather than a chemical reaction triggered by a catalyst. Epoxy esters are less durable than catalyzed epoxies.

INTUMESCENT PAINTS

Intumescent paints slow the rate at which fire spreads by delaying the ignition of the surface that has been coated. They are used on combustible materials such as wood to achieve the required flame-spread ratings. These paints delay but do not prevent a fire from spreading. Fire-retardant paints are intumescent and protect the substrate from burning by swelling to form a charred layer of blisters when exposed to extremely high heat.

Intumescent paint is a foamlike material made with either a water-based or solvent-based thinner. Requisite fire ratings are achieved with this material based on the number of coatings applied to the substrate at a prescribed thickness. Intumescent paint manufacturers certify painters to ensure that their products are correctly applied.

FIRE-RETARDANT PAINTS

Fire-retardant paints resist the spread of fire by not contributing to the flame. They are, however, less effective at controlling the spread of fire than intumescent coatings.

MULTICOLOR COATINGS

Multicolor coatings are durable and scratch-resistant. They add a three-dimensional quality to a surface, similar to hand-sponge techniques. Multicolor coatings can be water-thinned or solvent-thinned. Traditional solvent-thinned multicolor coatings are composed of tiny bubbles of different sizes and colors suspended in a nonpigmented solution. The separated beads of pigment remain separate until they are spray-applied. They burst upon impact with the surface.

STAINS

Stains made from dyes dissolved in either drying oil or water provide translucent or transparent coatings for wood. Oil-based stains use drying oil made from various plants. The oil dries by absorbing oxygen from the surface, and the air creates a tough elastic film that protects wood. Wood surfaces can be filled before staining in order to affect surface porousness and smoothness, but fillers may cause stains to be absorbed unevenly. Stain may be applied with a brush, spray, roller, or rag pad.

WALL COVERINGS

Wall coverings offer improved durability over paint finishes while providing texture and pattern to the wall surface. Wall covering types include vinyl, textile, wallpapers, fiberglass, and wood veneer. The most popular wall covering for commercial use is vinyl, favored for its affordability and durability.

VINYL WALL COVERINGS

The two vinyl wall covering manufacturing processes are calendering and plastisol methods:

- *Calendering* squeezes liquid vinyl over a series of hot metal rollers, flattening the compound into a sheet. The vinyl is then laminated under heat and pressure to a backing material. Calendered vinyl wall covering is harder, tougher, and usually much thicker than wall covering manufactured by the plastisol method.
- The *plastisol* method spreads liquid vinyl onto a backing material, which are then fused together under high temperatures. Plastisol technology is used primarily for residential wall coverings.

TEXTILE WALL COVERINGS

Not all textiles are suitable for use as wall coverings, nor are textile wall coverings appropriate in applications where wear resistance is a concern.

Textiles must be backcoated to be installed as wall covering. The backing provides a barrier to prevent adhesives from bleeding through and ruining the finish face of the fabric. Backings also provide the dimensional stability required for a textile to withstand the stretching and smoothing operations of wall covering installation. Two types of backcoating treatments are paper backing and acrylic latex backing:

- *Paper backing* involves laminating paper to the reverse side of the textile, which stiffens the textile for easier installation. The textile assumes properties similar to those of wallpaper.
- *Acrylic latex coating* involves stretching the textile in a frame and applying a latex compound. The textile retains some of its inherent flexibility but is much less dimensionally stable than paper-backed textiles and may increase installation costs. Latex backings do, however, improve ravel resistance and seam slippage. Often, due to its lack of rigidity, the adhesive used with this wall covering must be applied to the wall, rather than to the back of the wall covering. Consequently, this process is more labor-intensive and requires a higher degree of skill.

FIBERGLASS WALL COVERINGS

Fiberglass wall covering is composed of fiberglass yarns adhered together. Fiberglass wall covering is inherently flame-resistant and is suitable for use in reinforcing fragile or deteriorating wall surfaces. It is permeable, making it intrinsically mold- and mildew-resistant. Fiberglass wall coverings must be painted after installation; and, typically, a latex paint is selected to maintain the breathability of the wall. This wall covering type provides a textured pattern only, not a color.

WOOD VENEER WALL COVERINGS

Wood veneer wall covering is made by bonding veneer slices, about 1/64-in. thick, to a woven backing material. The resulting wall covering is thin enough to be pliable along the grain lines but too thick to be flexible in the horizontal direction (perpendicular to the wood grain). The inherent flexibility of wood veneer wall covering makes installation easy around columns and other curved surfaces.

The thinness of wood veneer wall covering does, however, raise three major concerns:

- Finishing operations after installation.
- Proper substrate preparation.
- Moisture.

Moreover, wood veneer wall covering is too thin to be sanded. Therefore, care must be taken during installation to prevent the surface from being stained or damaged. Also, wall surface imperfections tend to telegraph through the thin veneer, so in areas where the substrate cannot be prepared to a smooth, level surface, veneered plywood panels are a better choice. Buckling and warpage caused by moisture can be additional significant problems for this kind of wall covering; therefore, it is not recommended for application to the interior surface of an exterior wall, unless the finish face of the wall is furred out and dampproofed.

Wood veneer wall coverings are available prefinished or unfinished. Unfinished veneers must be stained and finished after they are installed. Some finishes, for example, penetrating oils, can have an adverse effect on the wall covering adhesive. Coatings applied to the surface of installed wood veneer should be approved by the wall covering manufacturer.

The installation of wood veneer wall covering is similar to the installation of other types of wall covering; however, the sheets must be butted together and cannot be overlapped and trimmed.

WALL PREPARATION

There are four traditional ways to prepare a wall surface for a wall covering: prime, seal, size, or apply a wall liner.

- *Primers* ensure proper adhesion and are the most commonly required wall preparation for commercial installations.
- *Sealers* are usually oil-based, made either of an alkyd or shellac. They provide stain-sealing properties; for example, walls that have suffered water damage must typically be sealed before they can be finished with either paint or wall covering. Sealers also promote strippability without damage to the wall surface.
- *Sizing* a wall surface lowers the absorbency of the wall by reducing the penetration of the paste. However, sizing does not necessarily improve the bond between the adhesive and the wall surface.
- *Wall liners* are nonwoven sheets; their installation is similar to that of wall covering. They are sometimes required where wall surfaces cannot be prepared by conventional means. Wall liners can be used to prevent cracks, holes, and gaps from telegraphing through the wall covering. They may also be used in lieu of primer/sealers to mask contrasting colors or areas of light and dark on the substrate.

FLOOR FINISHES

All flooring in rooms required to be accessible and on accessible routes must be firm, stable, and slip-resistant.

TILE FLOOR FINISHES

Many types of tile are used as floor finishes including: ceramic, quarry, glass mosaics, plastic, metal. Ceramic tile is fabricated from clay or a mixture of clay and ceramic materials. Natural clay is most commonly used, but porcelain is also available. Porcelain tile is fine-grained and smooth and can be formed into sharply detailed designs. Tile dimensions are typically nominal. Refer to manufacturers' data for specific tile and trim piece dimensions.

SIX WALL COVERINGS CATEGORIZED BY PERFORMANCE[a]
3.95

CATEGORY	DESCRIPTION	USE	COMMENTS
I	Decorative only	For decorative purposes	Wall coverings are not tested. Wallpaper and other primarily residential wall coverings fall into this category.
II	Decorative, with medium serviceability	Primarily decorative but more washable and colorfast than Category I wall coverings	In addition to the testing required for minimum washability and colorfastness, wall coverings are tested for maximum flame spread and smoke development. Primarily for residential use.
III	Decorative, with high serviceability	For medium use, where abrasion resistance, stain resistance, scrubbability, and increased colorfastness are necessary	In addition to the testing required for Category II wall coverings, in this category wall coverings are tested for minimum scrubbability, stain resistance, and crocking resistance. They meet more stringent requirements for colorfastness than Category II wall coverings. Primarily for residential use.
IV	Type I (Light Duty) commercial serviceability	For use where higher abrasion resistance, stain resistance, and scrubbability are necessary in heavy consumer and light commercial use	In addition to the testing required for Category III wall coverings, these wall coverings are tested for maximum shrinkage and minimum abrasion resistance, breaking strength, tear resistance, blocking resistance, coating adhesion, cold-cracking resistance, and heat-aging resistance. All test methods listed in the standard apply to Category III wall coverings, but these wall coverings meet more stringent requirements for colorfastness and scrubbability than those in Category III. Appropriate for private offices, hotel rooms, and areas not subject to unusual abrasion or heavy traffic.
V	Type II (Medium Duty) commercial serviceability	For use where better wearing qualities are required and exposure to wear is greater than normal	Tested according to more stringent requirements for scrubbability, abrasion resistance, stain resistance, tear resistance, and coating adhesion than Category IV wall coverings. Appropriate for public areas such as lounges, dining rooms, public corridors, and classrooms.
VI	Type III (Heavy Duty) commercial serviceability	For use in heavy-traffic areas	Category VI wall coverings are tested for the highest scrubbability, abrasion resistance, breaking strength, tear resistance, coating adhesion, and maximum shrinkage. Category VI, Type III wall coverings are commonly used in high-traffic service corridors where carts may bump into the walls.

TILE COMPOSITION AND GLAZE

Ceramic tile is made from either natural clay or porcelain, and is glazed or unglazed.

- *Porcelain tile* is a ceramic mosaic or paver tile generally made by the dust-pressed method. It is dense, impervious, fine-grained, and smooth, with a sharply formed face.
- *Natural clay* tile is a ceramic mosaic or paver tile with a distinctive, slightly textured appearance. It is made by the dust-pressed or plastic method from clays that have a dense body.
- *Glazed tile* has an impervious facial finish of ceramic materials that is fused to the body of the tile. The body may be nonvitreous, semivitreous, vitreous, or impervious.
- *Unglazed tile* is a hard, dense tile of uniform composition that derives color and texture from the materials used in its fabrication.

WATER ABSORPTION OF CERAMIC TILE
3.96

TYPE	WATER ABSORPTION	CERAMIC MATERIAL	USE
Nonvitreous	More than 7.0%	Natural clay	Not for use in continually wet locations
Semivitreous	More than 3.9%, but not more than 7.0%	Natural clay	Not for use in continually wet locations
Vitreous	0.5% to 3.0%	Natural clay	For use in continually wet locations
Impervious	0.5% or less	Porcelain	For use in continually wet locations; superior wear resistance

TILE TYPES

There are a variety of tile types, including ceramic mosaic, quarry, paver, decorative, mounted, and conductive tile.

CERAMIC MOSAIC TILE

Ceramic mosaic tile is formed either by the dust-pressed or the plastic method. Usually 1/4- to 3/8-in. thick with a facial area of less than 6 sq in., it may be made of either porcelain or natural clay and may be plain or have an abrasive mixture throughout.

QUARRY TILE

Quarry tile is glazed or unglazed tile made by the extrusion process from natural clay or shale. It usually has a facial area of 6 sq in. or more. Quarry tile may be specified with abrasive grit embedded in the surface, for use in areas where slip resistance is a concern.

PAVER TILE

Paver tile is glazed or unglazed porcelain or natural clay tile formed by the dust-pressed method with a facial area of 6 sq in. or more.

DECORATIVE THIN-WALL TILE

Decorative thin-wall tile is a glazed tile with a thin body that is usually nonvitreous. It is suitable for interior decorative residential use when breaking strength is not a requirement.

MOUNTED TILE

Mounted tile is assembled into units or sheets to facilitate handling and installation. Tile may be face-mounted, back-mounted, or edge-mounted. Material applied to the face of the tile is usually easily removed, but material bonded to the back is integrated to the tile installation.

CONDUCTIVE TILE

Conductive tile has specific properties of electrical conductivity but retains other normal physical properties of tile.

NOTES

3.95 [a]. Per ASTM F 793, "Standard Classification of Wall Covering by Use Characteristics." The backing material, sometimes called the substrate, is the major component in determining the strength and dimensional stability of a wall covering.

WALL TILE TRIM SHAPES
3.97

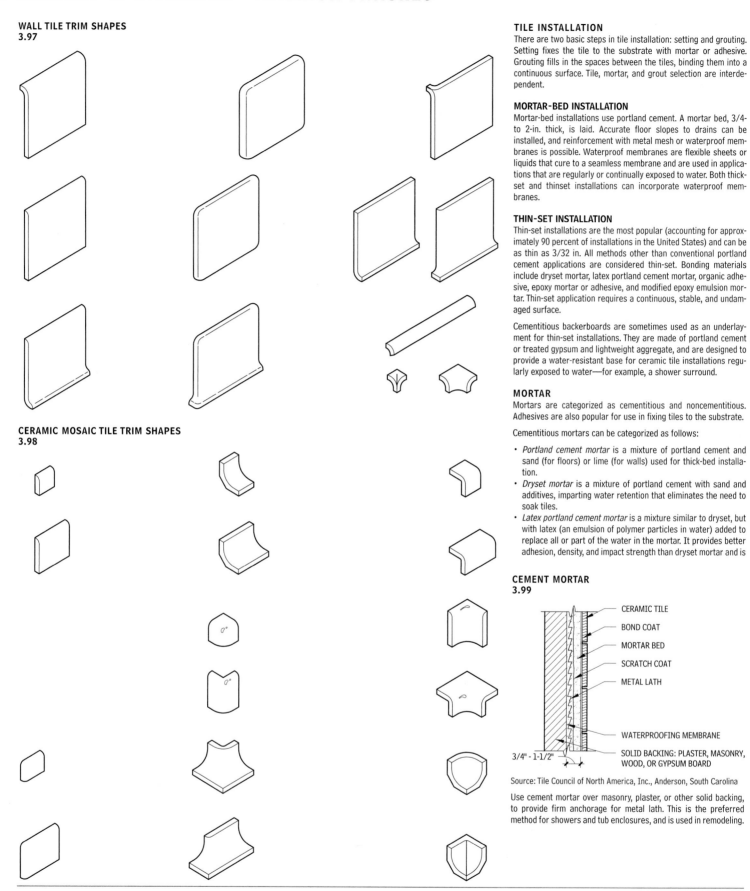

CERAMIC MOSAIC TILE TRIM SHAPES
3.98

TILE INSTALLATION

There are two basic steps in tile installation: setting and grouting. Setting fixes the tile to the substrate with mortar or adhesive. Grouting fills in the spaces between the tiles, binding them into a continuous surface. Tile, mortar, and grout selection are interdependent.

MORTAR-BED INSTALLATION

Mortar-bed installations use portland cement. A mortar bed, 3/4- to 2-in. thick, is laid. Accurate floor slopes to drains can be installed, and reinforcement with metal mesh or waterproof membranes is possible. Waterproof membranes are flexible sheets or liquids that cure to a seamless membrane and are used in applications that are regularly or continually exposed to water. Both thickset and thinset installations can incorporate waterproof membranes.

THIN-SET INSTALLATION

Thin-set installations are the most popular (accounting for approximately 90 percent of installations in the United States) and can be as thin as 3/32 in. All methods other than conventional portland cement applications are considered thin-set. Bonding materials include dryset mortar, latex portland cement mortar, organic adhesive, epoxy mortar or adhesive, and modified epoxy emulsion mortar. Thin-set application requires a continuous, stable, and undamaged surface.

Cementitious backerboards are sometimes used as an underlayment for thin-set installations. They are made of portland cement or treated gypsum and lightweight aggregate, and are designed to provide a water-resistant base for ceramic tile installations regularly exposed to water—for example, a shower surround.

MORTAR

Mortars are categorized as cementitious and noncementitious. Adhesives are also popular for use in fixing tiles to the substrate.

Cementitious mortars can be categorized as follows:

- *Portland cement mortar* is a mixture of portland cement and sand (for floors) or lime (for walls) used for thick-bed installation.
- *Dryset mortar* is a mixture of portland cement with sand and additives, imparting water retention that eliminates the need to soak tiles.
- *Latex portland cement mortar* is a mixture similar to dryset, but with latex (an emulsion of polymer particles in water) added to replace all or part of the water in the mortar. It provides better adhesion, density, and impact strength than dryset mortar and is

CEMENT MORTAR
3.99

CERAMIC TILE
BOND COAT
MORTAR BED
SCRATCH COAT
METAL LATH
WATERPROOFING MEMBRANE
SOLID BACKING: PLASTER, MASONRY, WOOD, OR GYPSUM BOARD
3/4" - 1-1/2"

Source: Tile Council of North America, Inc., Anderson, South Carolina

Use cement mortar over masonry, plaster, or other solid backing, to provide firm anchorage for metal lath. This is the preferred method for showers and tub enclosures, and is used in remodeling.

more flexible and resistant to frost damage.

Noncementitious mortars can be categorized as follows:

- *Epoxy mortar* is a two-part mixture (resin and hardener with silica filler) used where chemical resistance is important. It has high bond strength and high resistance to impact. This mortar and furan mortar are the only two types that can be recommended for use over steel plates.
- *Modified epoxy emulsion mortars* are similar to epoxy mortars. This mixture contains a resin and hardener along with portland cement and sand. Although it is not as chemically resistant as epoxy mortar, it binds well. Compared with mortar created from portland cement exclusively, it allows little or no shrinkage.
- *Furan mortars* are two-part mixtures, composed of furan resin and hardener. Excellent for chemical-resistant uses, they tolerate high temperatures up to 350°F. Epoxy adhesive is a mixture similar to epoxy mortar in bonding capability, but it is not as chemical- or solvent-resistant.

LATEX PORTLAND CEMENT MORTAR
3.100

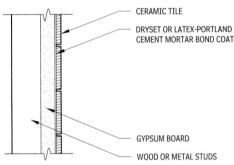

CERAMIC TILE
DRYSET OR LATEX-PORTLAND CEMENT MORTAR BOND COAT
GYPSUM BOARD
WOOD OR METAL STUDS

Source: Tile Council of North America, Inc., Anderson, South Carolina

Latex portland cement mortar is used in dry areas in schools, institutions, and commercial buildings. It should not be used in areas where temperatures exceed 125°F.

ONE-COAT METHOD
3.101

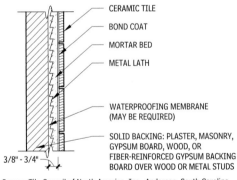

CERAMIC TILE
BOND COAT
MORTAR BED
METAL LATH
WATERPROOFING MEMBRANE (MAY BE REQUIRED)
SOLID BACKING: PLASTER, MASONRY, GYPSUM BOARD, WOOD, OR FIBER-REINFORCED GYPSUM BACKING BOARD OVER WOOD OR METAL STUDS

3/8" - 3/4"

Source: Tile Council of North America, Inc., Anderson, South Carolina

The one-coat method is used for remodeling or on surfaces that present bonding problems. It is the preferred method of applying tile over gypsum plaster or gypsum board in showers and tub enclosures.

DRYSET MORTAR (CEMENTITIOUS BACKER)
3.102

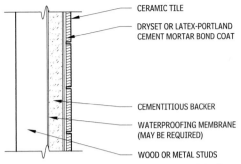

CERAMIC TILE
DRYSET OR LATEX-PORTLAND CEMENT MORTAR BOND COAT
CEMENTITIOUS BACKER
WATERPROOFING MEMBRANE (MAY BE REQUIRED)
WOOD OR METAL STUDS

Source: Tile Council of North America, Inc., Anderson, South Carolina

Use dryset mortar in wet areas over well-braced wood or metal studs. Stud spacing should not to exceed 16 in. o.c., and metal studs must be 20-gauge or heavier.

COATED GLASS-MAT BACKERBOARD
3.103

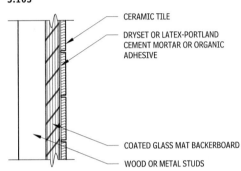

CERAMIC TILE
DRYSET OR LATEX-PORTLAND CEMENT MORTAR OR ORGANIC ADHESIVE
COATED GLASS MAT BACKERBOARD
WOOD OR METAL STUDS

Source: Tile Council of North America, Inc., Anderson, South Carolina

Coated glass-mat backerboard is used in wet areas over dry, well-braced wood or metal studs. Stud spacing should not exceed 16 in. o.c., and metal studs must be 20-gauge or heavier.

ADHESIVES
Organic adhesives are one-part mastic mixtures that require no mixing. They remain somewhat flexible (as compared with portland cement mortar) and have good bond strength, but should not be used for exterior or wet applications.

GROUT
Grout is used to fill joints between tiles and is selected with a compatible mortar. Grout is either a portland-cement-based mixture or a mixture of other compounds to enhance its performance or ease its installation. The type and size of tile, service level, climatic conditions, tile spacing, and individual manufacturer's recommendations are factors to consider when selecting grout.

- *Portland-cement-based grout* is a mixture of portland cement and sand (for floors) or lime (for walls) and is used for thickset installations. These grouts include commercial portland cement grout, sand-portland, cement grout, dryset grout, and latex portland cement grout.
- *Nonportland-cement-based* grouts include solid epoxy, furan, silicone, and mastic grouts. Mastic grout eliminates the need for mixing on-site.
- *Epoxy grout* is a two- or three-part mixture (epoxy resin hardener with silica sand filler) that is highly resistant to chemicals and has great bond strength. This grout and furan grout are made for different chemical and solvent resistance.
- *Furan resin grout* is two-part furan mixture (similar to furan mortar) that resists high temperatures and solvents.
- *Silicone rubber grout* is an elastomeric mixture of silicone rubber. It has high bond strength, is resistant to water and staining, and remains flexible under freezing conditions.

SETTING MATERIALS
3.104

TYPE	DESCRIPTION	FEATURES
CEMENTITIOUS		
Portland cement mortar	Portland cement and sand, in proportions of 1:5 for floors; portland cement, sand, and lime, in proportions of 1:5:1/2 to 1:7:1 for walls	Most surfaces, ordinary installations
Dryset mortar	Portland cement with sand and additives imparting water retentivity, which is used as a bond coat for setting tile	Thinset installations
Latex-portland cement mortar	Portland cement, sand, and special latex additive, which is used as a bond coat for setting tile	Latex additives improve adhesion, reduce water absorption, and provide greater bond strength and resistance to shock and impact. Required for large-unit porcelain-bodied tile.
NONCEMENTITIOUS		
Epoxy mortar	Epoxy resin and epoxy hardeners	Chemical-resistant
Modified epoxy emulsion mortars	Emulsified epoxy resins and hardeners with portland cement and silica sand	High bond strength; little or no shrinkage; not chemical-resistant
Furan resin mortar	Furan resin and furan hardeners	Chemical-resistant
Epoxy adhesives	Epoxy resin and epoxy hardeners	High bond strength and ease of application; less than optimal chemical resistance
Organic adhesive	For interior use only; ready to use (no addition of liquid); cures by evaporation	Not suitable for continuously wet applications or temperatures exceeding 140°F

MORTAR-BED—CHEMICAL-RESISTANT EPOXY MORTAR AND GROUT INSTALLATION (LEVELING REQUIRED)
3.105

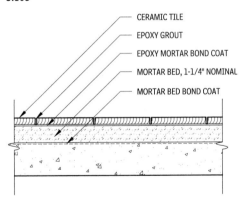

CERAMIC TILE
EPOXY GROUT
EPOXY MORTAR BOND COAT
MORTAR BED, 1-1/4" NOMINAL
MORTAR BED BOND COAT

Epoxy mortar and grout are used where leveling of the subfloor is required and where moderate chemical exposure and severe cleaning methods are used, such as in food-processing plants.

Contributor:
Tile Council of North America, Inc., Anderson, South Carolina.

TERRAZZO FLOOR FINISHES

Terrazzo is a very low-maintenance, seamless floor finish with the luxurious look of stone mosaic and durability comparable to that of concrete. Often selected for its decorative possibilities, terrazzo artistry can produce striking medallions or intricate inlaid patterns.

Terrazzo is a mixture of a binder and crushed aggregate, typically marble. Other aggregate types, such as glass, are available to vary the appearance of the terrazzo. Divider strips of brass, white alloy of zinc, or plastic, are used functionally as control joints, and aesthetically as design elements, to separate fields of color.

AGGREGATE

Aggregate, or stone chips used in terrazzo, includes all calcareous serpentine and other rocks capable of taking a good polish. Marble and onyx are the preferred materials. Quartz, granite, quartzite, and silica pebbles are used for rustic terrazzo and textured mosaics not requiring polishing.

INTERIOR TERRAZZO SYSTEMS
3.106

SYSTEM	DESCRIPTION	ADVANTAGES	TOTAL THICKNESS	WEIGHT PSF
Sand cushion	1/2″ terrazzo topping over 2-1/2″ underbed, reinforced with wire mesh, over an isolation membrane over 1/16″ of sand, on a concrete slab. For interior use only.	The best available cement terrazzo system, because it is the only system that completely separates the finish from the subfloor. This protects against minor substrate defects telegraphing through to the finish surface.	3″, including 1/2″ terrazzo topping	30
Bonded	1/2″ terrazzo topping over 1-1/4″ underbed, on a concrete slab. Interior use only.	Requires less thickness than sand cushion. Can be used for walls.	1-3/4 to 2-1/4″, including 1/2″ terrazzo topping	18
Monolithic	1/2″ terrazzo topping on a concrete slab. Performance dependent on the quality of the substrate. A level concrete slab must be provided.	Most economical system, ideal for large areas such as shopping malls, schools, and stores.	1/2″ terrazzo topping	7
Thinset (Epoxy)	1/4 to 3/8″ terrazzo topping over a concrete slab. Thinnest and, typically, most expensive system. Considered to be a resinous flooring type. Epoxy or polyester matrix is used.	Good for renovation work. Both epoxy and polyester resist many types of chemicals, making them suitable for labs, hospitals, and manufacturing facilities.	1/4 to 3/8″	4
Precast	Fabricated custom units for steps, bases, planters, benches, and wall panels.	Variety of uses	Custom	Varies

Source: Reprinted courtesy of the National Terrazzo and Mosaic Association (NTMA). The NTMA, an association of terrazzo contractors, material suppliers, and distributors, publishes the *NTMA Technical Manual*, which contains complete specifications for all terrazzo systems.

TERRAZZO
3.107

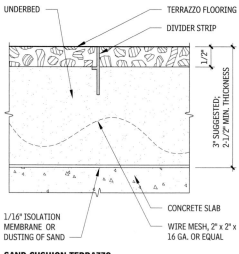

SAND CUSHION TERRAZZO

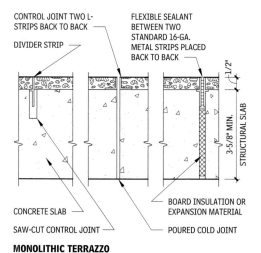

MONOLITHIC TERRAZZO

Contributor:
National Terrazzo and Mosaic Association, Inc., Leesburg, Virginia.

TERRAZZO BASES
3.108

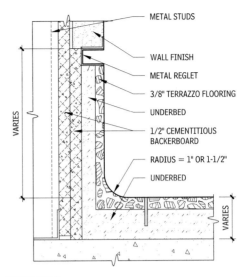

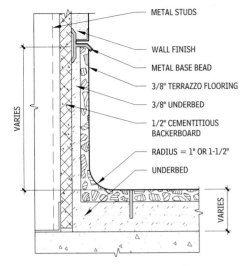

FLUSH BASE

RECESSED BASE

REVEAL BASE

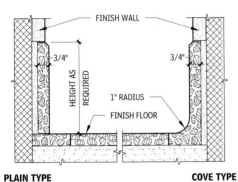

PLAIN TYPE   **COVE TYPE**

PRECAST TERRAZZO BASE

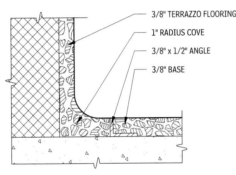

POLYACRYLATE TERRAZZO FLOOR AND BASE

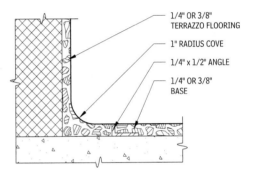

EPOXY OR POLYESTER TERRAZZO FLOOR AND BASE

WOOD FLOORING

Wood flooring consists of solid or engineered wood products and is available in strip, plank, and parquet. All wood floors require regular maintenance to maintain their appearance. Wood flooring industry organizations and suppliers provide detailed information on product specifications.

SOLID WOOD FLOORING

Solid wood flooring is available in many hardwood and softwood species. It can be refinished multiple times. It should not be installed below grade, due to the possibility of moisture damage to the wood floor.

WOOD STRIP FLOORING

Wood strip flooring for normal use is typically a nominal 3/4-in. thick, with an actual thickness of 25/32 in., in widths ranging from 1-1/2 to 2-1/4 in. Lengths are random.

WOOD PLANK FLOORING

Wood plank flooring is also typically a nominal 3/4-in. thick, in widths ranging from 3 to 10 in., and is available in random lengths.

SELECTION OF WOOD FLOORING

Wood flooring should be selected after considering pedestrian and vehicular (cart) traffic, durability required, and potential damage to floors; typical usage, exposure to moisture and sunlight, maintenance, wood floor appearance expectations, and other criteria specific to the project.

The majority of woods specified for commercial flooring are hardwoods such as oak or maple. Best overall appearance, uniformity of color, limited amounts of character marks, and minimal sap marks indicate the most desirable wood flooring.

Table 3.109 lists the typical grades and sizes of boards by species or regional group. Grade classifications vary, but in each case it can be assumed that the first grade listed is the highest quality and that the quality decreases with each succeeding grade. The best grade typically minimizes or excludes features such as knots, streaks, spots, checks, and torn grain, and will contain the highest percentage of longer boards. Grade standards have been reduced in recent years for most commercially produced flooring, hence a thorough review of exact grade specifications is in order when selecting wood flooring.

Contributors:
Trey Klein, AIA, Crayfish Design, Belmont, Massachusetts; Jason Dickerson, Rhode Island School of Design, Providence, Rhode Island; John C. Lunsford, AIA, Varney, Sexton Syndor Architects, Phoenix, Arizona.

TYPICAL GRADES AND SIZES OF BOARDS BY SPECIES OR REGIONAL GROUP
3.109

GROUP	INDUSTRY ORGANIZATION	GRADE	THICKNESS (IN.)	WIDTH (IN.)	NOTES
Oak, ash, black cherry, and walnut; also beech, birch, hard maple, pecan, and hickory	National Oak Flooring Manufacturers Association (NOFMA), Memphis, Tennessee: (901) 526-5016; www.nofma.org	Oak, ash, black cherry, and walnut	Strip	Face	Factory-finished oak flooring is available in Prime, Standard, and Tavern grades, 3/4" thick with a face width of 1-1/2" or 2-1/4". NOFMA grades hickory/pecan as first grade, first grade red, first grade white; second grade, second grade red; and third grade.
		Clear	3/4"	1-1/2" 2"	
				2-1/4", 3-1/4"	
		Select	1/2"	1-1/2", 2"	
		Common (Nos. 1 and 2)	Maple, beech, birch only		
		Beech, birch, and hard maple	3/4", 25/32"	1-1/2", 2"	
		First (including red and white)	33/32"	2-1/4", 3-1/4"	
		Second	Plank	3", 4", 5", 6", 7"	
		Third	3/4"	8"	
		(See notes in last column for other species.)			
Hard maple (Acer saccharum, not soft maple); also beech and birch	Maple Flooring Manufacturers Association, Northbrook, Illinois: (847) 480-9138; www.maplefloor.org	First, Second, and Better Third	25/32", 33/32"	Face	The Maple Flooring Manufacturers Association states that beech and birch have physical properties that make them fully suitable as substitutes for hard maple. Consult manufacturers for available width and thickness combinations.
				1-1/2"	
				2-1/4"	
				3-1/4"	
Southern pine	Southern Pine Inspection Bureau, Pensacola, Florida: (850) 434-2611; www.spib.org	B and B	3/8", 1/2", 5/8"	Nominal Face	Grain may be specified as edge (rift), near-rift, or flat. If not specified, manufacturer will ship flat or mixed-grain boards. Check with manufacturers for available width and thickness combinations.
		C	1", 1-1/4", 1-1/2"	2" 1-1/8"	
		C and Better		3" 2-1/8"	
		D		4" 3-1/8"	
		No. 2		5" 4-1/8"	
				6" 5-1/8"	
Western woods (Douglas fir, hemlock, Englemann spruce, Idaho white pine, incense cedar; lodgepole pine, ponderosa pine, sugar pine, western larch, western red cedar)	Western Wood Products Association, Portland, Oregon: (503) 224-3930; www.wwpa.org	All but Idaho white pine	2" and thinner	Nominal	Flooring is machined tongue-and-groove, and may be furnished in any grade. Grain may be specified as vertical (VG), Flat (FG), or mixed (MG). Basic size for flooring is 1" × 4" × 312'; standard lengths are 4' and longer. The moisture content of these grades is 15% MC, with 85% of the pieces less than 12% MC.
		B and Better Select		3"	
		C Select		4"	
		D Select		6"	
		Idaho white pine			
		Supreme			
		Choice			
		Quality			

Source: National Oak Flooring Manufacturers Association, Memphis, Tennessee

ENGINEERED WOOD FLOORING

Engineered wood flooring is available in strip, plank, or parquet tiles. Hardwood face veneers are laminated to a dimensionally stable, multiple-ply substrate. Engineered wood floors are not as susceptible to moisture as solid wood flooring, and may be used in below-grade areas, with the proper installation techniques.

BAMBOO FLOORING

Bamboo is a grass product (not a wood product, strictly defined). The bamboo is harvested, cut into strips, boiled in water with a preservative, and pressed flat. The strips are dried and laminated vertically into solid boards. Because bamboo matures in just three years, this product is an excellent renewable resource. The bamboo flooring is manufactured in tongue-and-groove strips approximately 3-1/2 in. wide, 3/4 in. thick, and in lengths up to 6 ft.

A 3/8-in.-thick material is available for glue-down application. It is available in vertical grain and flat grain. Bamboo flooring is very durable; hardness tests indicate similarity to red oak floors.

INSTALLATION

Wood flooring requires particular care in handling and installation. Prior to installation, the wood flooring should be allowed to acclimate to the space in which it is to be installed, at the humidity level of the final occupancy. Minimize moisture damage to wood floors by avoiding installation in close proximity to wet areas. In addition, to ensure constant temperature and humidity, and install wood floors after all "wet" jobs have been completed and after the heating plant and all permanent lighting have been installed.

Wood flooring is subject to expansion and contraction; therefore, perimeter base details that allow for movement and ventilation are recommended. Wood structures require adequate ventilation in basements and crawl spaces. Under a slab on or below grade, moisture control can be further enhanced by use of a vapor barrier; this provision should be carefully considered for each installation.

Wearing properties of wood flooring vary from species to species and should be considered along with appearance when specifying wood floors. In addition, grain pattern affects the durability of a given species. For example, industrial wood blocks are typically placed with the end grain exposed because it presents the toughest wearing surface. The thickness of the wood above the tongues in tongue-and-groove flooring may be increased for extra service.

Wood floors are installed over a plywood subfloor or over wood sleepers. Strips or planks are blind-nailed in tongue-and-groove installations and face-nailed in butt-jointed installations; parquet floors are commonly set in mastic. Vapor barriers are installed when the installation is slab-on-grade or below grade. Ventilation is required in certain installation conditions where moisture is a concern. Special conditions require additional detailing for proper installation.

Contributor:
Rippeteau Architects, PC, Washington, DC.

FASTENING
3.110

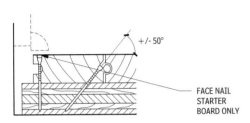

- FACE NAIL ALL BOARDS
- SUBFLOOR, TYPICAL

JOINTED

+/- 50°

- FACE NAIL STARTER BOARD ONLY

TONGUE AND GROOVE

Jointed flooring must be face-nailed, usually with fully barbed flooring brads. Tongue-and-groove boards are blind-nailed with spiral floor screws, cement-coated nails, cut nails, or machine-driven fasteners. Follow the manufacturer's recommendations.

STRIPS OVER PLYWOOD UNDERLAYMENT
3.111

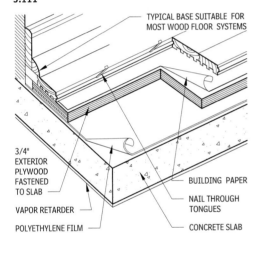

- TYPICAL BASE SUITABLE FOR MOST WOOD FLOOR SYSTEMS
- 3/4" EXTERIOR PLYWOOD FASTENED TO SLAB
- VAPOR RETARDER
- POLYETHYLENE FILM
- BUILDING PAPER
- NAIL THROUGH TONGUES
- CONCRETE SLAB

STRIPS OVER SUBFLOOR ON WOOD JOISTS
3.112

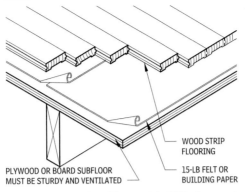

- WOOD STRIP FLOORING
- 15-LB FELT OR BUILDING PAPER
- PLYWOOD OR BOARD SUBFLOOR MUST BE STURDY AND VENTILATED

For parquet flooring, the subfloor must be 3/4-in. tongue-and-groove plywood, minimum, with a mastic coating.

STRIPS OVER STAGGERED TWO-BY-FOUR SLEEPERS
3.113

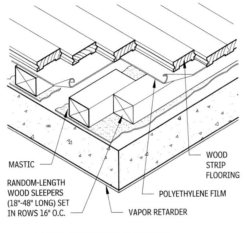

- MASTIC
- RANDOM-LENGTH WOOD SLEEPERS (18"-48" LONG) SET IN ROWS 16" O.C.
- WOOD STRIP FLOORING
- POLYETHYLENE FILM
- VAPOR RETARDER

STRIPS OVER CUSHIONED SLEEPERS
3.114

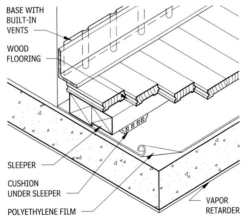

- BASE WITH BUILT-IN VENTS
- WOOD FLOORING
- SLEEPER
- CUSHION UNDER SLEEPER
- POLYETHYLENE FILM
- VAPOR RETARDER

THRESHOLD AT DOORWAY
3.115

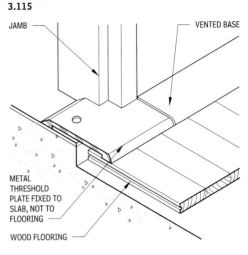

- JAMB
- VENTED BASE
- METAL THRESHOLD PLATE FIXED TO SLAB, NOT TO FLOORING
- WOOD FLOORING

INDUSTRIAL WOOD BLOCK
3.116

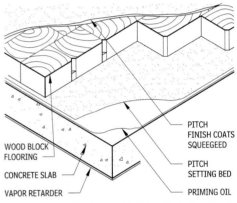

- PITCH FINISH COATS SQUEEGEED
- WOOD BLOCK FLOORING
- CONCRETE SLAB
- VAPOR RETARDER
- PITCH SETTING BED
- PRIMING OIL

Typical blocks are 3 by 6 in. up to 4 by 8 in., with depths of 2 to 4 in. Urethane finish coats are available for nonindustrial uses.

Contributors:
Tonn Lensment, Rhode Island School of Design, Providence, Rhode Island; Rippeteau Architects, PC, Washington, DC; Annica S. Emilsson; Rippeteau Architects, PC, Washington, DC; National Oak Flooring Manufacturers Association, Memphis, Tennessee; National Wood Flooring Association, Manchester, Missouri.

RESILIENT FLOORING

Resilient flooring provides a dense, nonabsorbent, pliant surface that is generally quiet, comfortable to walk on, and easy to maintain.

VINYL FLOORING

The five basic ingredients used in the manufacture of vinyl flooring are:

- *Polyvinyl chloride (PVC)*, which imparts wear resistance and durability. PVC is the basis of the binder, which constitutes most of the wear surface. The binder consists of PVC compounded with plasticizers and stabilizers.
- *Plasticizers*, which increase flexibility.
- *Stabilizers*, which provide color permanence and stabilize the pigments against heat and light deterioration.
- *Fillers*, which are added to supplement the bulk and thickness of the flooring. Mineral fillers, the most common, improve fire resistance. Natural fillers increase slip resistance.
- *Pigments*, which are used for color.

SHEET VINYL

Sheet vinyl flooring, either solid vinyl or backed, forms a continuous finished floor covering. Because sheet vinyl flooring has fewer joints, it is used for applications where spills, dirt, or bacterial growth are of concern. It is commonly specified in hospital operating rooms or other areas where resistance to bacterial growth or water penetration is required.

There are two types of seams for sheet vinyl installations: heat-welded and chemically welded.

- *Heat-welded seams* are formed by melting a vinyl rod between sheets. Solid-color or patterned welding rods can either accent or camouflage seams. Heat welding requires special equipment and trained installers.
- *Chemical welding* is accomplished with the application of a one- or two-part solvent that is mixed on-site. This softens the edges of the vinyl, essentially melting them together. Chemical welding is more economical than heat welding.

RESILIENT FLOORING SIZES
3.117

TYPE	COMPONENTS	THICKNESS (IN.)	SIZES
Vinyl sheet	Vinyl resins with fiber back	0.065–0.160	6', 10', 12'
Solid vinyl tile	Vinyl resins	1/16–1/8	9" × 9"
			12" × 12"
Vinyl composition tile	Vinyl resins with filler	0.050–0.095	9" × 9"
			12" × 12"
Rubber tile	Rubber compound	3/32–3/16	9" × 9"
			12" × 12"
Cork tile	Raw cork and resins	1/8–1/4	6" × 6"
			9" × 9"
Cork tile with vinyl coating	Raw cork with vinyl resins	1/8–3/16	9" × 9"
			12" × 12"

VINYL TILE

Two types of vinyl tile are *solid vinyl tile* and the less expensive *vinyl composition tile (VCT)*. Solid vinyl tile, or *homogeneous vinyl tile*, contains much more PVC than VCT, making it more resilient and resistant to abrasion. Homogeneous vinyl tile has superior indentation and rolling/load resistance. Because the pattern is continuous through the thickness of the flooring, its appearance will remain consistent when worn.

Three classes of VCT are defined by ASTM F 1066, "Standard Specification for Vinyl Composition Floor Tile": Type 1, solid-color tiles; Type 2, through-pattern tiles; and Type 3, surface-pattern tiles.

RUBBER FLOORING

Rubber sheet or rubber tile flooring is composed of natural rubber or synthetic rubber (styrene butadiene), mineral fillers, and pigments. Two types of rubber floor tile are homogeneous and laminated.

- *Homogeneous rubber tile* has coloring uniform throughout the tile thickness.
- *Laminated rubber tile* has coloring or patterning in the wear layer only.

LINOLEUM

Linoleum (derived from the Latin terms for "flax," *linum*, and "oil," *oleum*) is composed primarily of linseed oil, obtained from the flax plant. The oil is oxidized and mixed with a natural resin, such as rosin tapped from pine trees, and combined with powdered cork for flexibility and limestone for strength and hardness. Wood flour and pigments are added for color and colorfastness. For dimensional stability, this mixture is bonded to a fiber backing (typically burlap) for linoleum sheets, or to a polyester backing for tile. Felt backings are used for linoleum countertop or tack surface sheets.

CORK FLOORING

Cork flooring is harvested from the outer layer of cork oak trees grown in Mediterranean regions. When the bark becomes loose, approximately every nine years, it is cut away. Composition cork is the most common form of cork flooring. The bark material of the cork oak is granulated, pressed with binders such as synthetic resins, and then baked. The quality of composition cork varies according to the quality and size of granules, the type and quantity of the binder, and the density (compression) of the mix.

RESILIENT FLOORING PERFORMANCE ATTRIBUTES
3.118

ATTRIBUTE	RESILIENT FLOORING TYPE
Resilience and quietness	Cork tile, rubber tile
Resistance to indentation	Solid vinyl tile
Stain resistance	Vinyl sheet and tile
Alkali resistance	Vinyl sheet and tile
Grease resistance	Vinyl sheet and tile, cork tile with vinyl coating
Durability	Vinyl sheet and tile

MATERIALS

Resilient wall base and flooring accessories are available in three materials:

- *Vinyl* can be susceptible to shrinking when exposed to heat.
- *Thermoplastic rubber* is a vinyl compound with a comparatively small amount of rubber added for flexibility. Because of the high vinyl content, it performs similarly to vinyl, but is more flexible. It is commonly more expensive than vinyl but less expensive than vulcanized, thermoset rubber.
- *Thermoset rubber* is vulcanized natural rubber. It is the most flexible resilient base material and thus is easier to install and better at hiding surface imperfections in walls and floors. Thermoset rubber base is susceptible to color degradation due to UV exposure; however, it can be specially manufactured with UV inhibitors. White and dark-colored thermoset rubber base tends to hold color best. Lighter colors, especially gray, tend to be prone to color degradation. Thermoset rubber base also tends to be more vulnerable to scuffing than vinyl or thermoplastic rubber. Lighter colors tend not to show scuff marks as much as darker colors.

Although most building codes do not have flammability requirements for wall trim that constitutes less than 10 percent of the wall surface, the flame-spread ratings and the smoke generated from burning resilient flooring accessories differ among the three materials. Thermoset rubber, when burned, generates less smoke and toxic fumes than vinyl or thermoplastic rubber.

RESILIENT BASE MATERIALS
3.119

	RESPONSE TO HEAT	FLEXIBILITY	RESISTANCE TO GREASE AND OIL	RELATIVE COST
Vinyl	Shrinks	Good	Excellent	$
Thermoplastic Rubber	Expands	Better	Good	$$
Thermoset Rubber	Expands	Best	Fair	$$$

WALL BASE

Wall base conceals the joint where the wall meets the floor. Premolded inside and outside corners are available from some manufacturers, but they may differ in texture and color from straight sections. Straight sections of resilient wall base are available in precut lengths (4 ft long) and coils (approximately 100 ft long). Coils minimize the number of joints and may reduce installation costs.

There are three basic wall base profiles:

- *Straight base* is meant to be used with carpet.
- *Cove base* is meant to be used with resilient flooring.
- *Butt-to base*, sometimes referred to as *sanitary base*, is available from a limited number of manufacturers. It is installed prior to the finish floor covering. The finish floor covering must be the same thickness as the butt-to-base flange. The base is sealed to the floor and wall, creating an easy-to-clean, more sanitary joint, which is popular for health care applications.

Cove moldings support sheet vinyl, sheet linoleum, or other flexible floor coverings when coved up the wall. Cap moldings help to finish the exposed edges of coved floor coverings, ceramic tile, or wood paneling.

COVE BASE
3.120

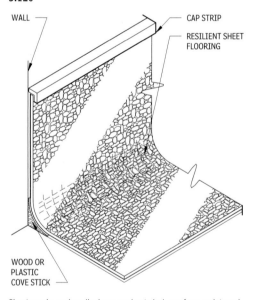

WALL

CAP STRIP

RESILIENT SHEET FLOORING

WOOD OR PLASTIC COVE STICK

Sheet goods, such as linoleum or sheet vinyl, can form an integral, monolithic cove base to simplify maintenance.

Contributors:
Faith Baum, AIA, IIDA, Faith Baum Architect, Lexington, Massachusetts; Mia Alwen, Rhode Island School of Design, Providence, Rhode Island; Lerlux Sophonpanich, Rhode Island School of Design, Providence, Rhode Island.

CARPET FLOORING

The specification of carpet and carpet tile requires evaluation of the following:

- Carpet construction, which includes tufted, fusion-bonded, woven, hand-tufted, knitted, and needle-punched processes
- Carpet fiber
- Carpet performance characteristics, including face and total weight, pile density, and appearance retention
- Density
- Thermal and acoustic considerations
- Installation
- Carpet cushion

CARPET CONSTRUCTION

Carpet construction refers to the carpet manufacturing method. The three most popular construction methods for commercial carpet construction are tufting, weaving, and fusion bonding. Knitted and needlepunched carpets are available but less often specified.

- *Tufted carpets* account for as much as 95 percent of the carpet produced in the United States.
- *Woven carpets* are made on a loom using the original carpet construction method.
- *Knitted carpets* use more face yarn than tufting.
- *Needlepunched carpets* are formed by hundreds of barbed needles punching through blankets of fiber.

TUFTED CARPET

Since its introduction in the early 1950s, tufting has transformed the carpet industry. Compared to other carpet construction methods, tufting does not require skilled labor and requires less expensive equipment to manufacture. It is also far less expensive and faster to produce than woven carpet. This process has enabled the mass production of an affordably priced, wide-width textile floor covering.

The tufted construction process is similar to sewing. Hundreds of needles stitch simultaneously through a backing material. To hold the tufted loops in place, the underside of the primary backing is coated with latex backing adhesive, a rubbery substance that dries hard but remains bendable. A secondary backing material is then applied.

- *Primary backing materials* are the woven or nonwoven fabrics into which the tufts are inserted. They are typically olefin-based, either plain-woven or spunbonded. A thin polymer coating is often applied to bond the warp and weft threads and to minimize unraveling. Spunbonded olefin is inherently resistant to fraying or unraveling. During the tufting process, the olefin fibers are pushed aside, minimizing the distortion of the backing. This helps ensure a uniform pile height. Backings made of olefin are impervious to moisture and are mildew-resistant.
- *Adhesives* used in tufted carpet are usually synthetic latex, although molten thermoplastic compounds are also used. Adhesives permanently anchor the tufts to the primary backing, preventing snags and unraveling.
- *Secondary backing materials*, sometimes referred to as scrims, provide dimensional stability to the finished tufted carpet. A secondary backing is added for strength and stability. Secondary backing materials are often made of polypropylene, which is popular because it is moisture-resistant. Alternatives to secondary backings are attached carpet cushions, solid vinyl composites, and coatings referred to as *unitary backings*.

The standard dimension of most manufactured tufted carpet is a 12-ft width, although some manufacturers provide 6 and 15-ft widths for special applications.

ACCESSIBLE ROUTE CHANGES IN LEVEL UP TO 1/4 IN.
3.121

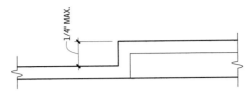

Changes in level up to 1/4 in. may be vertical and without edge.

ACCESSIBLE ROUTE CHANGES IN LEVEL BETWEEN 1/4 IN. AND 1/2 IN.
3.122

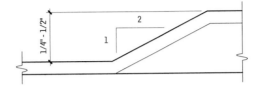

Changes in level between 1/4 in. and 1/2 in. should be beveled with a slope no greater than 1:2. Changes in level greater than 1/2 in. should be accomplished by means of a ramp.

ACCESSIBLE CARPET PILE THICKNESS
3.123

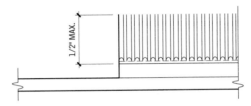

Pile heights over 1/2 in. are not allowed in spaces required to be accessible. Carpet having a pile height of 1/2 in. measured from the bottom of the tuft is allowed. Exposed edges should be secured and have a transition strip.

CARPET TILE

Carpet tiles provide ready access to a raised floor or easy replacement when soiled or worn. Carpet tile backing systems provide moisture barriers from the base of the pile yarn to the floor, preventing spills from penetrating to the subfloor. Backing materials include polyvinyl chloride (PVC), amorphous resins, and polyurethane cushion. The "hard backs" (PVC and amorphous resin) offer dimensional stability and seam and edge integrity for easy pattern matching. PVC backings are used most often for modular tiles.

Carpet tiles are installed with standard adhesives, releasable adhesives, and mill-applied peel-and-stick adhesives. Carpet tile installation is easier and causes less downtime and productivity loss than traditional carpet installation. Systems furniture divider panels and office furniture do not have to be removed, but are simply lifted with a "jack" system. The tiles are then installed underneath the furniture while it remains in place.

WOVEN CARPET

Weaving, the traditional carpet construction method, produces carpet on a loom, integrating the pile and backing yarns during the carpet construction. Most woven carpet is dimensionally stable as a result of the weaving process and does not require a secondary backing, as tufted carpet does. Weaving accounts for less than 2 percent of the carpet market in the United States. Its primary use is in the hospitality industry, where long-term durability and intricate pattern detail are primary considerations. The three basic types of weaving processes are velvet, Wilton, and Axminster.

KNITTED CARPET

As in the construction of woven carpet, the knitting process integrates pile and backing yarns in one operation. Needles are used to interlace yarns in a series of connecting loops, similar to the hand-knitting process. Knitted carpets are known for their plush piles, because there is more yarn in the wear surface than tufted carpets. Knitted carpet has a tendency to stretch, however, especially on the diagonal, and is difficult to seam during installation. Knitted carpet represents a very small percentage of the carpet produced in the United States.

NEEDLEPUNCHED CARPET

Needlepunching is achieved by layering thick fiber batts, typically polypropylene, over a support fabric. Hundreds of barbed needles punch through the support fabric, compressing and entangling the fibers. Needlepunched carpets are permeable, which presents a problem when liquids are spilled on a wall-to-wall interior installation. The most common application of needlepunched carpet is outdoor carpet.

CARPET FIBER TYPES

Several types of carpet fibers are used.

ACRYLIC

Acrylic was one of the first synthetic fibers to be used successfully in the production of carpet. However, because the color and texture of acrylic fiber can be glossy and harsh, and because acrylic carpet pile crushes easily, it is no longer recommended for use as a commercial carpet fiber.

NYLON

Nylon is the most popular carpet fiber. It has excellent wearability, abrasion resistance, and resilience, and solution-dyed nylon is also resistant to harsh cleaning chemicals and sunlight fading. However, because of nylon's excellent durability, appearance retention is a concern. Long before a nylon carpet wears out, its appearance may be permanently ruined.

POLYPROPYLENE

Polypropylene is the lightest commercial carpet fiber. Polypropylenes are known for their excellent stain and mildew resistance, low moisture absorbency, excellent colorfastness in sunlight, and high strength. They also minimize static electricity. Olefin is a polypropylene. Polypropylene is commonly used in outdoor carpeting.

POLYESTER

Polyester fibers are known for their color clarity and their capability to retain color. More popular for residential carpet applications than for commercial uses, polyester has a luxurious feel.

WOOL

Used for centuries in the manufacturing of carpet, wool is still the standard against which other carpet fibers are judged. It is generally the most expensive carpet fiber and is commonly used in woven carpets. When exposed to flame, wool chars, rather than melting like most synthetic fibers, making it naturally flame-resistant. It also dyes well and has good resistance to soil and wear.

SISAL

Sisal is a strong, woody fiber produced from the leaves of the agave plant, which is found in Central America, the West Indies, and Africa. Used mostly in twine and rope, it has become a popular contemporary flooring fiber.

CARPET DENSITY

Density, the amount of pile yarn in unit volume of carpet, is influenced by gauge—stitches per inch across the width—yarn size or thickness, and pile height. A larger yarn can be tufted at a wider gauge and receive the same density as a fine yarn at a small gauge. For areas where heavy foot traffic is likely, a density of 5000 to 7000 or more may be necessary. Office spaces with moderate traffic require a density of 4000 to 6000. Because of the fundamental differences in the manufacturing processes, different terms are used to describe carpet density for each type of carpet construction.

CEILING FINISHES

ACOUSTICAL PANEL CEILINGS

Acoustical panel ceilings are composed of manufactured units, installed in a metal suspension assembly. They are used where sound attenuation and accessibility to the above-ceiling interstitial or plenum space are desired. Acoustical ceilings are large visual elements within a space, and so are considered design elements as well as acoustical features. Partitions, light fixtures, ceiling diffusers, sprinklers, and other devices are attached to or installed within these ceilings, so coordination with the ceiling layout is critical.

Acoustical panels are installed on an exposed metal grid system suspended from the underside of the structure above. In contrast, acoustical tiles are inserted to a concealed suspension system and are generally 12 by 12 in. and 24 by 24 in.. Common acoustical panel sizes range from 24 by 24 in. to 24 by 48 in. up to 60 by 60 in., and are available in rectangular shapes as well as square. Thicknesses range from 5/8 in. to 3/4 in. to 1 in., with other thicknesses available for special applications. Most manufacturers provide hard metric-size acoustical panels to address global needs for their products.

Acoustical panel ceiling products are available to meet special project requirements, including the need for greater durability, light reflectance, and humidity resistance. Fire-resistant acoustical ceiling assemblies are available, when used with applicable UL designs.

SOUND ABSORPTION AND SOUND ISOLATION

In open office areas, the installation of an acoustical panel ceiling will improve the amount of privacy between partial-height partitioned workstations. Within closed areas, an acoustical panel ceiling can improve the transmission of noise from one room to another, if used with appropriate partition types. Manufacturers of acoustical tile ceilings categorize the acoustical features of their products according to industry standard designations for the ratings of sound absorption. Ceiling Attenuation Class (CAC) and Noise Reduction Coefficient (NRC) both rate sound absorption.

- *CAC (formerly known as CSTC, Ceiling Sound Transmission Class)* rates a ceiling's efficiency as a barrier to airborne sound transmission between adjacent spaces and from above-ceiling elements. Shown as a minimum value, a ceiling with a high CAC may have a low NRC.
- *NRC* rates average sound absorption coefficient measured at four frequencies: 250, 500, 1000, and 2000 Hz, and rates the capability of a ceiling to absorb sound, measured from 0.0 to 1.00. The higher the number, the greater the capability of the tile to absorb sound.
- *AC* rates the listener's ability to understand the spoken word within a space, expressed as a decimal, with 1.0 being perfectly intelligible. The AC rating measures the sound attenuation of a ceiling in open office areas with partial-height partitions and workstation furniture panels, without the use of a sound-masking system.

LIGHT REFLECTANCE

The quantity of light reflected by a surface, defined in ASTM E 1477, "Standard Test Method for Luminous Reflectance Factor of Acoustical Materials by Use of Integrating-Sphere Reflectometers," is known as *light reflectance*.

Illuminance is measured in footcandles, or *lux* (metric measure). One footcandle is approximately 10 lux. A *footcandle* is the average illumination resulting when one lumen of light falls on 1 sq ft of surface. The total number of lumens on a surface divided by the area of the surface equals footcandles.

High-light reflectance (*LR*) acoustical tiles provide greater reflected light from the ceiling plane. LR is measured in values from 0.00 to 1.00. High LR ceiling tiles are particularly effective in open office areas with indirect light sources, where glare is reduced at the work plane and where spaces incorporate daylight as a light source. Usable light is increased and is more evenly distributed.

Acoustical ceilings that have a light reflectance above 0.83 are considered to be high light-reflectance ceilings, but some products are available that exceed this number and reflect more light. After review of the planned illumination levels, it may be possible to reduce the number of light fixtures within a space, thereby reducing initial installation costs and long-term energy costs.

Light-reflectance values are generally lower for those acoustical tiles with textured and embossed patterns. Integrally colored tiles may affect the LR value. Unless the ceiling surface is to be used as a distributor of illumination, lower LR values may not be of concern.

CEILING TYPES

ASTM E 1264, "Classification for Acoustical Ceiling Products," provides a classification system for ceiling panels that describes various attributes of the panels; this is a very useful standard when using the descriptive method of specifying.

CEILING PANEL COMPOSITION

Several of the same types of acoustical tile are also employed as acoustical panels: water-felted, cast, or molded and nodular. Special acoustical panels composed of a ceramic and mineral fiber composite are used where increased durability, cleanliness, and resistance to humidity and fumes are required. Mylar-faced acoustical panels are used in cleanroom areas, food service, and other applications where cleanability is important.

Fiberglass panels are processed from a molten state into fibrous glass strands, then formed into sheet/board stock. A separate dimensionally stable facing material is laminated to the fiberglass core to provide texture and pattern. Backings are available to improve acoustical qualities of the fiberglass panels.

The availability of recycled content is increasing within acoustical panel manufacturers' product lines, depending on the product selected. To address the issue of sustainability within the manufacturing process many manufacturers are now recycling old ceiling panels.

EDGE DETAILS

Common edge details are square or reveal shapes. Acoustical panels with these edge details are easily dropped in place within the suspension system and are pushed up to access the ceiling plenum.

SQUARE EDGE

Square-edge acoustical panels are economical and are installed on the exposed ceiling suspension grid flanges. Square-edge panels do not conceal the suspension grid.

REVEAL EDGE

Reveal edge acoustical panels allow the panels to extend below the suspension system, partially concealing the metal grid. Tegular edges can be square, angled, beveled, stepped, or other special shapes, and are generally selected for their aesthetic appearance. When installed within an exposed tee suspension system, the acoustical panels "read" as modular elements, due to the reveals between the panels. Other suspension system profiles fill the tegular-edge reveal, providing a more flush, monolithic appearance to the ceiling.

FIRE-RESISTANCE-RATED ACOUSTICAL PANEL CEILING ASSEMBLY
3.124

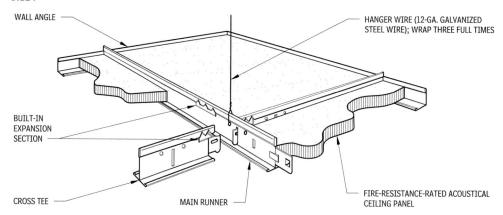

ACOUSTICAL PANEL CEILING ASSEMBLY
3.125

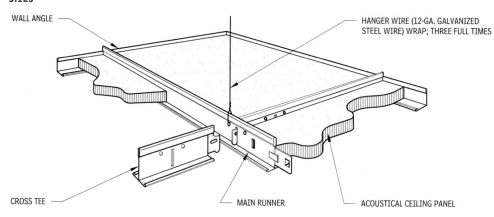

Contributors:
Setter, Leach & Lindstrom, Inc., Minneapolis, Minnesota; Blythe & Nazdin Architects, Ltd., Bethesda. Maryland.

BEVELED EDGE

Beveled edges, often found on reveal-edged units, form an eased-edge condition, which softens the line of the perimeter of the panel. When moving panels after the initial installation, beveled edges can minimize edge damage due to accidental bumping of the panel on the grid.

SPECIAL-USE PANELS

Acoustical ceiling panels are available to address special needs. Food service areas often require products that are accepted by the USDA for food preparation areas. Nonperforated mylar-faced or vinyl-faced acoustical panels with appropriate suspension systems can be installed in food service areas as well as in cleanrooms of certain classes. Acoustical properties of these mylar- or vinyl-faced products are less than those of nonfaced products; therefore, a check of the local regulations for these installations is recommended.

Composite ceramic and mineral fiber panel products perform well in areas such as indoor pool areas, hydrotherapy areas, laboratories, and other spaces where corrosive materials may be present. The suspension system grid and hangers should be of a corrosion-resistant material such as aluminum or stainless steel, to minimize deterioration.

SUSPENSION SYSTEMS

Exposed acoustical ceiling panel suspension systems are composed of main and cross-tee components, installed at the desired height by hanger wires. The suspension system is typically fabricated from factory-coated steel. Additional types include galvanized steel systems for improved resistance to moisture, and aluminum and stainless steel for other special installation requirements. Fire-rated suspension systems are available, with prenotched expansion relief segments to resist suspension system failure resulting from heat expansion of the grid.

COMPONENTS

The visible components of an exposed ceiling suspension system include interlocking main beams and cross tees, installed in a prescribed grid to accept the acoustical panels. Main beams are typically installed on hanger wires spaced at 4 ft o.c. along the beam. Angle or channel-shaped moldings are used for perimeter acoustical panel support.

Hanger wires support the main and cross tees from the structure above and are spaced per the manufacturer's recommendations and as project conditions require.

Other special accessory components of the exposed suspension system include stiffeners, clips, spacers, covers, and adapters. Although it may be difficult to identify all of the specific accessory components, the major items anticipated on a project, such as hold-down clips, stiffening braces, partition clips, and so on, should be identified, if possible. Specifications should cover accessories as well as the overall suspension system and acoustical panels.

FIRE-RESISTANCE-RATED SUSPENSION SYSTEMS

Fire-resistance-rated suspension systems conform to the UL design for fire-rated performance. Expansion points are provided at specific intervals to alleviate stresses on the grid in case of fire. Cross-tee end clips and other devices must be used as required by UL and local codes. The acoustical panels installed within the fire-resistance-rated suspension system must also be of a fire-resistive nature.

SEISMIC DESIGN

For the installation of an acoustical panel ceiling with seismic design requirement locations, review suspension systems with cross-tee end details that accommodate lateral movement. Check with ceiling suspension system manufacturers to determine the seismic capabilities of a particular system.

ACOUSTICAL TILE CEILINGS

Acoustical tile ceilings are composed of prefabricated ceiling units, which are installed in a concealed or semiexposed metal suspension system. Also known as *concealed spline ceilings*, they are directly installed on a substrate by stapling or adhesive bonding. Although acoustical tile installations provide a monolithic ceiling surface, installation can be more costly, and maintenance of the tile ceiling is more difficult than with acoustical panel installations. An acoustical tile ceiling is not as easily accessible to above-ceiling areas as acoustical panel ceilings with lay-in units. If accessibility is not an issue, an acoustical tile ceiling is an option when the aesthetics and other conditions of the installation are appropriate for the project.

Acoustical tiles are typically 12 by 12 in.; however, larger sizes are available. Thicknesses range from 1/2 in. to 5/8 in. to 3/4 in.. Hard metric sizes are available on a more limited basis from manufacturers. Acoustical panels are generally larger than 12-by-12-in. ceiling tiles, and are installed in exposed or semiconcealed grids.

Fire-resistant acoustical tile assemblies are available when used with applicable UL design criteria. Consult a manufacturer's product information for specific recommendations on acoustical panel ceiling data.

CEILING TILE COMPOSITION

Composition of the various acoustical tile types used in commercial construction include mineral fiber base and glass fiber base. Cellulose base, used primarily in residential construction, is not as durable as the commercial-grade panel construction. Construction of the mineral fiber base acoustical panels is cast, wet-felted, and nodular, and is available in a number of textures and acoustical properties.

WATER- OR WET-FELTED TILES

Water- or wet-felted tiles are fabricated from mineral wool, perlite, fillers, and binders, which are mixed into a loose slurry that is formed into sheets by draining, compressing, drying, and cutting to size. Fissured, perforated, or stippled textures are added to the tiles prior to painting the units.

CAST OR MOLDED TILES

Cast or molded tiles are fabricated from mineral fibers, fillers, and binders, then mixed into a pulp and poured into paper or foil-lined molds of the desired size. Surface textures are created by the manipulation of the surface of the molds. Integral colors can be added for a through-color product. The tiles are oven-dried, trimmed, and then painted.

NODULAR TILES

Nodular tiles are fabricated from mineral fibers wound into balls, combined with perlite, fillers, and binders, then mixed into a slurry. The mixture is formed into sheets, oven-dried, and cut to size. The tiles, which are inherently porous, are then textured with fissures and painted.

SUSPENSION SYSTEMS

Concealed acoustical tile ceiling suspension systems are installed at the desired height by hanger wires, which support the metal T- or Z-shaped grid components. The suspension system is typically fabricated from factory-coated steel or as galvanized steel systems for improved resistance to moisture.

Concealed suspension systems for acoustical tiles integrate above-ceiling access areas into the system. Access is upward or downward, depending on the system. Care should be taken to prevent damage to the ceiling tile during installation and maintenance of the system and above-ceiling elements.

STRUCTURAL PERFORMANCE

Ceiling suspension systems for acoustical tiles are designated as light-, intermediate-, or heavy-duty. Light-duty systems are used where there will be no additional loads other than the acoustical tiles; therefore, these systems are typically used only in residential and light commercial applications. Intermediate-duty systems are capable of supporting a moderate amount of additional load, such as light fixtures and ceiling diffusers. Intermediate-duty systems are commonly used in standard commercial applications. Heavy-duty systems can accommodate additional loads suspended from or installed within the ceiling system. Prior to specifying a suspension system, the anticipated loads on the ceiling should be reviewed to determine the most suitable type.

COMPONENTS

The concealed suspension system is composed of interlocking 15/16-in.- wide double-web main beams and cross tees. Main beams are typically installed on hanger wires spaced at 4 ft on center along the beam. Angle or channel-shaped moldings are used for perimeter acoustical tile support. Hanger wires support the main and cross tees from the structure above and are spaced per the manufacturer's recommendations and as project conditions require. Accessory components such as clips and concealed angles are available to allow access to the plenum space above the ceiling.

KERFED-EDGE ACOUSTIC CEILING TILE
3.126

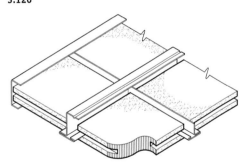

ACOUSTICAL CEILING TILE ASSEMBLY
3.127

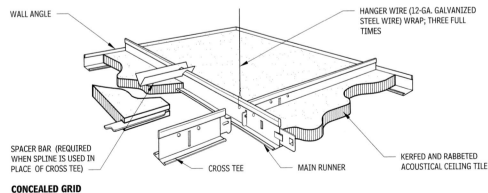

WALL ANGLE

HANGER WIRE (12-GA. GALVANIZED STEEL WIRE) WRAP; THREE FULL TIMES

SPACER BAR (REQUIRED WHEN SPLINE IS USED IN PLACE OF CROSS TEE)

CROSS TEE   MAIN RUNNER

KERFED AND RABBETED ACOUSTICAL CEILING TILE

CONCEALED GRID

Contributors:
Setter, Leach & Lindstrom, Inc., Minneapolis, Minnesota; Blythe & Nazdin Architects, Ltd., Bethesda, Maryland.

PARTITION CLIP
3.128

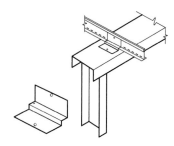

Partition clips fasten the partition top track to the ceiling grid.

STIFFENING BRACE
3.129

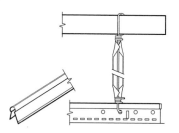

Vertical attachment of the stiffening brace to the hanger wire between grid and deck holds the suspension system in place during wind uplift and in high-security areas.

HOLD-DOWN CLIP
3.130

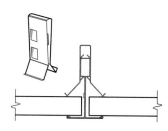

A hold-down clip attaches to the top bulb of the grid to hold lay-in panel in place, and helps prevent ceiling panels from fluttering at entryways.

ISOLATION HANGERS

Isolation hangers isolate ceilings from noise traveling through the building structure. Hangers are also available for isolating ceiling systems to shield spaces from mechanical equipment and aircraft noise.

When it is necessary to isolate a high-noise area from a building, or a "quiet room" from a high surrounding noise level, floors, walls, and ceilings should be built free of rigid contact with the building structure, to reduce sound and vibration transmission.

ISOLATION HANGER
3.131

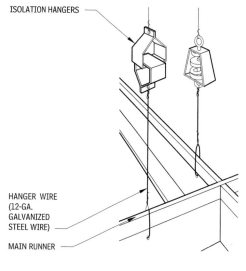

ISOLATION HANGERS

HANGER WIRE (12-GA. GALVANIZED STEEL WIRE)

MAIN RUNNER

SEISMIC DESIGN

For the installation of an acoustical tile ceiling with seismic design requirement locations, review suspension systems with cross-tee end details that accommodate lateral movement. Check with ceiling suspension system manufacturers to determine the seismic capabilities of a particular system.

LINEAR METAL CEILINGS

Linear metal ceilings are distinctive in appearance and are used where strong linear aesthetic, durability, and ease of maintenance are desired. Metal surfaces are available with many finishes and colors, which allow for a number of design options for the metal ceiling. Special suspension systems allow custom radius configurations, as well as flat horizontal ceilings, to be installed. Linear metal ceilings are typically installed as snap-in units on a concealed suspension system, and some can accept companion integrated light fixtures.

CEILING TYPES

Linear metal ceilings are fabricated from aluminum, steel, or stainless steel. Options include metal panel (slat) sizes, metal coating types, colors, textures, and acoustical insulation. Linear baffle ceilings are also available, but typically are not installed with acoustical insulation.

SIZES

Linear metal panel dimensions vary by manufacturer, but a common module width range is from 2 in. wide to 8 in. wide. Additional slat panel widths are available from manufacturers. Standard lengths are commonly 12 and 16 ft, but can be tailored to a particular installation with custom lengths. Depths of panels vary, with deeper panels providing a stronger linear effect to the ceiling. Overall size is regulated by the suspension method capacity and installation parameters of the project.

MATERIALS

The most common material for linear metal ceilings is roll-formed aluminum, with typical thicknesses of 0.020 in., 0.025 in., and 0.032 in. Aluminum linear panels are preferred for high-humidity areas and in spaces where the environment fluctuates, as well as for exterior applications. Roll-formed steel linear panels are available, and they can be more economical than aluminum, but are not as commonly used due to concerns about maintenance over time. Stainless steel also performs well but is typically more costly than aluminum or steel panels.

LINEAR BAFFLE CEILING SYSTEM
3.132

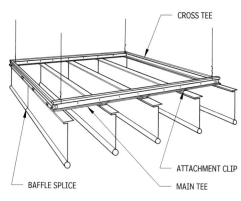

CROSS TEE

ATTACHMENT CLIP

MAIN TEE

BAFFLE SPLICE

LINEAR METAL PAN CEILING
3.133

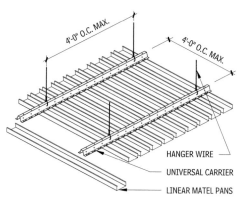

4'-0" O.C. MAX.

4'-0" O.C. MAX.

HANGER WIRE

UNIVERSAL CARRIER

LINEAR MATEL PANS

LINEAR METAL CEILING WITH ACOUSTICAL INSULATION
3.134

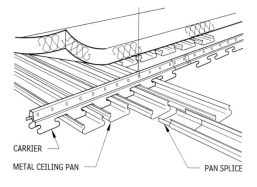

CARRIER

METAL CEILING PAN

PAN SPLICE

Contributors:
Keith McCormack, CSI, CCS, RTKL Associates, Baltimore, Maryland; USG Interiors, Inc., Chicago, Illinois; Setter, Leach & Lindstrom, Inc., Minneapolis, Minnesota.

LINEAR METAL CEILING AND FASCIA ASSEMBLY
3.135

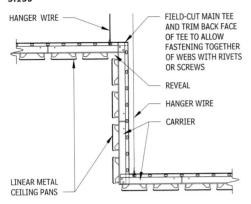

LINEAR METAL CEILING PERIMETER CONDITION
3.136

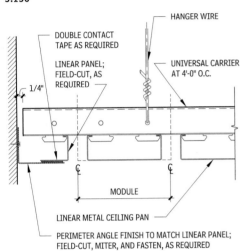

ACOUSTIC PROPERTIES

Acoustic properties of linear metal ceilings vary, depending on the type of metal pan used, type of sound attenuation used, and project conditions. Sound waves pass through the reveals between the panels, so the use of sound attenuation will reduce the sound transmitted. Sound passes through the ceiling plenum if ceiling-height partitions are installed in the areas with linear metal ceilings; therefore, sound attenuation batting above the ceiling will improve acoustics slightly. Microperforations are available on some metal panel products, and improve the acoustic qualities of the system, especially if used in conjunction with sound attenuation batting. NRC ratings average around 0.70 to 0.90, depending on installation conditions.

Fiberglass is the most common material for sound attenuation batting, but it should be wrapped so that the fibers do not escape into the space and compromise the indoor air quality. Reveal filler strips reduce sound transmission. A review with an acoustical consultant and the metal pan ceiling manufacturer may be beneficial when selecting a linear metal ceiling.

SUSPENSION SYSTEMS

Concealed suspension systems for linear metal ceilings are similar to those used for acoustical tile installations. Classifications of the suspension systems are typically intermediate- and heavy-duty, depending on the type and weight of the linear metal panels. Carrier suspension systems are hung from the structure above by hanger wires, with main tees usually located at 48 in. o.c., maximum. Special carriers, which require additional support, are available to provide radius configurations of the ceiling. Expansion carriers increase the centerline-to-centerline dimension of the panels to accommodate a nonstandard module installation. Stabilizer bars snap into slots every 4 in. o.c., and provide additional strength and rigidity to the suspension system.

ACCESSORIES

Accessories include cross-connector clamps, which are installed at grid intersections of main and cross-tees to provide added strength. Wind-uplift struts, seismic clips, and other devices are available to address the requirements of local codes regarding the installation of linear metal ceilings. Trim pieces and moldings are available for perimeter conditions, and access panels provide above-ceiling access.

FIRE RESISTANCE

Some linear metal ceiling systems are listed as UL fire-resistance-rated assemblies. Check with manufacturers for specific information regarding the fire resistance of a particular product. Currently, as with metal pan ceilings, linear metal ceilings are not identified as having specific fire-resistive qualities and are not listed in the *UL Fire Resistance Directory*.

RECYCLED CONTENT

Many manufacturers have integrated recycled material to their metal pan ceiling fabrication, although the percentage of recycled content varies among manufacturers and products.

SEE ALSO

Acoustical Panel Ceiling
Carpeting
Gypsum Lath
Joint Sealants
Linear Metal Ceilings
Metal Lath
Metal Pan Stairs
Resilient Base
Resilient Flooring
Resilient Wood Flooring
Suspension Systems
Terrazzo Flooring
Thinset Tiling
Tiling
Wood Block Flooring
Wood Flooring

Contributors:
Keith McCormack, CSI, CCS, RTKL Associates, Baltimore, Maryland; USG Interiors, Inc., Chicago, Illinois.

4

ELEMENT D: SERVICES

INTRODUCTION

To approach the discussions of this chapter, the following issues offer perspective.

Scale: Service elements comprise roughly 15 percent of overall project resources (construction cost, floor space, or building volume) of a residential project but may require up to 50 percent for a complex laboratory facility. Scale is affected if extra capacity is required for infrequent high-occupancy periods or emergency backup. However, with proper design, the incorporation of passive systems, and technical integration, some service elements may be minimized and as a result, resources allocated to other features.

Operation: Service elements consume resources and produce waste as long as the building is in operation. Furthermore, service equipment must be maintained, repaired, upgraded, and eventually replaced. These ongoing requirements are in addition to the suggested 15 to 50 percent project resource figure indicated in scale.. From a life-cycle perspective, operation and maintenance costs often exceeds construction costs.

Failures: Poor performance or temporary failure of facility services is seldom catastrophic. Small inefficiencies can, however, become expensive over long-term operation. More serious problems occur when conditions are poorly maintained and unsanitary, or when pollution results in the so-called sick building syndrome.

Dynamics: Equipment operation is matched to human needs by control systems. Thus, unlike static building elements, services provide a complex and variable response to changing conditions and fluctuating demands. Bimodalities of flux include summer/winter, day/night, and occupied/unoccupied modes.

Continuous commissioning: Occupant use, the environment, and service equipment are in constant motion and interrelated change. This dynamic condition must be routinely reconfigured to match the operation of equipment to current use patterns.

Facility services require equipment space and clearance. Vertical and horizontal distribution paths lead from equipment rooms through the building to delivery points in occupied space. Utility service entrances should be coordinated with large equipment spaces. Connections between indoor equipment and the outdoor environment may include exhaust flues, exhaust air ducts, combustion air ducts, and ventilation air intake grilles. Central location of services or close proximity to major loads can facilitate ease of distribution. Service systems may be divided into separate zones that are controlled independently.

Service elements become visual fixtures at their delivery point in occupied spaces. Visually exposing other distribution components such as ducts, conduit, and piping can increase room volume by eliminating ceilings; but this requires careful attention to the resulting aesthetic, functional and maintenance impacts of their presence in occupied space. For example, outdoor and rooftop equipment can compromise views from adjoining sites.

Facility services impact each other, such as heat from light fixtures and equipment affecting cooling loads, or the use of air-handling equipment to provide compartmentalization in case of a fire. Services may also be affected by other building components such as thermal mass of structure or sunlight and solar heat through fenestration. Service components produce noise that negatively impacts interior and exterior spaces, including air friction, fan noise, water flow, fixture noise, valve noise, electrical transformer hum, and vibration from motors and pumps.

Service elements should be selected by the design team and may require coordination with the owners design. Construction sequence is affected because many components are large and others are concealed behind construction assemblies. During construction, use of service elements may be required on a temporary basis, so as to provide electrical power for construction work, or humidity control for protection of interior finishes as they are installed. Services and controls should be tested, adjusted, and balanced before occupancy.

Contributor:
Leonard R. Bachman, RA, University of Houston, Houston, Texas.

CONVEYING

Conveying equipment may include elevators, escalators and moving walks, dumbwaiters, lifts, turntables, scaffolding, conveyors, and facility chutes, and pneumatic tube systems.

Conveying equipment is used to move people, equipment and freight along horizontal and vertical paths. Conveying equipment makes access within large buildings practical by minimizing effort and travel time and can also be used to control access for privacy and security. Their physical area and typical expense usually impact the basic planning of the building and control some aspects of the overall design. The speed at which these mechanized systems operate must be balanced against the occupants' waiting time in conjunction with the potential physical unease of rapid or jerky movement.

Conveying systems are also important elements of universal access for occupants of differing physical abilities and so must comply with relevant accessibility standards. Safety is critical, in particular where shafts, openings, or operating parts may pose a danger to occupants; therefore maintenance procedures require frequent inspection and, potentially, regular recertification by building authorities. Regulations are especially critical for elevators.

Other general design factors relate to matching equipment size, speed, and capacity with occupant type, demand load, and level of convenience.

DESIGN CONSIDERATIONS

Mechanized movement of occupants and materials within a building enables designers to organize, divide, and compartmentalize areas into distinctly separate zones that are accessible only through controlled portals of elevators or escalators. This separation can increase security, provide individual occupancies, and structure the sequences, such as arrival, greeting, and destination. These systems are typically surrounded by public physical space such as landings, foyers, and lobbies.

Conveying equipment also permit large plan areas to be folded upon themselves so that the shortest distance between two points is not a straight line from one area of the floor to another area of the same floor, but rather a mechanized path between adjacent or widely dispersed floor levels. In very large facilities such as airport terminals and high-rise buildings, conveying equipment facilitate rapid and easy communication between widely separated points that might otherwise be impractical to traverse, such as the sequence of passenger dropoff, baggage conveying, ticketing, passenger loading bridges, and departure lobbies.

CONFIGURATIONS

Elevators are generally used for longer-distance trips, while escalators are normally limited to five or fewer adjoining floor levels. Sky lobbies can be used to divide buildings into vertical subbuildings, and smaller elevators, escalators, stairs, or any combination can provide circulation among the divisions.

CONTROLS

Careful and expert consideration is required in the strategic design and automated operation of conveying equipment; therefore appropriate consultants should be engaged early in the design process.

INTERFACES

Conveying equipment interfaces directly with the general circulation system and planning organization of a facility. Mechanized passenger pathways should be supplemented by modes of emergency egress. To the extent that vertical conveyance equipment permits high-rise building designs, they may also impact site planning and building utilization.

ELEVATOR

Components of an elevator system include a hoistway, a machine room, an elevator car, and waiting lobbies for passenger, equipment or freight loading.

HOISTWAY

The hoistway is an open vertical shaft for the travel of one or more elevator cars. It includes a pit and usually terminates at the underside of the machine room in a traction assembly, and at the underside of the roof over the hoistway in a hydraulic assembly. Typically, access to the elevator car and hoistway is through hoistway doors at each floor, serviced by the elevator. Hoistway design is determined by the characteristics of the elevator system selected, along with requirements for fire separation, ventilation, soundproofing, and nonstructural elements.

MACHINE ROOMS

Both electric traction and hydraulic elevators require a location for elevator operating machinery. Due to current technology advances, operating machinery for hydraulic elevators has become smaller and often can be located within the hoistway. When a designated machine room is required, for either electric traction or hydraulic systems, fire separation; adequate ventilation and soundproofing are required, along with self-closing and self-locking doors. The machine room for an electric traction elevator is usually located directly above the hoistway, but could also be situated below, to the side, or to the rear of the hoistway and contains elevator hoisting machinery and electronic control equipment. Machine rooms for hydraulic elevators, normally located near the base of the hoistway contain a hydraulic pump unit and electronic controls. Codes may forbid placement of equipment not associated with the elevator in the machine room.

ELEVATOR CAR

Guided by vertical rails on each side, the elevator car conveys passengers or freight between floors. It is constructed within a supporting platform and frame. Design of the cab focuses on ceiling, wall, floor, and door finishes and accompanying lighting, ventilation, and elevator signal equipment.

The car and frame of a hydraulic elevator are supported by a piston or cylinder. The car and frame of an electric traction elevator are supported by the hoist machine. The elevator and its counterweight are connected with steel ropes or belts.

LOBBIES

Elevator waiting areas are designed to allow free circulation of passengers, rapid access to elevator cars, and clearly visible elevator signals. Dependent upon facility design elevator lobbies may be required to be enclosed.

ELEVATOR TYPES AND USES

Generally there are two types of elevators, hydraulic and electric traction. Both of these elevator types elevators can be used in various applications including passenger, service, freight and residential.

ELEVATOR TYPES

- *Hydraulic elevators:* Use a hydraulic oil driven machine to raise and lower the elevator car and its load. Lower speeds and piston length restrict the use of this type. Travel distances vary between 35 and 60 ft dependent upon configuration and capacity. Although

ELEVATOR TRAVEL DISTANCES
4.1

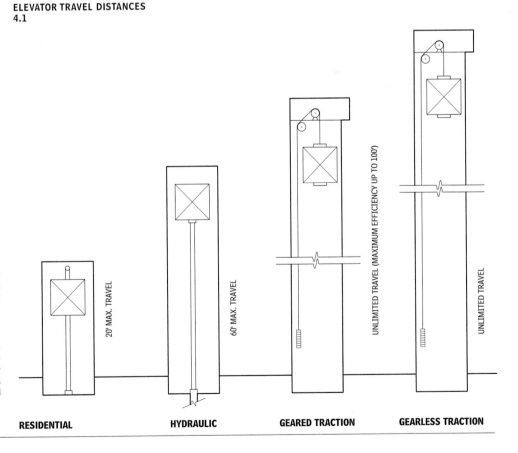

RESIDENTIAL   HYDRAULIC   GEARED TRACTION   GEARLESS TRACTION

20' MAX. TRAVEL

60' MAX. TRAVEL

UNLIMITED TRAVEL (MAXIMUM EFFICIENCY UP TO 100')

UNLIMITED TRAVEL

NOTE

4.1 These dimensions are general guidelines for selecting an elevator, using height as a criterion.

Contributor:
Leonard R. Bachman, University of Houston, Houston, Texas.

it generally requires the least initial installation expense, this elevator type requires more power to operate and will cost more over the life cycle.

- *Electric traction elevators:* Elevators in which the energy is applied by means of an electric driven machine. Medium to high speeds and virtually limitless rise allow this elevator type to serve high-rise, medium-rise, and low-rise buildings. Electric traction elevators can be further divided into geared and gearless categories.
- *Geared traction elevators:* Designed to operate within the general range of 100 to 450 ft/min, restricting their use to medium-rise buildings.
- *Gearless traction elevators:* Available in units with speeds of 500 to 1200 ft/min. They offer the advantages of a long life and a smooth ride.

ELEVATOR USE TYPES

- *Passenger elevators:* Used to convey people from floor to floor. Elevator cab are available in standard and custom designs.
- *Service elevators:* In industrial, residential, and commercial buildings, service elevators are often standard passenger elevator packages modified for service use.
- *Freight elevators:* Usually classed as general freight loading, motor vehicle loading, industrial truck, or concentrated loading elevators. General freight loading elevators may be electric drum type or traction or hydraulic elevators.
- *Residential elevators:* Installed only in a private residence or to serve a single unit in a building with multiple dwelling units. By code, elevators in private residences are limited in size, capacity, rise, and speed.

ELEVATOR PLANNING

ELEVATOR PLANNING DETAILS
4.2

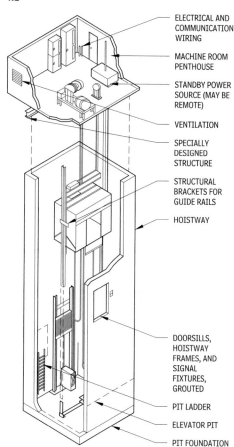

ELECTRICAL AND COMMUNICATION WIRING

MACHINE ROOM PENTHOUSE

STANDBY POWER SOURCE (MAY BE REMOTE)

VENTILATION

SPECIALLY DESIGNED STRUCTURE

STRUCTURAL BRACKETS FOR GUIDE RAILS

HOISTWAY

DOORSILLS, HOISTWAY FRAMES, AND SIGNAL FIXTURES, GROUTED

PIT LADDER

ELEVATOR PIT

PIT FOUNDATION

BUILDING CHARACTERISTICS

Physical building characteristics such as building height and hoistway location are considered in conjunction with population characteristics to determine the size, capacity, speed, type, and location of elevator components. These characteristics in particular affect elevator design:

- *Height:* Determine the distance of elevator travel from lowest stop to uppermost stop, the total number of stops, and the distance between stops.
- *Building use:* Identify the location of heavily used entrance areas, such as those leading to cafeterias, restaurants, auditoriums, and service areas. Typically, plan a facility so that no prospective passengers must walk more than 200 ft to reach an elevator.

The elevator selection process must begin with a thorough analysis of how people will occupy the facility. Four issues are pertinent:

- *Total population and density:* Determine these figures for each floor or for portion of floors.
- *Peak loading:* Identify the periods when elevators will carry the highest traffic loads.
- *Waiting time:* This is the length of time a passenger is expected to wait for the next elevator to arrive.
- *Demand for quality:* Smooth operation may be as important as fancy finishes.

PREPARATION FOR ELEVATOR INSTALLATION

The following preparatory work is required to be in place prior to the installation of the elevator and related equipment:

- An enclosed elevator equipment room with electrical outlets, adequate lighting, and heating and ventilation sufficient to maintain the room at a temperature between 50°F (minimum) and 100°F (maximum)
- Adequate supports and foundations to carry the loads of all equipment, including supports for guide rail brackets
- Connections from facility electric power to each controller, including necessary circuit breakers and fused main-line disconnect switches

ELEVATOR TYPES BY USE
4.3

NEED/USE	ELEVATOR TYPE			
	PRIVATE RESIDENTIAL	HYDRAULIC	GEARED TRACTION	GEARLESS TRACTION
Private houses	X			
Low-rise, low speed		X		
Medium-rise, moderate speed			X	
High-rise, high speed				X
Low initial cost		X		
No penthouse, lightweight construction		X		
Freight, low-rise		X	X	
Freight, high-rise			X	

- Electric power of the same characteristics as the permanent supply for construction, testing, and adjusting
- Trenching and backfilling for any underground piping or conduit
- Divider beams for rail bracket support, as required
- Cutting of walls, floors, and other construction, and removal of any obstructions; setting of anchors and sleeves
- Hoist beam for installation. Dependent on the installation and use, the hoist beam may be able to be removed after elevator installation.
- Temporary enclosures, barricades, or other protection from open hoistways and elevator work areas while the elevator is being installed
- Adequate storage facilities for elevator equipment before and during installation

ELEVATOR INSTALLATION

The following work may be required to be completed prior to use of the elevators for either temporary or permanent use:

- Grouting of doorsills, hoistway frames, and signal fixtures after installation of elevator equipment
- Temporary elevator service prior to completion
- Heat and smoke sensors, as required by authority having jurisdiction, which may include requirements of the National Fire Protection Association (NFPA) or National Elevator Code
- Telephone wiring to machine room control panel, and installation of telephone instruments
- A standby power source when elevator operation from an alternate power supply is required
- A means to disconnect the elevator's main-line power supply automatically, to protect the machine room equipment from damage
- A plumb and legal hoistway; a pit of proper depth with a pit ladder for each elevator; drains, lights, access doors, waterproofing, and hoistway ventilation, as required

Contributor:
Rippeteau Rollins Architecture + Design, Washington, DC.

ELEVATOR LOBBY PLANNING
4.4

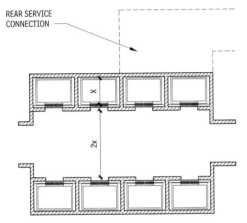

SINGLE CAR

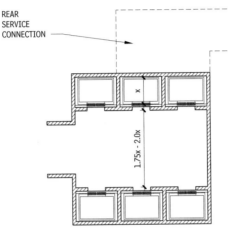

PAIRED CARS

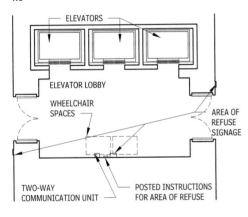

FOUR–EIGHT CAR ARRANGEMENT

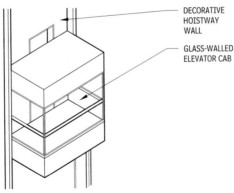

THREE–SIX CAR ARRANGEMENT

ELEVATOR LOBBY DESIGNED AS AN AREA OF REFUGE
4.5

GLASS-WALLED ELEVATOR CAB
4.6

Observation and glass-walled elevators travel outside of a hoistway or in a partially glass enclosed hoistway. Generally machinery is concealed or located to be inconspicuous. Elevators may be hydraulic or electric traction; the electric traction elevators may be geared or gearless. Cabs can be custom-designed with more than 75 percent of wall area as glass. Safety barriers must be provided at floor penetrations and the ground floor, completely surrounding that part of the elevator not enclosed by the hoistway. This is a very specialized application, so consultation is advised.

ELECTRIC TRACTION ELEVATORS

Electric traction elevators may be either geared or gearless systems. The main differences between the two systems lie in travel speed and travel height. General design considerations involving hoistway, machine room, and elevator planning are similar.

Both geared and gearless drive units are governed by electronic controls, which coordinate car leveling, passenger calls, collective operation of elevators, door operation, car acceleration and deceleration, and safety applications. A broad range of control systems is available to meet individual facility requirements.

Structural requirements call for the total weight of the elevator to be supported by the machine beams and transmitted to the building (or hoistway) structure. Coordination with elevator consultants and structural engineers is important for proper design.

Keep the following in mind when designing for traction elevator:

- Pit depths, clear overhead dimension, and machine room penthouse sizes should be in accordance with American Society of Mechanical Engineers Safety Code for Elevators and Escalators (ASME A17.1). Local codes may vary from these requirements along with requiring fire-resistance rated enclosures.
- Minimum clear overhead dimensions are based on manufacturer standard cab heights.
- Capacity may be considered in terms of passengers or pounds, dependent upon what will be moved.
- Elevator configuration will be dependent on capacity and also entrance size and location.
- Travel distance, speed, and number of stops are all factors that will affect the design of the elevator and associated equipment.
- The machine room for traction elevators is usually located directly above the hoistway in a penthouse, but may be located in other spaces adjacent to the hoistway. Space must be provided for the elevator drive, electronic control equipment, and governor; provide sufficient clearance for equipment installation, repair, and removal. Adequate lighting and heating, ventilation and sound insulation should be provided. An elevator consultant can be an valuable asset to the design team, during the early phases of a project.

ELECTRIC TRACTION ELEVATOR WITH BASEMENT MACHINE ROOM
4.7

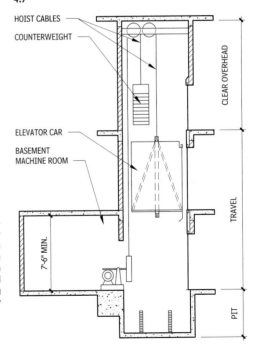

4.4 a. Passenger elevators should be centrally located, near the main entrance, and easily accessible on all floors. Groups of elevators should be arranged to minimize walking distance between cars. Lobby space must be sufficient to accommodate group movement. In general elevators may not open into a corridor.

b. The largest practical grouping of elevators in a building is eight cars. One row of more than four cars is generally not recommended. With groupings of four or six cars, lobbies may be closed at one end, forming an alcove, or open at both ends.

c. In buildings with several elevator groupings, one group may serve lower floors, while others serve as express elevators to upper floors.

d. When four or more elevators serve all or the same part of a building, they must be located in a minimum of two hoistways, but no more than four elevators can be located in any one hoistway.

e. The use of elevators with front and rear openings may provide an option for building service applications.

4.5 a. Refer to applicable codes, standards, and regulations for specific Area of Refuge requirements.

b. The elevator lobby and shaft must be pressurized for smokeproof enclosure, as required by the authority having jurisdiction.

c. The pressurization system must be activated by smoke detectors in locations approved by the authority having jurisdiction.

d. The system's equipment and ducts must be enclosed within 2-hour fire-resistance-rated construction.

4.7 This is a very specialized application, so consultation with experts is advised. Electric traction elevators with basement machine rooms are used in new and existing buildings where overhead clearance is limited.

Contributor:
Rippeteau Rollins Architecture + Design, Washington, DC.

GEARLESS ELEVATOR MACHINE ROOM
4.8

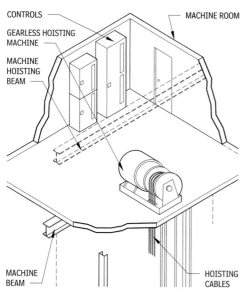

ELEVATOR HOISTWAY TYPES
4.9

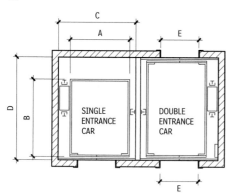

SIDE-MOUNTED COUNTERWEIGHT

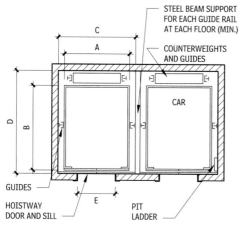

REAR-MOUNTED COUNTERWEIGHT

ELECTRIC TRACTION ELEVATOR DIMENSIONS (FT-IN.)
4.10

RATED LOAD (LB)	A	B	C	D	E
2000	5-8	4-3	7-4	6-11	3-0
2500	6-8	4-3	8-4	6-11	3-6
3000	6-8	4-7	8-4	7-5	3-6
3500	6-8	5-3	8-4	8-1	3-6
4500	5-8	7-10	8-2	10-5	4-0

HYDRAULIC ELEVATORS

Hydraulic elevators are used primarily in low- and mid-rise installations, where moderate car speed (up to 150 ft per minute) is acceptable. A car is connected to the top of a long piston that moves up and down in a cylinder. The car moves up when hydraulic fluid is pumped into the cylinder from a reservoir, raising the piston. The car is lowered when the hydraulic fluid returns to the reservoir. The up and down motions of the elevator car are controlled by the hydraulic valve.

The main space planning elements of a hydraulic elevator are the machine room, usually located at the base, and the hoistway, which serves as a fire-protected, ventilated passageway for the elevator car. Adequate structure must be provided at the base of the hoistway to bear the load of the elevator car and its supporting piston or cylinder.

There are three configurations of hydraulic elevators holed, holeless, and roped hydraulic. The cylinder in a holed hydraulic elevator is centered below the car and bored into the earth. The cylinder depth will be approximately equal to the travel distance plus the pit depth. Holeless hydraulic elevator cylinders are located on one or both side of the car and do not penetrate below the elevator pit. Holeless hydraulic elevators have substantially less travel than holed types. With roped hydraulic elevators, the plunger moves the cables or ropes, which then moves the elevator car. All three configurations can be used in commercial applications, but holed and holeless are the most common types.

When designing for hydraulic elevators, follow these guidelines:

- Ensure that pit depths and overhead clearances are in accordance with ASME A17.1 requirements; and note that local codes may vary from these requirements.
- Use car and hoistway dimensions of units for reference purposes only. A variety of units are available. Consult with manufacturers for specific dimensions.
- Hoistway walls serve primarily as fire-resistant enclosures. Check local codes to determine required fire-resistance ratings.
- Guide rails extend from the floor of the pit to top of the hoistway to guide the car inside the hoistway.
- Rail brackets attach the guide rails to the hoistway walls and typically are located at each floor level. A bracket is required at the top of the hoistway, and an intermediate bracket may be required for excessive floor-to-floor heights.
- Holed hydraulic applications require a jack hole in the floor of the pit.

TRACTION ELEVATOR (GEARED)
4.11

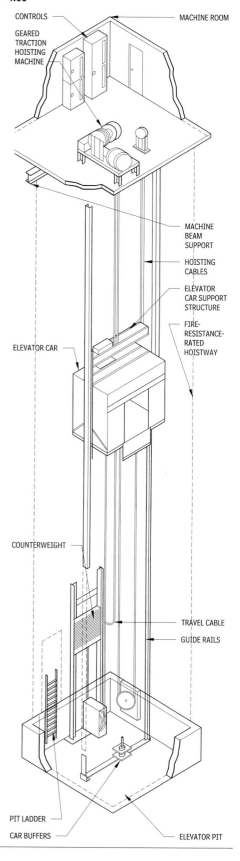

NOTES

4.9 Side-mounted counterweights allow an optional rear entrance door.
4.10 Indicated dimensions should be used only for preliminary planning. Actual dimensions are dependent on mounting location of counterweights and manufacturer standard elevator dimensions.

Contributor:
Rippeteau Architects, PC, Washington, DC.

PISTON AND CYLINDER DETAIL
4.12

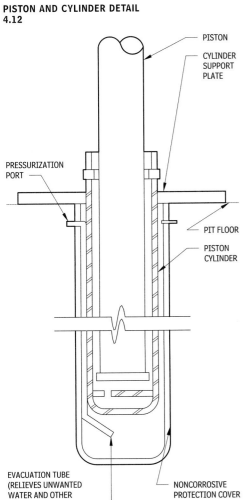

PISTON

CYLINDER SUPPORT PLATE

PRESSURIZATION PORT

PIT FLOOR

PISTON CYLINDER

EVACUATION TUBE (RELIEVES UNWANTED WATER AND OTHER LIQUIDS FROM CYLINDER)

NONCORROSIVE PROTECTION COVER FOR CYLINDER

HOLED HYDRAULIC ELEVATOR
4.13

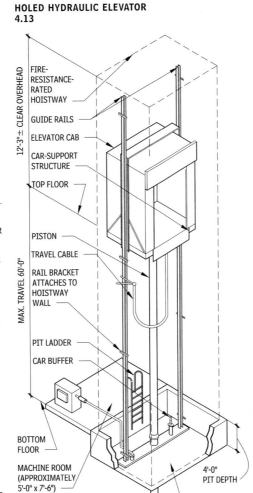

12'-3"± CLEAR OVERHEAD

MAX. TRAVEL 60'-0"

FIRE-RESISTANCE-RATED HOISTWAY

GUIDE RAILS

ELEVATOR CAB

CAR-SUPPORT STRUCTURE

TOP FLOOR

PISTON

TRAVEL CABLE

RAIL BRACKET ATTACHES TO HOISTWAY WALL

PIT LADDER

CAR BUFFER

BOTTOM FLOOR

MACHINE ROOM (APPROXIMATELY 5'-0" x 7'-6")

JACK HOLE (DEPTH = MAX. RISE + 4'-0", APPROXIMATELY)

4'-0" PIT DEPTH

ELEVATOR PIT

HOLED HYDRAULIC ELEVATOR DIMENSIONS (FT-IN.)
4.14

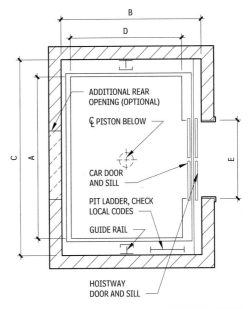

ADDITIONAL REAR OPENING (OPTIONAL)

$\mathcal{C}$ PISTON BELOW

CAR DOOR AND SILL

PIT LADDER, CHECK LOCAL CODES

GUIDE RAIL

HOISTWAY DOOR AND SILL

RATED LOAD (LB)	A	B	C	D	E
2000	5-8	4-3	7-4	5-11	3-0
2500	6-8	4-3	8-4	5-11	3-6
3000	6-8	4-7	8-4	6-3	3-6
3500	6-8	5-3	8-4	6-11	3-6
4500	5-8	7-10	7-5	10-0	4-0

NOTES

4.14 a. Indicated dimensions should be used only for preliminary planning. Actual dimensions are dependent on mounting location of counterweights and manufacturer standard elevator dimensions.

Contributor:
Rippeteau Architects, PC, Washington, DC.

HOLELESS HYDRAULIC ELEVATOR
4.15

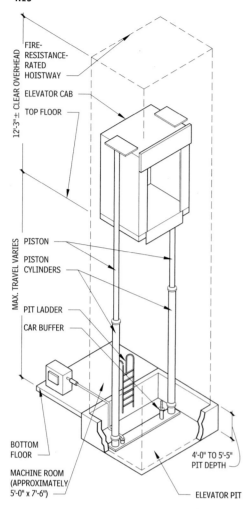

- FIRE-RESISTANCE-RATED HOISTWAY
- ELEVATOR CAB
- TOP FLOOR
- 12'-3" ± CLEAR OVERHEAD
- MAX. TRAVEL VARIES
- PISTON
- PISTON CYLINDERS
- PIT LADDER
- CAR BUFFER
- BOTTOM FLOOR
- MACHINE ROOM (APPROXIMATELY 5'-0" x 7'-6")
- 4'-0" TO 5'-5" PIT DEPTH
- ELEVATOR PIT

MACHINE ROOM
4.16

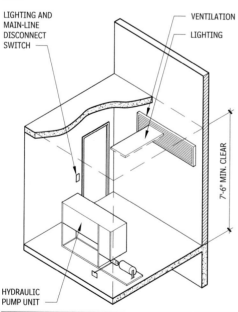

- LIGHTING AND MAIN-LINE DISCONNECT SWITCH
- VENTILATION
- LIGHTING
- 7'-6" MIN. CLEAR
- HYDRAULIC PUMP UNIT

FREIGHT ELEVATORS

General freight elevators with capacities of 2000 to 8000 lbs satisfy a variety of material-handling requirements. Industrial truck freight elevators require special design considerations to handle truckloads of 10,000 to 20,000 lbs or more.

General freight or industrial truck elevators may have either hydraulic or traction drive systems, similar to those of other elevator However, the units are usually custom-designed with vertical bipart doors and special structural support to accommodate heavy loads and eccentric loading conditions. Freight elevators usually have simple control systems and operate at slower speeds than other elevators. Their capacity must be sized for the largest expected load.

There are five classes of loading for freight elevators; Class A: General Freight Loading; Class B: Motor Vehicle Loading; Class C1: Industrial Truck Loading (where truck is carried by the elevator); Class C2: Industrial Truck Loading (where truck is used only for loading and unloading); Class C3: Other Loading with Heavy Concentrations. Refer to ASME A17.1 for additional information regarding loading and design of freight elevators.

HYDRAULIC FREIGHT ELEVATOR
4.17

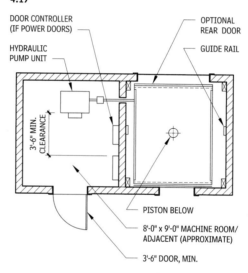

- DOOR CONTROLLER (IF POWER DOORS)
- HYDRAULIC PUMP UNIT
- OPTIONAL REAR DOOR
- GUIDE RAIL
- 3'-6" MIN. CLEARANCE
- PISTON BELOW
- 8'-0" x 9'-0" MACHINE ROOM/ADJACENT (APPROXIMATE)
- 3'-6" DOOR, MIN.

TRACTION FREIGHT ELEVATOR
4.18

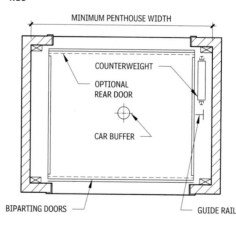

- MINIMUM PENTHOUSE WIDTH
- COUNTERWEIGHT
- OPTIONAL REAR DOOR
- CAR BUFFER
- BIPARTING DOORS
- GUIDE RAIL

FREIGHT ELEVATOR KEY PLAN
4.19

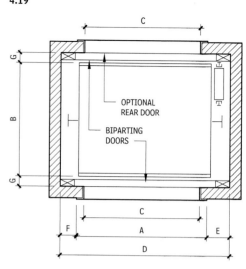

- OPTIONAL REAR DOOR
- BIPARTING DOORS

TRACTION FREIGHT ELEVATORS
4.20

CAPACITY (LB)	DIMENSIONS (FT-IN.)					
	A	B	C	D	E	F
2500	5–4	7–0	5–0	7–10	1–7	0–11
4000	6–4	8–0	6–0	8–10	1–7	0–11
8000	8–4	10–0	8–0	10–10	1–7	0–11
12,000	10–4	14–0	10–0	13–6	1–7	0–11
20,000	12–4	20–4	12–0	16–6	1–7	0–11

HYDRAULIC FREIGHT ELEVATORS
4.21

CAPACITY (LB)	DIMENSIONS (FT-IN.)				
	A	B	C	D (MANUAL DOORS)	D (POWER DOORS)
2000	5–0	6–0	4–8	6–4	6–10
4000	6–6	8–0	6–2	7–10	8–4
8000	8–6	12–0	8–2	10–6	10–6
12,000	10–6	14–0	10–2	12–6	12–6
20,000	12–6	20–0	12–2	14–6	14–6

NOTES

4.16 a. A machine room, meeting code requirements and ventilated for temperatures between 65°F and 100°F, must be provided for all elevators. It is usually located next to the hoistway at or near the bottom terminal landing. Room size may vary depending on the number of cars, capacity, and speed.
b. Machinery consists of a pump and motor drive unit, hydraulic fluid storage tank, and electronic control panel. Adequate ventilation, lighting, and entrance access (recommended 3 ft-6 in. wide) should be provided.

4.19 For regular counterbalanced hoistway doors, G = 5 in.; for pass-type counterbalanced hoistway doors, 6-3/4 in. Pass-type doors are required when floor heights are less than 11 ft for 7-ft openings, and less than 12 ft-6 in. for 8-ft openings.
4.20 and 4.21 Indicated dimensions should be used for preliminary planning. Consult elevator manufacturer for specific sizes and load capacities.

Contributor:
Rippeteau Architects, PC, Washington, DC..

FREIGHT ELEVATOR
4.22

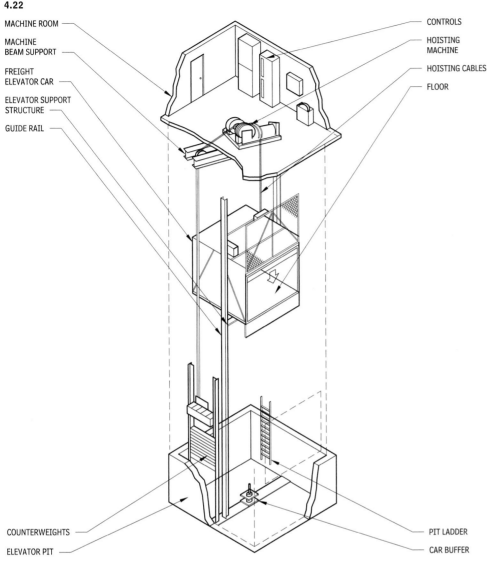

MACHINE ROOM

MACHINE
BEAM SUPPORT

FREIGHT
ELEVATOR CAR

ELEVATOR SUPPORT
STRUCTURE

GUIDE RAIL

CONTROLS

HOISTING
MACHINE

HOISTING CABLES

FLOOR

COUNTERWEIGHTS

ELEVATOR PIT

PIT LADDER

CAR BUFFER

ESCALATORS AND MOVING WALKS

Escalators are a very efficient form of vertical transportation for very heavy traffic where the number of floors served is limited (normally a maximum of five to six floors). Escalators are not usually accepted as a required exit and are not allowed as part of an accessible route.

Dimensions indicated in Table 4.25 are typical for commercial type escalators with two flat steps, dimensions will vary with the manufacturer, and other available configurations. Consult manufacturers for structural support, electrical supply, and specific dimensional requirements.

ESCALATORS
4.23

	DESCRIPTION	MANUFACTURER DIMENSIONS								
		KONE			OTIS			SCHINDLER		
SYMBOL	NOMINAL ESCALATOR WIDTH	32"	40"	48"	32"	40"	48"	32"	40"	48"
A	Centerline to centerline of handrail	2'-10-1/8"	3'-5-7/8"	4'-1-11/16"	N/A			2'-9"	3'-4-7/8"	4'-3/4"
B	Nominal step width	24"	32"	40"	24"	32"	40"	24"	32"	40"
C	Wellway rough opening	4'-1-1/16"	4'-8-7/8"	5'-4-5/8"	4'-3/16"	4'-8-3/16"	5'-4-1/8"	3'-11-1/4"	4'-7-1/8"	5'-3"
T	WP to end of lower truss	7'-0-11/16"			7'-8-3/4"			7'-1/2"		
U	Top of handrail	3'-3-3/8"			3'-3-3/8"			3'-3-3/8"		
V	Depth of lower pit	3'-8-7/8" Min.			3'-5-5/8"			4'-0"		
W	Top of handrail	2'-10-1/8"			2'-9-1/8"			2'-7"		
X	Depth of truss	3'-0-13/16"			3'-2-11/16"			2'-11-3/8"		
Y	Depth of upper pit	3'-5-3/16"			3'-5-5/8"			3'-3-3/4"		
Z	WP to end upper truss	8'-2-1/2"			8'-5"			8'-3"		

NOTES

4.22 a. Hoistway walls: Authorities having jurisdiction govern design characteristics; consult with appropriate agencies to determine requirements such as fire-resistance.

b. Traction elevators: The hoisting machine may be mounted directly overhead or at the side of the hoistway at any level, including the lowest landing. Special structural design considerations are necessary based on forces created by the use of traction equipment.

c. Guide rail bracket support: Freight elevators create horizontal forces greater than those created by passenger elevators. Vertical steel is installed within the hoistway to provide bracket support at elevations with bracket locations.

d. Truckable sills: At the edge of the building floor (leading into the elevator hoistway), a structural steel angle must be in place to avoid deterioration of the building floor through continued use of hand trucks, battery-operated pallet lifts, forklifts, and other heavy equipment.

e. Flooring: A variety of materials may be used for flooring in a freight elevator, including checkered steel plate, nonskid materials, galvanized steel, or high-density wood.

Contributors:
Rippeteau Architects, PC, Washington, DC; Alan H. Rider, AIA, Daniel, Mann, Johnson, and Mendenhall, Washington, DC.

ESCALATOR PROFILE
4.24

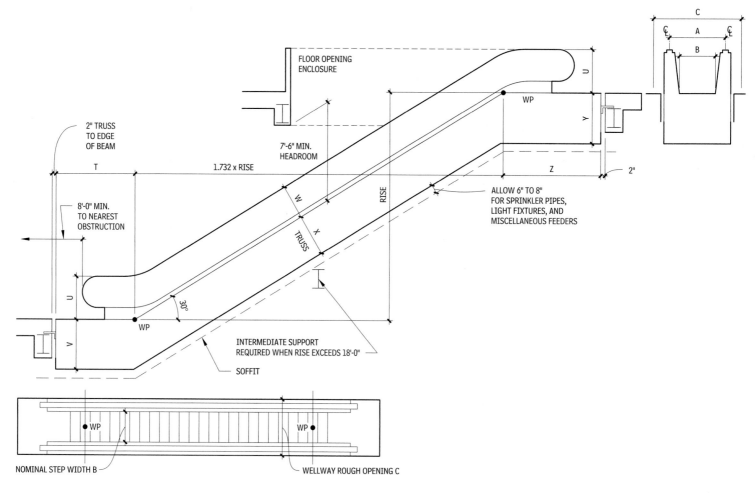

MOVING WALKS

Moving walks are particularly useful in transportation terminals, sports arenas, and exposition centers where large numbers of people must move long distances horizontally. The moving walks may be arranged in any combination of horizontal runs and inclines with a practical maximum of 12°.

It is generally not economical to provide moving walks for distances less than 100 ft. When conditions require distances longer than 300 ft, a series of units are often provided with transition areas allowing passengers to ingress and egress. Narrow units accommodate one adult; wider units allow for both walking and standing passengers. The most common pallet widths are most 32 in. and 40 in., but some manufacturers do have other size units including 48 in. and 56 in widths.

MOVING WALKS
4.25

SYMBOL	DESCRIPTION	MANUFACTURER DIMENSIONS					
	NOMINAL MOVING WALK WIDTH	KONE		OTIS		SCHINDLER	
		40″	48″	40″	48″	40″	48″
A	Centerline to centerline of handrail	3′-7-3/16″	4′-3-3/16″	3′-7-1/2″	4′-3-1/2″	3′-4-7/8″	4′-0-3/8″
B	Nominal pallet width	32″	40″	32″	40″	32″	40″
C	Wellway rough opening	5′-1-1/8″	5′-8-15/16″	4′-10-1/8″	5′-6-1/8″	4′-7-1/8″	5′-3″
X	Minimum pit depth (ends)	4′-0″		3′-5-5/8″		3′-8″	
Y	Minimum pit opening (control)	18′-10″		19′-4-1/2″		3′-3-3/4″	
Z	Minimum pit depth (middle)	1′-3″		1′-7-11/16″		N/A	

Contributor:
Alan H. Rider, AIA, Daniel, Mann, Johnson, and Mendenhall, Washington, DC.

PLUMBING

DESIGN CONSIDERATIONS

A plumbing system is used to safely transfer liquids and gasses to and from a building and its site. Water supply, plumbing fixtures, and waste piping may be the most common type of plumbing system within a building. But other types of plumbing systems may be required, including plumbing for gas service, and, dependent on the facility type, services such as medical gasses in a hospital.

Plumbing design usually will affect the overall design of a facility. Determining the fixture count, space requirements and location of toilet rooms within the building should be an early planning consideration of the design team. When sustainable design is a concern, addressing rain water and site drainage issues should also be part of the early planning process. Existing utility conditions and infrastructure (storm drainage, water utilities and sanitary sewage utilities) need to be considered. These utilities may need to be addressed on a site, facility or campus basis, or at a municipal scale when services do not exist. Spacing and location of plumbing fixtures and toilet rooms should respond to occupant needs and code requirements. The design professional should be aware of how water is piped to plumbing fixtures, how waste is plumbed from fixtures, along with general venting requirements. Even during preliminary design the design team should begin to address the requirements for accumulation and flow of waste through horizontal and vertical piping.

Other issues that should be considered in the design of the facility plumbing system, include the control of noise, vibration, and piping condensation.

- *Noise* is a factor of high-velocity liquid flow in pipes or of fixture noise (such as flush valves).
- *Vibration* is the result of mechanically coupling pipes to moving equipment (such as pumps), as well as the manner in which piping is physically isolated from the building structure. Structure-borne noise can propagate very efficiently.
- *Condensation* occurs when exposed or insufficiently insulated pipes cooled by their contents pass through warm, moist air and the exterior of the pipe reaches the dew point temperature.

The potential flow of unhealthy and dangerous sewer gasses back into the building requires the use of water-filled traps at each fixture, as well as a system of venting to open air. Exterior openings of these vents should be placed away from direct view, and must be remote from any outdoor air intakes to the building. Additionally, there are code requirements for the location in relationship to roofs.

Plumbing fixtures provide the most visible design elements in this system; they are the parts of the building that occupants actually touch and feel. Most other plumbing components are concealed within the building construction.

The basic components of a plumbing installation (water distribution and sanitary waste drainage system) are as follows:

1. Service tap
2. Meter
3. Shutoff valve
4. Service entry
5. Fixture supply tree
6. Fixture
7. Trap
8. Drain
9. Venting
10. Waste piping
11. Cleanouts
12. Building trap
13. Sewer connection

INTERFACES

Plumbing and piping connect to a building structure and may require vibration isolation to avoid structure-borne noise transmission. Acoustical considerations are necessary when routing of plumbing or piping near occupied spaces. Fixture noise (such as flush valves) is also a design consideration (such as flush valves) in buildings. Other design issues needing to be considered include coordination of plumbing fixture location with toilet compartments and urinal screens, toilet and bath accessories, tub and shower doors.

CODES AND STANDARDS

Plumbing codes establish minimum acceptable standards for the design and installation of plumbing systems and selection of the components they comprise. Model building codes and the plumbing codes associated with them have found general acceptance in large areas of the country. However, some jurisdictions have adopted their own codes or adopted modifications of one of the model codes. Verify the plumbing code used by the authority having jurisdiction and any amendments; for each specific project.

Requirements for plumbing system design should based on the adopted code the jurisdiction of the project. Tables and charts provided in this chapter are for preliminary planning purposes and should not be used for actual design.

The word "approved" is often used in conjunction with components and devices that come in contact with potable water and products used for human consumption or use. Nonetheless, a responsible code official or agency must examine and test these items to determine whether they are suitable for a particular intended use. Only materials and devices approved by the local jurisdiction can be used in plumbing systems. Plumbing design drawings and utility services also must be examined and found to be in compliance with local codes, rules, and regulations.

PLUMBING FIXTURES

A plumbing fixture is a device or appliance that is designed to supply water or receive waterborne waste, and may discharge into a sanitary waste system. Ideal fixture materials should be nonabsorbent, nonporous, nonoxidizing, smooth, and easy to clean.

Plumbing codes usually mandate the number and type of fixtures that must be provided for specific occupancy based on the capacity. Provisions for people with disabilities have been made an integral part of code requirements, mandating the quantity and design of spaces utilizing plumbing fixtures.

FIXTURE UNITS

Every plumbing fixture is assigned a value know as a fixture unit (FU). FU values represent the probable flow of water the fixture will discharge into a sanitary waste system or use (demand) from a potable water supply system. The base value of 1 is assigned to a lavatory for both water demand and waste discharge; other fixtures are assigned comparative values as they relate to the lavatory. Waste discharge and water demand FUs are different; therefore the designations DFU, for drainage fixture units, and WFU, for potable water fixture units, can be used to differentiate them.

WATER CLOSETS, URINALS, AND BIDETS

Water closets, urinal and bidets general have two parts - a receptor for waste, which includes the drain trap and a flushing or water supply mechanism. Most are made of vitreous china. These plumbing fixtures are generally grouped according to their flushing action, which affects the bowl type, flushing mechanism, and mounting method.

FLUSHING ACTION

Common water closet flushing action include:

- *Reverse trap:* Water is introduced into the fixture only through the rim by a gravity flush tank. This flushing action is low-cost and used mostly for residential projects. Reverse traps may be used with flush tanks or valves.
- *Blowout:* Water is introduced at high velocity through jets at the bottom of the waterway in. This action type is used for public facilities and industrial projects because of its capability to remove larger objects thrown into the fixture. Blowouts are used with a flush valve water supply only.
- *Siphon jet:* Water is introduced into the fixture both through the rim and by a jet at the bottom of the waterway. Quiet flushing and moderate cost make this the most common flushing action. Less costly variations include "washout" and "washdown," which do not use the jet. The siphon jet can be used with flush valves or tanks.

FIXTURE FLUSHING ACTION TYPES
4.26

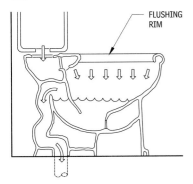

REVERSE TRAP

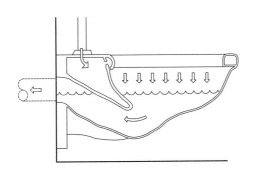

BLOWOUT

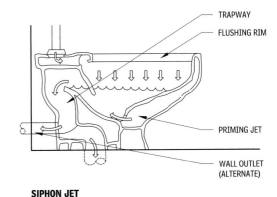

SIPHON JET

Contributors:
American Society of Plumbing Engineers (ASPE), Westlake, California; Michael Frankel, CIPE, Utility Systems Consultants, Somerset, New Jersey; Jacqueline Jones, American Standard, Piscataway, New Jersey; Philip Kenyon, Kohler, Kohler, Wisconsin.

FLUSHING MECHANISMS
4.27

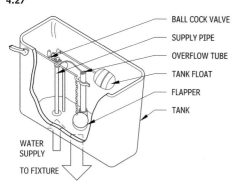

- BALL COCK VALVE
- SUPPLY PIPE
- OVERFLOW TUBE
- TANK FLOAT
- FLAPPER
- TANK

WATER SUPPLY

TO FIXTURE

GRAVITY FLUSH TANK

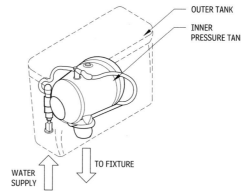

- OUTER TANK
- INNER PRESSURE TANK

WATER SUPPLY

TO FIXTURE

PRESSURE-ASSISTED FLUSH TANK

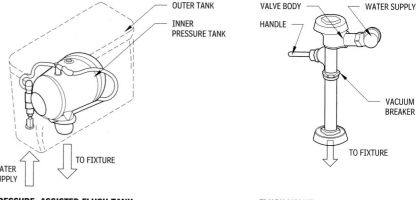

- VALVE BODY
- WATER SUPPLY
- HANDLE
- VACUUM BREAKER

TO FIXTURE

FLUSH VALVE

FLUSHING MECHANISMS

Common plumbing fixture water supply types include the following flushing mechanisms:

- *Gravity Flush Tank:* Water enters the tank through a ball cock and is stopped when the float valve reaches a predetermined level. The handle raises the flapper to release the water in the tank into the fixture and stops when the flapper closes. Gravity flush tanks require 10 psi water pressure.
- *Pressure-Assisted Flush Tank:* Water enters a pressure tank installed inside an outer tank, partially filling the tank and compressing the air inside. When flushing is started, the air pressure causes the quick release of water into the fixture. Pressure-assisted flush tanks require 30 psi water pressure.
- *Flush Valve:* Flush valves are available in a wide variety of manual and automatic operation fixtures, some with infrared and other proximity sensors. Once flushing has started, a measured quantity of water is quickly introduced into the fixture. Flush valves require 25 psi water pressure.

MOUNTING TYPES

Water closets may be either wall-hung or floor mounted, and one or two pieces.

WATER CLOSET MOUNTING TYPES
4.28

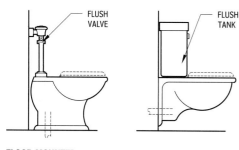

- FLUSH VALVE
- FLUSH TANK

FLOOR MOUNTED   **WALL HUNG**

BIDET
4.29

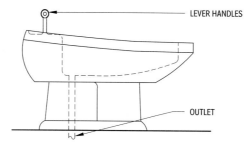

- LEVER HANDLES
- OUTLET

URINALS
4.30

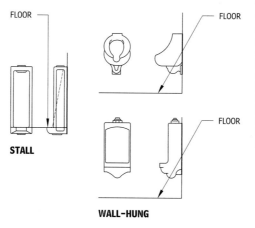

- FLOOR
- FLOOR
- FLOOR

STALL   **WALL-HUNG**

LAVATORIES AND SINKS

Lavatories have a shallow receptor designed primarily for washing hands, arms and face; sinks are generally deeper and designed for general washing and disposal of liquid waste. Sinks can include residential, commercial and service applications.

Lavatories are generally one of three types wall-hung, installed in or as a part of a countertop and pedestal. Vitreous china is the most common material used in lavatories, though they are also available in cast acrylic resin and enameled cast iron, enameled steel, stainless steel, and other metals.

Sink materials include stainless steel, enameled iron or steel, and cast resin. The underside of stainless steel sinks typically is coated with a sound-deadening material. Sink accessories may include pull out faucets, instant hot or chilled water dispensers, soap dispensers, and disposers.

WALL-HUNG LAVATORIES AND SINKS

Wall-hung lavatories are available in many sizes, shapes and designs the illustrations represent common design configurations, exact dimensions and design will very by manufacturer. Lavatories often have a raised back ledge that serves as a backsplash; deep ledges may serve as a shelf. They may be mounted on brackets or concealed arms and some units are designed for corner applications. Supports and brackets for wall-hung lavatories and sinks are discussed as a part of plumbing fixture supports later in this chapter. Some wall-hung lavatories are designed for compliance with ADA Accessibility Guidelines for Buildings and Facilities (ADAAG). Coordinate installation requirements of the fixture with applicable code.

NOTES

4.28 a. Flush valves and tanks can be installed on either floor mounted or wall hung water closets.
b. For rough-in dimensions for water supply and sanitary waste, refer to fixture manufacturer.
4.29 The bidet is often designed to sit next to a water closet, which it resembles, but is a form of lavatory.
4.30 a. Urinals require flush valves as the water supply source.
b. If used, urinal tanks should be 92 to 94 in. above the floor.
c. Install urinals 21 to 24 in. on center, except accessible units.

d. For styles and rough-in dimensions, refer to manufacturer.

Contributors:
American Society of Plumbing Engineers, Westlake, California; Michael Frankel, CIPE, Utility Systems Consultants, Somerset, New Jersey; Jacqueline Jones, American Standard, Piscataway, New Jersey; Philip Kenyon, Kohler, Kohler, Wisconsin.

BATHTUBS AND SHOWERS

BATHTUBS

Bathtubs are available in many shapes, sizes and styles, including, rectangular, corner and oval. Three types of installation are common including recessed, drop-in, and freestanding. Bathtub surrounds can be various materials, for example ceramic tile, solid surfacing, molded fiberglass or acrylic one-piece units, the surround material is important for coordination purposes during installation. Bathtubs are available in the following materials, though the fiberglass and acrylic units are the most common.

- *Fiberglass*: An economical and common choice, gel-coated fiberglass (also known as FRP) is lightweight and easy to install. Because the material can be molded, fiberglass tubs are available in a variety of shapes. Although not as durable as cast iron or acrylic, fiberglass can easily be repaired.
- *Acrylic*: Fiberglass reinforced acrylic is more durable than units constructed solely of fiberglass,. Because acrylic is light and easily formed into various shapes, it is a good choice for whirlpools and other large tubs that would be too heavy in cast iron. Acrylic is a good insulator and, thus, keeps water warm longer.
- *Cast iron*: Very heavy and extremely durable, traditional enamel-coated cast iron resists staining and scratching. It cannot be molded as freely as acrylic or fiberglass, so there are fewer shapes and styles from which to choose.
- *Enameled steel*: Because enameled steel is lighter weight it is a less expensive alternative to cast iron.

Whirlpool bathtubs, usually made of fiberglass-reinforced acrylic, which can be fabricated in a variety of shapes. Air mixed with water streams through jets in the side of the tub, giving the whirlpool its soothing, therapeutic character. Models may have 3 to 10 jets, including some aimed to massage feet, back, and neck. Jet direction can usually be adjusted; some jets can also be adjusted to deliver a pulsating or steady stream or to regulate intensity. Pumps range from 1/2 to 3 horsepower, and the intensity of the flow varies accordingly. In-line heaters are recommended to keep the water warm without refilling the tub.

Built-in bathtubs have an integral apron and tiling flange, for installation in a 3-wall alcove. Drop-in designs are intended for deck-mounted installations and typically have integral feet that support the weight of the unit. Many whirlpool bathtubs are drop-in units, though manufacturers may offer built-in units with removable apron for access to pump.

BUILT-IN BATHTUB
4.31

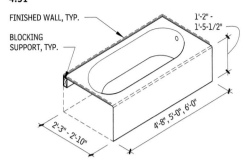

DROP-IN WHIRLPOOL BATHTUB
4.32

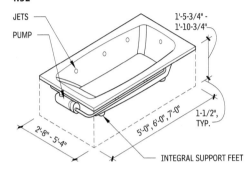

FREESTANDING BATHTUB
4.33

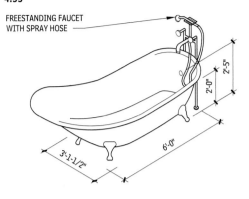

CLEAR FLOOR SPACE FOR ACCESSIBLE BATHTUBS
4.34

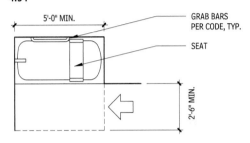

SIDE APPROACH

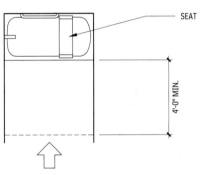

FRONT APPROACH

NOTES

4.34 For tubs with a built-in seat at the head of the tub, the seat must be 15 in. wide, and clear floor space must be provided in front of the seat.

Contributors:
American Society of Plumbing Engineers, Westlake, California; Michael Frankel, CIPE, Utility Systems Consultants, Somerset, New Jersey.

SHOWERS

Showers may tub showers, shower stalls or emergency showers. Tub showers are showers installed over a bathtub and usually share its water supply valve. The shower surround may be integral to the bathtub or site-built. Site-built shower enclosures are generally three-sided with an impervious finish with either a shower door or curtain completing the enclosure.

Shower stalls consist of a floor receptor topped by water-resistant walls either self-supporting or attached to wall framing. Receptors sloping to a drain and may be manufactured or site-built. Manufactured shower stalls may also be one-piece plastic units with integral grab bars, seat and other accessories.

Emergency showers and eyewash stations may be necessary or required in industrial, institutional, or other occupancies where people may come in contact with corrosive or hazardous material.

SHOWER RECEPTOR
4.35

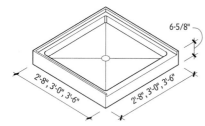

SQUARE

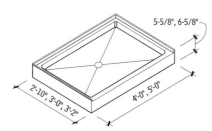

RECTANGULAR

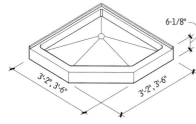

CORNER

COMMON SHOWER SIZES AND CONFIGURATIONS
4.36

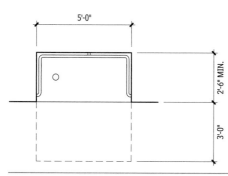

MANUFACTURERED ONE-PIECE SHOWER STALL
4.37

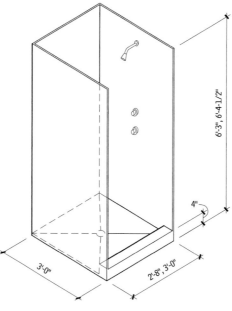

TYPICAL SITE-BUILT SHOWER CONSTRUCTION
4.38

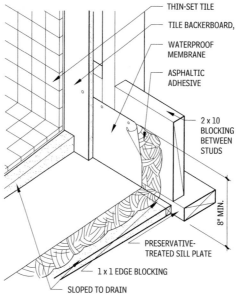

THIN-SET TILE
TILE BACKERBOARD,
WATERPROOF MEMBRANE
ASPHALTIC ADHESIVE
2 x 10 BLOCKING BETWEEN STUDS
8" MIN.
PRESERVATIVE-TREATED SILL PLATE
1 x 1 EDGE BLOCKING
SLOPED TO DRAIN

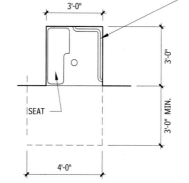

CONTROL WALL
SEAT

COMBINATION EMERGENCY SHOWER AND EYEWASH
4.39

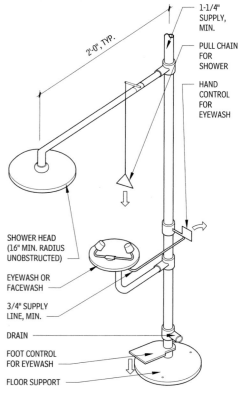

1-1/4" SUPPLY, MIN.
PULL CHAIN FOR SHOWER
HAND CONTROL FOR EYEWASH
2'-0", TYP.
SHOWER HEAD (16" MIN. RADIUS UNOBSTRUCTED)
EYEWASH OR FACEWASH
3/4" SUPPLY LINE, MIN.
DRAIN
FOOT CONTROL FOR EYEWASH
FLOOR SUPPORT

DRINKING FOUNTAINS AND ELECTRIC WATER COOLERS

Drinking fountains (DF) only use water at ambient temperatures; electric water coolers (EWC) use an integral or remote chiller to cool water for drinking. Design guidelines include:

- Use air-cooled condensers for normal room temperatures and water-cooled units for high room temperatures and larger capacities. Many models are available with hot and cold water supplies, a cup-filling spout, or refrigerated compartments.
- Install half of required fountains or water coolers as accessible, but design the layout so accessible fountains do not obstruct movement of the visually impaired.
- Explosion-proof electric water coolers are recommended for use in hazardous locations. Corrosion-resistant fountains are available for harsh environments.
- Consult local building codes for the number of drinking fountains or water coolers required.

TYPICAL EXTERIOR DRINKING FOUNTAINS
4.40

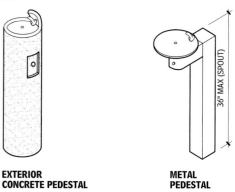

36" MAX (SPOUT)

EXTERIOR CONCRETE PEDESTAL   **METAL PEDESTAL**

NOTES

4.35 Materials for bases include acrylic with fiberglass reinforcement, enameled steel, and terrazzo.
4.36 Variations in shapes and designs are prevalent in one-piece shower units; consult manufacturers.

Contributors:
Michael Frankel, CIPE, Utility Systems Consultants, Somerset, New Jersey; K. Shahid Rab, AIA, Friesen International, Washington, DC; American Society of Plumbing Engineers, Westlake, California.

DOMESTIC WATER DISTRIBUTION

A building service is that portion of the supply piping on private property that extends below frost depth from the public utility main into the building. It includes the connection to the main, valves, pressure-reducing devices, backflow prevention devices, meters, and other requirements specific to the individual utility company.

Because of different requirements the water supply service for commercial buildings is often divided into two separate services at the public main: potable water and fire protection water. However, a single, combined service is sometimes used.

BACKFLOW PREVENTION

It is extremely important for a utility company to protect the public water supply from contamination flowing from any building to which it is supplying water. The device used to accomplish this is the backflow preventer (BFP), which prevents contaminated water from flowing backward into the potable water supply.

There are four types of BFP, and the degree of hazard in a particular situation determines which type to select and install:

- *Air gap*: This BFP provides a physical separation between the supply of potable water and the storage tank or piping distribution network. This is a passive method and is considered the only absolutely safe concept.
- *Reduced-pressure zone (RPZ)*: This type of BFP is a mechanical device used when a high hazard is present. Liquids attempting to flow in reverse discharge out of the BFP instead. When installed in a building water supply, the RPZ backflow preventer should be located as close to the public water main as is practical.
- *Double check valve*: This is a mechanical device often used on fire protection water supplies and for smaller-size piping that supplies equipment that has a back pressure and is not considered a high hazard.
- *Vacuum breaker*: This mechanical device is used when there is no back pressure, such as for a submerged water supply to a water closet. It uses a flexible diaphragm that allows water to flow through in only one direction; it closes on itself, stopping flow in the reverse direction.

After connecting a plumbing system to the public water main, it is necessary to provide a method to shut off the water supply to the building without entering it. A curb valve installed close to the property line is used to serve this function. A second shutoff valve is provided inside the building at the service entrance.

For high hazard occupancies, a reduced-pressure zone BFP should be installed as close to the public main as is reasonable to protect the public water supply from contamination. Because of the potentially large discharge of water, an aboveground, heated enclosure is recommended. For less hazardous locations, a double check valve assembly may be permitted. No water is discharged from a double check valve.

Water meters are necessary to measure the amount of water used in a facility. The arrangement of the water meter assembly is specific to each utility. The meter could be located in an outside pit or exposed inside the building. The meter used should be selected for accuracy. A compound meter, consisting of separate sections for low and high flows, is often used for applications such as multiple dwellings and dormitories.

A strainer may be required before the meter, if solids are present in the water supply. A second backflow preventer may be required on individual water branches supplying specific equipment inside a building.

WATER SUPPLY PIPING
4.41

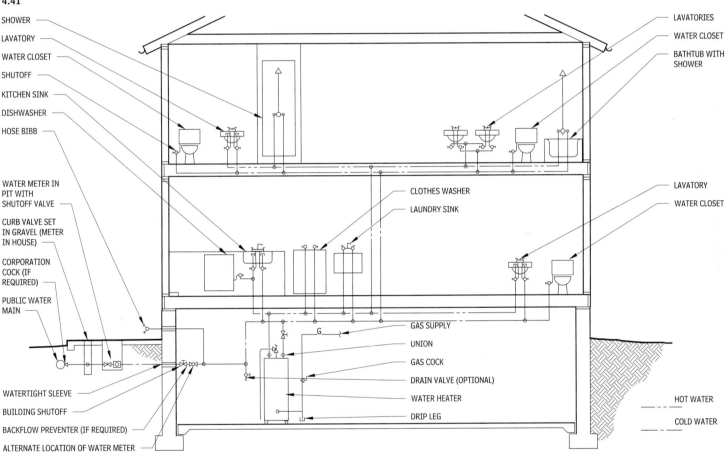

Contributors:
American Society of Plumbing Engineers, Westlake, California; Michael Frankel, CIPE, Utility Systems Consultants, Somerset, New Jersey; Brent Dickens, AIA, Architecture & Planning, San Rafael, California.

DRAINAGE AND VENT PIPING
4.42

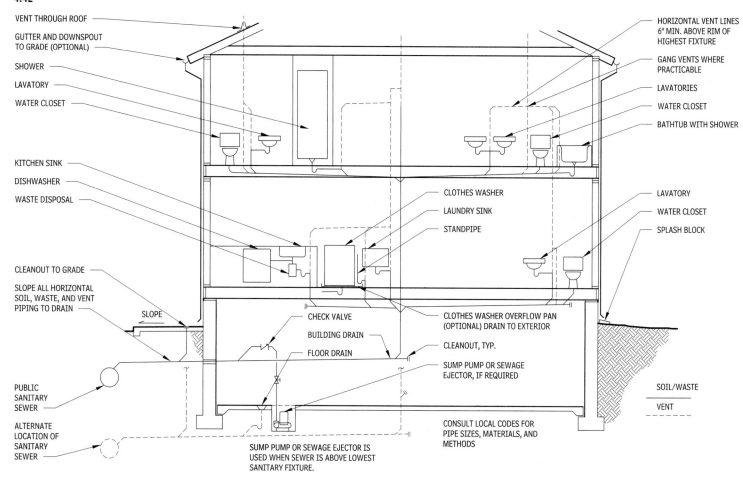

VENT THROUGH ROOF

GUTTER AND DOWNSPOUT TO GRADE (OPTIONAL)

SHOWER

LAVATORY

WATER CLOSET

KITCHEN SINK

DISHWASHER

WASTE DISPOSAL

CLEANOUT TO GRADE

SLOPE ALL HORIZONTAL SOIL, WASTE, AND VENT PIPING TO DRAIN

SLOPE

PUBLIC SANITARY SEWER

ALTERNATE LOCATION OF SANITARY SEWER

HORIZONTAL VENT LINES 6" MIN. ABOVE RIM OF HIGHEST FIXTURE

GANG VENTS WHERE PRACTICABLE

LAVATORIES

WATER CLOSET

BATHTUB WITH SHOWER

CLOTHES WASHER

LAUNDRY SINK

STANDPIPE

LAVATORY

WATER CLOSET

SPLASH BLOCK

CHECK VALVE

BUILDING DRAIN

FLOOR DRAIN

CLOTHES WASHER OVERFLOW PAN (OPTIONAL) DRAIN TO EXTERIOR

CLEANOUT, TYP.

SUMP PUMP OR SEWAGE EJECTOR, IF REQUIRED

CONSULT LOCAL CODES FOR PIPE SIZES, MATERIALS, AND METHODS

SUMP PUMP OR SEWAGE EJECTOR IS USED WHEN SEWER IS ABOVE LOWEST SANITARY FIXTURE.

SOIL/WASTE

VENT

TYPICAL BUILDING TRAP PIT DETAIL
4.43

GRADE

REMOVABLE COVER WITH LIFTING LUGS

LADDER

VARIES

8"

SECTION

14" – 31"

21" – 50"

CLEANOUTS

RUNNING TRAP

TRAP ELEVATION

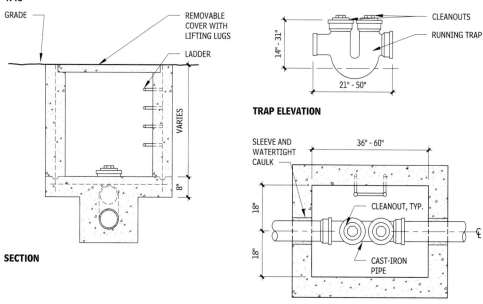

SLEEVE AND WATERTIGHT CAULK

36" – 60"

18"

18"

CLEANOUT, TYP.

CAST-IRON PIPE

PLAN

BUILDING DRAINS AND SEWERS[a]
4.44

MAXIMUM NUMBER OF FIXTURE UNITS THAT MAY BE CONNECTED TO ANY PORTION OF BUILDING DRAIN OR BUILDING SEWER[b]	SLOPE PER FOOT			
DIAMETER OF PIPE (IN.)	1/16"	1/8"	1/4"	1/2"
2			21	26
1-1/2			24	31
3			42[c]	50[c]
4		180	216	250
5		390	480	575
6		700	840	1000
8	1400	1600	1920	2300
10	2500	2900	3500	4200
12	2900	4600	5600	6700
15	7000	8300	10000	12000

NOTES

4.44 a. On-site sewers that serve more than one building may be sized according to current standards and specifications of the administrative authority for public sewers.
b. Consult local building codes for exact requirements.
c. No more than two water closets or two bathroom groups (except in single-family dwellings, no more than three water closets or three bathroom groups) may be installed.

Contributors:
Brent Dickens, AIA, Architecture & Planning, San Rafael, California; Michael Frankel, CIPE, Utility Systems Consultants, Somerset, New Jersey; American Society of Plumbing Engineers, Westlake, California.

RAIN WATER DRAINAGE

FACILITY STORM DRAINS

Facility storm drains include roof, area, and trench drains. A roof drain removes rainwater from roofs. Drains in other areas exposed to the weather such as balconies or canopies are called area drains. Both types of drain discharge the effluent into the storm drainage system. Specialized drain types are available for installation in specific exposed or interior locations; consult drain manufacturers for details.

- *Grate or dome:* This is the component that allows liquid into a drain body while excluding larger solids. Grates are available in a wide variety of shapes, slot configurations, materials, and load-bearing capability, from light to extra heavy. The high dome on the drain allows rainwater to enter the drain if some debris accumulates at the bottom. A generally accepted practice has the open area of a grate twice that of the discharge pipe. Generally, an adjustable grate allows the grate top to be adapted to the finished level.
- *Flange:* This is the part of the drain body that anchors the drain into roof or walking surface.
- *Flashing* ring: This is provided to secure any flashing directly to the drain body, to prevent leakage around the drain. Often, roof drains are provided with an integral gravel stop to prevent gravel from ballasted roofing from entering the drain.
- *Under-deck clamp:* This is used to secure the drain body to a slab through an opening prior to the installation of any roof, slab finish, or piping.

ROOF DRAIN
4.45

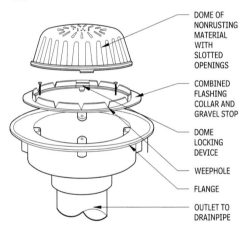

- DOME OF NONRUSTING MATERIAL WITH SLOTTED OPENINGS
- COMBINED FLASHING COLLAR AND GRAVEL STOP
- DOME LOCKING DEVICE
- WEEPHOLE
- FLANGE
- OUTLET TO DRAINPIPE

STORM DRAINAGE BOOT DETAIL
4.46

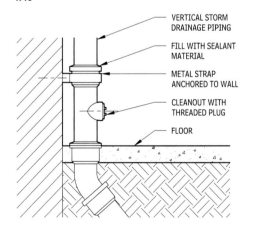

- VERTICAL STORM DRAINAGE PIPING
- FILL WITH SEALANT MATERIAL
- METAL STRAP ANCHORED TO WALL
- CLEANOUT WITH THREADED PLUG
- FLOOR

RAIN WATER HARVESTING SYSTEMS

Rain water harvesting is experiencing a renewed interest due to the following:

- Escalating environmental and economic costs of providing water by centralized water systems or by well drilling.
- The relatively pure, soft, low-sodium water source that rain water harvesting offers.
- Health concerns over the source and treatment of polluted waters.
- A perception that there are cost efficiencies associated with reliance on rain water.

Collecting rain water is not only a way to conserve water but also to conserve energy, as the energy input required to operate a centralized water system designed to treat and pump water over a vast service area is bypassed. Rain water harvesting also lessens local erosion and flooding caused by runoff from impervious cover such as pavement and roofs, as some rain is instead captured and stored.

CONCEPTS

Rain water quality almost always exceeds that of ground or surface waters: it does not come into contact with soil and rocks, where it dissolves salts and minerals, and it is not subject to many of the pollutants that often are discharged into surface waters such as rivers, and which can contaminate groundwater. However, rain water quality can be influenced by where it falls, as localized industrial emissions affect its purity. Thus, rain water falling in nonindustrialized areas can be superior to that in cities dominated by heavy industry, or in agricultural regions where crop dusting is prevalent.

PRIMARY WATER QUALITY CRITERIA: HEALTH CONCERNS

Once rain comes in contact with a roof or collection surface, it can wash many types of bacteria, molds, algae, protozoa, and other contaminants into the cistern or storage tank. Health concerns related to bacteria, such as salmonella, E coli, and legionella, and to physical contaminants, such as pesticides, lead, and arsenic, are the primary criteria for drinking water quality analysis.

If the rain water is intended for potable uses such as drinking and cooking or for nonpotable uses including showering and toilet flushing, appropriate filtration and disinfection practices should be employed. If the rain water is to be used exclusively for outside landscape irrigation, the presence of contaminants may not be of major concern, thus treatment requirements may be less stringent.

SECONDARY WATER QUALITY CRITERIA: AESTHETIC CONCERNS

Concerns such as color, taste, smell, and hardness comprise the secondary testing criteria used to evaluate publicly supplied water. When assessed according to these characteristics, rain water often proves to be of better quality than well or municipal tap water. Inorganic impurities such as suspended particles of sand, clay, and silt contribute to the water's color and smell. Proper screening and removal of sedimentation help to decrease problems caused by these impurities.

Rainwater is the softest natural occurring water available, with a hardness of zero for all practical purposes. It naturally contains almost no dissolved minerals and salts, and is near distilled-water quality. The pH of rain water would be 7.0 if there were nothing else in the air. However, as rain falls, it dissolves carbon dioxide that is naturally present in the air and, thus, becomes slightly acidic. The resultant pH is 5.6; however, any sulfates or nitrates dissolved from the air can lower this number.

COMPONENTS

Rain water harvesting systems are composed of six basic components:

- *Catchment area/roof:* The surface upon which the rain falls
- *Gutters and downspouts:* The transport channels from catchment surface to storage
- *Leaf screens and roof washers:* The systems that remove contaminants and debris
- *Cisterns:* Where collected rain water is stored
- *Conveying:* The delivery system for the treated rain water, either by gravity or pump
- *Water treatment:* Filters and equipment, and additives to settle, filter, and disinfect

CATCHMENT AREA/ROOF

The catchment area is the surface on which the rain that will be collected falls. Although this discussion focuses on roofs as catchment areas, it's important to point out that channeled gullies along driveways or swales in yards can also serve as catchment areas, collecting and then directing the rain to a French drain or bermed detention area. Rain water harvested from catchment surfaces along the ground should only be used for lawn irrigation because of the increased risk of contamination. For potable use, the roofs of buildings are the primary catchment areas, which, in rural settings, can include outbuildings such as barns and sheds.

For systems intended as potable water sources, no lead should be used as roof flashing or as gutter solder. The slightly acidic quality of rain can dissolve the lead and, thereby, contaminate the water supply. Existing houses and buildings should be fully examined for any lead content in the planning stages of any rain water harvesting project.

RAINWATER HARVESTING SYSTEM—MAIN COMPONENTS
4.47

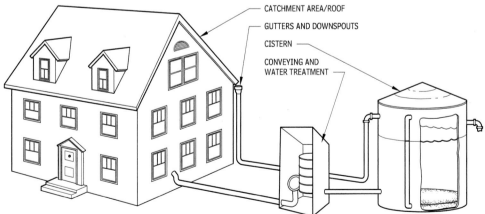

- CATCHMENT AREA/ROOF
- GUTTERS AND DOWNSPOUTS
- CISTERN
- CONVEYING AND WATER TREATMENT

Contributors:
American Society of Plumbing Engineers, Westlake, California; Michael Frankel, CIPE, Utility Systems Consultants, Somerset, New Jersey.

LEAF SCREENS AND ROOF WASHERS

EXAMPLE OF A COMMERCIALLY AVAILABLE ROOF WASHER WITH FILTER SYSTEM
4.48

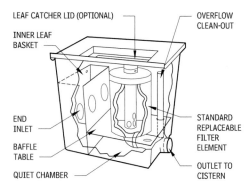

- LEAF CATCHER LID (OPTIONAL)
- INNER LEAF BASKET
- END INLET
- BAFFLE TABLE
- QUIET CHAMBER
- OVERFLOW CLEAN-OUT
- STANDARD REPLACEABLE FILTER ELEMENT
- OUTLET TO CISTERN

EXAMPLE OF A STANDPIPE-TYPE ROOF WASHER
4.49

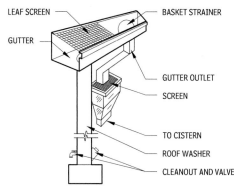

- LEAF SCREEN
- GUTTER
- BASKET STRAINER
- GUTTER OUTLET
- SCREEN
- TO CISTERN
- ROOF WASHER
- CLEANOUT AND VALVE

SEE ALSO

Bathtubs
Disposers
Facility Storm Drains
Firestopping
Lavatories and Sinks
Plumbing
Plumbing Fixtures
Roof Drainage
Toilet Compartments
Tub and Shower Doors
Water Closets, Urinals, and Bidets

HEATING, VENTILATING, AND AIR-CONDITIONING (HVAC)

HVAC includes energy supply, equipment, distribution, instrumentation and controls to provide climate control for facilities.

DESIGN CONSIDERATIONS

Although shelter from the weather and protection from harsh climates are historic reasons for constructing buildings, the mere act of building does not in itself result in desirable and acceptable interior environments. Thus, climate control is a critical performance attribute of a successful facility, and the creation of a comfortable, healthy environment for occupants is an important goal of the design process. HVAC also may include refrigeration for manufacturing, processing and storage.

HVAC is a requirement in virtually all types and sizes of buildings. Second only to structural, HVAC represent a technical area of design that must be generally understood and properly coordinated during the design process.

HVAC has a significant impact on the budget and space of a facility because they:

- Represent a substantial percentage of the construction budget for most facility types.
- Can consume up to 10 percent of the floor area of a building.
- Reach into and affect aesthetically most building spaces.

- Contribute greatly to facility energy use and operating expense.
- Account for the majority of occupant complaints.
- In processing, manufacturing, and storage facilities, HVAC may be critical to the basic function and operation of the facility.

HVAC has a major impact on occupant satisfaction, on facility construction and operating costs, and, often, on building layout and spatial efficiency.

The American Society of Heating, Refrigerating, and Air-conditioning Engineers (ASHRAE) definition of HVAC describes a system that must be able to simultaneously control:

- Temperature
- Relative humidity
- Air Speed
- Quality of air in occupied spaces

These four factors generally overlay the factors that define thermal comfort and indoor air quality—mean radiant temperature (MRT) being the critical exception.

Increasing demands for control of indoor air quality tend to require the design and installation of quality HVAC. Of the three primary means of mitigating indoor air pollutants—source control, filtration, and dilution—dilution (through ventilation and exhaust) and filtration (through system and equipment selection) are directly related to HVAC design, installation, and operation.

DESIGN ISSUES

The design of HVAC should follow a process similar to that used for overall facility design. The first steps in the design process are non-technical and generally independent of the system solution eventually chosen. Active involvement of the design professional in these first steps is critical to a successful design.

DESIGN INTENT

HVAC design should begin with a clear and explicit statement of what the system is expected to do. Design intent should ideally be defined during the programming phase of a project but certainly no

COMPARISON OF MANAGEMENT, OPERATION, AND DESIGN PROBLEMS IN COMMERCIAL FACILITIES
4.50

BASIS OF PROBLEM	RELATIVE FREQUENCY
Heating, ventilating, and air-conditioning	5.4
Elevators	2.7
Building design	1.5
Loading docks	1.2
Indoor air quality	1.0
Cleaning services	1.0

NOTES

4.50 Relative frequency suggests that problems with HVAC are twice as prevalent as problems with elevator systems and five times as prevalent as problems with cleaning services.

Contributors:
Peter Pfeiffer, Barley & Pfeiffer Architects, Austin, Texas; Michael Frankel, CIPE, Utility Systems Consultants, Somerset, New Jersey; Walter T. Grondzik, PE, Florida A&M Univeristy, Tallahasee, Florida.

later than the early stage of schematic design. Design intent should examine the operation of HVAC under all possible conditions (weekdays, weekends, emergencies, and predictable renovations). The process of defining the intent will lead to explicit design criteria—measurable targets for system performance—that can be used to select an appropriate system.

ZONING

An HVAC zone is an area of a facility (not necessarily coincident with a room or rooms) that requires a separate controller to provide conditions amenable to thermal comfort. Such control is typically provided by a thermostat that senses room air temperature. Thus, each thermal zone has its own thermostat.

Ideally, any area of a facility that responds to loads differentially across time from other areas should be considered for separate control. Such differential response usually is caused by the timing of loads, with solar orientation, fenestration, occupant, and equipment loads affecting this timing. For example, an office with east-facing glazing should not be controlled from a thermostat in an office (even if adjacent) with south-facing glazing. A conference room should not be controlled from an office, even if solar exposures are the same, as the occupancy schedules and loads are different.

Zoning is a critical part of the HVAC design process and should involve the active participation of the design professional. Using too many zones wastes money, while too few, may cause discomfort. Establishing appropriate zones is as much a qualitative as a quantitative process, one that requires a clear understanding of facility function and owner expectations. Zones are so critical to HVAC success that many systems are defined primarily by their zoning capabilities. As zoning depends on building layout, it should occur during schematic design.

SYSTEM SELECTION

HVAC selection is a sophisticated process. Normally, several system types would function adequately in a given facility application. Careful matching of system characteristics to design criteria can help achieve the best match for the system intent. The earlier in the design process that a system can be selected, the greater the opportunity for system coordination.

Characteristics to consider during the selection process include: life-cycle cost (including purchase, installation, and operating costs), energy consumption, space and volume requirements, noise, vibration, locational flexibility, operational flexibility, adaptability to changes in occupancy and/or room layout, ventilation capabilities, smoke control capabilities, aesthetics, reliability, maintainability, appropriateness to owner/operator personnel resources, and capability to provide thermal comfort. The relative importance of these characteristics, as well as system capabilities, will vary from project to project. Use of a project-specific, weighted selection matrix, such as the one shown in Table 4.170, can assist in the selection process.

SAMPLE SYSTEM SELECTION MATRIX
4.51

SELECTION CRITERION	RELATIVE WEIGHT	SYSTEM 1 RATING/ POINTS	SYSTEM 2 RATING/ POINTS
First cost	9	5/45	8/72
Space requirements	10	7/70	8/80
Energy use	7	9/63	5/35
Reliability	6	8/48	7/42
Noise	8	7/56	4/32
Aesthetics	4	10/40	8/322
Overall evaluation		322 points	293 points

HVAC DESIGN

The specifics of HVAC design are normally assigned to a mechanical engineer with the appropriate expertise. The detailed design, normally conducted during the design development phase, involves

selection of a number of manufactured equipment items (such as chillers, cooling towers, air-handling units, diffusers) to meet load and performance requirements, as well as design of numerous field-fabricated components (such as ductwork and piping) to connect and support the major equipment items.

In a typical building, most of the HVAC components are hidden from view behind mechanical room walls or above suspended ceilings. Thus, detailed design is driven by considerations of functionality and economics. Two exceptions to this "no-see" situation are the air supply and return devices (and/or water terminal units) and the exterior condenser.

COMMISSIONING

Commissioning is a systematic process of ensuring that facility systems are designed, installed, and operating so they meet design intent. The dynamic and complex nature of HVAC, as well the direct impact on occupant satisfaction and facility operating costs, makes them a good candidate for commissioning.

HVAC commissioning process typically involves functional testing of equipment and performance testing of systems and system interactions. For complex HVAC, commissioning may involve peer review of design concepts and solutions. Whatever the scope of commissioning, planning for this activity should begin as early in the design process as possible.

DESIGN COORDINATION

HVAC may place substantial space and volume demands on the design process and tend to interact with virtually all other building elements, key activities for coordinating these elements include the following:

- Ensuring HVAC design intent supports overall facility design intent.
- Coordinating HVAC zones with other system zones (fire suppression and alarm, lighting, and smoke control).
- Locating major equipment components to minimize distribution length and size, and to minimize negative aesthetic impacts.
- Locating major equipment components to minimize negative impacts on room acoustics, circulation patterns, and facility flexibility.
- Coordinating air distribution with elements of other systems, such as structural beams and columns, lighting fixtures, and plumbing and fire protection piping.
- Locating terminal devices (such as VAV or mixing boxes) and control devices (such as valves, dampers, and actuators) so they are accessible for regular maintenance.
- Giving more than rudimentary consideration to selection of air supply and return devices, such as diffusers, registers, and

HVAC AS A PERCENTAGE OF TOTAL BUILDING ENERGY USE
4.52

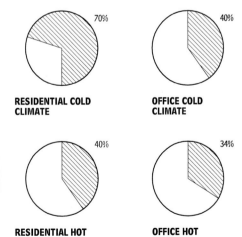

RESIDENTIAL COLD CLIMATE 70%

OFFICE COLD CLIMATE 40%

RESIDENTIAL HOT CLIMATE 40%

OFFICE HOT CLIMATE 34%

grilles. (These devices can have a dramatic effect on thermal and acoustical comfort and on aesthetics.)
- Coordinating controls with design intent. (Although controls are highly technical in implementation, failures are often conceptual.)
- Providing operations and maintenance manuals and procedures to assist the owner in operating the HVAC.

HVAC COST AS A PERCENTAGE OF TOTAL BUILDING CONSTRUCTION COST
4.53

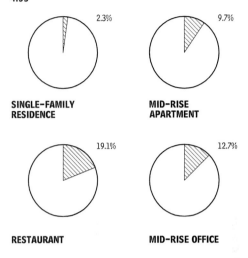

SINGLE-FAMILY RESIDENCE 2.3%

MID-RISE APARTMENT 9.7%

RESTAURANT 19.1%

MID-RISE OFFICE 12.7%

HVAC SYSTEM TYPES

Climate control systems may be classified as either active or passive in nature. Passive systems use no purchased energy resources, normally are assembled of "architectural" building elements doing double duty (such as glazings, walls, floors, finishes), and require design coordination.

Active climate control systems use purchased energy resources and employ task-specific, single-purpose elements (such as pumps, fans, ducts, and diffusers). Although mechanical engineers usually design HVAC systems, they must be coordinated with the entire project team.

HVAC systems are categorized by scale and by means of energy transfer to and from occupied spaces of a facility:

- *Local system*: This serves only a single space, and all of the system components are usually located in or directly adjacent to the space being conditioned.
- *Central system*: This serves multiple spaces, and the major components are usually located in a dedicated mechanical room or rooms.
- *District system*: This serves multiple buildings (as in a campus or central business district heating-cooling loop), with major components located in a dedicated plant.

CENTRAL SYSTEMS

Central systems are further categorized by the means of heat transfer used to convey heat to and from the spaces served by the system. Two primary media are used for this purpose: water and air.

Water is a very effective means of transferring heat, requiring substantially less volume to move a given quantity of heat than is possible with air as a medium. For the same heating or cooling load, the water distribution piping will be several times smaller than an equivalent air distribution duct. On the other hand, air distribution is convenient, because the air used to transport heating or cooling from a central location can simply be dumped into the space. Water distribution systems require some type of terminal device to exchange heat between the water and the air in the space to be cooled.

HVAC SYSTEM SPACE REQUIREMENTS AS A PERCENTAGE OF GROSS BUILDING FLOOR AREA
4.54

GROSS FLOOR AREA (SQ FT)	RESIDENTIAL OCCUPANCIES (%)	INSTITUTIONAL OCCUPANCIES (%)	ASSEMBLY OCCUPANCIES (%)	LABORATORY OCCUPANCIES (%)
10,000	6	8	9	11
50,000-100,000	4	6	7	10
500,000	3	4	5	8

LOCAL SYSTEMS
4.55

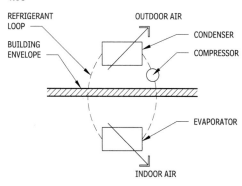

SPLIT SYSTEM

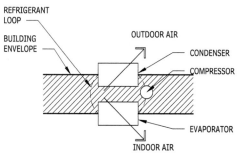

THROUGH WALL UNIT

CENTRAL SYSTEM WITH CHILLER AND COOLING TOWER
4.56

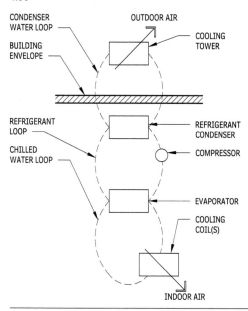

Those central systems that use only air to distribute heating and cooling effects to the occupied spaces are called all-air systems, and require a ductwork distribution tree. An all-water system uses only water to supply and remove heat from the spaces; such a system requires a piping distribution network. Air-water systems deliver both air and water to the occupied spaces and require both ductwork and piping distribution networks.

Central systems are secondarily classified by the location of the primary comfort control mechanism relative to the occupied spaces. In a number of systems, control resides at the air-handling unit, which makes changes in zoning and distribution layout difficult or impossible. Other systems use control mechanisms located adjacent to occupied spaces, which provide greater flexibility for change but require distribution of more equipment throughout the building, often in tight or hard-to-reach places.

CENTRAL SYSTEM WITH PACKAGED CHILLER
4.57

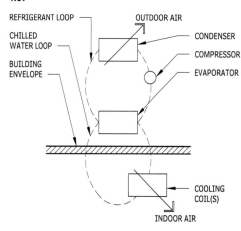

SYSTEM COMPONENTS

A number of components are required for the operation of typical HVAC. The components of a local system are generally packaged into a single unit that is installed through a wall or roof; air supply is usually introduced to the space directly from openings in the unit. The implications of installing potentially noisy mechanical equipment in or directly adjacent to an occupied space must be considered when selecting local HVAC.

Central system components are distributed throughout a facility, with a range of equipment choices available for most systems. The typical central system requires an air-handling unit, ductwork, air supply and return devices, a chiller, a boiler, an exterior condenser, and controls. Some of the many options for locating these components are illustrated in the Figures 4.56 and 4.57.

It is sometimes helpful to organize HVAC components into subsystems, including source, distribution, delivery, and control components.

- *Source subsystem:* Source components involve the generation of a heating or cooling effect and typically include chillers (vapor compression or absorption), boilers (electric, gas, oil, coal), cooling towers or air-cooled condensers, heat pumps, and solar collectors.
- *Distribution subsystem:* Distribution components involve transfer of a heating/cooling effect from the source to occupied

spaces, and typically include ductwork, piping, air-handling units (with fans, filters, coils, and accessories), pumps, stand-alone fans, and air terminal units.
- *Delivery subsystem:* Delivery components are used to introduce a heating/cooling effect into the occupied spaces, and typically include baseboard radiators, unit heaters, convector cabinets, fan-coil units, induction units, diffusers, and radiant panels.

HVAC SYSTEM FUNDAMENTALS

In the broadest sense, the term "air-conditioning" means that a quantity of air is

- mixed with the required amount of outside (fresh) air;
- filtered to remove specified amounts of particulate and/or gaseous elements;
- heated and/or cooled by an appropriate temperature control system;
- humidified or dehumidified;
- ionized, ozonated, or otherwise treated; or
- delivered to the conditioned spaces and distributed in a quiet, draft-free manner.

Conditioning of the air is basically performed within an enclosure called an air-handling unit, refer to Figure 4.58. The components need not be located within the central air-handling unit to perform their functions effectively. Space limitations, the operating and control results desired, and energy optimization considerations may affect where the components are situated.

Sources of electric power, heating and cooling media, water, steam, and natural gas, are often remote from the air-handling unit. However, in packaged air-conditioning equipment (such as air-heating units, room air conditioners, and many rooftop units), the heating and/or cooling "plant" is part of the package.

To the extent that an air-conditioning system does not provide all of the functions described here, it may not be furnishing the total space air-conditioning required for optimum comfort and health. The tendency to use the term "air-conditioning" synonymously with "cooling" should be altogether discouraged, as it falsely implies that the other functions of air-conditioning (such as proper filtration and humidification) are less important to total health and comfort, and may be eliminated.

The types of air-conditioning systems used and the selection and organization of their components is critical to the proper design of HVAC. For the optimum health, safety, and comfort of occupants and materials within the air-conditioned spaces, and to ensure the optimum life-cycle economics for a particular installation, this process should be entrusted to only experienced and knowledgeable mechanical engineers.

ALL-AIR SYSTEMS

In an all-air system, the heating and refrigerating plants may be located in a central mechanical room some distance from the conditioned space, or may be contained within the all-air system as packaged units in the air-conditioned spaces or on the roof. The air-handling unit is designed to mix outside and return air as desired, then to filter, heat, cool, and humidify the air before it is delivered to conditioned spaces. It may also exhaust portions of the return air based on how much return air is brought in.

Air-conditioning functions do not necessarily occur within the air-handling unit. Depending on the specific design criteria and space conditions, some air-conditioning components may be remote from the air-handling unit.

Some common all-air systems are single-duct, constant or variable volume airflow; dual duct (rarely used); multizone; single-duct with powered terminal and either constant or variable volume airflow; and a single-duct system with self-contained airflow volume controls and thermostats in each diffuser in the conditioned space.

Components of a basic all-air system include:

- *Minimum outside air damper:* Usually two positions.
- *Variable outside air damper:* Closed when only minimum outside air is desired (e.g. when outside air temperature is extremely high or low). Designed to open in response to the capability of

NOTE

4.54 The values for HVAC in this table include space for central equipment (chillers, boilers, pumps) and air circulation equipment (fans). HVAC space requirements tend to increase with increased load density and complexity, whereas the percentage space requirements tend to decrease with increased building size.

Contributor:
Walter T. Grondzik, PE, Florida A&M University, Tallahassee, Florida.

COMPONENTS OF A BASIC ALL-AIR SYSTEM
4.58

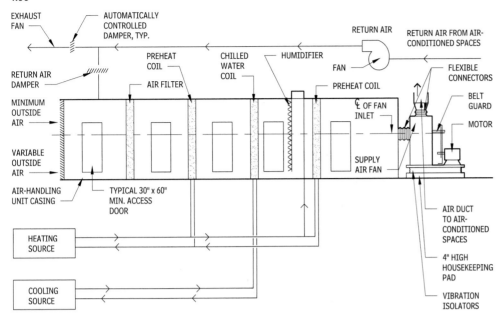

outside air to contribute to a building's heating or cooling needs. Exhaust and return air dampers are controlled to operate in accordance with the setting of the variable outside air damper.

- *Preheat coil (PHC):* Required only if the temperature and distribution of the return air mixture could cause freezing temperatures within the casing.
- *Air-handling unit (AHU):* May be field- or factory-fabricated. Pitch the floor of the AHU casing between components, as required, and provide piped floor drains to remove any moisture that develops.
- *Direct expansion coil (DXC):* Cooling coil may be a DXC if refrigerant is used instead of chilled water.
- *Humidifier (H):* May use steam or water as the humidification medium.
- *Reheat coil (RHC):* Used in the air-handling unit only when a fixed discharge air temperature is to be supplied to all areas served by the duct system. If different spaces require varying temperatures, a separate reheat coil may be placed in each duct serving a different temperature zone.

DIRECT-EXPANSION SYSTEMS

The term "direct expansion" means that a chemical refrigerant is used in the refrigeration circuit to remove heat and reject it, usually to the outdoors. Direct-expansion systems come in "cooling only" mode or in specially designed heat pumps that can furnish either heating or cooling.

The most common direct-expansion system is the packaged unit installed through the wall or in a window. These can also be floor-mounted in or out of the air-conditioned space, or located on the roof.

Another type of direct-expansion system is the "split" system, in which the heat rejection components of the condenser and compressor are packaged separately and can be located remotely from the evaporator and fan, which must be in the air-conditioned space. The two subassemblies, which are attached to the system with refrigerant piping, may be as close as on opposite sides of a wall or up to 100 ft away.

ALL-WATER SYSTEMS

The term "all-water system" is a misnomer, as all air-conditioning systems furnish conditioned "fresh" air to the air-conditioned spaces. All-water systems may have fan coil or radiant panel terminal units with separate all-air systems to supply the fresh air.

DIRECT-EXPANSION SYSTEM
4.59

SPLIT SYSTEM WITH COMPRESSOR/ CONDENSER ON ROOF AND MULTIPLE AIR HANDLERS

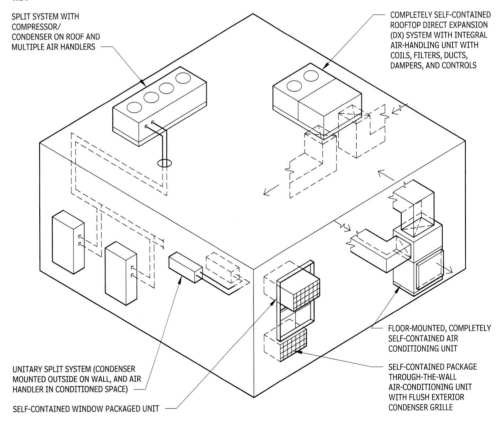

COMPLETELY SELF-CONTAINED ROOFTOP DIRECT EXPANSION (DX) SYSTEM WITH INTEGRAL AIR-HANDLING UNIT WITH COILS, FILTERS, DUCTS, DAMPERS, AND CONTROLS

FLOOR-MOUNTED, COMPLETELY SELF-CONTAINED AIR CONDITIONING UNIT

SELF-CONTAINED PACKAGE THROUGH-THE-WALL AIR-CONDITIONING UNIT WITH FLUSH EXTERIOR CONDENSER GRILLE

UNITARY SPLIT SYSTEM (CONDENSER MOUNTED OUTSIDE ON WALL, AND AIR HANDLER IN CONDITIONED SPACE)

SELF-CONTAINED WINDOW PACKAGED UNIT

Contributor:
Alfred Greenberg, PE, CEM, Murray Hill, New Jersey.

ALL-WATER SYSTEM
4.60

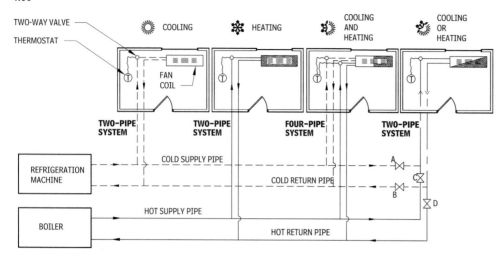

Fresh air furnished through openings in the walls behind the fan coil units is not considered properly conditioned, because most fan coil units are not designed to provide satisfactory filtering and humidity control or to prohibit the entry of outdoor noise.

In the vast majority of all-water systems, water is used to provide either heating or cooling through a two-pipe distribution system. A freeze protection chemical can be added to some systems when needed. When clients demand simultaneous heating or cooling everywhere, the piping will be either a two- or four-pipe distribution system, and the heating and cooling plants must be able to run at all times. The three-pipe system is seldom used because it is difficult to operate properly and to run efficiently.

MULTIPLE INTERIOR-ZONE HVAC SYSTEMS

The figures accompanying this discussion (Figures 4.60 to 4.66) on multiple interior-zone HVAC systems describe systems found in K-12 schools and small commercial office buildings.

FOUR-PIPE, SINGLE-ZONE AIR-HANDLING UNIT

Zonal air-handling units (AHUs) in this system provide heating and cooling for specific zones. Each AHU has a blower, filter, and heating and cooling coils. A fixed amount of fresh air to the units is pretempered to 55°F in a preconditioning unit. Both chilled and hot water are simultaneously provided to zonal and preconditioning units to carry the loads on the cooling and heating coils. Chilled water is provided by a chiller located in a central mechanical room (which contains a heat-rejecting condensing unit), and hot water is provided by a boiler, often located in the same mechanical room. Some single-zone AHUs run continuously. Newer units may have a variable volume fan that regulates airflow according to zone loads. The chiller or boiler must operate when any single zonal unit requires cooling or heating.

Each unit is controlled by a zone thermostat that adjusts the supply-air temperature to meet heating or cooling loads. The preconditioning unit is controlled to maintain 55°F by preheating air in winter and precooling it in the summer. The temperatures of the chilled water and hot water supplied to the units may be controlled with an outside reset thermostat.

ADVANTAGES

- This system can provide heating and cooling as needed.
- The system offers good dehumidification.
- The boiler and chiller are installed at a central location.
- The system operates with minimal distribution ductwork.
- Zonal air-handling units can be shut down without affecting adjacent areas.
- Chiller efficiency is higher than for individual heat pumps.
- The boiler and chiller have a long life (25 years).

DISADVANTAGES

- A four-pipe system is slightly more expensive than a two-pipe system.
- The hot water and chiller water loop must run even if only one zone needs heating or cooling.
- The entire system is shut down when the loop fails.
- The water-cooled condenser tower needs frequent service and water quality checks.
- The temperature is higher in an air-cooled condenser than a water-cooled condenser, making chillers less efficient.
- This system may require more energy than others because of the energy needed to run a four-pipe central loop.
- The system has no humidification.

FOUR-PIPE, SINGLE-ZONE AIR-HANDLING UNIT
4.61

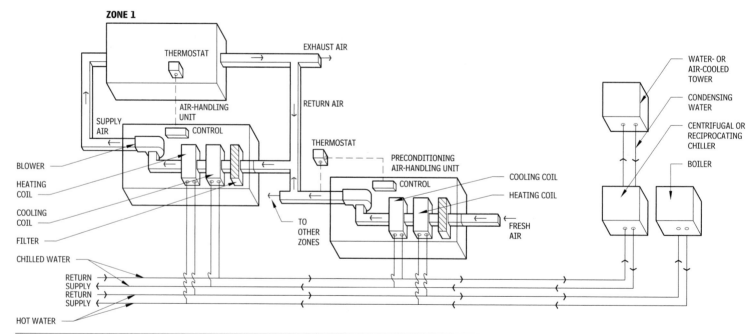

NOTES

4.60 a. Valves A and B are closed during the heating season.
b. Valves C and D are closed during the cooling season.
c. A majority of existing buildings with central heating and cooling use the two-pipe distribution system.

Contributor:
Alfred Greenberg, PE, CEM, Murray Hill, New Jersey.

PACKAGED SPLIT SYSTEM WITH INDIVIDUAL HEAT PUMPS

This system provides heating and cooling for individual zones with zonal heat pumps. Each heat pump unit contains a blower, filter, and heating/cooling coil. A fixed amount of fresh air to the units is pretempered to 55°F in a preconditioning heat pump unit. Each heat pump has its own heat rejection (or ambient heat source during cold weather). Emergency electric resistance heating is often provided for severe conditions.

The zonal heat pumps cycle on and off when the zone thermostat calls for heating or cooling. Airflow to the zones also cycles on and off according to zone demand. In general, the heat pump that preconditions outside air must run continuously to provide adequate preconditioned fresh air.

ADVANTAGES
- Installation, system operation, and maintenance are simple.
- No mechanical room is required.
- Ductwork is only required for fresh air.
- The initial cost is low.
- This system is well-suited to spaces that require many zones of individual temperature control.

DISADVANTAGES
- The noise level of this system is generally high.
- Maintenance costs are high.
- Overall efficiencies of individual heat pumps are less than that of one large chiller.
- The system needs electric resistance heating when the outside air temperature is below 35°F.
- Humidity control can be problematic if there is no preconditioning unit and zonal heat pumps are oversized.
- Wall penetration is required for refrigerant lines to and from the condenser/evaporator.
- Equipment life may be relatively short (typically, 10 years).
- The system has no humidification.

TWO-PIPE WATER LOOP HEAT PUMP WITH PACKAGED SPLIT

In this system, zonal heat pumps provide heating and cooling for individual zones. Each heat pump unit has a blower, filter, and heating/cooling coil. A fixed amount of fresh air to the units is pretempered to 55°F in a preconditioning heat pump unit. The system has a heat rejection loop, and each heat pump is connected to it with a heat exchanger. The heat rejection loop is maintained within a preset temperature range (e.g., 40°F to 100°F) using a central boiler in the winter and one or more heat-rejecting cooling towers in the summer. Usually, this type of system does not need emergency electric resistance heating for severe conditions. The heat rejection loop must operate when one or more heat pumps are running. In some cases, a variable speed loop can be used, although care must be taken to provide adequate flow to keep the heat pump heat exchangers from freezing up and/or to avoid heat transfer problems in the boiler caused by low flow.

The zonal heat pumps cycle on and off when the zone thermostat calls for heating or cooling. Airflow to the zones also cycles on and off according to zone demand. In general, to provide an adequate source of preconditioned fresh air, the outside air preconditioning heat pump must run continuously. An air-cooled condenser can be provided for the preconditioning units to allow for the main loop to be shut down during unoccupied periods.

TWO-PIPE, GROUND-COUPLED WATER LOOP HEAT PUMP WITH PACKAGED SPLIT SYSTEM

This system has zonal air-handling units (AHUs) that provide heating and cooling for individual zones. Each zonal heat pump contains a blower, filter, and heating/cooling coil. A fixed amount of fresh air to the units is pretempered to 55°F in a preconditioning heat pump unit. Each heat pump is connected to the system heat rejection loop with a heat exchanger. However, in contrast to the water loop system that has an auxiliary boiler and heat rejection tower, this water loop rejects heat in a series of wells or trenches that put it in direct contact with the earth. This heat rejection loop is also maintained within a preset temperature range (e.g., 40°F to 100°F) using the thermal mass of the earth it contacts. This type of system does not

PACKAGED SPLIT SYSTEM WITH INDIVIDUAL HEAT PUMPS
4.62

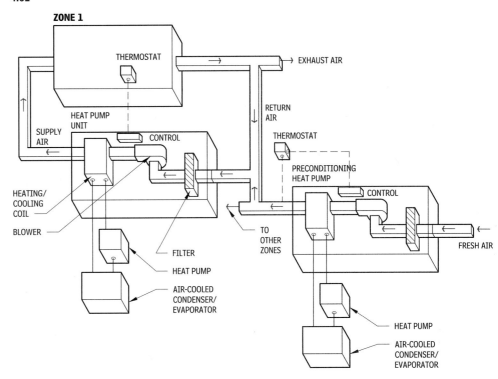

TWO-PIPE WATER LOOP HEAT PUMP WITH PACKAGED SPLIT SYSTEM
4.63

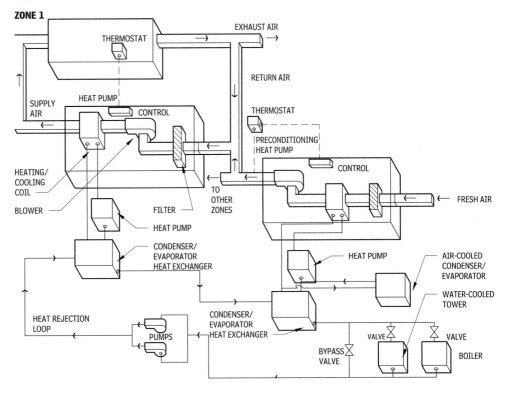

Contributor:
Jeff Haberl, PhD, PE, Texas A&M University, College Station, Texas.

need emergency electric resistance heating for severe conditions. The ground-coupled heat rejection loop must operate when one or more heat pumps are running. A variable speed heat rejection loop can be used, although care must be taken to provide adequate flow to avoid freeze-up of the heat pump heat exchangers.

Zonal heat pumps cycle on and off whenever the zone thermostat calls for heating or cooling. Airflow to the zones also cycle on and off according to zone demand. In most cases, the outside air pre-conditioning heat pump runs continuously to provide an adequate source of preconditioned fresh air. An air-cooled condenser can be provided for the preconditioning units to allow for the main loop to be shut down during unoccupied periods.

EVALUATION OF WATER LOOP HEAT PUMP SYSTEM FEATURES

These are the advantages and disadvantages, respectively (unless otherwise noted), that apply to the two-pipe water loop heat pump with packaged split system and the two-pipe, ground-coupled water loop heat pump with packaged split system.

ADVANTAGES

- The systems conserve energy by recovering heat from interior zones and/or waste heat.
- The systems do not require wall penetrations to provide for the rejection of heat from air-cooled condensers.
- Air-cooled preconditioning allows fresh air to be supplied without running the main loop.
- The noise level may be lower than that of air-cooled equipment because individual condenser fans are eliminated and the compression ratio is lower.
- The systems can be maintained locally, as specialized maintenance technicians are not are required for the heat pumps (specialized maintenance and repair technicians are required for the boiler in the system without ground coupling).
- Units have a longer service life than air-cooled heat pumps.
- The entire system does not shut down when a zonal unit fails.
- Ground-coupled systems normally do not need a boiler and cooling tower. The size of the mechanical room for the loop pumps can be minimized.
- The life-cycle cost of the two-pipe water loop heat pump with packaged split system (without ground coupling) compares favorably with that of central systems when life-cycle costs are considered.

DISADVANTAGES

- The initial cost for these systems may be higher than for systems that use multiple unitary HVAC equipment.
- Cleanliness of the piping loop must be maintained.
- The water-cooled tower needs frequent service and water quality checks (this does not usually apply to the ground-coupled system).
- If air-cooled preconditioning is not used, the loop must run 24 hours/day when any zone needs cooling or heating.
- The entire system shuts down when the loop fails.
- More maintenance will be required than for some other systems since the heat-pump equipment and air-handling units are decentralized.
- These systems have no humidification.
- In the ground-coupled system, soil type, moisture content, composition, density, and uniformity affect the success of this method of heat exchange.
- In the ground-coupled system, the pipe material and the corrosiveness of the local soil and groundwater may affect heat transfer and service life.
- In the ground-coupled system, a large area is needed in which to drill wells or dig trenches.
- Zonal heat pumps and preconditioning heat pumps need a sanitary sewer connection to drain condensate. These drains can be a maintenance concern.

FOUR-PIPE MULTIZONE SYSTEM WITH COLD DECK BYPASS

Multizone air-handling units (AHUs) provide heating and cooling for several zones (typically 4 to 10). Each multizone unit contains a blower, filter, heating coils, cooling coils, and bypass dampers. Chilled water and hot water are simultaneously provided to the

TWO-PIPE, GROUND-COUPLED WATER LOOP HEAT PUMP WITH PACKAGED SPLIT SYSTEM
4.64

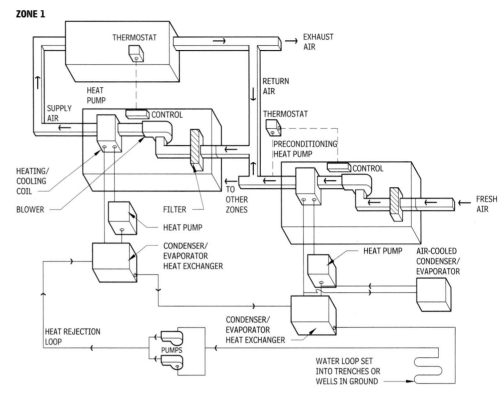

FOUR-PIPE MULTIZONE SYSTEM WITH COLD DECK BYPASS
4.65

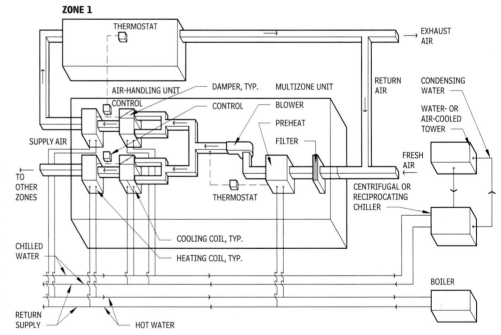

Contributor:
Jeff Haberl, PhD, PE, Texas A&M University, College Station, Texas.

zonal units to carry loads on the cooling and heating coils, respectively. Chilled water is provided by a chiller located in a central mechanical room (which contains a heat-rejecting condensing unit), and hot water is provided by a boiler (often located in the same mechanical room). The multizone units operate continuously. The chiller or boiler must operate when any multizone unit or preconditioning unit requires heating or cooling. Newer units may contain a variable volume fan that regulates the airflow according to the zone loads.

Each zone is controlled by a zone thermostat that changes the temperature of the supply air to meet heating or cooling loads. The supply air is conditioned by an arrangement of dampers that allow the correct portion of air either to flow across or to bypass the cold deck. A reheat coil can be provided for locations with extremely humid conditions. A preheat coil can be provided for extreme winter conditions. The temperature of the chilled water and hot water supplied to the units may be controlled with an outside reset thermostat.

ADVANTAGES
- The system supplies several zones from centrally located AHUs.
- No pipes are required that could leak in occupied zones.
- The system can provide heating and cooling as needed.
- The boiler and the chiller are centrally located.
- Chiller efficiency is often higher than that of individual heat pumps.
- The system offers good dehumidification. Much of the year, this can be provided with the cooling coil bypass damper.

DISADVANTAGES
- The hot water and chiller water loop must run when only one zone needs heating or cooling.
- The chiller and boiler require service by specially trained technicians.
- A water-cooled condenser tower needs frequent service and water quality checks.
- Additional space is required for distribution ductwork.
- The air-cooled condenser temperature (if used) is higher than that of a water-cooled condenser, making the chiller less efficient.
- The central system may use more energy because the loop has to operate more often.
- The system has no humidification.

FOUR-PIPE FAN COIL UNITS

In this system, fan coil units in each zone provide heating or cooling for that zone. Each fan coil unit contains a blower, filter, and heating/cooling coil. A fixed amount of fresh air to the units is pretempered to 55°F in a preconditioning unit that serves a number of zones. Chilled water and hot water are simultaneously provided to the zonal units and the preconditioning units to carry loads on the cooling and heating coils, respectively. Chilled water is provided by a chiller located in a central mechanical room (which contains a heat-rejecting condensing unit), and hot water is provided by a boiler (which is often located in the same mechanical room). The zonal fans can either operate continuously and modulate temperature or turn on and off as needed to satisfy the zone thermostat. Newer units may contain a variable volume fan that regulates the airflow depending upon zone loads.

FOUR-PIPE FAN COIL UNITS
4.66

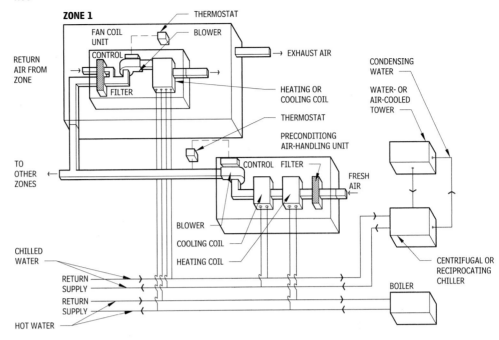

Each zonal fan coil unit is controlled by a zone thermostat, which changes the temperature of the supply air to meet heating or cooling loads. The preconditioning maintains a temperature of 55°F by preheating the air in the winter and precooling it in the summer. The temperature of the chilled water and hot water supplied to the units may be controlled with an outside reset thermostat.

ADVANTAGES
- The system provides all-season heating and cooling at each unit.
- The boiler and chiller are installed at a central location.
- The only ductwork needed is for preconditioned air (approximately 10 to 20 percent of fan coil air).
- Chiller efficiency is higher than that of individual heat pumps.
- The zonal fan coil unit can be shut down for maintenance without affecting adjacent areas.
- No summer/winter changeover is required.
- This system operates more simply than the others described in this discussion on multiple interior-zone HVAC systems.
- Cooling of preconditioned air may not be required in climates with hot, dry summers.

DISADVANTAGES
- Four-pipe systems are slightly more expensive to install than two-pipe systems.
- The hot water and chilled water loop must operate when only one zone needs heating or cooling.
- The chiller and boiler need servicing by specially trained technicians.
- Noise from individual units may be a problem.
- The water-cooled condenser tower needs frequent service and water quality checks.
- The air-cooled condenser temperature (if used) is higher than that of a water-cooled condenser, making the chiller less efficient.
- This central system may use more energy because of frequent operation of the loop.
- Decentralized maintenance of zonal units can require additional maintenance time.
- Zonal units need a sanitary sewer connection to drain condensate. These drains can be a maintenance concern.
- The system has no humidification.

Contributor:
Jeff Haberl, PhD, PE, Texas A&M University, College Station, Texas.

REFRIGERATION

Kitchen refrigerators move heat from the storage compartment to the surrounding room. Air conditioners move heat from a room to the outdoors. The efficiency of residential air-conditioning equipment is indicated by a seasonal energy efficiency rating (SEER), an index of the Btus moved per watt of electrical input energy. The higher its SEER, the more efficient and less costly a piece of equipment is to operate.

A large quantity of heat is required to boil or evaporate a liquid. This latent heat is the key to moving large quantities of heat with a small amount of refrigerant. To move heat from an area of low temperature to an area of high temperature (e.g., a building at 75°F to its surrounding environment at 95°F), the refrigeration equipment or air conditioner utilizes a fluid that boils and condenses within a limited range of temperatures and operating pressures.

During a cooling cycle, an evaporator coil absorbs heat from the building interior. This heat is absorbed by the refrigerant as it changes from a low-pressure liquid to a vapor. This low-pressure refrigerant vapor is then drawn into a package compressor and condenser unit, where it is compressed into a high-pressure vapor at high temperature. The resulting high-pressure refrigerant vapor is discharged into a condenser coil, where it gives up the latent heat absorbed in the evaporator and the heat added during compression and returns to a high-pressure liquid state. This high-pressure liquid is forced through an expansion device in which the pressure and temperature are rapidly decreased, making it possible for the evaporator to again absorb heat from the building.

The cooling cycle may be reversed to extract heat from a low-temperature source, such as outside air, to heat a building. The basic equipment is unchanged, with the exception of a four-way reversing valve and controls that permit the condenser and evaporator to exchange functions. A heat pump is more efficient than electric resistance heating because the only action required is to pump the refrigerant from a low-pressure vapor to a high-pressure vapor. The efficiency of a heat pump, measured as a coefficient of performance (COP), is a function of the temperature of the heat source.

CONDENSING UNIT
4.68

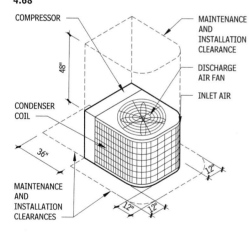

REFRIGERATION AND HEAT TRANSFER PRINCIPLES

A large building air-conditioning system typically includes a packaged water chiller, cooling tower, and one or more air-handling units. The arrangement shown in Figure 4.71 offers substantial flexibility in equipment location and distribution. Chilled water is generated in a chiller (vapor compression or absorption) and circulated to air-handling units strategically located in the building. Condensing water from the chiller is circulated to an exterior cooling tower, where heat from the building is rejected to the outside environment. The chiller and air handler(s) may be located virtually anywhere in the building, and the cooling tower at an appropriate exterior location.

TYPICAL BUILDING APPLICATION
4.67

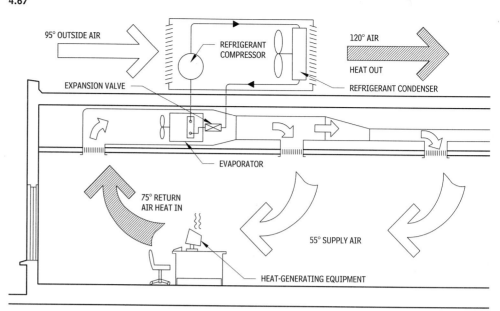

TYPICAL COOLING CYCLE TEMPERATURES AND PRESSURES
4.69

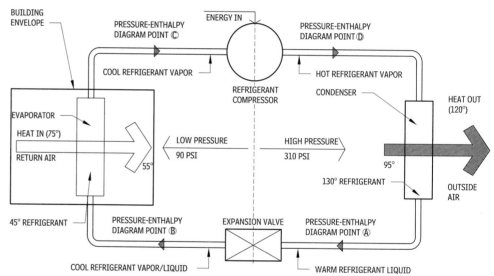

In large buildings, it is impractical to move heat with air only because duct sizes would have to be excessively large. Therefore, a heat exchanger is added to the evaporator, and chilled water is circulated to air-handling units throughout the building. Cooling towers are typically installed in such large systems to increase efficiency. Air-conditioning equipment transferring heat to 85°F water in a cooling tower will require less input energy to the compressor than the same equipment transferring heat to 95°F outside air.

In an absorption cooling cycle, cooling is generated by absorbing and desorbing water in a salt solution. Just as common table salt absorbs water on a damp day, a strong salt solution (e.g., lithium bromide) will draw water out of moist air when it is sprayed into an enclosed tank (absorber). If this moist air is connected to another tank that contains water that is evaporating, it will transfer water vapor to the absorber tank to replace the water that was drawn into the lithium bromide solution. Eventually, this strong lithium bromide solution becomes diluted and is pumped into a generator tank, where excess water is boiled off. The strong solution is then

cooled in a heat exchanger and expanded back into the absorber, where it can absorb more water. The water that was driven off in the generator is passed into a condenser, where it cools, condenses, and is then expanded back into the evaporator.

The refrigeration effect then draws off the (low-pressure) evaporator at 45°F to 55°F to produce chilled water. The absorption cycle accomplishes cooling without compressing a vapor, so it can operate with reduced amounts of electricity as long as adequate amounts of heat are available for the generator, and cooling for the condenser and absorber, and a reduced amount of electricity for the solution pumps.

Because an absorption cooling cycle does not use a vapor compressor, it is quieter and vibrates less than a vapor compression chiller. It also uses less electricity for solution pumps than a vapor compressor uses to do its work. Absorption refrigeration is ozone-friendly and can be configured to operate in systems with limited or no electricity (e.g., recreational vehicles).

Contributor:
Jeff Haberl, PhD, PE, Texas A&M University, College Station, Texas.

HEAT PUMP
4.70

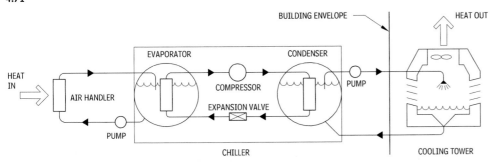

PACKAGED WATER CHILLER AND COOLING TOWER
4.71

ABSORPTION CYCLE
4.72

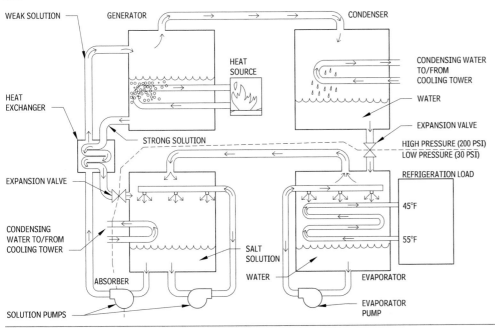

WATER CHILLERS

Chilled water is the most common medium for transferring heat from any type of cooling equipment, such as cooling coils and heat exchangers, to some source of refrigeration.

A chilled water system is a closed-circuit system that recirculates water between a mechanical refrigeration water-chilling unit and remote cooling equipment, usually operating with water temperatures in the range between 40°F and 55°F. There are five types of refrigeration units used in chilled water systems:

- Centrifugal water chiller, with electric motor or steam turbine drive
- Reciprocating water chiller, with electric motor drive
- Rotary-screw water chiller, with electric drive
- Indirect-fired water absorption water chiller
- Direct-fired water absorption chiller, using fuel oil or gas for firing
- Scroll water chiller

When a chilled water piping system also is used to circulate hot water for winter heating, it is called a dual-temperature water system. The design water temperature of chilled water systems usually falls in a rather narrow range because of the necessity for dehumidification and to avoid a possible freeze-up in the chiller. Chilled water supply temperatures usually range from 42°F to 60°F for normal comfort applications.

Design flow rates depend on the type of terminal apparatus and the supply temperature. In general, a higher temperature rise (or a greater temperature difference between supply and return temperatures) reduces the initial cost and the operating cost of the distribution system, as well as pumps required, and increases the efficiency of the chillers. In a given chilled water system, the selection of the design flow rate and the supply temperature, therefore, are closely related.

Although lower chilled water temperatures permit higher rises (or greater temperature difference), lower chiller efficiencies result. Water treatment may be required in chilled water systems to control corrosion rate, scaling, or algae growth.

Layout of piping for chilled water distribution varies greatly depending on system capacity, extent of distribution, type of terminals used, and control scheme to be employed.

Refrigerants that attack the ozone layer above the earth are being phased out and replaced with refrigeration systems that do not degrade the ozone layer, such as R-123, R-134A, and ammonia. This concern has also expanded the use of absorption chillers, both indirect (steam) and direct-fired types.

RECIPROCATING WATER CHILLER
4.73

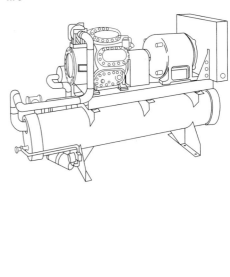

NOTE

4.73 Reciprocating water chiller, ideally suited to smaller jobs requiring less than 200 tons of cooling. Rotary screw chillers also operate in this capacity range.

Contributor:
Jeff Haberl, PhD, PE; Texas A&M University; College Station, Texas.

ABSORPTION WATER CHILLER
4.74

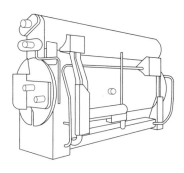

CENTRIFUGAL WATER CHILLER
4.75

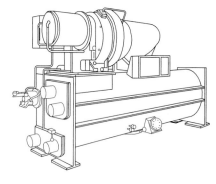

COOLING-ONLY AND HEATING/COOLING SYSTEMS

Cooling-only and heating/cooling systems include:

- Elementary chilled water system
- Primary/secondary chilled water pumping and distribution system
- Two-pipe dual-temperature system

ELEMENTARY CHILLED WATER SYSTEM

A chilled water system basically consists of a refrigeration water-chilling unit, a chilled water recirculating pump, terminal cooling

ELEMENTARY CHILLED WATER SYSTEM
4.76

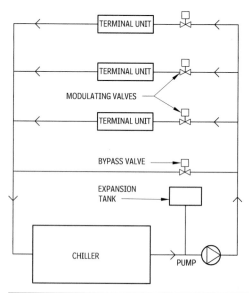

equipment, and an expansion tank. A chilled water bypass valve may be required in systems with two-way modulating valve control at the terminal units. As the cooling load on the terminal equipment decreases, the modulating valve closes and reduces the flow through the terminal. When the water flow through the terminal units is significantly throttled, the bypass valve opens gradually to prevent system pressure buildup and to maintain the water flow required for the proper operation of the chiller.

PRIMARY/SECONDARY CHILLED WATER PUMPING AND DISTRIBUTION SYSTEM

In large campus-type applications, the chilled water system consists of multiple chillers and primary and secondary system pumps. The terminal cooling equipment may be a chilled water cooling coil of a central air-conditioning unit, a closed-loop heat exchanger, or any other secondary or terminal cooling water system.

The primary loop does not require a pressure control device. The secondary loop pressure control valve operates as described under "Elementary Chilled Water System."

PRIMARY/SECONDARY CHILLED WATER PUMPING AND DISTRIBUTION SYSTEM
4.77

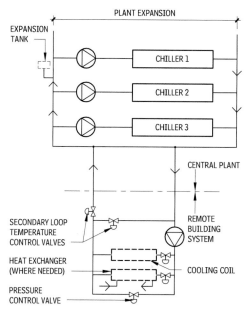

TWO-PIPE DUAL-TEMPERATURE SYSTEM

In a two-pipe dual-temperature system, hot water is circulated through the terminal units during cold weather and chilled water is circulated during the hot weather. The distribution system may be divided into zones, each of which is capable of changeover from heating to cooling, independent of the other zones.

When the hot and chilled water supply to each terminal unit is in two separate pipes but the return is in a common pipe, the system is called a three-pipe system. In a four-pipe system, separate supply and return mains for both hot and chilled water are run to each terminal unit.

TWO-PIPE DUAL-TEMPERATURE SYSTEM
4.78

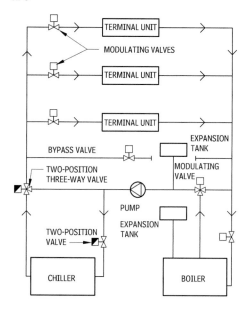

COOLING TOWERS

Water flows from the pump to the tower basin and is discharged under pressure to the condenser and back to the tower, where it is cooled through the spray deck. It is usually desirable to maintain condenser water temperature above a predetermined minimum, so return water is partially bypassed around the tower through a control valve to maintain desired supply water temperature.

In this condenser water system, air is continuously in contact with the water. Special consideration is then required for chemical treatment and allowance for impurities, scale, and corrosion in the condenser and piping system.

The amount of water flow required depends on the refrigeration system used and the available temperature of the condenser water. Lower condenser water supply temperature results in increased refrigeration machine efficiency.

COOLING TOWER
4.79

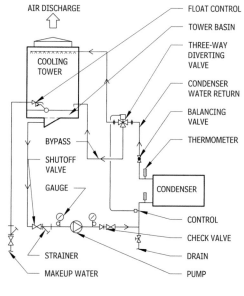

NOTES

4.74 Absorption water chiller, steam-powered for efficient production of 200 to 800 tons of cooling.
4.75 Centrifugal chiller with a flooded cooler and condenser. Typically to produce 150 to 1200 tons of cooling.

Contributors:
Joseph R. Loring & Associates, Inc., Consulting Engineers, New York City, New York; Jeff Haberl, PhD, PE, Texas A&M University, College Station, Texas.

Cooling towers cool water for reuse in refrigeration condensers or other heat exchangers. Standard ratings are in tons of refrigeration when cooling 3 gal/min per ton from 95°F to 85°F with ambient air at 78°F wet bulb. Cooling tower design should be based on performance at local conditions. Package cooling towers operate by fans moving air horizontally (crossflow) or up (counterflow) against water falling and wetting the fill or packing to expose maximum water surface to the air. Reduced airflow reduces tower performance. Architectural enclosures should minimize obstruction to airflow.

Warm water is distributed at the top of the cooling tower by spray nozzles or basins with multiple orifices, and cooled water is collected in a basin at the bottom and pumped to condensers. Water is cooled by evaporating a very small portion. Water droplets may also be carried out by the airstream. Minerals and impurities present in all water increase concentration as pure water evaporates, so a little water is "bled" and chemicals are added to minimize scaling, corrosion, or biological fouling of condenser tubes. Towers for critical or large systems should be multicell, for maintenance without shutdown.

Fan, motor, and water-splashing noise may be a nuisance. Fan noise is reduced by two-speed motors (about 8 dB at half speed, 15 percent power, and 60 percent capacity) and by intake and discharge attenuators (about 12 dB) with 10 percent power increase. Tower noise is louder in line with fan discharge and intake than in other directions. Each doubling of distance decreases noise about 6 dB. Barriers can reflect some noise from critical directions. For design purposes:

- Locate towers for free air movement.
- Avoid hot air recirculation, long piping from pumps and condensers, and inadequate substructures.
- Locate cooling towers so that noise and water droplet carryover and fog at air discharge in cold weather will not be a nuisance.
- Consider seismic and wind load in anchoring tower to supports; towers are usually designed to withstand 30 psf wind load. The basin may be heated for winter use.

ENCLOSURE CONSIDERATIONS

Provide liberal wall openings on air inlet side and mount tower so that air outlet is at top of enclosure. Consider the effect of wind on nearby structures and enclosures to minimize hot, moist discharge air from being recirculated into inlet.

CROSSFLOW-INDUCED, DRAFT-PACKAGED COOLING TOWER—
4.80

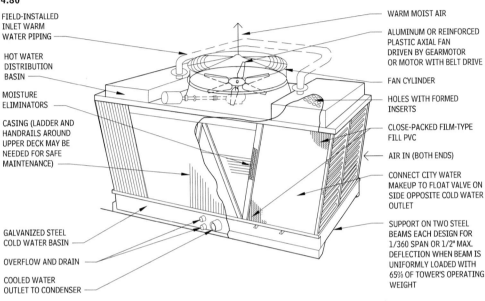

FIELD-INSTALLED INLET WARM WATER PIPING

HOT WATER DISTRIBUTION BASIN

MOISTURE ELIMINATORS

CASING (LADDER AND HANDRAILS AROUND UPPER DECK MAY BE NEEDED FOR SAFE MAINTENANCE)

GALVANIZED STEEL COLD WATER BASIN

OVERFLOW AND DRAIN

COOLED WATER OUTLET TO CONDENSER

WARM MOIST AIR

ALUMINUM OR REINFORCED PLASTIC AXIAL FAN DRIVEN BY GEARMOTOR OR MOTOR WITH BELT DRIVE

FAN CYLINDER

HOLES WITH FORMED INSERTS

CLOSE-PACKED FILM-TYPE FILL PVC

AIR IN (BOTH ENDS)

CONNECT CITY WATER MAKEUP TO FLOAT VALVE ON SIDE OPPOSITE COLD WATER OUTLET

SUPPORT ON TWO STEEL BEAMS EACH DESIGN FOR 1/360 SPAN OR 1/2" MAX. DEFLECTION WHEN BEAM IS UNIFORMLY LOADED WITH 65% OF TOWER'S OPERATING WEIGHT

ENCLOSURE CONSIDERATIONS
4.83

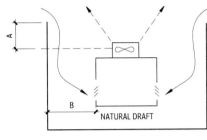

A

B

NATURAL DRAFT

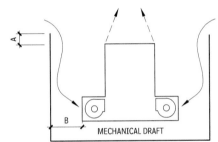

A

B

MECHANICAL DRAFT

NATURAL-DRAFT-PACKAGED COOLING TOWER
4.81

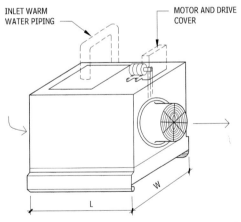

INLET WARM WATER PIPING

MOTOR AND DRIVE COVER

W

L

COOLING TONS	OVERALL DIMENSIONS (IN.)			OPERATING WEIGHT (LB)	MOTOR (HP)
	L	W	HT.		
5	69	33	60	940	1/4
25	75	46	80	1600	1
50	84	64	92	2500	3
100	93	100	92	4200	5
150	100	144	112	8000	7-1/2

MECHANICAL-DRAFT-PACKAGED COOLING TOWER
4.82

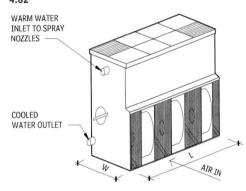

WARM WATER INLET TO SPRAY NOZZLES

COOLED WATER OUTLET

W

L

AIR IN

COOLING TONS	OVERALL DIMENSIONS (IN.)			OPERATING WEIGHT (LB)	MOTOR (HP)
	L	W	HT.		
20	36	36	78	950	2
50	72	36	96	1700	7-1/2
150	144	56	122	4800	20
400	140	118	192	14,000	50

EVAPORATIVE CONDENSERS

In refrigeration systems larger than 50-ton capacity, water-cooled condensers are used to cool the recirculating condenser water. Both the closed-circuit evaporative cooler and the cooling tower operate on the principle of evaporative cooling, which depends on the wet bulb temperature of the air. Closed-circuit evaporative coolers are available in sizes up to 300 tons and are used when contamination of the condenser water by direct contact with outdoor air cannot be tolerated.

Use of a cooling tower is generally acceptable in most installations in the building construction industry. The temperature of the water leaving the cooling tower is about 7°F to 10°F above the wet bulb temperature of the outside air entering the tower. In cold winter climates the cooling towers can be used directly to make chilled water, thereby eliminating mechanical refrigeration.

Evaporative condensers combine the functions of a cooling tower and a water-cooling condenser. Latent heat transfer is more effective as a means of heat dissipation. This permits a smaller-sized unit than an equivalent tonnage air-cooled unit and considerable energy savings in fan horsepower.

Installations can be either within an equipment room with appropriate ducts or ground- or roof-mounted outdoors. Adequate protection from freezing must be provided for exterior installations.

For sizing of condensing units, the manufacturer's rating is the only reliable method of determining unit capacity.

Multiple evaporative condensers may be connected in parallel, or an evaporative condenser may be connected in parallel with a shell and tube condenser. Proper piping and traps must be installed in these cases to prevent unequal loading or overloading.

NOTES

4.80 a. 200–700 ton capacity pumps available in dual cells with twice the capacity.
b. Field-erected custom-designed cooling towers with casings of masonry or concrete used to enhance building aesthetics.
4.81 Cooling 3 gal/min per ton from 95°F to 85°F with ambient air at 78°F wet bulb.
4.82 a. Cooling 3 gal/min per ton from 95°F to 85°F with ambient air at 78°F wet bulb.

b. Figure indicates single module. Units available in end-to-end and back-to-back double inlet configurations.
4.83 a. A = Height of enclosure above tower outlet. Minimize or extend shroud up from tower.
b. If enclosure walls have no opening, the horizontal distance from the tower inlet must increase greatly. (Power for fan must be increased.) Consult cooling tower manufacturers for minimum B dimension.

The condenser water is circulated inside the tubes of the unit's heat exchanger. Heat flows from the condenser water through the heat-exchanger tubes to the spray water outside, which cascades downward over the tubes. Air is forced upward through the heat exchanger, evaporating a small percentage of the spray water, absorbing the latent heat of vaporization, and discharging the heat to the atmosphere.

The remaining water falls to the sump to be recirculated by the pump. The water consumed is the amount evaporated plus a small amount that is bled off to limit the concentration of impurities in the pan.

The condenser water circulates through the clean, closed loop of the heat exchanger and is never exposed to the air stream or the spray water outside the heat-exchanger tubes.

REFRIGERANT COMPRESSORS AND CONDENSERS

The process of removing heat from a refrigerant is called condensing. In a refrigerant cycle, it is during the condensing process that the refrigerant rejects heat absorbed during the evaporation and compression processes, is reconverted to liquid state, and becomes ready to repeat the cycle.

To convert the refrigerant from gaseous to liquid state, heat exchangers called condensers are used. Air-cooled and water-cooled condensers are the predominant types used in the building construction industry.

In the less than 50-ton-capacity range, water-cooled condensers can be used where water sources such as a lake, river, or well are available for once-through use without recirculation of water.

DRY COOLER

Dry coolers of up to 25-ton capacity are normally used where water is scarce, as well as in computer rooms and other special air-conditioning applications. In areas where the winter ambient temperature is below the water freezing temperature, glycol is added to the condenser water. The heat rejection to the outdoor air is by sensible heat transfer, which depends on the dry bulb temperature of the air.

In the dry cooler, the condenser water-glycol solution is circulated inside the finned tubes of the dry cooler's heat exchanger. Heat flows from the condenser water-glycol solution through the heat-exchanger tube walls to the fins. Propeller fans draw air over the fins, and the heat from the fins is transferred to the air passing over them.

An aquastat that senses the temperature of the solution as it leaves the dry cooler cycles the fans to maintain the desired temperature.

DRY COOLER
4.85

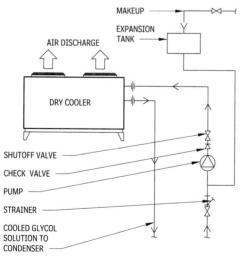

EVAPORATIVE CONDENSERS
4.84

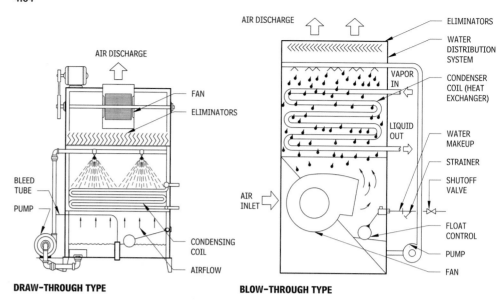

DRAW-THROUGH TYPE

BLOW-THROUGH TYPE

OTHER REFRIGERATION SYSTEMS

HVAC DISTRIBUTION

HVAC AIR DISTRIBUTION

OVERHEAD AIR SYSTEM WITH DUCTED RETURN
4.86

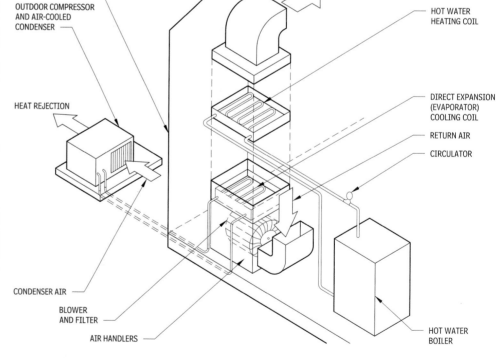

Contributor:
Walter T. Grondzik, PE, Florida A&M University; Tallahassee, Florida.

COMMON DUCT SYSTEM LAYOUTS
4.87

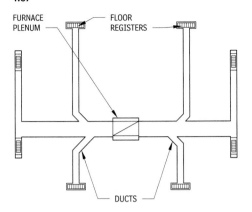

EXTENDED PLENUM SYSTEM

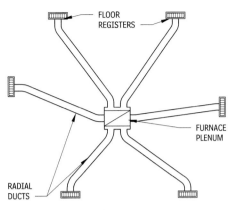

PERIMETER RADIAL SYSTEM

There are several HVAC distribution systems commonly used in medium to large buildings, including single duct with terminal reheat, single duct with variable volume, dual duct, and multizone; each of these systems is discussed in greater detail.

CONSTANT-VOLUME SINGLE-DUCT WITH TERMINAL REHEAT

This system provides a constant flow of air to the zones served by the HVAC system. Zone temperature is maintained by changing the temperature of the constant airflow. Dehumidification is provided by the combination of a cooling coil and a reheat coil in the terminal mixing box in each zone. Cooling is provided by a cooling coil that uses either direct expansion of the refrigerant or chilled water provided by a central plant. Heating is provided in the outside air preheat coil and in the reheat coil, using hot water from a boiler. Normally, the amount of outside air provided corresponds to the amount of ventilation appropriate for anticipated occupancy levels.

Winter and summer operation of the system is best understood by tracing the system state points on a psychrometric chart. The state points for summer conditions of 95°F, 50 percent relative humidity (RH) outdoor conditions, zonal conditions of 78°F and 50 percent RH, and system set points of 10 percent outside air, cooling coil set point of 55°F, and a maximum reheat coil set point of 110°F. The preheat coil is assumed to be inactive in the summer, and the cooling coil to be inactive in the winter when the mixed air is less than 55°F.

During summer conditions, the mixed airstream (point C, 80°F, 50 percent RH), which consists of 10 percent outside air (points B and B[1], 95°F, 50 percent RH) and 90 percent return air (point A, 78°F, 50 percent RH), is cooled to 55°F and 90 to 100 percent RH as it passes through the cooling coil (point D). This 55°F air is then provided to the terminal box in each zone, where it is reheated to meet the zonal cooling load; in this case, the 55°F, 90 to 100 percent RH air is reheated to 65°F and 70 percent RH in the terminal mixing box before it enters the zone.

During the winter, the preheat coil heats outside air (point B[1], 35°F, 50 percent RH) to 45°F (point B[1], 45°F, 35 percent RH). The mixed airstream (point C, 69°F, 50 percent RH), which consists of 10 percent outside air (point B[1], 45°F, 35 percent RH) and 90 percent return air (point A, 72°F, 50 percent RH), passes through the cooling coil, where it is cooled to 55°F and 80 percent RH (point D). The air is then heated in the terminal box to 90°F and 25 percent RH (point E).

ADVANTAGES
- Can provide heating and cooling as needed.
- Provides good dehumidification.
- Boiler and chiller can be installed at a central plant.
- Air-handling unit runs continuously, providing good ventilation.
- Equipment life is long.
- An economizer can be added to take advantage of free cooling during appropriate conditions.

CONSTANT-VOLUME SINGLE-DUCT SYSTEM WITH TERMINAL REHEAT
4.88

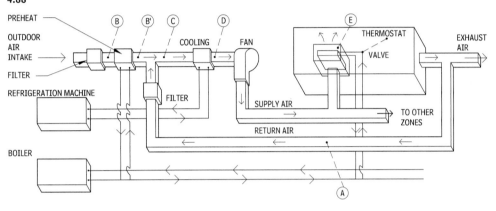

DISADVANTAGES
- There is no humidification, so this type of system may produce very dry conditions indoors during winter.
- Requires distribution ductwork to each zone.
- Air-handling unit runs continuously, which can cause excessive energy consumption.
- Reheat coils require piping run to each zone or electric resistance heating.
- Use of reheat during dehumidification uses unnecessary heating in the summer.
- Chiller and boiler both must operate except in extreme winter conditions.

VARIABLE-VOLUME SINGLE-DUCT SYSTEM WITH REHEAT
4.89

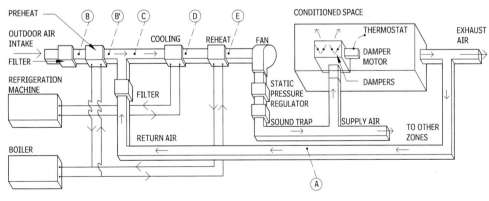

VARIABLE-VOLUME SINGLE-DUCT WITH REHEAT

This system provides a variable flow of air to the zone or zones served by the HVAC system. The amount of air is regulated by opening and closing individual terminal mixing boxes in each zone. Static pressure is maintained by varying the fan speed. During cooling, the temperature in each zone is maintained by changing the flow rate of the air. During heating, the cooling coil is inactive and the heating coil heats the main supply air to the minimum temperature necessary to meet the maximum load of any zone served. In the winter, a thermostat in each zone regulates the heated airflow to meet the zone load. Dehumidification is provided by the combination of a cooling coil and a reheat coil. Humidification is not provided, but can be added by inserting a humidification device immediately after the fan. Cooling is provided by a cooling coil that uses either direct expansion of the refrigerant or chilled water provided by a central plant. Hot water from a boiler provides heating in the outside air preheat coil and in the main reheat coil. Normally, a fixed amount of outside air is provided, corresponding to the amount of ventilation appropriate for anticipated occupancy levels.

Winter and summer operation of the system is best understood by tracing the system state points on a psychrometric chart. The state points for summer conditions of 95°F and 50 percent RH outdoors, zonal conditions of 78°F and 50 percent RH, and system set points of 10 percent outside air, cooling coil set point of 55°F, and a maximum reheat coil set point of 110°F. The preheat coil is assumed to be inactive in the summer; the cooling coil is inactive in the winter when the mixed air is less than 55°F.

In summer conditions, the mixed airstream (point C, 80°F, 50 percent RH), which consists of 10 percent outside air (points B and B[1], 95°F, 50 percent RH) and 90 percent return air (point A, 78°F, 50 percent RH), is cooled to 55°F and 90 to 100 percent RH as it passes through the cooling coil (point D). This 55°F air is then reheated to 65°F and 70 percent RH in the main reheat coil. Reheating must be controlled to maintain RH at or below 60 percent in all zones served in summer conditions. The amount of air entering each zone is then modulated to meet the cooling load.

During the winter, the preheat coil heats outside air to 45°F; the cooling coil is inactive. The mixed airstream (point C, 69°F, 50 percent RH), which consists of 10 percent outside air (point B, 35°F, 50 percent RH) that has been preheated to 45°F and 35 percent RH (point B[1]) and 90 percent return air (point A, 72°F, 50 percent RH), passes through the cooling coil unaffected and is heated in the main reheat coil to 110°F, 15 percent RH.

ADVANTAGES
- Can provide heating and cooling as needed.
- Provides average dehumidification.
- Boiler and chiller can be installed at a central plant.
- Air-handling unit runs continuously at variable volume, which provides adequate ventilation.
- Equipment life is long.
- An economizer can be added to take advantage of free cooling during appropriate ambient conditions.
- Does not require piping into individual zones.

DISADVANTAGES
- There is no humidification, so this type of system may produce very dry conditions indoors during winter.
- Requires distribution ductwork to each zone.
- Volume of air provided to air-handling units varies, which can result in inadequate ventilation if not properly balanced.
- One main reheat coil for the entire system can result in a very cold building in extremely humid climates. Could require humidity sensor to moderate supply air temperature, to maintain humidity at or below 60 percent RH.
- Use of reheat during dehumidification uses unnecessary heating in the summer.
- One main heating coil may cause hot interior zones when internal loads require year-round cooling.

CONSTANT-VOLUME DUAL-DUCT SYSTEM
4.90

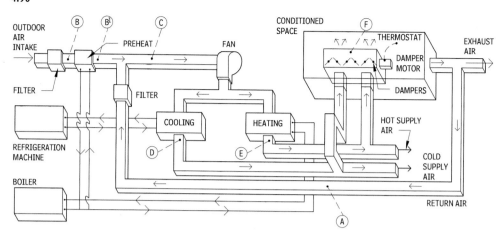

CONSTANT-VOLUME DUAL-DUCT

A constant-volume dual-duct (CVDD) system provides a constant flow of air to zones served by the HVAC system. Zone temperature is maintained by changing the temperature of the constant airflow that leaves the terminal mixing box in each zone. Dehumidification is provided by the cooling coil and any remixing of air in the terminal mixing boxes. Humidification is not provided in the system shown in Figure 4.235, but can be added by inserting a humidification device immediately after the main heating coil. Cooling is provided by a cooling coil that uses either direct expansion of the refrigerant or chilled water provided by a central plant. Heating is provided in the outside air preheat coil and in the main heating coil, using hot water from a boiler. Normally, the fixed amount of outside air provided corresponds to the appropriate amount of ventilation for anticipated occupancy levels. However, in a dual-duct system, both hot and cold airstreams are always available to each terminal mixing box. The temperature of the air leaving the cooling coil is always between 45°F (winter) and 55°F (summer). Air leaving the heating coil is either fixed at 110°F or can be moderated by an outside reset thermostat. Varying amounts of hot and cold air are mixed in the terminal boxes to achieve the required cooling or heating load.

Winter and summer operation of the system is best understood by tracing system state points on a psychrometric chart. The state points for summer and winter are the same as those indicated previously for the constant volume single-duct system with reheat.

In summer conditions, the mixed airstream (point C, 80°F, 50 percent RH), which consists of 10 percent outside air (points B and B[1], 95°F, 50 percent RH) and 90 percent return air (point A, 78°F, 50 percent RH), is either cooled to 55°F and 90 to 100 percent RH as it passes through the cooling coil (point D) or heated to 110°F and 20 percent RH as it passes through the main heating coil. Both the 55°F cold air and 110°F hot air are then made available to the terminal mixing box, where the two airstreams are mixed to produce a constant-flow variable-temperature airstream to meet the cooling and dehumidification load (point F, 65°F, 72 percent RH).

During winter conditions, the preheat coil heats outside air to 45°F. The mixed airstream (point C, 69°F, 50 percent RH), which consists of 10 percent outside air (point B, 35°F, 50 percent RH) that has been preheated to 45°F and 35 percent RH (point B[1]) and 90 percent return air (point A, 72°F, 50 percent RH) passes through the cooling coil, where it is cooled to 55°F and 82 percent RH, or is heated in the main heating coil to 110°F and about 15 percent RH. Both the 45°F cold air and 110°F hot air are then made available to the terminal mixing box, which mixes the two to produce a constant-flow variable-temperature airstream to meet the heating load (point F). This type of system does not provide humidification so it may produce extremely dry conditions indoors during the winter.

ADVANTAGES
- Can provide heating and cooling as needed.
- Provides good dehumidification.
- Boiler and chiller can be installed at a central plant.
- Air-handling unit runs continuously, providing good ventilation.
- Equipment life is long.
- CVDD systems do not require piping run to each zone.

DISADVANTAGES
- There is no humidification, so this type of system may produce very dry conditions indoors during winter.
- Requires distribution ductwork to each zone.
- Volume of air provided to air-handling units varies, which can result in inadequate ventilation if not properly balanced.
- One main heating coil may cause hot interior zones when internal loads require year-round cooling.

MODIFICATIONS
This system can easily be modified to make a variable-volume dual-duct system by installing a variable-speed controller on the main fan and modifying the terminal mixing boxes to allow for varying airflow rates.

Contributor:
Jeff Haberl, PhD, PE, Texas A&M University, College Station, Texas.

CONSTANT-VOLUME MULTIZONE SYSTEM
4.91

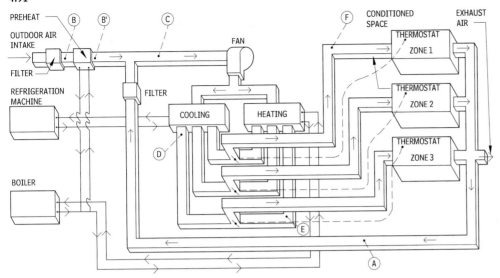

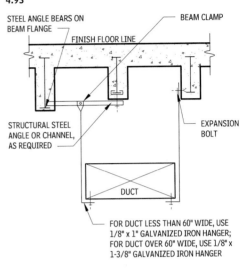

Supply ducts should be constructed entirely of noncombustible material in commercial construction. Single-family residential ducts need not meet this requirement, with the exception of the first 3 ft from the unit, provided they are used in conjunction with listed heating units, are properly constructed from a base material of metal or mineral, and are properly applied. Ducts passing through unconditioned spaces or located in exposed walls should have 1 to 2 in. of insulation.

Ducts must be securely supported by metal hangers, straps, lugs, or brackets. No nails should be driven through duct walls, and no unnecessary holes should be cut in them.

CONSTANT-VOLUME MULTIZONE

A constant-volume multizone (CVMZ) system provides a constant flow of air to the zones served by the system. Zone temperature is maintained by changing the temperature of the constant airflow that leaves the multizone unit. Dehumidification is provided by the cooling coil and any remixing of air from the heating coil before it enters a zone. The system shown does not provide humidification, but a dehumidification device can be added just after the main heating coil for each zone. Cooling is provided by a cooling coil that uses either direct expansion of the refrigerant or chilled water provided by a central plant. Heating is provided in the outside air preheat coil and in the main heating coil, using hot water from a boiler. Normally, a fixed amount of outside air corresponds to the amount of ventilation appropriate for the occupancy level. In a multizone system, both hot and cold airstreams are always available to each zone. The temperature of the air leaving the cooling coil is always between 45°F (winter) and 55°F (summer). Air leaving the heating coil is fixed at 110°F; or it can be moderated by an outside reset thermostat. Varying amounts of hot and cold air are mixed according to the required cooling or heating load in each zone.

Summer and winter operation of the system is best understood by tracing system state points on a psychrometric chart. The state points for summer and winter conditions are the same as those indicated for the constant-volume single-duct system with reheat described previously.

During summer conditions, the mixed airstream (point C, 80°F, 50 percent RH), which consists of 10 percent outside air (points B and B', 95°F, 50 percent RH) and 90 percent return air (point A, 78°F, 50 percent RH), is either cooled to 55°F and 90 to 100 percent RH as it passes through the cooling coil (point D) or is heated to 110°F and 20 percent RH as it passes through the main heating coil. Both the 55°F cold air and 110°F hot air are then made available to each zone to meet the cooling and dehumidification load.

During winter conditions, the preheat coil heats outside air to 45°F. The mixed airstream (point C, 69°F, 50 percent RH), which consists of 10 percent outside air (point B, 35°F, 50 percent RH) that has been preheated to 45°F and 35 percent RH (point B[1]) and 90 percent return air (point A, 72°F, 50 percent RH) passes through the cooling coil, where it is cooled to 55°F and 82 percent RH, or is heated in the main heating coil to 110°F and about 15 percent RH. Both the 55°F cold air and 110°F hot air are then made available to the individual zones to meet the heating load (point F, 90°F, 25 percent RH). This type of system does not provide humidification and so may produce extremely dry conditions indoors in the winter.

ADVANTAGES

- Can provide heating and cooling as needed.
- Provides good dehumidification.
- Boiler and chiller can be installed at a central plant.
- Air-handling unit runs continuously, providing good ventilation.
- Equipment life is long.
- CVMZ systems can be equipped with variable-volume fans for reduced energy use.

DISADVANTAGES

- There is no humidification, so this type of system may produce very dry conditions indoors during winter.
- Requires distribution ductwork to each zone.
- Air-handling unit runs continuously, which can cause excessive energy consumption.
- Use of reheat during dehumidification uses unnecessary heating in the summer.
- Chiller and boiler both must operate except in extreme winter conditions.

HVAC DUCTS AND CASINGS

Ducts must be permanent, rigid, nonbuckling, and nonrattling. Joints in ducts should be airtight. Steel or aluminum sheets are the most common materials used in the construction of ducts, which are generally round, flat-oval, or rectangular in cross section.

DUCT INSULATION DETAIL
4.92

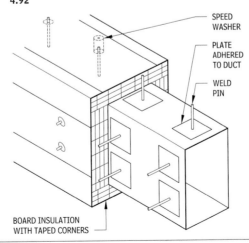

DUCT SUPPORT DETAIL
4.93

Supply ducts should be equipped with an adjustable locking type damper for air volume control. The damper should be installed in the branch duct as far from the outlet as possible, where it is accessible.

Automatic smoke dampers are required wherever ducts pass through a rated smoke barrier partition.

Return air ducts having more than one return intake may be equipped with balancing dampers.

Attention should be given to minimizing noise transmission. Metal ducts should be connected to the unit by strips of flexible fire-resistant material. Electrical conduit and piping, if directly connected to the unit, may increase noise transmission. Return air intakes immediately adjacent to the unit may also increase noise transmission. Installation of a fan directly under a return air grille should be avoided.

NOTE

4.93 On ducts over 48 in. wide, hangers must turn under and fasten to bottom of duct. When cross-sectional area exceeds 8 sq ft, duct will be braced by angles on all four sides.

Contributor:
Jeff Haberl, PhD, PE, Texas A&M University, College Station, Texas.

DUCT SYSTEMS

SINGLE-ZONE AIR DISTRIBTUION

Single-zone air distribution systems have only one point of control (one thermostat equals one zone). The system operates with a constant airflow from the air-handling unit and through the diffusers, with the thermostat controlling supply air temperature in response to load. Any number of diffusers may be provided to meet air distribution needs. Numerous air-handling unit configurations are available. This type of system may be found in residential, retail, and industrial buildings, and in interior (core) spaces of complex buildings. Multiple systems may be used to provide multiple zones.

MULTIZONE AIR DISTRIBTUION

A multizone air distribution system can serve approximately 10 zones per air-handling unit. The system operates with constant airflow from the air-handling unit and through the diffusers, with thermostats controlling the supply air temperature of individual zones in response to load. A dedicated supply duct serves each zone and can provide good control of space conditions at moderate energy cost. Because zone control occurs at the air-handling unit, this is not a flexible system. The numerous supply ducts make system layout and coordination critical. Multiple air-handling units may be used to provide additional zoning capability.

VARIABLE AIR VOLUME (VAV) AIR DISTRIBUTION

A variable air volume air distribution system can serve a virtually unlimited number of zones. The system meets loads by providing a varying airflow through the diffusers in each zone under the control of zone thermostats. VAV systems are very flexible because zone control occurs at VAV boxes located near the conditioned spaces. But a VAV system is essentially a cooling-only system, so some means of space heating must be provided (an independent heating system; fan-powered or induction terminals with electric or hot water heating). VAV systems can provide excellent comfort with good energy efficiency, but air quality issues must be seriously examined during system design. Several fan/air supply control options are available to minimize system energy use at part loads.

SINGLE-ZONE AIR DISTRIBUTION
4.94

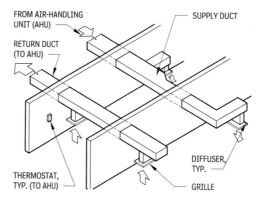

ABBREVIATIONS

AHU = AIR-HANDLING UNIT
VAV = VARIABLE AIR VOLUME

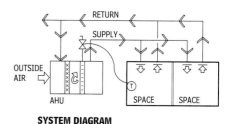

SYSTEM DIAGRAM

MULTIZONE AIR DISTRIBUTION
4.95

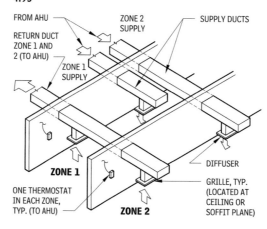

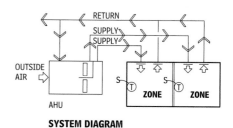

SYSTEM DIAGRAM

VARIABLE AIR VOLUME (VAV) AIR DISTRIBTUION
4.96

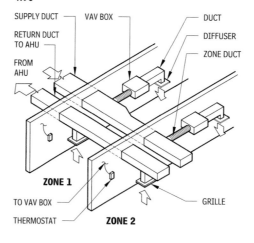

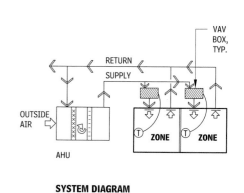

SYSTEM DIAGRAM

Contributor:
Walter T. Grondzik, PE, Florida A&M Univeristy, Tallahassee, Florida.

TERMINAL REHEAT AIR DISTRIBTUION

A terminal reheat air distribution system can serve virtually an unlimited number of zones. The system meets loads by varying the supply air temperature through the diffusers in each zone under the control of zone thermostats. The system is very flexible because zone control occurs at coils (electric or hot water) located near the conditioned spaces. A terminal reheat system can provide excellent comfort conditions (by providing constant airflow and humidity control) and simultaneous heating and cooling. Unfortunately, the reheat approach wastes substantial energy and is generally to be avoided unless the reheat comes from renewable energy sources (waste or reclaimed heat or solar energy). Terminal heating may be combined with variable volume air delivery.

DUAL-DUCT AIR DISTRIBUTION

A dual-duct air distribution system can serve a virtually unlimited number of zones. The system meets loads in the various zones by mixing hot and cold airstreams from the air-handling unit in response to zone thermostats. The system is very flexible because zone control occurs in mixing boxes located near the conditioned spaces. A dual-duct system provides good comfort and air quality conditions at reasonable energy cost. The need for two separate supply air distribution ducts, however, requires excellent coordination between air distribution and other services. Dual-duct systems may be designed with either a constant or variable-volume air supply.

FAN-COIL AIR DISTRIBUTION

A fan-coil air distribution system, either all-water or air-water, can serve a virtually unlimited number of zones. The system meets loads in the various zones by controlling the flow of chilled or hot water to the fan-coil unit in response to zone thermostats (often located integral to the fan coil). Design coordination must address the location of units within (or directly adjacent to) occupied spaces. All-water configurations are not true air-conditioning systems, and their use will generally be limited to exterior spaces; with a separate central air supply, however, the system can provide control of conditions as expected on full air-conditioning, and be used in both interior and exterior zones.

TERMINAL REHEAT AIR DISTRIBUTION
4.97

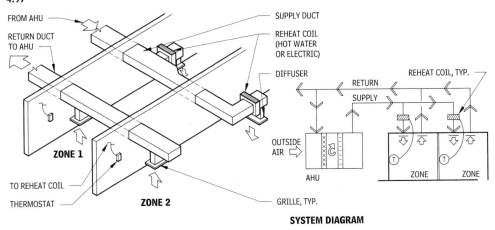

SYSTEM DIAGRAM

DUAL-DUCT AIR DISTRIBUTION
4.98

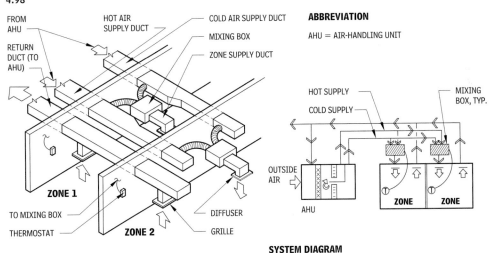

ABBREVIATION

AHU = AIR-HANDLING UNIT

SYSTEM DIAGRAM

FAN-COIL AIR DISTRIBTUION
4.99

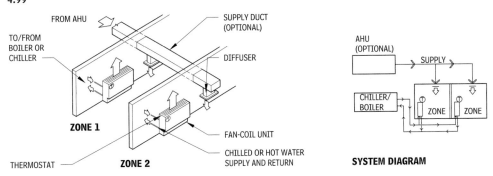

SYSTEM DIAGRAM

Contributor:
Walter T. Grondzik, PE, Florida A&M Univeristy, Tallahassee, Florida.

TYPICAL FLAT-PLATE SOLAR THERMAL COLLECTOR
4.100

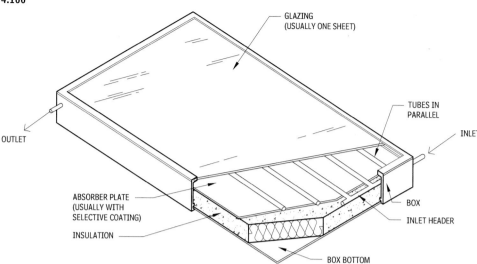

For systems having electric auxiliary heating, an electric element is typically located about one-third from the tank top, as shown in Figure 4.102, and the reentry line from the collector issues slightly below this element. The element thermostat is set at typically about 135°F to keeps the upper third of the tank heated. The lower two-thirds of the tank is reserved for solar, and if solar input is high and/or demand is low, the auxiliary element remains off and demand is met entirely by solar. For the case where gas is the auxiliary, it is necessary to use a two-tank design, wherein the gas heats a small tank and a second tank is heated by solar; and this serves as a preheat for the supply water to the gas water heater.

Scaling due to calcium carbonate or silica in some waters may be a serious problem. In such cases, a conventional closed loop system (Figure 4.102) can be used; but rather than the external heat exchanger, a better option is either a wraparound tank heat exchanger, a mantle-tank heat exchanger, or heat exchanger coil immersed in the tank. The system is simplified because Pump No. 2 is eliminated. When scaling occurs, it is on the inside of the tank wall or outside of the immersed coil, and though it may slightly reduce performance, it does not clog and impede flow.

INTEGRATED COLLECTOR-STORAGE (ICS)
While the solar domestic hot water systems described here are all active systems (i.e., they have pumped fluid circulation) and have the collector located on the roof and the tank below, the integrated collector-storage (ICS) system is a fairly common design. In such systems, the solar storage vessel is typically a horizontal vessel integrated with the collector and located at its upper end. Heat

OTHER SPECIAL HVAC SYSTEMS AND EQUIPMENT

SOLAR ENERGY UTILIZATION SYSTEMS

A system for using solar energy consists of an array of collectors; a thermal storage unit; and piping or ducting to distribute fluid between the collectors, storage, and the load. Pumps or blowers are used to circulate the heat transfer fluid, and control devices are used to actuate the circulators. Auxiliary or standby heat sources are generally needed to carry part to the load when demand is heavy and/or the weather has been unfavorable.

SOLAR ENERGY HEATING SYSTEMS

Figure 4.101 shows a simple system for providing space heating and domestic hot water, using a drain-down design in which the collectors are emptied to the storage tank whenever Pump No. 1 stops. A controller senses the temperature difference between the collector plate and the tank water and starts the circulation in Pump No. 1 when this difference exceeds a set value. This set difference is such that negligible thermal energy is collected for values below the set value.

Since solar thermal collectors work more efficiently when the temperature difference between the collector and the ambient is low, fan-coil units with large areas of finned-tube heat transfer surface are generally selected for the space heating assignment. These can be used with water temperatures as low as 90°F. The auxiliary heat source in solar installations could be electricity, fuel oil, or natural gas.

SOLAR DOMESTIC HOT WATER SYSTEMS.

Solar hot water (by itself) is one of the most attractive and cost-effective of solar applications. Figure 4.102 depicts the closed-loop design with an external heat exchanger, which isolates the domestic water from the collector loop fluid. In this case, antifreeze is likely the collector loop fluid, and an expansion tank is incorporated as appropriate. Other designs incorporate a smaller drain-down tank in the collector loop, which permits water, instead of antifreeze, to be used in the collector loop.

Domestic hot water is typically provided by an immersed coil located near the top of the main storage tank. The domestic hot water system operates under full line pressure, whereas the main tank is at essentially atmospheric pressure. Because of the remote possibility of a backflow from the main tank into the public water supply, some plumbing codes require a double-walled heat exchanger in isolating the collector loop fluid from the potable water. An auxiliary heater is provided to ensure an adequate supply of domestic hot water at all times.

DRAIN-BACK SOLAR SPACE AND DOMESTIC HOT WATER SYSTEM.
4.101

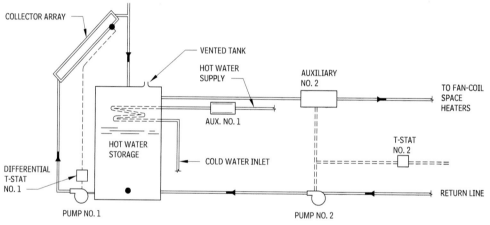

SOLAR DOMESTIC HOT WATER SYSTEM WITH COLLECTOR LOOP HEAT EXCHANGER
4.102

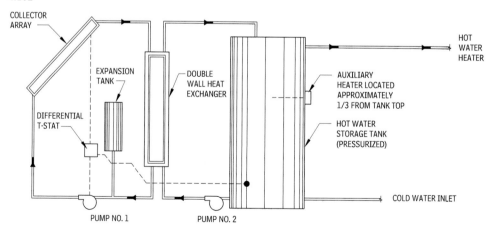

NOTES

4.100 a. The design shown is an example of a typical liquid-cooled collector. Air-cooled collector design varies somewhat.
b. For further information on collector design and performance, see manufacturers' specifications.
4.101 Differential T-Stat No. 1 is outside the tank. There are two sensors, one on the collector (dot) and one in the tank near the bottom (dot).

Contributors:
Charles Culp, CEMCS, Energy Systems Laboratory, Texas A&M University, College Station, Texas; R. Wilkinson, "Establishing Commissioning Fees," ASHRAE Journal 42(2), 2000:41-47; E. Mills, et al., "The Cost-Effectiveness of Commercial-Buildings Commissioning," Lawrence Berkeley laboratory Report # 56637, December 15, 2004.

is transported by natural circulation from the collector to the vessel. Some designs are open-loop (no heat exchanger in the vessel) and others are closed-loop (a heat exchanger in the vessel). The vessel serves as a preheater to the conventional water heater located in the semiconditioned space below. Such designs are very common in temperate locations such as Hawaii and south Florida.

It is becoming fairly common for domestic hot water systems to incorporate a PV-powered circulation pump in place of the common AC-powered pump. The pump operates when the sun shines, eliminating the differential thermostat; it also circulates water faster the higher the solar input, a desirable feature.

FREEZE PROTECTION FOR LIQUID SYSTEMS
When water is used for the heat transport fluid, freeze protection must be provided for essentially all locations within the continental United States. The drain-down system shown in Figure 4.102 is a fail-safe method to provide such protection, but it has certain disadvantages that, in many applications, make the use of an antifreeze fluid advisable. Figure 4.102 shows a widely used system in which water plus ethylene glycol or propylene glycol, or some similar antifreeze fluid, is circulated through the collector array by Pump No. 1. A double-walled heat exchanger is used to transfer the collected heat to the service hot water, which is under full line pressure.

SOLAR SWIMMING POOL HEATING SYSTEMS
The swimming pool heating application is a low-temperature one (80° to 90°F) and, as such, can use a much simpler collector for spring through fall use. As noted, the collectors are often unglazed with a plastic absorber, and are much less expensive than glazed collectors. The pool serves to the storage vessel, and the collector pump controls are similar to those described previously, except that there is an upper-limit temperature control to prevent the pool from overheating.

SOLAR ENERGY COOLING SYSTEMS
There are several means for providing cooling by solar power, including absorption cooling, desiccant cooling, and vapor compression cooling. Most installations have used the absorption or desiccant concepts, whereas, in general, solar cooling has not seen much success. The primary reasons are that these systems require relatively high-performance collectors and the systems themselves are more complex, making them generally less cost-effective than space heating and domestic hot water applications. Additionally, the duration of the cooling season tends to reduce cost-effectiveness in many applications. Of course, for commercial applications where cooling demand may be year-round, this doesn't apply.

AIR SOLAR HEATING SYSTEMS
Systems having collectors with air as the heat-transfer fluid have both advantages and disadvantages. The primary disadvantages are the necessarily large ducting systems and the typically higher parasitic power requirements for air circulation. Advantages include the absence of a freezing problem, negligible concern for minor leakage of properly designed systems, and minimal concern with corrosion. These systems have primary merit for space heating, where the load is the conditioned air, thus eliminating the load-side heat exchanger. Most frequently, rock (pebble-bed) thermal storage is incorporated.

Figure 4.103 shows the basic air solar heating system, and Figure 4.104 shows the damper positions for the three modes of operation: collector-to-load, collector-to-storage, and storage-to-load. Components that are inactive for any mode are "dashed" in. Note that the hot water coil is located downstream of the collectors so that water heating is achieved for all modes and is the first priority. Not shown on Figure 4.104 are components to accommodate summer operation when the heated space and storage are bypassed; but there is collector loop circulation to provide domestic water heating. In space and domestic hot water systems, it is the contribution to meet domestic hot water load that markedly improves the economics of the system, so it is important that there is contribution to domestic water heating year round.

Key issues in air system design are the large ducting components and the parasitic demands for air circulation. The larger ducting

BASIC SOLAR AIR HEATING SYSTEM
4.103

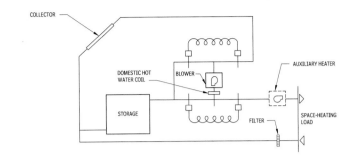

AIR SOLAR HEATING SYSTEM OPERATION MODES
4.104

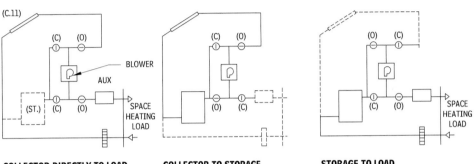

COLLECTOR DIRECTLY TO LOAD   **COLLECTOR TO STORAGE**   **STORAGE TO LOAD**

size can impact architectural decisions because of space considerations. Additionally, it is preferable to minimize externally located ducting due to heat losses, air leakage, and weatherization. An effective installation approach entails mounting the collectors integrally with the roof to keep all ducting below the roof. Whenever ducting is located externally, weather-resistant materials and airtight joints are essential.

Because of the large volume of air that must be circulated, pressure drops must be kept to a minimum, typically tenths of inches of water, compared to a few psi for liquid systems. It is this consideration that dictates large duct components and properly sized thermal storage.

The thermal storage unit usually uses rock aggregate (approximately golf-ball size) and the bin depth is typically about 6 ft, which is readily accommodated in a standard-story building. Flow is from

top to bottom for charging and from bottom to top for discharge. The bin volume is proportional to collector area, and varying size is accommodated by varying the cross section while keeping the depth constant. The golf-ball size aggregate is small enough to achieve good heat transfer but large enough to provide reasonable pressure drops and, thus, reasonable parasitic power demand.

Though rock storage is by far the most used, some designs have used a hydrated salt (Glauber's salt: sodium sulfate-decahydrate) to reduce storage volume. The salt is typically encapsulated in egg-carton-type containers.

Some problems with mold have been experienced in storage media, so such systems should be examined periodically.

In summary, air systems make sense for applications where space heating loads are large relative to domestic hot water loads, and of long duration.

TYPICAL GRID-CONNECTED PHOTOVOLTAIC SYSTEM
4.105

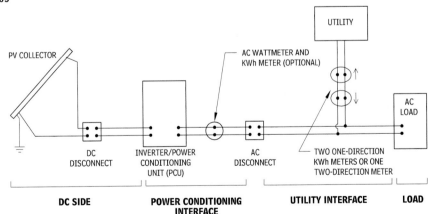

Contributors:
John I. Yellott, PE, and Gary Yabumoto, College of Architecture, Arizona State University, Tempe Arizona; Gary Vliet, PE, Mechanical Engineering, University of Texas at Austin, Austin Texas.

PHOTOVOLTAIC SYSTEMS

Photovoltaic (PV) systems convert sunlight into direct current (DC) electricity, which can subsequently be "inverted" to AC electricity to meet an AC load. Their rapidly decreasing cost and rising conventional energy costs will likely make these systems competitive with conventional sources of electricity within the decade. They are currently competitive with many off-grid applications where power line extension is costly or use of a diesel generator is undesirable.

The basic collection component of a PV system is the photovoltaic cell, a layered semiconductor that is generally fabricated from crystalline silicon. A group of cells interconnected in series is encapsulated to form a module. An array is an assembly of modules.

TYPICAL SILICON PHOTOVOLTAIC CELL
4.106

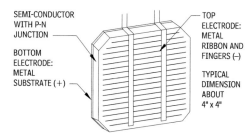

SEMI-CONDUCTOR WITH P-N JUNCTION

BOTTOM ELECTRODE: METAL SUBSTRATE (+)

TOP ELECTRODE: METAL RIBBON AND FINGERS (−)

TYPICAL DIMENSION ABOUT 4" x 4"

TYPICAL PHOTOVOLTAIC MODULE
4.107

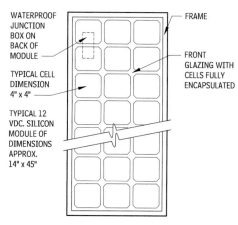

WATERPROOF JUNCTION BOX ON BACK OF MODULE

FRAME

TYPICAL CELL DIMENSION 4" x 4"

FRONT GLAZING WITH CELLS FULLY ENCAPSULATED

TYPICAL 12 VDC. SILICON MODULE OF DIMENSIONS APPROX. 14" x 45"

ALL (APPROX. 30 TO 36) CELLS CONNECTED IN SERIES TO PROVIDE A NOMINAL 12 VOLT, 50-60 WATT MODULE

The most common PV material is crystalline silicon, and currently the efficiency of commercial cells/modules is somewhat above 15 percent. Significant advances are being made in silicon technology and it is expected that the efficiency of commercial modules will exceed 20 percent in the near future. A variety of other PV technologies (including thin films and amorphous materials) are available, generally with somewhat lower efficiencies than current silicon technology. An important parameter for PV is the cost per watt of energy, and modules of different efficiencies may have comparable dollars per watt. The module efficiency is important to the designer in that the installed capacity (power) for a given area is directly proportional to efficiency.

A major component of a grid-connected PV system is the inverter, or power conditioning unit (PCU), which converts the DC power generated by the PV array into AC power used by the load and synchronizes the PV array's power output to make it compatible with the local utility output.

PV MODULE INSTALLATION

PV module installation typically involves one of three forms:

- Standoff or rack-mounted away from the roof or walls, and either parallel or inclined with the mounting surface. The standoff module design is currently the most common in residential applications and has the advantages of allowing convection cooling on the back side, ease of installation (particularly for retrofit), less impact on roof integrity, and ease of service/repair.
- Set directly on the roof sheathing or into the wall and made integral with that surface.
- PV shingles, which may replace conventional roofing. PV shingles have lower efficiencies and are currently much less common.

BUILDING-INTEGRATED PHOTOVOLTAICS (BIPV)

For commercial/institutional structures in particular, the use of building-integrated photovoltaics (BIPV) is becoming rather common. In such cases, PV modules may be sufficiently integrated into the roof or walls of the structure so that they provide the exterior barrier to the elements. Because of this integration of the PV system with the building envelope, it is particularly important that the architect be intimately involved in the design and specification of such a system.

STAND-ALONE (OFF-GRID) SYSTEMS

For residential and commercial buildings, the architect will most likely deal with grid-connected systems, since the loads will most likely be AC. However, some applications, such as vacation homes, offshore facilities, and so on, will be off-grid, and loads may be DC. In such cases, there is no need for the inverter; but for the system be stand-alone, a battery bank must be incorporated. In such systems, the battery bank should provide 5 to 10 "days of autonomy"—that is, have a capacity to meet the load for that many days.

LOCATING AND ORIENTING COLLECTOR ARRAYS

The most optimal orientation for solar collectors, whether thermal or PV, is on a south-sloping structure and inclined approximately at the local latitude or at a slightly greater tilt. For space heating systems, latitude plus about 15° favors the high winter season heating demand. Although these angles are recommended, if within even 10° or 15° for either azimuth or tilt, the collector's performance degradation is small. For locations where electric utility demand peaks in the late afternoons during summer, it may be best to face PV systems approximately to the southwest.

Shading is detrimental to collector performance and, as such, wherever possible collectors should be installed on the least shaded location of the building. Shading can arise from nearby trees and other buildings and from the building itself. For thermal collectors, the degradation is approximately proportional to the fraction of the collector array in shade, and so shading is not as significant a problem. However, for PV collectors, shading is very critical, as in an array possibly all cells are series-connected, and shading of even a few cells out of many hundreds will very seriously degrade performance. A good rule of thumb for PV collectors is that if any portion of a subarray of series-connected cells is shaded, then the output of that subarray will be negligible. Thus, PV modules should not be located proximate to any roof section elevated above it.

MOUNTING AND SUPPORTING COLLECTOR ARRAYS

The issues of collector mounting and support for truly BIPV designs are so site-specific that they will not be dealt with here. However, it is possibly even more important for the architect's involvement in BIPV designs than for the applications discussed here, which are restricted to standoff collector arrays.

The design of the support structure of a solar collector array can have an important influence on overall building appearance and design. It is also the aspect of the system that the architect can most easily control. If the collector array is to be selected as part of a total bid package, for example, sizing and coordination problems may result, and the architect may lose control of the array's

structural underpinnings and the building's overall appearance. In most cases, collector manufacturers (thermal and PV) will offer one or more support concepts that are compatible with their particular collectors. However, the means for the final anchoring to the structure will be the design professional's decision.

When mounting a collector array on a roof or other structure, the underlying supporting structure must be capable of meeting both the downward weight of the array as well as the uplift and sideward forces due to wind loadings. In retrofit applications, this may mean beefing up the substructure and special treatment for roof penetrations. Rooftop collector supports should be anchored directly to structural members, not to wood or metal decking; otherwise, wind-induced uplift forces and point loading may cause roofing and, possibly, structural failure. In steel buildings, vertical collector array supports must be secured directly to joists or beams. In wood buildings, securing the collectors to structural members will normally require the installation of some form of blocking, under the decking and between rafters, to adequately transfer the load.

On flat composition roofs, a fairly common approach is "gravity mounting," where the support posts are anchored to pans filled with sufficient aggregate to overcome wind forces. Of course, this adds to the weight of the system, which must be accommodated in the substructure. If anchored supports are used for a collector array on a light steel-framed roof, the supports should be anchored to the roof beams, and it is not uncommon to increase the capacity of the roof structure. Some roofs cannot support such loads and, thus, must be clear-spanned. However, long-span space-frame structures are invariably costly.

ANCHORING TO WOOD ROOF RAFTERS
4.108

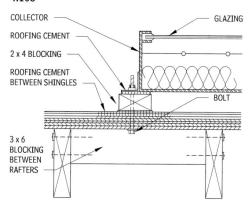

COLLECTOR

ROOFING CEMENT

2 x 4 BLOCKING

ROOFING CEMENT BETWEEN SHINGLES

3 x 6 BLOCKING BETWEEN RAFTERS

GLAZING

BOLT

GRAVITY MOUNTING FOR FLAT COMPOSITION ROOFS
4.109

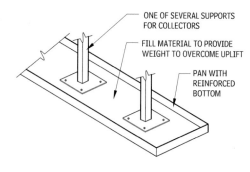

ONE OF SEVERAL SUPPORTS FOR COLLECTORS

FILL MATERIAL TO PROVIDE WEIGHT TO OVERCOME UPLIFT

PAN WITH REINFORCED BOTTOM

Contributors:
Stephen Weinstein, AIA, The Ehrenkrantz Group, New York City, New York; Gary Vliet, PE Mechanical Engineering, University of Texas at Austin, Austin, Texas.

COLLECTOR SPACING AND SUPPORT FOR LARGE ARRAYS AND MULTIPLE ROWS
4.110

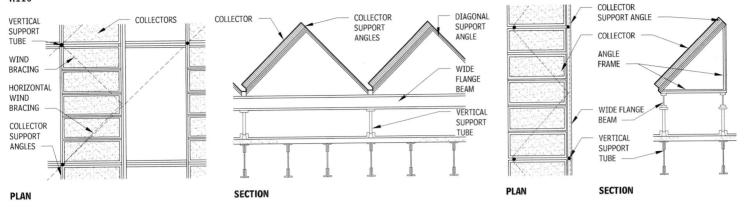

PLAN   SECTION   PLAN   SECTION

AVOIDING ROOFING PROBLEMS

Roof leaks can be a persistent and major problem in solar installations. The following guidelines will help to minimize such problems:

- Minimize roof penetrations by beefing up supports and increasing span lengths above the roof.
- Properly design the vertical supports at the roof line. Wood-blocking bolted directly through the roofing cannot be relied on even if sealed with roofing cement. Preferable approaches are: use of neoprene roofing sleeves, base flashings and canopies, and properly installed pitch pockets.
- Avoid the creation of dams. Continuous blocking, unless parallel to the slope, will cause damning and eventual leakage.
- Specify that all flashing work be performed by a roofing contractor, rather than the steel or plumbing contractor.
- On sloped roofs, mount collectors at the roof slope unless the pitch is such that the loss of year-round efficiency will be too great. When roof and collectors are parallel, leave at least 1-1/2-in. air space to reduce roofing deterioration. In snow-prone regions mount collectors as close to the roof ridge as possible and allow adequate roof clearance at the lower edge to reduce snow damning.

COLLECTORS ON SLOPED ROOFS IN SNOW-PRONE LOCATIONS
4.111

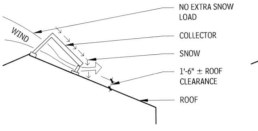

SAFE CONDITION

UNSAFE CONDITION

- On flat roofs, mount collectors 2 to 3 ft above the roof, rather than directly on the roof to prevent snow buildup, permit adequate slopes in pipe runs, allow installation of proper roof penetrations, and facilitate service. Also install proper roof walkways to protect roof from wear.

FIRE PROTECTION

DESIGN CONSIDERATIONS

The purpose of fire protection is to extinguish or mitigate the effects of a fire. Selection of the extinguishing medium most appropriate for a project is based on availability, compatibility, cost, and code requirements.

CODES AND STANDARDS

Most model, state, and local codes have a separate fire-protection section that mandates certain types of fire-suppression systems based on occupancy types, potential fire hazards, height, and area of the structure. Insurance companies, such as Factory Mutual Global, American Risk Insurers, and American Risk Management, have developed design standards to be followed by the clients they insure. In addition, the National Fire Protection Association (NFPA) has developed consensus standards for various suppression systems that are referenced by most building codes.

It is important that an adequate code search be made before the design phase of any project, to ensure compliance with the proper codes.

BASIC DEFINITIONS

Although the exact nature of fire and the combustion process is still not completely understood, it is known that three components are necessary for a fire to be maintained: fuel, oxygen, and a temperature high enough to start ignition or maintain combustion. All fire-extinguishing methods remove one or all of these components, causing the fire to be extinguished.

Fires are classified as:

- Class A fires, which occur in solid, combustible materials (such as wood and paper).
- Class B fires, which occur in combustible liquids (such as oil and gasoline).
- Class C fires are electrical in nature (such as a short circuit that causes a spark capable of igniting other substances).
- Class D fires occur in metals with their own fuel supply.

Building occupancy and other specific areas within a building are classified as follows, according to the potential for fire:

- *Light hazard* occurs in office buildings, schools, and public buildings.
- *Ordinary hazard* is similar to warehouses and stores with large amounts of combustible material.
- *Extra hazard* occurs where there is considerable potential for easily started, large fires.

These classifications are more fully explained in the applicable NFPA standards.

The term "automatic" is often used when referring to fire-suppression systems. In this context, "automatic" means operation of the system without human intervention when fire conditions occur.

SYSTEM TYPES

Three general types of systems are used for suppression and extinguishing of fires: water-based, chemical-based (either liquid or powder), and gas-based.

- *Water-based fire-suppression systems*: These use either water mixed with chemicals, which add fire-extinguishing characteristics, or undiluted water, to cool the fire below ignition temperature or deprive it of oxygen.
- *Gas-based fire-extinguishing systems*: These interfere with the combustion process and deprive the fire of oxygen.
- *Chemical-based fire-extinguishing systems* (either liquid or powder): These interfere with the combustion process and deprive the fire of oxygen.

WATER-BASED FIRE-SUPPRESSION SYSTEMS

The medium most often used to extinguish fires is water. It is readily available, inexpensive, and easy to apply. The most important factor in the use of water-based fire-suppression systems is adequate water pressure. When pressure from the building water supply is inadequate to supply fire standpipe and sprinkler systems, fire pumps, manufactured and installed specifically for fire-suppression systems, is used to increase water pressure. The fire pump is installed in strict conformance with NFPA-20.

Contributors:
Stephen Weinstein, AIA, The Ehrenkrantz Group, New York City, New York; Gary Vliet, PE Mechanical Engineering, University of Texas at Austin, Austin, Texas.

TYPICAL FIRE PUMP SCHEMATIC
4.112

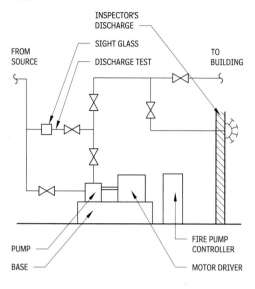

GAS-BASED SYSTEMS

Some gas-based systems use inert gasses, and others use chemical gasses.

TYPICAL GAS SYSTEM
4.113

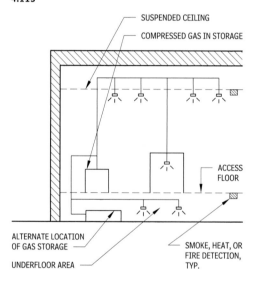

TYPICAL GAS DISCHARGE NOZZLES
4.114

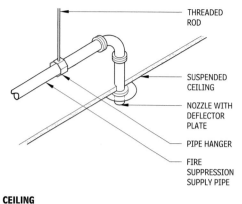

CEILING

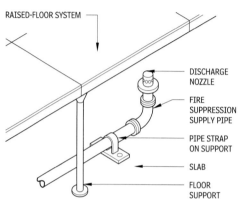

UNDERFLOOR

INERT GASSES

These systems are used when chemicals that may react to water are present or when water will cause unacceptable damage. The gasses (generally carbon dioxide or nitrogen) are discharged either directly onto a fire or are used to reduce the oxygen level in a room or area to a point below that required to sustain combustion. (Note, however, that this low level will not sustain life.)

The gas is stored compressed in high-pressure cylinders or tanks and is connected to a piping system with open heads. A quick-opening valve at the storage location detects heat, fire, or smoke at the hazard being protected, then opens to allow gas to enter the piping system and discharge out all the heads.

OTHER GASSES (HALON ALTERNATIVES)

Chemical gasses interfere with the combustion process, and chemical gas systems are often used to protect computer and electronic equipment and areas. The systems operate in the same way as inert gas systems, but a lower concentration of gas is usually required. Halon is no longer permitted because of environmental concerns. Many halon alternatives are available, but authorities having jurisdiction must approve their use.

Because of the force exerted by the discharging gas, hung ceilings should be reinforced in areas where heads are located and the heads mounted so they can resist the force of discharge.

CHEMICAL SYSTEMS

Both wet and dry chemical fire-extinguishing systems require extensive cleanup after a fire has been extinguished.

DRY-CHEMICAL FIRE-EXTINGUISHING SYSTEMS

This system is used to protect areas for which water is not a suitable extinguishing medium, such as chemical storage areas and cooking areas with exhaust ductwork that vents grease. A powdered chemical is stored in high-pressure cylinders or tanks connected to a piping system with open heads. Upon detecting heat, fire, or smoke at the hazard being protected, a quick-opening valve at the storage location opens, allowing the powder to enter the piping system and discharge from all of the heads simultaneously.

WET-CHEMICAL FIRE-EXTINGUISHING SYSTEMS

The recent shift from animal fats to vegetable fats for cooking requires a different medium for fighting fires in kitchens. This medium is a wet chemical, which operates in the same manner as the dry chemical system.

DRY OR WET CHEMICAL SYSTEM FOR KITCHENS
4.115

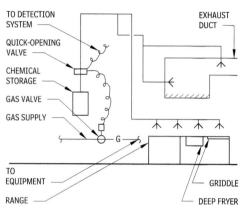

SPRINKLERS

A fire-suppression sprinkler system uses water distributed through a network of valves, piping, and nozzles, whose primary purpose is to set off an alarm and mitigate the effects of a fire, not necessarily to extinguish it. When a fire condition is present, the heat of the fire melts the element of a closed sprinkler head, allowing water to discharge automatically onto the fire.

The sprinkler piping system is sized using one of two methods:

- The schedule method uses pipe sizes based on a minimum available water pressure and the number of heads connected to the piping, given in NFPA-13.
- The *hydraulic method* uses a remote area (that farthest from the water supply source) based on occupancy type, flow of water over the remote area, flow of water at each design point, and pressure available in the system.

MAJOR SYSTEM COMPONENTS

The major operating components of a sprinkler system are the operating valve assembly, piping, and nozzles (referred to as *heads* for some systems).

The operating valve assembly admits water to or sends an alarm upon the flow of water in the system. There are many types of operating valves; the type of system installed determines the type of valve used.

Heads or nozzles distribute water in a special, predetermined pattern based on the requirements of the system. They are available in a wide variety of configurations, including upright, pendant, or sidewall, and can be closed or open. They have different temperature ratings to open the head, various orifice diameters for the discharge of water, standard or quick response, and standard or extended coverage. They can be installed in a hung ceiling as concealed, flush, or exposed fixtures.

Contributors:
Stephen Weinstein, AIA, The Ehrenkrantz Group, New York City, New York; Gary Vliet, PE Mechanical Engineering, University of Texas at Austin, Austin, Texas.

SPRINKLER SYSTEM TYPES

There are six common types of fire-suppression sprinkler systems.

- *Wet-pipe sprinkler systems*: This automatic system uses piping filled with water under pressure and closed heads. The operating valve assembly, called an *alarm check valve*, initiates an alarm when water flows and prevents the reverse flow of water into the building service if the system is supplied with water from a fire department connection. When a fire condition exits, the heat melts (fuses) a temperature-sensitive element in the head, causing the head to open and water to flow.
- *Dry-pipe sprinkler systems*: This automatic system uses piping filled with air under pressure and closed heads. The operating valve assembly is called a *dry pipe valve*. An air compressor is required to make up air lost through leakage. Both water and compressed air are supplied only to the dry pipe valve. When a head fuses due to a fire condition, it lowers the air pressure, opens the valve, and permits water to enter the piping; the water then flows only from the open heads.
- *Preaction sprinkler systems*: This automatic system uses closed heads and piping filled with air under atmospheric pressure. Water is supplied to the operating valve assembly, called a *pre-action valve*. An ancillary smoke or fire detection system initiates a signal upon detection of heat, fire, or smoke. The signal causes the preaction valve to open, allowing water to enter the piping system. Water will not flow out of the heads unless they fuse due to a fire condition.
- *Deluge fire-suppression sprinkler systems*: Used to protect high-hazard areas and specific equipment, this automatic system uses piping filled with air under atmospheric pressure and open heads. Water is supplied to the operating valve assembly, called a *deluge valve*. An ancillary smoke or fire-detection system is required to initiate a signal upon detection of heat, fire, or smoke at the hazard being protected. This signal will open the deluge valve, admitting water throughout the piping system and allowing water to discharge out of all the heads connected to the piping network.
- *Antifreeze sprinkler system*: A wet-pipe automatic system is filled with an antifreeze solution instead of water to protect areas subject to freezing but too small for a dry pipe system. Operations are similar to those of the standard wet pipe system.

TYPICAL SPRINKLER CONNECTION
4.116

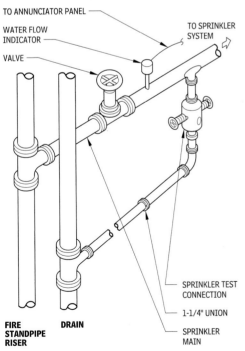

SPRINKLER SYSTEM TYPES
4.117

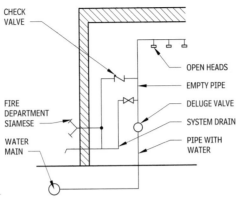

DELUGE SYSTEM

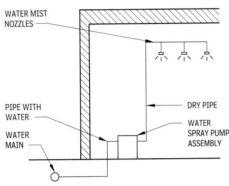

WATER SPRAY SYSTEM

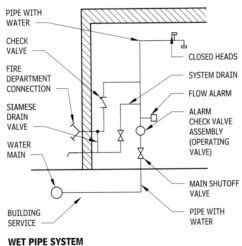

WET PIPE SYSTEM

- *Water spray fixed system*: This automatic system uses high-pressure water flowing through nozzles designed to discharge very small droplets of water directly onto a fire. A water pump is required to produce the high system pressure. Water is supplied to the pump, which is activated by ancillary heat, fire, or smoke detectors adjacent to the hazard protected.

STANDPIPES

Fire-suppression standpipes are a network of water-filled pipes, hose valves, and fire hose that allows the direct application of water onto a fire. The most common system configuration has hose valves only, which are connected to system piping to allow fire department personnel to connect their hose to the system. Mains are installed in high fire-resistance-rated areas such as stairwells. Hose valves are located so that all parts of the building can be reached with a 100-ft length of hose and a 20-ft water stream from the hose nozzle.

It is accepted practice to supply sprinkler heads from standpipes in various areas throughout a building. Each connection point is provided with a flow alarm. A test connection is installed at each point to permit authorities to visually verify that the water discharged from one sprinkler head is actually flowing and will initiate an alarm. This test connection is combined with a drain line to permit the entire branch to be drained for maintenance and repair.

FIRE-SUPPRESSION HOSES, RACKS, AND CABINETS

Recommended hose size for use with building fire-suppression standpipes should not exceed 1-1/2 in. in diameter and 100 ft in length. A larger hose used by amateurs is likely to tangle, cause excessive water damage, and cause injuries.

A connection for a 2-1/2-in. hose should be available to each station for the use of firefighters. Many codes require 2-1/2-in. outlets at all standpipes.

By using a reducing coupling, a 1-1/2-in. hose can be attached. When a 2-1/2-in. stream is required, the coupling may be removed. Industrial installations use 2-1/2-in. hoses and train personnel in the use of the heavier equipment. Valves may be located 5 ft-6 in. above floor (check local code).

Lined synthetic fiber plastic hoses are recommended for use on standpipe installations. Cotton-rubber-lined hoses are standard for fire department and heavy equipment use.

NOTE

4.117 Coverage varies with mounting height and water pressure.

Contributor:
Michael Frankel, CIPE, Utility Systems Consultants, Somerset, New Jersey.

FIRE HOSE AND EXTINGUISHER CABINETS
4.118

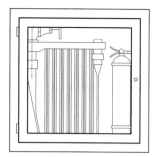

**75'-1-1/2" LINED HOSE, RACK,
AND ANGLE VALVE; 2-1/2 GAL
EXTINGUISHER**
2'-9" x 2'-9" x 8-1/2" TO
2'-11" x 2'-11" x 9"

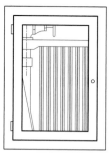

**75'-1-1/2" LINED HOSE,
RACK, AND ANGLE VALVE**
1'-9" x 2'-5" x 8" TO
1'-4" x 2'-7" x 8-1/2"

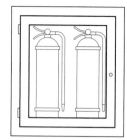

**TWO 2-1/2 GAL
EXTINGUISHERS**
1'-11" x 2'-9" x 7" TO
2'-2" x 2'-11" x 8"

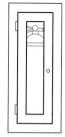

ONE 2-1/2 GAL EXTINGUISHER
1'-0" x 2'-6" x 8" TO
1'-4" x 2'-7" x 8-1/2"
RESIDENTIAL EXTINGUISHER
CABINET 1'-5" x 7" x 2"

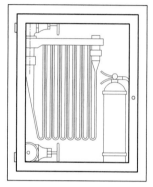

**75'-1-1/2" LINED HOSE AND RACK;
1-1/2" AND 2-1/2" ANGLE VALVE;
2-1/2" GAL EXTINGUISHER**
2'-9" x 3'-4" x 8-1/2" TO
2'-10" x 3'-7" x 9"

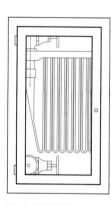

**75'-1-1/2" LINED HOSE AND RACK;
1-1/2" AND 2-1/2" ANGLE VALVE**
1'-11" x 3'-3" x 8-1/2" TO
2'-4" x 3'-4" x 9"

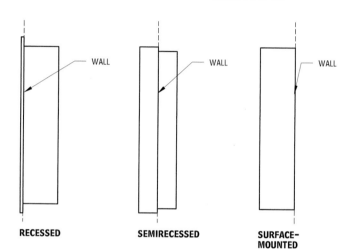

RECESSED   **SEMIRECESSED**   **SURFACE-
MOUNTED**

FIRE PROTECTION SPECIALTIES

FIRE EXTINGUISHERS

Portable fire extinguishers can serve as a first line of defense against fires of limited size, even for property equipped with automatic sprinklers or other fixed protection equipment. The following are criteria for selecting fire extinguishers:

- Type and severity (size, intensity, and speed of travel) of potential fire hazard
- Environmental conditions of potential fire hazard (ambient temperature conditions, presence of fumes, etc.)
- Effectiveness of extinguisher on potential fire hazard
- Ease of use
- Suitability for its environment
- Any anticipated adverse chemical reactions between the extinguishing agent and the burning materials
- Any health and operational safety concerns (exposure of operators during fire control efforts)
- Training and physical capabilities of available personnel to operate extinguisher
- Upkeep and maintenance requirements

General guidelines for fire extinguishers state that:

- Fire extinguishers on accessible routes must be configured so that they do not protrude more than 4 in.
- The authority with jurisdiction over the location dictates the number, type, and placement of fire extinguishers and fire-extinguisher cabinets.

- All extinguishers without wheels must be installed on hangers or brackets, mounted in cabinets, or set on shelves. Extinguishers weighing up to 40 lb should be no more than 5 ft above the floor. The top of extinguishers with a gross weight greater than 40 lb should be no more than 3 ft-6 in. above the floor. All operable parts must be within accessible-reach ranges.

It's also important to note that halon-type extinguishers are no longer manufactured as a result of an international environmental agreement.

These standards and classifications are taken from the National Fire Protection Association Publication 10, "Portable Fire Extinguishers" (1994). Always check local code requirements before specifying fire extinguishers.

DISTRIBUTION OF FIRE EXTINGUISHERS

The minimum number of fire extinguishers needed to protect a property from Class A fires is determined by Table 4.294; and, frequently, additional extinguishers are installed. Fire extinguishers rated for Class B fires are placed a maximum travel distance of 50 ft from the hazard (smaller rated extinguishers are placed no more than 30 ft from the hazard). Fire extinguishers rated for Class C fires are required in locations with energized electrical equipment that would require a nonconducting extinguishing medium. For Class D fires, extinguishers are located not more than 75 ft from the Class D hazard.

FIRE EXTINGUISHER SIZE AND PLACEMENT FOR CLASS A HAZARDS
4.119

	LIGHT-HAZARD OCCUPANCY	ORDINARY-HAZARD OCCUPANCY	EXTRA-HAZARD OCCUPANCY
Minimum rated single extinguisher	2-A[a]	2-A[a]	4-A[b]
Maximum floor area per unit of A	3000 sq ft	1500 sq ft	1000 sq ft
Maximum floor area for extinguisher	11,250 sq ft	11,250 sq ft	11,250 sq ft
Maximum travel distance to extinguisher	75 ft	75 ft	75 ft

NOTES

4.118 a. Cabinets are #18-gauge steel with glass doors, as shown, or with doors of metal, wood, mirror, and others.
b. Consult manufacturers' literature for cabinets with special features such as revolving door, twin doors, pivoting door with attached extinguisher, and curved door.
c. Cabinets are obtainable for 25-, 50-, 75-, and 100-ft hose racks. Rough dimensions are shown.
4.119 a. Up to two water-type extinguishers with 1-A rating can be used to fulfill the requirements of one 2-A-rated extinguisher for light-hazard occupancies.

b. Two 2-1/2 gal water-type extinguishers can be used to fulfill the requirements of one 4-A-rated extinguisher.

Contributor:
William G. Miner, AIA, Architect, Washington, DC.

MULTIPURPOSE DRY CHEMICAL (CLASS A, B, AND C FIRES)
4.120

Capacity (lb)	2-1/2	5	6	10	20
Height (in.)	14	14-1/2	16	20	24
Diameter (in.)	3	4-1/4	5	5	7
Class	1A-10B:C	2A-10B:C; 3A-40B:C	3A-40B:C	4A-60B:C	20A-120 B:C
Effective range (ft)	5 to 20				
Discharge time	10 to 25 sec for 10 to 20 lb				
Recharge	After use				
Pressure source	Compressed gas				
Temperature effect	Will operate at -65°F				
Electrical conductivity	Will not conduct				

CARBON DIOXIDE (CLASS B AND C FIRES ONLY)
4.121

Capacity (lb)	5	10	15	20
Height (in.)	17-3/4	24	30	30
Diameter (in.)	5-1/4	7	7	8
Class	5B:C	10B:C	10B:C	10B:C
Effective range (ft)	3 to 8			
Discharge time (sec)	10	10	12-1/2	19
Recharge	After use			
Pressure source	Compressed gas			
Temperature effect	Will operate at -40°F			
Electrical conductivity	Will not conduct			

REGULAR DRY CHEMICAL (CLASS B AND C FIRES)
4.122

Capacity (lb)	2-1/2	5-1/2	6	10	20
Height (in.)	15-1/2	15-1/4	16-1/4	20	23-1/4 to 24
Diameter (in.)	3	4-1/4	5	5	7
Class	10B:C	40B:C	40B:C	60B:C	120B:C
Effective range (ft)	9-21				
Discharge time	10; 30 lb, 34 sec	14	14	18	28
Recharge	After use				
Pressure source	Compressed gas				
Temperature effect	Will operate at -40°F				
Electrical conductivity	Will not conduct				

FIRE CLASSIFICATIONS FOR SELECTING FIRE EXTINGUISHERS
4.123

LETTER SYMBOL AND COLOR	PICTURE SYMBOL	DESCRIPTION
Green **A**		Class A: Fires involving ordinary combustible materials (such as wood, cloth, paper, rubber, and many plastics) that require the heat-absorbing (cooling) effects of water or water solutions, or the coating effects of certain dry chemicals that retard combustion.
Red **B**		Class B: Fires involving flammable or combustible liquids, flammable gasses, greases, and similar materials that are best extinguished by excluding air (oxygen), inhibiting the release of combustible vapors, or interrupting the combustion chain reaction.
Blue **C**		Class C: Fires involving energized electrical equipment where safety to the operator requires the use of electrically nonconductive extinguishing agents.
Yellow **D**		Fires involving combustible metals (such as magnesium, titanium, zirconium, sodium, lithium, and potassium).

PRESSURIZED WATER
4.124

Capacity (gal)	2-1/2
Height (in.)	24-1/2
Diameter (in.)	7
Weight (lb)	28
Class	2A
Effective range (ft)	30
Discharge time	50 seconds
Recharge	Weigh cylinder and check annually; in all cases, follow instructions on label.
Pressure source	Compressed air
Temperature effect	Will freeze
Electrical conductivity	Will conduct

SODIUM CHLORIDE
4.125

Capacity (lb)	30
Height (in.)	27-3/4
Diameter (in.)	7
Class	FM
Effective range (ft)	4 to 6
Discharge time	28 seconds
Recharge	After use
Pressure source	Compressed gas
Temperature effect	-40 to +120
Electrical conductivity	Will not conduct

OTHER FIRE PROTECTION SYSTEMS

FOAM EXTINGUISHING SYSTEMS

A foam system consists of a water supply, chemical additive injector, piping, and heads placed to discharge foam. The system uses an additive injected into the water supply to produce a discharge similar to soapsuds. This system is used to extinguish fires in flammable liquids that are lighter than water. The foam floats on top of the liquid and deprives the fire of oxygen.

SEE ALSO

Antifreeze Sprinkler System
Deluge Fire-Suppression Sprinkler System
Dry-Chemical Fire-Extinguishing Systems
Dry-Pipe Sprinkler System
Fire Extinguisher
Fire Extinguisher Cabinets
Fire Protection
Fire Protection Specialties
Fire Pumps
Fire-Suppression Sprinkler System
Fire-Suppression Standpipes
Portable Fire Extinguishers
Preaction Sprinkler System
Water-Based Fire-Suppression Systems
Water Spray Fixed System
Wet-Chemical Fire-Extinguishing Systems
Wet-Pipe Sprinkler System

FOAM SYSTEM
4.126

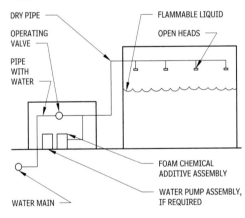

NOTES

4.120 Fluidized and siliconized monoammonium phosphate powder is dispersed then smothers and breaks the chain reaction of the fire.
4.121 Pressurized liquid carbon dioxide is released, changed into a gas, and appears as a cloud of white "snow," smothering the fire.
4.122 A siliconized sodium bicarbonate base (the traditional dry chemical design) extinguishes the fire. A base of potassium bicarbonate is also available.
4.123 Water quenches fire and cools area.
4.125 a. Sodium chloride dry powder is dispersed over a burning combustible metal or alloy; heat from the fire causes dry powder to cake and form exterior crust that excludes air and dissipates heat.
b. For lithium and lithium alloy Class D fires, a copper-based extinguishing agent is used.

Contributors:
Mark Conroy, National Fire Protection Association, Quincy, Massachusetts; Michael Frankel, CIPE, Utility Systems Consultants, Somerset, New Jersey.

ELECTRICAL

SUBSTATIONS, SWITCHBOARDS, MOTOR STARTERS, AND BUSWAYS

SECONDARY UNIT SUBSTATION

A secondary unit substation, sometimes called a *power center,* is a close-coupled assembly consisting of three-phase power transformers, enclosed high-voltage incoming line sections, and enclosed secondary low-voltage outgoing sections encompassing these electrical ratings:

- *Transformer kVA:* 112.5 through 2500 (self-cooled rating) liquid-filled, dry-type, or cast coil
- *Primary voltage:* 2.4 kV thru 34.5 kV
- *Secondary voltage:* 208, 240, 480, or 600 V (maximum)

For information on aisle space, ventilation, servicing area, and special building condition requirements, refer to the National Electrical Code.

MOTOR STARTERS

Four types of starters are described here: manual single-phase starters, magnetic motor starters, magnetic combination starters, and solid-state units.

- *Manual single-phase starters* are designed to give positive, accurate, trouble-free overload protection to single-phase motors rated up to 1 HP. Typical applications are fans, machine tools, motors, HVAC, and so on. Maximum voltage is 240 V AC.
- *Magnetic motor starters* are designed for across-the-line control of squirrel cage motors or as primary control for wound rotor motors. Starters can be furnished for nonreversing, reversing, and two-speed applications. Maximum voltage is 600 V AC; maximum horsepower is 200 HP.
- *Magnetic combination starters* are designed for across-the-line control of squirrel cage motors, or as primary control for wound rotor motors. In addition, they provide a disconnect means and short-circuit protection. They are available for nonreversing or reversing applications.
- A *solid state unit* is a reduced voltage motor starter, used to reduce starting current and high starting torque. Typical applications for controllers are in motors used in cranes, belt-driven equipment, conveyors, materials-handling facilities, compressors, and woodworking equipment. These units are available for AC motors in 5 to 900 HP.

SWITCHBOARD

Figure 4.128 shows a metering compartment, a main disconnect, check meters, and a low-voltage distribution section. See manufacturers' literature for type, size, and arrangements; and refer to the National Electrical Code for required aisle space, servicing area, and room layout.

SWITCHBOARD
4.128

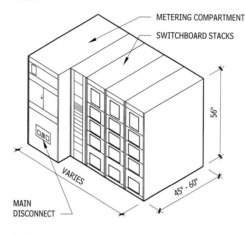

LOW-VOLTAGE MOTOR CONTROL CENTER

Motor control centers provide a method for grouping motor control, associated control, and distribution equipment. These centers are designed to operate machinery, industrial processes, and commercial building systems.

BUSWAY SYSTEM

Plug-in and feeder busways carry current from 50 to 5000 amps. They are utilized when large blocks of low-voltage power (up to 600 V) must be transmitted over long distances, or when taps must be made at various points, as in vertical risers in office buildings.

Codes limit locations in buildings where different types of busways may be installed. Consult an electrical engineer before using this system. Busway housing may be hung from an overhead support, mounted to a wall, or braced to the structure in vertical riser installation.

BUSWAY SYSTEM
4.129

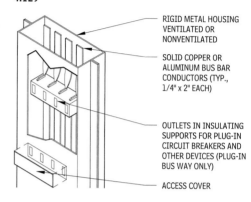

ELECTRICAL PANELBOARDS, CIRCUIT BREAKERS, DISCONNECT SWITCHES, AND FUSES

RESIDENTIAL AND COMMERCIAL PANELBOARD
4.130

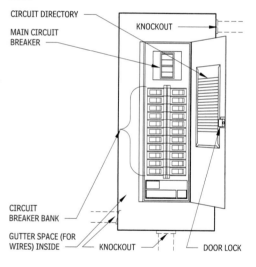

PANELBOARD DIMENSIONS
4.131

MAXIMUM NUMBER OF CIRCUITS	BOX DIMENSIONS (IN.)		
	WIDTH	HEIGHT	DEPTH
12	9–15	13–20	3-3/4–4-5/8
20	9–15	20-1/4 –24	3-3/4–4-5/8
30	12–15	30–33	3-3/4–4-5/8
40	14–15	34–39	4–4-5/8

SECONDARY UNIT SUBSTATION
4.127

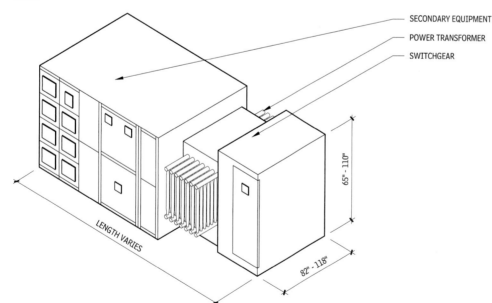

NOTE

4.130 Knockout holes allow conduit connections from all sides.

Contributor:
Charles B. Towles, PE, TEI Consulting Engineers, Washington, DC.

LIGHTING AND BRANCH WIRING

RESIDENTIAL ELECTRICAL WIRING

The general requirements described here for residential electrical wiring systems are intended to be used in conjunction with Figure 4.132, as the numbers in parentheses following each requirement refer to an aspect of the drawing.

- A minimum of one wall-switch-controlled lighting outlet is required in every habitable room, hallway, stairway, attached garage, and outdoor entrance. An exception is in habitable rooms other than kitchens and bathrooms, where one or more receptacles controlled by a wall switch are permitted in lieu of lighting outlets. (1)
- In every kitchen, family room, dining room, den, breakfast room, living room, parlor, sunroom, bedroom, recreation room, and similar rooms, convenience outlets must be installed so that no point along the floor line is farther than 12 ft (measured horizontally, from an outlet), including any wall space 2 ft or more wide, and the wall space occupied by sliding panels in exterior walls. (2)
- A minimum of two #12 wire 20-A small-appliance circuits are required to serve only small convenience outlets, including refrigeration equipment, in the kitchen, pantry, dining room, breakfast room, and family room. Both circuits must extend to the kitchen; the other rooms may be served by one or both of them. No other convenience outlets may be connected to these circuits, except a receptacle installed solely for an electric clock. In kitchen and dining areas, convenience outlets must be installed at each and every counter space wider than 12 in. (3)
- A minimum of one #12 wire 20-A circuit must be provided to supply the laundry receptacle(s), and it may have no other convenience outlets. (4)
- At least one convenience outlet must be installed in the bathroom near the basin and must be provided with ground-fault circuit-interrupter protection. (5)
- Code requires sufficient 15- and 20-A circuits to supply 3 watts of power for every square foot of floor space, not including garage and open porch areas. Minimum code suggestion is one circuit per 600 sq ft, but one circuit per 500 sq ft is desirable. (6)
- A minimum of one exterior convenience outlet is required (two are desirable) and must be provided with ground-fault circuit-interrupter protection. (7)
- A minimum of one convenience outlet is required in the basement and garage, in addition to the one in the laundry. In attached garages it must be provided with ground-fault circuit-interrupter protection. (8)
- Many building codes require a smoke detector in the hallway outside bedrooms or above the stairway leading to upper-floor bedrooms. (9)
- Disconnect switches are required for equipment. (10)

**SCHEMATIC DIAGRAM OF TYPICAL RESIDENTIAL ELECTRICAL LAYOUT
4.132**

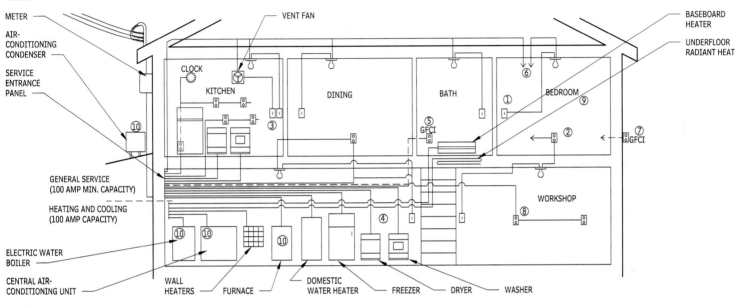

NOTE

4.132 Refer to the National Electrical Code (NEC) for further information on residential requirements.

FIRST-FLOOR PLAN OF ELECTRICAL EQUIPMENT AND DEVICES
4.133

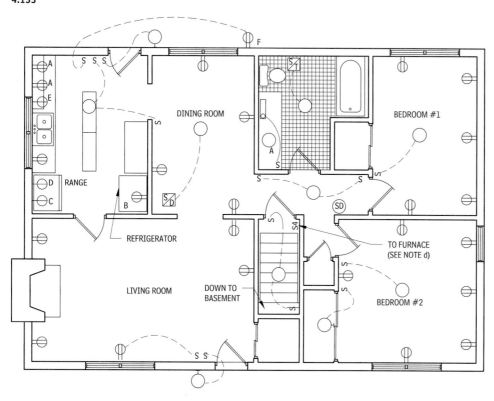

BASEMENT PLAN OF ELECTRICAL EQUIPMENT
4.134

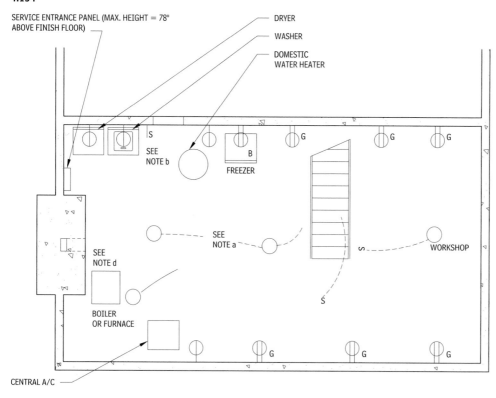

LEGEND FOR FIRST-FLOOR AND BASEMENT PLANS

A: Mount convenience outlets at countertop locations 2 inches above backsplash.

B: Mount convenience outlets 48 in. above finish floor (AFF).

C: Range and oven outlet boxes should be wall-mounted, 36 in. AFF. Use flexible connections to units.

D: Switch and outlet for exhaust fan. The switch should be wall-mounted above the sink backsplash, and the outlet blank should be cover-mounted adjacent to the fan wall opening. A separate switch may be omitted if the fan is supplied with an integral switch.

E: Dishwasher outlet is wall-mounted behind unit, 6 in. AFF.

F: Equipped with self-closing waterproof cover with gasket.

G: Mount 42 in. AFF.

AVERAGE WATTAGES OF COMMON ELECTRICAL DEVICES
4.135

TYPE	WATTS
Air conditioner, central	2500–6000
Air conditioner, room type	800–2500
Blanket, electric	150–200
Clock	2–3
Clothes dryer	4000–6000
Dishwasher	1000–1500
Fan, portable	50–200
Food blender	500–1000
Freezer	300–500
Frying pan, electric	1000–1200
Furnace blower	380–670
Garbage disposal	500–900
Hair dryer	350–1200
Heater, portable	1000–1500
Heating pad	50–75
Heat lamp (infrared)	250
Iron, hand	600–1200
Lamp, incandescent	10 upward
Lamp, fluorescent	15–16
Lights, Christmas tree	30–150
Microwave oven	1000–1500
Mixer	120–250
Power tools	up to 1000
Projector, slide or movie	300–500
Radio	40–150
Range (all burners and oven)	8000–14,000
Range top (separate)	4000–8000
Range oven (separate)	4000–5000
Refrigerator	150–300
Refrigerator, frostless	400–600
Sewing machine	60–90
Stereo (solid-state)	30–100
Television	50–450
Vacuum cleaner	250–1200
Washer, automatic	500–800
Water heater	2000–5000

BRANCH CIRCUIT PROTECTION
4.136

Lighting (general purpose)	#14 wires	15 A
Small appliances	#12 wires	20 A
Individual appliances	#12 wires	20 A
	#10 wires	30 A
	#8 wires	40 A
	#6 wires	50 A

NOTES

4.133 and 4.134 a. Wiring shown as exposed indicates absence of finished ceiling in basement level. All BX cable is run through framing members. Attachment below ceiling joists is not permitted.

b. Connect to two incandescent porcelain lamp holders with pull chain. Mount two evenly spaced ceiling fixtures in crawl space.

c. Connect to shutdown switch at top of stairs.

d. Boiler wiring safety disconnect switch should have red wall plate, clearly marked "BOILER ON/OFF."

Contributor:
Charles B. Towles, PE, TEI Consulting Engineers, Washington, DC.

LOADS, CIRCUITS, AND RECEPTACLES FOR RESIDENTIAL ELECTRICAL EQUIPMENT
4.137

APPLIANCE	TYPICAL CONNECTED VOLT-AMPERES[a]	VOLTS	WIRES[b]	CIRCUIT BREAKER OR FUSE[c]	OUTLETS ON CIRCUIT	NEMA[k] DEVICE[d] AND CONFIGURATION
KITCHEN						
Range[e]	12,000	115/230	3 # 6	60 A	1	14-60R
Oven (built-in)[c]	4500	115/230	3 # 10	30 A	1	14-30R
Range top[c]	6000	115/230	3 # 10	30 A	1	14-30R
Dishwasher[c]	1200	115	2 # 12	20 A	1	5-20R
Waste disposer[c]	300	115	2 # 12	20 A	1	5-20R
Broiler[e]	1500	115	2 # 12	20 A	1 or more	5-20R
Refrigerator[f]	300	115	2 # 12	20 A	1 or more	5-20R
Freezer[f]	350	115	2 # 12	20 A	1 or more	5-20R
LAUNDRY						
Washing machine	1200	115	2 # 12	20 A	1 or more	5-20R
Dryer[c]	5000	115/230	3 # 10	30 A	1	14-30R
Hand iron; ironer	1650	115	2 # 12	20 A	1 or more	5-20R
LIVING AREAS						
Workshop	1500	115	2 # 12	20 A	1 or more	5-20R
Portable heater[g]	1300	115	2 # 12	20 A	1	5-20R
Television[g]	300	115	2 # 12	20 A	1 or more	5-20R
FIXED UTILITIES						
Fixed lighting	1200	115	2 # 12	20 A	1 or more	5-20R
Air conditioner, 3/4 hp	1200	115	2 # 12	20 A or 30 A	1	5-20R
Central air conditioner[i]	5000	115/230	3 # 10	40 A	1	
Sump pump[j]	300	115	2 # 12	20 A	1 or more	5-20R
Heating plant—forced-air furnace[h, j]	600	115	2 # 12	20 A	1	
Attic fan[j]	300	115	2 # 12	20 A	1 or more	5-20R

TYPICAL WIRING IN WOOD CONSTRUCTION
4.138

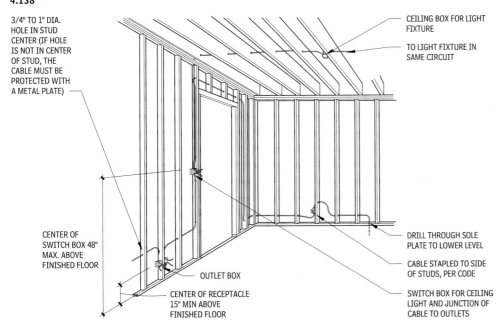

3/4" TO 1" DIA. HOLE IN STUD CENTER (IF HOLE IS NOT IN CENTER OF STUD, THE CABLE MUST BE PROTECTED WITH A METAL PLATE)

CENTER OF SWITCH BOX 48" MAX. ABOVE FINISHED FLOOR

OUTLET BOX

CENTER OF RECEPTACLE 15" MIN ABOVE FINISHED FLOOR

CEILING BOX FOR LIGHT FIXTURE

TO LIGHT FIXTURE IN SAME CIRCUIT

DRILL THROUGH SOLE PLATE TO LOWER LEVEL

CABLE STAPLED TO SIDE OF STUDS, PER CODE

SWITCH BOX FOR CEILING LIGHT AND JUNCTION OF CABLE TO OUTLETS

NOTES

4.137 a. Wherever possible, use actual equipment rating.
b. Number of wires does not include equipment grounding wires. Ground wire is No. 12 AWG for 20-A circuit and No. 10 AWG for 30-A and 50-A circuits.
c. May be direct-connected. For a discussion of disconnect requirements, see NEC Article 422.
d. Equipment ground is provided in each receptacle.
e. Heavy-duty appliances regularly used at one location should have separate circuits. Only one such unit should be attached to a single circuit.
f. A separate circuit serving only one other outlet is recommended.

g. Should not be connected to a circuit with appliances or other heavy loads
h. A separate circuit is recommended.
i. It is recommended that all motor-driven devices be protected by a local motor-protection element, unless motor protection is built into the device.
j. Connect through disconnect switch equipped with motor-protection element.
k. National Electrical Manufacturers Association (NEMA).
4.138 In metal stud construction, cables are passed through precut openings in place of field-drilled holes.

Contributor:
Charles B. Towles, PE, TEI Consulting Engineers, Washington, DC.

OUTLETS, SWITCHES, AND PLATES

RECEPTACLES AND SWITCHES
4.139

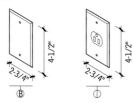

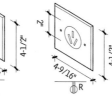
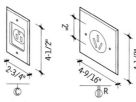

BLANK DEVICE PLATE

SINGLE RECEPTACLE

DUPLEX RECEPTACLE

DOUBLE DUPLEX RECEPTACLE

CLOCK HANGER OUTLET

RANGE OUTLET 125/250V

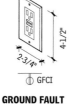

COMBINATION SWITCH AND RECEPTACLE

GROUND FAULT CIRCUIT INTERRUPTER DUPLEX

HINGED COVER

WEATHERPROOF (GFCI) DUPLEX

DIMMER SWITCH

SINGLE–POLE TOGGLE SWITCH

SWITCH AND PILOT LAMP

LOW VOLTAGE SWITCH

TELEPHONE JACK

CABLE TELEVISION OUTLET

COMPUTER DATA/ LAN OUTLET

Outlets and switches shown are those most commonly used. The number of gangs behind one wall plate depends on the type of devices used.

SWITCH AND OUTLET LOCATIONS
4.141

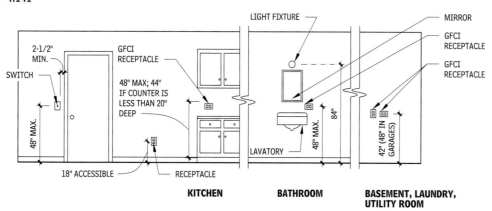

KITCHEN   **BATHROOM**   **BASEMENT, LAUNDRY, UTILITY ROOM**

GANG SIZE
4.140

GANG	HORIZONTAL (IN.)	
	HEIGHT	WIDTH
2	4-1/2	4-9/16
3	4-1/2	6-3/8
4	4-1/2	8-3/16
5	4-1/2	10
6	4-1/2	11-13/16

MONUMENT FLOOR OUTLET
4.142

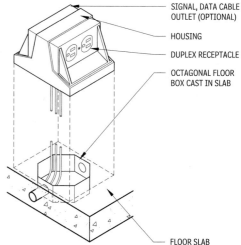

SIGNAL, DATA CABLE OUTLET (OPTIONAL)

HOUSING

DUPLEX RECEPTACLE

OCTAGONAL FLOOR BOX CAST IN SLAB

FLOOR SLAB

POKE-THROUGH ELECTRICAL BOX
4.143

ELECTRICAL CONDUIT MAY BE ADAPTED TO FLOOR FITTING

RAISED-FLOOR FITTING (MONUMENT FLOOR OUTLET, OPTIONAL)

INSERT LOCK

INTUMESCENT (SMOKE AND FIRE) BARRIER RINGS

FLOOR SLAB (FIRE-RATED)

3" DIA. CORE

JUNCTION BOX FOR POWER/ TELEPHONE/DATA CABLES

BX/MC SERVICE

The unit is adjustable to accommodate varying floor thickness. When abandoned, the floor fitting is replaced with a flat plate.

NOTES

4.139 a. Outlets and switches shown are those most commonly used. Number of gangs behind one wall plate depends on the type of devices used.
b. Symbols used are ASA standard.
c. Interchangeable devices (miniature devices) are available in various combinations using any of the following in one gang: switch, convenience outlet, radio outlet, pilot light, bell button. Combined gangs are available.

4.140 a. Add 1-13/16 in. for each added gang. Screws are 1-13/16 in. o.c.
b. Plates are made in plastic, brass (.04 to .06 in. thick), stainless steel, and aluminum.
c. All devices to be approved by Underwriters Laboratories and to comply with the National Electrical Code.
d. All devices to be of NEMA configuration.
e. Ground fault circuit interrupter or circuits are required in baths, garages, unfinished basements, outdoors at grade level, and within 6 ft of kitchen sinks.

Contributor:
Charles B. Towles, PE, TEI Consulting Engineers, Washington, DC.

FLAT-CABLE WIRING SYSTEM

Under-carpet flat cable wiring has developed into a viable system to serve workstations. By code, it can be used only with carpet squares to afford an acceptable degree of access. Although there are some limitations in performance for flat communications (telephone) and computer (data) cables, improvements are continually being made. Flat cables are now available for local area network (LAN) distribution, applicable where communications and data requirements are extensive.

Cables originate at transition boxes located at various intervals along core corridor walls and/or columns that are individually served from distribution centers in utility closets. Boxes can also be cast in the floor or atop a poke-through insert. Cables are not permitted to pass under fixed partitions, and must be carefully mapped out to minimize crossovers and clutter.

To install a service fitting, an interface base assembly must first be secured directly to the concrete floor at the flat-cable location. The base assembly stabs into conductors of the flat cable and converts them to round wire. When the service fitting is attached, it is activated and ready for use.

Careful consideration must be given to the application of this system based on limitations that may or may not be acceptable under different conditions. For example, it may be ideal for small areas or in renovations of existing buildings where the poke-through or power pole systems are unacceptable or cannot be used. In new buildings where poke-through has been chosen as the base system, the flat-cable system is a viable solution in areas where poke-through outlets cannot be installed, such as slab-on-grade.

Where frequent changes and additions are contemplated, the resulting wear and tear on expensive, glued-down carpet tiles may become a distinct disadvantage.

Although this system appears to be simple and inexpensive, it is highly labor-intensive, and actual installed initial costs and outlet relocation costs are comparable to cellular deck with trench header ducts.

LIGHTING TERMINOLGY

These terms and concepts are commonly used in the field of lighting and branch wiring:

- *Ballast*: Device providing a controlled electrical current, voltage, and waveform to gas-discharge-type lamps. Ballasts provide the energy necessary to start lamp operation, and limit the current that flows through them during operation afterward. Incandescent and halogen incandescent lamps are resistive-type sources and do not use ballasts; other lamps such as fluorescent and high-intensity discharge (HID) are gas-discharge types and do need ballasts. Low-voltage incandescent and halogen lamps do use a transformer to provide proper voltage, but do not require the level of circuit control provided by ballasts for fluorescent and HID lamps.
- *Blackbody*: An idealized radiator of energy that is at a uniform temperature and whose emitted color spectrum is the maximum that can be emitted by any substance at the same temperature. Blackbody radiation is more simply understood as the characteristic color spectrum emitted from a perfect radiator at a given temperature. Its basic definition is requisite to understanding qualitative measures of color rendering.
- *Bulb* or *tube*: The glass envelope of a lamp.
- *Color Rendering Index (CRI)*: Measure of the color shift in the appearance of objects when lit by a light source, as compared to being lit by a reference light source of the same color temperature. CRI is measured in percentage, with higher numbers being closer to color rendering of the reference light source. CRI should not be used to compare color rendering between light sources of different color temperatures. Even among lamps with similar color temperatures, a significant difference takes a 3 to 5 percentage point margin in CRI.
- *Color temperature*: A standard of light source color that is also referred to as *correlated color temperature (CCT)*. This is the absolute temperature in degrees Kelvin required for a blackbody to radiate a color spectrum most similar to that of a given light source. As color temperature increases, the general color-ren-

dering effect of light sources moves from red (low color temperature) to blue (high color temperature). The human visual expectation of what looks natural also varies with intensity: dim lighting scenes seem more natural in low color temperatures (such as firelight), whereas bright lighting scenes appear more natural in high color temperatures (such as the blue sky). Standard T8 fluorescent lamps have a CCT of about 4100°K, which appears cool. Generically, this temperature is seen as desirable in office settings, whereas warmer colored lamps with CCT of 3000°K or less are recommended for residences and hospitality environments. Natural daylight corresponds to a CCT of about 6000°K, an overcast sky to 7000°K, and a blue sky to something between 10,000 and 30,000°K.

- *Efficacy (LPW)*: Lumens of light output for each watt of electricity consumed. This is a measure of how efficient a lamp is, but not necessarily how efficient a lighting system (including fixtures and room conditions) will be. Total system efficacy should also include the energy of lamp ballasts in systems other than incandescent lighting. Be aware that lumen ratings are much like the EPA's miles-per-gallon ratings on automobiles; that is, rated lumens for a lamp are measured under ideal conditions. Electrical power, waveform, air temperature, operating position, and other conditions are constrained in standard tests so that accurate comparison to other lamps can be made on equal basis. The ballast used in testing is an extremely sensitive laboratory version and typically produces more light from lamps than commercially available ballasts do. In most cases, installed combinations of lamps and ballasts will not produce as much light as the rated lumens, even under initial conditions.
- *Illuminance*: Density of light on a surface, measured as candela per square foot or *footcandles (fc)*, and represented by the symbol "E." This is analogous to the gallons of water delivered on a square foot of lawn. Multiply fc by 10.76 to obtain the metric unit, lux.

- *Illumination*: The common term for footcandles of illuminance, but also used in a more general sense to describe the means of lighting a space. For clarity, when used to refer to footcandle levels, the term *level of illumination* is preferred.
- *Lamp*: Lighting source used in a fixture to generate visible energy. Many fixtures use more than one lamp.
- *Luminaire*: Lighting fixture including housing, lamp, ballast, lens, reflectors, and louvers or baffles. Some of these components are optional or may be part of the lamp.
- *Luminance*: Brightness of light transmitted by, reflected from, or transmitted through a surface. Brightness is measured as *foot-lamberts (fL)*, though that unit of measure is no longer commonly used. Brightness as *reflected luminance* is the product of incident footcandles on a surface multiplied by the percentage of visible light reflected from it. *Transmitted luminance* is, similarly, the product of incident footcandles on a surface multiplied by the percentage of visible light it transmits. The units of luminance are cd/ft^2.
- *Luminous flux*: Flow of light from a source, measured in *lumens (lm)*. This is analogous to the flow rate of water through a garden hose.
- *Luminous intensity*: Radiant energy emitted by a source, measured in *candela (cd)*, and represented with the symbol "I." This is analogous to water pressure in a hose.

Organizations to contact for more information in this subject area include:

- *American National Standards Institute (ANSI)*: ANSI publishes a system of nomenclature for the designation of lamps, including their electrical characteristics, performance, and physical specifications. These designations and specifications help ensure interchangeability among different manufacturers' lamps and ballasts.

FLAT-CABLE WIRING SYSTEM
4.144

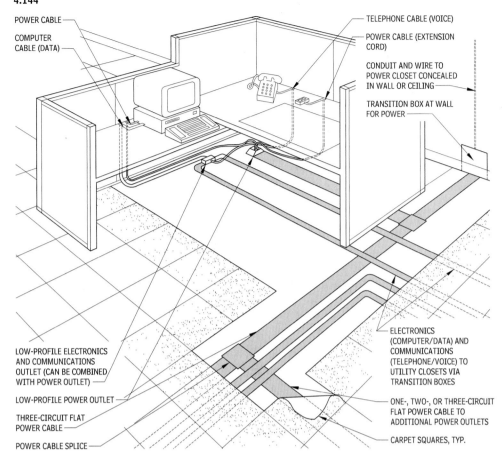

POWER CABLE
COMPUTER CABLE (DATA)
TELEPHONE CABLE (VOICE)
POWER CABLE (EXTENSION CORD)
CONDUIT AND WIRE TO POWER CLOSET CONCEALED IN WALL OR CEILING
TRANSITION BOX AT WALL FOR POWER
LOW-PROFILE ELECTRONICS AND COMMUNICATIONS OUTLET (CAN BE COMBINED WITH POWER OUTLET)
LOW-PROFILE POWER OUTLET
THREE-CIRCUIT FLAT POWER CABLE
POWER CABLE SPLICE
ELECTRONICS (COMPUTER/DATA) AND COMMUNICATIONS (TELEPHONE/VOICE) TO UTILITY CLOSETS VIA TRANSITION BOXES
ONE-, TWO-, OR THREE-CIRCUIT FLAT POWER CABLE TO ADDITIONAL POWER OUTLETS
CARPET SQUARES, TYP.

Contributors:
Richard F. Humenn, PE, Joseph R. Loring & Associates, Inc., Consulting Engineers, New York City, New York; Gary A. Hall, Hammel, Green, and Abrahamson, Minneapolis, Minnesota.

- *Illuminating Engineering Society of North America* (*IESNA*): IESNA is an organization of lighting professionals that provides the recognized technical authority on illumination. Its stated mission is "to improve the lighted environment by bringing together those with lighting knowledge and by translating that knowledge into actions that benefit the public." See www.iesna.org/ for more details.
- *International Commission on Illumination* (*CIE*): Promotes international cooperation and information exchange among member countries as a technical, scientific, and cultural organization. See www.cie.co.at/cie/home.html for more details.
- *National Electrical Manufacturer Association* (*NEMA*): NEMA publishes test standards for lamps, bulbs, lamp bases, and holders, as well as for ballasts, as part of its lighting standards program.

LIGHTING DESIGN CONSIDERATIONS

As in most architectural pursuits, lighting design has both quantitative and qualitative objectives, such as whether there is enough light and whether it is of appropriate character. Lighting design also engages both artistic and scientific thinking. Form, texture, and space are rendered by a combination of light and shadow. Color and composition are also direct artifacts of lighting. The methods selected to achieve these results are technical in nature, and are the most rapidly changing technology in buildings.

Technical considerations begin with the following:

- Footcandle (fc) illuminance levels
- Lighting efficacy (lumens per watt, LPW)
- Color Rendering Index (CRI)

These three basic factors correspond to having sufficient light, using energy-efficient lighting sources, and providing a color spectrum from the light source that is broad enough and balanced correctly for the visual task. These three fundamental decisions, therefore, require an understanding of the lighting task being considered and the means of matching the task to appropriate lighting methods.

LIGHT SOURCE SELECTION GUIDE
4.145

APPLICATIONS	
LAMP CCT[a] (KELVIN, OR °K)	
<2500	Bulk industrial and security (HPS) lighting
2700–3000	Low light levels in most spaces (<10 FC); general residential lighting; hotels, fine dining and family restaurants; theme parks
2950–3200	Display lighting for retail and galleries; feature lighting
3500–4100	General lighting in offices, schools, stores, industry, medicine; display lighting; sports lighting
4100–5000	Special-application lighting where color discrimination is very important; not commonly used for general lighting
5000–7500	Special-application lighting where color discrimination is critical; uncommon for general lighting
MINIMUM LAMP CRI[b]	
<50	Noncritical industrial, storage, and security lighting
50–70	Industrial and general illumination, where color is not important
70–79	Most office, retail, school, medical, and other work and recreational spaces
80–89	Retail, work, and residential spaces, where color quality is important
90–100	Retail and workspaces, where color rendering is critical

Beyond these three basic factors, however, there are a host of related lighting design issues and corresponding features of lighting systems to incorporate. Each lighting situation will prioritize these differently, but following are a few fundamental considerations, some of which are discussed in more detail later in this section.

HUMAN FACTORS

The physiology of human vision and the notion of visual comfort both influence lighting design in several ways.

- The healthy human eye can accommodate to different scene brightness levels by contracting or expanding the pupil, meaning that contrast level is more important in some aspects than is the quantitative illumination level.
- Accommodation is also important in planning for distinctions between day and night illuminance levels because occupants are accommodated to outdoor brightness levels by day, so higher interior illumination levels are needed for their level of adaptation. Nighttime lighting power levels can, therefore, be considerably lower. Dimming devices or stepped switching can help control lighting levels accordingly.
- The perceptive sensitivity of the human eye is essentially a logarithmic response to brightness. Generally, a 50 percent increase of brightness level is required to produce a subjective impression of one order of magnitude level change in illumination. So, for the same lighting situation, the difference between 10 fc and 15 fc of illuminance is perceptually the same as the change from 50 fc to 75 fc and 100 fc to 150 fc.
- Not all brightness is equally perceived. To appear as bright to the human eye as 50 fc from a 3500°K fluorescent lamp or a 2850°K incandescent, a low-pressure sodium lamp would need to produce almost a 100 fc; a high-pressure sodium lamp would likewise need to produce about 90 fc; and a mercury lamp around 60 fc. On the other end of the scale, a 6500°K fluorescent would produce the same subjective level of illuminance at only 40 fc; sunlight would be equivalent at 37 fc; and a 7500°K fluorescent lamp would need only 36 fc.
- Vision has a pronounced ability to discriminate detail in shadow within the narrow cone of foveal vision, as opposed to the wider cone of peripheral vision. This means that photographic or virtual representations of space are never quite the same as a direct experience of them.
- The human aging process decays the eye's ability to focus and even to perceive brightness. With aging, the lens inevitably becomes denser and less elastic, so the human ability to focus on objects within 2 ft is lessened (presbyopia). Presbyopia is progressive between a person's age in the 40s and 60s. Gradual yellowing of the lens also reduces the amount of light entering the eye. At the age of 60, the average healthy human eye receives only a third of what a 20-year-old eye does. Similar symptoms of aging include loss of acuity in fine details, slower accommodation to sudden changes in light level, degradation of color discrimination, glare caused by lens opacities, and a visual field that narrows some 1° to 3° per decade. Some of these factors of aging can be offset with additional light, of course, but others require high-quality light, proper contrast ratios, and considerate design.
- Enlightened designers and building owners are continually taking a broader perspective and life-cycle economics view of lighting. Quality lighting is now more frequently seen as a design opportunity and an investment in human productivity and occupant comfort.

ENERGY ECONOMICS

Lighting accounts for about 35 percent of the electricity use in a typical commercial building, about 8 percent in the residential sector, and about 10 percent of industrial energy consumption. Relating site energy consumption to the inefficiencies of source energy production involves a ratio of about 3.3 units of source energy used per 1.0 unit of energy consumed. Overall, then, lighting was about 8 percent of the total primary energy used in the United States in 2001, and consumed about 22 percent of all U.S. electricity generated that year.

ENERGY CODES

The ANSI/ASHRAE/IESNA 90.1 "Energy Standard for Buildings except Low-Rise Residential Buildings" is part of the Model Energy Code. It was published in December 2004 and supplements earlier versions. Compliance varies with adoption by state and local jurisdictions, but all code enforcement agencies are required to develop a set of regulations at least as stringent as the 90.1 Model Code. The regulation is based on a maximum power budget of allowable watts of lighting power per square foot, lineal foot, or individual installation. This ratio of watts per square foot is termed the *lighting power density* (*LPD*), or alternately called *unit power density* (*UPD*) or *lighting power allowance* (*LPA*). Allowable LPD under the Model Code is dependent on the building type, occupancy, or area use category. Exceptions are provided as appropriate to critical installations.

BEAM PATTERN

Distribution of light from a bare lamp or a luminaire can basically be thought of as having spot, normal, or flood patterns, depending on the beam spread. This photometric data is usually indicated in the manufacturer's product data as a *candlepower distribution curve* (*CDC*). The CDC is a polar coordinate plot graphically showing the candela output from a fixture at any angle relative to one fixture axis. The CDC also indicates the cutoff angle or shielding angle, above which no light is emitted.

TASK LIGHTING VERSUS AMBIENT LIGHTING

Task lighting and general illumination are often best considered and rendered separately. Task light is provided by direct point-to-point illumination from a fixture or fixtures onto a single point on a surface such as the center of a desk. Ambient light is the uniform level of illuminance provided in a room from a uniformly spaced grid of fixtures. It is generally wasteful to provide task level illuminance with ambient lighting if high footcandle levels are needed only in a small percentage of the space. Sometimes, however, it is acceptable to provide task-level lighting to work surfaces with the general illumination system, and then rely on spill light from these same fixtures to supply a lower level of background ambient light between task surfaces in areas such as circulation paths.

DIRECT VERSUS INDIRECT AMBIENT ILLUMINATION

Indirect lighting comes from suspended luminaires that radiate 90 to 100 percent of their light upward, where it is then reflected around the room. Direct lighting fixtures, on the other hand, radiate 90 to 100 percent of their light down onto the task surface or in the general direction of the surface to be illuminated. Indirect lighting results in a uniform distribution of light with reduced shadowing and glare. It is especially well regarded where the work surface is predominantly computer screens, so that direct glare from exposed lamps is less likely to be bouncing off the vertical visual task surface. Direct downlighting is more efficient than indirect lighting because it does not rely on the tactic of bouncing light off of multiple room surfaces; but direct lighting is decidedly more prone to create glare. Direct-indirect luminaires, which provide some balance of both techniques, can also be advantageous compromises that capture the best attributes of each.

DAYLIGHT INTEGRATION

Daylighting systems only provide energy savings and cooling load reductions if artificial lighting is switched or dimmed in proportion to received natural light. Photocell-controlled dimming can automate this process, but it is also possible to manually switch electrical lighting in separate rows parallel to the daylighting aperture or window. In either case, electrical lighting should generally be considered as supplemental to natural daylight. Another form of daylight integration is that of blending daylight and electrical light together before they enter the space. Where daylighting is used, it is also necessary to provide adequate illumination for nighttime use.

DIMMING AND CONTROLS

Beyond manual switching and dimming, there is a trend toward more dynamic controls that automate the operation of lighting and allow for the programming and on-demand use of different lighting scenes that might be required in a space. There is also an increasing number of practical ways to conserve energy by way of controls that sense the presence of daylight or the absence of occupants.

NOTES

4.145 a. CCT—Correlated Color Temperature
b. CRI—Color Rendering Index

Contributors:
James Robert Benya, PE, FIES, IALD, Pacific Lightworks, Portland, Oregon; Robert Sardinsky, Rising Sun Enterprises, Basalt, Colorado.

GLARE AND CONTRAST CONTROL

Glare is to light as noise is to acoustics. Excess brightness ratios measured between foreground and background surfaces is defined as *glare*. Direct source glare from lamps is controlled by the cutoff angle of the luminaire housing or louvers. Reflected glare is controlled by limiting the geometry of the cone of light that leaves a luminaire and by the absence of glossy or otherwise highly reflective task surfaces. Glare from veiling reflections is experienced when direct glare from a reflective surface is mixed with diffuse reflections from the same surface, such as off a glossy magazine page or from a plate of window glass.

LIGHT TRESPASS AND THE CAMPAIGN FOR DARK SKIES

Indiscriminate or careless use of exterior lighting in the name of security or landscape illumination leads directly to light trespass in neighboring properties and contributes to urban "skyglow" that pollutes views of the night sky. Light trespass infringes on other people's rights by intruding into their spaces. It also creates the experience of outdoor "glare bombs" in the form of exposed lamps and very bright luminaires. Ironically, such horizontal distribution of light has also been shown to provide sheltering glare for criminal activity even where it is intended to provide security lighting. Similarly, night-sky pollution ruins the view of stars, threatens wildlife habitat, and wastes energy on light that never touches its intended target surfaces.

Countermeasures focus on aiming all exterior light down onto low horizontal surfaces where the illumination is useful and not intrusive to others. It is recommended that no luminaire source brightness be visible from areas other than directly below its aperture opening. In terms of light distribution patterns, this fixture type has a narrow beam of light aimed downward with low cutoff or shielding angles that prevent light from being visible to the side of the fixture.

HEAT OF LIGHTING AS A THERMAL COOLING LOAD

All energy used to power electrical lighting is instantly converted to heat. In conditioned spaces during warm months, this means that lighting electricity used inefficiently or excessively is paid for twice: first to power luminaires and then remove the resulting heat by mechanical cooling. Even in cold weather, where waste heat from lighting might seem useful for warming the interior, it is more economical to provide the same heat with an efficient heating system than with what amounts to a very inefficient electrical resistance heating system of unneeded electrical light.

LAMP LIFE, LAMP REPLACEMENT SCHEDULE, AND FIXTURE MAINTENANCE

These factors are interwoven in a number of ways that impact lighting economics. First, proper maintenance and lamp replacement schedules will allow for the design of a smaller lighting system, as compared to a system that is less well maintained. Second, this resulting smaller system will cost less initially, and less to operate, and may also reduce the size of the cooling system that must be installed and operated to offset the waste heat of light.

LAMP LUMEN DEGRADATION (LLD)

Different lamp types have characteristic degradation curves. In point-to-point task lighting, it is therefore advisable to use average lamp lumen ratings rather than new lamp ratings. For ambient lighting calculations, LLD is one of several factors that make up the overall light loss factor (LLF) used to predict the average maintained level of light over the operation of the system. In either case, it is important to understand that the lighting level attained in a new system is not the same as the average operating conditions of the system.

LAMP COLOR STABILITY (OR CONSISTENCY)

Most lamp types will undergo some shift in color temperature over their life of operation. There is also some variation in actual color temperature among a random sample of any one given lamp product.

LIGHTING DESIGN OPPORTUNITIES

The architect is in the best position to integrate light sources within a building's structure. If a lighting consultant or designer is part of a design team, it is the lighting designer's task to assist the architect by recommending the appropriate luminaires to manifest

the architect's luminous image. It is also the lighting designer's task to refine the positioning of the luminaires for maximum comfort and efficiency in revealing structure and space and providing appropriate task lighting for activities within the space.

The lighting design process follows a path similar to that of architectural design:

1. Programming
2. Schematic design
3. Design development
4. Construction documents
5. Construction procurement
6. Construction administration

Lighting design can also include the additional finishing steps of final adjustment of adjustable luminaries and the programming of lighting controls after final client move-in and occupation of the space.

The lighting designer should start this process by meeting with the client/owner to determine the functional and aesthetic requirements of the end user of the project. The list should include the overall image (preferences and impressions) desired by the owner and design team, as well as the different tasks that are to be performed within the project's scope. As a result of this exercise, the designer will be able to order the priorities of initial cost, life-cycle cost, energy use, visual comfort, and aesthetics. The exercise should also educate the client about the lighting design possibilities.

Designers have many options in considering how lighting design influences a space:

- Effect: spot lighting, floodlighting, backlighting, footlighting, and other dramatic or theatrical effects
- Composition of the lighting scene: focus, balance, sequence, and so forth, as rendered by patterns of brightness and shadow
- Glitter and sparkle: small points of light used as visual elements without the introduction of source glare
- Beam play and shadow play as figural elements
- Fixture hardware as design elements, furniture, or architectural hardware
- Configurations: ways in which lighting systems are deployed
- Task lighting: work surfaces, lighting accents, artworks, retail displays
- Ambient lighting: background fill light
- Fixture mounting options: surface, recessed, pendant, cove, valiance
- Applications: general, task, high-bay, display, accent, signage, façade, landscape, emergency, security
- Controls: ways in which lighting is regulated to match changing requirements
- Local manual on/off switching
- Local manual dimming
- Occupant sensors for automated switching in periodically unoccupied spaces, especially small offices
- Multizone dimming and switching for manual selection of preset lighting "scenes" as set in a programmable scene controller
- Photocell for automated on/off operation tied to natural light levels
- Astronomical time clock for automated on/off tied to sunrise/sunset and time of day

LIGHTING INTERFACES

Lighting systems most commonly connect with other interior systems, especially ceilings. Recessed luminaires must be checked for clearance and for code compliance with fire-rated assemblies that they penetrate, as well as their insulation contact (IC) rating. The size of the lighting system, with some diversity factor, also has a direct impact on the size of the required mechanical cooling system. Most importantly, lighting design is usually a direct response to furniture arrangement, circulation paths, and other occupant use patterns. The luminous zoning of an entire building might be organized around the use of daylight, distance from a window, unfavorable east and west summer sun, and the distinct qualitative and quantitative needs of visual tasks that are performed in different areas.

A significant performance enhancement is achieved by the use of air-handling light fixtures. Fluorescent fixtures are commonly available as either air-handling or static devices. When used as return-air

devices, these air-handling fixtures remove some of the waste heat from the fixture before it ever becomes part of the room load, thus reducing the amount of cooling air needed to flush the room. This also keeps the lamp cooler and operating more efficaciously, makes it less prone to dust accumulation, and provides an extended lamp life. Air-handling fluorescent fixtures are estimated to have a 10 percent greater system efficiency than static fixtures, meaning that the average static luminaire will, on average, provide 10 percent less light-level output across its lifetime than an identically configured and maintained air-handling fixture. Consequently, the two systems would provide the same initial footcandle levels when they were new, but the air-handling system could be sized at 10 percent fewer fixtures to provide the same level of maintained illumination.

LIGHTING DESIGN DETAILS

Definitive lighting design standards are difficult to establish. Continual advances in lighting technology and the consequent rapid updating of lighting products are likely to make this so for the foreseeable future. Color, efficacy, control, and lamp life are the primary measures of lighting technology, and these continue to advance with every product catalog published. The shelf life of printed technical data and product information on lighting is now so short that all but the most current is open to question. Moreover, the voluminous new information being published is difficult to catalog, digest, evaluate, and use. Written guidelines should, therefore, convey something of the dynamic advances and dramatic changes that can be expected to continue, rather than offering up a static picture of one specific point in time.

The architect is well advised to keep in mind how fluid this industry is and to carefully consider the most current available information for a wide range of current products. Today's best decisions may well be different from other recent ones in this area. It is also advisable to use both manufacturer-specific performance data (such as from current catalogs) and independent evaluations of lighting technology (such as those available from relevant government agencies and the IESNA). Because competitive product ranges often use proprietary terms and labeling information, it may also be necessary to consult the appropriate product literature to make comparisons with similar products from other suppliers.

ILLUMINANCE TARGET VALUES FOR VARIOUS INDOOR ACTIVITIES

Selection of footcandle levels (or lux, in the metric system) should be made with several factors in mind:

- Illuminance category of the visual task
- Age of the occupants
- Contrast level of the task
- Duration of the task
- Critical importance level of visual error

Use the illuminance category as a center-value guideline and adjust accordingly to accommodate all occupants and tasks of the space. Remember that quality is just as critical as quantity but that the solution should work for all individuals. Consult the most current recommendations for the parameters of any specific application.

ILLUMINANCE TARGET VALUES FOR VARIOUS INDOOR ACTIVITIES
4.146

GROUP	CATEGORY	VISUAL TASK	FC
Task only occasionally involves reading or close visual scrutiny	A	Public spaces	3
	B	Simple orientation	5
	C	Simple tasks	10
Normal visual tasks as found in most buildings	D	Task of high contrast and large size	30
	E	Either low contrast or small size	50
	F	Low contrast and small size	100
Critical visual tasks	G	Task lighting for difficult or critical visual demands	300

NOTE

4.146 Illuminance categories and general footcandle recommendations for different visual demands. Multiply fc by 10.76 to obtain lux.

Contributors:
James Robert Benya, PE, FIES, IALD, Pacific Lightworks, Portland, Oregon; Robert Sardinsky, Rising Sun Enterprises, Basalt, Colorado; Robert Prouse, IALD, IES, HM Brandston & Partners, Inc., New York City, New York.

TASK METHOD OF CALCULATING ILLUMINANCE (POINT-TO-POINT LIGHTING)

For estimating lighting from one or more fixtures directly onto the center of a visual task area such as the middle of a desktop, use the inverse square law:

(candela of source) ÷ (distance from source to task)^2 × cos (incidence angle between ray of light from luminaire and line extending normal from task surface), or $fc = cd/d^2 \times \cos(\theta)$

Note that the candela output from a luminaire varies according to its candlepower distribution curve (CDC) and the aiming angle of the fixture. Lighting of one task point from multiple luminaires is simply the sum of the individual fc levels provided by each fixture.

Task-lighting calculations should be made with the understanding that the initial output of the fixture and its lamp(s) will degrade with age and that room surfaces are not considered as light-reflecting areas that contribute to illumination on the task.

LUMINAIRE LIGHT DISTRIBUTION PATTERN 4.147

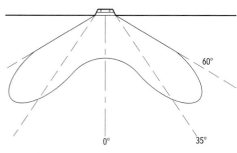

Any one of these dimensions may be the cavity height (H), which is the distance from the light fixture to the work plane of interest.

LUMEN METHOD OF CALCULATING ILLUMINANCE (UNIFORM BACKGROUND LIGHTING)

The lumen or zonal cavity method is used to estimate the maintained levels of uniform illumination from a room of uniformly spaced light fixtures. This estimation allows for the contribution of reflected light from room surfaces and, thus, considers the room itself, along with its geometry and reflectance levels, to be part of the lighting system. Maintained illumination is differentiated from initial fc levels by including light loss factors (LLF) for estimated recoverable light loss factors, which include:

- Area dirtiness
- Room surface dirt depreciation
- Lamp percentage burnout
- Lamp lumen depreciation
- Luminaire dirt depreciation

Unrecoverable light loss factors include:

- Luminaire ambient temperature
- Luminaire voltage
- Ballast efficiency factor
- Luminaire surface depreciation

Light loss factors are the mathematical product of all these different maintenance considerations, each of which can be determined by a detailed procedure. LLF usually ranges from 0.6 to 0.8 and can be estimated for very preliminary purposes with some knowledge of the room conditions and the parameters of lighting system operation.

Light output from luminaires in the lumen method is not taken from lamp candela as in the task-lighting method, but rather as the total lumens from the fixture multiplied by the efficiency of the fixture. This fixture efficiency is termed the *coefficient of utilization* (CU) and is determined from manufacturers' photometric test data as published in their product literature.

Generally:

footcandles (fc) = (number of fixtures × lumens per lamp × lamps per fixture × CU × LLF) ÷ (room square feet)

If there is only one lamp in each fixture this simplifies to:

fc = (fixtures × lumens × CU × LLF) ÷ (room square feet)

If the desired illuminance level is known and the number of fixtures is not, then the terms can be rearranged as:

(number of fixtures) = (fc × room square feet) × (lumens per fixture × CU × LLF)

Further, to assure uniform illumination at the task, it is necessary to check the final fixture layout against the allowable spacing ratio given by the manufacturer for the fixture being used. Exceeding the spacing ratio will result in gaps between the fixtures where the task will not be lit to the predicted average fc level. Note also that asymmetric fixtures such as linear fluorescents have two different spacing ratios to indicate the beam spread across the fixture width, as opposed to along the fixture length.

Determination of CU is key to this process, and involves a succession of calculations based on room geometry, fixture mounting height, and room surface reflectances. For very preliminary estimation purposes and typical room conditions, a CU can usually be assumed in the range of 0.5 to 0.8. Note that a CU of 0.6 indicates that only 60 percent of the light generated in the fixture will ever reach the intended task surface. Coupled with a hypothetical LLF of 0.7, this means that only 0.6 × 0.7 = 42 percent of the fixture output would be effectively utilized and that the average operating fc level would only be 70 percent of the illuminance when the system is new. All energy used for light is instantly converted to heat in a room, but light that never reaches the task surface is doubly problematic. It should be apparent that detailed ambient lighting design should never be initiated until CU and LLF values are well established. Equally obvious, better maintenance and quality component design results in higher CU and LLF factors that provide the same maintained illuminance levels with less wasted lighting energy and interior heat gain.

BALLASTS

Control of gas discharge lamps during starting and operation requires a ballast device. Many fixtures are available with either 120V or 277V ballast options. Higher-voltage fixtures allow for a simplified and more economical building electrical distribution system with smaller (lower ampacity) conductors. Ballasts consume some 10 to 20 percent as much energy as the lamp they control.

For some 50 years the standard ballast was the wire-wound magnetic type. Electronic ballast technology is now commonplace. Electronic ballasts are generally more efficient at operating discharge lamps and also have lower energy losses associated with their own power draw. The more sophisticated electronic ballasts also have other advantages:

- High-frequency ballasts can be used to drive fluorescent lamps at 20,000 Hz or more (40,000 pulses per second) and, thus, eliminate the eyestrain causing flicker associated with standard 60 Hz (120 pulses per second) ballasts. This high frequency also causes fluorescent lights to operate even more efficaciously than standard electronic ballasts.
- Additionally, electronic ballasts are available in dimmable configurations to allow for control of stepped or continuously variable illuminance levels.

On the downside, electronic ballasts are more heat-sensitive than magnetic ballasts. Electronic ballasts are designed for ambient temperatures below 105°F with an inside temperature of the ballast of less than 167°F. Magnetic ballasts, on the other hand, have a maximum interior temperature of 194°F. Electronic ballasts are fitted with thermal protection circuitry that shuts down when overheating occurs, but repeated overheating can lead to ballast failure.

Another critical factor is that ballast characteristics are tailored to a limited number of lamp applications. Mismatched lamp and ballast combinations can result in more than just poor performance; it can also cause immediate to near-term catastrophic failure.

Catastrophic failure can occur because discharge lamps tend to have negative electrical impedance once they reach operating temperature after start-up, and so a mismatched ballast may cause a sudden circuit failure if it is not programmed for the lamp in use.

Dimming electronic ballasts can incorporate low-voltage controls, and can be grouped into custom-sized and independently controlled zones. Low-voltage wiring for this purpose avoids the necessity of expensive conduit and is readily modified when use patterns change. Low-voltage controls also work with other control components such as photocells, occupant sensors, and energy management systems.

LAMPS

This section addresses design considerations for lamps and describes different types of lamps.

DESIGN CONSIDERATIONS

Even though color rendering, lamp life, and efficacy ratings will normally dictate the general choice among incandescent, fluorescent, and HID lamp families, there remain other detailed factors to consider when selecting a specific lamp.

SMALL LIGHT SOURCES

Smaller light sources are much easier to focus, whereas large diffuse sources such as fluorescent tubes are quite difficult to direct. The smallest conventional lamp source is the filament of a low-voltage halogen MR lamp. With a small filament it is much easier to design and build a reflector profile into the lamp bulb or fixture housing that will produce the desired beam spread, from very narrow spot to very wide flood. Small lamps with small filaments are, thus, usually better suited to task-lighting applications where precise control of beam pattern is more important. Larger light sources are more appropriate for ambient background illumination where light levels are fairly uniform.

LUMEN MAINTENANCE AND LAMP LIFE

The typical decline of lumen output from a lamp corresponding to age in operating hours is termed the *lamp lumen depreciation* factor (*LLD*). LLD is measured as a percent of the original lamp lumens and is rated as the percentage of original lumens still remaining at 40 percent of the rated life of the lamp. Lamp life in turn is established by the number of operating hours at which 50 percent of a large sample of lamps will burn out completely. Because lamps have a variety of expected life hours, the LLD degradation cannot be compared directly from one lamp to another. LLD and lamp life are also influenced by various factors depending on the lamp technology being considered; lamp position, operating voltage, operating temperature, and hours per on/off operating cycle also may have a significant impact. Another productive use of dimming is the graduated compensation for lamp lumen depreciation, where lamp power is increased over time to compensate for lumen depreciation.

SPECTRAL COLOR DISTRIBUTION AND PHOSPHOR BULB COATINGS

Gas-discharge lamps rely on a conductive vapor such as mercury, metal halide, or sodium to emit photon energy when subjected to a current flowing through the gasses held in the lamp bulb or arc capsule. In the case of mercury, these photons produce mostly invisible ultraviolet energy. As the photons leave the lamp, however, they are intercepted by a phosphor coating on the bulb surface, where they are absorbed and exchanged for photon energy in the visible spectrum. This photon exchange happens very efficiently. Different phosphors emit different spectrums of visible light, and so the lamp color balance can be tailored to specific applications. Halophosphor types are used in warm and cool-white fluorescent lamps. Triphosphor blends contain one phosphate each for reinforcing the red, green, and blue portions of the spectrum. Halophosphor and triphosphor coatings are combined and tuned in the design of lamps to vary color output across the spectrum by adjusting the specific type and amount of selected phosphors.

COMPONENTS

Although the fundamental function of a lamp is to convert electrical energy to visible light, lamp construction can also incorporate reflectors, lenses, and internal ballasts. These additional features allow for the use of less expensive fixtures and more flexible retro-fitting of room lighting.

MERCURY CONTENT AND LAMP DISPOSAL

Many lamp types contain the heavy metal mercury, which is a neurotoxin that can impair brain function, fetal health, and child development. Compact fluorescent lamps contain as little as 1.4 milligrams. On the other end of the spectrum, HID stadium lamps can contain as much as 225 milligrams. Linear fluorescent lamps range from 1.4 to 60 milligrams of mercury. Businesses were banned from disposing of lamps that contain mercury in the mid-1980s. In January 2000, the U.S. Environmental Protection Agency reclassified these lamps as "universal waste," a subset of hazardous waste. This reclassification was intended to simplify the recycling of said lamps by anyone who handles them in bulk. Most states already have their own more stringent and detailed methods for dealing with mercury lamps. Each year, however, an estimated 30,000 lb of mercury waste still makes its way into the U.S. environment, possibly into the groundwater, and potentially then into the food chain. About 1 percent of that mercury is thought to come from discarded lamps.

Designers can mitigate some of this risk by considering the mercury content of the lamps specified and the expected life of the lamp before it needs to be recycled.

LABEL DESIGNATIONS

Selecting a lamp also means interpreting their various label designations. All lamps have a great deal of information coded into their labeling, but different lamp families use different codings. This information may variously include the lamp shape, the wattage, the base type and size, the lamp tube length in inches, the lamp diameter in one-eighth-inch increments, the reflector shape, color temperature, and the beam spread pattern. An incandescent A-19 is just the common 2.375-in. diameter lamp. Likewise, an F25T8SPX30 is a 25-watt fluorescent lamp with a T-pin base and a 1-in. diameter bulb operating at a 3000°K color correlated temperature. A halogen 250PAR38SP designates a 250-watt lamp with a parabolic aluminized reflector, a 4.75-in. diameter, and a spot beam spread pattern, as opposed to a FL flood pattern.

Because manufacturers use slightly different coding, and new products are constantly being introduced, appropriate technical information should always be consulted. Some manufacturers also offer a comparison chart of competing product brand equivalencies.

TYPES OF LAMPS

Examined here are these common types of lamps:

- Incandescent
- Halogen incandescent
- High-intensity discharge (HD)
- Mercury vapor (MV)
- High-pressure sodium (HPS)
- Low-pressure sodium (LPS)
- Induction
- Light-emitting diode (LED)

INCANDESCENT LAMPS

Incandescent lamps generate light by heating a thin tungsten metal filament with electrical current. To prevent oxidation, the filament is sealed in a bulb of inert gas.

The typical A-lamp incandescent has a color temperature range from 2750 to 3200°K, which is warm and emphasizes reds while dulling blue tints. They have a short life of about 750 to 1500 hours, but are very inexpensive and easy to replace.

Because incandescent lamps have a small point source of light generated at the filament, effective reflector profiles can be designed into a reflective lamp bulb enclosure or into the fixture housing. This ease of control translates into good match of beam spread and beam pattern for task and display lighting because light can be put more specifically where it is wanted. Also, because the filament works in proportion to electrical current, incandescents can be readily dimmed. Dimming reduces the efficacy and color temperature of incandescent nonhalogen lamps slightly, but it does greatly increase lamp life. Solid-state dimmers reduce lamp buzz

noise, and lamp debuzzing coils (LDC) can be added to the circuit to reduce filament vibration even further.

Incandescent lamps come in several sizes and shapes. Their generic label takes the form WWSDDBB. Other terms may be used for colored lamps, lamp base, or manufacturer-specific features.

- *W:* Watts of power
- *S:* Shape, including general-service A-lamps, reflector lamps, elliptical reflectors, PAR (pressed aluminized reflector), candle, globe, and decorative shapes
- *D:* Diameter of the lamp bulb in eighths of an inch
- *B:* Beam spread characteristic, if applicable: spot or flood

REPRESENTATIVE INCANDESCENT LAMP SHAPES
4.148

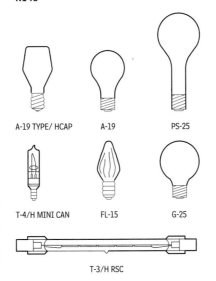

A-19 TYPE/ HCAP   A-19   PS-25

T-4/H MINI CAN   FL-15   G-25

T-3/H RSC

AREA SOURCES

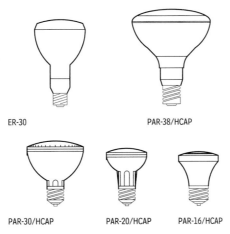

ER-30   PAR-38/HCAP

PAR-30/HCAP   PAR-20/HCAP   PAR-16/HCAP

REFLECTOR SOURCES

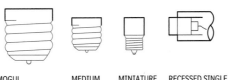

MOGUL   MEDIUM   MINIATURE CANDE-LABRA   RECESSED SINGLE CONTACT RSC

BASES

HALOGEN INCANDESCENT LAMPS

Both line-voltage and low-voltage halogen lamps differ from standard incandescent lamps in that they use an iodine or bromine gas within the bulb to protect against tungsten filament burnout and bulb blackening, which contributes to extended lamp life. During lamp operation, the halogen gas combines with tungsten that is evaporated off of the lamp filament. When the lamp is switched off and the gas mixture cools, tungsten is redeposited on the filament rather than on the bulb. This effect greatly retards filament weakening and lamp lumen degradation.

Halogen lamps have a rated life of about 2000 to 3000 hours with a 90 to 95 percent lamp lumen depreciation factor. They offer a CRI of 100 at CCTs of 2600°K to 3200°K. The regenerative halogen evaporation/cooling cycle necessitates a higher operating temperature, which slightly increases efficacy and improves the color rendering, as well as increasing the CCT. The bulb of halogen lamps is usually made of quartz to resist these high internal temperatures. Note, however, that quartz is very sensitive to oil and dirt, so direct handling of the bulb is to be avoided. Premature lamp failure can occur if contamination is allowed to deteriorate the quartz surface.

The most impressive advance in incandescent lighting technology in many years is that of the halogen infrared reflecting lamp (HIR). These lamps encapsulate the lamp filament in a quartz capsule, which is coated with a multilayered infrared reflecting film. Ninety percent of the energy consumed by incandescent lamps is converted to invisible infrared energy, so the energy reflected from the quartz capsule raises the filament temperature without drawing extra power. The added incandescence of the HIR lamp filament raises its efficacy into the 40 LPW range. HIR lamps are considerably more expensive than standard incandescent lamps, however, and with the advent of low-priced compact fluorescent lamps, HIR has a limited popularity.

Like conventional incandescent lamps, halogen lamps have a small filament point source of light that is readily controlled. Halogens are also dimmable, just as conventional incandescents are. Halogen lighting is most appropriate to applications where precise control and ease of dimming are important, such as display and accent lighting. But fluorescent and other gas-discharge lamps have a higher efficacy, so halogen should normally not be used where energy consumption and general room lighting are priorities.

Halogen multimirror reflecting lamps, labeled MR, are popular low-voltage lamps that have a compact filament and precision reflector for excellent beam control such as that required for projection lamps. MR lamps also have a dichroic coating on a faceted glass reflector that allows most infrared energy to pass through the back of the lamp but reflects visible light forward through the lens. The dichroic filtering gives the projected light a cooler hue and lower heat content. Some MR lamps have an infrared reflecting capsule around the filament, which increases efficacy. Typically, MR lamps are rated by center-of-beam candlepower, rather than initial lumens, but MR efficacy is generally around 30 LPW.

FLUORESCENT LAMPS

General fluorescent lamps pass an electrical current through an inert and electrically nonconductive gas by first evaporating a small drop of mercury held within the tube (typically, 10 to 23 milligrams) each time the lamp is started. The evaporation is accomplished by a high-voltage starting current from the fixture ballast. Once the mercury is evaporated and electrical current begins to flow through the lamp, a mostly invisible ultraviolet (UV) spectrum of light is produced. Photons of this UV light are then absorbed by special phosphor coatings on the lamp bulb that replaces them very efficiently by photons of visible light. The ballast then provides reduced current that maintains the discharge of light.

Although fluorescent lamps do not have the control or color-rendering capability of incandescents, nor the efficacy of HID lamps, they do offer good compromises of efficacy, color, and lamp life at a very reasonable first cost. This middle ground of good performance and economy have given fluorescent lamps a strong market advantage. Lamp life ranges from 6000 to 30,000 hours at an industry standard on/off cycle of 3 hours of operation per start. Many fluorescents offer about 20,000 life hours. Color Correlated

Contributor:
Fred Davis, CLEP, Fred Davis Corp., Energy and Lighting, Medfield, Massachusetts.

Temperature ratings are available from 2200°K to 7500°K with a CRI of 50 to 92 and typical CRI of about 80. Efficacy in some fluorescents approaches 100 lumens per watt with typical LPW values ranging from 75 to 90 LPW. The combination of these factors in any single example is highly dependent on the exact lamp and ballast combination selected.

Fluorescent lamps are identified by designations such as F40T12CW. The labeling format is generically FSWWTDD-CCC and is coded as follows:

- *F:* Fluorescent lamp. Germicidal shortwave UV lamps are designated G.
- *S:* Shape or style of lamp. No letter indicates the typical straight tube; circline lamps are designated C.
- *WW:* Power in watts.
- *CCC:* CW = cool white (about 4100°K), color. W = white (about 3500°K), WW = warm white (about 3000°K). Manufacturers may use special designations for specific products such as SPX.
- *T:* Tubular bulb.
- *DD:* Diameter of tube in eighths of an inch

Control of beam pattern and beam spread from incandescent sources is difficult, given the relatively large and diffuse surface of their bulb envelopes. This usually relegates fluorescent sources to general or uniform ambient lighting situations, rather than to task- or display-lighting applications. Dimming control of fluorescents is less problematic than beam control, especially with the advent of electromagnetic ballasts that can provide full range dimming from 10 to 100 percent brightness. Additionally, some electronic ballasts can be used with photosensors and other low-voltage controls for daylight integration.

The newest fluorescent lamp technology is that of T5 lamps, which have a peak lumen output at 95°F operating temperature, as compared to much lower peak operating temperatures for T12 and T8 lamps. This makes T5 lamps beneficial in closed luminaires where air circulation is restricted. Although the bulb wall is only 0.625-in. diameter, the T5 does have a high surface brightness and should, therefore, be carefully shielded from direct view, or used in indirect lighting applications to avoid glare.

Compact fluorescent lamps (CFL) come in a wide variety of sizes and shapes, as well as base mounting configurations, and may be either self-ballasted or require an external ballast. The use of triphosphors in CFL gives them satisfactory color rendering with a CRI over 80 and CCT in the general range of 2700 to 5000. CFLs are popular replacements for incandescent lamps because they offer light of about 4 times the efficacy and 10 times the lamp life. They are increasingly competitive on cost, efficiency, and color, even compared with some HID lamp technologies.

REPRESENTATIVE COMPACT FLUORESCENT LAMP SHAPES
4.149

GLASS SHAPES	PLUG-IN VERSION (FOR BALLASTED FIXTURE)			SCREW-IN VERSION (FOR USE IN MEDIUM SOCKET)	
	LAMP ALONE	BASE		MODULAR ASSEMBLY (LAMP AND BALLAST)	INTEGRAL (ONE-PIECE)
		2-PIN	4-PIN		
GLOBE, TUBE					
TWIN					
QUAD					
TRIPLE					
OCTIC					
HELICAL					
CIRCLINE					
2-D					
FLAT					
REFLECTOR					
LONG CFL					

Contributor:
Fred Davis, CLEP, Fred Davis Corp., Energy and Lighting, Medfield, Massachusetts.

STRAIGHT-TUBE FLUORESCENT LAMP SHAPES AND TYPICAL NOMINAL LENGTHS
4.150

TUBE SHAPE	BASE
T2 RIGHT ANGLE, 20"	
T5 MINIATURE BIPIN, 46"	
T8 MEDIUM BIPIN, 48"	
T8 MEDIUM BIPIN U-BENT, 22-7/16"	
T10 MEDIUM BIPIN, 48"	
T12 MEDIUM BIPIN, 48"	
T8 SINGLE-PIN SLIMLINE, 96"	
T12 SINGLE-PIN SLIMLINE, 96"	
T12 RECESSED DOUBLE CONTACT, 96"	

REPRESENTATIVE HID SHAPES
4.151

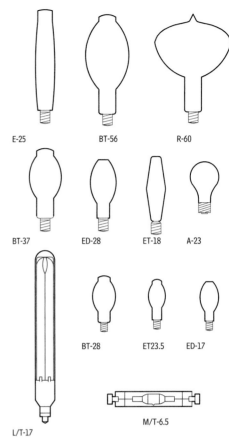

E-25   BT-56   R-60

BT-37   ED-28   ET-18   A-23

BT-28   ET23.5   ED-17

L/T-17   M/T-6.5

HIGH-INTENSITY DISCHARGE (HID) LAMPS

HID technology includes mercury, metal halide, and sodium-gas discharge lamps. In general, they have high efficacy and low to average color rendering. Their most common applications are industrial, commercial, roadway, and security lighting. HIDs are similar in operation to fluorescent lamps. All of them use a ballast to initiate and control a flow of electrical current through a gas-filled envelope. The gas emits photon energy when excited, just as in fluorescent lamps. Each of the different HID lamp types does, however, have individual efficacy, color, and control characteristics that make each of them better suited to a particular range of applications.

According to the U.S. Department of Commerce, sale of all HID technology lamps increased from 20 million units in 1990 to a peak of 37 million in 1999, and by 2002 was still near 34 million lamps. Despite the continued improvement in some HID lamp efficacy and color rendering, however, the relative share of the HID market by lamp wattage remained unchanged from 1993 to 2001. The total number of HID luminaires shipped has remained constant at about 12 million since 1996, with outdoor fixtures accounting for about 8 million, industrial fixtures for 3.5 million, and commercial fixtures for some 0.5 million. The only trends in fixture shipments indicate a slight increase in the commercial, and a similar small decrease in outdoor fixtures.

HID lamps can be dimmed by either step-level or continuous dimming ballasts. Dimming HID is important for more than daylight harvesting, illuminance flexibility, and energy savings; it also avoids the necessity of switching the lamps on and off. Given the strike and restrike time needed for HID lamps to warm up before reaching or returning to full brightness, dimming can thus help extend HID lamp life by maintaining the 10-hour operating cycle for which they are designed and rated. Note that the efficacy of an HID lamp will decrease when dimmed and that dimming below 50 percent of the lamp's rated power may degrade the life, efficacy, lumen maintenance, color, and warranty coverage.

MERCURY VAPOR (MV) LAMPS

Clear MV lamps have a very low CRI of approximately 15. Generally, even with phosphor coatings the CRI is still low, around 50 at CCTs of 3200 to 6700. Efficacy is also limited, to a low 25 to 32 LPW for small lamps of less than 100 watts to perhaps 50 to 60 LPW for MV lamps of 1000 watts. Efficacy at 40 percent of the lamp life (LLD) is about 75 percent of the initial efficacy. Lamp life is quite long, with 24,000 hours being quite common. Brightness and efficacy tend to slowly degrade over the life of an MV lamp, but they are known to be rugged and durable. Mercury lamps do require a five- to seven-minute warm-up strike time and an equal restrike time.

The bluish cast of uncoated mercury lamps is beneficial to the appearance of green vegetation in night scenes. Generally, however, mercury lighting has few applications where good vision is important. Small MV lamps of around 50 watts contain about 15 milligrams of mercury, and a 1000-watt MV lamp might contain as much as 250 milligrams, so all MV lamps should be recycled and treated as hazardous waste.

Mercury vapor lamps are essentially unchanged since their introduction in the 1930s. The sole development has been the invention of a type B self-ballasted incandescent/mercury hybrid lamp that uses a tungsten filament to regulate current in the absence of ballast control. An arc discharge within the B lamp tube generates light. Next, a filament is heated to incandescence. Together, the arc tube and the filament form a self-regulating series circuit. The B-lamp efficacy is comparable to incandescent lamps of the same wattage. B-lamps have about a three-minute strike time start-up with a five-minute restrike.

Overall, MV lamps have fallen from popularity because of the technical improvements in other lamp families. It is estimated that MV lamp shipments fell from 5.5 million units in 1993 to fewer than 3.0

million in 1999, alone. Projections indicate that this number could decrease to less than 1.0 million by 2008.

METAL HALIDE (MH)

MH lamps were developed from mercury vapor lamp technology by the addition of metal halides to the mercury and argon in the arc tube. Continual improvements have made MH technology an excellent match of color, efficacy, and lamp life. CRIs of 70 to 90 are common at CCTs of 2500˚K to 5000˚K; and lamp efficacies are in the range of 75 to 125 LPW.

Probe-start and pulse-start MH lamps differ in gas pressure within the arc capsule. Pulse-start lamps have improved life (15,000 to 30,000 hours) and lumen maintenance (as much as a 33 percent improvement, from about 65 percent to perhaps 80 percent), as well as higher efficacy (typically, 90 versus 100 LPW and varying with lamp wattage).

Note that metal halide lamp life is rated at a standard 10 hours per start. Pulse-start lamps start faster than probe-start metal halides, with a strike and restrike time of 1 to 4 minutes and 2 to 8 minutes, respectively, compared to probe-start times of 2 to 15 minutes and 5 to 20 minutes. Pulse-start MH lamps can also be used with electronic dimming ballasts to provide variable illuminance control and energy savings. These ballasts are also compatible with low-voltage controls systems for daylight integration and occupancy sensors.

The addition of ceramic arc tube technology, CMH, in lamps under 400 watts improves the small lamp metal halide efficacy to about 90 LPW, with a life of 9000 to 15,000 hours, a CRI approaching 95 at CCTs of 3000˚K to 4200˚K, and LLD factors of 80 percent.

Metal halide lamps are quickly gaining in popularity and their share of the HID market has basically doubled since 1991. The Department of Energy and the National Electrical Manufacturer's

NOTE

4.150 Lamps are not to scale; nominal length is from back of socket to back of socket.

Contributor:
Fred Davis, CLEP, Fred Davis Corp., Energy and Lighting, Medfield, Massachusetts.

Association estimated that MH lamp sales rose quickly from 5.7 million in 1990 to 18.1 million in 1999 and then increased more slowly to 18.8 million lamps in 2002.

HIGH-PRESSURE SODIUM (HPS)

HPS lamps discharge an arc current through a small ceramic arc tube in the center of the lamp. The arc tube is filled with xenon, sodium, and mercury vapor, but the larger outer bulb volume is drawn down to vacuum pressure. Efficacy is dependent on the vapor pressure of sodium in the arc tube, but 35-watt sources are in the range of 65 LPW, 100 watts at 100 LPW, and 1000 watts at 130 LPW. Standard HPS life is 24,000 hours with long-life lamps rated up to 40,000 hours. CCT is normally 2100°K with a very low CRI of 22. Maintenance is usually taken as LLD = 90 percent and the sample of HPS lamps included in Figures 4.408 through 4.410 follow that value. Higher color-rendering HPS lamps are also available, but their CRI of 60 to 85 at CCTs of 2200°K to 2700°K come with reduced efficacy, in the range of 50 to 95 LPW. Cold HPS lamps require a three- or four-minute strike time and a one- to three-minute restrike time.

The monochromatic yellow cast of standard HPS restricts its usage; thus, although HPS sales have remained relatively steady, at around 11.0 million lamps per year since 1994, their HID market share has slipped continually since 1991.

As discussed earlier, as for human factors in lighting design, designers are increasingly finding that lower illuminance levels of fuller-spectrum light provided by other sources such as metal halide are more desirable and actually provide greater visual acuity than higher illuminance levels with less color rendering. In technical terms, at low-light levels, human vision shifts to "scotopic visibility function," whereby the spectral distribution and higher CCT of metal halide lamps provide better peripheral visibility, even at lower footcandles. As long as the reduced lighting level is acceptable and compensates for reduced efficacy, this is probably a reasonable trade-off.

LOW-PRESSURE SODIUM (LPS)

Although LPS lamps have very high efficacy, on the order of 100 to 150 LPW, they have no color rendering capability due to their strictly monochromatic light, with a very low CRI at a CCT of 2000°K. LPS ballasts add another 30 or 40 watts of required system power and reduce the overall system efficacy. The most common LPS application might be that of replacement lamps in mercury vapor fixtures, where replacement wattages of 18 to 180 are available and offer life ratings of 16,000 to 18,000 hours, with a maintenance factor LLD of 87 percent. There are other environmental considerations in favor of LPS, however. First, the narrow bandwidth of LPS lamps is easily filtered out by astronomers who have increasing night "skyglow" from unshielded lighting to deal with; second, some animals such as sea turtles are not as attracted to these lamps as they are to full-spectrum lamps. Many animals are accidentally destroyed when leaving their habitat to approach full-spectrum lighting.

INDUCTION LAMPS

Induction lighting is a rapidly emerging and revolutionary lighting technology. It is essentially fluorescent technology without lamp cathodes. Induction lighting provides approximately 100,000 hours of lamp life, which is about 10 times the life of HID sources at about three times the cost. Efficacy is about 75 LPW, and a characteristic LLD of 0.70 means less than 30 percent lumen degradation after 60,000 hours of operation. Induction also features a CRI of 80 or better at CCTs of 3000°K or 4000°K. Due to their high cost and long life expectancy, induction lighting systems should be purchased with a warranty against premature failure.

Induction lamps resemble general-service incandescent A-lamps, but operate like gas-discharge lamps. At the center of the lamp itself is an induction coil, which produces a magnetic field and excites a mercury electron-ion plasma material on an inner glass assembly, producing ultraviolet light. Phosphor coatings on the lamp bulb envelope replace the ultraviolet energy photons with ones of visible light. Induction lamps have no strike or restrike time, no color shift with age, and low sensitivity to operating temperature. Induction lamps do require special fixtures, are not currently dimmable, and may have a pink hue in the first few minutes

of operation. At the end of the rated 100,000-hours life, it may be necessary to replace the entire induction system with its lamp, power coupler, and high-frequency generator.

LIGHT-EMITTING DIODE (LED) LAMPS

LED lighting uses the semiconductor diode lamps that have been around since 1962. Originally, gallium arsenide devices were used to produce red light. Developments in new material compounds have recently made other colors possible, but single LEDs emit a narrow spectrum of color. Combining the relatively wide-bandwidth blue gallium nitride LEDs with red and green ones would, in principle, allow for the production of white light. Most full-spectrum LEDs in current production, however, use the blue gallium nitride LED with a yellow phosphor lens coating.

LED lamps operate on direct-current voltage and are polarity-sensitive; improper connection can destroy them. Otherwise, they have an extremely long life, typically about 10 years. LEDs usually fail by gradual dimming rather than sudden burnout. They are also insensitive to vibration and temperature.

As replacements of incandescent and fluorescent lighting, LEDs are termed solid-state lighting (SSL) devices and are clustered in arrays of several semiconductors to form a single lamp. SSLs currently have efficacies of about 32 lumens per watt but are predicted to eventually reach 80 LPW.

LUMINAIRES

Light fixture performance, as an artifact of industrial design, has been greatly augmented by advancements in computer simulation and CAD design. The ability to use ray tracing for the design of reflectors, for example, and the parallel advent of precision manufacturing makes it possible to devise and craft luminaires that have finely controlled photometric performance.

Luminaires have the following functional components. Some of these are optional elements that are not included in every luminaire, or may be incorporated into the lamp used in the fixture. In the case of PAR incandescent lamps, for example (parabolic aluminized reflector lamps), the reflector and a lens are built into the reflective lamp bulb enclosure and a Fresnel lens is pressed into the lamp aperture.

- *Lamp*: The source of light used to convert supplied energy into visible light energy.
- *Reflector*: Interior surface around the lamp used to control the spread of light from the fixture or to diffuse it as widely as possible. Reflector profiles can be designed for converging or diverging patterns of light in parabolic or elliptical shapes. This level of control is only possible where a small lighting filament is used, such as incandescent lamps have. Larger sources such as fluorescent lamps can be diffused easily, but cannot be focused. Most reflectors are of white enamel or an aluminized surface. Cones of various color and material that are inserted into fixtures also fit this function, but cones are often dulled or darkened to reduce the apparent brightness of the fixture when viewed from the side.
- *Lens*: Optical element used to control the direction and diffusion of light from the fixture; to protect the lamp from physical damage, moisture, or weather; and, optionally, to color the light as it exits the fixture. Lenses can focus or spread a controlled beam or cone of light from the fixture by optical diffraction, and they can also diffuse light by having translucent properties or a diffuse rather than a transparent surface.
- *Louvers and baffles*: Shielding elements used to hide the lamp from direct view and/or to diffuse light from the fixture in a wide pattern.

COMMUNICATIONS AND SECURITY

This section discusses communications and security systems.

FIRE ALARM SYSTEMS

The simplest fire alarm system is a self-contained, UL-approved residential smoke detector. It senses products of combustion, sounds an alarm, and signals when the battery needs replacement.

Most municipalities require the use of smoke detectors in houses, apartments, and motel/hotel rooms. Check local codes for requirements.

More complex systems are needed in buildings where public safety is an issue, such as schools, hospitals, office buildings, and other commercial establishments or institutions. Although there are still applications for small hard-wired and relay-operated alarm signaling systems, the trend is to use microprocessor-based digital multiplex systems that not only signal the presence of a fire but also initiate other measures, including conditioning fans and dampers for smoke control, closing fire doors and shutters, releasing locked doors, capturing elevators, and transmitting voice messages. Voice communication may be required in high-rise buildings of specific group occupancies. It is also recommended for large low-rise buildings to enhance life safety.

Fire alarm systems can either function alone or be integrated with security and building management functions. Processors and their peripheral equipment are generally located in a manned central command center accessible to firefighters. Depending on the degree of reliability desired, redundancy can be provided in wiring and processors, along with battery backup.

Alarm system control cabinets can be 36 in. wide by 8 in. deep. They must have battery backup, be UL-approved, and conform to NFPA No. 72, and may also require local approval. In small systems where only one cabinet may be required, all the functions required at the command center can be incorporated in the same cabinet and located in the main entrance lobby. In larger systems, remote cabinets are generally located in wiring closets throughout the building and can be programmed to function independently of the central processor, should it fail.

SIGNALING SYSTEM TYPES

Common system types are defined as:

- *Noncoded*: Evacuation signal sounds continuously.
- *Master coded*: Signal repeats four rounds.
- *Selective coded*: Same as master coded, except individual and assigned number code of up to three groups per round.
- *Presignal*: Same as selective coded, except signals sound only at selected areas to prompt investigation. If a hazard is determined, an evacuation signal is initiated by key.
- *Voice*: Direct (by microphone) or automatic prerecorded messages are transmitted over speakers, following an alert signal.

AUDIBLE ALARMS

Audible alarms must have an intensity and frequency that attract the attention of those with partial hearing loss. Such alarms should produce a sound that exceeds the prevailing sound level in the space by at least 15 dBA or exceeds maximum sound level with a duration of 60 seconds by 5 dBA, whichever is louder. Sound levels should not exceed 120 dbA.

VISUAL ALARMS

Visual alarm signals should be integrated into the building alarm system. Alarm stations should give both audible and visual signals. Visual alarm signals should have the following characteristics:

Lamp: Xenon strobe type or equivalent.
Lamp color: Clear or nominal white (i.e., unfiltered or clear filtered white light).
Maximum pulse duration: 0.2 sec with a maximum duty cycle of 40 percent. The pulse duration is defined as the time interval between initial and final points of 10 percent of maximum signal.
Intensity: 75 candela minimum.
Flash Rate: 1 Hz minimum, 3 Hz maximum.

Place the alarm 80 in. above the highest floor level within the space or 6 in. below the ceiling, whichever is lower. In any space required to have a visual alarm, generally all areas must be within 50 ft of the signal (measured horizontally). In large spaces, such as auditoriums, exceeding 100 ft across, with no obstructions over 6 ft high, devices may be placed around the perimeter, spaced a maximum of 100 ft apart, in lieu of suspending devices from the ceiling.

Contributors:
Michael J. Smith, AIA, Michael John Smith Lighting Design, Houston, Texas; Leonard Bachman, University of Houston, Houston, Texas.

ELEMENT E: EQUIPMENT AND FURNISHINGS

5

INTRODUCTION

Understanding the spatial requirements of equipment and furnishings is essential to the planning and design of buildings. Proper layout of equipment and interior furnishings is an important contributor to the overall perception of interior space, not to mention its functionality. Furniture that is sensitively scaled and located to provide ease of access ensures that the overall design is coherent and successful.

In program-driven building types such as hospitals, laboratories, and libraries, the layout of equipment and furnishings begins at the programming level, as it is the accommodation of such items that determines the ultimate allocation of space. In other building types, the ultimate success of a project often rests on the proper allocation of space for the intended furnishings and equipment.

This chapter considers equipment and furnishings under a single heading. For many building types, most notably health care, laboratories, libraries, health clubs, and auditoriums/performance spaces, the equipment issues are presented in the context of overall planning and design data because the planning is often determined by such equipment considerations. Where it is furniture layout that determines such space planning, as is the case in restaurants and corporate offices, the furniture is presented in an overall planning and design context.

This chapter does not make specific reference to equipment or furniture by manufacturer; the information presented is generic in nature. You are encouraged to use the Web-based resource lists to investigate the particulars of furnishings and equipment elements presented here, as there may be considerable variation in availability of products to address specific needs. Likewise, planning data is presented as generically as possible, to encourage you to explore design possibilities.

Contributor:
Robin Guenther, Guenther 5 Architects, PLLC, New York City, New York.

EQUIPMENT

LIBRARY EQUIPMENT

This section on library equipment covers these areas of design:

- Automated book storage and retrieval systems
- Book theft protection equipment
- Book depositories
- Microreaders

AUTOMATED BOOK STORAGE AND RETRIEVAL SYSTEMS

Automated book storage and retrieval systems utilize computer-controlled automated storage and retrieval equipment, whose components are similar to those of automated warehousing storage systems.

Library systems are designed to work in temperature- and dust-controlled environments that are required for the storage of rare and valuable book collections. Automated systems utilize a bin system, with individual items tagged to indicate the bin placement. Items are requested through a computerized order entry system, which interfaces with the automated system to retrieve the bin. Operators remove and replace items from the bins.

Automated systems are estimated to achieve book storage in less than 15 percent of the space required by conventional stack book shelving and retrieve books in minutes. They are increasingly used to replace off-site storage of large collections of print materials.

Automated book storage installations are custom designed for each project application. Manufacturers of automated systems often design and install automated materials-handling systems for a range of product and service applications.

BOOK THEFT PROTECTION EQUIPMENT

Libraries utilize a wide range of equipment to intercept unauthorized removal of library materials. Many facilities employ electronic article surveillance (EAS) systems, with walk-through detection devices and magnetic inventory tags that are deactivated at checkout. Alternatively, libraries may install library security and checkout systems based on radio-frequency identification (RFID) technology. These systems, which are available hard-wired or wireless, employ magnetic IDs in each article, point-of-service (POS) self-checkout stations, and EAS sensors.

These systems work as follows:

1. Patrons bring materials to a self-checkout station or circulation desk.
2. Using an ID card, the computer system registers the article (scanning the internal RF code device), and prints a receipt indicating the patron's name, list of articles, and due dates.
3. When the patron exits the library, EAS sensor equipment detects and interrogates the library materials, communicates with the computer system, and determines the status of the items.

These computer systems are generally separate and distinct from the library circulation system.

BOOK DEPOSITORIES

Book depositories, book returns, or book drops provide for the safe return of library materials. Freestanding units are available in a wide variety of sizes, based on book capacity. In-wall units generally include pull-down doors and chute equipment to deliver the materials safely to a cart or bin on the building interior.

LIBRARY SECURITY AND CHECKOUT SYSTEM COMPONENTS—WIRED
5.1

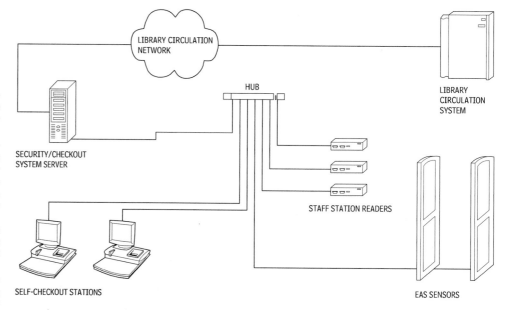

IN-WALL BOOK RETURN
5.2

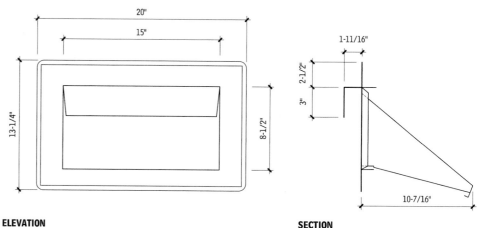

ELEVATION

SECTION

Contributors:
Norman Jaffe, FAIA, Bridgehampton, New York; Gulzar Haider, Carleton University, Ottawa, Canada.

THEATER AND STAGE EQUIPMENT

DESIGN CONSIDERATIONS

PERFORMANCE THEATERS

In performance halls used for concerts, the stage and audience seating area should be treated as one volume. In multiple-use halls, this is achieved with a hard orchestra shell, which must be demountable to allow for full use of the stage for scenery and stage sets. Acoustical requirements may dictate that reflective surfaces at the ceiling of the orchestra enclosure extend out above audience seating.

CONFIGURATION FOR LIVE PERFORMANCE
5.3

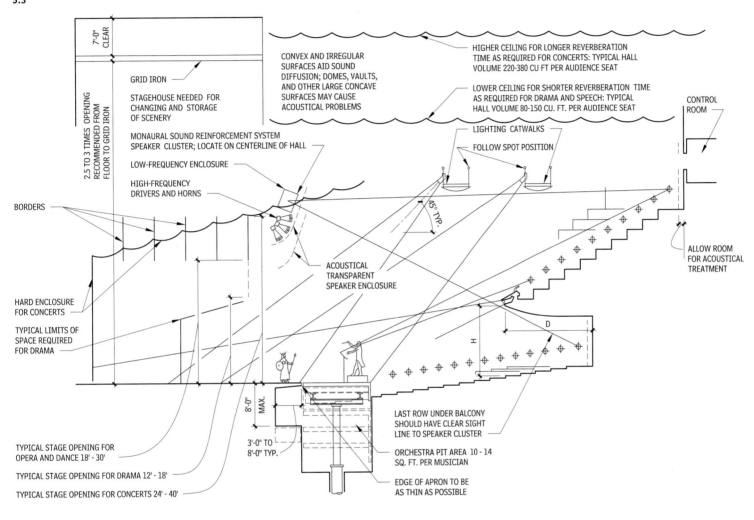

7'-0" CLEAR

2.5 TO 3 TIMES OPENING RECOMMENDED FROM FLOOR TO GRID IRON

GRID IRON

STAGEHOUSE NEEDED FOR CHANGING AND STORAGE OF SCENERY

MONAURAL SOUND REINFORCEMENT SYSTEM SPEAKER CLUSTER; LOCATE ON CENTERLINE OF HALL

LOW-FREQUENCY ENCLOSURE

HIGH-FREQUENCY DRIVERS AND HORNS

BORDERS

CONVEX AND IRREGULAR SURFACES AID SOUND DIFFUSION; DOMES, VAULTS, AND OTHER LARGE CONCAVE SURFACES MAY CAUSE ACOUSTICAL PROBLEMS

HIGHER CEILING FOR LONGER REVERBERATION TIME AS REQUIRED FOR CONCERTS: TYPICAL HALL VOLUME 220-380 CU FT PER AUDIENCE SEAT

LOWER CEILING FOR SHORTER REVERBERATION TIME AS REQUIRED FOR DRAMA AND SPEECH: TYPICAL HALL VOLUME 80-150 CU. FT. PER AUDIENCE SEAT

CONTROL ROOM

LIGHTING CATWALKS

FOLLOW SPOT POSITION

45° TYP.

ALLOW ROOM FOR ACOUSTICAL TREATMENT

ACOUSTICAL TRANSPARENT SPEAKER ENCLOSURE

HARD ENCLOSURE FOR CONCERTS

TYPICAL LIMITS OF SPACE REQUIRED FOR DRAMA

D

H

8'-0" MAX.

LAST ROW UNDER BALCONY SHOULD HAVE CLEAR SIGHT LINE TO SPEAKER CLUSTER

TYPICAL STAGE OPENING FOR OPERA AND DANCE 18' - 30'

TYPICAL STAGE OPENING FOR DRAMA 12' - 18'

TYPICAL STAGE OPENING FOR CONCERTS 24' - 40'

3'-0" TO 8'-0" TYP.

ORCHESTRA PIT AREA 10 - 14 SQ. FT. PER MUSICIAN

EDGE OF APRON TO BE AS THIN AS POSSIBLE

Contributor:
Peter H. Frink, Frink and Beuchat Architects, Philadelphia, Pennsylvania.

SEATING AREA DESIGN

The floor area efficiency in square feet per seat is a function of the row spacing, the average chair width, and the space allocation per seat for aisles, as shown in this equation:

Efficiency (F) = seat factor + aisle factor

$$F \, [\text{sq ft/seat}] = (W_s T) \div (144) + (IT) \div (144) \, (1) \div (S_{avg})$$

where:

W_s = Average seat width in inches

T = Row-to-row spacing (tread) in inches

I = Average aisle width in inches (42-in. width, typical)

S_{avg} = Average number of seats in a row per single aisle: 8 or fewer—inefficient layout; 14 to 16—maximum efficiency (multiple-aisle seating); 18 to 50 and more—continental seating

SEATING CAPACITY AND AUDIENCE AREA

The equation for determining seating capacity and audience area is:

Audience area = capacity × efficiency

Minimum seat row spacing reduces maximum distance to the stage.

EASE OF PASSAGE IN FRONT OF SEATED PERSONS

Guidelines for spacing seats to provide comfortable passage in front of seated patrons are as follows:

- *32 to 34 in.*: Seated person must rise to allow passage.
- *36 to 38 in.*: Some seated persons will rise.
- *40 in. and greater*: Passage in front of seated persons is possible.

ROW-TO-ROW SPACING CRITERIA

Consult local codes for required minimum row spacing. Codes typically stipulate a minimum clear plumb line distance measured between the unoccupied chair and the rear of the back of the chair in front, as follows:

- *32 to 33 in.*: Typical minimum for multiple-aisle seating.
- *34 to 37 in.*: Typical minimum for modified continental seating.
- *38 to 42 in.*: Typical minimum for continental seating.

COMFORT FOR THE SEATED PERSON

Guidelines for enough legroom to provide seated comfort are as follows:

- *32 in.*: Knees will touch the chair back—uncomfortable.
- *34 in.*: Minimum spacing for comfort.
- *6 in.*: Ideal spacing for maximum comfort.
- *38 in. and greater*: Audience cohesiveness may suffer.

THEATER SAFETY

Excessive plumb line distance may entice exiting persons to squeeze ahead and cause a jam. Consult applicable codes for aisle and exit path widths.

MULTIPLE-AISLE SEATING
5.4

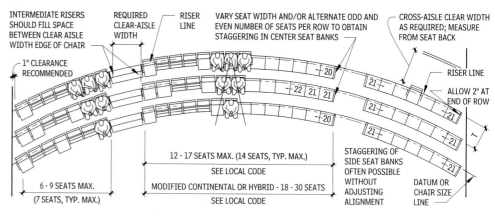

CONTINENTAL SEATING
5.5

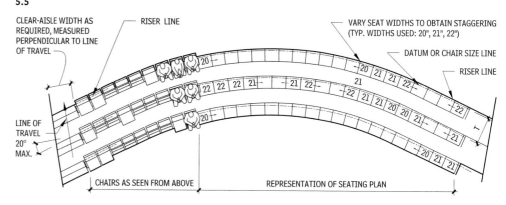

Contributor:
Peter H. Frink, Frink and Beuchat Architects, Philadelphia, Pennsylvania.

THEATER SIGHT LINES

SIGHT LINES FOR ISCIDOMAL (EQUAL-SEEING) FLOOR SLOPE
5.6

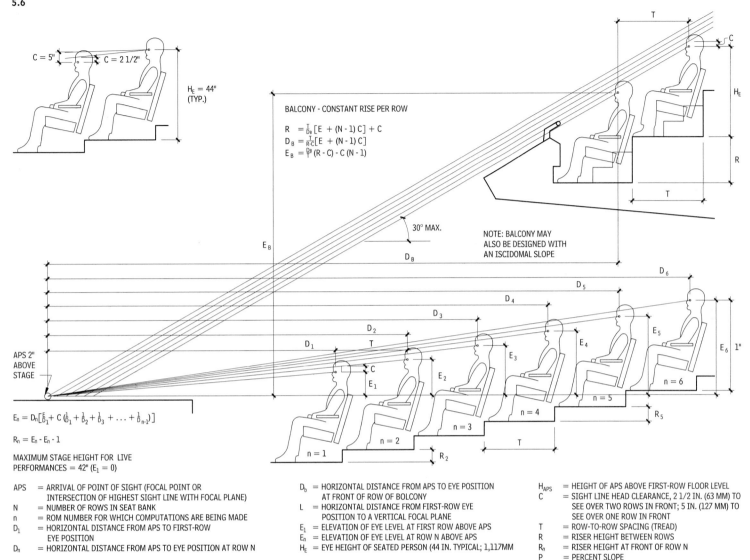

BALCONY - CONSTANT RISE PER ROW

$$R = \frac{L}{D_B}[E + (N-1)C] + C$$
$$D_B = \frac{T}{R-C}[E + (N-1)C]$$
$$E_B = \frac{D_B}{T}(R-C) - C(N-1)$$

30° MAX.

NOTE: BALCONY MAY ALSO BE DESIGNED WITH AN ISCIDOMAL SLOPE

$$E_n = D_n\left[\frac{E}{D_1} + C\left(\frac{1}{D_1} + \frac{1}{D_2} + \frac{1}{D_3} + \ldots + \frac{1}{D_{n-1}}\right)\right]$$

$$R_n = E_n - E_{n-1}$$

MAXIMUM STAGE HEIGHT FOR LIVE
PERFORMANCES = 42" ($E_1 = 0$)

APS	=	ARRIVAL OF POINT OF SIGHT (FOCAL POINT OR INTERSECTION OF HIGHEST SIGHT LINE WITH FOCAL PLANE)
N	=	NUMBER OF ROWS IN SEAT BANK
n	=	ROW NUMBER FOR WHICH COMPUTATIONS ARE BEING MADE
D_1	=	HORIZONTAL DISTANCE FROM APS TO FIRST-ROW EYE POSITION
D_n	=	HORIZONTAL DISTANCE FROM APS TO EYE POSITION AT ROW N

D_b	=	HORIZONTAL DISTANCE FROM APS TO EYE POSITION AT FRONT OF ROW OF BOLCONY
L	=	HORIZONTAL DISTANCE FROM FIRST-ROW EYE POSITION TO A VERTICAL FOCAL PLANE
E_1	=	ELEVATION OF EYE LEVEL AT FIRST ROW ABOVE APS
E_n	=	ELEVATION OF EYE LEVEL AT ROW N ABOVE APS
H_E	=	EYE HEIGHT OF SEATED PERSON (44 IN. TYPICAL; 1,117MM

H_{APS}	=	HEIGHT OF APS ABOVE FIRST-ROW FLOOR LEVEL
C	=	SIGHT LINE HEAD CLEARANCE, 2 1/2 IN. (63 MM) TO SEE OVER TWO ROWS IN FRONT; 5 IN. (127 MM) TO SEE OVER ONE ROW IN FRONT
T	=	ROW-TO-ROW SPACING (TREAD)
R	=	RISER HEIGHT BETWEEN ROWS
R_n	=	RISER HEIGHT AT FRONT OF ROW N
P	=	PERCENT SLOPE

SIGHT LINES FOR SLIGHTLY SLOPED FLOOR—VERTICAL FOCAL PLANE
5.7

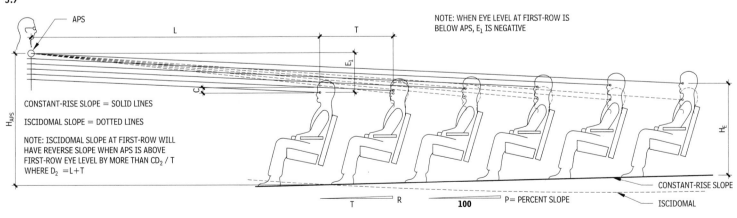

NOTE: WHEN EYE LEVEL AT FIRST-ROW IS BELOW APS, E_1 IS NEGATIVE

CONSTANT-RISE SLOPE = SOLID LINES

ISCIDOMAL SLOPE = DOTTED LINES

NOTE: ISCIDOMAL SLOPE AT FIRST-ROW WILL HAVE REVERSE SLOPE WHEN APS IS ABOVE FIRST-ROW EYE LEVEL BY MORE THAN CD_2 / T WHERE $D_2 = L+T$

CONSTANT-RISE SLOPE

ISCIDOMAL

P = PERCENT SLOPE

Contributor:
Peter H. Frink, Frink and Beuchat Architects, Philadelphia, Pennsylvania.

DETERMINING OPTIMUM VIEWING AREAS
5.8

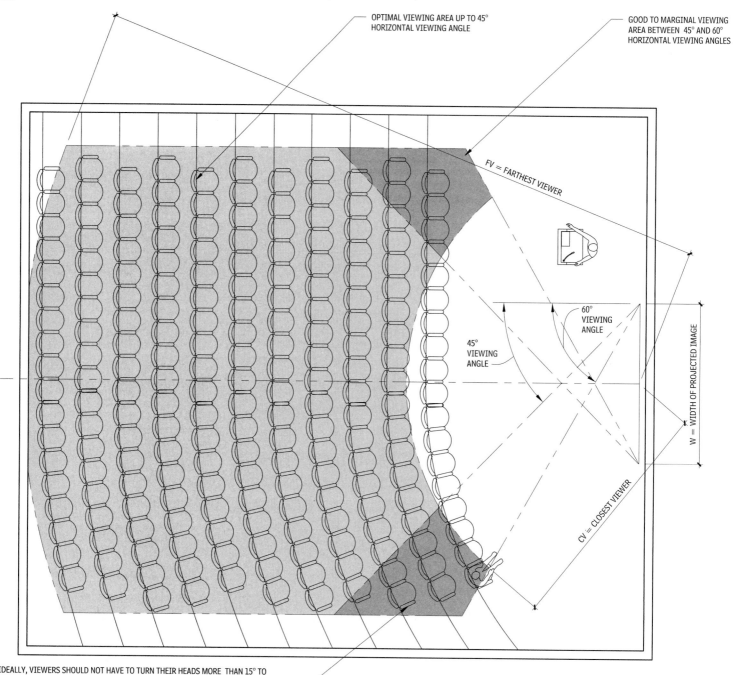

OPTIMAL VIEWING AREA UP TO 45°
HORIZONTAL VIEWING ANGLE

GOOD TO MARGINAL VIEWING
AREA BETWEEN 45° AND 60°
HORIZONTAL VIEWING ANGLES

FV = FARTHEST VIEWER

60°
VIEWING
ANGLE

45°
VIEWING
ANGLE

W = WIDTH OF PROJECTED IMAGE

CV = CLOSEST VIEWER

IDEALLY, VIEWERS SHOULD NOT HAVE TO TURN THEIR HEADS MORE THAN 15° TO
VIEW THE PROJECTED IMAGE. IN A WIDE ROOM, USE A MATTE WHITE SCREEN WITH
NO GRAIN AND SEATS THAT ARE ARRANGED IN CURVED ROWS TO ACHIEVE THIS GOAL.

OPTIMUM VIEWING AREA
5.9

	COMPUTER VIDEO	HDTV	STANDARD (NTSC) VIDEO	35MM SLIDES	16MM MOTION PICTURE FLIM	OVERHEAD TRANSPARENCIES
IMAGE ASPECT RATIO (W:H)	4:3	16:9	4:3	1:1.493	4:3	1:1
H	0.75 X W	0.5626 X W	0.75 X W	M	0.4255 X W	-
W	1.33 X H	1.78 X H	1.33 X H	-	2.35 X H	-
FV	≤ 4 X W	≤ 6 X H	≤ 8 - 10 X H	≤ 6 X H	≤ 4 X W	≤ 6 X H
CV	≥ 1.5-2 X W	≥ 1.5-2 X W	≥ 1.5-2 X W	≥ 1.5-2 X W	≥ 1.5-2 X W	≥ 1.5-2 X W

VIEWING ANGLES FOR A SINGLE FLAT SCREEN
5.10

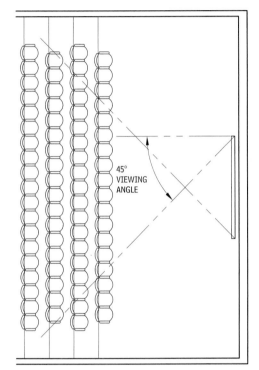

45° VIEWING ANGLE

VIEWING ANGLES FOR MULTIPLE SCREENS— PARALLEL ORIENTATION
5.11

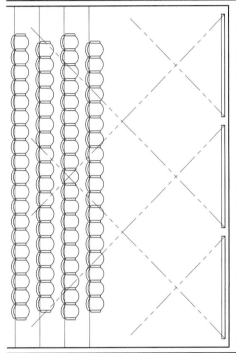

VIEWING FOR MULTIPLE SCREENS – ROTATED ORIENTATION
5.12

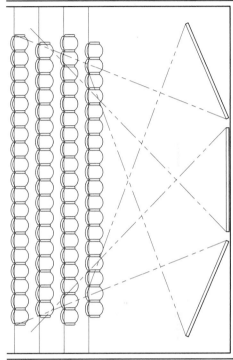

PROJECTION EQUIPMENT AND SCREENS

Single-lens LCD and digital light processing (DLP) video projectors offer some flexibility in placement. They may be placed at varying distances from the screen and be focused by adjustment of their lens, within the limits offered by the lenses available for the particular projector.

PROJECTION SCREENS

Rear projection screens or large-screen flat-panel displays (plasma or LCD) may be used for videoconferencing. When using a rear projection screen, it is possible to use brighter lights in the conference room during viewing than with a regular video monitor.

Front projection screens are not usually recommended for use in videoconferencing applications, as lighting levels in the room must be sufficient for the video camera to provide good video pickup, and the tendency for the higher light levels to wash out the image projected on the screen.

PROJECTORS AND DISPLAYS

Videoconference room rear projection systems employ video projectors and rear projection screens made of special material that provides uniform, high-brightness images. Usually, a mirror system is also employed, allowing the projector to be located closer to the rear screen and minimizing the space required behind the rear screen. Projectors employ either LCD or DLP technology and have a single lens.

Flat-panel displays (LCD or plasma) are used because they provide good brightness and resolution images and can easily be mounted in or on walls.

The choice of which display type to use is largely based on the size of the videoconference room and the distance between the display and the farthest viewer. Rear projection screens can be much larger than LCD or plasma displays and, therefore, can serve larger rooms. However, most videoconference rooms are small enough to be well served by LCD or plasma displays.

NOTES

5.10 Single flat screen provides poor viewing for front corner seats.
5.11 All projection screens are mounted parallel to front wall. This results in poor viewing for seats on the opposite side of the room from the screens.
5.12 Side projection screens are angled toward the audience. This results in improved viewing for people across the room from the screen.

Contributors:
Jeffery E. Bollinger and Jason Martinez, Acentech, Inc., Cambridge, Massachusetts; Cerami & Associates, Inc., New York City, New York.

MEDICAL EQUIPMENT

GENERAL ACUTE CARE

Patient rooms must be accessible, easy to maintain, and spacious enough to contain high-tech life-support and monitoring equipment. Entry doors should be a minimum of 48 in. wide. Wider openings are sometimes required to accommodate large equipment and surgical teams during emergency situations. A clear area of 48 in. should be maintained at the foot of patient beds.

Equip patient rooms with basic amenities such as a patient chair, visitor chair, television set (VCR and computer with Internet access, optional), wardrobe for full-length garments and luggage, drawers for clothing and personal items, and countertop or open shelving for flowers and cards. Patient rooms include toilet facilities with direct access, although central bathing areas may be provided in lieu of individual showers.

Doors to accessible toilet rooms must provide a clear opening of 32 in. minimum when opened 90°. If doors swing in, equip them with hardware that permits emergency access. Universal precautions require a lavatory in or near the entrance to each patient room for clinical use and a place to store gloves, masks, and gowns. Space for electronic equipment, such as a patient data terminal and printer, may be required.

Semiprivate patient rooms should contain cubicle curtains for visual privacy.

INTENSIVE CARE

Patients in an intensive care unit (ICU) are under continuous observation, therefore each room should be visible from the nurse station or a staffed corridor workstation, and unit must contain equipment for continuous monitoring. Provide a nurse call at each bed for summoning assistance.

Beds should be within view of an exterior window, preferably an operable window, although this is not required. If operable windows are provided, restrict degree of opening width to prevent escape or suicide attempts. Provide bedside space for visitors and a curtain for visual privacy.

Doors should be a minimum of 48 in. wide. Sliding doors may be used for access to rooms or cubicles within a suite.

Provide at least one private room or cubicle in each ICU for patients requiring isolation and/or separation.

Toilet units can be provided in each bed area, along with a sink, countertop for preparing medications, and universal precautions storage. IV tracks and exam lights are typically placed above each bed. Because of the illness acuity of these patients, rolling life-support equipment often occupies space at the side and foot of the bed. Maintain a minimum of 48 in. on three sides of each bed. Utility columns containing power outlets and medical gas and communications devices allow 360° access around the patient.

FINISHES AND HEADWALLS

Finishes in patient rooms should be durable and easy to maintain; resilient flooring, wallcoverings or painted gypsum board partitions, and so on, are typically used. Epoxy paint is sometimes used at wet or medication preparation areas. Some hospitals provide less institutional patient rooms with carpeted floors and other homelike finishes, to reduce stress by helping patients feel more comfortable during their stay. Consult local codes for restrictions on finishes in patient rooms.

Depending on the room type, bed headwalls may include a nurse call button; reading light; room light switches; television controls; electrical outlets; central monitoring capabilities; and suction, vacuum, and various medical gas outlets. Headwalls are available as prefabricated units or can be built into the partition with accessible cabinetwork, to render the devices less threatening. Wall thicknesses may vary depending on the type of equipment used.

Consult applicable codes, standards, and regulations for accessibility requirements.

PRIVATE PATIENT ROOM
5.13

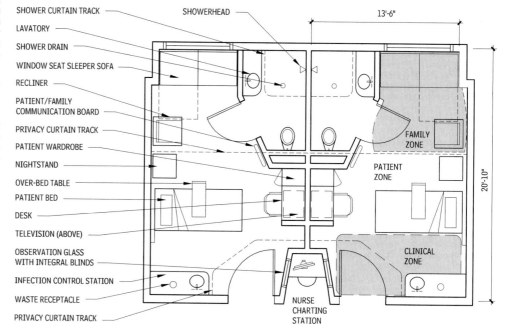

SHOWER CURTAIN TRACK
LAVATORY
SHOWER DRAIN
WINDOW SEAT SLEEPER SOFA
RECLINER
PATIENT/FAMILY COMMUNICATION BOARD
PRIVACY CURTAIN TRACK
PATIENT WARDROBE
NIGHTSTAND
OVER-BED TABLE
PATIENT BED
DESK
TELEVISION (ABOVE)
OBSERVATION GLASS WITH INTEGRAL BLINDS
INFECTION CONTROL STATION
WASTE RECEPTACLE
PRIVACY CURTAIN TRACK

SHOWERHEAD
13'-6"
FAMILY ZONE
PATIENT ZONE
CLINICAL ZONE
20'-10"
NURSE CHARTING STATION

Contributors:
Don Tapert, Tapert Architecture, New York City, New York; Timothy J. Cowan, Burt Hill Kosar Rittelmann Associates, Pittsburg, Pennsylvania.

SEMI-PRIVATE ROOM
5.14

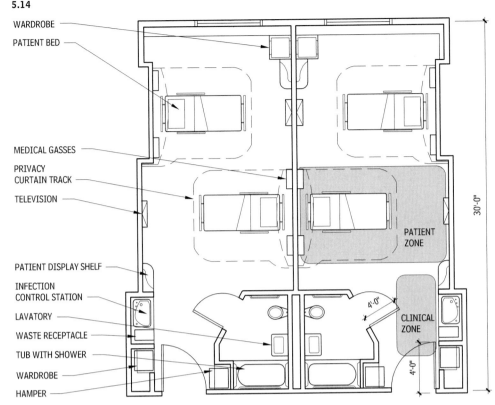

WARDROBE
PATIENT BED
MEDICAL GASSES
PRIVACY CURTAIN TRACK
TELEVISION
PATIENT DISPLAY SHELF
INFECTION CONTROL STATION
LAVATORY
WASTE RECEPTACLE
TUB WITH SHOWER
WARDROBE
HAMPER

PATIENT ZONE
CLINICAL ZONE
30'-0"
4'-0"
4'-0"

INTENSIVE CARE ROOM
5.15

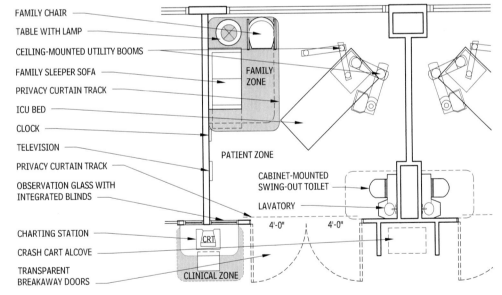

FAMILY CHAIR
TABLE WITH LAMP
CEILING-MOUNTED UTILITY BOOMS
FAMILY SLEEPER SOFA
PRIVACY CURTAIN TRACK
ICU BED
CLOCK
TELEVISION
PRIVACY CURTAIN TRACK
OBSERVATION GLASS WITH INTEGRATED BLINDS
CHARTING STATION
CRASH CART ALCOVE
TRANSPARENT BREAKAWAY DOORS

FAMILY ZONE
PATIENT ZONE
CABINET-MOUNTED SWING-OUT TOILET
LAVATORY
CRT
CLINICAL ZONE
4'-0"
4'-0"

EXAMINATION AND TREATMENT ROOMS

EXAM ROOMS

General-purpose exam rooms comprise the building blocks of out-patient facility design. Room configuration varies, but the minimum room dimension is generally 8 ft. The size for exam rooms needs to be a minimum of 80 sq. ft., but 110 sq ft is recommended. Typically, medical providers work from the patient's right side (see Figure 5.16); therefore, rooms should be planned to permit this. In pediatric facilities, the exam table is often located with the patient's left against the wall, to increase safety. In women's health facilities, the table is positioned to face away from the room entrance door. Often, cubicle curtains are included to screen the patient from the corridor when the door is opened.

AMBULATORY CARE EXAMINATION ROOM
5.16

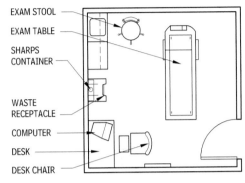

EXAM STOOL
EXAM TABLE
SHARPS CONTAINER
WASTE RECEPTACLE
COMPUTER
DESK
DESK CHAIR

DIALYSIS MODULES

Outpatient dialysis facilities generally include open treatment positions. In Figure 5.17, a reclining chair is positioned against a service wall in an arrangement where privacy is achieved through a cubicle curtain arrangement. A minimum of 80 sq ft is required for each treatment station, and 145 sq ft is recommended with an aisle between stations.

Space requirements for chemotherapy/oncology patients are similar. Often, the cubicle curtain is replaced by a fixed screen or partition to increase privacy.

DIALYSIS MODULE
5.17

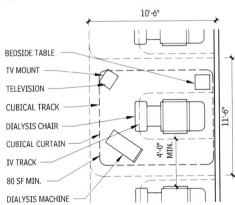

BEDSIDE TABLE
TV MOUNT
TELEVISION
CUBICAL TRACK
DIALYSIS CHAIR
CUBICAL CURTAIN
IV TRACK
80 SF MIN.
DIALYSIS MACHINE

10'-6"
11'-6"
4'-0" MIN.

Contributors:
WHR Architects, Houston, Texas; Timothy J. Cowan, Burt Hill Kosar
Rittelmann Associates, Pittsburg, Pennsylvania.

VEHICULAR EQUIPMENT

LOADING DOCK EQUIPMENT

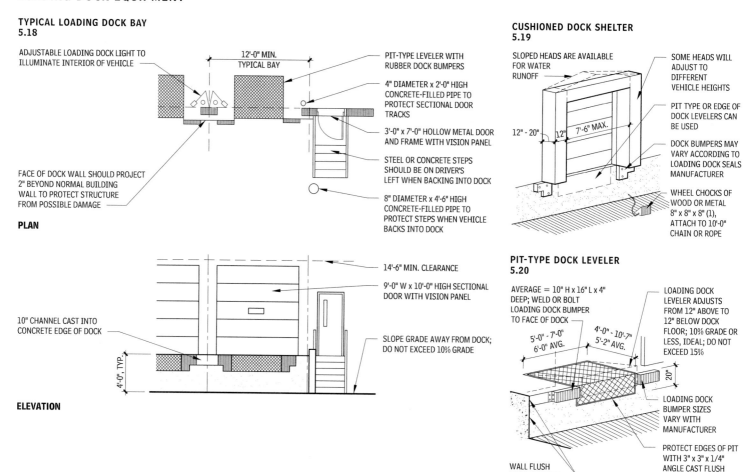

TYPICAL LOADING DOCK BAY
5.18

ADJUSTABLE LOADING DOCK LIGHT TO ILLUMINATE INTERIOR OF VEHICLE

12'-0" MIN. TYPICAL BAY

FACE OF DOCK WALL SHOULD PROJECT 2" BEYOND NORMAL BUILDING WALL TO PROTECT STRUCTURE FROM POSSIBLE DAMAGE

PLAN

PIT-TYPE LEVELER WITH RUBBER DOCK BUMPERS

4" DIAMETER x 2'-0" HIGH CONCRETE-FILLED PIPE TO PROTECT SECTIONAL DOOR TRACKS

3'-0" x 7'-0" HOLLOW METAL DOOR AND FRAME WITH VISION PANEL

STEEL OR CONCRETE STEPS SHOULD BE ON DRIVER'S LEFT WHEN BACKING INTO DOCK

8" DIAMETER x 4'-6" HIGH CONCRETE-FILLED PIPE TO PROTECT STEPS WHEN VEHICLE BACKS INTO DOCK

10" CHANNEL CAST INTO CONCRETE EDGE OF DOCK

4'-0", TYP.

ELEVATION

14'-6" MIN. CLEARANCE

9'-0" W x 10'-0" HIGH SECTIONAL DOOR WITH VISION PANEL

SLOPE GRADE AWAY FROM DOCK; DO NOT EXCEED 10% GRADE

CUSHIONED DOCK SHELTER
5.19

SLOPED HEADS ARE AVAILABLE FOR WATER RUNOFF

SOME HEADS WILL ADJUST TO DIFFERENT VEHICLE HEIGHTS

PIT TYPE OR EDGE OF DOCK LEVELERS CAN BE USED

DOCK BUMPERS MAY VARY ACCORDING TO LOADING DOCK SEALS MANUFACTURER

WHEEL CHOCKS OF WOOD OR METAL 8" x 8" x 8" (1), ATTACH TO 10'-0" CHAIN OR ROPE

12" - 20"   12"   7'-6" MAX.

PIT-TYPE DOCK LEVELER
5.20

AVERAGE = 10" H x 16" L x 4" DEEP; WELD OR BOLT LOADING DOCK BUMPER TO FACE OF DOCK

LOADING DOCK LEVELER ADJUSTS FROM 12" ABOVE TO 12" BELOW DOCK FLOOR; 10% GRADE OR LESS, IDEAL; DO NOT EXCEED 15%

5'-0" - 7'-0"   4'-0" - 10'-7"
6'-0" AVG.   5'-2" AVG.

20"

LOADING DOCK BUMPER SIZES VARY WITH MANUFACTURER

PROTECT EDGES OF PIT WITH 3" x 3" x 1/4" ANGLE CAST FLUSH INTO CONCRETE

WALL FLUSH WITH CHANNEL

NOTES

5.18 Dock height will vary dependent on trucks that will utilize the facility.
5.19 a. A cushioned dock shelter provides a positive weather seal; protects the dock from wind, rain, snow, and dirt. It also retains a constant temperature between dock and vehicle.
b. Many different types of dock shelters are available.
5.20 a. Dock levelers may be automatic or manually operated, where incoming vehicle heights vary widely.
b. Recessed levelers must be installed in a concrete pit.
c. Levelers vary by manufacturer, contact manufacturer for available dimensions and capacity.

Contributors:
Larsen Shein Ginsberg Snyder, New York City, New York; Robert H. Lorenz, AIA, Preston Trucking Company, Inc., Preston, Maryland.

OTHER EQUIPMENT

COMMERCIAL FOOD SERVICE EQUIPMENT

COMMERCIAL KITCHEN PLAN
5.21

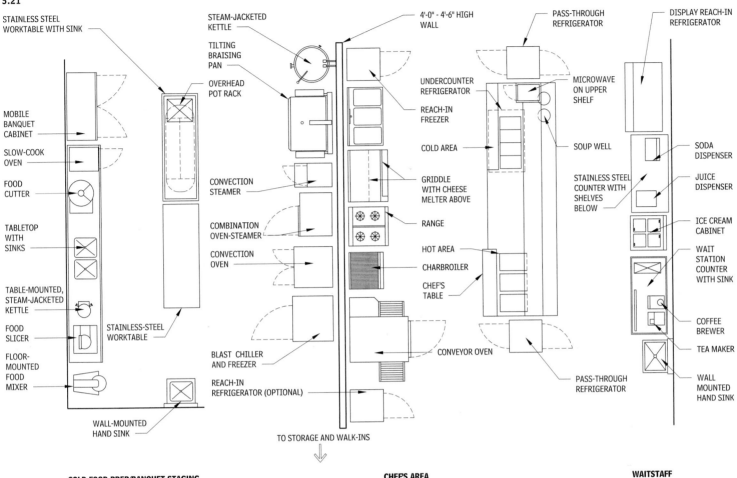

TO STORAGE AND WALK-INS

COLD FOOD PREP/BANQUET STAGING

CHEF'S AREA

WAITSTAFF

COUNTER WITH SNEEZE GUARD
5.22

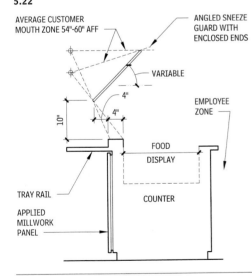

GAUGE AND USE OF GALVANIZED STEEL
5.23

GAUGE	RECOMMENDED USE
12	Support channels and bracing
14	Undershelves and partitions (optional)
16	Undershelves and side panels (optional)
18	Utensil drawers, hoods, body panels, interior partitions (optional)

GAUGE AND USE OF STAINLESS STEEL
5.24

GAUGE	TYPICAL USE
8 and 10	Support elements for heavy equipment or at stress points
12	Heavily used tabletops, pot sinks, or other surfaces that will receive a great amount of wear
14	Tabletops, sinks, shelves, and brackets that will be used frequently or that will hold heavy objects
16	Small equipment tops and sides that will carry light objects; shelves under equipment and heavily used side panels
18	Side panels that are not exposed to much wear and equipment doors, hoods, and partitions
20	Covers for supported or insulated panels, such as refrigerators or insulated doors

Contributors:
Tim Shea, AIA, Richard Meier & Partners, Los Angeles, California; Ji-Seong Yun, Rhode Island School of Design, Providence, Rhode Island; Jim Johnson, Wrightson, Johnson, Haddon & Williams, Inc., Dallas, Texas; Janet B. Rankin, AIA, Rippeteau Architects, PC, Washington, DC; Cini-Little International, Inc., Food Service Consultants, Washington, DC; Henry Grossbard & Cody Hicks, Post & Grossbard, Inc., Piermont, New York; John Birchfield, Birchfield Food Systems, Inc., Annapolis, Maryland.

FABRICATED WORKTABLE
5.25

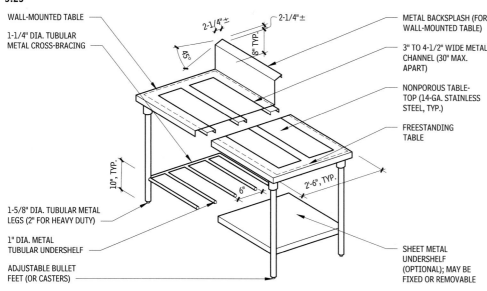

Tubular metal pieces should be welded, coved together, and sanded smooth. A layer of cork-based sound-deadening material may be applied to the underside of tabletops and finished with aluminum lacquer. Consult health codes for types of lacquer permitted.

FABRICATED SINK
5.26

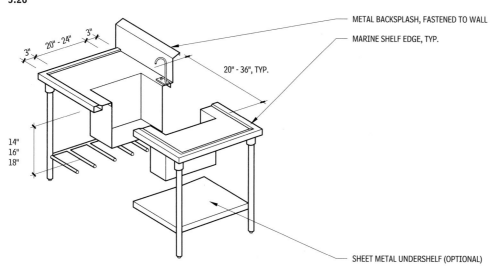

WORKTABLE EDGE PROFILES
5.27

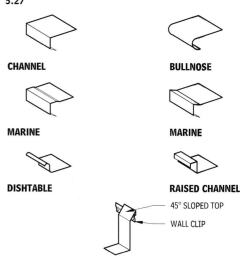

CHANNEL   BULLNOSE

MARINE   MARINE

DISHTABLE   RAISED CHANNEL

45° SLOPED TOP
WALL CLIP

DISH TABLE BACKSPLASH

- A *conveyor oven* moves food through a heated cavity at a pre-determined speed, ensuring even cooking time and allowing high-volume production. Heating, which is by convection or radiant heat, is on one or both sides of the belt. Pizzas, cookies, hamburgers, and seafood can by cooked using this method.
- *Combination oven-steamers*, shorthanded as *combi*, blend a convection oven with a steamer in one piece of equipment. It is popular because of its versatility.
- *Slow-cook ovens*, which are primarily used to roast meats, can also be used to warm hot foods and proof bread or dough. Designed to cook at 200°F to 240°F, these ovens reduce shrinkage of roast meats up to 40 percent—and save energy.

RESIDENTIAL EQUIPMENT

This section discusses equipment commonly used in residences, in particular, kitchens and laundry rooms.

KITCHENS
An ideal home kitchen design depends on a number of factors but, in particular, the living habits and possessions of the kitchen users. A design that is considered excellent for one user may be unsuitable for another.

The major components of a well-planned kitchen are traffic and workflow; cabinets and storage; appliance placement and use/clearance space; counter surface and landing space; and room, appliance, and equipment controls.

KITCHEN DESIGN CONSIDERATIONS
Important design guidelines for working with residential kitchens include that:

- No entry door, appliance door, or cabinet door should interfere with another door.
- All major appliances used for surface cooking should have a ventilation system, with a fan rated at 150 CFM minimum.
- No two primary work centers (the primary sink, refrigerator, preparation, or cooktop/range center) should be separated by a full-height, full-depth tall cabinet (measured from floor to top of wall cabinets).
- Work aisles (passages between vertical objects, both of which are work counters or appliances) should be at least 42 in. wide in one-cook kitchens, and at least 48 in. wide in multiple-cook kitchens.
- Open countertop corners should be clipped or radiused, and countertop edges should be eased to eliminate sharp edges.
- Controls, handles, and door/drawer pulls should be operable with one hand; they require only a minimal amount of strength for operation, without tight grasping, pinching, or twisting of the wrist.

FOOD PREPARATION EQUIPMENT
A food cutter, also called a "buffalo chopper," is used for chopping meats and vegetables. It is similar in function to a food processor. A larger type is a vertical cutter mixer (VCM), with a capacity of 30 to 45 quarts.

Food mixers are used to mix/process large quantities of food, especially if a variety of attachments are required.

COOKING EQUIPMENT
Nine types of cooking equipment are briefly described here.

- *Fryers* cook food when it is immersed in the hot fat they contain. Powered by either gas or electricity, fryers can be freestanding, table mounted, modular (electric only), or drop-in (electric only). Typical capacities range from 15 to 75 lb of shortening or fat. Two modular units with a filter dump station between them is a common fryer configuration.
- *Griddles*, also called *grills*, have a flat, heated surface that cooks food quickly. They can be freestanding units, part of a range,

table models, or part of a modular unit, and are either gas or electric powered.

- The *range* is often the most heavily used piece of equipment in a food service facility. Cooks prefer open-top gas ranges, especially for sautéing because the flame is visible and easy to adjust. However, electric models are also available.
- A *charbroiler* cooks food rapidly, one side at a time, usually with radiant heat produced by gas or electricity. There are many types: freestanding top-burner broilers, charbroilers, salamanders (small above-the-range broilers for last-minute browning), conveyor broilers, and rotisseries.
- A *tilting braising pan*, also called a *tilting skillet* or *tilting frying pan*, is used for grilling, steaming, braising, sautéing, or stewing a large volume of food, typically 20 to 40 gallons. The pan tilts down so that liquids can be poured off; this also aids in cleaning.
- *Convection steamers*, low-pressure (5 lb per sq in.) and no-pressure versions, efficiently prepare vegetables, seafood, eggs, rice, and pasta. Steamers are typically powered by gas, electricity, direct steam, or a steam coil.

NOTE

5.27 Channel edges and bullnose edges are used only when water will not be spilled on the table surface.

Contributors:
John Birchfield, Birchfield Foodsystems, Inc., Annapolis, Maryland; Henry Grossbard & Cody Hicks, Post & Grossbard, Inc., Piermont, New York.

- Ground fault circuit interrupters should be specified on all receptacles in a kitchen.
- A fire extinguisher should be visibly located in the kitchen, away from cooking equipment and 15 to 48 in. above the floor; smoke alarms should be included near the kitchen.
- The window/skylight area should equal at least 10 percent of the total square footage of a separate kitchen or of a total living space that includes a kitchen.
- Every work surface in a kitchen should be well lit by appropriate task and/or general lighting.

REFRIGERATOR WORK AREA
5.28

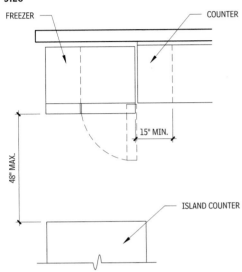

PLAN

In an enclosed configuration, allow a minimum at least a 3-in. clearance from the side wall, with flame-retardant surfacing material. The cooking surface and the adjacent counter area should be the same height.

A measurement of 24 in. minimum from the adjacent counter to the centerline of the sink makes possible a clear floor space of 30 by 48 in. centered on the sink. If the kitchen has only one sink, it should be located between or across from the cooking surface, preparation area, or refrigerator.

CENTERS OF ACTIVITY

Although the kitchen has evolved around three basic appliances—the sink, the range, and the refrigerator—a kitchen usually has many more centers of activity. Other considerations are primary and secondary cleanup sinks, preparation centers, cooking centers, microwave oven centers, pantry centers, a serving centers, dining areas, laundry areas, home office centers, or a media centers.

- A primary cleanup sink center houses a recycling center, dishwasher, and food waste disposer.
- The secondary sink center may serve cleanup functions as well, but is generally associated with a food preparation center.
- A preparation center is a long, uninterrupted counter that may be placed between the sink and the cooking surface or the sink and the refrigerator. In a kitchen for multiple cooks, there will be more than one preparation area.
- A cooking center revolves around the cooking surface. A separate built-in oven need not be a part of this center unless it includes a microwave oven.
- A microwave oven should be located close to the major areas of activity because of frequency of use.
- A pantry center for storing foodstuffs, including storage cabinetry from floor to soffit or floor to ceiling, should be located near the preparation area.

SURFACE COOKING WORK AREA
5.29

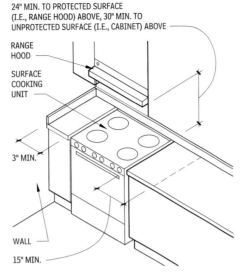

SURFACE COOKING AT ENCLOSED CONFIGURATION

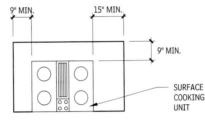

SURFACE COOKING AT OPEN (ISLAND) CONFIGURATION

KITCHEN LAYOUTS

Kitchen layouts may be customized to suit the needs of each user; thus, endless variations are possible.

- The U-shaped kitchen is usually considered the most efficient plan. In it, steps are saved because the cook is surrounded on three sides with a continuous countertop and storage system. Traffic is also naturally directed around the work area.
- The L-shaped kitchen with work centers on two adjacent walls forms a natural triangle that allows traffic to pass by the work area. The L shape gives the cook a generous amount of continuous counter space. If an L shape is combined with a freestanding central structure, all of the benefits of a U-shaped kitchen are available, with a more open, free-flowing plan. The island invites interaction between the cook and visitors and helpers because more than one person can work around this open counter.
- A corridor kitchen offers one cook the advantage of an efficient, close grouping of work centers on parallel walls. Disadvantages are that household traffic may cross back and forth through the area and that the shape is typically too small for two cooks. The single-wall kitchen type is only acceptable in small apartments or efficiency units.

SINK WORK AREA
5.30

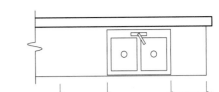

LINEAR COUNTER FRONTAGE

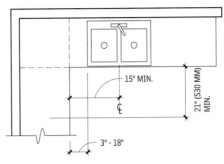

SINK ADJACENT TO CORNER

PREPARATION CENTER
5.31

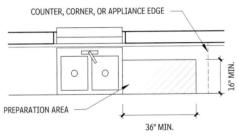

PREPARATION AREA--ONE PERSON

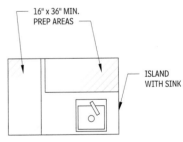

PREPARATION AREA--TWO PERSONS

NOTE

5.31 The preparation area should be immediately adjacent to a sink.

Contributors:
J. T. Devine, AIA, and Robert E. Anderson, AIA, Santa Rosa, California; National Kitchen and Bath Association, Hackettstown, New Jersey.

COMMON KITCHEN LAYOUTS
5.32

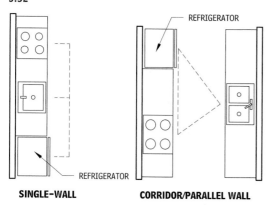

SINGLE-WALL   **CORRIDOR/PARALLEL WALL**   **L-SHAPED**

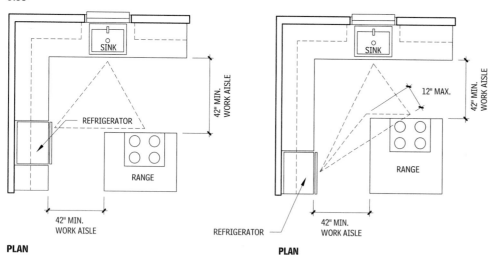

U-SHAPED   **L-SHAPED WITH ISLAND**

KITCHEN WORK TRIANGLE

The work triangle is the shortest walking distance between the refrigerator, primary food prep sink, and primary cooking surface, and is measured from the center front of each. Walkways and traffic patterns should not interfere with the primary work triangle, and cabinetry should not intersect any one triangle leg by more than 12 in. Each leg of a triangle length should be between 4 and 9 ft, and the total sum of the three legs should equal less than 26 ft.

WORK TRIANGLE—ONE COOK
5.33

PLAN   **PLAN**

WORK TRIANGLE—TWO COOKS
5.34

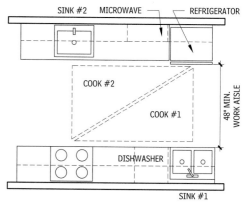

PLAN

If two or more people cook simultaneously, a work triangle should be placed for each cook. One leg of the primary and secondary triangles may be shared, but the two should not cross one another. Appliances may be shared or separate.

TRAFFIC FLOW ADJACENT TO WORK TRIANGLE
5.35

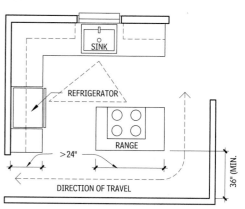

Walkways are passages between vertical objects that are greater than 24 in. deep in the direction of travel, of which not more than one is a work counter or appliance. Walkways should be at least 36 in. wide and should not cross through the work triangle.

RESIDENTIAL KITCHEN EQUIPMENT

RANGES, OVENS, COOKTOPS, AND VENT HOODS

Residential kitchen equipment dimensions and features vary for these items; consult manufacturers for specific features and dimensions.

Ranges are available in electric and gas models. Smooth-surface electric cooktops have radiant and halogen heating elements or an induction coil below a glass-ceramic top.

Radiant-heating elements (below surface or surface units, plug-in, coil, or solid plate) provide heat directly from resistance elements. Halogen-type elements usually combine radiant elements with a halogen light source, which allows the element to heat up faster than a radiant element alone. Other range options include griddles and charbroilers. Induction elements consist of a high-frequency induction coil beneath a glass-ceramic surface. Metal cooking utensils are heated by magnetic friction without directly heating the cooktop surface. Induction elements are considered energy-efficient.

Ovens are available in gas or electric, either as conventional, combination radiant/convection, or microwave models. Convection ovens

Contributors:
National Kitchen and Bath Association, Hackettstown, New Jersey;
Richard J. Vitullo, AIA, Oak Leaf Studio, Crownsville, Maryland.

UTILITY CONNECTION BOX (RECESSED)
5.50

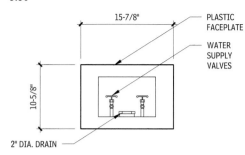

15-7/8"

PLASTIC
FACEPLATE

WATER
SUPPLY
VALVES

10-5/8"

2" DIA. DRAIN

ELEVATION

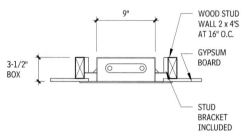

9"

3-1/2"
BOX

WOOD STUD
WALL 2 x 4'S
AT 16" O.C.

GYPSUM
BOARD

STUD
BRACKET
INCLUDED

PLAN

STACKED WASHER-DRYER COMBINATION
5.51

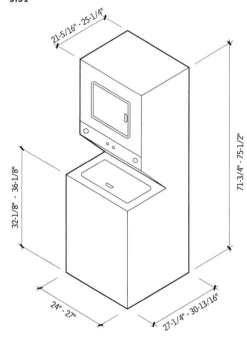

21-5/16" - 25-1/4"

71-3/4" - 75-1/2"

32-1/8" - 36-1/8"

24" - 27"

27-1/4" - 30-13/16"

FREESTANDING TOP-LOADING WASHER
5.52

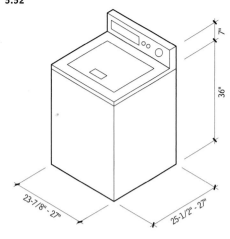

7"

36"

23-7/8" - 27"

25-1/2" - 27"

FRONT-LOADING DRYERS
5.53

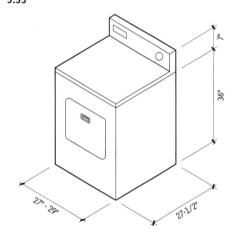

7"

36"

27" - 29"

27-1/2"

ATHLETIC EQUIPMENT

ARENA FOOTBALL GOALPOST AND REBOUND NET
5.54

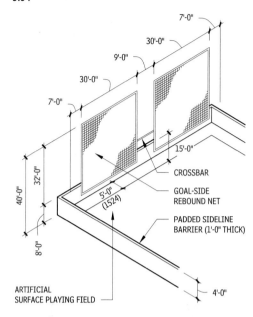

7'-0"

30'-0"

9'-0"

30'-0"

7'-0"

15'-0"

32'-0"

40'-0"

5'-0"
(1524)

8'-0"

CROSSBAR

GOAL-SIDE
REBOUND NET

PADDED SIDELINE
BARRIER (1'-0" THICK)

4'-0"

ARTIFICIAL
SURFACE PLAYING FIELD

BASKETBALL

The equipment illustrated in Figures 5.55–5.58 includes common forms of hydraulic goals and backboards.

Electronic scoreboard equipment is available in a wide range of sizes and configurations. For more information and the names of manufacturers, conduct an Internet keyword search on "athletic scoreboard equipment."

Contributors:
R. E. Powe, Jr., AIA, and Robin Andrew Roberts, AIA, Washington, DC; Arthur J. Pettorino, AIA, Hicksville, New York; Hugh Newell Jacobsen, FAIA, Washington, DC; Richard J. Vitullo, AIA, Oak Leaf Studio, Crownsville, Maryland; Dean Cox, AIA, Collins, Rimer, Gordon Architects, Cleveland, Ohio.

PORTABLE GOAL
5.55

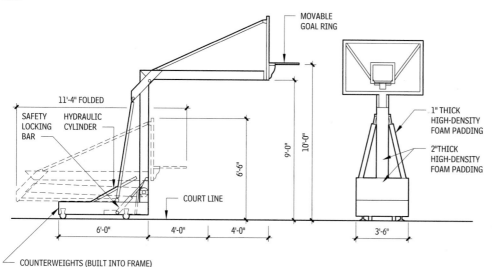

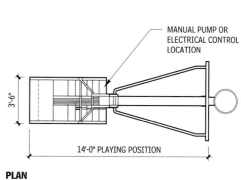

MOVABLE GOAL RING

MANUAL PUMP OR ELECTRICAL CONTROL LOCATION

11'-4" FOLDED

SAFETY LOCKING BAR

HYDRAULIC CYLINDER

9'-0"

10'-0"

6'-6"

COURT LINE

1" THICK HIGH-DENSITY FOAM PADDING

2"THICK HIGH-DENSITY FOAM PADDING

3'-6"

6'-0"   4'-0"   4'-0"

3'-6"

14'-0" PLAYING POSITION

PLAN

COUNTERWEIGHTS (BUILT INTO FRAME)

ELEVATION

BASKETBALL COURT DIMENSIONS
5.56

COURT	LENGTH (FT)	WIDTH (FT)	THREE-POINT LINE RADIUS (FT-IN.)
NBA	94	50	23-9
International	94	50	20-7
NCAA (men)	94	50	19-9
WNBA, NCAA (women)	94	50	19-9
High school (women)	84	50	19-9
High school (men)	84	50	19-9

BACKBOARD
5.57

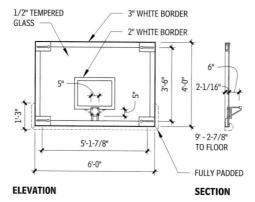

1/2" TEMPERED GLASS

3" WHITE BORDER

2" WHITE BORDER

5"

5"

3'-6"

4'-0"

1'-3"

5'-1-7/8"

6'-0"

ELEVATION

6"

2-1/16"

9' - 2-7/8" TO FLOOR

FULLY PADDED

SECTION

PORTABLE BASKETBALL RACKS
5.58

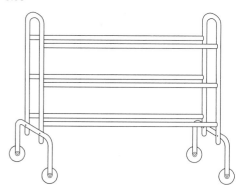

NUMBER OF BASKETBALLS	NUMBER OF TIERS	WIDTH (IN.)	DEPTH (IN.)	HEIGHT (IN.)
12	3	41	14	39-3/4
16	4	41	14	51-3/4
30	3	45	24	33

FURNISHINGS

FIXED FURNISHINGS

FIXED CASEWORK

This section examines custom millwork standards and the details of cabinet construction.

SHOP-FABRICATED CABINETS

WALL-HUNG AND BASE CABINETS
5.59

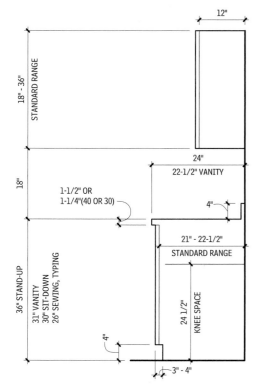

ACCESSIBLE WALL-HUNG AND BASE CABINETS
5.60

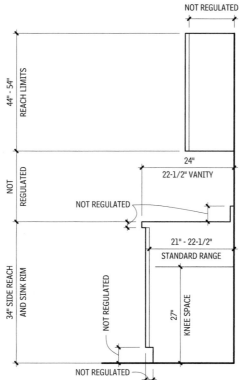

KNEE AND TOE CLEARANCES
5.61

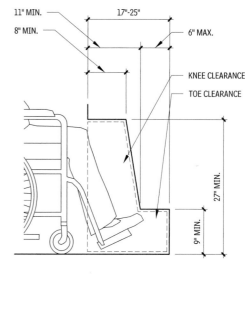

BARS AND COUNTERS
5.62

LOW COUNTER DIMENSIONS

A = 4'-11" TO 5'-6"
B = 3'-1" TO 3'-3"
C = 1'-10" TO 2'-0"
D = 17" TO 25"
E = 1'-6" TO 2'-0"
F = 2'-4" TO 2'-8"
G = 2'-3" MIN.
H = 4" - 8"

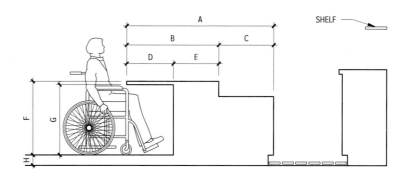

CABINET DETAILS

The Architectural Woodwork Institute (AWI) Quality Standards classify architectural cabinets in three categories: premium, custom, and economy. The materials, joinery, and finish quality are delineated for casework shops to follow.

- Premium is the highest grade, with close tolerances reserved for only the finest cabinets.
- Custom-grade cabinets, the most common, are made from very good materials with durable joinery.
- Economy-grade cabinets are used for utilitarian and inexpensive residential cabinets.

The AWI Quality Standards further classify cabinet parts as exposed, semiexposed, and concealed, and specify a minimum grade for each. The finish to be used is specified as paint grade or stain grade, or whether plastic laminate or other material will be used.

To prevent movement caused by wood shrinkage, use only kiln-dried solid lumber or panel product for base supports.

Contributors:
Kelsey Kruse, AIA, George Vaeth Associates, Inc., Columbia, Maryland;
Architectural Woodwork Institute, Reston, Virginia.

TYPICAL CABINET ELEVATION
5.63

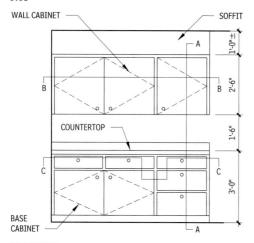

ELEVATION

FLUSH OVERLAY CONSTRUCTION—VERTICAL SECTION A-A
5.64

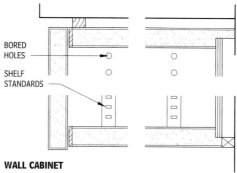

WALL CABINET

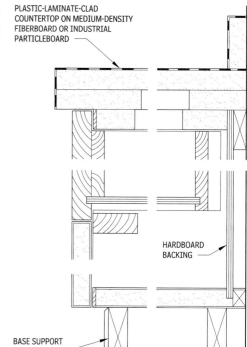

PLASTIC-LAMINATE-CLAD COUNTERTOP ON MEDIUM-DENSITY FIBERBOARD OR INDUSTRIAL PARTICLEBOARD

HARDBOARD BACKING

BASE SUPPORT BLOCKING

BASE CABINET

FLUSH OVERLAY CONSTRUCTION

Flush overlay construction offers a clean, contemporary design because only the doors and drawer fronts are visible in elevation. The grain between doors and drawer fronts can be matched by cutting all pieces from the same panel. This cabinet style lends itself well to the use of plastic laminate for exposed surfaces. Conventional and concealed hinges are available for a variety of door thickness. Door and drawer joinery and materials may vary from the selection shown in the details.

FLUSH OVERLAY CONSTRUCTION—HORIZONTAL SECTIONS
5.65

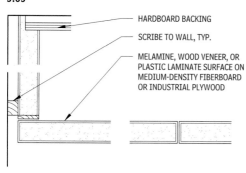

HARDBOARD BACKING

SCRIBE TO WALL, TYP.

MELAMINE, WOOD VENEER, OR PLASTIC LAMINATE SURFACE ON MEDIUM-DENSITY FIBERBOARD OR INDUSTRIAL PLYWOOD

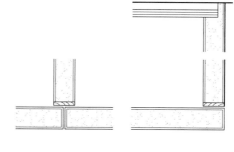

WALL CABINET - SECTION B-B

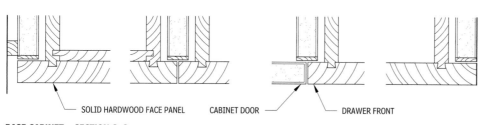

SOLID HARDWOOD FACE PANEL   CABINET DOOR   DRAWER FRONT

BASE CABINET - SECTION C-C

Contributor:
Greg Heuer, Architectural Woodwork Institute, Reston, Virginia.

REVEAL OVERLAY CONSTRUCTION

In this style of cabinet construction, the separation between doors and drawer fronts is accented by the reveal. The style is suited equally to either wood or plastic laminate construction. Figure 5.63 indicates a reveal at vertical and horizontal joints, but the designer may vary this arrangement.

A reveal wider than 1/2 in. requires the addition of a face frame, which would change the hinge requirements. With or without a face frame, this style allows the use of conventional or concealed hinges. Door/drawer joinery and materials may vary from selections shown in Figure 5.66.

FLUSH INSET CONSTRUCTION WITHOUT FACE FRAME

In this style of construction, all door and drawer faces are flush with the face of the cabinet. This style allows the use of door and drawer fronts with different thicknesses.

Conventional as well as concealed hinges are available for a variety of door thicknesses. The material chosen for the case, doors, and drawers influences the choice of hinges. In general, avoid conventional butt hinges when hinge screws would be attached to the edge grain of panel products.

Flush inset construction without any face frame is generally an expensive style because increased care is necessary to fit and align the doors and drawers. The design features of this casework style are the same as for conventional flush construction with face frame, except that, here, the face frame has been eliminated.

This style does not lend itself to the economical use of plastic laminate covering finishes. Door/drawer joinery and materials may vary from Figure 5.67.

REVEAL OVERLAY CONSTRUCTION—HORIZONTAL SECTIONS
5.66

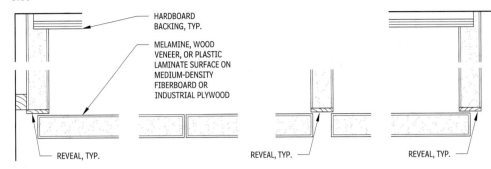

HARDBOARD BACKING, TYP.

MELAMINE, WOOD VENEER, OR PLASTIC LAMINATE SURFACE ON MEDIUM-DENSITY FIBERBOARD OR INDUSTRIAL PLYWOOD

REVEAL, TYP.

REVEAL, TYP.

REVEAL, TYP.

WALL CABINET SECTION B-B

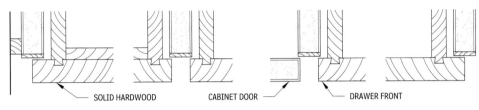

SOLID HARDWOOD

CABINET DOOR

DRAWER FRONT

BASE CABINET SECTION C-C

FLUSH INSET CONSTRUCTION WITHOUT FACE FRAME—HORIZONTAL SECTIONS
5.67

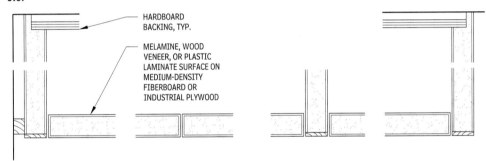

HARDBOARD BACKING, TYP.

MELAMINE, WOOD VENEER, OR PLASTIC LAMINATE SURFACE ON MEDIUM-DENSITY FIBERBOARD OR INDUSTRIAL PLYWOOD

WALL CABINET – SECTION A-A

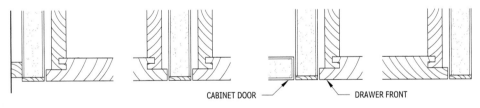

CABINET DOOR

DRAWER FRONT

BASE CABINET – SECTION B-B

Contributor:
Greg Heuer, Architectural Woodwork Institute, Reston, Virginia.

FLUSH INSET CONSTRUCTION WITH FACE FRAME

In this style of construction, all door and drawer faces are flush with the face of the cabinet. This style allows the use of different thicknesses for door and drawer fronts.

Conventional as well as concealed hinges are available for a variety of door thicknesses. The hinges chosen depend on the case and door/drawer material. In general, avoid conventional butt hinges when hinge screws would be attached to the edge-grain of panel products.

Flush inset construction with face frame is generally the most expensive cabinet door style because, in addition to the cost of providing the face frame, there is the cost of the increased care needed to fit and align the doors and drawers.

This style does not lend itself well to the economical use of plastic laminate surfaces. Door/drawer joinery and materials may vary from Figure 5.68.

CABINET HINGES AND CATCHES

Self-closing hinges spring-close the cabinet door when it is within 28° of being closed. When it is opened beyond 30°, the self-closer does not function, allowing the door to be left open. The self-closing feature eliminates the need for catches. Butt hinges are the only listed hinges not available with the self-closing feature.

FLUSH INSET CONSTRUCTION WITH FACE FRAME—HORIZONTAL SECTIONS
5.68

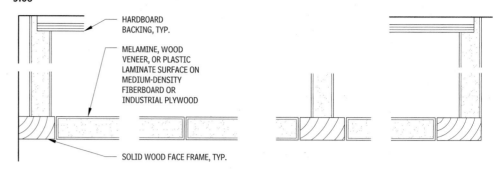

- HARDBOARD BACKING, TYP.
- MELAMINE, WOOD VENEER, OR PLASTIC LAMINATE SURFACE ON MEDIUM-DENSITY FIBERBOARD OR INDUSTRIAL PLYWOOD
- SOLID WOOD FACE FRAME, TYP.

WALL CABINET SECTION B-B

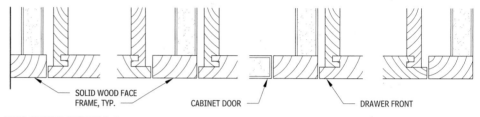

- SOLID WOOD FACE FRAME, TYP.
- CABINET DOOR
- DRAWER FRONT

BASE CABINET SECTION C-C

CABINET HINGES
5.69

	BUTT	WRAPAROUND	PIVOT (KNIFE)	EUROPEAN (CONCEALED)	FACE-MOUNT
Hinge type					
Elevation of cabinet face					
Door swing	180°	180°	180°	95°, 125°, OR 170°	180°
Easily adjusted after installation	No	No	No	Yes	Yes
Strength	High	Very high	Moderate	High to moderate	Moderate
Requires mortising	Yes	Occasionally	Usually	Yes	No
Cost of hinge	Low	Moderate	Low	High	Low
Ease of installation	Moderate	Easy	Moderate	Very easy	Easy
Adjustability	No	One-way	Two-way	Three-way	No
Easily adjusted after installation	No	No	No	Yes	No

Contributors:
Greg Heuer, Architectural Woodwork Institute, Reston, Virginia; Kelsey Kruse, AIA, George Vaeth Associates, Inc., Columbia, Maryland.

BASE CABINET CONSTRUCTION

BASE CABINET
5.70

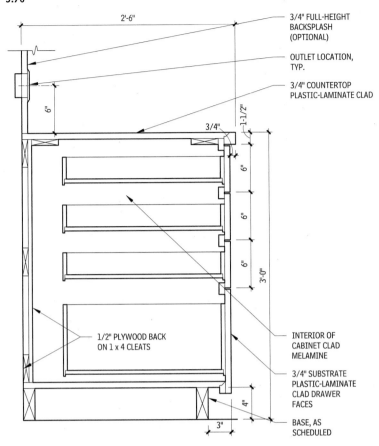

2'-6"

6"

3/4"

6"

6"

6"

3'-0"

1-1/2"

1/2" PLYWOOD BACK
ON 1 x 4 CLEATS

4"

3"

3/4" FULL-HEIGHT
BACKSPLASH
(OPTIONAL)

OUTLET LOCATION,
TYP.

3/4" COUNTERTOP
PLASTIC-LAMINATE CLAD

INTERIOR OF
CABINET CLAD
MELAMINE

3/4" SUBSTRATE
PLASTIC-LAMINATE
CLAD DRAWER
FACES

BASE, AS
SCHEDULED

COUNTERTOPS

COUNTER AND BACKSPLASH DETAILS
5.71

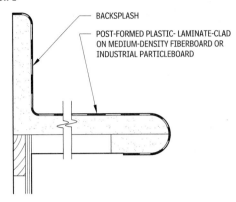

BACKSPLASH

POST-FORMED PLASTIC-LAMINATE-CLAD
ON MEDIUM-DENSITY FIBERBOARD OR
INDUSTRIAL PARTICLEBOARD

POST-FORMED PLASTIC-LAMINATE CLAD COUNTERTOP

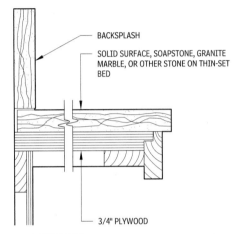

BACKSPLASH

SOLID SURFACE, SOAPSTONE, GRANITE
MARBLE, OR OTHER STONE ON THIN-SET
BED

3/4" PLYWOOD

STONE COUNTERTOP

SELF-EDGE NOSING
5.72

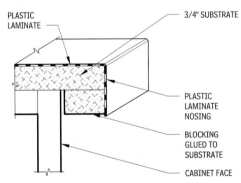

PLASTIC
LAMINATE

3/4" SUBSTRATE

PLASTIC
LAMINATE
NOSING

BLOCKING
GLUED TO
SUBSTRATE

CABINET FACE

Contributor:
Architectural Woodwork Institute, Reston, Virginia.

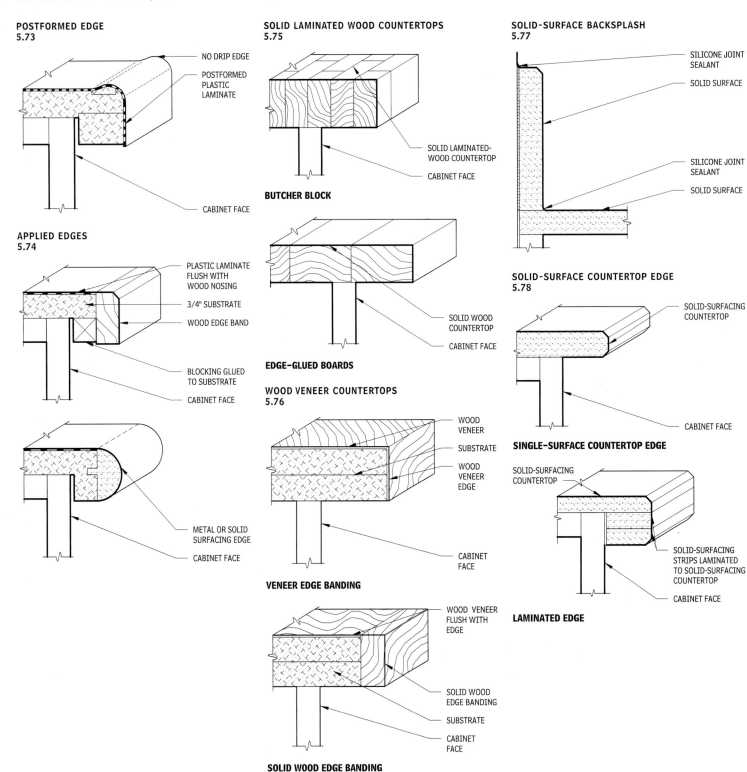

POSTFORMED EDGE
5.73

- NO DRIP EDGE
- POSTFORMED PLASTIC LAMINATE
- CABINET FACE

APPLIED EDGES
5.74

- PLASTIC LAMINATE FLUSH WITH WOOD NOSING
- 3/4" SUBSTRATE
- WOOD EDGE BAND
- BLOCKING GLUED TO SUBSTRATE
- CABINET FACE

- METAL OR SOLID SURFACING EDGE
- CABINET FACE

SOLID LAMINATED WOOD COUNTERTOPS
5.75

- SOLID LAMINATED-WOOD COUNTERTOP
- CABINET FACE

BUTCHER BLOCK

- SOLID WOOD COUNTERTOP
- CABINET FACE

EDGE-GLUED BOARDS

WOOD VENEER COUNTERTOPS
5.76

- WOOD VENEER
- SUBSTRATE
- WOOD VENEER EDGE
- CABINET FACE

VENEER EDGE BANDING

- WOOD VENEER FLUSH WITH EDGE
- SOLID WOOD EDGE BANDING
- SUBSTRATE
- CABINET FACE

SOLID WOOD EDGE BANDING

SOLID-SURFACE BACKSPLASH
5.77

- SILICONE JOINT SEALANT
- SOLID SURFACE
- SILICONE JOINT SEALANT
- SOLID SURFACE

SOLID-SURFACE COUNTERTOP EDGE
5.78

- SOLID-SURFACING COUNTERTOP
- CABINET FACE

SINGLE-SURFACE COUNTERTOP EDGE

- SOLID-SURFACING COUNTERTOP
- SOLID-SURFACING STRIPS LAMINATED TO SOLID-SURFACING COUNTERTOP
- CABINET FACE

LAMINATED EDGE

NOTES

5.73 No-drip edge helps to contain spills.
5.74 Applied edges can be wood, metal, or solid-surfacing and can be
adhered to the countertop substrate. Depending on the edge detail, the
applied edge can protect the plastic laminate surface from damage.

Contributors:
Don Tapert, Setu Shah, Tapert Architecture, New York City, New York.

CERAMIC TILE COUNTERTOPS
5.79

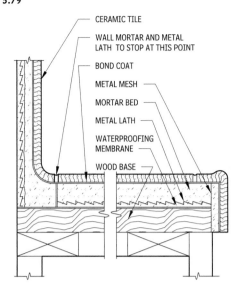

MORTAR–BED SET

Labels: CERAMIC TILE; WALL MORTAR AND METAL LATH TO STOP AT THIS POINT; BOND COAT; METAL MESH; MORTAR BED; METAL LATH; WATERPROOFING MEMBRANE; WOOD BASE

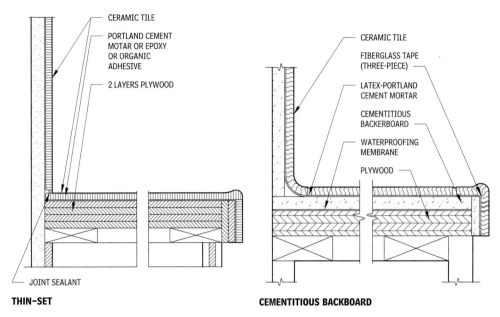

THIN-SET

Labels: CERAMIC TILE; PORTLAND CEMENT MOTAR OR EPOXY OR ORGANIC ADHESIVE; 2 LAYERS PLYWOOD; JOINT SEALANT

CEMENTITIOUS BACKBOARD

Labels: CERAMIC TILE; FIBERGLASS TAPE (THREE-PIECE); LATEX-PORTLAND CEMENT MORTAR; CEMENTITIOUS BACKERBOARD; WATERPROOFING MEMBRANE; PLYWOOD

RESTAURANT AND BAR SEATING

The dining rooms and bars in restaurants must be efficiently planned to optimize revenue. Upscale restaurants generally require more space between tables for privacy. The restaurant concept, menu, and operation style also influence space allocation. Depending on the type of restaurant and menu, kitchen areas range from 30 to 45 percent of the total restaurant area.

Building codes identify restaurants as assembly spaces. Comply with local code requirements for construction, including plumbing fixture counts.

The local department of health reviews restaurants for compliance with regulations for general sanitation in food handling and proper food storage.

Dimensions shown in Figure 5.81 are minimum clearances, and seating layouts indicate general configurations; they are not intended to depict any specific type of operation. Tables may be converted from square to round to enlarge seating capacity. Booth seating makes effective use of corner space. An accessible route, at least 36 in. wide, is required to connect the entrance, accessible fixed seating, and restrooms.

PRELIMINARY GUIDE FOR FRONT-OF-HOUSE AREAS
5.80

FOOD SERVICE VENUE	SUGGESTED AREA PER PATRON (SQ FT)
Banquet facility	10–11
Fast food	11–14
Full-service	15–18
Cafeteria	6–18
Upscale gourmet	17–22

DINING AND BAR AREA

Restaurant patrons typically form their first impression of a restaurant from the main dining room and bar areas. The restaurant concept may offer a variety of space types, including open or multilevel dining areas, secluded alcoves, private dining rooms, or features such as display cooking areas. A mix of seating and table types, adequate aisle and serving areas, and well-chosen materials and lighting combine to create a comfortable, inviting dining environment.

SEATING ARRANGEMENTS FOR PERSONS USING WHEELCHAIRS
5.81

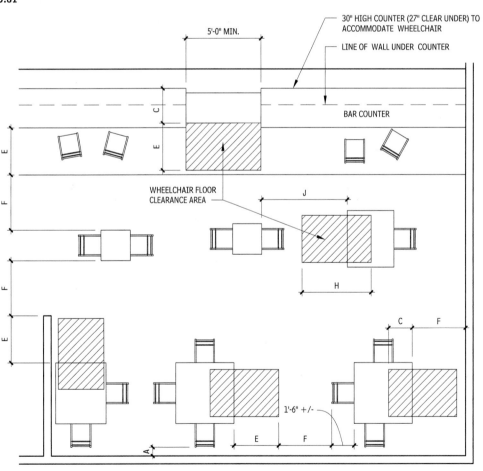

Labels: 5'-0" MIN.; 30" HIGH COUNTER (27" CLEAR UNDER) TO ACCOMMODATE WHEELCHAIR; LINE OF WALL UNDER COUNTER; BAR COUNTER; WHEELCHAIR FLOOR CLEARANCE AREA; 1'-6" +/-

NOTE

5.81 Refer to Table 5.83 for clearances.

Contributors:
Janet B. Rankin, AIA, Rippeteau Architects, PC, Washington, DC; Cini-Little International, Inc., Food Service Consultants, Washington, DC.

**TYPICAL SEATING ARRANGEMENTS
5.82**

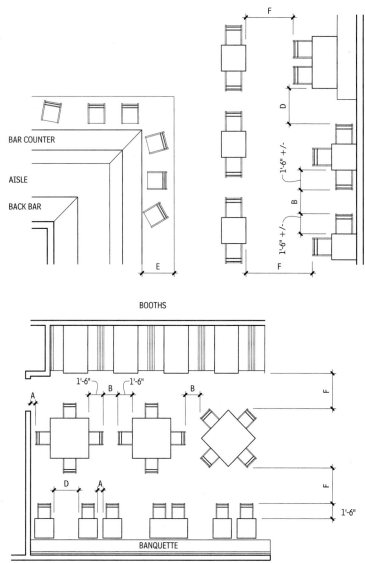

BOOTHS

BANQUETTE

Integrate 5 percent accessible seating allocation, distributed among various seating types, to accommodate both large and small groups. Consult codes, standards, and regulations for specific requirements for accessible seating and distribution. Tables, which should have rounded ends, are often 2 in. shorter than the booth seating.

Flexibility in dining spaces is an asset. Private dining and compartmentalization of the main dining areas provide a means of accommodating large or small groups of diners without disrupting the general dining area.

Bar areas may be open to the dining area or separate, possibly with a different design aesthetic from the main dining area. Hours of use, smoking areas (if allowed), and acoustics influence the location and adjacency of the bar to the dining area.

CLEARANCES
5.83

	DIMENSION (IN.)
A	6 Minimum (NO PASSAGE)
B	18 (LIMITED PASSAGE)
C	19
D	30
E	30
F	42
G	48
H	54
I	72

WAITSTAFF SERVICE STATIONS

Waitstaff service stations are located between the front of the house and the back of the house. Service stations are typically furnished with equipment, supplies, and selected beverages. Many service stations include a point-of-service (POS) terminal to calculate patron bills and process credit card receipts, depending on the operations preference of the restaurant owner. The size and configuration of the space may determine the number of waitstaff stations/POS terminals.

FIXED BOOTHS AND BANQUETTES

Banquettes can be used to provide comfortable, flexible seating arrangements and to serve as midheight privacy screens. The table size mix can vary at banquette areas by locating tables next to one another or separately. Two tops, for example, can be combined to create a table for four or more diners. Booths are desirable for comfort, privacy, and intimacy.

Note that booth sizes may be determined by local building codes.

RESTAURANT FIXED COUNTERS AND STOOLS

The design of restaurant counter service areas must allow for adequate workspace clearance behind the counter. The clearance from the top of the seat to the underside of the countertop and the depth of the countertop overhang are critical. Often, footrests that are applied to the counter are located such that the patron's leg is not supported; it is more likely to be successful for seated patrons when the footrest is integral to the stool. Standing patrons will often use the counter-mounted footrest. Footrests prevent accessibility and should not be included at accessible portions of counters.

NOTE

5.82 Refer to Table 5.83 for clearances.

Contributors:
Janet B. Rankin, AIA, Rippeteau Architects, PC, Washington, DC; Cini-Little International, Inc., Food Service Consultants, Washington, DC.

MOVABLE FURNISHINGS

BEDS

For wheelchair users who can independently transfer themselves between bed and chair, bed heights should facilitate their movement back and forth in a sitting position. Transfer is easiest for these users if the mattress top approximately matches their wheelchair seat height (typically, 18 to 20 in.). Wheelchair users who cannot independently transfer themselves between bed and chair are assisted by attendants, who use a portable lift mounted on a metal stand. The lift base requires approximately 8 in. of clearance below the bed.

BED ACCESSIBILITY
5.84

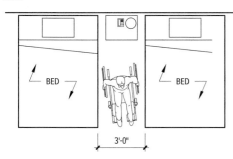

PLAN

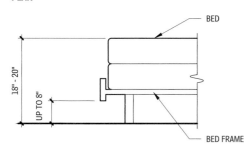

ELEVATION

CONVERTIBLE FURNITURE

SIDE (MURPHY) BED
5.86

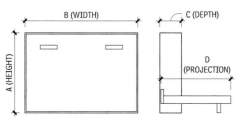

FRONT ELEVATION

SIDE ELEVATION

COMMON SIDE AND WALL BED SIZES
5.87

	SIDE BED		WALL BED			
	TWIN	DOUBLE	TWIN	DOUBLE	QUEEN	KING
A (IN.)	44-1/2	59	80	80	84	84
B (IN.)	79	79	42	57	63	79
C (IN.)	16	16	13-19	13-19	13-19	13-19
D (IN.)	43-1/2	57	82	82	88	88

TYPICAL BED SIZES
5.85

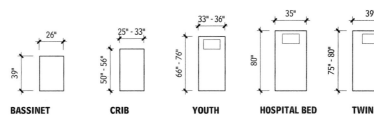

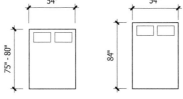

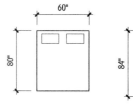

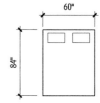

BASSINET   **CRIB**   **YOUTH**   **HOSPITAL BED**   **TWIN**   **TWIN EXTRA-LONG (DORM) OR TWIN WATER BED**

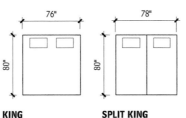

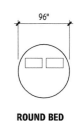

DOUBLE/FULL   **DOUBLE/FULL EXTRA-LONG OR FULL WATER BED**   **QUEEN**   **QUEEN EXTRA-LONG OR WATER BED**

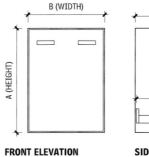

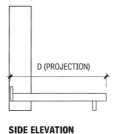

KING   **SPLIT KING**   **CALIFORNIA KING**   **KING WATER BED**   **ROUND BED**

WALL (MURPHY) BED
5.88

FRONT ELEVATION

SIDE ELEVATION

QUEEN-SIZE SLEEPER SOFA
5.89

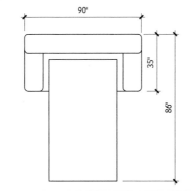

SLEEP CHAIR
5.90

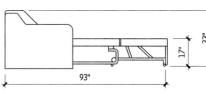

HOSPITALITY FURNITURE

The dimensional requirements of the guest room modules and guest corridor are set by the owner. These dimensions establish the depth of the guest floor bay, which is approximately 60 ft for double-loaded floors and 30 ft for single-loaded floors. The double-loaded guest floor is the most efficient layout. However, because of the popularity of atrium environments, single-loaded corridor schemes are often utilized.

NOTES

5.86 and 5.88 Refer to dimensions in Table 5.87.
5.87 Consult manufacturer for specific sizes.

Contributors:
Kim A. Beasley, AIA, and Thomas D. Davies, Jr., AIA, Paralyzed Veterans of America Architecture, Washington, DC.

CONFIGURATIONS FOR GUEST ROOMS
5.91

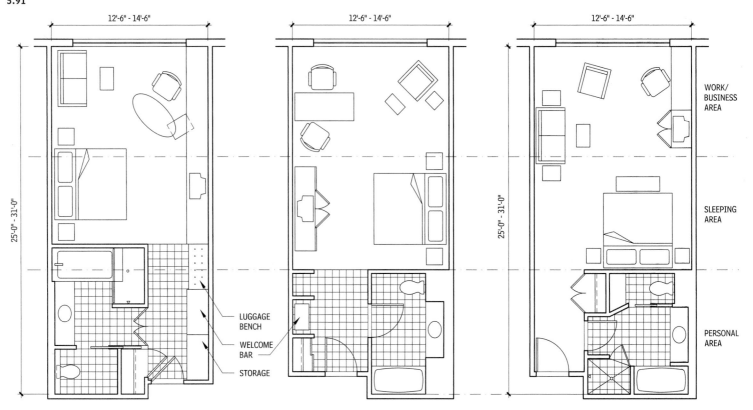

12'-6" - 14'-6"

12'-6" - 14'-6"

12'-6" - 14'-6"

25'-0" - 31'-0"

WORK/
BUSINESS
AREA

SLEEPING
AREA

PERSONAL
AREA

LUGGAGE BENCH

WELCOME BAR

STORAGE

ROOM COMBINATIONS
5.92

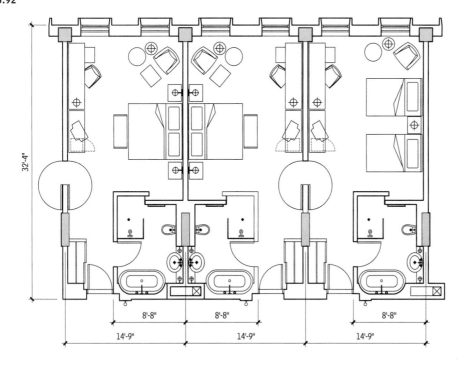

32'-4"

8'-8"   8'-8"   8'-8"

14'-9"   14'-9"   14'-9"

CABINETS, CHESTS, AND DRESSERS

Desks, armoires, dressers, chests, and cabinets come in a variety of shapes and sizes. Consult manufacturers for options and dimensions.

Dressers and chests for wheelchair users should be situated so there is a clear access aisle, of approximately 42 in., in front.

Cabinets, tables, stands, and other furniture with doors should have relatively narrow leaves so the arc of the swing is small when they are opened.

TV ARMOIRE
5.93

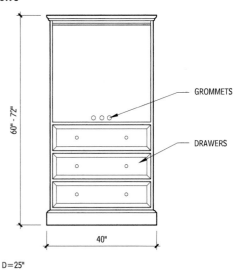

GROMMETS

DRAWERS

60" - 72"

40"

D=25"

NOTES

5.91 and 5.92 Accessible rooms must be provided for each type of accommodation (singles, doubles, suites, views, smoking, nonsmoking, etc.).

CREDENZA
5.94

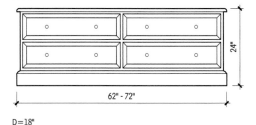

D=18"

DESK
5.95

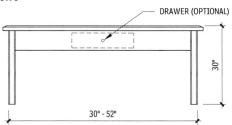

DRAWER (OPTIONAL)

LIBRARY FURNITURE

Libraries now link digital information, paper information, resources, and print collections. Consequently, libraries are now places where people not only read and borrow books but also use computers to find information and access online services. Traditional library furnishings for accommodating printed volumes range from 13-1/2 to 19 books per square foot, with the average of 16 books per square foot of gross area. The average additional dead load is 25-lb/cu ft.

Consult the following references:

- American Library Association (ALA) www.ala.org
- Association of College and Research Libraries (ACRL) www.ala.org
- Library Administration and Management Association (LAMA) www.ala.org/lama
- International Federation of Library Associations and Institutions (IFLA) www.ifla.org

Specific furniture designed for library use, includes library tables, shelves, carrels, card catalogs, and so on. Specialized furniture may include dictionary stands, atlas cases, book trucks, display cases, and the like.

Design guidelines for workspaces include the following:

- About 5 percent of fixed tables and carrels should be accessible.
- Reading tables and study carrels often should incorporate power outlets and, possibly, Internet connections.
- Reading tables and study carrels should be sized large enough so that library patrons can spread out their materials, particularly in areas where oversized materials are viewed.
- The recommended height of study carrel partitions is at least 52 in. above the floor.
- Tables or podiums with slanted tops should be provided for more convenient reading of oversized materials or newspapers.

Seating guidelines are as follows:

- Comfortable seating, such as upholstered chairs and sofas, is generally best for informal reading or lounge areas.
- Pull-up chairs with metal or wood arms are typically used at reading tables and carrels.
- Mechanically adjustable chairs are rarely selected for libraries because they are subject to heavy use and frequent maintenance.
- Library furniture is subject to extremely heavy wear, and frequent cleaning and reupholstery is required; thus, fabrics should be the wear-resistant because they may have a life span of only four to five years.

LIBRARY SHELVING

Shelving may be fixed or mobile/high-density. Shelving may be specialized to accommodate electronic media (CD/DVD), periodicals, or other print materials. A 36-in. minimum clear width aisle is required between stacks/shelving, although 42 in. is recommended.

LIBRARY READING ROOM TABLE LAYOUT
5.96

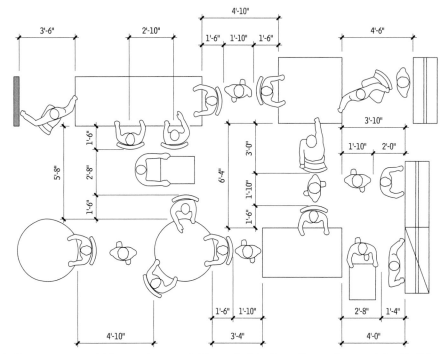

Round tables are not recommended for research purposes, but they may be desired in a staff room or in an area designed for light reading.

LOUNGE CHAIRS, TABLES, AND SHELVING LAYOUT
5.97

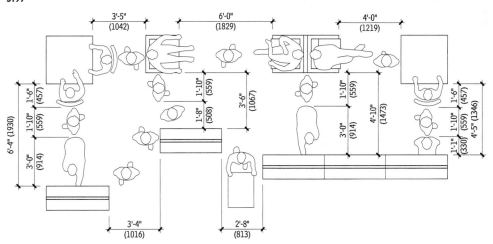

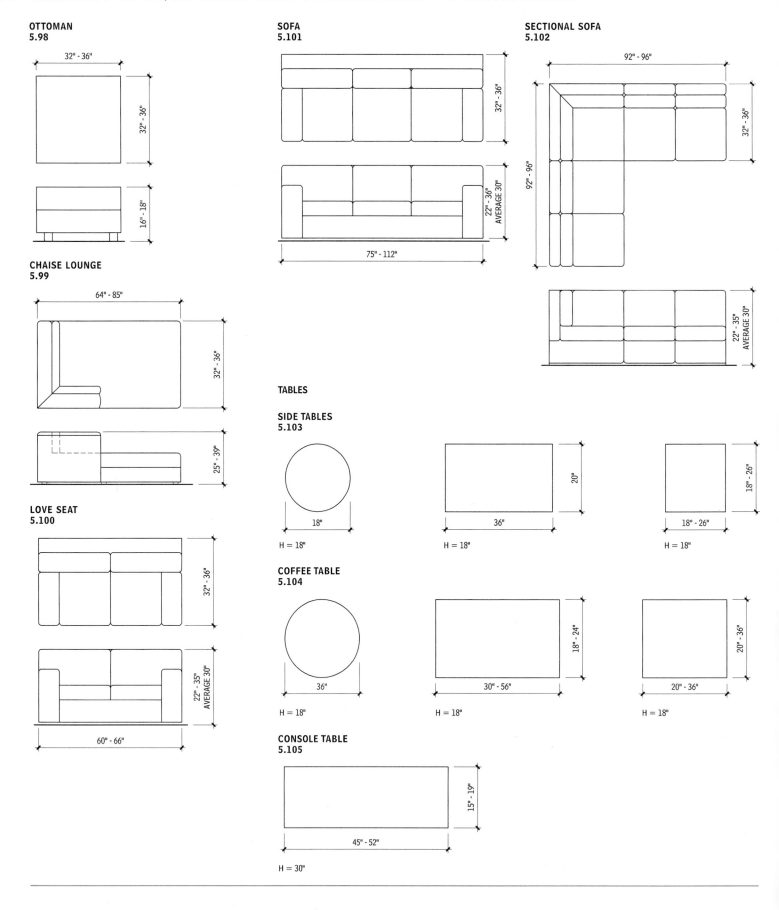

OTTOMAN
5.98

32" - 36"

32" - 36"

16" - 18"

CHAISE LOUNGE
5.99

64" - 85"

32" - 36"

25" - 39"

LOVE SEAT
5.100

32" - 36"

22" - 35"
AVERAGE 30"

60" - 66"

SOFA
5.101

32" - 36"

22" - 36"
AVERAGE 30"

75" - 112"

TABLES

SIDE TABLES
5.103

18"

H = 18"

20"

36"

H = 18"

18" - 26"

18" - 26"

H = 18"

COFFEE TABLE
5.104

36"

H = 18"

18" - 24"

30" - 56"

H = 18"

20" - 36"

20" - 36"

H = 18"

CONSOLE TABLE
5.105

15" - 19"

45" - 52"

H = 30"

SECTIONAL SOFA
5.102

92" - 96"

32" - 36"

92" - 96"

22" - 35"
AVERAGE 30"

OFFICE FURNITURE

OFFICE FURNISHINGS DESIGN CONSIDERATION

When planning the furnishing of office spaces, use these guidelines:

- The standard height for surfaces in an office is 28 to 30 in.
- The standard height for work surfaces that will accommodate a computer and/or a keyboard range from 25 to 30 in. Keyboards can be accommodated on a work surface either by lowering the work surface or installing an articulating keyboard arm under a standard-height work surface.
- Work surface depths typically range from 18 to 45 in., depending on the type and size of work being completed: 18 in. is used for storage, 30 in. is the standard desk depth, and 45 in. is used to accommodate conferencing.
- Occasionally, an office must accommodate stand-up work surfaces. The height of the work surfaces range from 36 to 52 in.
- Overhead storage above a work surface is standard, with 15- to 18-in. clearance.
- Knee space is integral to the use of desks, tables, and workstations. To serve wheelchair users, knee space with a clear height of approximately 2 ft-3 in. is sufficient.

INTERIOR OFFICE—100 SQ FT
5.106

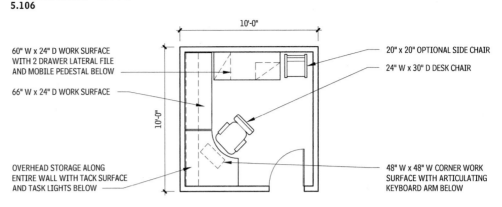

60" W x 24" D WORK SURFACE WITH 2 DRAWER LATERAL FILE AND MOBILE PEDESTAL BELOW

66" W x 24" D WORK SURFACE

OVERHEAD STORAGE ALONG ENTIRE WALL WITH TACK SURFACE AND TASK LIGHTS BELOW

20" x 20" OPTIONAL SIDE CHAIR

24" W x 30" D DESK CHAIR

48" W x 48" W CORNER WORK SURFACE WITH ARTICULATING KEYBOARD ARM BELOW

PERIMETER OFFICE, TRADITIONAL LAYOUT—150 SQ FT
5.107

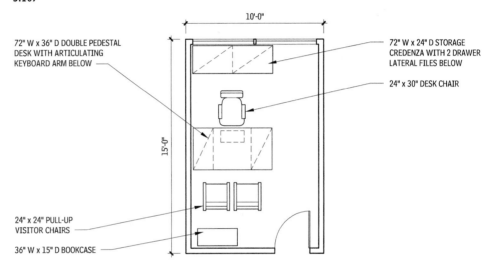

72" W x 36" D DOUBLE PEDESTAL DESK WITH ARTICULATING KEYBOARD ARM BELOW

24" x 24" PULL-UP VISITOR CHAIRS

36" W x 15" D BOOKCASE

72" W x 24" D STORAGE CREDENZA WITH 2 DRAWER LATERAL FILES BELOW

24" x 30" DESK CHAIR

PERIMETER OFFICE, INTENSIVE LAYOUT—150 SQ FT
5.108

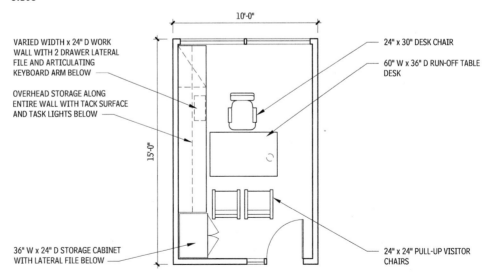

VARIED WIDTH x 24" D WORK WALL WITH 2 DRAWER LATERAL FILE AND ARTICULATING KEYBOARD ARM BELOW

OVERHEAD STORAGE ALONG ENTIRE WALL WITH TACK SURFACE AND TASK LIGHTS BELOW

36" W x 24" D STORAGE CABINET WITH LATERAL FILE BELOW

24" x 30" DESK CHAIR

60" W x 36" D RUN-OFF TABLE DESK

24" x 24" PULL-UP VISITOR CHAIRS

Contributors:
Joan Blumenfeld, Perkins & Will, New York City, New York; Sonya Dufner, Perkins & Will, New York City, New York.

PERIMETER OFFICE, COLLABORATIVE LAYOUT—150 SQ FT
5.109

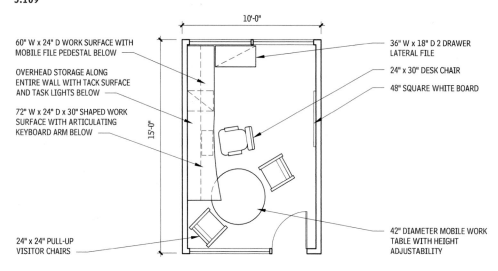

60" W x 24" D WORK SURFACE WITH MOBILE FILE PEDESTAL BELOW

OVERHEAD STORAGE ALONG ENTIRE WALL WITH TACK SURFACE AND TASK LIGHTS BELOW

72" W x 24" D x 30" SHAPED WORK SURFACE WITH ARTICULATING KEYBOARD ARM BELOW

24" x 24" PULL-UP VISITOR CHAIRS

36" W x 18" D 2 DRAWER LATERAL FILE

24" x 30" DESK CHAIR

48" SQUARE WHITE BOARD

42" DIAMETER MOBILE WORK TABLE WITH HEIGHT ADJUSTABILITY

CORNER OFFICE, TRADITIONAL LAYOUT—225 SQ FT
5.110

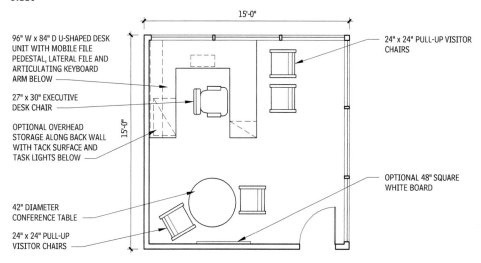

96" W x 84" D U-SHAPED DESK UNIT WITH MOBILE FILE PEDESTAL, LATERAL FILE AND ARTICULATING KEYBOARD ARM BELOW

27" x 30" EXECUTIVE DESK CHAIR

OPTIONAL OVERHEAD STORAGE ALONG BACK WALL WITH TACK SURFACE AND TASK LIGHTS BELOW

42" DIAMETER CONFERENCE TABLE

24" x 24" PULL-UP VISITOR CHAIRS

24" x 24" PULL-UP VISITOR CHAIRS

OPTIONAL 48" SQUARE WHITE BOARD

CORNER OFFICE, CONFERENCE/MEETING LAYOUT—225 SQ FT
5.111

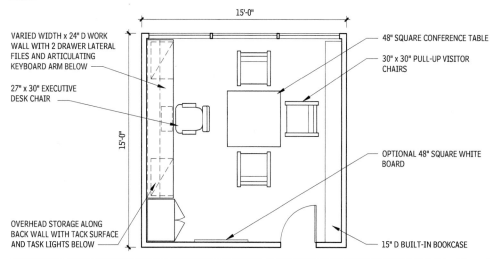

VARIED WIDTH x 24" D WORK WALL WITH 2 DRAWER LATERAL FILES AND ARTICULATING KEYBOARD ARM BELOW

27" x 30" EXECUTIVE DESK CHAIR

OVERHEAD STORAGE ALONG BACK WALL WITH TACK SURFACE AND TASK LIGHTS BELOW

48" SQUARE CONFERENCE TABLE

30" x 30" PULL-UP VISITOR CHAIRS

OPTIONAL 48" SQUARE WHITE BOARD

15" D BUILT-IN BOOKCASE

Contributors:
Joan Blumenfeld, Perkins & Will, New York City, New York; Sonya Dufner, Perkins & Will, New York City, New York.

OFFICE SPACE DIMENSIONS (IN.)
5.112

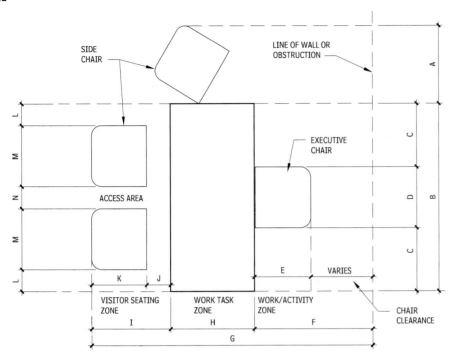

A	30–42
B	60–84
C	18–28
D	24–30
E	23–29
F	36 minimum
G	96–126
H	30–45
I	30–44
J	10–14
K	20–30
L	4–16
M	20–30
N	8–16

CONFERENCE ROOMS

Conference rooms should be located in proximity to user groups. A conference room typically serves multiple groups or departments; therefore, rooms in a high-rise office building may be organized near elevator banks on crossover floors for ease of access by many users. When a conference room functions as a flexible space, the location of entry/exit doors is positioned so that acoustical folding partitions or movable walls may be used to divide a larger space into smaller meeting areas.

FINISHES

Acoustic concerns dictate that finishes in conference rooms be chosen with adequate sound-absorption qualities, to prevent echo, particularly in rooms where teleconferencing or videoconferencing will occur. For this reason, carpet is a common floor finish in conference rooms; and some walls are covered with acoustical wall panels or fabric wallcoverings. Ceilings are generally a combination of acoustical material, either ceiling tile or fabric-wrapped panels and gypsum board. In more functional and less formal rooms, tackable surfaces or magnetic whiteboard writing surfaces should be provided to facilitate presentations, along with chart

CONFERENCE ROOM DESIGN RECOMMENDATIONS
5.113

	OPTIMAL	MINIMUM
Chair spacing	3'-0"	2'-6"
Clearance around table	5'-0"	3'-6"
Clearance at head of table	7'-0"	5'-0"
Chair width (including arms)	26"	22"
Chair depth	25"	21"
Credenza depth	24"	18"
Table width (single seat at end)	60"	30"
Table width (double seat at end)	72"	60"
Round table seating capacity	$(3.1425 \times D) \div 36"$	$(3.1415 \times D) \div 30"$

rails for presentation boards and writing tools. The color of the wall surface is generally a neutral color when the walls are used for display or projection. If a room will be used for videoconferencing or meetings that are captured on video, it is generally recommended that a medium-tone wall color be use so that the people projected on monitors do not appear in shadow. Finishes should be carefully examined for flame spread and smoke-generated ratings.

LIGHTING

Conference room lighting should be selected based on the tasks performed in the space. In rooms that offer flexibility, lighting that can be switched separately is optimal so that the users have control over the environment. Directional fixtures are appropriate over the conference table, with dimmable lamps near the front and sides of the room, so that display areas and the presenter at the head of the table can be highlighted, or fall into the background, as desired.

Contributors:
Tammy Cavin and Tama Duffy Day, Perkins+Will, Washington, DC.

SMALL CONFERENCE ROOMS
5.114

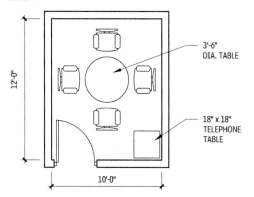

3'-6"
DIA. TABLE

18" x 18"
TELEPHONE
TABLE

12'-0"

10'-0"

TEAM ROOM: 120 SQ. FT.
TOTAL SEATS: 4

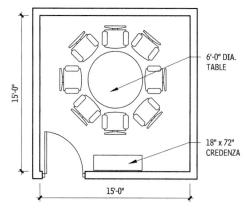

6'-0" DIA.
TABLE

18" x 72"
CREDENZA

15'-0"

15'-0"

SMALL CONFERENCE ROOM: 225 SQ. FT.
TOTAL SEATS: 8

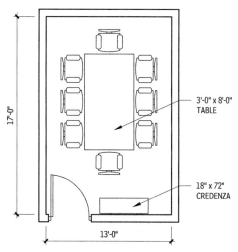

3'-0" x 8'-0"
TABLE

18" x 72"
CREDENZA

17'-0"

13'-0"

SMALL CONFERENCE ROOM: 225 SQ. FT.
TOTAL SEATS: 8

MEDIUM CONFERENCE ROOMS
5.115

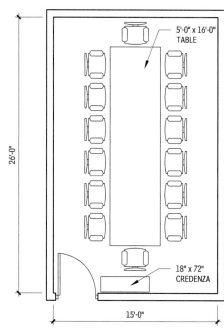

5'-0" x 16'-0"
TABLE

18" x 72"
CREDENZA

26'-0"

15'-0"

MEDIUM CONFERENCE ROOM: 400 SQ. FT.
TOTAL SEATS: 12 - 14

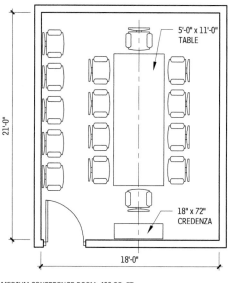

5'-0" x 11'-0"
TABLE

18" x 72"
CREDENZA

21'-0"

18'-0"

MEDIUM CONFERENCE ROOM: 400 SQ. FT.
TOTAL SEATS: 10 - 15

SCHOOL FURNITURE

This section describes furniture for preschool, elementary, middle, and high schools.

EARLY CHILDHOOD AND KINDERGARTEN CLASSROOMS

The design of schools for early childhood education has always been geared toward comfortable, supportive, and adaptive settings that are conducive to a learning process derived from familiar play and hands-on activities. Specific features associated with home as well as school are considered in developing an appropriate transitional setting. The type, size, scale, and variety of more public and private spaces underlie appropriate design and planning.

Among the general goals that all early childhood and kindergarten programs should strive to achieve are the following:

- Create a visually rich, fun, and surprising environment.
- Provide spaces and surfaces for display of children's work.
- Provide a variety of settings for work-in-progress.
- Introduce a variety of social settings for small and large groups.
- Make strong connections between the indoors and the outdoors; use daylighting as much as possible.
- Connect spaces to promote communication, orientation, and flexible programming and staffing.
- Build in flexibility of space to accommodate evolving teaching practices.
- Create a distinctive, pleasing entrance.
- Pay special attention to the scale and height of typical elements (such as windows, doors, doorknobs and pulls, sinks, toilets, counters, furnishings, mirrors, steps, shelving and storage, light switches, towel dispensers, and other accessories).

CHILDREN'S FURNISHINGS

Age-appropriate materials and equipment of sufficient quantity, variety, and durability should be readily accessible to children and be arranged on low, open shelves to promote independent use. Individual spaces for children to store their personal belongings should be provided.

PRESCHOOL DESIGN CONCEPT

The space for children three years and older should be arranged to facilitate a variety of small group and individual activities, including block-building, sociodramatic play, art, music, science, math, manipulatives, and quiet reading and writing. Other activities such as sand play and woodworking are also often accommodated. Soft spaces as well as hard surfaces, such as wood floors and ample crawling and toddling areas, are typically provided for infants and young toddlers. Sturdy furniture is required to enable nonwalkers to pull themselves up or balance themselves while walking. School-age children should be provided separate space that is arranged to facilitate a variety of age-appropriate activities and permit sustained work on projects.

PRIVATE AREAS

Private areas should be made available indoors and outdoors so that children can have occasional solitude. Soft elements such as rugs, cushions, or rocking chairs should be provided for the comfort of the children, in addition to sound-absorbing materials to minimize noise.

STAFF WORK AREA

The work environment for staff should include a place for adults to take a break or work away from children, an adult-size bathroom, a secure place for staff to store their personal belongings, and an administrative area that is separated from the children's areas for planning or preparing materials.

Contributors:
Joan Blumenfeld, Perkins & Will, New York City, New York; Sonya Dufner, Perkins & Will, New York City, New York.

KINDERGARTEN AND GRADE 1 CLASSROOM
5.116

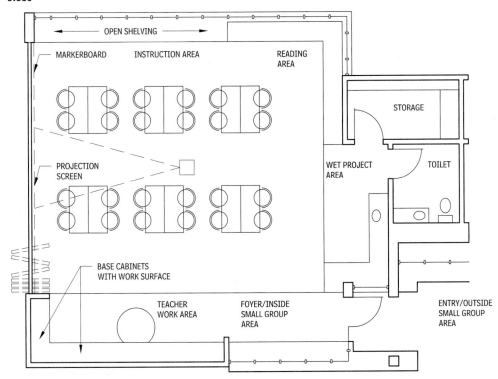

This classroom accommodates a variety of group and individual activities, with specific areas for instruction, group reading, wet projects, and small groups.

SPACE REQUIREMENTS FOR COMMON MIDDLE SCHOOL PROGRAM ELEMENTS
5.118

PROGRAM ELEMENT	TYPICALLY REQUIRED BY CODE	NET RANGE (SQ FT)
Computer center	No	850–1200 (1 per 250 students)
Music instruction room	No	850–1200 (1 per 250 students)
Laboratory spaces	No	1000–1200 (1 per 125 students)
Art instruction room	No	1000–1200 (1 per 250 students)
Gymnasium	Yes	3500 (equals one station; 1 station per 250 students)
Cafeteria	Yes	School population x 50% x 10 (recommended) (provides two lunch periods, total)
Kitchen	No	Depends on food program and equipment; typically equal to one-third the size of the dining area
Auditorium	No	School capacity x 50% x 7 (recommended) (based on seating one-half of the school population)
Library	Yes	10 per student (recommended)
Special-use rooms	No	500–750 per use
Media/video center	No	750–1000
Exhibition/ display areas	No	Standards developed on a school-by-school basis

ELEMENTARY AND MIDDLE SCHOOLS

For general-purpose classrooms, it is common to size rooms for approximately 28 students. Note that most schools attempt to keep the number of students per classroom lower than that, usually 22 to 24 students. Nonetheless, unless otherwise established, it is prudent to design for 28 to account for population growth, unbalanced section sizes, and similar contingencies.

Classroom sizes typically range from 750 to 1000 net sq ft. Adequate space must be allowed for classroom materials and student storage. Storage should be sized for coats, briefcases, purses, backpacks, and other paraphernalia. Most elementary schools do not have lockers in corridors, so storage areas must be accommodated within the classroom.

Many states have minimum standards for classroom size, so consult local requirements.

MIDDLE SCHOOL AND JUNIOR HIGH SCHOOL

For most school districts in the United States, the middle school is still evolving, but typically it includes grades 6 through 8. Students are introduced to departmental teaching, interdisciplinary teaching, flexible scheduling, block scheduling, collaborative learning, and flexible groupings.

Typically, fundamental instruction spaces include general classrooms, library, and gymnasium spaces. Many school programs include large common areas that have been developed to offer flexible and multifunction opportunities within the same space. The gymnasium, auditorium, and cafeteria are combined in some fashion (sometimes for two of these functions only).

CLASSROOM FOR GRADES 2 THROUGH 5
5.117

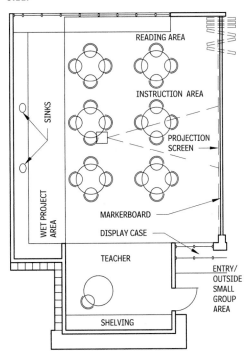

This classroom is smaller than the pre-K and K-1 classroom. It accommodates a variety of group and individual activities, with specific areas for instruction, group reading, wet projects, and small groups.

Contributor:
Robert Staples, Staples & Charles, Ltd., Washington, DC.

STUDENT LEARNING SPACES
5.119

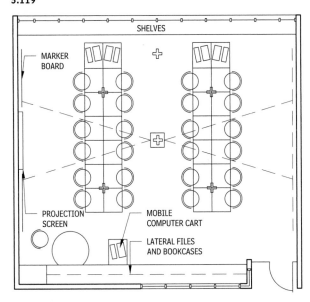

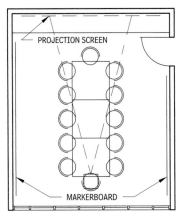

SMALL GROUP SPACES

LARGE GROUP SPACES

Classrooms are planned to have integrated technology available in a variety of configurations, to enable simulations research and streaming videos. Small group rooms are designed as breakout areas for the shared use of the middle school.

CLASSROOM SECTION
5.120

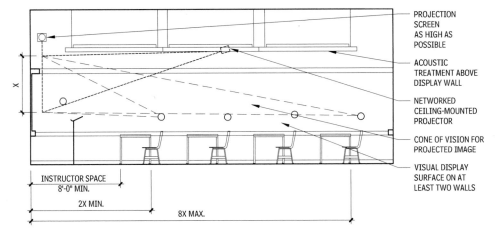

HIGH SCHOOL

High schools are dedicated to the concept of group instruction with an emphasis on the importance of individual learning. Many campuses are considered "open," allowing students to move freely on and off campus and to have flexible scheduling of classes and independent studies. Many courses of study are offered, thus, creating the need for more specialized rooms and, often, requiring larger, more flexible spaces.

DESIGN OF CLASSROOMS

The design objective for general-use classrooms should be to assist students to clearly see and hear any presentation. Therefore, special attention should be given to angles of view to the display wall or the projected image.

The integration of electronic media, especially overhead projectors and networked resources, has supplemented the traditional tools of the chalkboard and tablet armchair but has also presented new challenges for planning classrooms.

A heightened emphasis on teaching methodologies that stress discussion and interaction has created the need for furniture arrangements that are more flexible than traditional lecture-format row seating. Loose chairs and tables can be reconfigured for both discussion-style rooms and for lecture formats. Both table-and-chair and tablet armchair arrangements are used. Similarly, the need to accommodate students' laptops and other mobile technologies has increased the need for individual student workspace areas in both situations.

Planning issues vary according to the size of the room. As the capacity increases, it becomes more reasonable to build fixed-furniture configurations. Smaller classrooms may be reconfigured more easily.

To plan a successful classroom, pay special attention to integrating various critical interrelated components, including:

- *Electrical lighting*: Equal emphasis should be placed on quality of light as on quantity: low-glare, flexible switching for note-taking levels during presentations, and direct lighting of display surfaces.
- *Natural lighting*: Daylight should be introduced in every classroom, preferably perpendicular to the primary display wall.
- *Acoustics:* The basic purpose of a classroom is clear communication; to that end, limit background noise, isolate sound between rooms, and accommodate appropriate reverberation time.
- *Audio/visual technology*: Provision of a networked projector, along with the ability to control it from a wired lectern, is a basic level of media integration.
- *Display media writing and projection surfaces*: These should cover as much of the teaching walls as is economically and spatially feasible.
- *Furniture*: The ability to reconfigure loose furniture makes it possible to use the same room for different modes of learning—lectures, discussions, seminars, and small-group activities.

ELEMENT F: SPECIAL CONSTRUCTION

6

INTRODUCTION

The planning, design, and construction of a building requires many unique considerations, ranging from site planning to design and, ultimately, to the unique technical considerations required to implement the design through well thought-out construction details that will allow the design to be built in the most efficient, time-effective, and cost-effective manner. Technical documentation of a project involves the incorporation of special detailing of materials, whereby multiple materials are put together in a way to provide for ease of construction while achieving performance criteria to allow for such aspects as structural loading, waterproofing, thermal insulation, sustainability, and other technical criteria.

The assembly of these various materials can be based on standard, time-proven details modified for a particular condition required for a unique building, site, or performance criteria that must be achieved. However, there is another process that can be used to put a building together. That process makes use of the careful selection of fabricated, engineered, and manufactured building components to achieve a building design or programmatic requirement.

To that end, this chapter addresses various manufactured assemblies to achieve a building design. These assemblies are differentiated from fabricated furniture or equipment items, such as hospital equipment, that have a different intent and are usually installed near completion of a project space. The fabricated and manufactured components discussed in this chapter are integrated early in the construction process, with the significant difference being that they comprise a complete assembled component and are not assembled as a series of pieces, as is, for example, roof flashing.

The topic "Special Structures" describes portable buildings that can arrive at the project site already assembled, as well as a greenhouse glazed structure where a number of manufacturer engineered pieces arrive on a site to be field-assembled from a particular model.

This chapter does not make specific references to available products by manufacturers; rather, the information presented here is non-proprietary. You are encouraged to use Web-based resources and specific manufacturers' product catalogs. Availability, product selection, and details may vary. Likewise, planning information is presented as generically as possible to encourage you to explore alternatives.

Contributor:
William Sarama, AIA, Skidmore Owings & Merrill, New York City, New York.

SPECIAL CONSTRUCTION

SPECIAL STRUCTURES

AIR-SUPPORTED STRUCTURES

Air-supported structures are lightweight, totally free-span structures that maintain stability in space and resist loads with a pressure differential between the interior and exterior. This method of support leaves the interior free of support devices that could interfere with the efficient use of space. The roof and sidewalls can be a single structural element in pure tension, a fabric envelope. The only compression members are the slightly pressurized air inside and the rigid base of the membrane.

Most air-supported structures are primarily designed to resist wind loads. Mechanical blowers must maintain 3 to 5 psf pressure inside the structure at all times. Architectural elements of the building must be detailed to avoid loss of air pressure.

Consult building codes to determine requirements for all air-supported structures.

STRUCTURAL MEMBRANE

The structural membrane is usually a nylon, fiberglass, or polyester fabric coated with polyvinyl chloride (PVC). Such membranes have a life span from 7 to 10 years and offer fire-resistance-ratings that pass NFPA 701 requirements. A urethane topcoat will reduce dirt adhesion and improve service life. Fluorocarbon top finishes further enhance characteristics and can double service life. Teflon-coated fiberglass membranes have a life expectancy of more than 25 years. This material is not combustible, passing ASTM E84, with a flame spread rating of 10, smoke developed <50, and fuel contributed, 10. An acoustical liner (NRC = 0.65) is also available.

Figure 6.1 illustrates three common membrane configurations:

- *Single membrane*: This is the most common type of air-supported structure. The internal pressure (P_1) is kept approximately 0.03 psi above the external atmospheric pressure (P_0). It is this pressure difference that keeps the dome inflated.
- *Double membrane*: The air space between the two membranes

AIR-SUPPORTED FABRIC STRUCTURES
6.1

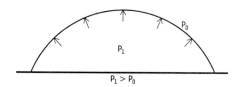

SINGLE MEMBRANE

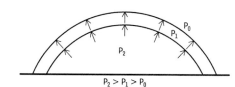

DOUBLE MEMBRANE

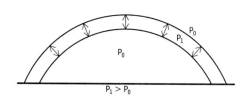

DUAL MEMBRANE

TYPICAL GROUND-MOUNTED AIR-SUPPORTED FABRIC STRUCTURE
6.2

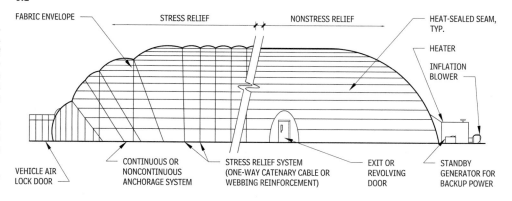

is used for insulation and security. If the outer skin is punctured, the inner skin will remain supported. Both single- and double-membrane air-supported structures require the constant use of blowers to keep them inflated.

- *Dual membrane*: The internal and external pressures are the same in a dual-membrane structure. Only the area between the skins is pressurized. This inflated area can be sealed, eliminating the need for constant use of blowers, although blowers are recommended to make up losses from leakage.

GROUND-MOUNTED AIR STRUCTURES

The shape of ground-mounted air structures permits the structure to meet the ground vertically, allowing gravity loads to resist the membrane tension. The semicircular cross section of the membrane structure has a curvature radius large enough to allow the fabric alone to carry wind forces that may affect the structure. If lightweight fabrics are used, catenary cables or webbing may be required for stabilization as well. Webbing is typically sewn into the fabric seams, forming a one-way system; cables are incorporated into pockets in a one-way system or formed into a cable net harness that is placed over the fabric in a two-way system.

BASIC CONFIGURATIONS OF GROUND-MOUNTED AIR-SUPPORTED FABRIC STRUCTURES
6.3

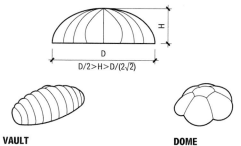

VAULT   **DOME**

SPAN LIMITATIONS	VAULT	DOME
Without cables	D = 120'	D = 150'
With cables	D = 400' t	D = 600'

CONTINUOUS ANCHORAGE DETAILS
6.4

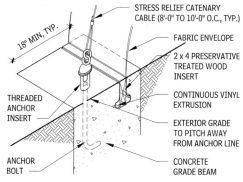

WEDGE INSERT

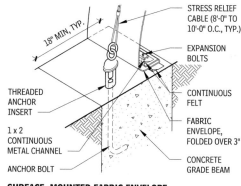

SURFACE-MOUNTED FABRIC ENVELOPE

NOTES

6.2 For temporary structures, anchorage system may be water tanks, sandbags, earth screw anchors, and so on, depending on conditions.
6.4 Beam design is based on actual uplift of air structure at the design inflation pressure and wind load.

Contributor:
Paul Gossen, Geiger Engineers, PC, Suffern, New York.

LONG-SPAN DOME STRUCTURE
6.5

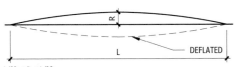

$L/20 < R < L/10$
$200 < L < $ NO UPPER LIMIT

The membrane in a long-span dome structure must be patterned to carry loads without wrinkling. Structural behavior is nonlinear with large displacements. The roof shape must be established so that under maximum load the horizontal components of the cable forces result in minimum bending moment in the compression ring. Consult an air-supported structure specialist to integrate structural and architectural requirements.

LONG-SPAN STRUCTURE SUPPORT DETAIL
6.6

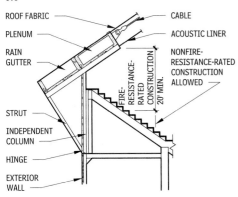

The perimeter compression ring in a long-span structure must be independent of the support structure to prevent radial restraint.

PRE-ENGINEERED STRUCTURES

METAL BUILDING SYSTEMS

Metal building systems are available in standard framing sizes and types from various manufacturers. Commonly used terms in the metal building industry:

- *Bay:* The dimension along a wall between the centerlines of wall columns and the dimension from the outside of an end wall corner column to the centerline of the first adjacent wall column. Spacings range from 18 to 30 ft, with 20 to 25 ft most common.
- *Width:* Measured from the surface of the outside wall girts. Inside clearance varies.
- *Eave height:* Measured from the bottom of a wall column to the top of an eave strut. Nominal 2-ft increments vary from 10 to 30 ft.
- *Diagonal bracing:* Normally required in the plane of the columns and beams in one or more bays to prevent racking and to resist lateral loading perpendicular to the span of the frames.
- *Girts:* Horizontal structural members that transmit lateral loads (pressure and suction) from the exterior walls to the columns. Sag rods may be needed to support the girts about the weak axis and to achieve design economy.
- *Anchor bolts:* Necessary to resist reactions at column bases. Foundations must be designed for reactions transmitted by the column bases and anchor bolts.

Designers should verify that individual manufacturer's standard practice and any special design considerations meet or exceed established engineering principles, local practice, and applicable building codes.

The letters enclosed in parentheses identify the respective components in Figure 6.7.

METAL BUILDING SYSTEM
6.7

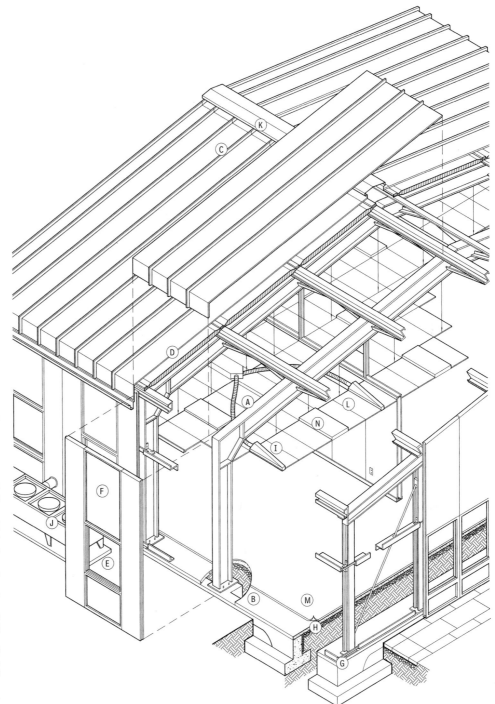

STRUCTURAL COMPONENTS
Rigid steel frame (A)
Cast-in-place concrete foundation and slab (B)

ENVELOPE COMPONENTS
Roof: Standing seam metal roof (C); blanket insulation (D)
Walls: Window assembly (E); insulated metal wall panels (F)

Floor: Dampproofing (G) and vapor barrier (H)

MECHANICAL COMPONENTS
HVAC: Ducts and diffusers (I); heat pump (J); ridge vent (K)

INTERIOR COMPONENTS
Ceilings: Suspended acoustical tile ceiling (L)
Floors: Carpet (M)
Lighting: Fluorescent light fixtures (N) and natural light

Contributor:
Richard D. Rush, AIA, *The Building Systems Integration Handbook* (John Wiley & Sons, 1986).

Metal building systems are predominantly used for single-story warehouse, agricultural, and light industrial facilities, though there is increasing demand of there use for office and retail facilities, and even expansion into the multistory market. This construction approach is particularly advantageous for applications requiring large interior clear spans, the support of heavy overhead cranes, or substantial expanses of roof, the metal buildings systems industry is able to respond to highly specialized needs, while still employing standardized structural components and factory fabrication.

Metal building systems take advantage of factory assembly techniques and quality control. The structural integration of frame components with the building skin, for strength and rigidity, permits economy in the size and number of steel framing components. Primary and secondary framing members, fasteners, and panels interact to produce a light, stable building envelope. Framing and cladding components are designed, engineered, and fabricated in a plant, then shipped to the project site for erection. Often, the same company designs, engineers, and builds the system.

The metal building system integrates lightweight structural and envelope components, each of which add strength and rigidity to the overall form. The light weight of the envelope system, which is an asset for shipping, is, however, especially vulnerable to wind uplift requiring care in design. Building corners and edges are particularly subject to wind-induced uplifting and suction. Additionally, the thin sheet steel wall panels may present acoustical issues when privacy or sound isolation are an issue.

The standing seam metal roof system requires less maintenance than other alternatives, and its long-term performance record is excellent. Most standing seam metal roofs provide a free-floating monolithic membrane, connected by a series of slotted clips that allow movement. This method freely accommodates expansion/contraction cycles caused by thermal changes. In addition, a variety of details, colors, and finishes are available. The standing seam metal roof may present several areas of concern to architects: the modularity of roof panels and seams, important for locating plumbing stacks, skylights, and other roof equipment.

Although the structural and envelope systems of metal buildings are usually highly integrated, metal building system manufacturers rarely consider the mechanical and interior components in any detail.

When using a metal building system a variety of exterior cladding alternatives are available, including lightweight corrugated metal, insulated sandwich panels that provide both interior and exterior finishes, masonry, and stucco. Metal building system manufacturers also offer door, window, and skylight components as integral parts of the envelope and interior. Designating responsibility for engineering, fabrication, and construction may allow better cost control. Architects working with metal building systems can rely on technical support from the manufacturer, including the preparation of fabrication and subsystem engineering documents.

The typical rectilinear nature of metal building systems frequently results in buildings that are more easily expanded. Mechanical and interior components are integrated in the ceilings or in the structure, but the mechanical equipment is normally kept on the exterior, sometimes presenting difficulty with visual integration.

BUILDING TYPES AND WIDTHS
6.8

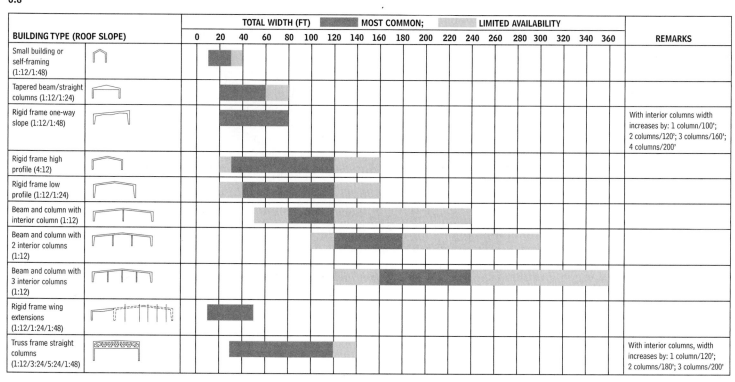

BUILDING TYPE (ROOF SLOPE)	TOTAL WIDTH (FT) — MOST COMMON; LIMITED AVAILABILITY	REMARKS
Small building or self-framing (1:12/1:48)		
Tapered beam/straight columns (1:12/1:24)		
Rigid frame one-way slope (1:12/1:48)		With interior columns width increases by: 1 column/100'; 2 columns/120'; 3 columns/160'; 4 columns/200'
Rigid frame high profile (4:12)		
Rigid frame low profile (1:12/1:24)		
Beam and column with interior column (1:12)		
Beam and column with 2 interior columns (1:12)		
Beam and column with 3 interior columns (1:12)		
Rigid frame wing extensions (1:12/1:24/1:48)		
Truss frame straight columns (1:12/3:24/5:24/1:48)		With interior columns, width increases by: 1 column/120'; 2 columns/180'; 3 columns/200'

Scale headings: 0 20 40 60 80 100 120 140 160 180 200 220 240 260 280 300 320 340 360

Contributors:
Based on Richard D. Rush, AIA, *The Building Systems Integration Handbook,* (John Wiley & Sons, Inc., 1986); Robert P. Burns, AIA, Burns and Burns, Architects, Iowa City, Iowa.

FRAMING SYSTEM COMPONENTS
6.9

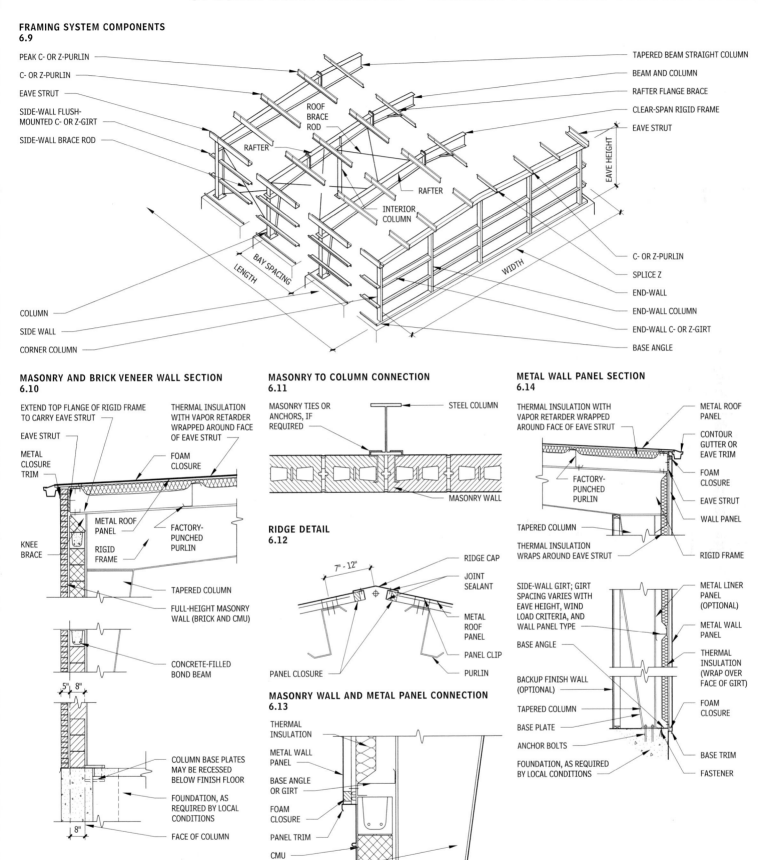

Labels (clockwise from top left):
PEAK C- OR Z-PURLIN
C- OR Z-PURLIN
EAVE STRUT
SIDE-WALL FLUSH-MOUNTED C- OR Z-GIRT
SIDE-WALL BRACE ROD
ROOF BRACE ROD
RAFTER
TAPERED BEAM STRAIGHT COLUMN
BEAM AND COLUMN
RAFTER FLANGE BRACE
CLEAR-SPAN RIGID FRAME
EAVE STRUT
EAVE HEIGHT
INTERIOR COLUMN
RAFTER
WIDTH
C- OR Z-PURLIN
SPLICE Z
END-WALL
END-WALL COLUMN
END-WALL C- OR Z-GIRT
BASE ANGLE
BAY SPACING
LENGTH
COLUMN
SIDE WALL
CORNER COLUMN

MASONRY AND BRICK VENEER WALL SECTION
6.10

Labels:
EXTEND TOP FLANGE OF RIGID FRAME TO CARRY EAVE STRUT
THERMAL INSULATION WITH VAPOR RETARDER WRAPPED AROUND FACE OF EAVE STRUT
EAVE STRUT
METAL CLOSURE TRIM
FOAM CLOSURE
METAL ROOF PANEL
FACTORY-PUNCHED PURLIN
KNEE BRACE
RIGID FRAME
TAPERED COLUMN
FULL-HEIGHT MASONRY WALL (BRICK AND CMU)
CONCRETE-FILLED BOND BEAM
5"   8"
COLUMN BASE PLATES MAY BE RECESSED BELOW FINISH FLOOR
FOUNDATION, AS REQUIRED BY LOCAL CONDITIONS
8"
FACE OF COLUMN

MASONRY TO COLUMN CONNECTION
6.11

Labels:
STEEL COLUMN
MASONRY TIES OR ANCHORS, IF REQUIRED
MASONRY WALL

RIDGE DETAIL
6.12

Labels:
7" - 12"
RIDGE CAP
JOINT SEALANT
METAL ROOF PANEL
PANEL CLIP
PURLIN
PANEL CLOSURE

MASONRY WALL AND METAL PANEL CONNECTION
6.13

Labels:
THERMAL INSULATION
METAL WALL PANEL
BASE ANGLE OR GIRT
FOAM CLOSURE
PANEL TRIM
CMU
COLUMN

METAL WALL PANEL SECTION
6.14

Labels:
THERMAL INSULATION WITH VAPOR RETARDER WRAPPED AROUND FACE OF EAVE STRUT
METAL ROOF PANEL
CONTOUR GUTTER OR EAVE TRIM
FACTORY-PUNCHED PURLIN
FOAM CLOSURE
EAVE STRUT
WALL PANEL
TAPERED COLUMN
THERMAL INSULATION WRAPS AROUND EAVE STRUT
RIGID FRAME
SIDE-WALL GIRT; GIRT SPACING VARIES WITH EAVE HEIGHT, WIND LOAD CRITERIA, AND WALL PANEL TYPE
METAL LINER PANEL (OPTIONAL)
METAL WALL PANEL
BASE ANGLE
BACKUP FINISH WALL (OPTIONAL)
THERMAL INSULATION (WRAP OVER FACE OF GIRT)
TAPERED COLUMN
BASE PLATE
ANCHOR BOLTS
FOAM CLOSURE
FOUNDATION, AS REQUIRED BY LOCAL CONDITIONS
BASE TRIM
FASTENER

NOTE

6.14 A sidewall girt may be inset between columns, attached by clip angles to the steel frame.

Contributors:
Based on Richard D. Rush, AIA, *The Building Systems Integration Handbook,* (John Wiley & Sons, Inc., 1986); Robert P. Burns, AIA, Burns and Burns, Architects, Iowa City, Iowa.

EXTERIOR ALUMINUM SPHERE DOMES

There are a number of manufacturers of planetarium interior projection domes that also manufacture, design, engineer, and install exterior modular dome assemblies. Components are modular and can be delivered to the site ready for assembly in conjunction with modular structural framing. Detailing is unique to each project and must be developed with the manufacturer.

The exterior skin is usually lightweight aluminum or stainless steel with a custom aluminum frame. The aluminum rib-frame consisting of hubs plates, ribs, and headers made from aluminum tubes and plates supports the exterior aluminum panels and seams. Major seam may be as wide as 1 in. and minor seams 1/4 in., when a seamless appearance is desired, the joints can narrower. The rib-frame is attached with threaded rod anchors and washers to a second spherical dome made of fire-resistance-rated, curved plywood panels attached to a curved aluminum structural tube-framing system. A sheet waterproofing and sprayed foam roofing is applied to the curved wood panels. A "zenith hub" on top of the dome connects the aluminum panel units. The aluminum exterior surface has concealed fasteners attaching the panels to the tube supports, and the connections form a watertight dome roof.

SPACE FRAME DOMES

A space frame is a three-dimensional truss with linear members that form a series of triangulated polyhedrons. It can be seen as a plane in constant depth that can sustain fairly long spans and varied configurations of shape, including dome shapes.

Space frames usually are engineered, fabricated modules, assembled on-site.

Dome roof modules can be a single-layer lattice membrane, a double layer with deep diagonals, or a double layer with vertical posts in Vierendeel truss configuration. Each manufacturer has many geometry patterns, such as geodesic, lamella, and others with unique names to the manufacturer; consult vendors for available dome structural patterns. Domes can be circular, parabolic, elliptical, compound parabolic, and inverted parabolic. Because of the inherent strength of double-curved surfaces, domes can span as far as 1000 ft. Space frame domes are made of galvanized or plated steel, stainless steel, or lightweight aluminum, and can be painted. Structural sections can be tubes, I-beams, or even angle or channel shapes. Node connections can be bolted bent plate, bolted

ALUMINUM EXTERIOR SPHERE DOME
6.15

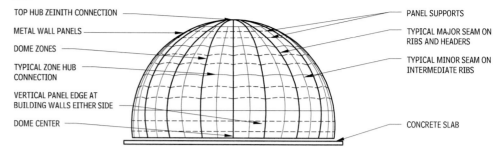

ELEVATION

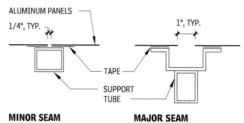

MINOR SEAM MAJOR SEAM

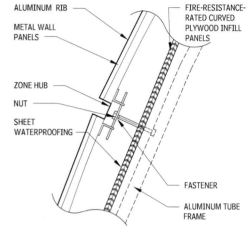

TYPICAL ZONE HUB CONNECTION

flat gusset plate, and full sphere or partial sphere with screw-in or welded connections and cylindrical hubs.

Systems are offered with glass or thermally insulated aluminum panels connected directly to the structural members, using extruded shapes and materials to receive the panels. Glass panels can have flush-glazed or batten-cap glazing connections. Numerous exterior cladding surfacing options are available, including insulated glass, metal panel decks, and thermal insulate sandwich panels.

The benefits of space frame domes are their light weight, inherent rigidity; variety of form, sizes, and spans; and compatible interaction with building mechanical infrastructure support systems.

SPACE FRAME DOMES
6.16

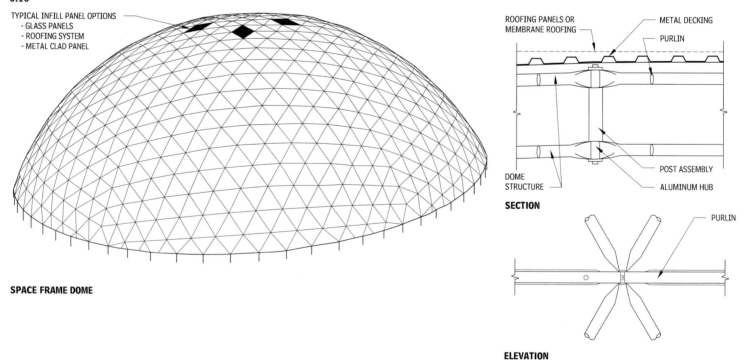

SPACE FRAME DOME

Contributor:
William Sarama, AIA, Skidmore, Owings & Merrill LLP, New York City, New York.

CABLE-SUPPORTED STRUCTURES

Cables and chains are structural elements unique in their load-carrying characteristics; they are capable only of resisting loads in tension, not compression or flexure. Steel is a material that is most efficient at resisting loads in tension, so very efficient structures can be formed if structural elements can be arranged such that many or all of the structural elements are in tension. The delicate, lightweight structures that can be created from cable-supported systems are a natural choice for the structural support of glazed façades and roofs, surfaces where the resulting potential for transparency is most advantageous.

LOADING AND VIBRATION PERCEPTION

Wind loads are often the controlling conditions for lightweight facade and roof systems, and are often of a similar magnitude in an inward and outward direction. Lightweight structural systems typically require a similar stiffness in both directions. For lightweight roof systems, the uplift wind load often exceeds the weight of the roof. Façade and roof systems can also accommodate more flexible supporting structures than floor framing due to the reduced ability of occupants to perceive movements through sight alone.

VERTICAL WALL SYSTEMS—CABLE TRUSSES

Cable truss systems are often used for wind bracing of tall, glass façades, and less conventionally, for the support of roof skylights. Trusses can be formed using a structural steel compression chord and a cable as the tension chord (Figure 6.17). This form of truss is lightweight and visually unobtrusive, but is capable only of resisting load in one direction. This truss type is, therefore, only appropriate for specific applications where it is known that the total load on the surface will be applied from only one direction.

When two of the trusses described above are connected back-to-back, to form a lightweight truss assembly it can support loads in both directions as shown in Figure 6.18. The figure shows a configuration with two compression chords forming a frame containing the two curved cables. An alternate but structurally similar configuration can be achieved with two curved cables outboard of a single compression chord. If the support points are immovable, the compression chords can be eliminated and the cable truss can support loads by each chord acting as hanging cable (Figure 6.54), similar to the main cable of a suspension bridge.

The cable-truss-supported glass walls at the Tokyo International Forum, designed by Rafael Viñoly are dramatic examples of the transparent walls that can result from the use of this type of cable support assembly.

CABLE SUPPORTED VERTICAL WALL ASSEMBLIES

When arranged in a rectilinear grid and tensioned to approximately one-quarter to one-third of their breaking strengths, a planar "cable-net" has significant resistance to being deformed out of plane. This characteristic makes for an ideal structural solution for highly transparent glass walls.

Cable-nets can be arranged as two-way systems consisting of horizontal and vertical systems (Figure 6.20) or as one-way systems consisting only of vertical cables (Figure 6.21). Two-way systems allow for longer spans to be constructed (100 by 100 ft can be achieved; larger spans are possible, but may require specialized solutions). Two-way systems also allow for simple detailing at boundary conditions, as the deflection of the cable-net is always zero at the perimeter. One-way systems are efficient for relatively short (less that 50 ft), wide walls, where the addition of horizontal cables does not add significantly to the stiffness of the wall.

Rectangular glass panels approximately 5 by 5 ft are attached to the cable-net, typically by being clamped at the glass corners by node castings, which also connect to the cable intersections (Figure 6.22). The only visible structural elements are the cables that align with the joints between the glass panels. The assembly is flexible, with maximum deflections in a 50-year return period wind event typically limited to L/45 to L/50, where L is this shortest span of the cable-net wall. The node castings are typically detailed in a manner that allows some rotation of the glass at the clamp point, allowing the cable-net to deform without breaking the glass panels. The vertical cables are typically located close to the glass, to minimize eccentric gravity loading on the cables, which otherwise

causes each course of glass panels to lean outward from the vertical plane. Joints are typically sealed to maintain weatherproofing.

The most notable early application of this system is the 70-ft-tall, 150-ft-wide cable-net wall at the Kempinski Hotel in Munich, Germany, completed in 1993 More recently, a significant development in the achievable size of cable-net walls is the 300-ft-tall, 200-ft-wide cable-net wall at the New Beijing Poly Plaza in Beijing, China, completed in 2005.

NODE CASTINGS USED TO CLAMP CABLE-NET
6.22

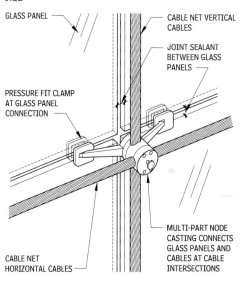

CABLE SUPPORTED ROOF ASSEMBLIES

Cable-supported roof assemblies have been utilized in a variety of configurations and scales, varying from the enclosure of courtyards to the roof assembly of sport stadiums. Roof assemblies supported by cable trusses are often utilized using a conventional beam-and-joist concept, but with heavier structural steel beams or trusses being replaced with cable trusses.

Cable-nets can also be used to support roof assemblies, although a planar cable-net is generally not the used. A planar cable-net will sag under the weight of the roof glazing; and when in this permanent deformed position, it has very little resistance to upward movement due to wind uplift. A cable-net can be stiffened for use as a roof assembly by deforming the net into a hyperbolic paraboloid or saddle shape. In this configuration, the cables in one direction curve upward, and in the other downward, therefore providing stiffness in both directions.

CABLE TRUSSES
6.17

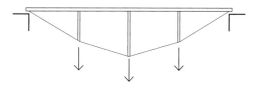

LIGHTWEIGHT TRUSS SYSTEM
6.18

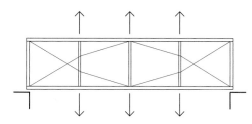

CABLE TRUSS SUPPORTING LOADS BY EACH CHORD
6.19

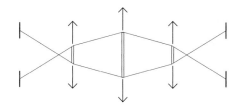

HORIZONTAL AND VERTICAL CABLE-NET
6.20

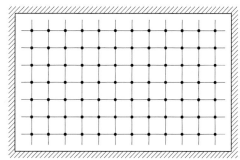

ONE-WAY CABLE-NET WITH VERTICAL CABLES
6.21

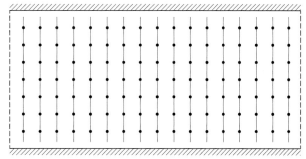

Additional structural systems employed in stadium roofs include tension or inverted domes (where the cladding may form a convex dome, but the structure is effectively a concave dome of cable elements in tension), and suspended roofs hung from support points on pylons above the roof level. All roof forms possible using fabric roofs can also be formed with a mesh of cables replacing the structural fabric, then clad with fabric, wood, or other materials.

CABLE MATERIALS

The cables are typically architecturally exposed and difficult to apply coatings to, therefore cable elements are generally manufactured from corrosion-resistive materials. Stainless steel cables are the most common material used in cable-supported structures, though galvanized steel cables can also be used. Stainless steel cables from 1/8 to 1-1/2 in. in diameter are commonly available, and galvanized steel cables can be manufactured in diameters exceeding 6 in. Stainless steel cables are typically connected to other elements through swaged end fittings, a technology that allows for relatively small end fittings (fitting diameter is approximately twice the cable diameter) but that is difficult to employ on cables larger than 1-1/2 in. diameter. Larger-diameter galvanized cables are typically connected to other elements using zinc-poured end fittings.

CABLE FIREPROOFING

It is possible but difficult to fireproof cable elements. Cable-supported structures are generally most suitable for use in conditions where fireproofing of the cables is not required by code or can be shown to be unnecessary through the use of engineering analysis. Typically, the principal attraction of the use of cables in structures, being the minimal dimensions of structural elements, is lost when cables are required to be fireproofed.

ENGINEERING

Due to the unconventional nature of these structural systems, an engineer familiar with the design of cable structures or a specialty manufacturer is typically consulted when designing cable-supported façade and roof assemblies of this type.

INSTALLATION

The construction tolerances required, both in terms of geometrical tolerances and tolerances on the installed cable tensions required in the final configuration, make it important that the installation of cable-supported façade and roof assemblies are performed by a qualified installer contractor.

FABRIC STRUCTURES

There are two types of nonpneumatic fabric structures. One supports the fabric membrane with a rigid frame, usually constructed of metal, the other is a self-supporting fabric membrane kept in tension with a supporting structure of steel or concrete. The rigid frame structures typically form pyramidal or long, continuous geometric shapes like sheds or barrel vaults. The self-supporting structures rely on opposing curves to distribute the necessary tension and typically form saddle, conical, or hyperboloid (anticlastic) shapes.

The structure that creates and maintains tension on the fabric can consist of cables and masts, a compression ring, trussed gridwork, or tied edges. These mechanisms create tension in the fabric sufficient to keep it taut. Any compressive loads imposed on the fabric will be balanced or, at most, reduced by the prestress created by the structure.

FABRIC STRUCTURE MATERIALS

The intended life span of the structure is an important factor in design decisions, fabrication details, and the cost of architectural fabric structures. The life span is most affected by the fabric material or membrane selected. Fabric is a directional material and does not have the same strength or elongation in all directions under a load. Materials with little creep are preferable for tensioned structures, as original prestress can be lost if the fabric stretches or deforms. Details allowing for retensioning must be incorporated if materials with moderate to high creep are used. Generally, the materials used in a membrane are composites consisting of a woven substrate protected with an applied coating.

The membrane is the principal structural component of a self-supporting or tensioned fabric structure. Two materials are generally used for membranes: polyvinyl chloride (PVC)-coated materials and fluorocarbon- (Teflon-) coated glass fiber fabric.

- *PVC-coated polyester* is a composite material composed of vinyl coating over both faces of a woven polyester fabric. The material is inexpensive, strong, translucent, and easy to fabricate, but has a limited life span and is only fire-resistant. For these reasons, it is used only in temporary or semipermanent structures.
- *Fluorocarbon-coated glass fiber fabric* is classified as a noncombustible material. Besides its advantages in fire safety, this fabric is extremely long-lasting, self-cleaning, and translucent, and is the accepted material for most permanent installations.

Development continues in fabric technology, and new products such as silicon-coated glass fiber may offer an improvement in the range of material characteristics.

FABRIC STRUCTURE DESIGN

In recent years, the structural design of fabric structures has improved due to the increased use of the computer in the engineering process. The first step in the design process aided by computer modeling is the definition of an acceptable surface geometry, such as the hyperboloid. A membrane mesh or network is then developed, representing the surface as a grid of lines. This graphic model is "prestressed," and the reactions are analyzed in an iterative, or repetition-based, process. Live loads such as wind, rain, or snow are applied to the model, and the stresses calculated n order to select the fabric and design the supporting structure or foundation.

The design, fabrication, and construction of fabric structures require close coordination among the architect, engineer, fabricator, and installer throughout the process, to ensure the strict quality control this technology requires. However, because most of the work is completed in the factory, minimizing on-site construction time, it is not unreasonable to maintain tight specifications.

FABRIC STRUCTURE DESIGNS
6.23

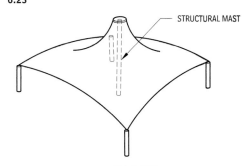

STRUCTURAL MAST

CONICAL-TYPE SURFACE GEOMETRY

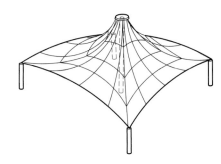

MEMBRANE MESH OVERLAY

TYPICAL CONE-SHAPED TENSILE FABRIC STRUCTURE
6.24

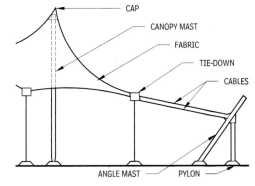

CAP
CANOPY MAST
FABRIC
TIE-DOWN
CABLES
ANGLE MAST
PYLON

Contributor:
Aaron Mazeika PE, Skidmore, Owings & Merrill LLP, San Francisco, California; Industrial Fabrics Association, Roseville, Minnesota; Adapted with permission from *Architectural Fabric Structures: The Use of Tension Fabric Structures by Federal Agencies* (Washington National Academy Press, 1985); Kathleen O'Meara, OM Architecture, Baltimore, Maryland; David Campbell, Geiger Engineers, Suffern, New York.

FABRIC STRUCTURE ANCHORAGE DETAILS
6.25

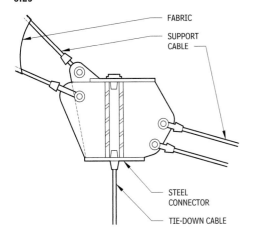

TIE-DOWN SECTION

FABRIC EDGE CLAMP—ATTACHMENT DETAIL
6.26

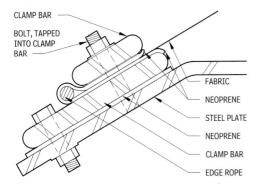

EDGE OR CATENARY CABLE—ATTACHMENT DETAIL
6.27

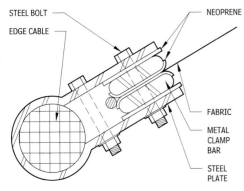

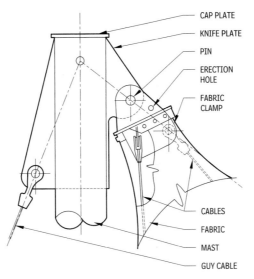

ALTERNATE EXTERIOR MAST TOP DETAIL

The two primary ways of attaching fabric to anchorages are with edge catenary cables or clamps. Catenaries allow free-form design. When a tighter connection between fabric and building structure is required (e.g., on roofs, skylights, and air structures), a clamp system is used, in which the fabric is sandwiched between clamping bars or plates, which are bolted to the structure. Some membrane structures use both kinds of attachment. Air structures sometimes have sleeves and cables, plus a fabric closure panel that extends beyond the cable.

Tensile structures usually are custom-designed; anchoring and connection details also are customized. However, basics, such as clamping systems, have become more standardized. Some frame and connection materials have been adapted from other industries, such as space frames and marine rigging. To determine the appropriate design aesthetic for a project, consider the following aspects:

- Tensile structures are flexible, and the details must be designed to move under loads.
- Tensile structures weigh a fraction of the amount of other buildings, and many of the materials are translucent.
- Lateral forces play a much greater role in tensile structures than in conventional structures.
- It is essential that the physical resolution of each element's force vector (the angle of direction and magnitude) be accurate.
- Details, material specifications, and reaction forces affecting interfacing structures should be developed with an engineer or fabricator with the expertise in the design of fabric structures.

LOG STRUCTURES

Residential log buildings have become a significant part of the home construction industry. The log house industry comprises two main segments: kit build, which are manufactured, or milled, and custom-built log houses.

- Houses built from kits use logs that have been machined or milled to a uniform shape in a variety of profiles. Although kit-built houses can be put together quickly and with few construction skills, the finished product tends to look artificial.
- Custom-built log houses are produced from hand-peeled, hand-notched logs in their natural profile. These structures more closely resemble a traditional log construction. Kits for hand-hewn houses are also available, but their reconstruction on-site is often complicated because of longer log lengths and the heavier weight of the logs. A hydraulic crane is usually required. Many building officials require a structural engineer's approval to accompany the plans, whether the log house an architect hired by the owner generates the construction documents

DESIGN CONSIDERATIONS

A number of design issues are important to consider when building log structures:

- Hewing logs into square members removes most of the sapwood, which reduces the weight of the log and its susceptibility to insect damage and rot. The flat surfaces of square logs are also easy to work with.
- Damage from rot (fungal decay) can be prevented or controlled in three ways: remove sapwood, which is high in cellulose and lignum on which fungi feed; reduce the log's moisture content to 20 percent or less by air or kiln dying; or provide proper air circulation under floors and around foundations. Generous roof overhangs and properly maintained gutters help keep water off the sides of the building.
- Insect damage from termites, beetles, and carpenter ants can be prevented by properly seasoning the wood (kiln or air drying) and by providing continuous vapor retarders at grade. Also, good air circulation can help prevent infestations.
- Exposed interior logs must be coordinated carefully with placement of plumbing, electrical wiring, and mechanical equipment.
- Good drainage around the building is important, as log buildings are susceptible to rot.
- Manufacturers of fabricated log structures offer milled log details to reduce air leakage and improve weatherability of the wall. Such details include tongue-and-groove joints, dovetailing, use of steep splines, and butyl gaskets.
- Spaces between individual logs (*chink area*) are filled with chinking, which can vary in width.

Contributor:
David Campbell, Geiger Engineers, Suffern, New York.

LOG FRAMING
6.28

WOOD PRESERVATION—DETAIL
6.30

SCRIBED OR CHINKLESS LOG JOINERY
6.31

CHINKING DETAILS
6.29

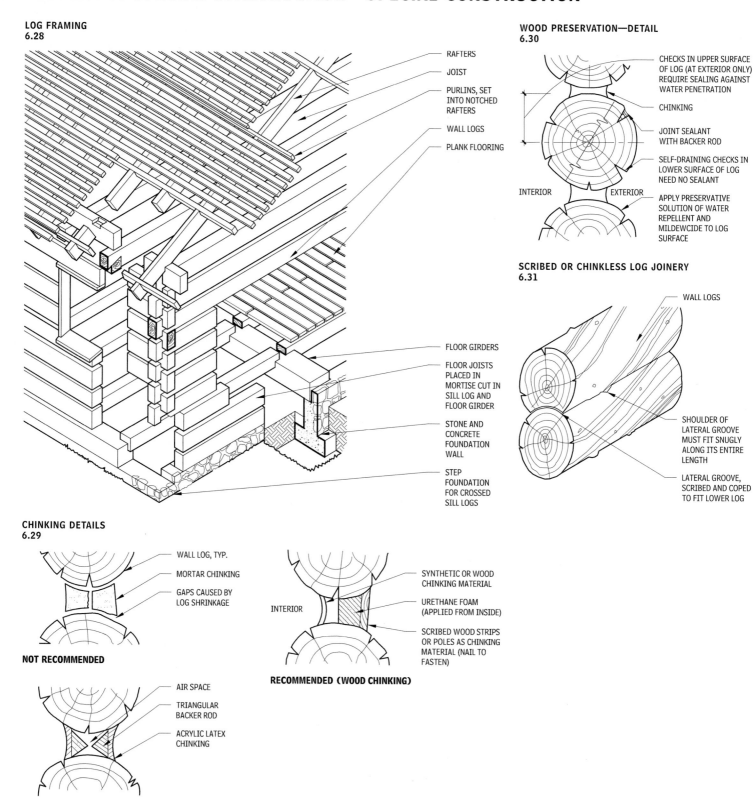

RAFTERS

JOIST

PURLINS, SET INTO NOTCHED RAFTERS

WALL LOGS

PLANK FLOORING

FLOOR GIRDERS

FLOOR JOISTS PLACED IN MORTISE CUT IN SILL LOG AND FLOOR GIRDER

STONE AND CONCRETE FOUNDATION WALL

STEP FOUNDATION FOR CROSSED SILL LOGS

CHECKS IN UPPER SURFACE OF LOG (AT EXTERIOR ONLY) REQUIRE SEALING AGAINST WATER PENETRATION

CHINKING

JOINT SEALANT WITH BACKER ROD

SELF-DRAINING CHECKS IN LOWER SURFACE OF LOG NEED NO SEALANT

APPLY PRESERVATIVE SOLUTION OF WATER REPELLENT AND MILDEWCIDE TO LOG SURFACE

INTERIOR   EXTERIOR

WALL LOGS

SHOULDER OF LATERAL GROOVE MUST FIT SNUGLY ALONG ITS ENTIRE LENGTH

LATERAL GROOVE, SCRIBED AND COPED TO FIT LOWER LOG

WALL LOG, TYP.

MORTAR CHINKING

GAPS CAUSED BY LOG SHRINKAGE

NOT RECOMMENDED

SYNTHETIC OR WOOD CHINKING MATERIAL

URETHANE FOAM (APPLIED FROM INSIDE)

SCRIBED WOOD STRIPS OR POLES AS CHINKING MATERIAL (NAIL TO FASTEN)

INTERIOR

RECOMMENDED (WOOD CHINKING)

AIR SPACE

TRIANGULAR BACKER ROD

ACRYLIC LATEX CHINKING

RECOMMENDED (SYNTHETIC CHINKING)

Contributor:
Arthur Theide, Log Homes Connect, Hailey, Idaho.

TYPICAL LOG WALL PROFILES
6.32

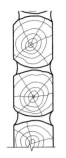

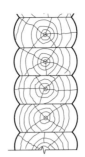
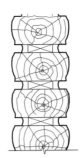

2-SIDED SAWN OR HEWN, STACKED WITH CHINKING

ROUND LOG WITH CHINKING

ROUND LOG, CHINKLESS OR SCRIBED

2-SIDED LOG, STACKED FLAT

2-SIDED SAWN LOG, STACKED FLAT WITH SPACERS AND CHINKING

TYPICAL CORNERS
6.33

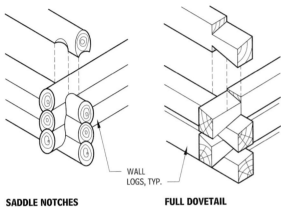
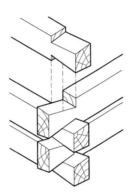
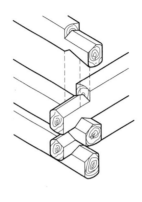
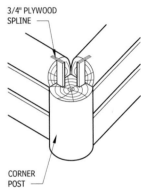

WALL LOGS, TYP.

3/4" PLYWOOD SPLINE

CORNER POST

SADDLE NOTCHES   **FULL DOVETAIL**   **HALF DOVETAIL**   **V-NOTCHES**   **POSTED CORNER**

LOG END PROFILES
6.34

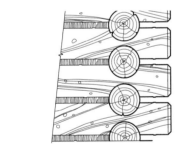
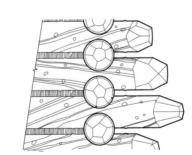

PLUMB LOG ENDS   **BEAVER-CUT LOG ENDS**

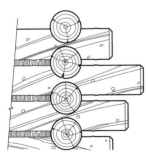
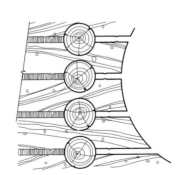

STAGGERED LOG ENDS   **ARCHED LOG ENDS**

Contributor:
Arthur Theide, Log Homes Connect, Hailey, Idaho.

7

ELEMENT G: BUILDING SITEWORK

INTRODUCTION

The site may be defined in many ways.

- The site is frequently regarded as real estate, a commodity that can be bought and sold, invested in, and developed.
- The site may be seen as a legal entity, an area of land geographically located, registered, and identified by coordinates within the survey grid.
- The site may be seen with respect to how it fits into a zoning pattern and for its potential use.
- The site may be seen as a plane, or surface, on which to build a building or facilities.
- The site may be regarded as the setting, foreground, or functional area for a building.
- Of course, many see their land, or site, as their possession, their private place of retreat, their domain and kingdom.

All of these common perceptions are true, yet they don't capture the complete essence of site. Every site is a part of a larger continuous landscape, or region, and really can't be contained by artificial or legal boundaries. As a biophysical entity, the land interacts with environmental systems such as sunlight, precipitation, and hydrology, wind, air temperature, and airborne particles. The site represents a dynamic interaction between the surface, the atmosphere above, and the earth below. The site, then, is not two-dimensional, but a three-dimensional entity. As a space of culture, the site is a place of human interaction. It serves social, psychological and experiential needs; accommodates behavior patterns, rituals, and movement; has a history; sits within a contextual land pattern; and establishes its own character and identity. In short, the site is a landscape—a complex idea with deep geographic, biological, and cultural meaning.

What, then, are the opportunities of the site? Of course, at a fundamental level, it must function in accordance with its program, incorporate elements of safety and security, and acknowledge regulatory issues.

Moving beyond that is the idea of the site as a generator of form. Orientation and aspect, topography, existing geological or other natural features, history and evidence of human use and occupation, views, edge conditions, and the site's relationship to the surrounding landscape all have the potential to become form and compositional determinants for buildings and site development.

The site can also be a mediator between interdependent cultural and environmental systems and between the past, the present, and the future. Just as a good building can adapt to different uses and needs over time, a good site is flexible and adaptable to changing conditions. The site can mediate between the forces of human society and the forces of nature to facilitate a healthy coexistence.

The site should age gracefully through time. Its materials should be enriched and not deteriorated by the forces acting upon them, and the spaces should address issues of scale, proportion and light in timeless ways. The site is a dynamic, evolutionary process, and this should be revealed in design.

The site can also be a regenerative system; it should be able to cycle and transform energy and materials and should provide for continuous energy replacement. In this way, the site works with, not against, the forces of the environment. Psychological regeneration is also important. A site that continually redesigns itself in response to external stimuli becomes a monitor of change, a source of information, and an environment of delight. A well-designed site can be experienced in remarkably different ways depending on the time of day and the time of year.

With this in mind, the site ought to become a critical part of the building process from the early conceptual design phases through the construction, and on into the evolutionary phases of the project.

SITE PREPARATION

SITE EARTHWORK

SLOPE PROTECTION AND EROSION CONTROL

Slope protection and erosion control is required when steep slopes are subject to erosion from stormwater runoff or flowing streams. Erosion can damage the site and pollute waterways with sediment.

The need for mechanical stabilization can be reduced through careful site gradings that divert or slow the velocity of runoff and by avoiding disturbances to stable, natural streambanks. Check with regulatory agencies before planning to grade streambanks, wetlands, or floodplains.

Numerous proprietary products are available for streambank stabilization and erosion control, so consult manufacturers.

Follow these general design guidelines:

- Control erosion during construction with silt fences, straw bales, sediment ponds, and seeding and mulching. Adhere to local and state guidelines and regulations.
- Line channels with erosion-resistant material (sod, stone riprap, erosion-control blanket). Channel dimensions and lining should be designed for expected runoff.
- At the bottom of the slope drain channel, convey the flow to a storm sewer, detention pond, constructed wetland, or other control method that meets regulations.

GRADING AND EROSION CONTROL
7.1

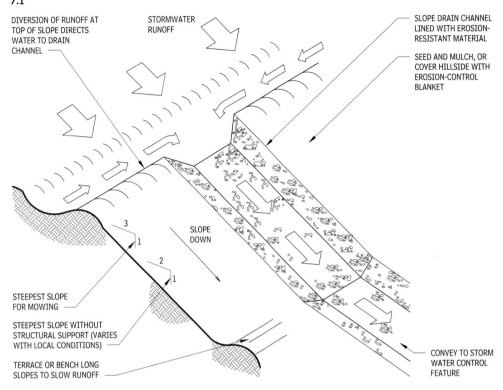

DIVERSION OF RUNOFF AT TOP OF SLOPE DIRECTS WATER TO DRAIN CHANNEL

STORMWATER RUNOFF

SLOPE DRAIN CHANNEL LINED WITH EROSION-RESISTANT MATERIAL

SEED AND MULCH, OR COVER HILLSIDE WITH EROSION-CONTROL BLANKET

SLOPE DOWN

STEEPEST SLOPE FOR MOWING

STEEPEST SLOPE WITHOUT STRUCTURAL SUPPORT (VARIES WITH LOCAL CONDITIONS)

TERRACE OR BENCH LONG SLOPES TO SLOW RUNOFF

CONVEY TO STORM WATER CONTROL FEATURE

Contributor:
James E. Sekela, PE, Pittsburgh, Pennsylvania.

**STREAMBANK STABILIZATION
7.2**

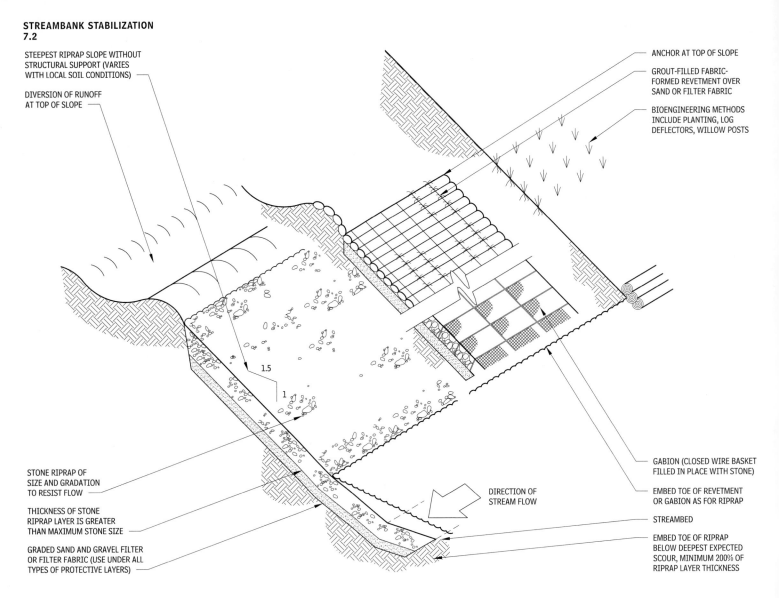

STEEPEST RIPRAP SLOPE WITHOUT
STRUCTURAL SUPPORT (VARIES
WITH LOCAL SOIL CONDITIONS)

DIVERSION OF RUNOFF
AT TOP OF SLOPE

ANCHOR AT TOP OF SLOPE

GROUT-FILLED FABRIC-
FORMED REVETMENT OVER
SAND OR FILTER FABRIC

BIOENGINEERING METHODS
INCLUDE PLANTING, LOG
DEFLECTORS, WILLOW POSTS

1.5

1

STONE RIPRAP OF
SIZE AND GRADATION
TO RESIST FLOW

THICKNESS OF STONE
RIPRAP LAYER IS GREATER
THAN MAXIMUM STONE SIZE

GRADED SAND AND GRAVEL FILTER
OR FILTER FABRIC (USE UNDER ALL
TYPES OF PROTECTIVE LAYERS)

DIRECTION OF
STREAM FLOW

GABION (CLOSED WIRE BASKET
FILLED IN PLACE WITH STONE)

EMBED TOE OF REVETMENT
OR GABION AS FOR RIPRAP

STREAMBED

EMBED TOE OF RIPRAP
BELOW DEEPEST EXPECTED
SCOUR, MINIMUM 200% OF
RIPRAP LAYER THICKNESS

SITE IMPROVEMENTS

POROUS PAVEMENTS

Porous pavements reduce or eliminate urban storm water problems at the source by changing the way urban structures are built and the way they operate hydrologically. They restore the landscape's natural water-retaining function by bringing water back into contact with the underlying soil, or emulate it by filtering and storing water in the pavement structure. By combining pavement stormwater control functions into a single structure, they reduce costs, compared with dense pavements that require downstream storm water control facilities.

Properly applied porous pavements can also enlarge urban tree rooting space, reduce the urban heat island effect, reduce traffic noise, increase driving safety, and improve appearance. Therefore, their selection and implementation are integral parts of the multifaceted concerns of urban design, and all of their effects are considered together in evaluations of benefits and costs. As porous paving materials become increasingly used, their potential cumulative effect is great, because pavements are the most ubiquitous man-made structures—they occupy two-thirds of the constructed surfaces in urban watersheds.

This section briefly reviews the types of porous paving materials that are available and some provisions necessary in their installation. Considerably more scope and detail on this subject are covered in the book *Porous Pavements*, by Bruce K. Ferguson (Boca Raton, FL: CRC Press, 2005).

POROUS PAVEMENT CONSTRUCTION

To make a successful porous pavement, it must be selected right, designed right, installed right, and maintained right. Failures—clogging and structural degradation—result from neglecting one or more these steps. Construction of porous pavements is not more difficult than that of dense pavements, but it is different, and its different specifications and procedures must be strictly adhered to.

The dominant component in most porous paving materials is aggregate, such as crushed stone. It is crucial that this aggregate be "open-graded"—that is, have a narrow range of particle sizes. The void space between single-sized particles typically amounts to 30 to 40 percent of the aggregate's volume; the aggregate's permeability is commonly over 1000 in. per hour. As long as the particles are angular, open-graded aggregate obtains structural stability from particle-to-particle interlock.

To protect a pavement's surface from sedimentary clogging, surface drainage should be away from the pavement edge in every possible direction, so that sediment is prevented from washing on and, conversely, being allowed to wash off. On the downhill side, large, numerous curb cuts should be added, if necessary. On the uphill side, a swale should be added, if necessary, to divert potentially sediment-laden runoff. These provisions limit most porous pavements to infiltrating the stormwater that falls directly upon the pavement, not runoff from surrounding earthen slopes.

Contributor:
James E. Sekela, PE, Pittsburgh, Pennsylvania.

POROUS PAVEMENT CONSTRUCTION WITH FLUSH CURB
7.3

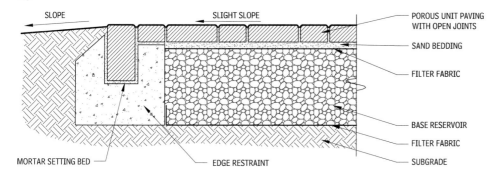

SLOPE — SLIGHT SLOPE

POROUS UNIT PAVING WITH OPEN JOINTS

SAND BEDDING

FILTER FABRIC

BASE RESERVOIR

FILTER FABRIC

SUBGRADE

MORTAR SETTING BED — EDGE RESTRAINT

POROUS PAVEMENT CONSTRUCTION WITH RAISED CURB
7.4

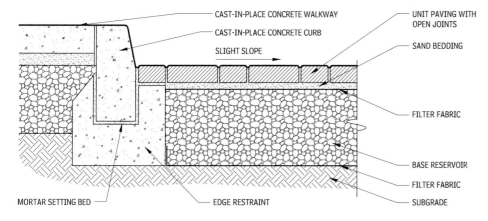

CAST-IN-PLACE CONCRETE WALKWAY

CAST-IN-PLACE CONCRETE CURB

SLIGHT SLOPE

UNIT PAVING WITH OPEN JOINTS

SAND BEDDING

FILTER FABRIC

BASE RESERVOIR

FILTER FABRIC

SUBGRADE

MORTAR SETTING BED — EDGE RESTRAINT

Each porous paving material has its own advantages and disadvantages for specific applications, and its own requirements for design, construction, and maintenance. A development site should be analyzed in detail to distinguish pavement settings where different, optimally suited materials can be placed. In all pavements, areas can be distinguished with different needs for hydrology, appearance, subsurface tree rooting, and cost.

PAVEMENT SETTINGS: TYPES OF PAVEMENT SETTINGS THAT CAN BE DISTINGUISHED FOR SELECTING DIFFERENT APPROPRIATE PAVING MATERIALS
7.5

TYPE OF AREA	DISTINGUISHED TYPE OF AREA
Universally accessible pedestrian routes requiring firm, smooth surface	General pedestrian routes
Turning lanes in parking lots requiring surface stability for braking and turning	Parking stalls
Heavily used parking stalls near the entrance of commercial buildings	Seldom-used parking stalls distant from entrances
Street traveling lanes requiring surface stability for braking and turning	Street parking lanes
Streets with swiftly, smoothly moving traffic requiring smooth, quiet surface	Streets with "calmed" traffic, where coarse texture and perceptible noise may be desirable
Steeply sloping pavements (>5%±) requiring stable surface and subsurface	Gently sloping pavements
Reliable turf maintenance routines	Unreliable maintenance routines

ALTERNATIVE POROUS PAVING MATERIALS

There are a number of alternative porous paving materials, among them:

- *Porous aggregate* is unbound gravel, crushed stone, crushed recycled brick, or decomposed granite. In most regions, unbound aggregate is both the least expensive of all firm surfacing materials and the most permeable. It is suitable for very light traffic such as that in residential driveways, lightly used portions of parking lots, and lightly used walkways. Annual maintenance for weeding or to replace lost material may be necessary.
- *Porous turf* makes a "green" open space where transpiration actively cools urban heat islands. It is suitable for bearing very light traffic, such as that in parking spaces used once per week or during seasonal peak shopping periods. The rooting-zone soil should be sandy, to resist compaction. Porous turf must be regularly mowed, fertilized, and irrigated; and because maintenance must be scheduled, it should be used only where traffic can be controlled or predictably scheduled.
- *Plastic geocells* are latticelike products that hold aggregate or topsoil in their cells, inhibiting displacement and compaction. The surface permeability, temperature, and visual appearance are essentially that of the grass or aggregate fill.
- *Open-jointed blocks and open-celled grids* are units of concrete, brick or stone, with open joints or cells. Porous aggregate or turf in the openings gives the pavement its porosity and permeability. Many block products can bear remarkably heavy traffic, but absorbs water intended for turf and holds heat in warm climates.
- *Porous concrete* is portland cement concrete made with single-sized aggregate. A qualified installer is required. The durability of porous concrete in cold climates can be enhanced by air entrainment and polymer fiber reinforcing. Properly installed porous concrete can bear heavy traffic loads, and the surface is universally accessible by most measures.
- *Porous asphalt* is bituminous concrete made with single-sized aggregate. Polymer fibers and liquid polymer additive can reduce drainage of the binder down through the pores—without them, the binder would leave surface aggregate particles unbound while accumulating into a clogging layer inside the structure. Properly installed porous asphalt can bear heavy traffic loads, and the surface is universally accessible by most measures.
- *"Soft" paving materials* include granular organic or recycled materials such as bark mulch, crushed shells, and rubber granules. They are suitable for very light traffic such as that in pedes-

CONSTRUCTION OF TRAFFIC-BEARING TURF
7.6

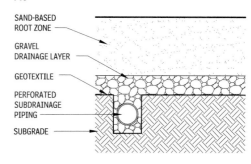

SAND-BASED ROOT ZONE

GRAVEL DRAINAGE LAYER

GEOTEXTILE

PERFORATED SUBDRAINAGE PIPING

SUBGRADE

POROUS UNIT PAVING
7.7

TYPE	TYPICAL SURFACE PATTERN
Unit Pavers with indentations (e.g., Uni Eco-Stone)	
Unit Pavers with spacers (e.g., SF-Rima)	
Unit Pavers laid in open-jointed pattern (e.g., brick)	
Open-celled grids (e.g., Turfstone)	
Widely spaced Unit Pavers (e.g., fieldstone)	

Contibutor:
Bruce K. Ferguson, FASLA, University of Georgia, Athens, Georgia.

trian walkways, residential driveways, equestrian ways, and very lightly used parking stalls. Materials with durable single-sized particles have the highest infiltration rates and are the least susceptible to displacement, crushing, and compaction.

- *Decks* are surrogates for pavements. They are completely permeable to air and water as long as their decking components are perforated or spaced apart from each other. Their footings leave the soil below almost entirely free for infiltration and tree rooting. Decks are uniquely suited to sites with steep slopes or where native tree roots or ecosystem dynamics are to be very conscientiously protected. They are made from a variety of natural, manufactured, and recycled materials; hence, their durability varies with the material and its preservative treatment.).

PARKING LOTS

DESIGN CONSIDERATIONS FOR PARKING LOTS

Creating vital places is the job of those of who design, build, finance, and plan the built environment. Unfortunately, too often, as acres of asphalt attest, engineering standards are applied cavalierly; they are not used properly to help design the place. Even "just a parking lot" can be made into a place of delight.

Some strategies to employ that go beyond bare-bones engineering are:

- *Parking courts*: Like the forecourt of a grand English manor, a parking place can serve as the introduction to a building. It may be a formal garden, an entrance hall, or a place to display art.
- *Multiple uses*: For many of the hours in a year, even a busy parking lot stands empty or underused. Find and design for other activities such as youth basketball, or the summer yard of a garden store.
- *Design for pedestrians*: Make the pedestrian activities the highest priority in the placement, size, location, and other details of the site design. Virtually everyone who drives to a parking lot walks out of it.
- *Reduce parking*: Find a means for multiple uses to share a lot over the course of the day or week. Design so that people can park once and go to multiple destinations. Design so that the parking does not impede other modes of transport such as walking, bicycles, or buses.

The tables and diagrams in this section provide the basic guidelines for the size and layout of stalls, grades in parking lots, the geometry of end islands, and the number of accessible stalls. For more detailed information on the design of access driveways, circulation patterns, calculating parking demand, safety, sustainability, and other aspects, refer to *Parking Spaces: A Design, Implementation, and Use Manual for Architects, Planners, and Engineers,* by Mark C. Childs (New York: McGraw-Hill, 1999).

END ISLANDS
7.9

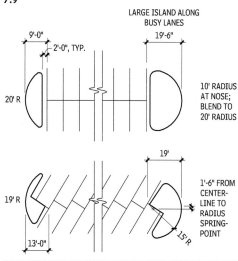

LARGE ISLAND ALONG BUSY LANES

9'-0"
19'-6"
2'-0", TYP.
20' R
10' RADIUS AT NOSE; BLEND TO 20' RADIUS

19'
19' R
1'-6" FROM CENTER-LINE TO RADIUS SPRING-POINT
15' R
13'-0"

SPACE LAYOUTS
7.8

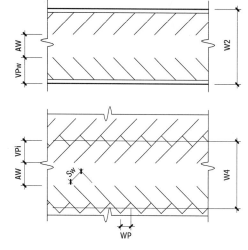

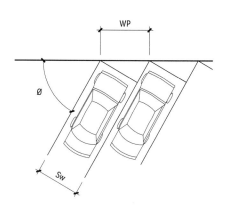

STALL AND MODULE DIMENSIONS
7.10

ANGLE	CAR TYPES	TURNOVER	STALL WIDTH		STALL DEPTH PARALLEL TO AISLE		AISLE WIDTH	MINIMUM MODULES	
			PARALLEL TO CAR	PARALLEL TO AISLE	TO WALL	TO INTERLOCK	MINIMUM	WALL TO WALL	INTERLOCK TO INTERLOCK
			(SW) (FT)	(WP) (FT)	(VP^w) (FT)	(VP^i) (FT)	(AW) (FT)	(W2) (FT)	(W4) (FT)
90	Mix	A	9.00	9.0	18.4	18.4	24.0	60.8	60.8
		B	8.75	8.8	18.4	18.4	24.0	60.8	60.8
		C	8.50	8.5	18.4	18.4	24.0	60.8	60.8
		D	8.25	8.3	18.4	18.4	24.0	60.8	60.8
	Small	A	8.00	8.0	15.1	15.1	22.3	52.4	52.4
		B	7.75	7.8	15.1	15.1	22.3	52.4	52.4
		C	7.50	7.5	15.1	15.1	22.3	52.4	52.4
		D	7.25	7.3	15.1	15.1	22.3	52.4	52.4
75	Mix	A	9.00	9.3	19.4	18.6	21.0	59.9	58.2
		B	8.75	9.1	19.4	18.6	21.0	59.9	58.2
		C	8.50	8.8	19.4	18.6	21.0	59.9	58.2
		D	8.25	8.5	19.4	18.6	21.0	59.9	58.2
	Small	A	8.00	8.3	16.2	15.4	20.0	52.5	50.8
		B	7.75	8.0	16.2	15.4	20.0	52.5	50.8
		C	7.50	7.8	16.2	15.4	20.0	52.5	50.8
		D	7.25	7.5	16.2	15.4	20.0	52.5	50.8
70	Mix	A	9.00	9.6	19.5	18.4	18.6	57.5	55.3
		B	8.75	9.3	19.5	18.4	18.6	57.5	55.3
		C	8.50	9.0	19.5	18.4	18.6	57.5	55.3
		D	8.25	8.8	19.5	18.4	18.6	57.5	55.3
	Small	A	8.00	8.5	16.4	15.3	17.9	50.6	48.4
		B	7.75	8.2	16.4	15.3	17.9	50.6	48.4
		C	7.50	8.0	16.4	15.3	17.9	50.6	48.4
		D	7.25	7.7	16.4	15.3	17.9	50.6	48.4
65	Mix	A	9.00	9.9	19.4	18.0	16.1	54.9	52.2
		B	8.75	9.7	19.4	18.0	16.1	54.9	52.2
		C	8.50	9.4	19.4	18.0	16.1	54.9	52.2
		D	8.25	9.1	19.4	18.0	16.1	54.9	52.2
	Small	A	8.00	8.8	16.4	15.0	15.7	48.5	45.8
		B	7.75	8.6	16.4	15.0	15.7	48.5	45.8
		C	7.50	8.3	16.4	15.0	15.7	48.5	45.8
		D	7.25	8.0	16.4	15.0	15.7	48.5	45.8

Contributor:
Mark Childs, University of New Mexico, Albuquerque, New Mexico.

STALL AND MODULE DIMENSIONS (continued)
7.10

ANGLE	CAR TYPES	TURNOVER	STALL WIDTH PARALLEL TO CAR (SW) (FT)	STALL WIDTH PARALLEL TO AISLE (WP) (FT)	STALL DEPTH PARALLEL TO AISLE TO WALL (VPʷ) (FT)	STALL DEPTH PARALLEL TO AISLE TO INTERLOCK (VPⁱ) (FT)	AISLE WIDTH MINIMUM (AW) (FT)	MINIMUM MODULES WALL TO WALL (W2) (FT)	MINIMUM MODULES INTERLOCK TO INTERLOCK (W4) (FT)
60	Mix	A	9.00	10.4	19.1	17.5	13.7	51.9	48.7
		B	8.75	10.1	19.1	17.5	13.7	51.9	48.7
		C	8.50	9.8	19.1	17.5	13.7	51.9	48.7
		D	8.25	9.5	19.1	17.5	13.7	51.9	48.7
	Small	A	8.00	9.2	16.3	14.7	13.6	46.1	42.9
		B	7.75	8.9	16.3	14.7	13.6	46.1	42.9
		C	7.50	8.7	16.3	14.7	13.6	46.1	42.9
		D	7.25	8.4	16.3	14.7	13.6	46.1	42.9
55	Mix	A	9.00	11.0	18.7	16.9	11.2	48.7	45.1
		B	8.75	10.7	18.7	16.9	11.2	48.7	45.1
		C	8.50	10.4	18.7	16.9	11.2	48.7	45.1
		D	8.25	10.1	18.7	16.9	11.2	48.7	45.1
	Small	A	8.00	9.8	16.0	14.2	11.5	43.5	39.8
		B	7.75	9.5	16.0	14.2	11.5	43.5	39.8
		C	7.50	9.2	16.0	14.2	11.5	43.5	39.8
		D	7.25	8.9	16.0	14.2	11.5	43.5	39.8
50	Mix	A	9.00	11.7	18.2	16.2	11.0	47.4	43.3
		B	8.75	11.4	18.2	16.2	11.0	47.4	43.3
		C	8.50	11.1	18.2	16.2	11.0	47.4	43.3
		D	8.25	10.8	18.2	16.2	11.0	47.4	43.3
	Small	A	8.00	10.4	15.7	13.6	11.0	42.4	38.2
		B	7.75	10.1	15.7	13.6	11.0	42.4	38.2
		C	7.50	9.8	15.7	13.6	11.0	42.4	38.2
		D	7.25	9.5	15.7	13.6	11.0	42.4	38.2
45	Mix	A	9.00	12.7	17.5	15.3	11.0	46.1	41.5
		B	8.75	12.4	17.5	15.3	11.0	46.1	41.5
		C	8.50	12.0	17.5	15.3	11.0	46.1	41.5
		D	8.25	11.7	17.5	15.3	11.0	46.1	41.5
	Small	A	8.00	11.3	15.2	12.9	11.0	41.4	36.9
		B	7.75	11.0	15.2	12.9	11.0	41.4	36.9
		C	7.50	10.6	15.2	12.9	11.0	41.4	36.9
		D	7.25	10.3	15.2	12.9	11.0	41.4	36.9

Sources: Adapted and recalculated from Parking, Robert D. Weant and Herberts Levinson, 1990, Eno Foundation; Parking Structures: Planning, Design, Construction, Maintenance and Repair, Anthony P. Chrest, Mary S. Smith, Sam Bhuyan, Chapman & Hall, 1996; Ricker, 1957.

STALL DIMENSIONS FOR SPECIAL CONDITIONS
7.11

	WIDTH (FT)	LENGTH (FT)	CLEAR HEIGHT (FT)
Designated large	9	18.5 to 20	
Passenger truck[a]	9	18.5	
Accessible car[b]	8 + 5 for aisle	17.5	
Accessible van[b]	8 + 8 for aisle	17.5	8.16
Universal[c] (accessible car or van)	11 + 5 for aisle		8.16
Valet[d]	7.5	17	
Europe typical[e]	7.83 to 8.16	15.58 to 16.42	
Bicycle[e]	2.5	6	
Motorcycle[e]	3.33	7	

CURB PARKING
7.12

	STALL LENGTH	STALL OTHER	SOURCE
Accessible loading	22' minimum	Platform 5' wide, 20' long, 9.5' clear height	ADAAG 4.6.5 and 4.6.6
Truck loading	30'–60'	Add truck length per additional truck.	Weant & Levinson
Drop-offs/ taxi	50'	Add 25' per additional vehicle.	Weant & Levinson
Paired (length per pair)	44'–50'	20' stalls	Hunnicutt, p. 666
Compact	19'		Hunnicutt, p. 666
End stall	20'		Hunnicutt, p. 666
Interior stall	22'–24'		Hunnicutt, p. 666

CURBSIDE BUS LOADING

	WHEEL POSITION FROM CURB 6"	WHEEL POSITION FROM CURB 1'		
			One 40' bus	Additional per bus
Upstream of intersection	L + 85' +	L + 65' +	105'–125'	L + 5' +
Downstream of intersection				
Street width >39'	L + 55' +	L + 40' +	80'–95'	L
Street width 32'–39'	L + 70' +	L + 55' +	95'–110'	L
Midblock				
Street width >39'	L + 135' +	L + 100' +	140'–175'	L
Street width 32'–39'	L + 150' +	L + 115' +	155'–190'	L

GRADES IN PARKING LOTS
7.13

GRADE	CONDITION
6% maximum	Continuous slope in parking lot
12% maximum, 30' long	Nonparking automobile ramps with pedestrians allowed
15% maximum	Nonparking automobile ramps with signs banning pedestrians
> 6% change	A vertical curve transition is required; see Figure 7.
1% minimum/2% rec.	Slope to drain asphalt
.5% minimum/2% rec.	Slope to drain concrete
2% (1:50) maximum	Slope within accessible stalls in any direction
5%	Accessible route running slope (2% cross slope)

NOTES

7.10 a. Turnover categories: A = very high turnover, such as at a post office or convenience store; B = high turnover, such as at a general retail store; C = medium turnover, such as at airports or hospitals; D = low turnover, such as at an employee parking lot.
b. Figure 7.11 defines the dimensions used in this table
c. Stalls at angles between 90° and 60° are confusing as to whether the aisle is one-way or two-way. Do not use angles between 90° and 75°. Stalls at a 75° angle with two-way aisles are advocated by some because the right-hand side parking maneuver is easier into an angled stall; however, making a left-hand turn to park in a 75° stall is difficult. A minimum of 22 ft is necessary for two-way aisles, and 24 to 25 ft allows ample walking space and occasional left-hand parking. Stalls at angles between 45° and 0° (parallel parking) are not generally advisable because they are space-inefficient and confusing.

d. Stall stripes are often painted 6 to 10 in. shorter than the stall depth to encourage drivers to pull fully into the stall.
e. The table uses a minimum aisle width of 11 ft. This dimension is minimally sufficient to allow passage of cars and pedestrians. In high turnover or special situations such as lots primarily serving the elderly or children, a pedestrian walkway and/or a wider aisle should be provided.
7.11 a. From Charles E. Dare, "Consideration of Special Purpose Vehicles in Parking Lot Design." ITE Journal, May 1985.
b. (ATBCB) Architectrual and Transportation Barriers Compliance Board, Americans with Disabilities Act Accessibilities Guidelines for Buildings and Facilities; Final Guidelines (ADAAG). 36 CFR Part 1191, 1991.
c. (ATBCB) Architectural and Transportation Barriers Compliance Board, Bulletin #6: Parking, 1994.

d. From Robert H. Burrage and Edward G. Morgen, Parking (Eno Foundation for Highway Traffic Control, 1957), p. 242.
e. From James Hunnicutt, "Parking, Loading, and Terminal Facilities" in Transportation and Traffic Engineering Handbook (Prentice Hall, 1982, p.50).
f. From Robert Weant and Herbert Levinson, Parking (Eno Foundatiuon for Highway Traffic Control, 1990), p. 167.
7.12 a. Bus-loading statistics adapted from First name or initials Homburger and First name or initials Quinby, "Urban Transit," in Transportation and Traffic Engineering Handbook, 2nd ed. (Prentice Hall, 1982).
b. L = length of bus.
7.13 Adapted from Chrest, Smith & Bhuyan, 1996; ITE, 1982; and Untermann, 1984.

Contributors:
Mark Childs, University of New Mexico, Albuquerque, New Mexico.

REQUIRED NUMBER OF ACCESSIBLE STALLS
7.14

GENERAL CASE	
TOTAL IN PARKING LOT	**REQUIRED MINIMUM NUMBER OF ACCESSIBLE SPACES**
1–25	1
26–50	2
51–75	3
76–100	4
101–150	5
151–200	6
201–300	7
301–400	8
401–500	9
501–1000	2% of total
1001 and over	20 + 1 per 100 over 1000
Number of accessible spaces	Required minimum number of van-accessible spaces
1–8	1
33 and over	1 additional van-accessible per 8 accessible spaces

SPECIAL CASES	
PLACE	**REQUIREMENT**
Medical outpatient units	10% of total stalls in lots serving visitors and patients
Medical units that specialize in persons with mobility impairments	20% of total stalls in lots serving visitors and patients
Valet parking	No stalls required; however, an accessible loading zone is required, and it is strongly recommended that self-park stalls be provided.
Residential	1 for each accessible dwelling unit and 2% for all additional units. Guest, employee, and nonresident parking must comply with table.

LOTS ACCESSIBLE TO THE MOBILITY IMPAIRED

Parking is a critical element of accessibility. In fact, the first federal court case that resulted in a civil penalty under Title III of the Americans with Disabilities Act (ADA) was for failure to make parking accessible.

The ADA is a civil rights law, meaning that the Department of Justice is charged with enforcing the law. People who believe they have been discriminated against may sue the property owner. The ADA Accessibility Guidelines for Buildings and Facilities (ADAAG) issued by the government are not building codes subject to state or local approval or variances.

The information in this section was compiled from publications of the United States Architectural and Transportation Barriers Compliance Board (United States Access Board) and other sources, as noted. Note, however, that the law and best practices continue to evolve, so designers are cautioned to review materials and conditions specific to the project at hand. Note that lots owned by government agencies generally follow Title II rules, which are usually more stringent than the Title III rules for privately owned lots discussed in this section.

REQUIRED NUMBER OF ACCESSIBLE STALLS

Whenever parking is supplied, no matter how the total amount is determined, a portion of the stalls must be accessible to people with mobility impairment (hereafter called *accessible stalls*). Local codes may exceed the federal requirement for required number of accessible stalls listed in Table 7.14; the more stringent rule governs. When a facility has more than one parking lot, the required number of stalls is determined lot by lot. In employee or contract lots, accessible stalls must be provided, but "accessible spaces may be used by persons without disabilities when they are not needed by (persons) with disabilities" (Bulletin #6: Parking, Architectural and Transportation Barriers Compliance Board, 1994). When the use of a facility—for example, a senior center—indicates that more accessible stalls are needed than are required according to Table 7.14, a study should be conducted to determine an adequate supply of accessible stalls.

LOCATION OF ACCESSIBLE STALLS

The location of accessible stalls must give mobility-impaired persons preferential treatment in terms of access, and must not discriminate against them in terms of amenities (e.g., if the general stalls have hail protection canopies, the accessible stalls must also). The shorthand rule is that accessible stalls should be located with the shortest possible route to the entrance(s). Relevant U.S. regulations include the following:

- "Accessible parking spaces serving a particular building shall be located on the shortest route of travel from adjacent parking to an accessible entrance. In parking facilities that do not serve a particular building, accessible parking shall be located on the shortest accessible route of travel to an accessible pedestrian entrance of the parking facility. In buildings with multiple accessible entrances with adjacent parking, accessible parking shall be dispersed and located closest to the accessible entrances."
- "Accessible spaces can be provided in other lots or locations, or in the case of parking garages, on one level only when equal or greater access is provided in terms of proximity to an accessible entrance, cost and convenience. The minimum number of spaces must still be determined separately for each lot…"

VAN-ACCESSIBLE STALLS

Van-accessible stalls must be marked as such, but this does not restrict the stall to use by vans (Bulletin #6, Parking, Architectural and Transportation Barriers Compliance Board, 1994).

ACCESSIBLE STALL LAYOUT GUIDELINES

Design guidelines for the layout of parking stalls are as follows:

- Two accessible stalls may share an access aisle. However, this should be done only when the stalls are at 90° and allow both front-in and back-in parking.
- Curb ramps or other obstructions may not be within the stall's access aisle, but may begin at the curb face when vehicles overhang a curb (Chrest, Smith & Bhuyan, 1996, p. 212).
- Car overhang may not obstruct the clear width of a sidewalk access route. Wheel stops and/or a reinforced sign post may help limit car overhang.

ACCESSIBLE SIGNAGE

Parking spaces that are to be accessible should be designated by signage indicating the spaces are reserved. Van-accessible spaces should have the words "van-accessible" printed below the universal symbol of accessibility. The ADAAG requires that the sign not be obscured by a car or parked van. Centering the sign on the access aisle may improve its visibility.

ACCESSIBLE EQUIPMENT

Equipment such as parking meters, automated teller machines, pay stations, and ticket dispensers must have accessible controls. Most such equipment is now designed with operating mechanisms that are considered accessible, so the designer's major role is to place the controls at a proper level and to provide clear access to them.

Specifically, parking meters for accessible stalls should be placed at or near the head or foot of the parking space, to ensure that no obstruction occurs for the operation of a side lift or a passenger side transfer. The meter should be placed a maximum of 42 in. above the public sidewalk. The accessible stall should be a minimum of 30 in. by 48 in.

ACCESSIBILITY OF EXISTING LOTS

Existing lots must be made accessible when it is possible to do so. "ADAAG established minimum requirements for new construction or alterations. However, existing facilities not being altered may be subject to requirements for access. This requirement is addressed by regulations issued by the Department of Justice. Under these regulations, barrier removal must comply with ADAAG requirements to the extent that is readily achievable to do so. For example, when restriping a parking lot to provide accessible spaces, if it is not readily achievable to provide the full number of accessible spaces required by ADAAG, a lesser number may be provided. The requirement to remove barriers, however, remains a continuing obligation; what is not readily achievable at one point may become achievable in the future."

When alternations are made (e.g., realigning striping or resurfacing, but not routine maintenance), whatever is altered must be made accessible unless technically infeasible and improvements to the path of travel to the lot must be made, up to a cost equal to 20 percent of the project budget.

PASSENGER LOADING ZONES

There must be at least one passenger loading zone for the mobility impaired whenever designated loading zones are provided. There must also be an access aisle at least 5 ft wide and 20 ft long adjacent and parallel to the vehicle pull-up space. A clear height of 9 ft-6 in. is required at the loading zone and along the vehicle route, to, from, and within the zone. The vehicle space and the access aisle must be level with surface slopes not exceeding 1:50 (2 percent) in all directions. Neither curb ramps nor street furniture may occupy the access aisle space.

PEDESTRIAN PAVING

DESIGN CONSIDERATIONS

Additional design guidelines for working with unit paving systems include the following:

- Drainpipes may be omitted at well-drained areas.
- Provide positive outflow for drainpipes.
- Do not use unsatisfactory soil (expanding organic). Satisfactory soil must be compacted to 95 percent.
- Hand-tight paving joints are preferred over mortar joints. However, when mortar joints are required, and freezing and thawing are frequent, use latex-modified mortar.
- Install concrete footing for edging 10 to 14 in. wide and 6 to 8 in. deep. It is preferable to place the bottom of the footing at freezing depth. If the freezing depth is deeper than the bottom of the footing, provide 4 in. of gravel below the footing.
- Interlocking pavers are available in concrete, hydraulically pressed concrete, asphalt, and brick in different weight classifications, compressive strengths, surface textures, finishes, and colors. Consult local suppliers for availability.
- Subject to the manufacturer's recommendations and local code requirements, use interlocking concrete pavers in areas subject to heavy vehicle loads at speeds of 30 to 40 mph.
- Be aware that concrete interlocking unit paver sizes may be based on metric dimensions. When paver shape permits, use the herringbone pattern for paving that is subject to vehicular traffic.
- Continuous curb or other edge restraint is required to anchor pavers in applications subject to vehicular traffic.

Contributors:
Mark Childs, University of New Mexico, Albuquerque, New Mexico, from *Parking Spaces: A Design, Implementation, and Use Manual for Architects, Planners, and Engineers* (New York: McGraw-Hill, 1999).

PEDESTRIAN CONCRETE WALK-ON GRADE
7.15

MEDIUM BROOM FINISH, UNLESS OTHERWISE SPECIFIED

CONCRETE PAVING

1/2" x 1" DEEP CONTROL JOINT (MINIMUM ACCEPTABLE DEPTH IS ONE-FIFTH OF SLAB THICKNESS)

JOINT SEALANT OVER BACKER ROD AND 1/2" EXPANSION JOINT FILLER MATERIAL

4"

COMPACTED SUBGRADE

COMPACTED AGGREGATE BASE COURSE (SOIL CONDITIONS MAY NOT REQUIRE AGGREGATE BASE)

WELDED WIRE FABRIC (WWF) BREAK AT EXPANSION JOINTS (MANY MUNICIPALITIES DO NOT PERMIT WWF WITHIN THE RIGHT-OF-WAY)

PEDESTRIAN CONCRETE WALK-ON STRUCTURE
7.16

MEDIUM BROOM FINISH, UNLESS OTHERWISE SPECIFIED

CONCRETE PAVING

1/2" x 1" DEEP CONTROL JOINT (MINIMUM ACCEPTABLE DEPTH IS ONE-FIFTH OF SLAB THICKNESS)

JOINT SEALANT OVER BACKER ROD AND 1/2" EXPANSION JOINT FILLER MATERIAL

LIGHTWEIGHT STRUCTURAL FILL

VARIES   4"

STRUCTURAL SLAB

WELDED WIRE FABRIC (WWF) BREAK AT EXPANSION JOINTS (MANY MUNICIPALITIES DO NOT PERMIT WWF WITHIN THE RIGHT-OF-WAY)

PLANTING AREA

DRAINAGE MAT CONTINUOUS OVER PROTECTION BOARD AND WATERPROOFING

BITUMINOUS WALK/BIKE PATH SECTION
7.17

BITUMINOUS PAVING BASE COURSE

BITUMINOUS PAVING SURFACE COURSE

FINISH GRADE

GEO-GRID TO ALLOW ROOTS ACCESS TO WATER AND AIR

4"

GEONET ROOT PROTECTION MAT IN TREE AREAS

COMPACTED AGGREGATE BASE COURSE

DO NOT COMPACT SUBGRADE

CRUSHED STONE PAVING
7.18

STEEL OR ALUMINUM LANDSCAPE EDGING

CRUSHED STONE OR DECOMPOSED GRANITE

COMPACTED SUBGRADE

4"

UNIT PAVER PATTERNS
7.19

RUNNING BOND

OFFSET BOND

MIXED RUNNING AND STACK BOND

BASKET WEAVE

BASKET WEAVE

STACK BOND

DIAGONAL STACK

DIAGONAL BOND

HERRINGBONE

ROMAN COBBLE

HEXAGON

BASKET WEAVE OR PARQUET

OCTAGON AND DOT

NOTES

7.15 a. Install expansion joints with joint sealant when paving is adjacent to vertical faces, curbs, steps, any fixed object, or other rigid paving material, and at maximum 20 ft o.c., unless otherwise noted on plans.
b. Meet flush with adjacent hardscape finish grades.
7.16 a. Install expansion joints with joint sealant when paving is adjacent to vertical faces, curbs, steps, any fixed object, or other rigid paving material, and at maximum 20 ft o.c., unless otherwise noted on plans.

b. Meet flush with adjacent hardscape finish grades.
7.17 Detail usually requires an arborist's input to detail connections from bed grid to finish grade.

Contributor:
Dennis Carmichael, EDAW, Inc., Alexandria, Virginia.

INTERLOCKING UNIT PAVER PATTERNS
7.20

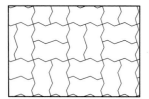

BASKET WEAVE

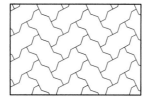

HERRINGBONE

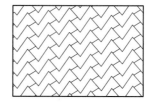

DIAGONAL RUNNING BOND

RUNNING BOND

COMBINED HEXAGON

TYPICAL PAVER SHAPES
7.21

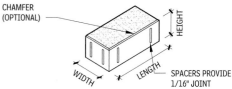

CHAMFER (OPTIONAL)

SPACERS PROVIDE 1/16" JOINT

RECTANGULAR

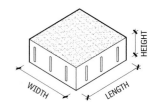

SQUARE

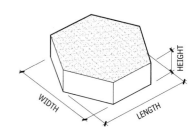

HEXAGONAL

UNIT PAVING

Unit paving assemblies are used principally for applications such as shopping plazas, building entrances, walkways, patios, residential driveways, and residential parking areas. But they may also be used for streets with heavy vehicular traffic and for industrial floors or other special conditions.

There are several types of unit pavers:

- Precast Concrete Unit Pavers
- Brick Unit Pavers
- Wood Pavers
- Recycled-Rubber Pavers
- Stone Pavers
- Porous Unit Pavers

PEDESTRIAN AND LIGHT-TRAFFIC BRICK PAVERS

Because of its more vulnerable exposure to weathering, and the constant stress of traffic, even light-traffic brick pavers must maintain higher compressive strength and lower porosity than face brick. ASTM C 902, "Standard Specification for Pedestrian and Light Traffic Paving Brick," establishes the criteria for pedestrian and light-traffic brick pavers. *Light-traffic* refers to frequency or pavements that receive limited vehicular traffic at low speeds, such as driveways and arrival courts (*light* does not refer to the weight of a vehicle). An arrival court may normally receive automobile traffic, but the occasional moving van will not damage an ASTM C 902 paver. The classification of light-traffic brick pavers is dependent on its intended application and use. There are three weathering classes of pavers and three types of pavers, based on anticipated traffic and the required levels of resistance to abrasion by traffic.

CLASSES
- *Class SX* (severe exposure) should be specified where pavements may encounter freezing while saturated with water. In contract to face brick, class SX pavers must have a minimum average compressive strength of 8000 psi. An individual unit may not have strength below 7000 psi.
- *Class MX* (moderate exposure) may be called for in southern climates where freezing is not expected.
- *Class NX* (negligible exposure) is for interior use only.

TYPES
- *Type I* bricks are recommended where highly abrasive traffic is anticipated, such as in driveways or heavily concentrated pedestrian zones.
- *Type II* bricks are best suited for typical pedestrian environments such as public walkways.
- *Type III* bricks offer the least resistance to abrasion and should be used in low-traffic residential applications.

HEAVY VEHICULAR PAVING BRICK

Where vehicular traffic is greater in speed, volume, and weight, a stronger brick is naturally required. Brick in heavy-traffic situations not only must tolerate the added structural load, but is also subjected to greater abrasion and the tendency for both horizontal and twisting forces. ASTM C 1272, "Standard Specification for Heavy Vehicular Paving Brick," establishes the standard. ASTM list two types and three application classifications for heavy vehicular paving brick.

TYPES
- *Type R* is intended for situations where a rigid or semirigid setting bed and base are provided (such as concrete or asphalt). With Type R pavers, the minimum average compressive strength is set at 8,000 psi, with the rigid setting bed and base contributing to the overall compressive strength of the cross section. Type R pavers carry a minimum thickness dimension of 2-1/4 in.
- *Type F* brick is stronger and better suited for use with a flexible base (such as compacted aggregate), along with an adequately compacted subgrade. Type F pavers are required to have a higher overall compressive strength than Type R pavers, with a minimum average of 10,000 psi. Type F pavers must have a thickness of no less than 2-5/8 in.

APPLICATIONS
- *Application PS* refers to heavy paving brick for general, all-purpose use. Where there is a greater concern for overall uniformity, including precision in dimension, degree of warping, and chipping, application PX should be specified.
- *Application PA* deals with paving bricks with specific visual characteristics, such as size and color.

Consult with a landscape architect or engineer for appropriate design guidelines.

PAVER SELECTION

Paver units are selected according to color, texture, abrasion resistance, and resistance to weathering. The texture of the unit affects slip resistance (the coarser the texture, the better the slip resistance). *Abrasion resistance* refers to the wear and tear an assembly is subjected to under normal use. According to ASTM C 902 (brick pavers) and ASTM C 936 (concrete pavers), an abrasion index classification determines the type of unit required for an intended exposure. A dense, hard-burned extruded brick with 8000 psi compressive strength that conforms to ASTM C 902, Class SX, Type 1 (water absorption of less than 5 percent, meets/exceeds ASTM C 67 freeze/thaw) resists both abrasion and weathering and is adequate for most heavy-traffic exterior applications. Molded brick with 4000 psi compressive strength that conforms to ASTM C 902, Class SX, Type 2, and may be adequate for most exterior pedestrian applications only. Some manufacturers recommend

TYPICAL PAVER SIZES (IN.)[b]
7.22

RECTANGULAR[a]		SQUARE	HEXAGONAL	
		WIDTH AND		
WIDTH	LENGTH	LENGTH	WIDTH	LENGTH
4	8	4	6	6
3-5/8	7-5/8	6	8	8
3-1/2	7-1/2	8	12	12
7-5/8	7-5/8	12		
8	8	16		

8000 psi pavers for both vehicular and pedestrian applications. Consult the manufacturer to learn which products are suitable for use as pavers in a particular application.

For all light or heavy vehicular traffic applications, 3-1/8-in. paver thickness is recommended; 2-3/8-in. thickness is recommended for pedestrian applications. Assess potential traffic loads when planning unit paving installations. Heavy vehicular loads require a rigid or semirigid continuous base, whereas a flexible base and flexible paving are suitable for light vehicular loads (residential type). Use either base type for pedestrian traffic. Appropriate base courses for heavy traffic would include asphalt over roadbase (Class 6), concrete over Class 6 roadbase, and just Class 6 roadbase. When using only roadbase under heavy loads, it should be at least twice as thick as the recommended 6-in. roadbase for pedestrian traffic.

Choose a bond pattern based on expected traffic patterns—traffic should travel perpendicular to the long dimension of the paving unit. For vehicular areas, use a gravel subbase (minimum 6 in. of crushed gravel) compacted to 95 percent, and paver sizes 8 in. square or smaller. Consult a civil engineer to accurately define paver sizes, shapes, gravel depth, concrete base depth, and concrete reinforcement requirements.

NOTES

7.22 a. Check with manufacturers for availability of chamfers.
b. The height of pavers varies with the manufacturer and application, but is usually 1-1/4, 2-1/4, 2-5/8, or 2-3/4 in.

Contributor:
Dennis Carmichael, EDAW, Inc., Alexandria, Virginia.

PAVER PREPARATION

Proper subgrade preparation of areas to be paved is important. Here are relevant guidelines:

- Remove all vegetation and organic material, and consider the location of existing or proposed underground utilities and storm drainage, as well as user convenience.
- Plan for surface and subsurface drainage. Slope paving away from buildings, retaining walls, and so on, at 1/8 to 1/4 in. per foot. Rigid paving always requires adequate surface drainage, with the long dimension of the mortar joints running parallel to the direction of runoff. Flexible paving requires both surface and subsurface drainage.
- Prevent horizontal movement of all types of mortarless unit paver assemblies—this is imperative. If the pavers are on an aggregate base, provide a rigid plastic edge restraint using spikes driven into the stone base designed for this purpose. A flush concrete curb works as well. If the paving system is over a concrete base, regardless of the setting bed (sand or bituminous), the pavers along the edge can be mortared to the base, but take care to ensure this method does not trap water which will seep into the setting bed. Another method is to secure an angle iron to the concrete base with anchor bolts, allowing for gaps on a regular basis to permit seepage. Cover vertical gaps with a small perforated metal sheet for bituminous setting beds, or filter fabric for sand beds, to prevent erosion.

In addition, be aware that chamfers on both clay and concrete pavers are required for heavy driving applications (e.g., public streets and parking lots). Chamfered edges avoid the splintering of edges that can occur.

There are three major types of unit paver joint material:

- Mortar
- Grout (portland cement and sand without hydrated lime)
- Dry mixture of grout

UNIT PAVER INLAY IN CONCRETE
7.23

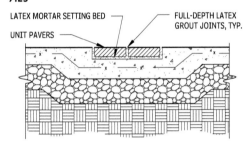

UNIT PAVERS ON SAND WITH CONCRETE BASE
7.24

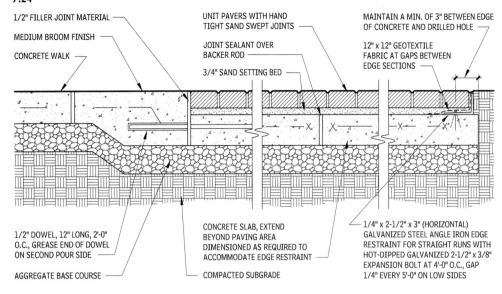

UNIT PAVERS ON BITUMINOUS WITH CONCRETE BASE
7.25

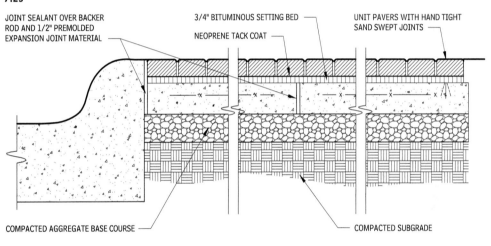

UNIT PAVERS ON AGGREGATE BASE
7.26

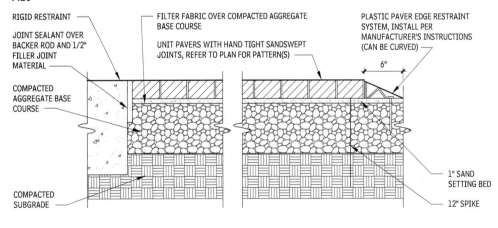

NOTES

7.23 a. Install expansion joints with joint sealant at all building faces, curbs, walls, steps, or when adjacent to any fixed object and changes in paving material, and at maximum 20 ft o.c., if not otherwise shown on plans.
b. For curved conditions, use a manufactured angle-edge restraint with same-size expansion bolts at preset openings. No anchor may be greater than 6 in. from the gap or end of run. Spacing of gaps may increase depending on design of restraint. Recommend spacing of gaps should not exceed 5 ft o.c.
c. If the landscape edging is aluminum, paint the area that comes in contact with the concrete slab with bituminous paint.
d. Meet flush with adjacent finish grades.

7.24 a. For curved conditions, use a manufactured angle-edge restraint with same-size expansion bolts at preset openings. No anchor may be greater than 6 in. from the gap or end of run. Spacing of gaps may increase depending on design of restraint. Recommend spacing of gaps should not exceed 5 ft o.c.
b. If the landscape edging is aluminum, paint the area that comes in contact with the concrete slab with bituminous paint. Also, provide an insulating fiber washer.
c. Meet flush with adjacent hardscape finish grades.
d. Refer to drainage detail if unit pavers slope to restraint.
7.25 a. Install expansion joints with joint sealant at all building faces, curbs, walls, steps, or when adjacent to any fixed object and changes in paving material, and at maximum 20 ft o.c., if not otherwise shown on plans.

b. For curved conditions, use a manufactured angle-edge restraint with same-size expansion bolts at preset openings. No anchor may be greater than 6 in. from the gap or end of run. Spacing of gaps may increase depending on design of restraint. Recommend spacing of gaps should not exceed 5 ft o.c.
c. If the landscape edging is aluminum, paint the area that comes in contact with the concrete slab with bituminous paint.
d. Meet flush with adjacent finish grades.
7.26 a. The thickness of the aggregate base varies depending on soil conditions and loading.
b. Pedestrian areas are approximately 6 to 8 in.; vehicular areas are approximately 8 to 12 in.

GRASS PAVING

GRASS PAVING SYSTEM
7.27

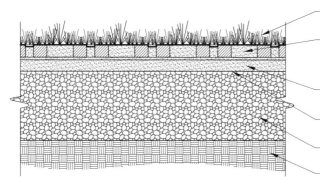

PLAN

NOTE: THERE ARE VARIOUS MANUFACTURERS OF THESE SYSTEMS. MOST ARE MADE IN SECTIONS WHICH EASILY FASTEN TOGETHER TO FACILITATE INSTALLATION. HOWEVER, SOME ARE RIGID AND DO NOT WORK WELL IN AREAS WITH AN UNDULATING GRADE. OTHER PRODUCTS ACCOMMODATE GRADE CHANGES DUE TO THE FLEXIBILITY OF THE MATRIX HOLDING THE SUPPORTS TOGETHER.

NOTE: DEPTH OF THE AGGREGATE BASE WILL VARY ACCORDING TO THE ANTICIPATED TRAFFIC, USUALLY FROM 6" TO 12". CONSULT A CIVIL ENGINEER.

HIGH DENSITY POLYETHYLENE PLASTIC

LAY SOD TURF ON TOP OF RINGS AND ROLL INTO SUPPORT SYSTEM.

BACK FILL ENTIRE GRASS PAVING SYSTEM TO APPROXIMATELY 50-75% OF ITS DEPTH WITH CLEAN, SHARP SAND. 10% ORGANICS MAY BE MIXED IN

1" MAX. SAND LEVELING COURSE WITH HYDROGROW MIX

FILTER FABRIC OVER AGGREGATE BASE COURSE

AGGREGATE BASE, COMPACT TO 95%

COMPACTED SUBGRADE

SECTION

RISER AND TREAD PROPORTIONAL DETAIL
7.28

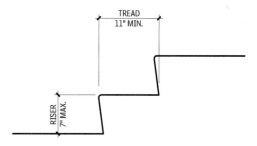

RISER HEIGHT (IN.)	TREAD DEPTH (IN.)
4	18
4-1/2	17
5	16
5-1/5	15
6	14
6-1/2	13
7	12

STAIR JOINT DETAIL
7.29

RECOMMENDED KEY JOINT OR SLIP DOWELS TO ADJACENT MATERIALS TO PREVENT DIFFERENTIAL SETTLEMENT

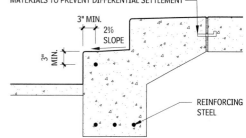

REINFORCING STEEL

EXTERIOR STAIRS AND RAMPS

Throughout the centuries, stairs and ramps have been used to address elevation changes in the landscape. They can be heroic or modest, nuanced or straightforward, detailed or plain. They represent for designers opportunities to create delight, variety, viewpoints, and accents in the movement of people across a landscape. They are also zones for heightened access and safety consideration. This section leaves for the designer's imagination the full potential of stairs and ramps as artistic design elements, and concentrates instead on access and safety design issues.

REGULATIONS

Stairs and ramps as components of the pedestrian walkway system are regulated for minimum design standards at federal, state, and local levels. With the Americans for Disabilities Act (ADA), the role of stairs and ramps in creating accessibility for all became a specific design focus. For designers, the first requirement is to thoroughly review the relevant jurisdiction's accessibility and safety codes related to stairs and ramps. Any discrepancies between the information presented in this discussion and any regulation should always be resolved in the favor of the regulation.

There are differences in the design requirements between local, state, and federal accessibility and safety regulations. Identifying and determining the relevant regulations for a project requires research and discussion with the project client. Private and local government projects usually must adhere to local, state, and federal requirements. State and federal projects usually exempt themselves from application of regulations enacted by lower jurisdictional levels.

A review meeting early in the design process with the relevant building code enforcement group is advisable. Determining the

applicable regulations with the client is a professional liability responsibility of the design professional.

EXTERIOR VERSUS INTERIOR DESIGN STANDARDS

Exterior stairs and ramps must deal with climatic issues that interior situations do not—obvious examples being rain and snow. In addition, the design and spatial variety of exterior landscape spaces make the location of stairs and ramps less predictable for pedestrians. Thus, in exterior design factors such as tread depth and slope, traction and detectable warning zones become important issues to consider. Directly applying interior stair and ramp standards to exterior locations is generally not a good practice.

EXTERIOR STAIR DETAILS

A rule of thumb for tread depths and riser heights for exterior stairs can be translated to this equation:

Height of two risers + depth of one tread = 26 inches

For exterior locations, a recommended range for risers is between 4 and 7 in., with recommended tread depth of 12 to 18 in.

Stairs in exterior locations require a slope on the tread to shed rain and snow melt. A generally recommended slope is a 2 percent slope from front to back of tread, or a 1/4-in. on a 12-in.-wide tread.

The leading edge of a step is called the *step nose*. Stairs nose details vary depending on the material used. Detailing of the stair nose is an important safety detail. The current accessibility standard is that step noses should have a radius of 1/2 in., with no overhang deeper than 1/2 in. on the step. The goal is to reduce the potential points where a person's shoe could become trapped or tripped, such as a toe under a step overhang or a heel at a sharp nose edge.

CONSTRUCTION OF EXTERIOR STAIRS

A construction concern for concrete stairs is the placement of reinforcing bars. Reinforcing steel should be placed a minimum of 3 in. back from any exposed surface of the step. Maintaining a minimum 3-in. clearance reduces the potential for breakup of the step due to differential freeze/thaw expansion between the reinforcing steel and the concrete. This is especially important in the stair nose zone. Adding slip dowels and keyed joints at the top of concrete stairs to adjacent concrete paving or subsurface layers is a good construction detail, to avoid differential settlement and tripping hazards. The bottom step footing on concrete stairs or concrete subsurface for stairs should extend down, at a minimum, to the local freeze depth.

Manufactured metal stair nosings are sometimes used in heavily trafficked locations to reduce the wear and tear on step noses. In climates with freezing temperatures, selecting a product and installation method that accounts for deferential freeze/thaw effects between the metal and the step material is important.

Metal stairs in exterior locations should be built with open-mesh metal grating or with embossed or raised patterning on the tread surface, to provide traction and the ability to release rain or snow quickly from the surface of the step. When open-mesh metal materials are used on steps, the rule of 1/4-in. maximum clear opening to provide safety for shoe heels is a good safety standard to follow.

Exterior raised steps made with wood, plastics or composites do not require a tread slope if there is a 1/4- to 1/2-in. gap between each wood member. This gap helps to release rain and snow buildup that can cause slipperiness.

NOTES

7.27 a. Voids may be filled with grass, ground cover, or gravel.
b. Grass pavers may be used to control erosion.
c. Preformed lattice unit grids are used for storm runoff control, pathways, parking areas, and soil conservation.

Contributors:
Dennis Carmichael, FASLA, EDAW, Inc., Alexandria, Virginia; Jon Pearson, EDAW, Inc., Alexandria, Virginia; John Rowe, Pavestone Company, Dallas, Texas; Faith Okuma, Design Workshop, Santa Fe, New Mexico.

For timber steps that are laid on grade, selecting wood varieties and installation methods that resist moisture rot is important to achieve long-term durability. Cedar, redwood, and preservative treated woods are generally considered reliable selections for ground-laid timber steps. A gravel subsurface is often used in high-moisture environments to reduce the moisture buildup beneath ground-laid timber steps.

Stone, when used in ground-laid steps, should be selected for flat tops and be large enough so that they do not overturn when pressure is applied at the step nose. Lapping each stone step by approximately one-fourth to one-third of their tread depth helps to prevent this overturning. If laid with spacing between each stone step, each stone should be buried up to one-third the thickness of the stone, and be level on its top surface.

Gravel beds or designed structural soil mixes such as base course should be considered whenever high moisture content or poor structural soil conditions exist. A solid subsurface contributes to the long-term durability and stability of a set of steps.

EXTERIOR STAIR RUNS, WIDTHS, AND LANDINGS

Single steps should be avoided, as they create a tripping hazard because of their lack of visibility. Stairs and steps in general should be distinguished from surround paving by a difference in material, color, or pattern, to highlight and make them more prominent. In most jurisdictions, when there are more than three steps, handrails must be provided.

As a general rule, exterior stair landings should, at a minimum, match the width of the stairs and be a minimum of 3 ft deep. Exterior stairs when located at main entries or emergency exits of buildings should, at a minimum, be the width of the exiting doorways. This helps to maintain a safe emergency egress zone. Providing a landing at doorways and gates that are served by stairs makes using doorways safer and more convenient. The swing of the door should be accounted for in scaling the depth of a landing, to avoid having to be on a step to open or close a door or gate.

Installing intermediate stair landings where an elevation change of between 2.5 and 5 ft has been reached on a run of stairs creates a comfortable resting place for users. When longer runs of stairs are used consideration for larger landings with opportunities for sitting should be given. Landings should be built with a minimum 2 percent slope toward the downhill edge.

RAMPS

Accessible ramp slope standards initially were based on research using disabled adult males as the test population. This means that, perhaps, it is not the best standard for the elderly, children, or the frail. Thus, for the greatest universal access of a project, designers should target for the lowest ramp slope rate practical. Research based on the elderly and children is beginning to show that a better slope rate for those populations is 1:16 or lower. The 1:12 or 8.333 percent slope rate should be considered the maximum rate, not the goal.

As a practical cost consideration, any ramp that is flatter than 1:20 does not require handrails and, thus, can avoid that cost.

STREET RAMPS

There are two common locations for exterior ramps: at street corners and crossings, and where grade changes occur. The design of street ramps is highly regulated by local, state, and federal ordinances. This discussion does not provide street ramp standards because the design requirements are diverse and undergo frequent review and modification. Thus, for street ramp standards, the design professional is referred directly to the relevant ordinance determined by discussion with the relevant code enforcement agency and the client.

EXTERIOR RAMP DETAILS

The most important design feature of an exterior ramp is the surface of the ramp. Ensuring that it is not slick in wet weather is critical for safety. Follow these guidelines:

- On concrete ramps, the surface should be, at minimum, a medium broom finish, with the broom strokes being perpendicular to the flow of traffic.

RAMP SLOPE RATIOS
7.30

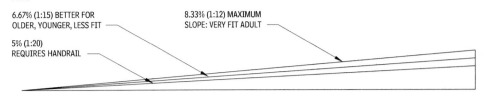

6.67% (1:15) BETTER FOR OLDER, YOUNGER, LESS FIT

5% (1:20) REQUIRES HANDRAIL

8.33% (1:12) MAXIMUM SLOPE: VERY FIT ADULT

RAMP SECTION
7.31

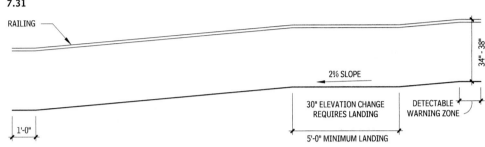

RAILING

34" - 38"

2% SLOPE

30" ELEVATION CHANGE REQUIRES LANDING

DETECTABLE WARNING ZONE

1'-0"

5'-0" MINIMUM LANDING

- Stone clad ramp designs should consider honed or scored surfaces, and avoid any smooth, flat finish.
- Metal ramps designs should consider structural grille/grate panels or embossed or patterned metal, and avoid any smooth finish.
- Installing slip dowels or keyed joints at the tops and bottoms of ramps to adjacent paving helps to avoid differential movement that causes tripping hazards at the entries to the ramp.

RAMP WIDTHS AND LANDINGS

Design guidelines for ramp widths and landings are as follows:

- An accessible ramp should have a clearance between ramp handrails of at least 36 in., to allow a person in a wheelchair room for his or her hands to turn the wheels.
- A ramp landing should occur at a maximum of 30 ft. of run of a ramp. The ramp landing must be a minimum of 60 in. clear depth.
- If ramps change direction at landings, the minimum landing size must be 60 by 60 in.
- If an exterior doorway is located at a ramp landing, the landing must comply with safety and access requirements for the door.

STAIRS AND RAMPS HANDRAILS

As part of the accessible system, stair and ramp handrails are covered under access and safety regulations. Their placement, height, length, strength, and safety details fall under the design guidance of these regulations. Thus, familiarity with the relevant codes is paramount.

General requirements for all handrails are:

- The top of handrail to stair nose or ramp surface distance should be constant—a height between 34 to 38 in.
- The diameter or width of the handrail must be 1-1/4 to 1-1/2 in.
- Structurally, the handrail must be able to withstand 250 lb of downward pressure per inch.
- The ends of handrails should not be sharp at the ends.

General standards for stair handrails are:

- At the top of the stair run, the rail must be level for 12 in. before the first step nose.
- At the bottom of stair run, the rail must extend for one tread length at the same slope as over the majority of the stairs, then remain level for an additional 12 in.

General standards for ramp handrails are:

- At the top of the ramp, the rail must be level for 12 in. before the top of the ramp.
- At the bottom of the ramp, the rail must remain level for 12 in. beyond the end of the ramp.

STAIR RAIL DETAIL
7.32

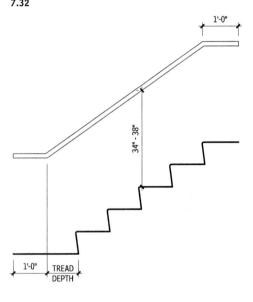

1'-0"

34" - 38"

1'-0" TREAD DEPTH

Contributor:
Faith Okuma, Design Workshop, Santa Fe, New Mexico.

SITE DEVELOPMENT

RETAINING WALLS

Retaining walls are designed and constructed to resist the thrust of the soil, which can cause the wall to fail by overturning, sliding, or settling. In stone walls, resistance to soil thrust can be helped by battering the stonework (i.e., recessing or sloping the masonry back in successive courses).

Garden-type retaining walls, usually no higher than 4 ft, are generlly made from small building units of stone, masonry, or wood. For higher walls, reinforced concrete is more commonly used. Terracing may be built with walls of wood, stone, brick, or concrete.

Walls less than 2 ft high do not require drains or weepholes. Preservative-treated wood is recommended for any design in which wood comes in contact with the ground. Redwood may be substituted if desired.

FORCES RESISTED BY RETAINING WALLS
7.33

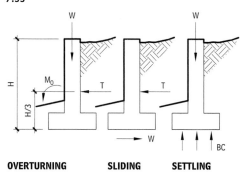

OVERTURNING **SLIDING** **SETTLING**

DRY-PLACED STONE RETAINING WALL
7.34

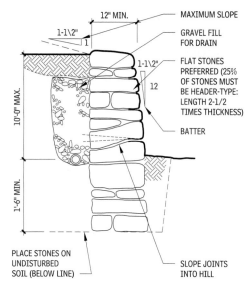

MAXIMUM SLOPE
GRAVEL FILL FOR DRAIN
FLAT STONES PREFERRED (25% OF STONES MUST BE HEADER-TYPE: LENGTH 2-1/2 TIMES THICKNESS)
BATTER
12" MIN.
1-1\2"
10'-0" MAX.
1'-6" MIN.
PLACE STONES ON UNDISTURBED SOIL (BELOW LINE)
SLOPE JOINTS INTO HILL

Stagger vertical joints from course to course 6 in. minimum horizontally. The thickness of the wall at any point should not be less than half the distance from that point to the top of the wall

BRICK UNIT MASONRY RETAINING WALL
7.35

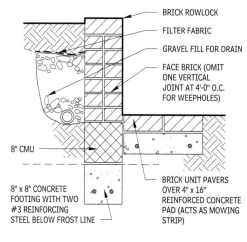

BRICK ROWLOCK
FILTER FABRIC
GRAVEL FILL FOR DRAIN
FACE BRICK (OMIT ONE VERTICAL JOINT AT 4'-0" O.C. FOR WEEPHOLES)
8" CMU
8" x 8" CONCRETE FOOTING WITH TWO #3 REINFORCING STEEL BELOW FROST LINE
BRICK UNIT PAVERS OVER 4" x 16" REINFORCED CONCRETE PAD (ACTS AS MOWING STRIP)

STONE BANK RETAINING WALL
7.36

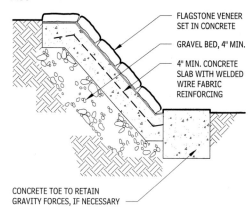

FLAGSTONE VENEER SET IN CONCRETE
GRAVEL BED, 4" MIN.
4" MIN. CONCRETE SLAB WITH WELDED WIRE FABRIC REINFORCING
CONCRETE TOE TO RETAIN GRAVITY FORCES, IF NECESSARY

STONE/BRICK VENEER UNIT MASONRY RETAINING WALL
7.37

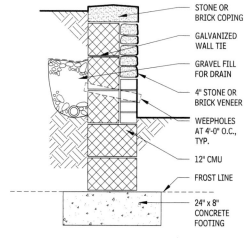

STONE OR BRICK COPING
GALVANIZED WALL TIE
GRAVEL FILL FOR DRAIN
4" STONE OR BRICK VENEER
WEEPHOLES AT 4'-0" O.C., TYP.
12" CMU
FROST LINE
24" x 8" CONCRETE FOOTING

NOTES

7.33 a. H = height of wall, A = area of footing, W = composite weight of wall, T= lateral thrust of soil on wall, d = width of base of wall; M_0 = overturning moment of a retaining wall; MR = resisting moment; W = lateral force on wall in psf; BC = bearing capacity of soil.

b. The overturning moment of a retaining wall (equal to T × H/3) is resisted by the resisting moment of the wall. For symmetrical sections, the resisting moment equals W × d/2. Using a safety factor of 2, MR 2 × M_0 (assume 33° angle of repose of soil).

c. The lateral (sliding) thrust of soil on a wall must be resisted. The resisting force is the weight of the wall multiplied by the coefficient of soil friction. Using a safety factor of 1.5, W 1.5T, where T = (w × H2)/2.

d. The bearing capacity of the soil must resist vertical forces (settling)—the weight of the wall plus any soil bearing on the base plus any vertical component of the soil thrust for a wall with any surcharge. Using a safety factor of 1.5, BC 1.5 W/A.

Contributors:
Dennis Wilkinson, Morrow Reardon Wilkinson Miller, Albuquerque, New Mexico; Donald Neubauer, PE, Neubauer Consulting Engineers, Potomac, Maryland.

TIMBER RETAINING WALL
7.38

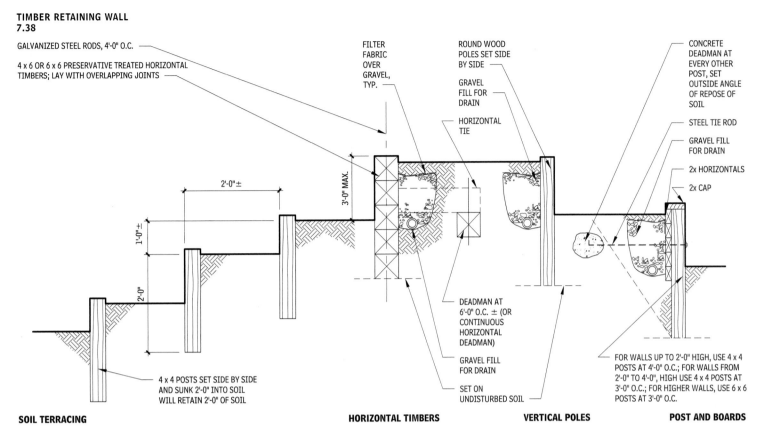

GALVANIZED STEEL RODS, 4'-0" O.C.

4 x 6 OR 6 x 6 PRESERVATIVE TREATED HORIZONTAL TIMBERS; LAY WITH OVERLAPPING JOINTS

FILTER FABRIC OVER GRAVEL, TYP.

ROUND WOOD POLES SET SIDE BY SIDE

GRAVEL FILL FOR DRAIN

HORIZONTAL TIE

CONCRETE DEADMAN AT EVERY OTHER POST, SET OUTSIDE ANGLE OF REPOSE OF SOIL

STEEL TIE ROD

GRAVEL FILL FOR DRAIN

2x HORIZONTALS

2x CAP

2'-0"±

1'-0"±

2'-0"

3'-0" MAX.

4 x 4 POSTS SET SIDE BY SIDE AND SUNK 2'-0" INTO SOIL WILL RETAIN 2'-0" OF SOIL

DEADMAN AT 6'-0" O.C. ± (OR CONTINUOUS HORIZONTAL DEADMAN)

GRAVEL FILL FOR DRAIN

SET ON UNDISTURBED SOIL

FOR WALLS UP TO 2'-0" HIGH, USE 4 x 4 POSTS AT 4'-0" O.C.; FOR WALLS FROM 2'-0" TO 4'-0", HIGH USE 4 x 4 POSTS AT 3'-0" O.C.; FOR HIGHER WALLS, USE 6 x 6 POSTS AT 3'-0" O.C.

SOIL TERRACING   **HORIZONTAL TIMBERS**   **VERTICAL POLES**   **POST AND BOARDS**

CAST-IN-PLACE CONCRETE RETAINING WALLS

When designing cast-in-place concrete retaining walls, keep these guidelines in mind:

- Provide control and/or construction joints in concrete retaining walls approximately every 25 ft. Every fourth control and/or construction joint should be an expansion joint. Coated dowels should be used if average wall height on either side of a joint is different.
- Consult with a structural engineer for final design of all concrete retaining walls.
- Concrete keys may be required below retaining wall footing to prevent sliding in high walls and those built on moist clay.

L-TYPE RETAINING WALLS
7.39

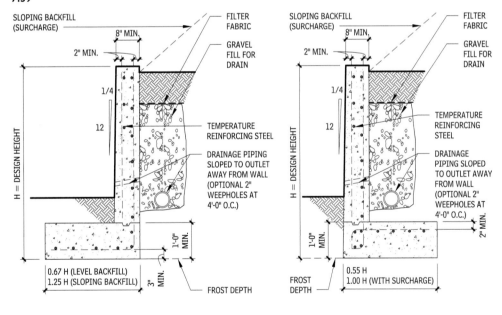

SLOPING BACKFILL (SURCHARGE)

FILTER FABRIC

8" MIN.

2" MIN.

GRAVEL FILL FOR DRAIN

1/4

12

H = DESIGN HEIGHT

TEMPERATURE REINFORCING STEEL

DRAINAGE PIPING SLOPED TO OUTLET AWAY FROM WALL (OPTIONAL 2" WEEPHOLES AT 4'-0" O.C.)

0.67 H (LEVEL BACKFILL)
1.25 H (SLOPING BACKFILL)

1'-0" MIN.

3" MIN.

FROST DEPTH

SLOPING BACKFILL (SURCHARGE)

FILTER FABRIC

8" MIN.

2" MIN.

GRAVEL FILL FOR DRAIN

1/4

12

H = DESIGN HEIGHT

TEMPERATURE REINFORCING STEEL

DRAINAGE PIPING SLOPED TO OUTLET AWAY FROM WALL (OPTIONAL 2" WEEPHOLES AT 4'-0" O.C.)

1'-0" MIN.

2" MIN.

FROST DEPTH

0.55 H
1.00 H (WITH SURCHARGE)

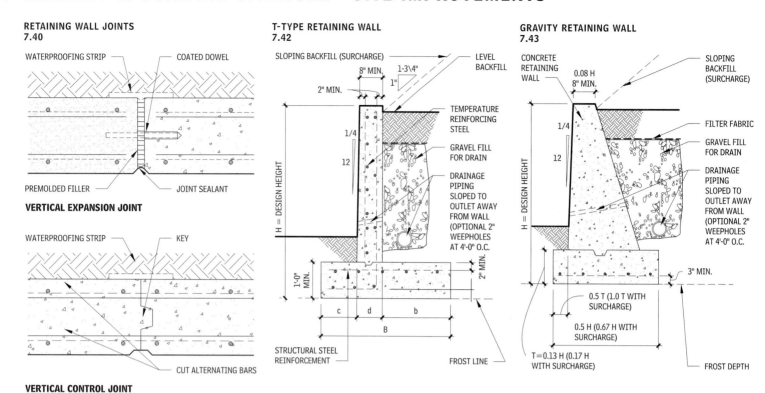

RETAINING WALL JOINTS
7.40

VERTICAL EXPANSION JOINT

VERTICAL CONTROL JOINT

T-TYPE RETAINING WALL
7.42

GRAVITY RETAINING WALL
7.43

PRELIMINARY DIMENSIONS FOR CAST-IN-PLACE CONCRETE RETAINING WALLS
7.41

APPROXIMATE CONCRETE DIMENSIONS (FT-IN.)									
BACKFILL SLOPING DIAMETER = 29" 45′ (13/4:1)					BACKFILL LEVEL—NO SURCHARGE				
HEIGHT OF WALL (H)	WIDTH OF FOOTING (B)	WIDTH OF WALL (d)	HEEL (b)	TOE (c)	HEIGHT OF WALL (H)	WIDTH OF BASE (B)	WIDTH OF WALL (A)	HEEL (b)	TOE (c)
3-0	2-8	0-9	1-5	0-6	3-0	2-1	0-8	1-0	0-5
4-0	3-5	0-9	2-0	0-8	4-0	2-8	0-8	1-7	0-5
5-0	4-6	0-10	2-6	1-2	5-0	3-3	0-8	2-2	0-5
6-0	5-4	0-10	2-11	1-7	6-0	3-9	0-8	2-5	0-8
7-0	6-3	0-10	3-5	2-0	7-0	4-2	0-8	2-6	1-0
8-0	7-0	1-0	3-8	2-4	8-0	4-8	1-0	2-8	1-0
9-0	7-6	1-0	4-2	2-4	9-0	5-2	1-0	3-2	1-0
10-0	8-6	1-0	4-9	2-9	10-0	5-9	1-0	3-7	1-2
11-0	11-0	1-1	7-2	2-9	11-0	6-7	1-1	4-1	1-5
12-0	12-0	1-2	7-10	3-0	12-0	7-3	1-2	4-7	1-6
13-0	13-0	1-4	8-5	3-3	13-0	7-10	1-2	5-0	1-8
14-0	14-0	1-5	9-1	3-6	14-0	8-5	1-3	5-5	1-9
15-0	15-0	1-6	9-9	3-9	15-0	9-0	1-4	5-9	1-11
16-0	16-0	1-7	10-5	4-0	16-0	9-7	1-5	6-2	2-0
17-0	17-0	1-8	11-1	4-3	17-0	10-3	1-6	6-7	2-2
18-0	18-0	1-10	11-8	4-6	18-0	10-10	1-6	7-1	2-3
19-0	19-0	1-11	12-4	4-9	19-0	11-5	1-7	7-5	2-5
20-0	20-0	2-0	13-0	5-0	20-0	12-0	1-8	7-10	2-6
21-0	21-0	2-2	13-7	5-3	21-0	12-7	1-9	8-2	2-8
22-0	22-0	2-4	14-4	5-4	22-0	13-3	1-11	8-7	2-9

NOTE

7.43 T = the lateral thrust of the soil on the wall.

Contributor:
Donald Neubauer, PE, Neubauer Consulting Engineers, Potomac, Maryland.

MASONRY SITE STEPS
7.44

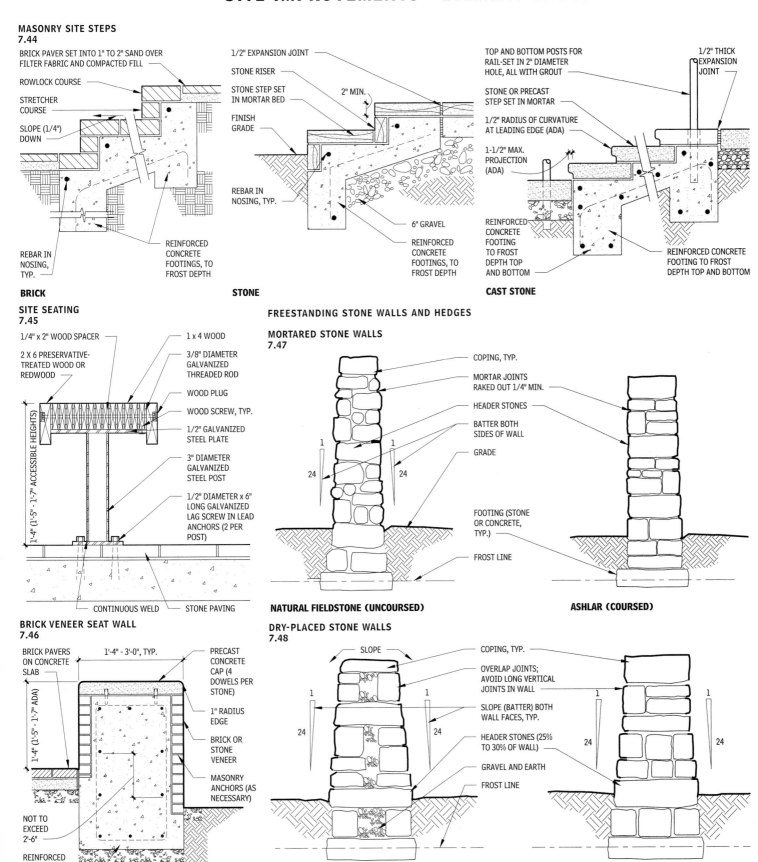

BRICK PAVER SET INTO 1" TO 2" SAND OVER FILTER FABRIC AND COMPACTED FILL

ROWLOCK COURSE

STRETCHER COURSE

SLOPE (1/4") DOWN

REBAR IN NOSING, TYP.

REINFORCED CONCRETE FOOTINGS, TO FROST DEPTH

BRICK

1/2" EXPANSION JOINT

STONE RISER

STONE STEP SET IN MORTAR BED

2" MIN.

FINISH GRADE

REBAR IN NOSING, TYP.

6" GRAVEL

REINFORCED CONCRETE FOOTINGS, TO FROST DEPTH

STONE

TOP AND BOTTOM POSTS FOR RAIL-SET IN 2" DIAMETER HOLE, ALL WITH GROUT

STONE OR PRECAST STEP SET IN MORTAR

1/2" RADIUS OF CURVATURE AT LEADING EDGE (ADA)

1-1/2" MAX. PROJECTION (ADA)

REINFORCED CONCRETE FOOTING TO FROST DEPTH TOP AND BOTTOM

1/2" THICK EXPANSION JOINT

REINFORCED CONCRETE FOOTING TO FROST DEPTH TOP AND BOTTOM

CAST STONE

SITE SEATING
7.45

1/4" x 2" WOOD SPACER

2 X 6 PRESERVATIVE-TREATED WOOD OR REDWOOD

1 x 4 WOOD

3/8" DIAMETER GALVANIZED THREADED ROD

WOOD PLUG

WOOD SCREW, TYP.

1/2" GALVANIZED STEEL PLATE

3" DIAMETER GALVANIZED STEEL POST

1/2" DIAMETER x 6" LONG GALVANIZED LAG SCREW IN LEAD ANCHORS (2 PER POST)

1'-4" (1'-5" - 1'-7" ACCESSIBLE HEIGHTS)

CONTINUOUS WELD

STONE PAVING

BRICK VENEER SEAT WALL
7.46

BRICK PAVERS ON CONCRETE SLAB

1'-4" - 3'-0", TYP.

PRECAST CONCRETE CAP (4 DOWELS PER STONE)

1" RADIUS EDGE

BRICK OR STONE VENEER

MASONRY ANCHORS (AS NECESSARY)

1'-4" (1'-5" - 1'-7" ADA)

NOT TO EXCEED 2'-6"

REINFORCED CONCRETE, SET TO FROST DEPTH

FREESTANDING STONE WALLS AND HEDGES

MORTARED STONE WALLS
7.47

COPING, TYP.

MORTAR JOINTS RAKED OUT 1/4" MIN.

HEADER STONES

BATTER BOTH SIDES OF WALL

GRADE

FOOTING (STONE OR CONCRETE, TYP.)

FROST LINE

1 / 24

1 / 24

NATURAL FIELDSTONE (UNCOURSED)

ASHLAR (COURSED)

DRY-PLACED STONE WALLS
7.48

SLOPE

COPING, TYP.

OVERLAP JOINTS; AVOID LONG VERTICAL JOINTS IN WALL

SLOPE (BATTER) BOTH WALL FACES, TYP.

HEADER STONES (25% TO 30% OF WALL)

GRAVEL AND EARTH

FROST LINE

1 / 24

1 / 24

1 / 24

1 / 24

DOUBLE-TIER WALL

SINGLE-TIER WALL

NOTES

7.46 a. Provide handrails on both sides of all stairs along accessible routes.
b. Slope step surfaces so water will not accumulate on the walking surface.
c. These details are for reference only. Consult the applicable codes accessibility requirements.

Contributor:
Dennis Carmichael, FASLA, EDAW, Inc., Alexandria, Virginia.

LANDSCAPING

IRRIGATION

Irrigation system design considerations include the water supply, site conditions, climate, and plant material selection. The available volume of the water supply is measured in gallons per minute (gpm). The available pressure of the water supply is measured in pounds per square inch (psi). Water supply can be from a public or private utility system, or can be pumped from a well or pond. Selection of irrigation equipment and sizing of distribution piping is based on available volume and pressure of the water supply.

Site conditions that must be considered are topography, drainage, soil type, and solar exposure. Important climatic conditions include predominant wind direction, annual rainfall, and temperature variations. When irrigation systems are subject to freezing temperatures, precaution against damage to the system components from freezing must be built into the design.

Planting materials have different requirements for water. In fact, variations of turf grass may have vastly different watering needs. Plant water requirements include water lost by evaporation into the atmosphere from the soil and soil surface, and by transpiration, which is the water actually used by the plan. The combination of these is called *evapotranspiration* (E.T.).

Because turf grass has the highest rate of E.T. of any planting materials in the landscape, and because the E.T. of turf varies depending on the seasons, irrigation systems are designed to replace water lost at the highest level of E.T. for the turf grass in the landscape.

IRRIGATION SYSTEM COMPONENTS

There are a number of common irrigation system components, among them:

- *Backflow preventer*: Prevents water from the irrigation system from backflowing into the potable water supply.
- *Controller*: Acts as a timer that maintains status of the day of the week and time of the day in order to activate electric control valves at a specific day, time of day, and duration.
- *Main line*: The primary pipe supply line that distributes water from the point of connection of the source of supply to the electric control valves. Main line piping of sizes 2-1/2 in. in diameter and larger are typically class 200 PVC. Piping of sizes 2 in. and smaller are typically schedule 40 PVC.
- *Electric control valve*: Low-voltage solenoid-actuated valves that control the flow of water from the main line into the lateral line piping. Electric control valves are activated by the controller. Signals are sent from the controller to the valves through direct burial wires.
- *Lateral line piping*: The pipe supply line that distributes water from an electric control valve to a sprinkler head or a drip emitter. Depending on the application, lateral line piping can be schedule 40 PVC, class 200 PVC, or class 160 PVC. Lateral line piping for drip irrigation is typically polyethylene tube.
- *Sprinkler head*: A water distribution device attached to the lateral line piping. Rotary and impact sprinkler heads are used to irrigate large areas and can be spaced from 20 to 80 ft o.c. Pop-up spray sprinkler heads are used to irrigate smaller areas and can be spaced from 5 to 20 ft o.c. Sprinkler heads are used to irrigate turf grass or broad areas of low-growing shrubs or ground covers. For optimum efficiency, sprinkler heads are spaced to provide overlapping head-to-head coverage.
- *Bubbler head*: A water-distribution device used to irrigate shrubs and ground covers by placing water immediately adjacent to the plant, or by flooding a planting bed.
- *Drip emitter*: A water distribution device that distributes water very slowly, in increments measured in gallons per hour. Drip emitters are used to water individual plants.

COORDINATION CONSIDERATIONS

Check the contract to ascertain that an irrigation system is to be provided. On rare occasions, it is an option, which should have been determined when signing the contract.

An irrigation plan should show:

- Limits of irrigation
- Approximate limits of grass versus shrub and ground cover areas
- Point of connection (POC) for the water
- Controller location
- Grading plan
- Any out-of-the-ordinary conditions (e.g., underground obstructions, areas over structure, isolated planting areas, tree pits, or pots) with a note clarifying whether these areas are or are not to be irrigated

Coordination with the plumbing engineer should occur near the start of the construction documents phase, mainly because the services needed to supply an irrigation system are the same as those for the domestic water system for a building. These include the location of the water meter and any calculations for the gallons per minute (gpm) and pounds per square inch (psi).

When working on a project that has a water meter room within the building, it is wise to let the plumbing engineer know (even as early as the design development phase) that a backflow preventer and an irrigation meter separate from the domestic water meter will be needed.

Ask the plumbing engineer to show the POC 2 ft beyond the outside face of the exterior wall, or vault at a depth of 18 in. below finish grade and with a cap. This is particularly important for commercial jobs where the water meter room is below grade and the exterior wall is likely cast-in-place concrete. If the irrigation main supply shows on the plumbing drawings, this will ensure the pipe is installed in the wall properly, with a waterstop, and has a tight seal around the pipe.

There is no need for the water and electrical power sources to be located near each other; they only have to meet at the remote control valves.

There needs to be a series of wires (one for each valve, plus a neutral wire) going through an exterior building wall 18 in. below grade or through the bottom of the pedestal, which has to be mounted on a concrete pad. These wires should always be enclosed in a "sleeve," which is usually PVC. Once outside, the

IRRIGATION SYSTEM SCHEMATIC
7.49

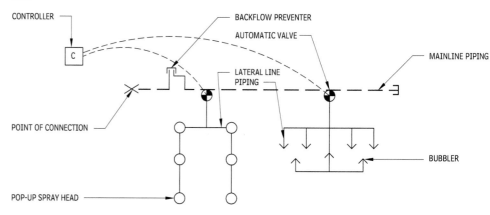

AUTOMATIC VALVE ASSEMBLY
7.50

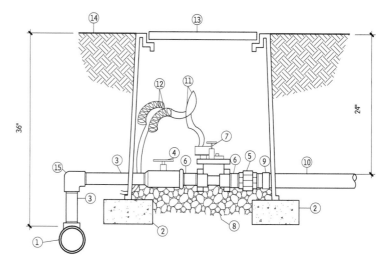

① MAINLINE SERVICE TEE	⑤ SCH 80 PVC UNION	⑨ SCH. 40 PVC BALL ADAPTER	⑬ BODY VALVE BOX WITH BOLT-DOWN COVER AND 8" EXTENSIONS, AS REQUIRED
② SOLID CMU BLOCK (FOUR)	⑥ SCH 80 PVC NIPPLE, 3" LENGTH	⑩ LATERAL PIPING	
③ SCH 80 PVC NIPPLE, LENGTH AS REQUIRED	⑦ AUTOMATIC VALVE	⑪ WATERPROOF WIRE CONNECTOR	⑭ FINISH GRADE
④ SCH 80 PVC BALL VALVE WITH UNIONS	⑧ 1" ROUND GRAVEL, 3 CU FT	⑫ 36" WIRE EXPANSION LOOPS	⑮ SCH 80 PVC THREADED ELL

NOTE

7.50 The contractor must install one automatic valve assembly per valve box.

Contributors:
Dennis Wilkinson, Morrow Reardon Wilkinson Miller, Albuquerque, New Mexico; John Pearson, EDAW, Inc., Alexandria, Virginia.

wires should remain encased in PVC pipe until they reach a mainline trench. From there they go off in all directions to the remote control valves, which should be buried under the pipe in the same trench.

Irrigation sleeves should be installed prior to paving operations, but after final subgrade elevation has been established.

The controller is best located in a place out of view from the general public.

POP-UP SPRAY ASSEMBLY
7.51

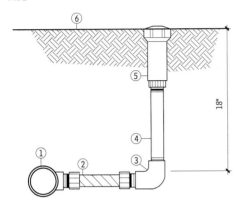

1. PVC LATERAL PIPE FITTING
2. 1/2" x 6" FLEX NIPPLE
3. 1/2" SCH 40 PVC THREADED ELBOW
4. 1/2" SCH 80 PVC THREADED NIPPLE, LENGTH AS REQUIRED
5. POP-UP SPRINKLER
6. TOP OF MULCH OR TOP OF SOD BED

BUBBLER ASSEMBLY
7.52

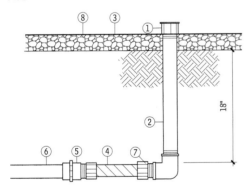

1. PRESSURE-COMPENSATING BUBBLER
2. 1/2" SCH 80 THREADED NIPPLE, LENGTH AS REQUIRED
3. FINISH GRADE
4. 1/2" x 6" PVC FLEX NIPPLE
5. 3/4" x 1/2" SCH 40 PVC FEMALE ADAPTER
6. PVC LATERAL PIPING
7. 1/2" SCH 40 PVC THREADED ELBOW
8. TOP OF MULCH

REDUCED PRESSURE BACKFLOW PREVENTER
7.53

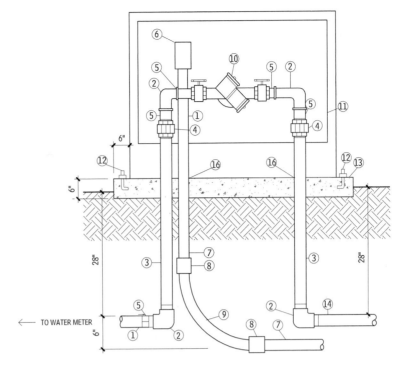

← TO WATER METER

1. PVC MAIN LINE
2. GALVANIZED ELBOW
3. GALVANIZED NIPPLE, 42" LENGTH
4. GALVANIZED UNION
5. GALVANIZED NIPPLE, 3" LENGTH
6. JUNCTION BOX FOR HEAT TAPE
7. RIGID STEEL CONDUIT
8. WATERTIGHT CONNECTOR
9. RIGID STEEL SWEEP ELL
10. REDUCED-PRESSURE BACKFLOW PREVENTER OR APPROVED EQUAL
11. INSULATION ENCLOSURE
12. ANCHOR BOLTS
13. 3000 PSI CONCRETE PAD WITH TOOLED EDGES
14. GALVANIZED NIPPLE, 36" LENGTH
15. SCH 40 PVC MALE ADAPTER
16. PVC SLEEVE

PLANTING OF TREES AND SHRUBS

TREES PLANTS AND GROUND COVERS

The physical environment of the site, the design needs of the project, and the design character of the trees are all factors that must be considered in selecting trees and preparing a landscape plan for a building.

Soil conditions (acidity, porosity) at the site, the amount and intensity of sunlight and precipitation, and the seasonal temperature range in the area create the physical environment in which trees must be able to survive. In addition, it is essential to consider how the location and topography of the site will direct the wind, resulting in cold winds and cooling breezes that can affect the health of trees.

Trees can be used to address the design needs of a project by directing pedestrian or vehicle movement, framing vistas, screening objectionable views, and defining and shaping exterior space. Trees can also be used to modify the microclimate of a site and to help conserve building energy use from heating, cooling, and lighting systems.

The design character of the trees themselves plays a part in which species are best suited for a particular application. The shape of a tree can be columnar, conical, spherical, or spreading, and the resulting height and mass will change over time as the tree matures. Some trees grow quickly, and others more slowly, and their color and texture varies from coarse to medium to fine, affecting their character. The appearance of deciduous trees changes with the seasons, while the effect of an evergreen remains relatively constant.

Contributors:
Dennis Wilkinson, Morrow Reardon Wilkinson Miller, Albuquerque, New Mexico; John Pearson, EDAW, Inc., Alexandria, Virginia.

PHYSICAL CHARACTERISTICS OF TREES
7.54

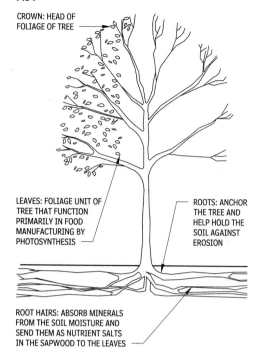

CROWN: HEAD OF FOLIAGE OF TREE

LEAVES: FOLIAGE UNIT OF TREE THAT FUNCTION PRIMARILY IN FOOD MANUFACTURING BY PHOTOSYNTHESIS

ROOTS: ANCHOR THE TREE AND HELP HOLD THE SOIL AGAINST EROSION

ROOT HAIRS: ABSORB MINERALS FROM THE SOIL MOISTURE AND SEND THEM AS NUTRIENT SALTS IN THE SAPWOOD TO THE LEAVES

HEARTWOOD: NONLIVING CENTRAL PART OF TREE, GIVING STRENGTH AND STABILITY

ANNUAL RINGS: REVEAL AGE OF TREE BY SHOWING YEARLY GROWTH

OUTER BARK: AGED INNER BARK THAT PROTECTS TREE FROM DESSICATION AND INJURY

INNER BARK (PHLOEM): CARRIES FOOD FROM LEAVES TO BRANCHES, TRUNK, AND ROOTS

CAMBIUM: LAYER BETWEEN XYLEM AND PHLOEM WHERE CELL-ADDING GROWTH OCCURS, NEW SAPWOOD TO INSIDE AND NEW INNER BARK OUTSIDE

SAPWOOD (XYLEM): CARRIES NUTRIENTS AND WATER TO LEAVES FROM ROOTS

GLARE PROTECTION
7.55

TREES PROTECT VIEWER FROM GLARE OF SURFACES SUCH AS WATER, PAVING, AND GLASS

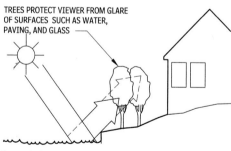

The vertical angle of the sun changes seasonally; therefore, the area of a building subject to the glare of reflected sunlight varies. Plants of various heights can screen sun (and artificial light) glare from adjacent surfaces.

AIR FILTRATION
7.56

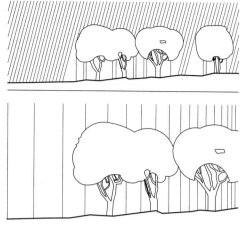

Large masses of plants physically and chemically filter and deodorize the air, reducing air pollution. Top: Particulate matter trapped on the leaves is washed to the ground during rainfall. Gaseous pollutants are assimilated by the leaves. Bottom: Fragrant plants can mechanically mask fumes and odors. Also, these pollutants are chemically metabolized in the photosynthetic process.

WIND PROTECTION
7.57

CONSTANT WIND VELOCITY=100%

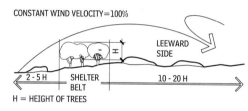

LEEWARD SIDE

2 - 5 H   SHELTER BELT   10 - 20 H

H = HEIGHT OF TREES

Shelter belt wind protection reduces evaporation at ground level, increases relative humidity, lowers the temperature in summer and reduces heat loss in winter, and reduces blowing dust and drifting snow. The amount of protection afforded is directly related to the height and density of the shelter belt.

SHADE PROVISION
7.58

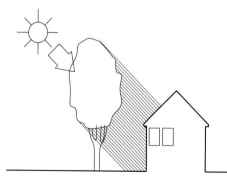

In summer, trees obstruct or filter the strong radiation from the sun, cooling and protecting the area beneath them. In winter, evergreen trees still have this effect, whereas deciduous trees, having lost their leaves, do not.

SOUND ATTENUATION
7.59

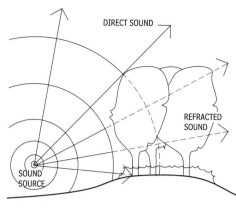

DIRECT SOUND

REFRACTED SOUND

SOUND SOURCE

A combination of deciduous and evergreen trees and shrubs reduces sound more effectively than deciduous plants alone. Planting trees and shrubs on earth mounds increases the attenuating effects of a buffer belt.

RUNOFF REDUCTION
7.60

LEAVES AND BRANCHES ARE COATED WITH THIN FILM OF WATER, HOLDING IT FROM RUNNING OFF

ROOTS ABSORB WATER RUNOFF FROM BRANCHES

BRANCH STRUCTURE CHANNELS WATER TO DRY AREA UNDER TREE TO BE ABSORBED

Mature trees absorb or delay runoff from stormwater at a rate four to five times that of bare ground.

PLANTING DETAILS

Planting details for trees and shrubs, tips on soil improvement, and general design considerations are the topics addressed in this section.

TREE PLANTING DETAILS

These three guidelines will aid in the successful planting of trees:

- For container-grown trees, use fingers or small hand tools to pull the roots out of the outer layer of potting soil; then cut or pull apart any roots circling the perimeter of the container. Incorporate commercially prepared mycorrhiza spores in the soil immediately around the root ball at rates specified by the manufacturer.
- During the design phase, confirm that water drains out of the soil; design alternative drainage systems as required.
- Thoroughly soak the tree root ball and adjacent prepared soil several times during the first month after planting, and regularly throughout the following two summers.

Contributor:
James Urban, ASLA, James Urban Landscape Architecture, Annapolis, Maryland.

Note that the planting process is similar for deciduous and ever-green trees.

SHRUB PLANTING DETAILS

For successful shrub planting, follow these guidelines:

- For container-grown shrubs, use fingers or small hand tools to pull the roots out of the outer layer of potting soil; then cut or pull apart any roots that circle the perimeter of the container. Incorporate commercially prepared mycorrhiza spores in the soil immediately around the root ball at rates specified by the manufacturer.
- Confirm that water drains out of the soil during the design phase; design alternative drainage systems as required.

SOIL IMPROVEMENT

The quality of soil available for planting varies widely from site to site, especially after construction activity has occurred. The nature of construction results in compaction, filling, contamination, and grading of the original soil on a site, rapidly making it useless for planting. Previous human activity at a site can also affect the ability of the soil to support plants.

During the design phase, assumptions must be made regarding the probable condition of the soil after construction is complete. The health of existing or remaining soil determines what types of soil preparation will be required and the volume of soil to be prepared. Conditions will vary from location to location within a project, and details must be condition-specific. For large projects or extreme conditions, it is useful to consult an expert experienced in modifying planting soils at urban sites.

To ensure good soil health at a project site, follow these guidelines:

- Whenever possible, connect the soil improvement area from tree to tree.
- Always test soil for pH and nutrient levels, and adjust these as required.
- Loosen soil with a backhoe or other large coarse-tilling equipment, when possible. Tilling that produces large, coarse chunks of soil is preferable to tilling that results in fine grains uniform in texture.
- Make sure that the bottom of planting soil excavations is rough, to avoid matting of soil layers as new soil is added. It is preferable to till the first lift (2 to 3 in.) of planting soil into the subsoil.

CONSTRUCTION AROUND EXISTING TREES

Great care should be taken not to compact, cut, or fill the earth within the crown area of existing trees. Most tree roots are located in the top 6 to 18 in. of the soil, and often spread considerably farther than the drip line of the tree. Compaction can cause severe root damage and reduce the movement of water and air through

STANDARD ROOT BALL SIZES FOR NURSERY-GROWN SHADE TREES
7.64

CALIPER[a] (IN.)	HEIGHT RANGE (FT-IN.)	MAXIMUM HEIGHT (FT)	MINIMUM BALL DIAMETER (IN.)	MINIMUM BALL DEPTH (IN.)
1/2	5–6	8	12	9
3/4	6–8	10	14	10-1/2
1	8–10	11	16	12
1-1/4	8–10	12	18	13-1/2
1-1/2	10–12	14	20	13-1/2
1-3/4	10–12	14	22	14-1/2
2	12–14	16	24	16
2-1/2	12–14	16	28	18-1/2
3	14–16	18	32	19-1/2
3-1/2	14–16	18	38	23
4	16–18	22	42	25
5	18–20	26	54	32-1/2

TREE PLANTING DETAIL (BALLED AND BURLAPPED PLANTS)
7.61

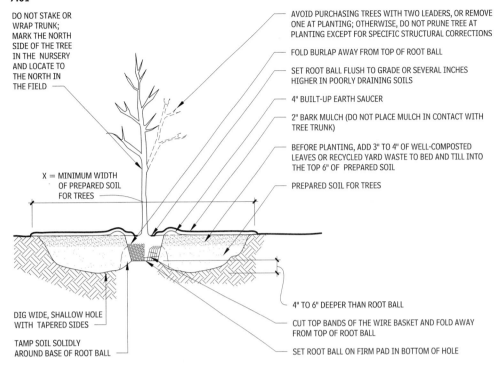

DO NOT STAKE OR WRAP TRUNK; MARK THE NORTH SIDE OF THE TREE IN THE NURSERY AND LOCATE TO THE NORTH IN THE FIELD

X = MINIMUM WIDTH OF PREPARED SOIL FOR TREES

DIG WIDE, SHALLOW HOLE WITH TAPERED SIDES

TAMP SOIL SOLIDLY AROUND BASE OF ROOT BALL

AVOID PURCHASING TREES WITH TWO LEADERS, OR REMOVE ONE AT PLANTING; OTHERWISE, DO NOT PRUNE TREE AT PLANTING EXCEPT FOR SPECIFIC STRUCTURAL CORRECTIONS

FOLD BURLAP AWAY FROM TOP OF ROOT BALL

SET ROOT BALL FLUSH TO GRADE OR SEVERAL INCHES HIGHER IN POORLY DRAINING SOILS

4" BUILT-UP EARTH SAUCER

2" BARK MULCH (DO NOT PLACE MULCH IN CONTACT WITH TREE TRUNK)

BEFORE PLANTING, ADD 3" TO 4" OF WELL-COMPOSTED LEAVES OR RECYCLED YARD WASTE TO BED AND TILL INTO THE TOP 6" OF PREPARED SOIL

PREPARED SOIL FOR TREES

4" TO 6" DEEPER THAN ROOT BALL

CUT TOP BANDS OF THE WIRE BASKET AND FOLD AWAY FROM TOP OF ROOT BALL

SET ROOT BALL ON FIRM PAD IN BOTTOM OF HOLE

SHRUB PLANTING DETAILS
7.62

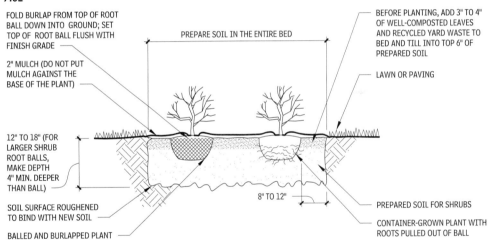

FOLD BURLAP FROM TOP OF ROOT BALL DOWN INTO GROUND; SET TOP OF ROOT BALL FLUSH WITH FINISH GRADE

2" MULCH (DO NOT PUT MULCH AGAINST THE BASE OF THE PLANT)

12" TO 18" (FOR LARGER SHRUB ROOT BALLS, MAKE DEPTH 4" MIN. DEEPER THAN BALL)

SOIL SURFACE ROUGHENED TO BIND WITH NEW SOIL

BALLED AND BURLAPPED PLANT

PREPARE SOIL IN THE ENTIRE BED

BEFORE PLANTING, ADD 3" TO 4" OF WELL-COMPOSTED LEAVES AND RECYCLED YARD WASTE TO BED AND TILL INTO TOP 6" OF PREPARED SOIL

LAWN OR PAVING

8" TO 12"

PREPARED SOIL FOR SHRUBS

CONTAINER-GROWN PLANT WITH ROOTS PULLED OUT OF BALL

GENERAL RANGE OF SOIL MODIFICATIONS AND VOLUMES FOR VARIOUS SOIL CONDITIONS
7.63

POSTCONSTRUCTION SOIL CONDITION	MINIMUM WIDTH PREPARED SOIL FOR TREES (X)	TYPE OF PREPARATION
Good soil (not previously graded or compacted; topsoil layer intact)	6' or twice the width of the root ball, whichever is greater	Loosen the existing soils to the widths and depths shown in Figures 7.101 and 7.102.
Compacted soil (not previously graded; topsoil layer disturbed but not eliminated)	15'	Loosen the existing soils to the widths and depths shown in Figures 7.101 and 7.102; add composted organic matter to bring the organic content up to 5% dry weight.
Graded subsoils and clean fills with clay content between 5% and 35%	20'	Minimum treatment: loosen existing soil to widths and depths shown in Figures 7.101 and 7.102; add composted organic matter to bring organic content up to 5% dry weight.
		Optimum treatment: remove top 8–10" or the existing material, loosen existing soils to the widths and depths shown in Figures 7.101 and 7.102; add 8"–10" of loam topsoil.
Poor-quality fills, heavy clay soils, soils contaminated with rubble ortoxic material	20'	Remove existing soils to the widths and depths shown in Figures 7.101 and 7.102; replace with loam topsoil.

NOTE

7.64[a]. Up to and including the 4-in. caliper size, the caliper measurement indicates the diameter of the trunk 6 in. above ground level. For larger sizes, the caliper measurement is taken 12 in. above ground level.

Contributors:
James Urban, ASLA, James Urban Landscape Architecture, Annapolis, Maryland; American Nursery & Landscape Association, Washington, DC.

the soil. To avoid compacting the earth, do not operate equipment or store materials within the crown spread.

Before construction begins, inject the soil within the crown area of nearby mature trees with commercially prepared kelp-based fertilizer and mycorrhiza fungus developed to invigorate tree roots. Prune tree roots at the edge of the root save area, as roots pulled during grading can snap or split well into the root save area. Rot and disease that enters dying roots in compacted or filled areas can move into the tree if root pruning has not been carried out. Install tree protection fencing and silt protection at the limits of construction activity near trees.

During construction, apply additional water in the canopy area to compensate for any root loss beyond the crown spread. Have all mature trees inspected by a certified arborist before construction begins, to identify any special problems. Remove all deadwood, and treat all trees for existing insect and disease problems. When possible, begin fertilization and problem treatments at least one full growing season before construction.

Removal of significant portions of the crown will affect the health of a tree by reducing its ability to photosynthesize in proportion to the mass of its trunk. Younger, healthier trees withstand construction impacts better than older trees.

ROOT PRUNE TRENCH
7.65

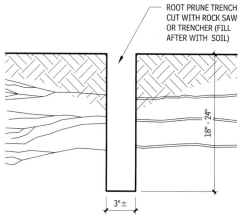

A root prune trench severs roots with a clean cut, protecting remaining roots from cracking, rot, and disease.

UNDERGROUND UTILITY LINE NEAR EXISTING TREES
7.66

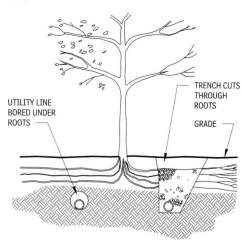

Fewer roots are severed by tunneling under a tree than by digging a trench beside it.

FILLING AROUND EXISTING TREE
7.67

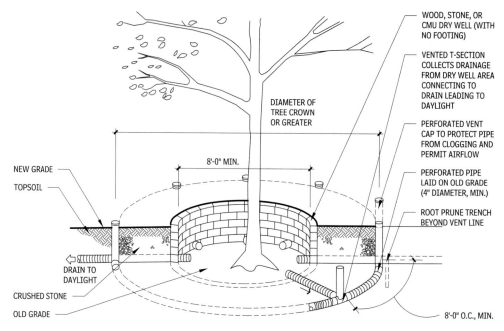

TREE AND ROOT PROTECTION
7.68

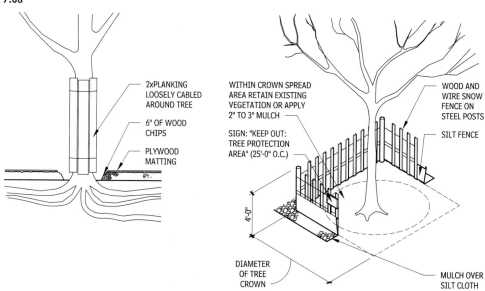

If construction operations must take place within the crown spread area, install 6 in. of wood chips on top of the soil to protect it. Use plywood matting over mulch in areas where equipment must operate. Protect the trunk of the tree with planking loosely cabled around the tree to reduce scarring by equipment. Remove planking, matting, and mulch as soon as operations are finished. A barrier such as that illustrated can keep construction equipment and personnel from compacting the soil around tree roots.

Contributors:
James Urban, ASLA, James Urban Landscape Architecture, Annapolis, Maryland; American Nursery & Landscape Association, Washington, DC.

CUTTING GRADE AROUND EXISTING TREE
7.69

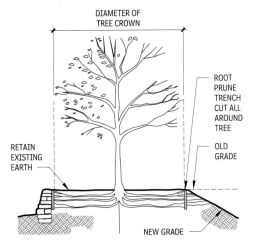

DIAMETER OF TREE CROWN

RETAIN EXISTING EARTH

ROOT PRUNE TRENCH CUT ALL AROUND TREE

OLD GRADE

NEW GRADE

FILLING GRADE AROUND EXISTING TREE
7.70

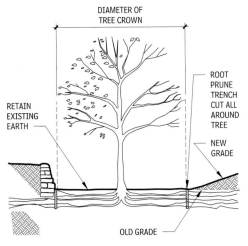

DIAMETER OF TREE CROWN

RETAIN EXISTING EARTH

ROOT PRUNE TRENCH CUT ALL AROUND TREE

NEW GRADE

OLD GRADE

TREE STRUCTURE—PARTS AND GROWING CHARACTERISTICS
7.71

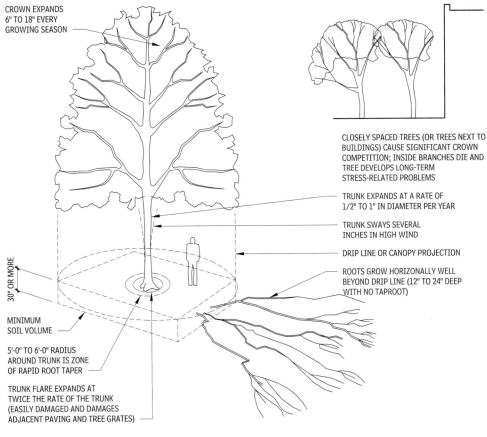

CROWN EXPANDS 6" TO 18" EVERY GROWING SEASON

CLOSELY SPACED TREES (OR TREES NEXT TO BUILDINGS) CAUSE SIGNIFICANT CROWN COMPETITION; INSIDE BRANCHES DIE AND TREE DEVELOPS LONG-TERM STRESS-RELATED PROBLEMS

TRUNK EXPANDS AT A RATE OF 1/2" TO 1" IN DIAMETER PER YEAR

TRUNK SWAYS SEVERAL INCHES IN HIGH WIND

DRIP LINE OR CANOPY PROJECTION

ROOTS GROW HORIZONALLY WELL BEYOND DRIP LINE (12" TO 24" DEEP WITH NO TAPROOT)

30" OR MORE

MINIMUM SOIL VOLUME

5'-0" TO 6'-0" RADIUS AROUND TRUNK IS ZONE OF RAPID ROOT TAPER

TRUNK FLARE EXPANDS AT TWICE THE RATE OF THE TRUNK (EASILY DAMAGED AND DAMAGES ADJACENT PAVING AND TREE GRATES)

For more information, on these topics, refer to the American Standard for Nursery Stock, ANSI Z60.1, which contains a complete list of nursery standards for other types and sizes of trees and shrubs. Also see the International Society of Arboriculture's "Principles and Practices of Planting Trees and Shrubs" (1997).

TREE PLANTING IN URBAN AREAS

Traditional urban designs in which trees are regularly spaced in small openings within paved areas generally result in poor tree performance because such designs generally do not provide adequate soil for root growth, and ignore the fact that trees must significantly increase trunk size every year. Moreover, competition for space, both at ground level and below, is intense in urban areas.

Although it is possible to design uncompacted soil volumes for trees under pavement, this is very expensive and the soil is never as efficient as that in open planting beds. Increasing trunk size can only be accommodated by using flexible materials that can change configuration over time. Urban designs that have flexible relationships between trees, paving, and planting beds and large areas of open planting soil offer the best opportunity for long-term tree health and lower maintenance costs.

Areas of dense urban development leave little room for tree roots to develop. Large areas of pavement, competition with foundations and utilities for space belowground, and extensive soil compaction and disruption limit the amount of soil available for trees. When the area of ground around the tree is open to the rain and sun is less than 400 to 500 sq ft per tree, the following design guidelines should be followed to encourage the growth of large healthy trees.

Five major parts of the tree structure must be accommodated in the design process:

- *Crown growth*: The tree crown expands every growing season at a rate of 6 to 18 in. per year. Once the crown reaches a competing object such as a building or another tree canopy, the canopy growth in that area slows and then stops. Eventually the branches on that side of the tree die. As the canopy expansion potential is reduced, the overall growth rate and tree health are also reduced.
- *Trunk growth*: The tree trunk expands about 1/2 to 1 in. per year. As the tree increases in size, the lower branches die and the trunk lengthens. Tree trunks move considerably in the wind, especially during the early years of development, and are damaged by close objects.
- *Trunk flare*: At the point at which the trunk leaves the ground, most tree species develop a pronounced swelling or flare as the tree matures. This flare grows at more than twice the rate of the main trunk diameter and helps the tree remain structurally sta-

ble. Any hard object placed in this area, such as a tree grate or confining pavement, will either damage the tree or be moved by the tremendous force of this growth.
- *Zone of rapid root taper*: Tree roots begin to form in the trunk flare and divide several times in the immediate area around the trunk. In this area, about 5 to 6 ft away from the trunk, the roots rapidly taper from about 6 in. in diameter to about 2 in. Most damage to adjacent paving occurs in this area immediately around the tree. Keeping the zone of rapid taper free of obstructions is important to long-term tree health. Once a tree is established, the zone of rapid taper is generally less susceptible to compaction damage than the rest of the root zone.
- *Root zone*: Tree roots grow radially and horizontally from the trunk and occupy only the upper layers (12 to 24 in.) of the soil. Trees in all but the most well-drained soils do not have taproots. A relationship exists between the amount of tree canopy and the volume of root-supporting soil required (see Figure 7.71). This relationship is the most critical factor in determining long-term tree health. Root-supporting soil is generally defined as soil with adequate drainage, low compaction, and sufficient organic and nutrient components to support the tree. The root zone must be protected from compaction both during and after construction. Root zones that are connected from tree to tree generally produce healthier trees than isolated root zones.

Contributors:
James Urban, ASLA, James Urban Landscape Architecture, Annapolis, Maryland; American Nursery and Landscape Association, Washington, DC.

SOIL VOLUME FOR TREES
7.72

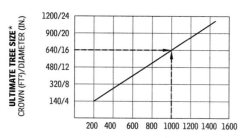

*THE ULTIMATE TREE SIZE IS DEFINED BY THE PROJECTED SIZE OF THE CROWN AND THE DIAMETER OF THE TREE AT BREAST HEIGHT

SOIL VOLUME FOR TREES

The ultimate tree size is defined by the projected size of the crown and the diameter of the tree at breast height. For example, a 16-in. diameter tree requires 1000 cu ft of soil.

SOIL MODIFICATIONS

To improve the soil's ability to retain water and nutrients:

- Thoroughly till organic matter into the top 6 to 12 in. of most planting soils. (Do not add organic matter to soil more than 12 in. deep.) Use composted bark, recycled yard waste, peat moss, or municipal processed sewage sludge. All products should be composted to a dark color and be free of pieces with identifiable leaf or wood structure. Recycled material should be tested for pH and certified free of toxic material by the supplier. Avoid material with a pH higher than 7.5.
- Modify heavy clay or silt soils (more than 40 percent clay or silt) by adding composted pine bark (up to 30 percent by volume) and/or gypsum. Coarse sand may be used if enough is added to bring the sand content to more than 60 percent of the total mix.
- Improve drainage in heavy soils by planting on raised mounds or beds and including subsurface drainage lines.
- Modify extremely sandy soils (more than 85 percent sand) by adding organic matter and/or dry, shredded clay loam up to 30 percent of the total mix.

SOIL VOLUME—REQUIREMENTS FOR TREES
7.73

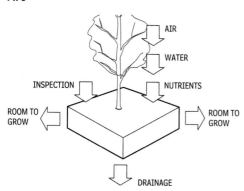

Soil volume provided for trees in urban areas must be sufficient for long-term maintenance.

SOIL VOLUME—INTERCONNECTION
7.74

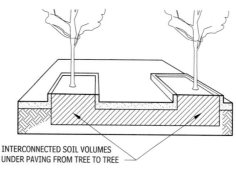

INTERCONNECTED SOIL VOLUMES UNDER PAVING FROM TREE TO TREE

The interconnection of soil volumes from tree to tree has been observed to improve the health and vigor of trees.

SOIL PROTECTION FROM COMPACTION AND DEGRADATION
7.75

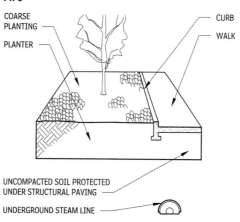

Coarse plantings keep pedestrians out of planters. Curbs protect planters from pedestrians and deicing salts. Underground steam lines must be insulated or vented to protect planter soil.

VISUALLY SYMMETRICAL TREES
7.76

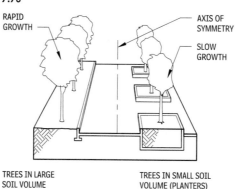

If visually symmetrical tree planting is required, symmetrical soil volumes are also required to produce trees of similar crown size.

SIDEWALK PLANTING OPTIONS
7.77

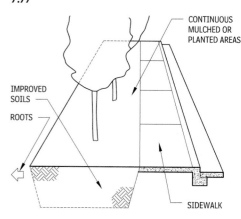

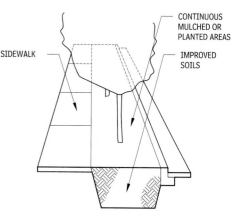

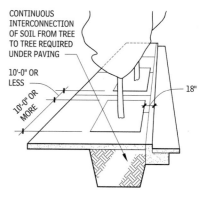

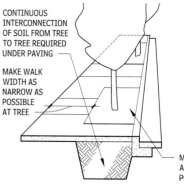

NOTES

7.77 a. Best design option: Planting trees between sidewalks and buildings causes the fewest conflicts between roots and paving by permitting rooting activity on adjacent property.
b. Acceptable design option: Planting between curbs and sidewalks in a continuous unpaved planting bed provides good soil levels for trees, but contributes to root/paving conflicts as trees mature.
c. Difficult design option: In highly developed areas with parking adjacent to the curb, planting in long narrow tree openings with an 18-in.-wide walk along the curb accommodates pedestrians exiting cars. Root/paving conflicts are probable.
d. Most difficult (and most expensive) design option: Tree openings are undersized for future trunk/root development. Severe root/paving conflicts are very likely.

Contributor:
James Urban, ASLA, James Urban Landscape Architecture, Annapolis, Maryland.

PLAZA TREE PLANTING OPTIONS
7.78

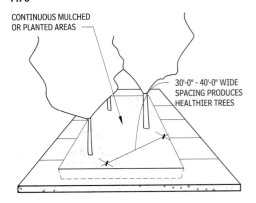

CONTINUOUS MULCHED OR PLANTED AREAS

30'-0" - 40'-0" WIDE SPACING PRODUCES HEALTHIER TREES

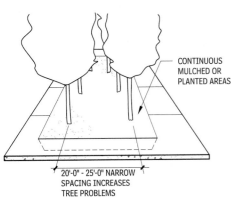

CONTINUOUS MULCHED OR PLANTED AREAS

20'-0" - 25'-0" NARROW SPACING INCREASES TREE PROBLEMS

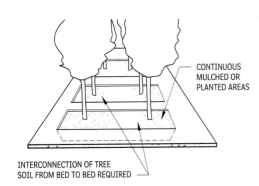

CONTINUOUS MULCHED OR PLANTED AREAS

INTERCONNECTION OF TREE SOIL FROM BED TO BED REQUIRED

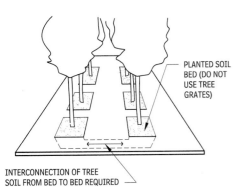

PLANTED SOIL BED (DO NOT USE TREE GRATES)

INTERCONNECTION OF TREE SOIL FROM BED TO BED REQUIRED

TREE SOIL INTERCONNECTION OPTIONS UNDER PAVING
7.79

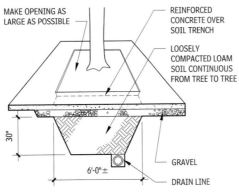

MAKE OPENING AS LARGE AS POSSIBLE

REINFORCED CONCRETE OVER SOIL TRENCH

LOOSELY COMPACTED LOAM SOIL CONTINUOUS FROM TREE TO TREE

30"

6'-0"±

GRAVEL

DRAIN LINE

CONTINUOUS SOIL TRENCH

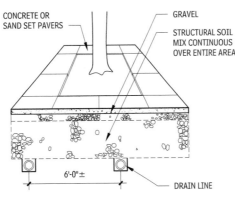

CONCRETE OR SAND SET PAVERS

GRAVEL

STRUCTURAL SOIL MIX CONTINUOUS OVER ENTIRE AREA

6'-0"±

DRAIN LINE

STRUCTURAL SOIL

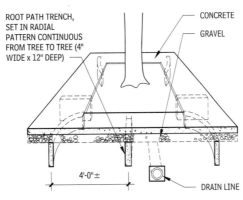

ROOT PATH TRENCH, SET IN RADIAL PATTERN CONTINUOUS FROM TREE TO TREE (4" WIDE x 12" DEEP)

CONCRETE

GRAVEL

4'-0"±

DRAIN LINE

ROOT PATH TRENCH

TREES PLANTED IN LAWNS
7.80

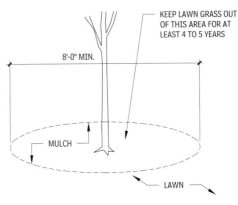

KEEP LAWN GRASS OUT OF THIS AREA FOR AT LEAST 4 TO 5 YEARS

8'-0" MIN.

MULCH

LAWN

Young trees planted in lawn areas face substantial competition from the roots of grasses.

TREE GUARDS
7.81

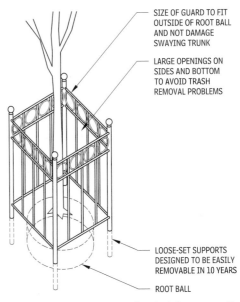

SIZE OF GUARD TO FIT OUTSIDE OF ROOT BALL AND NOT DAMAGE SWAYING TRUNK

LARGE OPENINGS ON SIDES AND BOTTOM TO AVOID TRASH REMOVAL PROBLEMS

LOOSE-SET SUPPORTS DESIGNED TO BE EASILY REMOVABLE IN 10 YEARS

ROOT BALL

Tree guards can protect young trees from trunk damage caused by bicycles. If made too small, however (less than 30 in. in diameter), they can damage the tree as it grows and are difficult to remove. The high cost and potential harm to trees outweigh the minor protection tree guards afford a trunk. They should be used only in areas with particularly high traffic.

NOTES

7.78 a. Best design option: Separate planting and walking areas. Avoid small disconnected soil volumes, to minimize too/paving conflicts.
b. Acceptable design option: Each tree has a smaller canopy with less yearly growth. More disease and insect problems are likely. Ground plantings are eliminated by shade, over time.
c. Difficult design option: Shading, slow tree growth, and poor health are problems. Root/paving conflicts are likely.
d. Most difficult (and most expensive) design option: Slow tree growth and severe root/paving conflicts are to be expected.

7.79 a. In urban areas where the pavement subgrade is compacted soil that is free from rubble, toxic, or poorly drained fills, a system of root paths can be installed to guide roots under the pavement, where they have room to grow. These roots grow deeper in the soil, causing fewer root/paving conflicts than roots left to exploit the normal minor weaknesses in paving and subgrades.
b. A root path trench is made by installing a length of strip drain material (a 12-in.-wide by 1-in.-thick plastic drain core wrapped in filter fabric) in a narrow trench and backfilling with loam topsoil. This allows air and water to flow more freely into the soil under the pavement. Install geotextile fabric and the gravel base material, then the paving.

c. Root paths cannot replace larger soil trenches or structural planting soil in areas in which existing soil conditions are extremely poor for root exploration.

Contributor:
James Urban, ASLA, James Urban Landscape Architecture, Annapolis, Maryland.

TREE BASE PROTECTION
7.82

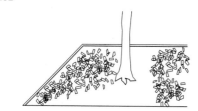

BARK MULCH

GROUND COVER PLANTS

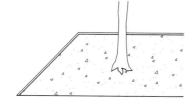

STONE DUST OR GRAVEL

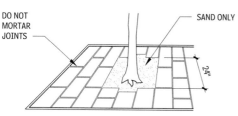

DO NOT
MORTAR
JOINTS

SAND ONLY

24"

SAND-SET PAVERS

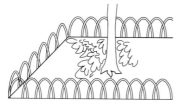

LOW FENCE AND GROUND COVER

Alternatives to tree grates (and guards) include softer, organic coverings that suit the purpose better, are less expensive, and require less maintenance over the life of the tree.

SELECTING PLANTS FOR ROOFTOP PLANTING

When choosing plants for a rooftop setting, consider the factors outlined here:

- *Wind tolerance*: Higher elevations and exposure to wind can cause defoliation and increase the transpiration rate of plants. High parapet walls with louvers can reduce wind velocity and provide shelter for plants.
- *High evaporation rate*: The drying effects of wind and sun on the soil in a planter reduce soil moisture rapidly. Irrigation, mulches, and moisture-holding soil additives (diatomaceous earth or organic matter) help reduce this moisture loss.
- *Rapid soil temperature fluctuation*: The variation in conduction capacity of planter materials results in a broad range of soil temperatures in planters of different materials. Cold or heat can cause severe root damage in certain plant species. Proper drainage helps alleviate this condition.
- *Topsoil*: Improve topsoil in planters to provide optimum growing conditions for the plants selected. A general formula calls for adding fertilizer (determined by soil testing) and one part peat moss to five parts sandy loam topsoil. More specific requirements for certain varieties of plants or grasses should be considered.
- *Root capacity*: Choose plant species carefully, considering their adaptation to the size of the plant bed. If species with shallow, fibrous roots are used instead of species with a coarse root system, consult with a nursery advisor. Consider the ultimate maturity of the plant species when sizing a planter.

ROOFTOP PLANTING DETAILS
There are five factors when designing rooftop plantings:

- *Soil depth*: Minimum soil depth in a planter varies with the plant type: for large trees, the soil should be 36 in. deep or 6 in. deeper than the root ball; for small trees, 30 in. deep; for shrubs, 24 in. deep; and for lawns, 12 in. deep (10 in. if irrigated).
- *Soil volume*: To determine sufficient soil volume, refer to the chart included in Figure 7.72, "Soil Volumes for Trees."
- *Soil weight*: The saturated weight of normal soil mix ranges from 100 to 120 pcf, depending on soil type and compaction rate. Soils can be made lighter by adding expanded shale or perlite. Soils lighter than 80 pcf cannot provide structure adequate to support trees.
- *Drainage fabric*: Plastic drainage material should be a minimum of 1/2 in. thick. Most drainage material comes with a filter fabric attached, but the overlap joints provided are not wide enough for the unconsolidated soils found in planters. A second layer of woven filter fabric, delivered in rolls greater than 10 ft in width, should be installed. Tuck the fabric over the exposed top of the drainage material to keep soil out of the drainage layer.
- *Insulation*: Most planters do not require insulation; however, in colder climates planters with small soil volumes located over heated structures may require insulation. Consult local sources for a list of cold-hardy plants.

ROOFTOP PLANTER
7.83

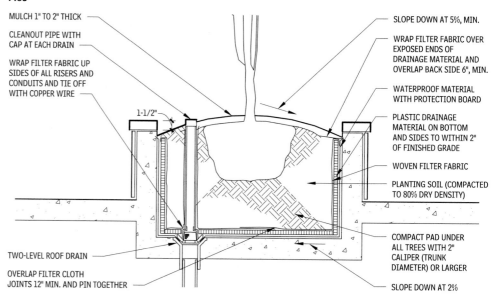

MULCH 1" TO 2" THICK

CLEANOUT PIPE WITH CAP AT EACH DRAIN

WRAP FILTER FABRIC UP SIDES OF ALL RISERS AND CONDUITS AND TIE OFF WITH COPPER WIRE

1-1/2"

TWO-LEVEL ROOF DRAIN

OVERLAP FILTER CLOTH JOINTS 12" MIN. AND PIN TOGETHER

SLOPE DOWN AT 5%, MIN.

WRAP FILTER FABRIC OVER EXPOSED ENDS OF DRAINAGE MATERIAL AND OVERLAP BACK SIDE 6", MIN.

WATERPROOF MATERIAL WITH PROTECTION BOARD

PLASTIC DRAINAGE MATERIAL ON BOTTOM AND SIDES TO WITHIN 2" OF FINISHED GRADE

WOVEN FILTER FABRIC

PLANTING SOIL (COMPACTED TO 80% DRY DENSITY)

COMPACT PAD UNDER ALL TREES WITH 2" CALIPER (TRUNK DIAMETER) OR LARGER

SLOPE DOWN AT 2%

Contributor:
James Urban, ASLA, James Urban Landscape Architecture, Annapolis, Maryland.

SITE CIVIL/MECHANICAL UTILITIES

SUBSURFACE DRAINAGE SYSTEMS

Subsurface drainage systems are very different engineering designs from surface drainage systems. Surface drainage systems intercept and collect stormwater runoff and convey it away from a building and site with the use of large inlets and storm drains. Subsurface drainage systems typically are smaller in size and capacity and designed to intercept the slower underground flows of a natural groundwater table, underground stream, or infiltration of soils from surface sources. Surface and subsurface systems typically require discharge either through a pumping station or by gravity drainage to an adequate outfall.

FOUNDATION DRAINAGE PIPING
7.84

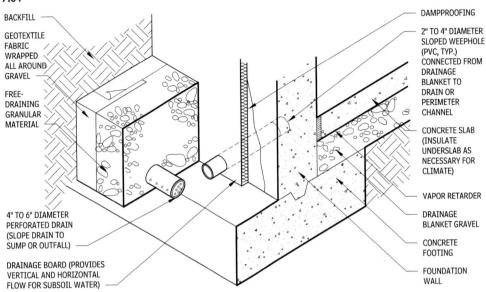

BACKFILL

GEOTEXTILE FABRIC WRAPPED ALL AROUND GRAVEL

FREE-DRAINING GRANULAR MATERIAL

4" TO 6" DIAMETER PERFORATED DRAIN (SLOPE DRAIN TO SUMP OR OUTFALL)

DRAINAGE BOARD (PROVIDES VERTICAL AND HORIZONTAL FLOW FOR SUBSOIL WATER)

DAMPPROOFING

2" TO 4" DIAMETER SLOPED WEEPHOLE (PVC, TYP.) CONNECTED FROM DRAINAGE BLANKET TO DRAIN OR PERIMETER CHANNEL

CONCRETE SLAB (INSULATE UNDERSLAB AS NECESSARY FOR CLIMATE)

VAPOR RETARDER

DRAINAGE BLANKET GRAVEL

CONCRETE FOOTING

FOUNDATION WALL

SUBDRAINAGE PIPING
7.85

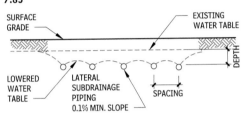

SURFACE GRADE

EXISTING WATER TABLE

DEPTH

LOWERED WATER TABLE

LATERAL SUBDRAINAGE PIPING 0.1% MIN. SLOPE

SPACING

SECTION

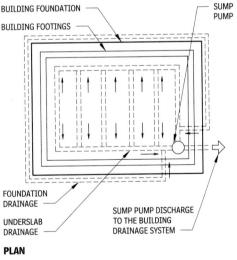

LATERAL SUBDRAINAGE PIPING 0.1% MIN. SLOPE

AREA FOR LOWERED WATER TABLE

TO ADEQUATE OUTFALL

PLAN

UNDERSLAB DRAINAGE
7.86

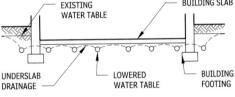

EXISTING WATER TABLE

BUILDING SLAB

UNDERSLAB DRAINAGE

LOWERED WATER TABLE

BUILDING FOOTING

SECTION

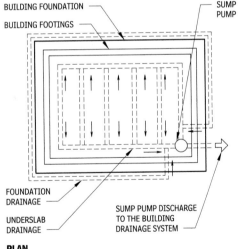

BUILDING FOUNDATION

BUILDING FOOTINGS

SUMP PUMP

FOUNDATION DRAINAGE

UNDERSLAB DRAINAGE

SUMP PUMP DISCHARGE TO THE BUILDING DRAINAGE SYSTEM

PLAN

TYPICAL SUBDRAINAGE DETAIL
7.87

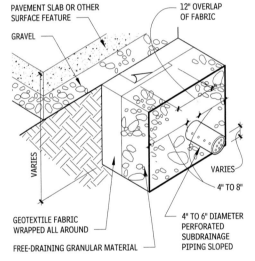

PAVEMENT SLAB OR OTHER SURFACE FEATURE

GRAVEL

VARIES

12" OVERLAP OF FABRIC

VARIES

4" TO 8"

GEOTEXTILE FABRIC WRAPPED ALL AROUND

FREE-DRAINING GRANULAR MATERIAL

4" TO 6" DIAMETER PERFORATED SUBDRAINAGE PIPING SLOPED

NOTES

7.84 a. Subdrainage is laid out to meet the needs of a site. A grid, parallel line, or random pattern at low points in the topography is used to collect subsurface water.
b. Depth and spacing of subsoil drainage pipes depend on soil conditions. Geotechnical design may be required to ensure effective operation of a subsoil drainage system.
7.87 a. The depth of subdrainage piping determines by how much subsurface water levels will be reduced.
b. When a perforated drain pipe is used, install it with the holes facing down.

c. When used to intercept hillside seepage, the bottom of a trench should be cut a minimum of 6 in. into underlying impervious material.

Contributor:
James Urban, ASLA, James Urban Landscape Architecture, Annapolis, Maryland; Joseph P. Mensch, PE, Wiles Mensch Corporation, Reston, Virginia; Kurt N. Pronske, PE, Restons, Virginia; Harold C. Munger, FAIA, Munger, Munger + Associates, Toledo, Ohio.

STORM DRAINAGE UTILITIES

Storm drainage utilities are designed to collect and dispose of rainfall runoff to prevent the flow of water from damaging building structures (through foundation leakage), site structures, and the surface grade (through erosion). The two basic types of surface drainage are the open system and the closed system.

- The open system, which utilizes a ditch/swale and culvert, is used in less densely populated, more open areas where the flow of water above grade can be accommodated fairly easily.
- The closed system, which utilizes pipes, an inlet/catch basin, and manholes, is used in more urban, populated areas, where land must be used efficiently and water brought below the surface quickly to avoid interference with human activity.

The two systems are commonly combined where terrain, human density, and land uses dictate.

A pervious or porous paving is often used for parking and other hard site surfaces. This drainage system allows water to percolate through the paved surface into the soil, similar to the way the land would naturally absorb water.

DESIGN CONSIDERATIONS FOR SURFACE DRAINAGE SYSTEMS

When designing surface drainage systems, follow these guidelines:

- Lay out all slopes, grates, swales, and other drainage features according to the ADA, without restricting accessible routes for persons with disabilities. Refer to applicable codes, standards, and regulations for accessibility requirements.

- Lay out grades so runoff can safely flow away from buildings. If drains become blocked, do not allow backed-up water to accumulate around the foundation.
- Keep in mind that an open system, or one in which water is kept on top of the surface as long as possible, is generally more economical than a closed system.
- Consider the effect of ice forming on the surface when determining slopes for vehicles and pedestrians.
- Consult local codes on such criteria as intensity and duration of rainstorms and allowable runoff for the locality.

Note that formulas given in this discussion are meant for approximation only. Consult a qualified engineer or landscape architect to design a site-specific system.

RUNOFF VELOCITY
7.89

VELOCITIES (CHANNEL)	MINIMUM (FT/SEC)	MAXIMUM (FT/SEC)
Grass—athletic field	0.5	2
Walks—long	0.5	12*
Walks—transverse	1	4
Streets—long	0.5	20
Parking	1	5
Channels—grass swale	1	8
Channels—paved swale	0.5	12

CALCULATION OF RUNOFF
7.90

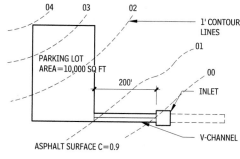

$$AREA = \frac{10,000 \text{ SQ FT}}{43,560 \text{ SQ FT/ACRE}} = 0.23 \text{ ACRES}$$

STORM DRAINAGE UTILITIES (IMPERVIOUS PAVING)
7.88

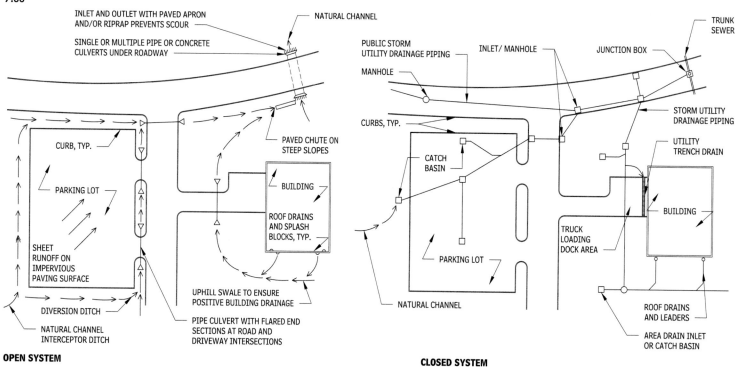

OPEN SYSTEM

CLOSED SYSTEM

NOTES

7.89 For accessibility, 8.3 percent maximum.
7.90 Here is a simplified method for calculating the approximate runoff of areas less than 100 acres:

$Q = C \times I \times A$
Q = flow (cu ft/sec)
C = surface runoff value (see Table 7.91)
I = intensity (in./hr; obtain from weather services)
A = area of site (acres)

For example, assume the local code requires I = 5 in./hr:

$Q = C \times I \times A$
$Q = 0.9 \times 5 \times 0.23$
$Q = 1.04$ cu ft/sec
Q = approximate volume of water per second entering the V-channel from the parking lot

Contributors:
Joseph P. Mensch, PE, Wiles Mensch Corporation, Reston, Virginia; Kurt N. Pronske, PE, Reston, Virginia; Harold C. Munger, FAIA, Munger Munger + Associates Architects, Toledo, Ohio; Pearse O'Doherty, ASLA, Graham Landscape Architecture, Annapolis, Maryland.

SURFACE RUNOFF VALUES (C)
7.91

SURFACE	VALUE*
Roofs	0.95–1.00
Pavement	0.90–1.00
Roads	0.30–0.90
Bare soil—sand	0.20–0.40
Bare soil—clay	0.30–0.75
Grass	0.15–0.60
Commercial development	0.60–0.75
High-density residential development	0.50–0.65
Low-density residential development	0.30–0.55

SLOPES
7.93

DESCRIPTION	MINIMUM %	MAXIMUM %	RECOMMENDED %
Grass—mowed	1	25	1.5 –10
Grass—athletic field	0.5	2	1
Walks—long	0.5	12a	1.5
Walks—transverse	1	4	1–2
Streets—long	0.5	20	1–10
Parking	1	5	2–3
Channels—grass swale	1	8	1.5–2
Channels—paved swale	0.5	12	4–6

n VALUES FOR MANNING FORMULA
7.94

CHANNEL SURFACE	n
Cast iron	0.012
Corrugated steel	0.032
Clay tile	0.014
Cement grout	0.013
Concrete	0.015
Earth ditch	0.023
Cut rock channel	0.033
Winding channel	0.025

POROUS PAVING SYSTEMS

Porous paving materials, methods for sizing channels, and design considerations for porous paving systems are the topics of this section.

POROUS PAVING MATERIALS

The two principal types of porous paving are monolithic surfacing material and unit pavers.

- *Monolithic porous paving* is stone aggregate bound with asphalt or portland cement. The aggregate must be sorted to exclude the "fines" or sand-sized particles that normally fill the voids between larger pieces. Without the fines, water is able to run through the paving material. Generally, porous asphalt and concrete are both strong enough for parking and roadway surfaces and pedestrian uses.
- *Precast concrete unit pavers*, with shapes that allow water to flow through them, can also give surface stability for parking or driveways. Paver types are available for exposed placement, or for burial just below the surface. In the latter case, the soil-pea gravel or vegetation in the pavers is exposed and can help percolate precipitation into the ground.

To reduce runoff and increase water absorption, porous paving must be underlaid with a bed of unbound aggregate. The unbound aggregate acts as a structural support and forms a reservoir to hold precipitation until it can percolate into the soil. Use of porous paving may permit use of a significantly smaller and simpler storm drainage system.

METHOD FOR SIZING CHANNELS

Channels and pipes for handling water runoff may be sized by determining the flow of water (Q) with the formula $Q = Va$. V is the velocity of the runoff water in ft/sec as determined by the Manning formula, and *a* is the cross-sectional area of water given in square feet. For a given Q, adjust the channel or pipe shape, size, and/or slope to obtain the desired velocity (one that will not erode earth, grass ditches, or other features).

The Manning formula is $V = 1.486/n \times r\ 0.67 \times S0.5$, in which *n* = values relating to surface characteristics of channels (see Table

HYDRAULIC PROPERTIES OF TYPICAL CHANNEL SECTIONS
7.95

TYPE SECTION	WIDTH (W)	BASE (b)	DEPTH (d)	AREA OF WATER SECTION (a)	WETTED PERIMETER (P)	HYDRAULIC RADIUS (r)
RECTANGULAR	b or $\dfrac{a}{d}$	W or $\dfrac{a}{d}$	$\dfrac{a}{b}$	wd	$W + 2d$	$\dfrac{d}{1+\dfrac{2d}{W}}$
TRIANGULAR	$2e$	—	$\dfrac{a}{e}$	ed	$e\sqrt{e^2 + d^2}$	$\dfrac{ed}{2\sqrt{e^2 + d^2}}$
TRIANGULAR (curb and gutter)	$\dfrac{2a}{d}$	—	$\dfrac{2a}{W}$	$\dfrac{Wd}{2}$	$d + \sqrt{d^2 + W^2}$	$\dfrac{2\,Wd}{d + \sqrt{W^2 + W}}$
TRAPEZOIDAL (even sides)	$b + 2e$	$W - 2e$	$\dfrac{a}{b + e}$	$d(b + e)$	$b + 2\sqrt{e^2 + d^2}$	$\dfrac{d(b + e)}{b + 2\sqrt{e^2 + d^2}}$
PARABOLIC	$\dfrac{a}{0.67d}$	—	$\dfrac{a}{0.67W}$	$0.67\,Wd$	$W + \left(\dfrac{8d^2}{3W}\right)$	$\dfrac{a}{W + \left(\dfrac{8d^2}{3W}\right)}$

POROUS PAVING TYPES
7.92

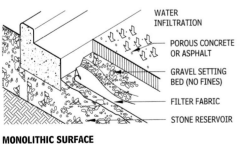

MONOLITHIC SURFACE

- WATER INFILTRATION
- POROUS CONCRETE OR ASPHALT
- GRAVEL SETTING BED (NO FINES)
- FILTER FABRIC
- STONE RESERVOIR

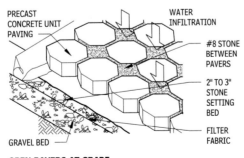

OPEN PAVERS AT GRADE

- PRECAST CONCRETE UNIT PAVING
- WATER INFILTRATION
- #8 STONE BETWEEN PAVERS
- 2" TO 3" STONE SETTING BED
- FILTER FABRIC
- GRAVEL BED

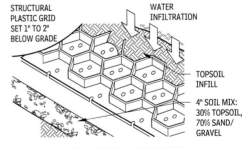

STRUCTURAL GRID/PAVERS BELOW GRADE

- STRUCTURAL PLASTIC GRID SET 1" TO 2" BELOW GRADE
- WATER INFILTRATION
- TOPSOIL INFILL
- 4" SOIL MIX: 30% TOPSOIL, 70% SAND/GRAVEL

NOTES

7.91 All values are approximate.
7.93 a. For accessibility, 8.3 percent maximum.
7.95 For freeboard (F), 0.3–0.5 ft is recommended.

Contributor:
Pearse O'Doherty, ASLA, Graham Landscape Architecture, Annapolis, Maryland.

7.94), r = hydraulic radius (see Table 7.95), and S = slope (the drop in ft/length).

For example, assume a 200-ft concrete V-channel for which

$$W = 2\ \text{ft}$$
$$h = 0.5\ \text{ft}$$
$$S = 0.005\ (1\ \text{ft}/200\ \text{ft})$$
$$r = 0.37\ \text{(calculated using V-channel properties)}$$
$$V = (1.486/0.015) \times 0.250.67 \times 0.0050.5$$
$$= 2.6\ \text{ft/sec (see Table 7.141)}.$$

To check flow, follow these steps:

$$Q = Va\ (a\ \text{from channel properties})$$
$$= 2.6 \times 0.5 = 1.3\ \text{cu ft/sec}$$

Use the formula for calculating runoff ($Q = C \times I \times A$) to determine the flow required for a site; compare it to the capacity of a channel sized according to the Manning formula to determine whether the channel design is satisfactory.

DESIGN CONSIDERATIONS FOR POROUS PAVING SYSTEMS

Design considerations for working with porous paving systems include the following:

- Soils around porous paving installations must have a minimum percolation rate of about 1/2 in./hr, and should not be more than about 30 percent clay. On sites where the slope is greater than 3 percent, terracing the paved areas allows the bottom of each reservoir to remain level.
- Proper specification and supervision are important in the installation of porous paving materials. Soil under the reservoir must not be unduly compacted during construction.
- Porous concrete can withstand heavier loads than porous asphalt. Because it does not soften in hot weather and may be more susceptible to freeze/thaw damage, it is better suited to warmer climates. Additives may be introduced to improve cold climate performance.
- Porous asphalt has good freeze/thaw resistance, but is best suited for areas in which traffic is limited, such as employee parking.
- While clogging of monolithic porous paving is generally not a problem, recommended maintenance may include use of a hydrovac once or twice a year, as well as the prompt removal of leaves and windblown sand.
- The reservoir below porous paving has no fixed depth but is designed according to the slope of the site, the soil percolation rate, and the size of the design storm. Consult a civil engineer or landscape architect.

RUNOFF CONTROL SYSTEMS

NATURAL WETLAND SYSTEMS

Wetlands naturally detain and filter water. Scattered throughout the United States, from tropical areas to tundra, they form in depressions in the landscape where the water table is near or at the surface of the soil. They may be as small as a tabletop or span tens of thousands of acres. There is no single, correct, ecologically sound definition for wetlands, primarily because of their diversity. These systems are an important part of the ecosystem because they produce food and timber, purify drinking water, absorb and store floodwater, suppress storm surges, and help maintain biodiversity. Water is supplied to a wetland either by surface sources (e.g., streams or rivers) or by groundwater.

The sensitivity of wetlands determines appropriate buffer distances between them and developed areas. Buffers, which may range from 30 to 300 ft or more, should respond to the effect runoff may have on the wetland ecosystem. (Consult a wetlands scientist to formulate buffer distances.)

In general, four wetland sensitivity issues should be taken into account:

- *Hydrology:* The wetland's source of water could be altered by development.

POROUS PAVING AND STONE RESERVOIR DETAIL
7.96

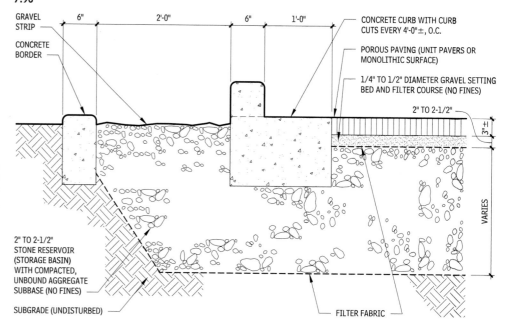

ON-SITE RUNOFF CONTROL MEASURES

Architects can use several on-site measures to control runoff in development projects. One of the most commonly used is a simple open storage area for runoff. The configuration of such open systems varies, depending on the desired level of pollutant treatment. Typically called *storage ponds*, *retention basins*, or (when made to resemble a natural environment) a *constructed stormwater wetland*, open systems generally operate more thoroughly with increased retention time.

Simple storage ponds are typically dry between storms after runoff has evaporated or infiltrated the groundwater. Dry ponds sometimes include a wet lower area for additional runoff retention. Wet ponds are permanently wet, allowing pollutants to settle to the bottom. Wet ponds that extend runoff retention time with control devices can remove a very high percentage of particulate pollutants.

Constructed stormwater wetlands (engineered, shallow marshlike areas) retain runoff for long periods, allowing pollutants to settle out of the water column and providing biological, chemical, and physical processes for breaking down pollutants. Wetland vegetation slows the velocity of stormwater, reducing erosion and allowing pollutants to settle. Many organic and inorganic compounds are removed from wetlands by the chemical processes of absorption, precipitation, and volatilization.

Constructed stormwater wetlands can also filter excess nutrients such as nitrogen and phosphorus contained in runoff from gardens and septic tanks. To correctly size a wetland used for stormwater runoff control, consider the total volume and velocity of water entering and leaving the system.

Potential advantages of using constructed stormwater wetlands are that they have relatively low capital and operating costs, offer consistent compliance with permit requirements, and greatly reduce operational and maintenance costs.

- *Vegetation:* The plant species in a wetland have different levels of hardiness.
- *Ecological state:* More pristine systems are more sensitive to development and runoff pollution.
- *Animal species:* Nesting birds, for example, need greater buffer distances than wintering waterfowl.

CROSS SECTION OF NATURAL FRESHWATER, NONTIDAL WETLANDS
7.97

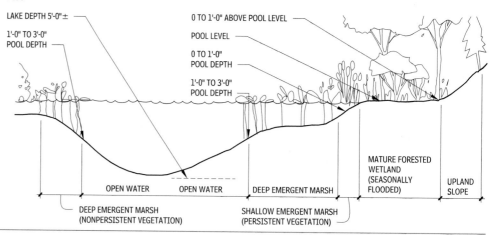

Contributors:
Pearse O'Doherty, ASLA, Graham Landscape Architecture, Annapolis, Maryland; Carrie Fischer, "Design for Wetlands Preservation," topic II.A.1 in *Environmental Resource Guide* (The American Institute of Architects, Washington, DC, 1992); Thomas Schueler, Metropolitan Washington Council of Governments, Washington, DC.

EFFECTIVENESS COMPARISON OF URBAN BEST MANAGEMENT PRACTICES (BMPS)[a]
7.98

URBAN BMP OPTIONS	POLLUTANT REMOVAL RELIABILITY	LONGEVITY[b]	APPLICABILITY TO MOST DEVELOPMENTS	WILDLIFE HABITAT POTENTIAL	ENVIRONMENTAL CONCERNS	COMPARATIVE COSTS	SPECIAL CONSIDERATIONS
Stormwater wetlands	Moderate to high, depending on design	20+ years expected	Applicable to most sites if land is available	High	Stream warming, natural wetland alteration	Marginally higher than wet ponds	Recommended with design improvements and with the use of micropools and wetlands
Extended detention ponds	Moderate but not always reliable	20+ years, but frequent clogging and short detention common	Widely applicable but requires at least 10 acres of drainage area	Moderate	Possible stream warming and habitat destruction	Lowest cost alternative in size range	Recommended with design improvements and with the use of micropools and wetlands
Wet ponds	Moderate to high	20+ years	Widely applicable but requires drainage area of more than 2 acres	Moderate to high	Possible stream warming, tropic shifts, habitat destruction	Moderate to high, compared to conventional	Recommended, with careful site evaluation
Multiple pond systems	Moderate to high (redundancy increases reliability)	20+ years	Widely applicable	Moderate to high	Selection of appropriate pond option minimizes overall environmental impact	Most expensive pond option	Recommended
Infiltration trenches	Presumed moderate	50% failure rate within 5 years	Highly restricted (soils, groundwater, slope, area, sediment input)	Low	Slight risk of groundwater contamination	Cost-effective on smaller sites, but rehab costs can be considerable	Recommended with pretreatment and geotechnical evaluation
Infiltration basins	Presumed moderate, if working	60–100% failure within 5 years	Highly restricted (soils, groundwater, slope, area, sediment input)	Low to moderate	Slight risk of groundwater contamination	Construction cost moderate, but rehab cost high	Not widely recommended until longevity is improved
Porous pavement	High, if working	75% failure within 5 years	Extremely restricted (traffic, soils, groundwater, slope, area, sediment input)	Low	Possible groundwater impacts, uncontrolled runoff	Cost-effective, compared to conventional asphalt when working properly	Recommended in highly restricted applications with careful construction and effective maintenance
Sand filters	Moderate to high	20+ years	Applicable for smaller developments	Low	Minor	Comparatively high construction costs and frequent maintenance	Recommended, with local demonstration
Grassed swales	Low to moderate, but unreliable	20+ years	Low-density development and roads	Low	Minor	Low compared to curb and gutter	Recommended, with check dams, as one part of a BMP system
Filter strips	Unreliable in urban settings	Unknown but may be limited	Restricted to low-density areas	Moderate, if forested	Minor	Low	Recommended as one element of a BMP system
Water quality inlets	Presumed low	20+ years	Small, highly impervious catchments (less than 2 acres)	Low	Resuspension of hydrocarbon loadings, disposal of hydrocarbon and toxic residuals	High, compared to trenches and sand filters	Not currently recommended as a primary BMP option

STORMWATER WETLANDS

Stormwater wetlands can be defined as constructed systems explicitly designed to mitigate the effects of stormwater quality and quantity on urban development. They temporarily store stormwater runoff in shallow pools that create growing conditions suitable for emergent and riparian wetland plants. In combination, the runoff storage, complex microtopography, and emergent plants in the constructed wetland form an ideal matrix for the removal of urban pollutants.

Unlike natural wetlands, which often express the underlying groundwater level, stormwater wetlands are dominated by surface runoff. Storm water wetlands can best be described as semitidal, in that they have a hydroperiod characterized by a cyclic pattern of inundation and subsequent drawdown, occurring 15 to 30 times a year, depending on rainfall and the imperviousness of the contributing watershed.

Storm water wetlands usually fall into one of four basic designs:

- *Shallow marsh system*: The large surface area of a shallow marsh design demands a reliable groundwater supply or base flow to maintain sufficient water elevation to support emergent wetland plants. Shallow marsh systems take up a lot of space, requiring a sizable contributing watershed (often more than 25 acres) to support a shallow permanent pool.

- *Pond/wetland system*: A pond/wetland design utilizes two separate cells for stormwater treatment, a wet pond and a shallow marsh. The multiple functions of the latter are to trap sediments, reduce incoming runoff velocity, and remove pollutants. Pond/wetland systems consume less space than shallow marsh systems because the bulk of the treatment is provided by a deep pool rather than a shallow marsh.

- *Extended detention wetland*: In extended detention wetlands, extra runoff storage is created by temporarily detaining runoff above the shallow marsh. This extended detention feature enables the wetland to occupy less space, as temporary vertical storage partially substitutes for shallow marsh storage. A growing zone is created along the gentle side slopes of extended detention wetlands, from the normal pool level to the maximum extended detention water surface.

- *Pocket wetlands*: Pocket wetlands are adapted to serve small sites (from 1 to 10 acres). Because the drainage area is small, pocket wetlands usually do not have a reliable base flow, creating a widely fluctuating water level. In most cases, water levels in the wetland are supported by excavating down to the water table. In drier areas, a pocket wetland is supported only by storm water runoff, and during extended periods of dry weather it will have no shallow pool at all (only saturated soils). Due to their small size and fluctuating water levels, pocket wetlands often have low plant diversity and poor wildlife habitat value.

The selection of a particular wetland design usually depends on three factors:

- Available space
- Contributing watershed area
- Desired environmental function

However, storm water wetlands are not typically located within delineated natural wetland areas, which provide critical habitat and ecosystem services, and are protected under local, state, and federal statutes. It's also important to point out that storm water wetlands should not be confused with constructed wetlands, which are used to mitigate the permitted loss of natural wetlands under wetland protection regulations. The primary goal of wetland mitigation is to replicate the species diversity and ecological function of the lost natural wetland, whereas the more limited goal of storm water wetlands is to maximize pollutant removal and create generic wetland habitat.

Storm water wetlands are also distinguished from natural wetlands that receive storm water runoff as a consequence of upstream development. Although not intended for stormwater treatment, wetlands influenced by stormwater are common in urban settings. Storm water runoff that becomes a major component of the water balance of a natural wetland can severely alter the functional and structural qualities of the wetland. The end result is a storm water-influenced natural wetland that is more characteristic of a storm water wetland than a natural one.

NOTES

7.98 [a]. The variety of urban BMPs available to remove pollutants from urban runoff differs widely in performance, longevity, feasibility, cost, and environmental impact. As the matrix shows, stormwater wetlands are an attractive BMP choice at many development sites.
[b]. Based on current designs and prevailing maintenance practices.

Contributors:
Carrie Fischer, "Design for Wetlands Preservation," topic II.A.1 in *Environmental Resource Guide* (Washington, DC: American Institute of Architects, 1992); Thomas Schueler, Metropolitan Washington Council of Governments, Washington, DC.

SHALLOW MARSH SYSTEM
7.99

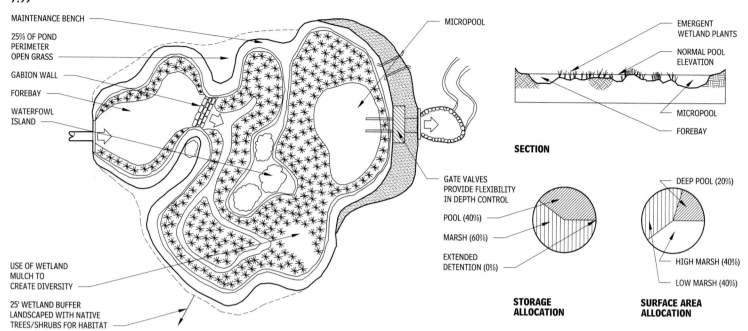

MAINTENANCE BENCH

25% OF POND PERIMETER OPEN GRASS

GABION WALL

FOREBAY

WATERFOWL ISLAND

USE OF WETLAND MULCH TO CREATE DIVERSITY

25' WETLAND BUFFER LANDSCAPED WITH NATIVE TREES/SHRUBS FOR HABITAT

MICROPOOL

GATE VALVES PROVIDE FLEXIBILITY IN DEPTH CONTROL

EMERGENT WETLAND PLANTS

NORMAL POOL ELEVATION

MICROPOOL

FOREBAY

SECTION

POOL (40%)

MARSH (60%)

EXTENDED DETENTION (0%)

STORAGE ALLOCATION

DEEP POOL (20%)

HIGH MARSH (40%)

LOW MARSH (40%)

SURFACE AREA ALLOCATION

Most of the shallow marsh system is 0 to 18 in. deep, a depth that creates favorable conditions for the growth of emergent wetland plants. A deeper forebay is located at the major inlet, and a deep micropool is situated near the outlet.

POND/WETLAND SYSTEM
7.100

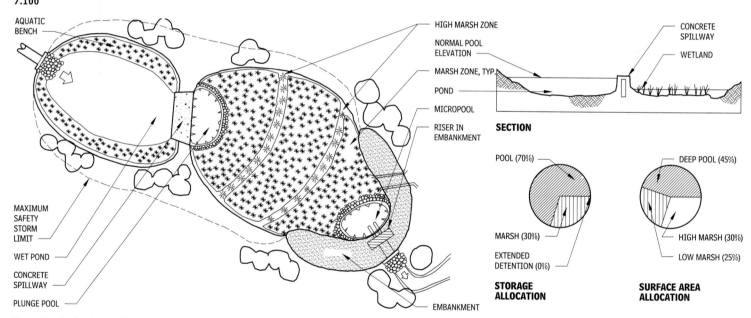

AQUATIC BENCH

MAXIMUM SAFETY STORM LIMIT

WET POND

CONCRETE SPILLWAY

PLUNGE POOL

HIGH MARSH ZONE

NORMAL POOL ELEVATION

MARSH ZONE, TYP.

POND

MICROPOOL

RISER IN EMBANKMENT

EMBANKMENT

CONCRETE SPILLWAY

WETLAND

SECTION

POOL (70%)

MARSH (30%)

EXTENDED DETENTION (0%)

STORAGE ALLOCATION

DEEP POOL (45%)

HIGH MARSH (30%)

LOW MARSH (25%)

SURFACE AREA ALLOCATION

The pond/wetland system consists of a deep pond that leads to a shallow wetland. The pond removes pollutants and reduces the space required for the system.

Contributors:
Carrie Fischer, "Design for Wetlands Preservation," topic II.A.1 in *Environmental Resource Guide* (The American Institute of Architects, Washington, DC, 1992); Thomas Schueler, Metropolitan Washington Council of Governments, Washington, DC.

COMPARATIVE ATTRIBUTES OF FOUR STORMWATER WETLAND DESIGNS
7.101

ATTRIBUTE	SHALLOW MARSH	POND/WETLAND	EXTENDED DETENTION WETLAND	POCKET WETLAND
Pollutant removal capability	Moderate; reliable removal of sediments and nutrients	Moderate to high; reliable removal of nutrients and sediment	Moderate; less reliable removal of nutrients	Moderate; can be subject to resuspension and groundwater displacement
Land consumption	High; shallow marsh storage consumes space	Moderate, as vertical pool substitutes for marsh storage	Moderate, as vertical extended detention substitutes for marsh storage	Moderate, but can be shoehorned into site
Water balance	Dry weather base flow normally recommended to maintain water elevations; groundwater not recommended as primary source of water supply to wetland			Water supply provided by excavation to groundwater
Wetland area/watershed area	Minimum ratio of .02	Minimum ratio of .01	Minimum ratio of .01	Minimum ratio of .01
Contributing watershed area	Drainage area of 25 acres or more, with dry weather Q*	Drainage area of 25 acres or more, with dry weather Q*	Minimum of 10 acres required for extended detention	1–10 acres
Deepwater cells	Forebay, channels, micropool	Pond, micropool	Forebay, micropool	Micropool, if possible
Outlet configuration	Reversed slope pipe extending from riser, withdrawn approximately 1' below normal pool; pipe and pond drain equipped with gate valve			Broadcrested weir with half-round trash rack and pond drain
Sediment cleanout cycle (approximate)	Cleanout of forebay every 2–5 years	Cleanout of pond every 10 years	Cleanout of forebay every 2–5 years	Cleanout of wetland every 5–10 years, on-site disposal and stockpile mulch
Native plant diversity	High, if complex microtopography is present	High, with sufficient wetland complexity and area	Moderate; fluctuating water levels impose physiological constraints	Low to moderate, due to small surface area and poor control of water levels
Wildlife habitat potential	High, with complexity and buffer	High, with buffer, attracts waterfowl	Moderate, with buffer	Low, due to small area and low diversity

EXTENDED DETENTION WETLAND
7.102

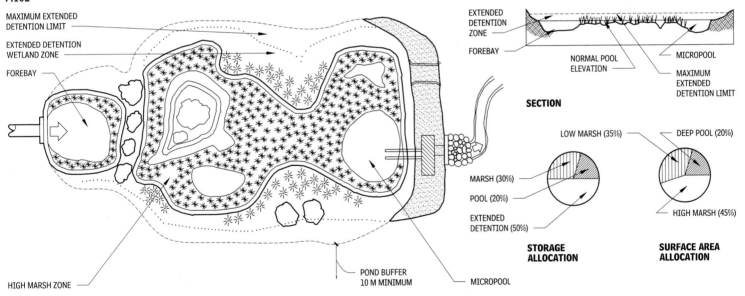

The water level in an extended detention wetland can increase by as much as 3 ft after a storm, returning to normal levels within 24 hours. As much as half the total treatment volume can be provided as extended detention storage, which helps protect downstream channels from erosion and reduces the space needed for the wetland.

NOTE

7.101 Q = coefficient of runoff

Contributors:
Carrie Fischer, "Design for Wetlands Preservation," topic II.A.1 in *Environmental Resource Guide* (The American Institute of Architects, Washington, DC, 1992); Thomas Schueler, Metropolitan Washington Council of Governments, Washington, DC.

SITE ELECTRICAL UTILITIES

This section addresses site lighting as a component of site electrical utilities.

SITE LIGHTING

SITE LIGHTING DESIGN CONSIDERATIONS

Creating good design for site lighting is not just about picking the latest technology or the best fixture. It is about using lighting to convey the overall story of a project. The story may be one of safety in a casino parking lot or it may be one of excitement in an outdoor mall where visitors can gather with their families for an evening to have dinner and see a movie.

Site lighting design requirements vary from project to project, and so need to be defined with the individual project team prior to preparing a design. Site lighting requirements typically include lighting pedestrian pathways, landscaping, landscape features, water features, and architectural features such as statuary and adjacent public roadways, parking areas, and nearby facades.

Site lighting design, at its core, is about lighting the environment in a manner that responds to the desired function of the guests within the space. There may be multiple functions such as wayfinding, creating gathering spaces, interacting with the organic and built environments, and meeting security requirements, which all must be taken into account. The overall design intent of the space must allow for these functions to coexist seamlessly, or the guest experience will be negative.

As a part of the design preparation, designers will want to familiarize themselves with the landscape design and current foliage specifications on the project. Lighting fixtures can be used to highlight trees, accent shrubbery, and be mounted in trees to light the path below. It is important to know which trees are deciduous and which trees retain their canopies when making these determinations. It is also highly recommended that lighting designers work closely with the landscape architect to understand which trees will allow the attachment of lighting hardware and mounting straps.

Once the site lighting tasks and requirements have been determined, the designer can begin selecting fixtures, determining lamp types, and preparing the layout.

SITE LIGHTING REGULATIONS AND CODES

Other factors to consider when designing site lighting are local and national energy codes, any locality-specific dark-sky ordinances, and the current lighting levels in the surrounding and adjacent areas. The International Dark-Sky Association (IDA) is a nonprofit group whose mission is "to preserve and protect the nighttime environment and our heritage of dark skies through quality outdoor lighting." This association (www.darksky.org) has been an active voice in the creation of many of the local dark-sky ordinances.

Several calculation programs are available to help verify the illuminance levels are being met in the site lighting design. AGI32 (www.agi32.com) is commonly used for site lighting studies, as is LumenMicro by Lighting Technologies (www.lighting-technologies.com).

The most difficult part of creating a good lighting design is to meet all of the functional and code requirements of a site while mixing in the desired aesthetics of the project. Providing the right nighttime identity for a site is key to making any project a success.

SITE LIGHTING DOCUMENTATION

Required documentation for the lighting design submittal will vary from project to project, but the basic elements will remain the same. A minimum of suggested documentation would include:

- A layout depicting the design intent
- Fixture cut sheets and specifications showing fixtures desired on the project
- Mounting details showing any special integration requirements

RELATIONSHIP OF OUTDOOR LIGHTING TO SITE AND ARCHITECTURE
7.103

| AC ARM MOUNT | BOUNCE© | LIGHTVAULT© | BOLLARD | ARCHITECTURAL FLOODLIGHT | WALL FORMS© | SITE WALLFORMS | WALL DIRECTOR© |

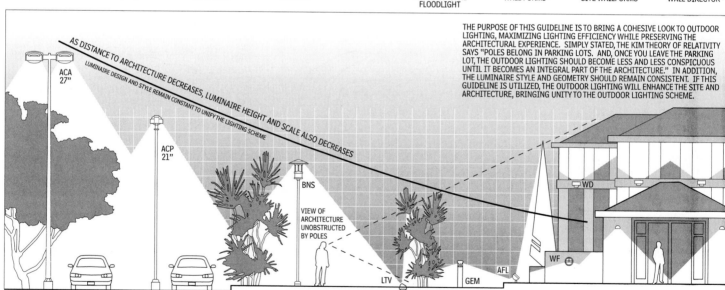

THE PURPOSE OF THIS GUIDELINE IS TO BRING A COHESIVE LOOK TO OUTDOOR LIGHTING, MAXIMIZING LIGHTING EFFICIENCY WHILE PRESERVING THE ARCHITECTURAL EXPERIENCE. SIMPLY STATED, THE KIM THEORY OF RELATIVITY SAYS "POLES BELONG IN PARKING LOTS. AND, ONCE YOU LEAVE THE PARKING LOT, THE OUTDOOR LIGHTING SHOULD BECOME LESS AND LESS CONSPICUOUS UNTIL IT BECOMES AN INTEGRAL PART OF THE ARCHITECTURE." IN ADDITION, THE LUMINAIRE STYLE AND GEOMETRY SHOULD REMAIN CONSISTENT. IF THIS GUIDELINE IS UTILIZED, THE OUTDOOR LIGHTING WILL ENHANCE THE SITE AND ARCHITECTURE, BRINGING UNITY TO THE OUTDOOR LIGHTING SCHEME.

SITE/ROADWAY ZONE
PARKING LOTS AND ROADWAYS REQUIRE LUMINAIRES ON 20' - 40' POLES TO EFFICIENTLY LIGHT THESE LARGE AREAS. THEREFORE, THIS LIGHTING BECOMES DOMINANT, AND SETS THE DESIGN AND STYLE FOR ALL OTHER LIGHTING AS YOU PROGRESS TOWARDS THE BUILDING.

PEDESTRIAN ZONE
AS YOU LEAVE THE PARKING LOT AND TRANSITION TO PEDESTRIAN AREAS, POLES SHOULD DECREASE IN HEIGHT TO 10' - 16'. IN ADDITION, LUMINAIRES SHOULD DECREASE IN SCALE, AND CAN HAVE MORE DECORATIVE FEATURES TO BE APPRECIATED AT THE PEDESTRIAN LEVEL.

LANDSCAPE/PATH ZONE
NEAR THE BUILDING, LUMINAIRES SHOULD BEGIN TO DISAPPEAR, BLENDING INTO THE LANDSCAPE AND HARDSCAPE ELEMENTS.

BUILDING/PERIMETER ZONE
NO POLE MOUNTED LUMINARIES SHOULD EVER BE USED NEAR THE BUILDING, AS THEY WILL DOMINATE THE ARCHITECTURE. THE ONLY EXCEPTION WOULD BE THE USE OF DECORATIVE LUMINARIES TO DELINEATE ENTRANCES TO THE STRUCTURE. BUILDING MOUNTED, ARCHITECTURALLY COMPATIBLE FIXTURES SHOULD BE ALMOST INVISIBLE.

Contributors:
Lisa Passamonte Green, Visual Terrain, Van Nuys, California; Kim Lighting, City of Industry, Californai; Resource Lighting, Inc., Albuquerque, New Mexico.

AREA LIGHTING

Path lighting fixtures generally include pole/post lighting, bollards, and step lights. Pole lighting can be decorative to match the architecture, make a statement, or be purely functional. Pole, post, and bollard heights and spacing are determined by calculating the desired and/or required illuminance values, along with creating a layout that meets the aesthetic qualities as determined by the project design team. As a general rule, the minimum mounting height should be no less than one-half the maximum projection distance from a single fixture head.

When using poles, posts or bollards, designers should be prepared to coordinate anchor bolt details and the need for any additional foundations required to meet local wind-loading requirements. Project engineers should be consulted, as well as the fixture manufacturer, to confirm the product can meet the wind-loading requirements.

Mounting details should be customized for any site-specific requirements, and the specified manufacturer should be treated as a valuable resource for the information needed to complete this effort. It is also highly recommended that the Illuminating Engineering Society of North America (IESNA) be a key resource for all projects located within North America. The IESNA has compiled a series of recommended lighting requirements and illuminance values for many of the tasks involved in creating the site lighting. There is a variety of lighting illuminance levels, depending on the adjacent architecture. For example, a bank parking lot may require higher levels of illuminance, due to security issues, than those of a library parking lot on the same street.

Recommended reading such as the ED-100.8 Course Book can be found at www.iesna.org.

SEE ALSO:

Area Lighting
Cast-in-Place Concrete Retaining Walls
Composites
Dry-Placed Stone
Earthwork
Erosion Control
Grading
Irrigation
Metal Grating
Metal Stair Nosings
Mulching
Preservative Treatment
Retention Basins
Seeding
Site Seating
Stone
Storm Drainage Utilities
Timber Retaining Wall
Trees
Underslab Drainage
Unit Masonry Retaining Wall

SECTION 2

MATERIALS

CONCRETE

8

INTRODUCTION

Concrete is present in almost every modern-day structure. Most foundations and floors are concrete, and concrete structural frames for buildings of all heights are common. Add to this the concrete used in other facility services, sites and infrastructure, and process construction, and it is easy to understand why concrete is one of the most widely used human-made building materials.

Concrete can be a sustainable building material. Its durability ensures that fewer resources are needed to repair or replace concrete structures. Structures built with insulated concrete have optimal energy performance, and light-colored concrete absorbs less heat and reflects more light, thus reducing the heat-island effect in urban environments. Concrete producers now use recycled materials as part of the concrete mixture, and the concrete itself can be crushed and recycled once its initial useful "life" is over.

Concrete can also be an aesthetically pleasing choice for building, with properties that offer design professionals a nearly limitless choice of shapes, textures, and colors. Signature structures by some of the world's greatest architects—Frank Lloyd Wright, Santiago Calatrava, and Tadao Ando, among them—attest to the beauty of concrete.

The degree to which concrete fulfills its utilitarian, environmental, and aesthetic roles depends on the knowledge and skill of people working at every link in the construction chain, from conception to execution. These people include design professionals, materials producers, and contractors. Input from all these professionals helps the architect to design structures that fulfill their function, please the eye, serve the environment, and adequately safeguard occupants.

The architect must clearly define expectations for the concrete materials used and for the execution of the work. Especially important are design details showing the concrete elements as they interface with other building components such as structural steel frames, fenestration, partition walls, cladding, and floor coverings. Incompatibility of construction tolerances for interfacing materials can negatively affect a project's cost and schedule, whereas thoughtfully developed and well-conceived details, as shown throughout this book, will facilitate coordination among different trades, and ensure the best possible project.

Contributor:
American Concrete Institute, Farmington Hills, Michigan.

CONCRETE FORMING AND ACCESSORIES

Concrete forming and accessories includes permanent and temporary forms, anchors, inserts, expansion and control joints, and waterstops for structural and architectural cast-in-place concrete. Concrete forms include metal pan forms, wood forms, plastic forms, slip forms, and corrugated paper forms for placing concrete. These may also include form liners and void forms.

CONCRETE FORMWORK

GENERAL

Concrete formwork costs are a substantial part of the total expense of putting concrete in place. Thus, by developing design elements and details that simplify or standardize form requirements, design professionals can help contain construction costs. The following are recommendations for economy in concrete forming:

- *Form reuse.* This is crucial to economy of construction. The design professional can facilitate form reuse by standardizing the dimensions of openings, columns, beams, and footings, using as few different sizes of each as possible. For example, where columns must change size, hold one dimension constant (e.g., width) while varying the other (depth). This enables at least half of the form panels to be used many times. Repeat the same floor and column layout from bay to bay on each floor and from floor to floor. This improves labor productivity and permits reuse of forms.
- *Mockups.* The architect and contractor should agree on the location and desired appearance of architectural surfaces before the exposed concrete work begins. Specify mockups to help achieve this and to avoid disagreements during and after construction.
- *Large panel forms.* Wherever possible, make uninterrupted formed areas the same size. Increasing the size of such areas enables the contractor to combine form panels into gangs for efficient crane use.
- *Design details.* Intricacies and irregularities cost more and often do not add proportionately to the aesthetic effect.
- *Steel-framed plywood panels.* These are best when column heights or size varies widely. Ganged/hinged/custom column forms are utilized to improve labor efficiency when multiple reuse (10-plus) can be planned. The productivity gained with each cycle will offset the increased form costs.

WALL FORMS AND PANELS

Commonly made of steel-framed plywood, panels are also available in aluminum. Wall ties (typically flat ties) and wall forms are held together by slotted pins that run through adjoining holes. A wedge pushed down into the slot alongside the wall form tightens the joint. Formwork service life can be extended by turning or replacing the plywood facing. To produce patterned concrete, reusable plastic liners may be used. For maximum economy, panels can be assembled in large gangs and set in place by crane. Steel-framed plywood panels and/or flat-tie wall forms are predominately utilized for structural concrete. The breakage of the flat tie and the steel frame imprint in the concrete can detract from concrete appearance.

FORMWORK JOINTS

Formwork joints are inherent in concrete work because of plywood panels. Architectural concrete will usually require a more aesthetic joint. A compressible foam gasket should only be used when a rustication is added. Epoxy on 45° cut, tongued and grooved (with sealant), taped, splined (with sealant), and gasketed with closed-cell compressible material are frequently acceptable formwork joints for structural concrete. 2x joint backing is acceptable for plywood joints in a single direction but not practical for perpendicular joints.

A good joint solution is to add a second layer of plywood to the formwork, staggering the joints from the face sheet. Though, difficult to achieve with site-built forms, applying joint sealant at formwork

MANUFACTURED CONCRETE FORMWORK
8.1

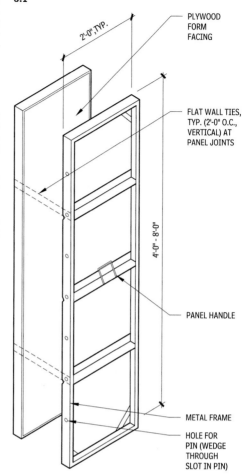

- PLYWOOD FORM FACING
- 2'-0", TYP.
- FLAT WALL TIES, TYP. (2'-0" O.C., VERTICAL) AT PANEL JOINTS
- 4'-0" - 8'-0"
- PANEL HANDLE
- METAL FRAME
- HOLE FOR PIN (WEDGE THROUGH SLOT IN PIN)

joints provides the most aesthetic joint. Because of limited access space, sealing formwork joints on both sides of a wall form is nearly impossible and will significantly increase the formwork cost.

BEAM-TO-COLUMN FORMWORK

In general, the least costly design to form has columns the same width or narrower than the beams they support, allowing the beam form to be erected in a continuous line. In midcost formwork design, the beam bottom forms are cut to fit around the column tops. In high-cost formwork design, the beam forms are fitted into pockets on both sides of the column forms.

FOOTINGS

When stepped footings are required, use fewer steps and design them to standard lumber and plywood dimensions or modular divisions of these dimensions.

TIE PATTERNS

Installing and removing ties and patching tie holes are some of the most labor-intensive operations in concrete forming. Also, getting a durable, inconspicuous patch often proves difficult. Avoid this problem by specifying smooth cone fittings at the tie ends, then either leaving the resulting uniform tie holes exposed or plugging them with preformed concrete plugs and a bonding agent. Corrodible metal must have coverage of a minimum 1-1/2 in. of

BEAM-TO-COLUMN FORMWORK
8.2

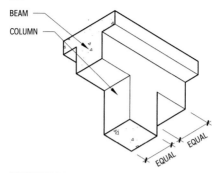

- BEAM
- COLUMN
- EQUAL EQUAL
- EQUAL

RECOMMENDED LOW-COST FORMWORK

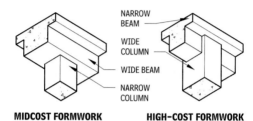

- NARROW BEAM
- WIDE COLUMN
- WIDE BEAM
- NARROW COLUMN

MIDCOST FORMWORK   **HIGH-COST FORMWORK**

STEPPED FOOTINGS
8.3

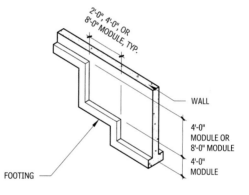

- 2'-0", 4'-0", OR 8'-0" MODULE, TYP.
- WALL
- 4'-0" MODULE OR 8'-0" MODULE
- 4'-0" MODULE
- FOOTING

FORM TIE PATTERN
8.4

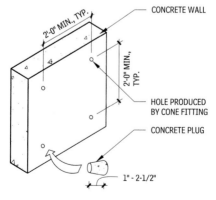

- 2'-0" MIN., TYP.
- CONCRETE WALL
- 2'-0" MIN., TYP.
- HOLE PRODUCED BY CONE FITTING
- CONCRETE PLUG
- 1" - 2-1/2"

Contributors:
Mary K. Hurd, Engineered Publications, Farmington Hills, Michigan; Portland Cement Association, Skokie, Illinois.

SPANDREL BEAM FORMWORK
8.5

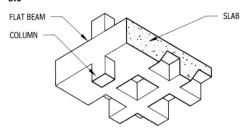

FLAT BEAM
COLUMN
SLAB

**RECOMMENDED
LOW-COST FORMWORK**

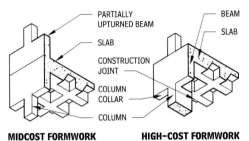

PARTIALLY
UPTURNED BEAM
SLAB
CONSTRUCTION
JOINT
COLUMN
COLLAR
COLUMN

BEAM
SLAB

MIDCOST FORMWORK　　　**HIGH-COST FORMWORK**

STANDARD LUMBER FORMS
8.6

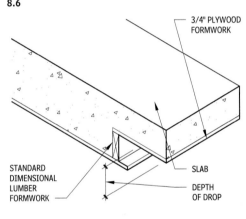

3/4" PLYWOOD
FORMWORK

STANDARD
DIMENSIONAL
LUMBER
FORMWORK

SLAB

DEPTH
OF DROP

TILT-UP CONCRETE WALL FORMWORK
8.7

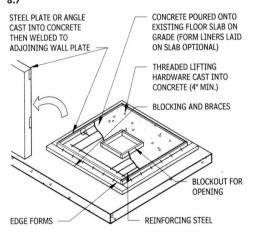

STEEL PLATE OR ANGLE
CAST INTO CONCRETE
THEN WELDED TO
ADJOINING WALL PLATE

CONCRETE POURED ONTO
EXISTING FLOOR SLAB ON
GRADE (FORM LINERS LAID
ON SLAB OPTIONAL)

THREADED LIFTING
HARDWARE CAST INTO
CONCRETE (4" MIN.)

BLOCKING AND BRACES

BLOCKOUT FOR
OPENING

EDGE FORMS

REINFORCING STEEL

---

concrete. Contractors may propose tie spacing wider than 2 ft. o.c. to reduce the total number of ties to save money, but this requires stronger ties and heavier form supports.

For tie patterns that are *not* gang-formed, due to limited reusage, a 2 ft. by 2 ft. tie pattern should be a maximum; a 1 ft. by 1 ft. pattern a corresponding minimum.

For tie patterns that *are* gang-formed, a 4 ft. by 4 ft. pattern is a minimum spacing utilizing the tie capacities. A corresponding maximum spacing is 6 ft. by 6 ft. Keep in mind the locations of vertical and horizontal construction joints when establishing tie locations. Exterior wall forms often require form anchors embedded in the concrete for each lift. The anchors can be patched but, doing so may detract from the concrete's appearance.

SPANDREL BEAMS

Flat beams designed to be equal in depth to the floor assembly are the least costly, as they most efficiently accommodate flying-form construction. Deeper, narrower beams cost more; but if deeper beams are required, costs can be controlled by making the beam the same thickness as the column depth and at least partially upturned. The upturned portion of the spandrel beam should be less than 30 in. for best economy. The most costly option is a col-

FORMED FOOTINGS
8.8

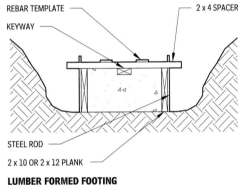

REBAR TEMPLATE
KEYWAY
2 x 4 SPACER

STEEL ROD
2 x 10 OR 2 x 12 PLANK

LUMBER FORMED FOOTING

WALL FOOTING FORMWORK PLAN
8.9

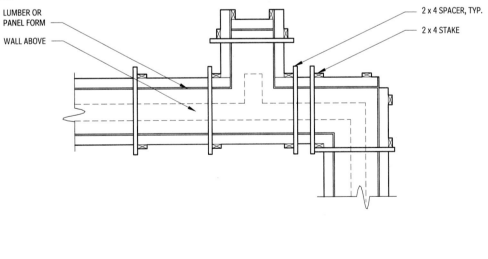

LUMBER OR
PANEL FORM
WALL ABOVE

2 x 4 SPACER, TYP.
2 x 4 STAKE

---

umn thicker than the beam. This requires a column collar with a construction joint.

LUMBER FORMS

Adapting design elements to the modular sizes of formwork lumber and plywood and dimensioning parts of the structure to fit the modules can save the expense of custom formwork. For example, to save the waste and time of sawing and piecing together the edge form, make the depth of the drop in a slab equal to the actual size of standard lumber, plus 3/4 in. for the plywood's thickness.

TILT-UP CONCRETE

In tilt-up concrete, walls are cast on the completed floor slab, which must be level, smoothly finished, and treated with a bond-breaking agent to permit easy separation. The wall is then tilted or lifted into vertical position and fastened to the structural frame. This method reduces formwork and labor and eliminates transportation requirements that may limit panel size.

CONCRETE FORMWORK FOR COLUMNS AND FOOTINGS

REBAR TEMPLATE
KEYWAY
2 x 4 SPACER
2 x 4 STAKE

PANEL OF 5/8" PLYFORM WITH 2 x 4
CLEATS (1-1/8" PLYWOOD, OFTEN
APPLIED WITHOUT 2 x 4 CLEATS)

PANEL FORMED FOOTING

Contributors:
Mary K. Hurd, Engineered Publications, Farmington Hills, Michigan;
Portland Cement Association, Skokie, Illinois; American Concrete
Institute, Farmington Hills, Michigan.

COLUMN FORMWORK PLANS
8.10

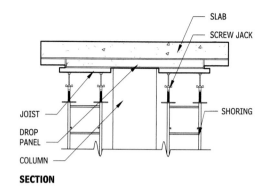

- COLUMN CLAMP
- PLYWOOD
- 2 x 4
- ADJUSTABLE CORNER
- 3/4"
- 3/4" CHAMFER STRIP

LUMBER/PANEL/COLUMN FORMWORK

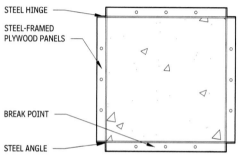

- STEEL HINGE
- STEEL-FRAMED PLYWOOD PANELS
- BREAK POINT
- STEEL ANGLE

MANUFACTURED COLUMN FORMWORK

COLUMN FOOTING FORMWORK
8.11

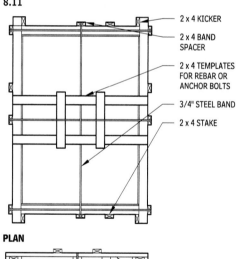

- 2 x 4 KICKER
- 2 x 4 BAND SPACER
- 2 x 4 TEMPLATES FOR REBAR OR ANCHOR BOLTS
- 3/4" STEEL BAND
- 2 x 4 STAKE

PLAN

- 2 x4
- 2 x 4 STAKE
- 3/4" STEEL BAND

ELEVATION

DROP PANELS AT COLUMN TOPS
8.12

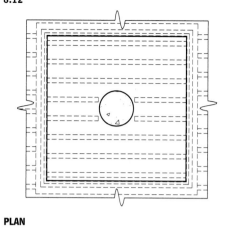

PLAN

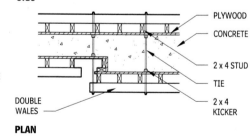

- SLAB
- SCREW JACK
- JOIST
- DROP PANEL
- COLUMN
- SHORING

SECTION

CONCRETE FORMWORK FOR WALLS

TYPICAL SITE-BUILT WALL FORMWORK
8.13

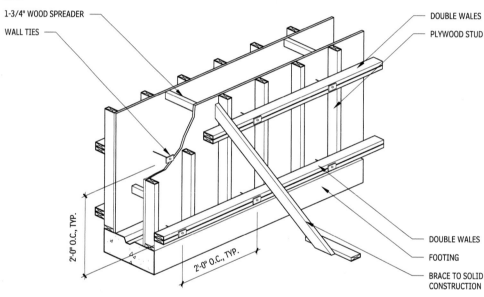

- 1-3/4" WOOD SPREADER
- WALL TIES
- DOUBLE WALES
- PLYWOOD STUD
- DOUBLE WALES
- FOOTING
- BRACE TO SOLID CONSTRUCTION
- 2'-0" O.C, TYP.
- 2'-0" O.C., TYP.

SITE-BUILT WALL FORMS
8.14

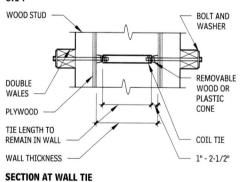

- WOOD STUD
- BOLT AND WASHER
- DOUBLE WALES
- REMOVABLE WOOD OR PLASTIC CONE
- PLYWOOD
- TIE LENGTH TO REMAIN IN WALL
- WALL THICKNESS
- COIL TIE
- 1" - 2-1/2"

SECTION AT WALL TIE

TYPICAL WALL WITH OFFSET
8.15

- PLYWOOD
- CONCRETE
- 2 x 4 STUD
- TIE
- 2 x 4 KICKER
- DOUBLE WALES

PLAN

NOTES

8.10 a. It is recommended that chamfer strips be used at all outside corners to reduce damage to concrete when forms are removed. Consult manufacturers' guides and catalogs for ideal materials, pour rate, and outside temperature.

b. Many form suppliers offer various gang column forms with hinged corners for columns up to 48 in. square. Beyond that size most column formwork resembles wall formwork, with some type of internal tie for lateral pressure.

8.14 Consult manufacturers' recommendations for safe working loads on ties.

Contributors:
Tucker Concrete Form Company, Stoughton, Massachusetts; Mary K. Hurd, Engineered Publications, Farmington Hills, Michigan; Portland Cement Association, Skokie, Illinois.

PILASTER
8.16

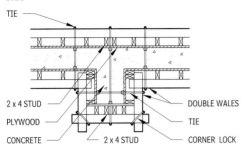

TIE
2 x 4 STUD
PLYWOOD
CONCRETE
DOUBLE WALES
TIE
2 x 4 STUD
CORNER LOCK

PLAN

TYPICAL T-WALL JUNCTION
8.17

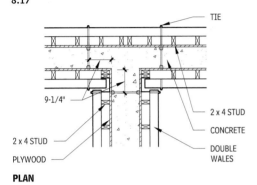

TIE
9-1/4"
2 x 4 STUD
CONCRETE
DOUBLE WALES
2 x 4 STUD
PLYWOOD

PLAN

TYPICAL CORNER
8.18

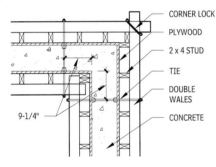

CORNER LOCK
PLYWOOD
2 x 4 STUD
TIE
DOUBLE WALES
CONCRETE
9-1/4"

PLAN

TYPICAL EXPOSED CONCRETE ELEVATION
8.19

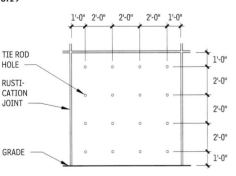

1'-0" 2'-0" 2'-0" 2'-0" 1'-0"

TIE ROD HOLE
RUSTICATION JOINT
GRADE

1'-0"
2'-0"
2'-0"
2'-0"
1'-0"

TYPICAL SITE-BUILT WALL SECTION
8.20

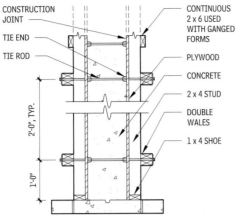

CONSTRUCTION JOINT
TIE END
TIE ROD
CONTINUOUS 2 x 6 USED WITH GANGED FORMS
PLYWOOD
CONCRETE
2 x 4 STUD
DOUBLE WALES
1 x 4 SHOE
2'-0", TYP.
1'-0"

TYPICAL PAN FORM FOR ONE-WAY SLAB
8.21

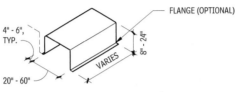

FLANGE (OPTIONAL)
4" - 6", TYP.
8" - 24"
VARIES
20" - 60"

TYPICAL PAN FORM

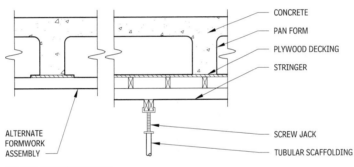

CONCRETE
PAN FORM
PLYWOOD DECKING
STRINGER
ALTERNATE FORMWORK ASSEMBLY
SCREW JACK
TUBULAR SCAFFOLDING

TYPICAL PAN FORMWORK

TYPICAL SLAB AND SHALLOW BEAM FORMING
8.22

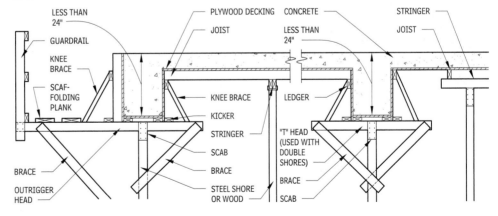

LESS THAN 24"
GUARDRAIL
KNEE BRACE
SCAFFOLDING PLANK
BRACE
OUTRIGGER HEAD
PLYWOOD DECKING
JOIST
KNEE BRACE
KICKER
STRINGER
SCAB
BRACE
STEEL SHORE OR WOOD
CONCRETE
LESS THAN 24"
LEDGER
"T" HEAD (USED WITH DOUBLE SHORES)
BRACE
SCAB
STRINGER
JOIST

CONCRETE FORMWORK FOR SLABS AND BEAMS

GENERAL

- Scaffolding, steel shores, or wood posts may be used under stringers, depending on loads and height requirements.
- For flat slabs of flat-plate forming, metal "flying forms" are commonly used.
- Patented steel forms or fillers can be special ordered for unusual conditions (see manufacturers' catalogs). Fiber forms are also on the market in similar sizes. Plyform deck is required for forming.
- Plywood decking is usually 5/8 in. minimum thickness, Exposure 1.

NOTES

8.19 a. Drawing illustrates typical site-built wall formwork for exposed structural concrete. Plywood is standard in 4 ft. by 8 ft. sheets. A line would be visible after removal of plywood; this is frequently rubbed out to make for a consistent appearance.
b. Rustication is preferred when plywood joints need to be disguised.
8.20 Verify size and spacing of components for each job. The combination of plywood, studs, walers, and ties must be chosen carefully to safely resist concrete pressure and limit deflection of the form face. Steel and aluminum studs and walers may be used in place of wood. Lateral pressure varies depending on the rate at which the form is filled, the temperature of the concrete, vibration procedures, and the type of admixtures used in the concrete.

8.21 a. Forms are available in steel and lightweight fiberglass. Consult manufacturers for dimensions and rib-form variations. Typically, two types are available: nail-down flange (simplest, but produces rough, nonarchitectural surface) and slip-in type (based on nail-down form but with board insert for smooth appearance).
b. The details are all for typical flange-form-type pans. Long-form-type pans require different forming details.

Contributors:
Tucker Concrete Form Company, Stoughton, Massachusetts; Mary K. Hurd, Engineered Publications, Farmington Hills, Michigan; Portland Cement Association, Skokie, Illinois.

TYPICAL SLAB AND HEAVY BEAM FORMING
8.23

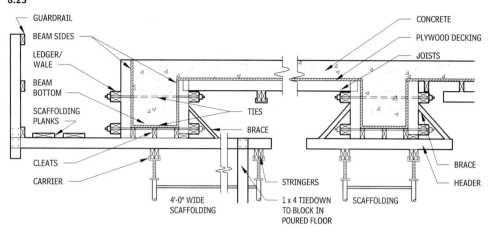

GUARDRAIL
BEAM SIDES
LEDGER/WALE
BEAM BOTTOM
SCAFFOLDING PLANKS
CLEATS
CARRIER
CONCRETE
PLYWOOD DECKING
JOISTS
TIES
BRACE
BRACE
HEADER
STRINGERS
4'-0" WIDE SCAFFOLDING
1 x 4 TIEDOWN TO BLOCK IN POURED FLOOR
SCAFFOLDING

TYPICAL DOME FORM FOR WAFFLE OR TWO-WAY SLAB
8.24

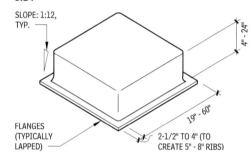

SLOPE: 1:12, TYP.
FLANGES (TYPICALLY LAPPED)
4" - 24"
19" - 60"
2-1/2" TO 4" (TO CREATE 5" - 8" RIBS)

TYPICAL SUSPENDED FORM WITH COIL SADDLE-TYPE HANGERS
8.26

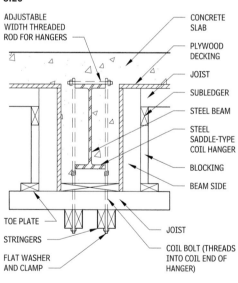

ADJUSTABLE WIDTH THREADED ROD FOR HANGERS
TOE PLATE
STRINGERS
FLAT WASHER AND CLAMP
CONCRETE SLAB
PLYWOOD DECKING
JOIST
SUBLEDGER
STEEL BEAM
STEEL SADDLE-TYPE COIL HANGER
BLOCKING
BEAM SIDE
JOIST
COIL BOLT (THREADS INTO COIL END OF HANGER)

SLAB FORMWORK WITH WATERSTOP
8.25

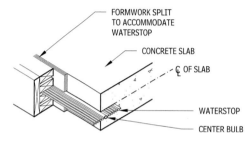

FORMWORK SPLIT TO ACCOMMODATE WATERSTOP
CONCRETE SLAB
℄ OF SLAB
WATERSTOP
CENTER BULB

CONCRETE FORMWORK ACCESSORIES

GENERAL

Concrete formwork accessories includes ties, anchors, hangers, and spacers used to hold forms and reinforcements in place against the forces of uncured concrete and other loads applied during construction. Concrete ties are tensile units used to hold concrete forms together and may be classified by use or by load-carrying capacity.

- *Use classification of formwork tie.* "Continuous single member," in which the entire tie rod extends through the wall and through both sides of the formwork (this can be a pullout tie or a snap-off tie), and "internal disconnecting," in which the tensile unit has an inner part with threaded connections to the removable external members.
- *Load-carrying classification of formwork ties.* Light-duty, which has safe working loads of up to 3750 lbs and heavy-duty, which will carry loads of more than 3750 lbs.

Safe working load should be set at no more than half the tie's ultimate strength. Other hardware assemblies and configurations may be available; consult manufacturers for complete details.

FORMWORK TIES

Consult ACI SP-4, Formwork for Concrete, for detailed design recommendations.

A wide variety of form ties are commercially available. For concrete surfaces exposed to weather, select ties that have no corrodible metal closer than 1-1/2 in. to the exposed concrete surface. Ties should be tight-fitting and sealed to prevent leakage at holes in the forms.

Ties fitted with wood or plastic cones should leave depressions at least as deep as the surface diameter of the cone. The holes may be filled with recessed plugs or left unfilled if noncorroding ties are used.

COIL TIES
8.27

FLAT WASHER

SECTION

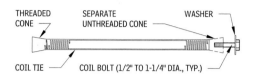

THREADED CONE
SEPARATE UNTHREADED CONE
WASHER
COIL TIE
COIL BOLT (1/2" TO 1-1/4" DIA., TYP.)

FLAT TIE
8.28

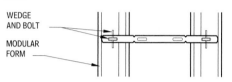

WEDGE AND BOLT
MODULAR FORM

SECTION

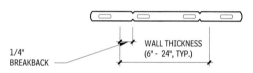

1/4" BREAKBACK
WALL THICKNESS (6" - 24", TYP.)

STEEL TAPER TIE
8.29

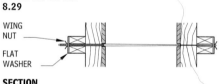

WING NUT
FLAT WASHER

SECTION

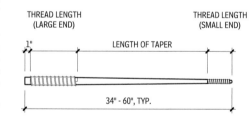

THREAD LENGTH (LARGE END)
THREAD LENGTH (SMALL END)
1"
LENGTH OF TAPER
34" - 60", TYP.

FIBERGLASS FORM TIE
8.30

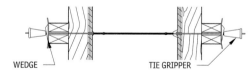

WEDGE
TIE GRIPPER

SECTION

1/4" TO 1/2" DIA. TIE ROD
TIE GRIPPER

NOTES

8.24 a. Standard waffle slab forms are square for ease of use and economy. Dimensions vary slightly by manufacturer.
b. Forms are available in steel and lightweight fiberglass. Consult the form manufacturer for options in materials, textures, and dimensions.
c. Steel domes may not be acceptable for exposed concrete applications due to the irregularities caused by the reuse of steel pans.
8.25 Waterstops are flexible barriers used to prevent the passage of liquids and gasses under pressure through joints in concrete slabs. Waterstops are typically made of polyvinyl chloride, and their shapes vary according to application. If a center bulb is specified, it must remain unembedded in the center of the joint.
8.26 a. This type of formwork is used to fireproof structural steel beams by wrapping them in concrete.
b. Most applications require 4x wood members for subledger, blocking, and toe plate.

Contributors:
Tucker Concrete Form Company, Stoughton, Massachusetts; Mary K. Hurd, Engineered Publications, Farmington Hills, Michigan; Portland Cement Association, Skokie, Illinois.

SNAP TIES
8.31

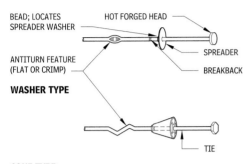

STUD
WALL THICKNESS
1", TYP. BREAKBACK
WEDGE
WALE
CONE (OPTIONAL)

SECTION

BEAD; LOCATES SPREADER WASHER
HOT FORGED HEAD
SPREADER
BREAKBACK
ANTITURN FEATURE (FLAT OR CRIMP)

WASHER TYPE

TIE

CONE TYPE

ANCHORS
8.32

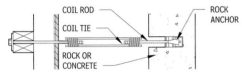

COIL ROD
COIL TIE
ROCK ANCHOR
ROCK OR CONCRETE

SECTION

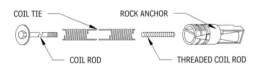

COIL TIE
ROCK ANCHOR
COIL ROD
THREADED COIL ROD

TIE ROD ACCESSORIES
8.33

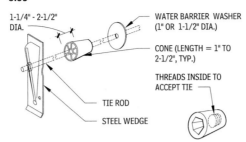

1-1/4" - 2-1/2" DIA.
WATER BARRIER WASHER (1" OR 1-1/2" DIA.)
CONE (LENGTH = 1" TO 2-1/2", TYP.)
THREADS INSIDE TO ACCEPT TIE
TIE ROD
STEEL WEDGE

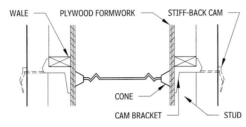

COIL TIE CONE

CAM LOCK BRACKET
8.34

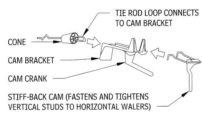

WALE
PLYWOOD FORMWORK
STIFF-BACK CAM
CONE
CAM BRACKET
STUD

SECTION

TIE ROD LOOP CONNECTS TO CAM BRACKET
CONE
CAM BRACKET
CAM CRANK
STIFF-BACK CAM (FASTENS AND TIGHTENS VERTICAL STUDS TO HORIZONTAL WALERS)

HE-BOLT WITH COIL ANCHOR
8.35

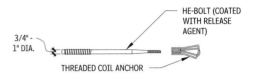

SCAF-FOLDING
HE-BOLT
CONCRETE
FORMWORK
SETBACK 6", MIN.
EDGE DISTANCE 9", MIN.
COIL-END LOOP ANCHOR

SECTION

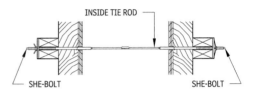

HE-BOLT (COATED WITH RELEASE AGENT)
3/4" - 1" DIA.
THREADED COIL ANCHOR

SHE-BOLT/TIE ROD
8.36

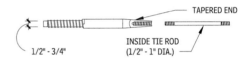

INSIDE TIE ROD
SHE-BOLT
SHE-BOLT

SECTION

TAPERED END
INSIDE TIE ROD (1/2" - 1" DIA.)
1/2" - 3/4"

REINFORCING BAR AND MESH SUPPORTS
8.37

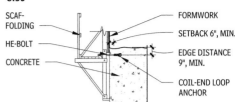

5'-0" - 40'-0"

SLAB BOLSTER

2" - 9"

HIGH CHAIR

SIDE-FORM SPACE

Coil ties are medium- to heavy-duty ties fabricated to accept a threaded bolt, which passes through the formwork lumber.

Flat ties are light-duty ties used with a wedge and bolt to secure and space modular wall forms.

Taper tie assemblies are generally used for heavy-duty loads of up to 50,000 lbs. Taper ties are versatile in that their parts are removed after the concrete cures and may be reused. Ties may be installed after forms are in place.

Fiberglass form ties are straight rods secured with reusable external metal grippers and have safe working loads ranging from 2,250 to 25,000 lbs. The ties are readily broken off or cut at the concrete surface, then ground flush.

Snap ties are for light-duty use, fabricated so the exposed ends of the tie can be snapped off at the breakback (a notch in the rod). The antiturn device makes it easy to break off the exposed end.

Anchors are used with coil ties to facilitate single-side forming of walls.

Steel wedges are placed at the outside threaded ends of pullout or snap tie rods, holding the formwork in place. Plastic or wood cones may be placed on the tie rod at the formwork wall surface so that when the formwork is removed, the tie rod ends are set back for subsequent finishing (with plugs, etc.).

The cam lock bracket is a light-duty assembly suitable for job-set forms.

When using he-bolts, the coil anchor is embedded near the top of a concrete lift to support the formwork of the succeeding lift. The reusable he-bolt is threaded into the coil.

She-bolts are reusable heavy-duty tie components threaded onto an internal tie rod that is permanently embedded in the concrete. They are typically used with crane-handled forms.

Bar supports are used to maintain the design location of the reinforcement away from the wall sides or slab bottom. They are typically made of stainless-steel epoxy- or plastic-coated steel, or plastic.

Contributors:
Mary K. Hurd, Engineered Publications, Farmington Hills, Michigan;
Portland Cement Association, Skokie, Illinois.

CONCRETE REINFORCING

PLACEMENT OF STEEL REINFORCING

CONCRETE FLOOR CONSTRUCTION
8.38

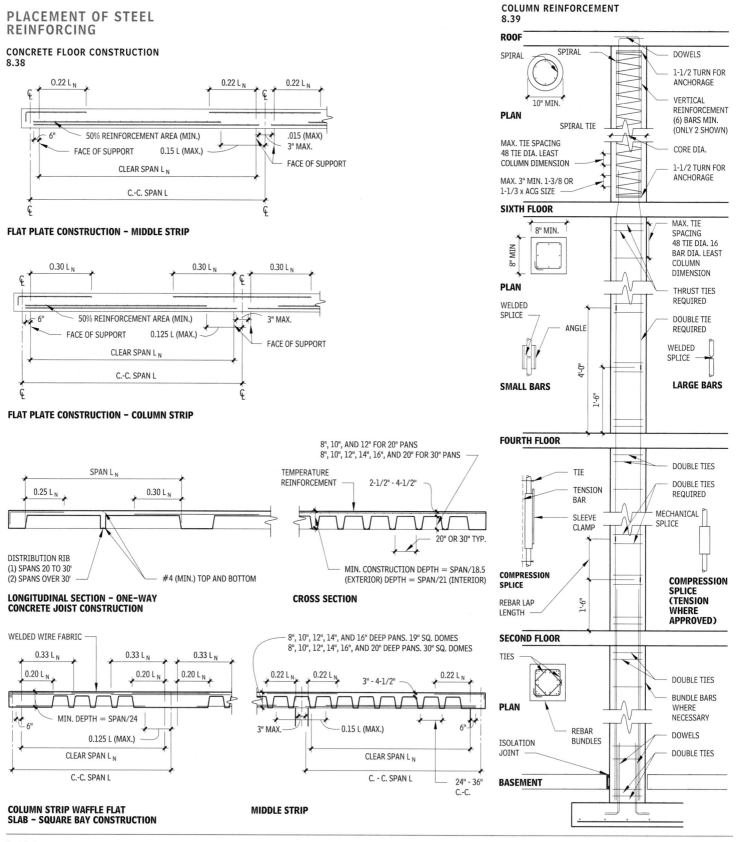

FLAT PLATE CONSTRUCTION – MIDDLE STRIP

0.22 L$_N$ ⋅ 0.22 L$_N$ ⋅ 0.22 L$_N$

6"
50% REINFORCEMENT AREA (MIN.)
FACE OF SUPPORT
0.15 L (MAX.)
.015 (MAX)
3" MAX.
FACE OF SUPPORT
CLEAR SPAN L$_N$
C.-C. SPAN L

FLAT PLATE CONSTRUCTION – COLUMN STRIP

0.30 L$_N$ ⋅ 0.30 L$_N$ ⋅ 0.30 L$_N$

6"
50% REINFORCEMENT AREA (MIN.)
FACE OF SUPPORT
0.125 L (MAX.)
3" MAX.
FACE OF SUPPORT
CLEAR SPAN L$_N$
C.-C. SPAN L

LONGITUDINAL SECTION – ONE-WAY CONCRETE JOIST CONSTRUCTION

SPAN L$_N$
0.25 L$_N$ ⋅ 0.30 L$_N$

DISTRIBUTION RIB
(1) SPANS 20 TO 30'
(2) SPANS OVER 30'
#4 (MIN.) TOP AND BOTTOM

CROSS SECTION

8", 10", AND 12" FOR 20" PANS
8", 10", 12", 14", 16", AND 20" FOR 30" PANS
TEMPERATURE REINFORCEMENT
2-1/2" - 4-1/2"
20" OR 30" TYP.
MIN. CONSTRUCTION DEPTH = SPAN/18.5
(EXTERIOR) DEPTH = SPAN/21 (INTERIOR)

COLUMN STRIP WAFFLE FLAT SLAB – SQUARE BAY CONSTRUCTION

WELDED WIRE FABRIC
0.33 L$_N$ ⋅ 0.33 L$_N$ ⋅ 0.33 L$_N$
0.20 L$_N$ ⋅ 0.20 L$_N$ ⋅ 0.20 L$_N$
MIN. DEPTH = SPAN/24
6"
0.125 L (MAX.)
CLEAR SPAN L$_N$
C.-C. SPAN L

MIDDLE STRIP

8", 10", 12", 14", AND 16" DEEP PANS. 19" SQ. DOMES
8", 10", 12", 14", 16", AND 20" DEEP PANS. 30" SQ. DOMES
0.22 L$_N$ ⋅ 0.22 L$_N$
3" - 4-1/2"
0.22 L$_N$
3" MAX.
0.15 L (MAX.)
6"
CLEAR SPAN L$_N$
C. - C. SPAN L
24" - 36" C.-C.

COLUMN REINFORCEMENT
8.39

ROOF

SPIRAL
SPIRAL
10" MIN.
PLAN
SPIRAL TIE

DOWELS
1-1/2 TURN FOR ANCHORAGE
VERTICAL REINFORCEMENT (6) BARS MIN. (ONLY 2 SHOWN)
CORE DIA.
1-1/2 TURN FOR ANCHORAGE

MAX. TIE SPACING 48 TIE DIA. LEAST COLUMN DIMENSION
MAX. 3" MIN. 1-3/8 OR 1-1/3 x ACG SIZE

SIXTH FLOOR

8" MIN.
8" MIN
PLAN

MAX. TIE SPACING 48 TIE DIA. 16 BAR DIA. LEAST COLUMN DIMENSION
THRUST TIES REQUIRED
DOUBLE TIE REQUIRED

WELDED SPLICE
ANGLE
SMALL BARS

4'-0"
1'-6"

WELDED SPLICE
LARGE BARS

FOURTH FLOOR

TIE
TENSION BAR
SLEEVE CLAMP

DOUBLE TIES
DOUBLE TIES REQUIRED
MECHANICAL SPLICE

COMPRESSION SPLICE
REBAR LAP LENGTH

1'-6"

COMPRESSION SPLICE (TENSION WHERE APPROVED)

SECOND FLOOR

TIES
PLAN

DOUBLE TIES
BUNDLE BARS WHERE NECESSARY
DOWELS
DOUBLE TIES

ISOLATION JOINT
REBAR BUNDLES

BASEMENT

Contributors:
Concrete Reinforcing Steel Institute, Schaumburg, Illinois; Kenneth D. Franch, AIA, PE, Phillips Swager Associates, Inc., Dallas, Texas; Portland Cement Association, Skokie, Illinois.

CAST-IN-PLACE CONCRETE

GENERAL

Cast-in-place concrete includes concrete mixture placement, finishing, and curing for structural, architectural, and specialty placed concrete. The concrete mixture generally includes aggregate, cement, and additives.

CONCRETE ADMIXTURES

Concrete admixtures are supplementary materials other than portland cement, water, and aggregates that are added to the mixture immediately before or during mixing. Admixtures can be classified by function as follows: air-entraining admixtures; water-reducing admixtures; retarding admixtures; accelerating admixtures; superplasticizers; hydration-control admixtures; and miscellaneous admixtures that aid workability, bonding, dampproofing, gas-forming, grouting (nonshrink), coloring, and admixtures that reduce permeability and inhibit corrosion.

Concrete should be workable, finishable, strong, durable, water-resistant, and wear-resistant. These qualities can usually be achieved by selecting suitable materials or by changing the mix proportions. Admixtures may be necessary to meet design performance or intent.

The major reasons for using admixtures are to reduce the cost of concrete construction; to achieve certain properties in concrete more effectively than by other means; to ensure the quality of concrete during mixing, transporting, placing, and curing in adverse weather conditions.

The effectiveness of an admixture depends on such factors as type, and amount of cement; water content; aggregate shape, gradation, and proportions; mixing time; slump; and concrete and air temperatures.

Concrete samples should be made with the admixture and the job materials at temperatures and humidity levels anticipated on the job, to ensure compatibility with other admixtures and job materials and to allow observation of how the properties of the fresh and cured concrete are affected by local conditions. The cost of using admixtures should be compared with the cost of changing the basic concrete mixture.

Recommended total air contents for different exposure conditions are shown for different aggregate sizes in the Table 8.40.

TOTAL TARGET AIR CONTENT FOR CONCRETE[a]
8.40

NOMINAL MAXIMUM AGGREGATE SIZE (IN.)	AIR CONTENT (PERCENT)[b]		
	SEVERE EXPOSURE[c]	MODERATE EXPOSURE[c]	MILD EXPOSURE[c]
< 3/8	9	7	5
3/8	7-1/2	6	4-1/2
1/2	7	5-1/2	4
3/4	6	5	3-1/2
1	6	4	1/2
1-1/2	5-1/2	4-1/2	2-1/2
2-1/2	5	4	2
3	4-1/2	3-1/2	1-1/2

SUPPLEMENTARY CEMENTITIOUS MATERIALS (SCM)

Fly ash, ground-granulated blast-furnace slag, silica fume, and natural pozzolans are materials that, when used in conjunction with portland cement, contribute to the properties of the cured concrete through hydraulic or pozzolanic activity, or both.

CONCRETE ADMIXTURES BY CLASSIFICATION
8.41

TYPE OF ADMIXTURE	DESIRED EFFECT	MATERIAL
Accelerators (ASTM C 494, Type C)	Accelerate setting and early strength development.	Calcium chloride (ASTM D 98); triethanolamine, sodium thiocyanate, calcium formate, calcium nitrate, calcium nitrite
Air detrainers	Decrease air content.	Tributyl phosphate, dibutyl phthalate, octyl alcohol, water-insoluble esters of carbonic and boric acid, silicones
Air-entraining admixtures (ASTM C 260)	Improve durability in environments of freeze-thaw, deicers, sulfate, and alkali reactivity. Improve workability.	Salts of wood resins some synthetic detergents, salts of sulfonated lignin, salts of petroleum acids, salts of proteinaceous material, fatty and resinous acids and their salts, alkylbenzene sulfonates, salts of sulfonated hydrocarbons
Alkali-aggregate reactivity inhibitors	Reduce alkali-aggregate reactivity expansion.	Barium salts, lithium nitrate, lithium carbonate, lithium hydroxide
Bonding admixtures	Increase bond strength.	Rubber, polyvinyl chloride, polyvinyl acetate, acrylics, butadiene-styrene copolymers
Coloring admixtures	Colored concrete.	Modified carbon black, iron oxide, phthalicyanine, umber, chromium oxide, titanium oxide, cobalt blue (ASTM C 979)
Corrosion inhibitors (ASTM C1582)	Reduce steel corrosion activity in a chloride environment.	Calcium nitrite, sodium nitrite, sodium benzoate, certain phosphates of fluosilicates, fluoaluminates
Dampproofing admixtures	Retard moisture penetration into dry concrete.	Soaps of calcium or ammonium stearate or oleate, butyl stearate, petroleum products
Fungicides, germicides, and insecticides	Inhibit or control bacterial and fungal growth.	Polyhalogenated phenols, dieldrin emulsions, copper compounds
Gas formers	Cause expansion before setting.	Aluminum powder, resin soap and vegetable or animal glue, saponin, hydrolyzed protein
Grouting agents	Adjust grout properties for specific applications (i.e., nonshrink grout for setting steel on masonry or concrete, fill reglets and cracks).	See air-entrained admixtures, accelerators, retarders, workability agents.
Permeability reducers	Decrease permeability	Silica fume; fly ash (ASTM C 618), ground slag (ASTM C 989), natural pozzolans, water reducers, latex
Pumping aides	Improve pumpability.	Organic and synthetic polymers; organic flocculents; organic emulsions of paraffin, coal tar, asphalt, acrylics; bentonite and pyrogenic silicas; natural pozzolans (ASTM C 618, Class N); fly ash (ASTM C 618, Classes F and C); hydrated lime (ASTM C 141)
Retarders (ASTM C 494, Type B)	Retard setting time to offset effect of hot weather, to delay initial set for difficult placement, or for special finishing, such as exposed aggregate.	Lignin, borax, sugar, tartaric acids and salts
Superplasticizers (ASTM C 1017, Type 1)	Increase slump to aid in pumping concrete; reduce water-cement ratio.	Sulfonated melamine formaldehyde condensates; sulfonated naphthalene formaldehyde condensates; lignosulfonates
Superplasticizer and retarder (ASTM C 1017,Type 2)	Increase slump to aid in pumping concrete with retarded set; reduce water.	See superplasticizers and water reducers.
Water reducer (ASTM C 494, Type A)	Reduce water demand at least 5%.	Lignosulfonates, hydroxylated carboxylic acids, carbohydrates (also tend to retard set, so accelerator is often added)
Hydration control admixtures	Suspend and reactivate cement hydration with stabilizer and activator.	Carboxylic acids, phosphorous-containing organic acid salts
Shrinkage reducers	Reduce drying shrinkage.	Polyoxyalkylene alkyl ether; propylene glycol
Water reducer and accelerator (ASTM C 494 and AASHTO M 194 Type E)	Reduce water content (minimum 5%) and accelerate set.	See water reducer, Type A (accelerator is added).
Water reducer and retarder (ASTM C 494 and AASHTO M 194 Type D)	Reduce water content (minimum 5%) and retard set	See water reducer, Type A (retarder is added)
Water reducer—high range (ASTM C 494 and AASHTO M 194 Type F)	Reduce water content (minimum 12%)	See superplasticizers
Water reducer—high range—and retarder (ASTM C 494 and AASHTO M 194 Type G)	Reduce water content (minimum 12%) and retard set.	See superplasticizers, and water reducers
Water reducer—midrange	Reduce water content (between 6% and 12%) without retarding.	Lignosulfonates, polycarboxylates

NOTES

8.40 a. Experience shows that cured concrete with the air contents specified in this table, as sampled and tested in the plastic state, performs satisfactorily. The air content of cured concrete may be somewhat different.

b. Project specifications often allow the air content of the delivered concrete to be within a range of the percentage points of the table target values.

c. Severe exposure is an environment in which concrete is exposed to wet freeze-thaw conditions, deicers, or other aggressive agents. Moderate exposure is an environment in which concrete is exposed to freezing but will not be continually moist, will not be exposed to water for long periods before freezing, and will not be in contact with deicers or aggressive chemicals. Mild exposure is an environment in which concrete is not exposed to freezing conditions, deicers, or aggressive agents.

8.41 Superplasticizers are also referred to as high-range water reducers or plasticizers. These admixtures often meet both ASTM C 494 and C 1017 specifications simultaneously.

Contributor:
Portland Cement Association, Skokie, Illinois.

Hydraulic materials will set and harden when mixed with water, whereas pozzolanic materials require a source of calcium, usually supplied by portland cement. Slags and some Class C fly ashes are hydraulic materials, and Class F fly ashes are typically pozzolanic. Collectively, these materials are referred to as supplementary cementitious materials (SCMs). Formally, a pozzolan is a siliceous or aluminosiliceous material that, in finely divided form and in the presence of moisture, chemically reacts with the calcium hydroxide released by the hydration of portland cement to form calcium silicate hydrate (similar to that produced by cement hydration). In very broad terms, the reactions may be considered to be:

Water + Cement → Calcium Silicate Hydrate + Calcium Hydroxide
Calcium Hydroxide + Pozzolan + Water → Calcium Silicate Hydrate

Calcium silicate hydrate is the primary compound that contributes to strength and impermeability of hydrated cement paste; in contrast, calcium hydroxide is not as strong and is more soluble. Conversion of calcium hydroxide to more calcium silicate hydrate may, therefore, be considered beneficial.

Supplementary cementitious materials in concrete mixtures may be used in addition to, or as a partial replacement for, portland cement in concrete, depending on the properties of the materials and the desired effect on the concrete.

Supplementary cementitious materials can be used to improve a particular concrete property such as resistance to alkali-aggregate reactivity. The optimum amount to use should be established by testing to determine: (1) whether the material is indeed improving the property; (2) the correct dosage rate, as an overdose or underdose can be harmful or fail to achieve the desired effect; and (3) whether unintended effects occur—for example, a significant delay in early strength gain. Supplementary cementitious materials may react differently with different cements.

SPECIFICATIONS FOR SUPPLEMENTARY CEMENTITIOUS MATERIALS
8.42

GROUND-GRANULATED IRON BLAST-FURNACE SLAGS	
ASTM C 989/AASHTO M 302	
Grade 80	Slags with a low activity index
Grade 100	Slags with a moderate activity index
Grade 120	Slags with a high activity index
FLY ASH AND NATURAL POZZOLANS	
ASTM C 618/AASHTO M 295	
Class N	Raw or calcined natural pozzolans including
	Diatomaceous earths
	Opaline cherts and shales
	Tuffs and volcanic ashes or pumicites
	Calcined clays, including metakaolin and shales
Class F	Fly ash with pozzolanic properties
Class C	Fly ash with pozzolanic and cementitious properties
SILICA FUME	
ASTM C1240	
HIGHLY REACTIVE POZZOLANS	
AASHTO M 341	

CONCRETE SURFACES, FINISHES, AND INTEGRAL COLOR

GENERAL

Architectural concrete and structural concrete are both made from portland cement, aggregate, and water, but they have entirely different concrete mix designs. A variety of architectural finishes and colors can be achieved by changing the mix of these three simple ingredients. The cost of production usually determines the limit of finish choices. There are three basic ways to change the appearance of a concrete surface finish:

VOID FORM FOR CORNER REVEAL
8.43

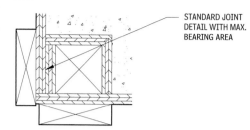

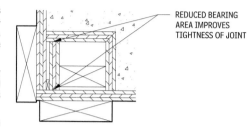

STANDARD JOINT DETAIL WITH MAX. BEARING AREA

REDUCED BEARING AREA IMPROVES TIGHTNESS OF JOINT

JOINTS IN FORMWORK
8.44

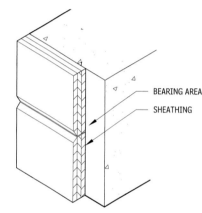

BEARING AREA
SHEATHING

HORIZONTAL FORMWORK JOINT

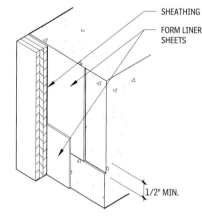

SHEATHING
FORM LINER SHEETS
1/2" MIN.

FORM LINER JOINT

CONTROL JOINTS
8.45

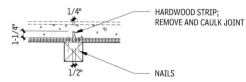

HARDWOOD STRIP; REMOVE AND CAULK JOINT
NAILS
1-1/4"
1/4"
1/2"

WOOD FORM INSERT

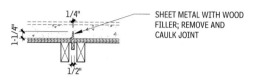

SHEET METAL WITH WOOD FILLER; REMOVE AND CAULK JOINT
1-1/4"
1/4"
1/2"

SHEET METAL FORM INSERT

KEYED CONSTRUCTION JOINT
8.46

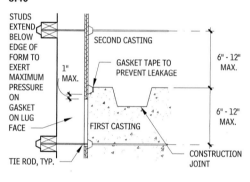

STUDS EXTEND BELOW EDGE OF FORM TO EXERT MAXIMUM PRESSURE ON GASKET ON LUG FACE
SECOND CASTING
1" MAX.
GASKET TAPE TO PREVENT LEAKAGE
FIRST CASTING
TIE ROD, TYP.
6" - 12" MAX.
6" - 12" MAX.
CONSTRUCTION JOINT

RUSTICATION AT CONSTRUCTION JOINT
8.47

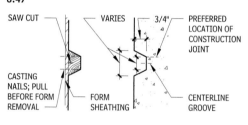

SAW CUT
VARIES
3/4"
PREFERRED LOCATION OF CONSTRUCTION JOINT
CASTING NAILS; PULL BEFORE FORM REMOVAL
FORM SHEATHING
CENTERLINE GROOVE

- *Material variation* involves changing the size, shape, texture, and color of the coarse and fine aggregate, particularly in exposed aggregate concrete, and choosing white or gray cement.
- *Mold or form variation* involves changing the texture or pattern of the concrete surface by means of form design, form liners, or joint/edge treatments.
- *Surface treatment* involves treating or tooling the surface after the concrete has cured.

Design drawings for architectural concrete should show form details, including openings, joints (control, construction, and rustication), and other important specifics. Other factors that affect concrete surfaces are mixing and placing techniques, slump control, curing methods, and release agents.

Choosing a placing technique (pumping, chute, bucket) is an important step toward achieving a desired architectural concrete surface and finish. Evaluate whether architectural concrete forms can also be used for structural concrete. Verify that the vibrators used are of the proper size, frequency, and power.

Shop drawings should be carefully checked to determine conformance with contact documents. Require approval of forms and finishes; field mockups are advised, to evaluate the appearance of the concrete panel and the quality of workmanship.

NOTES

8.44 a. A notch at the joint between two form members reduces the bearing area at the point of contact, improving the tightness of the joint. A nonnotched joint is acceptable, but a notch is recommended.
b. Placing the inner sheet above the outer sheet reduces shadows, particularly on smooth surfaces.
8.45 In flat concrete work, a rotary saw may be used to make a contraction joint.

Contributors:
D. Neil Rankins, RGA/Virginia, Richmond, Virginia; Portland Cement Association, Skokie, Illinois.

Release agents are chemical treatments applied to the liner or face of the form that react with the concrete to prevent it from sticking to the form. The best way to select a release agent is to evaluate several products on a test panel under actual job conditions. The curing compound, used to retard or reduce evaporation of moisture from concrete or to extend curing time, is typically applied immediately after final finishing of the concrete surface. Consult manufacturers and the American Concrete Institute for more detailed information about the compatibility of these treatments and the form surface material or other finishes and surfaces to be applied to the concrete.

AGGREGATE

Aggregate, one of five components of concrete, greatly affects the final appearance of the concrete surface. Aggregate should be selected on the basis of color, hardness, size, shape, gradation, method of exposure, durability, availability, and cost. Aggregate hardness and density must be compatible with structural requirements and weathering conditions.

Sources for coarse and fine aggregates should be kept the same for an entire job to avoid variations in the final surface appearance, particularly in light-toned concrete. Following are the common types of aggregate available:

- Quartz is available in clear, white, yellow, green, gray, and light pink or rose. Clear quartz is used as a sparkling surface to complement other colors and pigmented cements.
- Granite, known for its durability and beauty, is available in shades of pink, red, gray, dark blue, black, and white. Traprock such as basalt can be used for gray, black, or green.
- Marble probably offers the widest selection of colors—green, yellow, red, pink, gray, white, and black.
- Limestone is available in white and gray.
- Miscellaneous gravel, after being washed and screened, can be used for brown and reddish-brown finishes. Yellow ochers, umbers, buff shades, and pure white are abundant in riverbed gravels. Check local availability.
- Ceramic exhibits the most brilliant and varied colors when vitreous materials are used.
- Expanded lightweight shale may be used to produce reddish-brown, gray, or black aggregate. Porous and crushable, this shale produces a dull surface with soft colors. It should be tested for iron-staining characteristics and must meet ASTM C 330.
- Recycled concrete aggregate is produced when old concrete is crushed. Primarily used in pavement work, this material generally has a higher absorption rate and lower density than conventional aggregate. It should be tested for durability, gradation, and other properties, as with any new aggregate source.

EXPOSED AGGREGATE

An exposed aggregate surface is a decorative finish for concrete work, achieved by removing the surface cement to expose the aggregate. Aggregates suitable for exposure may vary from 1/4 in. to a cobblestone more than 6 in. in diameter. The extent to which the pieces of aggregate are revealed is largely determined by their size. Size is generally selected on the basis of the distance from which it will be viewed and the appearance desired.

Aggregates with rough surfaces have better bonding properties than those with smoother surfaces; bind is important, particularly when small aggregate is used. For better weathering and appearance, the area of exposed cement matrix between pieces of aggregate should be minimal, which makes the color of cement in exposed aggregate concrete less important.

EXPOSURE METHODS FOR ARCHITECTURAL CONCRETE SURFACES
8.48

METHOD	FINISH EFFECT	COLOR SOURCE	FORM SURFACE	CRITICAL DETAILS
1. As cast	Remains as is after form removal; usually exhibits board marks or wood grain.	Cement first influence; fine aggregate second influence	Smooth and textured	• Slump = 2-1/2″ to 3-1/2″ • Joinery of forms • Proper release agent • Point form joints to avoid marks
2. Abrasive blasted surfaces				
a. Brush blast	Uniform scour cleaning	Cement and fine aggregate have equal influence.	All smooth	• Scouring after 7 days • Slump = 2-1/2″ to 3-1/2″
b. Light blast	Blasted to expose fine and some coarse aggregate (sandblast, water blast, air blast, ice blast)	Fine aggregate primary; coarse aggregate and cement secondary	All smooth	• 10% more coarse aggregate • Slump = 2-1/2″ to 3-1/2″ • Blasting between 7 and 45 days • Water and air blasting used where sandblasting is prohibited. 1500 psi concrete compressive strength, min.
c. Medium exposed aggregate	Blasted to expose coarse aggregate (sandblast, water blast, air blast, ice blast)	Coarse aggregate	All smooth	• Higher than normal coarse aggregate • Slump = 2″ to 3″ • Blast before 7 days
d. Heavy exposed aggregate	Blasted to expose coarse aggregate (sandblast, ice blast); 80% visible	Coarse aggregate	All smooth	• Special-mix coarse aggregate • Slump = 0″ to 2″ • Blast within 24 hours. • Use high-frequency vibrator.
3. Chemical retardation of surface set	Chemicals expose aggregate.	Coarse aggregate and cement	All smooth; glass fiber best	• Chemical grade determines etch depth. • Stripping scheduled to prevent long drying between stripping and washoff
	Aggregate can be adhered to surface.			
4. Mechanically fractured surfaces, scaling, bush hammering, jackhammering, tooling	Varied	Fine and coarse cement and aggregate	Textured	• Aggregate particles 3/8″ for scaling and tooling • 2-1/2″ min. concrete cover over over reinforced steel • 4000 psi concrete compressive strength, min.
5. Combination/fluted	Striated/abrasive blasted/ irregular pattern Corrugated/abrasive Vertical rusticated/abrasive blasted Reeded and bush hammered Reeded and hammered Reeded and chiseled	The shallower the surface, the more influence fine aggregate and cement have.	Wood or rubber strips, corrugated sheet metal, or glass fiber	• Depends on type of finish desired. • Wood flute kerfed and nailed loosely.
6. Grinding and polishing	Terrazzolike finish	Aggregate and cement	All smooth	• Surface blemishes should be patched. • 5000 psi concrete compressive strength, min.

VISIBILITY OF EXPOSED AGGREGATE DEPENDENT ON AGGREGATE SIZE
8.49

AGGREGATE SIZE, IN.	DISTANCE AT WHICH TEXTURE IS VISIBLE, FT
1/4–1/2	20–30
1/2–1	30–75
1–2	75–125
2–3	125–175

SEE ALSO

Architectural concrete
Cast-in-place concrete
Concrete forming and accessories
Dampproofing
Fibrous reinforcing
Formwork
Grouting
Mockups
Openings
Reinforcing steel
Stressing tendons
Structural concrete
Tilt-up concrete
Waterstop
Welded wire fabric reinforcing

Contributors:
D. Neil Rankins, RGA/Virginia, Richmond, Virginia; Portland Cement Association, Skokie, Illinois.

9 MASONRY

INTRODUCTION

Mortar and grout are the cementitious bonding agents that integrate masonry units into masonry assemblies. Because concrete, masonry mortar, and grout contain the same principal components, some design professionals assume good practice for one will also be good practice for another. In reality, the three materials differ in proportions, working consistencies, methods of placement, and structural performance.

Mortar and grout structurally bind masonry units together, whereas concrete is usually itself a structural material. One of the most important functions of concrete elements is to carry load, whereas the principal function of mortar and grout is to develop a complete, strong, and durable bond with masonry units. Concrete is poured into non-absorbent forms with a minimum amount of water. Mortar and grout are placed, with much more water, between absorptive forms (masonry units). The water/cement ratio of the mix design is very important in concrete work, but it is less important with mortar or grout for masonry. When mortar or grout is placed with masonry units, the water/cement ratio rapidly decreases because of the clay or concrete unit masonry's absorbency. It is important to distinguish between the requirements for concrete, masonry mortar, and grout.

MASONRY MORTARING AND GROUTING

TYPES OF JOINTS

Mortar serves multiple functions:

- Joins and seals masonry, allowing for dimensional variations in masonry units.
- Affects overall appearance of wall color, texture, and patterns.
- Bonds reinforcing steel to masonry, creating composite assembly.

MORTAR JOINT FINISH METHODS

- Troweled: Excess mortar is struck off. The trowel is the only tool used for shaping and finishing.
- Tooled: A special tool is used to compress and shape mortar in the joint.

MORTAR JOINTS
9.1

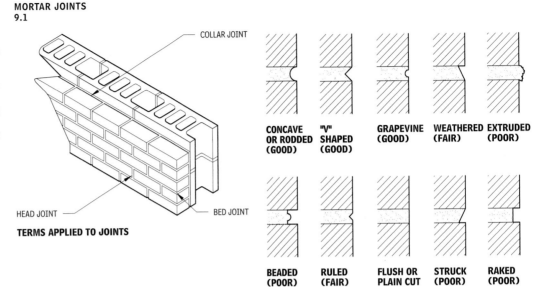

TERMS APPLIED TO JOINTS

CONCAVE OR RODDED (GOOD)   "V" SHAPED (GOOD)   GRAPEVINE (GOOD)   WEATHERED (FAIR)   EXTRUDED (POOR)

BEADED (POOR)   RULED (FAIR)   FLUSH OR PLAIN CUT (FAIR)   STRUCK (POOR)   RAKED (POOR)

TYPES OF JOINTS (WEATHERABILITY)

MASONRY ANCHORAGE, REINFORCING, AND ACCESSORIES

MASONRY ANCHORAGE AND REINFORCING

GENERAL

Masonry construction has not always required the inclusion of metal components. Historically, composite masonry construction consisted of multiple wythes of masonry bonded together by headers. However, contemporary masonry walls require ties between the inner and outer wythes, which are then anchored to the structural frame. Many design professionals use the terms "wall tie" and "anchor" interchangeably; in practice "ties" are of a lighter-gage material than anchors. Both ties and anchors transfer load to structural framing or other structural members.

Anchors and ties with flexible components may accommodate limited differential movement between the structural frame and the masonry wall by allowing for in-plane movement.

CORROSION PROTECTION

The durability of any metal component is usually based on its ability to resist corrosion. Since masonry walls are often subject to moisture, metal must be protected, either by galvanizing or by the use of corrosion-resistant metals. The following ASTM standards apply to corrosion protection of carbon steel components.

- ASTM A 123, "Standard Specification for Zinc (Hot-Dip Galvanized) Coatings on Iron and Steel Products"
- ASTM A 153, "Standard Specification for Zinc Coating (Hot-Dip) on Iron and Steel Hardware"
- ASTM A 641, "Standard Specification for Zinc-Coated Carbon steel Wire"

- ASTM A 653, "Standard Specification for Steel Sheet, Zinc-Coated (Galvanized) or Zinc-Iron Alloy-Coated (Galvannealed) by the Hot-Dip Process"

Corrosion protection is also provided by stainless-steel anchors and ties conforming to ASTM A 580, for Type 304.

ANCHORS AND REINFORCEMENT

Selection of anchors and reinforcement is determined by the relationship of the masonry element to the structural support.

Reinforcing bars may be placed horizontally and vertically in masonry. The reinforcement may be placed in the cores or cells of masonry units or between wythes of masonry. The use of dovetail slots welded on steel or concrete columns requires coordination during the steel or concrete fabrication stage. The type of anchor specified, including its size, diameter, and spacing, should be called out in the construction documents.

ASTM STANDARD REINFORCING BARS FOR MASONRY
9.2

BAR SIZE DESIGNATION	WEIGHT (LB/FT)	NOMINAL DIMENSIONS—ROUND SECTIONS		
		DIAMETER (IN.)	CROSS-SECTIONAL AREA (SQ IN.)	PERIMETER (IN.)
#3	0.376	0.375	0.11	1.178
#4	0.668	0.500	0.20	1.571
#5	1.043	0.625	0.31	1.963
#6	1.502	0.750	0.44	2.356
#7	2.044	0.875	0.60	2.749
#8	2.670	1.000	0.79	3.142
#9	3.400	1.128	1.00	3.544
#10	4.303	1.270	1.27	3.990
#11	5.313	1.410	1.56	4.430

NOTE

9.2 Bar sizes larger than #11 are not permitted in masonry work.

Contributors:
Grace S. Lee, Rippeteau Architects, PC, Washington, DC; Brian E. Trimble, PE, Brick Industry Association, Reston, Virginia; Stephen S. Szoke, PE, National Concrete Masonry Association, Herndon, Virginia.

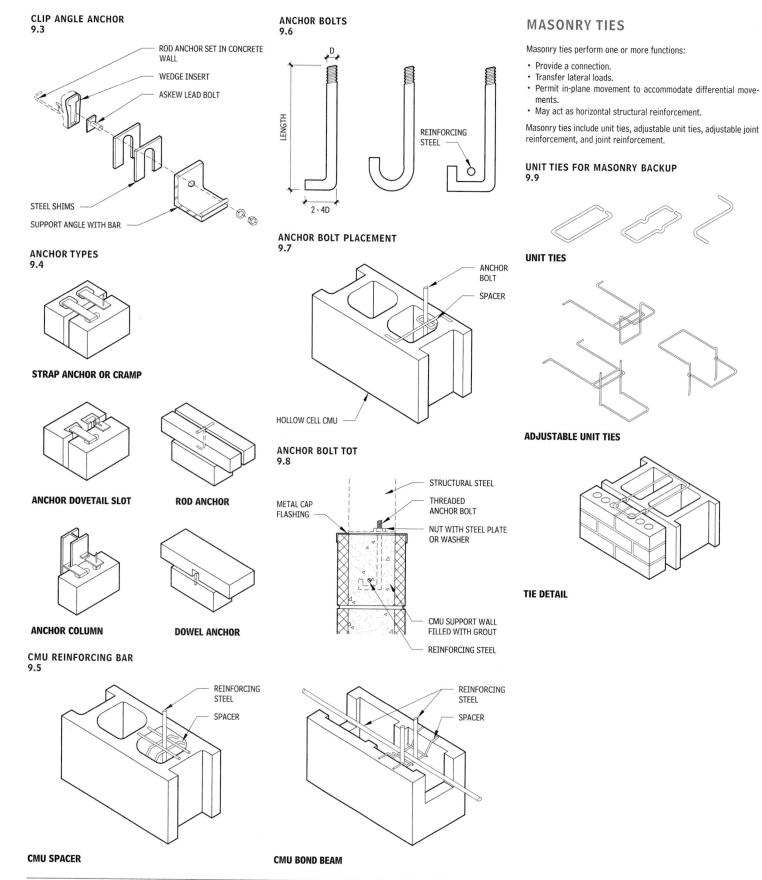

CLIP ANGLE ANCHOR
9.3

- ROD ANCHOR SET IN CONCRETE WALL
- WEDGE INSERT
- ASKEW LEAD BOLT
- STEEL SHIMS
- SUPPORT ANGLE WITH BAR

ANCHOR TYPES
9.4

STRAP ANCHOR OR CRAMP

ANCHOR DOVETAIL SLOT

ROD ANCHOR

ANCHOR COLUMN

DOWEL ANCHOR

CMU REINFORCING BAR
9.5

- REINFORCING STEEL
- SPACER

CMU SPACER

- REINFORCING STEEL
- SPACER

CMU BOND BEAM

ANCHOR BOLTS
9.6

D

LENGTH

2 - 4D

REINFORCING STEEL

ANCHOR BOLT PLACEMENT
9.7

- ANCHOR BOLT
- SPACER
- HOLLOW CELL CMU

ANCHOR BOLT TOT
9.8

- STRUCTURAL STEEL
- THREADED ANCHOR BOLT
- NUT WITH STEEL PLATE OR WASHER
- METAL CAP FLASHING
- CMU SUPPORT WALL FILLED WITH GROUT
- REINFORCING STEEL

MASONRY TIES

Masonry ties perform one or more functions:

- Provide a connection.
- Transfer lateral loads.
- Permit in-plane movement to accommodate differential movements.
- May act as horizontal structural reinforcement.

Masonry ties include unit ties, adjustable unit ties, adjustable joint reinforcement, and joint reinforcement.

UNIT TIES FOR MASONRY BACKUP
9.9

UNIT TIES

ADJUSTABLE UNIT TIES

TIE DETAIL

NOTES

9.9 a. Z-ties can be used only with solid masonry veneer units.
b. Tie must extend a minimum of 1-1/2 in. onto solid masonry units and be fully embedded in mortar on the outer face shell of hollow masonry units.

Contributor:
Brian E. Trimble, PE, Brick Industry Association, Reston, Virginia.

JOINT REINFORCEMENT FOR MASONRY BACKUP
9.10

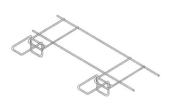
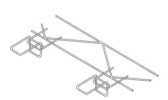

ADJUSTABLE JOINT REINFORCEMENT

TRUSS TYPE **LONGITUDINAL WIRE LADDER TYPE** **LONGITUDINAL TRUSS TYPE**

ADJUSTABLE UNIT TIE FOR FRAMING BACKUP
9.11

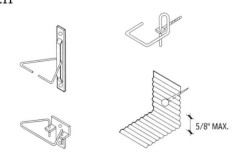

5/8" MAX.

ADJUSTABLE UNIT TIES – STUD

ADJUSTABLE UNIT TIE—STRUCTURAL STEEL BACKUP
9.12

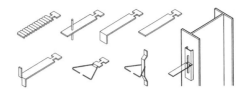

UNIT TIES - STEEL FRAME **WELD-ON TYPE CHANNEL SLOT (ANCHOR SHOWN)**

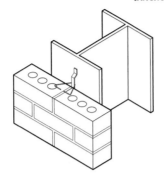

TIE DETAIL

ADJUSTABLE UNIT TIE FOR CONCRETE BACKUP
9.13

UNIT TIES - CONCRETE

DOVETAIL SLOT

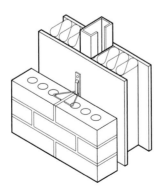

TIE DETAIL

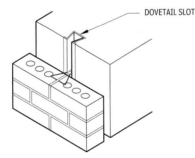

TIE DETAIL

TYPICAL ADJUSTABLE UNIT TIE
9.14

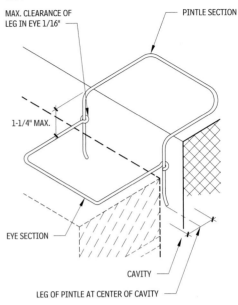

MAX. CLEARANCE OF LEG IN EYE 1/16"

PINTLE SECTION

1-1/4" MAX.

EYE SECTION

CAVITY

LEG OF PINTLE AT CENTER OF CAVITY

Masonry tie spacing recommendations are included Table 9.22. The ties should be staggered in alternate rows, and only one row of ties should be located in the same bed joint to allow proper embedment in the mortar.

In wall construction in which masonry wythes are built up together and the joints align, a single anchor is laid over both wythes. Where one wythe of masonry is laid up before the other wythe, or when joints do not align, adjustable ties may be necessary. Adjustable ties are advantageous for several reasons:

- Interior wythes can be constructed before the exterior wythe, allowing the structure to be enclosed faster.
- The risk of damage to the ties when the exterior wythe is constructed is reduced.
- Adjustable ties can more readily accommodate construction tolerances.
- Adjustable ties can accommodate larger differential movements.

However, adjustable ties must be installed properly or the tie may be rendered useless. Location of the channel is critical, as the tie must engage the channel and be properly embedded in the exterior wythe.

MASONRY TIE SPACING RECOMMENDATIONS
9.15

WALL TYPE	TIE AND GAUGE	MAXIMUM AREA PER PER TIE (SQ FT)	MAXIMUM VERTICAL SPACING (IN.)	MAXIMUM HORIZONTAL SPACING (IN.)
Multi-wythe walls	W 1.7 (9 gauge)	2-2/3	24	36
	W 2.8 (3/16 in. dia.)	4-1/2	24	36
Cavity walls	W 1.7 (9 gauge)	2-2/3	24	36
	W 2.8 (3/16 in. dia.)	4-1/2	24	36
	Adjustable W 2.8 (3/16 in. dia.)	1.77	16	16
Veneer	Wire tie	3-1/2	18	32
	Corrugated	2-2/3	18	32

NOTES

9.11 Differential movement must always be accounted for wall framing with adjustable ties.

9.15 Consult applicable building codes for spacing requirements and for allowable tie types for various construction. Corrugated ties may not be allowed by code.

Contributor:
Brian E. Trimble, PE, Brick Industry Association, Reston, Virginia.

RECOMMENDED MINIMUM TIE DIAMETERS AND GAUGES
9.16

MASONRY TIES			MINIMUM DIMENSION	
			DIAMETER (IN.)	GAUGE
Standard Ties	Unit	Rectangular and Z-tie	3/16	—
		Corrugated	—	22
	Joint reinforcement	Ladder and truss	—	9
		Tab	—	9
Adjustable Ties	Unit	Rectangular and Z-tie	3/16	—
	Dovetail/channel slot	Wire	3/16	—
		Corrugated	—	16
		Connector slot	—	22
	Slotted plate	Wire	3/16	—
		Slot plate	—	14
		Backer plate	—	14
	Joint reinforcement	Standard section	—	9
		Tabs	3/16	—

MASONRY ACCESSORIES

MASONRY CAVITY DRAINAGE, WEEPHOLES, AND VENTS

With proper design and installation, weepholes and vents discharge moisture trapped within the wall cavity. Weepholes are required in the head joint of the course of masonry immediately above all embedded flashing, and should be installed at all horizontal interruptions in the wall. Weepholes should never be located below grade and should be small enough to keep out rodents. Weepholes may be open head joints, holes formed with nylon rope or oiled rods, plastic or metal tubes, fibrous rope, cotton sash cord, or cellular material. Open head joints are often fitted with vents or screens to keep out insects or rodents. Formed and tube weepholes should have a minimum diameter of 1/4 inch, though it is important to take into consideration the type of weephole utilized in conjunction with the climate. Open head joints are a preferred type of weephole, occurring no more than 32 in. on center, although in clay unit masonry they should be spaced no more than 24 in. or in. on center. If cord or rope is, the material should be at least 16 in. long. Weepholes other than open head joints should be spaced no more than 16 in. on center.

MASONRY EMBEDED FLASHING Flashing in masonry construction is necessary to collect moisture that enters the wall system and to channel it to the exterior through weepholes. Moisture enters masonry walls through condensation, penetration of wind-driven rains, failed sealant joints, interfaces with other components, or other components themselves, such as windows or roofs.

There are two types of flashing. Exposed flashings can be applied to all masonry construction, while use of embedded flashing is usually limited to drainage-type walls. Masonry is a durable, long-lasting construction material. Thus, the flashing materials selected should also be durable and have a long life, especially embedded flashing materials, which are difficult to replace.

MATERIALS

Flashing may be made of sheet metal (copper, lead, stainless steel, galvanized steel, or aluminum), plastic, or composite materials (usually paper-backed, coated, metallic sheet, or fibrous glass mesh). When selecting flashing materials, avoid those that would have cathodic reactions with mortar, other metals, or other construction materials. The thickness of the flashing material specified should take into account the span between embedment, bends, or connections. Copper may cause a patina, which may be desirable. Lead and galvanized metal may result in some white staining, but this may be minimal if coated materials are used. Choose aluminum as an embedded flashing only if it is properly coated, so it will not react wit the mortar. Polyethylene should not be used as flashing unless it has been chemically stabilized so it will not deteriorate when exposed to sunlight (ultraviolet radiation). Asphalt-impregnated building paper (building felt) is not an acceptable flashing material. Adhered flashings must be held back from the face of the wall to avoid deterioration and staining caused by high temperatures.

INSTALLATION

Embedded flashing is typically used in drainage walls at the base, above all openings, at sills and shelf angles, and under copings. Continuous embedded flashing should be lapped at lease 6 in. and sealed with and appropriate sealer. Discontinuous flashing should have the ends turned up at lease 1 in. to form a dam. Dams prevent water collected on the flashing from draining off the ends of the flashing back into the wall system or into framing or mullions.

Embedded flashing should extend at least 8 in. vertically within the wall system; it should extend at least 1-1/2 in. into the interior wythe and through the exterior wythe at least 1/4 in. to form a drip. The drip minimizes possible staining. Sometimes, it may be necessary to avoid the drip, as with rough textured units and ribbed, scored, or fluted masonry units. The flashing must be carefully brought to the surface of the recessed portion of the masonry. Plastic flashing is often exposed and cut off flush with the face of the masonry. If the flashing is recessed and does not reach the surface, water collected on it may be channeled by mortar under the flashing and back into the wall system.

WEEPHOLE DETAILS
9.17

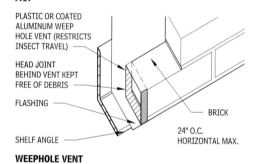

PLASTIC OR COATED ALUMINUM WEEP HOLE VENT (RESTRICTS INSECT TRAVEL)

HEAD JOINT BEHIND VENT KEPT FREE OF DEBRIS

FLASHING

SHELF ANGLE

BRICK

24" O.C. HORIZONTAL MAX.

WEEPHOLE VENT

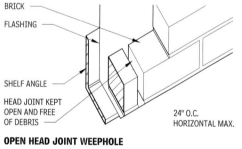

BRICK

FLASHING

SHELF ANGLE

HEAD JOINT KEPT OPEN AND FREE OF DEBRIS

24" O.C. HORIZONTAL MAX.

OPEN HEAD JOINT WEEPHOLE

BRICK OR BLOCK VENT
9.18

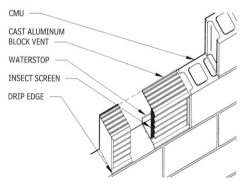

CMU

CAST ALUMINUM BLOCK VENT

WATERSTOP

INSECT SCREEN

DRIP EDGE

GALVANIC CORROSION (ELECTROLYSIS) POTENTIAL BETWEEN COMMON FLASHING MATERIALS AND SELECTED CONSTRUCTION MATERIALS
9.19

FLASHING MATERIALS	COPPER	ALUMINUM	STAINLESS STEEL	GALVANIZED STEEL	ZINC	LEAD	BRASS	BRONZE	MONEL	UNCURED MORTAR OR CEMENT	WOODS WITH ACID (REDWOOD AND RED CEDAR)	IRON/STEEL
Copper		●	●	◐	●	◐	◐	◐	◐	○	○	●
Aluminum			○	○	○	◐	●	●	○	●	●	◐
Stainless steel				◐	●	◐	●	●	●	○	○	◐
Galvanized steel					○	○	◐	◐	◐	○	◐	◐
Zinc alloy						○	●	●	●	○	●	●
Lead							◐	◐	◐	●	○	○

NOTES

9.16 Thicker diameters and gauges are available.

9.19
● Galvanic action will occur, hence direct contact should be avoided.
◐ Galvanic action may occur under certain circumstances and/or over a period of time.
○ Galvanic action is insignificant; metals may come into direct contact under normal circumstances.
a. Galvanic corrosion is apt to occur when water runoff from one material comes in contact with a potentially reactive material.

Contributors:
Brian E. Trimble, PE, Brick Industry Association, Reston, Virginia; Grace S. Lee, Rippeteau Architects, PC, Washington, DC; Stephen S. Szoke, PE, National Concrete Masonry Association, Herdon, Virginia.

WOOD BLOCKING AND METAL WALL PLUGS

The procedure for attaching other materials, and fixtures, to masonry is relatively simple and can be executed either during or after construction. Fasteners, such as lag bolts and shields, are commonly used because of their flexibility in placement. However, when the precise location of the fastener can be determined during construction, nailing blocks and metal wall plugs are the preferable means of attachment to masonry and are placed in the mortar joints as the masonry is laid.

Wood blocking should be of seasoned softwood to prevent shrinkage and be pressure treated to inhibit deterioration. They should be placed only in the head joint. Metal wall plugs are made of galvanized metal and may contain wooden or fiber inserts. Such plugs may be placed in either the head or bed joints of masonry.

METAL WALL PLUGS
9.20

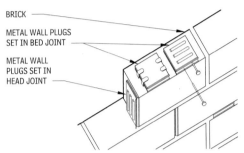

BRICK

METAL WALL PLUGS SET IN BED JOINT

METAL WALL PLUGS SET IN HEAD JOINT

METAL WALL PLUGS

MASONRY MOVEMENT JOINTS

GENERAL

The various materials and elements used to construct a building are in constant motion. All building materials change in volume in response to internal or external stimuli, such as temperature changes, moisture expansion, and elastic deformation due to loads or creep. Restraining such movements may cause stresses within the building elements, which in turn may result in cracks.

To avoid cracks, the building design should minimize volume change, prevent movement, or accommodate differential movement between materials and assemblies. Masonry control and expansion joints are types of movement joints that minimize cracks in of masonry construction. The design of joints should take into consideration the magnitude of each type of movement that may occur in masonry and other building materials.

MOVEMENTS OF CONSTRUCTION MATERIALS

The design and construction of most buildings does not allow precise movement prediction of building materials. Changes depend on material properties; therefore, they are highly variable. Material age and temperature at installation are two conditions that may also influence movement. When mean values of material properties are used in design, the actual movement may be underestimated or overestimated. Design professionals should use discretion when selecting the applicable values. Table 9.21 indicates the type of movements that affect common building materials.

MOVEMENT JOINTS

There are various types of movement joints in buildings: expansion joints, control joints, separation or isolation joints, and construction joints. Each type of movement joint is designed to perform a specific task; they should not be used interchangeably.

Control joints are used to separate masonry into segments to minimize cracking due to changes in temperature, moisture expansion,

MOVEMENT OF BUILDING MATERIALS
9.21

BUILDING MATERIAL	THERMAL	REVERSIBLE MOISTURE	IRREVERSIBLE MOISTURE	ELASTIC DEFORMATION	CREEP
Brick masonry	X	—	X	X	X
Concrete masonry	X	X	—	X	X
Concrete	X	X	X	X	X
Steel	X	—	—	X	—
Wood	X	X	—	X	X

elastic deformation due to loads, and shrinkage and creep in concrete-framed buildings. Control joints may be horizontal or vertical. They are formed of elastomeric materials placed in a continuous, unobstructed opening through the masonry wythe. This construction allows the joint to compress with movement of materials. Control joints must be located so the structural integrity of the masonry is not compromised.

Expansion (isolation) joints are used to separate a building into discrete structural sections so that stresses developed in one section, will not affect the integrity of the entire structure. The Expansion joint is a through-the-building joint, including the roof assembly.

CONCRETE UNIT MASONRY CONTROL JOINTS
9.22

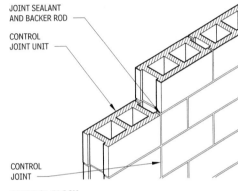

JOINT SEALANT AND BACKER ROD

CONTROL JOINT UNIT

CONTROL JOINT

CONTROL BLOCK

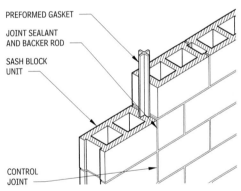

PREFORMED GASKET

JOINT SEALANT AND BACKER ROD

SASH BLOCK UNIT

CONTROL JOINT

GASKET TYPE

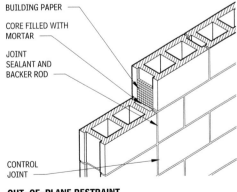

BUILDING PAPER

CORE FILLED WITH MORTAR

JOINT SEALANT AND BACKER ROD

CONTROL JOINT

OUT-OF-PLANE RESTRAINT

CLAY UNIT MASONRY CONTROL JOINTS
9.23

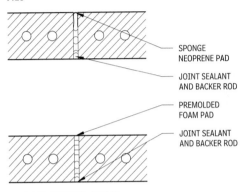

SPONGE NEOPRENE PAD

JOINT SEALANT AND BACKER ROD

PREMOLDED FOAM PAD

JOINT SEALANT AND BACKER ROD

VERTICAL CONTROL JOINTS

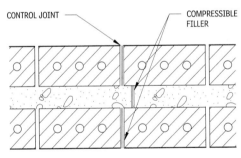

CONTROL JOINT

COMPRESSIBLE FILLER

GROUTED MULTIPLE-WYTHE MASONRY

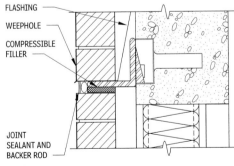

FLASHING

WEEPHOLE

COMPRESSIBLE FILLER

JOINT SEALANT AND BACKER ROD

HORIZONTAL EXPANSION JOINT

Contributors:
Grace S. Lee and A. Harris Lokmanhakim, AIA, Rippeteau Architects, PC, Washington, DC; Brian E. Trimble, PE, Brick Industry Association, Reston, Virginia; Stephen S. Szoke, PE, National Concrete Masonry Association, Herndon, Virginia

Separation or isolation joints are joints between dissimilar materials such as openings and adjacent masonry construction. These joints accommodate differential movement in building materials.

MASONRY CONTROL AND EXPANSION JOINTS
9.24

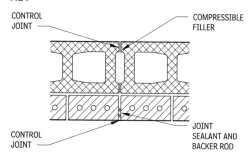

DOUBLE WYTHE MASONRY

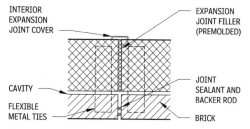

EXPANSION JOINT AT MASONRY CAVITY WALL

CONTROL JOINT SPACING FOR CONCRETE MASONRY UNITS
9.25

RECOMMENDED SPACING OF CONTROL JOINTS	VERTICAL SPACING OF JOINT REINFORCEMENT			
	NONE	24″	16″	8″
Expressed as ratio of panel length to height (L/H)	2	2-1/2	3	4
Panel length (L) not to exceed (regardless of height [H])	40′	45′	50′	60′

A construction (cold) joint is used primarily in concrete construction when construction work is interrupted. Construction joints are located where they will least impair the strength of the structure.

SPACING OF MASONRY CONTROL AND EXPANSION JOINTS

No single recommendation on the positioning and spacing of control and expansion joints can be applied to all structures. Each building should be analyzed to determine the extent of movement expected within that particular structure. Provisions should be made to accommodate these movements and their associated stresses with a series of control and expansion joints.

Generally, spacing of control joints is determined by considering the amount of expected wall movement and the size of the control joint. Recommended spacing of control joints in concrete unit masonry is addressed in Table 9.25. Control joints are often sized to resemble a mortar joint, usually 3/8 in. to 1/2 in.

Expansion joints may utilize sealant or preformed filler. Maximum sealant joint size is approximately 2 inches with 50 percent movement, thus when expansion joints are over 3 inches in width preformed fillers are common.

Control and expansion joints do not have to be aligned in cavity walls; however, they should be aligned in multiwythe walls.

LINTELS

STEEL LINTEL DETAILS
9.27

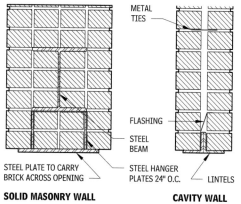

SOLID MASONRY WALL　　**CAVITY WALL**

MASONRY LINTEL DETAIL
9.28

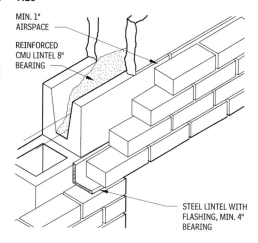

PRECAST CONCRETE LINTEL DETAIL
9.29

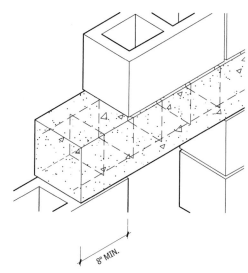

LINTEL LOADING CONDITIONS (CONSULT STRUCTURAL HANDBOOK FOR DESIGN FORMULAS)
9.26

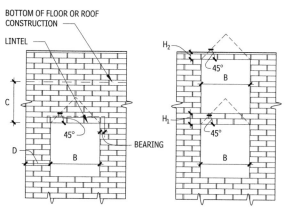

SIMPLE LINTEL WITH ARCH ACTION CARRIES WALL LOAD ONLY IN TRIANGLE ABOVE OPENING: C ≥ B AND D ≥ B

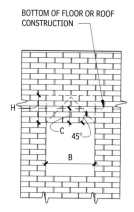

SIMPLE LINTEL WITHOUT ARCH ACTION CARRIES LESS WALL LOAD THAN TRIANGLE ABOVE OPENING: H_1 OR H_2 < 0.6B

LINTEL WITH UNIFORM FLOOR LOAD CARRIES BOTH WALL AND FLOOR LOADS IN RECTANGLE ABOVE OPENING: C < B

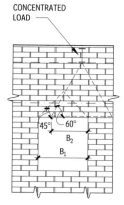

LINTEL WITH CONCENTRATED LOAD CARRIES WALL AND PORTION OF CONCENTRATED LOAD DISTRIBUTED ALONG LENGTH B_2.

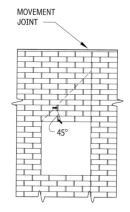

LINTELS AT MOVEMENT JOINTS REQUIRE SPECIAL DESIGN CONSIDERATIONS

NOTE

9.27 Steel members to be designed by structural engineer. Flashing details must be designed to suit job conditions.

Contributors:
Grace S. Lee, Rippeteau Architects, PC, Washington, DC; Brian E. Trimble, PE, Brick Industry Association, Reston, Virginia; Stephen S. Szoke, PE, National Concrete Masonry Association, Herndon, Virginia.

STEEL ANGLE LINTEL SIZING CHART
9.30

HORIZONTAL LEG	ANGLE SIZE	WEIGHT PER FT (LB)	SPAN (FT) (CENTER TO CENTER OF REQUIRED BEARING)									
			3	4	5	6	7	8	9	10	11	12
3-1/2	3 × 3-1/2 × 1/4	5.4	956	517	262	149	91	59				
	× 5/16	6.6	1166	637	323	184	113	73				
	3-1/2 × 3-1/2 × 1/4	5.8	1281	718	406	232	144	94	65			
	× 5/16	7.2	1589	891	507	290	179	118	80			
	4 × 3-1/2 × 1/4	6.2	1622	910	580	338	210	139	95	68		
	× 5/16	7.7	2110	1184	734	421	262	173	119	85	62	
	× 3/8	9.1	2434	1365	855	490	305	201	138	98	71	
	× 7/16	10.6	2760	1548	978	561	349	230	158	113	82	60
	5 × 3-1/2 × 1/4	7.0	2600	1460	932	636	398	264	184	132	97	73
	× 5/16	8.7	3087	1733	1106	765	486	323	224	161	119	89
	× 7/16	12.0	4224	2371	1513	1047	655	435	302	217	160	120
	6 × 3-1/2 × 1/4	7.9	3577	2009	1283	888	650	439	306	221	164	124
	× 5/16	9.8	4390	2465	1574	1090	798	538	375	271	201	151
	× 3/8	11.7	5200	2922	1865	1291	945	636	443	320	237	179

REQUIRED REINFORCING FOR SIMPLY SUPPORTED REINFORCED CONCRETE MASONRY LINTELS
9.31

TYPE OF LOAD	LINTEL SECTION NOMINAL SIZE (IN.)	REQUIRED REINFORCING CLEAR SPAN							
		3′-4″	4′-0″	4′-8″	5′-4″	6′-0″	6′-8″	7′-4″	8′-0″
Wall loads	6 × 8	1—#3	1—#4	1—#4	2—#4	2—#5			
	6 × 16					1—#4	1—#4	1—#4	1—#4
Floor and roof loads	6 × 16	1—#4	1—#4	2—#3	1—#5	2—#4	2—#4	2—#5	2—#5
Wall loads	8 × 8	1—#3	2—#3	2—#3	2—#4 2	2—#4	2—#5	2—#6	
	8 × 16							2—#5	2—#5
Floor and roof loads	8 × 8	2—#4							
	8 × 16	2—#3	2—#3	2—#3	2—#4	2—#4	2—#4	2—#5	2—#5

MAXIMUM DESIGN LOADS FOR PRECAST CONCRETE LINTELS (LB/LINEAR FT)
9.32

REINFORCEMENT	CLEAR SPAN											
	3′-4″	4′-0″	4′-8″	5′-4″	6′-0″	6′-8″	7′-4″	8′-0″	8′-8″	9′-4″	10′-0″	10′-8″
2—#3	1585	1150	850	625	475	365	285	225	180	145	115	90
2—#4	1855	1300	910	665	500	380	300	235	185	150	120	95
2—#5	1825	1410	1005	725	535	410	315	250	195	155	125	100

UNIT MASONRY

GENERAL

There are various types of bonding patterns that may be used when laying masonry. The most common bond pattern is the running bond for both exposed and unexposed masonry. Combination of various bonds patterns produce more aesthetically interesting construction and may be combined with various types, textures, and colors of masonry. Many of the most common bond patterns are indicated in the figure entitled Common Bond Patterns (Figure 9.33).

When a curved masonry wall is to be laid up in running bond, the projection of the corners of each unit beyond the face of the units on the courses above and below may need to be limited for aesthetic reasons. Generally, projections of approximately 1/8 in. for nominal 8-inch-long units and 1/4 in. for nominal 16-inch-long units are acceptable. If the wall surface is to be stuccoed or otherwise covered, projections of 1/2 to 3/4 in. may not be objectionable. However, if it is desirable to obtain a smooth appearance for the curve or to limit the shadows created by the projected corners, the projections should not exceed those indicated above. Projections of less than 1/8 in. are usually impractical because of construction tolerances. Dependent upon the aesthetic desired, use of other types of bonding patterns may allow for tighter radii, such as a header course in stacked bond. The Minimum Radii of Masonry table (Table 9.34) indicates radii related to the used of running bond patterns and common masonry sizes.

NOTES

9.30 a. Allowable loads to the left of the heavy line are governed by moment, and to the right by deflection. Fy = 36,000 psi. Maximum deflection 1/600. Consult structural engineer for long spans.
b. Allowable uniform loads indicated in pounds per linear foot.
9.31 a. Includes weight of lintel.
b. Wall loads assumed to be 300 lb per linear ft.
c. Floor and roof loads including wall loads assumed to be 1000 lb/linear ft.
d. Eight-inch lintels assumed to weigh 50 lb/ft.

e. Sixteen-inch lintels assumed to weigh 100 lb/ft.
9.32 Lintel properties: width = 7-5/8 in., height = 7-5/8 in., weight = 60 lb/linear ft, f′c = 2500 psi.

Contributors:
Grace S. Lee, Rippeteau Architects, PC, Washington, DC; Brian E. Trimble, PE, Brick Industry Association, Reston, Virginia; Stephen S. Szoke, PE, National Concrete Masonry Association, Herndon, Virginia.

COMMON BOND PATTERNS
9.33

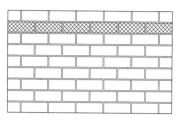

RUNNING

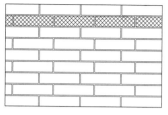

1/3 RUNNING

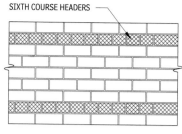

SIXTH COURSE HEADERS

COMMON

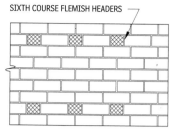

SIXTH COURSE FLEMISH HEADERS

COMMON

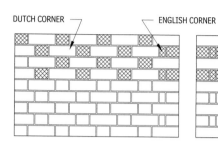

DUTCH CORNER   ENGLISH CORNER   DUTCH CORNER

FLEMISH

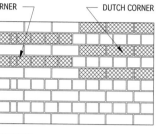

ENGLISH

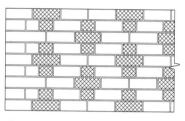

FLEMISH (CROSS)

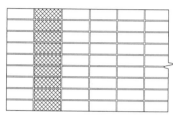

STACK

MINIMUM RADII OF MASONRY
9.34

NOMINAL LENGTH	NOMINAL WIDTH (IN.)	3/8-IN. EXTERIOR MORTAR JOINT			1/2-IN. EXTERIOR MORTAR JOINT		
		RADIUS OF WALL	NUMBER OF UNITS IN 360° WALL	PROJECTION OF UNIT (IN.)	RADIUS OF WALL	NUMBER OF UNITS IN 360° WALL	PROJECTION OF UNIT (IN.)
8 in. (uncut)	4	9'-9"	92	1/16	6'-6"	61	3/32
	8	20'-4"	192	1/32	13'-7"	126	1/16
	12	31'-1"	293	1/32	20'-8"	195	1/32
16 in. (uncut)	4	19'-6"	92	1/8	13'-1"	61	7/32
	8	40'-9"	192	1/16	27'-5"	128	3/32
	12	62'-2"	293	1/16	41'-9"	195	1/16
8 in. (3/4 in., cuts interior face, both ends)	4	1'-6"	14	7/16	1'-4"	13	1/2
	8	8'-0"	26	7/32	2'-9"	26	1/4
	12	4'-6"	42	5/32	4'-3"	40	5/32
16 in. (3/4 in., cuts interior face, both ends)	4	2'-11"	14	7/8	2'-9"	13	15/16
	8	5'-11"	26	7/16	5'-7"	26	1/2
	12	8'-11"	42	5/16	8'-6"	40	5/16

RADIAL WALLS AND BRICK PROJECTIONS
9.35

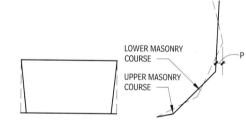

LOWER MASONRY COURSE

P

UPPER MASONRY COURSE

DOUBLE CORNER UNIT

PLAN VIEW

NOTE

9.34 Interior mortar joints maintained at approximately 1/8 in.

Contributors:
A. Harris Lokmanhakim, AIA, Rippeteau Architects, PC, Washington, DC;
Stephen S. Szoke, PE, National Concrete Masonry Association, Herndon, Virginia; Brian E. Trimble, PE, Brick Industry Association, Reston, Virginia.

CORNER LAYOUT SHOWING ALTERNATING COURSES
9.36

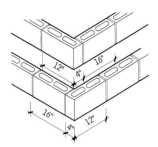

4-IN. WALL TO 4-IN. WALL

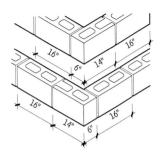

6-IN. WALL TO 6-IN. WALL

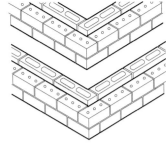

10-IN. CAVITY WALL

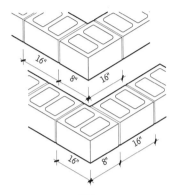

8-IN. WALL TO 8-IN. WALL

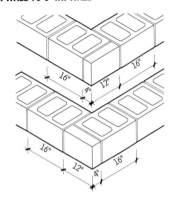

12-IN. WALL TO 12-IN. WALL

CLAY MASONRY UNITS

BRICK AND TILE CLASSIFICATION

Brick and tile are classified according to the specific location where they are used. Standard specifications have been developed to produce uniform requirements for brick. ASTM publishes the most widely accepted standards on brick. Standard specifications include strength, durability, and aesthetic requirements.

GENERAL REQUIREMENTS

Terms used in each standard for brick classification may include exposure, appearance, physical properties, efflorescence, dimen-

sional tolerances, distortion, chipping, core, and frogs. Brick may be classified by use, grade (exposure), and type (appearance). Properties should be identified, each ASTM standard has minimum requirements for grade and type, which will be used as the default property if a not specified.

GRADE REQUIREMENTS FOR FACE EXPOSURE

Specific grades of brick are required to accommodate the various climates in the United States and the different applications in which brick can be used. Brick grades include Severe Weathering (SW), Moderate Weathering (MW), and Negligible Weathering (NW), each is based on the weathering index and the exposure they will receive. The weathering index is the product of the average annual number of freezing cycle days and the average annual winter rainfall in inches (see Figure 9.38). The exposure is related

to whether the brick is used on a vertical or horizontal surface and whether the unit will be in contact with the earth (see Table 9.39). A higher weathering index or a more severe exposure will require face brick to meet the SW requirements. The grades for each specification are listed in Table 9.39.

CLAY MASONRY CLASSIFICATION TYPES
9.37

TYPE OF BRICK UNIT	ASTM DESIGNATION
Building brick	C 62
Facing brick	C 216
Hollow brick	C 652
Paving brick	C 902
Paving brick (heavy vehicular)	C 1272
Ceramic glazed brick	C 126
Thin brick veneer units	C 1088
Sewer and manhole brick	C 32
Chemical-resistant brick	C 279
Industrial floor brick	C 410
TYPE OF TILE UNIT	
Structural clay load-bearing tile	C 34
Structural clay nonload-bearing tile	C 56
Structural clay facing tile	C 212
Structural clay nonload-bearing screen tile	C 530
Ceramic glazed tile	C 126

U.S. WEATHERING INDEXES
9.38

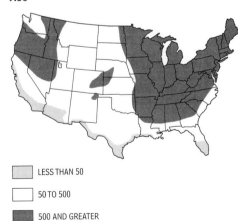

▢ LESS THAN 50

▢ 50 TO 500

▣ 500 AND GREATER

EXPOSURE
9.39

EXPOSURE	WEATHERING INDEX	
	LESS THAN 50	50 AND GREATER
In vertical surfaces		
In contact with earth	MW	SW
Not in contact with earth	MW	SW
In other than vertical surfaces		
In contact with earth	SW	SW
Not in contact with earth	MW	SW

GRADE REQUIREMENTS FOR FACE EXPOSURES
9.40

ASTM STANDARD	MORE SEVERE EXPOSURE		LESS SEVERE EXPOSURE
C 62 Grade	SW	MW	NW
C 216 Grade	SW	MW	—
C 652 Grade	SW	MW	—
C 902 Grade	SX	MX	NX
C 126[a]	—	—	—
C1088 Grade	Exterior	Interior	—
C 32 sewer[b]	SS	SM	—
Grade manhole	MS	MM	—

NOTES

9.39 See Figure 9.45 for U.S. weathering indexes
9.40 a. No requirements for durability.
b. Based on durability and abrasion.

Contributors:
Grace S. Lee, Rippeteau Architects, PC, Washington, DC; Stephen S. Szoke, PE, National Concrete Masonry Association, Herndon, Virginia; Brian E. Trimble, PE, Brick Industry Association, Reston, Virginia.

COLUMNS, PILASTERS, AND BEAMS

TYPICAL SPECIAL PILASTER UNIT FOR USE WITH CONTROL JOINTS
9.41

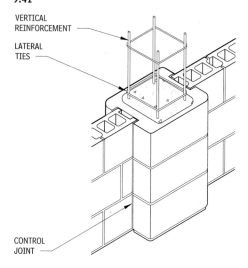

VERTICAL REINFORCEMENT

LATERAL TIES

CONTROL JOINT

REINFORCED BRICK COLUMNS
9.42

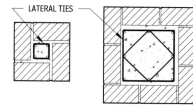

LATERAL TIES

12-IN. SQUARE BRICK COLUMN

20-IN. SQUARE BRICK COLUMN

CMU PILASTER AND EMBEDDED COLUMN
9.43

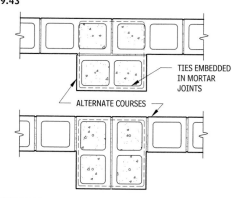

TIES EMBEDDED IN MORTAR JOINTS

ALTERNATE COURSES

CMU PILASTER

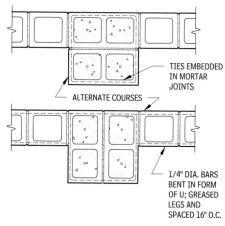

TIES EMBEDDED IN MORTAR JOINTS

ALTERNATE COURSES

1/4" DIA. BARS BENT IN FORM OF U; GREASED LEGS AND SPACED 16" O.C.

CMU EMBEDDED COLUMN

Contributors:
Brian E. Trimble, PE, Brick Industry Association, Reston, Virginia; Stephen S. Szoke, PE, National Concrete Masonry Association, Herndon, Virginia; Grace S. Lee, Rippeteau Architects, PC, Washington, DC.

REINFORCED CLAY MASONRY PILASTERS
9.44

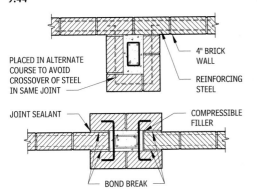

PLACED IN ALTERNATE COURSE TO AVOID CROSSOVER OF STEEL IN SAME JOINT

4" BRICK WALL

REINFORCING STEEL

JOINT SEALANT

COMPRESSIBLE FILLER

BOND BREAK

PRECAST CONCRETE AND CMU BEAMS OR LINTELS
9.45

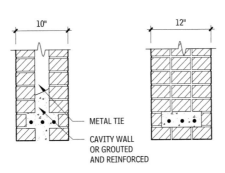

7-5/8"

3-5/8"

4"

1-1/8"

CONCRETE

GROUT FILL

COMMON U-BLOCK

REINFORCING STEEL BAR

DOUBLE CORE

CMU

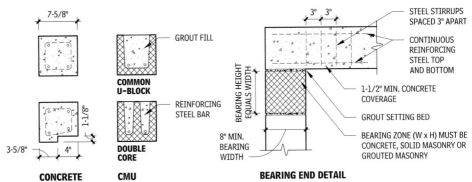

3" 3"

STEEL STIRRUPS SPACED 3" APART

CONTINUOUS REINFORCING STEEL TOP AND BOTTOM

1-1/2" MIN. CONCRETE COVERAGE

GROUT SETTING BED

BEARING ZONE (W x H) MUST BE CONCRETE, SOLID MASONRY OR GROUTED MASONRY

BEARING HEIGHT EQUALS WIDTH

8" MIN. BEARING WIDTH

BEARING END DETAIL

REINFORCED BRICK BEAMS OR LINTELS
9.46

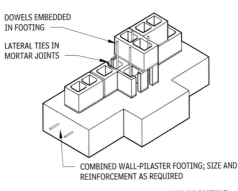

4"   6"   8"   10"   12"

METAL TIE

CAVITY WALL OR GROUTED AND REINFORCED

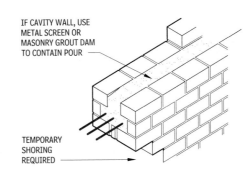

IF CAVITY WALL, USE METAL SCREEN OR MASONRY GROUT DAM TO CONTAIN POUR

TEMPORARY SHORING REQUIRED

COLUMN AND PILASTER CONSTRUCTION
9.47

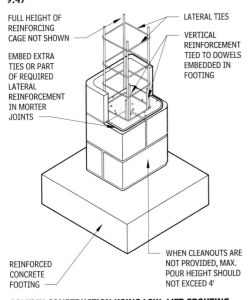

FULL HEIGHT OF REINFORCING CAGE NOT SHOWN

LATERAL TIES

VERTICAL REINFORCEMENT TIED TO DOWELS EMBEDDED IN FOOTING

EMBED EXTRA TIES OR PART OF REQUIRED LATERAL REINFORCEMENT IN MORTER JOINTS

REINFORCED CONCRETE FOOTING

WHEN CLEANOUTS ARE NOT PROVIDED, MAX. POUR HEIGHT SHOULD NOT EXCEED 4'

COLUMN CONSTRUCTION USING LOW-LIFT GROUTING TECHNIQUES

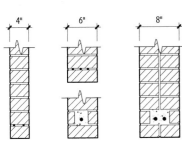

DOWELS EMBEDDED IN FOOTING

LATERAL TIES IN MORTAR JOINTS

COMBINED WALL-PILASTER FOOTING; SIZE AND REINFORCEMENT AS REQUIRED

PILASTER CONSTRUCTION USING LOW-LIFT GROUTING TECHNIQUES

LINTEL REINFORCING REQUIRMENTS
9.48

LINTEL TYPE	CLEAR SPAN (MAX.)	8" BRICK WALL (80 LB/SQ FT)	8" CMU WALL (50 LB/SQ FT)
Reinforced concrete (7-5/8" square section)	4'-0"	4—#3	4—#3
	6'-0"	4—#4	4—#3
	8'-0"	4—#5	4—#4
Concrete masonry unit (7-5/8" square section) nominal 8 × 8 × 16 unit	4'-0"	2—#4	2—#3
	6'-0"	2—#5	2—#4
	8'-0"	2—#6	2—#5

NOTES

9.47 Cut block in first course before laying to form cleanout openings at base of cells to be filled. Remove all mortar droppings, set and inspect vertical reinforcement, and form over opening before filling with grout or concrete. When cleanouts are not provided maximum pour should not exceed 4 ft.

9.48 a. For precast concrete and reinforced concrete masonry unit lintels with no superimposed loads.

b. f'c= 3000 psi concrete and grout; fy = 60,000 psi.

Contributors:
Grace S. Lee, Rippeteau Architects, PC, Washington, DC; Brian E. Trimble, PE, Brick Industry Association, Reston, Virginia; Stephen S. Szoke, PE, National Concrete Masonry Association, Herndon, Virginia

MASONRY ARCHES

MASONRY ARCHES
9.49

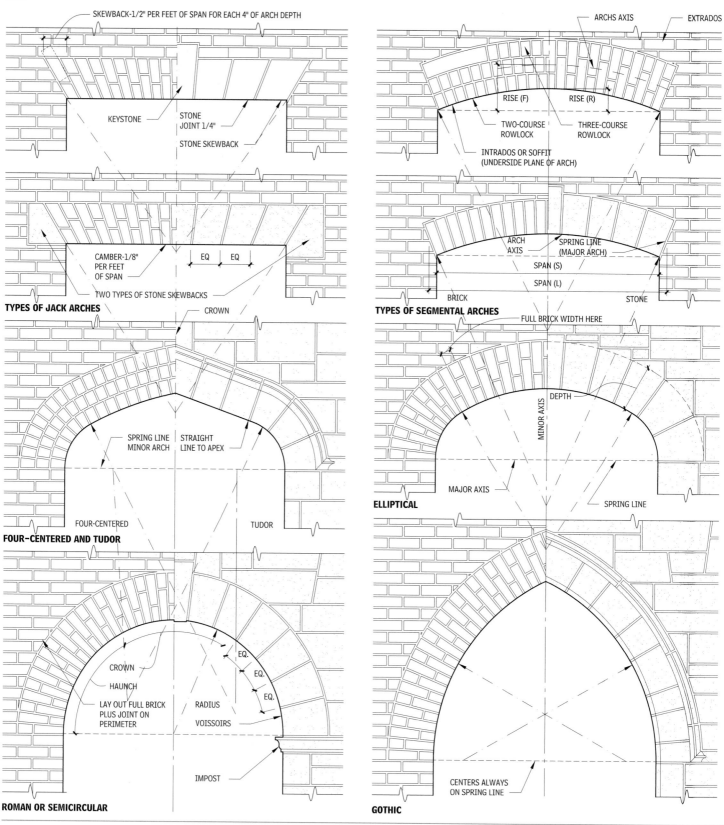

SKEWBACK-1/2" PER FEET OF SPAN FOR EACH 4" OF ARCH DEPTH

KEYSTONE

STONE JOINT 1/4"

STONE SKEWBACK

CAMBER-1/8" PER FEET OF SPAN

EQ   EQ

TWO TYPES OF STONE SKEWBACKS

TYPES OF JACK ARCHES

ARCHS AXIS

EXTRADOS

RISE (F)   RISE (R)

TWO-COURSE ROWLOCK

THREE-COURSE ROWLOCK

INTRADOS OR SOFFIT (UNDERSIDE PLANE OF ARCH)

ARCH AXIS

SPRING LINE (MAJOR ARCH)

SPAN (S)

SPAN (L)

BRICK

STONE

TYPES OF SEGMENTAL ARCHES

CROWN

SPRING LINE MINOR ARCH

STRAIGHT LINE TO APEX

FOUR-CENTERED

TUDOR

FOUR-CENTERED AND TUDOR

FULL BRICK WIDTH HERE

DEPTH

MINOR AXIS

MAJOR AXIS

SPRING LINE

ELLIPTICAL

CROWN

HAUNCH

LAY OUT FULL BRICK PLUS JOINT ON PERIMETER

RADIUS

VOISSOIRS

IMPOST

EQ.

EQ.

EQ.

ROMAN OR SEMICIRCULAR

CENTERS ALWAYS ON SPRING LINE

GOTHIC

NOTES

9.49 a. Walls, piers, or abutments adjacent to masonry must be of sufficient strength to resist horizontal thrusts.

b. Arch is called "pointed" when radii are equal to span, and called "lancet" when radii are greater than span.

Contributors:
Charles George Ramsey, AIA, and Harold Reeve Sleeper, FAIA, New York City, New York.

GLASS UNIT MASONRY

GLASS BLOCK: DESIGN DATA

GENERAL

Glass block is a diverse building material whose many applications exhibit its multifaceted characteristics. The varying forms of glass block—type, thickness, size, shape, and patterns—along with the method of installation can combine to create unique design solutions. Applications range from entire façades, windows, interior dividers, and partitions to skylights, floors, walkways, and stairways. In all applications, glass block units permit the control of light, both natural and artificial, for function or drama. Glass block also allows for control of thermal transmission, noise, dust, and drafts. Thick-faced glass block or solid 3 in. are impact resistant at assist in security applications.

MORTAR

An optimum mortar mix for installing glass block units is one part portland cement, one-half part lime, and four parts sand. Table 9.50 below gives the number of glass blocks that can be installed at that ratio.

GLASS BLOCK/MORTAR BATCH
9.50

SERIES	BLOCK SIZE[a]	BLOCK NUMBER[b]
Regular	4 × 8	350
	6 × 6	350
	8 × 8	260
	12 × 12	190
Thin	4 × 8	450
	6 × 6	450
	8 × 8	335

TYPES OF BLOCKS

The basic glass block unit is made of two halves fused together with a partial vacuum inside. Units may be transparent, translucent, or opaque, and may be also colored; and patterned. Other options may be available, consult the manufacturer.

SQUARE GLASS BLOCK UNITS
9.51

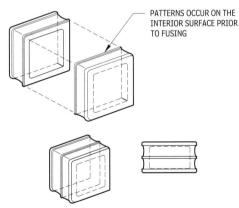

PATTERNS OCCUR ON THE INTERIOR SURFACE PRIOR TO FUSING

Glass block is available in thicknesses ranging from a minimum of 3 in. for solid units to a maximum of 4 in. (nominal) for hollow units.

Some manufacturers provide thick blocks for critical applications where a thick-faced, heavier glass block is needed. These blocks have superior sound transmission rating properties, as their faces are three times as thicker than standard units.

BLOCK FACE THICKNESS COMPARISON
9.52

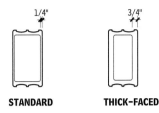

1/4"   3/4"

STANDARD   THICK-FACED

Solar control units have either inserts or exterior coatings to reduce heat gain. Coated units require periodic cleaning to remove alkali and metal ions that can harm the coating. Edge drips are required to prevent moisture rundown on the surface.

A few manufacturers have special shapes to execute corner designs. These units also may be placed together for varying patterns and forms.

Surface decoration may be achieved with fused-on ceramic, etching, or sandblasting.

SOUND TRANSMISSION[a]
9.53

STC[b]	SIZE	ASSEMBLY CONSTRUCTION
31	8″ × 8″ × 3″	Silicone
37[c]	8″ × 8″ × 4″	Mortar
40	8″ × 8″ × 4″ with fibrous filter	Mortar
50	8″ × 8″ × 4″ thick-faced block	Mortar
53	8″ × 8″ × 3″ solid units	Mortar

GLASS BLOCK INSERT OR COATING
9.54

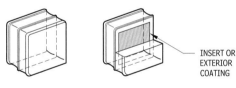

INSERT OR EXTERIOR COATING

TYPICAL THERMAL PERFORMANCE/LIGHT TRANSMISSION[a,c]
9.55

BLOCK TYPE	HEAT TRANSMISSION[b] U-VALUE (BTU/HR FT^2 °F)	THERMAL RESISTANCE[b] R-VALUE (HR FT^2 °F/BTU)	THERMAL EXPANSION COEFFICIENT(/°F)	VISIBLE LIGHT TRANSMISSION (%)	SHADING COEFFICIENT[d]
Standard (3-7/8 inch thick)	0.51 (0.48 with fibrous filter)	1.96 (2.08 with fibrous filter)	47 × 107	75	0.65
Reflective coated	0.51	1.96	47 × 107	5–20	0.20–0.25
Thin (3-1/8 inch thick)	0.57 (0.54 with fibrous filter)	1.75 (1.85 with fibrous filter)	47 × 107	75	0.65
Solid	0.87	1.15	47 × 107	80	
Monolithic glass	1.04	0.96	47 × 107	90	1.00

END BLOCK
9.56

EXPANSION MATERIAL

END BLOCK

2" MAX.

4" MAX.

NOTES

9.50 a. Includes 15 percent waste.
b. Based on a 1/4-in. exposed joint.
9.53 a. Tested in accordance with ASTM E 90, "Standard Test Method for Laboratory Measurement of Airborne Sound Transmission Loss of Building Partitions and Elements."
b. STC rating value in accordance with ASTM E 413, "Classification for Rating Sound Insulation."
c. Test method and STC rating value in accordance with ASTM E 90 and ASTM E 413, accordingly.

9.55 a. Values equal ± 5 percent.
b. Winter night values.
c. To calculate instantaneous heat gain through glass block panels, see *ASHRAE Handbook.*
d. Based on 8-in. square units: ratio of heat gain through glass block panels versus that through a piece of double-strength monolithic glass under specific conditions.
9.56 End block units have a rounded, finished surface on one edge. They may be used to end interior partitions or walls, or serve as space dividers when installed horizontally.

Contributor:
Grace S. Lee, Rippeteau Architects, PC, Washington, DC.

SPECIAL SHAPES (CORNERS)
9.57

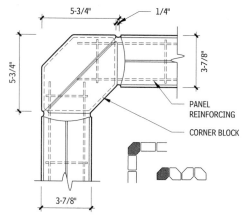

CORNER BLOCK

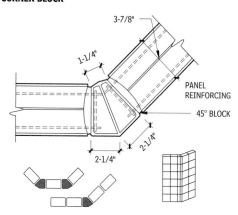

45° BLOCK

GLASS BLOCK PANELS
9.58

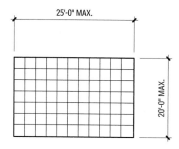

ELEVATION

NUMBER OF BLOCKS FOR 100 SQ. FT. PANEL			
BLOCK SIZE (NOMINAL)	6″	8″	12″
Number of blocks	400	225	100

MAXIMUM PANEL DIMENSIONS
9.59

PERIMETER SUPPORT METHOD	REGULAR			THIN		
	AREA (SQ FT)	HEIGHT (FT)	WIDTH (FT)	AREA (SQ FT)	HEIGHT (FT)	WIDTH (FT)
EXTERIOR						
Channel-type restraint	144	20	25	85	10	25
Panel anchors	144	20	25	85	10	25
Channels or panel anchors with intermediate stiffener	250	20	25	150	20	25
INTERIOR						
Channel-type restraint	250	20	25	150	20	25
Panel anchors	250	20	25	150	20	25

GLASS BLOCK INSTALLATION

Glass block can be used for both interior and exterior applications; connections to structure and the use of expansion material at the separation joints is critical to ensure glass block panels are not subject to loading from adjacent construction. Both interior and exterior panels must be designed for lateral loads. Glass block can be used in many applications including walls, roofs, and floors.

INSTALLATION REQUIREMENTS

- Area of exterior unbraced panel should not exceed 144 sq ft and 250 sq ft for interior unbraced installations. Refer to Figure 9.59 for maximum dimension.
- Indicated maximum exterior panel sizes are based on a design wind load of 20 lb./sq ft with a 2.7 safety factor. Evaluate panel sized and design wind load for specific projects.
- Panels are designed to be mortared at sill, with head and jambs providing for movement and settling. Deflection of lintel at head should be anticipated.
- Movement joints should be installed at change of direction of a multicurved wall, at points of curved wall intersection with straight walls, and at center of curvature in excess of 90 degrees.
- Consult manufacturers for specific design limitations of glass block panels. Thickness of block used also determines maximum panel size.

GLASS BLOCK PANEL COMPONENTS
9.60

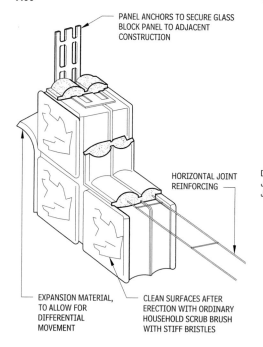

GLASS BLOCK CONTROL JOINT
9.61

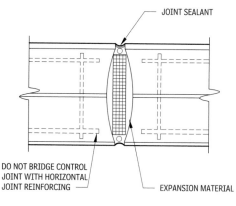

NOTE

9.60 Full bed of mortar typically 1/4 in. wide at face of wall. Mortar to be type S optimum mixture: one part portland cement, one-half part lime, four parts sand.

Contributor:
Grace S. Lee, Rippeteau Architects, PC, Washington, DC.

RADIUS MINIMUMS FOR CURVED PANEL CONSTRUCTION
9.62

BLOCK SIZE	INSIDE RADIUS (IN.)	NUMBER OF BLOCKS IN 90° ARC	JOINT THICKNESS (IN.)	
			INSIDE	OUTSIDE
4″ × 8″	32	13	1/8	5/8
6″ × 6″	48-1/2	13	1/8	5/8
8″ × 8″	65	13	1/8	5/8
12″ × 12″	98-1/2	13	1/8	5/8

CURVED PANEL CONSTRUCTION
9.63

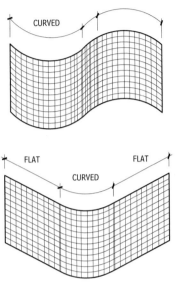

INTERMEDIATE CONTROL JOINTS AND SUPPORTS

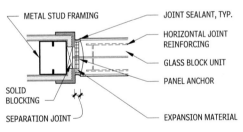

(32" MIN. RAD. 4" x 8" BLOCK)

90° ARC

(48-1/2" MIN. RAD. 6" SQUARE BLOCK)

(65" MIN. RAD. 8" SQUARE BLOCK)

(98-1/2" MIN. RAD. 12" SQUARE BLOCK)

HORIZONTAL JOINT REINFORCING

MINIMUM RADII

DOOR FRAME DETAILS
9.65

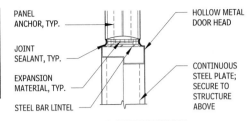

PANEL ANCHOR, TYP.

JOINT SEALANT, TYP.

EXPANSION MATERIAL, TYP.

STEEL BAR LINTEL

HOLLOW METAL DOOR HEAD

CONTINUOUS STEEL PLATE; SECURE TO STRUCTURE ABOVE

HEAD AT DOORFRAME SECTION/ELEVATION

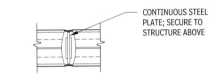

CONTINUOUS STEEL PLATE; SECURE TO STRUCTURE ABOVE

HEAD AT DOOR FRAME PLAN (JOINT ABOVE JAMB)

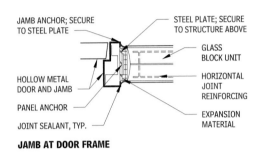

JAMB ANCHOR; SECURE TO STEEL PLATE

HOLLOW METAL DOOR AND JAMB

PANEL ANCHOR

JOINT SEALANT, TYP.

STEEL PLATE; SECURE TO STRUCTURE ABOVE

GLASS BLOCK UNIT

HORIZONTAL JOINT REINFORCING

EXPANSION MATERIAL

JAMB AT DOOR FRAME

INTERIOR CONNECTION DETAILS
9.64

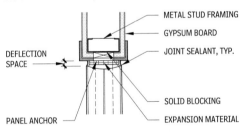

METAL STUD FRAMING

GYPSUM BOARD

JOINT SEALANT, TYP.

SOLID BLOCKING

EXPANSION MATERIAL

DEFLECTION SPACE

PANEL ANCHOR

HEAD AT INTERIOR PARTITION

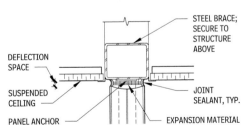

METAL STUD FRAMING

SOLID BLOCKING

SEPARATION JOINT

JOINT SEALANT, TYP.

HORIZONTAL JOINT REINFORCING

GLASS BLOCK UNIT

PANEL ANCHOR

EXPANSION MATERIAL

JAMB AT INTERIOR PARTITION

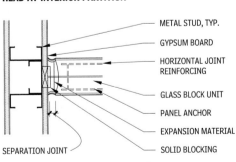

METAL STUD, TYP.

GYPSUM BOARD

HORIZONTAL JOINT REINFORCING

GLASS BLOCK UNIT

PANEL ANCHOR

EXPANSION MATERIAL

SOLID BLOCKING

SEPARATION JOINT

JAMB AT PERPENDICULAR PARTITION

DEFLECTION SPACE

SUSPENDED CEILING

PANEL ANCHOR

STEEL BRACE; SECURE TO STRUCTURE ABOVE

JOINT SEALANT, TYP.

EXPANSION MATERIAL

HEAD AT SUSPENDED CEILING

NOTES

9.63 a. It is suggested that curved areas be separated from flat areas by intermediate control joints and supports, as indicated in these drawings.
b. When straight ladder-type reinforcing is used on curved walls, the innermost parallel wire may be cut periodically and bent to accommodate the curvature of the wall.

Contributor:
Grace S. Lee, Rippeteau Architects, PC, Washington, DC.

STONE ASSEMBLIES

STONE USES AND PROPERTIES

GENERAL

Stone assemblies include both natural and cut stone that can be used in many construction applications. The major factors affecting the suitability and use of stone for construction fall under two broad, but overlapping, categories: physical and structural properties and aesthetic qualities. The three factors of building stone that most influence its selection by design professionals for aesthetic reasons are pattern, texture, and color. Consideration also should be given to cost, availability, weathering characteristics, physical properties, and size limitations.

Stone patterns are highly varied, and provide special features that make building stone a unique material. Texture ranges from coarse fragments to fine grains and crystalline structures. Texture also varies with the hardness of minerals composing the stone. To accurately compare stone colors, the rock color chart published by the Geological Society of America (Boulder, Colorado) is recommended. Samples also may be used to establish acceptable color ranges for a particular installation.

Pattern, texture, and color all are affected by how the stone is fabricated and finished. Granites tend to hold their color and pattern, whereas limestone color and pattern change with exposure. Textures may range from rough and flamed finishes to honed or polished surfaces. The harder the stone, the better it takes and holds a polish.

Stone is obtained by quarrying and has two general shapes: cut and rubble.

- Rubble is irregular in size and shape. Collected natural stone includes excavated stone, field stone and riverbed stone, it may be weathered smooth, but remains irregular and uneven. The second type of rubble, quarry rubble, includes the fragments of stone left over from the cutting and removal of large stone slabs at the quarry. It has freshly broken faces, which may be sharp and angular.
- Cut stone is either dimension stone or cleft-faced stone. Cut stone is delivered from fabricators who have cut and dressed the stone to a specific size, squared to dimension each way, and to a specific thickness. Surface treatments include a rough or natural split face, smooth, slightly textured, or polished finishes. Ashlar is a type of flat-faced dimension stone, generally in small squares or rectangles, with sawed or dressed beds and joints, while dimension stone is typically larger blocks.

PHYSICAL PROPERTIES OF STONE

The physical characteristics of a particular stone must be suitable for its intended use. It is important to determine the physical properties of the actual stone being used rather than using values from a generic table, which can be very misleading. Considerations of the physical properties of the stone being selected include modulus of rupture, shear strength, coefficient of expansion, creep deflection, compressive strength, modulus of elasticity, moisture resistance, and weatherability.

In addition to accessibility and ease of quarrying, building stone must satisfy requirements for strength, hardness, workability, porosity, durability, and appearance.

- Typically, the compressive strength of building stone is many times higher than required by the loads imposed on it in contemporary construction. Flexural and shear strength are relatively low. Both compressive strength and hardness are proportional to silica content.
- Hardness of stone is critically important only in horizontal planes such as flooring and paving, but hardness does have a direct influence on workability. Characteristics may vary from soft sandstone, which is easily scratched, to very hard stones such as granite.
- Workability refers to the ease with which a stone may be sawed, shaped, dressed, or carved, and will directly affect the cost of

production. Workability decreases as the percentage of silica increases. Limestone, for instance, which contains little silica, is easily cut, drilled, and processed. Granite, in contrast, has a high silica content, and is the most difficult stone to cut and finish.

- Porosity, the percentage of void content, affects a stone's absorption of moisture, thus influencing its ability to withstand frost action and repeated freeze/thaw cycles. Pore spaces are usually continuous, and often form microscopic cracks of irregular shape. Sandstone and limestone are more porous than granite and marble. Due to its porosity, stone selection should take into consideration both application and adjacent construction materials, such as sealant, that may cause staining of the stone.
- Closely linked to porosity are grain and texture, which influence the ease with which stones may be split, and for ornamental purposes contribute to aesthetic effects as much as color.
- Durability of stone, or its resistance to wear and weathering, is also considered analogous to silica content. This is perhaps the most important characteristic of stone because it affects the life span of a structure. Granite is more durable than other building stones because it contains more silica.

In terms of practicality and long-term cost, durability is the most important consideration in selecting building stones. Suitability will depend not only on the characteristics of the stone but also on local environmental and climatic conditions. Water is the most active agent in the destruction of stone. In warm, dry climates, almost any stone may be used with good results. Stones of the same general type such as limestone, sandstone, and marble differ greatly in durability based on softness and porosity. Soft, porous stones are more liable to absorb water and to flake or deteriorate in heavy frosts, and may not be suitable in the colder and moister northern climates.

Most stone used for exterior building construction is relatively volume-stable, returning to its original dimensions after undergoing thermal expansion and contraction through a range of temperatures. Some fine-grained, uniformly textured, relatively pure marbles, however, retain small incremental volume increases after each heating cycle. Marble is actually composed of layers of crystals, and repeated thermal and moisture cycles tend to make these crystals loosen and slide apart. The marble becomes less dense when it expands during heating, but does not return to its prior state during the cooling cycle. This irreversible expansion is called *hysteresis*. In relatively thick veneers, the greater expansion on the exposed exterior surface is restrained or accommodated by the unaffected interior mass. In thin veneers, however, dilation of the surface region can easily overcome the restraint of the inner layers, causing a "dishing" effect because the greatest expansion is across the diagonal axis. Expansion of the exterior face of marble panels also increases the porosity of the stone and its vulnerability to attack by atmospheric acids and cyclic freezing.

TYPES OF STONE

The three rock classes are igneous, sedimentary, and metamorphic. Despite their abundant variety, relatively few types of stone are suitable as building materials. Granite, marble, limestone, sandstone, and slate are the most common building stones in the United States. Many others, such as quartzite and serpentine, are used locally or regionally, but to a much lesser extent.

GRANITE

Granite is an igneous rock composed primarily of silica quartz, feldspar, mica, and hornblende. Colors vary from red, pink, brown, buff, gray, and cream to dark green and black. Granite is classified as fine, medium, or coarse grained. It is very hard, strong, and durable, and is noted for its weathering and abrasion resistance. Compressive strength may range from 7700 to 60,000 psi, but ASTM C 615, "Standard Specification for Granite Dimension Stone" requires a minimum of 19,000 psi for acceptable performance in building construction. While the hardness of the stone lends itself to a highly polished surface, it also makes sawing and cutting very

difficult. Granite is used for flooring, paneling, veneer, column facings, stair treads, flagstones, and in landscape applications. Carving or lettering on granite, which was formerly done by hand or pneumatic tools, is now performed by, computer-assisted stone-cutting equipment to achieve a high degree of precision.

LIMESTONE

Limestone is a sedimentary rock, which is durable and easily worked. It consists chiefly of calcium carbonate, but many contain magnesium carbonates in varying proportions, sand or clay, carbonaceous matter, or iron oxides, which may color the stone. The most "pure" form is crystalline limestone, in which calcium carbonate crystals predominate, producing a fairly uniform white or light gray stone of smooth texture. It is highest in strength and lowest in absorption of the various types of limestone. Dolomitic limestone is somewhat crystalline in form, and has a greater variety of texture. Oolitic limestone is noncrystalline, has no cleavage planes, and is very uniform in composition and structure.

The compressive strength of limestone varies from 1800 to 28,000 psi, depending on the silica content. ASTM C 568, "Standard Specification for Limestone Dimension Stone" classifies limestone in three categories: I (low-density); II (medium-density); and III (high-density), with minimum required compressive strengths of 1,800, 4,000, and 8,000 psi, respectively. Limestone is much softer, more porous, and more absorptive than granite. Although it is quite soft when first taken from the ground, limestone weathers hard upon exposure. Its durability is greatest in drier climates.

Impurities affect the color of limestone. Iron oxides produce reddish or yellowish tones, while organic materials such as peat give a gray tint. Limestone textures are graded as:

- A – Statuary
- B – Select
- C – Standard
- D – Rustic
- E – Variegated
- F – Old Gothic

Grades A, B, C, and D come in buff or gray, and vary in grain from fine to coarse. Grade E is a mixture of buff and gray, and is of unselected grain size. Grade F is a mixture of D and E and includes stone with seams and markings.

Limestone is used as cut stone for veneer, caps, lintels, copings, sills, and moldings, and as ashlar with either rough or finished faces. Veneer panels or slabs may be sliced in thicknesses ranging from 1 in. to 6 in. and face sizes from 3 ft by 5 ft to 5 ft by 14 ft. As panel size increases, panel thickness must increase as well. Collected and quarry rubble are often used as rustic veneers on residential and low-rise commercial buildings. Travertine is a porous limestone characterized by small pockets or voids. The pockets common to travertine may be filled to provide a consistent surface, prior to polishing. This natural and unusual texturing presents an attractive decorative surface highly suited to facing materials and veneer slabs.

The denser varieties of limestone, including travertine, can be polished, and for that reason are sometimes classed as marble. The dividing line between limestone and marble is often difficult to determine.

MARBLE

Marble is a crystallized, metamorphic form of noncrystalline limestone or dolomite. Its texture is naturally fine, permitting a highly polished surface. Marble is found in a wide range of colors, and its crystalline structure adds depth and luster to a polished surface. Pure marbles are white, without the pigmentation caused by mineral oxides. Brecciated marbles are made up of angular and rounded fragments embedded in a colored paste or cementing medium.

Marble often has compressive strengths as high as 20,000 psi, and when used in dry climates or in areas protected from precipitation,

---

Contributor:
Christine Beall, NCARB, CCS, Austin, Texas.

the stone is quite durable. Some varieties, however, deteriorate by weathering or exposure to industrial fumes and are suitable only for interior work. ASTM C 503, "Standard Specification for Marble Dimension Stone (Exterior)" covers four marble classifications, each with a minimum required compressive strength of 7500 psi: I, Calcite; II, Dolomite; III, Serpentine; and IV, Travertine. More than 200 imported and domestic marbles are available in the United States. Each has properties and characteristics that make it suitable for different types of construction.

Marbles are classified as A, B, C, or D on the basis of working qualities, uniformity, flaws, and imperfections. For exterior applications, only group A, highest-quality materials should be used. The other groups are less durable and therefore less suitable for use in exterior unprotected areas. Group B marbles have less favorable working properties than Group A, and will have occasional natural faults requiring limited repair. Group C marbles have uncertain variations in working qualities; contain flaws, voids, veins, and lines of separation; and will always require some repair (known as sticking, waxing, filling, and reinforcing). Group D marbles have an even higher proportion of natural structural variations requiring repair, and have great variation in working qualities.

Marble is available as rough or finished dimension stone, as thin veneer slabs for wall and column facings, flooring, partitions, tiles, and other decorative surface work. Veneer slabs may be cut in thicknesses from 3/4 in. to 2 in. Light transmission and translucence diminish as thickness increases.

SLATE

Slate is a metamorphic rock, formed from sedimentary deposits of clay and shale. Slates containing large quantities of mica are stronger and more elastic than clay slates. The texture of slate is fine and compact, with very minute crystallization. It is characterized by distinct cleavage planes, permitting easy splitting of the stone into slabs 1/4 in. or more in thickness. Used in this form, slate provides an extremely durable material for flooring, roofing, sills, stair treads, and facings. ASTM C 629, "Standard Specification for Slate Dimension Stone" requires that both Type I exterior and Type II interior slate have a minimum modulus of rupture of 9000 psi across the grain, and 7200 psi along the grain.

Small quantities of other mineral ingredients give color to the various slates. Carbonaceous materials or iron sulfides produce dark colors such as black, blue, and gray; iron oxide produces red and purple; and chlorite produces green tints. "Select" slate is uniform in color and more costly than "ribbon" slate, which contains stripes of darker colors.

SANDSTONE

Sandstone is a sedimentary rock formed of sand or quartz grains. Its hardness and durability depend primarily on the type of cementing agent present. If cemented with silica and hardened under pressure, the stone is light in color, strong and durable. If the cementing agent is largely iron oxide, the stone is red or brown, and is softer and more easily cut. Lime and clay are less durable binders subject to deterioration by natural weathering. Sandstone can be categorized by grain size and cementing agent. Siliceous sandstone is cemented together with silica. Many siliceous sandstones contain iron, which is oxidized by acidic pollutants (or acidic cleaners), which turn the stone brown. Ferruginous sandstone is cemented together with iron oxide, so it is naturally red to deep brown in color. Calcareous sandstone is cemented together with calcium carbonate, which is sensitive to acids and can deteriorate rapidly in a polluted environment. Dolomitic sandstone is cemented together with dolomite, which is more resistant to acid. Argillaceous sandstone contains large amounts of clay, which can quickly deteriorate simply from exposure to rain.

FORMS OF BUILDING STONE
9.66

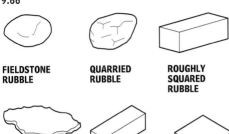

FIELDSTONE RUBBLE   **QUARRIED RUBBLE**   **ROUGHLY SQUARED RUBBLE**

MOSAIC FLAGSTONE   **ASHLAR CUT DIMENSION STONE**   **SQUARED FLAGSTONE**

ASTM C 616, "Standard Specification for Quartz-Based Dimension Stone" includes three stone classifications. Type I, sandstone, is characterized by a minimum of 60 percent free silica content; Type II, quartzite sandstone, by 90 percent free silica; and Type III, quartzite, by 95 percent free silica content. As a reflection of these varying compositions, minimum compressive strengths are 2000 psi, 10,000 psi, and 20,000 psi, respectively. Absorption characteristics also differ significantly, ranging from 20 percent for Type I to 3 percent for Type II and 1 percent for Type III. When first taken from the ground, sandstone contains large quantities of water, which make it easy to cut. As the moisture evaporates, the stone becomes considerably harder.

Sandstones vary in color from buff, pink, and crimson to greenish brown, cream, and blue-gray. Both fine and coarse textures are found, some of which are highly porous and therefore low in durability. The structure of sandstone lends itself to smooth and textured finishes for cut stone typically used in veneers, moldings, sills, and copings. Sandstone is also available in rubble masonry.

FINISHES

Much of the stone that is produced for building construction has a sawn finish, but stone may also be further dressed with hand or machine tools into hammered finishes, polished finishes, honed or rubbed finishes. Honing is accomplished by rubbing the stone surface with an abrasive after it has been planed. Larger surfaces are done by machine, smaller surfaces and moldings by hand. Polished surfaces require repeated rubbing with increasingly finer abrasives. Only granite, marble, and some very dense limestones will take and hold a high polish. Power-driven lathes have been developed for turning columns, balusters, and other members that are round in section.

Hand-tooling is the oldest method of stone dressing. Working with pick, hammer, and chisels, the mason dresses each successive face of a stone, giving it the desired finish and texture. Hand-applied finishes include the bush-hammered, patent-hammered, pick-pointed, crandalled, and peen-hammered surface. Many of these finishes are now applied with pneumatic rather than hand tools, resulting in a more uniform surface. Ornate carving is still done by hand, both for new construction and for restoration and rehabilitation projects, although it is sometimes aided by pneumatic chisels.

Granite can be fabricated with a flame cut, or thermal finish to produce a fractured surface texture. It is most often selectively applied to portions of a surface to contrast with polished finish areas.

STONE MASONRY PATTERNS AND VENEER

NOTES

- Structural bond refers to the physical tying together of load-bearing and veneer portions of a composite wall. Structural bond can be accomplished with metal ties or with stone units set as headers into the backup.
- Ashlar masonry is composed of squared-off building stone units of various sizes. Cut ashlar is dressed to specific design dimensions at the mill. Ashlar is often used in random lengths and heights.
- Ties and anchors must be made of noncorrosive material. Chromium-nickel stainless steel Types 302 and 304 and eraydo alloy zinc are the most resistant to corrosion and staining. Use stainless steel Type 316 in highly corrosive environments. Copper, brass, and bronze will stain under some conditions. Local building codes often govern the types of metal that may be used for stone anchors.
- Nonstaining cement mortar should be used on porous and light-colored stones. At corners use extra ties and, when possible, larger stones. Joints for rough work are usually 1/2 in. to 1-1/2 in. and 3/8 to 3/4 in. for ashlar. Prevent electrochemical reaction between different metals combined in the same assembly by properly isolating or coating them.

RUBBLE STONE MASONRY PATTERNS—ELEVATIONS
9.67

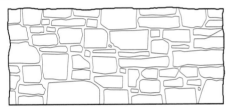

UNCOURSED ROUGHLY SQUARE PATTERN

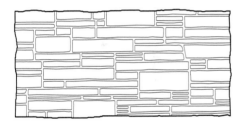

UNCOURSED LEDGE ROCK PATTERN

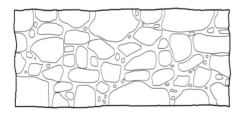

UNCOURSED FIELDSTONE PATTERN

Contributors:
The McGuire & Shook Corporation, Indianapolis, Indiana; Christine Beall, NCARB, CCS, Autsin, Texas.

**CUT STONE MASONRY PATTERNS—ELEVATIONS
9.68**

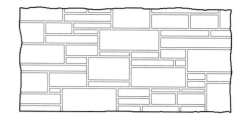

RANDOM BROKEN COURSED ASHLAR

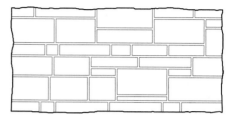

RANDOM COURSED ASHLAR

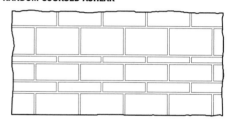

COURSED ASHLAR - RUNNING BOND

**CUT STONE MASONRY HEIGHT PATTERNS—
ELEVATIONS
9.69**

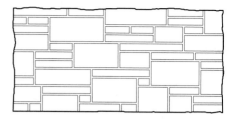

**THREE-HEIGHT PATTERN (15% AT 2-1/4 IN.;
40% AT 5 IN.; 45% AT 7-3/4 IN.)**

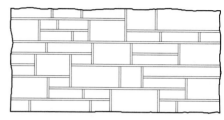

**TWO-HEIGHT PATTERN (40% AT 2-1/4 IN.;
60% AT 5 IN.)**

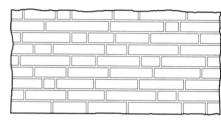

ONE-HEIGHT PATTERN (SINGLE RISE)

**INSTALLATION DETAILS
9.70**

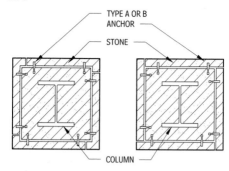

SQUARE COLUMNS

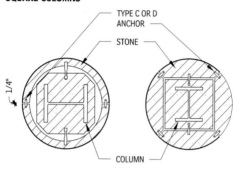

ROUND/QUADRANT COLUMNS

**ANCHORS
9.71**

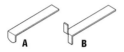

STONE TO STRUCTURE **STONE TO STONE**

**TYPICAL STONE VENEER SECTIONS
9.72**

CORROSION-RESISTANT
FASTENER LOCATED
WITHIN 1/2 IN. OF 90°
BEND IN ANCHOR

BACKUP WALL

AIR SPACE

WEATHER
BARRIER

NONCORROSIVE
ANCHOR

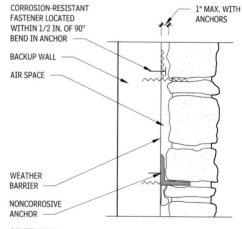

1" MAX. WITH
ANCHORS

CAVITY WALL

WEATHER
BARRIER

STONE
VENEER

METAL
LATH

BACKUP
WALL

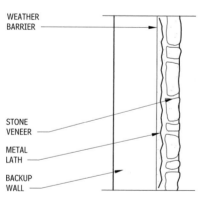

THIN VENEERED MASONRY ON METAL LATH

Contributors:
George M. Whiteside, III, AIA, and James D. Lloyd, Kennett Square,
Pennsylvania; Building Stone Institute, New York City, New York;
Alexander Keyes, Rippeteau Architects, PC, Washington, DC; Christine
Beall, NCARB, CCS, Austin, Texas.

STONE DETAILS

TYPICAL STONE JOINT DIMENSIONS
9.73

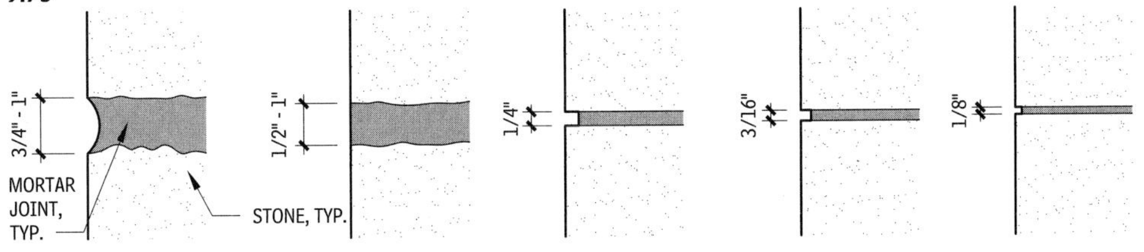

3/4" - 1"

MORTAR JOINT, TYP.

STONE, TYP.

1/2" - 1"

1/4"

3/16"

1/8"

RUBBLE   **CUT STONE**   **GENERAL USE**   **FINE WORK**   **SPECIAL INTERIOR**

RUSTICATED JOINTS
9.74

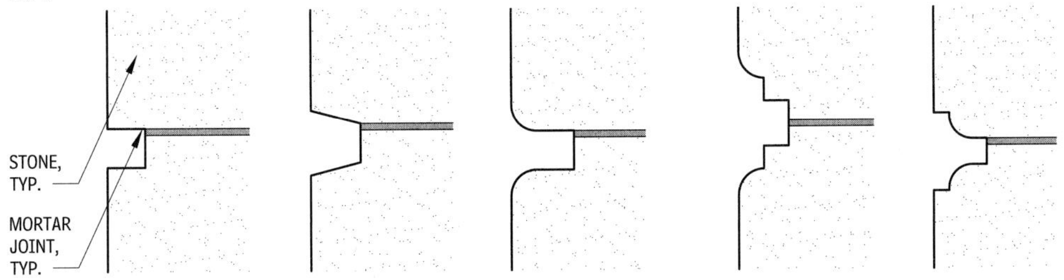

STONE, TYP.

MORTAR JOINT, TYP.

TYPICAL JOINT PROFILES
9.75

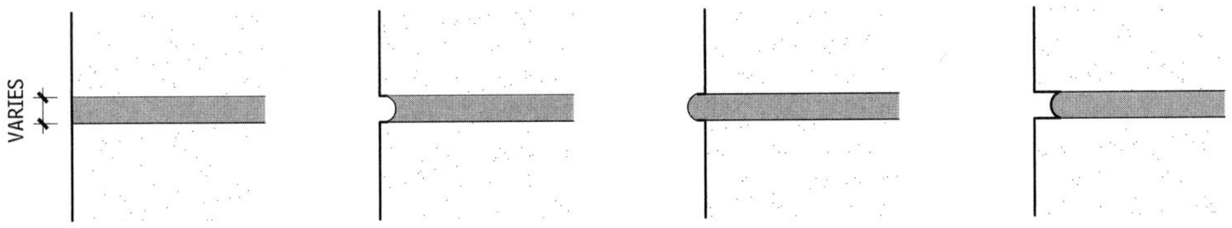

VARIES

FLUSH   **CONCAVE**   **BEAD**   **RECESS-GROOVED**

STONE SILL TYPES
9.76

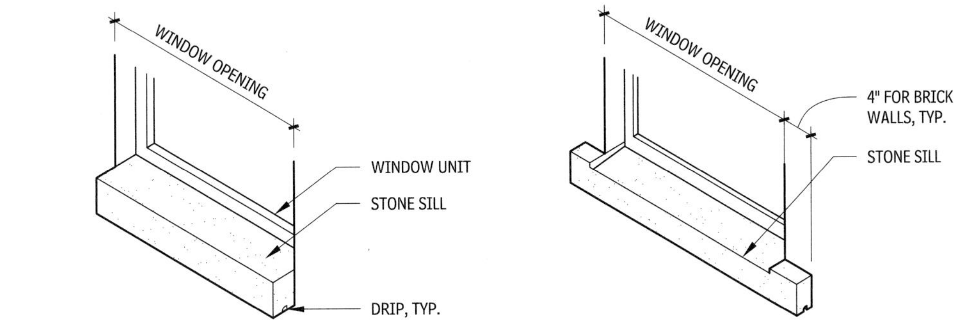

WINDOW OPENING

WINDOW UNIT

STONE SILL

DRIP, TYP.

SLIP SILL

WINDOW OPENING

4" FOR BRICK WALLS, TYP.

STONE SILL

LUG SILL

STONE LUG SILL PROFILES
9.77

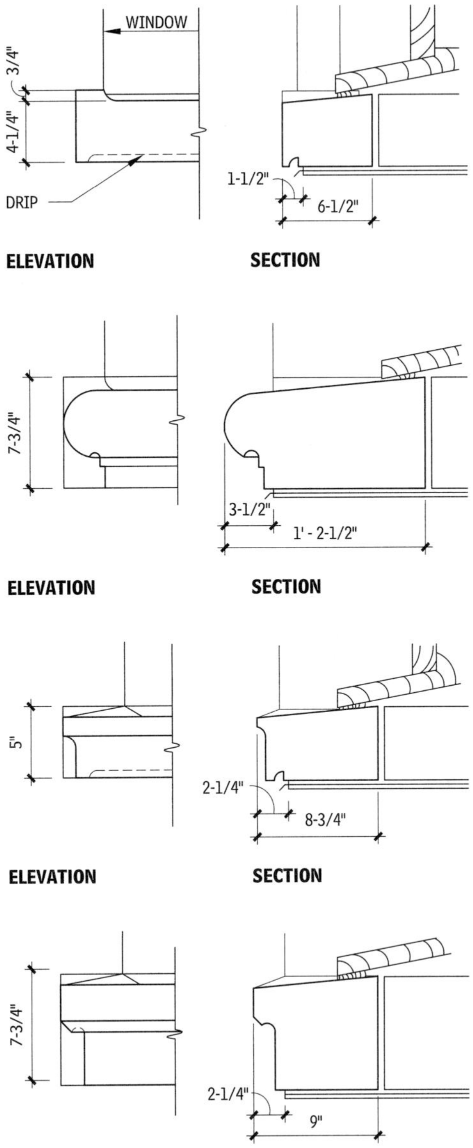

WINDOW

3/4"

4-1/4"

DRIP

1-1/2"

6-1/2"

ELEVATION   **SECTION**

7-3/4"

3-1/2"

1' - 2-1/2"

ELEVATION   **SECTION**

5"

2-1/4"

8-3/4"

ELEVATION   **SECTION**

7-3/4"

2-1/4"

9"

ELEVATION   **SECTION**

SEE ALSO

Architectural Concrete Unit Masonry
Clay Unit Masonry
Concrete Unit Masonry
Glass Unit Masonry
Masonry Anchorage and Reinforcing
Masonry Cavity Drainage, Weepholes, and Vents
Masonry Control and Expansion Joints
Masonry Embedded Flashing
Masonry Grouting
Masonry Mortaring
Prefaced Concrete Unit Masonry
Stone Assemblies
Unit Masonry

Contributor:
Christine Beall, NCARB, CCS, Austin, Texas.

10

METALS

INTRODUCTION

Metals are an integral part of world development. From the earliest discovery to the latest and most esoteric materials, knowledge of the properties and applications of metals has increased and created a continuing challenge to find new and improved uses.

Steel has evolved from the earliest cast iron and wrought iron, which still have applications and current usage, to a multitude of grades obtained by alloying and heat-treating. The properties of some grades depend on adding elements such as nickel and chromium to obtain a family of stainless steels; other grades rely on various chemicals to obtain strength characteristics. Desired ductility is obtained by controlling carbon content.

From the tiniest staple used to adhere sheets of paper to the huge columns installed to support skyscrapers, steel is available in many forms, including wire, rod, pipe, tube, sheet, plate, and rolled structural sections.

Hot-rolled steel is used for heavy structural members. Cold-formed steel applications include steel decking, cold-formed metal framing, cold-formed metal joist framing, structural metal stud framing, slotted channel framing, and cold-formed metal trusses. The high strength-to-weight ratio obtained with thin profiles is one of cold-formed steel's benefits.

Sheet and strip steel can be formed, providing lightweight structural properties for use in building components, door stiffeners, and vehicles. Expanded metal gratings, treads, and screens are made by slitting and stretching steel sheets. Sheets are also used with internal stiffeners to provide hollow metal doors. Thicker plates can be welded together to form shapes larger than those created by rolling. Plates and angles connected by rivets are still in use after many years of service, but now steel plates are welded together to obtain the desired shape.

Stainless steel may be a preferred metal when corrosion resistance is important. Hot-dip galvanizing, and a variety of coatings, are acceptable and proven methods to resist corrosion, when metal is not exposed to excess moisture or other chemicals. Many old steel structures that have been properly maintained are still in service.

Steel specifications are established by ASTM International (ASTM). These standards, as well as standards for the other metals, are developed by consensus committees comprised of producer, user, and general-interest members.

For years, sheet and strip thickness was designated by gauge. This designation does not, however, accurately reflect current industry terminology because gauge sizes may vary by material. Therefore, ASTM, American National Standards Institute (ANSI), American Iron and Steel Institute (AISI), National Association of Architectural Metal Manufacturers (NAAMM), and other standards organizations have discontinued the use of gauge to designate thickness, and instead, use a minimum thickness with tolerance.

Many of the sheet steel standards for hot-rolled, cold-rolled, and zinc-coated steels have been combined into three standards. Thus, the hot-rolled sheet steel standard now covers commercial steels, drawing steels, and high-strength, low-alloy steels. This requires the design professional to identify which designation, type, and grade is desired. The same applies to the cold-rolled steel sheet standard and the zinc-coated standard for galvanized and galvannealed steels. The new designations provide the necessary information, including chemical and mechanical properties, so the user can select the appropriate steel for the end application.

Based on their characteristics, all metals—steel, stainless steel, aluminum, copper alloys (bronze and brass), titanium, and other nonferrous metals—provide the design professional with an palette of materials, which when combined with a consideration of availability, cost, and effectiveness enable creation of either a simple or a complex structure.

The information in this chapter should be supplemented by literature available from many associations, among them: AISI, Aluminum Association, American Institute of Steel Construction, ANSI, ASTM, Copper Development Association, Nickel Development Institute, and NAAMM.

Contributor:
Edward R. Estes, Jr., PE, Techinical Concultant, National Association of Architectural Metal Manufacturers, Norfolk, Virginia.

METAL MATERIALS

PROPERTIES OF METALS

Metals and their alloys are classified in two broad categories: ferrous and nonferrous. Ferrous metals' main component is iron, and nonferrous metal alloys normally do not contain iron.

FERROUS METALS

Iron, steel, and their alloys are usually the most cost-effective metal choice for structural applications.

Iron that contains no trace of carbon is soft, ductile, and easily worked, but it rusts in a relatively short period of time and is susceptible to corrosion by most acids.

The characteristics of cast iron vary widely among the six basic types: gray, malleable, ductile, white, compacted graphite, and high-alloy iron. All cast irons have high compressive strengths, but tensile and yield strengths vary widely depending on basic type. Cast iron is relatively corrosion-resistant but cannot be hammered or beaten into shapes.

Gray irons are rather brittle because they have a high carbon and silicon content. However, castings of gray iron are excellent for damping purposes (i.e., absorbing vibrations). They are produced in eight ASTM classes or grades, with tensile-strength ratings from 20,000 to 60,000 psi. Applications include decorative shapes, such as fences and posts, gratings, and stair components, as well as utility uses such as manhole covers and fire hydrants.

Malleable iron, which is more expensive than gray iron, has been used for decades in applications that require durability and high ductility. This low-carbon white iron is cast, reheated, and slowly cooled, or annealed, to improve its workability.

Ductile iron is made by adding magnesium to molten iron shortly before the metal is poured into molds. The magnesium alters the surface-tension mechanism of the molten iron and precipitates the carbon out as small spheres, instead of flakes, which make the iron casting more ductile. Ductile iron is less brittle, stiffer, stronger, and more shock-resistant than gray iron. Ductile iron castings are more expensive than gray iron but usually less than malleable iron. Ductile iron is the fastest-growing segment of the metal casting industry.

Ductile irons are produced in strength ratings from 55,000 to 130,000 psi. Ductile castings using a special austempering heat-treating process offer much higher tensile strengths, ranging from 125,000 to 230,000 psi. Called ADI castings, they rival or surpass certain alloy steel castings in tensile and yield strengths.

White iron castings, which are extremely hard and brittle, are used primarily in industrial machinery parts that experience high wear and require abrasion resistance.

The characteristics of compacted graphite iron fall between those of gray and ductile iron. The properties of this metal are so difficult to control during production that very few metal casters manufacture it.

High-alloy irons are gray, ductile, or white irons with an alloy content of 3 percent to more than 30 percent. Their properties are significantly different from those of unalloyed irons.

Wrought iron or steel is relatively soft, corrosion- and fatigue-resistant, and machinable. It is easily worked, making it ideal for railings, grilles, fences, screens, and various types of decorative metal. It is commercially available in bars, rods, tubing, sheets, and plates.

Carbon steel is iron that contains low to medium amounts of carbon. Higher carbon content increases metal strength and hardness but reduces its ductility and weldability. The corrosion resistance of carbon steels is improved by galvanizing, which is a hot-zinc dipping process, or applying an organic coating. Some architectural uses include structural shapes such as welded fabrications or castings, metal framing and joists, fasteners, wall grilles, and ceiling suspension grids.

High-strength low-alloy (HSLA) steels have better corrosion resistance than carbon steels, and they are chosen when weight is a consideration and higher strength is specified. Low-alloy steels are seldom used in exterior architectural applications that involve water runoff because adjacent materials could become stained with rust.

Typical elements used to modify steel include the following:

- Aluminum, for surface hardening.
- Chromium, for corrosion resistance.
- Copper, for atmospheric corrosion resistance.
- Manganese in small amounts, for additional hardening; in larger amounts, for better wear resistance.
- Molybdenum, combined with other metals such as chromium and nickel, to increase corrosion resistance and raise tensile strength without reducing ductility.
- Nickel, to increase tensile strength without reducing ductility; in high concentrations, nickel improves corrosion resistance.
- Silicon, to strengthen low-alloy steels and improve oxidation resistance; larger amounts produce hard, brittle castings that are resistant to corrosive chemicals.
- Sulfur, for free machining.
- Titanium, to prevent intergranular corrosion of stainless steels.
- Tungsten, vanadium, and cobalt for hardness and corrosion resistance.

Stainless steels are at least 11.5 percent chromium. Nickel is added to boost atmospheric corrosion resistance; molybdenum is added when maximum corrosion resistance is needed, such as when iron will come into contact with saltwater. Stainless steel is used in construction for flashing, coping, fasciae, wall panels, floor plates, gratings, handrails, hardware, fasteners, and anchors. Decorative shapes and statuary can be cast in stainless steel.

NONFERROUS METALS

Nonferrous metals and their alloys can be categorized into seven major groups for architectural applications: those based on aluminum, copper (pure copper, brasses, and bronzes), lead, zinc, tin, nickel, and magnesium. Another approach is to divide nonferrous alloys into two groups: heavy metals (copper-, zinc-, lead-, and nickel-based) and light metals (aluminum- and magnesium-based).

ALUMINUM

The nonferrous metal workhorse for architectural applications is aluminum. It has good forming and casting characteristics and offers good corrosion resistance. When exposed to air, aluminum does not oxidize progressively because a hard, thin oxide coating forms on the surface and seals the metal from its environment.

Aluminum and its alloys, numbering in the hundreds, are widely available in common commercial forms. Aluminum alloy sheets can be formed, drawn, stamped, or spun. Many wrought or cast aluminum alloys can be welded, brazed, or soldered, and aluminum surfaces readily accept a wide variety of finishes, both mechanical and chemical.

Although it is light in weight, commercially pure aluminum has a tensile strength of about 13,000 psi. Most aluminum alloys lose strength at elevated temperatures. At subzero temperatures, on the other hand, aluminum is stronger than at room temperature but no less ductile. Cold-forming the metal may nearly double its tensile strength. Aluminum can be further strengthened by alloying it with other elements such as manganese, silicon, copper, magnesium, zinc, or lithium. The manganese-based aluminum alloy 3003 is used for roofing, sheet metal, siding, and electrical conduit.

BRASS, COPPER, AND BRONZE

Good thermal and electrical conductivity, corrosion resistance, and easy forming and joining make copper and its alloys useful in construction. However, copper and many of its alloys have relatively low strength-to-weight ratios, and their strength is even further reduced at elevated temperatures. These metals are offered in rod, plate, strip, sheet, and tube shapes; forgings; castings; and electrical wire.

These metals can be grouped according to composition in several general categories: copper, high-copper alloys, and many types of brass and bronze. Monel metal is a copper-nickel alloy that offers excellent corrosion resistance, and is often used for corrosion-resistant fasteners.

Bronze was originally a copper-tin alloy, but today aluminum bronzes, silicon bronzes, and leaded phosphor bronzes are more common. Phosphor bronze is a copper-tin-phosphorus alloy, and leaded phosphor bronze is composed of copper, lead, tin, and phosphorus.

Brass is copper with zinc as its principal alloying element. It is important to know that some brass alloys may be called bronzes even though they have little or no tin in them. Some common nonbronze brass alloys are commercial bronze (90 percent copper, 10 percent zinc), naval brass (60 percent copper, 29 percent zinc, and 1 percent tin), Muntz metal (60 percent copper, 40 percent zinc), and manganese bronze (58 percent copper, 39 percent zinc, and 1 percent tin and iron). When a metal is identified as bronze, the alloy may not contain zinc or nickel; if it does, it is probably brass. Architectural brasses and bronzes are actually all brasses; they are used for doors, windows, door and window frames, railings, trim and grilles, and finish hardware. Muntz metal, also called malleable brass, is a bronze alloy resembling extruded architectural bronze in color. It is available in sheet and strip and is used in flat surfaces in architectural compositions in connection with extruded architectural bronze.

Copper-based alloys characteristically form adherent films that are relatively impervious to corrosion and protect the base metal from

TYPES AND PROPERTIES OF BRASS
10.1

NAME	ARCHITECTURAL BRONZE	COMMERCIAL BRONZE	MUNTZ METAL
Composition (%)			
Copper (Cu)	56.5	90.0	60.0
Zinc (Zn)	41.25	10.0	40.0
Lead (Pb)	2.25		
Color	Bronze	Bronze	Light yellow
Cold workability	Very poor	Excellent	Fair
Machinability	Good	Poor	Good
Weldability	Poor	Gas, carbon arc, metal arc	Gas, carbon arc, metal arc, spot and seam welding for thin sheets
Hot workability (and soldering and polishing)	Very good	Very good	Very good
Other properties	Excellent forging and free-machining	Very ductile	High strength; low ductility

Contributors:
Edward R. Estes, Jr., PE, Technical Consultant, National Association of Architectural Metal Manufacturers, Norfolk, Virginia; Robert C. Rodgers, PE, Richmond Heights, Ohio.

further attack. In exterior applications certain alloys darken rather rapidly, from brown to black. Under most outdoor weather conditions, however, copper surfaces, such as roofs or statuary, develop a blue-green patina. Lacquer coatings can help retain the original alloy color.

LEAD

An extremely dense metal, lead is corrosion-resistant and easily worked. Alloys are added to it to improve properties such as hardness and strength. Typical applications of lead include roof and wall accessories, sound and vibration control, and radiation protection. It can be combined with tin alloy to plate iron or steel, which is commonly called terneplate.

It is important to note that lead vapors and dust are toxic if ingested, so care must be taken regarding how and where this metal is used.

ZINC

Although it is corrosion-resistant in water and air, zinc is brittle and low in strength. Its major use is in galvanizing (dipping hot iron or steel in molten zinc), although zinc is also used to create sand-cast or die-cast components. Major building industry uses are roofing, flashing, nails, plumbing hardware, galvanizing structural components, and decorative shapes.

TIN

Key properties of tin are its low melting point (450°F), relative softness, good formability, and readiness to form alloys. Principal uses for tin are as a constituent of solder, a coating for steel (tinplate, terneplate), and an alloy with other metals that can be cast, rolled, extruded, or atomized. Tin is most popular as an alloy for copper, antimony, lead, bismuth, silver, and zinc. Pewter alloys contain 1 to 8 percent antimony and 0.5 to 3 percent copper. Alloy metal in tin solders ranges from 40 percent lead to no lead and 3.5 percent silver.

NICKEL

Whitish in color, nickel is used for plating other metals or as a base for chromium plating. Nickel polishes well and does not tarnish. It is also widely applied as an additive in iron and steel alloys, as well as other metal alloys. Nickel-iron castings are more ductile and more resistant to corrosion than conventional cast iron. Adding nickel makes steel more resistant to impact.

CHROMIUM

A hard, steel-gray metal, chromium is commonly used to plate other metals, including iron, steel, brass, and bronze. Plated cast shapes can be brightly polished and do not tarnish. Several steel alloys, such as stainless plate, contain as much as 18 percent chromium. Chromium does not rust, which makes chromium alloys excellent for exterior uses.

MAGNESIUM

Lightest of all metals used in construction, pure magnesium is not strong enough for general structural functions. For comparison, if a block of steel weighs 1000 lbs, equal volumes of aluminum and magnesium weigh 230 lbs and 186 lbs, respectively. Combining other metals such as aluminum with magnesium results in lightweight alloy materials used in ladders, furniture, hospital equipment, and automobile wheels.

METAL CORROSION

Corrosion, which is caused by galvanic action, occurs between dissimilar metals or between metals and other materials when sufficient moisture is present to carry an electrical current. The galvanic series shown in Table 10.3 is a useful indicator of corrosion susceptibility caused by galvanic action. The metals listed are arranged in order from the least noble (most reactive to corrosion) to the most noble (least reactive to corrosion). The farther apart two metals are on the list, the greater the deterioration of the less noble metal will be if the two come in contact under adverse conditions.

Metal deterioration also occurs when metal comes in contact with chemically active materials, particularly when moisture is present. For example, aluminum corrodes when in direct contact with concrete or mortar, and steel corrodes when in contact with certain treated woods.

WEIGHTS OF METALS FOR BUILDINGS
10.2

MATERIAL	SPECIFIC GRAVITY	DENSITY	
		(LB/CU FT)	(LB/CU IN.)
Magnesium	1.76	110	0.064
Aluminum	2.77	173	0.100
Zinc	7.14	446	0.258
Cast iron	7.22	450	0.260
Wrought iron	7.70	480	0.278
Steel	7.85	490	0.283
Brass	8.47	529	0.306
Copper and bronze	8.92	556	0.322
Lead	11.35	708	0.410

THE GALVANIC SERIES
10.3

Anode (least noble) +	Magnesium, magnesium alloys
	Zinc
	Aluminum 1100
	Cadmium
	Aluminum 2024-T4
	Steel or iron, cast iron
	Chromium iron (active)
	Ni-Resist
	Type 304, 316 stainless (active)
	Hastelloy "C"
	Lead, tin
Electric current flows from positive (+) to negative (−)	Nickel (active)
	Hastelloy "B"
	Brasses, copper, bronzes, copper-nickel alloys, monel
	Silver solder
	Nickel (passive)
	Chromium iron (passive)
	Type 304, 316 stainless (passive)
	Silver
	Titanium
Cathode (most noble) −	Graphite, gold, platinum

Pitting and concentration cell corrosion are other types of metal deterioration. Pitting takes place when particles or bubbles of gas are deposited on a metal surface. Oxygen deficiency under these deposits sets up anodic areas, which cause pitting. Concentration cell corrosion is similar to galvanic corrosion; the difference is in the electrolytes. Concentration cell corrosion can be produced by differences in ion concentration, oxygen concentration, or foreign matter adhering to the surface.

SHAPING AND FABRICATION OF METALS

Many different manufacturing processes are applied to metal to produce structural forms and shapes required in the construction and ornamentation of buildings.

- Rolling hot or cold metal between pressurized rollers produces most of the readily available, standard construction material shapes. Baked enamel-coated aluminum is cold rolled to make siding and gutters.
- In the extruding process, heated metal ingots or bars are pushed through a die orifice to produce a wide variety of simple and complex shapes. Sizes are limited only by the size or capacity of the die.

- Casting is a process in which molten metal is poured into molds or forced into dies and allowed to solidify in the shape of the mold or die. The casting process is used with virtually all metals; however, surface quality and physical characteristics are greatly affected by the metal alloy and casting process selected. Almost all metals can be cast in sand molds. Only aluminum, zinc, and magnesium are ordinarily cast in metal dies in what is called either a die-casting or permanent-mold process. Round, hollow building products such as cast-iron pipe for plumbing and sewer applications are made by centrifugal casting machines.
- In the drawing process, either hot or cold metal is pulled through dies that alter or reduce its cross-sectional shape to produce architectural product configurations. Common drawn products are sheets, tubes, pipes, rods, bars, and wires. Drawing can be used with all metals except iron.
- Forging is the process of hammering hot metal or pressing cold metal to a desired shape in dies of a harder metal. The process usually improves the strength and surface characteristics of the metal. Aluminum, copper, and steel can be forged.
- Machining is used to finish areas of castings or forgings that require highly precise fits or contours. Shapes can also be machined from heavy plate or solid blocks of metal.
- Bending produces curved shapes in tubing, pipe, and extrusions.
- Brake forming of metal plate or sheet metal is a process of making successive pressings to achieve shapes with straight-line angles.
- In the spinning process, ductile types of sheet metal (usually copper or aluminum) are shaped with tools while being spun on an axis.
- Embossing and coining stamps metal with textured or raised patterns.
- Blanking shears, saws, or cuts metal sheets with a punch press to achieve a desired configuration.
- Perforating punches or drills holes through flat plate or sheet metal.
- Piercing punches holes through metal without removing any of the metal.
- Fusion welding is used to join metal pieces by melting filler metal (welding rod) and the adjacent edges briefly with a torch and then allowing the molten metal to solidify. Two common types of fusion welding are electric-arc and gas. Electric arc or metallic arc welding normally uses metal welding rods as electrodes in the welding tool.
- Gas welding is also known as oxyacetylene welding because it uses a mixture of oxygen and acetylene to fuel the flames produced by the blowtorch. Oxyacetylene blowtorches are widely used in construction work to cut through metal structural beams and metal plates.

MELTING TEMPERATURES OF METALS
10.4

BASE METAL	MELTING TEMPERATURES	
	DEGREES CELSIUS	DEGREES FAHRENHEIT
Aluminum	660	1220
Antimony	631	1168
Cadmium	321	610
Chromium	1857	3375
Cobalt	1495	2723
Copper	1083	1981
Gold	1064	1947
Iron	1535	2795
Lead	328	622
Magnesium	649	1200
Manganese	1244	2271
Nickel	1453	2647
Silver	962	1764
Tin	232	450
Zinc	420	788
Zirconium	1852	3366

Contributors:
Robert C. Rodgers, PE, Richmond Heights, Ohio; Edward R. Estes, Jr., PE, National Association of Architectural Metal Manufacturers, Norfolk, Virginia.

- Soldering is a metal joining process that uses either hard or soft solder. The metal pieces being joined together do not melt as they do in the welding process because solders melt at much lower temperatures. Soft solders consist of tin with a high percentage of lead, and melt at temperatures of 360° to 370°F. Hard solders are composed of tin and a low content of antimony or silver, and melt at temperatures ranging from 430° to 460°F.
- Brazing, which is sometimes called hard soldering, also joins two pieces of metal together by torch melting a filler rod material between them. The filler has a high content of copper and melts between 800° and 900°F.

FINISHES ON METALS

GENERAL

The finishes commonly used on architectural metals fall into three categories:

- Mechanical finishes are the result of physically changing the surface of the metal through mechanical means. The forming process itself or a subsequent procedure is performed either before or after the metal is fabricated into an end-use product.
- Chemical finishes are achieved by means of chemicals, which may or may not have a physical effect on the surface of the metal.
- Coatings are applied as finishes, either to the metal stock or to the fabricated product. These coatings either change the metal itself, through a process of chemical or electrochemical conversion, or they are simply applied to the metal surface.

Application environments, service requirements, and aesthetics together determine which metal finish or coating is best to specify. Finishes are usually selected for both appearance and function; chromium plating on metal bathroom water faucets and handles, or baked enamel on sheet metal lighting fixtures, for example, must be attractive as well as functionally protective.

For structural and exterior metal building products, such as structural metal framing, steel siding, and exterior lighting, function and operating environments are more important criteria. From a design standpoint, it is important to recognize how finishes and coatings resist wear, and corrosion. To choose the right coating or finish, design professionals must understand which material or process is best suited for a specific application.

MECHANICAL FINISHES
Mechanical finishes fall into the following five categories:

- As-fabricated finishes are the texture and surface appearance given to a metal by the fabrication process.
- Buffed finishes are produced by successive polishing and buffing operations using fine abrasives, lubricants, and soft fabric wheels. Polishing and buffing improve edge and surface finishes and render many types of cast parts more durable, efficient, and safe.
- Patterned finishes are available in various textures and designs. They are produced by passing an as-fabricated sheet between two matched-design rollers, embossing patterns on both sides of the sheet, or between a smooth roller and a design roller, embossing or coining on one side of the sheet only.
- Directional textured finishes are produced by making tiny parallel scratches on the metal surface using a belt or wheel and fine abrasive, or by hand-rubbing with steel wool. Metal treated this way has a smooth, satin sheen.
- Peened finishes are achieved by firing a stream of small steel shot at a metal surface at high velocity. The primary aim of shot-peening is to increase the fatigue strength of the component; the decorative finish is a by-product. Other nondirectional textured finishes are produced by blasting metal, under controlled conditions, with silica sand, glass beads, and aluminum oxide.

CHEMICAL FINISHES
Chemical finishes are produced in four ways.

- Chemical cleaning cleanses the metal surface without affecting it in any other way. This finish is achieved with chlorinated and hydrocarbon solvents and inhibited chemical cleaners or sol-

vents (for aluminum and copper) and pickling, chlorinated, and alkaline solutions (for iron and steel).
- Etched finishes produce a matte, frosted surface with varying degrees of roughness by treating the metal with an acid (sulfuric and nitric acid) or alkali solution.
- The bright finish process, not used widely, involves chemical or electrolytic brightening of a metal surface, typically aluminum.
- Conversion coating is usually categorized as a chemical finish, but since a layer or coating is produced by a chemical reaction, it could be considered a coating. Conversion coatings typically prepare the surface of a metal for painting or for receiving another type of finish, but they are also used to produce a patina or statuary finish. A component is treated with a diluted solution of phosphoric acid or sulfuric acid and other chemicals that convert the surface of the metal to an integral, mildly protective layer of insoluble crystalline phosphate or sulphate. Such coatings can be applied by either spray or immersion and provide temporary resistance in a mildly corrosive environment. They can be used for gray, ductile, and malleable iron castings as well as steel castings, forgings, or weldments, such as railings and outdoor furniture.

COATINGS
Organic coatings on metal can provide protection and may also be decorative. When protection is the sole purpose, primers or undercoats, pigmented topcoats in hidden areas, and clear finishes are used. Organic coatings used for decorative and protective applications include pigmented coatings, clear finishes used for gloss, and transparent or translucent clear finishes with dyes added.

Organic coatings usually fall under the general categories of paints, varnishes, enamels, lacquers, plastisols, organisols, and powders. Literally hundreds of different organic coating formulations offer an almost unlimited range of properties.

Many organic coatings are applied with brushes and rollers, but dipping and spraying of coatings account for most industrial and commercial building projects. Dipping is useful for coating complex metal parts, but spraying is used for most architectural applications. Spraying is fast and inexpensive, and new computer-controlled applicators can follow even complex curvatures. Conventional spraying, however, has two disadvantages. First, there is no easy, inexpensive way to collect and reuse the coating material. And, second, when solvent-based coatings are used, environmental restrictions need to be taken into consideration.

Electrodeposition, an increasingly popular alternative to spraying, is similar to electroplating, except that organic resins are deposited instead of metal. Electrodeposition is based on the principles of electrophoresis—the movement of charged particles in a liquid under the influence of an applied electrical charge. Electrodeposition offers several advantages: The coating builds up to a uniform thickness without runs or sags, very little paint is wasted, low levels of volatile organic compounds (VOCs) are emitted, and coatings can be deposited even into deeply recessed areas of a complex shape. Electrodeposition also has disadvantages: Coating thickness is limited, and because only one coat can be applied this way, subsequent coats must be sprayed.

Powder coating is perhaps the best known environmentally acceptable painting process. It offers three major advantages. One, because the paints are solventless, they are safer and sustainable; two, the paints cost less; and, three, they are more durable.

Powdered paints are formulated in much the same way as solvent-based paints, with the same pigments, fillers, and extenders, but are dry at room temperatures. Heat-reactive or "heat-latent" hardeners, catalysts, or cross-linking components are used as curing agents.

Powder coatings are either thermoplastic or thermosetting. Thermoplastic coatings (e.g., vinyl, polyethylene, and certain polyesters), as the term implies, are melted by heat during application. Before such coatings are applied, the surface must be primed to ensure adhesion. Thermosetting paints undergo a chemical change; they cannot be remelted by heat. Thermosets do not require a primer. Coating powders include epoxies, polyurethanes, acrylics, and polyesters.

The two most common methods of applying powdered finishes to metal are spraying and dipping, the same as those used for solvent-based paint. Electrostatic spraying is used to apply powder films 1 to 5 mil in thickness. A mixture of air and powder moves from a hopper to a spray applicator. The mixture is charged electrostatically as it passes through the applicator, causing it to stick to any grounded metal object. Powder that falls to the floor is recycled.

For coatings thicker than 5 mil, fluidized-bed dipping is used. The powder is placed in a special tank into which air is blown, turning the powder into a fluidlike mass. Objects are dipped in the "fluid" and then baked to cure the finish.

COMPARATIVE APPLICABILITY OF VARIOUS FINISHES FOR ARCHITECTURAL APPLICATIONS
10.5

TYPE OF FINISH OR TREATMENT	METAL			
	ALUMINUM	COPPER ALLOYS	STAINLESS STEEL	CARBON STEEL AND IRON
As-fabricated	Common to all of the metals (produced by hot rolling, extruding, or casting)			
Bright rolled	Commonly used (produced by cold rolling)			Not used
Directional grit textured	Commonly used (produced by polishing, buffing, hand-rubbing, brushing, or cold rolling)			Rarely used
Nondirectional matte textured	Commonly used (produced by sandblasting or shot blasting)			Rarely used
Bright polished	Commonly used (produced by polishing and buffing)			Not used
Patterned	Available in light sheet gauges of all metals			
CHEMICAL FINISHES				
Nonetch cleaning	Commonly used on all of the metals			
Matte finish	Etched finishes widely used	Seldom used	Not used	Not used
Bright finish	Limited uses	Rarely used	Not used	Not used
Conversion coatings	Widely used as pretreatment for painting	Widely used to provide added color variation	Not used	Widely used as pretreatment for painting
COATINGS				
Organic	Widely used	Opaque types rarely used; transparent types common	Sometimes used	Most important type of finish
Anodic	Most important type of finish	Not used	Not used	Not used
Vitreous	Widely used	Limited use	Not used	Widely used
Metallic	Rarely used	Limited use	Limited use	Widely used
Laminated	Substantial uses	Limited use	Not used	Substantial uses

NOTE

10.5 For more information, see the *Metal Finishes Manual for Architectural and Metal Products*, published by the Architectural Metal Products Division of the National Association of Architectural Metal Manufacturers.

Contributor:
Robert C. Rodgers, PE, Richmond Heights, Ohio.

STRUCTURAL METAL FRAMING

W AND M STEEL SHAPES

W SHAPES—DIMENSIONS FOR DETAILING 10.6

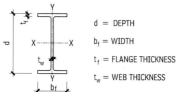

d = DEPTH
b_f = WIDTH
t_f = FLANGE THICKNESS
t_w = WEB THICKNESS

DESIGNATION	DEPTH (IN.)	FLANGE WIDTH (IN.)	FLANGE THICKNESS (IN.)	WEB THICKNESS (IN.)
W 36 × 300	36-3/4	16-5/8	1-11/16	15/16
× 280	36-1/2	16-5/8	1-9/16	7/8
× 260	36-1/4	16-1/2	1-7/16	13/16
× 245	36-1/8	16-1/2	1-3/8	13/16
× 230	35-7/8	16-1/2	1-1/4	3/4
W 36 × 210	36-3/4	12-1/8	1-3/8	13/16
× 194	36-1/2	12-1/8	1-1/4	3/4
× 182	36-3/8	12-1/8	1-3/16	3/4
× 170	36-1/8	12	1-1/8	11/16
× 160	36	12	1	5/8
× 150	35-7/8	12	15/16	5/8
× 135	35-1/2	12	13/16	5/8
W 33 × 241	34-1/8	15-7/8	1-3/8	13/16
× 221	33-7/8	15-3/4	1-1/4	3/4
× 201	33-5/8	15-3/4	1-1/8	11/16
W 33 × 152	33-1/2	11-5/8	1-1/16	5/8
× 141	33-1/4	11-1/2	5/16	5/8
× 130	33-1/8	11-1/2	7/8	9/16
× 118	32-7/8	11-1/2	3/4	9/16
W 30 × 211	31	15-1/8	1-5/16	3/4
× 191	30-5/8	15	1-3/16	11/16
× 173	30-1/2	15	1-1/16	5/8
W 30 × 132	30-1/4	10-1/2	1	5/8
× 124	30-1/8	10-1/2	15/16	9/16
× 116	30	10-1/2	7/8	9/16
× 108	29-7/8	10-1/2	3/4	9/16
× 99	29-5/8	10-1/2	11/16	1/2
W 27 × 178	27-3/4	14-1/8	1-3/16	3/4
× 161	27-5/8	14	1-1/16	11/16
× 146	27-3/8	14	1	5/8
W 27 × 114	27-1/4	10-1/8	15/16	9/16
× 102	27-1/8	10	13/16	1/2
× 94	26-7/8	10	3/4	1/2
× 84	26-3/4	10	5/8	7/16
W 24 × 162	25	13	1-1/4	11/16
× 146	24-3/4	12-7/8	1-1/16	5/8
× 131	24-1/2	12-7/8	15/16	5/8
× 117	24-1/4	12-3/4	7/8	9/16
× 104	24	12-3/4	3/4	1/2
W 24 × 94	24-1/4	9-1/8	7/8	1/2
× 84	24-1/8	9	3/4	1/2
× 76	23-7/8	9	11/16	7/16
× 68	23-3/4	9	9/16	7/16
W 24 × 62	23-3/4	7	9/16	7/16
× 55	23-5/8	7	1/2	3/8
W 21 × 147	22	12-1/2	1-1/8	3/4
× 132	21-7/8	12-1/2	1-1/16	5/8
× 122	21-5/8	12-3/8	15/16	5/8
× 111	21-1/2	12-3/8	7/8	9/16
× 101	21-3/8	12-1/4	13/16	1/2

DESIGNATION	DEPTH (IN.)	FLANGE WIDTH (IN.)	FLANGE THICKNESS (IN.)	WEB THICKNESS (IN.)
W 21 × 93	21-5/8	8-3/8	15/16	9/16
× 83	21-3/8	8-3/8	13/16	1/2
× 73	21-1/4	8-1/4	3/4	7/16
× 68	21-1/8	8-1/4	11/16	7/16
× 62	21	8-1/4	5/8	3/8
W 21 × 57	21	6-1/2	5/8	3/8
× 50	20-7/8	6-1/2	9/16	3/8
× 44	20-5/8	6-1/2	7/16	3/8
W 18 × 119	19	11-1/4	1-1/16	5/8
× 106	18-3/4	11-1/4	15/16	9/16
× 97	18-5/8	11-1/8	7/8	9/16
× 86	18-3/8	11-1/8	3/4	1/2
× 76	18-1/4	11	11/16	7/16
W 18 × 71	18-1/2	7-5/8	13/16	1/2
× 65	18-3/8	7-5/8	3/4	7/16
× 60	18-1/4	7-1/2	11/16	7/16
× 55	18-1/8	7-1/2	5/8	3/8
× 50	18	7-1/2	9/16	3/8
W 18 × 46	18	6	5/8	3/8
× 40	17-7/8	6	1/2	5/16
× 35	17-3/4	6	7/16	5/16
W 16 × 100	17	10-3/8	1	9/16
× 89	16-3/4	10-3/8	7/8	1/2
× 77	16-1/2	10-1/4	3/4	7/16
× 67	16-3/8	10-1/4	11/16	3/8
W 16 × 57	16-3/8	7-1/8	11/16	7/16
× 50	16-1/4	7-1/8	5/8	3/8
× 45	16-1/8	7	9/16	3/8
× 40	16	7	1/2	5/16
× 36	15-7/8	7	7/16	5/16
W 16 × 31	15-7/8	5-1/2	7/16	1/4
× 26	15-3/4	5-1/2	3/8	1/4
W 14 × 730	22-3/8	17-7/8	4-15/16	3-1/16
× 665	21-5/8	17-5/8	4-1/2	2-13/16
× 605	20-7/8	17-3/8	4-3/16	2-5/8
× 550	20-1/4	17-1/4	3-13/16	2-3/8
× 500	19-5/8	17	3-1/2	2-3/16
× 455	19	16-7/8	3-3/16	2
× 426	18-5/8	16-3/4	3-1/16	1-7/8
× 398	18-1/4	16-5/8	2-7/8	1-3/4
× 370	17-7/8	16-1/2	2-11/16	1-5/8
× 342	17-1/2	16-3/8	2-1/2	1-9/16
× 311	17-1/8	16-1/4	2-1/4	1-7/16
× 283	16-3/4	16-1/8	2-1/16	1-5/16
× 257	16-3/8	16	1-7/8	1-3/16
× 233	16	15-7/8	1-3/4	1-1/16
× 211	15-3/4	15-3/4	1-9/16	15/16
× 193	15-1/2	15-3/4	1-7/16	7/8
× 176	15-1/4	15-5/8	1-5/16	13/16
× 159	15	15-5/8	1-3/16	3/4
× 145	14-3/4	15-1/2	1-1/16	11/16
W 14 × 132	14-5/8	14-3/4	1	5/8
× 120	14-1/2	14-5/8	15/16	9/16
× 109	14-3/8	14-5/8	7/8	1/2
× 99	14-1/8	14-5/8	3/4	1/2
× 90	14	14-1/2	11/16	7/16
W 14 × 82	14-1/4	10-1/8	7/8	1/2
× 74	14-1/8	10-1/8	13/16	7/16
× 68	14	10	3/4	7/16
× 61	13-7/8	10	5/8	3/8
W 14 × 53	13-7/8	8	11/16	3/8
× 48	13-3/4	8	5/8	5/16
× 43	13-5/8	8	1/2	5/16

DESIGNATION	DEPTH (IN.)	FLANGE WIDTH (IN.)	FLANGE THICKNESS (IN.)	WEB THICKNESS (IN.)
W 14 × 38	14-1/8	6-3/4	1/2	5/16
× 34	14	6-3/4	7/16	5/16
× 30	13-7/8	6-3/4	3/8	1/4
W 14 × 26	13-7/8	5	7/16	1/4
× 22	13-3/4	5	5/16	1/4
W 12 × 336	16-7/8	13-3/8	2-15/16	1-3/4
× 305	16-3/8	13-1/4	2-11/16	1-5/8
× 279	15-7/8	13-1/8	2-1/2	1-1/2
× 252	15-3/8	13	2-1/4	1-3/8
× 230	15	12-7/8	2-1/16	1-5/16
× 210	14-3/4	12-3/4	1-7/8	1-3/16
W 12 × 190	14-3/8	12-5/8	1-3/4	1-1/16
× 170	14	12-5/8	1-9/16	15/16
× 152	13-3/4	12-1/2	1-3/8	7/8
× 136	13-3/8	12-3/8	1-1/4	13/16
× 120	13-1/8	12-3/8	1-1/8	11/16
× 106	12-7/8	12-1/4	1	5/8
× 96	12-3/4	12-1/8	7/8	9/16
× 87	12-1/2	12-1/8	13/16	1/2
× 79	12-3/8	12-1/8	3/4	1/2
× 72	12-1/4	12	11/16	7/16
× 65	12-1/8	12	5/8	3/8
W 12 × 58	12-1/4	10	5/8	3/8
× 53	12	10	9/16	3/8
W 12 × 50	12-1/4	8-1/8	5/8	3/8
× 45	12	8	9/16	5/16
× 40	12	8	1/2	5/16
W 12 × 35	12-1/2	6-1/2	1/2	5/16
× 30	12-3/8	6-1/2	7/16	1/4
× 26	12-1/4	6-1/2	3/8	1/4
W 12 × 22	12-1/4	4	7/16	1/4
× 19	12-1/8	4	3/8	1/4
× 16	12	4	1/4	1/4
× 14	11-7/8	4	1/4	3/16
W 10 × 112	11-3/8	10-3/8	1-1/4	3/4
× 100	11-1/8	10-3/8	1-1/8	11/16
× 88	10-7/8	10-1/4	1	5/8
× 77	10-5/8	10-1/4	7/8	1/2
× 68	10-3/8	10-1/8	3/4	1/2
× 60	10-1/4	10-1/8	11/16	7/16
× 54	10-1/8	10	5/8	3/8
× 49	10	10	9/16	5/16
W 10 × 45	10-1/8	8	5/8	3/8
× 39	9-7/8	8	1/2	5/16
× 33	9-3/4	8	7/16	5/16
W 10 × 30	10-1/2	5-3/4	1/2	5/16
× 26	10-3/8	5-3/4	7/16	1/4
× 22	10-1/8	5-3/4	3/8	1/4
W 10 × 19	10-1/4	4	3/8	1/4
× 17	10-1/8	4	5/16	1/4
× 15	10	4	1/4	1/4
× 12	9-7/8	4	3/16	3/16
W 8 × 67	9	8-1/4	15/16	9/16
× 58	8-3/4	8-1/4	13/16	1/2
× 48	8-1/2	8-1/8	11/16	3/8
× 40	8-1/4	8-1/8	9/16	3/8
× 35	8-1/8	8	1/2	5/16
× 31	8	8	7/16	5/16

Contributor:
American Institute of Steel Construction, Chicago, Illinois.

M SHAPES—DIMENSIONS FOR DETAILING
10.7

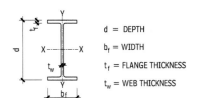

d = DEPTH
b_f = WIDTH
t_f = FLANGE THICKNESS
t_w = WEB THICKNESS

DESIGNATION		DEPTH (IN.)	FLANGE WIDTH (IN.)	FLANGE THICK-NESS (IN.)	WEB THICK-NESS (IN.)
M 14	× 18	14	4	1/4	3/16
M 12	× 11.8	12	3-1/8	1/4	3/16
	× 10.8	12	3-1/8	1/4	3/16
	× 10	12	3-1/4	3/16	3/16
M 10	× 9	10	2-3/4	3/16	3/16
	× 8	10	2-3/4	3/16	3/16
	× 7.5	10	2-3/4	3/16	1/8
M 8	× 6.5	8	2-1/4	3/16	1/8
M 6	× 4.4	6	1-7/8	3/16	1/8
M 5	× 18.9	5	5	7/16	5/16

S, HP, C, MC, AND L STEEL SHAPES

ANGLES—DIMENSIONS FOR DETAILING
10.8

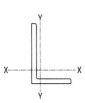

SIZE AND THICKNESS (IN.)		WEIGHT PER FT (LB)	SIZE AND THICKNESS (IN.)		WEIGHT PER FT (LB)
L8 × 8 ×	1-1/8	57.2	L6 × 6 ×	9/16	22
	1	51.3		1/2	19.6
	7/8	45.3		7/16	17.3
	3/4	389.2		3/8	14.9
	5/8	33.0		5/16	12.5
	9/16	29.8	L6 × 4 ×	7/8	27.1
	1/2	26.7		3/4	23.5
L8 × 6 ×	1	44.4		5/8	19.8
	7/8	39.3		9/16	17.9
	3/4	34		1/2	16
	5/8	28.6		7/16	14.1
	9/16	25.9		3/8	12.2
	1/2	23.2		5/16	10.2
	7/16	20.4	L6 × 3-1/2 ×	1/2	15.3
L8 × 4 ×	1	37.6		3/8	11.6
	3/4	28.9		5/16	9.72
	9/16	22.1	L5 × 5 ×	7/8	27.3
	1/2	19.7		3/4	23.7
L7 × 4 ×	3/4	26.2		5/8	20.1
	5/8	22.1		1/2	16.3
	1/2	17.9		7/16	14.4
	3/8	13.6		3/8	12.4
L6 × 6 ×	1	37.5		5/16	10.4
	7/8	33.2	L5 × 3-1/2 ×	3/4	19.8
	3/4	28.8		5/8	16.8
	5/8	24.3		1/2	13.6

SIZE AND THICKNESS (IN.)		WEIGHT PER FT (LB)	SIZE AND THICKNESS (IN.)		WEIGHT PER FT (LB)
L5 × 3-1/2 ×	7/16	12.0	L3-1/2 × 2-1/2 ×	1/2	9.4
	3/8	10.4		7/8	8.3
	5/16	8.7		3/8	7.2
	1/4	7.0		5/16	6.1
L5 × 3 ×	5/8	15.7		1/4	4.9
	1/2	12.8	L3 × 3 ×	1/2	9.4
	7/16	11.3		7/16	8.3
	3/8	9.8		3/8	7.2
	5/16	8.19		5/16	6.1
L4 × 4 ×	3/4	18.5		1/4	4.9
	5/8	15.7		3/16	3.71
	1/2	12.8	L3 × 2-1/2 ×	1/2	8.5
	7/16	11.3		7/16	7.6
	3/8	9.8		3/8	6.6
	5/16	8.2		5/16	5.6
	1/4	6.6		1/4	4.5
L4 × 3 1/2 ×	1/2	11.9		3/16	3.39
	7/16	10.6	L3 × 2 ×	1/2	7.7
	3/8	9.1		7/16	6.8
	5/16	7.7		3/8	5.9
	1/4	6.2		5/16	5.0
L4 × 3 ×	1/2	11.1		1/4	4.1
	7/16	9.8		3/16	3.07
	3/8	8.5	L2-1/2 × 2-1/2 ×	1/2	7.7
	5/16	7.2		3/8	5.9
	1/4	5.8		5/16	5.0
L3 1/2 × 3 1/2 ×	1/2	11.1		1/4	4.1
	7/16	9.8		3/16	3.07
	3/8	8.5	L2-1/2 × 2 ×	3/8	5.3
	5/16	7.2		5/16	4.5
	1/4	5.8		1/4	3.62
L3-1/2 × 3 ×	1/2	10.2		3/16	2.75
	7/16	9.1	L2 × 2 ×	3/8	4.7
	3/8	7.9		5/16	3.92
	5/16	6.6			
	1/4	5.4			

MISCELLANEOUS CHANNELS—DIMENSIONS FOR DETAILING
10.9

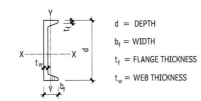

d = DEPTH
b_f = WIDTH
t_f = FLANGE THICKNESS
t_w = WEB THICKNESS

DESIGNATION		DEPTH (IN.)	FLANGE WIDTH (IN.)	FLANGE THICK-NESS (IN.)	WEB THICK-NESS (IN.)
MC 18	× 58	18	4-1/4	5/8	11/16
	× 51.9	18	4-1/8	5/8	5/8
	× 45.8	18	4	5/8	1/2
	× 42.7	18	4	5/8	7/16
MC 13	× 50	13	4-3/8	5/8	13/16
	× 40	13	4-1/8	5/8	9/16
	× 35	13	4-1/8	5/8	7/16
	× 31.8	13	4	5/8	3/8
MC 12	× 50	12	4-1/8	11/16	13/16
	× 45	12	4	11/16	11/16
	× 40	12	3-7/8	11/16	9/16
	× 35	12	3-3/4	11/16	7/16
	× 31	12	3-5/8	11/16	3/8

DESIGNATION		DEPTH (IN.)	FLANGE WIDTH (IN.)	FLANGE THICK-NESS (IN.)	WEB THICK-NESS (IN.)
MC 12	× 37	12	3-5/8	5/8	5/8
	× 32.9	12	3-1/2	5/8	1/2
	× 30.9	12	3-1/2	5/8	7/16
MC 12	× 10.6	12	1-1/2	5/16	3/16
MC 10	× 41.1	10	4-3/8	9/16	13/16
	× 33.6	10	4-1/8	9/16	9/16
	× 28.5	10	4	9/16	7/16
	× 25	10	3-3/8	9/16	3/8
	× 22	10	3-3/8	9/16	5/16
MC 10	× 8.4	10	1-1/2	1/4	3/16
MC 10	× 6.5	10	1-1/8	3/16	1/8
MC 9	× 25.4	9	3-1/2	7/16	9/16
	× 23.9	9	3-1/2	3/8	9/16
MC 8	× 22.8	8	3-1/2	7/16	1/2
	× 21.4	8	3-1/2	3/8	1/2
MC 8	× 20	8	3	3/8	1/2
	× 18.7	8	3	3/8	1/2
MC 8	× 8.5	8	1-7/8	3/16	5/16

HP SHAPES—DIMENSIONS FOR DETAILING
10.10

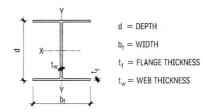

d = DEPTH
b_f = WIDTH
t_f = FLANGE THICKNESS
t_w = WEB THICKNESS

DESIGNATION		DEPTH (IN.)	FLANGE WIDTH (IN.)	FLANGE THICK-NESS (IN.)	WEB THICK-NESS (IN.)
MHP 14	× 117	14-1/4	14-7/8	13/16	13/16
	× 102	14	14-3/4	11/16	11/16
	× 89	13-7/8	14-3/4	5/8	5/8
	× 73	13-5/8	14-5/8	1/2	1/2
HP 13	× 100	13-1/8	13-1/4	3/4	3/4
	× 87	13	13-1/8	11/16	11/16
	× 73	12-3/4	13	9/16	9/16
	× 60	12-1/2	12-7/8	7/16	7/16
HP 12	× 84	12-1/4	12-1/4	11/16	11/16
	× 74	121/8	12-1/4	5/8	5/8
	× 63	12	12-1/8	1/2	1/2
	× 53	11-3/4	12	7/16	7/16
HP 10	× 57	10	10-1/4	9/16	9/16
	× 42	9-3/4	10-1/8	7/16	7/16

Contributor:
American Institute of Steel Construction, Chicago, Illinois.

METAL TUBING AND PIPES

RECTANGULAR TUBING—STEEL
10.11

SIZE (IN.	T = WALL THICKNESS (BW GAUGE OR IN.)						
11 × 1/2	18	16					
1-1/2 × 3/4	16	14	11				
1-1/2 × 1	16	14	11				
2 × 1	18	16	15	14	12	11	11
2 × 1-1/4	14						
2 × 1-1/2	14	11					
2-1/2 × 1	14						
2-1/2 × 1-1/4	14						
2-1/2 × 1-1/2	14	11	1/8″	9/16″	1/4″		
3 × 1	16	14					
3 × 1-1/2	14	13	12	11	1/8″	3/16″	1/4″
3 × 2	16	14	11	1/8″	3/16″	1/4″	5/16″
4 × 2	14	11	1/8″	3/16″	1/4″	5/16″	3/8″
4 × 2 1/2	1/8″						
4 × 3	11	1/8″	3/16″	1/4″	5/16″	3/8″	
5 × 2	11	1/8″	10	1/4″	5/16″		
5 × 2-1/2	1/8″	3/16″					
5 × 3	11	1/8″	1/4″	5/16″	3/8″	1/2″	
6 × 2	11	1/8″	1/4″	5/16″	3/8″		
6 × 3	11	1/8″	1/4″	5/16″	3/8″	1/2″	
6 × 4	1/8″	3/16″	1/4″	5/16″	3/8″	1/2″	
7 × 3	3/16″	1/4″	3/8″				
7 × 4	3/16″	1/4″	3/8″				
7 × 5	3/16″	1/4″	5/16″	3/8″	1/2″	3/8″	1/2″
8 × 2	3/16″	1/4″	3/8″				
8 × 3	3/16″	1/4″	5/16″	3/8″	1/2″		
8 × 4	3/16″	1/4″	5/16″	3/8″	1/2″		
8 × 6	3/16″	1/4″	5/16″	3/8″	1/2″		
9 × 5	3/8″						
9 × 7	1/4″	5/16″					
10 × 2	3/16″	1/4″					
10 × 4	3/16″	1/4″	5/16″	3/8″	1/2″		
10 × 5	1/4″						
10 × 6	1/4″	3/16″	5/16″	3/8″	1/2″		
10 × 8	1/4″	3/8″	1/2″				
12 × 2	3/16″	1/4″					
12 × 4	3/16″	1/4″	5/16″	3/8″	1/2″		
12 × 6	1/4″	5/16″	3/8″	1/2″			
12 × 8	1/4″	3/8″	1/2″				
ALUMINUM							
1 × 1-1/2	0.125″						
1 × 2	0.125″						
1-1/2 × 2	0.125″						
1-1/2 × 2-1/2	0.125″						
1-1/2 × 3	0.125″	0.188					
1-3/4 × 2-1/4	0.125″						
1-3/4 × 3	0.125″						
1-3/4 × 3-1/2	0.125″						
1-3/4 × 4	0.125″						
1-3/4 × 4-1/2	0.125″						
1-3/4 × 5	0.125″						
2 × 3	0.125″						
2 × 4	0.125″						
2 × 5	0.125″						
2 × 6	0.125″	0.250					
2 × 8	0.125″						
STAINLESS STEEL							
1 × 1-1/2	11						
1 × 2	11	16					
2 × 3	11	7					
2 × 4	11	7	1/4″				

RECTANGULAR AND SQUARE TUBING
10.12

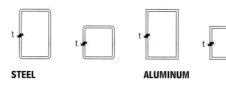

STEEL　　　　　　　ALUMINUM

RECTANGULAR ALUMINUM TUBING (IN.)
10.13

SIZE × t	SIZE × t	SIZE × t
1-1/2 × 1-1/2 × 1/8	1-3/4 × 3-1/2 × 1/8	2 × 4 × 1/8
1 × 2 × 1/8	1-3/4 × 4 × 1/8	2 × 5 × 1/8
1-1/2 × 2-1/2 × 1/8	1-3/4 × 4-1/2 × 1/8	3 × 5 × 1/8
1-3/4 × 2-1/4 × 1/8	1-3/4 × 5 × 1/8	
1-3/4 × 3 × 1/8	2 × 3 × 1/8	

SQUARE ALUMINUM TUBING (IN.)
10.14

SIZE × t	SIZE × t	SIZE × t
1/2 × 1/2 × 1/8	1-1/2 × 1-1/2 × 1/8	3 × 3 × 1/4
3/4 × 3/4 × 1/8	1-3/4 × 1-3/4 × 1/8	4 × 4 × 1/8
1 × 1 × 1/16	2 × 2 × 1/8	4 × 4 × 1/4
1-1/4 × 1-1/4 × 1/8	2 × 2 × 1/4	
1-1/2 × 1-1/2 × 5/64	3 × 3 × 1/8	

ROUND TUBING—COPPER
10.15

SIZE (IN.) NOMINAL INSIDE DIAMETER	OUTSIDE DIAMETER (IN.)	INSIDE DIAMETER (IN.)		
		TYPE K	TYPE L	TYPE M
1/4	0.375	0.305	0.315	
1/2	0.625	0.527	0.545	0.569
3/4	0.875	0.745	0.785	0.811
1	1.125	0.995	1.025	1.055
1-1/2	1.625	1.481	1.505	1.527
2	2.125	1.959	1.985	2.009
4	4.125	3.857	3.905	3.935

ROUND PIPE—STEEL
10.16

SIZE (IN.) NOMINAL INSIDE DIAMETER	OUTSIDE DIAMETER (IN.)	INSIDE DIAMETER (IN.)		
		STANDARD	EXTRA-STRONG	DOUBLE-EXTRA-STRONG
1/8	0.405	0.269	0.215	
1/4	0.540	0.364	0.302	
3/8	0.675	0.493	0.423	
1/2	0.840	0.622	0.546	
3/4	1.050	0.824	0.742	
1	1.315	1.049	0.957	
1-1/4	1.660	1.380	1.278	
1-1/2	1.900	1.610	1.500	
2	2.375	2.067	1.939	1.503
2-1/2	2.875	2.469	2.323	1.771
3	3.500	3.068	2.900	2.300
3-1/2	4.000	3.548	3.364	
4	4.500	4.026	3.826	3.152
5	5.563	5.047	4.813	4.063
6	6.625	6.065	5.761	4.897
8	8.625	7.981	7.625	6.875
10	10.750	10.020	9.750	
12	12.750	12.000	11.750	

ROUND TUBING AND PIPE
10.17

STDO　　　　EXTRA STRONG　　　DOUBLE EXTRA STRONG

PIPE – STEEL

K　　　　　　L　　　　　　M

TUBING – COPPER

NOTES

10.14 Rectangular and square tubing with sharp corners is usually used for metal specialties.

10.15 Round tubing, usually manufactured for mechanical purposes, is used for metal specialties. Round tubing is measured by the outside diameter and the wall thickness by gauge, fractions, or decimals of an inch. Round tubing is used where a high-grade finish is required and exact diameters are necessary.

Round tubing is available in steel, aluminum, copper, stainless steel, and other metals. Consult manufacturers for availability of materials and sizes.

10.16 Round pipe is made primarily in three weights: standard, extra-strong (or extra-heavy), and double-extra-strong (or double-extra-heavy). Outside diameters of the three weights of pipe in each size are always the same: extra wall thickness is always on the inside, and therefore reduces the inside diameter of the heavier pipe. All sizes are specified by what is known as the "nominal inside diameter." Round pipe is also available in aluminum and stainless steel. Consult manufacturer for sizes.

Contributor:
HMC Architects, Incorporated, Ontario, California.

SQUARE TUBING—STEEL
10.18

SIZE (IN.)	WALL THICKNESS (BW GAUGE OR IN.)												
1/2 × 1/2	20	18	16										
5/8 × 5/8	20	16											
3/4 × 3/4	20	18	16	13	11								
7/8 × 7/8	18	16	14	13									
1 × 1	20	18	16	15	14	13	12	11					
1-1/8 × 1-1/8	18	16											
1-1/4 × 1-1/4	18	16	14	13	12	11	0.135	3/16"					
1-1/2 × 1-1/2	18	16	15	14	13	12	11	0.145	3/16"	1/4"			
1-3/4 × 1-3/4	16	14	13	11									
2 × 2	18	16	15	14	13	12	11	1/8"	10	0.145	3/16"	1/4"	
2-1/4 × 2-1/4	16	0.109	1/4"										
2-1/2 × 2-1/2	16	12	1/8"	10	3/16"	0.238	1/4"						
3 × 3	14	0.109	11	1/8"	3/16"	1/4"	5/16"	3/8"					
3-1/2 × 3-1/2	1/8"	3/16"	1/4"	5/16"									
4 × 4	11	1/8"	3/16"	1/4"	5/16"	3/8"	1/2"						
4-1/2 × 4-1/2	3/16"	1/4"											
5 × 5	11	1/8"	7	3/16"	1/4"	5/16"	3/8"	1/2"					
6 × 6	3/16"	1/4"	5/16"	3/8"	1/2"								
7 × 7	3/16"	1/4"	5/16"	3/8"	1/2"								
8 × 8	3/16"	1/4"	5/16"	3/8"	1/2"	5/8"							
10 × 10	1/4"	5/16"	3/8"	1/2"	5/8"								
12 × 12	1/4"	5/16"	3/8"	1/2"									
14 × 14	3/8"	1/2"											
16 × 16	1/2"												

SIZE (IN.)	WALL THICKNESS (BW GAUGE OR IN.)				
ALUMINUM (IN.)					
3/4 × 3/4	0.125				
1 × 1	0.125				
1-1/4 × 1-1/4	0.125				
1-1/2 × 1-1/2	0.125				
1-3/4 × 1-3/4	0.125				
2 × 2	0.125	0.250			
2-1/2 × 2-1/2	0.125				
3 × 3	0.125	0.250			
4 × 4	0.250				
STAINLESS STEEL					
1 × 1	18	16	11		
1-1/4 × 1-1/4	16	14	11		
1-1/2 × 1-1/2	16	14	11	7	
2 × 2	16	14	11	7	1/4"
2-1/2 × 2-1/2		7			
3 × 3	14	11	7	1/4"	3/16"
4 × 4	11	7	3/16"		

GRATINGS

RECTANGULAR BAR GRATING (WELDED OR PRESSURE-LOCKED)
10.19

WITH SPACER BARS WELDED 4" O.C.

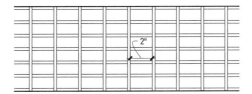

WITH SPACER BARS WELDED 2" O.C.

RETICULATED GRATING (RIVETED)
10.20

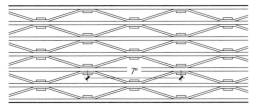

WITH SPACER BARS RIVETED APPROX. 7" O.C.
USED FOR AVERAGE INSTALLATION

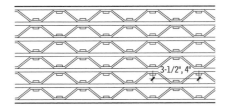

WITH SPACER BARS RIVETED 3-1/2" OR 4"
USED FOR HEAVY TRAFFIC AND WHERE WHEELED
EQUIPMENT IS USED

NOTE

Rectangular bar grating is fabricated from rectangular bearing bars of steel, stainless steel, or aluminum or aluminum I-bars, with cross bars at right angles. Cross bars may be square, rectangular, or of another shape, and be pressure-locked, swaged, or welded to the bearing bars. They may have open ends or ends banded with flats, approximately the same size as the bearing bars. Standard bar spacing include 7/16, 15/16, and 1-3/16 in. The 7/16-in. close mesh spacing which provides 1/4-in. clear opening may be more suitable for pedestrian traffic areas, eliminating openings too big for crutches, wheelchairs, and the heels on women's shoes. For sizes, tolerances, details, and load tables, refer to ANSI/NAAMM MBG 531, *Metal Bar Grating Manual,* published by the National Association of Architectural Metal Manufacturers.

NOTE

Reticulated grating is fabricated from rectangular bearing bars of steel, stainless steel, or aluminum, and continuous crimped connecting (reticuline) bars riveted to the bearing bars. They may have open ends or ends banded with flats, approximately the same size as bearing bars, welded across the ends. Normal bar spacing is 3/4, 1-1/8, or 2-5/16 in. For sizes, tolerances, details, and load tables, refer to ANSI/NAAMM MBG 532, *Heavy-Duty Metal Bar Grating Manual,* published by the National Association of Architectural Metal Manufacturers.

SEE ALSO

Cold-Formed Metal Framing
Cold-Formed Metal Joist Framing
Cold-Formed Metal Trusses
Metal Fastenings
Metal Gratings
Metal Specialties
Metals
Radiation Protection
Roof and Wall Accessories
Steel Decking
Slotted Channel Framing
Sound and Vibration Control
Steel Siding
Structural Metal Framing

Contributors:
HMC Architects, Inc., Ontario, California; Charles F. D. Egbert, AIA, Washington, DC; Vincente Cordero, AIA, Arlington, Virginia; Edward R. Estes, Jr., Norfolk, Virginia.

11

WOOD

INTRODUCTION

Wood is one of the most common and versatile building materials used today. Wood construction can include rough carpentry, finish carpentry, architectural woodwork, and structural composites.

Approximately 9 of every 10 buildings constructed in the United States each year are framed with wood, including most single-family and multifamily residences and a large percentage of commercial, institutional, and public buildings. Wood is favored as both a structural material and a finish material, for its economy, architectural flexibility, and visual qualities. Many contractors know how to build with it. Small work crews can handle most wood members without special lifting equipment, cutting and fastening can be accomplished on-site with hand or portable power tools, and the skills needed for wood construction are easily learned. Yet wood is one of the most difficult materials for the designer to master, because it is virtually the only building material whose origin is vegetable rather than mineral. With this origin comes a host of idiosyncrasies relating to directional properties, strength, stiffness, grain patterns, shrinkage, distortion, decay, insect damage, and fire resistance.

Today, most wood comes from younger forests, where trees are typically smaller than those harvested only a few decades ago. Large, solid timbers are increasingly difficult to obtain, and the general quality of lumber is declining. As a result, design professionals and contractors must depend more and more on shop-fabricated structural wood such as laminated veneer lumber, parallel strand lumber, fabricated wood I-joists, rim boards, and shop-fabricated wood trusses. These products tend to be straighter, stronger, stiffer, less prone to distortion, and more economical of trees than conventional solid lumber.

Wood is also one of the world's most environmentally friendly building materials. From framing to floors to other interior products, wood is renewable and recyclable, and continues to store carbon dioxide even as a finished product. Not only can wood be recycled, but it can be regenerated as well. In fact, North American forests have grown 20 percent since 1970. Although wood products make up 47 percent of all raw materials manufactured in the United States, wood's share of energy consumption is only 4 percent during manufacturing. Wood product manufacturing produces relatively fewer greenhouse gasses than alternative building materials, and has the lowest impact on air and water quality. Moreover, forest regeneration creates trees that benefit the environment while they grow, taking in carbon dioxide and releasing oxygen.

Wood structures can be designed and built to meet the code requirements to protect against earthquakes and hurricanes. Wood frame construction consists of numerous small connections. If one connection is overloaded, its share can be picked up by adjacent connections. Wood also has a high strength-to-weight ratio. Light, strong buildings tend to perform better during earthquakes.

Wood frame construction is generally finished with interior surfaces of gypsum board, which is more resistant to fire.

WOOD MATERIALS

TYPES OF WOOD CONSTRUCTION

Building codes generally categorize wood construction into two distinct types: heavy timber (Type IV) and light wood frame (Type V).

- Heavy timber construction, consisting of exposed columns, girders, beams, and decking large enough to be slow to catch fire and burn, is permitted for use in relatively large buildings across a broad spectrum of uses. Its large member dimensions and spans make heavy timber construction best suited to buildings with regular, repetitive bays. Heavy timber buildings are engineered in accordance with the National Design Specification for Wood Construction, published by the American Forest and Paper Associations of the American Wood Council (www.awc.org).
- Wood frame construction is made up of nominal 2-in. framing members spaced closely together and normally concealed by interior finish materials such as gypsum board or wood paneling. Wood frame construction, with its small members and close member spacings, adapts readily to even the most intricate spaces and architectural forms. However, because such construction is less resistant to fire than heavy timber construction, building codes limit the heights and areas of wood framed buildings. The maximum height generally permitted in residential wood frame buildings is three stories, although four or more stories are possible if an approved sprinkler system is installed. Under many conditions wood frame construction can utilize the International Code Council (ICC) International Residential Code, which has been widely adopted by states and municipalities.

WOOD AS A STRUCTURAL MATERIAL

On the basis of performance per unit weight, typical construction lumber is at least as strong and stiff as structural steel. Because of its microstructure of longitudinal cells, wood has different structural properties in its two principal directions: parallel to the grain, wood is strong and stiff; perpendicular to the grain, it is weak and deformable. The strength of wood varies with the duration of the load. For short-term loads, such as those from snow, wind, and impact, allowable stress values are 15 to 100 percent higher than those allowed for normal-term loads. Under very long-term loading, however, wood has a tendency to creep, and reduced stress values must be used.

WOOD AS A FINISH MATERIAL

Wood is used as a finish material in buildings of every kind. Even in the most fire-resistant types of construction limited quantities of wood finish may be used. With proper protection from fire, water, and sunlight, wood can serve as a durable exterior material for cladding, trim, and even roofing. For interior finishes, despite recent concerns regarding the depletion of rare or old-growth species, woods of many types remain commonly available in solid or veneer forms and exhibit a variety of properties, including hardness, grain, color, suitability for different finishes, and cost. Finish woods are readily available in many preformed shapes and are also easily shaped and cut in the field. Wood and wood products may be finished with transparent or opaque coatings or serve as a base for applied plastic laminates.

SELECTION OF INTERIOR FINISH WOOD MATERIALS

The major factors that influence lumber selection for finish wood applications, as specified by the Architectural Woodwork Institute (AWI) are:

- *Aesthetic characteristics*: Different species exhibit a variety of colors, grains (open or close grain), and figures (grain patterns) that are further distinguished by the sawing method (plain-sawn, quarter sawn, rift-sawn) and finishing characteristics (receptivity to finish processes, such as fillers, stains, etc.).
- *Availability*: The availability of particular species varies by season and popularity.
- *Size limitations*: Some species produce longer and/or wider members.

HEAVY TIMBER CONSTRUCTION
11.1

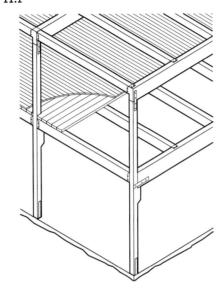

WOOD FRAME CONSTRUCTION
11.2

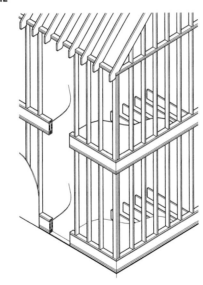

- *Strength, hardiness, and density*: The ability of selected lumber to sustain stress; resist indentation, abuse, and wear; and carry its anticipated load contributes to its suitability for particular uses.
- *Dimensional stability*: Swelling and shrinking due to relative humidity and moisture content changes vary according to the species and product type.
- *Adaptability for exterior use*: Certain species are more durable for use in exterior applications. Heartwood of all species is more resistant to damage by the elements than sapwood. The following species are rot-resistant and acceptable for exterior use: Eastern and Western red cedar, redwood, mahogany, and teak. For more information, see "Wood Treatment" in this chapter.
- *Fire retardance*: Natural fire-retardant qualities and acceptability of treatment vary with species. Flame spread classification is the generally accepted measurement for fire rating of materials.

Fire-retardant treatments and buildup of members can be used to improve the fire resistance rating of wood materials.

- *Preservative treatments*: Certain species used for architectural woodwork can be treated with preservative compounds to extend their life when exposed to the elements.

LUMBER PRODUCTION

Commercially marketed lumber includes trees of dozens of species roughly divided into softwoods, which are the evergreen species, and hardwoods, those species that drop their leaves in the fall. The majority of framing lumber comes from the comparatively plentiful softwoods. Hardwoods, with their greater range of colors and grain figures, are used primarily for interior finishes, flooring, cabinets, and furniture.

When examined under a low-power magnifier, wood is made up primarily of hollow tubular cells of cellulose that run parallel to the long axis of the tree trunk. When the tree is harvested, both the hollows and the walls of these tubes are full of watery sap. The tree is sawed into rough lumber while in this saturated, or "green," condition. Finish lumber is seasoned (dried of much of its moisture), either by stacking it in the open air for a period of months or, more commonly, by heating it in a kiln for a period of days. During seasoning, moisture evaporates first from the hollows of the tubes, and then from the cellulose walls of the tubes, causing the lumber to shrink. By the time the lumber leaves the kiln, it is considerably smaller. Further shrinkage usually occurs after the lumber has been incorporated into a building, as the moisture content in the wood comes gradually to equilibrium with the moisture content of the surrounding air. Wood absorbs moisture during damp weather and gives it off during dry weather in a never-ending cycle of

SHRINKAGE DUE TO DRYING
11.3

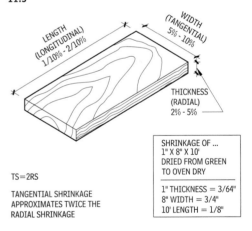

TS = 2RS

TANGENTIAL SHRINKAGE APPROXIMATES TWICE THE RADIAL SHRINKAGE

SHRINKAGE OF ...
1" X 8" X 10'
DRIED FROM GREEN
TO OVEN DRY

1" THICKNESS = 3/64"
8" WIDTH = 3/4"
10' LENGTH = 1/8"

EXPANSION DUE TO MOISTURE IN THE AIR
11.4

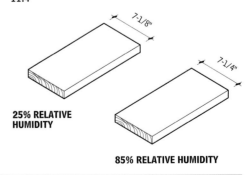

25% RELATIVE HUMIDITY

85% RELATIVE HUMIDITY

Contributors:
Edward Allen, AIA, South Natric, Massachusetts; Joseph Iano, Architect, Mercer Island, Washington; American Forest & Paper Association, Incorporated, Washington, DC; John Showalter, PE, American Wood Council, Washington, DC; Greg Hauer, Architectural Woodwork Institute, Potomac Falls, Virginia.

swelling and shrinking, a fact that must be taken into account when detailing wood components of buildings.

Most lumber is surfaced after seasoning to reduce it to its final dimensions and give it smooth faces.

TYPICAL SAWING OF A LARGE LOG
11.5

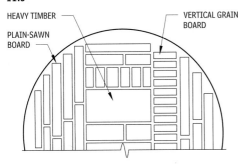

LUMBER THICKNESS
11.6

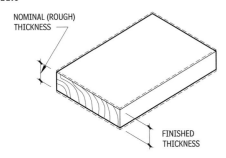

BEFORE MACHINING		AFTER MACHINING
NOMINAL (ROUGH) THICKNESS		FINISHED THICKNESS
INCHES	QUARTERS	HARDWOODS AND SOFTWOODS (IN.)
1	4/4	3/4
1-1/4	5/4	1
1-1/2	6/4	1-1/4
2	8/4	1-1/2
2-1/2	10/4	2
3	12/4	2-1/2

LUMBER GRADING

As a natural product wood varies greatly in appearance and structural properties. Consequently, elaborate systems of grading have been established to indicate the quality of each piece of lumber. Within each species of wood there are two grading systems, one based on structural strength and stiffness, the other on appearance. Appearance is graded visually. Structural grading is based either on visual inspection, the sizes and positions of knots and other defects, or structural properties as measured by machines that analyze each piece of lumber.

The strength and stiffness of wood varies considerably from one species and grade to another. When designing a wood structure, it is necessary to know which species and grade will be used. If in doubt, base structural calculations on the weakest species, and base grade on a locally available species.

JOINING WOOD

Nailing is the most common method of joining wood framing. Nails are inexpensive to buy and install and may be driven by hand or with pneumatic equipment. When applied in proper size, number,

and spacing, they form a strong, resilient joint. Sheet metal straps, anchors, and brackets can be nailed to connections where greater resistance to tension or shear is necessary. Detailed nailing requirements for wood frame construction are included in building codes. Heavy timber construction typically relies on bolts and lag screws, together with metal connecting devices.

In finish wood construction, nearly headless finish nails are used for improved appearance. Screws, concealed or embedded fasteners, splines, and fitted and glued joints provide greater mechanical stiffness and optimal appearance.

MOISTURE MOVEMENT IN WOOD

The shrinkage of wood as it dries is not uniform. Wood shrinks very little along the length of the grain, somewhat in the radial direction of a cylindrical log, and more in the tangential direction of the log, as shown in Figure 11.7. One consequence of the difference between the radial and tangential shrinkage is that radial splits, called checks, form during seasoning, especially in lumber of larger dimensions. In addition, pieces of lumber distort noticeably in accordance with their original positions in the tree trunk.

For pieces of lumber that must stay flat, such as flooring, outdoor decking, baseboards, casings, and paneling, vertical-grain lumber, which is sawn so the annual growth rings are more or less perpendicular to the broad face of the board, is desirable. One particular sawing pattern that produces vertical-grain lumber is called quarter sawn. For ordinary framing, seasoning distortions are of little consequence, so plain sawn boards are used.

A number of accepted wood detailing practices have been developed in response to the moisture movement that occurs in wood and the distortions that result from the differing rates of shrinkage along the three axes of the grain. In applying wood siding, it is nec-

MOISTURE SHRINKAGE OF TYPICAL SOFTWOOD
11.7

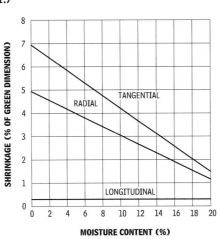

SHRINKAGE DISTORTIONS BY POSITION IN LOG
11.8

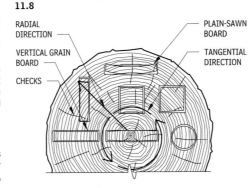

essary to use nailing patterns that do not restrain the cross-grain seasonal shrinking and swelling of the wood as indicated in Figure 11.9. Horizontal bevel siding is nailed so that each board is fastened by one row of nails only, creating a sliding joint at each overlapping edge to allow for movement. Tongue-and-groove siding boards are nailed at the tongue edge only, the other edge being restrained by the tongue of the adjacent board sliding freely in its groove. Vertical board-and-batten siding is nailed only at the centers of the boards and battens, allowing for free expansion and contraction of the wood.

SLIDING JOINTS IN WOOD SIDING
11.9

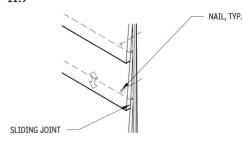

HORIZONTAL SIDING

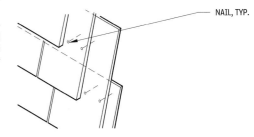

WOOD SHAKE SIDING

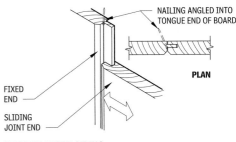

VERTICAL WOOD SIDING

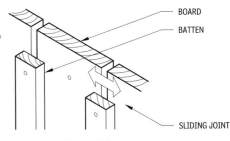

BOARD AND BATTEN SIDING

Contributors:
Edward Allen, AIA, South Natick, Massachusetts; Joseph Iano, Architect, Mercer Island, Washington; Greg Heuer, Architectural Woodwork Institute, Potomac Falls, Virginia; John Showalter, PE, American Wood Council, Washington, DC; American Forest & Paper Association, Incorporated, Washington, DC.

Because wood shrinkage is so much greater in the tangential direction than in the radial, plain-sawn boards tend to cup noticeably in a direction opposite to the curvature of the annual rings. Therefore, plain-sawn decking and flooring should be laid with the "bark side" of each board facing down, to reduce the raising of edges. On outdoor decks, this practice will also minimize puddling of water on the boards. Vertical-grain flooring and deck boards are preferable to plain-sawn boards, not only because they minimize cupping but also because the tighter grain pattern wears better.

**SHRINKAGE DISTORTION OF PLAIN-SAWN DECKING
11.10**

BARK SIDE DOWN IS
CORRECT ORIENTATION

DECAY AND INSECTS

Wood provides food and habitat to various insects and decay-causing fungi. For the most part, decay and insect attack can be minimized by detailing construction in ways that keep wood dry. Wood components should be kept a minimum of 6 in. away from the edge of soil. Details that trap and hold moisture, such as connections in exterior decks and railings, should be avoided unless preservative-treated wood or decay-resistant species such as redwood, cedar, or cypress are used.

FIRE

Wood burns easily, giving off highly toxic combustion products, so it is important to design wooden structures for fire safety. The first step is to follow the height and area restrictions of the building codes, along with code provisions for easy egress from wooden buildings. Smoke and heat alarms are essentials in wooden residential buildings. Heavy timber buildings have a natural resistance to fire because their massive timbers are slower to ignite and burn in comparison to the smaller framing members in wood frame construction. Wood framing has internal hollow passages that encourage the spread of fire.

WOOD TREATMENT

PRESERVATIVE WOOD TREATMENT

GENERAL

Wood may be destroyed by decay caused by fungi, by insects such as carpenter ants and termites, and by marine borers in saltwater exposures. Four conditions must exist before many of these organisms can destroy wood: (1) a free oxygen supply, (2) a moisture content in the wood above the fiber saturation point (20 percent), (3) a temperature in the range of 50 to 90°F, and (4) the presence of a food source, in this case, the wood. Some insects, such as dry-wood termites and carpenter ants, are able to destroy wood that has very low moisture content.

In most indoor environments, where relative humidity levels are generally low, wood will last for a very long time. In certain indoor environments, however, and in many exterior environments, wood cannot be kept dry or out of the proximity of moisture. Most building codes recognize this by requiring the use of preservative wood treatment or naturally resistant wood species in building components that come into contact with concrete, masonry, or exposed soil. This requirement also covers floor joists and crawl space support members within 12 to 18 in. of exposed soil.

**TERMITE SHIELD DETAIL
11.11**

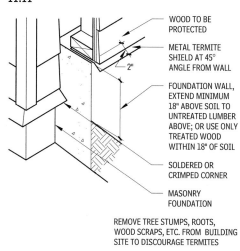

WOOD TO BE
PROTECTED

METAL TERMITE
SHIELD AT 45°
ANGLE FROM WALL

2"

FOUNDATION WALL,
EXTEND MINIMUM
18" ABOVE SOIL TO
UNTREATED LUMBER
ABOVE; OR USE ONLY
TREATED WOOD
WITHIN 18" OF SOIL

SOLDERED OR
CRIMPED CORNER

MASONRY
FOUNDATION

REMOVE TREE STUMPS, ROOTS,
WOOD SCRAPS, ETC. FROM BUILDING
SITE TO DISCOURAGE TERMITES

DECAY-RESISTANT WOOD

When specifying a wood that will resist decay, the choice is between naturally decay-resistant wood and wood treated with preservatives. The first requires use of the heartwood of naturally decay-resistant woods such as western red cedar, bald cypress, redwood, and others that contain natural poisons called extractives, which are not palatable to decay-causing organisms. However, not all grades or species of these woods are suitable for some structural situations. The process for treating wood with preservatives is to impregnate the wood with chemicals through a pressure treatment process. Nonpressure treatments, such as spraying, dipping, and brushing, are commonly used for the treatment of millwork components during manufacture, field treatment of wood during construction, or remedial treatment of existing wood that is already in service.

PRESERVATIVE TREATED WOOD

Several processes are commonly used for preservative treating wood, including the full-cell, modified-full-cell, and empty-cell pressure processes. The method chosen depends on the desired amount of preservative retention. During treatment, the wood is placed in a large, cylindrical pressure vessel and, depending on the process, a vacuum or low pressure is applied. The preservative is pumped into the cylinder and forced under pressure into the wood cells. After the proper amount of preservative has been injected, the preservative is pumped out of the cylinder and, in most cases, a vacuum is applied to remove excess preservative. Regardless of which process is used, the wood is generally dried prior to treatment to a moisture content that will permit the specified penetration and retention of the preservative.

PENETRATION AND RETENTION OF PRESERVATIVES

Penetration and retention are the two measures that define the effectiveness of preservation methods. Penetration depends on the species of wood, the type of preservative, and the size of the lumber member being treated. Some species that resist preservative penetration, such as Douglas fir, are usually incised with small slits to make treatment more effective. Others, such as Southern pine, are easily treated without incisions. While the sapwood of some species is readily penetrated, the heartwood of most resists penetration (although the heartwood of all species naturally resists decay to varying degrees).

Penetration and retention are determined by using a hollow drill bit to remove a "core" from a representative sample of wood treated in each batch. Penetration is determined by visual examination of each core, and retention is determined through chemical analysis of the core. Penetration and retention standards are established by

the American Wood Preservers' Association (AWPA) in an open, consensus-based process; these standards are enforced by an independent third-party agency approved by the American Lumber Standard Committee (ALSC). A quality mark outlining pertinent information can be found on complying wood stock.

**RELATIVE HEARTWOOD DECAY RESISTANCE OF
NATURALLY RESISTANT UNTREATED WOODS
11.12**

RESISTANT OR VERY RESISTANT	MODERATELY RESISTANT	SLIGHTLY OR NONRESISTANT
Bald cypress (old-growth), cedar, white oak, redwood	Bald cypress (new-growth), Douglas fir, Western larch, old-growth longleaf, slash, and Eastern white pines, tamarack	Pines other than those listed under "Moderately Resistant," spruces, true firs

PRESERVATIVE TYPES

Two primary classes of preservatives are in use today: oil-borne (organic and organometallic) and waterborne (inorganic).

OIL-BORNE PRESERVATIVES

Organic and organometallic oil-borne preservatives either are used alone or are carried in hydrocarbon solvents such as mineral spirits or fuel oil, and are used to treat most softwoods and hardwoods. Some of the more common oil-borne preservatives include creosote, pentachlorophenol (penta), copper naphthenate, and copper 8-quinolinolate.

- Creosote-treated wood is often used for industrial products such as railroad crossties, piling, utility poles, and heavy timbers in exterior applications. Creosote is especially effective in deterring the attack of marine borers when used to treat piles and timbers that will be immersed in salt or brackish water. Wood treated with creosote is colored dark brown to black, and usually has a strong mothball odor when freshly treated. Due to the oily residue sometimes found on the surface of creosote-treated wood, paint may not adhere satisfactorily. Also, creosote contains volatile organic compounds (VOCs) and, as such, should not be specified for interior locations without adequate ventilation.

- Penta-treated wood is primarily used for utility poles, heavy timbers, and glue-laminated timbers. For these applications, penta is dissolved in a heavy hydrocarbon solvent, which leaves the wood with an oily surface until the solvent evaporates, at which time it is possible to paint the wood—although oils may bleed through the paint at a later date. When penta is dissolved in a

---

NOTE

11.12 *Wood Handbook: Wood as an Engineering Material,* developed by the USDA Forest Products Laboratory.

Leaf Studio, Crownsville, Maryland; Engineered Wood Association, Tacoma, Washington; American Wood Preservers' Association, Selma, Alabama.

Contributors:
Edward Allen, AIA, South Natick, Massachusetts; Joseph Iano, Architect, Mercer Island, Washington; Greg Heuer, Architectural Woodwork Institute, Potomac Falls, Virginia; John Showalter, PE, American Wood Council, Washington, DC; Richard J. Vitullo, AIA, Oak

light hydrocarbon solvent and is used to treat millwork items, oil-based paints and primers may adhere adequately after all of the solvents have evaporated from the wood. The color of penta-treated wood depends on the color of the hydrocarbon solvent. Lighter oils darken the wood slightly, while darker oils make the wood very dark in color.

- Copper naphthenate, which is often dissolved in a heavy hydro-carbon solvent, is used for the treatment of utility poles and rail-road crossties. Wood treated with copper naphthenate is typi-cally greenish-brown in color and has an oily odor. Some oil-based paints may adhere to copper-naphthenate-treated wood after the solvent has evaporated, but some oils may subse-quently bleed through the finish. Because it is not a restricted-use pesticide, copper naphthenate may be purchased at many paint or building supply stores and applied to cut ends and drilled holes in pressure-treated wood.
- Copper 8-quinolinolate (also called oxine copper) is normally dissolved in light hydrocarbon solvents and is most often used for the treatment of wood that comes into contact with food-stuffs. Wood treated with copper-8 is frequently used for agri-cultural crates and containers.

WATERBORNE PRESERVATIVES

Inorganic waterborne preservatives are the most popular and commonly available types of preservatives used for treating wood. They include alkaline copper quaternary (ACQ), both copper boron azole type A (CBA-A) and copper azole type B (CA-B), chromated copper arsenate (CCA), ammoniacal copper zinc arsenate (ACZA), and inorganic boron (SBX). All of these preservatives are dissolved in water, so after the wood is permitted to dry, the surface readily accepts paints and stains.

ACQ (types A, B, C, and D) are composed of copper and a quater-nary ammonium compound dissolved in an aqueous solution of ammonia and/or ethanolamine.

FINISHING OF PRESERVATIVE TREATED WOOD

Waterborne preservatives are recommended when clean, odorless, and paintable wood products are required. Wood treated with such preservatives may be used indoors if sawdust and construction debris are cleaned up. Painting wood treated with oil-borne preser-vatives is not recommended, as it is difficult to use, requiring exten-sive care and an aluminum-based paint. For certain interior appli-cations in commercial, industrial, or farm buildings, creosote- or penta-treated wood may be used if exposed surfaces are sealed with two coats of urethane or epoxy paint or shellac. Guidelines for precautions in these cases are outlined in an EPA-approved con-sumer information sheet for each preservative treatment.

FASTENING PRESERVATIVE TREATED WOOD

Wood treated with most waterborne preservatives can be corro-sive to metal fasteners and connectors. For aboveground con-struction, hot-dip galvanized steel and stainless steel fasteners are typically recommended. Joist hangers and framing anchors should also be hot-dip galvanized steel or stainless steel. For below-grade construction, such as treated wood foundation systems, types 304 and 316 stainless steel Type H silicon bronze, ETP copper, and monel fasteners are required. Adhesives work well with wood treated with waterborne preservatives. Phenolresorcinol, resorci-nol, and melemine-formaldehyde structural adhesives are used in glulam beams made from treated wood members. On job sites, use adhesives recommended for use with treated wood.

Other issues important to design professionals:

- Never mix galvanized steel with stainless steel in the same con-nection. When these dissimilar metals are in physical contact with each other, galvanic action will increase the corrosion rate of the galvanized part (the zinc will migrate off the galvanized part onto the stainless part at a faster rate). Refer to Table 10.3 in Chapter 10 Metals.
- Galvanizing provides a sacrificial layer to protect the steel con-nector or fastener. Greater thicknesses (coating weights) gen-erally provide longer protection in corrosive environments.

- Most commonly available electrogalvanized fasteners do not have a sufficient coating of zinc for these new chemicals.
- Aluminum should not be used in direct contact with CCA, ACQ, copper azole or ACZA.

PRECAUTIONS FOR USE AND HANDLING

The chemical formulations used for preservative treatment of wood are registered with the EPA, which has approved certain uses for various types of pressure-treated wood to ensure safe handling and avoid environmental or other health hazards. Some guidelines for use and handling follow:

- Dispose of treated wood by ordinary trash collection or burial. Never burn treated wood in open fires or in stoves, fireplaces, or residential boilers.
- Avoid frequent inhalation of sawdust from treated wood. Whenever possible, perform sawing and machining of treated wood outdoors.
- Avoid frequent or prolonged skin contact with penta- or cre-osote-treated wood.
- After handling treated wood products, wash skin thoroughly before eating or drinking.

SPECIFICATION OF TREATED WOOD

Most building codes require the use of preservative treated wood in certain applications. AWPA has established a use category sys-tem and has published these standards in a document entitled *U1—Use Category System: User Specification for Treated* Wood. Wood processing and treatment is regulated by a number of organ-izations, and not all regulatory bodies recognize or permit the use of the particular preservatives, processes or the wood species list-ed in the standard. The following is a summary of the AWPA–U1 categories:

- *Use Category UC1*: Wood used in interior construction, not in contact with the ground or foundations, and protected from water.

- *Use Category UC2*: Wood used in interior construction not in contact with ground, but may be subject to occasional damp-ness.
- *Use Category UC3*: Wood used in exterior construction, not in contact with ground. UC3 can be divided into two subcategories: UC3A, is wood that is coated and used in a way that permits water to quickly drain from the surface, typically used in vertical applications.; UC3B is wood that is not coated (except for aes-thetic purposes) and may be used either vertical or horizontal applications.
- *Use Category UC4*: Wood used in exterior construction and in contact with the ground or other conditions that support poten-tial deterioration. UC4 can be divided into three subcategories: UC4A is wood used in ground- or freshwater contact; UC4B is wood used in contact with the ground in severe environments or as critically important structural components; and UC4C is wood used in contact with the ground in extremely severe environ-ments or climates with an extremely high potential for deterio-ration.
- *Use Category UC5*: Wood exposed to Saltwater and brackish water exposure. UC5 is divided into three subcategories, which depend on the types of marine borers present in various areas in North America: UC5A is for wood exposed to waters north of New Jersey or north of San Francisco, UC5B is for wood exposed to waters south of San Francisco or from New Jersey south to Georgia, and UC5C is for waters south of Georgia , the Gulf Coast, Puerto Rico, and Hawaii. Prior to specifying a UC5 subcategory, it is necessary to determine which marine borers are present in the area before consulting AWPA Standard U1.

Once the use category for each component has been determined, the specifier should consult the tables found in commodity specifi-cation for the type of component, to determine the appropriate species and preservative and retention combinations for that com-ponent. Table 11.13 provides examples of applications from AWPA Standard U1.

EXAMPLES OF APPLICATIONS AND PRESERVATIVE RETENTION VALUES FROM AWPA STANDARD U1 11.13

APPLICATION	USE CATEGORY	COMMODITY SPECIFICATION	SPECIES	PRESERVATIVE	RETENTION (PCF)
Residential decks	UC3B	A	Southern pine	ACQ	0.25
			Douglas fir	CBA-A	0.21
Fascia boards	UC3A	A	Ponderosa pine	ACQ	0.25
			Southern pine	CA-B	0.10
Glulam beams, interior	UC2	F	Southern pine	ACQ	0.25
Glulam beams, exterior	UC4A	F	Douglas fir	Penta	0.30
Molding	UC1	A	Spruce Pine Fir	SBX	0.17
Permanent wood foundation	UC4B	A	Southern pine	CCA	0.60
			Douglas fir	ACZA	0.60
Piles, foundation	UC4C	E	Southern pine	Creosote	12.0
Piles, marine	UC5B	G	Douglas fir	ACZA	2.5 outer
					1.5 inner
Plywood subfloor	UC2	F	Southern pine	CCA	0.25
			Southern pine	SBX	0.17
Poles, building and utility	UC4B	D	Western red cedar	Penta	1.0
			Southern pine	CCA	0.60
Posts, fence, round	UC4A	B	Jack pine	CCA	0.40
Sill plates	UC2	A	Southern pine	SBX	0.17
			Douglas fir	ACQ	0.25

NOTE

11.13 Many other species and preservative combinations are available for each application; the table listing is intended only as a sample from AWPA Standard U1. For more information on the AWPA's Use Category System visit www.awpa.com.

Contributors:
Richard J. Vitullo, AIA, Oak Leaf Studio, Crownsville, Maryland; Engineered Products Association, Tacoma, Washington; Colin McCown, American Wood Preservers' Association, Selma, Alabama; John Showalter, PE, American Wood Council, Washington, DC

TYPICAL QUALITY MARK FOR TREATED LUMBER
11.14

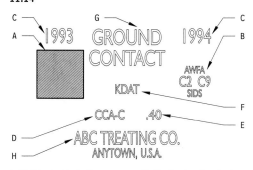

A: Trademark of inspection agency certified by the American Lumber Standard Committee (ALSC). Contact the Southern Pine Council (SPC) or the ALSC for a list of certified inspection agencies.
B: Applicable American Wood Preservers' Association (AWPA) standard
C: Year of treatment
D: Preservative used for treatment
E: Retention level
F: Dry or KDAT (kiln-dried after treatment), if applicable
G: Proper exposure conditions
H: Treating company and location

FIRE-RETARDANT WOOD TREATMENT

GENERAL

Building construction materials are tested for four criteria related to performance during a fire: fire resistance, flame spread, fuel contributed, and smoke developed.

- Fire resistance is the material's ability to resist burning while retaining its structural integrity.
- Flame spread measures the rate at which flames travel along the surface of a material.
- Fuel contributed is a measure of how much combustible matter a material furnishes to a fire.
- Smoke developed is a measure of the surface-burning characteristics of a material.

How fire spreads through wood structures depends on the size and arrangement of wood members and the details that restrict or encourage air movement around them. Larger cross sections take longer to burn. As wood burns, it develops an outer layer of charcoal, which insulates the wood beneath and slows burning. This "char" layer proceeds through the burning wood at an average rate of 1-1/2 in. per hour. Various design strategies can be used to resist fire damage to a wood structure and its spread to adjacent areas, but the most important is to protect the wood members by means of coverings, coatings, or treatments.

Modern fire-retardant treatment (FRT) of wood consists of pressure treatment with aqueous solutions of various organic and inorganic chemicals, followed by kiln drying to reduce moisture content to 19 percent or less for lumber under 2 in. thick, and 15 percent or less for plywood. All proprietary FRTs must conform to Underwriters Laboratory (UL) classifications. FRT wood is commonly used in plywood sheathing, roof trusses, rafters, floor joists, studs, staging, and shingles and shakes. Fire-retardant chemical combinations include zinc chloride, ammonium sulfates, borax or boric acid, and smaller amounts of sodium dichromate. Ammonium phosphates are no longer used because they cause rapid disintegration of wood.

Fire retardants work when chemicals react with the tars and gasses normally produced by burning wood. The resultant carbon char acts as thermal insulation (greater than on untreated wood), slowing the rate of burning. Gasses released from the FRT wood are diluted with carbon dioxide and water vapor, lessening the chance of flashover, in which wood gases are ignited by high temperatures and then explode.

FRT STANDARDS AND CLASSIFICATIONS

Interior fire retardants meet Class I ratings, which are required by code for vertical exits and special areas. Class II ratings are required for horizontal exits, but this rating is rarely reached with untreated wood. FRT lumber and plywood are recognized substitutes for noncombustible materials for insurance purposes. Many codes allow FRT wood products for a variety of applications.

Both the flame spread index and smoke developed index give numerical scales for a material's fire classification. The flame spread index is the primary test for fire performance, according to ASTM E 84. In the International Building Codes, flame spread ratings are classified as 0-25 (Class I or A), 26-75 (Class II or B), and 76-200 (Class III or C).

A smoke developed index of 450 or less is permitted for FRT wood used for interior wall and ceiling finishes. The UL FR-S listing applies only to treated products with a UL-723 (ASTM E 84) flame and smoke classification not exceeding 25 in a 30-minute test. The classification applies to the species tested and does not pertain to the structures in which the materials are installed.

Fire retardants come in interior and exterior types. Interior fire retardants are used on wood trusses and studs; exterior retardants protect exterior lumber, siding, roof shakes and shingles, and scaffold planking. The latter type offers durable, nonleachable, long-term fire protection in outdoor or moist (relative humidity of 95 percent or greater) conditions.

Class C or Class B FRT shingles and shakes may be considered non-combustible materials. For wood exposed to the weather, specify exterior-type retardants that retain their protective properties under the standard rain test.

Interior Type A wood is appropriate for interior and weather-protected applications with less than 95 percent relative humidity. In rare instances, when relative humidity is less than 75 percent, Type B can be specified. Interior Type A is used when a wood with low hygroscopicity (the rate at which the chemical draws moisture from the air) is required.

FRT INTERIOR WOODWORK

Instead of solid lumber, it is often desirable to build members of treated cores clad with untreated veneers 1/28-inch thick or less. Most codes discount this narrow finishing in determining the flame spread index of the wood, permitting the use of untreated wood in about 10 percent of the combined wall and ceiling surface area. Sizes and species currently being treated (flame spread index less than 25) include red oak and Western red cedar up to 4/4 and yellow poplar up to 8/4. Color and finishes are affected by FRTs.

FINISHING AND FINISHES

FRT lumber and plywood can be lightly sanded for cosmetic cleaning after treatment. Painting and staining are possible but not always successful, particularly transparent finishes. Test finishes for compatibility before application.

FRT lumber may be end-cut, but ripping and extensive surfacing will normally void the treating agency certification. To the extent possible, materials should be precut before treatment, otherwise a wood treater should be consulted. Treated plywood can be cut in either direction without loss of fire protection.

Intumescent coatings are sometimes used to reduce flammability of wood surfaces in both opaque and transparent finishes. Under high heat, these coatings expand or foam, creating an insulating effect that reduces flame spread. Check local codes before specifying these coatings because they tend to be less durable, softer, and more hygroscopic than standard finishes.

FRT FACTS

- These standards apply to FRT wood: ASTM E 84, ASTM D 2898, ASTM D 3201, ASTM E 108, AWPA C 20, AWPA C 27, and the *ULI Building Materials Directory* (current edition). For more information, contact the American Wood Preservers' Association (AWPA), American Wood Preservers' Institute, USDA Forest Service, Southern Forest Products Association, Western Wood Preservers Institute, and American Forest and Paper Association.
- FRT wood has increased weight and decreased strength. Consult a structural engineer and the wood treater for actual design values for structural applications.
- FRT wood fasteners must be hot-dipped, zinc-coated galvanized stainless steel, silicon bronze, or copper; other materials deteriorate upon contact with FRT chemicals.

TYPICAL FIRE-RETARDANT TREATED WOOD IDENTIFICATION MARK
11.15

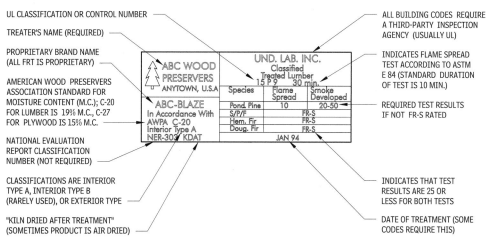

UL CLASSIFICATION OR CONTROL NUMBER

TREATER'S NAME (REQUIRED)

PROPRIETARY BRAND NAME
(ALL FRT IS PROPRIETARY)

AMERICAN WOOD PRESERVERS ASSOCIATION STANDARD FOR MOISTURE CONTENT (M.C.); C-20 FOR LUMBER IS 19% M.C., C-27 FOR PLYWOOD IS 15% M.C.

NATIONAL EVALUATION REPORT CLASSIFICATION NUMBER (NOT REQUIRED)

CLASSIFICATIONS ARE INTERIOR TYPE A, INTERIOR TYPE B (RARELY USED), OR EXTERIOR TYPE

"KILN DRIED AFTER TREATMENT" (SOMETIMES PRODUCT IS AIR DRIED)

ALL BUILDING CODES REQUIRE A THIRD-PARTY INSPECTION AGENCY (USUALLY UL)

INDICATES FLAME SPREAD TEST ACCORDING TO ASTM E 84 (STANDARD DURATION OF TEST IS 10 MIN.)

REQUIRED TEST RESULTS IF NOT FR-S RATED

INDICATES THAT TEST RESULTS ARE 25 OR LESS FOR BOTH TESTS

DATE OF TREATMENT (SOME CODES REQUIRE THIS)

NOTE

11.15 Wood shakes and shingles are further classified as Class B or C. Rather than stamp each piece, each bundle is tagged with an identification mark.

Contributors:
Richard J. Vitullo, AIA, Oak Leaf Studio, Crownsville, Maryland; Southern Pine Council, Kenner, Louisiana; Colin McCown, American Wood Preservers' Association, Selma, Alabama; Engineered Wood Association, Tacoma, Washington.

FLAME SPREAD INDEX
11.16

MATERIAL[a]		ASTM E 84 FLAME SPREAD	SOURCE[b]
Lumber	Birch, yellow	105-110	UL
	Cedar, Western red	70	HPMA
	Douglas fir	70-100	UL
	Maple (flooring)	104	CWC
	Oak, red or white	100	UL
	Pine, Ponderosa	105-230[c]	UL
	Pine, Southern yellow	130-195	UL
	Poplar	170-185	UL
	Redwood	65	CRA
	Spruce, Northern	65	UL
Softwood plywood (exterior glue)	Douglas fir, 1/4"	118	CWC
	Douglas fir, 5/8"	95	APA
	Southern pine, 1/4"	95-110	APA
Hardwood plywood	Lauan, 1/4"	150	HPMA
Particleboard	1/2", 47 lb/cu ft	156	NBS
	5/8", 44 lb/cu ft	153	NBS
Flakeboard	Red oak, 1/2", 42-47 lb/cu ft (four types)	71-189	FPL
Shakes	Western red cedar, 1/2"	69	HPMA
Shingles	Western red cedar, 1/2"	49	HPMA

FLAME SPREAD INDEX OF FACTORY-FINISHED PRODUCTS
11.17

MATERIAL[a]			ASTM E 84 FLAME SPREAD
Particleboard	1/32"	Factory finish printed	118-178
	1/2"	Paper overlay	175
	5/8"	Vinyl overlay	100
Medium-density fiberboard (MDF)	3/16"	Factory finish printed	167
Hardboard	1/8"	Factory finish printed	158-194
		Paper overlay	155-166
Flakeboard	Aromatic cedar, 3/16"		156
Hardwood plywood	Aspen, 1/4"	Factory finished	196
	Birch, 5/32"	Factory finished	160-195
	Cherry, 1/4"	Factory finished	160
	Hickory, 1/4"	Factory finished	140
	Lauan, 1/4"	Factory finish printed	99-141
	Maple, 1/4"	Factory finished	155
	Oak, 1/4"	Factory finished	125-185
	Pine, 1/4"	Factory finished	120-140
	Walnut, 1/4"	Factory finished	138-160

FASTENINGS

WOOD ADHESIVES

GENERAL

Adhesives have been used for bonding wood for centuries, but until the 1930s they were limited to only a few naturally derived substances—those based on animal or vegetable proteins, gums, or resins. It wasn't until World War II that stepped-up materials research efforts spurred the development of synthetic adhesives for bonding metals, concrete, glass, rubber, plastics, and wood. Many of these synthetic adhesives are used to manufacture products such as plywood, oriented-strand board (OSB), and laminated timbers. They can also be used during construction to attach plywood subfloors to floor joists, adhere ceramic tiles to floors or walls, attach gypsum board, and other construction products. In addition to their structural use, adhesives also can be used to eliminate squeaks in floors and for some mechanical fastening.

Adhesives are composed of a base component, dispersion medium, and various additives that impart specific properties. The elastomeric base of a construction-type adhesive accounts for 30 to 50 percent of its weight. Depending on its intended application, this base is made of natural rubber (isoprene) or synthetic rubbers such as neoprene, butyl, polyurethane, polysulfide, nitrile, styrene-butadiene, or butadiene acrylonitrile. Additives include tackifiers, flow and extrusion modifiers, curing agents, antioxidants, and fillers. Together, the base and the additives are dispersed (or dissolved) in a liquid, typically an organic solvent or water.

Currently, most adhesives use organic solvents, but water-based adhesives are gaining in popularity because they do not emit harmful vapors, are easy to clean up, and can be discarded as regular trash. The design professional should consider requirements for disposal of the containers containing from organic solvents. Many jurisdictions are enacting clean air statutes that, among other things, target organic solvents as air pollutants. Organic solvents also can have adverse affects on the workers who apply them, as well as on future building occupants. One drawback to most water-based adhesives, however, is that they tend only to resist water, whereas the solvent-based adhesives are waterproof.

CONSTRUCTION ADHESIVES

Construction adhesives are defined as elastomer-based extrudable mastics, which means that the main adhesive component is elastic and will continue to maintain some of its flexibility indefinitely. Mastics are a type of adhesive with high viscosity, or resistance to flow. A construction adhesive is a substance capable of holding materials together by surface attachment.

Adhesives used for building have been formulated to tolerate many of the often-adverse conditions that exist at most job sites, such as extreme temperatures and temperature fluctuations. They are excellent for filling gaps, and thus work on both smooth and rough surfaces. The degree of adhesion depends on the surface conditions of the materials; ice, dirt, grease, or other contaminants will have a negative effect.

Many of the characteristics of modern adhesives are described in Table 11.18. Note that most adhere to wood, but performance depends on careful consideration of the physical and chemical compatibility of glue and wood, processing requirements, mechanical properties, and durability under design conditions.

NOTES

11.16 a. Unless indicated, thickness of material is 1 in. nominal.
b. The Engineered Wood Association (APA), California Redwood Association (CRA), Canadian Wood Council (CWC), USDA Forest Products Laboratory (FPL), Hardwood Plywood Manufacturers Association (HPMA), National Bureau of Standards (NBS), Underwriters Laboratories (UL).
c. Average of 18 tests was 154 with three values over 200.
11.17 Hardwood Plywood Manufacturers Association test records.

Contributors:
Richard J. Vitullo, AIA, Oak Leaf Studio, Crownsville, Maryland; Colin McCown, American Wood Preservers' Association, Selma, Alabama.

ADHESIVE SUMMARY[a]
11.18

CLASS	FORM	PROPERTIES	TYPICAL USES
Urea resin	Dry powders or liquids; may be blended with melamine or other resins	High strength under both wet and dry conditions; moderately durable under damp conditions; moderate to low resistance to temperatures above 120°F; white or tan color	Hardwood plywood for interior use and furniture; interior particleboard; flush doors; furniture core stock
Phenol resin[b]	Dry powders or liquids	High strength under both wet and dry conditions; very resistant to moisture and damp conditions; dark red in color	Primary adhesive for exterior softwood plywood and flakeboard
Resorcinol resin and phenol-resorcinol resins	Liquid; hardener supplied separately	High strength under both wet and dry conditions; very resistant to moisture and damp conditions; dark red color	Primary adhesive for laminated timbers and assembly joints, to withstand severe service conditions
Polyvinyl acetate resin emulsions	Liquid; ready to use	Generally high strength in dry conditions; low resistance to moisture and elevated temperatures; joints tend to yield under continued stress; white or yellow color	Furniture assembly, flush doors, bonding of plastic laminates, architectural woodworking
Cross-linkable polyvinyl acetate resin emulsions	Similar to polyvinyl acetate resin emulsions but includes a resin capable of forming linkage	Improved resistance to moisture and elevated temperatures; improved long-term performance in moist or wet environment; color varies	Interior and exterior doors, molding and architectural woodworking
Contact adhesives	Typically an elastomer base in organic solvents or water emulsion	Initial joint strength develops immediately upon pressing, increases slowly over a period of weeks; dry strength generally lower than those of conventional woodworking glues; water resistance and resistance to severe conditions variable; color varies	For some nonstructural bonds; high-pressure decorative laminates to substrates; useful for low-strength metal and some plastic bonding
Mastics (elastomeric construction adhesives)	Puttylike consistency; synthetic or natural elastomer base, usually in organic solvents	Gap filling; develops strength slowly over several weeks; water resistance and resistance for severe conditions vary; color varies	Lumber and plywood to joists and studs; gypsum board; styrene and urethane foams
Thermoplastic synthetic resins (hot melts)	Solid chunks, pellets, ribbons, rods, or films; solvent-free	Rapid bonding; gap filling; lowerstrength than conventional woodworking adhesives; minimal penetration; moisture resistant; white to tan color	Edge banding of panels; films and paper overlays
Epoxy resins	Chemical polymers, usually in two parts, both liquid; completely reactive; no solvents	Good adhesion to metals, glass, certain plastics, and wood products; permanence in wood joints not adequately established; gap-filling	Used in combination with other resins for bonding metals, plastics, and materials other than wood; a fabrication of cold-molded wood panels
Protein glues (casein and hide)	Dry powders or reconstituted liquid	Bonds extremely well to wood; moisture resistant	Interior applications; laminating beam

ADHESIVE APPLICATORS
11.19

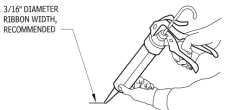

3/16" DIAMETER RIBBON WIDTH, RECOMMENDED

ADHESIVE GUN

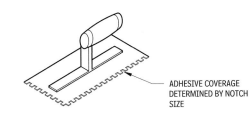

ADHESIVE COVERAGE DETERMINED BY NOTCH SIZE

NOTCHED TROWEL (TO SPREAD ADHESIVE OVER LARGE AREAS)

RECOMMENDED ADHESIVE BEAD PATTERNS
11.20

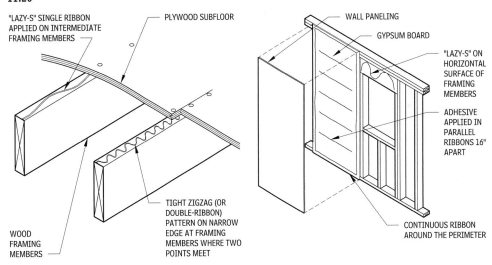

"LAZY-S" SINGLE RIBBON APPLIED ON INTERMEDIATE FRAMING MEMBERS

PLYWOOD SUBFLOOR

TIGHT ZIGZAG (OR DOUBLE-RIBBON) PATTERN ON NARROW EDGE AT FRAMING MEMBERS WHERE TWO POINTS MEET

WOOD FRAMING MEMBERS

WALL PANELING

GYPSUM BOARD

"LAZY-S" ON HORIZONTAL SURFACE OF FRAMING MEMBERS

ADHESIVE APPLIED IN PARALLEL RIBBONS 16" APART

CONTINUOUS RIBBON AROUND THE PERIMETER

NOTES

11.18 a. Data adapted from *Architectural Woodwork Quality Standards*.
b. Most types of resin used in the United States are alkaline-catalyzed. The general statements refer to this type.
11.20 Adhesive is applied to one surface only.

Contributor:
Richard J. Vitullo, AIA, Oak Leaf Studio, Crownsville, Maryland.

NAILS

GENERAL

Nails are made of many types of metal for diverse uses. When selecting nails, follow the recommendations of the manufacturer of the material to be fastened, as well as applicable building codes. General guidelines include:

- Select nails so as to avoid galvanic action between the nail and the nailed material.
- Select nail head size according to the strength and area of the material to be held.
- In wood framing use the correct size and number of nails to withstand stress. Procedures for calculating nailed connections can be found in the *National Design Specifications for Wood Construction.*
- Base nail selection on the type(s) of wood or other materials to be assembled, joined, or connected.
- Be aware that nails with serrated or helically threaded shanks have increased holding power, but such nails are difficult to remove without destroying the surrounding material.
- Where nails are exposed to moisture or weather—for example, in exterior stucco lath—use nonferrous (aluminum) or zinc-coated nails.
- Choose nails for automatic nailing equipment specifically for the equipment used. See ANSI's "Safety Requirements for Power-Actuated Fastening Systems," and OSHA regulations.

COMMON NAIL SIZES
11.21

LENGTH	PENNY (D)	GAUGE	DIAMETER OF HEAD (IN.)	NAILS/LB
1	2	15	11/64	847
1-1/4	3	14	13/64	543
1-1/2	4	12-1/2	1/4	296
1-3/4	5	12-1/2	1/4	254
2	6	11-1/2	17/64	167
2-1/4	7	11-1/2	17/64	150
2-1/2	8	10-1/4	9/32	101
2-3/4	9	10-1/4	9/32	92.1
3	10	9	5/16	66
3-1/4	12	9	5/16	66.1
3-1/2	16	8	11/32	47.4
4	20	6	13/32	29.7
4-1/2	30	5	7/16	22.7
5	40	4	15/32	17.3
5-1/2	50	3	1/2	13.5
6	60	2	17/32	10.7

NAILS FOR ROUGH CARPENTRY
11.22

NAME	SHAPE	MATERIAL	FINISH
Common		Steel or aluminum	Smooth
Annular		Steel, hardened steel, copper, brass, bronze, silicon bronze, nickel silver, aluminzum, monel, or silver, aluminum, monel,	Bright, hardened
Helical		Steel, hardened steel, copper, brass, bronze, silicon bronze, nickel silver, aluminum, monel, or stainless steel	Bright, hardened
Common cut strike		Steel or iron	Bright or zinc-coated
Double-headed		Steel	Bright or zinc-coated
		Aluminum	Bright
Square		Steel	Smooth, bright, zinc-coated
Round wire		Steel	Smooth, bright, zinc-coated
Annular		Aluminum	Bright or hard

ROOFING NAILS
11.23

NAME	SHAPE	MATERIAL	FINISH
Siding and shingle		Steel, copper, or aluminum	Smooth, bright, zinc- or cement-coated
Roofing (barbed)		Steel or aluminum	Smooth, bright, zinc- or cement-coated
Roofing		Steel	Bright or zinc-coated
Nonleaking		Steel	Bright or zinc-coated
Shingle nail		Steel or cut iron	Plain or zinc-coated
Cut slating (nonferrous)		Copper, muntz metal, or zinc	
Gutter spike (round)		Steel	Bright or zinc-coated
Gutter spike (annular)		Copper	Bright

NAILS FOR FINISH WORK
11.24

NAME	SHAPE	MATERIAL	FINISH
Wallboard		Steel or aluminum	Smooth, bright, blued, or cement-coated
Fine nail		Steel	Bright
Lath		Steel	Blued or cement-coated
Lath		Steel or aluminum	Smooth, bright, blued, or cement-coated
Casing or brad		Steel or aluminum	Bright or cement-coated
Finishing		Steel	Smooth

Contributors:
Charles F. D. Egbert, AIA, Washington, DC; American Forest & Paper Association, Incorporated, Washington, DC; John Showalter, PE, American Wood Council, Washington, SC.

SHEATHING

PLYWOOD DESIGN DATA

APA TRADEMARKS
11.25

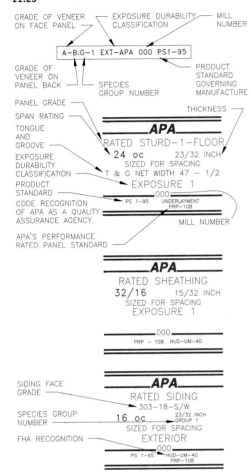

GRADE OF VENEER ON FACE PANEL — EXPOSURE DURABILITY CLASSIFICATION — MILL NUMBER

A–B.G-1 EXT–APA 000 PS1–95

GRADE OF VENEER ON PANEL BACK — SPECIES GROUP NUMBER — PRODUCT STANDARD GOVERNING MANUFACTURE

PANEL GRADE
SPAN RATING
TONGUE AND GROOVE
EXPOSURE DURABILITY CLASSIFICATION
PRODUCT STANDARD
CODE RECOGNITION OF APA AS A QUALITY ASSURANCE AGENCY
APA'S PERFORMANCE RATED PANEL STANDARD

APA
RATED STURD–1–FLOOR
24 oc   23/32 INCH
SIZED FOR SPACING
T & G NET WIDTH 47 – 1/2
EXPOSURE 1
000
PS 1–95   UNDERLAYMENT PRP–108
MILL NUMBER
THICKNESS

APA
RATED SHEATHING
32/16   15/32 INCH
SIZED FOR SPACING
EXPOSURE 1
000
PRP – 108   HUD–UM–40

SIDING FACE GRADE
SPECIES GROUP NUMBER
FHA RECOGNITION

APA
RATED SIDING
303–18–S/W
16 oc   23/32 INCH GROUP 1
SIZED FOR SPACING
EXTERIOR
000
PS 1–95   HUD–UM–40 PRP–108

GRADE DESIGNATIONS

Structural panel grades are generally identified in terms of the veneer grade used on the face and back of the panel (e.g., A-B, B-C, etc.) or rated by a name suggesting the panel's intended end use (e.g., APA Rated Sheathing, APA Rated Sturd-I-Floor, etc.).

VENEER GRADES

Veneer grades define veneer appearance in terms of natural unrepaired growth characteristics and the number and size of repairs allowable during manufacture. The highest quality veneer grades are N and A. The minimum grade of veneer permitted in exterior plywood is C-grade. D-grade veneer is used only for backs and inner plies of panels intended for interior use or applications protected from exposure to permanent or severe moisture.

- *N*: Smooth surface "natural finish" veneer. Select all heartwood or all sapwood. Free of open defects. Allows not more than six repairs, wood only, per 4 by 8 panel, made parallel to grain and well matched for grain and color.

- *A*: Smooth, paintable. Not more than 18 neatly made repairs; boat, sled, or router type; parallel to grain permitted. May be used for natural finish in less demanding applications. Synthetic repairs permitted.
- *B*: Solid surface. Shims, circular repair plugs, and tight knots to 1 in. across grain permitted. Some minor splits and synthetic repairs permitted.
- *C*: Plugged, improved. C-grade veneer with splits limited to 1/8-in. width; knotholes and borer holes limited to 1/4 by 1/2 in. Admits some broken grain. Synthetic repairs permitted.
- *C*: Tight knots to 1-1/2 in. Knotholes to 1 in. across grain and some to 1-1/2 in., if total width of knots and knotholes is within specified limits. Synthetic or wood repairs. Discoloration and sanding defects that do not impair strength permitted. Limited splits allowed. Stitching permitted.
- *D*: Knots and knotholes to 2-1/2 in. width across grain and 1/2 in. larger within specified limits. Limited splits allowed. Stitching permitted. Limited to interior and Exposure 1 panels.

SPAN RATINGS

APA Rated Sheathing, APA Rated Sturd-I-Floor, and APA Rated Siding carry numbers in their trademarks called span ratings. These denote the maximum recommended center-to-center spacing, in inches, of supports for the panels in construction applications. Except for APA Rated Siding panels, the span rating in the trademark applies when the long panel dimension is across supports, unless the strength axis is otherwise identified. The span rating in the trademark of rated siding panels applies when installed vertically.

The span rating in APA Rated Sheathing trademarks appears as two numbers separated by a slash, such as 32/16 and 48/24. The Span Rating for APA Rated Siding panels is for vertical installation; for lap siding, the rating applies with the long dimension across supports. An exception is APA Rated Sheathing intended for use on walls only. The trademarks for these contain a single number similar to the span rating for APA Rated Siding. The left-hand number denotes the maximum recommended spacing of supports when the panel is used for roof sheathing, with the long dimension or strength axis of the panel across three or more supports. The right-hand number indicates the maximum recommended spacing of supports when the panel is used for subflooring, with the long dimension or strength axis of the panel across three or more supports. A panel marked 32/16, for example, may be used for roof decking over supports 32 in. o.c. or for subflooring over supports 16 in. o.c.

The span ratings in the trademarks on APA Rated Sturd-I-Floor and Siding panels appear as a single number. APA Rated Sturd-I-Floor panels are designed specifically for single-floor (combined subfloor underlayment) applications under carpet and pad and are manufactured with span ratings of 16, 20, 24, 32, and 48 in. The span ratings for APA Rated Sturd-I-Floor panels, like those for APA Rated Sheathing, are based on application of the panel, with the long dimension or strength axis across three or more supports.

APA Rated Siding is available with span ratings of 16 and 24 in. Span-rated panels and lap siding may be applied directly to studs, over nonstructural wall sheathing (Sturd-I-Wall construction), or over nailable panel or lumber sheathing (double wall construction). Panels and lap siding with a span rating of 16 o.c. may be applied directly to studs spaced 16 in. o.c and similarly with 24 in. o.c for panel and span rating of 24. All rated siding panels may be applied horizontally direct to studs 16 or 24 in. o.c., provided horizontal joints are blocked. When used over nailable structural sheathing, the span rating of rated siding panels refers to the maximum recommended spacing of vertical rows of nails, rather than to stud spacing.

BOND CLASSIFICATIONS

APA-trademarked panels may be produced in three bond classifications: Exterior, Exposure 1, and Interior. (Note: All-veneer APA-rated Sheathing, Exposure 1, commonly called CDX in the trade, is frequently mistaken as an Exterior panel and is erroneously used in applications for which it does not possess the required resistance to weather. CDX should only be used for applications as outlined under Exposure 1, below. For sheathing grade panels that will be exposed permanently to the weather, specify APA Rated Sheathing Exterior (C-C Exterior under Product Standard PS 1 for manufacturing).

- Exterior panels have a fully waterproof bond and are designed for applications subject to permanent exposure to the weather.
- Exposure 1 panels have a fully waterproof bond and are designed for applications where long construction time may delay permanent protection or where high-moisture conditions may be encountered in service. Exposure 1 panels are made with the same adhesives used in Exterior panels. However, because other compositional factors may affect bond performance, only Exterior panels should be used for permanent exposure to the weather.
- Interior panels that lack further glueline information in their trademarks are manufactured with interior glue and are intended for interior applications only.

SANDED, UNSANDED, AND TOUCH-SANDED PANELS

Panels with B-grade or better veneer faces are sanded smooth in manufacture to fulfill the requirements of their intended applications (cabinets, shelving, furniture, built-ins, etc.). APA Rated Sheathing panels are unsanded because a smooth surface is not required for their intended use. Other APA panels—Underlayment, Rated Sturd-I-Floor, C-D Plugged, and C-C Plugged—require only touch-sanding for "sizing," to make the panel thickness more uniform.

Unsanded and touch-sanded panels and panels with B-grade or better veneer on one side only usually carry the APA trademark on the panel back. Panels with both sides of B-grade or better veneer, or with special overlaid surfaces (such as medium-density overlay), carry the APA trademark on the panel edge.

GROUP NUMBER

Plywood can be manufactured from more than 70 species of wood. These species are divided, on the basis of bending strength and stiffness, into five groups under U.S. Product Standard PS 1. Strongest species are in Group 1, the next strongest in Group 2, and so on. The group number that appears in the trademark on some APA trademarked panels—primarily sanded grades—is based on the species of face and back veneers. Where face and back veneers are not from the same species group, the higher group number is used, except for sanded and decorative panels 3/8 in. thick or less. These are identified by face species because they are chosen primarily for appearance and used in applications where structural integrity is not critical. Sanded panels greater than 3/8 in. are identified by face species if C or D grade backs are at least 1/8 in. and are no more than one species group number larger. Some species are used widely in plywood manufacture, others rarely. Check local availability before specifying if a particular species is desired.

Contributors:
BSB Design, Des Moines, Iowa; APA—The Engineered Wood Association, Tacoma, Washington.

CLASSIFICATION OF SPECIES
11.26

GROUP 1		GROUP 2				GROUP 3		GROUP 4		GROUP 5
Apitong[a,b]		Cedar, Port Orford		Maple, Black		Alder, Red		Aspen		Basswood
Beech, American		Cypress		Mengkulang[a]		Birch, Paper			Bigtooth	Poplar, Balsam
Birch		Douglas-fir, No. 2[c]		Meranti, Red[a,d]			Cedar, Alaska		Quaking	
	Sweet	Fir		Mersawa[a]		Fir, subalpine		Cativo		
	Yellow		Balsam	Pine		Hemlock, Eastern		Cedar		
Douglas-fir, No. 1[c]			California Red		Pond	Maple, Bigleaf			Incense	
Kapur[a]			Grand		Red	Pine			Western red	
Keruing[a,b]			Noble		Virginia		Jack	Cottonwood		
Larch, Western			Pacific Silver		Western White		Lodgepole	Eastern		
Maple, Sugar			White	Spruce			Ponderosa		Black (Western poplar)	
Pine		Hemlock, Western			Black		Spruce	Pine		
	Caribbean	Lauan			Red	Redwood			Eastern White	
	Ocote	Almon			Sitka	Spruce			Sugar	
Pine, Southern		Bagtikan		Sweetgum			Engelmann			
	Loblolly	Mayapis		Tamarack			White			
	Longleaf	Red Lauan		Yellow Poplar						
	Shortleaf	Tangile								
	Slash	White Lauan								
Tanoak										

PLYWOOD PANEL TYPES

APA RATED SIDING PANELS

APA Rated Siding Panels can be used for exterior siding, fencing, and other external applications. They can be manufactured as conventional veneered plywood or as an overlaid oriented-strand board siding. Both panel and lap siding are available. They are intended for use with a special surface treatment such as V-groove, shallow channel groove, deep groove (such as APA Texture 1-11), kerfed groove, brushed, rough-sawn, and texture-embossed medium density overlay (MDO). Span Rating (stud spacing for siding qualified for APA Sturd-I-Wall applications) and face grade classification (for veneer-faced siding) are indicated in the trademark. Bond Classification: Exterior. Common thicknesses are 11/32, 3/8, 15/32, 1/2, 19/32, and 5/8 in.

303-PLYWOOD SIDING GRADES
11.27

CLASS	GRADE[a]	WOOD PATCHES	SYNTHETIC PATCHES
Special Series 303	303-OC[b,c]	Not permitted	Not permitted
	303-OL[d]	Not applicable for overlays	
	303-NR[e]	Not permitted	Not permitted
	303-SR[f]	Not permitted	Permitted as natural defect shape only
303-6	303-6-W	Limit 6	Not permitted
	303-6-S	Not permitted	Limit 6
	303-6-S/W	Limit 6, any combination	
303-18	303-18-W	Limit 18	Not permitted
	303-18-S	Not permitted	Limit 18
	303-18-S/W	Limit 18, any combination	
303-30	303-30-W	Limit 30	Not permitted
	303-30-S	Not permitted	Limit 30
	303-30-S/W	Limit 30, any combination	

SPECIALTY SIDING

APA publishes minimum requirements that plywood panels must meet to qualify for classification as Specialty Siding. APA classifies materials that meet the requirements as, APA 303 Series Specialty Siding. These materials much meet requirements related to gluebond, veneer grade, workmanship, panel thickness, and number of plies and layers, as well as type and number of repair patches. Table 11.50 indicates the allowable patches for various types of specialty siding.

Texture 1-11 is a groove detail for 303 Special Siding siding panel. Texture 1-11 pattern details include: 1/4 in. deep groove, 3/8 in. wide, spaced 4 or 8 in. o.c., overall panel thickness is limited to five-plies with a nominal thickness of 19/32 inch minimum.

MARINE-GRADE PLYWOOD

Ideal for boat hulls. Made only with Douglas fir or Western larch. Special solid-jointed core construction for water resistance. Subject to special limitations on core gaps and face repairs. Also available with high-density overlay (HDO) or MDO faces. Bond Classification: Exterior. Common thicknesses: 1/4, 3/8, 1/2, 5/8, 3/4 in. A common misconception, involves the use of marine-grade plywood in place of exterior panels. Marine-grade plywood is uniquely situated for marine applications and is not treated to enhance its resistance to decay. Marine-grade plywood and exterior panels have the same APA Exterior Exposure Durability, and both are designed for extended exposure to weather and moisture. Marine-Grade plywood has a sanded face and will not be as visually acceptable after weathering.

APA RATED STURD-I-FLOOR 48 OC (2-4-1)

For combination subfloor underlayment on 32- and 48-in. spans and for heavy timber roof construction. Manufactured only as conventional veneered plywood. Available square-edged or tongue-and-grooved. Bond Classifications: Exposure 1. Thickness: 1-1/8.

NOTES FOR SANDED AND PERFORMANCE-RATED PANELS

- Specify performance-rated panels by thickness and span rating. Span ratings are based on panel strength and stiffness. These properties are a function of panel composition and configuration as well as thickness, therefore the same span rating may appear on panels of different thicknesses. Conversely, panels of the same thickness may be marked with different span ratings.
- All plies in Structural I panels are limited to Group 1 species. Structural II panels are seldom available.
- Exterior sanded panels, C-C Plugged, C-D Plugged, and Underlayment grades can also be manufactured in Structural I (all plies limited to Group 1 species).
- Some manufacturers also produce panels with premium N-grade veneer on one or both faces. They are available only by special order.
- Available in thicknesses of 11/32, 15/32, 19/32, 23/32 in.

NOTES

11.26 a. Each of these names represents a trade group of woods consisting of a number of closely related species.

b. Species from the genus *Dipterocarpus* are marketed collectively: Apitong if originating in the Philippines, Keruing if originating in Malaysia or Indonesia.

c. Douglas fir from trees grown in the states of Washington, Oregon, California, Idaho, Montana, and Wyoming, and the Canadian provinces of Alberta and British Columbia are classed as Douglas fir No. 1. Douglas fir from trees grown in the states of Nevada, Utah, Colorado, Arizona, and New Mexico are classed as Douglas fir No. 2.

d. Red Meranti is limited to species having a specific gravity of 0.41 or more, based on green volume and oven-dry weight.

11.27 a. Limitations on grade characteristics are based on 4 by 8 ft panel sizes. Limits on other sizes vary in proportion. All panels except 303-NR allow restricted minor repairs such as shims. These and other face appearance characteristics such as knots, knotholes, and splits, are limited by both size and number, in accordance with panel grades; 303 OC is the most restrictive and 303-30 the least. Multiple repairs are permitted only on 303-18 and 303-30 panels. Patch size is restricted on all panel grades. For additional information, including finishing recommendations, refer to the APA Product Guide: 303 Plywood Siding, E300.

b. Check local availability.

c. Clear.

d. Overlaid (e.g., medium-density overlay siding).

e. Natural rustic.

f. Synthetic rustic.

Contributors:
BSB Design, Des Moines, Iowa; APA—The Engineered Wood Association, Tacoma, Washington.

PLYWOOD USES

EXTERIOR-TYPE PANELS
11.28

APPEARANCE[a]		VENEER			THICKNESS (IN.)					
GRADE[b]	COMMON USES	F	M	B	1/4	5/16	11/32 3/8	15/32 1/2	19/32 5/8	23/32 3/4
A-A Ext	For use where appearance of both sides is important for exterior applications such as fences, signs, boats, shipping containers, tanks, ducts, etc.	A	C	A	●		●	●	●	●
A-B Ext	For use where appearance of one side is less important but where two solid surfaces are necessary	A	C	B	●		●	●	●	●
A-C Ext	For use where appearance of only one side is important in exterior applications, e.g., soffits, fences, structural uses, boxcar and truck linings, farm buildings, tanks, trays, commercial refrigerators, etc.	A	C	C	●		●	●	●	●
B-B Ext	Utility panels with two solid sides; for protected applications.	B	C	B	●		●	●	●	●
B-C Ext	Utility panel for farm service and work buildings, boxcar and truck linings, containers, tanks, agricultural equipment, as a base for exterior coatings and other exterior uses.	B	C	C	●		●	●	●	●
HDO Ext	Has a hard semiopaque resin-fiber overlay on both sides; abrasion-resistant. For concrete forms, cabinets, countertops, signs, tanks. Suitable for permanent exterior exposure without further finishing Also available with skid-resistant screen-grid surface.	A B	C	A B			●	●	●	●
MDO Ext	Medium-density overlay with smooth, opaque, resin-fiber overlay, one or both sides. Recommended for siding and other outdoor applications. Ideal base for paint, indoors and outdoors. Available as a 303 Siding.	B	C	B C			●	●	●	●
Panel Siding Ext[c]	Special surface treatment, such as V-groove, channel groove, striated, brushed, rough sawn	C	C			●	●	●	
T1-11 Ext[c]	Special 303 panel having grooves 1/4 in. deep, 3/8 in. wide, spaced 4 or 8 in. o.c.; other spacing optional. Edges shiplapped. Available unsanded, textured, and medium-density overlay.	A B C	C	C				●		
Plyron Ext	Hardboard face on both sides. Faces tempered, untempered, smooth, or screened. For countertops, shelving, cabinet doors, flooring, etc.	HB	C	HB				●	●	●
Underlayment C-C Plugged Ext	For application over structural subfloor. Provides smooth surface for application of carpet and pad. Touch-sanded.	C	C	C			●	●	●	●
C-C Plugged Ext	For use as underlayment over structural subfloor, in severe moisture conditions, including refrigerated or controlled atmosphere storage rooms, pallet bins, tanks, truck floors, linings, and other exterior applications. Touch-sanded.	C-Plugged	C	C			●	●	●	●
B-B Plyform Class I and Class II Ext[d]	Concrete form grades with high reuse factor. Sanded both sides and mill-oiled, unless otherwise specified. Special restrictions on species. Class I panels are stiffest, strongest, and most commonly available. Also available in HDO for very smooth concrete finish, in Structural I (all plies limited to Group 1 species), and with special overlays.	B	C	B					●	●

PERFORMANACE RATED[a]		VENEER			THICKNESS (IN.)					
GRADE[b]	COMMON USES	F	M	B	1/4	5/16	11/32 3/8	15/32 1/2	19/32 5/8	23/32 3/4
Sheathing Ext	Specially designed for subflooring and wall and roof sheathing, and siding on service and farm buildings. Also good for a broad range of other construction and industrial applications. Can be manufactured as a conventional veneered plywood, as a composite, or as a nonveneered panel. For special engineered applications, veneered panels conforming to PS 1 may be required.	C	C	C		●	●	●	●	●
Structural I and II Sheathing Ext	Unsanded all-veneer PS 1 or PS 2 plywood grades are used where strength is of maximum importance; for example, for box beams, gusset plates, stressed-skin panels, containers, and pallet bins. Structural I is more commonly available. For engineered applications in construction and industry where full exterior-type panels are required. Unsanded.	C	C	C		●	●	●	●	●
Sturdi-I-Floor Ext	Specially designed as combination subfloor underlayment, where severe moisture conditions exist (e.g., balcony decks). Provides smooth surface for application of carpet and pad, and possesses high concentrated and load-impact resistance. Can be manufactured as a nonveneered panel. Available square-edged or tongue-and-grooved. Touch-sanded.	C	C[e]	C					●	●

NOTES

11.28 a. Standard 4 by 8 panel sizes; other sizes available.
b. Available in Group 1, 2, 3, 4, or 5, unless otherwise noted.
c. Maximum recommended support spacing for roofs and floors is indicated in sheathing and single-layer floor trademarks. Wall span ratings are included in rated siding panels.
d. Also available in Structural I.
e. Special construction to resist indentation from concentrated loads.
f. Interior type panels with exterior glue are identified as Exposure I.

g. Special improved grade for structural panels.
h. Also available as nonveneer panels.

Contributors:
David S. Collins, FAIA, Preview Group, Inc., Cincinnati, Ohio; APA—The Engineered Wood Association, Tacoma, Washington.

INTERIOR TYPE PANELS
11.29

APPEARANCE[a]			VENEER			THICKNESS (IN.)					
GRADE[b, f]	COMMON USES		F	M	B	1/4	5/16	11/32 3/8	15/32 1/2	19/32 5/8	23/32 3/4
A-A Int	Use where appearance of both sides is important for interior applications, such as built-ins, cabinets, furniture, partitions. Smooth surfaces suitable for painting.		A	D	A	●	●	●	●	●	
A-B Int	For use where appearance of one side is less important but where two solid surfaces are necessary.		A	D	B	●		●	●	●	●
A-D Int	For use where appearance of only one side is important in interior applications, e.g., paneling, built-ins, shelving, partitions, etc.	Interior Exposure 1	A	D	D	●		●	●	●	●
B-B Int	Utility panels with two solid sides.		B	D	B	●		●	●	●	●
B-D Int	Utility panel for backing, sides of built-ins, industry shelving, slip sheets, separator boards, bins, and other interior or protected applications.		B	D	D	●		●	●	●	●
Decorative Panels-Int	Rough-sawn, brushed, grooved, or other faces. For paneling, interior accent walls, built-ins, counter facing, and exhibit displays. Can also be made by some manufacturers in exterior for siding, gable ends, fences, etc. Use recommendations for exterior panels vary with the particular product; check with manufacturer.		A B C	D	D		●	●	●	●	
Plyron-Int	Hardboard face on both sides. Faces tempered, screened, untempered, smooth, or for countertops, shelving, cabinet doors, flooring, etc.		HB D	C	HB				●	●	●
Underlayment-Int	For application over structural subfloor. Provides smooth surface for application of carpet and pad, and has high concentrated and impact-load resistance. Touch-sanded. Also available with exterior glue.		C D	C	D			●	●	●	●
C-D Plugged Int	For open soffits, built-ins, wall and ceiling tile backing, cable reels, walkways, separator boards, and other interior or protected applications. Not a substitute for underlayment or APA Rated Sturd-I-Floor, as it lacks puncture resistance. Touch-sanded. Also made with exterior glue.		C	D	D			●	●	●	●

PERFORMANACE RATED[a, g]			VENEER			THICKNESS (IN.)					
GRADE	COMMON USES		F	M	B	1/4	5/16	11/32 3/8	15/32 1/2	19/32 5/8	23/32 3/4
Sheathing Exp 1	Specially designed for subflooring and wall and roof sheathing. Also good for broad range of other construction and industrial applications. Can be manufactured as a conventional veneered plywood, as a composite, or as a nonveneered panel. For special engineered applications, veneered panels conforming to PS 1 may be required. Commonly available with exterior glue for sheathing and subflooring. Specify Exposure 1 treated wood foundations.		C	D	D		●	●	●	●	●
Structural 1 and II Sheathing Exp 1	Unsanded all-veneer PS 1 or PS 2 plywood grades for use where strength is of maximum importance; for example, box beams, gusset plates, stressed-skin panels, containers, pallet bins. Structural I is more commonly available. Made only with exterior glue for beams, gusset plates, and stressed-skin panels.		C[g]	D[g]	D[g]					●	●
Floor Exp 1	For combination subfloor and underlayment under carpet and pad. Specify Exposure 1 where moisture is present. Available in tongue-and-groove.		C D[e]	C	D					●	●
Floor 48 in. o.c. Exp 1	Combination subfloor underlayment on 32- and 48-in. spans and for heavy timber roofs. Touch-sanded or fully sanded.		C D	C	D					1-1/8	

NOTES

11.29 a. Standard 4 by 8 panel sizes; other sizes available.
b. Available in Group 1, 2, 3, 4, or 5, unless otherwise noted.
c. Maximum recommended support spacing for roofs and floors is indicated in sheathing and single-layer floor trademarks. Wall span ratings are included in rated siding panels.
d. Also available in Structural I.
e. Special construction to resist indentation from concentrated loads.
f. Interior type panels with exterior glue are identified as Exposure I.

g. Special improved grade for structural panels.
h. Also available as nonveneer panels.

Contributors:
David S. Collins, FAIA, Preview Group, Inc., Cincinnati, Ohio; APA—The Engineered Wood Association, Tacoma, Washington.

WALL AND ROOF SHEATHING

FIBERBOARD SHEATHING
11.30

WOOD FRAMING OR CFS

STRUCTURAL SHEATHING INSTALLED VERTICALLY AT CORNERS FOR BRACING (SPACE NAILS 6" O.C., 3" O.C. AT EDGES)

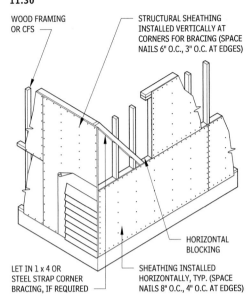

HORIZONTAL BLOCKING

LET IN 1 x 4 OR STEEL STRAP CORNER BRACING, IF REQUIRED

SHEATHING INSTALLED HORIZONTALLY, TYP. (SPACE NAILS 8" O.C., 4" O.C. AT EDGES)

STRUCTURAL WALL SHEATHING
11.31

APA RATED SHEATHING INSTALLED WITH LONG DIMENSION ACROSS STUDS; STAGGER VERTICAL JOINTS

LEAVE 1/8" GAP AT EDGES AND ENDS UNLESS OTHERWISE RECOMMENDED BY MANUFACTURER

DOUBLE TOP PLATE LAP ENDS

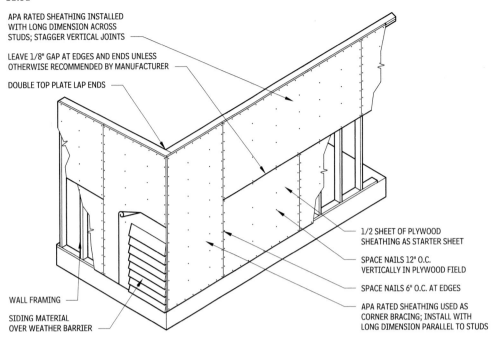

WALL FRAMING

SIDING MATERIAL OVER WEATHER BARRIER

1/2 SHEET OF PLYWOOD SHEATHING AS STARTER SHEET

SPACE NAILS 12" O.C. VERTICALLY IN PLYWOOD FIELD

SPACE NAILS 6" O.C. AT EDGES

APA RATED SHEATHING USED AS CORNER BRACING; INSTALL WITH LONG DIMENSION PARALLEL TO STUDS

GYPSUM BOARD SHEATHING
11.32

SPACE STUDS 24" O.C. MAX.

SPACE STUDS 16" O.C. FOR CORNER BRACING

HORIZONTAL BLOCKING

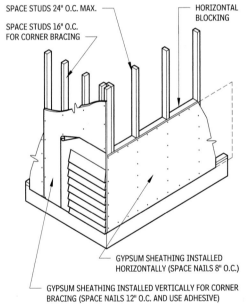

GYPSUM SHEATHING INSTALLED HORIZONTALLY (SPACE NAILS 8" O.C.)

GYPSUM SHEATHING INSTALLED VERTICALLY FOR CORNER BRACING (SPACE NAILS 12" O.C. AND USE ADHESIVE)

STRUCTURAL ROOF SHEATHING
11.33

PANEL CLIPS, TONGUE-AND-GROOVED EDGES, OR BLOCKING UNDERNEATH IF REQUIRED

SPACE NAILS 12" O.C., 6" O.C. AT ENDS

ROOFING FELT

GUTTER

SHINGLES OR SHAKES ON ROOFING. FOLLOW ROOFING MANUFACTURER'S RECOMMENDATIONS FOR ROOFING FELTS

PROTECT EDGES OF EXPOSURE 1 AND 2 PANELS AGAINST EXPOSURE TO WEATHER OR USE EXTERIOR PANEL STARTER STRIPS

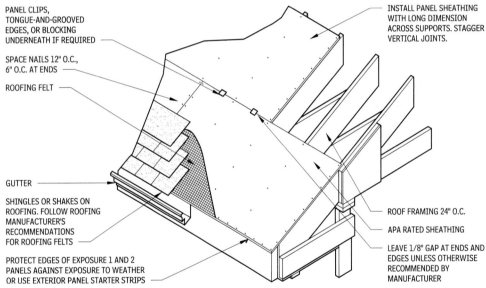

INSTALL PANEL SHEATHING WITH LONG DIMENSION ACROSS SUPPORTS. STAGGER VERTICAL JOINTS.

ROOF FRAMING 24" O.C.

APA RATED SHEATHING

LEAVE 1/8" GAP AT ENDS AND EDGES UNLESS OTHERWISE RECOMMENDED BY MANUFACTURER

NOTES

11.32 Nail siding through gypsum board to studs; refer to manufacturer's recommendations for specific installation instructions.
11.33 Before roofing is applied cover roof sheathing as soon as possible with roofing felt for protection from moisture.

Contributors:
David S. Collins, FAIA, Preview Group, Incorporated, Cincinnati, Ohio; American Forest & Paper Association.

SHEATHING MATERIALS
11.34

CHARACTERISTICS	STRUCTURAL SHEATHING	GYPSUM	FIBERBOARD	PLASTIC
Nailable base	Yes	No	Only high-density	No
Vapor retardant	No	No	If asphalt-treated	Yes
Insulation R-value (1/2-in. thickness)	1.2	0.7	2.6	Varies with manufacturer
Corner bracing provided	Yes	Yes (see manufacturer's recommendations)	Only high-density	No
Panel sizes (in.)	48 × 96, 48 × 108, 48 × 120	24 × 96, 48 × 96, 48 × 120, 48 × 144, 48 × 168	48 × 96, 48 × 108, 48 × 120, 48 × 144	2′ × 96, 24 × 48, 224 × 96, 48 × 96, 48 × 108
Panel thickness (in.)	5/16, 3/8, 7/16, 15/32, 1/2, 19/32, 5/8, 23/32, 3/4, 7/8, 1, 11/8	1/4, 3/8, 1/2, 5/8	1/2, 25/32	1/2 to 6 (for roof)
Other remarks	Plywood grades commonly used for roof and wall sheathing have span ratings of 12/0, 16/0, 20/0, 24/0, 24/16, 32/16, 40/20, and 48/24; exposure durability classifications are Exposure 1 and Exterior. For unsupported edges, refer to manufacturer's recommendations.	Fire-resistance-rated panels are available in 1/2- and 5/8-in. thicknesses.	Also called insulation board. Can be treated or impregnated with asphalt. Available in regular and high-density panels.	Considered an effective vapor barrier, so walls must be well vented. Some products emit toxic fumes when burned; refer to manufacturer's specifications.

GYPSUM SHEATHING
11.35

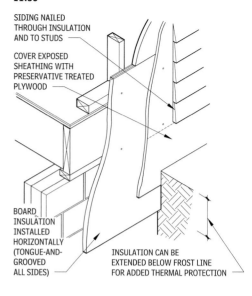

SIDING NAILED THROUGH INSULATION AND TO STUDS

COVER EXPOSED SHEATHING WITH PRESERVATIVE TREATED PLYWOOD

BOARD INSULATION INSTALLED HORIZONTALLY (TONGUE-AND-GROOVED ALL SIDES)

INSULATION CAN BE EXTENDED BELOW FROST LINE FOR ADDED THERMAL PROTECTION

PLYWOOD SUBFLOORING ON WOOD FRAMING

APA RATED STURD-I-FLOOR
11.36

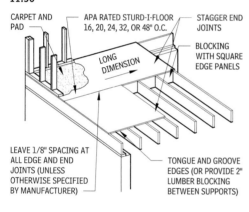

CARPET AND PAD

APA RATED STURD-I-FLOOR 16, 20, 24, 32, OR 48" O.C.

STAGGER END JOINTS

BLOCKING WITH SQUARE EDGE PANELS

LONG DIMENSION

LEAVE 1/8" SPACING AT ALL EDGE AND END JOINTS (UNLESS OTHERWISE SPECIFIED BY MANUFACTURER)

TONGUE AND GROOVE EDGES (OR PROVIDE 2" LUMBER BLOCKING BETWEEN SUPPORTS)

SPAN RATING (MAXIMUM JOIST SPACING, IN.)	PANEL THICKNESS (IN.)	NAIL SIZE AND TYPE	FASTENING			
			PANEL EDGE SPACING (IN.)		INTERMEDIATE SPACING (IN.)	
			GLUE/NAILED	NAILED ONLY	GLUE/NAILED	NAILED ONLY
16	19/32, 5/8, 21/32	6d ring or screw shank[c]	12	6	12	12
20	19/32, 5/8, 23/32, 3/4	6d ring or screw shank[c]	12	6	12	12
24	11/16, 23/32, 3/4	6d ring or screw shank[c]	12	6	12	12
	7/8, 1	8d ring or screw shank[c]	12	3	12	12
48	1-1/8	8d ring or screw shank[d]	6	6		

PLYWOOD UNDERLAYMENT
11.37

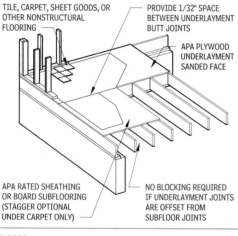

TILE, CARPET, SHEET GOODS, OR OTHER NONSTRUCTURAL FLOORING

PROVIDE 1/32" SPACE BETWEEN UNDERLAYMENT BUTT JOINTS

APA PLYWOOD UNDERLAYMENT SANDED FACE

APA RATED SHEATHING OR BOARD SUBFLOORING (STAGGER OPTIONAL UNDER CARPET ONLY)

NO BLOCKING REQUIRED IF UNDERLAYMENT JOINTS ARE OFFSET FROM SUBFLOOR JOINTS

PLYWOOD GRADES AND SPECIES GROUP	APPLICATION	MINIMUM PLYWOOD THICKNESS (IN.)
Groups 1, 2, 3, 4, and 5 Underlayment Int-APA (with interior or exterior glue), or Underlayment Ext-APA (C-C Plugged) Ext	Over smooth subfloor.	1/4
	Over lumber subfloor or other uneven surfaces.	11/32
Same grades as above, but Group 1 only	Over lumber floor up to 4 in. wide. Face grain must be perpendicular to boards.	1/4

UNDERLAYMENT NAILING SCHEDULE

Use 3d ring shank nails for underlayment up to 1/2-in. thickness, 4d for 19/32 in. and thicker. Use 16-gauge staples; however 18-gauge may be used with 1/4-in. thick underlayment. Crown width should be 3/8 inch for 16-gauge staples, 3/16 in. for 18-gauge. Length should be sufficient to penetrate subflooring at least 5/8 in. or extend completely through. Space fasteners at 3 in. along panel edges and 6 in. each way in the panel interior, except for 11/32 in. or thicker underlayment applied with ring shank nails; in this case, use 6-in. spacing along edges and 8-in. spacing each way in the panel interior. Unless subfloor and joists are of thoroughly seasoned material and have remained dry during construction, countersink nail heads below surface of the underlayment just prior to laying finish floors, to avoid nail popping. Joints should be 1/32 in. wide to allow for expansion and contraction. If thin resilient flooring is to be used to cover underlayment, fill and thoroughly sand joints.

NOTES

11.36 a. For conditions not listed, see APA literature.
b. Use only APA Specification AFG-01 adhesives, properly applied. Use only solvent-based glues on nonveneered panels with sealed surfaces and edges.
c. If ring or screw-shank nails are not available, 8d common nails may be substituted.
d. If supports are well seasoned, 10d common nails may be substituted with 1-1/8-in. panels.
e. Space nails 6 in. for 48-in. spans and 12 in. for 32-in. spans.

11.37 a. For carpeting, sheet goods, or other nonstructural flooring (consult the Tile Council of America for recommendations regarding ceramic tile).
b. Where floors may be subject to unusual moisture conditions, use panels with exterior glue (Exposure 1) or Underlayment C-C Plugged EXT-APA. C-D Plugged is not an adequate substitute for underlayment grade, since it does not ensure equivalent dent resistance.
c. Recommended grades have a solid surface backed with a special inner-ply construction that resists punch-through and dents from concentrated loads.

Contributor:
David S. Collins, FAIA Preview Group, Inc., Cincinnati, Ohio.

APA PANEL SUBFLOORING[a]
11.38

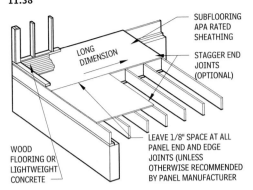

SUBFLOORING APA RATED SHEATHING

LONG DIMENSION

STAGGER END JOINTS (OPTIONAL)

LEAVE 1/8" SPACE AT ALL PANEL END AND EDGE JOINTS (UNLESS OTHERWISE RECOMMENDED BY PANEL MANUFACTURER)

WOOD FLOORING OR LIGHTWEIGHT CONCRETE

APA PANEL SUBFLOORING

PANEL SPAN RATING (OR GROUP NUMBER) (IN.)	PANEL THICKNESS (IN.)	MAXIMUM SPACING[b, c, e]
24/16	7/16, 1/2	16
32/16	15/32, 1/2, 5/8, 23/32	16[d]
40/20	19/32, 5/8, 23/32, 3/4	20[d]
48/24	23/32, 3/4, 7/8	24
1-1/8 in., Groups 1 and 2	1-1/8	48

SUBFLOORING NAILING SCHEDULE

For 7/16-in. panel, use 6d common nails at 6 in. o.c. at panel edges and 12 in. o.c. at intermediate supports. For 15/32- to 7/8-in. panels, use 8d common nails at 6 in. o.c. at panel edges and 12 in. o.c. at intermediate supports. For 1-1/8- and 1-1/4-in. panels up to 48-in. span, use 10d common nails 6 inch. o.c. at panel edges and 6 inch o.c. at intermediate supports.

GLUED FLOOR SYSTEM

- For complete information on glued floors, including joist span tables (based on building code criteria and lumber sizes), application sequence, and a list of recommended adhesives, contact the Engineered Wood Association.
- Place APA Sturd-I-Floor tongue-and-groove (T&G) across the joists with end joints staggered. Leave 1/8 in. space at all end and edge joints.
- Although T&G is used more often, square edge panels may be used if 2 by 4 blocking is placed under panel edge joints between joists.
- Based on live load of 40 psf and total load of 50 psf, deflection is limited to 1/360 at 40 psf.
- Glue to joists and at T&G joints. If square edge panels are used, block panel edges and glue between panels and between panels and blocking.

GLUED FLOOR NAILING SCHEDULE

Panels should be secured with power-driven fasteners or nailed per APA Sturd-I-Floor Table 11.36.

PLYWOOD SHEATHING FOR ROOFS AND SOFFITS

OPEN SOFFIT
11.39

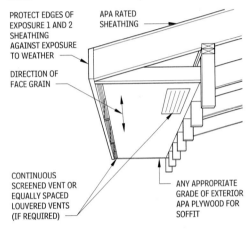

APA RATED SHEATHING

SHIM AT EACH RAFTER FOR FLUSH JOINT AT CHANGE OF PANEL THICKNESS

DIRECTION OF LONG DIMENSION

ANY APPROPRIATE EXTERIOR OR EXPOSURE PANEL GRADE OF ADEQUATE SPAN RATING TO CARRY DESIGN ROOF LOADS

CLOSED SOFFIT
11.40

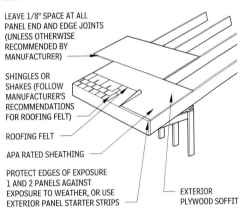

PROTECT EDGES OF EXPOSURE 1 AND 2 SHEATHING AGAINST EXPOSURE TO WEATHER

APA RATED SHEATHING

DIRECTION OF FACE GRAIN

CONTINUOUS SCREENED VENT OR EQUALLY SPACED LOUVERED VENTS (IF REQUIRED)

ANY APPROPRIATE GRADE OF EXTERIOR APA PLYWOOD FOR SOFFIT

GABLE ROOF
11.41

LEAVE 1/8" SPACE AT ALL PANEL END AND EDGE JOINTS (UNLESS OTHERWISE RECOMMENDED BY MANUFACTURER)

SHINGLES OR SHAKES (FOLLOW MANUFACTURER'S RECOMMENDATIONS FOR ROOFING FELT)

ROOFING FELT

APA RATED SHEATHING

PROTECT EDGES OF EXPOSURE 1 AND 2 PANELS AGAINST EXPOSURE TO WEATHER, OR USE EXTERIOR PANEL STARTER STRIPS

EXTERIOR PLYWOOD SOFFIT

EXTERIOR OPEN SOFFITS/COMBINED CEILING DECKING[a]
11.42

PANEL DESCRIPTIONS, MINIMUM RECOMMENDATIONS	GROUP	MAXIMUM SPAN (IN.)
15/32" APA 303 siding	1, 2, 3, 4	16
15/32" APA sanded and MDO	1, 2, 3, 4	
15/32" APA 303 siding	1	24
15/32" APA sanded and MDO	1, 2, 3	
19/32" APA 303 siding	1, 2, 3, 4	32[b]
19/32" APA sanded and MDO	1, 2, 3, 4	
19/32" APA 303 siding	1	
19/32" APA sanded and MDO	1	
23/32" APA 303 siding	1, 2, 3, 4	
23/32" APA sanded and MDO	1, 2, 3, 4	
1-1/8" APA textured	1, 2, 3, 4	48[b]

EXTERIOR CLOSED PLYWOOD SOFFITS
11.43

NOMINAL PLYWOOD THICKNESS	GROUP	MAXIMUM SPAN (IN.) ALL EDGES SUPPORTED
11/32" APA 303 Siding or APA sanded	All species groups	24
15/32" APA 303 Siding or APA sanded32		32
19/32" APA 303 Siding or APA sanded		48

FLAT LOW-PITCHED ROOF
11.44

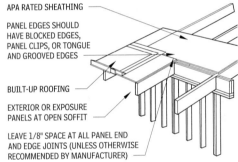

APA RATED SHEATHING

PANEL EDGES SHOULD HAVE BLOCKED EDGES, PANEL CLIPS, OR TONGUE AND GROOVED EDGES

BUILT-UP ROOFING

EXTERIOR OR EXPOSURE PANELS AT OPEN SOFFIT

LEAVE 1/8" SPACE AT ALL PANEL END AND EDGE JOINTS (UNLESS OTHERWISE RECOMMENDED BY MANUFACTURER)

NOTES

11.38 [a.] Applies to APA Rated Sheathing grades only.
[b.] The spans assume plywood is continuous over two or more spans, with the long dimension across supports.
[c.] In some nonresidential buildings, special conditions may require construction in excess of minimums given.
[d.] May be 24 in. if 3/4-in. wood strip flooring is installed at right angles to joists.
[e.] Spans are limited to the values shown because of the possible effect of concentrated loads.

11.42 [a.] Plywood is assumed to be continuous across two or more spans with face grain across supports.
[b.] In open soffit construction, for spans of 32 or 48 in., provide adequate blocking, tongue-and-groove edges, or other support such as panel clips. Minimum loads are at least 30 psf live load, plus 10 psf dead load.
11.43 Plywood is assumed to be continuous across two or more spans with face grain across supports.

Contributors:
BSB Design, Des Moines, Iowa; APA—The Engineered Wood Association, Tacoma, Washington.

APA PANEL ROOF SHEATHING
11.45

PANEL SPAN RATING	PANEL THICKNESS (IN.)	MAXIMUM SPAN (IN.)		NAIL SPACING (IN.)		
		WITH EDGE SUPPORT	WITHOUT EDGE SUPPORT	NAIL SIZE AND TYPE	PANEL EDGES	INTERMEDIATE
12/0	5/16	12	12	6d common	6	12
16/0	5/16, 3/8	16	16			
20/0	5/16, 3/8	20	20			
24/0	3/8, 7/16, 15/32, 1/2	24	20			
24/16	7/16, 15/32, 1/2	24	24			
32/16	15/32, 1/2	32	28			
32/16	19/32, 5/8	32	28	8d common		
40/20	19/32, 5/8, 23/32, 3/4, 7/8	40	32			
40/24	23/32, 3/4, 7/8	48	36			

			STAPLING SPACES (IN.)		
			LEG LENGTH	PANEL EDGES	INTERMEDIATE
(See above)	5/16	(See above)	1-1/4"	4	8
	3/8		1-3/8"		
	7/16, 15/32, 1/2		1-1/2"		

NOTES
- Applicable to APA Rated Panel Sheathing.
- All panels will support at least 30 psf live load plus 10 psf dead load at maximum span. Uniform load deflection limit is 1/180 span under live load plus dead load, or 1/240 under live load only.
- Special conditions may require construction in excess of the given minimums.
- Panel is assumed to be continuous across two or more spans, with long dimension across supports.

CONNECTIONS TO OPEN WEB STEEL JOIST
11.46

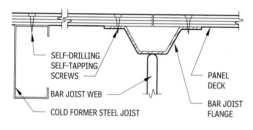

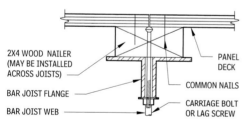

NAILING SCHEDULE
For closed soffits, use nonstaining box or casing nails: 6d for 11/32-in. and 15/32-in. panels, and 8d for 19/32-in. panels. Space nails 6 in. at panel edges and 12 in. along intermediate supports for spans less than 48 in.; 6 in. at all supports for 48-in. spans.

Use 6d common smooth, ring shank, or spiral thread nails for plywood 1/2-in. thick or thinner and 8d for plywood to 1-in. thick. Use 8d ring shank or spiral thread or 10d common smooth for 2-4-1 and 1-1/8-in. panels. Space nails 6 in. at panel edges and 12 in. at intermediate supports, except for 48-in. or longer spans, where nails should be spaced 6 in. at all supports.

ORIENTED-STRAND BOARD

GENERAL

Oriented-strand board (OSB) is manufactured from rectangular-shaped wood strands that are oriented length-wise and then arranged in layers at right angles to one another, laid up into mats, and bonded together with waterproof, heat-cured adhesives. This results in a structural engineered wood product that shares many of the strength and performance characteristics of plywood.

In the first phase of OSB manufacture, logs are debarked and cut to a uniform length. The logs are then turned into strands or wafers. The strands are dried with heat in a large rotating drum, which is screened to grade for strands that are the correct size. The dried strands are sprayed with liquid or powder resin and then transported in layers on a conveyer system to a forming line, where the layers are cross-oriented into mats. For face layers, the strands generally run along the panel; for core layers, the strands are randomly oriented or run across the panel. The mats are trimmed to a workable size and then moved to a press where the wood strands and glue are bonded together under heat and pressure to create a structural panel. Finally, the panels are cut to size. Panels can be manufactured in many sizes simply by altering the cutting pattern.

OSB uses the wood resource very efficiently, in part because sheathing panels can be made using smaller, younger fast-growing tree species such as aspen and Southern yellow pine. Plus, about 85 to 90 percent of a log can be used to make high-quality structural panels, and the remainder—bark, saw trim, and sawdust—can be converted into energy, pulp chips, or bark dust.

OSB is most commonly used for traditional applications such as sheathing for roofs and walls, subfloors, and single-layer flooring. Its superior performance has allowed OSB to gain popularity in a variety of other areas, including structural insulated panels, webs for wood I-joists, materials-handling applications, furniture, and a variety of do-it-yourself projects.

COMMON SIZES

OSB panels manufactured in North America are typically 4 by 8 feet in size. Panels for use as exterior siding are also available in narrow lap widths of 6 or 8 in. and 16-ft lengths. Because OSB is typically manufactured in large sizes, many manufacturers can custom-make panels in almost any size simply by altering the cutting pattern. Most OSB manufacturers make oversized panels, up to 8 by 24 feet, which are typically used for panelized roof systems or modular floors. In operations where oversized panels can be handled, they provide the advantage of reducing the total number of panels required to do a job, and thus speed installation time and cost.

OSB can be manufactured with square edges or with T&G edges. Panel surface treatments may include texturing or sanding. Overlaid OSB for use as exterior siding also may be surface textured or grooved.

APA PANEL GRADE AND THICKNESS

Two common panel grades for OSB are APA Rated Sheathing and APA Rated Sturd-I-Floor. OSB APA Rated Sheathing is intended for subflooring, wall sheathing, and roof sheathing. APA Rated Sheathing/Ceiling Deck can also be made using OSB; it is made so that one surface has an overlay, texturing, or grooving. Common thicknesses for sheathing panels are: 5/16, 3/8, 7/16, 15/32, 1/2, 19/32, 5/8, 23/32, and 3/4 in.

OSB APA Rated Sturd-I-Floor is intended for single-layer flooring under carpet and pad. APA Rated Sturd-I-Floor panels often have tongue-and-groove edges. Common thicknesses for flooring panels are: 19/32, 5/8, 23/32, 3/4, 7/8, 1, and 1-1/8 in.

BOND CLASSIFICATION OF OSB

APA Performance Rated oriented-strand board panels have a designated bond classification, which identifies the panel's resistance to moisture exposure. Panels are classified into the following two groups:

- Exterior panels have a fully waterproof bond and are designed for applications subject to permanent exposure to the weather or to moisture.
- Exposure 1 panels have a fully waterproof bond and are designed for applications where long construction delays may be expected prior to providing protection. Approximately 95 percent of Performance Rated Panels are manufactured with this designation.

APA'S PERFORMANCE RATED PANEL STANDARD FOR OSB

OSB panels that bear the APA trademark are manufactured under APA's rigorous quality assurance program and are recognized by the major U.S. and Canadian building codes, as well as many international building codes. Each panel is "performance rated," which means the panel meets the performance requirements necessary for its end-use application.

Most North American OSB panels are manufactured in conformance with Voluntary Product Standard PS-2 or APA PRP-108 performance standards. Panel applications described in PS-2 and APA PRP-108 include floors, walls, and roofs. These standards are recognized by the building codes in the United States, including the International Building Code and International Residential Code, and by National Evaluation Service Report NER-108.

Contributors:
BSB Design, Des Moines, Iowa; APA—The Engineered Wood Association, Tacoma, Washington.

ARCHITECTURAL WOODWORK

WOOD PANELING

Wood paneling includes shop-fabricated wall paneling, fabricated as solid lumber paneling, wood-veneer paneling, and plastic-laminate-faced wood paneling. Board paneling fabricated from standard profile boards is considered finished carpentry, and should not be confused with wood paneling, classified as architectural woodwork. Wood paneling consists of a series of thin sheets of wood panels framed together by strips of wood, vertical stiles, and horizontal rails.

Paneling was first used as a wallcovering in England in the thirteenth century. Up to the sixteenth century, the framing was almost as massive as halftimber construction over time the framing has become lighter and less massive. Today, wood panels 1-in. thick or less in thickness may be solid lumber panels or made from veneer over plywood or composition boards. The stiles and rails are typically made from solid wood or veneered boards. Rim and lip moldings and other trims are made almost exclusively from solid wood.

SECTION—WAINSCOT WITH RAISED PANEL AND FLUSH MOLDING
11.47

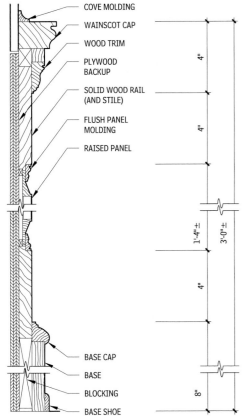

- COVE MOLDING
- WAINSCOT CAP
- WOOD TRIM
- PLYWOOD BACKUP
- SOLID WOOD RAIL (AND STILE)
- FLUSH PANEL MOLDING
- RAISED PANEL
- BASE CAP
- BASE
- BLOCKING
- BASE SHOE

SECTION—WAINSCOT WITH FLUSH PANEL AND RAISED MOLDING
11.48

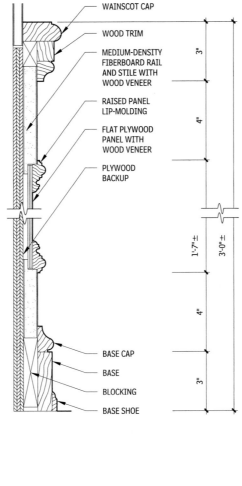

- WAINSCOT CAP
- WOOD TRIM
- MEDIUM-DENSITY FIBERBOARD RAIL AND STILE WITH WOOD VENEER
- RAISED PANEL LIP-MOLDING
- FLAT PLYWOOD PANEL WITH WOOD VENEER
- PLYWOOD BACKUP
- BASE CAP
- BASE
- BLOCKING
- BASE SHOE

SECTION—FULL-HEIGHT WALL PANEL
11.49

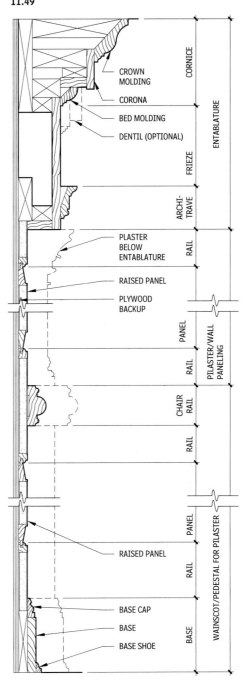

- CROWN MOLDING
- CORONA
- BED MOLDING
- DENTIL (OPTIONAL)
- PLASTER BELOW ENTABLATURE
- RAISED PANEL
- PLYWOOD BACKUP
- RAISED PANEL
- BASE CAP
- BASE
- BASE SHOE

- CORNICE
- ENTABLATURE
- FRIEZE
- ARCHI-TRAVE
- RAIL
- PANEL
- RAIL
- CHAIR RAIL
- RAIL
- PANEL
- RAIL
- BASE
- PILASTER/WALL PANELING
- WAINSCOT/PEDESTAL FOR PILASTER

NOTES

11.49 a. Because of its stability, plywood is preferable to solid lumber or other materials as backup.
b. To join stile to rail, mortise and tenon or dowelled joints are used. Stile-to-stile joints at outside corners are spline joints or lock miters; inside corners are butt-jointed.

Contributors:
Greg Heuer, Architectural Woodwork Institute, Potomac Falls, Virginia;
Richard J. Vitullo, AIA, Oak Leaf Studio, Crownsville, Maryland.

PANEL PRODUCTS AND WOOD VENEERS

GENERAL

Architectural wood panels are made from wood material that is cut or formed into sheet products that are referred to as the "panel core." These sheets are used alone (with or without a finish) or laminated together with other veneer products to make plywood. A wide variety of panels are manufactured using different core materials and adhesives or binders and various forming techniques and surface treatments. The characteristics of the panels vary with these differences in material and construction.

PANEL CORE TYPES

Panel cores, which serve as the substrate for laminates and veneers on the outer surface, are classified by products and methods of manufacture. The types of panel cores described below are suitable for architectural use.

INDUSTRIAL-GRADE PARTICLEBOARD CORE

This core type is made by using heat and pressure to bond together synthetic resin or binder and wood particles of various sizes.

Employed in a wide variety of architectural woodwork applications, industrial-grade particleboard is especially well suited as a substrate for high-quality veneers and decorative laminates. When used as panels without any surface layers, the product is called particleboard; when used with wood veneer on the surface, the panels are referred to as particle-core plywood. Particleboard core is classified into three densities, dependent on weight per cubic ft.:

- *Low-density*: less than 40 lb. per cubic ft.
- *Medium-density*: 40 to 50 lb. per cubic ft.
- *High-density*: more than 50 lb. per cubic ft.

MOISTURE-RESISTANT PARTICLEBOARD CORE

Some medium-density industrial particleboard is bonded with resins more resistant to swelling when exposed to moisture. The most common grades are Type M-2-Exterior Glue and M-3-Exterior Glue in accordance with ANSI 208.1.

FIRE-RETARDANT PARTICLEBOARD CORE

Medium-density industrial particleboard may be treated during manufacture to carry a UL Class A fire rating stamp (flame spread, 20; smoke developed, 25). This material can be used as a substrate for paneling, requiring a Class A rating.

MEDIUM-DENSITY FIBERBOARD (MDF) CORE

MDF is made from wood particles reduced to fibers in a moderate-pressure steam vessel, combined with resin, and bonded together under heat and pressure. The surface is flat, smooth, uniform, dense, and free of knots or grain pattern. MDF is useful as a substrate for paint, thin overlay materials, veneers, and decorative laminates. The homogeneous edge allows machining and paint finishes. MDF is one of the most stable mat-formed panel products and is widely used as an architectural panel.

MOISTURE-RESISTANT MDF CORE

Some MDF is bonded with a moisture-resistant resin to produce a water-resistant product.

VENEER CORE (PLYWOOD)

This panel product is made up of alternating layers of thin veneer. Adhesive is placed between the layers, and the panels are pressed until the adhesive is set; heat is often used to speed the cure. The two outside layers, often selected for species, grain, and appearance, are called the face veneers.

HARDBOARD CORE

Hardboard is made of interfelted fibers consolidated under heat and pressure to a density of 31 lbs. per cubic ft or more. Available with either one side (S1S) or two sides (S2S) smooth, hardboard is often used for casework backs, drawer bottoms, and divider panels. Architectural woodworkers typically use two types of hardboard core: standard (untempered) and tempered, which is standard hardboard that has been subjected to a curing treatment to increase its stiffness, hardness, and weight.

CHARACTERISTICS OF CORE MATERIAL

Characteristics of core material performance are influenced by the grade and thickness of the core and specific gravity of the core species. Visual edge quality is rated before treatment with edge bands or fillers and, for lumber core, assumes the use of "clear edge" grade. Surface uniformity is directly related to the performance of fine veneers placed over the surface. Dimensional stability is usually related to exposure to wide variations in relative humidity. Screw-holding and bending strength are influenced by proper design and engineering.

PLYWOOD

The term "plywood" is defines as a panel consisting of three or more layers (plies) of wood or wood products (veneers or overlays and/or core materials) generally laminated into a single sheet (panel). Plywood is separated into two groups, according to materials and manufacturing:

- Hardwood plywood panels are made from hardwood or decorative softwood veneers over a core material such as medium-density particleboard, medium-density fiberboard, low-density lumber and other veneers
- Softwood plywood panels are made with softwood face veneers, and are seldom incorporated into finished architectural woodworking projects because of the instability of the core material and core voids.

TYPES OF FACING MATERIAL

Wood product substrates are classified in two main facing material categories: decorative laminates/overlays and wood veneers.

DECORATIVE LAMINATES, OVERLAYS, AND PREFINISHED PANEL PRODUCTS

This finish surface category can be broken down into the following broad groups:

- High-pressure decorative laminates are formed under heat and pressure from resin-impregnated kraft paper substrates with decorative plastic face materials and a clear protective top sheet. This assembly, commonly called plastic laminate, offers resistance to wear and many stains and chemicals. Common uses include casework exteriors, countertops, and wall paneling.
- Thermally fused decorative panels are flat-pressed from a thermoset polyester or melamine resin-impregnated web, and most

HARDWOOD PLYWOOD CORE TYPES 11.50

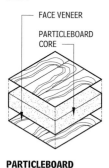

PARTICLEBOARD

FACE VENEER
PARTICLEBOARD CORE

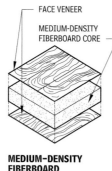

MEDIUM-DENSITY FIBERBOARD

FACE VENEER
MEDIUM-DENSITY FIBERBOARD CORE

VENEER

FACE VENEER
VENEER CORE

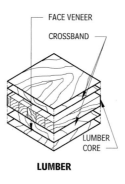

LUMBER

FACE VENEER
CROSSBAND
LUMBER CORE

CHARACTERISTICS OF CORE MATERIAL PERFORMANCE 11.51

PANEL CORE TYPE	FLATNESS	VISUAL EDGE QUALITY	SURFACE UNIFORMITY	DIMENSIONAL STABILITY	SCREW-HOLDING	BENDING STRENGTH	AVAILABILITY
Industrial Particleboard (medium)	Excellent	Good	Excellent	Fair	Fair	Good	Readily
Medium-density fiberboard (MDF)	Excellent	Excellent	Excellent	Fair	Good	Good	Readily
Veneer	Fair	Good	Fair	Excellent	Excellent	Excellent	Readily
Lumber	Good	Good	Good	Good	Excellent	Excellent	Limited
Combination Core with Composite Crossbands	Excellent	Good	Excellent	Good	Excellent	Excellent	Limited
Combination Core with Composite Innerply	Good	Fair	Good	Good	Good	Good	Limited
Moisture Resistant Particleboard	Excellent	Good	Good	Fair	Fair	Good	Limited
Moisture Resistant MDF	Excellent	Excellent	Excellent	Fair	Good	Good	Limited
Fire Rated Particleboard	Excellent	Fair	Good	Fair	Fair	Good	Limited

Refer to *Architectural Woodwork Quality Standards Illustrated* for additional information.

Contributors:
Greg Heuer, Architectural Woodwork Institute, Potomac Falls, Virginia;
Richard J. Vitullo, AIA, Oak Leaf Studio, Crownsville, Maryland.

have been laminated to industrial particleboard or medium-density fiberboard substrates when they arrive at the woodwork fabricator. Performance is similar to that of high-pressure decorative laminates. Common uses include casework interiors, furniture, shelving, display materials, and decorative paneling.

- Thermoplastic sheets are semi rigid sheets or rolls stock extruded from a nonporous acrylic/polyvinyl chloride (PVC) alloy. The materials are impact resistant and minor scratches and gouges are less conspicuous due to the through color property.
- Medium-density overlays are made from pressed resin-impregnated paper overlays, and are highly resistant to moisture. They are available applied to cores suitable for both interior and exterior uses. The seamless panel face and uniform density offer a sound base for opaque finishes and paint.
- Vinyl films, foils, and low-basis weight papers are decorative facing materials that, although they have limited use in custom architectural woodworking, are suitable for some installations.

WOOD VENEERS

Wood veneers are produced in a variety of industry standard thicknesses. The slicing process is controlled by a number of variables, but the thickness of the veneer has little bearing on the quality of the end product.

There are two types of veneers, hardwood and softwood. Hardwood veneers are available in many domestic and imported wood species and are normally plain sliced, but certain species can be rift-sliced, quarter sliced, or rotary cut. Softwood veneers are usually sliced from Douglas-fir, but pine and other softwoods are available. Most softwood veneer is rotary cut. Plain sliced and quarter sliced (vertical grain) softwoods may be obtained by special order.

Most veneers are taken from large trees, but some are sliced from fast-growing trees, dyed, and reglued in molds to create "grain" patterns. The color of these reconstituted veneers is established during manufacture because the high percentage of glue line resists staining.

The manner in which a log segment is cut with relation to the annual rings of the tree determines the appearance of the veneer. Individual pieces of veneer, referred to as "leaves," are kept in the order in which they were sliced for reference during installation. The group of leaves from one slicing is called a "flitch" and is identified by a number and the gross square feet it contains. The faces of the leaves with relation to their position in the log are identified as the "tight face" (toward the outside of the log) and the "loose face" (toward the inside or heart of the log).

NOTES

- To achieve balanced construction, panel products should be absolutely symmetrical from the centerline. Materials used on either side should contract and expand or exhibit moisture permeability at the same rate.
- In panel construction, the thinner the facing material, the less force it can generate to cause warping. The thicker the substrate, the more it can resist a warping movement or force.
- *Wood veneer standards*: For hardwood plywood, the face veneer characteristics of the Hardwood Plywood and Veneer Association (HPVA) have generally been adapted for use. These face grades apply to custom architectural woodwork.
- *Flame spread factors*: The fire rating of the core material determines the rating of the assembled panel. Fire-retardant veneered panels must have a fire-retardant core. Particleboard core is available with a Class I (Class A) rating. Some building codes, except where locally amended, provide that facing materials 1/28 in. or thinner are not considered in determining the flame spread rating of the panel. For more information, refer to the Architectural Woodwork Institute publication, *Quality Standards Illustrated*.

TYPES OF VENEER CUTS

The plain or flat slicing method is most often used to produce veneers for high-quality architectural woodwork. Slicing is done parallel to a line through the center of the log. A combination of cathedral and straight-grain patterns results, with a natural progression of pattern from leaf to leaf.

PLAIN-SLICED (FLAT-SLICED) VENEER
11.52

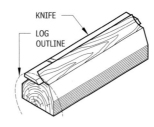

KNIFE

LOG
OUTLINE

**CATHEDRAL
PATTERN**

Quarter slicing, roughly parallel to a radius line through the log segment, simulates the quarter sawing process used with solid lumber. In many species, the individual leaves are narrow as a result. A series of stripes is produced, varying in density and thickness among species. In red and white oak, "fleck" (sometimes called flake) is a characteristic of this slicing method.

QUARTER-SLICED VENEER
11.53

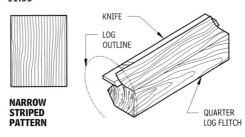

KNIFE

LOG
OUTLINE

**NARROW
STRIPED
PATTERN**

QUARTER
LOG FLITCH

Rift cut veneers are produced most often in red and white oak, rarely in other species. Note that rift veneers and rift sawn solid lumber are produced so differently that a "match" between them is highly unlikely. In both cases the cutting is done slightly off the radius lines, minimizing the "fleck" (sometimes called flake) associated with quarter slicing.

RIFT-SLICED (RIFT-CUT) VENEER
11.54

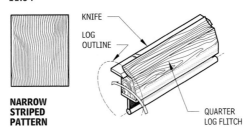

KNIFE

LOG
OUTLINE

**NARROW
STRIPED
PATTERN**

QUARTER
LOG FLITCH

To create rotary cut veneers, the log is center-mounted on a lathe and "peeled" along the path of the growth rings, like unwinding a roll of paper. This provides a bold, random appearance. Rotary veneers vary in width, so matching at veneer joints is extremely difficult. Most softwood veneers are cut this way. Rotary cut veneers are the least useful in fine architectural woodwork.

ROTARY VENEER
11.55

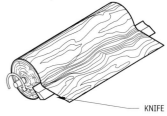

**VERY BROAD
PATTERN**

KNIFE

MATCHING BETWEEN ADJACENT VENEER LEAVES

It is possible to achieve certain visual effects by the manner in which the veneer leaves are arranged. Rotary-cut veneers are difficult to match; therefore, most matching is done with sliced veneers. Matching of adjacent veneer leaves must be specified. Consult the AWI woodworker for choices.

BOOK MATCHING

Book matching is the most commonly used match in the industry. In it, every other piece of veneer is reversed so adjacent pieces (leaves) are "opened" like the pages of a book. Because the "tight" and "loose" faces alternate in adjacent leaves, they reflect light and accept stain differently. The veneer joints match, creating a symmetrical pattern that yields maximum continuity of grain.

SLIP MATCHING

In this match method, adjoining leaves are placed (slipped out) in sequence without being turned; thus, all of the same face sides are exposed. The grain figure repeats but joints do not show grain match.

RANDOM MATCHING

In random matching, veneer leaves are placed next to each other in a random order and orientation, producing a casual board-by-board effect in many species. Conscious effort is made to mismatch the grain at joints.

END MATCHING

End matching is often used to extend the apparent length of available veneers for high wall panels and long conference tables. End matching occurs in two types:

- *Architectural end match*: Leaves are individually book or slip matched, alternating end to end and side to side. Architectural end matching yields the best continuous grain patterns for length as well as width.
- *Panel end match*: Leaves are book or slip matched on panel subassemblies, with sequenced subassemblies end matched, resulting in some modest cost savings on projects, where applicable. For most species, panel end matching yields a pleasing, blended appearance and grain continuity.

RUNNING MATCHING

Using this method, each panel face is assembled from as many veneer leaves as necessary. This often results in an asymmetrical appearance, with some veneer leaves of unequal width.

BALANCE MATCHING

In balance matching, each panel face is assembled from an odd or even number of veneer leaves of uniform width before edge trimming.

BALANCE AND CENTER MATCHING

Using this method, each panel face is assembled from an even number of veneer leaves of uniform width before edge trimming. Thus, there is a veneer joint in the center of the panel, producing horizontal symmetry.

Contributors:
Greg Heuer, Architectural Woodwork Institute, Potomac Falls, Virginia;
Richard J. Vitullo, AIA, Oak Leaf Studio, Crownsville, Maryland.

VENEER MATCH TYPES
11.56

SLIP MATCH

BOOK MATCH

RANDOM MATCH

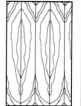
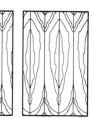

RUNNING MATCH

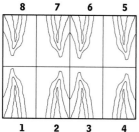

8 7 6 5

1 2 3 4

PANEL END MATCH

2 4 6 8

1 3 5 7

ARCHITECTURAL END MATCH

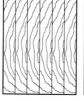

BALANCE AND CENTER MATCH

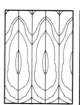
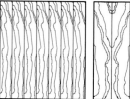

BALANCE MATCH

GENERAL CHARACTERISTICS OF SELECTED WOOD VENEER SPECIES
11.57

SPECIES		WIDTH TO (IN.)	LENGTH (FT)	FLITCH SIZE	COST[a]	AVAILABILITY
Mahogany	Plain-Sliced Honduras Mahogany	18	12	Large	Moderate	Good
	Quartered Honduras Mahogany	12	12	Large	High	Moderate
	Plain-Sliced African Mahogany	18	12	Large	Moderate	Moderate
	Quartered African Mahogany	12	12	Large	High	Good
Ash	Plain-Sliced American White Ash	12	10	Medium	Moderate	Good
	Quartered American White Ash	8	12	Small	High	Good
	Quartered- or Plain-Sliced European Ash	10[d]	10	Medium	High	Limited
Anegre	Quartered- or Plain-Sliced Anegre	12[d]	12	Large	High	Good
Avodire	Quartered Avodire	10	10	Large	High	Limited
Cherry	Plain-Sliced American Cherry	12	11	Medium	Moderate	Good
	Quartered American Cherry	4	10	Very small	High	Moderate
Birch	Rotary Cut Birch (Natural)	48	10	Large	Low	Good
	Rotary Cut Birch (Select Red or White)	36	10	Medium	Moderate	Moderate
	Plain-Sliced Birch (natural)	10	10	Small	Moderate	Limited
	Plain-Sliced Birch (Select Red or White)	5	10	Small	High	Limited
Butternut	Plain-Sliced Butternut	12	10	Medium	High	Limited
Makore	Quartered- or Plain-Sliced Makore	12[d]	12	Large	High	Good
Maple	Plain-Sliced (Half Round) American Maple	12	10	Medium	Moderate	Good[b]
	Rotary Birdseye Maple	20	10	Medium	Very high	Good
Oak	Plain-Sliced English Brown Oak	12	10	Medium	Very high	Limited
	Quartered English Brown Oak	10	10	Medium	Very high	Limited
	Plain-Sliced American Red Oak	16	12	Large	Moderate	Good
	Quartered American Red Oak	8	10	Small	Moderate	Good
	Rift-Sliced American Red Oak	10	10	Medium	Moderate	Good
	Comb Grain Rift American Red Oak	8	10	Small	Very high	Limited
	Plain-Sliced American White Oak	12	12	Medium	Moderate	Good
	Quartered American White Oak	8	10	Small	Moderate	Good
	Rift-Sliced American White Oak	8	10	Medium	High	Good
	Comb Grain Rift American White Oak	8	10	Small	Very high	Limited
Hickory or Pecan	Plain-Sliced American Hickory or Pecan	12	10	Small	Moderate	Good
Sapele	Quartered- or Plain- Sliced Sapele	12[d]	12	Large	High	Good
Sycamore	Plain-Sliced English Sycamore	10	10	Medium	Very high	Limited
	Quartered English Sycamore	6	10	Medium	Very high	Limited
Teak	Plain-Sliced Teak	12	12	Large	Very high	Limited[c]
	Quartered Teak	12	12	Medium	Very high	Limited[c]
Walnut	Plain-Sliced American Walnut	12	12	Medium	Moderate	Good
	Quarter-Sliced American Walnut	6	10	Very small	High	Rare

NOTES

11.57 a. Cost reflects raw veneer costs weighted for waste or yield characteristics and degree of labor difficulty.
b. Seasonal factors may affect availability.
c. Availability of blond teak is very rare.
d. When quartered or plain-sliced are listed on the same line, the width dimensions are listed with quartered first and plain sliced second.

Contributors:
Greg Heuer, Architectural Woodwork Institute, Potomac Falls, Virginia;
Richard J. Vitullo, AIA, Oak Leaf Studio, Crownsville, Maryland.

SPECIAL WOOD VENEER MATCHING OPTIONS
11.58

8-PIECE SUNBURST

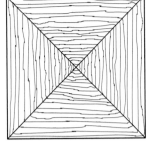

BOX MATCH

PARQUET MATCH

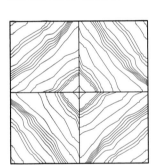

REVERSE OR END GRAIN BOX

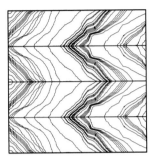

HERRINGBONE

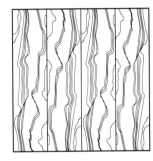

SWING MATCH

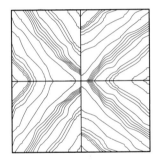

DIAMOND

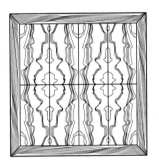

REVERSE DIAMOND

SKETCH FACE

COMMON FACE VENEER PATTERNS OF SELECTED COMMERCIAL SPECIES
11.59

PRIMARY COMMERCIAL HARDWOOD SPECIES	FACE VENEER PATTERNS			
	PLAIN SLICED (FLAT CUT)	QUARTERED	RIFT AND COMBGRAIN	ROTARY
Ash	Yes	Yes	No	Yes
Birch	Yes	No	No	Yes
Cherry	Yes	Yes	No	Yes
Hickory	Yes	No	No	Yes
Lauan	No	Yes	No	Yes
Mahogany, African	Yes	Yes	No	Yes
Mahogany, American Honduras	Yes	Yes	No	Yes
Maple	Yes	Yes	No	Yes
Oak, Red	Yes	Yes	Yes	Yes
Oak, White	Yes	Yes	Yes	Yes
Pecan	Yes	No	No	Yes
Walnut (black)	Yes	Yes	No	Yes
Yellow poplar	Yes	No	No	Yes
Typical methods of cutting	Plain Slicing or Half-Round on Rotary Lathe	QuarterSlicing	Off-set Quarter on Rotary Lathe	Rotary Lathe

Source: Chart reprinted with permission from the Hardwood Plywood and Veneer Association

NOTES

11.59 a. The headings refer to the face veneer pattern, not to the method of cutting. Face veneer patterns other than those listed are obtainable.

b. The method of cutting for a given face veneer pattern will be at mill option, unless otherwise specified by the buyer in an explicit manner to avoid the possibility of misunderstanding. For example, "plain-sliced veneer cut on a vertical slicer" or "plain-sliced veneer cut on a half-round rotary lathe" could be specified.

Contributors:
Greg Heuer, Architectural Woodwork Institute, Potomac Falls, Virginia;
Richard J. Vitullo, AIA, Oak Leaf Studio, Crownsville, Maryland.

SECTION 3

ISSUES OF CONTEMPORARY PRACTICE

SUSTAINABLE DESIGN

12

INTRODUCTION

Sustainable design, like all powerful ideas, is defined in diverse ways. The term has lost clarity amid the noble efforts of designers to create a healthier and better world. Even the accepted Bruntland Commission definition of sustainable development as "...meeting the needs of the present while allowing future generations to meet their own needs..." uses the undefined term *need*. What will "meet our needs" is not a quantitative standard that can be defined in this chapter—or anywhere else. David Orr, the noted educator and advocate of ecological literacy from Oberlin College, has defined the term more clearly than most when he offers that "ecological design is the careful meshing of human purposes with the larger patterns and flows of the natural world."

The idea of *sustainability*, which is that humans must intentionally coexist in a state of equilibrium with nature, grew out of the environmental movement in the last half of the twentieth century. The phrase "sustainable design" in current practice—where it is often used interchangeably with "green," "environmental" or "ecological" design—comprises wide ranging conceptions in planning and architecture of the actions needed to achieve sustainability. These include site ecology, alternative urban infrastructures, mobility, socially-responsible design, water conservation and treatment, heat island mitigation, energy efficiency, renewable energy integration, design for disassembly, adaptive reuse, recycled, recyclable and reclaimed materials, healthy material redesign, efficient construction protocols, daylighting, indoor air quality, commissioning, post-occupancy feedback, as well as the need for excellent architectural design and the process integration required to provide clarity amidst these often-competing parameters.

Environmentalists tell us that we confuse our needs and wants, and that we must learn to make do with less—to be "less bad." Architect William McDonough, FAIA, has asserted a positive agenda that will lead to a new paradigm in which we "...celebrate our interdependence with other living systems and make architecture itself a regenerative force." This is a call to architects and designers to first envision what it looks like to be more good, *not* less bad.

Sustainable design is design that asks the right questions. It requires us to understand the story behind what we create: Is it safe? How is it interdependent with living systems? Does it make life better? Sustainable design is, in essence, *good design*.

The following pages provide an initial framework for design that is based on a vision of a healthy and sustaining world.

Contributor:
Mark Rylander, AIA, William McDonough + Partners, Charlottesville, Virginia.

FRAMEWORK OF GOOD DESIGN: PRINCIPLES AND PROCESS

PRINCIPLES OF SUSTAINABLE DESIGN

Every act of design signals a vision of the world. Whether intentional or not, that vision of the world is supported by principles. Principles are basic generalizations intended as standards of good conduct. They define an ethical framework within which architects can practice with clarity, fairness, and sensitivity to the elements of the world that are affected by design. Principles in this sense are not design strategies but rather the basis for such strategies.

SUSTAINABLE DESIGN

In 1992, William McDonough, FAIA, and Michael Braungart authored the nine Hannover Principles, Design for Sustainability (Issued by the City of Hannover, Germany, 1992), which today serve as a guide to the design of products, communities, and architecture:

1. *Insist on rights of humanity and nature to coexist* in a healthy, supportive, diverse, and sustainable condition.
2. *Recognize interdependence.* The elements of human design interact with and depend upon the natural world, with broad and diverse implications at every scale. Expand design considerations to recognizing even distant effects.
3. *Respect relationships between spirit and matter.* Consider all aspects of human settlement, including community, dwelling, industry, and trade in terms of existing and evolving connections between spiritual and material consciousness.
4. *Accept responsibility for the consequences of design* decisions upon human well-being, the viability of natural systems and their right to coexist.
5. *Create safe objects of long-term value.* Do not burden future generations with requirements for maintenance or vigilant administration of potential danger due to the careless creation of products, processes, or standards.
6. *Eliminate the concept of waste.* Evaluate and optimize the full life cycle of products and processes, to approach the state of natural systems, in which there is no waste.
7. *Rely on natural energy flows.* Human designs should, like the living world, derive their creative forces from perpetual solar income. Incorporate this energy efficiently and safely for responsible use.
8. *Understand the limitations of design.* No human creation lasts forever and design does not solve all problems. Those who create and plan should practice humility in the face of nature. Treat nature as a model and mentor, not as an inconvenience to be evaded or controlled.
9. *Seek constant improvement by the sharing of knowledge.* Encourage direct and open communication between colleagues, patrons, manufacturers, and users to link long-term sustainable considerations with ethical responsibility and reestablish the integral relationship between natural processes and human activity.

The Hannover Principles provide a foundation for understanding a human interdependence with nature and, thus, provide a building block for the principle of sustainable design.

Sustainable design enables architects to determine the best course for integrating buildings, infrastructure, and natural systems. Architects should understand natural systems so that their designs remain environmentally friendly throughout the life of the structures and infrastructures.

SUSTAINABLE DEVELOPMENT

In 1987, the United Nations-appointed World Commission on Environment and Development published "Our Common Future" (more commonly known as the "Brundtland Report," after Norwegian Prime Minister Gro Harlem Brundtland, chair of the commission). A single phrase from this document has become the most widely quoted definition of sustainability, which, according to the report, "meets the needs of the present without compromising the ability of future generations to meet their own needs." This has

become a broadly accepted definition of sustainable development, one that evidences the political realities of its construction, as "needs" is not distinguished from the needs of current lifestyles. Defining what society needs is both a challenge and the key to a more sustaining world. Environmentalists often equate the solution with learning to make do with less. Indeed, one role of designers is to make less into more, so the future can be seen not as a time of scarcity, but as a world of sustained abundance.

ECOLOGICAL DESIGN

The American Institute of Architect's Committee on the Environment (AIA COTE) has cited a sustainable design definition from noted environmentalist David Orr, professor at Oberlin College. Orr prefers the term *ecological design*. In an article titled, "Environmental Literacy: Education as if the Earth Mattered" (1992), he wrote, "Ecological design requires the ability to comprehend patterns that connect, which means looking beyond the boxes we call disciplines to see things in their larger context. Ecological design is the careful meshing of human purposes with the larger patterns and flows of the natural world; it is the careful study of those patterns and flows to inform human purposes...."

ECONOMY-ECOLOGY-EQUITY

Sustainable design entails more than environmentally sensitive design or bioclimatic design. Many architects who follow the principles of sustainable design are aware that sustainability involves more than environment and energy, which form the substance of much of the green building movement to date.

Sustainable design and development can be seen as an optimization of economic, environmental, and social considerations—or economy, ecology, and equity.

This optimization can be represented as a triangular relationship between these considerations and, thus, can be used as a way of identifying the relationship of individual issues. For example, the manufacture of cost-effective environmentally friendly products, or "eco-efficiency," is an economy/ecology question. Finding a balance between fairness to a community and the surrounding natural landscape is an equity/ecology issue.

FRACTAL TRIANGLE: ECONOMY-ECOLOGY-EQUITY
12.1
Source: William McDonough, FAIA

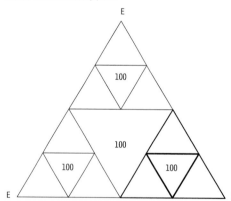

Historically, good architectural design has been defined as design that addresses commodity (program and project economics), firmness (performance), and delight (beauty). Environmental and social issues are not necessarily inherent in commodity, firmness, and delight, but some have attempted to identify a connection between the economy-ecology-equity (community) paradigm and the concepts of commodity, firmness, and delight.

MAPPING OF COMMODITY FIRMNESS AND DELIGHT ONTO ECONOMY-ECOLOGY-EQUITY
12.2
Source: National Council of Architectural Registration Boards

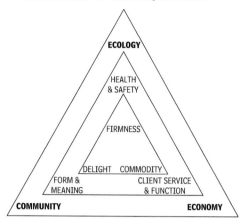

ARCHITECTS AS GUARDIANS OF HUMAN AND ECOLOGICAL HEALTH

Earlier editions of *Architectural Graphic Standards* clearly defined the role of the architect, narrowly defined style, and generally based the regulatory framework on a building tradition that architects understood at the time. Subsequent editions took into account how ongoing industrialization transformed much of how buildings were made and how new technologies were used to make and shape materials and products.

Not until design practices began to be affected by more than cost, performance, and aesthetics did these new technologies begin to be considered differently. In particular, issues related to human and environmental health have affected the building industry, among them:

- Asbestos and lung disease
- Chlorofluorocarbons (CFCs) and the ozone layer
- PCBs and cancer
- Radon and disease
- Second-hand smoke and disease
- Air pollution and allergies and asthma
- Suburban sprawl and sedentary lifestyles
- Junk food and diabetes
- Clear-cutting of forests and erosion and endangered species
- Industrial pollution of water and air and species depletion

Every aspect of design has become more complex because the connections between materials and practices are only beginning to be understood. Principles based on newly discovered connections between the health of the human and natural environment are transforming the architectural industry.

SUSTAINABLE DESIGN PROCESS

Architects are capable of solving complex problems through design synthesis. This skill has been formalized in a design process that, at its best, characterizes a kind of systems thinking that can be applied to any discipline. Systems thinking is characterized by identification of connections to and relationships between disparate items, combined with intensive analysis. Effective problem solving applies nonlinear thinking to find patterns, scales, and relationships, often against linear timelines, relationships, and known subsystems to find creative solutions. Architects are trained as three-dimensional problem solvers and, thus, architectural training can be seen as a form of systems thinking.

Contributor:
William McDonough, FAIA, William McDonough + Partners, Charlottesville, Virginia.

Architecture is constrained by functional, regulatory, and economic considerations, as well as the influence of multiple decision makers, all of which all can change the direction of a design unexpectedly. As this complexity increases, systems thinking is needed to bring clarity to the process, while linear thinking may be of value for certain specialized disciplines, critical path schedules, budgets, and engineering calculations and the like.

ITERATION

Linear thinking is not effective for a good design process, which approaches the problem over and over, almost going back to the beginning, to the initial project premises and program, revisiting them to confirm the design direction and determine whether the major pieces of the solution are appropriate.

Architectural design may be more complex than the process of other design disciplines. For example, materials design may be difficult and multidimensional but is essentially linear and is usually about meeting specifications. Automobile and product design have issues in common with building design. Less is likely to change between design and manufacturing of products, however, because most products are replicated within stringent limits of variation.

All design is iterative by nature, and usually the more iteration is allowed to take place, the higher the quality of the result. Stanford

University's Capital Planning and Management Department characterizes a structured iterative process over the life of the project, allowing approvals, checks, and balances at each phase along the way.

SYSTEMS THINKING

Ecology is about natural systems and good design attempts to replicate the effectiveness of these systems, identifying relationships that are essential. For example, a deep understanding of a project program ensures that every incorporated space will have value and the appropriate level of quality and furnishing. Understanding programs, formal design concepts, team structures, site and engineering parameters, schedules, and construction techniques and materials requires complex system thinking. Sustainable design adds new parameters to this equation and reframes many of the traditional elements.

MEETINGS

A sustaining design process reconsiders when and how meetings are held, who attends, and what fees are appropriate at each stage. Sustainable design requires more interaction at the beginning of design, with more stakeholders in attendance, and greater transparency of the design process. If community leaders, offi-

cials, and neighborhoods participate in the evolution of the design, the design will be better understood and of a higher quality.

ENGINEERS

Engineers provide knowledge that leads to low-energy buildings with optimized systems. Specialist consultants are more commonly found in sustainable design projects due to the relatively new nature of much of the information. This is a transitional phase for the engineering profession, as these new services are incorporated by primary architecture and engineering firms. Technological advances increasingly allow modeling of considerations such as energy flow and daylight to be performed as part of architectural services.

CHARACTERISTICS OF SUSTAINABLE DESIGN

As goals are set in the initial stages of the project, determining what represents a sustainable approach can be difficult. Particular circumstances of a site, its region, and project program will inform decisions. In addition, consideration of a set of sustainable design issues across disciplines can be helpful. A matrix of sustainable design published with the Hannover Principles, and adapted here in Table 12.4 (from a chart developed by Malcolm Wells and later Osama Salem in 1990), can help put issues on the table and begin to establish what is important in a particular project.

STANFORD PROCESS—HEARTBEAT
12.3

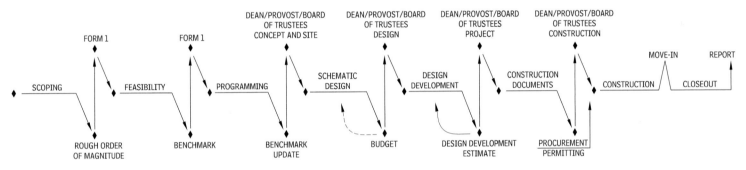

Contributor:
Stanford University Department of Project Management, Stanford, California.

MATRIX OF SUSTAINABILITY
12.4

NEGATIVE EXTREME MINUS 100	POSITIVE EXTREME PLUS 100
MATERIALS	
Imported materials	Indigenous materials
High-embodied energy materials	Low-embodied energy materials.
Nonrenewable materials	Renewable materials
Nonrecyclable materials	Recyclable materials
Toxic materials	Nontoxic materials
LAND USE	
Destroys rich soil	Protect/creates rich soil
Destroys nutrients	Creates/adds nutrients
Produces no food	Produces its own food
Destroys wildlife habitat	Provides wildlife habitat
Uses high-productivity land	Uses low-productivity land
URBAN CONTEXT	
Favors high-energy transport	Favors low-energy transport
Favors polluting transport	Favors nonpolluting transport
Excludes urban agriculture	Includes urban agriculture
Homogeneous building types	Mixed building types
No open space	Forever preserved open spaces
Destroys human habitat	Provides human habitat
No solar and wind access	Zoned for solar and wind access
WATER	
Destroys pure water	Creates pure water
Wastes rainwater	Stores and uses rainwater
Ignores graywater use	Uses graywater
Wastes runoffs	Creates percolation
Obtains water far away	Obtains water locally
WASTES	
Dumps blackwater	Recycles blackwater
Wastes embodied energy	Recycles embodied energy
Dumps solid waste	Recycles solid waste
AIR	
Destroys clean air	Creates clean air
Pollutes air thermally	Avoids thermal pollution
Pollutes indoor air	Purifies indoor air
ENERGY	
Wastes solar energy	Uses solar energy
Ignores buildings' thermal inertia	Uses buildings' thermal inertia
Dumps waste energy	Recycles waste energy
Wastes wind energy	Uses wind energy
Wastes biomass	Uses biomass
Ignores daylighting	Uses daylighting
Ignores natural ventilation	Uses natural ventilation
Intensifies microclimate	Moderates microclimate
RESPONSIBILITY	
Destroys silence	Creates silence
No participatory design	Participatory design
Needs frequent repair	Maintains itself
Addictive and enslaving	Enlightening and liberating
No response to nature	Responsive to nature
No response to change	Responsive to change
No response to culture	Responsive to culture

EXPANDED SCOPE OF SERVICES

Sustainable design brings with it opportunities for expanded services that benefit architects, owners, users, society, and the environment. Strategic facilities planning has always benefited from the input of architects. Traditionally, architects are hired once a decision to build has been made and a site has been selected.

Planning and architecture are coming together in emerging fields of community design and urban design. An array of new practices is presenting itself within the traditional phases of a project. Many architects are pursuing sustainability consulting as an alternative career path. Postoccupancy opportunities such as commissioning and facilities management are also becoming growth areas.

This expanded scope of services suggests that the process start earlier, when key strategic decisions are made; extend later, to assure performance goals and user satisfaction; and be more thorough along the way, to assure perfunctory examination of energy modeling, daylighting, acoustics, and other parameters typically seen as optional.

STRATEGIC ADVISORS
Sustaining design of buildings considers decisions that take place before a building is a building. The concept of sustaining design questions status quo assumptions and redefines design assignments. Should the building be built at all? How is site selection optimized for mobility and access to public transportation or alternatives? As the primary advisor to clients, architects can apply a framework of sustaining principles to optimize economy, ecology, and equity.

Guiding project principles and goals are essential to successful design. Other elements of "predesign," which are all part of a successful start to a solid program, include the following:

- Qualitative dimensions
- Financial analysis
- Environmental assessments
- Benchmarking
- Construction strategies

Sustaining design places greater emphasis on a successful start-up, nurturing community acceptance, managing risk, and considering social and ecological connections.

COMMUNITY DESIGN
Sustaining design of buildings alone will not affect the financial, environmental, and social costs of communities. Sustainability is fundamentally a question of cultural change. There is no single right answer for communities. Sustaining urban, suburban, and rural strategies to development are all possible. Unchecked growth into rural counties has burdened infrastructure and government primarily because effective community design has not been incorporated into the development process.

MAXIMIZING EARLY OPPORTUNITIES
The kinds of decisions that happen in each phase of a development project can be charted in a graph, as shown in Figure 12.5. Opportunities for optimizing economy, ecology, and equity exist at each stage, but more large-scale opportunities are apparent at the earliest stages.

SUSTAINABLE DESIGN OPPORTUNITIES AND QUESTIONS
12.5

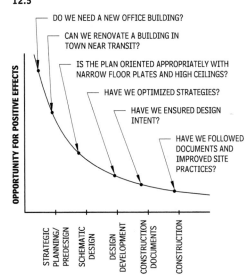

As an example, assume a new corporate office building is under consideration. A greenfield site for a new facility at an existing farm would provide desperately needed space, but the environmental and social impacts of the new building would be considerable. Renovating the existing facility would be an opportunity to avoid relocation of the workforce, with ripple effects involving relocation of family homes, new school districts, longer commute times, less access to public transit, and so forth. But the existing facility is too inefficient to reuse, so an existing building close to the original one is found near a major metro stop. A feasibility study shows that 20 percent of the workforce would be able to use public transportation; the site is near a hub, with many available apartments for new staff and plenty of nearby restaurants, eliminating the need for lunchtime car trips. The result is an improvement in the quality of life for employees and cost savings for the company. Moreover, there is no need for the materials that would have gone into the new construction, as there is no need for new house construction and related infrastructure; the land the farm is on is preserved; there is reduced burden on local schools and related taxes, and commute times are shortened, thus, reducing carbon emissions and related environmental degradation.

Comparing these consequences to the opportunities presented during the design development phase, which included material specifications and energy optimization of a new building, it is clear that better results can be achieved by making good early decisions. Rating systems developed for sustainable design may give credit for urban redevelopment, but most of the system is green-building-focused, with an emphasis on energy optimization and low-impact materials.

This example demonstrates that using a renovated building near transit produced better overall effects, even though it might not have been as highly rated in the system. Universal building-centric approaches to sustainability are limited. The unique design circumstances of a project like the one described here, show how a broader perspective creates greater opportunity.

Contributor:
Mark Rylander, AIA, William McDonough + Partners, Charlottesville, Virginia.

OPPORTUNITIES WITHIN THE PROCESS

The following list of activities and opportunities within the development process can be part of an enhanced scope related to sustainable design:

- Existing assessment—understanding existing conditions
- Goal setting—establishing project principles/goals
- Programming/growth assessment—understanding future needs
- Urban design/community design—considering larger civic and cultural context
- Environmental impact studies—understanding downstream impacts
- Site selection process—finding a site that both meets current needs and is mindful to future alternatives
- Conceptual design—allowing enough time in the design process
- Schematic design-defining program and testing goals as well as creating form
- Design development—refining design performance
- Construction documents—assuring incorporation of goals
- Bidding—communicating sustainable concepts
- Construction—employing sustainable practices and sourcing
- Commissioning—optimizing performance
- Occupancy/facilities operation—educating users in how to use facility
- Postoccupancy evaluation—educating design team in how well use was anticipated (i.e., lessons learned)

INTEGRATED DESIGN

Integrated design refers to a process whereby everyone associated with the design (also known as *stakeholders*) is brought into the design early enough to allow an integration of disciplines that can optimize the design.

Figure 12.6 shows Stanford University's approach to the expanded design team involved in a high-quality process. The project itself is at the center of the diagram, and stakeholders are "around the table." This project-centric approach differs from a "command and control" pyramid of authority or accountability. The structure of authority is still in place, but it is not used as a means of keeping important voices from being heard.

As it pertains to typical green building design, integrated design is centered on building performance, particularly energy efficiency and the kinds of interaction that should take place between designers, engineers, and specialists to improve performance. A broader view of integrated design, and one that is emerging in the profession, looks toward integration of the range of scales from region to site to building performance and quality.

ECOLOGICAL LITERACY

Today's educational system should include an ecological design-centered curriculum to teach students the benefits of sustainability. In design education, even at the professional level, this is already underway. Designers and ecologists are revealing connections between materials selection and environmental impact; and science is reinforcing the relationship between energy use and pollution, and between pollution, global climate change, and environmental degradation.

David Orr has called Vitruvius the first systems thinker in the Classical world and has said that architecture is itself a profound pedagogy, but without any formalized approach to translate its educational value to the broader world. He shares with many the view that the world will not be sustained if our system "fails to build a secure, durable civilization that operates within a recognizable moral framework and ecological limits."

STANFORD UNIVERSITY PROJECT TEAM: PRIMARY COMMUNICATIONS DIAGRAM
12.6

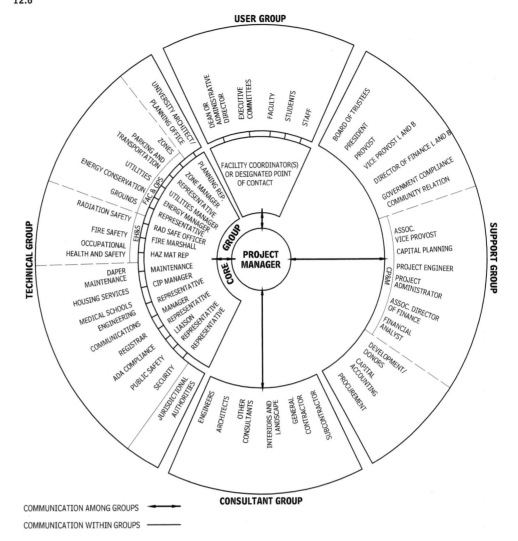

COMMUNICATION AMONG GROUPS ⟷
COMMUNICATION WITHIN GROUPS ⎯⎯⎯

In light of today's knowledge, architects must be prepared to consider their ethical responsibilities. Interns and students have been profoundly influenced by this perspective. Professionals must respond quickly to the needs of this next generation coming into architecture.

The topic of sustainable design education has been taken up by every major organization dealing with design. Valuable ideas common to all of these approaches include:

- Creation of professional courses in sustainable design
- Addition of foundation courses in ecology to core curriculum
- Establishment of resources within professional organizations
- Creation of ties to allied professions
- Creation of software and Web tools to allow assessment of building performance

Ecological literacy can be defined as interdisciplinary education centered on direct interaction with the environment in which it occurs. To achieve this, designers must understand the patterns and flows of the natural world.

Contributors:
Mark Rylander, AIA, William McDonough + Partners, Charlottesville, Virginia; Stanford University Department of Project Management, Stanford, California.

FLOWS IN NATURE

CONCEPT OF FLOWS

A simplistic definition of a building is a "shelter that offers protection from natural elements." Traditionally, elements in nature have been characterized as earth air, fire, and water, and a comprehensive sustainable design framework can be organized around these elements; thus, energy as fire; materials as earth, water, and air.

Because they often exist in a state of transition, all elements in nature "flow." It is easy to comprehend, water flows next to a rushing river, but evaporation, absorption, and other slow changes cannot be sensed as readily. Among these other less obvious flows are the following:

- *Solar flows,* which include all interaction between the sun, the atmosphere, and mass on earth. Radiation emitted by the sun that is beyond the spectrum of visible light is essential not only to living things but also to a range of emerging solar energy technologies. Solar flows vary by latitude, water in the atmosphere, time of year, and time of day. The element of fire incorporates solar flows, as well as all forms of thermal and electrical energy.
- *Water flows,* which include the interaction between water in the atmosphere, on land in the sea, and within the earth. Water is in a continuous cycle of evaporation and transpiration, precipitation, flow, and absorption. As a medium to support life, water requires flow to exchange air and nutrients with the environment. Types of water based on quality and related to human use include potable water, wastewater, irrigation water for agriculture and gardens, industrial process water, and stormwater. Water flows vary by climate, topography, and infrastructure.
- *Air flows,* which include all forms of air movement. Interaction of atmospheric pressure changes, topography, radiation, and water all affect wind flows. Air flow is essential to living things. Wind flow can create comfort and destroy buildings. For the purposes of this discussion, air flows in nature incorporate air movement through and around buildings. Air in buildings is almost always in motion, and its speed has profound effects on human comfort.

PHYSICS

Physics describes these elemental flows. Resources are now available to architects that map sun, wind, and light in a useful way. However, the element of time, the specificity of place, and the interaction of the elements is so complex that our ability to understand the forces acting on architecture at any one time is still relatively crude. More than analysis is needed for design to work well—to create safe, comfortable, responsive, and aesthetically pleasing buildings (shelter) that are effective most of the time and meet basic needs all of the time. Architects have the ability to respond to flows using a rational understanding provided by such tools as a starting point for design synthesis.

- *Buildings are subjected to remarkable extremes and patterns.* The temperature on a roof, for example, might be 100°F higher than the surrounding air. Wind chill from moving cold air and freeze/thaw cycles put the building envelope materials under extreme stress.
- *Design can harness flows or create even greater challenges to overcome.* Thanks to technology, today's cities can be built in places that were once considered uninhabitable. Any building in any style can be built anywhere at any time. Such buildings can even overheat in winter and require air conditioning. New technologies that seal building envelopes and provide substantially more insulation are creating additional stresses on materials even while creating responsive and energy-efficient envelopes. Condensation and mold can now appear in places that previously remained dry. Massive mud walls suited to New Mexico would not be effective in Minnesota or Miami. One size does not fit all.

SCALE

Design that responds to flows can occur in any scale, from the street layout of a new town to the overhang of a side porch.

SOLAR FLOWS

The sun was once the only energy source of the earth and will be the primary energy source of the future. Solar energy is taken in by plants and transformed by photosynthesis. That energy exists in a broad spectrum of radiation, and architectural technology can transform it in a number of ways: all infrared energy is heat and the basis of passive solar design and active solar hot water systems. The visible portion of the spectrum provides light, which along with nonvisible portions, empower photoelectric technology. The ultraviolet portion of the spectrum is essential to plant life but can damage architectural materials.

To make some choices in the implementation of electrical and plumbing technologies and equipment (which are covered elsewhere in this book), architects must become familiar with variations in solar resources and with the potential payback of the technologies and how they are used in buildings.

SOLAR ENERGY AND UTILITY COSTS

Solar resource maps identify parts of the country with the greatest opportunity for solar power. Solar resource data, in conjunction with electrical utility rates and the cost of photovoltaic collectors can reveal the payback for photovoltaic (PV) technology. For example, a 4 kilowatt system may cost $28,000 (at $7/installed watt) and be installed in a part of the country where electricity costs 5 cents per kilowatt hour, and the system is able to generate 6000 kWh per year. This system will save $400 per year but will take 70 years to pay for itself—using a simple payback calculation. In remote parts of the country, electricity costs 20 cents per kilowatt hour, reducing the payback to under 18 years.

EFFICIENCY AND SIZE OF PHOTOVOLTAIC COLLECTORS

Efficiency is still approximately 15 percent for polycrystalline silicon photovoltaic cells used in collectors. In other words, only 15 percent of the solar energy reaching the collector is converted to electricity. Six square feet of module area may be required to generate enough electricity to illuminate a 60 watt lightbulb. At $7 per watt, it would initially cost $420 to illuminate a standard incandescent light bulb with PV.

RENEWABLE ENERGY AND POLLUTION

A 60-watt light fixture used continuously over a 10-year period consumes about 5256 kWh of energy, costing $1051 at 20 cents per kWh over the period. This is not the only cost, however. Transmission line losses and the energy infrastructure required to extract and burn fossil fuels (or build nuclear fuel reactors) are far from efficient. Each watt of electricity used at the lamp requires several times that much energy to make it to the lamp. Accounting for these energy "externalities" is one way to link energy use to full environmental effects.

Some environmental literature promoting clean energy often explains the real cost of electricity in terms of pounds of carbon dioxide and other pollutants. For example, a family in Ohio with a monthly electric bill of $100 generates the following pollution annually, according to the Environmental Law and Policy Center of the Midwest (Ohio generates 88 percent of its electricity using coal):

- 2621 lb of carbon dioxide
- 10 lb of nitrogen oxide
- 28 lb of sulfur dioxide, nuclear waste, and mercury as a result of burning coal at the power plant

ENERGY EXTERNALITIES/ENVIRONMENTAL FOOTPRINT

Solar flows seen in this perspective offer a clean alternative to the pollution in the previous example. A full accounting of energy externalities would include:

- Disease caused by the pollution
- Environmental degradation caused by extraction of coal
- The transportation infrastructure, used for transporting the raw materials
- Environmental impacts on natural resources such as lakes, rivers, and so forth

DESIGN FOR ENERGY CONSERVATION

Regional design for energy conservation aims to minimize the use of conventionally powered heating, cooling, and lighting by using natural energy available at the building site. Site planning and building orientation, massing, and envelope design are the principal means for managing climate-driven conduction, convection, radiation, and vapor transfer. Climatic design strategies are selected in response to outdoor microclimatic conditions, defined as *underheated* or *overheated* with respect to indoor human comfort parameters.

Contributor:
Mark Rylander, AIA, William McDonough + Partners, Charlottesville, Virginia.

BASIC PRINCIPLES OF NATURAL VENTILATION
12.7

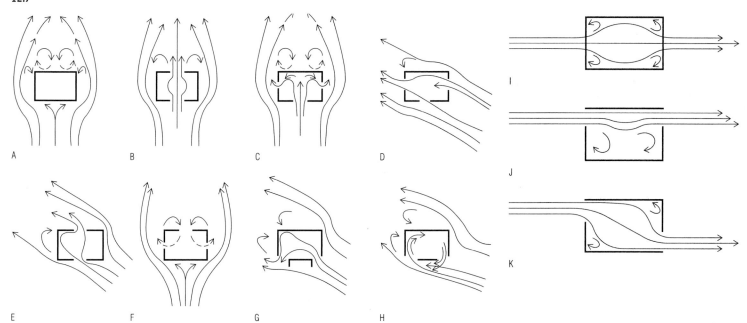

A   B   C   D

E   F   G   H

I

J

K

WINDOW SIZE

Airflow within a given room increases as window size increases, and to maximize airflow, the inlet and outlet opening should be the same size. Reducing the inlet size relative to the outlet increases inlet velocities. Making the outlet smaller than the inlet creates low but more uniform airspeed.

VENTILATION AIR CHANGE RATE

The natural air change rate within a building depends on several factors:

- Speed and direction of winds at the building site
- External geometry of the building and adjacent surroundings
- Window type, size, location, and geometry
- The building's internal partition layout

Each of these factors may have an overriding influence on the air change rate of a given building. Natural ventilation can be accomplished by wind-driven methods or by solar chimneys (stack effect). However, the stack effect is weak and works best during hours when air temperatures are highest and ventilation may not be desirable. In many areas, ventilation is best accomplished during the night hours when temperatures are lowest. The average night wind speed is generally about 75 percent of the 24-hour average wind speed reported by weather bureaus. Often, wind speeds are insufficient to accomplish effective people cooling; therefore, ventilating for structure cooling rather than people cooling should be the first design goal. As a rule of thumb, an average of 30 air changes per hour should provide adequate structure cooling, maintaining air temperatures most of the time within 1.5°F of outdoor temperatures.

EXTERNAL EFFECTS

The leeward wake of typical residential buildings extends roughly four and one-half times the ground-to-eave height. For buildings spaced greater than this distance, the general wind direction will remain unchanged. For design purposes, vegetation should be considered for its effect on wind speed, which can be as great as 30 to 40 percent in the immediate vicinity of the vegetation. Its effect on wind direction is not well established, however, and so should not be relied on in establishing ventilation strategies.

RULE-OF-THUMB EXAMPLE

First, determine an inlet window opening area to achieve 30 air changes per hour in a house of 1200 sq ft with a ceiling height of 8 ft and awning windows with insect screens.

Required airflow (CFM) = House volume × air changes per hr/60

Required airflow = 1200 × 8 × 30/60 = 4800 CFM

Next, from local National Oceanic and Atmospheric Administration (NOAA) weather data, determine site wind conditions for the design month. For this example, average wind speed at about 32.81 ft above ground level equals 7 mph, or 616 ft/min at 30-in. incidence angle to the house face. Note that site wind speeds are generally less than NOAA data, usually collected at airports.

To determine the required inlet area, divide the house airflow by the wind speed passing through openings on the windward building face. To establish this wind speed, the site wind speed must be modified by the effects of building angle relative to wind direction and porosity of the window opening.

Figure 12.8 charts the effect of the wind incidence angle on airflow rates (based on wind tunnel tests on model buildings with equal inlet and outlet areas equaling 12 percent of inlet wall areas). Table 12.9 establishes porosity factors for typical window arrangements. By multiplying the site wind speed by the window airspeed factor (WAF) and window porosity factor (WPF), the effective wind speed can be determined.

$$\text{Inlet window area} = \frac{\text{Airflow}}{\text{Wind speed} \times \text{WAF} \times \text{WPF}}$$

$$\text{Inlet window area} = \frac{4800}{616 \times 0.35 \times 0.75} = 29.7 \text{ sq ft}$$

In this example, therefore, providing a total of 60 sq ft of insect-screened awning windows will provide the required ventilation of 30 air changes per hour. For best results, the 60 sq ft of windows should be split equally between inlets and outlets. However, adequate airflows can be maintained for anywhere from 40/60 to 60/40 split between inlets and outlets.

EFFECTS OF WIND INCIDENCE ANGLE ON AIRFLOW RATES
12.8

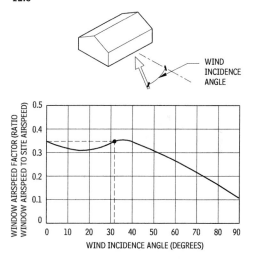

POROSITY FACTORS
12.9

WINDOW TYPE	FACTOR
Fully open awning or projecting window	0.75
Awning window with 60% porosity insect screen	0.65
60% porosity insect screen only	0.85

Contributor:
W. Fred Roberts Jr., AIA, Roberts Kirchner Architects, Lexington, Virginia.

TIME

Tuning well-designed buildings to the path of the sun and to the change in seasons is not a new idea. For design to become more sustaining, it must seek opportunities to respond to changes in the day through daylighting and other strategies, and to changes in the seasons through the integration of building and landscape.

DIURNAL RHYTHMS

The design and location of rooms based on daily (diurnal) use patterns and orientation are optimized in sustaining design. Outdoor lighting and transportation have eliminated the unique and restful qualities of night and have interrupted human biological circadian rhythms that have developed over millennia. Examples include placement of bedrooms to the east, cooking spaces to the north,

or gardens to the south. Architects address diurnal cycles with design that:

• Responds to the position of the sun throughout the day
• Responds to night conditions through the elimination of light trespass and pollution
• Responds to color temperature and intensity of light
• Responds to the biological (circadian) rhythms that are interrupted by work and school schedules, television, and travel

SEASONAL RHYTHMS

Architecture that responds to seasons has outdoor spaces that are used more frequently as weather allows. For example, porches, decks, and patios are a part of summer in most of the United States and are used even more of the year in the South; living spaces in

the interior of a house—such as at the hearth—are comfortable centers in cold weather.

At the heart of the best regional architecture is the idea that buildings and landscapes are designed to enable people to spend as much time as possible in the most comfortable place with the best views and best connection to the outdoors. Seasonal transformation and regional response are primary design drivers of sustaining design. Operability of windows and walls assists in this transformation. The design of primary indoor and secondary outdoor dining space both in close proximity to a kitchen is an example of adaptability in response to seasonal flows. In areas with extreme seasonal events such as hurricanes, architecture incorporates elements such as exterior shutters and movable storm panels that provide enhanced protection for doors and windows.

HEALTHY ECOSYSTEMS

A self-reliant perspective is often associated with sustainable design. The emergence in the 1970s of passive solar houses corresponded to a movement toward withdrawal from mainstream culture. Solar design has a reputation of independence, of "living off the land." However, *interdependence* has proven to be a more effective model of sustainability, and one based on the principle of ecology.

ECOSYSTEM CONCEPTS

An expanded concept of place includes physical attributes of a location and the flows described in the last section, as well as the more commonly accepted, if not understood, attributes of culture and human history. Less well understood are the communities of interdependent living things that are native to a place and give it a stability and unique character. This section explores how architects' decisions can have positive effects on these sensitive environments.

An ecosystem is defined as a naturally occurring community of organisms living together with their physical environment and functioning as a loose unit. *Ecosystem* is a twentieth-century term that emerged from the study of interdependence among communities of plants and animals within particular environments. Ecosystems exist at all scales, and more than one ecosystem can exist in one place. Ecosystems can blend together, and their boundaries can shift over time. Energy and matter flow between elements of an ecosystem, allowing it to maintain a state of equilibrium. Ecosystems can be as large as a forest or as small as a pond and are often separated by major geographic features, such as lakes, deserts, and mountain ranges.

An *ecotone* is the transitional zone between two or more ecosystems. It is a place where ecologies are in tension and often represents opportunities for life forms that can take advantage of multiple ecologies. The boundary can be sharp or broad. Shorelines and edges of forests are examples of ecotones.

DISRUPTION

New elements introduced into an ecosystem are disruptive to some extent, whether they are biotic (living) or abiotic (nonliving). Building disrupts the functioning of ecosystems, so efforts are made to restore or replace critical elements of these systems. For example, some regulations may require the restoration or replacement of disrupted wetlands, allowing related plant and animal families to reestablish balance.

BIOMES

A *biome* is a large biotic community comprising many smaller ecosystems with a prevailing climate; it is characterized by dominant forms of plant life. Examples of biomes are forests, deserts, tundra, and grasslands (there are also aquatic biomes). The major land biomes of the United States are tundra, deserts, deciduous forests, coniferous forests, rain forests, and grasslands.

**LAND BIOMES
12.10**

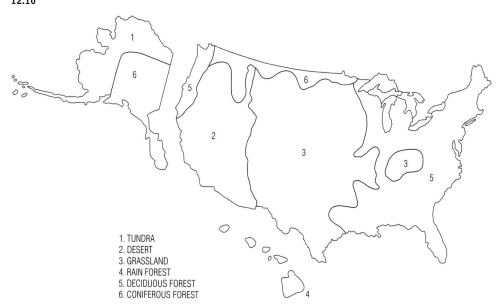

1. TUNDRA
2. DESERT
3. GRASSLAND
4. RAIN FOREST
5. DECIDUOUS FOREST
6. CONIFEROUS FOREST

MONOCULTURE

In agriculture, *monoculture* describes planting and cultivation of a single species over a substantial area, or the practice of relying on a very small number of species for agricultural purposes. The rise of monoculture in modern agriculture has been the result of improved technology; machinery for tilling, planting, pest control, and harvesting generally are much cheaper and more efficient than human labor. Examples of monocultures include lawns and most field crops, such as wheat or corn. Monocultures compromise ecological systems.

HEALTHY SOIL

Healthy soil is alive. Minerals and the porosity and soil structure are important, but fertility is a function of soil biota, including the effects of large animals such as moles and other rodents; smaller animals or macrofauna (0.08 to 0.8 inches in size) such as spiders, ants, earthworms, beetles, slugs, and snails and smaller animals; and microflora and microfauna. The latter groups include bacteria and fungi, which are essential to maintaining soil health.

ARCHITECTURAL PLANNING FOR REGENERATION OF ECOSYSTEMS

Architects are occasionally involved in site selection decisions with clients, or may even function as developers themselves. Existing

planning policies rarely take into account protections not already required by regulation, such as wetland remediation laws. As parcels of land available for development become larger and open space diminishes, collaborative decisions must be made, and architects are well trained to solve such complex problems.

Natural resources are not inexhaustible, and this culture of extraction and wasteful production can be redesigned. Ecosystem regeneration—beginning with the restoration of systems as they were before development and supplementing those systems to help them thrive—allows for the continual succession that takes place in natural systems.

BROWNFIELD REMEDIATION AND GREENFIELD DEVELOPMENT

One effective strategy that is increasingly brought to bear on urban development planning is brownfield remediation. Brownfields are previously developed lands that may require removal or treatment of toxic soil before they can be reoccupied. The U.S. EPA evaluates and rates such sites working with developers and local government to clean up and reuse land that is often close to city centers and neighborhoods. In some cities such as Portland, Oregon, the government provides incentives for developing on previously developed land within a growth boundary.

Contributor:
Mark Rylander, AIA, William McDonough + Partners, Charlottesville, Virginia.

Greenfield sites, in contrast, are either undeveloped lands that may contain portions of native ecosystems or agricultural land.

CONSERVATION LAND TRUSTS
Sensitive natural areas can be preserved in a number of ways, including purchase that holds the land in perpetual protection. This approach grew threefold in the 1990s and now protects more than 6 million acres.

ORGANIZATIONAL EFFORTS

Several key organizations within the industry have formally expressed policies and opinions related to the role of sustainable design and how it affects ecology. These organizations include the Forest Stewardship Council (FSC), the International Union of Architects (UIA), and the American Institute of Architects (AIA).

SUSTAINABLE FORESTRY
Few ecological issues related to the building industry have raised as much controversy as forest practices. In an effort to curtail clear-cutting and the devastating Third World wood practices that have caused ecological collapse in some regions including tropical rain forests, international organizations have been established and certification standards have been created.

One of the most stringent and best known of these is the FSC. The principles that govern FSC certification also apply to other certification systems, many of which are emerging or tailored to particular land holdings and parts of the wood and paper industry. FSC has developed a set of 10 principles and 57 criteria for forest management that are applicable to all FSC-certified forests throughout the world. They address legal issues, indigenous rights, labor rights, multiple benefits, and environmental impacts surrounding forest management.

The 10 principles are:

* *Principle 1—Compliance with Laws and FSC Principles*: Forest management shall respect all applicable laws of the country in which they occur, and international treaties and agreements to which the country is a signatory, and comply with all FSC Principles and Criteria.
* *Principle 2—Tenure and Use Rights and Responsibilities*: Long-term tenure and use rights to the land and forest resources shall be clearly defined, documented, and legally established.
* *Principle 3—Indigenous Peoples' Rights*: The legal and customary rights of indigenous peoples to own, use, and manage their lands, territories, and resources shall be recognized and respected.
* *Principle 4—Community Relations and Workers' Rights*: Forest management operations shall maintain or enhance the long-term social and economic well-being of forest workers and local communities.
* *Principle 5—Benefits from the Forest*: Forest management operations shall encourage the efficient use of the forest's multiple products and services to ensure economic viability and a wide range of environmental and social benefits.
* *Principle 6—Environmental Impact*: Forest management shall conserve biological diversity and its associated values, water resources, soils, and unique and fragile ecosystems and landscapes, and by so doing, maintain the ecological functions and the integrity of the forest.
* *Principle 7—Management Plan*: A management plan (appropriate to the scale and intensity of the operations) shall be written, implemented, and kept up to date. The long-term objectives of management, and the means of achieving them, shall be clearly stated.
* *Principle 8—Monitoring and Assessment*: Monitoring shall be conducted (appropriate to the scale and intensity of forest management) to assess the condition of the forest, yields of forest products, chain of custody, management activities, and their social and environmental impacts.
* *Principle 9—Maintenance of High Conservation Value Forests*: Management activities in high conservation value forests shall maintain or enhance the attributes that define such forests. Decisions regarding high conservation value forests shall always be considered in the context of a precautionary approach.
* *Principle 10—Plantations*: Plantations shall be planned and managed in accordance with Principles and Criteria 1 to 9, and Principle 10 and its Criteria. While plantations can provide an array of social and economic benefits and can contribute to satisfying the world's needs for forest products, they should complement the management of, reduce pressures on, and promote the restoration and conservation of natural forests.

DECLARATION OF INTERDEPENDENCE

At the UIA/AIA World Congress of Architects held in Chicago, Illinois in 1993, architects from around the world met to address the emergence of global environmental problems. One of the results of that meeting was an acknowledgment that architects must develop and apply innovative designs, technologies, and methods to achieve a sustainable future.

According to the document signed by Olufemi Majekodunmi (then president of the International Union of Architects) and Susan A. Maxman, FAIA (then president, American Institute of Architects), and entitled, "Declaration of Interdependence for a Sustainable Future," the architects recognized the following:

* "A sustainable society restores, preserves, and enhances nature and culture for the benefit of all life, present and future; a diverse and healthy environment is intrinsically valuable and essential to a healthy society; today's society is seriously degrading the environment and is not sustainable;
* "We are ecologically interdependent with the whole natural environment; we are socially, culturally, and economically interdependent with all of humanity; sustainability, in the context of this interdependence, requires partnership, equity, and balance among all parties;
* "Buildings and the built environment play a major role in the human impact on the natural environment and on the quality of life; sustainable design integrates consideration of resource and energy efficiency, healthy buildings and materials, ecologically and socially sensitive land use, and an aesthetic sensitivity that inspires, affirms, and ennobles; sustainable design can significantly reduce adverse human impacts on the natural environment while simultaneously improving quality of life and economic well-being."

The architects (individually and through professional organizations) committed to do the following:

* "Place environmental and social sustainability at the core of our practices and professional responsibilities;
* "Develop and continually improve practices, procedures, products, curricula, services, and standards that will enable the implementation of sustainable design;
* "Educate our fellow professionals, the building industry, clients, students, and the general public about the critical importance and substantial opportunities of sustainable design;
* "Establish policies, regulations, and practices in government and business that ensure sustainable design becomes normal practice;
* "Bring all existing and future elements of the built environment—in their design, production, use, and eventual reuse—up to sustainable design standards."

HEALTHY MATERIALS

ENVIRONMENTAL IMPACT/ MATERIAL LIFE CYCLE

The *AIA Environmental Resource Guide,* produced in the 1990s by the AIA and the EPA, contains a wealth of information on where today's materials come from and where they go after they serve their purposes in buildings. For such information to be meaningful, designers and their clients must work together to establish the priorities that will guide material choices. The discussion here is not intended as conclusive, but rather to provide perspective across a series of considerations. For example, an architect could determine that one material has very low-embodied energy (good) and defined toxicity; another could be shown to contribute significantly to acid rain but is durable; and a third could be made of recycled content, but the recycled materials are not entirely known. Without a framework, each decision would be impossible to make, and each would be structured as a search for the lesser evil.

As life-cycle tools become more accessible, architects will have access to even more information about upstream and downstream effects of materials. For the architect and owner willing to take the time to set goals and research life cycles, there are no shortcuts, Software programs and certifications will emerge that simply declare one material better than another. Designers must understand the criteria behind a given certification to make an informed selection as they would for any other aspect of material performance.

A proactive approach that voluntarily eliminates materials suspected of having adverse effects has proven to be extremely valuable and practical. By voluntarily eliminating asbestos or CFCs or PCBs from projects before they became regulated and banned, designers saved clients significant amounts of money and time. Once a designer is aware of a health concern, it becomes his or her ethical responsibility to share it with a client and propose alternatives proactively.

ENVIRONMENTAL CONSTRUCTION
ENVIRONMENTAL IMPACT ANALYSIS OF BUILDING MATERIALS
For years the building industry in the United States has depended on a seemingly endless supply of high-quality materials, supplies, and energy resources. Manufacturers have been producing building materials abundantly, and architects generally have been specifying them for reasons of aesthetics, budget, performance, code compliance, and availability. Consideration is rarely given to the environmental impact of using these materials—that is, what environmental "costs" go into extracting, producing, shipping, and installing them. These costs include depletion of nonrenewable raw materials and resources; production of waste by-products; and exposure of toxicity to the air, water, soils, and inhabitants of nearby areas.

For the building industry of the future, it will make good business sense to use materials that are environmentally friendly, sustainable, and renewable, and that contain recycled materials. A building industry that depends on depletable resources to manufacture its materials will become more and more costly as the resources are depleted. More important, the world in which we build will become more and more uninhabitable because of the toxins and waste left by our present materials and methods of construction. To do its part in keeping the world safe to live in, the architecture profession must incorporate procedures and standards of resource conservation into our design philosophies.

BUILDING MATERIALS ANALYSIS
LIFE CYCLE OF BUILDING MATERIALS
To analyze a building material from an environmental standpoint, an understanding of the life cycle of that material must be reached. This is achieved by examining the environmental burdens that accrue through extraction or acquisition of the raw materials and their processing/manufacture and the packaging, distribution, use, and ultimate recovery (reuse/recycling) or disposal of the finished product.

Contributors:
Mark Rylander, AIA, William McDonough + Partners, Charlottesville, Virginia; Forest Stewardship Council, Washington, DC.

**LIFE-CYCLE CHART
12.11**

Three aspects of the life of a building material are most significant in considering environmental impact:

* Is the raw material renewable or nonrenewable?
* How much total waste or how many toxic by-products are produced in its production and during the life of the product?
* How much energy is consumed in its life cycle?

A building material that is both environmentally "pure" and readily available—that is, one made from a 100 percent renewable raw material that uses only renewable energy in its extraction, production, and transport and can be infinitely reclaimed and recycled (as well as healthy to the occupants of a building)—will be hard to find. Even to have that "perfect" material as a goal, it is necessary to have a frame of reference from which to choose materials based on environmental concerns, something like ingredient and nutrition labeling on food products. If this information were available on materials for the building industry, it would be possible to specify materials that are healthy and "nutritious" for a sustainable planet.

EMBODIED ENERGY OF BUILDING MATERIALS
The embodied energy of a building material comprises all the energy consumed in acquiring and transforming the raw materials into finished products and transporting them to the building site. The life-cycle chart shown in Figure 12.20 details where energy is consumed in producing building materials. The embodied energy or energy "content" of a building material will act as a rough guide to its environmental friendliness. The energy content reflects the material's closeness to the earth; the more it is refined or processed, the more energy it contains, hence the more "expensive" it is environmentally.

If we must produce and use high-energy materials, it is important not to waste that energy by burying them in a landfill, but rather reuse or recycle them.

To compare one material to another, the following characteristics must be taken into account:

* Regional availability—local extraction/manufacture
* Recyclability (how many times the material can be recycled and retain viability)
* Reusability
* Durability and life span
* Toxicity of the product or of the materials used to maintain the product during its life
* Efficiency of product's performance as an architectural component
* Savings on other materials not used because this product is used
* Savings in energy not consumed over the life span of the building because this product is used
* Any combination of these factors

Some construction methods and systems bind materials together to render them difficult or costly to recycle or reuse. One example of this is reinforced concrete, which efficiently not only uses steel in its role of spanning distances but also makes it impractical to recycle after a building has outlived its usefulness. A structural

steel frame, although it uses a great deal more steel than a similar reinforced concrete frame, can be unbolted, disassembled, and reused or melted down and reformed infinitely.

Evaluating whether a certain material is used in construction is a complicated process involving many factors. Certain regions or markets may be more familiar with or more suitable for certain types of construction or materials, and this may be an unavoidable factor that nullifies all others in determining which structural or other material is used.

LIFE CYCLE CHECKLIST FOR BUILDING MATERIALS
This checklist can be used to analyze the environmental impact of building materials:

* Raw material acquisition (mining, harvesting, drilling, extraction)
  * Is the resource renewable or sustainable (reproducible indefinitely)?
  * How much nonrenewable waste is produced?
  * What is the amount and type of energy consumed? (Is it sustainable?)
  * How does acquisition affect the environment? (Does it destroy forests or other habitats, or produce silt or toxic runoff or air pollution?)
* Raw material processing and manufacturing
  * How much nonrecyclable waste is produced?
  * What is the type and amount of energy consumed to manufacture the product?
  * What toxicity to air, water, or soils is produced by processing?
* Product packaging and final packaging (for shipping)
  * Is packaging recyclable or made of recycled material?
  * Is packaging excessive?
  * Does packaging use nonrenewable resources (e.g., petroleum or materials harmful to the environment, such as CFC insulation packing material)?
* Product distribution
  * Would the product travel an excessive distance from the manufacturing site to the building site when more local products could be used?
  * What is the type and amount of energy consumed to transport the material?
* Product installation, use, and maintenance
  * Does installation produce excessive and/or nonrenewable site waste?
  * What energy is consumed to install and maintain the product?
  * Does installation, use, or maintenance of the product pollute the outdoor or indoor environment for installers or occupants?
  * How durable is the product and what is its rate of degradation?
  * Does the product add to the energy efficiency of the building?
* Disposal, recycling, and reuse
  * Does the product use virgin materials wisely?
  * Is it recyclable after use and, if so, to what degree?
  * Can the product be reused?
  * What energy is consumed to recycle the product?

APPROXIMATE VALUE OF EMBODIED ENERGY IN BUILDING MATERIALS
12.12

MATERIALS		ENERGY CONTENT (BTU/LB)
Low-energy materials	Sand/gravel	18
	Wood	185
	Sand-lime brick	730
	Lightweight concrete	940
Medium-energy materials	Gypsum board	1830
	Brick	2200
	Lime	2800
	Cement	4100
	Mineral fiber insulation	7200
	Glass	11,100
	Porcelain	11,300
High-energy materials	Plastic	18,500
	Steel	19,200
	Lead	25,900
	Zinc	27,800
	Copper	29,600
	Aluminum	103,500

* What energy is consumed to dispose of its nonrecyclable elements?
* What is the toxicity to the environment when the product is thrown away?

ENVIRONMENTAL IMPACT OF MATERIALS
Table 12.13 is intended as a guide to selecting environmentally friendly materials. As a rule of thumb, use locally produced environmentally friendly materials to save transportation-related energy.

In comparing building materials, the choice that promotes resource conservation may not always be as straightforward as it appears. For example, wood may seem a better choice than plastic for a park bench, as it is a natural, renewable material rather than a petroleum-based one. However, in an outdoor usage, where durability and good maintenance characteristics are preferred, offgassing from plastic may be less critical. When the aesthetics of wood are not important, plastic made from recycled soda bottles may be an appropriate solution. Choosing recycled plastic would conserve wood materials—old-growth cedar, redwood, or chemically treated pine—and reuse something made from a nonrenewable resource, making it an acceptable solution sympathetic with resource conservation principles. At issue is the definition of a "resource" that must be conserved. A great deal of material and embodied energy are tied up in existing plastic. The reuse of these materials not only allows those resources to continue a useful life but also saves the embodied energy that would have been used to create a new product in its place. Plastic, particularly, is very durable and very slow to degrade.

NOTE

12.11 Energy consumption considerations of building materials should not override basic respect for the earth. Degradation of the landscape in materials extraction, transport, and manufacturing, as well as in construction, should be minimized.

Contributors:
Richard J. Vitullo, AIA, Oak Leaf Studio, Crownsville, Maryland; *AIA Environmental Resource Guide* (John Wiley & Sons, Inc., 1998); Bradley Guy, Building Materials Reuse Association, State College, Pennsylvania; Mark Rylander, AIA, William McDonough + Partners, Charlottesville, Virginia.

BUILDING MATERIALS COMPARISON CHART
12.13

MASTER FORMAT DIVISION	PRODUCTS	ENVIRONMENTAL IMPACT	TOXICITY TO INDOOR ENVIRONMENT	ENVIRONMENTALLY SOUND ALTERNATIVE PRODUCTS OR SUGGESTIONS	ENVIRONMENTAL IMPACT	TOXICITY TO INDOOR ENVIRONMENT
Concrete	Concrete material	• Concrete has high-embodied energy content.		• Uses fly ash, a by-product of coal combustion • Autoclaved cellular concrete (ACC)	• No harmful by-products	• Aluminum powder additive reacts with lime to create hydrogen bubbles and a lightweight, cellular cementitious material (provides high strength-to-weight ratio); also self-insulating (R-10 for 8-in. wall).
Metals	Steel studs/framing members	• Reduces depletion of old- and new-growth timber. • Consumes more energy to produce (high-embodied energy content). • Steel production pollutes air, water, and soil.	• Inert; produces no harmful by-products	• Use materials with less-embodied energy content if recycled steel not available		• Can be made from recycled scrap into identical product
Wood, Plastics, and Composites	Wood framing	• Depletes old- and new-growth timber. • Can be recycled into particleboard and other wood products.	• Produces no significant harmful by-products • Preservative-treated woods contain toxic inorganic arsenates (site waste needs to be contained).	• Interior: Engineered lumber; finger-jointed structural lumber; plastic framing members • Exterior: Decking—pao lope; mudsills—douglas fir treated with resin oil, beechwood distillates, and other treatments	• Engineered lumber is made from recycled wood fiber and small-diameter trees. • Finger-jointed wood is made from small wood pieces. • Plastic members made from recycled soda bottles. • Pav lope, a plantation-grown, rot-resistant hardwood. • Natural wood treatments are not toxic.	• Engineered lumber may offgas formaldehyde. • Plastic members may offgas chemical fumes and give off toxic fumes when burned.
	Plywood	• Made from large-diameter, old-growth peeler logs	• Interior-grade offgasses high-emitting levels of urea formaldehyde. • Exterior-grade offgasses low-emitting phenol formaldehyde. • Formaldehyde is a possible carcinogen and is irritating to respiration. • Offgassing half-life is ± 6 months.	• Lumber-core plywood • Cellulose fiberboard underlayment • Exterior-grade plywood • With sealing finishes • Tongue-and-groove pine sheathing	• All plywood still is made from old-growth peeler logs. • Cellulose fiberboard is made from recycled newspapers. • Tongue-and-groove pine usually is locally grown and can be from smaller-diameter trees.	• Lumber core and exterior-grade plywoods have reduced levels of formaldehyde offgassing. • Cellulose fiberboard and tongue-and-groove pine have no harmful offgassing.
	Particleboard: oriented strandboard (OSB), medium-density fiberboard (MDF)	• Can be made from recycled wood scrap, sustainable woods, and cellulose fibers	• Same characteristics as plywood	• Laminated or sealed MDF		• Covering finishes or sealers reduce offgassing.
	Finish woods	• Use of exotic tropical woods depletes rain forests.	• Produces no harmful by-products	• Domestic temperate hardwoods (plum, cherry, alder, black locust, and persimmon) • Veneer woods with recycled backup • Reclaimed and reused woods	• Domestic woods can be managed as sustainable tree farms. • Use of veneers instead of solid woods saves tree resources. • Use of reused woods saves tree resources.	• Some finishes may be harmful to indoor air.
Thermal and moisture protection	Blanket insulation	• Can be made from recycled glass	• Airborne fibers can be irritating to skin, lungs, and nasal passages. • Offgasses formaldehyde.	• Cellulose insulation • Cotton insulation • Cementitious foam insulation • Mineral fiber insulation	• Cellulose insulation is made from recycled newsprint. • Cotton blanket insulation is made from recycled cotton denim fibers. • Cementitious foam is made from silicate-based magnesium (CFC-free). • Mineral fiber is made from mineral slag, a waste by-product of steel production.	• Cotton and cellulose insulation may be treated with chemical fire treatment.
	Board insulation	• Many types are made from nonrenewable petrochemicals.	• Gives off toxic fumes when burned. • Those made with isocyanurate, polyurethane, and phenolic foam offgas chemical fumes.	• Recycled, extruded polystyrene insulation • CFC-free insulation • Expanded polystyrene	• Reuse of recycled plastic does not deplete oil resources. • HCFC foaming agent 1/20 is as damaging to ozone as CFC. • Expanded polystyrene only R-3.6 per inch (extruded polystyrene R-4.4 per inch).	• Some recycled plastic materials may offgas chemical fumes. • Plastics give off toxic fumes when burned.
	Siding	• Vinyl siding is made from nonrenewable petrochemical source. • Wood siding and shakes deplete mature slow-growth cedar and redwood trees.		• Hardboard siding • Mineral-fiber cement siding • Composite trim	• Hardboard siding is made from recycled wood fiber. • Mineral-fiber cement siding is made from wood sawmill chips and portland cement. • Composite trim is made from recycled plastic and recycled wood fiber.	

Contributors:
Richard J. Vitullo, AIA, Oak Leaf Studio, Crownsville, Maryland; *AIA Environmental Resource Guide* (John Wiley & Sons, Inc., 1998).

BUILDING MATERIALS COMPARISON CHART (continued)
12.13

MASTER FORMAT DIVISION	PRODUCTS	ENVIRONMENTAL IMPACT	TOXICITY TO INDOOR ENVIRONMENT	ENVIRONMENTALLY SOUND ALTERNATIVE PRODUCTS OR SUGGESTIONS	ENVIRONMENTAL IMPACT	TOXICITY TO INDOOR ENVIRONMENT
	Wood and asphalt roof shingles	• Asphalt is derived from nonrenewable petrochemicals.	• Many contain fiberglass fibers (mostly harmful to installers), an irritant.	• Fiber-cement composite shingles	• Fiber-cement shingles are made from recycled wood sawmill chips or paper and portland cement (also recyclable).	• Plastic offgasses harmful fumes (negligible to indoor air) and gives off toxic fumes when burned.
	Wood shingles, either cedar or redwood, are made from old-growth, slow-growth tree stands.		• Chemical treatment of wood shingles is harmful to installers.	• Natural slate and terra-cotta • Recycled aluminum shingles • Recycled plastic shingles • Metal roofing of recycled steel or copper	• Recycled aluminum from soda cans and scrap • Recycled plastic from computer housings	
Openings	Doors	• Some doors are made with endangered old-growth woods, such as teak or mahogany (lauan) veneers and solids.	• Few harmful by-products in wood; finishes may contain offgassing materials.	• Recycled-content doors • Fiberglass doors	• Some doors are made from recycled plastic and wood waste; also recycled steel. • Fiberglass uses a few petrochemicals in production.	• Recycled wood may be bound by urea formaldehyde resin. • Recycled plastic offgasses and gives off toxic fumes when burned.
	Windows	• Many windows in older structures are not energy-efficient.	• Vinyl windows offgas harmful fumes and give off toxic fumes when burned.	• Recycled-content windows • High-efficiency, low-E glass windows • Argon-filled insulated glass windows	• Fiberglass has same coefficient of expansion as glass. • See doors, above.	• See doors, above.
Finishes	Gypsum board	• Many types use predominantly virgin gypsum mineral, depleting resources.	• Many carcinogens in standard joint compounds	• Gypsum board is made with recycled or reclaimed materials.	• Some alternative "gypsum" board cores contain recycled scrap wallboard; by-product gypsum (from emissions of fossil-fueled factories); recycled cellulose fiber, perlite, ryegrass straw (an agricultural by-product); and mixed waste papers. Some wallboard facings are made with recycled paper.	• Nontoxic joint compounds contain no harmful agents (they must be site-mixed and may be difficult to use).
	Flooring	• PVC and vinyl tiles are made from nonrenewable petrochemicals.	• PVC and vinyls contain additives that offgas harmful fumes.	• Natural linoleum tile • Recycled-content tile • Natural grouts • Reclaimed and reused wood floors	• Linoleum is made from linseed oil, pine resins, softwood flour, cork, and jute. • Tile is made from recycled light bulbs and auto glass. • Tile is made from recycled auto tires. • Grouts are made from silica, calcium rock, and iron-oxide pigments.	• Use low-VOC adhesives
	Carpet	• Many are made from petrochemicals, a nonrenewable resource.	• Plastic fibers, backing, mastics, and treatments offgas many gasses harmful to respiratory systems (major component of "sick building syndrome"). • All carpets may harbor dust and mites, both respiratory irritants. • Plastic gives off toxic fumes when burned.	• Natural fiber carpets • Recycled-content carpets	• Choose untreated carpets made with natural fibers and backing such as wool or cotton. • Some carpets are made from recycled plastic (soft drink bottles). • Choose natural jute padding.	• Use tackable edging instead of adhesives, or just edge- and seam application of adhesives. • Use low-VOC adhesives. • Recycled plastic offgasses harmful fumes and gives off toxic fumes when burned.
	Paint, finishes, and wood treatments	• Unused paint and so forth can cause groundwater and soil pollution if disposed of improperly. • Volatile organic compounds (VOCs) can cause smog and ground level ozone pollution.	• Many enamels, varnishes, and polyurethanes contain VOCs and offgas these, causing harmful respiratory reactions.	• Citrus-based paints • Acrylic-based stains • Natural wood treatments and finishes	• Citrus-based paints have low-biocide content but contain some petrochemicals. • More organic-type finishes present less disposal problems.	• Citrus-based paints have low-biocide, nonirritating content (it must be thinned and color-mixed by the installer). • Acrylic-based stains are low-VOC. • Natural wood treatments of tung oil, ointment of beeswax, and so forth contain no harmful irritants (more maintenance is required).
	Adhesives and mastics	• Unused containers can cause groundwater and soil pollution if disposed of improperly. • Many types of adhesives are flammable and give off toxic fumes when burned.	• Some adhesives and mastics offgas hazardous fumes to installers and occupants.	• Low-VOC, environmentally safer adhesives and mastics	• Some adhesives and mastics are nontoxic, nonflammable, and safer for disposal (water-soluble).	• Low-VOC content emits less toxic fumes.
Electrical	Electrical power cables		• Electromagnetic fields are created around any electrical source and may cause cancer.	• Electromagnetic shielding		• Install shielding for wiring at spaces that will have prolonged exposure to occupants (e.g., bedrooms).

Source: Adapted from *AIA Environmental Resource Guide* (John Wiley & Sons, Inc., 1998)

Contributor:
Richard J. Vitullo, AIA, Oak Leaf Studio, Crownsville, Maryland.

RESOURCE CONSERVATION AND NONTOXIC MATERIALS

RESOURCE CONSERVATION METHODS AND SYSTEMS

Choosing building materials containing recycled materials is but one step in the process of environmentally conscious design. Sensitive environmental design takes the holistic view, regarding every aspect of how a building works in its context. Consideration must be given to how a building performs and relates to its surroundings throughout its life, before (design and specification), during (construction), and after (lifetime maintenance and energy costs) it is built. The following guidelines can be used for designing with resource conservation goals:

1. Design with nature's patterns in mind so the building works with them and the resources of its site, rather than overpowering and controlling them. The following methods will help you achieve this goal:
   - *Building and site planning*: To achieve the goal of overall environmental design, it is critical to orient the building to the landscape at the site. Working with site features makes it possible to take advantage of natural systems, such as ventilation by means of windows and chimneys or full-spectrum light sources.
   - *Earth-sheltered design*: Solar heat and light can be used to reduce the nonrenewable energy requirements of a building. The temperature-moderating feature of the earth is an aspect of the surrounding environment, often ignored. Through earth berms, earth-covered roofs, and underground design, a building can make use of the consistent 55°F± of the earth below the local frost line, or at least the inherent R-value of earth material. A well-designed earth-sheltered structure also reduces the need for exterior maintenance of building materials.

2. Preserving existing site features may benefit the local habitat and make the building harmonize with the site.
   - *Tree, plant, and soil preservation*: Establish environmental priorities for the building site. Inventory natural features such as viable trees and shrubs and wetland areas. Trees provide an enormous environmental benefit to the health of buildings (shading), sites (e.g., soil enrichment from leaves), and birds and other wildlife. Locate buildings, driveways, and land to be disturbed during construction far enough from existing trees to avoid root compaction. A good rule of thumb is to stay out of the drip line of a tree during construction. Have a landscape architect, arborist, forester, or environmental consultant assist in the survey.
   - *Construction and demolition site waste recycling or reuse*: The construction of a single-family home in the United States generates 2.5 tons of waste. Because landfill overcrowding has caused dumping fees to increase significantly, it is becoming economically feasible to recycle construction and demolition wastes. Identify materials that could be used more efficiently, salvaged, reused on site, or recycled. Common materials that generally can be recycled from construction sites are (with percentages based on total site waste volume): wood (27 percent), cardboard/paper (18 percent), gypsum board (15 percent), thermal insulation (9 percent), roofing (8 percent), metals (7 percent), concrete/asphalt rubble (6 percent), landscaping debris (5 percent), and miscellaneous (5 percent). These are national averages, and each site will be

ENERGY-SAVING SYSTEMS
12.14
Source: Rocky Mountain Institute, Snowmass, Colorado

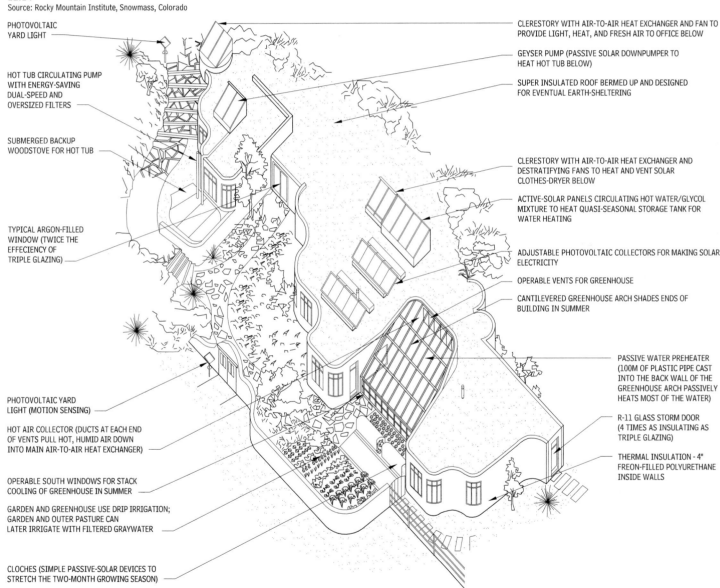

PHOTOVOLTAIC YARD LIGHT

HOT TUB CIRCULATING PUMP WITH ENERGY-SAVING DUAL-SPEED AND OVERSIZED FILTERS

SUBMERGED BACKUP WOODSTOVE FOR HOT TUB

TYPICAL ARGON-FILLED WINDOW (TWICE THE EFFECIENCY OF TRIPLE GLAZING)

PHOTOVOLTAIC YARD LIGHT (MOTION SENSING)

HOT AIR COLLECTOR (DUCTS AT EACH END OF VENTS PULL HOT, HUMID AIR DOWN INTO MAIN AIR-TO-AIR HEAT EXCHANGER)

OPERABLE SOUTH WINDOWS FOR STACK COOLING OF GREENHOUSE IN SUMMER

GARDEN AND GREENHOUSE USE DRIP IRRIGATION; GARDEN AND OUTER PASTURE CAN LATER IRRIGATE WITH FILTERED GRAYWATER

CLOCHES (SIMPLE PASSIVE-SOLAR DEVICES TO STRETCH THE TWO-MONTH GROWING SEASON)

CLERESTORY WITH AIR-TO-AIR HEAT EXCHANGER AND FAN TO PROVIDE LIGHT, HEAT, AND FRESH AIR TO OFFICE BELOW

GEYSER PUMP (PASSIVE SOLAR DOWNPUMPER TO HEAT HOT TUB BELOW)

SUPER INSULATED ROOF BERMED UP AND DESIGNED FOR EVENTUAL EARTH-SHELTERING

CLERESTORY WITH AIR-TO-AIR HEAT EXCHANGER AND DESTRATIFYING FANS TO HEAT AND VENT SOLAR CLOTHES-DRYER BELOW

ACTIVE-SOLAR PANELS CIRCULATING HOT WATER/GLYCOL MIXTURE TO HEAT QUASI-SEASONAL STORAGE TANK FOR WATER HEATING

ADJUSTABLE PHOTOVOLTAIC COLLECTORS FOR MAKING SOLAR ELECTRICITY

OPERABLE VENTS FOR GREENHOUSE

CANTILEVERED GREENHOUSE ARCH SHADES ENDS OF BUILDING IN SUMMER

PASSIVE WATER PREHEATER (100M OF PLASTIC PIPE CAST INTO THE BACK WALL OF THE GREENHOUSE ARCH PASSIVELY HEATS MOST OF THE WATER)

R-11 GLASS STORM DOOR (4 TIMES AS INSULATING AS TRIPLE GLAZING)

THERMAL INSULATION - 4" FREON-FILLED POLYURETHANE INSIDE WALLS

Contributors:
Richard J. Vitullo, AIA, Oak Leaf Studio, Crownsville, Maryland; *AIA Environmental Resource Guide* (John Wiley & Sons, Inc., 1998).

LIFE-CYCLE FLOWCHART
12.15

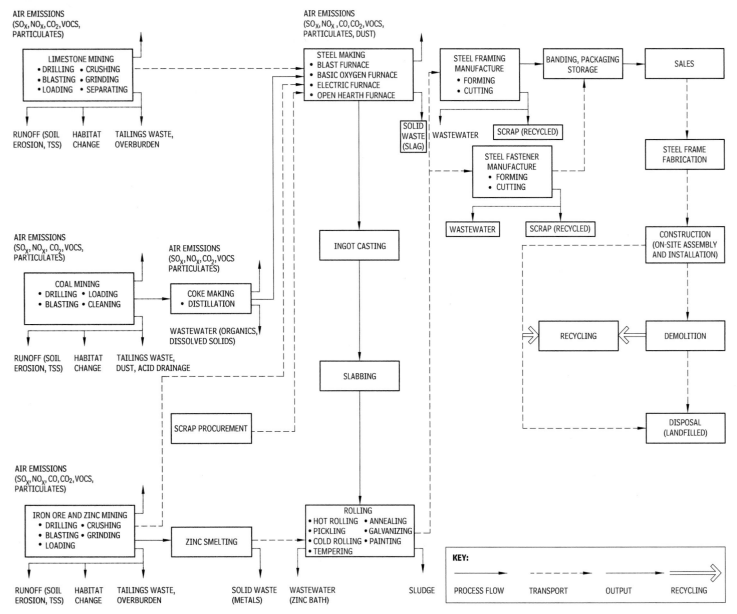

SAMPLE LIFE-CYCLE FLOWCHART (STEEL FRAMING AND FASTENERS)

different. Identify positions for recycling bins on-site so materials can be separated as they are recovered. Prevent storm sewer and groundwater pollution and reduce soil erosion with sensitive design and site construction methods.

3. Energy-efficient design should reduce or eliminate nonrenewable fossil fuel consumption for heating, cooling, and lighting. Although it is good to create a building with resource-conservative materials, it is critical to ensure that once the building is built it either continues to conserve energy resources or uses renewable ener-

gy resources throughout its life. Consider using durable, low-maintenance materials. Where practical, design full-cycle systems such as solar water heating that will capture renewable energy onsite. The following equipment can help achieve this goal:

- *Heat recovery ventilators:* This system extracts the heat from the air as it is exhausted and transfers that to incoming air (or the reverse in the summer). This system allows a tight, energy-efficient building to be ventilated but still retains the heat-energy used to maintain the indoor environment. Depending

on the climate, this system can be up to 80 percent efficient in recovering energy and is recommended for either very cold or very hot, humid climates. Consult with a mechanical engineer or equipment manufacturer.

- *Ground-source heat pump:* Like earth-sheltered building design, this system takes advantage of the stability of underground temperatures. Long lengths of copper tubing are buried either horizontally or vertically in the earth and circulated with a heat-exchanging medium.

Contributors:
David Natella and Joel Ann Todd, Scientific Consulting Group, Inc., Gaithersburg, Maryland; Chart reprinted from *AIA Environmental Resource Guide* (John Wiley & Sons, Inc., 1998).

HEALTHY COMMUNITY DESIGN

Community design and planning, or lack of planning, have a greater effect on the natural environment than the design of individual buildings. The goal of lower-impact buildings certainly makes a difference, but it will not be enough; creative redesign of communities is needed to improve the quality of life and create potential for regeneration of natural systems. Part of the solution is personal, part is a household commitment, part is neighborhood-based, and part requires involvement of government at all scales.

Healthy communities are a sign of ecological health. Public policy planning, including Smart Growth, and cultural trends such as New Urbanism are transforming the American landscape. This section briefly summarizes key definitions and concepts.

COMMUNITY FORM AND SUSTAINABLE INFRASTRUCTURE

Community form and character can be defined as urban, suburban, or rural.

The physical form of cities and towns, which has been researched and defined by Kevin Lynch and others, includes urban centers, edges, and nodes. Each element of traditional community form offers opportunities to be reconceived as more sustaining infrastructure. Rights-of-way for utilities can begin to incorporate water treatment and energy technologies. Street widths and overall street patterns can be considered with respect to water, material, energy, and future use.

The center of a community, depending on scale, may be a city, town, village center, or neighborhood. That highest-density area may be able to employ different kinds of infrastructure solutions than its surrounding area. Cities, for example, can more easily consider combined heat and power generation or decentralized wastewater treatment, saving the large-scale conveyance infrastructure.

Sustaining design begins to see form in an even more integrated way than traditional urban design in the relationship of a community to flows and natural features. Infrastructure is an opportunity for significant improvement in communities, and new towns and cities are particularly good candidates for rethinking conventional assumptions on water, energy, and transportation. In general, sustaining community design seeks to manage and reuse water that falls on sites and neighborhoods, rather than conveying it in pipes to remote treatment plants, lakes, or rivers.

Recent developments in community design have allowed for defined areas and special planned districts and regional initiatives, such as:

- *Pedestrian-oriented development*, which seeks to reduce dependence on automobiles for commuting, school, shopping, and activities.
- *Transit-oriented development*, which seeks to place major transit hubs near areas of greatest density and create new development in conjunction with light rail and other mass-mode mobility systems.
- *Enterprise zones*, which encourage economic development in particular ways.
- *Eco-industrial parks*, which identify synergies between industry types to eliminate the concept of waste through full utilization of by-products.
- *Traditional town planning*, which seeks to use higher-density forms of the past.
- *Mixed-use development*, which seeks to integrate residential and commercial uses to create neighborhoods that are full of activity throughout the day and evening.
- *Special-use permits and planned unit developments*, which allow variation from prescribed zoning if it improves the community.
- *Urban growth boundaries*, which limit sprawl by restricting growth within a prescribed area.

The effectiveness and meaning of these concepts can vary as much as the term *sustainability* itself. Designs for new towns can be highly prescriptive, such as design guidelines for some new urban-ist developments. The sustainable design section of such guidelines often draws from LEED or reference standards for individual building performance. Additional, perhaps greater opportunities lie in the planning itself because planning affects orientation, infrastructure and paving and so has a dramatic impact on water and energy flow.

INVOLVEMENT IN COMMUNITY DESIGN

Successful community design projects bring the government, neighborhood residents, and concerned citizens together for conversations that envision the best possible future. Community design centers now exist in major cities. These organizations provide a place for designers and citizens to participate in discussions about the future of streets and neighborhoods and seek approval of proposed new development.

COMMUNITY GROWTH AND CHANGE

Changes in planning and zoning require political will and a general acceptance that growth and change can be positive. Parts of the United States are staunchly antigrowth; others areas, unprepared for out-of-control growth are struggling; in others still, growth is taking place without any form of planning. In all of these places, the unique character of a place may be lost if growth is not directed. Active engagement by architects in the community—whether engaged as professionals or citizens—is critical to the sustainability of communities. Unique buildings, landscapes, and other attributes of a place often need to be identified and preserved as communities grow.

DENSITY AND SUSTAINABLE COMMUNITIES

The concept of density is important for architects to understand and has, in general, been an area architects are familiar with through understanding the scale of buildings. The ability of a community to support retail-lined streets successfully or to implement mass transit or facilitate walking to work and school is primarily a function of density.

Certain technologies require an appropriate scale of community to succeed. Efficient space conditioning plants, chilled water loops, water treatment, fuel cells, and other technologies all require a relatively large module.

Environmental benefits of higher residential densities have been calculated by the San Francisco League of Conservation Voters (www.sflcv.org). The comparison detailed in Table 12.16 identifies the higher environmental costs of low-density development. A typical new subdivision with three households per residential acre requires more than 30 times the area of roads and sidewalks compared to a higher-density city neighborhood, such as Telegraph Hill in San Francisco.

MOBILITY

The term *mobility* expands the notion of *transportation* to include all forms of moving through communities for all ages at all scales. Sustaining community design addresses accessibility for youth and elderly who may not have access to either automobiles or conventional mass transit and seeks to find solutions that reduce unnecessary travel for errands and other activities. Mobility is essential to healthy communities.

Considerations for good mobility include:

- Maximum five-minute walks from residential areas to neighborhood centers
- Short wait times for public transportation
- Appropriate scale and routing of transit options
- Accessible sidewalks, landscapes, and buildings
- Plans that consider all age groups, including youth and elders
- Bike paths, greenways, and wide sidewalks
- Strategic locations for schools and public buildings

PERMACULTURE

One approach to sustainable living is the permaculture movement. The original meaning of the term *permaculture*, derived from *permanent agriculture*, now is applied to culture, in general, address-

ENVIRONMENTAL EFFECTS OF RESIDENTIAL DENSITIES
12.16

IMPACT ON	SPRAWL NEIGHBORHOOD	DENSE CITY NEIGHBORHOOD	MEASURE
Density	3	90	households per residential acre
Land used	333	11	acres/1000 households
Roads plus sidewalks	233,333	7777	sq yd/1000 households
Water use	1031	194	gallons/household each day
Local shopping	1	43	service and retail employees/acre
Transit service	0	233	average buses 2
AUTOS AND DRIVING (PER HOUSEHOLD EACH YEAR)			
Vehicles	2.03	0.75	average number of vehicles
Parking	14	5	parking places
Mileage	22,844	7865	average vehicle miles traveled
Fuel use	1142	393	gallons of gasoline
Gasoline cost	$3426	$1179	$US
Auto costs	$22,439	$8,043	$US
AIR POLLUTION FROM DRIVING (PER HOUSEHOLD EACH YEAR)			
Volatile organic compounds (VOCs) 60	60	20	pounds of volitile organic compounds
Nitrogen oxides	150	51	pounds of nitrous oxides
Particulates	13.70	4.71	pounds of particulates (pm10)
Greenhouse gasses	15.99	5.50	tons CO_2 per 1000 households

Source: San Francisco League of Conservation Voters

NOTES

12.16 a. Average daily number of buses/hour at each bus stop within a 1/4 mile walk of home, or railcars (10 car BART train = 10 railcars) or ferries within a 1/2 mile walk. Walks are measured on gridded street pattern.

b. 3 households/residential acre: typical of single-family dwellings in sprawl.

c. 10 households/residential acre: row houses, older suburbs.

d. 100 households/residential areas: mostly three- to five-story apartment houses with occasional mid- to high-rise and single-family dwellings. Examples: northeast San Francisco (Russian, Nob Hill and Telegraph Hill, North Beach); River North in Chicago; Beacon Hill in Boston, along Connecticut Avenue in Washington, DC; and compact neighborhoods throughout the country.

e. 500 households/residential acre: mostly mid- to high-rises. Examples: the Upper East Side and West Side in Manhattan.

Contributors:
Mark Rylander, AIA, William McDonough + Partners, Charlottesville, Virginia; Arkin Tilt Architects, Berkeley, California.

ing in particular the social aspects of sustainability. An accepted definition of permaculture includes the following concepts:

- An ethical approach to the environment that includes limits to population growth and consumption, fair distribution of resources, and personal responsibility.
- Ecological principles derived by the observation of natural systems by ecologists such as L.C. Birch and Howard Odum, as well as from successful pretechnological societies.
- A design approach or plan of action that can be implemented and maintained with minimal resources.
- Holistic care for local people and ecologies in a local energy-based economy.

SMART GROWTH

Concern for the effects of development on the environment led to the creation in 1996 of the Smart Growth Network (SGN). The U.S. EPA and several non-profit and government organizations drafted a set of principles that are now widely accepted as a guide to good practice in low-impact development. The Urban Land Institute and others have also addressed the issue with guidelines and studies. SGN was formed in response to increasing community concerns about the need for environmental protection and economic growth that also supports community vitality. The Network's partners include environmental groups, historic preservation organizations, professional organizations, developers, real estate interests, and local and state government entities.

AIA'S 10 PRINCIPLES FOR LIVABLE COMMUNITIES

The AIA's Center for Communities by Design offers a broad range of services for architects and communities including the organization of assistance teams for needy communities who are trained in urban design or sustainable design. The following principles are a coherent summary of strategies for planning and restoring communities of all scales:

1. *Design on a human scale*: Compact, pedestrian-friendly communities allow residents to walk to shops, services, cultural resources, and jobs and can reduce traffic congestion and benefit people's health.
2. *Provide choices*: People want variety in housing, shopping, recreation, transportation, and employment. Variety creates lively neighborhoods and accommodates residents in different stages of their lives.
3. *Encourage mixed-use development*: Integrating different land uses and varied building types creates vibrant, pedestrian-friendly, and diverse communities.
4. *Preserve urban centers*: Restoring, revitalizing, and infilling urban centers takes advantage of existing streets, services, and buildings and avoids the need for new infrastructure. This helps to curb sprawl and promote stability for city neighborhoods.

5. *Vary transportation options*: Giving people the option of walking, biking, and using public transit, in addition to driving, reduces traffic congestion, protects the environment, and encourages physical activity.
6. *Build vibrant public spaces*: Citizens need welcoming, well-defined public places to stimulate face-to-face interaction, collectively celebrate and mourn, encourage civic participation, admire public art, and gather for public events.
7. *Create a neighborhood identity*: A "sense of place" gives neighborhoods a unique character, enhances the walking environment, and creates pride in the community.
8. *Protect environmental resources*: A well-designed balance of nature and development preserves natural systems, protects waterways from pollution, reduces air pollution, and protects property values.
9. *Conserve landscapes*: Open space, farms, and wildlife habitat are essential for environmental, recreational, and cultural reasons.
10. *Design matters*: Design excellence is the foundation of successful and healthy communities.

Visit the AIA Center for Communities by Design (http://www.aia.org/ liv_about) for more information on how architecture can influence the quality of life in communities.

HEALTHY BUILDINGS

EFFECTIVE STRATEGIES

CLEAN ENERGY

ENERGY CONSERVATION STRATEGIES FOR NONRESIDENTIAL BUILDINGS

Energy-conserving design for nonresidential buildings can be justified by savings in operating costs, which result in a lower life-cycle investment. For large buildings of all types, the best opportunities are most likely to be found in electricity costs; depending upon the demand charges of the local utility, peak load reduction and/or shifting (diurnal or seasonal) measures may prove to be cost-effective. Concurrently, reducing electric use by effective daylighting and cooling load reduction (window orientation and sun shading devices) will be cost-effective because these loads are typically interrelated and use expensive forms of energy. When these loads and costs are reduced, heating load reduction by solar and energy-conserving techniques also applies to larger buildings. Energy-conserving opportunities are best addressed by a whole-systems team approach of architecture, HVAC, lighting, and integrated automation. For example, high levels of thermal insulation or of thermal mass may be cost-justified when these also result in substantially reduced mechanical system sizes and power requirements.

The architect should consider the following items in designing an energy-efficient nonresidential building, regardless of size and building type. (Note that the numbers in the lists that follow refer to items in Figures 12.17 to 12.22.)

SITE PLANNING AND ORIENTATION
1. *Orient the longer walls of a building to face north-south*: Walls that face the equator (e.g., the noonday sun) are ideal for windows oriented to admit daylighting, with minimum cost for shading (i.e., relatively small horizontal overhangs create effective shading). Walls and windows facing east and west, however, are sources of undesirable overheating and are difficult to shade effectively. In a cool climate, windows facing the equator can gain useful wintertime heating from the sun. (See also "Daylighting" criteria, next.)
2. *Provide sunshading to suit climate and use variations*: Buildings can be located in groups to shade one another. Landscaping and sun screens can be used to shade building surfaces, especially

SITE PLANNING AND ORIENTATION 12.17

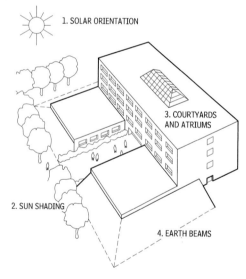

1. SOLAR ORIENTATION
2. SUN SHADING
3. COURTYARDS AND ATRIUMS
4. EARTH BEAMS

windows, during overheated hours. Functions can be located within a building to coincide with solar gain benefit or liability. For example, cafeterias are ideally exposed to noontime winter sun in cool and temperate climates, or placed in the midday shade in warm climates; low-use areas (storage areas) can be used as climatic buffers placed on the east or west in hot climates, or on the north in cool climates.
3. *Create courtyards and enclosed atriums*: Semienclosed courtyards (in warm climates) and enclosed atriums (in temperate and cool climates) can be formed by groups of buildings to provide areas for planting, sun shading, water fountains, and other microclimatic benefits. Atriums can also be used as light courts and ventilating shafts. Indoor or outdoor planted areas provide evaporative cooling for local breezes when located near buildings.

4. *Use earth berms for climatic buffering*: Earth berms (sloped or terraced, formed simply by grading earth against the wall of a building) help to buffer the building against temperature extremes of both heat and cold.

DAYLIGHTING
5. *Place windows high in the wall of each floor*: Windows placed high in the wall near the ceiling provide the most daylight for any given window area, permitting daylight to penetrate more deeply into the interior.
6. *Use light shelves*: Light shelves are horizontal projections placed on the outside and below a window to reflect sunlight into the interior. Typically placed just above eye level, the light shelf reflects daylight onto the interior ceiling, making it a light-reflecting surface (instead of a dark, shaded surface typical of a conventional interior ceiling). At the same time, the light shelf shades the lower portion of the window, reducing the amount of light near the window, which is typically overlit. The result is more balanced daylighting with less glare and contrast between light levels in the interior.
7. *Size windows according to use and orientation*: Because window glass has little or no resistance to heat flow, it is one of the primary sources of energy waste and discomfort. Window areas should be shaded against direct solar gain during overheated hours. Even when shaded, windows gain undesired heat when the outdoor temperature exceeds the human comfort limit. Window areas should, therefore, be kept to a reasonable minimum, justified by clearly defined needs for view, visual relief, ventilation, and/or daylighting.
8. *Use skylighting for daylighting, with proper solar controls*: Skylighting that is properly sized and oriented is an efficient and cost-effective source of lighting. Consider that for most office buildings, sunlight is available for nearly the entire period of occupancy and that the lighting requirement for interior lighting is only about 1 percent of the amount of light available outside. Electric lighting costs, peak charges, and work interruptions during power brownouts can be greatly reduced by using daylight. Cost-effective, energy-efficient skylights can be small, spaced widely, with "splayed" interior light wells that help reflect and diffuse the light. White-painted ceilings and walls further improve the efficiency of daylighting (by as much as 300 percent, when compared with dark interior finishes).

Contributors:
Mark Rylander, AIA, William McDonough + Partners, Charlottesville, Virginia; Ronald L. Gobbell, FAIA, Gobbell Hays Partners, Inc., Nashville, Tennessee; Donald Watson, FAIA, Rensselaer Polytechic Institute, Troy, New York.

DAYLIGHTING
12.18

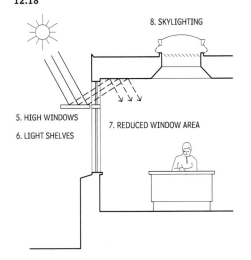

8. SKYLIGHTING

5. HIGH WINDOWS

6. LIGHT SHELVES

7. REDUCED WINDOW AREA

Skylights should include some means to control undesired solar gain by one or more of the following means: (a) Face the skylight to the polar orientation; (b) provide exterior light-reflecting sun shading; (c) provide movable sunshades on the inside, with a means to vent the heat above the sunshade.

ENERGY-EFFICIENT LIGHTING

9. *Use task lighting, with individual controls*: Lamps for task lighting are ideally located near the work surface and are adjustable to eliminate reflective glare. The energy-efficient advantages are that less light output is required (reduced geometrically as a function of its closer distance to the task), and the lamp can be switched off when not needed.

10. *Use the ceiling as a light-reflective surface*: By using uplights, either ceiling pendants or lamps mounted on partitions and/or cabinets, the ceiling surface can be used as a light reflector. This has three advantages: First, fewer fixtures are required for general area (ambient) lighting; second, the light is indirect, eliminating the sources of visual discomfort due to glare and reflection; and, third, if light shelves are used, the ceiling is the light reflector for both natural and artificial light, an advantage for the occupant's sense of visual order.

11. *Employ a variety of light levels*: In any given interior, a variety of light levels improves visual comfort. Light levels can be reduced in low-use areas, storage, circulation, and lounge areas. Daylighting can also be used to provide variety of lighting, thereby reducing monotone interiors.

12. *Provide switching choices, to accommodate schedule and daylight availability*: Areas near windows that can be naturally lit should have continuous dimming controls to dim lights that are not needed. Other areas should have separate switching to coincide with different schedules and uses. Consider occupant-sensing light switches in areas of occasional use, such as washrooms, storage, and warehouse areas.

ENERGY-EFFICIENT LIGHTING
12.19

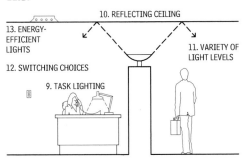

10. REFLECTING CEILING

13. ENERGY-EFFICIENT LIGHTS

11. VARIETY OF LIGHT LEVELS

12. SWITCHING CHOICES

9. TASK LIGHTING

13. *Use energy-efficient lights and luminaires*: Use the most efficient light source for the requirement: these might be fluorescent lamps, high-intensity discharge lamps, or high-voltage/high-frequency lights. Compact fluorescent lights with high-efficiency ballasts have advantages of low wattage, low waste heat, long life, and good color rendering. Incandescent lights use less energy when switched on, so these are appropriate for occasional use and short-term lighting. Luminaires should also be evaluated for how efficiently they diffuse, direct, or reflect the available light.

THERMAL CONSTRUCTION
12.20

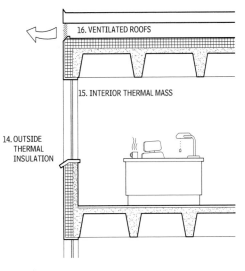

16. VENTILATED ROOFS

15. INTERIOR THERMAL MASS

14. OUTSIDE THERMAL INSULATION

THERMAL CONSTRUCTION

14. *Place thermal insulation on the outside of the structure*: Thermal insulation is one of the most cost-effective means of energy conservation. Insulation placed on the outer face of a wall or roof protects the structure from the extremes of the outside temperature (with the added benefit of lengthening the life of the roof waterproofing membrane) and adds the massiveness of the structure to the thermal response of the interior (see strategy 15). In localities where *resistance insulation* is not available, the combination of airspaces and high-capacitance materials such as masonry and/or earth berms should be designed for effective thermal dampening or time lag (the delay and diffusion of outside temperature extremes that are transmitted to the interior). As an alternative to insulating roof structures in hot climates, a *radiant barrier* consisting of a continuous sheet of reflective foil with a low-emissivity (low-E) coating and an airspace around it serves as an effective shield against undesired heat gain.

15. *Utilize thermal mass on building interior*: In office buildings, thermally massive construction (such as masonry and concrete, which have good heat storage capacity) benefits the energy-efficient operation of heating and cooling equipment as follows:
   - *Cooling benefits*: Thermal mass absorbs the overheating that is inevitable in an office space due to the buildup of heat from people, equipment, lighting, rising afternoon temperature, and solar gain. The more thermal mass that is effectively exposed to an interior space ceiling and walls, the greater is the saving on air conditioning in the afternoon, with the potential to delay the overheating until early evening, when electric rates may be lower and/or outdoor air may be low enough to cool the mass by night ventilation. (The night cooling option is especially favorable in warm, dry climates due to predictably cooler nighttime temperatures.)
   - *Heating benefits*: In temperate and cool climates, thermal mass helps absorb and store wintertime passive heat. This is especially effective if the thermal mass is on the building interior and directly heated by the sun (made possible by

design of various corridor, stairway, and half-height partition arrangements).

16. *Use light-constructed ventilated roofs in hot climates*: In hot climates, the roof is the primary source of undesired heat gain. Energy-efficient roof designs should be considered. One of the best for hot climates is a ventilated double roof wherein the outside layer is a light-colored and lightweight material that shades the solar heat from the inner roof, which should be well insulated. As described in strategy 14, a *radiant barrier* can be considered as an alternative to resistance insulation to serve as a shield against thermal transfer through the ceiling portion of the roof structure.

ENERGY-EFFICIENT MECHANICAL SYSTEMS

17. *Use decentralized and modular systems*: Heating and cooling equipment is most efficient when sized to the average load condition, not the peak, or extreme, condition. Use modular-unit boilers, chillers, pumps, and fans in series so that the average operating load can be met by a few modules operating at peak efficiency rather than a single unit that is oversized for normal conditions. Zone the distribution systems to meet different loads due to orientation, use, and schedule. Use variable-air-volume (VAV) systems to reduce fan energy requirements and to lower duct sizes and costs (the system can be designed for the predominant load, not the sum of the peak loads). Decentralized air-handling systems have smaller trunk lines and duct losses. Dispersed air handlers, located close to their end use, can be reduced in size from conventional system sizes if hot and chilled water is piped to them (a decentralized air-handling system with a centralized plant).

18. *Use economizer/enthalpy cycle cooling*: Economizer/enthalpy cycle cooling uses outdoor air when it is cool enough for direct ventilation and/or when the outdoor air has a lower heat content than indoor air, so that it can be cooled evaporatively without raising indoor humidity. Although useful in all climates, direct or indirect evaporative cooling systems are especially effective in hot, dry climates.

19. *Use energy-efficient equipment*: The energy efficiency of mechanical equipment varies greatly. Consider heat pumps for cooling and for heating to replace separate chiller and boiler units. Heat pumps can also use local water sources or water storage (see strategy 20).

20. *Use energy storage for cooling*: Chilled water storage has two advantages: First, it permits water chilling or ice making at night under more favorable ambient conditions and possible lower electric rates. Second, and perhaps more important, it reduces or eliminates peak-hour energy consumption, thereby reducing demand charges.

21. *Use heat recovery for heating*: In cool and temperate climates, heat can be recovered from warm zones of a building and

ENERGY-EFFICIENT MECHANICAL SYSTEMS
12.21

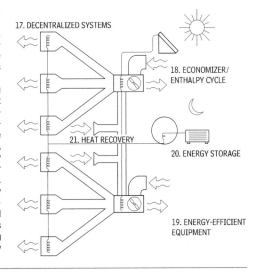

17. DECENTRALIZED SYSTEMS

18. ECONOMIZER/ ENTHALPY CYCLE

21. HEAT RECOVERY

20. ENERGY STORAGE

19. ENERGY-EFFICIENT EQUIPMENT

Contributor:
Donald Watson, FAIA, Rensselaer Polytechnic Institute, Troy, New York.

SMART BUILDING CONTROLS
12.22

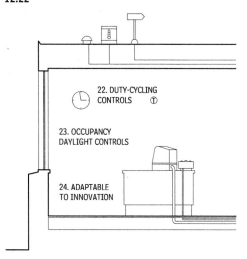

22. DUTY-CYCLING
CONTROLS   Ⓣ

23. OCCUPANCY
DAYLIGHT CONTROLS

24. ADAPTABLE
TO INNOVATION

recirculated to underheated areas. Recoverable heat sources include equipment, process heat, and passive solar gain. Heat recovery wheels or coils can be used where indoor air needs to be ventilated, transferring heat into the incoming fresh airstream. In all climates, process heat or active solar heat (e.g., from solar collectors) can be used for domestic hot water or for tempering incoming fresh air.

SMART BUILDING CONTROLS

22. *Use smart thermostats*: *Duty-cycling* temperature controls can be programmed for different time schedules and thermal conditions, the simplest being the day/night setback. Newer controls are predictive, sensing outdoor temperature trends and then selecting the system operation most appropriate to the condition.

23. *Use occupancy- and daylight-sensing lighting controls*: Automatic switching of lights according to the building occupant schedule and the daylight condition is recommended, with manual override for nighttime occupancy. Photosensors should be placed in areas that can be predictably lit by natural light.

24. *Be prepared for rapid innovation in building control systems*: Newly developing "smart" building systems include microprocessing for thermal and light control, fire and air-quality precautions, equipment failure, and operations/ maintenance requirements (along with new communication and office management systems). These innovations require that electric wiring be easily changed, such as through double-floor construction.

ENERGY-EFFICIENT ATRIUM DESIGN

In its original meaning, an atrium was the open courtyard of a Roman house. Today, an atrium is a glazed courtyard on the side of or within a building. If issues of heating, cooling, and lighting are ignored, atrium designs can add significantly to the energy cost of the building, as well as require above-average energy to maintain comfort within them. In contrast, energy-efficient atrium spaces can contribute savings through natural lighting, passive heating, and natural cooling strategies. (Any multistoried space raises concerns for fire safety and requires special attention.)

Atrium spaces are more responsive to the influence of the outside climate than conventional buildings, and their design, therefore, will follow local climate requirements. Design also will depend on the specific function and goals of the atrium: to supply daylight for itself or to adjacent spaces; to provide comfort for human occupancy or to serve only as a semiconditioned space for circulation. The challenge of energy-efficient atrium design is to combine various and perhaps conflicting requirements for passive heating, natural cooling, and daylighting using the geometry of the atrium, its orientation, and solar and insulation controls at the glazing surfaces. These architectural choices need to be integrated with the mechanical engineering to assure that the passive energy opportunities will, in fact, effectively reduce building energy use.

PASSIVE SOLAR HEATING OPPORTUNITIES

Atriums designed with large glass areas overheat during the day, providing potentially recoverable heat to parts of the adjacent building, such as its outer perimeter, which can be transferred by air or by an air-to-water heat pump. In cool climates and in buildings with a predominant heat load (such as a residential or hotel structure), using this solar heat gain can be cost-effective. In such a case, vertical glass facing the south captures winter sun while incurring minimum summer heat gain liability. If the atrium space requires sedentary occupant comfort, heat storage within the space and energy-efficient glazing also are beneficial.

NATURAL COOLING OPPORTUNITIES

To reduce required cooling in an atrium, protection from the summer sun is essential. Natural cooling can be accomplished by glass orientation, protective coatings as part of the glazing, and shading devices, which may or may not be movable. In hot, sunny climates, relatively small amounts of glass can meet daylighting objectives while reducing the solar gain liability. In warm, humid climates with predominantly cloudy skies (the sky is nonetheless a source of undesirable heat gain), the north-facing orientation should be favored for large glazed areas. Mechanical ventilation should facilitate the upward flow of natural ventilation. Spot cooling by air-conditioning in lower atrium areas is a relatively efficient means of keeping some areas comfortable for occupancy without fully conditioning the entire volume of air.

DAYLIGHTING OPPORTUNITIES

An atrium with the predominant function to provide natural lighting takes its shape from the predominant sky condition. In cool, cloudy climates, ideally, the atrium cross section would be stepped outward as it gets higher, to increase overhead lighting. In hot, sunny locations with clear sunny skies, the cross section is like a large lighting fixture designed to reflect, diffuse, and make the light from above usable. Daylighting design is complicated by the movement of the sun, as it changes position with respect to the building throughout the day and the year.

WINTER GARDEN ATRIUM DESIGN

Healthy greenery can be incorporated in atrium design. The designer needs to know the unique horticultural requirements for the plant species for lighting, heating, and cooling, which could be quite different from those for human occupancy. Generally, plants need higher light levels and cooler temperatures than might be comfortable for humans. The most efficient manner to keep plants heated is with plant bed or root heating, as with water tubes or air tubes in gravel or earth. Plants also benefit from gentle air movement, which reduces excessive moisture that might rot the plants and circulates carbon dioxide needed for growth.

PASSIVE SOLAR HEATING DESIGN PROCEDURE

The focus of this section is on winter heating between U.S. latitudes 32°N and 48°N. This design and calculation procedure is applicable to:

- Building types that have space heating requirements dominated by heat loss through the exterior enclosure of the building.
- Buildings with a small internal heat contribution from lights; people; and equipment such as residences, small commercial, industrial and institutional buildings; and large daylit buildings whose internal heat gain is only a small portion of their total heating requirement.

Passive solar heating systems are integral to building design. The concepts relating to system operation must be applied at the earliest stages of design decision making.

Passive systems demand a skillful integration of all the architectural elements within each space—glazing, walls, floor, roof, and, in some cases, even interior surface colors. The way in which the glazing and thermal mass (heat storage materials, that is masonry, water) are designed generally determines the efficiency and level of thermal comfort provided by the system. Two concepts are critical to understanding the thermal performance of passively heated space:

- That the quantity of south glazing, insulating properties of the space, and the outdoor climatic conditions will determine the number of degrees the average indoor temperature in a space is above the average outdoor temperature on any given day.
- That the size, distribution, material, and in some cases—direct gain systems—surface color of thermal mass in the space will determine the daily fluctuation above and below the average indoor temperature (see Figure 12.25).

Calculating heat gain and loss is a relatively straightforward procedure. The storage and control of heat in a passively heated space, however, is the major problem confronting most designers. In the process of storing and releasing heat, thermal mass in a space will fluctuate in temperature, yet the object of the heating system is to maintain a relatively constant interior temperature. For each system, the integration of thermal mass in a space will determine the fluctuation of indoor temperature during the day.

For example, in a direct gain system with masonry thermal mass, the major determinant of fluctuations of indoor air temperature is the amount of exposed surface area of masonry in the space; in a thermal storage wall system, it is the thickness of the material used to construct the wall. The following is a procedure for sizing both direct gain and thermal storage wall systems.

Contributor:
Donald Watson, FAIA, Rensselaer Polytechnic Institute, Troy, New York.

12.23

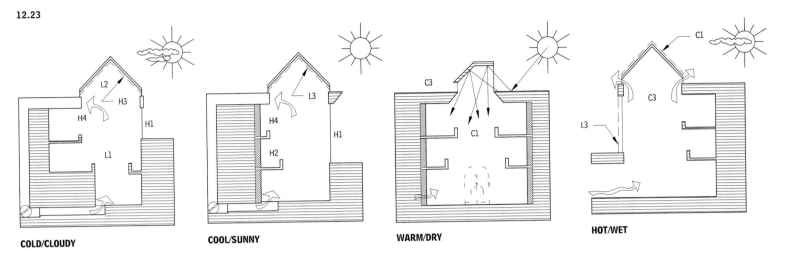

COLD/CLOUDY **COOL/SUNNY** **WARM/DRY** **HOT/WET**

RELATIVE IMPORTANCE OF DESIGN PRINCIPLES IN VARIOUS CLIMATES
12.24

ATRIUM ENERGY-DESIGN PRINCIPLE[a]	HEATING	COLD/CLOUDY (SEATTLE, CHICAGO, MINNEAPOLIS)	COOL/SUNNY (DENVER, ST. LOUIS, BOSTON)	WARM/DRY (LOS ANGELES, PHOENIX, MIDLAND, TEXAS)	HOT/WET (HOUSTON, NEW ORLEANS, MIAMI)
H1	To maximize winter solar heat gain, orient the atrium aperture to the south.	V	P	D	
H2	For radiant heat storage and distribution, place interior masonry directly in the path of the winter sun.	P	V		
H3	To prevent excessive nighttime heat loss, consider an insulating system for the glazing.	V	P		
H4	To recover heat, place a return air duct high in the space, directly toward the sun.	P	V	D	
	COOLING				
C1	To minimize solar gain, provide shade from the summer sun.	P	P	V	
C2	Use the atrium as an air plenum in the mechanical system of the building.	P	P	P	P
C3	To facilitate natural ventilation, create a vertical chimney effect with high outlets and low inlets.	P	P	P	V
	LIGHTING				
L1	To maximize daylight, use a stepped section (in predominantly cloudy areas).	P	D		
L2	To maximize daylight, select skylight glazing for predominant sky condition (clear and horizontal in predominantly cloudy areas).	P	P	P	P
L3	Provide sun and glare control.	P	P	V	P

V Very important; P Positive benefit; D Discretionary use

DAILY TEMPERATURE FLUCTUATIONS
12.25

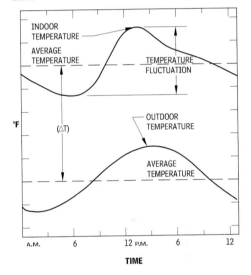

NOTE

12.24[a] These atrium energy-design principles are illustrated in Figure 12.23, using the letter/number indicators given here.

Contributor:
Donald Watson, FAIA, Rensselaer Polytechnic Institute, Troy, New York.

DIRECT GAIN

Direct gain systems are characterized by daily fluctuations of indoor temperatures, which range from only 10°F to as much as 30°F. The heating system cannot be turned on or off, as there is little control of natural heat flows in the space. To prevent overheating, shading devices are used to reduce solar gain, or excess heat is vented by opening windows or activating an exhaust fan.

The major glass areas (collector) of each space must be oriented to the south (+30°) for maximum solar heat gain in winter. These windows can serve other functions as well, such as openings for light and for views.

Each space must also contain enough mass for the storage of solar heat gain. This implies masonry in the building, but the masonry can be as thin as 4 in. in cold climates and 1 1/2 in. to 2 in. in very mild climates.

SOUTH GLAZING

One criterion for a well-designed space is that it gains enough solar energy on an average sunny day in winter to maintain an average space temperature of +68°F over the 24-hour period. By establishing this criterion, it is possible to develop ratios for the preliminary sizing of south glazing. Table 12.27 lists ratios for various climates.

In a direct gain system, sunlight can also be admitted into a space through clerestories and skylights, as well as vertical south-facing windows. This approach may be taken: (1) for privacy, (2) because of shading on the south façades, (3) because spaces are located along façades other than south, and (4) to avoid direct sunlight on people and furniture. Use the following guidelines when designing clerestories and skylights:

- *Clerestory*: Locate the clerestory at a distance in front of the interior mass wall of roughly 1 to 1.5 times the height of the clerestory above the finished floor. Make the ceiling of the clerestory a light color to reflect and diffuse sunlight down into the space. In regions with heavy snowfall, locate the sill of the clerestory glazing 18 in. or more above the roof surface (see Figure 12.25).
- *Sawtooth clerestories*: Make the angle (as measured from horizontal) equal to or smaller than the altitude of the sun at noon on December 21, the winter solstice. Make the underside of the clerestories a light color (see Figure 12.25).
- *Roof windows and skylights*: Use a south-facing or horizontal skylight with a reflector to increase solar gain in winter and shade both horizontal and south-facing skylights in summer to prevent excessive solar gain (see Figure 12.25).

THERMAL STORAGE MASS

The two most common materials used for storing heat are masonry and water. Masonry materials transfer heat from their surface, to the interior, at a slow rate. If direct sunlight is applied to the surface of a dark masonry material for an extended period of time, it will become uncomfortably hot, thereby, giving much of its heat to the air in the space rather than heat conducting it away from the surface for storage. This results in daytime overheating and large daily temperature fluctuations in the space. To reduce fluctuations, direct sunlight should be spread over a large surface area of masonry. To accomplish this:

1. Construct interior walls and floors of masonry at least 4-in. thick.
2. Diffuse direct sunlight over the surface area of the masonry either by using a translucent glazing material—placing a number of small windows so that they admit sunlight in patches—or by reflecting direct sunlight off a light-colored interior surface first (see Figure 12.26).
3. Use the following guidelines for selecting interior surface color and finishes:
   - Masonry floors of a medium to dark color
   - Masonry walls of any color
   - Lightweight construction (little thermal mass) of a light color to reflect sunlight onto masonry surfaces
   - No wall-to-wall carpeting over masonry floors

By following these recommendations, it is possible to control temperature fluctuations in the space on clear winter days to approximately 10°F to 15°F. These temperature fluctuations are for clear winter days and for at least 6 sq ft of exposed masonry surface area for each square foot of south glazing.

Thermal Storage Walls

The predominant architectural expression of a thermal storage wall building is south-facing glass. The glass functions as a collecting surface only; it admits no natural light into the space. However, windows can be included in the wall to admit natural light and direct heat and to permit a view.

Either water (see Figure 12.26) or masonry can be used for a thermal storage wall. Because the mass is concentrated along the south face of the building, there is no limit to the choice of construction materials and interior finishes in the remainder of the building.

SOUTH GLAZING

The criterion for a double-glazed thermal storage wall is the same as for a direct gain system: that it transmits enough heat on an average sunny winter day to supply a space with all its heating needs for that day. Table 12.28 lists, guidelines for sizing the glazing of vented Trombe and water wall systems, and Table 12.27 lists guidelines for sizing solar glazing for unvented masonry thermal storage wall systems.

DIRECT GAIN SYSTEMS
12.26

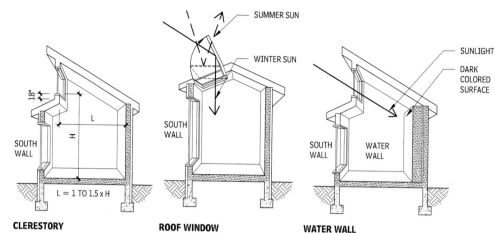

CLERESTORY **ROOF WINDOW** **WATER WALL**

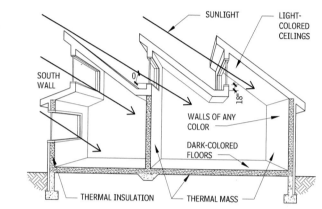

SAWTOOTH CLERESTORIES

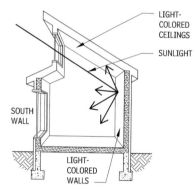

REFLECTING DIRECT SUNLIGHT

Contributors:
Donald Watson, FAIA, Rensselaer Polytechnic Institute, Troy, New York;
Huber H. Buehrer, AIA, PE, Buehrer Group, Maumee, Ohio.

SIZING SOLAR GLAZING FOR UNVENTED MASONRY THERMAL STORAGE WALL SYSTEMS
12.27

	AMOUNT OF GLAZING NEEDED (SQ FT) FOR EACH SQUARE FOOT OF FLOOR AREA			
	36°F NET LOSS (NL)		44°F NET LOSS (NL)	
AVERAGE WINTER TEMPERATURE (CLEAR DAY)	LOW HEAT LOSS	HIGH HEAT LOSS	LOW HEAT LOSS	HIGH HEAT LOSS
Cold climates				
20°F	0.33	0.66	0.43	0.85
25°F	0.30	0.60	0.35	0.70
30°F	0.26	0.52	0.30	0.60
Temperate climates				
35°F	0.20	0.40	0.23	0.46
40°F	0.15	0.30	0.17	0.34
45°F	0.12	0.23	0.13	0.26

SIZING SOLAR GLAZING FOR DIRECT GAIN VENTED TROMBE AND WATER WALL SYSTEMS
12.28

	AMOUNT OF GLAZING NEEDED (SQ FT) FOR EACH SQUARE FOOT OF FLOOR AREA			
	36°F NET LOSS (NL)		44°F NET LOSS (NL)	
AVERAGE WINTER TEMPERATURE (CLEAR DAY)	LOW HEAT LOSS	HIGH HEAT LOSS	LOW HEAT LOSS	HIGH HEAT LOSS
Cold climates				
20°F	0.23	0.46	0.30	0.60
25°F	0.18	0.37	0.23	0.46
30°F	0.15	0.30	0.17	0.34
Temperate climates				
35°F	0.12	0.23	0.13	0.26
40°F	0.09	0.18	0.10	0.20
45°F	0.06	0.13	0.08	0.15

WALL DETAILS

The preceding procedure gives guidelines for the overall size (surface area) of a thermal storage wall, but the efficiency of the wall as a heating system depends mainly on its thickness, material, and surface color (see Table 12.29). If the wall is too thin, the space will overheat during the day and be too cool in the evening; if it is too thick, it becomes inefficient as a heating source because little energy is transmitted through it. The greater the absorption of solar energy at the exterior face of a thermal wall, the greater the quantity of incident energy transferred through the wall in the building. Therefore, make the outside face of the wall dark (preferably black) with a solar absorption of at least 85 percent.

The choice of wall thickness, within the range given for each material in Table 12.29 will determine the air temperature fluctuation in the space during the day. As a general rule, the greater the wall thickness, the smaller the indoor fluctuation. Table 12.30 can be used to select a wall thickness.

SUGGESTED MATERIAL THICKNESS FOR INDIRECT GAIN THERMAL STORAGE WALLS
12.29

MATERIAL	RECOMMENDED THICKNESS (IN.)
Brick (common)	10 to 14
Concrete (dense)	12 to 18
Water	6 or more

APPROXIMATE SPACE TEMPERATURE FLUCTUATIONS AS A FUNCTION OF INDIRECT GAIN THERMAL STORAGE WALL MATERIAL AND THICKNESS
12.30

	THICKNESS (IN.)					
MATERIALS	4	8	12	16	20	24
Brick (common)	—	24°	11°	7°	—	—
Concrete (dense)	—	28°	16°	10°	6°	5°
Water (31°F)	—	18°	13°	11°	10°	9°

PRIORITIES FOR SUSTAINABLE BUILDINGS

It is rarely possible for architects to do everything they would like to reduce the environmental impact of building projects. It takes time to research alternative design and construction systems, new materials may lack proven track records, costs may be excessive, or clients may not be interested. Therefore, it makes sense to determine which efforts will do the most good.

Materials selection is one of the most visible green building strategies, and often the easiest to point to, but it is not usually the most important. Therefore, outlined here are other factors to consider and a list of priorities in green design.

BASIS FOR ESTABLISHING PRIORITIES

To make objective decisions about which investments of time and money will contribute the most toward reducing environmental impact, consider several related factors:

- *Most significant environmental risks of the project*: These may be global in nature or more specific to the region or site. Prioritizing them is difficult, as they often are unrelated and so cannot be compared directly, but determining how buildings contribute to these risks and how significantly the measures adopted can help the situation are essential.
- *Specific opportunities presented by each individual project*: For some projects, an architect can dramatically affect building performance in one area with little investment, while addressing other environmental impacts may prove very expensive and only minimally effective.
- *Available resources and agenda of the client*: Often, measures can be taken at no additional cost—some may even save money—to reduce environmental impacts. Other measures might increase the first cost of a building but save money over time.

All the measures described in the following sections are important and should be implemented whenever feasible within the constraints of a particular project.

SAVE ENERGY

Design and build energy-efficient buildings. Ongoing energy use is the single greatest source of environmental impact from a building; thus, buildings designed for low energy use can have a significant effect on the environment. An integrated design approach takes advantage of energy savings that result from interaction between separate building elements (e.g., windows, lighting, and mechanical systems).

Sample strategies include:

- In buildings with skin-dominated energy loads, incorporate high levels of insulation and high-performance windows to make buildings as airtight as possible.
- Minimize cooling loads through careful building design, glazing selection, lighting design, and landscaping.
- Meet energy demand with renewable energy resources.
- Install energy-efficient appliances, lighting, and mechanical equipment.

RECYCLE BUILDINGS

Reuse existing buildings and infrastructure instead of developing open space. Existing buildings often contain a wealth of materials and cultural resources and contribute to a sense of place. Moreover, the workmanship and quality of materials that went into them is almost impossible to replicate today.

Sample strategies include:

- Maximize energy efficiency when restoring or renovating buildings.
- Handle any hazardous materials appropriately (lead paint, asbestos, and so on).

CREATE COMMUNITY

Design communities to reduce dependence on the automobile and foster a sense of community. Address transportation as part of the effort to reduce environmental impacts. Even the most energy-efficient, state-of-the-art passive solar house will carry a heavy environmental burden, if its occupants have to get in a car to commute 20 miles to work.

Sample strategies include:

- Design communities that provide access to public transit, pedestrian corridors, and bicycle paths.
- Work to change zoning to permit mixed-use development so homeowners can walk to the store or to work.
- Plan home offices in houses to enable telecommuting.
- Site buildings to enhance the public space around them and maximize pedestrian access.

REDUCE MATERIAL USE

Optimize design to make use of smaller spaces and utilize materials efficiently. Smaller is better relative to the environment. For all materials, using less is almost always preferable, provided the durability or structural integrity of a building is not compromised. Reducing the surface area of a building reduces energy consumption. Reducing waste both helps the environment and reduces cost.

NOTES

12.27 a. No convective connections to building.
b. Temperatures listed are for December and January (usually the coldest months) and are monthly averages.
c. Low heat loss: Space with a net load coefficient (NLC) = Btu/day/sq ft/°F—a space with little exposed external surface area.
d. High heat loss: Space with an NLC = 6 Btu/day/sq ft/°F—a space with a large amount of exposed external surface area.
e. The NLC is the total building heat loss less the loss through the solar aperture.

12.28 a. Convective connections to building.
b. Temperatures listed are for December and January (usually the coldest months) and are monthly averages.
c. Low heat loss: Space with a net load coefficient (NLC) = 3 Btu/day/sq ft/°F—a space with little exposed external surface area.
d. High heat loss: Space with an NLC = 6 Btu/day/sq ft/°F—a space with a large amount of exposed external surface area.
e. The NLC is the total building heat loss less the loss through the solar aperture.
12.29 When using water in tubes, cylinders, or other types of circular containers, have a container of at least a 9-1/2 in. diameter or holding 1/2 cu ft (31 lb, 3.7 gal) of water for each 1 sq ft of glazing.
12.30 Assumes a double-glazed thermal wall. If additional mass is located in the space, such as masonry walls and/or floors, then temperature fluctuations will be less than those listed. Values are given for clear winter days.

Contributor:
Edward Mazria, FAIA, Architect, Edward Mazria & Associates, Albuquerque, New Mexico.

Sample strategies include:
- Reduce the building footprint and use space more efficiently.
- Simplify building geometry to save energy and materials.
- Design building dimensions to optimize material use and reduce waste.

PROTECT AND ENHANCE THE SITE
Preserve or restore local ecosystems and biodiversity. In fragile ecosystems or ecologically significant environments, such as old-growth forests or remnant stands of native prairie, this might be the highest priority.

Sample strategies include:
- Protect wetlands and other ecologically important areas on a parcel of land to be developed.
- On land that has been ecologically damaged, work to reintroduce native species.
- Protect trees and topsoil during construction.
- Avoid pesticide use. Provide construction detailing that minimizes the need for pesticide treatments.
- With on-site wastewater systems, provide responsible treatment to minimize groundwater pollution.

SELECT LOW-IMPACT MATERIALS
Specify safe, low-environmental-impact, resource-efficient materials. Most environmental impacts associated with building materials occur before installation. Raw materials have been extracted from the ground or harvested from forests, pollutants have been emitted during manufacture, and energy has been invested during production.

Sample strategies include:
- Avoid materials that generate a lot of pollution (VOCs, HCFCs, and so on) during manufacture or use.
- Specify materials with low-embodied energy (energy used in resource extraction, manufacturing, and shipping).

- Specify materials salvaged from other uses.
- Avoid materials that unduly deplete limited natural resources.
- Avoid materials made from toxic or hazardous constituents (benzene, arsenic, and so on).

MAXIMIZE LONGEVITY
Design for durability and adaptability. The longer a building lasts, the longer the period over which to amortize its environmental impacts. Designing and building a structure that will last a long time necessitates consideration of how the building can be modified to satisfy changing needs.

Sample strategies include:
- Specify durable materials. This is usually even more important than selecting materials with low-embodied energy.
- Assemble the materials to prevent premature decay.
- Design for easy maintenance and replacement of less durable components.
- Design for adaptability, especially in commercial buildings.
- Allocate an appropriate percentage of building funds for ongoing maintenance and improvement.

SAVE WATER
Design buildings and landscapes that use water efficiently. This is largely a regional issue. In some parts of the country, reducing water use is much higher on the priority list.

Sample strategies include:
- Install water-efficient plumbing fixtures and appliances.
- Collect and use rainwater.
- Provide low water-use landscaping (xeriscaping).
- Separate and use graywater for landscape irrigation where codes permit.
- Provide for groundwater recharge through effective stormwater infiltration designs.

MAKE THE BUILDING HEALTHY
Provide a safe, comfortable indoor environment. Although some people separate the indoor and outdoor environments, the two are integrally related and the health of its occupants should be ensured in any sustainable building.

Sample strategies include:
- Design air distribution systems for easy cleaning and maintenance.
- Avoid mechanical equipment that could introduce combustion gasses into the building.
- Avoid materials with high rates of VOC offgassing such as standard particleboard, some carpets and adhesives, and certain paints.
- Control moisture to minimize mold and mildew.
- Provide for continuous ventilation in all occupied buildings. In cold climates, heat recovery ventilation will reduce the energy penalty of ventilation.
- Give occupants some control of their environment with such features as operable windows, task lighting, and temperature controls.

MINIMIZE CONSTRUCTION AND DEMOLITION WASTE
Return, reuse, and recycle job-site waste. For more and more materials, sorting and recycling job-site waste pays off economically. It also can generate a good public image.

Sample strategies include:
- Sort construction and demolition waste for recycling.
- Donate reusable materials to nonprofit or community groups that can use them to build or improve housing stock.

METRICS

RATING SYSTEMS AND AWARDS

Sustainable design in architecture is typically defined using a collection of attributes across a spectrum of environmental criteria. To measure these attributes, rating systems and performance standards have been developed that combine and cross-reference standards from a variety of disciplines.

Whole building design must be highly energy efficient and/or use renewable energy sources. It must be similarly efficient or productive with water use, materials, and land. Whole building design integrates the planning and interior quality such that the whole is greater than the sum of the parts.

Because most building owners want concrete proof that such design distinguishes itself from conventional design, there is often an emphasis on quantitative criteria. Two of the many systems now in use are described here.

- The U.S. Green Building Council (USGBC) Leadership in Energy and Environmental Design (LEED) certification is becoming an industry standard for large scale green buildings. It requires proof across a rigorous series of measures and awards certification only after an internal review team has completed the examination of submitted documents.
- The Top Ten Green Projects program of the AIA's Committee on the Environment (COTE) is an annual award for 10 projects that complete a detailed application, with as much quantitative data as possible to enable a qualified architectural jury to make awards to the best designs. In this case, design quality and narrative responses are critical to success, so the highest performers from an energy-efficiency perspective may not receive awards if the jury determines other aspects of the design are not as successful as other candidates.

USGBC AND LEED
The USGBC's LEED program is a leading green building rating system in the United States. This system, which develops through a consensus-based process of its members, has branched out from its basis in office buildings to address new and existing structures of the most common types.

Submitted projects are evaluated against criteria in five areas of environmental design: energy, water, site design, materials, and indoor environment. The checklist in Table 12.32, for New Construction (NC), tracks credits in each category and, after review, the USGBC awards a design team with basic, silver, gold, or platinum certification.

AIA COTE TOP TEN GREEN PROJECTS
This set of 10 measures and supporting metrics comprise the foundation of the COTE Top Ten Green Projects, an annual awards program initiated in 1996, and the basis of the COTE theory of sustainable design. While not a rating system like LEED, the metrics employed in the COTE Top Ten program are a reliable indicator of sustainable design quality. COTE recognizes that great design includes environmental, technical, and aesthetic excellence. Stewardship, performance, and inspiration are essential and inseparable.

Top Ten entrants are asked to provide narratives responding to specific categories and indicating an understanding of the connections between sustainable design strategies and design, quantifying features when possible using the suggested metrics. This set of measures and metrics evolves each year, making it one of the most flexible rating systems currently in use. The COTE Top Ten links to the EPA Energy Star program, and entries are automatically entered into the Department of Energy (DOE) High-Performance Buildings Database.

DEMAND VERSUS BIOCAPACITY
Source: Global Footprint Network
12.31

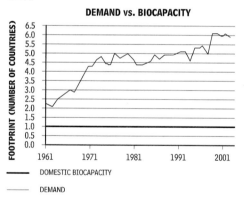

Although emphasis should be placed on measurable results whenever possible, the narrative format recognizes that qualitative goals are often subjective and, therefore, cannot always be evaluated quantitatively. The brief essays allow the entrants to describe in their own words how the project's goals were pursued and achieved. Narrative and metrics should refer only to the final built project, without regard to design measures that were not implemented.

Selection favors beautifully designed solutions that exhibit an integration of natural systems and appropriate technology, verified through building systems modeling, analysis, and best practices. (Entrants also provide descriptions of key environmental features, project economics, and details about the process and results.)

Contributors:
Arkin Tilt Architects, Berkeley, California; *Environmental Building News*, Brattleboro, Vermont, Real Goods Solar Living Center, Hopland, California; Mark Rylander, AIA, William McDonough + Partners, Charlottesville, Virginia.

TOP TEN MEASURE 1: SUSTAINABLE DESIGN INTENT AND INNOVATION

• *Narrative:* Sustainable design embraces the ecological, economic, and social circumstances of a project. How did these circumstances drive the project's design? Did they influence the architectural expression? Describe the most important sustainable design ideas for your project as well as the specific circumstances or constraints that generated those ideas. (This should not be a list of sustainable design measures.) Describe any unique sustainable design innovations. How does the architectural expression demonstrate the sustainable design intent? How did the sustainable design effort lead to a better overall project design?

TOP TEN MEASURE 2: REGIONAL/COMMUNITY DESIGN AND CONNECTIVITY

• *Narrative:* Sustainable design recognizes the unique cultural and natural character of a given region. Describe how the design promotes regional and community identity and an appropriate sense of place. Describe how the project contributes to public space and community interaction. Does the project's selected location reduce automobile travel from home, work, shopping, or other frequent destinations? Does the project make use of any alternative local or regional transportation strategies as well as successful efforts to reduce locally mandated parking requirements?

• *Metrics:* Indicate percentage of the building population traveling to the site by public transit (bus, subway, light rail, or train), carpool, bicycle, or on foot. Please indicate in the narrative whether there are company transportation policies and incentives and efforts made to provide a quality experience for those using transportation alternatives (enhancements to bikeway or pedestrian streets, and so on).

And: Divide the total number of parking spaces available by the total building population (occupants and visitors). Parking spaces that are dedicated to the building use but not part of the building project must be counted. Please indicate in narrative if project is successful in providing fewer parking spaces than zoning requirements through proactive measures.

Percent of building population using transit options other than the single occupancy vehicle: _____ %

Number of parking spaces per person: _____

TOP TEN MEASURE 3: LAND USE AND SITE ECOLOGY

• *Narrative:* Sustainable design reveals how ecosystems can thrive in the presence of human development. Describe how the development of the project's site responds to its ecological context. How does the site selection and design relate to ecosystems at different scales, from local to regional? How does the development of the immediate site and its buildings relate to a larger master plan and/or land use guidelines for the area?

Describe the landscape design and the creation, recreation or preservation of open space, permeable groundscape, and/or on-site ecosystems. Briefly describe any strategies for habitat creation and regionally appropriate planting. (Water will be addressed elsewhere.)

Describe any density or land use assessments and objectives. Is the site rural, suburban or urban, brownfield or other previously developed land, infill or greenfield? (Or can its land use be best characterized in other terms?) How does the project address sustainable land use practices within its given context?

TOP TEN MEASURE 4: BIOCLIMATIC DESIGN

• *Narrative:* Sustainable design conserves natural resources and maximizes human comfort through an intimate connection with the natural flows and cycles of the surrounding bioclimatic region. Describe how the building responds to these conditions through passive design strategies. What are the most important issues to address for your climate and building type? Describe your site analysis and how the building footprint, section, orientation, and massing respond to this analysis and to regional and local climate conditions, the sun path, prevailing breezes, and seasonal and daily cycles. Discuss design strategies and energy-conserving techniques that reduce or eliminate the need for active systems or mechanical solutions. Describe how passive ventilation and solar design strategies shaped the building.

LEED-NC VERSION 2.2 REGISTERED PROJECT CHECKLIST
12.32

YES	?	NO	SUSTAINABLE SITES	14 POINTS	
Y			Prerequisite 1	Construction Activity Pollution Prevention	Required
			Credit 1	Site Selection	1
			Credit 2	Development Density and Community Connectivity	1
			Credit 3	Brownfield Redevelopment	1
			Credit 4.1	Alternative Transportation, Public Transportation Access	1
			Credit 4.2	Alternative Transportation, Bicycle Storage, and Changing Rooms	1
			Credit 4.3	Alternative Transportation, Low-Emitting and Fuel-Efficient Vehicles	1
			Credit 4.4	Alternative Transportation, Parking Capacity	1
			Credit 5.1	Site Development, Protect or Restore Habitat	1
			Credit 5.2	Site Development, Maximize Open Space	1
			Credit 6.1	Stormwater Design, Quantity Control	1
			Credit 6.2	Stormwater Design, Quality Control	1
			Credit 7.1	Heat Island Effect, Nonroof	1
			Credit 7.2	Heat Island Effect, Roof	1
			Credit 8	Light Pollution Reduction	1
			WATER EFFICIENCY	**5 POINTS**	
			Credit 1.1	Water-Efficient Landscaping, Reduce by 50%	1
			Credit 1.2	Water-Efficient Landscaping, No Potable Use or No Irrigation	1
			Credit 2	Innovative Wastewater Technologies	1
			Credit 3.1	Water Use Reduction, 20% Reduction	1
			Credit 3.2	Water Use Reduction, 30% Reduction	1
			ENERGY AND ATMOSPHERE	**17 POINTS**	
Y			Prerequisite 1	Fundamental Commissioning of the Building Energy Systems	Required
Y			Prerequisite 2	Minimum Energy Performance	Required
Y			Prerequisite 3	Fundamental Refrigerant Management	Required
			Credit 1	Optimize Energy Performance	1 to 10
			Credit 2.1	On-Site Renewable Energy	1 to 3
			Credit 3	Enhanced Commissioning	1
			Credit 4	Enhanced Refrigerant Management	1
			Credit 5	Measurement and Verification	1
			Credit 6	Green Power	1
			MATERIALS AND RESOURCES	**13 POINTS**	
Y			Prerequisite 1	Storage and Collection of Recyclables	Required
			Credit 1.1	Building Reuse, Maintain 75% of Existing Walls, Floors, and Roofs	1
			Credit 1.2	Building Reuse, Maintain 100% of Existing Walls, Floors, and Roofs	1
			Credit 1.3	Building Reuse, Maintain 50% of Interior Nonstructural Elements	1
			Credit 2.1	Construction Waste Management, Divert 50% from Disposal	1
			Credit 2.2	Construction Waste Management, Divert 75% from Disposal	1
			Credit 3.1	Materials Reuse, 5%	1
			Credit 3.2	Materials Reuse,10%	1
			Credit 4.1	Recycled Content, 10% (postconsumer + half preconsumer)	1
			Credit 4.2	Recycled Content, 20% (postconsumer + half preconsumer)	1
			Credit 5.1	Regional Materials, 10% Extracted, Processed, and Manufactured Regionally	1
			Credit 5.2	Regional Materials, 20% Extracted, Processed, and Manufactured Regionally	1
			Credit 6	Rapidly Renewable Materials	1
			Credit 7	Certified Wood	1
			INDOOR ENVIRONMENTAL QUALITY	**15 POINTS**	
Y			Prerequisite 1	Minimum IAQ Performance	Required
Y			Prerequisite 2	Environmental Tobacco Smoke (ETS) Control	Required
			Credit 1	Outdoor Air Delivery Monitoring	1
			Credit 2	Increased Ventilation	1
			Credit 3.1	Construction IAQ Management Plan, During Construction	1

Contributors:
US. Green Building Council, www.usgbc.org; Global Footprint Network, wwwfootprintnetwork.org.

LEED-NC VERSION 2.2 REGISTERED PROJECT CHECKLIST (continued)
12.32

YES	?	NO	INDOOR ENVIRONMENTAL QUALITY	15 POINTS	
			Credit 3.2	Construction IAQ Management Plan, Before Occupancy	1
			Credit 4.1	Low-Emitting Materials, Adhesives, and Sealants	1
			Credit 4.2	Low-Emitting Materials, Paints, and Coatings	1
			Credit 4.3	Low-Emitting Materials, Carpet Systems	1
			Credit 4.4	Low-Emitting Materials, Composite Wood, and Agrifiber Products	1
			Credit 5	Indoor Chemical and Pollutant Source Control	1
			Credit 6.1	Controllability of Systems, Lighting	1
			Credit 6.2	Controllability of Systems, Thermal Comfort	1
			Credit 7.1	Thermal Comfort, Design	1
			Credit 7.2	Thermal Comfort, Verification	1
			Credit 8.1	Daylight and Views, Daylight 75% of Spaces	1
			Credit 8.2	Daylight and Views, Views for 90% of Spaces	1
			INNOVATION AND DESIGN PROCESS	**5 POINTS**	
			Credit 1.1	Innovation in Design: Provide Specific Title	1
			Credit 1.2	Innovation in Design: Provide Specific Title	1
			Credit 1.3	Innovation in Design: Provide Specific Title	1
			Credit 1.4	Innovation in Design: Provide Specific Title	1
			Credit 2	LEED Accredited Professional	1
			PROJECT TOTALS (PRECERTIFICATION ESTIMATES)	**69 POINTS**	
			Certified: 26–32 points		
			Silver: 33–38 points		
			Gold: 39–51 points		
			Platinum: 52–69 points		

TOP TEN MEASURE 5: LIGHT AND AIR

- *Narrative:* Sustainable design creates and maintains a comfortable interior environment while providing abundant daylight and fresh air. Outline design strategies that create a healthful and productive indoor environment through daylighting, lighting design, ventilation, indoor air quality, view corridors, and personal control systems. Describe how the project's design enhances connections between indoors and outdoors. Provide drawings or diagrams to illustrate these strategies.
- *Metrics:* Identify the percentage of the total building area that uses daylight as the dominant light source during daylight hours (with electric lights off or dimmed below 20 percent). This calculation should include all areas of the building, including stairways, restrooms, corridors, and so on. Identify the percentage of the total building area that can be adequately served by natural ventilation (with all HVAC systems shutdown) for all or part of the year.

Percent of total building area that is naturally lit: ____ %

Percent of building that can be ventilated or cooled with operable windows: ____ %

TOP TEN MEASURE 6: WATER CYCLE

- *Narrative:* Water is an essential resource for all life on earth. Describe how building and site design strategies conserve water supplies, manage site water and drainage, and capitalize on renewable sources (such as precipitation) on the immediate site. Outline water-conserving landscape and building design strategies, as well as any water-conserving fixtures, appliances, and HVAC equipment. List water reuse strategies for rainwater, graywater, and/or wastewater.
- *Metrics:* What percentage of precipitation from a typical (regularly occurring in spring/summer/fall) storm event falling on the site is retained and infiltrated/recharged on-site? Naturally occurring stormwater flows due to topography and soils inherent to the predevelopment conditions on the site (unaffected by development) can be deducted from this calculation.

And: This calculation must include all water use inside and outside of the building (e.g., plumbing fixtures, appliances, HVAC equipment, landscape irrigation, and so on). Potable water is defined as water that is extracted from municipal supply, wells, or irrigation ditches. Reclaimed graywater and harvested rainwater should not be deducted for this calculation, but note the percentage of reclaimed water used and note the source in the narrative. Please describe water-conserving strategies used and projected water savings in the narrative.

And: If wastewater is reused on site, rather than discharged to municipal treatment systems or conventional septic systems, identify the portion of wastewater that is reused on-site.

Precipitation managed on site: ____ %

Total water used indoors: ____ gal/yr

Total water used outdoors: ____ gal/yr

Percent of total water from reclaimed sources: ____%

Percent wastewater reused on-site: _____ %

TOP TEN MEASURE 7: ENERGY FLOWS AND ENERGY FUTURE

- *Narrative:* Good design of building mechanical and electrical systems and integration of those systems with passive design strategies is essential for conserving natural resources and improving building performance. Describe how the design of building systems contributes to energy conservation, reduces pollution, and improves building performance and comfort. Describe techniques for integrating these systems with other aspects of building design. Describe effective use of controls and technologies, efficient lighting strategies, and any on-site renewable energy systems.

Sustainable design carefully considers the long-term impact of current decisions in order to protect quality of life in the future. Describe how your project responds to the ongoing reduction and possible loss of fossil fuels. Does the project employ or encourage alternative energy sources? Describe strategies to reduce peak electrical demand through design, programming, use patterns, equipment selection, HVAC/lighting controls, and on-site energy generation. Describe how the building or parts of the building could function in a blackout (operable windows and daylight/independent power for life safety, and so on).

- *Metrics:* Use the Environmental Protection Agency's (EPA) Energy Star Target Finder tool and enter your score here. (Note that a limited number of building types are available for this analysis.) Use actual utility meter or billing data whenever possible. Go to: www.energystar.gov/index.cfm?c=new_bldg_design.bus_target_finder.

EPA Performance Rating ____

For residential projects, if you used the HERS rating system, enter your score here. Go to: www.energystar.gov/index.cfm?c=new_homes.hm_verification.

HERS Performance Rating ____

Determine percentage of annual energy cost savings achieved with the design, as compared to a minimally code compliant base model. Use ASHRAE 90.1, or the local code/standard, whichever is more stringent. Other, more stringent codes may be used as a baseline. However, the alternate code must be identified (including year of issue), and the calculation method (e.g., DOE-2 energy modeling, utility meter data, and so on) must be described. Also provide a PDF of the energy calculations (energy model summary, LEED energy sheet, Title 24 analysis, or other).

Percent total energy savings: ____ %

Provide the requested detailed information to the extent possible. Note that total energy (consumption) includes all purchased and site-generated energy and refers to all related loads including HVAC, lighting, and plug loads. Square footage (sf) refers to gross square footage. Provide building "standard design" or "base case" from building energy model.

TOTAL ENERGY SAVINGS
12.33

	BASE CASE	ACTUAL	
Total annual energy			Btu/sf/yr
Total annual energy by fuel			
Electricity			Btu/sf/yr
Natural Gas			Btu/sf/yr
Other (specify)			Btu/sf/yr
Heating			Btu/sf/yr
Cooling (if necessary)			Btu/sf/yr
Cooling capacity			sf/ton
Lighting load connected			W/sf
Lighting load after controls (estimate used in energy model)			W/sf
Plug load (estimate used in energy model)			W/sf

And: Identify peak electrical demand per net square footage of building area (subtract mechanical space and loading docks), and identify the extent to which you have reduced peak power demands through demand site management and renewable energy generation.

And: What percentage of total annual energy usage for the facility is provided by on-site renewable energy sources? Identify the mix from the following list: PV, solar thermal, wind, micro-hydro, biomass (define) electricity, biomass thermal, geothermal, biogas (define), electricity, passive solar, others.

And: What portion of the total annual energy usage for the facility is generated from grid supplied renewable sources that meet the Center for Resource Solutions (CRS) Green-E requirements? Please identify the sources used and the proportion from each source in the supplemental narrative.

Contributors:
Mark Rylander, AIA, William McDonough + Partners, Charlottesville, Virginia; AIA Committee on the Environment (COTE); US Green Building Council.

ENERGY DEMAND
12.34

	BASE CASE	DESIGN CASE	
Identify watt per net sf peak electricity demand			W/sf
Percent on-site renewable energy generation			
Percent grid-supplied renewable energy			

- *Supplemental Narrative:* Describe the standard or guideline used to develop the base case and actual or design case for the data provided above, and identify the software used to perform any simulations.

TOP TEN MEASURE 8: MATERIALS AND CONSTRUCTION
- *Narrative:* The careful selection of materials and products can conserve resources, reduce impacts of harvesting, production, and transportation, improve building performance, and enhance occupant health and comfort. Describe the most important selection criteria, considerations, and constraints (such as optimizing health, durability, maintenance, and energy use, and/or reducing the impacts of extraction, manufacturing, and transportation) for materials or building assemblies for your project. What were the most important considerations in developing the building envelope? What were the most important material or building assembly decisions or selections (no more than three) and how did they meet the criteria? Include consideration given to impacts on the environment over the full life cycle and the results of the life-cycle assessment, if available. Describe any materials that are part of a "green lease" program. Describe construction waste reduction and any strategies to promote recycling during occupancy.

TOP TEN MEASURE 9: LONG LIFE, LOOSE FIT
- *Narrative:* Sustainable design seeks to maximize ecological, social, and economic value over time. Describe how the project's design creates enduring value through long-term flexibility and adaptability. Why is this project likely to continue thriving far into the future? Identify the anticipated service life of the project and describe any components designed for disassembly. Describe materials, systems, and design solutions developed to enhance versatility, durability, and adaptive reuse potential. Describe efforts to "right size" the project and to reduce unnecessary square footage.

TOP TEN MEASURE 10: COLLECTIVE WISDOM
AND FEEDBACK LOOPS
- *Narrative:* Sustainable design recognizes that the most intelligent design strategies evolve over time through shared knowledge within a large community. Clearly and specifically describe how your design process enhanced the ultimate performance and success of the building. How did collaborative efforts between the design team, consultants, client, and community contribute to success?

What lessons were learned during the design, construction, and occupation of the building? If starting over today, how would your approach or emphasis change? Identify efforts to document and share these lessons with the larger community. Describe commissioning and any ongoing monitoring of building performance and occupant satisfaction. How do (or will) these contribute to building performance, occupant satisfaction, or design of future projects?

OTHER INFORMATION

Project Economics
- *Finance:* Describe innovative cost analyses, financing strategies and/or partnerships that contributed to the success of the project (<200 words).
- *Cost and Payback Analysis:* Describe atypical project cost issues and provide estimated payback of any investment in green measures (<200 words).

Process and Results
- Provide as much detail as you can on any notable aspects of the process of designing and building this project, especially as they relate to its environmental performance. Information is required for only the first two phases; the rest are optional (predesign, design, construction process, operations/maintenance, Commissioning, measurement, and verification/postoccupancy evaluation).

Rating System(s) Results
- If the project has been officially rated under LEED, BREEAM, or a local/regional green building program, please list rating system, rating date (MM-DD-YYYY), and score or rating level.

Minimum Informational Requirements: Context Plan showing the place, region, neighborhood (with North arrow); Site Plan (with North arrow); Floor Plans (with North arrow); Elevations; Sections and Details (including at least one section that illustrates daylighting, natural ventilation, or other sustainable design strategies); Photographs of completed project (interior and exterior).

STANDARDS AND CERTIFICATIONS SOURCES

High-performance building metrics are often employed to make the case for whether a building is sustainable. In fact, such metrics, many of which predate the emergence of a sustainable design movement, are simply performance standards that are higher than building codes. A variety of federal and state agencies, nongovernmental organizations, and professional and trade associations develop these standards and certifications, which are becoming key architectural (nongraphic) standards.

Some programs are very specific to one issue or material such as the Cool Roof Rating Council standards for roofing, which reduces the urban heat island effect. Wood certification programs, such as the Smartwood of the Rainforest Action Network, exist to provide clarity to claims of sustainability within the building materials marketplace. This ever-lengthening list of programs includes many that have incorporated LEED or elements of the preceding standards into building codes or as requirements for development of local projects. Refer to "Building Design & Construction White Paper on Sustainability" (*Building Design & Construction*, November 2003) for information on more than 50 programs.

WHOLE BUILDING CERTIFICATION, AWARDS, DATABASES
- U.S. Green Building Council LEED rating system
- Green Building Initiative Green Globes
- American Institute of Architects Committee on the Environment AIA COTE Top Ten Green Design Awards
- Department of Energy (DOE) High Performance Buildings Database

ENERGY, AIR QUALITY, AND SPACE-CONDITIONING STANDARDS
- ASHRAE (Association of Heating, Refrigeration, and Air-Conditioning Engineers) in collaboration with other organizations such as *IESNA* (Illuminating Engineering Society of North America)
- Standard 90.1 Energy Efficiency
- Standard 55 Thermal Comfort
- Standard 62 Indoor Air Quality
- U.S. Environmental Protection Agency (EPA), ENERGY STAR Program

WATER EFFICIENCY STANDARDS
- Energy Policy Act of 1992

MATERIAL STANDARDS AND CERTIFICATIONS
- U.S. Environmental Protection Agency (EPA) Environmentally Preferable Purchasing www.epa.gov/opptintr/epp
- South Coast Air Quality Management District Standard
- Scientific Certification Systems Environmentally Preferable Products and Services, Environmental Claims Certification Program
- McDonough Braungart Design Chemistry Cradle to Cradle Certification
- Green Seal
- Greenguard Environmental Institute Certification
- National Institute of Standards & Technology Building for Environmental and Economic Sustainability (BEES)

SEE ALSO

Awnings
Canopies
Exterior Shutters
Mineral-Fiber-Reinforced Cementitous Panels

13 INCLUSIVE DESIGN

INTRODUCTION

Inclusive design is an umbrella that acknowledges the diversity of human beings and in the process embraces a number of positions in relationship to people with disabilities and the built environment. Some positions are mandated and some are advocated (driven by public demand). The litany of terminology describing these positions can be perplexing and lead to an ineffectual blurring of the critical differences in meaning, derivation, and approach; therefore, a number of relevant terms are defined here as a preface to the discussions presented in this chapter:

- *Universal design*: "The design of products and environments to be usable by all people, to the greatest extent possible, without the need for adaptation or specialized design." (Ron Mace, architect and founder of the Center for Universal Design)
- *Accessible design*: Design focused on people with disabilities (primarily people with physical and sensory limitations) as a percentage of the population. Minimum standards are mandated via building codes and regulations, technical standards, and civil rights laws such as the Americans with Disabilities Act (ADA) and the Fair Housing Amendments Act (FHAA).
- *Americans with Disabilities Act (ADA)*: Federal civil rights law that prohibits discrimination on the basis of disability in employment, state and local government, places of public accommodation, transportation, and telecommunications. The ADA includes the Standards for Accessible Design.
- *Fair Housing Act*: Civil rights law that prohibits discrimination in housing on the basis of race, color, religion, sex, disability, familial status, and national origin. The Fair Housing Amendments Act includes the Fair Housing Accessibility Guidelines.

Many architects currently think that universal design and accessibility are synonymous. In fact, universal design is not accessibility, although it is underpinned by accessibility codes and standards, as well as all other required codes and standards. Accessibility standards use a prescriptive, technical approach based on a percentage framework required by law. Universal design is an approach to good design, which posits that by considering the full range of human ability across our lifetimes (small/big, young/old, with varying abilities across every size, every stage of life), we can design better environments for everyone.

This chapter will explain the differences and relationship between two very different approaches to design: one that addresses the full range of human experience and abilities, and is subsequently a condition of sustainability; the second that is derived from a percentage mentality and is subsequently more narrowly focused.

Contributors:
Karen J. King, RA, University of New Mexico, Albuquerque, New Mexico;
Rebecca Ingram Architect, Albuquerque, New Mexico.

UNIVERSAL DESIGN

Our individual physical realities are in a constant state of change across the human lifetime. We are not static. We are young and old, with many shades of in-between; we are small and big, with many variations; we are every ethnicity, in many combinations; we possess all abilities, with infinite variations. Our lives are constituted of differing and changing cadence. This is normal for our species, occurring naturally as well as by our exercise of free will. To design universally is to design for the human experience of the built environment.

The movement toward a design process that puts human experience at the beginning is not new. Universal design is most successful when fully integrated within a project, rendering it invisible and untitled. Its underpinnings as a design movement are attributed to a correlation between improved functional capability and

the removal of barriers in the built environment. In the 1970s, architect Michael Bednar suggested that the value in this correlation extends to all of us, not just the few. In the 1980s, Mace would define and give the movement its name and become one of its most recognizable faces. "Universal design is the design of products and environments to be usable by all people, to the greatest extent possible, without the need for adaptation or specialized design."

In the 1990s, Mace worked with a group of fellow advocates and designers (architects, product designers, engineers, and environmental design researchers) to create the Principles of Universal Design, providing a first step for increasing markets through the design of more widely usable products and environments. This marked a significant shift away from the prescriptive technical approach delineated in codes and standards and established

an alternative performance-based criteria focused on issues of usability.

The seven principles establish baseline performance criteria for a wide range of designed products and conditions. They still serve very well in many instances where a one-to-one correlation between improved functional capability and the removal of barriers can readily be employed and discerned. However, the making and experience of architecture rarely presents a one-to-one correlation. The assembly of a spatial experience described by materials and products often results in a more complex overlay of multiple principles and the emergence of universal attributes that expand the scope of the original seven principles. The authors of the original principles recognized that they were establishing an evolving

**SITE PLAN WITH INTEGRATED
UNIVERSAL CIRCULATION
13.1**

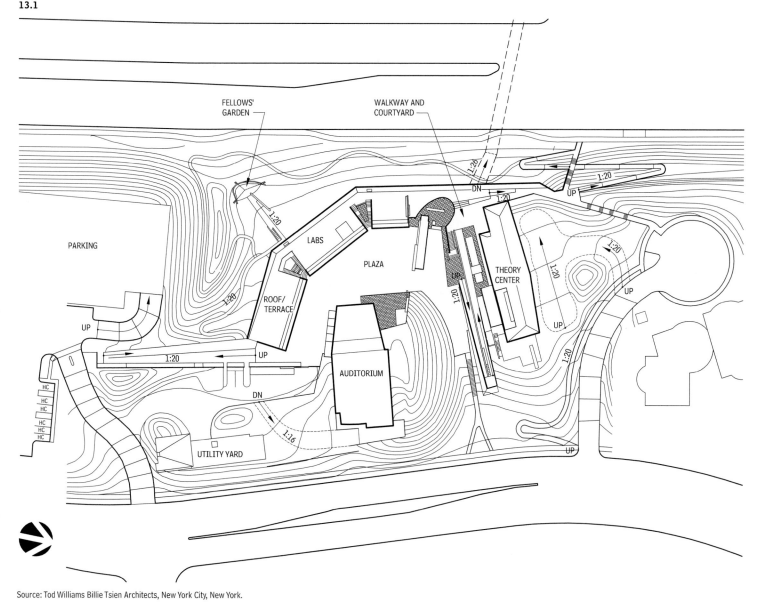

Source: Tod Williams Billie Tsien Architects, New York City, New York.

Contributors:
Karen J. King, RA, University of New Mexico, Albuquerque, New Mexico;
Rebecca Ingram Architect, Albuquerque, New Mexico.

SECTION AT CARVED-IN COURTYARD WITH TERRACE ABOVE
13.2

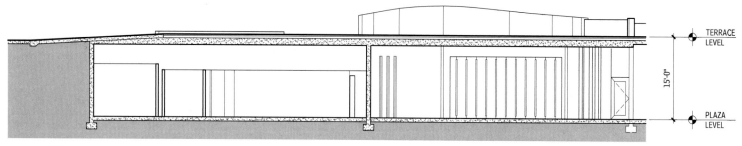

TERRACE
LEVEL

15'-0"

PLAZA
LEVEL

Source: Tod Williams Billie Tsien Architects, New York City, New York.

INCLINED WALKWAY—EAST ELEVATION AT LABS
13.3

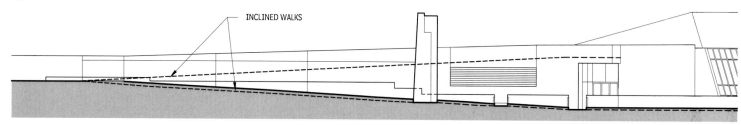

INCLINED WALKS

Source: Tod Williams Billie Tsien Architects, New York City, New York.

framework that could expand as each discipline seized upon and expanded the opportunities inherent in the original intent.

In keeping with the original intent (" . . . usable by all people, to the greatest extent possible, without the need for adaptation or specialized design"), the attributes of universal design presented here are sometimes a clean fit with the existing principles—sometimes a complex overlay and sometimes emergent. The presentation in this chapter of a particular attribute does not ensure that the project meets every principle or complies with every required code or standard that underpins it. Rather, the principles are presented as examples of critical thinking and detail execution that result in architectural experiences that enrich our lives—all our lives.

SEVEN PRINCIPLES OF UNIVERSAL DESIGN

PRINCIPLE ONE: EQUITABLE USE
The design is useful and marketable to people with diverse abilities.

- Provide the same means of use for all users: identical whenever possible; equivalent when not.
- Avoid segregating or stigmatizing any users.
- Make provisions for privacy, security, and safety equally available to all users.
- Make the design appealing to all users.

EXAMPLE: NEUROSCIENCES INSTITUTE
Tod Williams, FAIA and Billie Tsien, AIA blend ideas of program, topography, and motion in their design for the Neurosciences Institute in La Jolla, California. The buildings enclose a public outdoor space, into which a scientific auditorium is inserted. The auditorium, together with its planted berm, operates in a richly combined manner to set up one of the entries into the plaza, being read as an object, defining closure, and directing view. A series of inclined walks (1:20 or less) both take advantage of existing topographies and invent new ones, while connecting places internal (the plaza and the terraces above the labs) and external (parking and the Scripps Institute under the major roadway).

A laboratory building and one end of the theory building are carved into the topography to form an inhabitable retaining wall bordering the road above.

The inclined walks, along with a variety of stairs, are an integral part of a circuit designed to be a journey of discussion, contemplation, and discovery—a journey that anyone can take. As a matter of "ethics and aesthetics," the architects have seamlessly integrated universal access into a tectonic essay on movement, creating an ever-changing spatial experience.

INTEGRATED LIGHTING—INCLINED WALKWAY (TYPICAL)
13.4

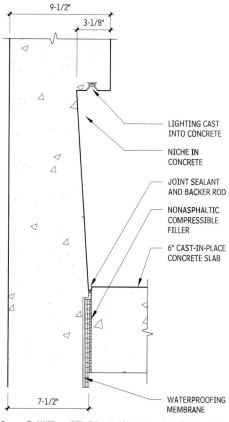

9-1/2"

3-1/8"

LIGHTING CAST INTO CONCRETE

NICHE IN CONCRETE

JOINT SEALANT AND BACKER ROD

NONASPHALTIC COMPRESSIBLE FILLER

6" CAST-IN-PLACE CONCRETE SLAB

WATERPROOFING MEMBRANE

7-1/2"

Source: Tod Williams Billie Tsien Architects, New York City, New York.

NOTE

13.4 All concrete this sheet to be sandblasted and sealed.

Contributors:
The Principles of Universal Design, North Carolina State University, Center for Universal Design, 1997. Compiled by advocates: Bettye Rose Connell, Mike Jones, AIA, Ron Mace, Jim Mueller, Abir Mullick, Elaine Ostroff, Honorary AIA, John Sanford, Ed Steinfeld, Molly Story, and Gregg Vanderheiden. Major funding provided by the National Institute on Disability and Rehabilitation Research, U.S. Department of Education.

**GRATE AND DRAIN DETAIL—AUDITORIUM PLAZA
(TYPICAL AT INCLINED WALKWAYS)
13.5**

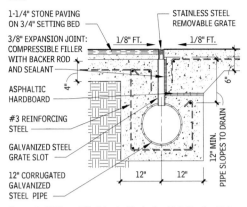

1-1/4" STONE PAVING
ON 3/4" SETTING BED

STAINLESS STEEL
REMOVABLE GRATE

3/8" EXPANSION JOINT:
COMPRESSIBLE FILLER
WITH BACKER ROD
AND SEALANT

ASPHALTIC
HARDBOARD

#3 REINFORCING
STEEL

GALVANIZED STEEL
GRATE SLOT

12" CORRUGATED
GALVANIZED
STEEL PIPE

1/8" FT.   1/8" FT.

4"   6"

12"   12"

12" MIN.
PIPE SLOPES TO DRAIN

Source: Tod Williams Billie Tsien Architects, New York City, New York.

**INCLINED WALK ELEVATIONS—THEORY BUILDING
13.6**

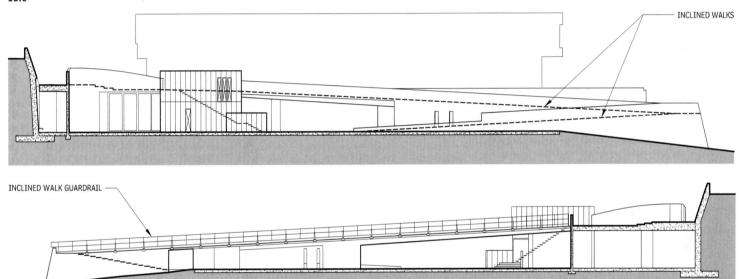

INCLINED WALKS

INCLINED WALK GUARDRAIL

Source: Tod Williams Billie Tsien Architects, New York City, New York.

INCLINED WALKWAY—TERRACE-LEVEL PLAN
13.7

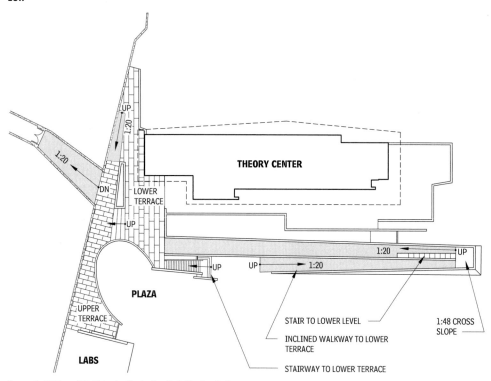

Source: Tod Williams Billie Tsien Architects, New York City, New York.

AUDITORIUM PLANS WITH INCLINED WALKS
13.8

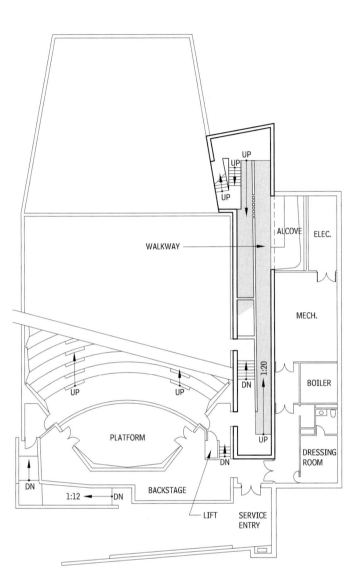

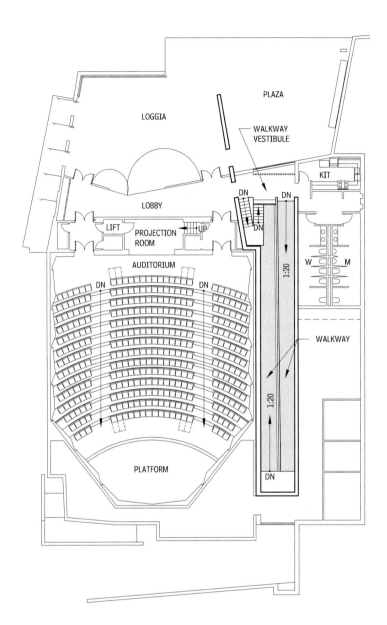

Source: Tod Williams Billie Tsien Architects, New York City, New York.

NOTE

13.8 Inclined walkways continue in the scientific auditorium, connecting
the upper and lower level seating.

**INCLINED WALKWAY AND VESTIBULE SECTION WITH BENCHES—AUDITORIUM
13.9**

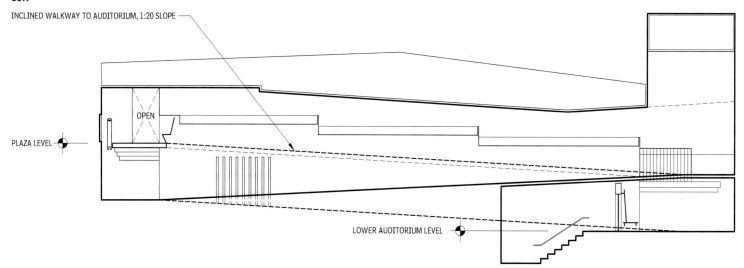

INCLINED WALKWAY TO AUDITORIUM, 1:20 SLOPE

OPEN

PLAZA LEVEL

LOWER AUDITORIUM LEVEL

Source: Tod Williams Billie Tsien Architects, New York City, New York.

PRINCIPLE TWO: FLEXIBILITY IN USE
The design accommodates a wide range of individual preferences and abilities.

- Provide choice in methods of use.
- Accommodate right- or left-handed access in use.
- Facilitate the user's accuracy and precision.
- Provide adaptability to the user's pace.

EXAMPLE: SCHALL RESIDENCE
Passing through the big wall and arriving at the car court of the Schall house reveals a hidden realm, an oasis in the desert climate of Phoenix, Arizona.

Guest quarters and gardens fill the entry level, effectively screening out the suburban world just beyond its walls. The primary living spaces are on the second level, and getting there is a matter of choice and options. A residential elevator, which passes from exterior to interior space, and a mysterious curving stair, provide passage in a manner that people with a range of abilities can use. The architecture, by Wendell Burnette, AIA, offers choice in how people move through the house, in keeping with the idea of creating multiple possibilities for living inside and outside, as well as on and above the ground plane.

**ENTRY-LEVEL PLAN WITH CIRCULATION CHOICES—STAIR AND ELEVATOR
13.10**

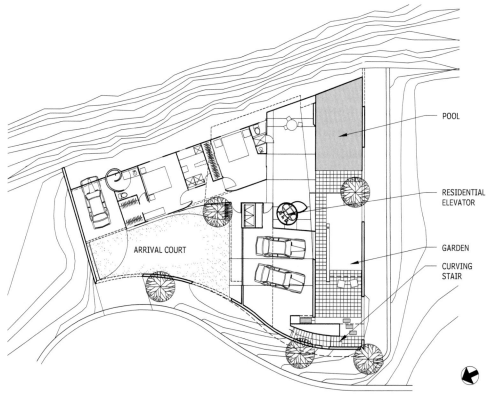

POOL

RESIDENTIAL ELEVATOR

GARDEN

CURVING STAIR

ARRIVAL COURT

Source: Wendell Burnette Architects, Phoenix, Arizona.

SECTION SHOWING DISAPPEARING STAIR
13.11

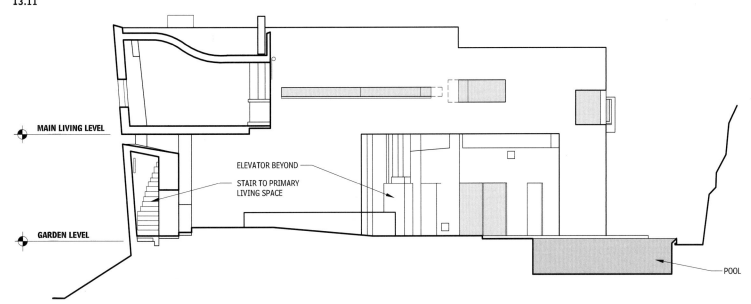

MAIN LIVING LEVEL

ELEVATOR BEYOND

STAIR TO PRIMARY
LIVING SPACE

GARDEN LEVEL

POOL

Source: Wendell Burnette Architects, Phoenix, Arizona.

PRINCIPLE THREE: SIMPLE AND INTUITIVE USE

Use of the design is easy to understand, regardless of the user's experience, knowledge, language skills, or current concentration level.

- Eliminate unnecessary complexity.
- Be consistent with user's expectations and intuition.
- Accommodate a wide range of literacy and language skills.
- Arrange information consistent with its importance.
- Provide effective prompting and feedback during and after task completion.

ELEVATOR SECTION AND PLANS
13.12

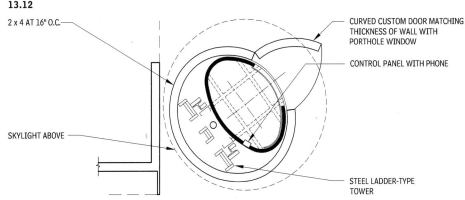

2 x 4 AT 16" O.C.

CURVED CUSTOM DOOR MATCHING
THICKNESS OF WALL WITH
PORTHOLE WINDOW

CONTROL PANEL WITH PHONE

SKYLIGHT ABOVE

STEEL LADDER-TYPE
TOWER

SECOND-LEVEL PLAN

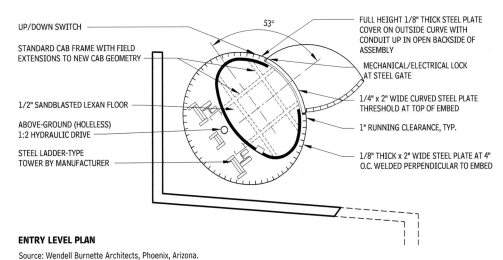

UP/DOWN SWITCH

53°

STANDARD CAB FRAME WITH FIELD
EXTENSIONS TO NEW CAB GEOMETRY

FULL HEIGHT 1/8" THICK STEEL PLATE
COVER ON OUTSIDE CURVE WITH
CONDUIT UP IN OPEN BACKSIDE OF
ASSEMBLY

MECHANICAL/ELECTRICAL LOCK
AT STEEL GATE

1/2" SANDBLASTED LEXAN FLOOR

1/4" x 2" WIDE CURVED STEEL PLATE
THRESHOLD AT TOP OF EMBED

ABOVE-GROUND (HOLELESS)
1:2 HYDRAULIC DRIVE

1" RUNNING CLEARANCE, TYP.

STEEL LADDER-TYPE
TOWER BY MANUFACTURER

1/8" THICK x 2" WIDE STEEL PLATE AT 4"
O.C. WELDED PERPENDICULAR TO EMBED

ENTRY LEVEL PLAN

Source: Wendell Burnette Architects, Phoenix, Arizona.

ELEVATOR SECTION AND PLANS (continued)
13.12

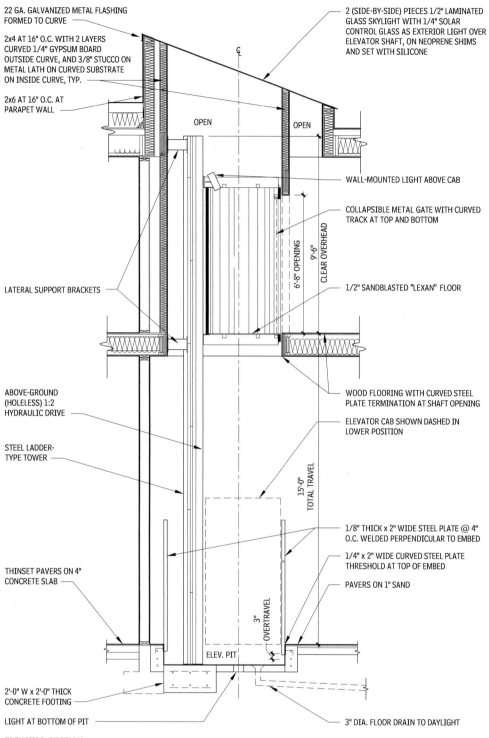

22 GA. GALVANIZED METAL FLASHING FORMED TO CURVE

2x4 AT 16" O.C. WITH 2 LAYERS CURVED 1/4" GYPSUM BOARD OUTSIDE CURVE, AND 3/8" STUCCO ON METAL LATH ON CURVED SUBSTRATE ON INSIDE CURVE, TYP.

2x6 AT 16" O.C. AT PARAPET WALL

LATERAL SUPPORT BRACKETS

ABOVE-GROUND (HOLELESS) 1:2 HYDRAULIC DRIVE

STEEL LADDER-TYPE TOWER

THINSET PAVERS ON 4" CONCRETE SLAB

2'-0" W x 2'-0" THICK CONCRETE FOOTING

LIGHT AT BOTTOM OF PIT

2 (SIDE-BY-SIDE) PIECES 1/2" LAMINATED GLASS SKYLIGHT WITH 1/4" SOLAR CONTROL GLASS AS EXTERIOR LIGHT OVER ELEVATOR SHAFT, ON NEOPRENE SHIMS AND SET WITH SILICONE

OPEN

OPEN

WALL-MOUNTED LIGHT ABOVE CAB

COLLAPSIBLE METAL GATE WITH CURVED TRACK AT TOP AND BOTTOM

6'-8" OPENING

9'-6" CLEAR OVERHEAD

1/2" SANDBLASTED "LEXAN" FLOOR

WOOD FLOORING WITH CURVED STEEL PLATE TERMINATION AT SHAFT OPENING

ELEVATOR CAB SHOWN DASHED IN LOWER POSITION

15'-0" TOTAL TRAVEL

1/8" THICK x 2" WIDE STEEL PLATE @ 4" O.C. WELDED PERPENDICULAR TO EMBED

1/4" x 2" WIDE CURVED STEEL PLATE THRESHOLD AT TOP OF EMBED

PAVERS ON 1" SAND

3" OVERTRAVEL

ELEV. PIT

3" DIA. FLOOR DRAIN TO DAYLIGHT

ELEVATOR SECTION

Source: Wendell Burnette Architects, Phoenix, Arizona.

EXAMPLE: PITTSBURGH CHILDREN'S MUSEUM

At the Pittsburgh Children's Museum, the architect, Koning Eizenberg Architecture, and the exhibit designers, Springboard Architecture Communication Design, turned a mundane hand dryer into something more. They took an object that is simple to use and clear in its utility, multiplied it, mounted it within multiple reach ranges, and transformed it into an experience.

PRINCIPLE FOUR: PERCEPTIBLE INFORMATION

The design communicates necessary information effectively to the user, regardless of ambient conditions or the user's sensory abilities.

- Use different modes (pictorial, verbal, tactile) for redundant presentation of essential information.
- Maximize "legibility" of essential information.
- Differentiate elements in ways that can be described (i.e., make it easier to give instructions or directions).
- Provide compatibility with a variety of techniques or devices used by people with sensory limitations.

PRINCIPLE FIVE: TOLERANCE FOR ERROR

The design minimizes hazards and the adverse consequences of accidental or unintended actions.

- Arrange elements to minimize hazards and errors: most used elements, most accessible; hazardous elements eliminated, isolated, or shielded. Make provisions for privacy, security, and safety equally available to all users.
- Provide warnings of hazards and errors.
- Provide fail-safe features.
- Discourage unconscious action in tasks that require vigilance.

PRINCIPLE SIX: LOW PHYSICAL EFFORT

The design can be used efficiently and comfortably and with a minimum of fatigue.

- Allow the user to maintain a neutral body position.
- Use reasonable operating forces.
- Minimize repetitive actions.
- Minimize sustained physical effort.

PRINCIPLE SEVEN: SIZE AND SPACE FOR APPROACH AND USE

Appropriate size and space is provided for approach, reach, manipulation, and use regardless of user's body size, posture, or mobility.

- Provide a clear line of sight to important elements for any seated or standing user.
- Make reach to all components comfortable for any seated or standing user.
- Accommodate variations in hand grip and size.
- Provide adequate space for the use of assistive devices or personal assistance.

EXAMPLE: ANDERSON RESIDENCE

The bathroom for the Anderson Remodel in Albuquerque, New Mexico, by Geoffrey C. Adams, AIA, with Rebecca Ingram Architect and Karen J. King, RA, addresses a number of issues in a relatively small space.

Often, a second bathroom must serve visitors as well as people who reside in the house. This bath connects to an adjacent bedroom and to a hallway that is lit by daylight and leads to the public space of the house. Pocket doors, designed as a variation on the shoji screen, allow private access from the bedroom, while borrowing daylight from the hall. Alternately, the bath can be open for visitors and closed off from the bedroom. An additional division of the shower and water closet from the lavatory and grooming area offers flexibility in use for family and people who are more familiar with one another; privacy with quick proximity for people who may require some assistance; a staging area for assistive equipment; and a transitional zone for hosting groups of people.

The shower and water closet form a wet room, lined with grab bars that read as just another layer to the space. This approach is becoming more common because the design of grab bars has

WATERPLAY ENVIRONMENT—WALL OF DRYERS
13.13

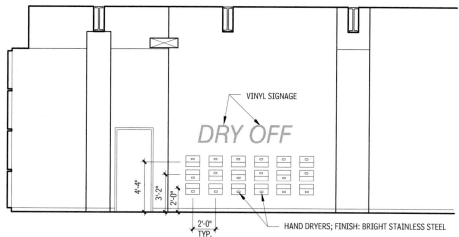

VINYL SIGNAGE

DRY OFF

4'-4"   3'-2"   2'-0"

2'-0" TYP.

HAND DRYERS; FINISH: BRIGHT STAINLESS STEEL

Source: Springboard Architecture Communication Design LLC, Pittsburgh, Pennsylvania.

evolved beyond institutional utilization. They double as towel bars, while increasing safety. Open shelving was designed with visual cueing in mind, and for multiple-reach ranges (tall to small).

The doors move easily on a caster system and are made of translucent plastic filled with blanket insulation. Being very lightweight, these doors reduce the likelihood of anyone being injured by a slamming door. Additionally, the use of sliding doors reduces the congestion associated with swinging doors; it also reduces the necessary maneuvering clearance for those using assistive devices.

ENLARGED BATHROOM PLAN AND ELEVATIONS
13.14

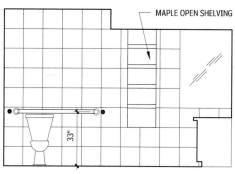

MAPLE OPEN SHELVING

33"

ENLARGED BATHROOM ELEVATION

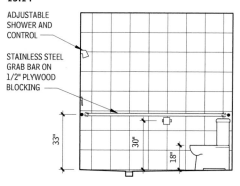

ADJUSTABLE SHOWER AND CONTROL

STAINLESS STEEL GRAB BAR ON 1/2" PLYWOOD BLOCKING

33"   30"   18"

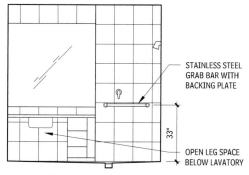

STAINLESS STEEL GRAB BAR WITH BACKING PLATE

33"

OPEN LEG SPACE BELOW LAVATORY

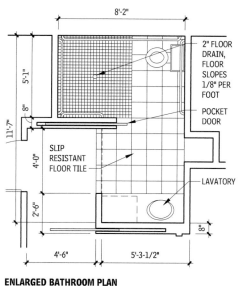

8'-2"

5'-1"   8"   11'-7"   4'-0"   2'-6"

2" FLOOR DRAIN, FLOOR SLOPES 1/8" PER FOOT

POCKET DOOR

SLIP RESISTANT FLOOR TILE

LAVATORY

8"

4'-6"   5'-3-1/2"

ENLARGED BATHROOM PLAN

Source: Geoffrey C. Adams, AIA, with Rebecca Ingram Architect and Karen J. King, RA, Albuquerque, New Mexico.

ACCESSIBLE DESIGN

Accessible is a design term that was first introduced in the 1950s to describe elements of the physical environment that can be used by people with disabilities. Originally, the term described facilities that could be accessed by wheelchair users, but it has evolved to include designs for a wider group of people with more diverse functional requirements.

Society's need for accessible design has increased as a result of continuing medical advances. Concurrent with the medical advances has been the development of new building technologies, such as residential elevators, wheelchair lifts, and power-door operators, that have made the provision of accessible facilities more practical and less expensive. Accessible design will continue to change as medical advances and building technologies continue to evolve.

From an architect's perspective, there is a difference between appropriate accessible design for public facilities and the best approach for private, custom, accessible projects. Public accessibility standards establish general design specifications that broadly meet the targeted population's needs. By contrast, custom accessible design should address the specific needs of an individual user.

CODES, LAWS, AND REGULATIONS

Although still an evolving field, there is already a proliferation of laws and codes governing the implementation of accessible design; therefore, architects must educate themselves, and stay current, in both the principles and the legal requirements of accessibility.

REGULATORY HISTORY OF ACCESSIBLE DESIGN

In 1961, the American National Standards Institute (ANSI) published "Accessible and Usable Buildings and Facilities," A117.1; the first national standard for accessible design. After its initial publication, many state and local jurisdictions began to adopt ANSI A117.1 as their accessibility code, although they often modified selected standards to suit their communities. ANSI A117.1 quickly became the most widely used accessibility standard in the United States.

ANSI A117.1 is periodically revised. In 1980, it was expanded to include housing standards focused primarily on the needs of wheelchair users (specifically paraplegics). In an effort to encourage states to adopt the standards and to promote uniformity; the 1986 revision eliminated all *scoping* requirements.

Scoping is the extent to which a standard is applied; for example, a standard may be applied to all project elements or to only a fraction of the elements. The 1980 ANSI A117.1 standard, for instance, requires provision of a "reasonable number" of wheelchair seating spaces in places of assembly but not fewer than two spaces. After publication of the 1986 ANSI A117.1 standard, scoping was left to the discretion of the local adopting authority, which usually based it on national model codes. ANSI A117.1 includes the "technical" requirement—or "how to"—make building elements accessible.

In 1998, ANSI A117.1 was expanded to include the technical requirements for dwelling and sleeping units consistent with the requirements in the Fair Housing Act (FHA).

As ICC/ANSI A117.1 has evolved to include new information and technologies, legislation has been passed in response, including:

- *Architectural Barriers Act (ABA):* Passed in 1968, the ABA was the first federal legislation that required accessible design in federal facilities.
- *Rehabilitation Act:* Congress enacted this act in 1973 to address the absence of federal accessibility standards, as well as the lack of an enforcement mechanism. In addition, the act required facilities built with federal funds, and facilities built by entities that receive federal funds, to be accessible to persons with disabilities. Section 502 of the 1973 Rehabilitation Act created a new federal agency, the Architectural and Transportation Barriers Compliance Board (Access Board) to develop and issue

minimum guidelines for design standards to be established by four standard-setting agencies.

- *Uniform Federal Accessibility Standards (UFAS):* In 1984, the Access Board issued the Uniform Federal Accessibility Standards (UFAS), which were established by the Department of Defense (DOD), the Department of Housing and Urban Development (HUD), the General Services Administration (GSA), and the U.S. Postal Service (USPS). UFAS is similar in format and content to the 1980 edition of A117.1.
- *Fair Housing Amendments Act (FHAA):* In 1988, Congress amended the Fair Housing Amendments Act (FHAA) to prohibit discriminating against individuals on the basis of disability. Although the Fair Housing Act Guidelines (FHAG) include design requirements, the FHAA is a civil rights law, not a building code. And because it is a federal law, neither state nor local building authorities can officially interpret the FHAG requirements, nor can local building inspectors enforce them. The 1988 FHAA was the first federal law to regulate private residential construction.
- *Americans with Disabilities Act (ADA):* In 1990, President George Herbert Walker Bush signed the ADA, a landmark piece of legislation that provided new civil rights protections for people with disabilities. Its guidelines included new federal accessibility standards and addressed the design and operation of privately owned public accommodations and state and local government facilities and programs.
- *ADA Accessibility Guidelines (ADAAG):* The ADAAG are very similar to the 1986 edition of ANSI A117.1 standards. ADA did not include housing design requirements because they were addressed in the earlier FHAA.

The Access Board is revising and updating its accessibility guidelines for buildings and facilities covered by the ADA of 1990 and the ABA of 1968. The final ADA/ABA Guidelines, dated July 23, 2004, will serve as the basis for the minimum standards when adopted by other federal agencies responsible for issuing enforceable standards. For the current status of this adoption process, visit the Access Board Web site (www.access-board.gov).

RELATIONSHIP BETWEEN CIVIL RIGHTS LAWS AND BUILDING CODES

The enactment of the 1988 FHAA and 1990 ADA created a complex relationship between federal laws and the local building codes that already existed throughout the United States. Although many of the accessible design requirements in the civil rights laws and the codes are similar, there have been considerable differences. During the last few years, however, there has been a significant effort to harmonize national model codes and ICC/ANSI A117.1 with the federal requirements.

Building codes are specific to a legal jurisdiction, such as a state, county, township, or city. These state/local regulations are usually based on national model codes developed by the International Code Council (ICC) (previously BOCA, ICBO, and SBCCI) and the National Fire Protection Association (NFPA). The state and local jurisdictions may modify the model codes and, as part of their review and enforcement process, make administrative rulings and interpretations. Over time, these modifications and interpretations make the design requirements of each municipality unique even though the underlying code is based on a national model.

Building officials use local codes to review architectural and engineering plans before they permit construction. They also perform on-site inspections to verify that the completed construction is in compliance.

Unlike municipal officials, federal agencies do not issue building permits and typically do not inspect construction. Furthermore, the federal government does not issue rulings or interpretations for individual projects. Civil rights law enforcement is a "complaint-based process" that HUD administers for fair housing and the Department of Justice (DOJ) administers for the ADA. These agencies may choose to act on a citizen complaint, or a complainant may elect to seek direct relief through federal courts. Legal decisions

regarding such complaints will gradually refine unclear design and construction components of federal civil rights laws. Architects must therefore monitor federal court rulings made throughout the United States to ensure they are apprised of the most current design standard information.

As civil rights laws, the FHAA and ADA include provisions for both facility design and construction and facility operation and management. Provisions that address operation and management create new legal responsibilities that are shared between facility designers and facility operators.

This arrangement changes the traditional architect-client relationship and alters the way architects must do business. For example, architects should carefully record programming decisions, as the intended use of a new space often establishes its accessibility requirements. ADA requirements for an employee workspace, for example, are different from those for a public space. If a facility operator later changes the use of a space, compliance becomes the owner's rather than the architect's responsibility. Another change is that architects must now evaluate an owner's project funding sources to determine the project's federal accessibility requirements. This precautionary step can prevent an architect's failure to comply with federal laws such as the 1973 Rehabilitation Act as a result of inaccurate funding information.

Terminology common to both civil rights law and building code standards can be confusing, because the same words may have different meanings. Because architects must deal with both types of standards, they should carefully review the definitions included in each.

ADA AND FHAA DESIGN REQUIREMENTS

The Americans with Disabilities Act (ADA) and the Fair Housing Amendments Act (FHAA) are the two broad federal civil rights laws that address accessible design and construction of both public and private facilities. The ADA applies to a wide range of public accommodations offered by private entities (Title III) and municipal facilities (Title II); the FHAA covers multifamily housing. Other federal laws such as the 1973 Rehabilitation Act may also apply to some projects. Architects should be aware that in many aspects federal civil rights laws are different from building codes. That means receiving a building permit does not indicate that a project design complies with these federal laws.

ADA REQUIREMENTS

The ADA includes design requirements for new facility construction, and for additions to and alterations of existing facilities that are owned, leased, or operated by both private entities and local governments. However, design standards and management responsibilities differ between the two owner groups.

Standards and responsibilities are described in the ADA, in Title III for private entities and in Title II for local governments. Title III includes design standards and scoping for general application and for certain specific building types, including transient lodging, medical care facilities, and libraries. Regulations issued by DOJ are contained in 28 CFR, Part 36.

Owners and operators of existing private facilities that serve the public have ADA construction responsibilities under what is called "barrier removal." Local governments also have the responsibility of making all their new and existing programs accessible. Meeting this ADA responsibility for municipal programs may sometimes require new construction or physical modifications to existing facilities. The ADA also prescribes employer responsibilities for changing their policies or modifying their facilities to accommodate employees with disabilities (Title I).

Several ADA concepts determine design requirements, such as "path-of–travel" components for renovation projects and the "ele-

Contributors:
Karen J. King, RA, University of New Mexico, Albuquerque, New Mexico; Rebecca Ingram Architect, Albuquerque, New Mexico; Kim A. Beasley, AIA, and Thomas D. Davies Jr., AIA, Paralyzed Veterans of America Architecture, Washington, DC.

vator exception" for small multistory buildings. It is imperative that architects familiarize themselves with all aspects of the law, as well as with the design standards.

ADA Title II requirements are based on the concept of "program accessibility," which is similar to Section 504 of the 1973 Rehabilitation Act for Federal Programs. ADA requires state and local governments to provide access to all their programs for people with disabilities. Local government program responsibility includes policies and operations as well as the built environment. To provide access to existing inaccessible programs, state and local governments must develop a "transition plan" that lists the necessary changes. Inaccessible programs can be addressed either by altering policies and procedures or by modifying physical structures or by a combination of both strategies.

FHAA REQUIREMENTS

The FHAA addresses new multifamily housing constructed either by private entities or local governments. Generally, the FHAA covers projects with four or more total dwelling or sleeping units in one structure that are built for sale or lease. This includes apartments and condominiums, as well as all types of congregate living arrangements such as dormitories, boarding houses, sorority and fraternity houses, group homes, assisted-living facilities and nursing homes. Typically, townhouses are exempted because they are multistory units. Existing housing structures and remodeling, conversion, or reuse projects are not covered by FHAA. The law's design standards include requirements for both individual dwelling units and common-use facilities such as lobbies, corridors, and parking.

The Fair Housing Accessibility Guidelines (FHAG) allow the exclusion of certain dwelling units because of site considerations such as steep topography and floodplains. The guidelines include site practicality tests for analyzing site constraints. Several major scoping issues such as multistory dwelling units and multiple ground-floor levels are discussed in the supplementary information included in the FHAG. Prior to project design, architects should carefully review this material as well as the guidelines themselves.

FEDERAL LEGISLATIVE PROCESS

To help understand current civil rights law design requirements and monitor the publication of new standards, architects should become familiar with the federal legislative process. Information on federal design standards is available within specific acts, in the resultant regulations, and in published guidelines. Additional information is available in the legislative history of an act and in the numerous documents issued during the "rule-making process."

The administrative process for implementing federal laws requires public notice (in the *Federal Register*) and a public comment period for any proposed new regulations or guidelines. Architects should monitor this ongoing process to track the new standards that are periodically added to the existing accessibility guidelines and to verify their adoption status. The architectural guidelines for laws such as the ADA are also periodically revised through the same rule-making process.

Technical assistance manuals (TAMs) are another design information source. Administering agencies such as the DOJ and HUD periodically publish these manuals to clarify existing guidelines or standards.

APPLICABLE FEDERAL STANDARDS FOR SPECIFIC PROJECTS

The first step in evaluating the accessibility requirements for a specific project is to determine which laws and regulations apply. Project accessibility requirements may be determined by answering the following questions:

- What type of building or structure will be built?
- Who owns the facility?
- Where will the construction funds originate?
- What other federal funding will the project's owner receive?
- Who are the intended users of a space or component?

Table 13.15 lists the applicable standards for many types of projects.

APPLICABLE ACCESSIBILITY STANDARDS FOR SAMPLE PROJECTS
13.15

PROJECT DESCRIPTION	FEDERAL LAWS	BUILDING CODES
Federally owned project of any type	1968 Architectural Barriers Act 1973 Rehabilitation Act Other standards as described by the agency	State and/or local building codes may apply.
Project that utilizes federal funds or is built by the recipient of federal funds (private or government)	1968 Architectural Barriers Act 1973 Rehabilitation Act, UFAS Other standards appropriate with ownership use and type	State and/or local building codes may apply.
Local government-owned commercial or public facility	ADA Title II 1973 Rehabilitation Act	State and/or local building codes may apply.
Local government-owned multifamily housing	ADA Title II 1973 Rehabilitation Act 1988 Fair Housing Amendments Act	State and/or local building codes may apply.
Privately owned public accommodation or commercial facility	ADA Title III	State and/or local building codes may apply.
Privately owned multifamily housing	1988 Fair Housing Amendments Act (Public accommodation spaces must meet ADA.)	State and/or local building codes may apply.
Privately leased, government-owned public accommodation	ADA Title III—Tenant ADA Title II—Owner	State and/or local building codes may apply.
Government-leased, privately owned public accommodation	1973 Rehabilitation Act—Tenant ADA Title II—Tenant ADA Title III—Owner	State and/or local building codes may apply.
Church-operated, church-owned facility	None	State and/or local building codes may apply.
Privately operated, church-owned facility	ADA Title III—Tenant None—Owner	State and/or local building codes may apply.
Church-operated, privately owned facility	None—Tenant ADA Title III—Owner	State and/or local building codes may apply.

FEDERAL RULE-MAKING PROCESS
13.16

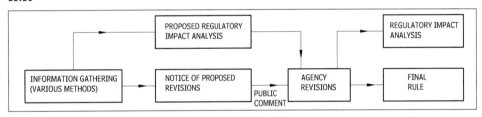

The technical material covered in the discussions here is drawn from the minimum legal standards required to make buildings, sites, and their constituent parts accessible. Note that these are "minimums" based on a calculated percentage of the population and, as such, are still quite challenging for many individuals. For many reasons, including deviations in finish material dimensions and construction errors, architects should consider exceeding the minimums and would be well advised to gain an understanding of how people with disabilities use spaces.

NOTES

13.15 Temporary facilities must meet the same federal standards as similar permanent facilities.
State and local building codes may apply for all types of projects.

Contributors:
Kim A. Beasley, AIA, and Thomas D. Davies Jr., AIA, Paralyzed Veterans of America Architecture, Washington, DC.

BUILDING BLOCKS

MANEUVERING CLEARANCES
13.17

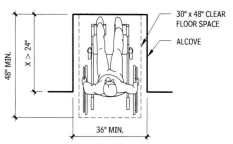

30" x 48" CLEAR FLOOR SPACE

ALCOVE

48" MIN.

X > 24"

36" MIN.

FORWARD APPROACH – ALCOVE

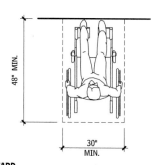

48" MIN.

30" MIN.

FORWARD

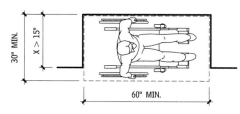

30" MIN.

X > 15"

60" MIN.

PARALLEL APPROACH – ALCOVE

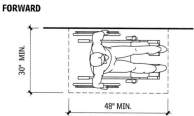

30" MIN.

48" MIN.

PARALLEL

MANEUVERING CLEARANCES
13.18

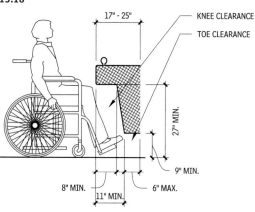

17" - 25"

KNEE CLEARANCE

TOE CLEARANCE

27" MIN.

9" MIN.

8" MIN.

11" MIN.

6" MAX.

KNEE AND TOE CLEARANCES

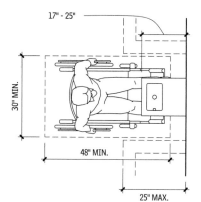

17" - 25"

30" MIN.

48" MIN.

25" MAX.

WHEELCHAIR TURNING SPACE
13.19

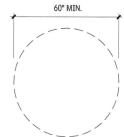

60" MIN.

CIRCULAR

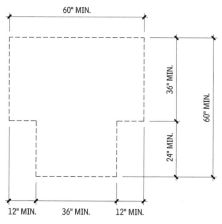

60" MIN.

36" MIN.

24" MIN.

60" MIN.

12" MIN.   36" MIN.   12" MIN.

T-SHAPED

Knee and toe clearance that is included as part of a T-shaped turning space is allowed only at either the base of the T or on one arm of the T. In some configurations, the obstruction of part of the T-shape may make it impossible for a wheelchair user to maneuver to the desired location. Floor surfaces of a turning space must have a slope that is not steeper than 1:48.

NOTES

13.17 a. Floor surfaces of a clear floor space must have a slope not steeper than 1:48.
b. One full, unobstructed side of the clear floor space must adjoin or overlap an accessible route or adjoin another clear floor space.

Contributors:
Kim A. Beasley, AIA, and Thomas D. Davies Jr., AIA, Paralyzed Veterans of America Architecture, Washington, DC.

REACH RANGES FOR ACCESSIBILITY

PARALLEL/SIDE REACH LIMITS
13.20

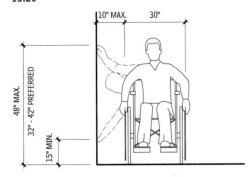

HIGH AND LOW SIDE REACH LIMITS – UNOBSTRUCTED

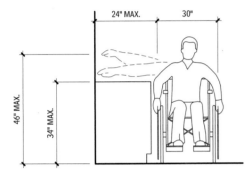

MAXIMUM SIDE REACH OVER OBSTRUCTION

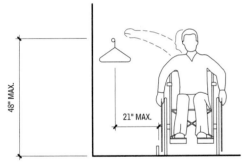

CLOSET

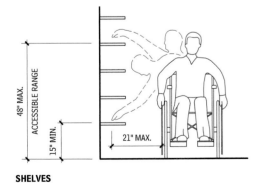

SHELVES

ICC/ANSI A117.1 requires the unobstructed side reach to be 15 in. minimum to 48 in. maximum, with these exceptions:

1. ICC/ANSI A117.1 provides exception for existing elements located 54 in. maximum above the floor or ground.
2. ICC/ANSI A117.1 provides exception for elevator car controls, allowing buttons at 54 in. maximum, with a parallel approach, where the elevator serves more than 16 openings. This exception

may be revisited in future editions, when the elevator industry has had an opportunity to develop alternate control configurations.
3. ICC/ANSI A117.1 does not apply the 48-in. restriction to tactile signs. Tactile signs must be installed so the tactile characters are between 48 and 60 in. above the floor. Below this height, tactile characters are difficult to read by standing persons, as the hand must be bent awkwardly or turned over (similar to reading upside down) to read the message.

REACH RANGES
13.21

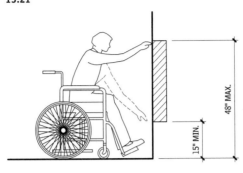

UNOBSTRUCTED FORWARD REACH

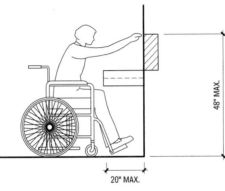

OBSTRUCTED HIGH FORWARD REACH

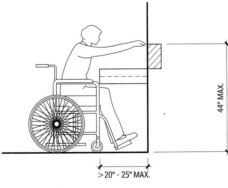

OBSTRUCTED HIGH FORWARD REACH

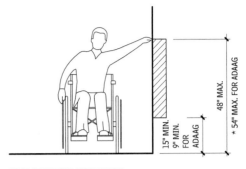

UNOBSTRUCTED SIDE REACH

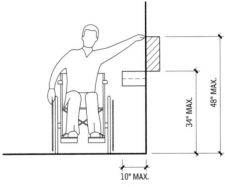

OBSTRUCTED SIDE REACH

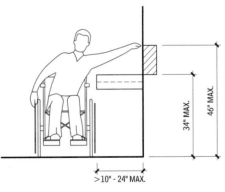

OBSTRUCTED SIDE REACH

CHILDREN'S REACH RANGES FROM A WHEELCHAIR (IN.)
13.22

FORWARD OR SIDE REACH	AGES 3 AND 4	AGES 5–8	AGES 9–12
High (maximum)	36	40	44
Low (minimum)	20	18	16

Contributor:
Lawrence G. Perry, AIA, Silver Spring, Maryland.

OPERABLE PARTS

Accessible controls and operating mechanisms should be operable with one hand and not require tight grasping, pinching, or twisting of the wrist. Operating force must not exceed 5 lb.

PROTRUDING OBJECTS IN CIRCULATION PATHS

FREESTANDING OBJECTS
13.23

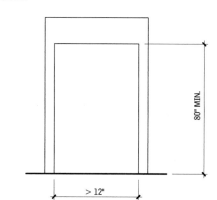

ELEVATION

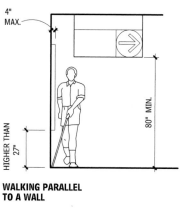

ELEVATION

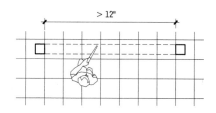

PLAN

POST-MOUNTED PROTRUDING OBJECTS

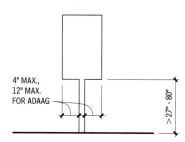

ELEVATION

REDUCED VERTICAL CLEARANCE
13.24

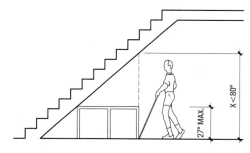

OVERHEAD HAZARD PROTECTION—EXAMPLES
13.25

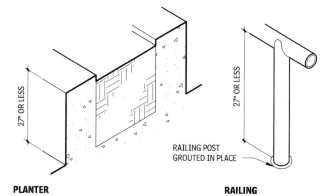

PLANTER   **RAILING**

RAILING POST GROUTED IN PLACE

DIMENSIONS OF PROTRUDING OBJECTS
13.26

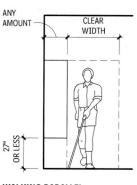

WALKING PARALLEL TO A WALL

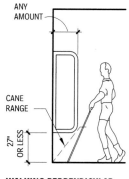

WALKING PARALLEL TO A WALL

WALKING PERPENDICULAR TO A WALL

NOTES

13.24 a. Protection from overhead hazards can be provided by built-in elements such as planters or railings, or curbs.
b. Designers can reduce or eliminate most overhead hazards (e.g., low-headroom hazards can be avoided by enclosing areas under stairs and escalators).
13.26 a. Wall sconces, fire extinguisher cabinets, drinking fountains, signs, and suspended lighting fixtures are examples of protruding objects.

b. Some standards allow doorstops and door closers 78 in. minimum above the floor.
c. Protruding objects are not permitted to reduce the required width of an accessible route.

Contributor:
Lawrence G. Perry, AIA, Silver Spring, Maryland.

ACCESSIBLE ROUTES AND WALKING SURFACES

CLEAR WIDTH OF AN ACCESSIBLE ROUTE
13.27

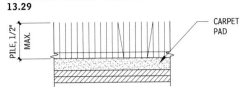

60" MIN.	48" MIN.
TWO WHEELCHAIRS	**ONE WHEELCHAIR AND ONE AMBULATORY PERSON**

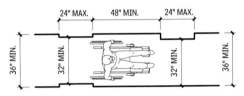

SINGLE WHEELCHAIR

CHANGES IN LEVEL
13.28

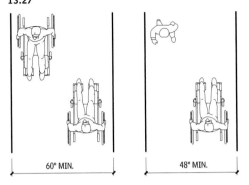

FLOOR AND GROUND SURFACES
13.29

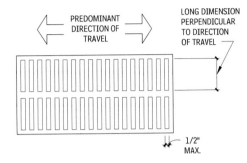

CARPET ON FLOOR OR GROUND SURFACES

PREDOMINANT DIRECTION OF TRAVEL

LONG DIMENSION PERPENDICULAR TO DIRECTION OF TRAVEL

1/2" MAX.

OPENING IN FLOOR OR GROUND SURFACES

CLEAR WIDTH AT TURNS
13.30
Source: ICC/ANSI A117.1.

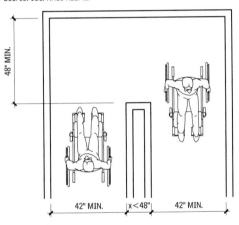

180° TURN

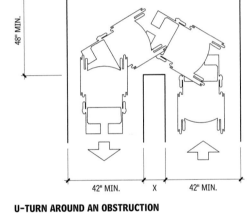

U-TURN AROUND AN OBSTRUCTION

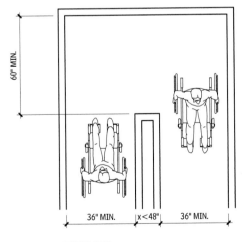

180° TURN – EXCEPTION

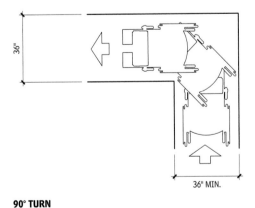

90° TURN

NOTES

13.27 Clear width of the accessible route must be 36 in.; however, it may be reduced to 32 in. for a distance of 24 in., as shown.
13.28 a. Changes in level greater than 1/2 in. must be ramped.
b. Some standards prohibit changes in level in clear floor space, maneuvering clearances, wheelchair turning space, and access aisles.
13.29 a. All surfaces must be firm, stable, and slip-resistant.
b. Carpets must be securely attached with a firm pad, or no pad, and a level loop, textured loop, level cut pile, or level cut/uncut pile texture.

c. Other openings, such as in-wood decking or ornamental gratings, must be designed so that a 1/2-in.-diameter sphere cannot pass through the opening. The potential for wood shrinkage should be considered.
13.30 If *x* is less than 48 in., the route must be 42 in. minimum, except where the clear width at the turn is 60 in. minimum.

Contributor:
Lawrence G. Perry, AIA, Silver Spring, Maryland.

REQUIREMENTS FOR ACCESSIBLE ROUTES

Accessible routes are generally required as follows:

- *Site arrival points:* From each type of site arrival point (public transportation stops, accessible parking spaces, passenger loading zones, and public streets or sidewalks) to an accessible entrance. Consult the applicable regulation to determine the required number of accessible entrances. Building codes generally require that at least 50 percent of the public entrances, but no less than one, be accessible. Under the Fair Housing Accessibility Guidelines (FHAG), site conditions may allow some buildings to be exempt from this requirement.
- *Within a site:* Between accessible buildings, facilities, elements, and spaces on the site.
- *Intent:* The intent of this requirement is not to require accessible routes where no "connection" is otherwise intended between buildings or facilities, but to ensure that where a connection is intended an accessible connection is also provided.
- *FHAG vehicular route exception:* FHAG allows a vehicular route to be provided in lieu of an accessible route between covered dwelling units and public and common-use site facilities where the slope of the site or other restrictions prevents the use of an accessible route. Accessible parking spaces are required at the covered dwelling units and at the facilities served only by the vehicular route.
- *Building code vehicular route exception:* Model building codes also allow the use of a vehicular route in lieu of an accessible route where the only means of access between two accessible facilities is "a vehicular way, not intended for pedestrian access." This exception is not limited to slope or other site restrictions.
- *Multilevel buildings and facilities:* Between all levels, including mezzanines, in multistory buildings, unless exempted.
- *ADA elevator exception:* Buildings with only two floors are exempt from providing an accessible route to the upper or lower level. Buildings with less than 3000 sq ft per floor, regardless of height, are exempt from providing an accessible route to upper or lower floor levels. Neither exception applies to shopping centers, offices of professional health care providers, public transportation terminals, or state and local government facilities.
- *Building code elevator exception:* Model building codes generally exempt a maximum aggregate area of 3000 sq ft, regardless of the number of levels. Similar to the ADA restrictions, this exception cannot be used in offices of health care providers, passenger transportation facilities, or mercantile occupancies with multiple tenants. Consult the applicable local code.
- *FHAG elevator requirements:* Model code and FHAG elevator requirements for buildings containing dwelling units, and not public or common-use spaces. The presence of an elevator determines the extent of units covered (and the floors required to be served by an accessible route). When elevators are provided, they generally must serve all floors; an exception is provided for elevators serving only as a means of access from a garage to the lowest floor with dwelling units. When elevators are not provided, only the "ground floor" units are subject to the FHAG and model code Type B requirements. In mixed-use construction, an accessible route is required to the first level containing dwelling units, regardless of its location. Consult FHAG and model codes for specific requirements.
- *Levels not containing accessible elements or spaces:* For facilities in which only a percentage of the spaces provided are required to be accessible (assembly, residential, institutional, and storage), the model codes do not require an accessible route to serve levels not containing required accessible spaces. For example, a motel would not require an accessible route to upper floors if all required accessible units or rooms and common areas were located on the accessible level. Separate requirements for dispersion of accessible elements and spaces may still require multiple accessible levels. Consult the applicable local code.
- *Accessible spaces and elements:* To all spaces and elements that are required to be accessible.
- *Toilet rooms and bathrooms:* ADA and the model codes generally require that all toilet and bathing rooms be accessible. This does not trigger a requirement for accessible routes if the floor level is not otherwise required to have an accessible route.

- *Alterations:* The ADA and the model building codes generally do not require that altered elements trigger a requirement for accessible routes to the elements, unless covered under specific "primary function" requirements. In alterations involving "primary function" areas, the accessible route obligation is triggered but is subject to specific limitations. Consult the ADA and the applicable local code.

COMPONENTS OF ACCESSIBLE ROUTES

Accessible routes are permitted to include the following elements:

- Walking surfaces with a slope of less than 1:20
- Curb ramps
- Ramps
- Elevators
- Platform (wheelchair) lifts (The use of lifts in new construction is limited to locations where they are specifically permitted by the applicable regulations. Lifts are generally permitted to be used as part of an accessible route in alterations.)

Each component has specific technical criteria that must be applied for use as part of an accessible route. Consult the applicable code or regulation.

LOCATION OF ACCESSIBLE ROUTES

Accessible routes should be located as follows:

- *Interior routes:* Where an accessible route is required between floor levels, and the general circulation path between levels is an interior route, the accessible route must also be an interior route.
- *Relation to circulation paths:* Accessible routes must "coincide with, or be located in, the same area as a general circulation path." Avoid making the accessible route a "second-class" means of circulation. Consult the applicable regulations for additional specific requirements regarding location of accessible routes.
- *Directional signs:* Where the accessible route departs from the general circulation path and is not easily identified, directional signs should be provided as necessary to indicate the accessible route. The signs should be located so that a person does not need to backtrack.

ACCESSIBLE CURB RAMP PLAN
13.31

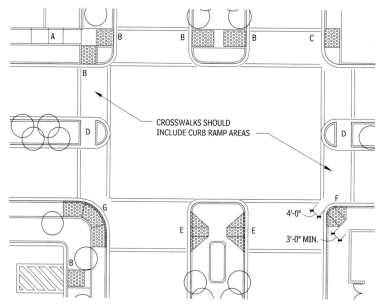

CROSSWALKS SHOULD INCLUDE CURB RAMP AREAS

4'-0"

3'-0" MIN.

CURBS AND PARKING

Follow these design guidelines for accessible curb ramps and passenger loading.

- Design storm drainage utilities to shed water away from curb ramps.
- The dimensions shown in Figures 13.31 to 13.33 are for new construction. For alterations when these dimensions are impractical, refer to guidelines and standards.
- Refer to applicable codes, standards, and regulations for detectable warning requirements and locations.

CURB RAMP SECTION
13.32

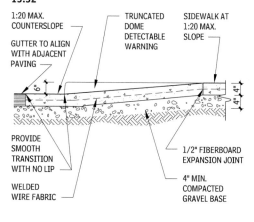

1:20 MAX. COUNTERSLOPE

TRUNCATED DOME DETECTABLE WARNING

SIDEWALK AT 1:20 MAX. SLOPE

GUTTER TO ALIGN WITH ADJACENT PAVING

6"

4" 4"

PROVIDE SMOOTH TRANSITION WITH NO LIP

WELDED WIRE FABRIC

1/2" FIBERBOARD EXPANSION JOINT

4" MIN. COMPACTED GRAVEL BASE

Contributor:
Lawrence G. Perry, AIA, Silver Spring, Maryland.

CURB RAMP TYPES
13.33

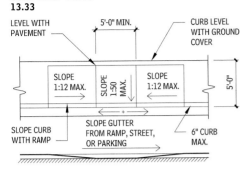

TYPE A

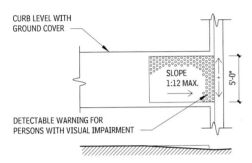

TYPE B

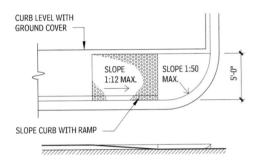

TYPE C

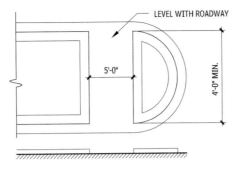

TYPE D

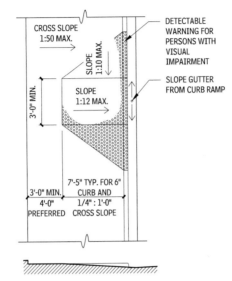

TYPE E

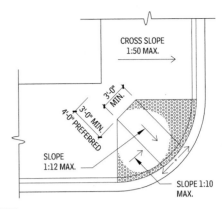

TYPE F

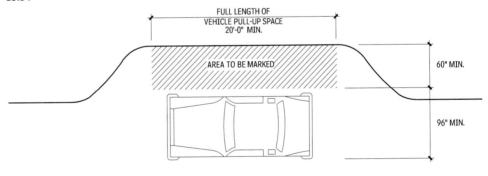

TYPE G

PASSENGER LOADING ZONES

Where passenger loading zones are provided, at least one accessible parking loading zone must be provided. An accessible parking loading zone is also required where there is valet parking.

Accessible passenger loading zones must have a 96-in.-wide, minimum, by 20-ft-long vehicle pull-up space, with an adjacent access aisle that is 60 in. wide and as long as the vehicle pull-up space. The access aisle must be marked, at the same level as the vehicle pull-up space, and adjoin an accessible route.

The vehicle pull-up space and access aisle must be level, with slopes no steeper than 1:48. The accessible parking loading zone and the vehicular route to the entrance and exit serving it must have a vertical clearance of 114 in. minimum.

ACCESSIBLE PASSENGER LOADING ZONE
13.34

NOTES

13.33 For types E and F, in alterations where there is no landing at the top of curb ramps, curb ramp side flares must not be steeper than 1:12.

Contributors:
Mary S. Smith, PE Walker Parking Consultants/Engineers, Inc., Indianapolis, Indiana; Mark J. Mazz, AIA, PA, Hyattsville, Maryland.

ACCESSIBLE PARKING

The information provided here conforms to the Americans with Disabilities Act Accessibility Guidelines for Buildings and Facilities (36 CFR 1191; July 26, 1991), also known as ADAAG, and Bulletin #6: Parking (August 2003), both issued by the Architectural and Transportation Barriers Compliance Board, and ICC/ANSI A117.1, 2003. State and local requirements may differ and the requirements providing the greater access apply.

- Accessible parking stalls should be 8 ft wide with an adjacent 5ft access aisle.
- Van-accessible stalls should be 11 ft wide with an adjacent 5-ft access aisle; or they are permitted to be 8 ft wide with an adjacent 8 ft access aisle. The access aisle must be accessible from the passenger side of the vehicle. Backing into 90° stalls from a two-way aisle is an acceptable method of achieving this; but with angled parking, the aisle must be on the right side. Vehicular clearance at the van-accessible stall, adjacent access aisle, and along the path of travel to and from a van-accessible stall should be 8 ft-2 in. In parking structures, van-accessible stalls may be grouped on a single level.
- Access aisles must be clearly marked and be the same length as the adjacent parking space. They also must be at the same level as parking stalls (not above, at sidewalk height). Required curb ramps cannot be located in access aisles.
- Parking spaces and access aisles should be level with surface slopes, not exceeding 1:50 (2 percent) in any direction.
- The stalls required for a specific facility may be relocated to another location if equivalent or greater accessibility in terms of distance, cost, and convenience is ensured.
- Accessible stalls in the numbers shown in Table 13.35 must be included in all parking facilities.
- The access aisle must join an accessible route to the accessible entrance. It is recommended that accessible routes be configured to minimize wheelchair travel behind parked vehicles.
- Signs with the International Symbol of Accessibility are required for accessible spaces, unless there are four or fewer total spaces provided. Signs must be mounted 60 in. minimum from the ground surface to the bottom of the sign.
- Accessible parking spaces must be on the shortest accessible route to the accessible building entrance. If there is more than one accessible entrance with adjacent parking, accessible parking must be dispersed and located near the accessible entrances.
- The accessible parking spaces must be located on the shortest route to an accessible pedestrian entrance in parking facilities that do not serve a particular building.
- When different types of parking are provided—for example, surface, carport, and garage spaces—the accessible parking spaces must be dispersed among the various types.

REQUIRED MINIMUM NUMBER OF ACCESSIBLE PARKING SPACES
13.35

TOTAL SPACES PROVIDED	REQUIRED MINIMUM NUMBER OF ACCESSIBLE SPACES[a]
1 to 25	1
26 to 50	2
51 to 75	3
76 to 100	4
101 to 150	5
151 to 200	6
201 to 300	7
301 to 400	8
401 to 500	9
501 to 1000	2% of total
More than 1000	20, plus one for each 100 over 1000

PARKING SPACE AND ACCESS AISLE LAYOUT
13.36

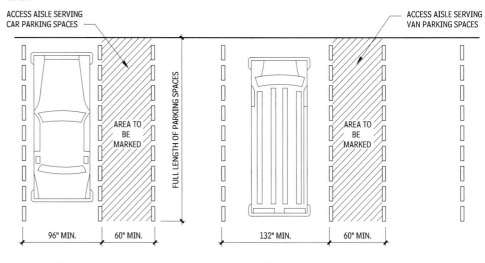

STANDARD ACCESSIBLE SPACE   **VAN-ACCESSIBLE SPACE**

ACCESSIBLE PARKING LAYOUTS
13.37

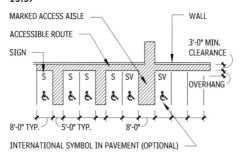

INTERNATIONAL SYMBOL IN PAVEMENT (OPTIONAL)

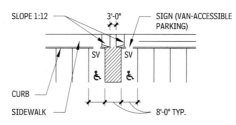

S = ACCESSIBLE PARKING SIGN
SV = VAN-ACCESSIBLE PARKING SIGN

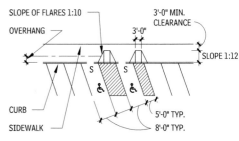

Following are exceptions to the requirements outlined in Table 13.98:

- At facilities providing outpatient medical care and other services, 10 percent of the parking spaces serving visitors and patients must be accessible.
- At facilities specializing in treatment or services for persons with mobility impairments, 20 percent of the spaces provided for visitors and patients must be accessible.
- The information in Table 13.35 does not apply to valet parking facilities, but such facilities must have an accessible loading zone. One or more self-park, van-accessible stalls are recommended for patrons with specially-equipped driving controls.
- The requirements for residential facilities differ slightly among applicable codes and guidelines, but generally 2 percent of the parking is required to be accessible. This parking must be dispersed among the various types of parking, including surface, covered carports, and detached garages.

ACCESSIBLE PARKING IN DEDICATED BAY
13.38

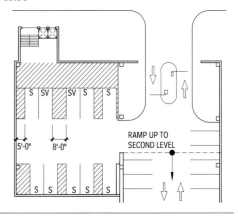

NOTES

13.35 a. For every six or fraction of six required accessible spaces, at least one must be a van-accessible parking space

Contributors
Mary S. Smith, PE, Walker Parking Consultants/Engineers, Inc., Indianapolis, Indiana; Mark J. Mazz, AIA, PA, Hyattsville, Maryland.

ACCESSIBLE RAMPS

RAMPS

- Accessible ramps must have running slopes of 1:12 or less; surfaces with a running slope greater than 1:20 are considered ramps. All design parameters shown on Figure 13.39 are based on ICC/ANSI A117.1. Provide ramps with the least possible running slope. Wherever possible, accompany ramps with stairs for use by those individuals for whom distance presents a greater barrier than steps.
- Design outdoor ramps and approaches so water will not accumulate on the surface. Maximum cross slope is 1:48.
- Landings should be level at top and bottom of ramp run and at least as wide as the run leading to it. A 60 by 60 in. landing is required where ramp changes direction. Provide level maneuvering clearances for doors adjacent to landings. If doors are subject to locking, landings must be sized to provide a wheelchair turning space.
- Handrails are required on both sides when rise is greater than 6 in.
- Edge protection is required at ramps and landings. Refer to local building codes for guard requirements.

COMPONENTS OF A RAMP
13.39

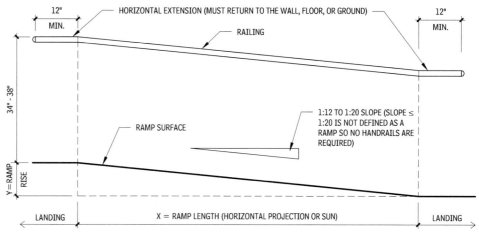

SLOPE = Y:X, WHERE X IS A LEVEL PLANE

HANDRAIL DESIGN
13.40

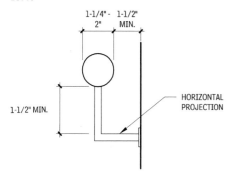

CIRCULAR

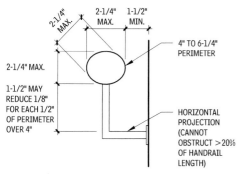

NONCIRCULAR

RAMP SECTIONS
13.41

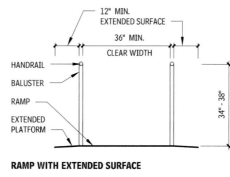

RAMP WITH EXTENDED SURFACE

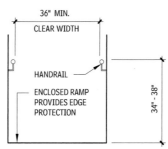

ENCLOSED RAMP

Dimensions are based on ICC/ANSI A117.1. Provide continuous handrails at both sides of ramps and stairs and at the inside handrail of switchback or dogleg ramps and stairs. If handrails are not continuous at bottom, top, or landings, provide handrail extensions as shown in the ramp example in Figure 13.39; ends of handrails must be rounded or returned smoothly to floor, wall, or post. Provide handrails of size and configuration shown and gripping surfaces uninterrupted by newel posts or other construction elements; handrails must not rotate within their fittings. The handrails and adjacent surfaces must be free from sharp or abrasive elements.

CURB OR BARRIER
13.42

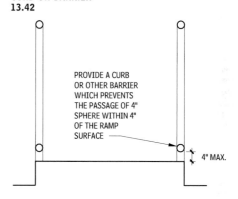

PROVIDE A CURB OR OTHER BARRIER WHICH PREVENTS THE PASSAGE OF 4" SPHERE WITHIN 4" OF THE RAMP SURFACE

Contributor:
Lawrence G. Perry, AIA, Silver Spring, Maryland.

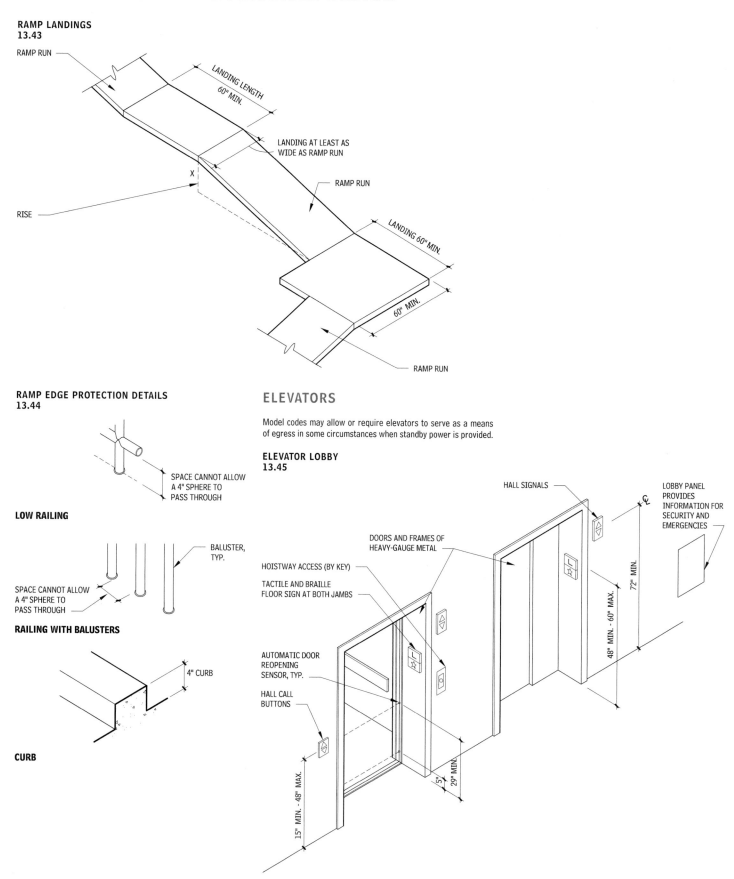

RAMP LANDINGS
13.43

RAMP RUN

LANDING LENGTH
60" MIN.

LANDING AT LEAST AS
WIDE AS RAMP RUN

RAMP RUN

X

RISE

LANDING 60" MIN.

60" MIN.

RAMP RUN

RAMP EDGE PROTECTION DETAILS
13.44

SPACE CANNOT ALLOW
A 4" SPHERE TO
PASS THROUGH

LOW RAILING

BALUSTER,
TYP.

SPACE CANNOT ALLOW
A 4" SPHERE TO
PASS THROUGH

RAILING WITH BALUSTERS

4" CURB

CURB

ELEVATORS

Model codes may allow or require elevators to serve as a means
of egress in some circumstances when standby power is provided.

ELEVATOR LOBBY
13.45

HALL SIGNALS

LOBBY PANEL
PROVIDES
INFORMATION FOR
SECURITY AND
EMERGENCIES

DOORS AND FRAMES OF
HEAVY-GAUGE METAL

HOISTWAY ACCESS (BY KEY)

TACTILE AND BRAILLE
FLOOR SIGN AT BOTH JAMBS

72" MIN.

48" MIN. - 60" MAX.

AUTOMATIC DOOR
REOPENING
SENSOR, TYP.

HALL CALL
BUTTONS

29" MIN.

5"

15" MIN. - 48" MAX.

NOTE

13.43 Required handrails and ramp edge protection are not shown in
this drawing. Building codes require a guard when the drop-off adjacent
to any walking surface is greater than 30 in. This would include ramps,
stairs, and landings.

Contributor:
Lawrence G. Perry, AIA, Silver Spring, Maryland.

Elevator doors must open and close automatically and have a reopening device that will stop and reopen the car and hoistway door if the door is obstructed. Although the device cannot require contact to activate, contact can occur before the door reverses direction. The device must remain effective for at least 20 seconds.

Tactile designations at each jamb of hoistway doors should be 2 in. high, a maximum of 60 in. above the floor. A five-pointed star should be included at the main entry level.

Hall call buttons should be raised or flush, 15 to 48 in. unobstructed above the floor measured to the center line of the highest operable part, with the up button located above the down button.

Audible hall signals should sound once for cars traveling in the up direction and twice for cars traveling down. Check the applicable regulations for required decibel level and frequency of audible signals. In-car signals are permitted in lieu of hall signals, as long as they meet all the requirements for visibility and timing.

DESTINATION-ORIENTED ELEVATOR SYSTEMS

Destination-oriented elevator systems assign passengers to specific cars by requiring them to enter their destination floor at a keypad or by other means, such as use of a coded identification card. ICC/ANSI A117.1 provides detailed accessibility criteria for this type of elevator system.

Destination-oriented elevator systems must provide both an audible and a visible signal to indicate the responding car. The audible signal is activated by pressing a tactile button identified by the International Symbol for Accessibility. The tactile button must be located immediately below the keypad or floor buttons. A visible display is required in the car to identify the registered destinations for each trip, and an automatic verbal announcement is required to announce the floor as the car stops. Tactile signs at hoistway jambs are required to identify not only the floor level but also each car.

ICC/ANSI A117.1 allows use of a telephone-style keypad in lieu of buttons for each floor. Keypads used for destination floor input must have a telephone keypad arrangement, with a tactile dot on the number-5 key.

ELEVATOR EMERGENCY COMMUNICATIONS

Elevator cars must provide an emergency two-way communication system between the car and a point outside the hoistway. Controls must be located within accessible reach ranges. When the system includes a handset, the cord must be at least 29 in. long. The system must provide both audible and visible signals; it cannot be limited to voice communication.

ELEVATOR CAR POSITION INDICATORS

Within elevator cars, audible and visible signals are required to identify the location of the car. Visible signals at least 1/2-in. high must be provided for each floor the car serves; these signals must illuminate to indicate the floors at which the car stops or passes.

Audible signals for new elevators must be automatic verbal announcements that indicate the floor at each stop. Exceptions allow the use of audible signals for some low-rise hydraulic elevators.

ELEVATOR CAR CONTROL PANELS

ICC/ANSI A117.1 requires all elevator car controls to be 15 in. minimum and 48 in. maximum above the floor. An exception is provided for elevator cars serving 16 or more openings, where a parallel approach is provided. Controls as high as 54 in. are allowed. When car control buttons are higher than 48 in. sequential step scanning must be provided. Existing elevators allow controls at 54 in. with a parallel approach until the panel is changed out. Buttons must be at least 3/4 in. in diameter and can be raised or flush. Existing recessed buttons are generally permitted to remain. Buttons for floor designations should be located in ascending order. Visual characters, tactile characters, and Braille are required to identify buttons. Tactile characters and Braille should be to the immediate left of each button.

CONTROL PANEL HEIGHT
13.46

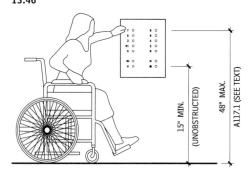

ASME A17.1, "Safety Code for Elevators and Escalators," applies to all elevators and escalators and covers general elevator safety and operational requirements. It has been adopted in virtually all jurisdictions. All sizes shown in this discussion are based on ICC/ANSI A117.1, which contains extensive accessibility provisions for passenger elevators, destination-oriented elevator systems, limited-use/limited-application elevators, and private residence elevators. The ASME A18.1, "Safety Standard for Platform Lifts and Stairway Chairlifts," applies to all lifts, along with other applicable codes and standards. Consult the applicable accessibility regulations for elevator, escalator, and lifts for exceptions and requirements.

INSIDE DIMENSIONS OF ACCESSIBLE ELEVATOR CARS
13.47

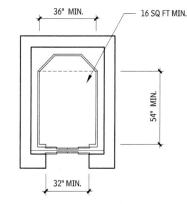

EXISTING CAR CONFIGURATION

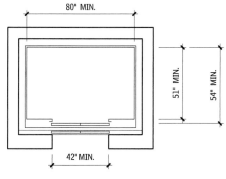

CENTERED DOOR LOCATION

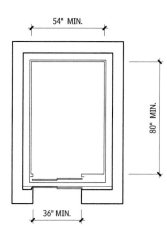

ANY DOOR LOCATION

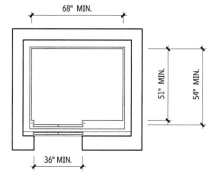

OFF-CENTER DOOR LOCATION

Contributor:
Lawrence G. Perry, AIA, Silver Spring, Maryland.

INSIDE DIMENSIONS OF ACCESSIBLE ELEVATOR CARS (continued)
13.47

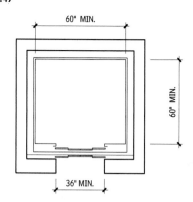

ANY DOOR LOCATION

A 5/8-in. tolerance is permitted at 36-in. elevator doors, allowing the use of standard 35-3/8 in. clear-width doors. Any other car configuration that provides a 36-in. door and either a 60-in. diameter or T-shaped wheelchair turning space within the car, with the door in the closed position, is permitted. Inside car dimensions are intended to allow an individual in a wheelchair to enter the car, access the controls, and exit.

PRIVATE RESIDENCE ELEVATOR
13.48

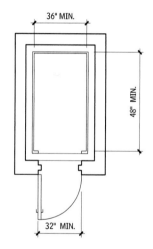

This type of elevator is permitted as part of an accessible route within dwelling units. Car size shown is per ICC/ANSI A117.1. Verify the car size requirements of applicable accessibility regulations. Controls are located in a side wall 12 in. minimum from an adjacent wall. Doors must be located on the narrow end of the car. Car door/gates are required to be power-operated. Cars with openings on only one end require a person in a wheelchair to either enter or exit by moving backward; therefore, in a single-opening configuration, the hoistway doors/gate must be low-energy, power-operated doors. Cars with openings on each end allow a wheelchair user to roll through (enter and exit in a forward direction); manual, self-closing hoistway doors/gates are permitted. A telephone with a cord length of 29 in. and signal device are required in the car.

LIMITED-USE/LIMITED-APPLICATION ELEVATOR
13.49

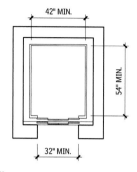

NEW

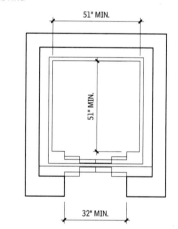

EXISTING

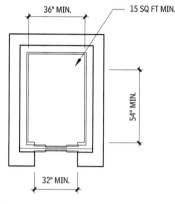

NEW CONSTRUCTION EXCEPTION 1

Limited-use/limited-application (LULA) elevators are permitted to be used as part of an accessible route in certain conditions. Check applicable accessibility regulations for permitted installations. LULAs must comply with ASME A17.1. LULA elevators have a smaller car size, requiring a person in a wheelchair to either enter or exit by moving backward, unless the car has openings on each end. Car size and vertical travel is limited by ASME A17.1. Because LULAs move more slowly than other passenger elevators, they may not be appropriate when large numbers of people must be served. Car controls are centered on a side wall. Low-energy, power-operated swing doors are permitted at the hoistway entrance, provided they remain open for 20 seconds when activated. See ICC/ANSI A117.1 for emergency communication, signage, control and signal requirements.

WHEELCHAIR LIFTS

VERTICAL WHEELCHAIR LIFTS

Vertical wheelchair (platform) lifts are generally permitted to be used as part of an accessible route in new construction only to reach limited access or small spaces, such as:

- Performing areas in assembly occupancies
- Wheelchair spaces in assembly occupancies
- Seating spaces in outdoor dining with A5 occupancy (bleachers, grandstands, stadiums, ect.)
- Courtrooms
- Spaces not open to the public with an occupant load of no more than five spaces within a dwelling unit

In some regulations, wheelchair lifts are permitted where site constraints prevent the use of ramps or elevators.

VERTICAL WHEELCHAIR LIFTS
13.50

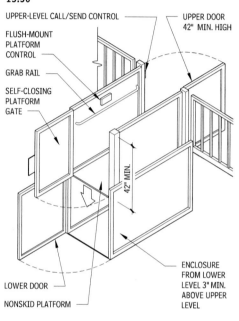

When vertical wheelchair lifts are used in new construction, an accessible means of egress may be required from the spaces served by the lifts. These lifts are not permitted to be used as part of an accessible means of egress except where allowed as part of an accessible route by model codes. In such circumstances, standby power is required.

Vertical Wheelchair lifts are generally permitted as part of an accessible route in alterations to existing buildings.

Vertical Wheelchair lifts that are part of an accessible route are required to comply with ASME A18.1 and must provide a wheelchair-sized clear floor space, level floor surfaces, and accessible operable parts. These lifts are not permitted to be attendant-operated; they must allow for unassisted entry and exit.

ICC/ANSI A117.1 allows self-closing manual doors or gates on lifts with doors or gates on opposite sides (a roll-through configuration). Other lifts must have low-energy, power-operated doors or gates that remain open for at least 20 seconds. Doors/gates located on the ends of lifts must provide 32 in. clear width; doors/gates located on the side of a lift must provide 42 in. clear width.

Contributor:
Lawrence G. Perry, AIA, Silver Spring, Maryland.

GENERAL

Not all lifts comply with ADAAG and ICC/ANSI A117.1 requirements. Verify applicable regulations before selecting a specific type of lift. Consult ASME 18.1, "Safety Standard for Platform Lifts and Stairway Chairlifts."

Wheelchair lifts are suitable for retrofits of buildings that are not barrier-free. Bridges are available from manufacturers for installation over stairs. Recommended speed is 10 to 19 fpm. Capacity should be 500 to 750 lb.

Lifts operate on standard household current and are suitable for interior or exterior applications.

VERTICAL WHEELCHAIR LIFT REQUIREMENTS
13.51

TYPICAL	PRIVATE RESIDENCE
42" high door for top and bottom landings; mechanical/electrical interlock, solid construction	36" high door for top landing; bottom landing can have guard (other requirements similar to 42" high door)
Platform sides: 42" high, solid construction	Platform sides 36" high, solid construction
Grab rails	Same
Enclosure or telescoping toe guard	Obstruction switch on platform
Maximum travel 12'	Maximum travel 10'
	Automatic guard 6" at bottom landing in lieu of door
Push button operation for rider	Push button operation for rider

WHEELCHAIR LIFTS
13.52

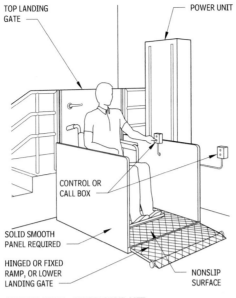
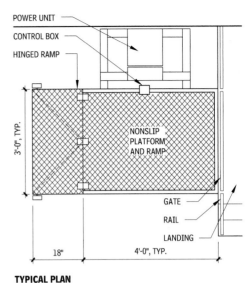

TYPICAL PLAN

OVERALL VIEW – WHEELCHAIR LIFT

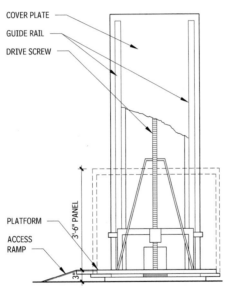

SCREW-DRIVEN LIFT PLATFORM IS LIFTED ALONG A THREADED ROD, WHICH IS ROTATED BY THE POWER UNIT

CUTAWAY SECTION

Inclined wheelchair lifts can be adapted to straight-run and spiral stairs. Standard types run along guide rails or tubes fastened to solid wall, stairs, or floor structure. Power units may be placed at the top or bottom of the lift run or in the lift chassis, depending on the manufacturer. Some inclined lift systems fold up out of the way for daily stair use.

Recommended speed is 20 to 25 fpm on straight runs, 10 fpm on curved sections. Capacity should be 500 lb. The typical platform size is 30 by 40 in. Check local code capacities. A chairlift cannot serve as part of a required accessible route.

INCLINED WHEELCHAIR LIFT REQUIREMENTS
13.53

TYPICAL RESIDENCE	PRIVATE
42" high self-closing door: solid construction, mechanical/electrical interlock, lower landing	36" high self-closing door: solid construction, mechanical/electrical interlock, upper landing
42" platform side guard: not used as exit; solid construction	36" platform side guard: not used as exit; solid construction
6" guard: permitted in lieu of side guard	6" guard: permitted in lieu of side guard
6" retractable guard: to prevent wheelchair rolling off platform	6" retractable guard: to prevent wheelchair rolling off platform
Door required at bottom landing	Underside obstruction switch bottom landing
Travel three floors maximum	Travel three floors maximum
Push button operation by rider	Push button operation by rider

Contributor:
Eric K. Beach, Rippeteau Architects, PC, Washington DC.

INCLINED WHEELCHAIR LIFT
13.54

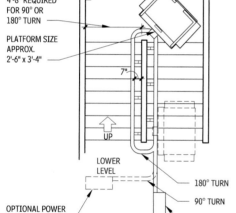

POWER UNIT

AUTOMATIC OR MANUAL DOWNSWING SAFETY BAR

CONTROLBOX, FIXED OR HAND HELD

OPTIONAL FOLD-DOWN CHAIR

NONSLIP PLATFORM

STEEL GUIDE RAIL BOLTED TO WALL OR SUPPORTED BY POSTS ALONG RUN

CALL BOX

CUSTOM-DESIGNED SUPPORT RAILS MAY TURN CORNER; FOLD-UP PLATFORMS ALSO AVAILABLE

INCLINED WHEELCHAIR LIFT PLAN WITH TURNS
13.55

CONTROL PANEL AT EACH LANDING

4'-8" REQUIRED FOR 90° OR 180° TURN

PLATFORM SIZE APPROX. 2'-6" x 3'-4"

7"

UP

LOWER LEVEL

OPTIONAL POWER UNIT LOCATION

180° TURN

90° TURN

POWER UNIT

ACCESSIBLE DOORS

ACCESSIBLE DOOR FEATURES
13.56

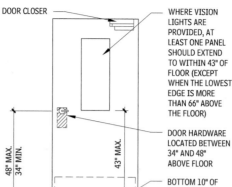

DOOR CLOSER

WHERE VISION LIGHTS ARE PROVIDED, AT LEAST ONE PANEL SHOULD EXTEND TO WITHIN 43" OF FLOOR (EXCEPT WHEN THE LOWEST EDGE IS MORE THAN 66" ABOVE THE FLOOR)

DOOR HARDWARE LOCATED BETWEEN 34" AND 48" ABOVE FLOOR

BOTTOM 10" OF DOOR SURFACE SHOULD BE SMOOTH

48" MAX.
34" MIN.

43" MAX.

CLEAR WIDTH OF ACCESSIBLE DOORWAYS
13.57

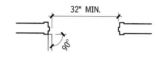

32" MIN.

90°

HINGED DOOR

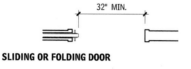

32" MIN.

SLIDING OR FOLDING DOOR

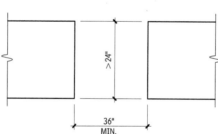

> 24"

36" MIN.

TWO DOORS IN SERIES – ANSI ONLY

PULL-SIDE MANEUVERING CLEARANCE AT SWINGING DOORS
13.58

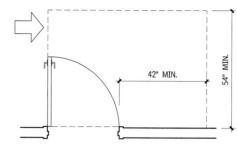

42" MIN.

54" MIN.

HINGE APPROACH

36" MIN.

60" MIN.

HINGE APPROACH

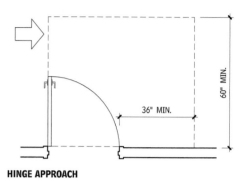

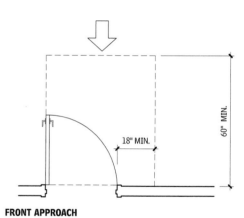

18" MIN.

60" MIN.

FRONT APPROACH

24" MIN.

48" MIN.

54" MIN.

IF CLOSER IS PROVIDED

LATCH APPROACH

NOTES

13.56 a. Door Hardware: Specify hardware that can be operated with one hand, without tight grasping, pinching, or twisting of the wrist.
b. Thresholds: Thresholds are typically limited to 1/2 in. maximum height; however, some standards allow a 3/4-in. height beveled at a 1:2 maximum slope for existing or altered thresholds and patio sliding doors in some dwelling units.
c. Opening force: Interior doors (other than fire doors) should be able to be operated with 5 lb of force. Exterior doors and fire doors may be regulated by the authority having jurisdiction.

d. Door closers must be adjusted so that there is at least a five-second interval from the time the door moves from 90° to 12° open.

Contributors:
Eric K. Beach, Rippeteau Architects, PC, Washington, DC; Lawrence G. Perry, AIA, Silver Spring, Maryland.

PUSH-SIDE MANEUVERING CLEARANCE AT SWINGING DOORS
13.59

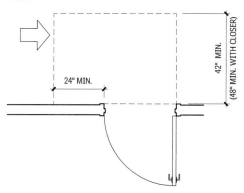

LATCH APPROACH

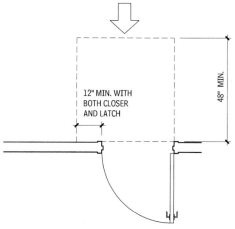

FRONT APPROACH

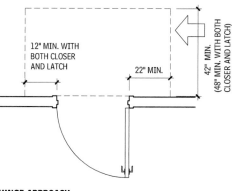

HINGE APPROACH

For a hinged door, the clear width is measured between the face of the door and the door stop with the door open at a 90° angle. For a sliding or folding door, the clear width is measured between the edge of the door and the jamb with the door fully open. Hardware must be accessible with the door in fully open position. Openings and doors without doorways more than 24 in. in depth must have a clear width of 36 in. minimum. Doors in dwelling units covered by FHAG are permitted to have a "nominal" 32-in. clear width. HUD allows a 2 ft-10 in. with 31–5/8-in. clear width swing door to satisfy this requirement. ICC/ANSI A117.1 allows a 31–3/4-in. clear width.

PROJECTIONS INTO CLEAR WIDTH
13.60

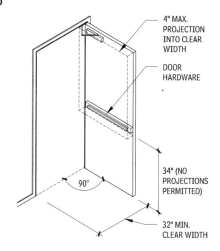

TWO DOORS IN SERIES—ICC/ANSI A117.1 ONLY
13.61

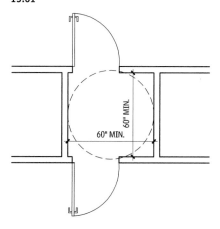

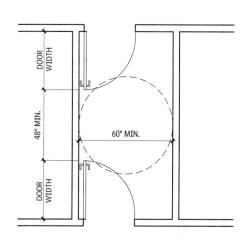

Source: ICC/ANSI A117.1.

Manual doors and doorways and manual gates on accessible routes must comply. With double-leaf doors and gates, at least one of the active leaves must comply. Maneuvering clearances include the full width of the door. Maneuvering clearances are also required at power-assisted doors. Maneuvering clearances are not applicable at full-powered automatic doors or low-energy power-operated doors. The floor and ground surface within the required maneuvering clearance of a door must not slope more than 1:48, and must be stable, firm, and slip-resistant. Where any obstruction within 18 in. of the latch side of a doorway projects more than 8 in. beyond the face of the door (e.g., a recessed door) maneuvering clearances for a forward approach must be provided. Maneuvering clearances are required only on the exterior side of the primary entry door of dwelling units covered by the Fair Housing Accessibility Guidelines (FHAG).

NOTES

13.60 Exceptions
a. Door closers and door stops are permitted 78 in. above the floor.
b. For alterations, a 5/8-in. maximum projection is permitted for the latch-side stop.

Contributor:
Lawrence G. Perry, AIA, Silver Spring, Maryland.

MANEUVERING CLEARANCE AT SLIDING AND FOLDING DOORS
13.62

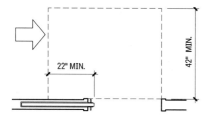

POCKET OR HINGE APPROACH

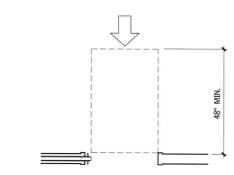

FRONT APPROACH

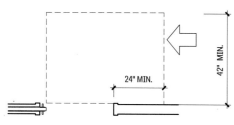

STOP OR LATCH APPROACH

ACCESSIBLE COMMUNICATIONS FEATURES

TACTILE SIGNS

Tactile signage with raised characters and Braille are required on signs provided as permanent designations of rooms and spaces. ICC/ANSI A117.1 allows either combined tactile/visual characters or separate tactile characters with redundant visual characters. By providing duplicate characters, the tactile characters can be made easier to read by touch, and a wider variety of visual characters can be used. Room numbers, room names, exit stairs, and restrooms are examples of spaces with "permanent" designations. Tactile characters must be located between 48 and 60 in. above the floor or ground.

Tactile signs at doors must be located so that a person reading the sign will not be hit by a door that is being opened. ICC/ANSI A117.1 allows door-mounted tactile signs on the push side of doors with closers, which do not have hold-open devices. Tactile signs located on the pull side of doors should be located so that an 18-in. by 18-in. "safe" zone, centered on the sign, is provided beyond the arc of any door swing between the closed position and the 45° open position. At double doors with two active leafs, signs must be located on the right-hand side or, if no wall space is available, on the nearest adjacent wall.

Signs that provide directional information to, or information about, permanent spaces are required to comply with specific requirements for visual characters. Minimum character heights are regulated both by the height of the sign above the floor and by the intended viewing distance. Consult the applicable regulations for signs required to identify specific accessible features, spaces, or elements.

FIRE PROTECTION ANS ALARM

Fire detection alarm systems are not required by accessibility regulations, but when they are provided they are required to include accessibility-related features. Visible-alarm notification appliances, intended to alert persons with hearing impairments, are the primary accessibility component of fire alarm systems. Criteria for the placement of visible alarms, the intensity of each appliance, the intensity of the signal throughout the covered area, and the cumulative effect of multiple appliances are all regulated in an attempt to ensure that the signal is immediately noticed, without creating light patterns that could trigger seizures in persons with photosensitivity.

The National Fire Alarm Code, NFPA 72, contains the criteria for visible alarms. ICC/ANSI A117.1 references this standard, and requires visible alarms to be:

- Powered by a commercial light and power source
- Permanently connected to the wiring of the premises electric system
- Permanently installed

Where alarms are provided, visible alarms are required in all public and common-use areas, including restrooms. Visible alarms are not required in individual employee workstations, but the wiring system must support the integrated addition of one, if required by an employee. Verify these and other requirements specific to the occupancy classification in the applicable building code and federal laws.

DETECTABLE WARNINGS
13.63

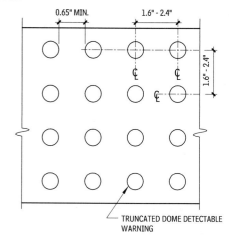

PLAN

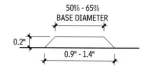

ELEVATION

TRUNCATED DOME SIZE AND SPACING

Detectable warnings are required at passenger transit platforms whose edges border a drop-off where no screen or guard is provided. The detectable warning should be a 24-in.-wide strip of truncated domes, contrasting with the adjacent walking surface.

Consult applicable codes and federal requirements regarding the current status of the requirements for detectable warnings at hazardous vehicular ways.

ASSISTIVE LISTENING SYSTEMS

Stadiums, theaters, auditoriums, lecture halls, and similar fixed-seating assembly areas are required to provide assistive listening systems when an audio amplification system is provided. Courtrooms are required to have assistive listening systems whether or not an audio application system is provided.

Check the applicable requirements for the number of receivers required, as they vary from just over 1 to 4 percent of the total capacity of the assembly area. At least 25 percent of the receivers should be hearing-aid compatible.

Signs should be provided at ticketing areas or other clearly visible locations, indicating the availability of the assistive listening system. Signs should include the International Symbol of Access for hearing loss.

Contributor:
Lawrence G. Perry, AIA, Silver Spring, Maryland.

AUTOMATIC BANKING SYSTEMS AND TRANSPORTATION FARE COLLECTION EQUIPMENT

Where automatic teller machines (ATMs) or fare collection equipment are provided, generally at least one machine is required to be accessible. ICC/ANSI A117.1 lists extensive criteria addressing the input and output requirements of these machines, which are intended to make them usable by someone with a vision or hearing impairment. A117.1 requires operable parts to be not more than 48 in. above the floor or ground.

TELEPHONES

Accessible public telephones are required where coin-operated public pay telephones, coinless public pay telephones, public closed-circuit telephones, courtesy phones, or other types of public telephones are provided. One wheelchair-accessible phone is required on each floor or level where phones are provided; where more than one bank is provided on a floor or level, at least one phone at each bank must be wheelchair-accessible. ICC/ANSI A117.1 requires that all operable parts of wheelchair-accessible phones be located a maximum of 48 in. above the floor or ground. Federal regulations require all new telephone equipment to be hearing-aid-compatible.

VOLUME-CONTROL TELEPHONES

Check applicable requirements for the number of and amplification requirements for telephones with volume control, which vary among the building code and federal requirements. Telephones with volume control must be identified by signs, unless all telephones have volume control.

TEXT TELEPHONES (TTYs)

Consult the applicable standards for the required number and location of TTYs. Model codes, based on the recommendations of the ADAAG Review Committee, provide for an increased number of TTYs based on whether the building is publicly or privately owned and the number of phones at the site, in the building, on each floor, and at each bank of phones. Additional requirements may apply for hospitals, transportation facilities, highway rest stops, emergency roadside stops, service plazas, and detention and correctional facilities. Public TTYs should be identified by the international TTY symbol. Directional signs to TTYs should be provided at banks of public telephones not providing TTYs. In addition, there may be requirements for shelves and outlets at banks of telephones without TTYs, to allow use of a portable TTY.

TELEPHONES
13.64

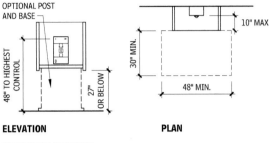
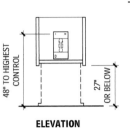
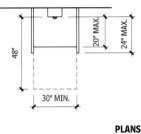
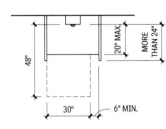

ELEVATION   **PLAN**

SIDE REACH POSSIBLE

ELEVATION

FORWARD REACH REQUIRED

PLANS

ACCESSIBLE TOILETS AND BATHROOMS

GRAB BARS

LOCATION OF ACCESSIBLE FIXTURES AND ACCESSORIES
13.65

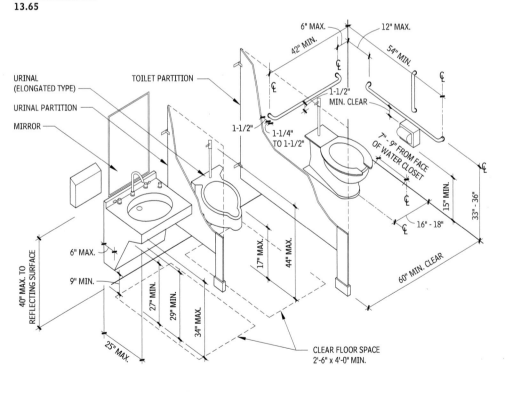

NOTES

13.65 a. If the partition is greater than or equal to 2 ft-0 in. deep, urinal clear floor spaces must be 3 ft wide.

b. Mirrors located above lavatories, sinks, and vanities must be mounted with the bottom edge of the reflecting surface 40 in. maximum above the floor. Other mirrors must be mounted with bottom edge of the reflecting surface 35 in. maximum above the floor.

c. Vertical grab bars are required by ICC/ANSI A117.1.

Contributor:
Lawrence G. Perry, AIA, Silver Spring, Maryland.

ACCESSIBLE BATHTUB AND SHOWER
13.66

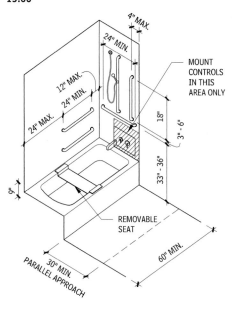

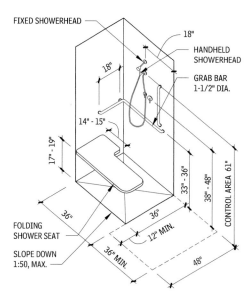

GRAB BAR ATTACHMENT DETAILS
13.67

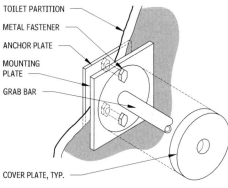

TOILET PARTITION

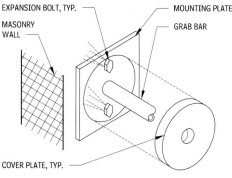

MASONRY WALL

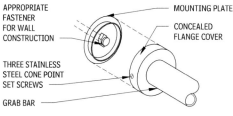

WOOD CONSTRUCTION

CONCEALED FLANGE

Size: 1-1/2 in. or 1-1/4 in. O.D. with 1-1/2 in. clearance at the wall.

Material: Stainless steel chrome-plated brass with knurled finish (optional).

Installation: Concealed or exposed fasteners; return all ends to the wall, intermediate supports at 3 ft maximum. Use heavy-duty bars and methods of installation.

Other grab bars are available for particular situations. Consult ICC/ANSI A117.1 and ADAAG requirements, as well as applicable local and federal regulations.

ACCESSIBLE TOILET ROOMS

All dimensional criteria in this discussion are based on ICC/ANSI A117.1, and on adult anthropometrics.

- In new construction, all public and common-use toilet rooms are generally required to be accessible.
- Where multiple single-user toilet rooms or bathing rooms are clustered in a single location and each serves the same population, 5 percent, but not less than one of the rooms must be accessible. The accessible room(s) must be identified by signs.
- Single-user toilet and bathing rooms provided within a private office are permitted to be adaptable. Making the room accessible is permitted to involve replacement of the water closet and lavatory, changing the swing of the door, and installing grab bars in previously reinforced walls.
- In accessible toilet and bathing rooms, at least one of each type of fixture and accessory provided must be accessible.
- A wheelchair turning space is required within accessible toilet and bathing rooms.
- Doors are not permitted to swing into the required clear floor space at any fixture, except in single-user rooms, where a clear floor space is provided beyond the swing of the door.

UNISEX TOILET AND BATHING ROOMS
ASSEMBLY AND MERCANTILE OCCUPANCIES

- Recent model codes require accessible unisex toilet and bathing rooms in certain assembly and mercantile occupancies. These unisex rooms are beneficial for parents with small children and for persons with disabilities who require personal assistance in using toilet facilities, as the assistant may be a person of the opposite sex. This requirement applies when a total of six or more water closets (or water closets and urinals) is provided in the facility or in certain occupancy areas.
- Fixtures provided in unisex rooms are permitted to be included in the number of required plumbing fixtures.
- Unisex facilities must be located within 500 ft, and within one floor, of separate-sex facilities. In facilities with security checkpoints, such as airport terminals, unisex facilities must be located on the same side of the checkpoint as the separate-sex facilities they serve.
- Unisex toilet rooms require a single water closet and lavatory, or as an exception, a urinal, in addition to the water closet.
- When bathing fixtures are provided in separate-sex facilities, an accessible shower or bathtub must be provided in the unisex bathing room.
- If storage is provided in separate-sex facilities, it must be provided in the unisex bathing room.
- Doors to unisex toilet and bathing rooms must be securable from within the room.

ALTERATIONS

- Accessible unisex toilet and bathing rooms are permitted in alterations in lieu of altering existing separate-sex facilities in certain conditions.
- Unisex rooms must be located in the same area and on the same floor as the existing inaccessible facilities.

TOILET ROOM LAYOUTS

- Variations are in the direction of the door swing and whether the width or depth is the more constraining dimension. Dimensions show comfortable minimums and preferred dimensions.
- Overall room dimensions include a 2-in. construction tolerance.
- Each layout shows the required clear floor space for the fixtures and the doors. Frequently, the clear floor space at the fixture is more stringent than the 60-in. diameter or the T-shaped maneuvering space required. Both must be considered.
- Door maneuvering clearances: Variables include direction of swing, direction of approach, size of door, and door hardware. See "Accessible Doors" in this chapter.
- Doors to bathrooms are assumed to be 36 in. wide, with a closer and latch for privacy. Where noted, the overall dimension may decrease if there is no closer.
- Maneuvering clearances at the base of water closets are based on American Standard models (floor-mounted tank type and wall-mounted, flush-valve type), mounted according to the manufacturer's recommendations. Confirm actual water closet dimensions.

NOTES

13.66 a. Vertical grab bars are required by ICC/ANSI A117.1.
b. The space in front of the transfer shower must also meet alcove provisions if the adjacent walls confine access to the clear floor space in front of the shower.

Contributors:
Mark J. Mazz, AIA, Hyattsville, Maryland; Lawrence G. Perry, AIA, Silver Spring, Maryland.

• Maneuvering clearances below lavatories are based on American Standard models (wall-hung and mounted in countertop). Confirm actual lavatory dimensions.

SHORT AND COMPACT PLANS
13.68

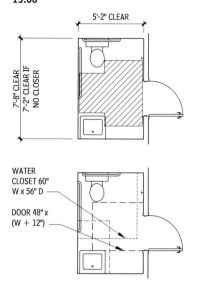

OUTSWINGING DOOR

LAVATORY ON SIDE WALL
13.69

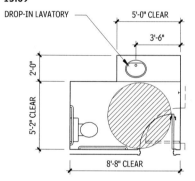

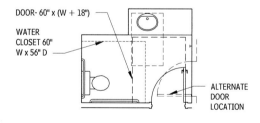

LAVATORY ON OPPOSITE WALL
13.70

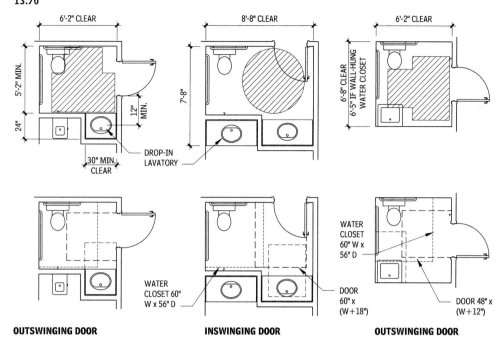

OUTSWINGING DOOR   **INSWINGING DOOR**   **OUTSWINGING DOOR**

TOILET COMPARTMENTS
• Where toilet compartments are provided, at least one compartment must be wheelchair-accessible.
• Where six or more toilet compartments are provided in a toilet room, in addition to the wheelchair-accessible compartment, a 36-in.-wide ambulatory accessible compartment is required.

ACCESSIBLE TOILET AND BATHING FIXTURES
Requirements for accessible residential fixtures are discussed throughout this chapter. All dimensional criteria are based on ICC/ANSI A117.1 and adult anthropometrics, unless otherwise indicated.

WATER CLOSETS AND URINALS
• ICC/ANSI A117.1 allow water closets to be located 16 to 18 in. from the side wall in wheelchair-accessible stalls, and 17 to 19 in. in ambulatory accessible stalls. Other regulations may require this dimension to be 18 in.

• ICC/ANSI A117.1 prohibits other fixtures within the required clearances for the water closet. Previous editions and other regulations allow other configurations with a lavatory within the water closet clearance.
• The top of the water closet seat must be 17 to 19 in. above the floor. Seats must not be sprung to return to a lifted position.
• ICC/ANSI A117.1 requires a vertical grab bar located on the side wall; previous editions and other regulations may not.
• The hatched area on Figure 13.97 indicates the allowable location of the toilet paper dispenser. Outlet must be within the range shown. Dispensers should allow continuous paper flow, not control delivery.
• ICC/ANSI A117.1 allows a stall-type urinal; it does not require an elongated urinal rim for a wall urinal. Other regulations may.
• Manually operated flush controls must be located 44 in. maximum above the floor.

WATER CLOSETS
13.71

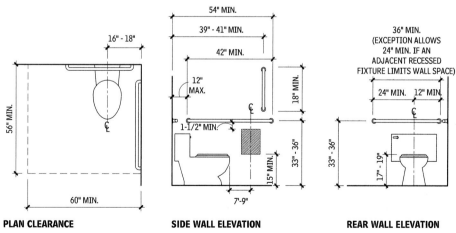

PLAN CLEARANCE   **SIDE WALL ELEVATION**   **REAR WALL ELEVATION**

Contributors:
Mark J. Mazz, AIA, P.A., Hyattsville, Maryland; Lawrence G. Perry, AIA, Silver Spring, Maryland.

URINALS
13.72

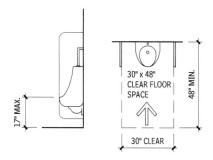

TOILET COMPARTMENTS
- Toe clearance 9 in. high and 6 in. deep is required at the front and at least one side of accessible toilet compartments. Toe clearance is not required when the compartment size exceeds the minimum dimension by 6 in. or more.
- Left- or right-handed configurations are permitted.
- The door to the toilet compartment must be self-closing and have a pull on both sides near the latch.

LAVATORIES
- Knee and toe clearance is required below accessible lavatories. The lavatory overflow is permitted to project into the knee clearance.
- All exposed pipes located beneath accessible lavatories must be insulated or located so as to protect users from contact with the pipes.
- Lavatory controls should be within accessible reach range, be operable with one hand, and not require tight grasping, pinching, or twisting of the wrist. Automatic controls are acceptable. Manually activated, self-closing faucets should operate for not less than 10 seconds.

BATHTUBS
- Bathtub controls, other than drain stoppers, must be located on an end wall between the tub rim and grab bar and between the open side of the tub and the midpoint of the tub width.
- A 59-in. minimum length shower spray unit is required.
- Tub enclosures must not obstruct controls or interfere with transfer from a wheelchair to the tub. Enclosures must not have tracks mounted on the tub rim.
- ICC/ANSI A117.1 does not allow a sink with knee clearance at the foot end of the tub. Other regulations may.
- ICC/ANSI A117.1 requires an 18-in. minimum long vertical grab bar on the control wall, 3 to 6 in. maximum above the horizontal grab bar, which is 4 in. maximum inward from the front edge of the bathtub. Other regulations may not have these requirements.

TOILET COMPARTMENTS
13.73

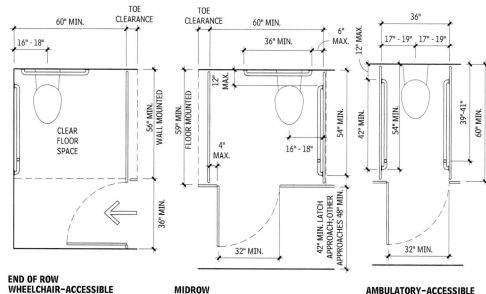

END OF ROW
WHEELCHAIR–ACCESSIBLE   **MIDROW**   **AMBULATORY–ACCESSIBLE**

LAVATORIES
13.74

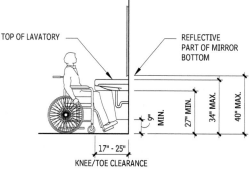

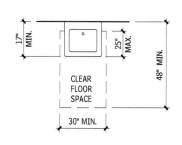

BATHTUBS
13.75

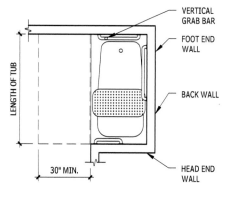
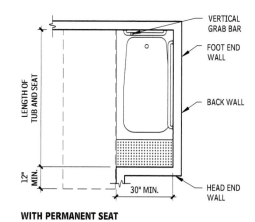

WITHOUT PERMANENT SEAT   **WITH PERMANENT SEAT**

Contributor:
Lawrence G. Perry, AIA, Silver Spring, Maryland.

SHOWER COMPARTMENTS

- Shower compartment thresholds are not permitted to exceed 1/2 in. Design should anticipate water escaping from the compartment.
- A fixed, folding, or removable seat is required in transfer-type compartments. Seats in roll-in showers, where provided, should be located on the wall adjacent to the control wall and should be folding-type seats. Seats can be rectangular or L-shaped; see ICC/ANSI A117.1 for details.
- A 59-in. minimum length shower spray unit is required.
- Shower enclosures, where provided, must not obstruct controls or interfere with transfer from a wheelchair.
- In transfer-type showers, ICC/ANSI A117.1 requires an 18-in. minimum long vertical grab bar on the control wall, 3 to 6 in. maximum above the horizontal grab bar, which is 4 in. maximum inward from the front edge of the bathtub. Other regulations may not have these requirements.

CHILDREN'S FIXTURES

ICC/ANSI A117.1 and ADAAG provide technical requirements based on children's dimensions and anthropometrics for water closets, toilet compartments, lavatories, and sinks, when used primarily by people 12 years old and younger. The dimensions should be applied consistently within the restroom.

Toilet compartments for children's use require a depth of 59 in. for both wall-hung and floor-mounted water closets, and a toe clearance of 12 in. high, 6 in. minimum, beyond the partition on the front and one side. Toilet compartments that are 65 in. minimum deep are not required to have toe clearance.

Table 13.77 lists dimensions for water closets serving children, and provides additional guidance specific to the age group served. The specifications chosen should correspond to the age group of primary user and should be applied consistently in the installation of the water closet and the related grab bars and dispensers.

Sinks and lavatories for children ages 6 to 12 with a 31-in. maximum rim or counter surface may have a knee clearance of 24 in. minimum. Parallel approach is permitted at lavatories and sinks used primarily by children ages 5 and younger.

WATER CLOSETS FOR CHILDREN
13.77

DIMENSION	PRE-K, K (AGES 3 AND 4)	FIRST-THIRD (AGES 5-8)	FOURTH-SEVENTH (AGES 9-12)
Water closet centerline	12"	12"-15"	15"-18"
Toilet seat height	11"-12"	12"-15"	15"-17"
Grab bar height	18"-20"	20"-25"	25"-27"
Dispenser height	14"	14"-17"	17"-19"

ACCESSIBLE RESIDENTIAL BATHROOMS

ACCESSIBILITY STANDARDS FOR BATHROOMS

Although toilet room and fixture design standards were an important part of the first ANSI A117.1 standards in 1961, bathroom standards with mobility features for residential dwellings were not included until the 1981 edition. Four years later, the Uniform Federal Accessibility Standard (UFAS) published nearly identical bathroom standards for dwellings included in federal projects. In most multifamily projects, whether privately or publicly funded, between 1 and 5 percent of the total dwellings must meet the ANSI or UFAS standards for full wheelchair accessibility. The exact scoping requirement depends on the specific codes or laws.

In 1988, the Fair Housing Amendments Act (FHAA) was amended to include protection against discrimination on the basis of disability. The FHAA applies to buildings with four or more dwelling units intended to be used as a residence, whether the housing is for rent or for sale, and whether it is privately or publicly funded.

SHOWERS
13.76

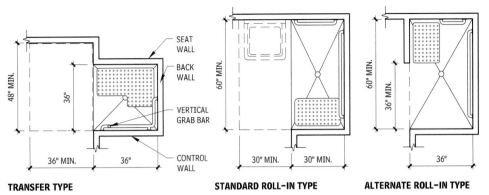

TRANSFER TYPE   **STANDARD ROLL-IN TYPE**   **ALTERNATE ROLL-IN TYPE**

This includes apartments, condominiums, residential shelters, and long-term care facilities. Although the requirements are less stringent than those found in ICC/ANSI A117.1 Accessible Units and UFAS, the FHAA requirements are more broadly applied to all units in buildings with one or more elevators, and ground floor units in buildings without elevators. The Fair Housing Accessibility Guidelines (FHAG) include two options for bathroom design, designated as Option A and Option B. The primary difference is that Option B provides a more accessible approach to the bathtub. In covered dwellings with two or more bathrooms, all bathrooms must comply with Option A, or at least one must comply with Option B requirements. In covered units with one bathroom, either Option A or B may be used.

The Americans with Disabilities Act (ADA) and the Americans with Disability Act Accessibility Guidelines (ADAAG) provide accessibility requirements for units in transient lodging, medical care and long-term care facilities, and detention and correction facilities. Some residential facilities may be covered by both the ADA and the FHAA, for example dormitories and nursing homes. The final ADA/ABA Guidelines dated July 23, 2004 revise ADAAG, and will serve as the basis for the minimum standards when adopted by other federal agencies responsible for issuing enforceable standards. These guidelines include updates to requirements for units and also include new requirements for "Residential Units" that are not included here. The ADAAG bathroom layouts accompanying this discussion reflect the ADAAG (Appendix A 28 CFR Part 36) criteria and the final ADA/ABA Guidelines for transient lodging. Refer to the Access Board Web site (www.access-board.gov) for the current status of this adoption process.

ICC/ANSI A117.1 includes the technical requirements for three types of dwelling and sleeping units with mobility features:

- *Accessible units:* The number of accessible units required by the building code typically is based on the total number of units provided in the facility.
- *Type A dwelling units:* Type A dwelling units are required by the building code in multifamily residential facilities, including apartment buildings, condominiums, monasteries, and convents. The number of units required to comply with these requirements is generally based on a percentage of the total number of units provided; refer to the applicable building code.
- *Type B dwelling units:* The requirements for Type B dwelling units are intended to be consistent with the technical requirements of the FHAA.

The technical requirements for the bathrooms vary significantly among these types. Accessible units are most accessible, and they are generally required by the building code in public and institutional residential facilities, including nursing homes, hospitals, detention facilities, dormitories, boarding houses and hotels.

There has been an effort in the code development community to make the technical requirements for residential units in ICC/ANSI A117.1 consistent with those found in the federal requirements. It should be noted that in addition to the guidelines, the regulations

are also an important part of these federal laws. To ensure compliance, architects should consult the codes, laws, and appropriate regulations, and carefully verify the requirements applicable to their projects before proceeding with the design and construction of residential housing.

MANEUVERING SPACE

An accessible bathroom must meet specified plan requirements, depending on the standards used. Each bathroom plan must provide the fixture clearances required by the applicable standard. In addition, general maneuvering space must be provided, although the amount of space varies by unit type.

ICC/ANSI A117.1 Accessible Unit and Type A, UFAS, and ADAAG require either a 5-ft diameter circle or a 5-ft T-shaped wheelchair turning area. Maneuvering space can generally include knee and toe space under fixtures and accessories.

Bathrooms in ICC/ANSI A117.1 Type B and FHAG must be "usable" rather than "accessible;" therefore, the minimum maneuvering clearance is less. In these units, there must be enough clear space to position a wheelchair clear of the door swing. This requirement is described as a rectangular space 30 by 48 in. All of the standards permit required floor space for fixtures to overlap with required maneuvering space. ADAAG standards, however, do not permit the bathroom door (even in single-user facilities) to swing into any fixture clearance. In almost all situations, this requirement effectively necessitates that the door swing out into the adjacent hall or bedroom. This has been revised in the final ADA/ABA Guidelines.

BATHROOM ENTRY DOORS

Different unit types require different-size bathroom entry doors. ICC/ANSI A117.1 Accessible Unit and Type A, UFAS, and ADAAG require installation of at least a 3-ft door to provide the full 32-in. clear opening. Additionally, they include requirements for maneuvering clearances. ICC/ANSI A117.1 Type B and FHAG permit a 2 ft 10 in. door clearance to provide a "nominal" 32-in. clear opening; door maneuvering clearances are not required.

GRAB BARS

The grab bar arrangement can influence the floor plan of an accessible bathroom. The grab bar requirements of ICC/ANSI A117.1 Accessible and Type A, UFAS, and ADAAG can become critical factors in water closet and bathroom arrangements. ICC/ANSI A117.1 Type B and FHAG unit grab bar standards permit a shorter side grab bar, and allow the installation of swing-up grab bars, so the wall adjacent to the water closet may be shorter or omitted entirely.

ADAPTABLE FEATURES

In residential bathroom design, *adaptability* was a new term when introduced in the 1980 ANSI edition. Adaptability, in this case, is defined as "the capability of certain . . . elements . . . to be altered or added so as to accommodate the needs of persons with or without disabilities, or to accommodate the needs of persons with different types or degrees of disabilities."

Contributor:
Lawrence G. Perry, AIA, Silver Spring, Maryland.

BATHROOM LAYOUTS
13.78

☐ 30" x 48" CLEAR FLOOR SPACE OUTSIDE DOOR SWING

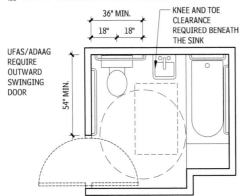

UFAS/ADAAG REQUIRE OUTWARD SWINGING DOOR

36" MIN.
18" | 18"
54" MIN.

KNEE AND TOE CLEARANCE REQUIRED BENEATH THE SINK

UFAS/ADAAG/ONE WALL

☐ 30" x 48" CLEAR FLOOR SPACE OUTSIDE DOOR SWING
▢ GRAB BAR REINFORCEMENT REQUIRED

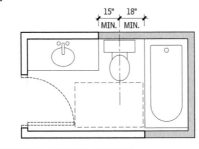

15" MIN. | 18" MIN.

ANSI TYPE B, OPTION A-ONE WALL

☐ 30" x 48" CLEAR FLOOR SPACE OUTSIDE DOOR SWING

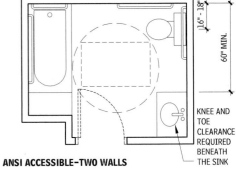

16" - 18"
60" MIN.

KNEE AND TOE CLEARANCE REQUIRED BENEATH THE SINK

ANSI ACCESSIBLE-TWO WALLS

☐ 30" x 48" CLEAR FLOOR SPACE OUTSIDE DOOR SWING

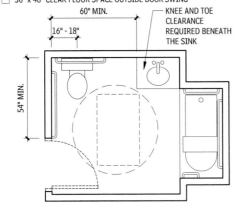

60" MIN.
16" - 18"
54" MIN.

KNEE AND TOE CLEARANCE REQUIRED BENEATH THE SINK

ANSI ACCESSIBLE/ADA-ABA/ONE WALL

☐ 30" x 48" CLEAR FLOOR SPACE OUTSIDE DOOR SWING
▢ GRAB BAR REINFORCEMENT REQUIRED

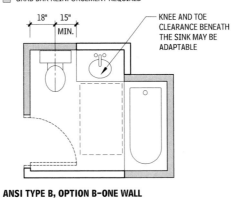

18" | 15" MIN.

KNEE AND TOE CLEARANCE BENEATH THE SINK MAY BE ADAPTABLE

ANSI TYPE B, OPTION B-ONE WALL

☐ 30" x 48" CLEAR FLOOR SPACE OUTSIDE DOOR SWING
▢ GRAB BAR REINFORCEMENT REQUIRED

18" 16" - 18"
18"

KNEE AND TOE CLEARANCE BENEATH THE SINK MAY BE ADAPTABLE

ANSI TYPE A-TWO WALLS

☐ 30" x 48" CLEAR FLOOR SPACE OUTSIDE DOOR SWING
▢ GRAB BAR REINFORCEMENT REQUIRED

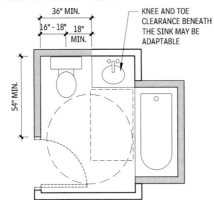

36" MIN.
16" - 18" | 18" MIN.
54" MIN.

KNEE AND TOE CLEARANCE BENEATH THE SINK MAY BE ADAPTABLE

ANSI TYPE A-ONE WALL

☐ 30" x 48" CLEAR FLOOR SPACE OUTSIDE DOOR SWING

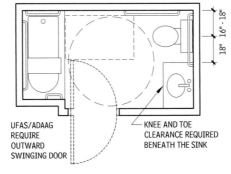

18" 16" - 18"
18"

UFAS/ADAAG REQUIRE OUTWARD SWINGING DOOR

KNEE AND TOE CLEARANCE REQUIRED BENEATH THE SINK

UFAS/ADAAG-TWO WALLS

☐ 30" x 48" CLEAR FLOOR SPACE OUTSIDE DOOR SWING
▢ GRAB BAR REINFORCEMENT REQUIRED

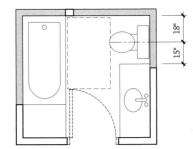

18"
15"

ANSI TYPE B, OPTION A OR OPTION B-TWO WALLS

NOTES

13.78 a. ANSI Accessible refers to ICC/ANSI A117.1 Accessible Units.
b. ANSI A refers to ICC/ANSI A117.1 Type A unit.
c. ANSI B refers to ICC/ANSI A117.1 Type B unit.

Contributors:
Kim A. Beasley, AIA, and Thomas D. Davies Jr., AIA, Paralyzed Veterans of America Architecture, Washington, DC.

In accessible bathrooms, adaptable elements might typically include "removable" base cabinets that can be eliminated, when necessary, to provide knee space below vanities, and hidden wall reinforcing that will facilitate later installation of grab bars around certain plumbing fixtures. It is important that cabinets be of the same quality as those in nonaccessible units and that the flooring and wall finishes be extended beneath and behind so that when the cabinet is removed, the bathroom maintains a finished appearance.

Although the term *adaptability* is not included in ICC/ANSI A117.1, this standard allows removable base cabinets and reinforcement for the later installation grab bars in ICC/ANSI Type A and Type B units.

OTHER RESIDENTIAL BATHROOMS
As with all custom design, the design of accessible bathrooms for single-family custom homes or remodeling projects should be tailored to the individual homeowners. For example, if a master bathroom is planned for a wheelchair user, the design should reflect that person's individual requirements and preferences.

PLUMBING FIXTURE REQUIREMENTS
Fixture requirements vary among the common accessibility standards and guidelines. The most significant differences are found between those required to comply with FHAA and the requirements for ICC/ANSI A117.1 Accessible Unit and Type A, UFAS, and ADAAG. The final ADA/ABA Guidelines dated July 23, 2004 revised ADAAG, and will serve as the basis for the minimum standards when adopted by other federal agencies responsible for issuing enforceable standards.

These guidelines include updates to requirements for units as well as new requirements for "Residential Units." The ADAAG fixture space diagrams shown in Figures 13.79 to 13.81 reflect the ADAAG

(Appendix A, 28 CFR Part 36) criteria, not the final ADA/ABA Guidelines. Refer to the Access Board Web site (www.access-board.gov) for the current status of this adoption process.

Approach clearance requirements for the different accessibility standards are illustrated in Figures 13.79 to 13.81. For other requirements, such as grab bar installations or faucet specifications, architects should refer to the code(s) or standard(s) that apply to their projects.

WATER CLOSET STANDARDS
The differences in the minimum clear floor space requirements for water closets are related to the allowed proximity of adjacent fixtures and required locations for grab bars. In ICC/ANSI A117.1 Accessible Units, no other fixture is permitted in the required clearance, and the water closet must be located adjacent to a side wall to accommodate grab bars.

UFAS, ICC/ANSI A117.1 Type A, and ADAAG also require an adjacent side wall, but allow a lavatory with knee clearance 18 in. minimum from the centerline of the water closet. ICC/ANSI A117.1 Type A allows "adaptable" cabinetry beneath the lavatory, provided it can be removed without removing or replacing the lavatory, the flooring extends under the cabinetry, and the walls surrounding the cabinetry are finished. ICC/ANSI A117.1 Type B/FHAA allow a sink or vanity with or without knee clearance 15 in. minimum from the centerline of water closet. The water closet is not required to be adjacent to the side wall, but it must have 18 in. minimum clearance to accommodate the future installation of swing-up or floor-mounted grab bars.

In addition to clearance requirements, UFAS, ICC/ANSI A117.1 Accessible Unit, and ADAAG include provisions for toilet seat height (17 to 19 in. AFF) and the location and operation of flush controls

and toilet paper dispensers. ICC/ANSI A117.1 Type A requirements also include seat height (15 to 19 in. AFF) and the location and operation of flush controls. ICC/ANSI A117.1 Accessible Unit, UFAS, and ADAAG specify the extent and location of the required grab bars; ICC/ANSI A117.1 Type A, ICC/ANSI A117.1 Type B, and FHAG require reinforcement for future installation of grab bars.

LAVATORY AND VANITY STANDARDS
The major differences between accessibility standards for lavatories and vanities are related to the need for forward-approach clearance with knee space. All unit types require this approach, with the exception of FHAG/ICC/ANSI A117.1 Type B, which allow a parallel approach centered on the basin. ADAAG, ICC/ANSI A117.1 Accessible Unit, ICC/ANSI A117.1 Type A, and UFAS also include requirements for faucets, mirror height, and pipe protection. ICC/ANSI A117.1 Accessible Unit includes a provision requiring comparable vanity space, in terms of size and proximity to the lavatory, in accessible units as provided in the nonaccessible units in a project.

BATHTUB AND TUB/SHOWER STANDARDS
The accessible bathtub standards also have subtle differences. For bathtubs without permanent seats, ICC/ANSI A117.1 Accessible Unit requires a 30-in. clearance parallel to the length of the bathtub. For bathtubs with permanent seats, ICC/ANSI A117.1 Accessible Unit requires 12 in. beyond the seat to allow room for a wheelchair user to align the wheelchair for transferring to the seat. ICC/ANSI A117.1 Type A requires these same clearances, but allows a countertop or cabinetry (not a sink) at the foot end, provided it can be removed and the flooring extends underneath. UFAS and ADAAG allow an accessible lavatory with knee clearance in the foot end clearance.

WATER CLOSET SPACE REQUIREMENTS
13.79

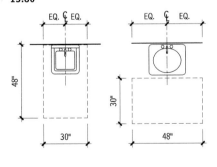

ANSI ACCESSIBLE A/B, UFAS, ADAAG, FHAG (EITHER APPROACH)

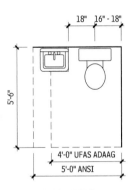

ANSI A, UFAS, ADAAG (FRONT APPROACH)

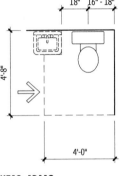

UFAS, ADAAG (SIDE APPROACH)

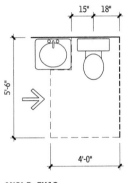

ANSI B, FHAG (EITHER APPROACH)

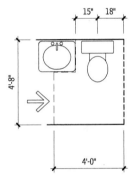

ANSI B, FHAG (SIDE APPROACH)

LAVATORY AND SHOWER SPACE REQUIREMENTS
13.80

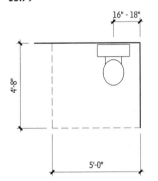

ANSI ACCESSIBLE, ANSI A, UFAS, ADAAG (WITH KNEE SPACE) | **ANSI B, FHAG (NO KNEE SPACE)**

ANSI ACCESSIBLE, ANSI A, UFAS, ADAAG (STALL SHOWER)

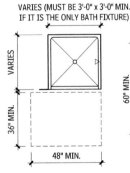

ANSI B, FHAG (STALL SHOWER)

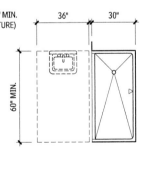

ANSI ACCESSIBLE, ANSI A, UFAS, ADAAG (ROLL-IN SHOWER)

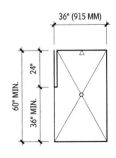

ANSI ACCESSIBLE, ANSI A, ADAAG (ALTERNATIVE ROLL-IN SHOWER)

Contributors:
Kim A. Beasley, AIA, and Thomas D. Davies Jr., AIA, Paralyzed Veterans of America Architecture, Washington, DC; Rebecca Ingram, Architect, Albuquerque, New Mexico.

BATHTUB SPACE REQUIREMENTS
13.81

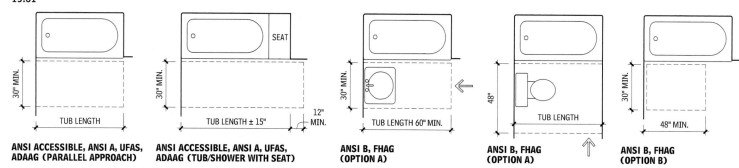

| ANSI ACCESSIBLE, ANSI A, UFAS, ADAAG (PARALLEL APPROACH) | ANSI ACCESSIBLE, ANSI A, UFAS, ADAAG (TUB/SHOWER WITH SEAT) | ANSI B, FHAG (OPTION A) | ANSI B, FHAG (OPTION A) | ANSI B, FHAG (OPTION B) |

FHAG and ICC/ANSI A117.1 Type B provide two bathroom options. Option A allows a parallel approach, which can include a lavatory with knee clearance, or a perpendicular approach into which a toilet may encroach. Option B requires a clear 30 by 48 in. approach parallel to the bathtub, beginning at the control wall. Of these alternatives, Option B is more accessible because it provides greater access to the controls. ICC/ANSI A117.1 Accessible Unit, ICC/ANSI A117.1 Type A, UFAS, and ADAAG all have additional requirements for the location and operation of the showerhead and faucet controls. ICC/ANSI A117.1 Accessible Unit, UFAS, and ADAAG specify the extent and location of the required grab bars; ICC/ANSI A117.1 Type A, ICC/ANSI A117.1 Type B, and FHAG require reinforcement for future installation of grab bars.

TRANSFER-TYPE STALL SHOWER AND ROLL-IN UNIT STANDARDS

Accessible showers include both transfer stalls (where a bather moves from a wheelchair to a bench or portable seat) and roll-in stalls (where a bather remains seated in a special shower chair and is either pushed by an attendant or self-propelled into the stall). ICC/ANSI A117.1 Accessible Unit, UFAS, and ADAAG require installation of a built-in stall seat in stall type and alternate roll-in type showers. ICC/ANSI A117.1 Type A requires reinforcement for future installation of a shower seat. ICC/ANSI A117.1 Type B and FHAG also require reinforcement, except in showers that are greater than 36 by 36 in. ICC/ANSI A117.1 Accessible Unit, ICC/ANSI A117.1 Type A, UFAS, and ADAAG include requirements regarding the location and operation of the showerhead and operating controls, threshold configuration, and water temperature. ICC/ANSI A117.1 Accessible Unit, UFAS, and ADAAG specify the extent and location of the required grab bars; ICC/ANSI A117.1 Type A, ICC/ANSI A117.1 Type B, and FHAG require reinforcement for future installation of grab bars.

ACCESSIBLE RESIDENTIAL KITCHENS

ACCESSIBILITY GUIDELINES

The 1980 ANSI A117.1 and the 1984 UFAS were the first to include kitchen design standards with features for wheelchair users. In most multifamily housing, between 1 and 5 percent of the total dwelling units must be wheelchair-accessible, depending on local building codes or federal standards. The kitchen standards in the 1988 Fair Housing Amendments Act (FHAA), a federal civil rights law, include requirements for "usable kitchens" in multifamily housing. Fair Housing standards must be applied to between 20 and 100 percent of the total project units, with some exceptions, depending on the configuration of the buildings, whether they are equipped with a passenger elevator, and the site topography.

The ADA/ABA Guidelines provide new requirements for "Residential Units," which are not included here. Refer to the Access Board Web site (www.access-board.gov) for the current status of this adoption process.

The ICC/ANSI A117.1 includes the technical requirements for three types of dwelling units with mobility features, and the technical requirements for the kitchens vary among these types:

- *Accessible units:* These units are most accessible and they are generally required by the building code in public and institutional residential facilities, including dormitories, boarding houses, and hotels.
- *Type A units:* These are typically required by the building code in multifamily residential facilities, including apartment buildings. The number of units required to comply with these requirements is based on a percentage of the total number of units provided.
- *Type B units:* These are intended to be consistent with the technical requirements of the Fair Housing Amendments Act.

Architects should carefully verify which kitchen requirements are appropriate for their specific projects because these unit types have very different design standards. HUD has designated "safe harbors" for compliance with the FHAA.

Accessible kitchens should reflect conventional layout principles with regard to proper workflow and functional adjacencies. As with conventional custom design, accessible kitchen designs for single-family custom homes or remodeling projects should suit the specific needs and preferences of the homeowners.

FIXTURE AND APPLIANCE REQUIREMENTS

The three general types of wheelchair standards for residential kitchens are:

- Overall kitchen maneuvering clearance
- Approach clearances for individual fixtures and appliances
- Other fixture specifications such as basin depths, switch locations, and faucet configurations

ICC/ANSI A117.1 Accessible Unit, ICC/ANSI A117.1 Type A, and UFAS standards for appliances and plumbing fixtures are much more accessible than ICC/ANSI A117.1 Type B/FHAG, as detailed in Table 13.108. All require that sufficient clear floor space be provided at fixtures or appliances to accommodate either a parallel or front approach, depending on the applicable design standard.

Fair Housing guidelines and most building code standards require a clear floor space at most kitchen fixtures and appliances. This space can permit a parallel or a perpendicular (front) wheelchair approach, depending on the fixture or appliance selected or the decision of the designer. HUD has interpreted its FHAA guidelines to require centering of the clear floor space on the appliance or fixture. This is not a requirement of ICC/ANSI A117.1.

Some clearance standards do not have a functional basis, however. For example, in order to be useful, a parallel approach to a dishwasher must be offset to allow the bottom-hinged door to be fully lowered. An adjacent knee space at either the kitchen sink or an open, end-of-counter location provides optimum wheelchair access to a dishwasher. A parallel approach to a refrigerator is more practical than a front approach because the user's longer horizontal reach will allow full access to the interior.

Appliance clearances may depend on specific appliance features. For example, oven clearances depend on whether the appliance is side- or bottom-hinged. Overall maneuvering clearances must take into consideration the depth of any projecting appliances. If the kitchen design is based on specific assumptions regarding appliances, the architect should carefully note that fact on the drawings to ensure compliance.

A critical point regarding clear floor space and kitchen fixtures and appliances is the requirement to precisely center the floor space on the centerline of the appliance or fixture. Although this requirement was not explicitly stated in the Fair Housing guidelines, HUD interprets this to be a Fair Housing kitchen and bathroom requirement. In a kitchen plan, the impact can be significant. For example, to provide a parallel approach, fixtures or appliances less than 48 in. wide must be offset from either an end wall or an inside counter corner. A 30-in. refrigerator, for example, must be located 9 in. away from an end wall, or a forward approach must be provided; a 24-in. dishwasher must be located 12 in. away from an inside counter corner.

FLOOR SPACE AND KNEE SPACE REQUIREMENTS FOR FIXTURES AND APPLIANCES
13.82

APPLIANCE	REQUIREMENT	ICC/ANSI A117.1 ACCESSIBLE UNIT	ICC/ANSI A117.1 TYPE A	ICC/ANSI A117.1 TYPE B/FHAG	UFAS
Sink	Approach Knee space	Front Yes	Front Yes[b]	Parallel or front Yes, with front approach[b]	Parallel or front Yes
Workspace	Approach Knee space	Front Yes[a]	Front Yes[b]	Not required	Front Yes
Storage		Parallel or front approach for 50%	Parallel or front	No requirements	
Range/cooktop	Approach Knee space	Parallel or front Yes, with front approach to cooktop	Parallel or front Yes, with front approach to cooktop	Parallel or front Yes, with front approach to cooktop	Parallel or front Optional
Refrigerator	Approach	Parallel (offset 24" maximum)	Parallel (offset 24" maximum)	Parallel or front	Parallel or front
Dishwasher	Approach	Parallel or front adjacent to dishwasher[c]	Parallel or front adjacent to dishwasher[c]	Parallel or front	Parallel or front
Oven	Approach	Parallel or front[d]	Parallel or front[e]	Parallel or front	Front
Trash compactor	Approach		Parallel or front	Parallel or front	Parallel or front

NOTE

13.81 ANSI A allows for removable cabinetry in the clearance at the foot end. ADAAG and UFAS allow a lavatory.
13.82 a. Unless there is no conventional cooktop or range.
b. Removable base cabinets permitted.
c. The door in the open position must not obstruct the sink or dishwasher approach clearances.
d. Side-hinged ovens are required to have a work surface with knee clearance adjacent to the latch side; bottom-hinged ovens may have the work surface with the clearance on either side.

e. Side-hinged ovens are required to have a counter adjacent to the latch side; bottom-hinged ovens may have the counter on either side.

Contributor:
Lawrence G. Perry, AIA, Silver Spring, Maryland.

Requirements for general maneuvering space within the kitchen and for counter heights also vary among standards. All require a minimum clearance between counters, countertops, appliances, or walls of (1) 40-in. in a galley aisle where a required fixture or work area knee space is provided or (2) a 60-in. aisle in U-shaped kitchens. In ICC/ANSI A117.1 Accessible Units, a pass-through kitchen must have two points of entry. If it is enclosed on three contiguous sides, it is considered a U-shaped kitchen and must have a wheelchair turning area. ICC/ANSI A117.1 Accessible Unit, ICC/ANSI A117.1 Type A, and UFAS require a work surface either with an adjustable-height counter or a fixed counter at a height of 34 in. ICC/ANSI A117.1 Type A allows removable base cabinets for this work surface and the sink. ICC/ANSI A117.1 Type B/ FHAG does not include requirements for counter heights.

ICC/ANSI A117.1 ACCESSIBLE PASS-THROUGH AND ACCESSIBLE U-SHAPED 13.83

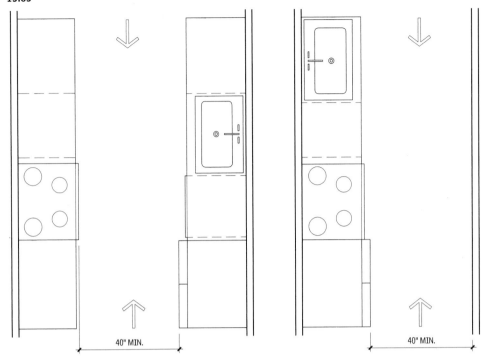

ACCESSIBLE PASS-THROUGH KITCHENS

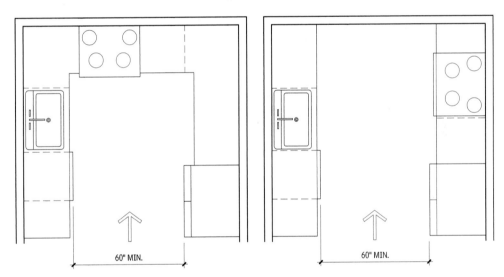

ACCESSIBLE U-SHAPED KITCHENS, SINK AND WORK SURFACE REQUIRED

NOTE

13.83 A wheelchair turning area and accessible sink and work surface are required. In pass-through kitchens, the required turning area may include knee and toe clearances under the sink or work surface.

ICC/ANSI A117.1 TYPE A MINIMUM CLEARANCE AND TYPE A U-SHAPED
13.84

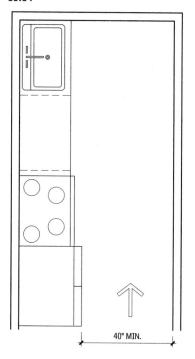

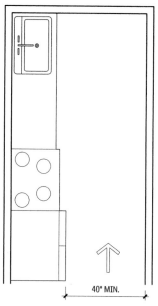

ACCESSIBLE KITCHENS

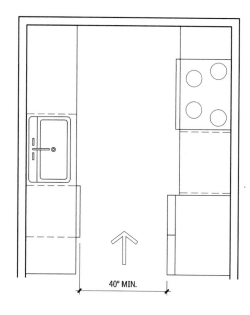

40" MIN.

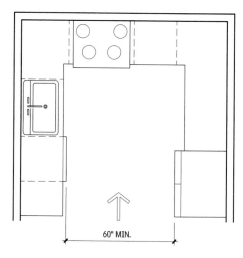

60" MIN.

ACCESSIBLE U-SHAPED KITCHEN

A wheelchair turning area and accessible or adaptable sink and work surface are required. In galley kitchens (minimum clearance) the required turning area may include knee and toe clearances under the sink or work surface.

ICC/ANSI A117.1 TYPE B MINIMUM CLEARANCE AND TYPE B U-SHAPED
13.85

40" MIN.

ACCESSIBLE KITCHENS

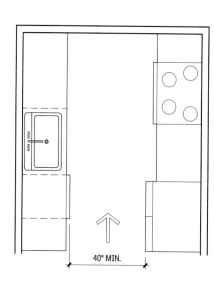

40" MIN.

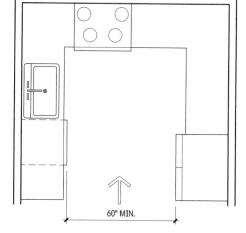

60" MIN.

ACCESSIBLE U-SHAPED KITCHEN

A U-shaped counter arrangement must include a 5-ft clearance between the opposing counters (or appliances or walls) to comply with ICC/ANSI A117.1 Accessible Unit, ICC/ANSI A117.1 Type A, and ICC/ANSI A117.1 Type B. FHAA guidelines require a 5-ft clearance if a sink, range, or cooktop is installed in the base leg of the U. If the base leg fixture includes a knee space or removable base cabinets, the 5-ft clearance is not required.

NOTE

13.85 A wheelchair turning area and accessible or adaptable sink and work surface are required.

APPROACH DIAGRAM FOR FIXTURES OR APPLIANCES
13.86

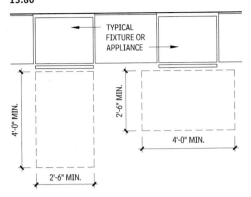

FRONT   **PARALLEL**

KITCHEN SINK AND DISHWASHER
13.87

Locating the kitchen sink next to the dishwasher has accessibility benefits as well as functional advantages. The sink knee space provides convenient access for a wheelchair user to the adjacent dishwasher. The sink itself should be a shallow unit with easy-to-operate faucets. A tall spout and a pullout spray attachment are also recommended. Garbage disposals must be offset in order to provide full knee space under the sink.

KITCHEN STORAGE
13.88

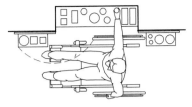

The design of kitchen storage space for wheelchair users should provide both visual and physical access to cabinets, drawers, and pantries. Base cabinets, for example, can be specified to include pullout shelves or drawers that will provide easy access to items stored in the back of the cabinets. Similarly, shelf racks on pantry doors make it easier for the user to find and reach stored items.

STOVES AND COOKTOPS
13.89

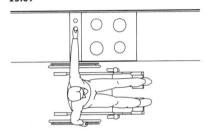

A range or cooktop should have front- or side-mounted controls so the seated user does not need to reach over the heated surfaces. A smooth cooktop surface allows pots to be slid, rather than lifted, on and off the burners. Separate cooktop and oven units allow the alternative of providing knee space below the cooking surface, although this arrangement can also create safety issues.

REFRIGERATORS
13.90

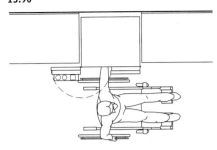

Side-by-side models offer the user both freezer and refrigerator storage at all height levels, from the floor to the top shelf. Over-and-under models can also be a satisfactory choice for many wheelchair users. Models with narrower doors are easier to operate, and the desired parallel access is easier to provide if the refrigerator doors swing back a full 180°.

ADAPTABLE FEATURES

The term *adaptability* is defined as "the capability of certain . . . elements . . . to be altered or added so as to accommodate the needs of persons with or without disabilities." For accessible kitchens, adaptable elements might include removable base cabinets that can be eliminated to provide knee space below countertops, or adjustable-height countertop sections that can be raised and lowered. With adaptable cabinets, the flooring must extend beneath, and the walls must be finished, so that when the base cabinet is removed, the kitchen maintains a finished appearance.

Contributors:
Lawrence G. Perry, AIA, Silver Spring, Maryland; Rebecca Ingram Architect, Albuquerque, New Mexico.

14 COMPUTING TECHNOLOGIES

491 **Building Information Modeling (BIM)**

INTRODUCTION

Computing technologies evolve rapidly, and their integration into the profession of architecture matches—if not exceeds—the pace of their development. Some technology-based tools are well established in architectural practice; others have unknown potential in their application to design, visualization, or project delivery.

Architects navigate between two attitudes toward computing technologies:

- *Technology facilitates*: It can help architects do what they have always done, but better, faster, and/or cheaper.
- *Technology transforms*: It can reshape what architects do, changing the premises upon which they operate.

An example of the first attitude are those firms that have changed the way they deliver services through building information modeling (BIM), but design within relatively conventional boundaries. An example of the second attitude are architects who use computing technology to explore design parameters too complex to study using analog techniques, which may include non-Euclidian geometries or precise airflows in and around a building. The project delivery for this second approach is not necessarily radically different from conventional delivery but is often altered because the highly specialized data can't be manipulated through conventional means.

Most practices experiment with a range of applications for computing technology depending on the project; sometimes technology facilitates, sometimes it transforms. The variety of approaches have one thing in common, however: the architect plays a crucial role in the creation, coordination, and general management of data. Judging which technology to use and deciding on which tool to apply toward what end has become one of the most critical activities in which architects engage.

This chapter outlines the fundamental tools found in building information modeling (BIM).

Renée Cheng, University of Minnesota

BUILDING INFORMATION MODELING (BIM)

A data model in any given domain describes the attributes of the entities in that domain, as well as how these entities are related to each other. All computer programs deal with some kind of data, so they must have some type of underlying data model. Traditional 2D CAD and generic 3D modeling programs such as AutoCAD, MicroStation, Autodesk VIZ, and form•Z internally represent data using geometric entities such as points, lines, rectangles, planes, and so forth. Thus, although these applications can accurately describe geometry in any domain, they cannot capture domain-specific information about entities. The drawings and models of buildings created with these applications don't carry much information about the building itself, and are essentially "dumb." They are used primarily for producing documentation and for visualization.

To overcome the limited intelligence of general-purpose geometric representations, every design-related industry has been developing and using object-based data models that are specific to their domains. In the case of the building industry, both researchers at universities and commercial software vendors have worked to develop a data model that is constructed around building entities and their relationships to one another. Geometry is only one of the properties, of these building entities; thus, its primacy is greatly reduced, even though the interface to create the model is still primarily graphic. Such a data model is rich in information about the building, which can be extracted and used for various purposes, be it documentation, visualization, or analysis.

Building information modeling, (BIM) is the term that has been coined to describe the use of such a model. Several software applications are now available that are built upon this concept, such as ArchiCAD, the Bentley Building suite, the Autodesk Revit suite, and others.

BIM in itself is not a new concept. It has been the subject of architectural CAD research since the mid-1970s, when the earliest attempts were made to develop integrated design systems that could support a suite of applications capable of operating together, rather than just individually. In the industry, Graphisoft's now 20-year-old solution, ArchiCAD, had building modeling capabilities right from its start. However, what is new is the push to replace CAD with BIM as the de facto standard in the building industry for integrating architecture, engineering, and construction. BIM is continuing to gain momentum rapidly in the building industry, and it is anticipated that most of the transition from CAD to BIM will be completed by the year 2010.

EXAMPLES OF APPLICATIONS THAT USE GEOMETRIC DATA MODELS. TOP: A BUILDING DRAWING IN AUTOCAD. BOTTOM: A ROOM INTERIOR MODELED USING FORM•Z
14.1

EXAMPLE OF USING A BIM APPLICATION, ARCHICAD, FOR BUILDING DESIGN: THE OPEN WINDOWS SHOW A PLAN, SECTION, AND 3D VIEW OF THE SAME BUILDING DATA MODEL
14.2

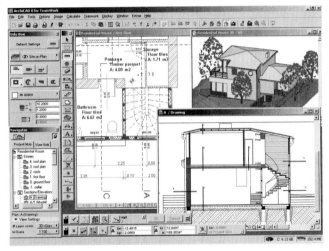

Source: Graphisoft

Source: Auto•Des•Sys, Inc.

HOW BIM OVERCOMES THE LIMITATIONS OF CAD

Traditional 2D CAD technology has dominated the construction industry for decades, and technological progress has been severely constrained by the limited intelligence of such applications in representing buildings and the capability to extract the relevant information from the representation that is needed for design, analysis, construction management, operation, and so on. Drawings are no longer done manually, but the ubiquitous use of CAD applications in creating drawings has not revolutionized the construction industry in any way. CAD continues to have all the problems associated with manual drafting:

- It is tedious and time-consuming to create separate plans, sections, elevations, details, and so forth, of the same building.
- Any change made must be manually updated in all drawings and reports.
- There is no guarantee of accuracy, consistency, or completeness.
- Coordinating work based on these drawings between the different professionals is extremely difficult.
- Conflicts and errors are detected in abundance at the construction site, necessitating expensive fixes.
- At the end of the process, the owner/operator has nothing but a nonintelligent 2D representation of the building on which to base a lifetime of management, operation, and maintenance.

Analysis and evaluations of energy efficiency, circulation, egress, and other aspects of the building, haven't really become an integral part of the design process as the building data is not available in any intelligent format and has to be tediously reentered into analysis tools. As a result, the quality of the building suffers. In short, CAD simply replicates the processes of manual drafting by reducing building representations to dumb graphic entities and does little to reduce the inefficiency, waste, errors, and escalating costs that are all too common in the design, construction, and operation of a building.

Unlike CAD, which is general-purpose, BIM is specific to building design: it represents a building using intelligent objects that know about their properties and about their relationship to other objects. Therefore, with BIM, a full 3D representation of the building can be created that simulates how it would be in real life; from this information-rich model, any kind of data needed for design, analysis, visualization, documentation, construction management, operation, and so on, can be derived.

The potential benefits of implementing BIM are manifold:

- Because it is customized for building design, it is faster and easier to create and edit a building model in a BIM application, compared to developing the drawings of the building in a CAD application.
- Once the model is created, all other requirements, including 2D documentation, schedules, reports, 3D renderings, and animations, can be automatically derived from it, improving speed and efficiency.
- All graphical and tabular views of the building are automatically synchronized when a change is made to the model, eliminating the inconsistencies found in construction documents created with conventional CAD software.
- The minimization of drafting allows greater focus on design.
- Interdisciplinary collaboration can be significantly improved, as it will be based on a shared building model.
- Better support for analysis and evaluation tools will allow the building to be thoroughly and vigorously tested before it is built, instituting much higher standards of quality control than those in place today.
- Conflicts are easier to identify in the building model and can be detected during the design phase, which can reduce the expensive fixes at construction time.
- The model created during the design phase can be reused for subsequent phases such as construction and facilities management, saving costs.
- The use of a "live" model for building maintenance can reduce operating costs significantly throughout the lifetime of the building.

In general, BIM is a technology that has the potential to integrate and dramatically streamline operations and processes in the architecture, building, and construction industries.

BIM AND RELATED TECHNOLOGIES

BIM does not work in isolation. What makes it particularly powerful in contrast to CAD is a host of related tools and technologies dealing with different aspects of building design and construction that work with it. This section provides an overview of various applications currently available that are either BIM applications or are complementary to BIM.

CORE BIM APPLICATIONS

The core tools for creating BIM models for architectural, structural, and HVAC, electrical, and plumbing design, as well as for constructability include the following commercially available applications.

BENTLEY BUILDING

The Bentley Building suite includes Bentley Architecture, Bentley Structural, Bentley Mechanical Systems, and Bentley Building Electrical Systems. All these solutions are built on top of Bentley's existing CAD platform, MicroStation, and its vertical extension for the building industry, Triforma. This coordinates with Bentley's belief in "not starting over" with a new solution for BIM, but providing an evolutionary ramp for users to transition from CAD to BIM.

EXAMPLE OF A BUILDING PROJECT WITH STEEL FRAMING AND CONCRETE FOUNDATIONS, DESIGNED USING BENTLEY STRUCTURAL. 14.4

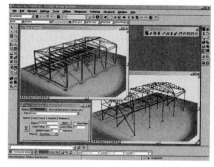

The upper-left window shows the physical model, while the lower-right window shows the analytical model, with finite elements in red, annotated section sizes, and boundary conditions at the bottom of the columns with nodes and node labels.

Source: Bentley

EXAMPLE OF HOW A CHANGE TO THE FOOTPRINT OF THE REAR WING MADE TO THE MODEL IN A BIM APPLICATION, REVIT (SHOWN IN THE UPPER IMAGE), IS AUTOMATICALLY REFLECTED IN ALL THE VIEWS (SHOWN IN THE LOWER IMAGE) 14.3

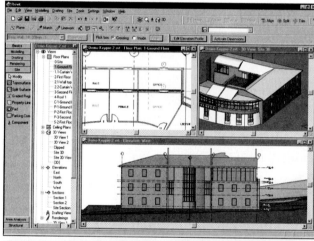

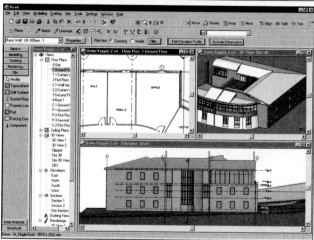

Bentley takes a "federated database" approach to BIM, meaning that not all the data related to the building is centralized in a single building model; instead, it is distributed across multiple applications and data stores in a coordinated fashion. Because the building data is decentralized rather than maintained as a monolithic block in a single model, it lends itself more easily to distributed work processes and sharing of information among design teams in multiple offices, as well as making the application more efficient for large projects.

ARCHICAD AND GRAPHICSOFT CONSTRUCTOR
Graphisoft offers ArchiCAD for architectural design, and Graphisoft Constructor for construction modeling. The core strengths of ArchiCAD are:

- A comprehensive feature set for the core architectural tasks of 3D building modeling, 2D documentation, and visualization
- A TeamWork module for collaboration that partitions the building model intelligently so that multiple users can work on it
- Support for openness with a full-fledged application programming interface (API), which allows the application to be customized, and add-ons to be developed to expand its capabilities
- Compatibility with Industry Foundation Classes (IFC) (see the later subsection, "Interoperability and the IFC Building Model"), which enables ArchiCAD to interoperate with other building applications for energy analysis, cost estimation, scheduling, and construction management.

ArchiCAD is based on the single model concept. The Constructor application includes the ArchiCAD modeling system for creating 3D construction models, a 4D sequencer for automatically linking the construction model to the project schedule, thus enabling different schedule alternatives to be analyzed, and a connector to a related estimating application.

EXAMPLE OF A CONSTRUCTION MODEL OF A PROJECT CREATED WITH GRAPHISOFT CONSTRUCTOR
14.5

Source: Graphisoft

ALLPLAN
Nemetschek's Allplan family of products includes Allplan Architecture for architectural design, Allplan Engineering for all areas of construction engineering, Allplan Steel for steel design, and Allplan Precast Concrete for the design, manufacture, and delivery of Shop fabricated concrete elements.

AUTODESK REVIT
The Autodesk Revit family of products includes Autodesk Revit Building for architectural design, Autodesk Revit Structure for structural design, and an application for HVAC, electrical, and plumbing design The highlights of the Revit products are:

- A single building model
- A simple, elegant, and intuitive interface
- Parametric building components that simplify the creation and editing of the building model
- Intelligent built-in relationships among building components, as well as the capability to define custom relationships and dimensional constraints, all of which are maintained when changes are made
- Automatic generation and coordination of all views and documents, including schedules
- Instant update of all views when any change is made to the model, eliminating inconsistencies
- Immediate availability of 3D views, contributing to a more interactive design experience

REAL-WORLD EXAMPLE: LOBLOLLY RESIDENCE
To illustrate the application of BIM software, a real-world example is included here. It demonstrates how the Revit family of products was used in the construction of a single-family residence, the Loblolly house, in Taylors Island, Maryland, on the Chesapeake Bay.

This 1,800 sq ft weekend house was designed by KieranTimberlake Associates (KTA) from Philadelphia, Pennsylvania. With a tight con-

LOBLOLLY HOUSE–EXTERIOR RENDERING FROM BAY
14.6

View of Loblolly House from Chesapeake Bay.

struction schedule and without access to skilled local labor, the architects embraced the precision of off-site shop fabricated, site assembled construction. This necessitated a three-dimensional understanding of the building and its components, which led to their use of BIM software.

KTA's systematic approach to Loblolly House allowed the architects to seamlessly combine standard on-site with unconventional off-site construction strategies. Use of Autodesk's BIM software, Revit, enabled them to improve communication among themselves, engineers, fabricators, and contractors, to collapse all phases of the project into a virtual snapshot. Design decisions were made in tandem with detailing, building system, fabrication, and shipping decisions.

The holistic nature of a single virtual model circumnavigated many of the unknowns that slow down traditional building processes. By understanding Revit's capabilities, as well as its limitations, KTA could customize the software in response to the specifics of the project. In many cases, they had to reteach the software how to "behave" with respect to issues of shop fabrication and modular construction. Proof of their mastery of the software is evident in the project's 30-day overall construction schedule.

Aside from the advantages of designing in three dimensions, this holistic approach allowed for more efficient coordination between systems and components, as well as more effective management of part schedules and cost models. With BIM software, one model is the sole source of all project information: it drives all details, fabrication drawings, finish schedules, and parts lists. As a shop fabricated project, this degree of control became very important for KTA in Loblolly House.

This example describes the attributes and benefits of Autodesk's Revit BIM software by examining each of the major construction components in the project: scaffolding, framing, cartridges, boxes, and skin.

LOBLOLLY HOUSE–EXTERIOR RENDERING FROM DRIVEWAY
14.7

View of the approach to Loblolly House from the driveway.

LOBLOLLY HOUSE–EXPLODED DRAWING OF COMPONENTS
14.8

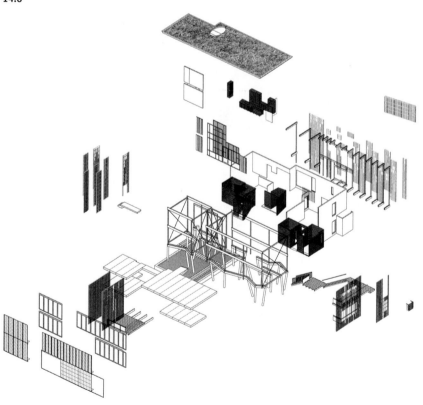

Exploded axonometric of Loblolly house with its four major components: scaffolding, cartridges, boxes, and exterior skin.

SCAFFOLDING

Fabricators extruded the aluminum profiles, which composed the structural frame, cut them to size, then shipped them to the site for assembly. The characteristics of these profiles required a great degree of accuracy, so KTA created a library of aluminum profiles within the Revit model. This enabled them to assemble the frame virtually, much as it would be erected on-site. Each aluminum component contained embedded data, including the size of the profile, length, manufacturer and distributor information, and cost.

Modeling the project in Revit also allowed KTA to accurately study sequencing, detailing, and tolerances during the early design phases of the project. In the case of the scaffolding and all of the project's construction components, BIM software shortened the on-site assembly of all building elements above the piling foundation to an astonishing two weeks.

LOBLOLLY HOUSE—FOUR PERSPECTIVES
14.9

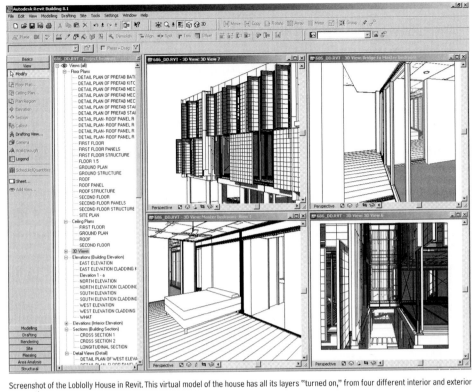

Screenshot of the Loblolly House in Revit. This virtual model of the house has all its layers "turned on," from four different interior and exterior perspectives.

LOBLOLLY HOUSE—FRAMING
14.1-0

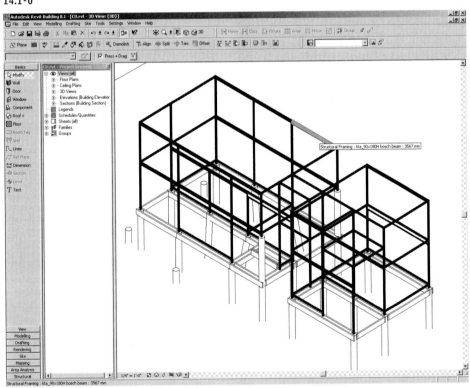

Revit screenshot shows the relationship of the light aluminum framing elements to the heavier framing members supported by randomly placed pilings.

FRAMING

KTA used the schedule produced from the embedded information in Revit for a number of important purposes: coordination with the structural engineer, development of a cost model, and, most importantly, as a parts list for purchasing this material. Having a single model to which all participants in the design, fabrication, and construction of Loblolly House could refer greatly simplified communication and coordination of changes. This meant that material, detailing, and cost considerations found their way into the project very early in its development. Traditional, two-dimensional construction drawings gave way to a holistic virtual model.

LOBLOLLY HOUSE–DETAIL OF ALUMINUM EXTRUSION
14.11

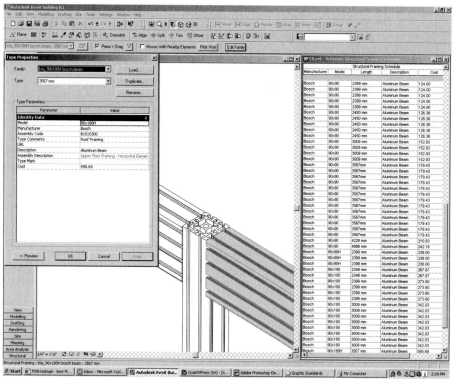

Revit parametrically associates numeric descriptions used for engineering and material tracking purposes to the virtual model of aluminum framing members.

LOBLOLLY HOUSE–FLOOR AND ROOF DECK
14.12

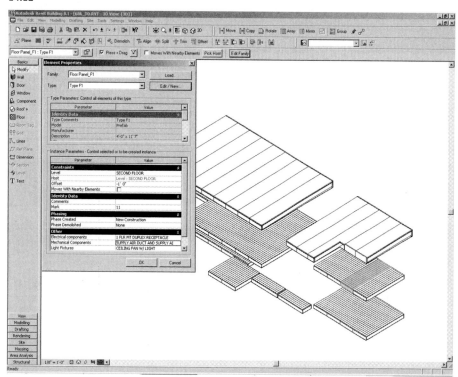

Figure 14.12 shows what KTA refers to as "cartridges," 12-in.-deep sandwich panels that form the floor and roof plates of the house and are fabricated with embedded lighting, electrical wiring, and radiant heating.

CARTRIDGES

Shop fabricated elements that KTA refers to as "cartridges" formed the floor, ceiling, and roof. These 12-in.-deep sandwiches arrived at the site with mechanical and electrical components installed, including lighting, floor receptacles, and radiant heating. The architects divided the 4-ft-wide panels into types according to their length dimension, which varied according to the floors and space. Models of these components, which included all building materials and finishes, informed KTA's approach to standardizing them.

This made the fabrication process more efficient. Because manufacturing limitations and the confinements of the structural frame dictated the dimensions of the panels, the components emerged almost as furniture, with restrictions built into their parameters. Within each floor/roof panel type, KTA embedded a schedule of facility service components. Again, this enabled them to produce a schedule that included the panel type, the number of recessed light fixtures within each panel, the number of floor receptacles, and so on. In addition to this information, the fabricator utilized the model as a base for fabrication drawings, eliminating the need for traditional construction drawings.

LOBLOLLY HOUSE—TWO FLOATING ROOMS
14.13

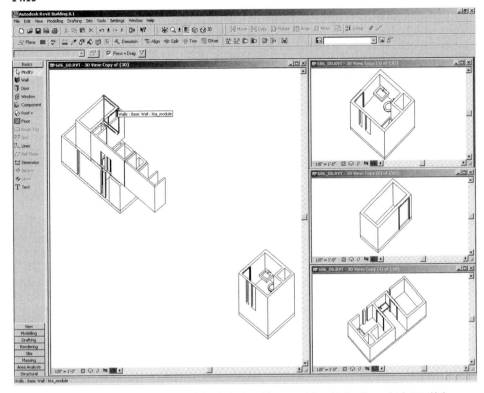

The boxes utilized by KTA contain complex plumbing and electrical systems. These were delivered to the site completely assembled.

LOBLOLLY HOUSE—WOOD RAINSCREEN
14.14

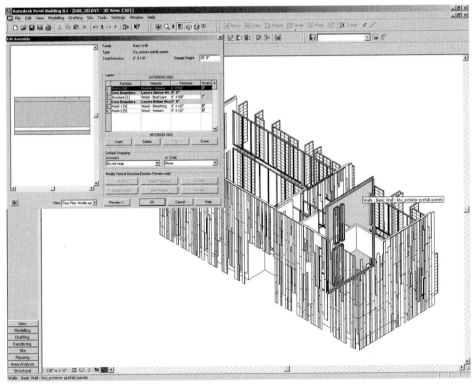

The house's wood rainscreen is held away from an operable glass wall by 16 in.

BOXES

KTA describes *boxes* as spatial units fabricated off-site that contain the most complex and intricate elements of the house. In the *kitchen box*, fabricators constructed all cabinetry and fixtures as large furniture with integrated fixtures and systems, connected on-site to waiting utility hookups in the lateral coffers. In *bathroom, closet, and mechanical boxes*, KTA conceived of floors, walls, ceilings, glazing, roofs, finishes, fixtures, drainage systems, power, and lighting as being finished within the factory and lifted into place at waiting utility hookups.

Modeling these objects in 3D informed KTA's approach to on-site erection. Because of aluminum frame conflicts, certain structural members were erected after modules were in place. The heightened understanding of interaction among systems informed the assembly strategy. As with other components, the Revit model enabled the architects to produce finish schedules, plumbing fixture schedules, and door schedules for the boxes. This was a beneficial communication tool for fabricators and manufacturers.

EXTERIOR SKIN

The construction team lifted and attached wood-framed, shop fabricated wall panels with a cedar rainscreen to the structural frame. Windows and glazing were also installed off-site. Transparent and translucent panels were off-the-shelf products designed with custom-hinged and sliding assemblies. Fabricators produced these off-site as multilevel units before attaching them to the structural frame on-site. Offset 16 in. from a fully retractable, double-glazed storefront, the whole assembly created a high-performance cavity wall.

Unlike typical walls built on-site, these wall modules had to respect the limitations of shipping. Therefore, awareness of their parameters was particularly useful during fabrication. KTA understood the performance requirements of constructing a functional rainscreen wall. Using Revit allowed them to closely monitor the relationship between off-the-shelf and custom components to render the screen operationally sound.

OTHER APPLICATIONS RELATED TO BIM

All component specification information is captured within a BIM model, which means that any kind of data needed for design, analysis, visualization, documentation, construction management, operation, and so on, can be derived from it, thus allowing the building to be simulated as it would be in real life. Some tools that work with the information in a BIM model are already available, and as the use of BIM becomes more widespread, future development is progressing for many more tools dealing with all aspects of design, construction, and operation.

BIM tools currently available include:

- *Tools that check a BIM model for design and modeling errors*: The best example of this tool category is the Solibri Model Checker, which "spell-checks" a BIM model to detect potential problems, conflicts, or design code violations, thereby ensuring the integrity of the model for downstream building analysis applications. It works primarily with a building model described in the IFC format (see the next subsection, "Interoperability and the IFC Building Model").
- *Tools that can detect conflicts and spatial interferences between the different disciplinary BIM models*: One of the key benefits of BIM is its capability to facilitate multidisciplinary collaboration, particularly when BIM is being used by all the different disciplinary professionals involved in a project. This category of tools includes the architectural, structural, and HVAC components. Leading examples of such tools are the Bentley Interference Manager, which works with all the Bentley Building solutions, and the Clash Detective module in NavisWorks, which is a suite of applications for 3D design publishing and review that works with many different file formats.
- *Tools for energy analysis*: These tools have a long history in the architecture, engineering, and construction (AEC) industry and have been used since the advent of computing. Prior to BIM, using these tools involved a great deal of manual entry of the building data, a tedious process that was prone to inaccuracy. With BIM, the building data is already available in a semantically meaningful form and the data can be directly input to an energy analysis tool. A leading example is Green Building Studio, a

SCREENSHOT SHOWING BIDIRECTIONAL LINKS
BETWEEN REVIT STRUCTURE AND STRUCTURAL
ANALYSIS AND DESIGN APPLICATIONS
14.15

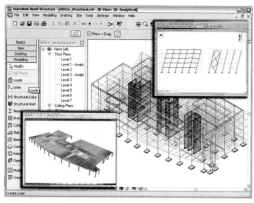

Source: Autodesk

NONCOMPLIANCE RESULTS DETECTED BY
E-PLANCHECK FOR A SPECIFIED CLAUSE IN A
BUILDING. WHEN VIEWED IN COLOR, THE PROBLEM
AREA IS HIGHLIGHTED IN RED IN THE VIEWER
14.16

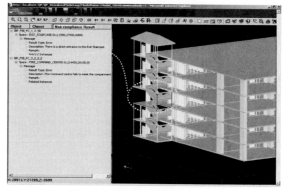

Source: Courtesy of Novacitynets Pte. Ltd., Singapore

Web-based application that works with a gbXML file exported from several BIM applications and uses the building information it needs to perform a DOE-2 energy simulation. It allows a proposed design to be quickly evaluated for energy performance and makes it easy to compare the simulation results for multiple options by displaying them together in one table. Another example is ECOTECT, which allows daylighting analysis, as well as thermal analysis.

- *Structural design and analysis tools:* Similar to energy analysis tools, these tools also have a long history of use in the industry and have also traditionally relied on manual reentry of the building data. Now, BIM structural modeling tools such as Bentley Structural and Autodesk Revit Structure automatically link to structural design and analysis tools such as ETABS, STAAD.Pro, RAM Structural System, and RISA-3D. Some BIM applications provide a bidirectional link to the structural analysis tools, which not only automatically input the analytical model of the structure to those tools but also use the results of the analysis to automatically update the physical model and all the related documentation.

- *Cost estimating tools:* For cost estimating, BIM again removes the need for tedious, manual entry of building data into estimating tools, and provides the capability to directly link to the building model for quantity takeoff. Examples include Timberline Precision Estimating and Graphisoft Estimator. Graphisoft Estimator includes not only a model-based estimating system, which extracts quantity information from the construction model for producing estimates quickly and accurately, but also a traditional estimating system for easing the transition from manual takeoff-based estimating to model-based estimating. Additionally, it includes modules that divide the resources created by the estimating application into production zones and generate procurement requirements. Cost estimating modules also contain a 5D reporting system (i.e., 3D model plus time sequence plus cost) that uses the construction model as the link between cost and time and produces cost-loaded schedules for financial analysis.

- *Specifications tools:* Still in its infancy, only one example exists of a specifications tool that works with BIM. This is e-SPECS by InterSpec, which automatically creates and updates preliminary project specifications of a Revit BIM model, ensuring their coordination and accuracy.

- *Code-checking tools:* Of the various analysis and evaluation tools that can be supported by BIM, code-checking stands near the top of the list as one of the areas ripe for automation. It is well known that the process of checking code manually has many problems. It is very labor-intensive and time-consuming, prone to inconsistency (because codes can be interpreted differently by different individuals), and is usually not comprehensive because of time constraints. Because a BIM model is so information-rich, it should be able to support at least a partial code check. A system for automated code checking called CORENET e-PlanCheck

has been under development in Singapore for several years. It is now being tested before a full public release. Like many of the analysis tools described in this section, it works on the basis of the IFC format.

INTEROPERABILITY AND THE IFC BUILDING MODEL

Most BIM applications by commercial vendors have proprietary internal data models and so cannot communicate their rich building information directly with each other unless the vendors develop specific translators for this purpose. Neither can they communicate with other third-party analysis or evaluation tools unless a link has been custom-developed or the product has an API. This inhibits the free flow of building information across the various applications used by the individual players, becoming an impediment to achieving the full potential of BIM. What is required is that these applications be able to easily "interoperate," which is where the Industry Foundation Classes (IFC) comes in.

THE IFC MODEL

The IFC is an object-based building data model similar to that of commercial BIM applications, except that it is nonproprietary. It has been developed by the International Alliance for Interoperability (IAI), a global consortium of commercial companies and research organizations founded, in 1995, as an industry-based not-for-profit organization. The IFC model is intended to support interoperability across the individual, discipline-specific applications that are used to design, construct, and operate buildings by capturing information about all aspects of a building throughout its life cycle. It was specifically developed as a means to exchange model-based data between model-based applications in the AEC and facilities management (FM) industries, and is now supported by all of the major CAD/BIM vendors, as well as an increasing number of downstream analysis application vendors. With 14 chapters in 19 countries and 650 member companies funding its development, it is a truly global effort.

Because the IFC is an open data exchange format that captures building information, it can be used by the commercial BIM applications to exchange data with each other. This requires the application to be IFC-compliant, which means that it is capable of importing and exporting IFC files. Applications are assigned the IFC-compliant tag by going through an IAI-supervised product certification process. The IFC model specification is posted publicly and is accessible to anyone, so developers can work with it and build the necessary IFC import and export capabilities into their applications.

Looking at the actual IFC model itself in some more detail, it represents not just tangible building components such as walls, doors, beams, ceilings, furniture, and so on, but also more abstract concepts such as schedules, activities, spaces, organization, construction costs, and others in the form of *entities*. All entities can have a number of *properties* such as name, geometry, materials, finishes, relationships, and so on. The latest release of the IFC has a

total of 623 entity definitions, which means that it represents 623 different kinds of components or concepts.

ARCHITECTURE OF THE IFC MODEL

The main architecture of the IFC model shows how the model has been designed. From the broadest perspective, the model is divided into four separate layers, representing four different levels. Each layer comprises several diverse categories, and it is within each category, or *schema*, that the individual entities are defined. For example, the Wall entity (called IfcWall) falls in the Shared Building Elements schema, which in turn belongs to the Interoperability layer. The layering system is designed in such a way that an entity

DIAGRAMS SHOWING DIFFERENCE BETWEEN
TRADITIONAL PROCESSES IN THE CONSTRUCTION
INDUSTRY AND THOSE ENABLED BY IFC-BASED BIM
14.17

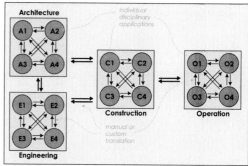

Traditional Fragmented Processes in the Construction Industry

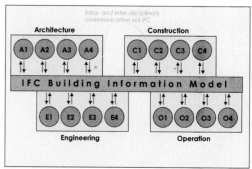

Integration Enabled by Building Information Modeling Based on IFC

at a given level can only be related to or reference an entity at the same or lower level, but not an entity at a higher level. The modular design of the overall architecture is intended to make the model easier to maintain and grow. Lower-level entities can be reused in higher-level definitions and a clear distinction can be made between the different AEC/FM disciplinary entities so that the model can be more easily implemented in individual, discipline-specific applications.

A brief description of the four main layers of the IFC model architecture is given here, from the lowest to the highest:

1. *Resource layer*: This contains categories of entities representing basic properties such as geometry, material, quantity, measurement, date and time, cost, and so on that are generic and not specific to buildings. They function as resources that are used in defining the properties of entities in the upper layers. Several of the resource definitions have been adapted from the STandard for the Exchange of Product model data (STEP) standard.

2. *Core layer*: This layer contains entities that represent specific nonindustry and industrywide abstract concepts that are used to define entities in the higher layers. For example, the Kernel schema defines core concepts such as actor, group, process, product, relationship, and so on, which are used in all the higher-level entities of the model. The Product Extension schema defines abstract building components such as space, site, building, building element, annotation, and so on. The other two Extension schemas define process and control-related concepts such as task, procedure, work schedule, performance history, work approval, and so on.

3. *Interoperability layer*: This level comprises entity categories that are commonly used and shared among multiple building construction and facilities management applications. Thus, the Shared Building Elements schema has entity definitions for a beam, column, wall, door, and so on; the Shared Building Services Elements schema defines entities such as a flow segment, flow controller, fluid flow properties, sound properties, and so on; the Shared Facilities Elements schema has entity definitions for an asset, occupant, and furniture type; and so on. Most common building entities would be defined in this layer.

4. *Domain layer*: This, the highest level of the IFC model, contains entity definitions for concepts specific to individual domains such as architecture, structural engineering, facilities management, and so on. Examples include a space program for architecture; footing, pile, and plate entities for structural engineering; boilers, chillers, and coils for HVAC, and so on.

In a color rendition of the architecture diagram, some of the schemas are shown in green, in contrast to the other schemas that are shown in orange. The green schemas are part of ISO/PAS 16739, meaning that these model definitions have been certified by the Organization for Standardization. To qualify for this certification, these model definitions must meet certain quality control standards. The ISO certification, which was awarded in 2002, is critical to the IFC because it implies a certain level of maturity and stability for that part of the model, which in turn makes it easier for commercial companies to justify its implementation.

FUTURE OF THE IFC EFFORT

The Model Support Group of the IAI continues to develop the IFC model. Although the base platform, comprising the green-colored ISO-certified schemas shown in the overall architecture diagram, is now frozen, work continues on stabilizing the entity definitions in the other schemas, and on extending the capability of the model to represent more concepts in the different domains of building design, construction, and operation. The IFC model aims to serve the entire building community throughout the life cycle of a facility—a massive undertaking, by any standards—therefore it is likely that the development effort will continue for several years. At the same time, efforts will also be made to receive ISO certification for larger parts of the model, to establish more of it as a stable standard for continued commercial development.

The entire IFC effort itself has reached a critical juncture. The model has matured, and the ISO-certification in late 2002 for a large part of the model was a major achievement. With the industry slowly but irrevocably moving toward BIM, the IFC has become all the more critical as an exchange format for model-based data. At the same time, efforts are underway to utilize its information-rich description of a building in more advanced ways then as an exchange mechanism.

Examples of such ongoing IFC-based projects include ifc-mBomb in the United Kingdom, which is focused on IFC model-based operation and maintenance of buildings; the CORENET e-PlanCheck project in Singapore, described previously; and the IFC Model Server project in Finland, which stores the IFC model data in an Internet-enabled database system, allowing IFC-compatible applications to communicate with each other via Web services.

SEE ALSO

Concrete Forming
Glazing
Metal Wall Panels
Precast Concrete

Contributors:
Text: Lachmi Khemlani, PhD, Founder, AECbytes and Arcwiz Consulting, Union City, California; Real-world examples: Marc Swackhamer, Assistant Professor, School of Architecture, University of Minnesota, Minneapolis, Minnesota.

15 ARCHITECTURAL RESEARCH

INTRODUCTION

Architectural practitioners conduct research all the time to:

- Stay abreast of client trends
- Gather data on project programs and sites
- Survey the relevant work of colleagues
- Investigate the performance and availability of products and systems
- Evaluate options during construction
- Monitor building performance after its completion

Despite the prevalence of research in practice, however, relatively few architects have training in research methods or a full understanding of the range of architectural research being done. The goal of this chapter is to begin to fill that gap.

Architectural research has characteristics of both scientific or technical research, on one hand, and artistic or humanistic research, on the other. Christopher Frayling, rector of London's Royal College of Art, has argued that all research in architecture revolves around one of two prepositions.

- Research "into" design encompasses the social sciences and humanities, such as historical and environment behavior research.
- Research "through" design embraces creative production, with the design process itself as a form of discovering new knowledge.

Among these two types of architectural research exist different methods of investigation. Whereas scientific researchers ask testable questions, conduct replicable experiments, draw general conclusions, and communicate through peer-reviewed journals or databases, architectural practitioners engage primarily in a far more applied form of research. They ask questions particular to a project, gather information mostly from existing sources, make decisions based on these findings, and communicate them through such vehicles as memos, drawings, models, and contract documents.

If architects can be said to do "basic" research, it typically occurs through design. But unlike the basic research of science or social science, design discovers new knowledge in a less linear, more iterative way, based less on experiment than on experience, and conveyed less through written papers and more through competitions, exhibitions, magazines, and monographs.

Although research pervades architectural practice, it remains relatively invisible for a couple of reasons. The field does not have a long tradition of documenting and communicating the research that goes into the work of its practitioners, as opposed to publishing the results of investigations in the form of completed buildings. Most architectural publications, for example, give scant attention to the design process, the critical thinking, or the detailed discoveries that often occur in the act of designing and constructing buildings. And even if publications welcomed such material, many architects hesitate sharing it, given the strong sense in the field of the proprietary nature of the work. Perhaps because of the close working relationship architects have with the construction industry and product suppliers, they sometimes act like a trade, keeping secrets, rather than a profession, sharing knowledge. That distinction has become particularly important now that designing and building have begun to merge in a variety of new delivery methods in response to changing market forces. As architects look for ways to distinguish themselves from their increasingly close contractor colleagues, research becomes a primary form of differentiation. By conducting and communicating research of all sorts, they increase their knowledge, raise their value, sharpen their identity, and improve the quality and performance of what they do.

Tom Fischer

NATURE OF RESEARCH

A user-centered POE focuses on the extent to which a building meets the needs of its users, according to environmental psychologists Kathleen Harder and John Bloomfield at the University of Minnesota. The evaluation centers on the people who use the building—both the primary users and those who visit the building. Their perceptions are needed to obtain a comprehensive understanding of a building's strengths and weaknesses.

TYPES OF DATA

In a user-centered POE, two kinds of data are obtained: subjective and objective data.

- *Subjective data* are acquired by querying a variety of people who work in or visit the building about their perceptions of various aspects of the building. Two approaches are used to obtain subjective data: surveys and focus groups.
- *Objective data* are obtained by measuring physical characteristics of the building such as air quality, temperature, sound levels, and lighting levels.

The subjective and objective data are compared—where appropriate—and any mismatches are explored to identify potential solutions to problems.

TYPES OF QUESTIONS

Before acquiring the survey data, the client should be interviewed about the intended purpose and functionality of the building prior to construction. In addition, a walk-through should be conducted to gain an understanding of the layout and flow of activity in the building. This information assists in the development of a survey that addresses specific characteristics and dynamics of the building.

The survey questions should be carefully crafted to be neutral and unambiguous. For example,

- "Do you agree that the facility meets your needs?" is a leading question likely to result in an affirmative answer.
- "How does the facility meet your needs?" is ambiguous because it is not focused on any particular dimension. The problem with ambiguous questions is that the researcher may have one dimension in mind (e.g., how well does the facility meet job performance needs), while the respondent might respond to another dimension (e.g., whether the facility has easily accessible food). Consequently, the data will be difficult to interpret correctly.

Rather than either of these formulations, the question should be "How well does the facility meet your needs for performing your job?" because it focuses the respondent on a specific dimension without forcing a particular response. This neutral question is given with a seven-point category response scale, with "not at all well" anchoring one end of the continuum and "very well" anchoring the other end.

Develop different sets of questions for the various groups of people who access the building for different reasons. Different versions of the survey, each with slightly different content, are administered to individuals within the relevant groups. A multiple survey approach yields more comprehensive and accurate data. It also allows for the comparison of the responses between the different groups.

Survey data are analyzed and interpreted. Also, where appropriate, the survey and physical data are compared. The results of this process aid in determining the areas to be explored in the focus groups.

FOCUS GROUPS

Several focus groups are formed. Each group is composed of people from similar levels in the organization. Do not recommend a mix of hierarchical levels because the presence of a supervisor can inhibit frank and valuable discussion. If there is a mix of hierarchical levels, then the discussion may be skewed toward what participants believe their superiors want to hear, rather than their actual perceptions. Custodians should comprise one focus group. They provide valuable insights into the building's functionality and the way in which others are using it.

As a general rule, there should not be more than seven participants in any one focus group. Numbers larger than this tend to be unwieldy and can limit the input of some participants.

It is important to note that the person convening the focus group should be a facilitator, who must not regard him- or herself as a participant. In other words, the facilitator should not offer opinions; rather, the facilitator should encourage discussion in particular areas, listen carefully to the responses, and make notes.

FINAL REPORT

Based on the results obtained from the surveys, physical data, and focus groups, a report is generated noting building strengths and weaknesses. The report is useful for the current occupants and facilities management people, who may be able to make adjustments. It is also instructive for the building's architects so they become aware of what works and does not work from the perspective of the users of the building.

HISTORICAL RESEARCH

Whether or not the project is a historic building or in a historic district, historical research plays an important role in architecture. The research can include investigation of the history of the site, the community, the client's organization, the building type, the existing fabric of a structure, or a particular material or system.

Historical research depends greatly on the range and quality of sources, according to Otakar Macel in *Ways to Study and Research Urban, Architectural, and Technical Design* (DUP Science, 2002). These include:

- *Literature*: The studies that have already been written about a subject
- *Sources*: The documentary material, printed or not, from the era of study

The sources are categorized in one of two ways:

- *Primary*: These include a building itself and the drawings and models of it.
- *Secondary*: These include what others said or wrote about the building, either at the time of its design and construction or afterward.

As in the design process, historical research demands an ongoing critique of the sources.

- *Correctness*: Is a source possibly false or biased toward or against the subject?
- *Provenance*: Where did the source come from, and is it reliable?
- *Time*: What is the date of the source and how does that relate to the subject?
- *Origin*: Who was the author of the source?
- *Originality*: Is the source or the information in it original form?

The sources also need to be ordered, of which several ways exist:

- *Elementary information*: Order the material according to time, place, subject, author, or any combination.
- *Thematic organization*: This orders the information according to type, based on function use or form or based on material and construction, for example.

The literature, too, needs to be ordered in a way that is useful. The ways of doing so include:

- *Topographical ordering*: Material is ordered according to published descriptive lists and inventories.
- *Chronological ordering*: Literature is sorted according to the era or date it was produced.
- *Bibliographical ordering*: The lists of books and other bibliographical materials dictate the way the information is organized.
- *Monographic ordering*: Material is ordered according to specific projects or people.

In terms of a building itself, the analysis of it takes two forms:

- *Morphological analysis*: This involves looking at the specific characteristics (what and how) of the work in order to compare it to others and to put it in a broader perspective (why). This can include the formal, functional, and structural aspects of the work, or its stylistic or conceptual aspects.
- *Technical analysis*: This can include looking at the site or material of a building or the construction methods used in it.

Evaluating the physical fabric of a historic building, says Barry Richardson in *Defects and Deterioration in Buildings* (Spon, 2001), involves its own particular investigative process that involves the following tools:

- Moisture meter to assess moisture content of wood and other materials and assemblies
- Borescope and a small mirror to look into inaccessible or hard-to-see places
- Utility knife, claw hammer, crowbar, chisel, screwdrivers, saw, and electric drill
- Camera, plastic sealable bags or sealable envelopes for samples
- Sectional ladder, flashlight, notebook, waterproof pens or pencils

Research into the history and conditions of existing structures constitutes one of the largest areas of architectural research because of the widespread reuse of buildings. The following case study, by Harry Hunderman and Richard Weber of Wiss, Janney, Elstner Associates, offers some insight into how this is done.

TECHNICAL RESEARCH

CASE STUDY: BUILDING DIAGNOSTICS

The development of appropriate repair methods arises from a thorough understanding of the condition and behavior of structures and construction materials. For each project, this understanding is gained through the use of selected diagnostic techniques. A wide variety of tools exist to help in the evaluation of existing conditions, diagnosis of problems, and development of appropriate methods of repair. The case study described here illustrates the diagnostic process.

BACKGROUND

An investigation was performed to determine the causes of masonry distress and water leakage observed on a midrise building constructed in the 1990s in the northern United States. The exterior walls consisted principally of cavity wall construction with brick masonry cladding backed up by cold-formed metal framing. The steel studs were covered with exterior gypsum sheathing with a building paper weather barrier. A drainage cavity existed between the brick veneer and the building paper, with the weight of the brick supported by the foundation and by shelf angles at floor slabs. Precast concrete lintels and sills occurred at all windows. In this

system, water that penetrated the brick veneer was intended to flow down within the drainage cavity behind the masonry to flashings installed at the shelf angles and lintels, and drain to the exterior through weep installed on the flexible flashing.

The windows consisted of a thermally improved, aluminum-framed system, with fixed insulating glass (IG) units. The window assembly typically had two IG units with an intermediate vertical mullion and a thermally improved aluminum subsill, with end dams extending beneath the full length of the window. Aluminum and glass curtain walls extending several stories in height also interrupted the brick masonry cladding at several areas.

TYPICAL OVERALL WALL SECTION AT WINDOW AND SHELF ANGLE
15.1

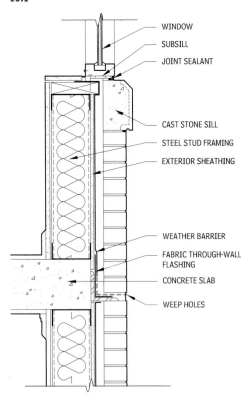

- WINDOW
- SUBSILL
- JOINT SEALANT
- CAST STONE SILL
- STEEL STUD FRAMING
- EXTERIOR SHEATHING
- WEATHER BARRIER
- FABRIC THROUGH-WALL FLASHING
- CONCRETE SLAB
- WEEP HOLES

TYPICAL WALL ELEVATION AT WINDOW AND SHELF ANGLE
15.2

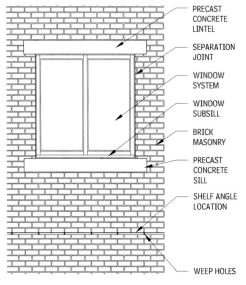

- PRECAST CONCRETE LINTEL
- SEPARATION JOINT
- WINDOW SYSTEM
- WINDOW SUBSILL
- BRICK MASONRY
- PRECAST CONCRETE SILL
- SHELF ANGLE LOCATION
- WEEP HOLES

SECTION THROUGH SHELF ANGLE SHOWING BULGING
15.4

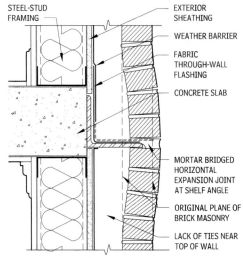

- STEEL-STUD FRAMING
- EXTERIOR SHEATHING
- WEATHER BARRIER
- FABRIC THROUGH-WALL FLASHING
- CONCRETE SLAB
- MORTAR BRIDGED HORIZONTAL EXPANSION JOINT AT SHELF ANGLE
- ORIGINAL PLANE OF BRICK MASONRY
- LACK OF TIES NEAR TOP OF WALL

SECTION THROUGH SHELF ANGLE AS ORIGINALLY CONSTRUCTED
15.3

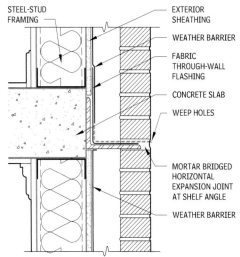

- STEEL-STUD FRAMING
- EXTERIOR SHEATHING
- WEATHER BARRIER
- FABRIC THROUGH-WALL FLASHING
- CONCRETE SLAB
- WEEP HOLES
- MORTAR BRIDGED HORIZONTAL EXPANSION JOINT AT SHELF ANGLE
- WEATHER BARRIER

INVESTIGATION

Problems observed in the exterior cladding included outward displacement (bulging) and cracking of the masonry and water leakage into the interior at various locations. The purpose of the investigation was to determine the causes of distress and leakage, evaluate the extent of the problems, and provide direction for repairs.

REVIEW OF DOCUMENTS

Prior to the field investigation, original architectural and structural documents were reviewed, as well as shop drawings and submittals from original construction. In addition, the review of maintenance records helped to understand the nature of existing construction and past problems and repairs.

VISUAL SURVEY

Following review of available documents, a visual survey of the building exterior walls was performed from grade, using binoculars and from the roof areas. This visual survey provided a general understanding of existing conditions and permitted the investigators to select the range and extent of further investigation required.

The visual survey of the brick veneer revealed numerous bond separations between masonry units and mortar. The extent of bond separations also suggested poor workmanship and tooling of the mortar joints during installation. These separations, as well as cracks and voids in the mortar, allowed an increased amount of water to enter into the drainage cavity behind the masonry. Efflorescence, observed on the brick masonry at several isolated locations, primarily above the shelf angles, results from the deposition of soluble salts on the masonry surface and usually indicates water moving through the masonry. In addition, cracking and bulging were observed at shelf angle locations, and control joints had completely compressed in areas where there appeared to be blockage of the horizontal control joint.

Visual observation also revealed a widespread failure of sealant joints at window perimeters and curtain walls, including both adhesive and cohesive failures. A visual survey of the interior, performed in conjunction with the exterior survey, showed water damage to interior finishes at numerous windows, primarily at the ends of the sill member. Based on the results of the visual survey, locations were selected for close-up inspection, inspection openings, and water leakage testing.

CLOSE-UP INSPECTION

A close-up inspection was performed at representative locations from suspended scaffolding (swing stages) and personnel lifts. The close-up inspection provided the opportunity for inspection openings, field-testing, removal of samples, and implementation of a variety of diagnostic techniques. Evaluating the precast concrete units demanded nondestructive test methods, which included

sounding techniques (tapping with a hammer) to identify delaminations and voids, and a metal detector survey to identify the presence and general location of metal elements. A borescope, which uses a fiberoptic light source, was used to examine concealed conditions within the masonry wall through very small openings made in mortar joints. Sample removals included brick and mortar for laboratory testing, as discussed later in this section. During the metal detector survey for embedded brick ties, a lack of brick ties was detected near the floor lines. This allowed the masonry to displace outward at the shelf angles.

Inspection openings were performed at selected locations to permit examination of concealed conditions and to verify as-built construction. Inspection openings were made in the brick veneer at suspected sources of leakage and observed distress and at other locations of interest to expose the underlying construction to view. For example, inspection openings made at the shelf angle locations revealed that the through-wall flashing at the shelf angles consisted of paper-coated copper. The laminated sheet flashing was terminated at or behind the toe of the angle, rather than extending to the face of the masonry. The flashing was not sealed down to the steel angle. Because the flashing terminated at the edge of the steel and was not sealed down, any water flowing off the end of the flashing could contact the steel angle.

As another example of conditions revealed at inspection openings, the flashing at the window heads was found not to extend beyond the precast concrete lintel. Instead, flashing at these locations terminated approximately 2 in. beyond the window opening without end dams. Water collected by this flashing flowed laterally and would drop onto the top of the masonry at the jamb, as observed during testing.

WATER LEAKAGE TESTING

A visual survey on the building interior was completed to identify evidence of moisture infiltration. Water spray testing was performed at selected exterior locations to evaluate the resistance of wall construction and windows to water leakage. Four test methods were used.

In *spray rack testing*, water is introduced against the surface of the masonry with a rack of nozzles calibrated to deliver water at a rate of 5 gallons per square foot per hour. The spray rack was built and calibrated in accordance with ASTM E 1105, "Standard Test Method for Field Determination of Water Penetration for Installed Windows, Curtain Walls, and Doors by Uniform or Cyclic Static Pressure Difference." The test was performed without an applied air pressure difference across the wall system. In water permeance testing, a 3-ft-wide by 4-ft-high chamber is mounted on the masonry surface. Water is applied as a sheet across the specimen within the chamber while air pressure is also applied. This test was performed in accordance with ASTM C 1601, "Standard Test Method for Field Determination of Water Penetration of Masonry Wall Surfaces." The test determines the rate water penetrates the masonry during heavy, wind-driven rain conditions. The amount of water flowing into the masonry, rather than being circulated by the chamber and supply tank, is measured as the amount of water penetration into the wall. The tests were run for a period of four hours each at an applied air pressure of 10 psf across the exterior of the test area.

In *wall drainage testing*, water is applied through plastic tubing directly into the drainage cavity behind the brick veneer to evaluate the performance of the wall drainage system and its effectiveness in handling water that penetrates into the wall system. As specified in the American Architectural Manufacturers Association (AAMA) test method 501.2, "Quality Assurance and Diagnostic Water Leakage Field Check of Installed Storefronts, Curtain Walls, and Sloped Glazing Systems," a calibrated hand-held nozzle is used to test the resistance of nonmoving joints to water penetration and to help isolate, or pinpoint, sources of water leakage.

Prior to performing water infiltration testing, finishes were removed to allow monitoring for leakage. This included the removal of the interior stool and gypsum board at leakage locations and surrounding windows to be tested. In this fashion, leakage occurring during testing could be readily observed and the sources pinpointed.

Water permeance testing was performed at two areas where the condition of the masonry was judged visually to be relatively good and exhibited few bond separations. The results of the testing indicated that the brick masonry had a relatively high permeance for a building of this age. The high permeance results in an increased amount of water that must be handled and drained by the wall flashing system, especially during heavy, wind-driven rains.

During testing of the through-wall flashing at the shelf angle, water leakage occurred at the intersection of the shelf angle and the curtain wall system. Water flowed onto the interior finishes and ran down the interior of the curtain wall frame. Water leakage also occurred at the underside of the concrete slab. This leakage occurred near splices in the shelf angles.

During testing of the masonry, water flowed behind the masonry at the window jamb and bypassed the window subsill/masonry intersection and flowed onto the interior sill framing. Water was directed into the subsill in many cases; however, at some locations, leakage occurred onto the wood blocking at the sill due to defects in the subsill end dam or poorly sealed joints between the end dam and the adjacent rough opening materials.

TYPICAL WINDOWSILL DETAIL
15.5

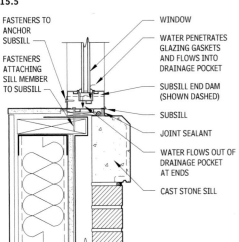

FASTENERS TO ANCHOR SUBSILL

FASTENERS ATTACHING SILL MEMBER TO SUBSILL

WINDOW

WATER PENETRATES GLAZING GASKETS AND FLOWS INTO DRAINAGE POCKET

SUBSILL END DAM (SHOWN DASHED)

SUBSILL

JOINT SEALANT

WATER FLOWS OUT OF DRAINAGE POCKET AT ENDS

CAST STONE SILL

FLASHING AND END DAM LEAKAGE
15.6

WINDOW NOT SHOWN FOR CLARITY

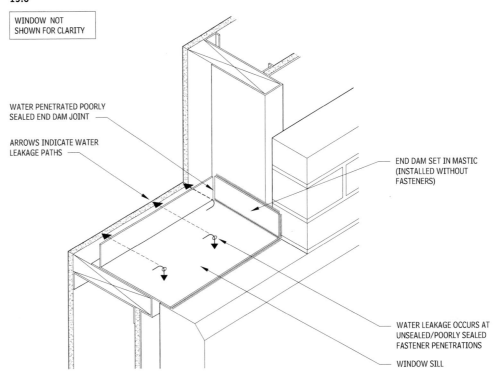

WATER PENETRATED POORLY SEALED END DAM JOINT

ARROWS INDICATE WATER LEAKAGE PATHS

END DAM SET IN MASTIC (INSTALLED WITHOUT FASTENERS)

WATER LEAKAGE OCCURS AT UNSEALED/POORLY SEALED FASTENER PENETRATIONS

WINDOW SILL

During *spray rack testing* of the window system, water leakage readily occurred at the subsill. At locations where nozzle testing was performed to pinpoint leak locations, observation from the interior during the testing indicated that the leakage at the sill of the test windows was the result of water penetration at the subsill, particularly at fastener penetrations and at incompletely sealed end dams.

Because of the need to confirm paths of water movement at the windowsill, the window system was disassembled at several representative locations. The subsill was found to be fastened to the wood blocking below, with screws that penetrate the subsill; however, joint sealant was not present at some of these screw penetrations. Aluminum end dams were present at the terminations in the subsill; however, the seals between the end dams and the subsill were not complete in all areas. The end dams were not mechanically fastened to the subsill. Also, subsill fasteners penetrated the horizontal legs of the end dams at a number of locations.

Subsequently, laboratory testing of selected materials was performed to provide specific information about materials characteristics and causes of failure. For example, petrographic examination was performed on samples of precast concrete to confirm that no compositional problems appeared to be present. Petrographic studies involved a standardized microscopic examination of materials samples based on the methods outlined in ASTM C 856, "Petrographic Examination of Hardened Concrete," to evaluate the overall quality and soundness of the materials. Compositional analysis of the mortar using methods of ASTM C 1324, "Standard Test Method for Examination and Analysis of Hardened Masonry Mortar," including chemical methods to supplement petrographic examination, was performed to confirm that the mortar composition was in accordance with specification requirements. Absorption and saturation coefficient testing of brick was performed in accordance with ASTM C 216, "Standard Specification for Facing Brick (Solid Masonry Units Made from Clay or Shale)." Per ASTM C 216, five bricks were included in each test, and half of each brick was used as a test specimen. The results were obtained for the individual specimens and averages calculated, to compare the brick to requirements of ASTM C 216 performance. The information gathered through research and investigation was analyzed to determine the causes of observed distress and to inform decision making about appropriate repairs.

Contributors:
Harry Hunderman and Richard Weber, Wiss, Janney, Elstner Associates, Inc., Northbrook, Illinois.

CURTAIN WALL TYPES
15.7

	CONVENTIONAL	STRUCTURAL SILICONE GLAZING		HIGH TECH ASIA	HIGH TECH EUROPE	POINT SUPPORT GLAZING	DOUBLE SKIN FACADE
		STRUCTURAL SILICONE ON	HORIZONTAL RIBBON WINDOW				INTERACTIVE ENVELOPES: COMBINED TECHNOLOGY OF CURTAIN WALL & HVAC SYSTEMS TO CONTROL INDOOR CLIMATE
MANUFACTURER	WASAU METALS, YKK AP AMERICA	WASAU METALS, YKK AP AMERICA	YKK AP JAPAN		PERMASTEEUSA (ITALY)	PILKINGTON (UK), MERO GERMANY	PERMASTEEUSA (ITALY) JOSEF GARTNER & SONS (GERMANY)
AESTHETIC	2*-2½-3*SIGHTLINES GRID WITH EXPOSED METAL MULLIONS	½ SIGHTLINE VERT. & HORIZ.) ALL GLASS & MONOLITHIC APPEARANCE	½ VERT. SIGHTLINE ½ HORIZ. SIGHTLINE HORIZONTAL RIBBON WINDOW	2*-2½-3-3½ SIGHTLINES ½-1* SIGHTLINE FOR SSG SIMILAR TO CONVENTIONAL BUT MORE ELEGANT & REFINED	DISTINCE & UNIQUE METAL & GLASS FACADES	ALL GLASS FLUSH SURFACE WITH MAXIMUM TRANSPARENCY	SLEEK FACADE TRANSPARENT WALL "HIGH-TECH" LOOK
TECHNICAL	GLASS CLAMPED TO METAL FRAME WITH A PRESSURE BAR THERMAL BREAK TECHNOLOGY USES THERMOPLASTICS GLAZING VIA INTERIOR OR EXTERIOR	GLASS BONDED TO METAL W/ STRUCTURAL SILICONE ON ALL 4 SIDES ½ SILICONE WEATHER SEAL NO THERMAL BRIDGING	GLASS BONDED TO METAL FRAME W/ STRUCTURAL SILICONE ONLY ON VERTICAL SIDES ½ SILICONE WEATHER SEAL	COMPARABLE TO CONVENTIONAL &SSG COMPLEX MULLION GEOMETRY UNITIZED SYSTEM ASSEMBLY METHOD	ENVELOPES ARE TYPICALLY UNITIZED SYSTEM W/ CONCEALED ALUM. PROFILES, THESE REQUIRE SPECIAL JOINT DETAILS SINCE THIS SYSTEM IS AN INTERLOCKING TYPE.	PATENTED GLASS FITTINGS CONNECTED TO STAINLESS STEEL CONNECTORS DESIGNED TO ATTACH TO SUPPORT STRUCTURES CONSISTING OF SPACE FRAMES, TENSION SYSTEMS, OR GLASS FINS. SILICONE SEALANT FUNCTIONS AS WEATHERPROOFING BETWEEN LITES	OUTER LAYER OF SINGLE GLAZING MIDDLE LAYER OF COMPUTER CONTROLLED METAL BONDS INNER LAYER OF INSULATED GLASS INTEGRATION W/ BUILDING HVAC
TYPICAL INSTALLATION	USED IN LOW, MID, & HIGH RISE APPLICATIONS TYPICAL LEAD TIME	USED IN LOW & MID RISE APPLICATIONS TYPICAL LEAD TIME	USED IN LOW & MID RISE APPLICATIONS TYPICAL LEAD TIME	USED IN LOW, MID, & HIGH RISE APPLICATIONS LONG LEAD TIME	USED IN LOW, MID, & HIGH RISE APPLICATIONS LONG LEAD TIME	USED IN LOW, MID, & HIGH RISE APPLICATIONS ATRIUM WALLS, LONG SPAN GLASS WALLS MODERATE LEAD TIME IF STANDARD FITTINGS USED	USED IN MID, & HIGH RISE APPLICATIONS LONG LEAD TIME
ANALYSIS	STANDARD WALL CLADDING SYSTEM MANUFACTURED EXTENSIVELY & WIDELY AVAILABLE IN THE U.S. POSSIBLE CUSTOMIZATION OF MANUF. STANDARD COMPONENTS EXTRUSION OF CUSTOM SHAPES AVAILABLE	LIMITED CUSTOMIZATION APPLICATION OF WEATHER SEAL & STRUCTURAL SEALANT IN FIELD SUBJECT TO WORKMANSHIP CAN BE UNITIZED & FACTORY GLAZED		STANDARD RANGE OF COMPONENTS DIFFER CONSIDERABLY FROM CONVENTIONAL IN TERMS OF EXTRUSION SHAPES & SIZES & ASSEMBLY OF FRAME MORE VISUALLY INTERESTING PROFILES FABRICATION TO TIGHTER TOLERANCES MANUF. MORE INCLINED TO CUSTOMER	INNOVATIVE AND SOPHISTICATED SOLUTIONS TO TECHNICALLY CHALLENGING DESIGNS ARE THE NORM	PROPRIETARY SYSTEM, MANUF. ENGINEERS THE SYSTEM AS A WHOLE PACKAGE UNLIMITED CUSTOMIZATION SINCE FACADES CAN BE ON ANY PLANE, VERTICAL, HORIZ., OR ANGLED	HIGHLY CUSTOMIZED & ENGINEERED SYSTEM IMPROVES BUILDING PERFORMANCE & OCCUPANT COMFORT SIGNIFICANT ENERGY SAVINGS ADVANCED BUILDING TECHNOLOGY USED PRIMARILY IN EUROPE
COST	LOW END: $28-35/SF HIGH END: $50-75/SF	$60-100/SF		$75-100/SF	$75-100/SF	$150-300/SF	$100-25

CLASSIFICATION OF WALL SYSTEMS

NOTES

1. ALL THE SYSTEMS ILLUSTRATED ABOVE INCORPORATE THE RAINSCREEN/PRESSURE EQUALIZED WALL DESIGN, THE ONLY EXCEPTIONS ARE THE 4-SIDED SSG AND POINT SUPPORT GLASS SYSTEMS, WHICH RELY ON THE SEALANT BETWEEN EXTERIOR GLASS LITES TO KEEP MOISTURE OUT.

2. OF THE FOUR SYSTEMS SHOWN AT LEFT, THE STICK SYSTEM IS THE MOST COMMONLY EMPLOYED INSTALLATION METHOD FOR CONVENTIONAL SYSTEMS. THE HIGH TECH SYSTEMS ARE EXCLUSIVELY ASSEMBLED USING THE UNITIZED SYSTEM.

3. GLAZING TYPES HAVE A SIGNIFICANT EFFECT ON THE APPEARANCE AND THERMAL PERFORMANCE OF A CURTAIN WALL, RANGING FROM HIGHLY REFLECIVE (MIRROR) TO COMPLETELY TRANSPARENT AS VIEWING FROM THE EXTERIOR.

KieranTimberlakeAssociates
ARCHITECTS

Levine Hall
UNIVERSITY OF PENNSYLVANIA
IAST PHASE II SCHOOL OF ENGINEERING AND APPLIED SCIENCES

Not To Scale
18 February 2000

Contributor:
KieranTimberlake Associates LLP, Philadelphia, Pennsylvania.

ACTIVE CURTAIN WALL SECTION
15.8

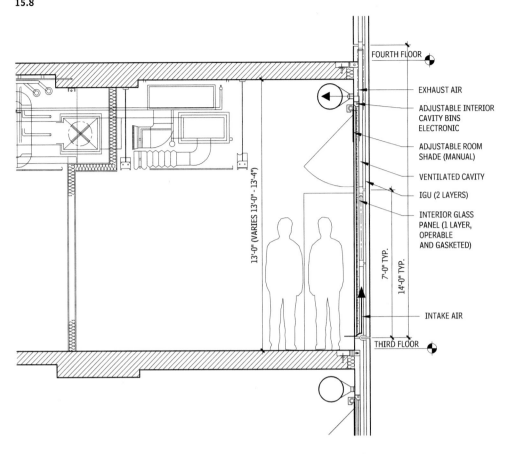

FOURTH FLOOR

EXHAUST AIR

ADJUSTABLE INTERIOR
CAVITY BINS
ELECTRONIC

ADJUSTABLE ROOM
SHADE (MANUAL)

VENTILATED CAVITY

IGU (2 LAYERS)

INTERIOR GLASS
PANEL (1 LAYER,
OPERABLE
AND GASKETED)

13'-0" (VARIES 13'-0" - 13'-4")

7'-0" TYP.

14'-0" TYP.

INTAKE AIR

THIRD FLOOR

GLAZING DETAIL
15.9

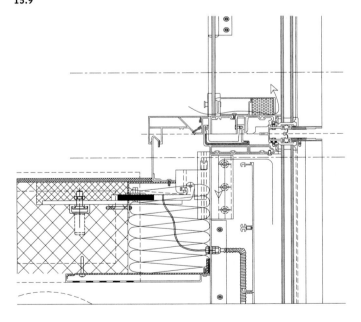

APPENDICES

INTRODUCTION

GENERAL

There are numerous ways of organizing facility and construction information, from various points of view starting with project conception throughout the facility's life cycle. The *OmniClass Construction Classification System™*, *UniFormat™*, *MasterFormat™*, and *SectionFormat™* are the four primary structures for classifying and organizing facility information.

OMNICLASS CONSTRUCTION CLASSIFICATION SYSTEM™

The *OmniClass Construction Classification System™* (OCCS) is designed to provide a standardized basis for classifying information created and used by the North American architectural, engineering, and construction (AEC) industry, throughout the full facility life cycle, from conception to demolition, and encompassing all of the different types of construction that make up the built environment. Created by the OCCS Development Committee, an all-volunteer cross-industry coalition of organizations, firms, and individuals, *OmniClass™* is intended to be the means for organizing, sorting, and retrieving information and deriving relational applications.

Industry organizations are beginning to realize that a greater degree of harmonization in classifying information is now necessary and possible. The classification tables in the industry-created *OmniClass™* address these criteria in an effort to make this harmonization a reality.

OmniClass's™ scope is designed to encompass objects at every scale of the built environment, from completed structures, large projects, and multi-structure complexes to individual products and component materials. Deviating from many of the systems that have preceded it, *OmniClass™* also addresses actions, people, tools, and information that are used or take part in the design, construction, and maintenance of these structures. It is anticipated that *OmniClass™* will be used throughout a facility's life cycle, starting with facility conception, continuing through design and construction, and finally to demolition and the recycling of its components. The means to address classification throughout the life cycle are provided through both a table to track and document the stages and the properties to describe dating information for components and for modifications to the facility as a whole.

OmniClass™ Table 22—Work Results is based on the concepts incorporated into *MasterFormat™* 2004. Conversely, the indexes and explanations of *MasterFormat™* 2004 draw information from *OmniClass™* Table 21—Elements and Table 23—Products, making it an application of *OmniClass™*. For information on *OmniClass™*, visit the OCCS Web site at http://www.omniclass.org.

UNIFORMAT™

CSI/CSC *UniFormat™* is designed to provide a standardized basis for classifying the physical elements of a facility by their primary function without regard to the particular work results that will be used to achieve the function. Substructure, shell, interiors, and services are examples of basic functional elements. The functional elements are often systems or assemblies. The shell element can be broken down into superstructure (structural frame), exterior enclosure (exterior wall assemblies), and roofing (roofing assemblies). The services element can be broken down into conveying (elevator systems); plumbing (domestic water distribution); heating, ventilating, and air-conditioning (heat generation); fire protection (fire sprinkler systems); and electrical (lighting systems). *UniFormat™* is an application of Table 21—Elements of *OmniClass™*.

UniFormat™ is a companion organizational tool to *MasterFormat™*. *UniFormat™* is most commonly used at the early stages of a project before particular work results have been selected. *UniFormat™* provides a means to organize design criteria, performance requirements, cost data, and descriptive requirements for systems and assemblies before a solution has been selected. *UniFormat™* is often used to organize preliminary project descriptions, preliminary cost estimates, and reference details. It is appropriate to change from *UniFormat™* to *MasterFormat™* to classify the physical elements of a project at the time in the project development when particular work results are being designated.

MASTERFORMAT™

CSI/CSC *MasterFormat™* is an organizational structure used to arrange information by traditional construction practices or "work results." The primary uses of *MasterFormat™* include organization of the project manual, detailed cost estimating, and drawing notations, including reference keynotes.

SECTIONFORMAT™

CSI/CSC *SectionFormat™* provides a uniform approach to organizing specification text within specification sections contained in a project manual. *SectionFormat™* is a companion organizational tool to *MasterFormat™*. *MasterFormat™* provides a standardized system for sequence, numbers, titles, and scope of the elements, including sections, of a project manual. *SectionFormat™* provides a standardized system to organize the data within each specification section.

OMNICLASS CONSTRUCTION CLASSIFICATION SYSTEM™

INTRODUCTION

The *OmniClass Construction Classification System™* (known as *OmniClass™* or OCCS) is a new classification system for the con-

struction industry. *OmniClass™* is a classification scheme useful for numerous applications, from organizing library materials, structuring product literature, and structuring project information to providing a classification structure for databases. It incorporates existing systems as the basis of many of its tables—*MasterFormat™* for work results, *UniFormat™* for elements, and EPIC (Electronic Product Information Co-operation) for structuring products.

OmniClass™ is a strategy for classifying the entire built environment.

The activities conducted throughout the life cycle of any structure generate an enormous amount of data that needs to be stored, retrieved, communicated, and used by all parties involved. Advances in technology have increased the opportunities for gathering, providing access to, and exchanging this information.

OmniClass™ is a publication of the OCCS Development Committee which has continually been updating and refining the *OmniClass™* tables. This manuscript references the 2005 edition of the tables, published in late 2005.

HISTORY

The concept for *OmniClass™* is derived from internationally accepted standards developed by the International Organization for Standardization (ISO) and the International Construction Information Society (ICIS) subcommittees and workgroups from the mid-1990s to the present.

ISO Technical Committee 59, Subcommittee 13, Working Group 2 (TC59/SC13/WG2) was established in 1988 to explore classification of construction information. In 1994, ISO Technical Report 14177 *Classification of Information in the Construction Industry* was published which provided guidelines for organizing industry information with recommendations aimed at improving the information flow within particular countries, and also from country to country.

Recognizing the growing need for such an organizational structure, the OCCS Development Committee held its inaugural meeting in 2000. CSI initially acted as the organizational body, though the committee has established its own organizing body, and is currently not directly affiliated with any other professional organization.

Based on its earlier recommendations, TC59/SC13/WG2 produced two new standards in 2001, one addressing a framework for the classification of information (ISO 12006-2) and the other addressing a framework for object-oriented information exchange (ISO/PAS 12006-3).

The Construction Industry Project Information Committee (CPIC) of the United Kingdom, which was formed to create an organizational framework, has utilized these standards most successfully with its 1997 publication of Uniclass.

In addition to the application of ISO 12006-2 in *Uniclass*, the object-oriented framework standardized by ISO/PAS 12006-3 has been adopted by ICIS members in their Lexicon program, and both standards are followed by groups in several other countries that are developing similar classification standards, including Germany and Sweden, in concert with the Nordic chapter of the International Alliance for Interoperability (IAI), and the Japan Construction Information Center (JACIC), which is currently working to develop the Japanese Construction Classification System (JCCS), modeled in part on *OmniClass™*.

The development of *OmniClass™* will be an ongoing process, accessible to all interested parties and designed to allow its content to expand over time to address unmet needs as they arise.

A preliminary draft for review and comment was published in October 2001 designated as the *Overall Construction Classification System*. Upon industry review and comment, Version 1 was published in 2006.

OMNICLASS STRUCTURE

The *OmniClass™ Construction Classification System* (OCCS) Development Committee believes that following these standards will promote the ability to map between localized classification systems developed worldwide. It is the Committee's hope that organizations in other countries pursuing initiatives similar to *OmniClass™* will also strive to be ISO compatible, thereby enabling smoother exchange of information between them.

ISO 12006-2: *Organization of Information about Construction Works - Part 2: Framework for Classification of Information*: This standard provides a basic structure of information about construction that is grouped into three categories composing the process model: construction resources, construction processes, and construction results. These are then broken down into 17 suggested "tables" for organizing construction information. The *OmniClass™* tables correspond to this arrangement of information:

- Tables 11 through 22 organize construction results.
- Tables 23, 33, 34, and 35, and to a lesser extent 36 and 41, organize construction resources.
- Tables 31 and 32 classify construction processes, including the phases of construction entity life cycles.

ISO 12006-2: *Organization of Information about Construction Works - Part 2: Framework for Classification of Information*, and ISO/PAS 12006-3: *Organization of Information about Construction Works - Part 3: Framework for Object-Oriented Information* define methods of organizing the information associated with the construction and affiliated industries, and also promote a standard object-modeling definition for concepts addressed. Of these two standards, ISO 12006-2 has more immediate impact on *OmniClass™*, and the OCCS Development Committee has closely adhered to this standard in establishing and defining the tables that make up *OmniClass™*.

OmniClass™ consists of 15 distinct tables, each of which represents a different facet of construction information. Each table can be used independently for the classification of a particular type of information, or be combined to classify more complex subjects.

The 15 interrelated *OmniClass™* tables are:

- Table 11—Construction Entities by Function
- Table 12—Construction Entities by Form
- Table 13—Spaces by Function
- Table 14—Spaces by Form
- Table 21—Elements (Including Designed Elements)
- Table 22—Work Results
- Table 23—Products
- Table 31—Phases
- Table 32—Services
- Table 33—Disciplines
- Table 34—Organizational Roles
- Table 35—Tools
- Table 36—Information
- Table 41—Materials
- Table 49—Properties

APPLICATION OVERVIEW

Many facility owners and managers insist on having access to all information generated during a developing project, updated throughout the life of the facility. They want to have access to the data that was used to prompt decisions, the options that were considered, the records of those options and decisions, and the information used to support the decisions made. They need that information to better manage their facilities, and the information will likely become an expected or saleable asset that will be transferred to future owners.

Coordinating the production, storage, and retrieval of that information is a daunting task, to which *OmniClass™* is perfectly suited.

CLASSIFICATION TABLE CONCEPT—OVERVIEW

The organization of the *OmniClass™* tables is based on the segregation of information types to be classified into a set of distinct, coordinated tables. The information contained in each table exists, and is organized, based on a specific facet or view of the total information that exists in the built environment.

Work has already begun on defining the ways that classification table entries can be combined to refine the classification of an object or concept by the International Alliance for Interoperability (IAI). It is expected that the entries from *OmniClass™* tables will also help to define (and refine) the characteristics used in IAI's Industry Foundation Classes (IFC), XML metadata entries, and other means of information distribution, storage, and retrieval. This will enable industry users to classify and store information in uniform ways so that other users can locate that information from a number of facets or viewpoints in consistent ways, using standardized terminology.

The ease of implementation is important in addressing *OmniClass™'s* table structure, as well as the definitions and facets of the tables that make it up. Although it is designed so that it can be used for hard copy classification, the real power of *OmniClass™* is dependent upon its implementation in computer, primarily relational or object-oriented database technology, using that technology's ability to relate information from a variety of perspectives, and to produce reports from all perspectives. The end result is an information management system that is more flexible and powerful than any simple flat-file storage system.

The subjects addressed at any level within a table are sufficiently broad in their definitions and dispersed in their organization that they will allow for subject expansion for new or innovative products or technologies that may be introduced to the industry. This can all be accomplished without any disruption to existing categories and to permit reasonably deep subordinate expansion of any heading.

Perhaps most importantly, the *OmniClass™* tables are designed to work together to provide specific classification. Depending on the complexity of the object being classified, and the level of detail desired, an object could have occurrences in one or more tables.

NUMBERING SYSTEMS

The OCCS Development Committee has assigned numbers to all entries in *OmniClass™* tables, and will continue to assign numbers throughout its development. The *OmniClass™* numbers will be selected to correspond to a broader numbering strategy.

The numbering of *OmniClass™* entries is chiefly a convenience for human interface; however, it is possible, and indeed preferable, for database applications to use the published *OmniClass™* numbers as data locations, to enable more reliable information exchange.

CLASSIFYING THE SCALE OR COMPLEXITY OF CONSTRUCTION WORKS

With *OmniClass™*, different scales or complexities of construction works are recognized. In order of decreasing scale or complexity, these are:

- Construction complexes
- Construction entity
- Spaces
- Elements

RETRIEVING INFORMATION CLASSIFIED BY *OMNICLASS™*

To retrieve information classified by *OmniClass™*:

- Find the class number in *OmniClass™* that best describes the information being sought;
- Check that the context is correct and that there is not another position in the *OmniClass™* table that better describes what you are looking for; and
- Go to the point in the classified collection of information which corresponds to your *OmniClass™* code.

UNIFORMAT™

INTRODUCTION

UniFormat™ is an arrangement of construction information based on physical parts of a facility called elements or systems and assemblies. These elements are characterized by their function without identifying the products that compose them. Elements render a view of a constructed facility different from the view rendered by a breakdown of building materials, products, and activities. *UniFormat™* is primarily used to organize preliminary project descriptions, preliminary cost estimates, and standard drawing detail filing. It is intended to complement *MasterFormat™*.

The Construction Specifications Institute (CSI) and Construction Specifications Canada (CSC) jointly produce *UniFormat™*. *UniFormat™* is updated periodically; the information given here reflects the 2001 edition.

HISTORY

Construction information arranged according to functional building elements was first introduced outside of the United States. Elements were included in one of five tables in a comprehensive Swedish classification system known as "SfB." In 1947, Sweden formed a committee of 32 major building industry organizations, called Samarbetskommittén för Byggnadsfr Çgor, thus the initials for the classification. Its first work was published in 1950 in the form of general material and work specifications for buildings. This was a collection of codes and practices arranged according to SfB.

The Royal Institute of Chartered Surveyors published a standard list of elements in 1969, *Standard Form of Cost Analysis*, which was reprinted in December 1995. The Canadian Institute of Quantity Surveyors published *Elemental Cost Analysis Method of Measurement and Pricing*. In the early 1970s, the first element-based classification in the United States was developed by the American Institute of Architects (AIA) for the General Services Administration (GSA). *UniFormat™* has since been used by U.S. Federal agencies, R. S. Means (in its *Means Assemblies Cost Data*), and others. In 1993, the American Society for Testing and Materials (ASTM) published ASTM E 1577, *Standard Classification for Building Elements and Related Sitework Uniformat II*.

In 1990, CSI became active on the working group of this ASTM subcommittee. Other participating organizations include the American Association of Cost Engineers, American Society of Professional Estimators, GSA, Naval Facilities Engineering Command, U.S. Air Force, and U.S. Army Corps of Engineers.

Working in cooperation with the ASTM Working Group, a Department of Defense (DoD) Tri-Service Committee on Work Breakdown Structure established a similar building element–based arrangement to classify DoD building project cost information.

The ASTM Working Group and DoD Tri-Service Committee each prepared versions of an element-based format in the first half of 1992. The two formats were similar but not identical. In August 1992, the National Institute of Standards and Technology (NIST) published *UNIFORMAT II: A Recommended Classification for Building Elements and Related Sitework*. UNIFORMAT II was influenced greatly by discussions held at ASTM Working Group meetings.

The first edition of *UniFormat™* was published as an interim edition, based on the work of the ASTM Working Group and the DoD Tri-Service Committee. The *UniFormat™* Interim Edition was published with the 1992 edition of CSI *Manual of Practice* and included coordination with the 1988 edition of *MasterFormat™*. This interim edition was published for trial use and comment.

After the publication of NIST and CSI versions, ASTM balloted and accepted *UNIFORMAT™* II in 1993 as ASTM E 1557. The ASTM standard was based on NIST and DoD documents but did not include a numbering system or the low-level detail of other systems and assemblies classifications. In 1996, ASTM adopted the numbering scheme used in CSI's *UniFormat™* for the 1996 edition of ASTM E 1557.

In 1995, CSI and CSC began revising *UniFormat™*. Revisions were intended to align ASTM and CSI documents and to coordinate *UniFormat™* with the *MasterFormat™* 1995 edition. CSI and CSC actively solicited public comments on the *UniFormat™* Interim Edition and continued ongoing discussions with ASTM Subcommittee E06.81 to determine the direction for the 2001 edition.

The current 2001 edition of *UniFormat™* (Tables A.69 and A.70) and ASTM E 1557-02 have the same numbering scheme, and the titles from Levels 1 through 3 are identical. ASTM E 1557 does not include the levels of detail, Project Description, and Category Z—General.

The 2001 edition *UniFormat™* titles, which are published in this text, are the result of extensive public review and coordination with industry users. In coordination with *OmniClass™* a CSI/CSC task team was established in the spring of 2006 to begin the updating of *UniFormat™*. It is anticipated that this extensive update will be complete in 2008 and will expand *UniFormat™* to cover all construction and the entire facility life cycle.

UNIFORMAT™ STRUCTURE

UniFormat™ classifies information into the following nine Level 1 categories:

- Project Description
- A—Substructure
- B—Shell
- C—Interiors
- D—Services
- E—Equipment and Furnishings
- F—Special Construction
- G—Building Sitework
- Z—General

The nine categories can be used to arrange brief project descriptions and preliminary cost information. Category Z—General is designated by the last letter of the alphabet, so the system can expand beyond building construction. When so expanded, this category will remain at the end.

Titles in Levels 1 through 3 can be applied to most project descriptions and preliminary cost estimates. Levels 4 and 5 are available for use in detailed, complex projects. Level 4 and 5 titles and detailed listings provide a checklist to ensure the comprehensive and complete application of *UniFormat™*.

APPLICATION OVERVIEW

Not all *UniFormat™* titles will be used for a given project. *UniFormat™* is an expandable structure that can accommodate additional titles to meet specific requirements. However, the designated numbers and titles listed should not be changed. This helps set and maintain a consistent arrangement.

UniFormat™ titles are generic, descriptive titles independent of the design solution. *UniFormat™* titles are the starting point for systems and assemblies. When creating a user-defined Level 3, 4, or 5 title, it is best to incorporate the parent title, so systems and assemblies titles are complete, clear, and descriptive.

Additional systems and assemblies numbers and titles can be added by users for projects that include items that go beyond build-

ing construction. These projects include heavy civil engineering construction and process facilities.

Some users may want to add *MasterFormat™* materials and methods information to a document organized according to UniFormat. *MasterFormat™* numbers may be included if some materials and methods have been determined. For example, if the building structural frame will be steel but the design solutions for exterior walls have not been determined, *MasterFormat™* numbers could be included for B10 Superstructure but not for B20 Exterior Enclosure. Users may refine documents organized according to *UniFormat™* during subsequent design phases as materials and construction activities are determined.

The transition from a document organized according to *UniFormat™* to one organized according to *MasterFormat™* may be made easier by using *MasterFormat™* extensions. When *MasterFormat™* six-digit number extensions have been added, the document organized according to *UniFormat™* may be searched or sorted according to the *MasterFormat™* extension to regroup information. Sorting in this manner may help discover, for example, a list of elements common to cast-in-place concrete construction within the project.

USING *UNIFORMAT™* FOR ARRANGING COST INFORMATION

The list of elements or systems serves as a basis for a system to organize cost information. Cost information may be reported in varying degrees of detail. As design decisions are made, the information can be refined. This arrangement of cost information allows for the comparison of various building elements, particularly during early design phases. The *UniFormat™* cost model can evolve along with a cost model organized according to *MasterFormat™*.

These two models render a different view of the same project and provide details appropriate for different requirements. For example, a cost model organized by *UniFormat™* can provide information about the cost of a concrete structure compared with a steel structure, even though there will be more concrete and steel on the project. However, a cost model organized according to *MasterFormat™* can provide information about the cost of all the concrete and steel on a project regardless of the structural system chosen.

Value analysis requires a consistent naming scheme carried throughout the project. *UniFormat™* is particularly useful for value analysis, which requires attaching a cost to a particular use or facility function rather than to particular products and activities. Using *MasterFormat™* numbers as suffixes to element designations helps the value analyst evaluate change proposals to the final value analysis.

USING *UNIFORMAT™* FOR ARRANGING PRELIMINARY PROJECT DESCRIPTIONS

Preliminary project descriptions are described in CSI's *Project Resource Manual*, Module 4 Design, 4.8.1, "Use of Preliminary Project Descriptions." A preliminary project description helps the owner understand the various components and systems proposed by the A/E for the project. It also serves a requirement normally included in a design services agreement in which the A/E must submit a report after completing the schematic design before proceeding to design development. These descriptions may be supported by, and serve as a basis of, an estimate of probable construction costs.

UniFormat™ provides a logical sequence of systems and assemblies to describe a construction project before all materials and methods have been determined. *UniFormat™* is used to organize, and serves as a checklist for preparing, preliminary project descriptions at various levels of detail.

As the design progresses, both descriptions and the estimate of probable construction cost can be refined.

USING *UNIFORMAT™* FOR ARRANGING PROJECT MANUALS

Most project manuals are arranged using *MasterFormat™*. Specifications using both *MasterFormat™* and *UniFormat™* should not be combined into a single project manual.

Performance specifying can be used at many levels, from a single product to major subsystems or entire projects. The choice of using either *MasterFormat™* or *UniFormat™* allows the architect to access a range of options. Performance specifying encourages competitive bidding based on nonproprietary requirements and, in its broadest application, is used for design-build projects. CSI's *Project Resource Manual*, Module 5, 1.5—"Performance Specifying," provides detailed discussions about this application.

USING *UNIFORMAT™* FOR ORGANIZING DRAWINGS

UniFormat™ numbers and titles can be used as a file-naming convention for library files of standard details and schedules. The *U.S. National CAD Standard's* UDS Set Organization Module provides a detailed description for this application.

Library files are named differently from project files because the classification and indexing requirements are different. Library file naming should be grouped by building systems, assemblies, or use because that is the most natural way to search for them. Project detail files must also be organized to make it easy to produce project contract documents, record documents, and facility management documents from several files. Naming a detail file for a project requires the sheet identification coordinates on the document, and a detail identifier.

The UDS Set Organization Module recommends an eight-character designator for naming library schedule files. A numbering system based on *UniFormat™* can be used for preliminary phases of a project. *UniFormat™* numbers can be used during the construction documents phase for schedules made up of assemblies of materials that might otherwise have separate *MasterFormat™* numbers.

USING *UNIFORMAT™* FOR ARRANGING FACILITIES MANAGEMENT INFORMATION

As *UniFormat™* is used for preliminary project descriptions to communicate systems and assemblies concepts to a building owner, preliminary project descriptions can be refined and used to communicate the building's functional systems and assemblies for real estate due-diligence reports and organizing maintenance and operation programs and data.

UniFormat™ is an ideal organization concept to describe systems design intent for facility commissioning purposes. *UniFormat™* can be used to document how systems and assemblies function. Preliminary project descriptions can be refined and can evolve through all design phases, with the commissioning authority's making system performance testing and acceptance easier. Descriptions can then be used by the facility operators and maintenance personnel to store information about system maintenance and operations.

USING *UNIFORMAT™* FOR ARRANGING INFORMATION FOR DESIGN-BUILD APPLICATIONS

The design-build project delivery has created a need for an organizational structure for communicating functional performance requirements, including organizing design-build requests for proposals. To communicate project performance requirements to design-build entities in requests for proposals, owners or architects must describe those requirements. In turn, design-build contractors must use performance requirements to communicate their proposals. *UniFormat™* provides this organizational structure.

MASTERFORMAT™

INTRODUCTION

MasterFormat™ is a master list of numbers and titles classified by work results or construction practices, primarily used to organize project manuals, organize detailed cost information, and relate drawing notations to specifications.

Construction projects use many different kinds of delivery methods, products, and installation methods, but one thing is common to all—the need for effective teamwork by the many parties involved to ensure the correct and timely completion of work. The successful completion of projects requires effective communication among the people involved, and that in turn requires easy access to essential project information. Efficient information retrieval is only possible when everyone uses a standard filing system. *MasterFormat™* provides such a standard filing and retrieval scheme which can be used throughout the construction industry.

The Construction Specifications Institute (CSI) and Construction Specifications Canada (CSC) jointly produce *MasterFormat™*. *MasterFormat™* is updated periodically; the information in this text refers to the 2004 edition.

HISTORY

Since it was introduced in 1963, *MasterFormat™*, as it is now known, has been widely accepted as a standard format for organizing specifications in the United States and Canada, designed to fulfill, in the words of the original authors, "a pressing need for a national format for construction specifications." First published as part of the "CSI Format for Construction Specifications" it was later used as the basis for the "Uniform System for Construction Specifications, Data Filing and Cost Accounting—Title One Buildings" published in 1966. The "Uniform System" was developed and endorsed by the following organizations: American Institute of Architects, American Society of Landscape Architects, Associated General Contractors of America Inc., Associated Specialty Contractors, Construction Products Manufacturing Council, National Society of Professional Engineers, and Construction Specifications Institute. In 1966 a similar effort in Canada produced "The Building Construction Index" (BCI), based on the 16-Division format that had been introduced by the Specification Writers Association of Canada, renamed Construction Specifications Canada in 1974.

The U.S. and Canadian formats were merged into a single format in 1972 and published as the *Uniform Construction Index* (UCI). The UCI was a comprehensive framework for organizing information contained in project manuals, as well as providing a basis for data filing and project cost classification.

In 1978, Construction Specifications Canada joined with the Construction Specifications Institute to produce the first edition of *MasterFormat™*, introduced by CSI as MP-2-1 and by CSC as Document 004E. It incorporated a complete organizational format for project manuals by including bidding requirements, contract forms, and conditions of the contract in addition to the 16-Division list of five-digit section numbers and titles used primarily for specifications.

The first revised edition of *MasterFormat™* was published in 1983. It retained the basic principles of organization contained in the previous edition. However, revisions and additions recognized the needs of the engineering disciplines.

The 1988 edition included revisions and additions needed to recognize new products and developments in the construction industry, and was based on input from *MasterFormat™* users.

The 1995 edition of *MasterFormat™* underwent a more extensive public review and coordination with industry users than any previous edition. It incorporated many minor revisions in section numbers and titles, and several changes in style and presentation. There were also some significant rearrangements of section numbers and titles, particularly in Divisions 1, 2, 13, 15, and 16. This was done, to a certain extent, to address the overcrowding of these divisions. The applications guide was expanded to provide specific information on proper uses of *MasterFormat™*.

From 2001 to 2004, in an unprecedented attempt at obtaining industry-wide acceptance and participation in the development process, the CSI/CSC *MasterFormat™* Expansion Task Team (MFETT) drew members from many parts of the construction industry in North America. Participants included architects, engineers, specifiers, contractors, and subcontractors, representing a wide variety of professional, contractor, trade, and manufacturing organizations. Due to the expanded scope of *MasterFormat™*, special emphasis was placed on input for highway, telecommunications, and process engineering work.

The *MasterFormat™* Expansion Task Team made their work known, and solicited input, through a wide variety of activities: a series of Stakeholders' Symposia, over 120 presentations to construction industry groups, numerous articles in national construction industry magazines, and four Internet discussion forums. In each case, commentary and input was solicited and incorporated into the process, all to help arrive at the highest quality content and most logical organization for the 2004 edition of *MasterFormat™*.

The initial task for the *MasterFormat™* Expansion Task Team was to establish guiding principles. These principles included:

- Keep changes to a minimum where the current system appears to be adequate
- Make it more acceptable to the mechanical and electrical disciplines
- Expand as required to cover things other than buildings
- Follow recognized classification principles
- Provide room for future expansion
- Maintain organizational consistency
- Expand to cover life-cycle activities

The 2004 edition is the result of this extensive public review and coordination with industry groups. The changes from previous editions are revolutionary in the expansion of Divisions and changes in the numbering structure.

MASTERFORMAT™ STRUCTURE

GROUPS AND SUBGROUPS

All of the following *MasterFormat™* groups and subgroups can be included in project manuals:

- Procurement and Contracting Requirements Group (Division 00) contains:
  - *Introductory Information:* Indexing and general-information documents are found at the beginning of project manuals.
  - *Procurement Requirements and Contracting Requirements:* Referred to in *MasterFormat™* 95 as the "Zero Series Numbers and Titles" and now included in Division 00, they are to be used in the definition of the relationships, processes, and responsibilities for projects.
- Specifications Group: This Group contains the following five subgroups. Each Subgroup is broken down into Divisions as listed. This group has now grown from 16 Divisions to 49 Divisions, (16 of which are designated reserved for future expansion).
  - General Requirements Subgroup: Division 01.
  - Facility Construction Subgroup: Divisions 02 through 19.
  - Facility Services Subgroup: Divisions 20 through 29.
  - Site and Infrastructure Subgroup: Divisions 30 through 39.
  - Process Equipment Subgroup: Divisions 40 through 49.

Groups are not numbered, but are divided into *subgroups*. Subgroups are not numbered, but are divided into numbered *Divisions*. Divisions are the top Level (Level 1) in the hierarchy of the classification system. The Divisions include sets of numbered *Titles* (Levels 2 through 4). In a project manual application, the titles are called *Sections* that specify "work results" (Levels 2 through 4). Work results are permanent or temporary aspects of construction projects achieved in the production stage or by subsequent alteration, maintenance, or demolition processes through the application of a particular skill or trade to construction resources.

APPLICATION OVERVIEW

The principle application for *MasterFormat™* 2004 is for titling and arranging the parts of project manuals that contain any combination of procurement requirements, contracting requirements, or construction specifications. Participants in the construction process may use *MasterFormat™* for other applications by adapting the organizing principles to those applications, such as for organizing construction cost databases, drawings notations in coordination with specifications, collections of technical data, construction market data, facilities management data, and others. Although it provides a detailed and ordered listing of potential titles, *MasterFormat™* is designed to maximize flexibility for individual users. For any given project, a user is free to assign new numbers for new titles in appropriate locations.

USING *MASTERFORMAT™* FOR PROJECT MANUALS

DISCIPLINE AND TRADE JURISDICTIONS

MasterFormat's™ organizational structure used in a project manual does not imply how the work is assigned to various design disciplines, trades, or subcontractors. *MasterFormat™* is not intended to determine which particular elements of the project manual are prepared by a particular discipline. Similarly, it is not intended to determine what particular work required by the project manual is the responsibility of a particular trade. A particular discipline or trade is likely to be responsible for subjects from multiple divisions, as well as from multiple subgroups.

CONTRACT DOCUMENTS

MasterFormat's™ organizational structure does not determine what is and is not a contract document. Generally, the documents included in the contracting requirements will include a definition and listing of the contract documents for a particular project.

In the procurement requirements and contracting requirements, some owners may use different terminology for some of the documents from those listed in *MasterFormat™*. Users may alter the *MasterFormat™* terms in favor of appropriate synonyms required by the owner. See the Master List of Numbers, Titles, and Explanations for examples.

In the procurement requirements and contracting requirements, *MasterFormat™* 2004 numbers have been assigned to provide a consistent sequencing within the document. However, it is not necessary to renumber or re-title printed forms and standard documents published by various professional societies or contract issuing bodies to correspond with these numbers.

USING *MASTERFORMAT™* FOR NAMING DATA FILES

MasterFormat™ is not intended to provide a technical or product data filing system as there is not necessarily a single location at which any particular technical subject or product may be located in the system. A product that is used for multiple purposes or work results may be located in multiple locations in *MasterFormat™*. If *MasterFormat™* is used for product data filing, then the user should be aware that for some products an arbitrary choice of where to file the data among multiple locations must be made. Names of products may be included in the titles in *MasterFormat™* when they are synonymous with the work result. Products which might be included with a work result but not included in the title may be listed in the explanations column for the title, under the heading "Products."

Product data is identified using *MasterFormat™* numbers and titles to clarify the relationship between products and specifications. *OmniClass™* Table 23—Products, provides a tool for classifying product data as product data, with single locations provided for any given product type, regardless of how many different types of work results the product may be employed in.

MasterFormat™ numbers can be used as suffixes within another cataloging system, such as the Dewey-Decimal Classification, the Universal Decimal Classification, or the U.S. Library of Congress classification.

Suppliers' and subcontractors' data (such as qualification information or submittals) may be identified by the work result they supply or install. The work of suppliers and subcontractors often transcends section and division boundaries, so some method is required for multiple references to *MasterFormat™* titles. A recommended solution is to use other *OmniClass™* Tables such as Table 33—Disciplines or Table 32—Services.

The inventory of construction products is made simpler by using the specification section number, perhaps as a suffix to a project number. If more than one product is specified in a section, then some form of suffix to the section number is needed to distinguish the products. See Using *MasterFormat™* with Construction Market Data for examples. User-created Level 5 extension may also be used for this purpose. *OmniClass™* Table 23—Products is the recommended standard for classifying products; one that provides unique locations.

USING *MASTERFORMAT™* IN COST DATA APPLICATIONS

Cost classification requires identification of line items, which are often related to products and activities. An identification scheme based on *MasterFormat™* can be flexible, varying with each construction project, or more rigid and uniform, establishing a single number and location for similar costs in many projects. *OmniClass™* Table 21—Elements, is also recommended when dealing with construction costing applications in the earlier stages of a project before particular work results have been selected. Similar to the way that *OmniClass™* Table 22—Work Results is based on *MasterFormat™* 2004, the Elements Table is based on the existing legacy system UniFormat.

Organizing unit-price databases using the same numbering and titling format for specifying and naming data files benefits the user with increased uniformity and standardization. Familiarity with *MasterFormat™* allows users to relate specification requirements, product information, and cost data. Numbers and titles under "Procurement Requirements" and "Contracting Requirements" in Division 00 identify cost items related to bonds, insurance, permits, fees, and other general items. Numbers and titles in Division 01 identify unit costs for temporary construction facilities and controls, mobilization, project site administration, and other general requirement cost items. Numbers and titles in the other subgroups of the Specifications Group identify costs related to work results and their installation.

Organizing and tabulating cost reports may require indicating or summarizing products and activities. Using *MasterFormat™* numbers and titles will aid users in making inferences about material costs while analyzing the report.

Value analysis requires a consistent naming scheme carried throughout the stages of the project. *MasterFormat™* is not particularly useful for value analysis, which requires attaching a cost to a particular functional element, rather than to particular products and activities. *OmniClass™* Table 21—Elements and *UniFormat™* are more appropriate for this application, although using *MasterFormat™* numbers as suffixes to the element designation may assist the value analyst in evaluating change proposals from a contractor.

USING *MASTERFORMAT™* FOR ORGANIZING DRAWING NOTATIONS

An important strategy for naming drawing elements is related to the need to link requirements between complementary documents. One must examine the entire set of contract documents to determine all of the requirements for a single product. Notations on drawings should use terminology consistent with that used in other contract documents, such as the specifications, to identify the specified work results and activities.

Reference keynoting applications have adopted *MasterFormat™* as a base numbering system, to enhance cross-referencing and coordination between drawings and specifications. This formal method of linking between drawing objects and the specification is encouraging increased development of automated linking software. See the U.S. National CAD Standard, UDS Notations module for more information.

USING *MASTERFORMAT™* WITH CONSTRUCTION MARKET DATA

To develop a comparable database and optimize communication, an agency may have to report a product occurrence using a standard number that differs from the project specification section number. The agency may wish to identify specific products that are covered in a Level 2 Section by using the number associated with a narrower standard title.

Market data reporting agencies routinely use *MasterFormat™* to identify products specified in a project manual during the procurement stage. This practice allows users to quickly identify substitution and sales potential for their products and services on a particular project.

If the general subject is a Level 3 number and title, Level 4 numbers and titles can be used to differentiate product types. For example in 33 33 13 Sanitary Utility Sewerage, user-created Level 4 numbers might be used to distinguish different materials used for sanitary piping:

LEVEL 4 NUMBER USE
A.1

NUMBER	MATERIALS
33 33 13.11	cast-iron piping and fittings
33 33 13.12	ductile-iron piping and fittings
33 33 13.13	stainless-steel piping and fittings
33 33 13.21	ABS piping and fittings
33 33 13.22	PVC piping and fittings
33 33 13.23	fiberglass piping and fittings
33 33 13.31	concrete piping and fittings

If the general subject is a Level 4 number and title then an extended user-created Level 5 designation as described above under "Electronic Filing" might be used. *OmniClass™* Table 23—Products, is also recommended for this purpose.

USING *MASTERFORMAT™* FOR FACILITY MANAGEMENT

Facility managers use *MasterFormat™* numbers and titles to identify data associated with products incorporated into their buildings, and for identifying items that may be referenced in several documents. The added titles related to operation and maintenance will provide a scheme for recording general maintenance information as well. Usually the numbers and titles will be taken from the original project specifications and other documents. This enhanced information in *MasterFormat™* 2004 will allow and encourage facility managers to better track maintenance through the full life cycle of a facility.

SECTIONFORMAT™

INTRODUCTION

SectionFormat™ provides a uniform approach to organizing specification text within a section of a project manual. The organization structure is divided into three primary parts; each part is further divided into article subjects to standardize the location of information into a logical order.

The Construction Specifications Institute (CSI) and Construction Specifications Canada (CSC) jointly produce *SectionFormat™*. *SectionFormat™* is currently undergoing review and revision to reflect the current state of the industry. It is anticipated that the revised document will be published in late 2007; the information in this text refers to the current 1992 edition.

HISTORY

CSI and CSC both published *SectionFormat™* documents beginning in 1969, and each of the documents was periodically revised. *SectionFormat™* was published as a joint document for the first time in 1980, with subsequent revisions in 1985 and 1992.

Article titles in the 1992 edition were rearranged to align certain PART 1 and PART 3 with the sequence of *MasterFormat™* Division 01 subjects.

There are still a few article terms and title discrepancies that were recommended by the Technical Studies Committee, CSC, for specifications serving the Canadian construction industry.

STRUCTURE

SectionFormat™ consists of three primary parts: GENERAL, PRODUCT, and EXECUTION.

- PART 1—GENERAL: Describes administrative, procedural, and temporary requirements unique to the section. PART 1 expands on information covered in Division 1 with information specific to the section.
- PART 2—PRODUCTS: Describes materials, products, equipment, systems or assemblies that are required for incorporation into the project. Manufactured materials and products are included along with the quality level required.
- PART 3—EXECUTION: Describes preparatory actions and the method in which products are to be incorporated into the project. Site-built assemblies and site-manufactured products and systems are included.
- Each part is divided into articles, which are then further divided into paragraphs and subparagraphs. If a section does not require the use of one or two of the three PARTS, then the PART number and title is stated and the words "Not Used" are placed under the part title.

ARTICLE TITLES

Text within each of the three PARTS of any section is divided into articles and subordinate paragraphs and subparagraphs. All *SectionFormat™* articles are optional and should be selected from the listing for inclusion in a section only as required to categorize the information being presented. If a suggested article does not apply to a particular project, it should not be used.

APPLICATION

USING *SECTIONFORMAT™* FOR PROJECT MANUALS

The primary use of *SectionFormat™* is for the organization of specification sections. *SectionFormat™* provides a listing of typical article titles and a standard arrangement of article subjects in the three parts suitable for use in master specification systems. This document provides an industry-accepted standard for locating information within the specification section and therefore reduces the chance for omissions or duplication of information.

USING *SECTIONFORMAT™* FOR BUILDING INFORMATION MODELS

SectionFormat™ may also be used as a checklist of data tags for the building of information models. These data tags will contain information necessary for the creation, operation, and maintenance of a material, product, work result, or construction entity. The information contained in these data tags will evolve with the life cycle of the facility.

INTRODUCTION

The U.S. National CAD Standard (NCS) is a compilation of related documents published by several organizations for the purposes of creating a national standard for construction-related CAD documents. The demand for a national CAD standard came from two sources. First, major facility owners such as the federal government were looking to establish a mechanism for organizing graphic facility information so that it could be easily stored and retrieved. Whereas most architects think about drawings only as construction documents, many facility owners perceive them as the basis of facility management documents. This information is used throughout the life cycle of a facility for operation, renovations, additions, and, finally, facility decommissioning and demolition. What has now come to be known as the facility cycle was a major impetus in the participation by the U.S. Department of Defense (DoD) in the creation of the NCS.

The second major reason for the creation of the NCS was the demand by design professionals to develop standards to allow sharing of information and to minimize the need for each user group to create its own CAD standards, which required teams to adapt different CAD standards for each project, thus wasting time and money while achieving no benefit. The NCS was perceived as a method to provide uniformity from project to project and save time in production, thus allowing architects to spend more time on design. It was also viewed as a means to allow CAD software vendors to create tools around these standards that would make the production of the construction documents easier and faster.

The benefits of a national standard should be clear to all design professionals, as it allows information to be transfered throughout the project cycle from one design professional to another. Streamlining the manner in which information is shared results in better coordination between architects and engineers, as well as saving production time and improving the overall design of the project.

The National Institute of Building Sciences, the American Institute of Architects, the Construction Specifications Institute, and the Tri-Service CAD/GIS Technology Center are the contributing organizations to the NCS. The NCS is updated periodically; the information within reflects NCS version 3.1, updated in January 2005.

UNIFORM DRAWING SYSTEM MODULES 01-08

Published by the Construction Specifications Institute

- *Module 01: Drawing Set Organization*: Provides guidelines for the organization of a drawing set, drawing set order, and sheet identification system.
- *Module 02: Sheet Organization*: Provides guidelines for the layout of the drawing sheet, location and numbering of drawings on the sheet, sheet sizes, title block area, and supplemental drawing sheet layout.

- *Module 03: Schedules*: Provides guidelines for the layout of schedules and use of schedules, both on drawings and in the project manual.
- *Module 04: Drafting Conventions*: Provides guidelines for the production of construction drawings, including line weights, dimensioning, orientation, notations, and other graphic drawing conventions.
- *Module 05: Terms and Abbreviations*: Provides a searchable list of preferred and nonpreferred terms, as well as abbreviations used on drawings.
- *Module 06: Symbols*: Provides standard symbols organized by MasterFormat, 2004 edition, divisions, and symbol type classification structure.
- *Module 07: Notations*: Provides guidelines for locating and using notations on drawings, including general notes, general discipline notes, general sheet notes, reference keynotes, and sheet keynotes.
- *Module 08: Code Conventions*: Provides guidelines for presenting code-related data on drawings. This module establishes types of code-related information, preferred location, and format for display of the information.

AIA CAD LAYER GUIDELINES

Published by the American Institute of Architects

- Provides guidelines and organizational structure for creating CAD layer names for all disciplines.

TRI-SERVICE PLOTTING GUIDELINES

Published by the CADD/GIS Technology Center

Provides guidelines for pen color and line weight.

APPENDICES

Published by the National Institute of Building Sciences

- Appendix A—Statement of Substantial Conformance
- Appendix B—Optional and Recommended NCS Items
- Appendix C—Memorandum of Understanding
- Appendix D—Members of the NCS Project Committees
- Appendix E—NIBS Consensus Process
- Appendix F—NCS Rules of Governance
- Appendix G—Facility Information Council Board
- Appendix H—Implementation of U.S. National CAD Standard

APPLICATION OVERVIEW

Following are examples of a few of the many guidelines and standards included in the NCS.

DRAWING SET HIERARCHY
A.2

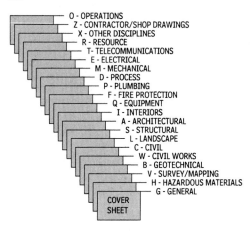

Source: Reprinted with permission from *The Architects Guide to the U.S. National CAD Standard*, Hall and Green, 2006.

DRAWING SHEET ORGANIZATION
A.3

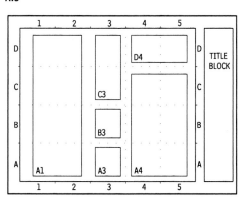

Source: Reprinted with permission from *The Architects Guide to the U.S. National CAD Standard* (Hall and Green, 2006).

TITLE BLOCK ORGANIZATION
A.4

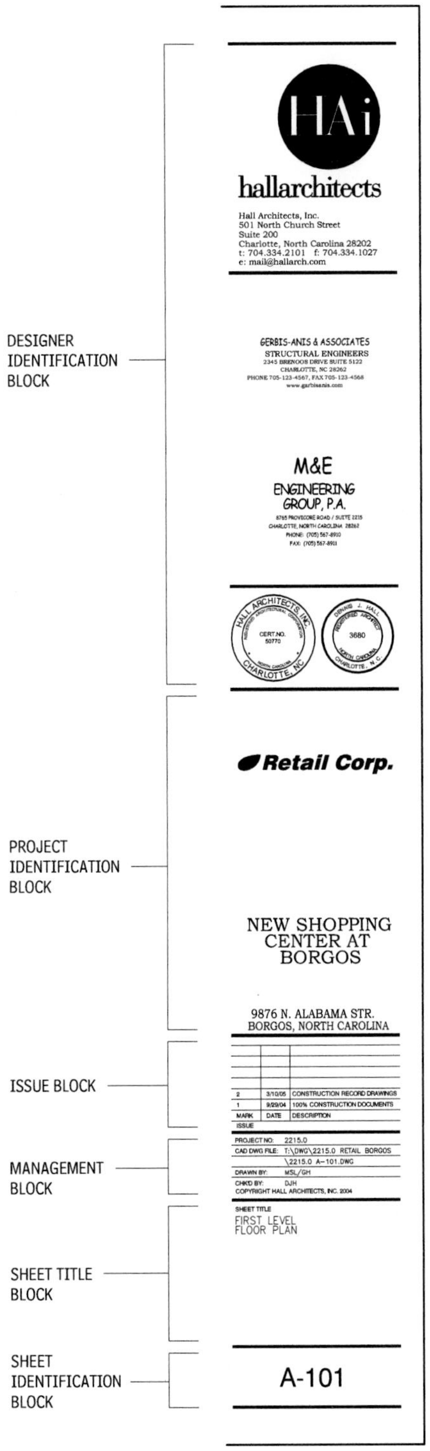

TITLE BLOCK FORMATS
A.5

DESIGNER
IDENTIFICATION
BLOCK

PROJECT
IDENTIFICATION
BLOCK

ISSUE BLOCK

MANAGEMENT
BLOCK

SHEET TITLE
BLOCK

SHEET
IDENTIFICATION
BLOCK

hallarchitects

Hall Architects, Inc.
501 North Church Street
Suite 200
Charlotte, North Carolina 28202
t: 704.334.2101 f: 704.334.1027
e: mail@hallarch.com

GERBIS-ANIS & ASSOCIATES
STRUCTURAL ENGINEERS
2345 BIRKWOOD DRIVE SUITE 5122
CHARLOTTE, NC 28262
PHONE 705-123-4567, FAX 705-123-4568
www.garbisanis.com

M&E
ENGINEERING
GROUP, P.A.
8765 PROVIDORE ROAD / SUITE 2215
CHARLOTTE, NORTH CAROLINA 28262
PHONE: (705) 567-8910
FAX: (705) 567-8911

Retail Corp.

NEW SHOPPING
CENTER AT
BORGOS

9876 N. ALABAMA STR.
BORGOS, NORTH CAROLINA

2	3/10/05	CONSTRUCTION RECORD DRAWINGS
1	9/29/04	100% CONSTRUCTION DOCUMENTS
MARK	DATE	DESCRIPTION
ISSUE		

PROJECT NO: 2215.0
CAD DWG FILE: T:\DWG\2215.0 RETAIL BORGOS
\2215.0 A-101.DWG
DRAWN BY: MSL/GH
CHKD BY: DJH
COPYRIGHT HALL ARCHITECTS, INC. 2004

SHEET TITLE
FIRST LEVEL
FLOOR PLAN

A-101

Source: Reprinted with permission from *The Architects Guide to the U.S. National CAD Standard* (Hall and Green, 2006).

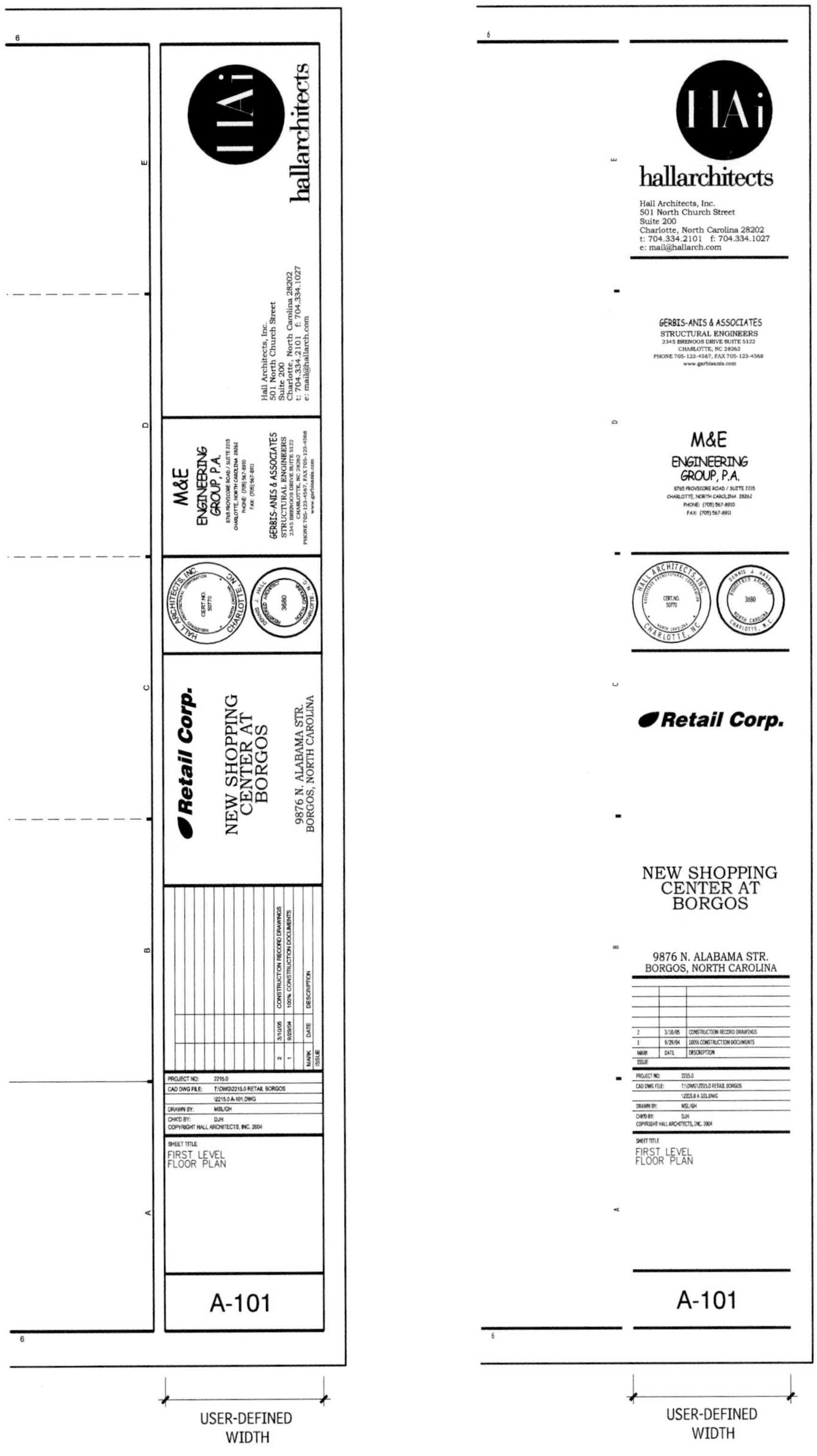

VERTICAL TEXT FORMAT

HORIZONTAL TEXT FORMAT

USER-DEFINED
WIDTH

USER-DEFINED
WIDTH

Source: Reprinted with permission from *The Architects Guide to the U.S. National CAD Standard* (Hall and Green, 2006).

SHEET IDENTIFICATION FORMAT
A.6

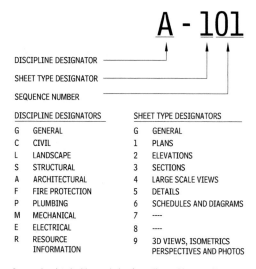

DISCIPLINE DESIGNATOR

SHEET TYPE DESIGNATOR

SEQUENCE NUMBER

DISCIPLINE DESIGNATORS		SHEET TYPE DESIGNATORS	
G	GENERAL	G	GENERAL
C	CIVIL	1	PLANS
L	LANDSCAPE	2	ELEVATIONS
S	STRUCTURAL	3	SECTIONS
A	ARCHITECTURAL	4	LARGE SCALE VIEWS
F	FIRE PROTECTION	5	DETAILS
P	PLUMBING	6	SCHEDULES AND DIAGRAMS
M	MECHANICAL	7	----
E	ELECTRICAL	8	----
R	RESOURCE INFORMATION	9	3D VIEWS, ISOMETRICS PERSPECTIVES AND PHOTOS

Source: Reprinted with permission from *The Architects Guide to the U.S. National CAD Standard* (Hall and Green, 2006).

GRAPHIC SYMBOLS

INTRODUCTION

Graphic symbols are representations of objects, materials, or words. Module 6—Symbols of the *Uniform Drawing System* (UDS), produced by the Construction Specifications Institute (CSI), is the portion of the *U.S. National CAD Standard* (NCS) that classifies, organizes, and presents graphic symbols used in construction documents. This Appendix is a summary of the information contained in the Symbols module. For more information on the *U.S. National CAD Standard*, see Appendix B.

The UDS Symbols module provides a hierarchy for the organization of symbols. Symbols are first organized by *MasterFormat™* 2004 Level 2 numbers, then by symbol classification type, and then alphabetically by description. For more information on *MasterFormat™* 2004, see Appendix A.

SYMBOL CLASSIFICATION STRUCTURE

The *U.S. National CAD Standard* provides six classifications of symbols. Following is a listing of the symbol types with description and examples of each.

IDENTITY SYMBOLS

Identity symbols are those symbols that indicate individual objects but are not representations of the objects. Identity symbols are generally used to indicate objects such as valves, fire alarms, light fixtures, and electrical outlets.

LINE SYMBOLS

Line symbols are symbols that indicate continuous objects and are drawn using either single or double lines. Line symbols are generally used to indicate objects such as walls, ductwork, and utility lines.

MATERIAL SYMBOLS

Material symbols are symbols that graphically indicate construction materials or material of existing conditions. Material symbols may be shown in elevation, section, or plan views. Material symbols are generally used to indicate objects such as brick, stone, earth, wood, concrete, and steel.

IDENTITY SYMBOLS
A.7

EXHAUST ROOF VENT FAN

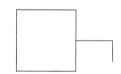

DISCONNECT SWITCH

LINE SYMBOLS
A.8

1-HOUR FIRE-RESISTIVE CONSTRUCTION

2-HOUR FIRE-RESISTIVE CONSTRUCTION

MATERIAL SYMBOLS
A.9

FINISH WOOD

END-GRAIN CONSTRUCTION LUMBER

S_3

THREE—WAY SWITCH

ROUND CATCH BASIN

3-HOUR FIRE-RESISTIVE CONSTRUCTION

STORM DRAINAGE

EARTH

OBJECT SYMBOLS

Object symbols are symbols that represent specific physical objects. Object symbols are generally used to indicate objects such as doors, windows, toilet fixtures, and furniture.

**OBJECT SYMBOLS
A.10**

LEFT SINGLE-HINGED DOOR

SQUARE TABLE WITH ARMLESS CHAIRS

SHOWER STALL

REFERENCE SYMBOLS

Reference symbols are symbols that refer the reader to information in another area of the set of drawings, or give basic information regarding the drawings or data on the sheet. Reference symbols include such symbols as elevation indicators, detail indicators, a north arrow, a graphic scale, section indicators, and revision clouds.

**REFERENCE SYMBOLS
A.11**

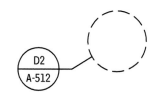

DETAIL INDICATOR

COLUMN GRID INDICATOR

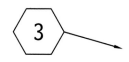

SHEET KEYNOTE

TEXT SYMBOLS

Text symbols are symbols that graphically indicate a word or words and may be in notations on drawings.

**TEXT SYMBOLS
A.12**

SYMBOL	MEANING
'	foot (feet)
"	inch (inches)
&	and
@	at
#	number, pound

MATHEMATICAL DATA

D

CONVERSION FACTORS
A.13

QUANTITY	FROM INCH-POUND UNITS	TO METRIC UNITS	MULTIPLY BY
Length	mile	km	1.609344[a]
	yard	m	0.9144[a]
	foot	m	0.3048[a]
	foot	mm	304.8[a]
	inch	mm	25.4[a]
Area	square mile	km^2	2.59000
	acre	m^2	4046.87
		ha (10,000m^2)	0.404687
	square yard	m^2	0.83612736[a]
	square foot	m^2	0.09290304[a]
	square inch	mm^2	645.16[a]
Volume	acre foot	M^3	1233.49
	cubic yard	M^3	0.764555
	cubic foot	M^3	0.0283168
		cm^3	28,316.85
		L (1000 cm^3)	28.31685
	100 board feet	m^3	0.235974
	gallon	L (1000 cm^3)	3.78541
	cubic inch	cm^3	16.387064[a]
		mm^3	16,387.064[a]
Mass	lb	kg	0.453592
	Kip (1000 lbs)	metric ton (1000 kg)	0.453592
Mass/unit length	plf	kg/m	1.48816
Mass/unit area	psf	kg/m^2	4.88243
Mass density	pcf	kg/m^3	16.0185
Force	lb	N	4.44822
Force/unit length	plf	N/m	14.5939
Pressure, stress, modulus of elasticity	psf	Pa	47.8803
	psi	kPa	6.89476
Bending moment, torque, moment of force	ft-lb	N.m	1.35582
Moment of mass	lb/ft	kg.m	0.138255
Moment of inertia	lb/ft^2	$kg.m^2$	0.0421401
Second moment of area	in^4	mm^4	416231
Section modulus	in^3	mm^3	16,387.064[a]
Mass/area (density)	lb/ft^2	kg/m^2	4.882428
Temperature	°F	°C	5/9(°F-32)
Energy, work, quantity of heat	kWh	MJ	3.6[a]
	Btu	J	1055.056
	ft/lbf	J	1.35582
Power	ton (refrig)	kW	3.517
	Btu/s	kW	1.055056
	hp (electric)	W	745.700
	Btu/h	W	0.293071
Heat flux	$Btu/ft^2/h$	W/m	3.152481
Rate of heat flow	Btu/s	kW	1.055056
	Btu/h	W	0.2930711

CONVERSION FACTORS (continued)
A.13

QUANTITY	FROM INCH-POUND UNITS	TO METRIC UNITS	MULTIPLY BY
Thermal conductivity (k value)	Btu/ft·h·°F	W/m/K	1.73073
Thermal conductance (U value)	Btu/ft²/h/°F	W/m²/K	5.678263
Thermal resistance (R value)	ft²/h/°F/Btu	m²/K/W	0.176110
Heat capacity, entrophy	Btu/°F	kJ/K	1.8991
Specific heat capacity, specific entropy	Btu/lb/°F	kJ/kg/K	4.1868[a]
Specific energy, latent heat	Btu/lb	kJ/kg	2.326[a]
Vapor permeance	perm (23 °C)	ng/(Pa/s/m²)	57.4525
Vapor permeability	perm/in	ng/(Pa/s/m)	1.45929
Volume rate of flow	ft³/s	m³/s	0.028316 8
	cfm	m³/s	0.0004719474
	cfm	L/s	0.4719474
Velocity, speed	ft/s	m/s	0.3048[a]
Acceleration	ft/s²	m/s²	0.3048[a]
Momentum	lb.ft/s	kg/m/s	0.1382550
Angular momentum	lb/ft²/s	kg/m²/s	0.04214011
Plane angle	degree	rad	0.0174533
Power, radiant flux	W	W	1 (same unit)
Radiant intensity	W/sr	W/sr	1 (same unit)
Radiance	W/(sr/m²)	W/(sr/m²)	1 (same unit)
Irradiance	W/m²	W/m²	1 (same unit)
Frequency	Hz	Hz	1 (same unit)
Electric current	A	A	1 (same unit)
Electric charge	A/hr	C	3600[a]
Electric potential	V	V	1 (same unit)
Capacitance	F	F	1 (same unit)
Inductance	H	H	1 (same unit)
Resistance	W	W	1 (same unit)
Conductance	mho	S	100[a]
Magnetic flux	maxwell	Wb	10-8[a]
Magnetic flux density	gamma	T	10-9[a]
Luminous intensity	cd	cd	1 (same unit)
Luminance	lambert	kcd/m²	3.18301
	cd/ft²	cd/m²	10.7639
	footlambert	cd/m²	3.42626
Luminous flux	lm	lm	1 (same unit)
Illuminance	footcandle	lx	10.7639

NOTE

A.13[a] Denotes an exact conversion.

SELECTED EQUATIONS AND CONSTANTS

SCIENTIFIC NOTATION

Scientific notation is used to abbreviate large numerical values in order to simplify calculations.

$$4.2 \times 10^4 = 4.2 \times (10 \times 10 \times 10 \times 10) = 42,000$$

$$1.0 \times 10^1 = 1 \times 10 = 10$$

$$6.0 \times 10^{-4} = 6.0 \times (1 / 10 \times 10 \times 10 \times 10) = 0.0006$$

MULTIPLYING AND DIVIDING POWERS

$$x^n x^m = x^{nm} \qquad (x^n)^m = x^{nm}$$

$$\frac{x^n}{x^m} = x^{n-m} \qquad \frac{1}{x^n} = \sqrt[n]{x}$$

PYTHAGOREAN THEOREM

$$c^2 = a^2 + b^2$$

PYTHAGOREAN THEOREM
A.14

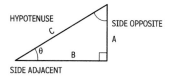

BASIC TRIGONOMETRY FUNCTIONS

$$\sin \theta \frac{\text{opposite}}{\text{hypotenuse}} = \frac{a}{c}$$

$$\cos \theta \frac{\text{adjacent}}{\text{hypotenuse}} = \frac{b}{c}$$

$$\tan \theta \frac{\text{opposite}}{\text{adjacenet}} = \frac{a}{b}$$

$$\cot \theta \frac{\text{adjacent}}{\text{opposite}} = \frac{b}{a}$$

RADIANS AND DEGREES

A radian is a way of measuring angles in addition to degrees. Radians are the primary unit of angular measurement used in calculations.

$$1 \quad \text{rad} = \frac{180°}{\pi} = 57.3 \quad \text{(approx)}$$

$$1° = \frac{\pi}{180°} = 0.01745 \quad \text{rad} \quad \text{(approx)}$$

LINEAR DISTANCE

The distance *s* that a point *p* on the rim of a rotating wheel covers is called linear distance. The angle θ, the intercepting angle, is measured in radians.

$$s = r\theta$$

LINEAR SPEED

The linear speed *v*, of the point *p* around the rim of a rotating wheel, is the time taken *t* for a point to travel the distance *s*.

$$v = \frac{s}{t}$$

ANGULAR SPEED

The angular speed ω, of the point **p** around the rim of a rotating wheel is the time taken, **t**, for the point to travel the angular distance, θ. The angular distance can be measured in degrees, revolutions, or radians. The resulting units of angular speed depend on the units used for angular distance and time.

$$\omega = \frac{\theta}{t}$$

LAW OF REFLECTION

A light ray reflects from a surface such that the angle of reflection equals the angle of incidence.

$$\theta' = \theta_2$$

**LAW OF REFLECTION
A.15**

LAW OF REFRACTION

When a light ray traveling through a transparent medium strikes another transparent medium, part of the ray is reflected and part is refracted, entering the second medium. The angle of the refracted ray depends on the angle of incidence and the index of refraction of both mediums.

$$n_1 \sin\theta_1 = n_2 \sin\theta_2$$

**LAW OF REFRACTION
A.16**

TOTAL INTERNAL REFLECTION

When light attempts to move from a medium with a high index of refraction to a medium with a low index of refraction, there is a particular angle of incidence large enough that the angle of refraction reaches 90°. The transmitted light ray moves parallel to the surface of the first medium, and no more light is transmitted.

This angle of incidence is called the critical angle and depends on the indexes of refraction of the two mediums. Any angle of incidence larger than the critical angle is reflected back into the first medium.

$$\sin\theta_c = \frac{n_2}{n_1}$$

**TOTAL INTERNAL REFLECTION
A.17**

SPEED OF LIGHT IN MEDIUM

$$c_{medium} = \frac{c_{vac}}{n_{medium}}$$

THERMAL EXPANSION OF LENGTH

An object of initial length L_0 at some temperature. With a change in temperature of ΔT, the length increases ΔL. The constant α is called the average coefficient of linear expansion for the given material.

$$\Delta L = \alpha L_0 \Delta T$$

THERMAL EXPANSION OF AREA

An object of initial area A_0 at some temperature. With a change in temperature of ΔT, the area increases ΔA. The constant γ is the average coefficient of area expansion for the given material.

$$\Delta A = \gamma A_0 \Delta T \qquad \gamma = 2\alpha$$

THERMAL EXPANSION OF VOLUME

A mass of initial volume V_0 at some temperature. With a change in temperature ΔT, the volume increases ΔV. The constant β is called the average coefficient of volume expansion for a given material.

$$\Delta V = \beta V_0 \Delta T \qquad \beta = 3\alpha$$

USEFUL CONSTANTS

INDEXES OF REFRACTION (N)
A.18

Air at 20°c, 1 atm.			1.000
SOLIDS AND LIQUIDS AT 20°C			
Water	1.333	Polystyrene	1.49
Ice (H$_2$O)	1.309	Glass, crown	1.52
Fused quartz	1.458	Glass, flint	1.66

LINEAR EXPANSION COEFFICENTS (A)
A.19

Aluminum	24×10^{-6}	Concrete	12×10^{-6}
Brass and bronze	19×10^{-6}	Lead	29×10^{-6}
Copper	17×10^{-6}	Steel	11×10^{-6}
Glass, ordinary	9×10^{-6}		

VOLUME EXPANSION COEFFICENTS (β) (β = 3α)
A.20

Air	3.67×10^{-3}

NATURAL CONSTANTS
A.21

Speed of light in a vacuum	$C = 3.0 \times 10^8$ m/s
Standard gravity	$g = 9.80$ m/s^2

WEIGHT OF MATERIALS

**WEIGHT OF MATERIALS
A.22**

BRICK AND BLOCK MASONRY		PSF
4" brickwork		40
4" concrete block, stone or gravel		34
4" concrete block, lightweight		22
4" concrete brick, stone or gravel		46
4" concrete brick, lightweight		33
6" concrete block, stone or gravel		50
6" concrete block, lightweight		31
8" concrete block, stone or gravel		55
8" concrete block, lightweight		35
12" concrete block, stone or gravel		85
12" concrete block, lightweight		55
CONCRETE		**PCF**
Plain	Cinder	108
	Expanded slag aggregate	100
	Expanded clay	90
	Slag	132
	Stone and cast stone	144
Reinforced	Cinder	111
	Slag	138
	Stone	150
FINISH MATERIALS		**PSF**
Acoustical tile unsupported per 1/2"		0.8
Building board, 1/2"		0.8
Cement finish, 1"		12
Fiberboard, 1/2"		0.75
Gypsum board, 1/2"		2
Marble and setting bed		25–30
Plaster, 1/2"		4.5
Plaster on wood lath		8
Plaster suspended with lath		10
Plywood, 1/2"		1.5
Tile, glazed wall 3/8"		3
Tile, ceramic mosaic, 1/4"		2.5
Quarry tile, 1/2"		5.8
Quarry tile, 3/4"		8.6
Terrazzo 1", 2" in stone concrete		25
Vinyl tile, 1/8"		1.33
Hardwood flooring, 25/32"		4
Wood block flooring, 3" on mastic		15
FLOOR AND ROOF (CONCRETE)		**PSF**
Flexicore, 6" precast lightweight concrete		30
Flexicore, 6" precast stone concrete		40
Plank, cinder concrete, 2"		15
Plank, gypsum, 2"		12
Concrete, reinforced, 1"	Stone	12.5
	Slag	11.5
	Lightweight	6–10
Concrete, plain, 1"	Stone	12
	Slag	11
	Lightweight	3–9
FUELS AND LIQUIDS		**PCF**
Coal, piled anthracite		47–58
Coal, piled bituminous		40–54

WEIGHT OF MATERIALS (continued)
A.22

Ice	57.2
Gasoline	75
Snow	8
Water, fresh	62.4
Water, sea	64
GLASS	**PSF**
Polished plate, 1/4"	3.28
Polished plate, 1/2"	6.56
Double strength, 1/8"	26 oz
Sheet A, B, 1/32"	45 oz
Sheet A, B, 1/4"	52 oz
Insulated glazing 5/8" plate with air space	3.25
Wire glass, 1/4"	3.5
Glass block	18
INSULATION AND WATERPROOFING	**PSF**
Blanket per 1" thickness	0.1–0.4
Corkboard per 1" thickness	0.58
Foamed board insulation per 1" thickness	2.6 oz
Five-ply membrane	5
Board insulation	0.75
LIGHTWEIGHT CONCRETE	**PSF**
Concrete, aerocrete	50–80
Concrete, cinder fill	60
Concrete, expanded clay	85–100
Concrete, expanded shale-sand	105–120
Concrete, perlite	35–50
Concrete, pumice	60–90
METALS	**PCF**
Aluminum, cast	165
Brass, cast, rolled	534
Bronze, commercial	552
Bronze, statuary	509
Copper, cast or rolled	556
Gold, cast, solid	1205
Gold coin in bags	509
Iron, cast gray, pig	450
Iron, wrought	480
Lead	710
Nickel	565
Silver, cast, solid	656
Silver, coin in bags	590
Tin	459
Stainless steel, rolled	492–510
Steel, rolled, cold drawn	490
Zinc, rolled, cast or sheet	449
MORTAR AND PLASTER	**PCF**
Mortar, masonry	116
Plaster, gypsum, sand	104–120
PARTITIONS	**PSF**
2 × 4 wood stud, gypsum board , two sides	8
4" metal stud, gypsum board, two sides	6
4" concrete block, lightweight, gypsum board	26
6" concrete block, lightweight, gypsum board	35

2" solid plaster	20
4" solid plaster	32
ROOFING MATERIALS	**PSF**
Built up	6.5
Concrete roof tile	9.5
Copper	1.5–2.5
Corrugated iron	2
Deck, steel without roofing or insulation	2.2–3.6
Fiberglass panels (2 1/2" corrugated)	5–8 oz
Galvanized iron	1.2–1.7
Lead, 1/8"	6.8
Plastic sandwich panel, 2 1/2" thick	2.6
Shingles, asphalt	1.7–2.8
Shingles, wood	2–3
Slate, 3/16" to 1/4"	7–9.5
Slate, 3/8" to 1/2"	14–18
Stainless steel	2.5
Tile, cement flat	13
Tile, cement ribbed	16
Tile, clay shingle type	8–16
Tile, clay flat with setting bed	15–20
Wood sheathing per inch	3
SOIL, SAND, AND GRAVEL	**PCF**
Ashes or cinder	40–50
Clay, damp and plastic	110
Clay, dry	63
Clay and gravel, dry	100
Earth, dry and loose	76
Earth, dry and packed	95
Earth, moist and loose	78
Earth, moist and packed	96
Earth, mud, packed	115
Sand or gravel, dry and loose	90–105
Sand or gravel, dry and packed	100–120
Sand or gravel, dry and wet	118–120
Silt, moist, loose	78
Silt, moist, packed	98
STONE (ASHLAR)	**PCF**
Granite, limestone, crystalline	165
Limestone, oolitic	136
Marble	173
Sandstone, bluestone	144
Slate	172
STONE VENEER	**PSF**
2" granite, 1/2" parging	30
4" granite, 1/2" parging	59
6" limestone facing, 1/2" parging	55
4" sandstone or bluestone, 1/2" parging	49
1" marble	13
1" slate	14
STRUCTURAL CLAY TILE	**PSF**
4" hollow	23
6" hollow	38
8" hollow	45

STRUCTURAL FACING TILE	**PSF**
2" facing tile	14
4" facing tile	24
6" facing tile	34
8" facing tile	44
SUSPENDED CEILINGS	**PSF**
Mineral fiber tile 3/4", 12" * 12"	1.2–1.57
Mineral fiberboard 5/8", 24" * 24"	1.4
Acoustic plaster on gypsum lath base	10–11
WOOD	**PCF**
Ash, commercial white	40.5
Birch, red oak, sweet and yellow	44
Cedar, northern white	22.2
Cedar, western red	24.2
Cypress, southern	33.5
Douglas fir (coast region)	32.7
Fir, commercial white, Idaho white pine	27
Hemlock	28–29
Maple, hard (blacks and sugar)	44.6
Oak, white and red	47.3
Pine, northern white sugar	25
Pine, southern yellow	37.3
Pine, ponderosa, spruce: eastern and sitka	28.6
Poplar, yellow	29.4
Redwood	26
Walnut, black	38

To establish uniform practice among designers, it is desirable to present a list of materials generally used in building construction, together with their proper weights. Many building codes prescribe the minimum weights of only a few building materials. It should be noted that there is a difference of more than 25 percent in some cases.

AREA AND VOLUME CALCULATION

ARCHITECTURAL AREA OF BUILDINGS

The architectural area of a building is the sum of the areas of the floors, measured horizontally in plan to the exterior faces of perimeter walls or to the center line of walls separating buildings. Included are areas occupied by partitions, columns, stairwells, elevator shafts, duck shafts, elevator rooms, pipe spaces, mechanical penthouses, and similar spaces having headroom of 6 ft and over. Areas of sloping surfaces, such as staircases, bleachers, and tiered terraces, should be measured horizontally in plan. Auditoriums, swimming pools, gymnasiums, foyers, and similar spaces extending through two or more floors should be measured once only, taking the largest area in plan at any level.

Mechanical penthouse rooms, pipe spaces, bulkheads, and similar spaces having a headroom less than 6 ft and balconies projecting beyond exterior walls, covered terraces and walkways, porches, and similar spaces shall have the architectural area multiplied by 0.50 in calculating the building gross area.

Exterior staircases and fire escapes, exterior steps, patios, terraces, open courtyards and light wells, roof overhangs, cornices and chimneys, unfinished roof and attic areas, pipe trenches, and similar spaces are excluded from the architectural area calculations. Interstitial space in healthcare facilities is also excluded.

ARCHITECTURAL VOLUME OF BUILDINGS

The architectural volume of a building is the sum of the products of the areas defined in the architectural area times the height from the underside of the lowest floor construction to the average height of the surface of the finished roof above, for the various parts of the building. Included in the architectural volume is the actual space enclosed within the outer surfaces of the exterior of outer walls and contained between the outside of the roof and the bottom of the lowest floor, taken in full: bays, oriels, dormers; penthouses, chimneys; walk tunnels; enclosed porches and balconies, including screened areas.

The following volumes are multiplied by 0.50 in calculating the architectural volume of a building; nonenclosed porches, if recessed into the building and without enclosing sash or screens; nonenclosed porches built as an extension to the building and without sash or screen; areaways and pipe tunnels; and patio areas that have building walls extended on two sides, roof over, and paved surfacing.

Excluded from the architectural volume are outside steps, terraces, courts, garden walls; light shafts, parapets, cornices, roof overhangs; footings, deep foundation, pilling cassions, special foundations, and similar features.

NET ASSIGNABLE AREA

The net assignable area is that portion of the area that is available for assignment to an occupant, including every type of space usable by the occupant.

The net assignable area should be measured from the predominant inside finish of enclosing walls in the categories defined below. Areas occupied by exterior walls, partitions, internal structural, or party walls are to be excluded from the groups and are to be included under "construction area."

1. *Net assignable area*: Total area of all enclosed spaces fulfilling the main functional requirements of the building for occupant use, including custodial and service areas such as guard rooms, workshops, locker rooms, janitors' closets, storerooms, and the total area of all toilet and washroom facilities.
2. *Circulation area*: Total area of all enclosed spaces that is required for physical access to subdivision of space such as corridors, elevator shafts, escalators, fire towers or stairs, stairwells, elevator entrances, public lobbies, and public vestibules.
3. *Mechanical area*: Total area of all enclosed spaces designed to house mechanical and electrical equipment and utility services such as mechanical and electrical equipment rooms, duct shafts, boiler rooms, fuel rooms, and mechanical service shafts.
4. *Construction area*: The area occupied by exterior walls, partitions, structure, and so on.
5. *Gross floor or architectural area*: The sum of areas 1, 2, 3, and 4 plus the area of all factored non- and semi-enclosed areas equal the gross floor area or architectural area of a building.

In commercial buildings constructed for leasing, net areas are to be measured in accordance with the "Standard Method of Floor Measurement," as set by the Building Owners and Managers Association (BOMA).

The net rentable area for offices is to be measured from the inside finish of permanent outer building walls, to the office or occupancy side of corridors and/or other permanent partitions, and to the center of partitions that separate the premises from adjoining rentable areas. No deductions are to be made for columns and projections necessary by the building.

The net rentable area for stores is to be measured from the building line in case of street frontages and from the inside finish of other outer building walls, corridor, and permanent partitions and to the center of partitions that separate the premises from adjoining rentable areas. No deductions are to be made for vestibules inside the building line or for columns that are projections necessary to the building. No addition is to be made for projecting bay windows.

If a single occupant is to occupy the total floor in either the office or store categories, the net rentable area would include the accessory area for that floor of corridors, elevator lobbies, toilets, janitors' closets, electrical and telephone closets, air-conditioning rooms and fan rooms, and similar spaces.

The net rentable area for apartments is to be measured from the inside face of exterior walls, and all enclosing walls of the unit.

Various governmental agencies have their own methods of calculating the net assignable area of buildings. They should be investigated if federal authority of funding applies to a project. Also, various building codes provide their own definitions of net and gross areas of building for use in quantifying requirements.

ARCHITECTURAL AREA DIAGRAM A.23

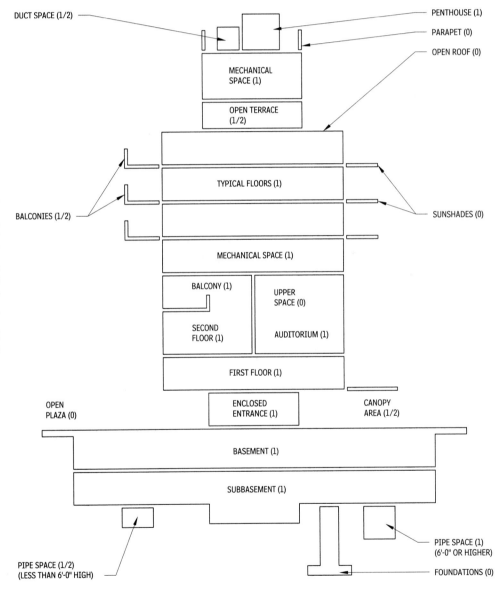

Contributor:
T. Edward Thomas, AIA, Hansen Lind Meyer, Inc., Orlando, Florida.

INDEX